MODERN ECONOMICS

Second Edition

MODERN ECONOMICS

Second Edition

David Heathfield
and
Mark Russell

New York London Toronto Sydney Tokyo Singapore

First published 1992 by
Harvester Wheatsheaf,
Campus 400, Maylands Avenue, Hemel Hempstead
Hertfordshire, HP2 7EZ
A division of
Simon & Schuster International Group

Typeset in 10/11pt Ehrhardt
by Advanced Filmsetters (Glasgow) Ltd
Text design by Lesley Stewart

Printed and bound in Great Britain by
Butler and Tanner Ltd, Frome

British Library Cataloguing in Publication Data

Heathfield, David
Modern economics. – 2nd ed.
I. Title II. Russell, Mark
330

ISBN 0–7450–1180–2
ISBN 0–7450–1181–0 pbk

1 2 3 4 5 96 95 94 93 92

Contents

Preface to the first edition

Familiarity breeds contempt, as the saying goes, and our economic environment is so familiar to us that we all tend to take it for granted. We take it for granted that when we walk into a supermarket there will be packets of tea for sale. Not only that, but we also expect a choice of teas – with several types and brands available. We take it for granted that when we switch on a light or a microwave oven, there will be electricity available to operate them. We have not forewarned the tea planter, the tea shipper, the packer or the supermarket manager, or anyone else about our intention to buy tea, nor have we specified a brand. Nor have we alerted the suppliers of electricity to the need for generators or power lines.

We take it for granted that when we want something, it will be available. This is true not only for tea and electricity, but for an enormous range of goods and services.

Were this not the norm, were this not so familiar, it would be amazing. If we asked strangers from another planet, or culture, to believe what we take for granted, then we would have to offer a fairly convincing account of how the economy worked. Many people expect it not only to work, but to work perfectly. They complain when they feel that it fails to meet these exacting standards. The complaint may be that there is too much inflation, or too much unemployment, or too few hospitals. They may well be right, but by concentrating on the apparent shortcomings of our economy, they seem to overlook the fact that it works at all.

It is part of the purpose of this book to awaken interest in the whole fascinating question of why and how the economy does work.

It is, of course, perfectly proper to be concerned when the economy seems not to be working well. There will always be room for improvement. But we should always be aware of success as well as of failure. Seeking to explain why the economy works successfully is as important as – perhaps more important than – seeking explanations of its failures. Understanding the reasons for success is important in its own right, but it also serves to help us understand failures too.

This is the approach taken in *Moden Economics*. I do not see economics as primarily a 'tool box' for solving 'problems'. Rather I attempt to explain the amazing fact that, largely, the economy works. By explaining how it works, we shall of course see how and why the economy may occasionally fail to work. We may even come to see what could be done about these failures. I am not, however, primarily concerned with focusing on economic problems.

My account of the workings of our economy is aimed partly at sharing with the reader the excitement and fascination of economic analysis. The main aim of *Modern Economics* is, however, to enable students to succeed in 'A' level examinations in economics. This examination requirement has been to the forefront throughout, and the content and emphasis has been chosen to reflect the requirements of the many separate examining boards. Any book is of course limited in what it can cover, but *Modern Economics* contains sufficient material to see the student through the 'A' level examinations of the various boards in the UK.

Economics is not an easy subject. It would be wrong to pretend it is easy by offering a trivialised account of it, even for beginners, and you will need to work at it. Some of the material in *Modern Economics* is a bit technical. This reflects the approach taken by examining boards, but also reflects the nature of economic analysis in the modern world. Again, to omit any technical chapters would be to mislead the student as to what economists currently do. However, the technical aspects have been kept within the requirement of examining boards. There is nothing unsurmountably difficult in the book and even the technical matters may prove fascinating for some readers. In any event, they will need working at. The rewards are, of course, great – not only from the point of view of succeeding in examinations, but also in coming to grips with the major issues of the day.

I have tried to make the material easily digestible by providing frequent summaries of the main points covered in each section. I have also provided a number of examination questions taken from previous examination papers set by the various boards. You are strongly urged to read, think about and attempt to answer at least some of these questions. It is not possible to provide 'specimen' answers to the questions, since they are designed to offer the student an opportunity to show what he or she knows about a particular topic. There is, however, a short account of how the student might approach the problem of answering examination questions. The usual difficulties are to do with interpreting the question and selecting the 'relevant' bits of economic theory or economic fact to put together an answer. In the final section of *Modern Economics* there are some hints as to how you may get round those difficulties.

Throughout the book I have used the universal 'he' rather than the more cumbersome 'he or she' in referring to readers. I am aware that there will be students of either sex and trust that neither will take it amiss.

In writing this book, I have received an enormous amount of help and advice. Special thanks are due to Professor D.C. Rowan, Professor Emeritus at Southampton University, Professor Roy Wilkinson, Chairman of the School of Economics and Management, University of Sheffield, and to Mr B. Gilman, Mr C. Rummings, Mr P.

Kewley, Mr P. Longhurst and Ms L. Allen, all of whom read and commented upon the manuscript at various stages. It has not been possible to include all their suggestions and hence any shortcomings or errors are mine alone. Thanks are also due to Marilyn Friend for typing and clerical assistance.

David Heathfield
1987

Preface to the second edition

The second edition of *Modern Economics* has built upon the structure and experience of the first edition. Those of you who are familiar with the first edition will find that this is a very different book. For a start it is twice as long, but thankfully not twice the price!

The main difference from the first edition is that we present a book that is much more strictly directed to the needs of the A-level syllabus, with numerous exercises, multiple-choice questions and data-response questions to provide exam practice and aid understanding. Those of you who wrote enthusiastically of the first edition will be pleased to see that we have retained the style of that book. The chapters are structured in a similar way and we have tried to present a *modern* approach to economics. It is here that our greatest difficulty lay.

Economics is a fast-changing subject. Since 1971 the traditional Keynesian macroeconomics has fallen from grace, monetarism has come and gone, and new areas of concern and theory arise every year. Examination syllabuses cannot change as quickly, so combining a modern approach with an introductory text is difficult. The result is that we have inevitably had to compromise. However, we believe that the result is a book that deals with many up-to-date issues, but which can be used by any student regardless of background.

Our compromise involves giving the student an insight into modern developments in the discipline, but clearly discriminating between these areas and what we might call the core material by starring the sections where non-core material is dealt with. We also use this approach on areas of the text that are more complex than the rest, and which may be omitted without lessening understanding of the basic principles.

The question of why we cover these areas at all has arisen with some readers. Our answer is that we have set out to write a book on *modern* economics at A-level standard. We feel that the gulf between A-level economics and university economics has grown too wide and hope that we can contribute to narrowing that gap. We do not seek to close the gap, that is the function of the universities, but by extending the coverage of the text at the same level of difficulty we believe those students who use our book will be better able to understand the events they see going on around them.

To the teacher

This edition of *Modern Economics* is designed to be a comprehensive text that will be suitable for use throughout an A-level BTEC, or degree-level course. The chapters have been designed to be comprehensive in topic areas, and there are therefore fewer of them than in many textbooks. This will, we hope, avoid the need for you to have to cover material from different chapters in the same lesson or section of your course.

The order of the chapters occupied our thoughts for many months. The final result is a book that aims to build on results discovered in previous chapters. Thus our decision to cover consumer and production theory before market demand and supply was made to allow us to explain why demand and supply curves are the shape they are without simply asking students to 'believe it for now'. We do realize that this approach may not match your own teaching programme and so we have tried to write the chapters so that they can be read in an order different from that in which they are written. The cost of this is some repetition of material, and we ask you to bear with us on this.

The book is organized into five parts. In Part I we provide an overview of economics for the reader. Recognizing that most readers will have no previous knowledge of economics and are eager to learn, we discuss the concept of economic growth and opportunity cost in Chapter 2. We hope that this will provide an immediate point of interest without requiring any technical knowledge.

In Part II we discuss microeconomics. The central theme of this part of the book is the use of the price mechanism as a method of resource allocation. Chapter 5 on market demand and supply builds directly on the results discovered in Chapters 3 and 4. In the rest of this part of the book we discuss the core aspects of neo-classical microeconomics, but try to provide as many opportunities to apply economic theory as possible. Hence the chapters on cost–benefit analysis and the distribution of income get rather more space than in traditional textbooks. We also reserve the subject of comparative systems for Chapter 8 to allow the use of some of the theory students have learned.

Part III discusses macroeconomics. We start with national accounts and then discuss the nature of money and the determination of national output. Chapter 15 provides a very simple exposition of the *IS*/*LM* system. We believe any A-level student can cope with this exposition, although we have starred the whole chapter so that students may avoid it if they wish. The chapter is included because it is clear from examiners' reports that *IS*/*LM* is widely taught, so far presumably with reference to more advanced texts.

From then on Chapters 16, 17 and 18 deal with inflation, unemployment and macroeconomic policy. We try to compare and contrast different views and provide an up-to-date treatment of this very difficult and confusing area of economics. In particular we stress the modern view of monetary policy i.e., the management of the structure of government debt. We also cover the more traditional treatment by which monetary policy is used to influence aggregate demand. You will find this a different, but we hope a contemporary and useful addition to an introductory level text. You will find a discussion of both rational expectations and supply-side economics in separate sections of Chapter 18. You may use these independently or as an integral part of the text.

Part IV deals with open economy issues. The balance of payments, the theory of trade and exchange rates are all discussed before we have a detailed look at the European Community and the European Monetary System.

Part V contains three chapters on current issues in economics. They are '1992', green economics and development economics. It is our intention that this part of the book will be revised considerably in subsequent editions to deal with topical issues.

It is possible to deal with macroeconomics first (Chapters 11 to 18) or to move from chapter to chapter at will. However, we do recommend that Chapters 3 and 4 are covered before Chapter 5, and that all three are covered before the other chapters in Part II. We also advise that Chapter 14 is covered before Chapters 16 to 18.

The basic structure of each chapter is the same. Each begins with a preview to indicate to the student the areas to be discussed. The chapters are broken down into major sections and then subsections for easy digestion. We have deliberately kept to a policy of putting in summaries where we felt them necessary to aid understanding. This was one of the features most welcomed in the first edition and so we have resisted the calls of our editor and broken up major headings with summaries where necessary. The loss of symmetry may be regrettable, but we believe it is a price worth paying. At the end of each chapter there are multiple-choice questions, exercises and, where appropriate, data-response or statistical questions. The data-response questions have been chosen with a view to extending knowledge as well as providing exam practice.

The provision of questions is new to this edition. The range of questions is not meant to be representative of any particular examining board. The aim has been to provide examination practice and a range of exercises that will enhance understanding. As the length of each chapter varies, so the number of questions varies. Again we felt this the preferable alternative to always providing a certain number of questions.

There are no answers to the exercises or data-response questions in this book. This has been on the advice of the many teachers we have consulted. We do provide answers and our own guidance to data-response questions in our Instructor's Manual, a free copy of which is available to adopters of the book. There is also a book of additional questions and exercises available. The *Modern Economics Workbook* follows the chapter structure of *Modern Economics* and provides a wide range of methods of learning and assessment.

Another new feature is the inclusion of case studies. These are intended to illuminate points raised in the text and to alert students to the wide range of sources of information available. There are also occasions where we do not designate a section as a case study, but continue with an in-depth discussion within the text. We have done this in the belief that case studies can be easily overlooked, and often do not exactly meet our needs in an A-level textbook. You will find our discussion of French indicative planning in Chapter 8 an early example of this approach.

You may be reassured to know that this edition has been thoroughly tested on an A-level group at Wycliffe College for the whole of their two-year course. This was very much a mixed-ability group, and their experience has led us to make many revisions on content and presentation. Should you have any comments on this edition, we would be delighted to hear from you.

To the student

This book is designed with your needs in mind. We know that economics is not easy, and that events in the outside world often serve to confuse rather than clarify the things you will learn in your course. Since economics is not an easy subject we have built in some features that should help you through.

- Frequent summaries of the material.
- Many diagrams.
- Alternative explanations where possible.
- Many examples and real-world applications.
- Case studies that demonstrate the application of economic theory and principles.
- A comprehensive glossary to explain key terms.
- Practice exam questions.
- Exercises that will allow you to develop your understanding of the material covered in the chapter.
- Advice on essay writing in examinations.
- Areas that are more difficult or an extension of traditional A-level teaching in starred sections.

The last feature on this list is designed to help you to select the material you read. If on the first reading you wish to leave the starred sections out then you may do so without any loss of understanding. You may wish to go back to these sections later, or you may choose to leave them completely. It really is up to you. This said, all of the material covered here is dealt with at an introductory level, and you will be able to cope with these sections if you choose. They will widen your knowledge and, we believe, improve your grade.

There is one area you may wish to leave out altogether: Chapter 15, which deals with a method of analysis known as the *IS/LM* model. This does not specifically appear on any A-level syllabus, but has appeared on one multiple-choice paper so far. The advantage of reading this chapter is that it is more comprehensive than the preceding analysis and will allow candidates who require grades A and B greatly to extend the scope of their outside reading, but we suspect most of you can safely ignore *IS/LM* if you wish.

If you are studying in a class with a teacher, or if you are studying alone, this book is designed to be a complete coursebook for you. The exercises will help you to understand the material; you should attempt them at some stage. The glossary will explain any terms you do not understand and you may use it as a dictionary if you wish. Like any textbook it cannot be completely up to date and so you should make sure that you pay close attention to current affairs through the newspapers and the television. An example is the developments occurring in the former Soviet Union and Eastern Europe as these former communist countries attempt to change the nature of their economies. The various case studies will show you how much information is available around you – make use of it! You will find publications like *The Economist* and *The Economic Review* useful.

Finally, we must stress that you will have to work very hard to succeed in the study of economics, but it really is worth it. Economics is a fascinating subject which, much to the annoyance of non-economists, goes through frequent revisions as the society we live in changes. Both of us are as enthusiastic about and interested in economics today as when we were undergraduates, and we hope we can convey our enthusiasm to you.

Acknowledgements

We have received much help and advice during the writing of this book. We are grateful for the tolerance and understanding of our families and friends who have suffered almost as much as we have. In the early stages the advice of Bernie Gilman was invaluable in setting the direction and tone of this edition. We are also grateful to the sixth-form economists at Wycliffe College 1989–91, who were our guinea-pigs for this edition. In particular, the detailed comments of Sean Collins, Jo Endacott, Olly Marsden and Richard Tubbs were extremely valuable. The final preparation of the manuscript was aided considerably by the comments of the readers, the detailed attention of Paul Lewis and the loan of an extra PC by Phil Brown. Chris Bessant's copy-editing made the book much more readable and ironed out many inconsistencies. A very tight proofreading schedule was met thanks to the assistance of Paul Lewis and William Tovey, both of Wycliffe College, and Mr and Mrs Mervyn Russell.

We are most grateful to the examination boards who have allowed us to reproduce past questions. Each board is acknowledged after its respective question according to the following key: LON. – University of London Schools Examinations Board; AEB – The Associated Examining Board; JMB – The Joint Matriculation Board; O&C – Oxford and Cambridge Schools Examination Board; CAM – University of Cambridge Local Examinations Syndicate; OXF – University of Oxford Delegacy of Local Examinations; and WJEC – Welsh Joint Education Committee. We are also grateful to the various newspapers and journals that have allowed us to reproduce their material for case studies. The source of each case study is acknowledged in the text.

We have not been able to include all of the suggestions that have been made to us and any shortcomings or errors are ours alone.

David Heathfield, University of Southampton
Mark Russell, Wycliffe College
September 1991

PART

I

INTRODUCTION

1 Economics: an overview

In this chapter we will discuss:

1. The scope and subject matter of economics.
2. How producers and consumers come together in markets.
3. How prices play a vital co-ordinating role in markets.
4. The methods used by economists to describe and explain the economy.

Introduction

To get some idea of what economists do, compare the economy with a bee hive. Inquisitive biologists would take the lid off the hive and observe the intricate patterns of behaviour within. They could then attempt to *describe* what was going on in the hive by identifying and naming certain patterns of repeated behaviour. They might even try to *explain* some of these behaviour patterns by examining their causes and consequences. They could go still further and try to *modify* the activities of the bees. They could, for example, try to increase the honey yield or reduce the tendency to swarm.

To be successful in any one of their aims (description, explanation or control) the biologists would have to undertake hours of patient study, testing out various theories and revising those which seem not to work very well. Even so some of the accepted theories may turn out to be mistaken or unreliable.

Economists of course are not biologists. We have 'taken the lid off' a far more complicated system than ever existed in a bee hive. We try to describe and explain what is going on in the whole economy. We also try to advise policy makers on how to modify it. We too will occasionally come up with wrong explanations and mistaken policies. We have, however, made substantial progress.

In order to make any headway at all we had to find ways of simplifying the ever-changing picture before us. We do this in two ways. First, we adopt a step-by-step approach. We take the economy a bit at a time and try to understand each bit. Then we gradually bring the bits together to see how they fit into a complete picture of the economy.

Second, we simply ignore some of the complexities. We know, for instance, that there are all sorts of things which influence people when they are deciding what to buy. The weather, the latest fashion, their friends, the amount they have to spend, prices and many other things all have a bearing when people are deciding what to buy. But, instead of trying to keep all these influences in mind when analysing the behaviour of buyers, we try to identify one or two of the most important influences and concentrate on them. Once we know how the simplified version works we can begin to deal with the more complicated real-world problems by adding back more and more of those things which we originally omitted. Even these simplified versions of the economy are surprisingly fruitful and offer many helpful insights into how the economy works.

The economic problem

As we have seen, the subject matter of economics is society itself – or at least one aspect of our social organization. Having 'taken the lid off' our society we confine ourselves to studying only those aspects of our society which are to do with the *creation and distribution of material wealth*. We do not, for example, investigate the religious, the sporting or the cultural activities of our society.

More simply, the economic problem can be defined as the problem of **scarcity**. Were it possible for us all to live off the land, there would be no such subject as economics. We would eat the fruit from the trees and the fish from the sea, drink water from the springs and enjoy the warmth of the sun. There would be nothing here to interest an economist. There would be no scarcity and nature would see to the creation and the distribution of our material wealth.

Most animals seem to be content with this and graze or hunt whatever nature provides. Human beings, however, are not content with what nature provides and have learned to manipulate nature and bend it to their will. Humans are the only inhabitants of this planet which seek to influence nature in this way (at least to any significant extent).

We found that by cultivating crops and by herding other animals we could improve our material welfare – we could have more to eat and could eat more regularly. This did not come about without effort. We had to learn what to do and be energetic enough to get on and do it. We learned that watering young plants improves their survival rate and their rate of growth. But, to reap any benefit from this knowledge, we had to collect the water and carry it to the plants.

This application of human knowledge and physical effort to the natural process is called **labour**.

As our knowledge increases and we learn more and more about the laws of nature, our labour becomes more and more effective and we become progressively better and better off. This steady improvement in our material welfare is called **economic growth**. Economic growth has its supporters and its detractors. Some see it as the path to freedom from material wants and an invitation to a life of leisure. Others see it as ultimately destroying the planet and in the meantime leading to the divorce of mankind from nature. These are ongoing debates which have yet to be settled, but there can be no doubt that economic growth has completely transformed our lives and is continuing to do so with every passing year.

Increasing and applying our knowledge is one source of economic growth, but another major contributing factor is our increasing tendency to specialize in what we produce. Adam Smith gives an example of the productive power of **specialization** in his *Inquiry into the Nature and Causes of the Wealth of the Nations* (1776). He reports that in the making of pins one worker working alone could make at most 20 pins per day. If ten workers co-operated in the production of pins so that one man merely straightened the wire and another cut it to length and yet another put a point on it and so on, then they could together produce 48,000 pins per working day. This is an increase in output per worker of 23,900 per cent.

Adam Smith called this specialization the **division of labour**. As the division of labour increased, so did the output of labour. Hence the division of labour, like the increase in our knowledge, has led to ever-increasing standards of material welfare.

The problem of scarcity therefore arose because we wanted more than nature alone provided. The natural supply failed to meet our wants. This was moderated by our applying our labour to the natural processes of production and thereby increasing the amount supplied. Also, by engaging in the division of labour, we can increase the output still further.

SUMMARY

1. Economists try to describe and explain how the whole economy works and advise policy makers.
2. Economists simplify their task by examining only part of the economy at a time and considering only the major influences on behaviour.
3. Economics is concerned with those aspects of human society to do with the creation and distribution of material wealth.
4. The economic problem is scarcity – nature does not provide all of the things society wants. We must decide what, how and for whom to produce.
5. To reduce scarcity human beings can apply their labour to manipulate nature, e.g. cultivating crops.
6. If human beings succeed in their efforts, they become better off in terms of material wealth. This steady improvement is called economic growth.
7. It is possible to increase production greatly by specialization and division of labour, where each person concentrates on just one small part of a productive process.

Exchange

The division of labour means that each group of workers will specialize in the production of one particular good (e.g. pins) and this in turn leads to the production of that good being concentrated in one place. In the case of the pin maker, for example, a very small factory could supply enough pins to serve a very large number of customers indeed. One pin maker in London could supply pins as far afield as Glasgow or Paris and still sell them cheaper than pins made locally by non-specialist producers.

In order to specialize to this extent, and hence to reap the benefits of the division of labour, the pin maker must be able to find and supply many buyers. To find enough buyers it may be necessary to seek customers a long way from the factory, which means that some pins will have to be transported over large distances. Eventually, of course, the distances become so great that the transport costs exceed the advantages of specialization and thereafter the division of labour can be taken no further. The corollary of this is that you would expect specialized production to occur where there were many customers within easy reach (i.e. near a city) or where the transport costs were small. At the dawn of manufacturing we would expect specialized production to occur near rivers or on coasts or on flat fertile plains where large populations could be sustained and where travelling was easy.

It would be a little too much to claim that the location of civilization was determined by mankind's answer to the scarcity problem, but it clearly had a bearing on it. Where specialization was possible the standard of living would rise and this would allow time for the pursuit of arts and time too for reflection and thought.

In sparsely populated regions where travelling is difficult most people would spend most of their time simply trying to stay alive. They would remain in this 'primitive' state until trade with a 'civilized' region became possible. Once trade developed they would have access to very cheap products and could in turn begin to specialize themselves.

With the continuing improvement in transportation more and more communities were able to exchange goods and so there was more and more specialization and higher and higher productivity.

Economic growth therefore depends in part on specialization, and specialization depends in turn on supplying more customers, and supplying more customers leads to ever-increasing costs of transporting the goods.

The cost of transport is not the only factor limiting our economic growth. Certainly the goods have to be delivered to the customers, but first it is necessary to find the customers (people who want what you have and who have what you want). In other words, the extent of the market will depend not only on transport costs but also on how difficult it is for producers and consumers to be brought together and how difficult it is for them to conduct their business. These are the problems of exchange and, like the problem of transport, they will limit the number of customers to any one supplier and hence limit the size of the supplier's market.

Markets

Markets address the difficulty of bringing would-be buyers and would-be sellers together. The sellers could just wander around the world calling out their wares and randomly looking for customers. This would clearly be a very time-consuming way of finding customers and would soon use up any time saved by specializing in production.

One way of improving on this would be to arrange a time and place where all those with something to exchange would meet. This arrangement is called a market. A market is a pooling of information on potential exchanges and greatly cuts down the time we spend searching for trading partners.

Originally a market was a time and place, and in many cases markets still are times and places. Street markets still exist and market towns hold cattle markets on particular days of the week. However, like everything else, markets have become more sophisticated over time. It is no longer necessary to form a market by everyone physically coming together at the same time and place. All that is necessary is a pooling of information on possible exchanges. This can be done in newspapers and trade papers, on telephones or Ceefax, or by any printed or electronic information system. All you need to make a market is a good number of potential traders pooling their offers.

Money

The creation of markets then is one very effective way of easing the problems of exchange. The second special social invention which helps with these problems is the introduction of **money.** In order to understand what money is and what it does to improve the efficiency of exchange it is necessary to look more closely at what is involved in exchange.

The market is a device for pooling information on potential exchanges. Traders are offering apples for pears, cloth for wine and so on. And markets where goods exchange directly for other goods constitute a **barter system**. One of the problems with barter systems is that if you have apples and want pears then you have to find someone who has pears and wants apples. Clearly it will often be difficult to find such traders since there may be traders with pears but who want cloth and there may be traders who want apples but who are offering wine. You need to find someone who needs what you have and who has what you want. This problem is compounded if you have something large to offer and yet require in exchange many different things. Say, for example, you have a cow and want some shoes, some cloth, some wine and some timber. It is extremely unlikely that you will ever find someone who wants a cow and is offering shoes, cloth, wine and timber. This perfect matching of swaps is called a **double coincidence of wants**, and its rarity is yet another barrier to easy exchange.

There is a very neat solution to this. Imagine if, instead of having to exchange the good they have for the good(s) they want, everyone agrees to first exchange their goods for gold. They then take the gold and exchange it for the goods they want. This means that if some traders brought bread to market and wanted some cloth and some wine they would first have to exchange their bread for gold and then they would exchange some of the gold for cloth and some of it for wine.

Instead or arranging only two exchanges (bread for cloth and bread for wine), as they would in a barter economy, the traders have now to exchange three times (bread for gold, gold for cloth and gold for wine). The fact that traders now have to do three deals rather than two is more than compensated for by avoiding the need for a double coincidence of wants.

In this system then every exchange goes through gold. To exchange the good you have for the goods you want you have to first exchange the good you have for gold. Then you can exchange the gold for the goods you want to consume. Because gold stands between the two sides of the exchange, it is said to be a **medium of exchange**.

The medium of exchange is called money and is used in order to reduce the information costs and search costs which arise in barter systems. In these markets goods are exchanged for money and the amount of money paid for a good is its market price or its exchange value or its market value.

SUMMARY

1. Specialization of production can only occur to the extent that it is possible to sell the increased output, i.e. to the extent of the market.
2. Transport costs and the ease with which buyers and sellers can meet are important determinants of the extent of the market. These are the problems of exchange.
3. Markets are where buyers and sellers can pool information. There is no longer a need for them to meet, as in street markets, since they may trade by electronic means, for example.
4. When traders swap their goods directly for the goods of others there is a barter system. This relies on two traders both wanting exactly what the other has to offer – a double coincidence of wants.
5. A market system is improved by the elimination of the need for barter. When every trader will accept one particular good in exchange for theirs, that good becomes a 'medium of exchange' or money.
6. In markets that use money, each good has a market price expressed in terms of that money. This is its exchange value or market value.

Economic systems

Although markets and money arose initially out of the need to make exchange as efficient as possible, they actually perform another vital role in our economy. Specialization not only gives rise to greater output, but it also leads to the fragmentation of production. In the manufacture of bread, for example, some producers will grow the wheat, others will grind the wheat into flour, and yet others will turn the flour into bread. These groups of workers are separate from each other and it is extremely unlikely that anyone is involved in every stage of the process. Despite being separate their tasks have to be co-ordinated. The farmers must grow the amount of wheat which the baker can eventually sell as bread. To grow more means a waste of effort and a waste of land. To grow less means that bakers are idle and we go short of bread. The question is: how is it that each of these producers manages to produce just the quantities required? On a larger scale the question is: how are all the millions of decisions by separate producers fitted together? To see the issue more clearly consider an economy which has no need of a co-ordinating mechanism.

Robinson Crusoe, all alone on his island, knows how much bread he will need and how much effort is involved in making the tools and in growing and processing the wheat. He can balance the costs of providing bread against his need for bread. He knows how much seed to plant and what size mill he will need to grind the wheat into flour. The co-ordination of all these decisions takes place inside Robinson's head.

But, with the division of labour, many of these decisions are taken by separate individuals. There must therefore be some communication system so that each decision taker knows what the others are planning to do. The grower of wheat needs to grow just the amount of wheat which the baker wants. The miller must mill that amount into flour and the baker must bake that amount into bread. The workers who make farm equipment and build the mill and the ovens must all supply the exact amount of equipment needed to process that amount of wheat. Finally, the amount of bread produced must meet the needs of the consumers.

Central planning

One form of co-ordination mechanism would be a series of committee meetings in which everyone involved in production and consumption had their say and voted on what was to be done. Under this system there would be little chance of ever reaching an agreement (or enforcing it) in any but the smallest, well-integrated communities. There are indeed few examples of any successful participatory economic decision systems.

An alternative would be to delegate the decisions to a small group of elected representatives. This is the system originally preferred by communist states. The Politburo would make the economic decisions – typically formulated as a five-year plan – and ask professional economists to put the plan into action. Production and price decisions would be made by these civil servants who would then send out instructions to the farms, factories and shops. The chain of command is via a structure of **central planning bureaux** and such systems are called **centrally planned** or **command economies.**

Whatever the political or social arguments in favour of central planning it has demonstrably failed to deliver the goods in eastern Europe. For example, the economic performance of the Federal Republic of Germany far outstripped that of the German Democratic Republic.

Market economies

Apart from those few economies which continue to use central planning bureaux, most economies seem to be self-regulating and in need of little or no help from governments. The apparent ability of quite complex economic systems to regulate themselves with only the minimum intervention by the state was one of the puzzles which Adam Smith addressed in his *Wealth of Nations* (1776). The solution he offered then laid the foundation for modern economics.

The self-regulation of an economy is a triumph of spontaneous social adaptation and development. It deserves to be better understood and more highly regarded – so too does Adam Smith's account of it.

The system which we have evolved and which was first analysed by Adam Smith is called the price mechanism and, as its name implies, grew out of the market system which was set up to solve the exchange problem.

In a money-using, exchange economy every good in the market has its market price. Say the price of the good goes up. How will the producer respond? Let us for the moment make the reasonable assumption that as the price of a good rises more of it will be produced and brought to market. That is to say, *supply increases with market price*. Conversely, of course, supply will be reduced when market price falls.

Let us go on to assume that when buyers come to market they will react to price changes by buying less when the price rises and by buying more when it falls. That is to say, *demand will decrease as market price rises*.

Given these responses to price changes we can show that the activities of each economic agent will be co-ordinated so that no one produces too much or too little and so that producers will supply more when people demand more and supply less when people demand less. The system is flexible enough to respond to changing patterns of demand and powerful enough to bring all the decisions into line with each other.

A market might seem a rather trivial invention, but it is a very simple solution to a very complex problem. Markets are absolutely essential to the efficient working of any modern economy. They are the key to the co-ordination problem and give rise to the expression 'a market economy'. Markets certainly provide information in exchanges, but they also facilitate *exchanges of information*. It is this exchange of information through which the millions of economic decisions are co-ordinated. The market, which was designed to provide efficient exchanges of goods, can also co-ordinate supply and demand decisions. All the producers need do is to respond to price changes in ways which increase their incomes. Thus the market provides the information and the incentives to ensure that producers respond to the needs of consumers. This ensures the sovereignty of the consumer.

When working properly the price mechanism so organizes our economy that it works exactly as if it were organized by a kind of composite Robinson Crusoe. On his own Robinson has no need of a price mechanism – he knows what the consumer wants and he knows what is being produced, and he can ensure that the necessary tasks are performed in the right order and in the right way. As more and more people join Robinson on his island it becomes possible to begin the division of labour. With only a few people on the island they can decide what to produce and who will do the jobs by group discussions. As the population grows these discussions will become impossibly complicated and absorb more and more of their time. Reaching agreements and ensuring that people really do the tasks allotted to them will become increasingly difficult. Ideally we want the group to behave as if it were simply a large Robinson Crusoe. Among the many claims being made for the free-market price mechanism is that it can co-ordinate the decisions and enforce the behaviour of very large populations so as to replicate the Robinson Crusoe world.

There are wide differences of opinion as to how well markets work. Those on the right of the political spectrum typically believe that markets work very well if left alone. These would be the supporters of the free market. Others – typically those on the left of the political spectrum – believe that markets either cannot work properly or are used by the rich and powerful to exploit the poor and the oppressed. These would try either to do away with the market altogether (centrally planned economies) or to moderate them by government intervention in the markets so as to get them to work more in the social interest. The latter would include the Greens, for example, who argue that markets are incapable of protecting the environment, and socialists, who argue that markets fail to protect the weak. Socialists advocate the social market, which is a free-market system moderated by state intervention to protect the weak. The Greens require legislation to override the market and penalize or tax those who pollute our air or water.

We have therefore a range of economic systems from free markets (*laissez-faire*) through social markets to central planning. A large part of economics deals with the operation of the market economy – its origins, its development, its successes and its shortcomings.

SUMMARY

1. Specialization leads to the fragmentation of production and to there being many different decision makers within each process. These decisions must be co-ordinated.
2. One way of co-ordinating decisions is to have a committee that issues directions. This system is known as central planning and is used in command economies.
3. Economies can be left to regulate themselves and they then rely on the working of markets.

Case Study 1.1 Right and left still vie to claim Adam Smith

A triumphalist air has crept into Edinburgh's celebrations of the 200th anniversary of the death of Adam Smith, the founder of classical economics, apostle of free markets and recently-adopted patron saint of Thatcherism.

But at a business conference which set the ball rolling this week, there was also a certain amount of confusion about exactly whose side Smith was on.

His master-work, *The Wealth of Nations*, was very much out of fashion during the years of the mixed economy. Over the last decade or so, he has been rehabilitated, alongside a very modern brand of right-wing economics. His name has been adopted by an economics institute credited with influencing some Thatcher policies, including poll tax. Now the collapse of the Soviet Union and the abandonment of central planning in Eastern Europe have put Smith back on his pedestal.

Opening a four-day business conference this week in Edinburgh called The Wealth of Nations 1990, Lord Sharpe, chairman of Cable & Wireless, summed up Smith's posthumous triumph. He said: 'The market economics and invisible hand of Adam Smith ... have demonstrated their dialectical superiority over totalitarian systems of both left and right, in winning both the cold war and the hot war of 1939–45.'

But was Smith quite the right-wing free marketeer he has been cracked up to be? Denis Healey, the former Labour Chancellor, who spoke stirringly at the conference on the decline of the Soviet Union, said: 'I think his views on economic matters were very much more balanced than some of his recent acolytes imagine.'

In reality, Adam Smith believed government should be involved in infrastructure and should ensure that the living standards of the poor rise with the rest, said Mr Healey. He would also have opposed the poll tax.

As if to demonstrate that he cannot be pigeon-holed, Smith has been claimed by both sides in the poll tax row. Defenders say the tax meets his conditions because it is reliable, convenient and cheap to collect (though that is now debatable). Enemies of the poll tax point to Smith's other condition, which is that a tax should be related to ability to pay.

Smith certainly believed that the economic system required a minimum of government interference, and that each free individual was 'led by an invisible hand to promote an end which was no part of his intention'.

But he was not quite the great defender of businessmen he had sometimes been made out to be: 'People of the same trade seldom meet together even for merriment and diversion, but the conversation ends in a conspiracy against the public, or in some contrivance to raise prices.' He would certainly sympathise with a tough competition policy.

But it was the former US Defence Secretary James Schlesinger, now senior adviser to Shearson Lehman, who best explained why Smith was cited by all sides. He said: 'No doctrinaire liberal he – in contrast to the caricature of him presented in this era. Indeed, he was not doctrinaire about anything – always being guided by solid practical sense.'

Smith was simultaneously a strong defender of empire and a pillar of the market system. Mr Schlesinger added: 'Sometimes we forget how radically altered and infinitely more complex the international economic system has become since the time of *The Wealth of Nations*. Consequently we may be inclined automatically to accept the simple precepts of free trade in circumstances that have become infinitely more complicated.'

For Mr Schlesinger, that meant the international economy today required 'continuous and careful management'. But free marketeers use Smith to justify not interfering at all.

Smith is also useful to blame. Tom Clausen, former president of the World Bank, attributed the $500bn (£295bn) savings and loans crisis to 'Adam Smith's self-interest which ran wild among both businessmen and politicians thanks to a badly managed process of deregulation'. And in Mr Clausen's view, 'the fact that Adam Smith fathered economics should not be held against him'.

1. In this book we shall present many theories of economics. Does this extract show that people sometimes misunderstand the theories, or that there is room for differing opinions?

Source: Peter Rodgers, *Independent*, 26 June 1990

Decisions are then co-ordinated by market prices which react to relative demand or supply.

4. Economies that allow market prices to co-ordinate decisions are known as market economies or free-enterprise economies.
5. Supporters of markets claim that they cause firms to produce what consumers require efficiently (consumer sovereignty). Opponents of markets say that markets cannot deal with important social problems.
6. A range of possible economic systems exist, from those with no co-ordination except markets, through to markets moderated by government intervention, to central planning.

Market failures

The study of markets lies at the very centre of economic analysis, but no one would want to argue that all economic decisions should be left to the market. Markets have their uses but they have their shortcomings too and cannot solve each and every economic problem. Economists are of course interested in how markets work. However, they are also interested in those problems which the markets cannot solve, why they cannot solve them and what alternative answers have been found. The technical term for these aspects of the economy is **market failure**.

One example of market failure is the case where market prices fail to send out the right signals to suppliers and consumers. Say there are two possible routes for a new motorway and we have to choose between them. One route runs through a spring of fresh water – our prime source of drinking water. The other route would destroy a diamond mine. If we were to follow the market, we would base our decision on market prices and destroy the 'least valuable' site.

Now water, although essential for life, commands a rather low market price, whereas diamonds, which have few practical uses, commands very high market prices. (Adam Smith called this the paradox of value.) Thus if we based our decision on market values we would choose to build over the spring. Since this would wipe out the population, it would seem rather a foolish thing to do.

Problems of this kind arise when market prices fail to reflect the value which we place on things. If asked whether we wanted a cup of water or a cup of diamonds, most of us would opt for the diamonds. This is what the market price reflects – we value diamonds more than water. But if asked to choose between giving up water altogether or giving up diamonds altogether, most of us would opt to give up diamonds. Thus for small amounts the market does reflect our valuations, but for very large changes the situation can be reversed.

Cost–benefit analysis

In **cost–benefit analysis** we try to look at those values which are not reflected by market prices. This is particularly necessary when looking at very large investment projects, but there are other circumstances when markets either cannot work or need a little help. This may arise because the market is simply unable to find a price (any price), and when there is no price the market signalling system breaks down entirely.

There are some goods, for example, which are made available to us all whether we pay for them directly or not. For most goods it is necessary to pay for what you consume – if you do not pay for a loaf then you do not eat bread. On the other hand, the provision of national defence – our army, navy and air force – is not paid for directly by individual citizens. The protection of our armed forces is provided for us all. It is simply not possible to protect some of our citizens and exclude others from protection. Goods such as defence as known as **public goods** and suffer from the problem of non-excludibility.

We might all want protection and be prepared to pay for it, but if each of us is protected whether we pay or not, it is difficult to see why anyone would actually pay for the protection. Those who do not want such protection are not allowed to opt out.

Decisions about how much protection to provide when everyone knows that they are going to be protected whether they pay or not are typically made by Parliament and we are forced to contribute to the cost by paying our taxes. The only way we can influence the amount spent on defence is through the ballot box not through the market. The government did not ask firms to bid for taking on the Gulf War. Parliament decided what should be done and how much should be spent.

Merit goods

Another reason for the government intervening in the market is in the provision of what are called **merit goods**. For example, the government seems to feel that if consumers had to bear the full costs of education and medical treatment then the nation would be undereducated and unfit. They clearly feel that education and health are 'good' things to be encouraged. The state therefore provides them at low or zero price to the user, the bulk of the costs being met out of taxation. Indeed, education is thought to be such a good thing that it is compulsory up to 16, so you have to have it whether you want it or not.

On the other hand, there are also **demerit goods**, such as tobacco and hard drugs. The consumption of tobacco is discouraged by placing heavy taxes on it; the consumption of hard drugs is illegal. This results in the market prices of these goods being much higher than would have been the case in free markets.

Quite what decisions should be left to the market and what should be organized directly by the state is a matter of continuing debate. There is no clear cut-off point up to which the market works and beyond which it fails completely. However, a general movement away from state control towards market forces is very apparent in the recent spate of privatizations. These remove things from public-sector control to the private sector.

Competition policy

Apart from displacing the market entirely or manipulating

market prices it is sometimes enough simply to give the market a helping hand. If we know the conditions under which markets work well, we can take steps to ensure that those conditions come about and are maintained.

It turns out, for instance, that markets must have many buyers and many suppliers if they are to work well. In other words, markets must be competitive. Misleading signals occur when one buyer or one seller becomes large enough to influence market price. Most free-market governments therefore try to watch over markets to see that no one is becoming too powerful.

In the United Kingdom the **Monopolies and Mergers Commission** has the power to ensure that no single supplier or demander can unduly influence the market. This means preventing them from growing too big or controlling them when they do grow too big.

In some cases it is simply not economically feasible to prevent the domination of a market by one or two very large firms. The state could take them over and run them like a centrally planned state would. This is what the **nationalized industries** are. Alternatively, the government could leave the firm in private hands but control the way it makes some decisions. This would mean overriding the firm's own commercial judgement of what was in the best interests of its shareholders in favour of a wider set of considerations involving the 'public interest'.

SUMMARY

1. Markets are unable to solve all economic problems and when this happens it is known as a market failure.
2. One type of market failure is when the market price fails to reflect values properly, e.g. diamonds have a very high price compared to water, but water is essential to life whereas diamonds are not. This is called a paradox of value.
3. Considerations not reflected in market prices can be allowed for by using cost–benefit analysis.
4. Some goods, once provided, benefit everybody even if they do not want them. This is a problem of non-excludibility and it applies to public goods, such as defence.
5. Some goods are considered important, but are provided by the market in insufficient quantities. These are known as merit goods and include education and health.
6. The provision of public and merit goods is decided by the government, which may also act to restrict the supply of bad or demerit goods, such as drugs.
7. For markets to work properly it is necessary that no buyer or seller dominates it. Thus governments are keen to regulate the degree of competition. In the UK this is done by the Monopolies and Mergers Commission.
8. Where important industries cannot be adequately regulated they are sometimes run by the state as nationalized industries.

Microeconomics and macroeconomics

So far we have considered the working and the problems of particular markets. This is called the study of **microeconomics** and is concerned with how the market system co-ordinates our individual decisions through the price mechanism, how it usually does this unaided, but also how the government intervenes in the market when it considers it necessary to do so.

There are other ways in which the government becomes involved in economics and these concern the economy taken as a whole. The analysis here is concerned not with the market for bread or the number of people working as bakers, but with the level of output and employment in the economy as a whole. Because this takes the large view it is called **macroeconomics**.

First, there is the question of controlling the money supply. We need to know how much medium of exchange is needed to carry out our exchanges efficiently, what happens if we have too little and what happens if we have too much. Providing and controlling our medium of exchange has long been a function of the state and is a legitimate economic task for government quite independently of the question of whether the market system is working well or not. Government decisions regarding the quantity of money in the economy are called **monetary policy**.

All markets use money and hence all markets are affected by the government's monetary policy. It is a matter which affects the whole economy and is therefore part of macroeconomics.

Secondly, and more problematically, is there a role for the state in determining the output of the economy as a whole? Should the state have a view on the level of national output and its rate of growth? There are basically two conflicting views and there is no clear way of deciding between them. One group of economists feels that the government should take responsibility for the level of national output, the level of unemployment, the rate of economic growth and so on. The other group argues that the state has neither the need nor the ability to seek to control the economy in this way. This is just one of many issues where economists disagree, but at the moment those who wish to limit the government's attempts at influencing output and employment are in the ascendancy.

International trade

Both in microeconomics and in macroeconomics the economist is looking inside one 'hive' – inside the national economy. But there are clearly many other 'hives' with which a country has dealings and these external relations form part of international trade.

Within one economy the price mechanism is judged in terms of its ability to replicate the Robinson Crusoe economy. But a slightly different problem arises when trade takes place between two economies. The citizens of one country may wish to pursue economic policies which bias the market in their favour at the expense of the foreign country. This slightly different policy angle and the fact that different countries use different media of exchange (different currencies) give international trade a distinctive role in economics.

More and more in recent years it has become apparent that the pursuit of domestic macroeconomic policies can have effects on other countries and, indeed, that they may depend for their success on the way other countries respond. This has led to work on the co-ordination of economic policy among different countries and the growth of trading groups such as the European Community (EC) and the Organization for Economic Co-operation and Development (OECD).

SUMMARY

1. The study of individual decisions of consumers or firms is known as the study of microeconomics.
2. The study of features of the economy as a whole, such as the level of unemployment, is known as the study of macroeconomics.
3. One area of macroeconomics is the conduct of monetary policy – the control of the money supply – and this is just one area where debate between economists continues to exist.
4. As different countries trade with one another, can affect one another and each has different currencies, the study of international trade is also an important area of economics.

Positive versus normative economics

As we have seen, different economists offer different descriptions of our economy and different explanations of how it works, and they prescribe different policies too. This raises a fundamental problem common to all sciences: if there is a diversity of accounts of one economy then at most only one can be the correct one – the 'truth'. If we can establish the truth then there is no diversity. If, on the other hand, we cannot establish the truth then anything goes and there is no demarcation between science and speculation, no way of saying what is science and what is science fiction, no way of saying whether a student's answer is correct or not.

These are matters which lie outside economics and constitute a branch of philosophy called the philosophy of science. The best-known philosophical response to this challenge of allowing anything to pass as the truth is called logical positivism. Logical positivists argue that 'truth' means correspondence to reality. Truth is an empirical matter and cannot be found by just thinking about things, by praying or by discussion. Thus theories should be judged according to how closely they correspond to the real world and it is part of a scientist's job to test theories and reject or modify them when they fail the tests.

Statements which cannot be subjected to empirical testing are not scientific (or even meaningful) and are consigned to the realms of metaphysics. This means that science can be demarcated from non-science by asking whether it can be subjected to empirical testing, If the answer is 'yes' then it is science, but if the answer is 'no' then it is not.

Statements which are admissable as science may not of course be correct. For example, we could have a number of conflicting theories about the effects of heat on metals. They are all testable and hence they all form part of science, but again at most only one of them can be true. So scientific theories can be true or false and many still await conclusive testing. When they are eventually tested these differences will disappear as false theories are discarded. Disagreements among economists can therefore arise because their various theories have yet to be convincingly tested.

The scientific part of economics comprises all those statements which can in principle be tested. These are called positive statements and together constitute **positive economics**. There may be disagreements within positive economics, but they are in principle resolvable and so will gradually disappear.

An example of a positive statement is 'Increasing the rate of income tax will decrease expenditure.' We may not all agree with this, but we could agree on a suitable test to prove which of us was correct.

Not all economic statements are positive statements. Economists are of course interested in what the economy *is* like, but they also make statements about what it *should be* like. These statements cannot be tested and so are not positive statements – they are called **normative statements**. Disagreements about normative statements cannot be resolved; the protagonists must simply agree to differ.

An example of a normative statement is 'We *should* increase the rate of income tax.' Our response to this statement depends in part on our understanding of the positive part of economics – what the effect will be. But it also depends on whether we think that effect is a 'good thing' or a 'bad thing', i.e. it will depend on the normative part of economics.

Whether we think it a good thing or a bad thing will depend on our personal preferences and hence is subjective. Whether the tax will or will not reduce expenditure is a matter of fact, independent of the observer, and is called objective.

Thus disagreements among economists arise from different views about what the economy is actually like and about what it should be like. Disagreements of the first kind are what drive the subject forward. When old explanations fail and new explanations are offered the subject progresses in an evolutionary way. Thus we should seek out these disagreements and test new theories. Disagreements of the second kind lead nowhere and generate more heat than light. When assessing economic statements then the first thing to do is to decide whether they are positive or normative. If normative, we simply note the statement and move on. If positive, we try to think of ways of testing it and so pushing the subject forward.

The distinctions drawn here rely heavily on testing. Testing is a major part of the physical sciences and involves conducting controlled experiments in laboratories. To find out what happens to metal when heated, a piece of metal is heated under controlled conditions so that there are no other influences on the metal other than the heat. Things are not so simple in economics. We have no laboratory and cannot experiment with the actual economy without risking permanent and painful damage. We can look back over our history and try to find examples of changes in which we are now interested. We certainly cannot control all other possible effects. If we examine what happened when we increased taxes before, we may find that something else changed at the same time. Deciding how much of the subsequent change can be ascribed to the tax change and how much to other causes presents economists with real problems. Economics is not an experimental discipline and hence takes a very long time to resolve even positive differences.

Being an economist means having a clear idea of the various theories currently under consideration, having some knowledge of the actual economy and forming a view about appropriate economic policy. This book aims to set you on your way.

SUMMARY

1. Economics is a science, and to proceed any economic theory must be able to be tested against observed facts – empirical testing.
2. If the truth of an economic theory can be tested then it belongs to the area of positive economics.
3. If the truth of an economic theory cannot be tested, i.e. it is opinion, then it belongs to the area of normative economics.
4. Economists are unable to conduct strictly controlled laboratory experiments and so disagreements often take a long time to resolve.

Exam Preparation and Practice

MULTIPLE-CHOICE QUESTIONS

1. The 'division of labour' refers to:
   A Splitting up jobs to reduce unemployment.
   B The formation of trade unions.
   C Labour specializing in certain tasks.
   D Those who perform more than one task for their employers.

2. Which of the following would be considered as a 'pure' public good?
   A Education.
   B Public health services.
   C Defence.
   D Water supply.

3. Which of the following is a normative statement?
   A The fight against inflation should be the most important economic policy objective of the UK government.
   B Entrepreneurs maximize profit when revenues exceed costs by the greatest extent.
   C Reducing income tax allows consumers greater disposable income.
   D The government could raise spending on the National Health Service to reduce waiting lists.

Answer key

Where there are three numbered alternatives

A	B	C	D	E
1, 2, 3 Correct	1, 2 Correct	2, 3 Correct	1 Correct	3 Correct

Where there are four numbered alternatives

A	B	C	D	E
1, 2 and 3 Correct	1 and 3 Correct	2 and 4 Correct	4 only Correct	1 and 4 Correct

4. Which of the following would concern an economist?
   1 The level of prices.
   2 The number of homeless.
   3 The amount of investment in the UK.
   4 The rehabilitation of released prisoners.

5. Which of the following are 'positive' statements?
   1 Alcohol can seriously damage your health.
   2 Increasing the tax on a good reduces the consumption of that good.
   3 The tax on alcohol should be raised to reduce consumption.

6. Which of the following are examples of merit goods?
   1 The provision of law and order.
   2 The provision of education.
   3 The provision of street lighting.

EXERCISES

1. The resources of Antarctica are said to be as bountiful as those of any other continent and are as yet untouched. If this is the case, why should anyone be worried about scarce resources?

2. A group of people live on a desert island and they each provide for themselves by hunting, fishing and gathering food. The people live under whatever naturally occurring shelter they can find. Under what circumstances and in what way would it pay these people to pool their efforts?

3. Money is unknown on the desert island described in exercise 2. After the initial success of specialization problems arise because of disputes over the distribution of the island's (higher) production. Could a system of money help? What might be suitable as money? Justify your answer.

2 Economic growth

In this chapter we will discuss:

1. How choices must be made about what to produce.
2. The characteristics of natural resources and the costs of economic growth.
3. The causes and sources of economic growth.

Introduction

We shall see in the microeconomic part of this book how capitalist economies allocate resources (land, labour and capital) to the production of various goods and services. We shall see in the macroeconomic section that it is possible for these scarce resources sometimes to be left idle. In this chapter we address a simpler question: what determines national output when all the resources are fully employed? What determines economic growth?

Production possibility and opportunity cost

The distinctions between microeconomics, macroeconomics and economic growth can perhaps best be illustrated by the **production possibility frontier** (PPF). By dividing national output into two subsets (say, manufactured goods and non-manufactured goods) we can draw a production possibility frontier which represents the maximum of these goods which can be produced in a fully employed economy. This is shown in Figure 2.1.

The slope of the PPF represents the rate at which an economy must give up one good to gain more of another. For example, in Figure 2.1 the economy is operating at point *A* and is producing *OC* manufactured goods and *OK* non-manufactured goods. If the people who live in the society represented by the PPF wish to obtain extra manufactured goods they must give up some non-manufactured goods. Suppose there is a desire for CC_1 more manufactured goods. This implies operating at point *B* on the PPF and producing only OK_1 non-manufactured goods. The PPF shows us what must be given up of one good to gain more of another and so it shows us the real cost of the extra goods. This is known as the **opportunity cost** of producing one good at the expense of another.

The concept of opportunity cost is a most important one in economics and arises because of scarcity. We have already stated that resources are scarce due to infinite wants and that, as shown by the PPF, only a certain amount can be produced in a given time with given resources. Thus all societies have to make a choice about what to produce.

Making a choice about what to produce means also deciding what not to produce. This is illustrated in Figure 2.1. By choosing point *B* the society chooses to produce OC_1 manufactured goods, but not to produce $K_{max} - K_1$ non-manufactured goods. Thus the opportunity of producing $K_{max} - K_1$ has been given up. We can then say that the opportunity cost of OC_1 manufactured goods is $K_{max} - K_1$ non-manufactured goods.

More formally, opportunity cost is defined as *the best alternative forgone* and it arises whenever there is a choice between two alternatives that involves not being able to follow one of them if the other is chosen. For example, a business may need a new delivery van and a new machine, but cannot afford both. If the delivery van is chosen then the opportunity cost of doing so is the new machine which is the best alternative forgone.

Microeconomics is concerned to explain this choice, i.e. to explain where on the production possibility frontier the economy will settle down. Will it choose many non-manufactured goods and few manufactured goods – (point *b*) or more manufactured goods (point *c* in Figure 2.2)? The position of the PPF or the possibility of being below it is not the concern of microeconomics.

Macroeconomics, on the other hand, focuses attention on

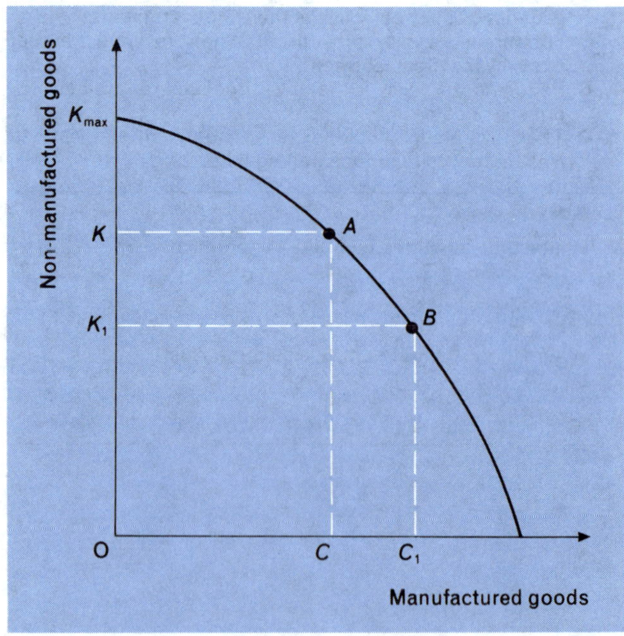

Figure 2.1 Production possibility frontier.

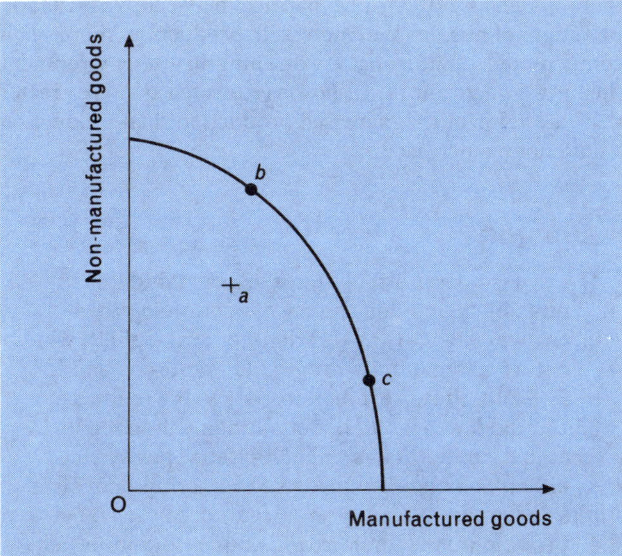

Figure 2.2 Choosing what to produce.

how to get on to the production possibility frontier. If the economy settles down at *a* then there will be some idle resources, and macroeconomics aims to explain why this may happen and how to get an economy back on to its frontier. Typically, macroeconomics is not concerned with the position of the PPF or with the choice of a point on the PPF. It is merely concerned to be somewhere on a given PPF.

Economic growth takes the third view: it is not concerned with the possibility of idle resources or with the choice of a point on the PPF. It is entirely concerned with questions relating to the position of the PPF. Clearly, as the PPF moves north-easterly we can have more of everything. That is economic growth.

In Chapter 1 it was shown that in order to produce output it is necessary to have land, labour and capital. These three inputs are combined in various ways to produce all the variety of goods available each year. It follows from this that in order to increase our productive potential it is necessary either to increase the amount of land, labour or capital available for productive use or to find better ways of using the current supplies of inputs. We therefore have four options: increasing land; increasing labour; increasing capital; and improving techniques. We shall take each of these in turn and then finally offer some assessment of their comparative contributions to the UK record of economic growth.

SUMMARY

1. A production possibility frontier (PPF) shows the maximum potential output of an economy when all resources are fully employed.
2. When the economy chooses to produce so much of one subset of goods, the PPF shows the maximum of the other subset that can be produced.
3. The slope of the PPF reflects how much of one good (or subset of goods) must be sacrificed to gain more of the other. The slope of the PPF therefore reflects the opportunity cost of production.
4. Opportunity cost arises because of scarcity. The opportunity cost of any choice is the loss of the best alternative forgone.
5. Microeconomics is concerned with the choice of where on the PPF an economy produces. Macroeconomics is concerned with how an economy reaches its PPF.
6. Economic growth is the expansion of productive potential, i.e. the movement of the PPF to the north-east.

Land

Recall that by land we mean all those natural resources which are supplied 'free' by nature. Land includes the soil, seeds, fish, fresh water, sunshine, coal, oil and so on. It is customary to divide land or natural resources into two types: renewable and non-renewable.

Renewable resources

Renewable resources are those such as fish or wheat. Each year there is a fresh crop of them and we can take and consume a certain percentage of the crop. The remaining (unconsumed) part will give rise to next year's harvest. Thus there are some things provided by nature which we can continue to consume for ever provided we leave enough to produce next year's crop.

Some forms of economic growth bear quite heavily on renewable resources and are thought by some to be reaching their limit. Over-fishing, for example, has led to the rapid decline of some species of fish and the whale. Since no one owns the seas or the fish, it is in no one's interest to hold back and allow the stocks to recuperate. International agreements and laws here replace the price mechanism as a regulator of use. Such regulations, or else the possibility of exhausting the resource altogether, limit the growth processes which rely on renewable resources.

Non-renewable resources

The other kind of land consists of **non-renewable resources**. Nature provides us with iron ore, coal, oil, etc. in finite amounts. There is just so much of each available on this planet and no matter how slowly we use them, the resources will inevitably run out eventually. Any growth process which therefore relies on non-renewable resources must eventually cease.

The problem of non-renewable resources is a major concern to economists and industrialists alike. If there is indeed only so much oil or coal to go around, how should it be allocated so as to be fair to future generations? And what happens when we finally run out of some essential material? Mineral oil, for example, is used as a source not only of fuels but also of herbicides, insecticides, fungicides and fertilizers. Modern methods of food production rely heavily on such aids, and if they were suddenly to become unavailable then food production would fall dramatically. Current populations, let alone those projected for the future, simply could not be sustained and growth would be negative rather than positive. This might then have serious consequences in terms of war and famine.

Adjustment problems

Some economists argue that this shortage of necessary inputs will occur suddenly. One day the oil wells will be pumping and the next they will run dry. There will be very little time to adjust and hence the adjustment will be extremely painful.

Others argue that as the oil runs out it will become progressively more expensive and hence will induce some economy of use, a gradual reduction in food supply and a consequent gradual decline in population. This is the way the price mechanism should operate in allocating scarce resources. They further argue that, as one resource becomes expensive, substitutes will be found for it. Thus shale oil would increasingly replace oil-well oil and nuclear fuels would replace petrol. This gradual process of adjustment is orchestrated by the price mechanisms, which will always be able to find some substitute for the scarce resource. The oil price shock of 1974 did indeed result in the more economical use of oil: car engines became smaller and more efficient, and buildings were fitted with heat insulation to conserve heating fuels.

Whichever adjustment eventually takes place, the fact remains that any economic growth which relies upon the easy exploitation of land will be limited by the need to conserve renewable resources and to find more and more substitutes for non-renewable resources.

Nature as a 'sink'

There is one other way in which land might be said to contribute to economic growth. Not only does nature provide us with certain commodities, but it also acts as a waste disposal unit. Factories and power stations discharge smoke and other materials into our skies and waters and, provided they are in small enough quantities, nature seems capable of absorbing them with no apparent ill effects.

However, as economic activity increases, more and more waste is produced and can begin to destroy the environment. Disposal of waste is therefore no longer a service provided free by nature. The costs fall on those whose environment is damaged. These costs of economic growth do not as yet appear in the balance sheets of the polluting companies and hence there is no economic incentive for them to moderate their emissions of waste material. That is not to say that all companies disregard their environmental responsibilities, only that there is no economic incentive for them to minimize emissions.

These attendant consequences of economic growth lead some economists to argue that we should aim at zero or even negative growth, rather than continue competing with other countries to get higher and higher growth rates. Other economists suggest that the preferred way forward is to impose some economic costs on the polluters so as to cause them to choose the right balance between growth and pollution. Thus, if the increased production more than compensated for the slight worsening in the environment then it would go ahead. If, however, the 'costs' were greater than the value of the increased production then production would not be increased.

SUMMARY

1. Land is an important factor in assessing the possibility and desirability of economic growth.
2. Growth will inevitably be limited by the ability of nature to sustain its renewable resources and to find substitutes for its non-renewable resources.
3. Should these limits occur suddenly then the adjustment process could be fraught with difficulties and may give rise to international strife and famine.
4. In deciding whether growth is unambiguously a 'good' thing it is necessary to consider the effects on the environment and the costs which are borne by those other than the producer.

Labour

The second input into production is labour, which may be defined as human effort and intelligence. The amount of labour which our economy has at its disposal will depend partly on population size, partly on what proportion of the population is normally regarded as the workforce, partly on the number of hours each worker supplies and finally upon the effort being put into the work.

Effort

No doubt by all working longer and harder we could push up our national output, but unless we go on increasing our work effort for ever it is unlikely to offer more than a once and for all increase in output. It is not therefore a source of economic growth in the sense of a sustained expansion in output. Furthermore, it is not clear that we would necessarily *want* to obtain more output in this way. One reason which is occasionally offered to explain the United Kingdom's relatively poor economic performance is that UK workers prefer more relaxed working conditions and are unwilling to change to conditions of harder work and higher pay.

However, it might still be possible to increase output by increasing the size of the working population. This might be done either by increasing the participation rate of the current population or by increasing the population itself.

Participation rates

The working population is usually defined as those in good health between school-leaving age (16) and retirement (60 for women and 65 for men). Married women traditionally often did not enter the job market but remained at home in the non-market sector. However, the participation rate of

Table 2.1 Working population and employment, 1988

Country	Civilian working population	
	000s	As % of total population
Belgium	4,132	41.8
Denmark	2,886	56.3
W. Germany[1]	26,914	47.5
Greece[2]	3,811	38.5
Spain	14,633	37.5
France	23,587	42.2
Ireland	1,297	36.7
Italy	23,718	41.3
Luxemburg	160.5	42.8
Holland	6,549	44.4
Portugal	4,604	44.8
United Kingdom	28,236	49.5
Turkey[3]	18,804	35.6
Norway	2,183	51.8
Sweden	4,471	53.0
Switzerland	3,297	49.8
Austria	3,430	45.2
Finland	2,536	51.3
USSR	131,300	46.4
USA	121,669	50.1
Canada	13,275	51.5
Japan	61,660	50.3

Notes:
1. Data for united Germany not available.
2. 1984.
3. 1987.
Source: Eurostat.

married women in the UK labour market has increased substantially over the years and hence the 'working population' has been growing. Table 2.1 shows the estimated size of the UK workforce as a proportion of the total population, and incidentally shows that the participation rate is higher in the UK than in most European countries.

One source of economic growth is therefore to encourage a switch out of non-market work (e.g. housework) into market work. It must be remembered that this expansion in 'recorded' economic activity will be somewhat moderated by a decline in 'unrecorded' economic activity. Nevertheless it will help to explain changes in recorded national income.

Population size

There remains the possibility of increasing the population size. This is problematic in two ways. First, every additional pair of hands brings an additional mouth. Thus, although output would increase, so would the number of consumers – and hence no one consumer may be any better off. A 10 per cent increase in population which gave a 10 per cent increase in output would clearly leave each individual's consumption unchanged. If the 10 per cent increase in population resulted in only 5 per cent growth in output, then each individual would become worse off. The principal argument for pursuing economic growth is that it makes us all better off without making anyone else worse off. For this to be true it must lead to increased output per capita, i.e. per member of the whole population. It is not clear that increasing the population will actually increase per capita income. Figure 2.3 shows output per head for some western economies and for Japan.

The second problem arises from the possible methods of increasing population. The obvious way is to encourage an increase in the birth rate. This will certainly have an effect on the population size, but it will have no positive effect on 'working population' until 16 years have elapsed. During those 16 years the increased population is an increase in mouths with no increase in hands. Furthermore, the time devoted to child carrying and child rearing may cause some working women to withdraw from the labour force. Thus increasing the population size by way of increasing the birth rate will initially reduce output and income per head. In the longer run the working population will increase, but unless the increase in output is greater than the increase in working population then per capita income will fall.

An alternative way of increasing population is by immigration. This enables new entrants into the population to be immediately set to work. This is the case, for example, if able-bodied persons between the ages of 16 and 65 are admitted. They will have been nurtured for their first 16 years by their original community and then, on reaching working age, will begin contributing to their host country. A similar result will occur if immigrant labour is replaced by 'guest workers' as has happened in (West) Germany. Such workers do not become citizens but merely work in the host country and retain their original nationality. The guest worker system means that when an economy enters a depression it can simply reduce the number of guest workers and preserve the employment opportunities for its own.

SUMMARY

1. Increasing the labour input into production will provide a source of economic growth but may not increase per capita income.
2. This may be done by increasing the participation rate so that a higher proportion of the population is in the workforce, or by increasing the size of the population.
3. Increasing the population by birth involves a long wait before the workforce increases. One solution is to import labour either as new citizens or as 'guest workers'.

Capital

Unlike labour and land, capital is a 'produced' means of production. It is that amount of past production which is being used to help with current production. Steel mills, lathes and office blocks have all been produced with past labour and land, and help the current production of steel, machined parts and services. The more steel mills and

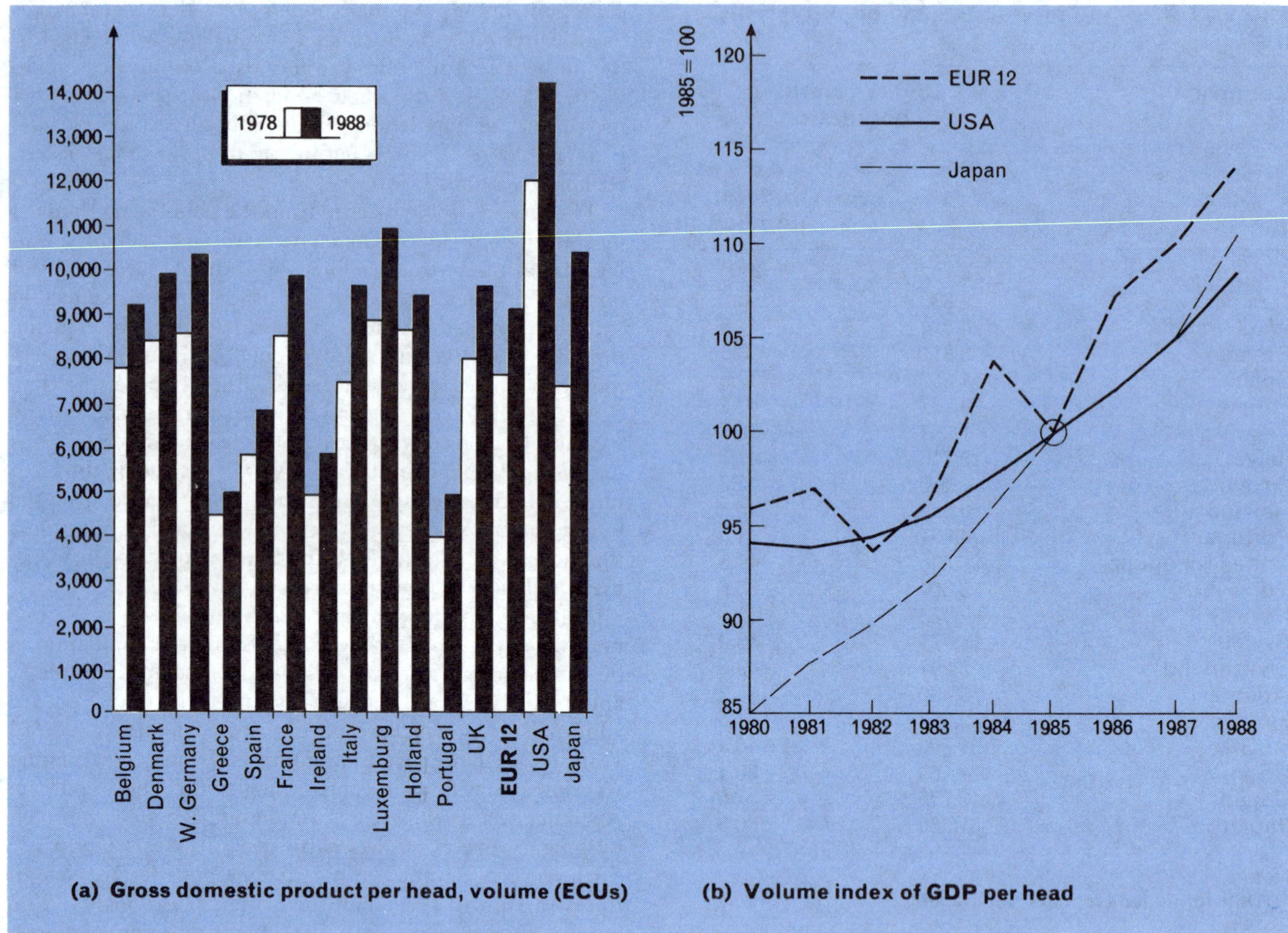

Figure 2.3 Output per head for western economies, 1979–88.

lathes we have, the more we are capable of producing. Thus increasing our 'capital stock' increases capacity output. Some economic growth can therefore be explained in terms of increased capital stock.

Changes in capital stock occur in two ways. First, some of the existing capital wears out or becomes unprofitable to use. This is called **depreciation** (wearing out) and obsolescence (becoming uneconomical). Second, every year some output is devoted to production (the rest is consumed). That part of current output which is devoted to production is called **investment**.

Investment

If the amount of investment exactly equals the amount of depreciation then capital stock will remain constant. If investment is less than depreciation then capital stock will decrease. Finally, if investment is greater than depreciation then capital stock will increase and will contribute to growth. Investment before allowing for depreciation is called gross investment; investment after allowing for depreciation is called net investment.

Increases in capital therefore depend upon net investment. Therein lies the problem of increasing economic growth by way of increasing investment. In order to increase investment it is necessary to consume less of our current output. The less we consume now, the faster capital will grow and hence the more we can produce and consume later. Investment decisions are therefore decisions about the distribution of consumption over time. This can be illustrated with the aid of Figure 2.4.

In the figure there are three possible time paths for consumption. If current output is Y_0 and if current consumption is equal to output then there is no net investment and hence capital stock and output remain constant. Path *a* shows this option.

If, however, current consumption is greater than output (say C_1) then we are not even replacing worn-out capital and hence capital stock and output decline. This is sometimes known as 'eating the seed corn'. It is clear from this that we can consume more now (C_1 as opposed to Y_0) but will eventually pay for this by having less to consume in future. Eventually such an economy will be extinguished altogether (see path *b* in Figure 2.4).

The third alternative is to consume less than is currently produced (say C_2). In this case investment is greater than depreciation, hence capital stock and output grow. This is shown by path *c*. Growth has come about because we chose to consume less now and more later.

The question is: how much are we prepared to give up

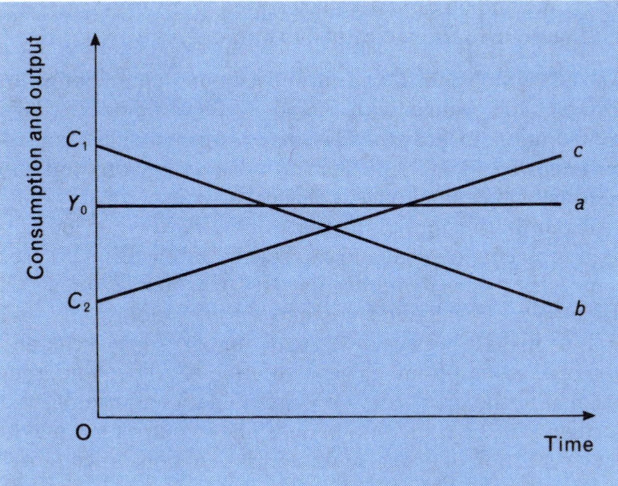

Figure 2.4 Current and future consumption.

now in order to benefit those who will be consuming in future? Growth can take place only at the expense of current consumption.

Take-off growth

For very rich countries this is often a matter of choosing between high and low growth since forgoing current consumption involves no real hardship. But for poor countries the problem is something of a catch-22 situation. Current output is so low that it can barely meet the basic subsistence requirements of the population. Growth is clearly one way of alleviating this desperate situation, but in order to get some growth it is necessary to cut consumption now. This may involve some proportion of the population falling below even the subsistence level. Some part of one generation is therefore being sacrificed in order to improve the lives of future generations. Once growth is achieved the choice is much less stark – it is possible to have both investment and sufficient current consumption.

Growth 'takes off' when output is more than is necessary to satisfy subsistence living standards. It is somewhat ironic that the poor who desperately need growth cannot afford it, whereas the rich who do not really need growth can. The rich therefore get richer and the poor get poorer.

One solution is for the poor countries to borrow or receive investment aid from a richer country. This aid is a form of pump priming, since it enables 'take-off' to be achieved so that a poor country's growth rate becomes self-sustaining. Aid is then no longer necessary.

SUMMARY

1. Capital contributes to output and increasing capital stock will lead to economic growth.
2. Capital stock comes from current output, so any increase can be achieved only by consuming less than is currently available.
3. For very poor countries this imposes very severe costs on growth. It may even result in the death of a proportion of the population.
4. This stark choice can be alleviated through aid, which can provide investment goods without a decrease in the already low consumption levels of the country receiving aid. Once begun growth is self-sustaining, but the problem is to reach this 'take-off' level of output.

Technological progress

We have seen that growth can be achieved by increasing either of the 'original' factors of production (land and labour) or by increasing the 'produced' factor of production (capital). These three inputs are combined in some way to produce output. The various ways of combining the three inputs are summarized by a **production function**, which relates the level of each input to the resulting level of output.

As we discover more and more about the physical world, we find new and better ways of combining land, labour and capital in the production of goods. We also discover new things to make. These changes in the production function are called **technological progress**. And technological progress may either be process oriented (how to make things with fewer inputs) or product oriented (how to make new products). Spinning machines, Bessemer converters and assembly line production are examples of new ways of making the existing products of thread, steel and motor cars. Colour TV sets, personal computers and nylon are new products, many of which replace existing products or enable us to do things we could not do before.

Technological progress is largely concerned with using existing resources more and more efficiently. Growth from this source may economize on land and postpone or avoid altogether the limits to growth imposed by finite resources. It is this last source of growth then which seems to offer the best way forward.

Research and development

Some new processes and some new products are stumbled upon more or less by accident, e.g. the steam engine and penicillin. But considerable effort is directed at discovering new ideas. This form of activity is called **research and development (R & D)** and is conducted by governments, large firms and universities. Some of our current resources are therefore devoted to R & D rather than to producing current goods for immediate consumption.

In this way R & D is rather like capital – it involves some current sacrifice. Unlike capital, however, the benefits of R & D do not always accrue to those who made the initial sacrifice. Once a new process or product is discovered or invented anyone can copy it – it virtually becomes public property. This is moderated to some extent by the granting of patent rights, which enable the discoverer or inventor to have exclusive use of the product or process for a fixed term of years. Such protection is difficult to enforce, however, and can often be quite legally circumvented.

SUMMARY

1. A production function summarizes the relationship between inputs and a given level of output.
2. Technical progress is concerned either with finding better ways of combining inputs, which may lead to producing existing goods with fewer inputs, or with producing new products.
3. The deliberate process to discover new and to improve existing products is known as research and development (R & D).

Contributions to economic growth

We have seen that there are four possible sources of economic growth: land, labour, capital and technological progress. The most obvious question to ask is: which of these factors has contributed most to growth over the past 20 years? Has growth been due primarily to an enlarged workforce, to greater capital stocks or to increased know-how?

Most of the work on this question has not been directed towards land as a contributory factor in growth. Attention has been focused almost exclusively on labour, capital and technological progress. It is not entirely clear why this should be so, but it means that in what follows we too will omit land from our considerations.

The first difficulty one faces in trying to ascribe growth to labour, capital or technological progress is that, whereas labour and capital are in principle measurable, technological progress is not. Labour can be measured in man-hours and capital can be measured in machine-hours, but in what units, on what scale, can technological progress be measured?

Fortunately, there is a way around this problem. If we can measure the contribution which labour makes to growth and which capital makes to growth, then any growth left over (i.e. unexplained by labour or capital) must be due to technological progress. We can therefore infer the contribution of technological progress from the residual. The first step then is to establish the contributions of labour and capital to growth.

The contribution of labour comes about in two stages. First, of course, is the expansion of the labour force. There is no doubt that a 10 per cent increase in man-hours will induce some increase in output. But by how much will output increase? This leads to the second stage. If labour makes a very small contribution to output, as compared, say, with the contribution made by capital, then quite large percentage changes in man-hours will result in rather small increases in output. If, on the other hand, labour makes a very large contribution to output then even small percentage increases in man-hours will have an appreciable influence on output. We therefore need to know:

1. By how much labour was increased.
2. The contribution of labour to output.
3. By how much capital was increased.
4. The contribution of capital to output.

Armed with 1 and 2 we can find labour's contribution to growth, and armed with 3 and 4 we can find capital's contribution to growth. Having established these contributions we can subtract them from actual growth and any residual will be due to technological progress.

1 and 3 are simply a matter of record. We can look up figures on employment and capital stock in the Blue Book or some other official publication (see Chapter 12 for a full discussion of available statistics on the economy). As to 2 and 4 it has been shown that, under some generally accepted assumptions, the contribution of labour to output is equal to the proportion of wages to national income, and further that the contribution of capital to output is equal to the proportion of profits and interest to national income.

Fortunately, UK national accounts also contain data on wages, profits, interest and national income. From these we know that labour receives about 75 per cent of national income (on average) and capital receives about 25 per cent. This means that labour contributes three times as much to national income as does capital. Thus a 10 per cent increase in man-hours would increase output by 7.5 per cent whereas a 10 per cent increase in capital would increase output by only 2.5 per cent.

Table 2.2 summarizes data for some western economies for the years 1950–62. The first thing to notice about this table is that, for each of the countries listed, the 'residual' or technological progress contribution to economic growth was far greater than that due to either labour or capital and, except for the United States, was greater even than the sum of the contributions of labour and capital.

The second thing to notice is the wide spread of growth rates from 7.26 per cent per annum for West Germany to 2.29 per cent for the UK. Here we can see the role played by technological progress. The German residual is 4.4 per cent per annum whereas the UK residual is only 1.18 per cent per annum. Thus the residual is the most important element in the growth of each country and a major part of the reason for differing growth rates.

It is not easy to see why the residual should differ so markedly among countries since know-how is generally available. German methods and German inventions are known by other countries and are largely imitable. Why then is technological progress not the same everywhere?

Table 2.2 Western economies compared, 1950–62 (% p.a.)

	Output growth	Due to labour	Due to capital	Residual
W. Germany	7.26	1.37	1.41	4.48
Italy	5.96	0.96	0.70	4.30
France	4.92	0.45	0.79	3.68
Netherlands	4.73	0.87	1.04	2.82
Denmark	3.51	0.59	0.96	1.96
Norway	3.45	0.15	0.89	2.41
United States	3.32	1.12	0.83	1.37
Belgium	3.20	0.76	0.41	2.03
United Kingdom	2.29	0.60	0.51	1.18

Note: All figures are annual averages.

The catch-up hypothesis

One explanation which has been offered is the so-called catch-up hypothesis. The idea is that one country in particular is responsible for most innovative activity – it is the 'technological leader'. This role was once ascribed to the UK and it then passed to the USA. It may now be passing on yet again to Japan. For the period covered by the data in Table 2.2 the USA was undoubtedly the leader and had already installed the latest techniques. Other countries, which were still using old-fashioned techniques, could therefore grow very quickly by switching from old to new techniques.

Some support for this hypothesis has come from studies which show that growth rates were correlated with the backwardness of the country concerned. West Germany, Italy and France, for example, were still largely agricultural economies, whereas the UK and the USA were comparatively heavily industrialized. Thus whereas West Germany, Italy and France had a lot of catching up to do, the UK did not.

The key to differing growth rates, according to the catch-up hypothesis, is the gradual diffusion of know-how from the leader to the followers. As an additional explanation it is sometimes claimed that the catch-up was made easier for West Germany by the destruction of its industries in the Second World War. The retooling was done with up-to-date capital and up-to-date techniques.

The embodiment hypothesis

This brings us to the second explanation of why growth rates differ. The idea behind the embodiment hypothesis is that technological progress is not truly separate from capital. Technological progress is available to everyone but often necessitates some rebuilding of capital, i.e. the improved technique is 'embodied' in capital.

The contribution of capital to growth therefore falls into two parts. First, more capital means more output can be produced simply because we have more machines. But secondly, more capital means more output because the new machines are better than the old. They are said to embody best-practice techniques.

This second contribution of capital is therefore ascribed to technological progress, but it is not available unless new investment occurs. Technological progress which can be had without buying new machines is called 'disembodied' and may accrue, for example, by rearranging existing machines so as to provide a more efficient flow of work through a factory.

Thus technological progress seems to provide the greater part of economic growth either via its embodied form (in partnership with capital) or in its disembodied form. It is something over which governments can exercise very little influence except by encouraging research and development.

So far we have spoken of growth as if we produced a homogeneous bundle of goods and simply produced more and more of them. In the long run, however, certain trends are discernible. In its earlier stages of economic development a country will expand its agriculture and be almost exclusively an agrarian economy. After a point the manufacturing sector begins to grow, often at the expense of agriculture, and so growth is dominated by the switch from agriculture to manufacturing. This continues until the third or tertiary stage of development is reached. This occurs when the service sector begins to outstrip the manufacturing sector. Banking, insurance, medicine, etc. become the growth points and manufacturing becomes relatively less important; it may decline in absolute as well as relative terms.

Growth therefore often implies structural change. New kinds of work are replacing old, and new regions expand at the expense of older industrial regions. Growth can therefore be a painful process for some and as the pace of change accelerates the adjustment costs increase. What is needed then is some way of moderating the pace of change so as to avoid overburdening some sectors but at the same time gaining at least some measure of progress and change.

In most countries economic growth is not left to the market mechanism. Population policies are widespread in the under-developed world, and in developed countries education of the workforce and the funding of research and development (R & D) are usually carried out by governments rather than entrepreneurs. The provision of new investment is probably the most market-oriented aspect of economic growth, but even here the government offers investment grants and itself provides the roads, bridges and so on which make up most of the investment in infrastructure.

This action on the part of national governments to influence economic growth is reinforced on the international level by the need for international agreements on the use of exhaustible natural resources and on the international effects of pollution.

SUMMARY

1. As land is fixed, the sources of economic growth are increases in the quantity of labour and capital, and technical progress.
2. The contributions of labour and capital can be measured. It is assumed that economic growth in excess of that due to increases in labour or capital is due to technical progress.
3. The contribution of labour to output can be measured by the proportion of wages to national income. The contribution of capital is equal to the proportion of profits and interest to national income.
4. A possible explanation for differing growth rates between countries is that there is not an equal diffusion of 'know-how'. Some countries therefore apply modern techniques later than others, and so appear to be growing very fast.
5. Technical progress can be acquired without new machinery, that is 'disembodied' from capital. Much technical progress is 'embodied' in machines, and so to acquire it requires investment.
6. Growth usually implies change, say from an agrarian to an industrial society. Governments often try to moderate or direct growth to avoid the worst effects of such adjustments.

Exam Preparation and Practice

MULTIPLE-CHOICE QUESTIONS

1.

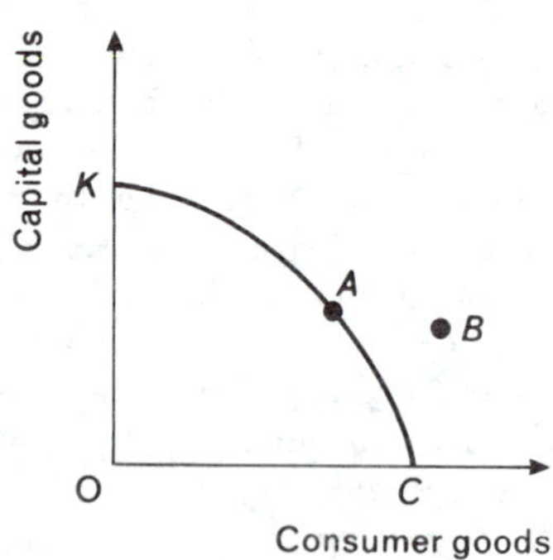

The production possibility frontier, *KC*, for an economy producing capital and consumer goods is shown in the diagram above. The economy is presently producing at point *A* and could move to point *B* by:

A Increasing the level of consumers' demand.
B Reallocating resources between firms.
C Improving the existing level of technology.
D Raising the level of government subsidies.

2.

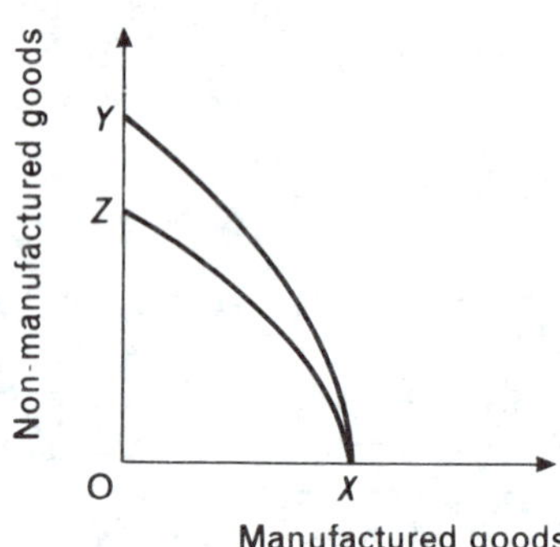

The diagram shows two production possibility frontiers (PPFs) for an economy. The movement of the PPF from *XY* to *XZ* may be due to:

A A reduction in unemployment.
B The intervention of government planners.
C A general increase in the productivity of labour.
D A fall in the productivity of labour in the non-manufactured goods sector.

3. A country has 100 units of capital and 200 units of labour which it can devote to the production of either capital or consumer goods. If the capital and labour requirements are as shown below, which of the diagrams represents the country's production possibility frontier?

	Capital units	Labour units
Capital goods	2	4
Consumer goods	2	2

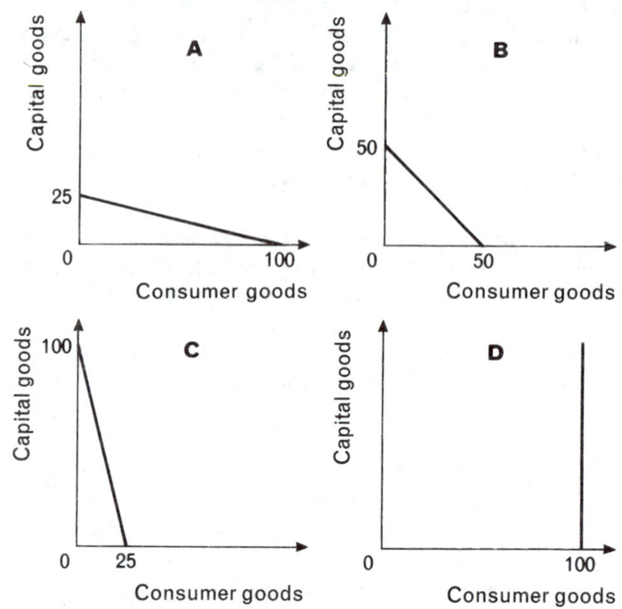

4. When people say 'There is no such thing as a free lunch', they are recognizing:
A The concept of opportunity cost.
B The price of restaurants today.
C The existence of money.
D The concept of land.

5. The working population can best be defined as:
A Those who are presently employed.
B All those over school age.
C All men over school age, but below 65.
D All those over school age, below retiring age and able to work.

Answer key

Where there are three numbered alternatives

A	B	C	D	E
1, 2, 3 Correct	1, 2 Correct	2, 3 Correct	1 Correct	3 Correct

Where there are four numbered alternatives

A	B	C	D	E
1, 2 and 3 Correct	1 and 3 Correct	2 and 4 Correct	4 only Correct	1 and 4 Correct

6. All economic problems involve the concept of choice because:
1 Resources have alternative uses.
2 Wants of consumers are finite.
3 Resources are limited in supply.
4 Economists have different views about how economies should be organized.

7. The diagram shows the production possibility frontier for an economy. If the economy moves from point *A* to point *B*:
1 More workers are employed.
2 There has been economic growth.

3 The efficiency of resource allocation has improved.
4 The opportunity cost of 1 unit of manufactured goods is 2 units of non-manufactured goods.

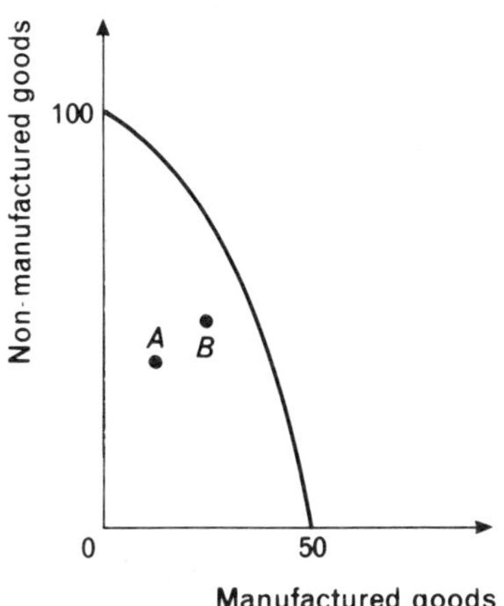

8. Which of the following would influence the rate of economic growth?
1 The birth rate.
2 Government support for research and development.
3 The importing of modern capital equipment.

EXERCISE

1. Draw a production possibility frontier for the economy of Little Trivilvania, which has 1,000 workers and 200 machines. The machines can produce capital goods or consumer goods and all of the workers can operate the machines in either sector. Each machine requires the attention of 5 workers and can produce 1 unit of capital goods (a new machine) or 3 units of consumer goods each year.

(a) From the diagram show how many new machines would be made if the people of Little Trivilvania decided to consume 525 units of consumer goods.

(b) If the people decided that they would like to consume another 30 units of consumer goods, what would the opportunity cost of this consumption be in terms of capital goods?

(c) Suppose no machines wore out during the year and the economy continued to produce 525 units of consumer goods. What would be the effect on the PPF of Little Trivilvania for the following year?

DATA-RESPONSE QUESTION

1. Suppose that ten individuals are shipwrecked on an isolated tropical island, on which there are two natural sources of food, coconuts and fish. Suppose that with their initial capital equipment each individual can collect 2 coconuts or catch 1 fish per hour.

(a) Assuming that initially it is agreed that each individual should work for 10 hours per day, illustrate the daily production possibility curve for coconuts and fish for this economy. *(5 marks)*

(b) Why is the form of the production possibility curve different from the usual concave curve typically portrayed in the economics textbooks? *(5 marks)*

(c) Suppose that, after some time, a new tree climbing technique is discovered which makes it possible for an individual to collect 4 coconuts per hour. How would this discovery shift the production possibility curve? *(5 marks)*

(d) Suppose that, following the introduction of the new climbing technique, the economy is observed to be producing 50 fish and 150 coconuts. Does this observation imply that the economy is producing at an inefficient point? *(5 marks)*

(e) Suppose that, alternatively, it was assumed that out of the ten workers, five could collect coconuts but were incapable of catching fish, while the other five could catch fish but were incapable of collecting coconuts. Assuming, again, that the five workers in each activity were equally productive, what would the production possibility curve look like in this case, and what are the implications for the costs of production of coconuts in terms of fish? *(5 marks)*

(WJEC)

PART II

MICROECONOMICS

3 A closer look at production

In this chapter we will discuss:

1. How land, labour and capital are brought together to allow production to take place.
2. How production may be organized in the most cost-effective manner.
3. How costs and productivity change with the level of output.

Introduction

It is possible to have a reasonable standard of living without producing anything, but most of us require more than just what nature provides. In order to produce anything it is necessary to bring together all of the factors of production and this is the job of the entrepreneur, a businessman or woman. Entrepreneurs may earn a reward for this task, profit, but they may make a loss. It is therefore vital that they find the best way to organize production.

The factors of production

Land

We have already seen in Part I that in an ideal world there would be no need for us to become involved in the process of production. We would eat fish from the sea, fruit from the trees and roots from the ground. We would be warmed by sunshine and our thirst would be slaked by the fresh water which literally rained down from above. Nature itself would therefore provide us with many goods and services. All such goods and services which are supplied by nature are called **land**.

This use of the word 'land' must be carefully distinguished from the way it is normally used. Normally the word 'land' simply means the ground – the earth. Economists, however, use the word 'land' to mean all natural endowments – all those goods and services which we get from nature. It includes what is normally called land but much more besides. It includes ores, coal, oil, fish, fowl, grains, fruit, sunlight, fresh air and fresh water.

In an ideal world this bounty of mother nature would provide all our needs and in some parts of the world this is very nearly the case. The South Seas, for example, are usually thought of as a close approximation to this ideal world. The climate is temperate, the sea contains plenty of fish and the vegetation is abundant. Islanders can therefore have a reasonable standard of living without doing much work. But equally there are parts of the world (the deserts and the poles) where nature is not quite so generous and, if we were to rely only on what nature provided, then life would be dire indeed.

On the whole we do not live in an ideal world and are not content with the natural status of things – we are not content to 'live off the land'. We want more than nature provides and we have found ways of getting more. We discovered very early in our history that we could manipulate nature. We learned how to select seeds and suppress weeds, how to till the soil and apply fertilizers, how to make metals, store grain and transport goods from one part of the world to another. In other words, we learned that we need not rely entirely on what nature provides. We could be *producers* as well as *consumers*.

Labour

We now need to look more closely at what is involved in production. We already know that people and land together can produce more than land alone, but there is more to it than that.

As far as our labour is concerned, it contributes to production in two ways. First, we can use our muscle power. This may be to remove weeds, till the soil and so on. But before we can use this muscle power we have to know how to improve crops, how to turn iron ore into iron, how to make fire, etc. This knowledge is also part of our labour. We therefore contribute both muscle power and brain power to production.

This application of *human effort* and *intelligence* to production is called **labour**. Instead of lazing in the sun or sleeping or playing games we engage in work – i.e. in labour – and we do so because we consider that the gains (in terms of increased production) more than outweigh our dislike of work.

The more we work, and the better we are at working, the more goods and services we will have at our disposal. Of course, those who live in the South Seas will get more for less work than those who live in the Arctic. But for any particular kind of land the more you work on it the more you can consume.

Capital

Unfortunately production is not quite as straightforward as that. There are many different ways of combining our labour with land and each has its own advantages and drawbacks. Let us take an example.

Imagine a community which lives by fishing. Imagine too that the people have nothing to catch fish with but their own hands; they catch very few fish per day. They know that they could catch a few more fish if they had spears, a lot more if they had fishing rods and even more fish if they had fishing nets. If they decided to make some spears, they would have to stop fishing for a few days while they made the spears. For those few days they would have little or no fish, but later, when they had the spears, they would catch more fish than they ever had before.

They may decide to make fishing rods rather than spears. This would take them longer and they would have to go without fish for many more days. Of course, when they eventually got their rods they would be able to catch a great deal of fish. Finally, if they wanted to use fishing nets they would have to go without fish for even longer while they made them, but again they would eventually have even more fish than they could catch with rods.

The point of this example is to show that there are many ways of applying our labour to the natural production process. In other words, there are many possible technologies. Some technologies use only direct labour: you simply walk into the sea and try to grab a fish. Some technologies use some labour and some simple tools. Finally, some technologies use a little labour and a lot of equipment.

This equipment, which is made as an aid to production, is called **capital**. Capital takes many forms (fishing rods and fishing nets, for example), but what all these things have in common is that they are produced means of production. Labour and land are also means of production, of course, but they are not produced – they are original means of production.

The amount of capital available has a great bearing on how labour affects production. It turns out that the more capital we use, the more output each worker can produce. This means that we have to consider three rather than two factors of production: land, labour and capital.

Modern, developed economies use enormous amounts of capital. In order to build a motor car, for example, it is necessary to dig mines for coal and iron ore, build steel-producing plants, drill for oil, make paint, make machines and build factories long before the first car rolls off the production line. Although the amount of capital involved are enormous and take so many different forms, the principle is the same as that for fishing nets. In order to increase the output per worker tomorrow, we have to spend some land and labour in making aids to production today.

SUMMARY

1. Land is the factor of production provided by nature. It includes all natural resources, such as coal, fresh water and sunlight.
2. The products of nature are usually insufficient to meet human needs without the application of human effort.
3. Labour is the application of human effort and intelligence to production.
4. Capital is the equipment which is made to aid production. To get capital it is necessary to give up the production of some consumer goods now in order to be able to produce more later.
5. The more capital a society has, the more it can produce.

Scarcity

If land, labour and capital were freely available, we could produce all that we wanted and there would be an infinite quantity of goods available, prices would fall to zero and economics would never have come into being. The fact that we do not have enough goods must mean that the supply of goods is restricted in some way. If the supply of goods is restricted (i.e. if they are scarce), it must be due to the scarcity of some (or all) factors of production. Thus in order to understand scarcity, we need to look at what it is that limits the availability of factors of production.

Scarcity of land

The flow of goods from nature, as we have seen, has a limit and in some parts of the world that limit is not far above subsistence level. The bounty of nature is therefore not infinite. We have only so much soil in which to plant vegetables or on which to raise livestock, only so much sunshine and so much rainfall. These are provided by nature but in quantities which in many cases are below our required levels.

The fact that land is often scarce implies that people will be competing among themselves for its use. In the case of the soil, for example, those who wish to grow wheat will be competing with those who wish to raise cattle.

These competitions may take the form of open warfare with the cattle ranchers fighting off the farmers or vice versa, but in our economic system competition is confined to the market place. The 'winners' are those who are prepared to pay most for something. If ranchers are prepared to pay a rent of £300 per acre and farmers are prepared to pay £301 then the farmers get to use the land. The problem with this allocation mechanism is that land is provided free by nature and nature has no way of conducting a land auction. There is no one to ensure that land will go to the highest bidder.

In market economies we overcome this problem by allowing individuals to own land. We use the institution of private property. This means that, although humans have had no hand in the provision of land, certain individuals (or groups) are granted ownership of it. People can own the coal lying beneath the ground, they can own rivers and the fish in those rivers. They can even own mountains and the animals which breed on those mountains.

Landowners can hold auctions and it is in their best interest to let the land to the highest bidders. This means that users of land do not see it as a free good. To society as a whole it is free, but because of private ownership and scarcity it has a price. This price is called **rent** and is any payment made for any of the natural endowments called land.

The use of the word 'rent' should not be confused with the rent which is paid for a house or for a television set on hire. Economists use the word in a very special way to mean *payment for land* and this use of the word is sometimes stressed by referring to it as **economic rent**.

Not all land attracts rent. Fishing for whales in the Atlantic, for example, does not mean paying rent to someone. This is because no one yet has managed to lay claim to the oceans and so the 'ownership' condition is not satisfied. The same applies to sunlight and many other gifts of nature which remain free of charge. But as far as our analysis of production is concerned, we are going to consider only those parts of land which do attract rent.

Those who own land and receive rent for it are called rentiers. Quite who they are or how they came to be rentiers and how much they own is beyond the scope of this book, but such rights were usually the result of conquest or gifts from a grateful monarch.

Not all countries allow the private ownership of property. In communist countries private property is illegal and all land is owned by the state. It is sufficient here to note that land is limited in supply and that in our economy it is rationed out among users by charging them rent.

Scarcity of labour

Labour, as we have seen, is the contribution of human effort and intelligence to the productive process. Some people have more to contribute than others, but most of us can contribute something. Those who do contribute are called labourers. This term is not confined only to those who carry out menial tasks, but includes all those who work with their hands and all those who work with their brains. By labourers we mean managers as well as machinists.

Since there are as many labourers as there are people, it might appear that a shortage of labour means a shortage of people. However, this is not the case. Worldwide it would be difficult to argue that there is a shortage of people. Many countries seem to think they have too many citizens rather than too few. The scarcity of labour comes about not because there are too few people but because there are only 24 hours in a day.

Doing work (labouring) typically means performing actions at times and places and under conditions which one would rather avoid: for example, tightening up nuts and bolts on a noisy production line for eight hours a day.

The opposite of working is doing what we want to do and is called leisure. Since there are only 24 hours in a day, every hour spent at work means one fewer hour of leisure. In order to persuade people to work it is necessary to compensate them for their loss of leisure. Their compensation comes in the form of wages.

Scarcity of capital

Capital is a produced factor of production and, as we have seen, in order to produce capital it is necessary to divert labour and land away from producing the things you actually want. The islanders, for example, had to leave their fishing in order to make the fishing nets. The time spent making nets represents fish forgone, fish which they could have had if they had not stopped fishing. One cost of capital then is forgone consumption.

Eventually, of course, the nets will improve their fishing and they will have far more fish than before. Giving up some fish today enables them to have more fish tomorrow – that is why they do it. But giving up fish today may cause considerable distress, particularly if they are very hungry or even perhaps near starvation level. For very poor countries to build up their capital they may have to allow some citizens to forgo even subsistence levels of consumption and starve to death.

Forgoing current consumption is not something which most people would choose to do, so there is a real cost associated with capital, and hence it is limited in supply.

Forgoing consumption today is a cost associated with the supply of capital, and the extra consumption you get tomorrow is partly to compensate you for bearing that cost. That compensation is called interest. Interest is paid to those who forgo consumption today in order to provide capital for production tomorrow. Those who supply capital are called capitalists.

There is a second cost to supplying capital which has nothing to do with forgone consumption. We have assumed that the fishing nets produced on the island actually turn out to be useful and time saving. There are, however, several possible reasons why this need not be the case. They might be made with a mesh which is too large so that the fish escape. They might rot away soon after being exposed to salt water. A new source of better food might be found. And so on and so on.

All these uncertainties about the eventual usefulness of the nets endow the project with a degree of risk. The piece of capital equipment may turn out to be useful, or it may not. In order to supply capital, therefore, it is necessary to find someone who is willing to bear the risk. Since people are generally supposed to be averse to risk, there will be a shortage of such people and so once again we have a restriction on the supply of capital.

Risk is unavoidably associated with capital, and in order to compensate for risk it is necessary to offer the possibility of **profit**. We say the *possibility* of profit because an absolutely certain profit would absolve the process from all risk. Sometimes the capital will work very well, save a lot of time and earn a lot of profit; sometimes it will not work at all and will involve a negative profit – a loss. The person who bears the risk and reaps any profit or bears any loss is called an **entrepreneur**.

Thus all three factors of production – land, labour and capital – are scarce, and therefore the output they produce will also be scarce. Those who contribute to production receive inducements in the form of rent, wages, interest and profit. These payments are made to the factors of production and are therefore called factor incomes.

SUMMARY

1. The supply of goods is limited by the scarcity of one or more of the factors of production.

Case study 3.1 The social classes

Throughout this section on the supply of factors of production we have associated particular functions with particular persons. The entrepreneur is the risk taker, the capitalist forgoes current consumption, the labourer forgoes leisure and the rentier is the owner of the land. There is really no need to make these associations. One person can embody all these functions. Some farmers, for example, own land, provide their own farm machinery (capital), take risks (by planting one crop rather than another) and work on their farms too. They therefore perform all the functions outlined above and will consequently earn all four kinds of income. It is customary, however, particularly in an advanced economy, to separate these functions. Typically, those who work do not own capital or land or take risks. Those who provide capital typically do not work, etc.

Thus each cost of production is borne by a separate group of people. There will, for example, be one group who live almost exclusively on wages; another group will live almost exclusively on interest; yet another will live on rent; and a fourth group will live on profits.

These groups are regarded by some commentators as social classes. Those who live principally by selling their labour for wages constitute the labouring class or the working class. Those who live principally on interest constitute the capitalist class. The profit earners are usually grouped with the capitalists since their risk bearing arises from the uncertain rewards of capital. The principal landowners make up the aristocracy.

The class to which someone belongs therefore depends on his or her relation to the means of production, rather than on education, religion, hobbies, age or any other characteristic. This definition of a class is a very powerful political idea.

Some economists (Marxists) argue that these classes are inevitably in conflict with each other. The capitalists try to increase their income at the expense of the labourers and the landowners try to outdo them both. This leads those countries which follow Marxist doctrine to abolish all classes except the labouring class. All land and capital is owned by the state and production is organized by the state via its central planning bureaux. Clause 4 of the Labour Party's constitution seeks public ownership of the means of production and distribution.

Free-market economists argue that in a property-owning democracy the price mechanism will ensure that any competition among the factors of production will prevent any one factor exploiting any other. Classes are therefore in competition but not in conflict.

We shall not deal with these questions in great depth, but we raise them here merely to illustrate some of the wider consequences which flow from this account of production.

2. The scarcity of land, together with the institution of private property, results in the payment of rent to landowners (rentiers) for the use of their land.
3. Labour means forgoing leisure and therefore labourers are paid wages to compensate for their loss of leisure.
4. Capital involves postponing consumption and bearing risk.
5. Those who postpone their consumption are called capitalists and they are paid interest.
6. Those who bear risk are called entrepreneurs and receive profits.
7. These four payments – rent, wages, interest and profit – are called factor payments or factor incomes.

Production decisions

There are many possible ways to make production decisions. We could invite the local priest to decide how much should be produced and how much capital and labour should be used to produce it. Alternatively, the government could set up a central planning bureau and let the bureau decide what to do. Or we could ask one of the factors of production to decide. We could, for example, set up a workers' co-operative and ask the workers to decide what should be done.

All these various possibilities have their attractions and at various times have been used. However, the usual practice in a market economy such as the UK is for those who bear the *risks* to make the decisions. In other words, the *entrepreneurs* decide how much of what to produce, and how much labour and how much capital to hire. The justification for this is that, since entrepreneurs bear the risk, they should have the last say in what is to be done. Typically, the entrepreneurs bring all the factors together into a **firm**. We are therefore describing how entrepreneurs organize their firms.

Having identified who has the power to make production decisions, we must now describe how that power is exercised.

In the Adam Smith world of the price mechanism every agent is assumed, indeed advised, to operate with an eye for only self-interest. If we each pursue our own self-interest then the price mechanism will work and work well. Therefore in order to know how the entrepreneurs will behave it

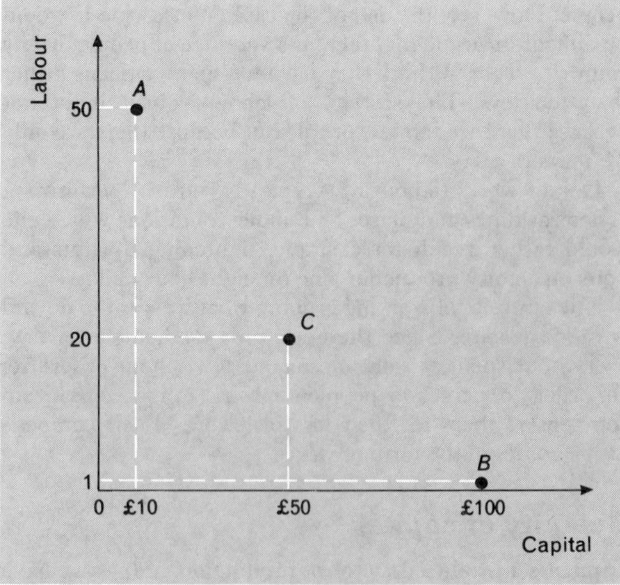

Figure 3.1 Factor combinations (technologies).

is necessary to know what is in their best interest. If we know the entrepreneurs' aims then we can say how they will behave in order to achieve those aims..

We know that entrepreneurs receive profits and so we assume that they will organize the productive process in such a way as to *maximize profits*. This may seem an oversimplified account of entrepreneurs' aims, but in fact maximizing profits turns out to be consistent with many other apparently different aims and objectives of entrepreneurs and hence is a good assumption to begin with.

SUMMARY

1. In a free-enterprise economy, decisions about production are made by entrepreneurs.
2. Entrepreneurs receive profits and so we assume that the aim of the entrepreneur is to maximize profits.
3. Production is therefore organized so as to maximize profits.

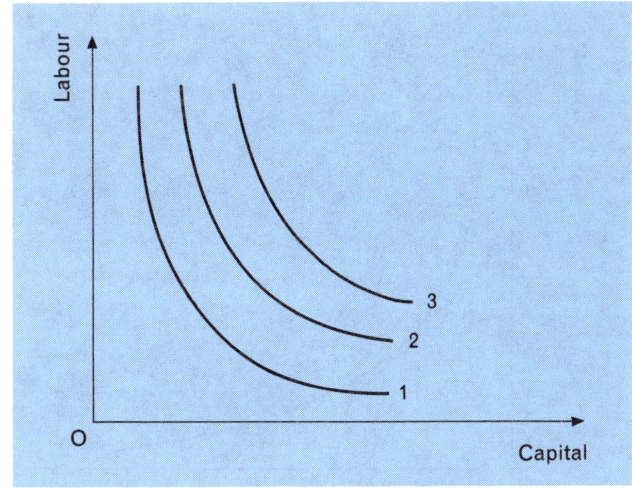

Figure 3.2 An isoquant map.

The production function

The point we have reached suggests that each of the factors of production is in limited supply and that this will in turn limit the supply of goods. We do not yet know, however, just how severe these limitations on the factors of production will prove to be. It might, for example, be possible to compensate for an acute shortage of one factor (say land) by a superabundance of some other factor (say capital). This would mean that the factors of production are **substitutes** for each other.

We can illustrate this idea by considering how two of the factors, labour and capital, can be used to plant a tonne of wheat. If labour and capital are substitutes for each other then we could plant the tonne of wheat with 50 workers using spades or one worker using a tractor. In the first case we are using a lot of labour and a little capital. In the second case we are using a lot of capital and a little labour. In between these two extremes there are many other combinations of capital and labour capable of planting the tonne of wheat. These various combinations of factors are called technologies.

Isoquants

One way of representing the range of possible technologies (factor combinations) is by a diagram. In Figure 3.1 labour is measured up the vertical axis and capital is measured along the horizontal axis. The many labourers/little capital combination is represented by point *A* (50 workers and £10 worth of capital). The single labourer/high capital combination is represented by point *B* (1 worker and £100 worth of capital). Each point in the diagram represents a particular combination of labour and capital. Thus in Figure 3.1 point *C* shows 20 workers and £50 worth of capital.

This means that all the possible combinations of capital and labour which are capable of planting a tonne of wheat can be represented as points on the diagram, and all these points can be joined up to form a line. Since this line represents all combinations of capital and labour capable of producing a fixed quantity of output it is called an **isoquant** ('iso' meaning the same and 'quant' being short for quantity).

If we plotted all the combinations of labour and capital capable of planting 2 tonnes of wheat we would generate another isoquant. This second isoquant would lie everywhere above the first isoquant, since in order to plant twice the amount of wheat we would need more labour or more capital or more of both. There will be one isoquant for each level of output and those representing more output will always and everywhere lie above those representing less output.

A number of isoquants are shown in Figure 3.2. Isoquant 3 requires more factors than isoquant 2, which in turn requires more factors than isoquant 1. Each isoquant is shown as downward sloping since the less labour is used, more capital is necessary to compensate. Not only are the isoquants shown sloping downwards, but they are also shown as bending towards the origin (*convex* to the origin). The convex shape of the isoquants reflects the assumption that labour can be substituted for capital but that substitution becomes progressively more difficult as less and less labour is used. Substitution becomes more difficult in the sense that we need more and more capital to replace each successive unit of labour saved.

Close to the vertical axis a great deal of labour can be saved (L_1 in Figure 3.3) for an additional unit of capital. Further away from the vertical axis only a modest amount of labour (L_2) can be saved by the addition of one more unit of capital. Close to the horizontal axis only a tiny amount of labour (L_3) is saved by adding another unit of capital. Every *point* on the isoquant represents a combination of capital and labour. The *slope* of the isoquant at that point represents the rate at which capital can be substituted for labour. The slope of the isoquant is called the marginal rate of technical substitution. The marginal rate of technical substitution decreases as we move along an isoquant.

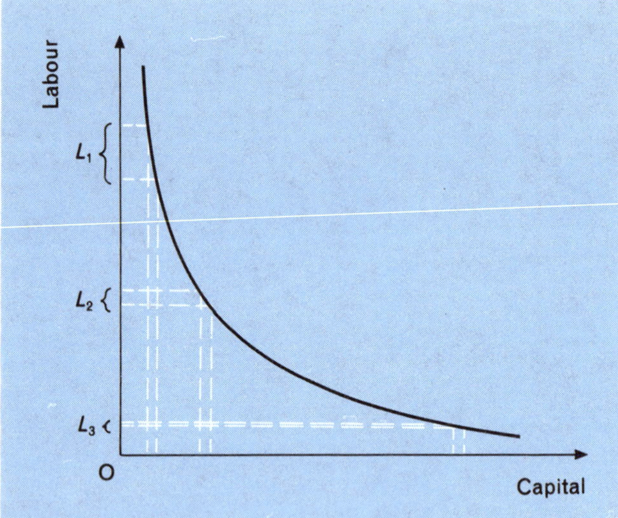

Figure 3.3 Marginal rate of technical substitution.

SUMMARY

1. For simplicity we assume that output is produced by labour and capital with no land.
2. There are many different combinations of labour and capital which are capable of producing a particular level of output.
3. A line joining up all such combinations is called an isoquant ('iso' meaning the same and 'quant' being short for quantity).
4. If output is to be increased, it is necessary to move to a new isoquant further away from the origin.
5. Isoquants are convex to the origin, which implies that, as more capital is substituted for labour, greater and greater increments in capital are needed to compensate for the successive (uniform) reductions in labour.
6. The slope of an isoquant is called the marginal rate of technical substitution.

Isocost lines

The complete set of isoquants represent all possible combinations of labour and capital capable of producing any level of output. Of all of these possible combinations only one will be chosen. The choice will determine the quantity of output and the amount of capital and labour used to produce it.

Choosing a quantity of output means choosing an isoquant. Choosing a combination of capital and labour means choosing a point on that isoquant. Every point in the diagram therefore represents both a level of output and a technology. How are these choices made?

To simplify things, imagine that an entrepreneur is just beginning to set up a business. She has already decided how many goods to produce and hence knows which isoquant she must be on. She now has to decide on a labour/capital combination – a technology. She knows the going wage rate and the going interest rate. What will she do?

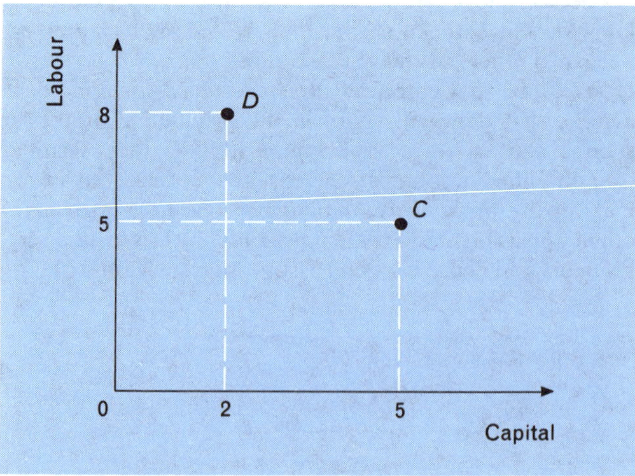

Figure 3.4 Alternative technologies.

One way forward would be for the entrepreneur to work out how the total cost (wages + interest) changes as the technology changes. This would indicate which technology had the lowest cost.

We can illustrate this in Figure 3.4. Point *D* in Figure 3.4 represents a combination of 8 units of labour and 2 units of capital. Let the wage rate be £10 per worker. Let each unit of capital (machine) cost £100 and let the interest rate be 10 per cent (0.1). The total cost of combination *D* will be £100:

8 (workers) × £10 (wage rate)	£80
2 (machines) × £100 (machine price) × 0.1 (interest rate)	£20
Total cost	£100

This sum of £100 could buy many other combinations apart from combination *D*. It could, for example, be spent on 5 workers at £10 each (£50) and 5 machines at (5 × £100 × 0.1 = £50). This is represented by point *C* in Figure 3.4. There would be many other combinations of labour and capital which, like *D*, would cost the entrepreneur £100.

Table 3.1 Labour and capital costing £100

Units of labour	Wage bill (£)	Units of capital	Interest bill (£)	Total cost (£)
10	100	0	0	100
9	90	1	10	100
8	80	2	20	100
7	70	3	30	100
6	60	4	40	100
5	50	5	50	100
4	40	6	60	100
3	30	7	70	100
2	20	8	80	100
1	10	9	90	100
0	0	10	100	100

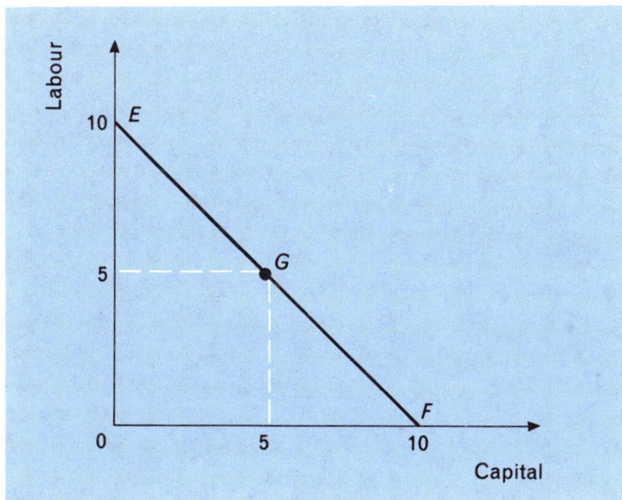

Figure 3.5 An isocost line.

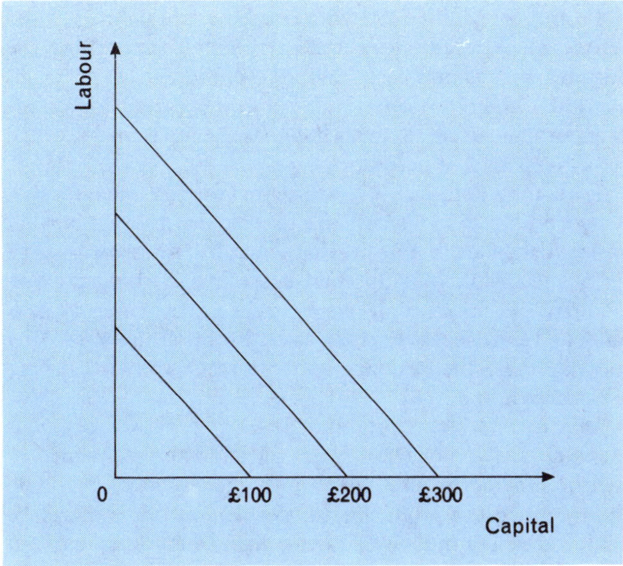

Figure 3.6 Isocosts with increasing resources.

Table 3.1 contains a number of combinations of labour and capital which can be bought for £100. If all these combinations of labour and capital were to be plotted out, we would have a line of them as in Figure 3.5. This line is called an **isocost line**.

An isocost line represents all those combinations of labour and capital which cost a given sum of money. Point *E* in Figure 3.5 is where all the £100 is spent on hiring labour and hence indicates 10 workers. Point *F* represents the case when all the £100 is spent on machines, and hence indicates 10 machines. Point *G* is the case when there are 5 workers and 5 machines. Any number of isocost lines can be constructed: one for £100, one for £200, one for £300, etc.

It will be clear from Figure 3.5 that each isocost line is a straight line. The slope of an isocost line represents how many workers have to be given up in order to afford another machine. Each additional machine adds £10 to costs (£100 × 0.1) so for every machine there has to be a saving of £10 on labour. Each worker costs £10 so we can save the cost of one machine by reducing the number of workers by one. In this case the slope of the isocost line will be 1 because you have to give up one worker for each additional machine – the fall in the number of workers (1) divided by the increase in the number of machines (1) equals 1.

Clearly, the number of workers given up per machine will depend on the cost of workers (the wage rate) and the cost of machines (the price × the interest rate). If the wage rate decreased to £5 then each additional machine would require 2 workers to be given up. Thus the slope would then be 2.

The slope of the isocost line depends only on the relative prices of labour and capital. Provided factor prices (the wage rate, the price of a machine and the interest rate) remain constant, all the isocost lines will have the same slope.

The position of each line depends on the sum it represents. The greater the sum, the more capital and/or the more labour can be hired. Thus the isocost lines move further away from the origin as the sum they represent increases. This is shown in Figure 3.6.

We now have two pieces of information: the isoquants, which represent all the production possibilities; and the isocost lines, which represent the various costs of those possible combinations of labour and capital. Both the isoquants and the isocost lines are drawn on diagrams with labour measured up the vertical axis and capital measured along the horizontal axis. To compare the costs of the various technologies it is necessary to bring the isoquants and the isocost lines together on the same diagram. This is done in Figure 3.7.

Each point in Figure 3.7 represents a point on an isoquant (a level of output) and a point on an isocost line (a level of cost). The level of output multiplied by the price of the output generates the entrepreneur's revenue. Thus each point in Figure 3.7 represents a level of revenue and a level of costs.

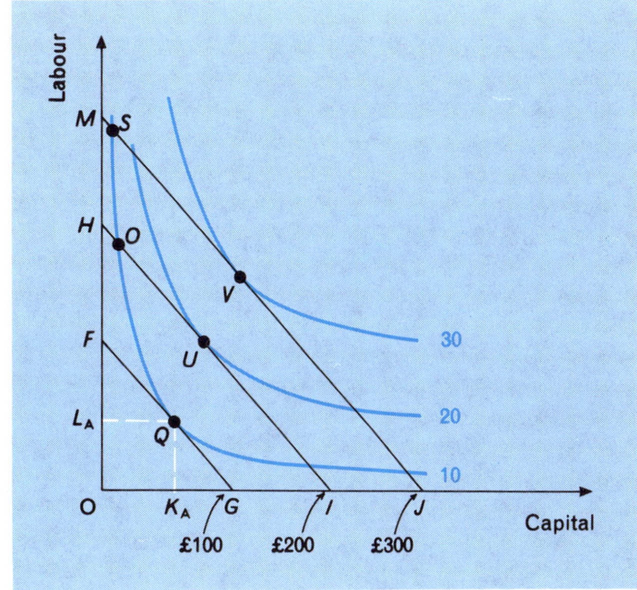

Figure 3.7 Minimum costs of different levels of output.

Profits, which motivate entrepreneurs, are defined as the difference between sales revenue (receipts from selling the output) and factor costs (wages + interest). In order to maximize their profits it is therefore necessary for entrepreneurs to choose a point which has the lowest isocost line for a given level of output.

Returning to Figure 3.7, we see that for any given level of output we must stay on a particular isoquant – that is what an isoquant means. But moving along the isoquant puts us on a succession of different isocost lines. Moving along isoquant 10, for example, we first cut isocost line *MJ* at *S* and then cut isocost line *HI* at *O*. Profit is maximized by moving along the isoquant until we reach the lowest possible isocost line.

In Figure 3.7 the minimum level of cost will occur at point *Q*. If we move still further around the isoquant, we will be moving up to higher and higher isocost lines. The minimum cost of producing this level of output is therefore achieved where the lowest isocost line is just touching, and tangential to, the isoquant (point *Q*). At this point we will be producing 10 units of output with L_A workers and K_A capital.

If we were to cut the wage rate by half then for every given amount spent on labour we would get twice the number of workers. This means that the slope of the isocost lines would alter. Being able to hire more workers for a given cost means that the isocost lines become steeper, as shown in Figure 3.8. Line *AB* is the isocost line at the original wage rate and line *CB* is the isocost line at the new lower wage rate.

If these new isocost lines are superimposed on the original isoquants then the points of tangency (lowest cost points) can be seen to have moved around the isoquants. This indicates that more labour and less capital should be used.

In Figure 3.9 we draw the original isoquant *II* and the old and the new isocost lines, *AB* and *CB* respectively. The point of tangency with the old isocost line requires L_1 workers and K_1 capital. To find the new least-cost combination of labour and capital to produce the output represented by *II* at the new wage rate it is necessary to find the point at which an isocost line with the *same slope* as line *BC* is tangential to isoquant *II*. If the line *BC* is drawn back towards the origin, parallel to *BC*, we find it is tangential to *II* where L_2 workers and K_2 capital are required.

Thus if there were a superabundance of workers, they would bid against each other for jobs and wage rates would fall. This would steepen the isocost lines and cause the profit-maximizing entrepreneur to hire more workers. This is just one more way in which the price mechanism works to clear markets.

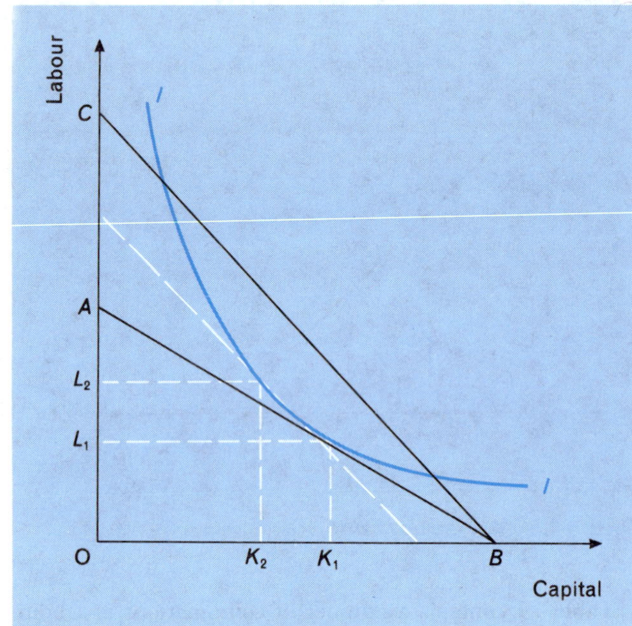

Figure 3.9 Effect of a cut in wages on factor combinations.

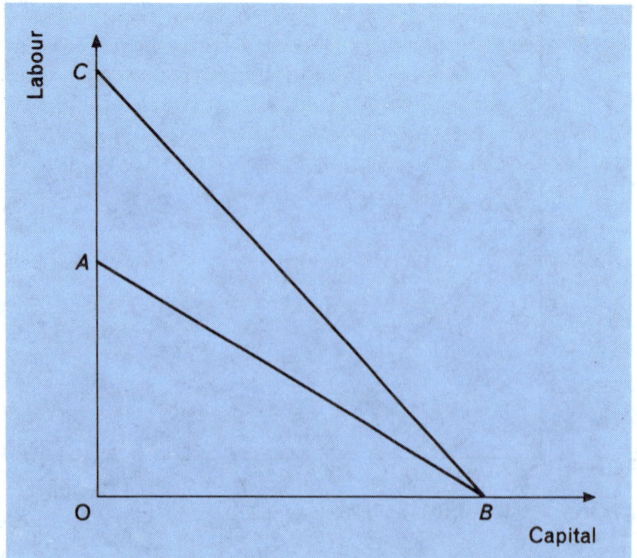

Figure 3.8 Effect of a cut in wages on the isocost line.

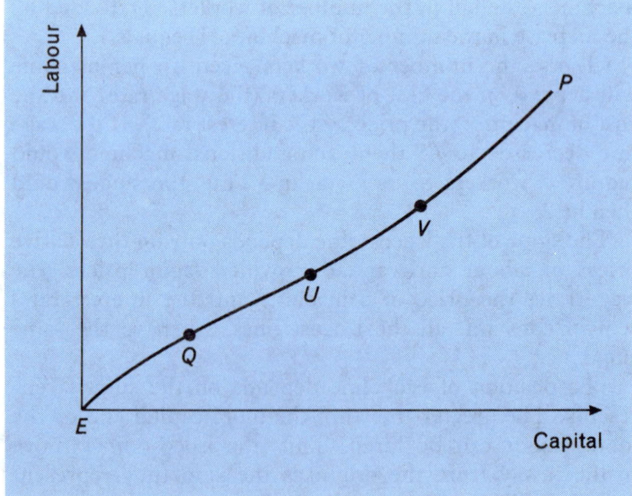

Figure 3.10 Expansion path.

SUMMARY

1. The costs of production are the payments made for labour and capital.
2. For any given level of cost, it is possible to buy a large number of different combinations of labour and capital.
3. A line joining up all these combinations is called an isocost line.
4. The higher the level of cost, the further the isocost line is from the origin.
5. The slope of the isocost line depends upon the ratio of the wage rate to the interest rate.
6. Profits are the difference between a firm's total revenue from selling a good and the total cost of producing it.
7. To achieve the lowest costs of producing a given level of output it is necessary to choose that combination of capital and labour at which the isoquant is tangential to the isocost line (i.e. just touching at one point only).
8. This uniquely determines the most profitable combination of capital and labour.

The expansion path

We have seen that for any given level of output the entrepreneur would choose that combination of labour and capital which minimizes costs. What is not yet clear is what level of output would be chosen. That is to say, we have seen how a *point* on an isoquant is chosen, but we have yet to see how the *isoquant* is chosen.

We saw that as we moved around an isoquant costs at first fell, then reached a minimum (at point *Q*) and then began to rise as we moved further round. This holds true for all levels of output, so if we jump to a higher isoquant we will choose that point on it at which the costs of production are at a minimum, i.e. the point where the new isocost line is tangential to the new isoquant.

These are shown as points *Q*, *U* and *V* in Figure 3.10 and represent the minimum-cost factor combinations for outputs 10, 20 and 30 respectively. The points *Q*, *U* and *V* can be joined up to yield the line *EP*. This line traces out the factor combinations (technologies) chosen so as to minimize costs as output expands. It is called the **expansion path**.

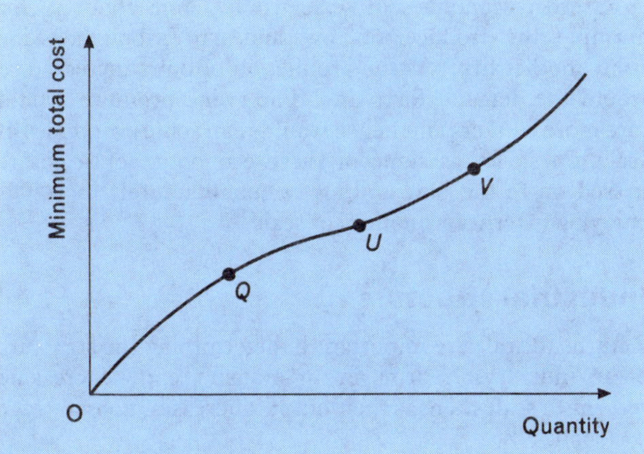

Figure 3.11 Total cost curve.

Each level of output will have its own minimum cost represented by the isocost line which is tangential to it. Thus each point on the expansion path represents a level of output and its corresponding level of costs. We therefore know the costs associated with each level of output and so can draw a graph of output against costs. This is shown in Figure 3.11 and is called a **total cost** curve.

SUMMARY

1. The profit-maximizing entrepreneur will choose that point on the isoquant (a combination of labour and capital) which is tangential to the lowest isocost line.
2. There will be one such point for each and every level of output.
3. If all these points are joined up they form an expansion path.
4. Each point on the expansion path represents a certain level of costs and a certain level of output. We can therefore work out the total cost associated with each level of output.
5. By drawing a curve of cost against output, we construct a total cost curve.

Returns to scale

As output increases it is necessary to hire more labour and/or more capital and so minimum costs must increase as output increases. The total cost curve will therefore be everywhere upward sloping.

Although we know that the curve must slope upwards, we can say very little about its actual shape, i.e. how its slope changes along its length. It could become progressively steeper and steeper as output increases. Or it could have the same slope all the way up. Or again it could get shallower and shallower as output increases. This all turns on whether costs increase faster than output, at the same rate as output or slower than output.

The costs of production depend on two things: the quantities of inputs necessary and the prices of those inputs. If for the moment we let prices remain constant as output expands then the only way to change costs is to change the quantities of inputs required. We need then to know by how much inputs have to change when output changes.

As we move from *Q* to *U* (in Figure 3.10) we double output from 10 to 20. If by doing so we more than double the amounts of labour and capital needed then the total cost curve will get steeper and steeper as output increases (Figure 3.12(a)). If, when output is doubled, the amounts of labour and capital also double then the total cost curve will be a straight line (Figure 3.12(b)). If labour and capital less than double as output is doubled then the total cost curve will become shallower and shallower as output increases (Figure 3.12(c)). Each of these cases is possible.

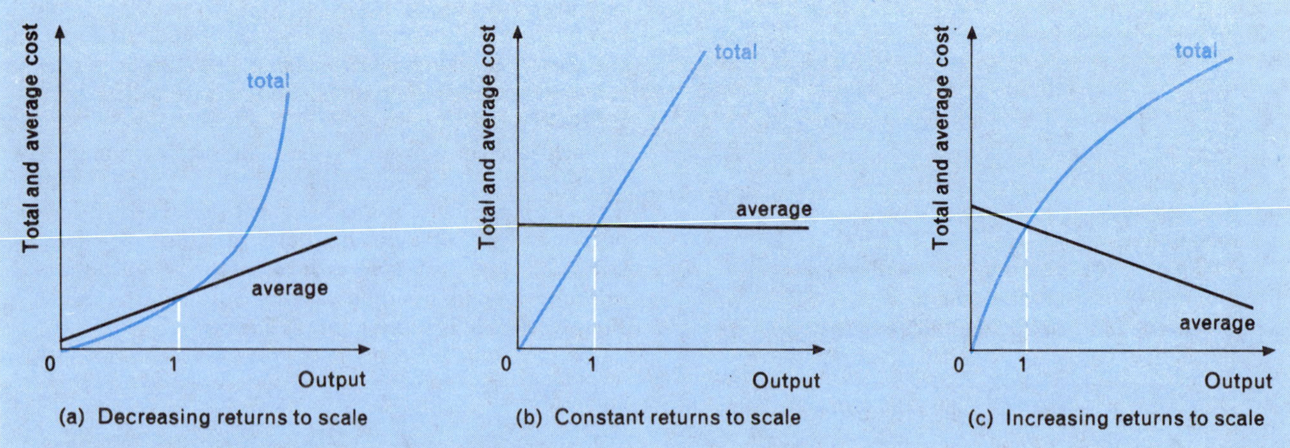

Figure 3.12 Returns to scale.

In the first case, where total costs increase by more than output, the *cost per unit of output* will increase as output increases. The cost per unit is called the **average cost** and is found by dividing the total cost by the total output.

In the second case, where total costs go up in line with output, the average cost will remain constant as output increases.

In the third case, where total costs go up by less than output, average costs fall as output increases.

The total cost curves and the average cost curves corresponding to these three cases are given in Figure 3.12 and describe what might happen to average costs as output is increased. Which of the three is actually experienced will depend on whether it is possible to double output without doubling inputs. That is to say, it all depends on what happens when we change the **scale** of production.

When output increases by more than inputs there are said to be **increasing returns to scale**. This is because as the scale of operation expands we can economize on inputs – fewer inputs are needed per unit of output.

When output increases by the same proportion as inputs increase there are said to be **constant returns to scale**.

When output increases by less than inputs have increased there are said to be **decreasing returns to scale**. This is because as the scale of operations expand we need *more inputs per unit of output*.

These three cases together describe all the ways in which the inputs of capital and labour change as output changes. **Returns to scale**, whether they be constant, increasing or decreasing, offer a very convenient way of describing how the efficiency of production changes as the scale of production changes.

With increasing returns to scale, the output per worker (and the output per machine) increases as the level of output increases. This, as we have seen, means that the average costs fall as output increases. Because these cost reductions are caused by what is happening in the production process itself, they are said to be the result of **internal economies of scale**.

There is another way in which altering the scale of production could affect average costs. We have assumed above that the prices of the firm's inputs do not change as its output changes. This may not be the case. As the output of a particular firm expands, it will need to buy more and more materials from other producers. If these other producers enjoy increasing returns to scale then their costs will fall as the demand for their output rises. If these cost reductions are passed on to the particular firm then its costs will fall too. Thus as it expands its costs fall not because it enjoys increasing returns, but because its suppliers do. Their increased efficiency is passed on in lower prices. Reductions in average costs due to increasing returns to scale of its suppliers are called **external economies of scale**.

Both internal and external economies of scale may be illustrated with a rather simple example. Consider a firm which produces bows and arrows. If it has enough customers to keep only one worker busy then that worker has to be able to do all the operations involved in making bows and arrows: bending the bow, whipping the cord, fitting the flights and making the arrowheads. Some of these tasks may prove particularly difficult and hold up progress. If the market expands and 10 workers are needed to produce the bows and arrows then different workers can be allocated to different tasks. The best flight fitter would only fit flights. The best arrowhead maker would only make arrowheads. This is called division of labour by process and has been shown greatly to improve the efficiency of production. Thus there will be internal economies of scale.

External economies of scale would come about if, for example, the producer of bows and arrows bought twine from another firm. As the production of bows increased so would the demand for twine. The twine producer would hire more workers and hence would reap some economies of scale. In so far as some of these economies of scale are passed on to the bow and arrow manufacturer, then it is enjoying external economies of scale.

Industrial structure

Returns to scale are important in determining the structure of an industry. If firms in an industry enjoy increasing returns to scale then, as their output increases, their average costs fall.

To see how this affects industrial structure, imagine six identical plants producing a particular good and each plant producing the same quantity of output. Since their outputs are equal, their costs are equal. Since they are all selling the same good, their revenues and profits are equal. Now let one firm slightly reduce its price. At first it suffers a slight reduction in profits. But it will attract customers away from the other five firms. Its own production will increase, and that of the other five will decrease. Its average costs will therefore fall, and their average costs will rise (due to increasing returns to scale). Its profits are restored and it has a bigger share of the market.

If this continued, and if the other firms did not respond by cutting their prices, then eventually there would be only one firm in the industry. In other words, it would be a **monopoly**. This one firm would have a monopoly of the market in that particular good. Or it might be that one or two firms would continue to fight it out while most of the original six firms went out of business. An example of this type of industry is motor car production. Gradually one or two firms emerge as dominant (Ford) and only by sustaining heavy losses can another firm hope to regain its place in the market (Austin Rover). By staying in the market, other firms simply keep the price of cars above the lowest possible, since this prevents the leading firm from reaping further economies of scale.

Of course, not all industries are characterized by increasing returns to scale. The building and construction industry, for example, has a very wide range of sizes of firms, from the smallest one-man jobbing builder to great national companies like Wimpey and Costain. They all seem to co-exist in relative harmony. This would be impossible without constant returns to scale.

An industry with decreasing returns to scale would be characterized by a total absence of large companies and a profusion of small ones. Two examples of this are hairdressers and horticulturalists. There is very little to be gained from having chains or huge centrally located hairdressers. It seems even less likely that a hairdresser could be organized so as to promote the division of labour – one person combs, another clips and cuts with scissors, another shampoos, etc. One person is expected to do all these things.

Monopoly production

Increasing returns to scale are not the only reason for there being monopolies. It may be that one firm has a patent or a copyright and hence prevents any other firm from entering the market.

It may be that it is simply silly to have a number of firms in an industry. Examples might be the telephone and railway networks. We could have a system in which there were ten separate telephone companies, each with its own repair crews, telegraph poles, holes in the ground and switchboards. Perhaps too they would have some very complicated way of allowing the customer of one company to ring up a customer from another company. This would be very inefficient. The obvious thing to do is to let one firm run the entire telephone system.

Similarly with railways: it may be possible to lay ten tracks between London and Manchester, with 10 sets of railway stations and ten separate train signalling systems, cafeterias and so on. But again the obvious thing to do is to put all the lines under the direction of one company.

Monopolies of this kind are called **natural monopolies** and are usually brought into being by legislation rather than by several companies starting up and battling for survival. A lot of wasteful duplication is avoided by there being only one producer who is granted a licence by the government.

Returns to scale and monopoly turn out to be important in a number of ways, as we shall see in later chapters.

SUMMARY

1. The shape of the total cost curve depends partly on the returns to scale of the plant:
   (a) For increasing returns to scale, costs increase less quickly than output and so average costs fall.
   (b) For constant returns to scale, costs increase *pari passu* (in line) with output, so average costs remain constant.
   (c) For decreasing returns to scale, costs increase faster than output, so average costs increase.
2. There are internal economies of scale and external economies of scale. The former arise from improved efficiency within the plant. The latter arise from improved efficiencies of the suppliers of materials to the plant.
3. Internal economies of scale will influence the number of independent producers in an industry:
   (a) With increasing returns to scale there will be a tendency for a single dominant producer to emerge. This is called a monopoly.
   (b) With constant returns to scale there will be both large and small firms co-existing in the industry.
   (c) With decreasing returns to scale there will be a large number of very small firms in the industry and no large firms.
4. Monopolies may also be formed by patent rights or due to legislation resulting from natural monopoly.
5. Natural monopolies occur when the duplication of services (necessary for there to be more than one supplier) are obviously and massively wasteful and inefficient.

Short- and long-run cost curves

Now let us return to our entrepreneurs who are trying to decide how much to produce and how to produce it. We saw that if they could choose the best combination of labour and capital to maximize their profits, they would choose a point of tangency between an isoquant and an isocost line. However, this freedom to choose any point on the expansion path is not always open to them. Once they have built their factories and bought their machinery, they are more or less stuck with them, for a while at least. They cannot, in other words, quickly change the amount of capital they have available. They can more easily change the amount of labour. This gives rise to a very important distinction in economics. It is the distinction between the long run and the short run.

The **short run** is defined as that period of time over which only some factors of production can be changed. Conversely, the **long run** is defined as that period of time over which all factors can be adjusted.

Some capital can be quite quickly changed – it does not take very long to make some more spades or hoes, for example. On the other hand, the electricity-generating industry takes several years to build a new power station. Thus the 'long run' and the 'short run' can be almost any actual time period, ranging from a few months to several years. All we need to know is that in the long run *all* factors are variable, but in the short run *at least one factor* is fixed.

Since, in the long run, all factors are assumed to be equally and easily variable, entrepreneurs can choose any combination of capital and labour they like. The most profitable combinations are those which minimize costs, i.e. lie on the expansion path. Thus, in the long run, as output expands entrepreneurs will simply move along their expansion paths.

In the short run, however, their range of choice is restricted. They can still choose any amount of labour, but they have to make do with a fixed amount of capital. In the short run, therefore, they cannot expand along their expansion paths.

What happens then if, instead of being able to choose any combination of labour and capital, entrepreneurs can choose only labour, capital being fixed? We can illustrate this new restricted set of choices in Figure 3.13.

In the long run we saw how entrepreneurs would choose a point on the expansion path. (Remember this is the path traced out by all the points of tangency of the isoquants and the isocost lines). Let us assume that they chose point *a*. Once there they are constrained to use at most *K* units of capital.

As they expand output in the short run they move up curve *KK*. They are using a fixed amount of capital, but they are employing more and more labour and so produce more and more output. This leads us to a fundamental law in economics: the law of diminishing returns.

The law of diminishing returns

The law of diminishing returns says that *if more and more of one factor is applied to a fixed quantity of another factor then eventually the additions to output will become smaller and smaller.*

This means that, as we go above *a* in Figure 3.13, the first additional labourer might result in, say, 10 more units of output. The second additional labourer might result in only 9 new units of output, the third additional labourer might cause output to increase by only 8 units, and so on. Eventually, as more and more labourers are added, there will be no further increase in output. There may even be a reduction in output as labourers begin to get in each other's way.

A fixed wage rate has to be paid to each additional worker, so labour costs are rising steadily as more and more workers are hired. Output, however, is rising less quickly than labour costs, so the labour cost of producing each unit of output increases too. Increasing output above *a* in the short run therefore increases the average costs of production.

If output is reduced below *a*, the number of workers is reduced but the capital stock is fixed. However, not all of the capital stock need be used. Instead of having 5 workers working 10 machines we could have 5 workers working 5 machines. Reducing the number of workers *and* the number of machines together means that diminishing returns will not operate. The amount of *active* capital is not fixed. Each worker and each active machine therefore continues to produce as efficiently as before. Labour costs per unit of output will therefore remain constant as output falls below *a*.

This means that, as output increases from zero, labour

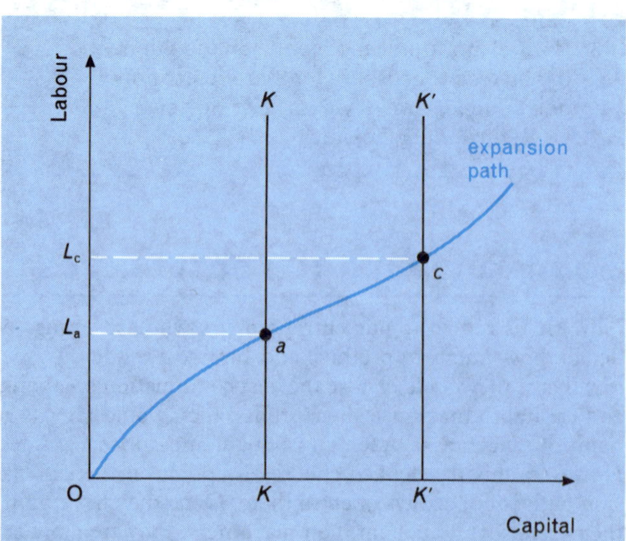

Figure 3.13 Expanding output with fixed capital.

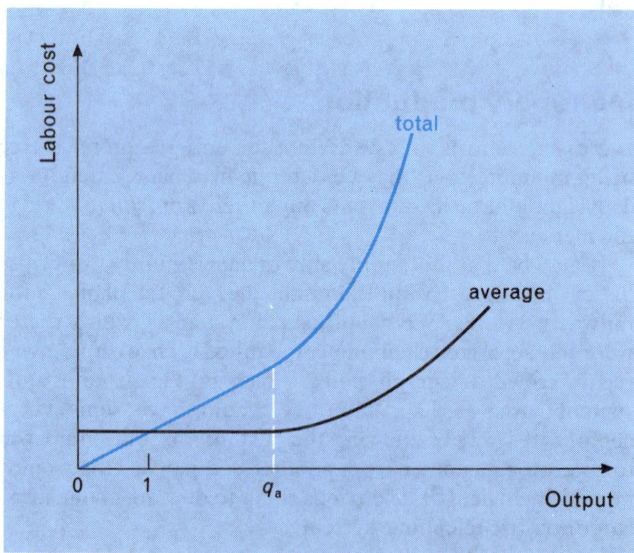

Figure 3.14 Total labour and average labour cost curves.

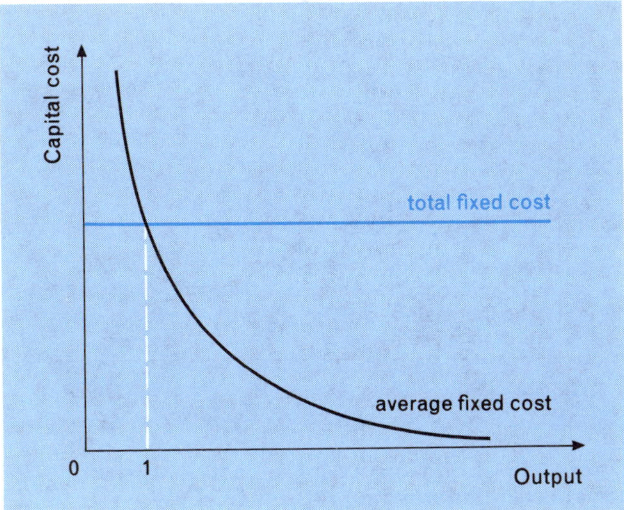

Figure 3.15 **Total fixed and average fixed cost curves.**

costs per unit are constant up to a point *a* and will increase after that. Costs which vary as output varies are called **variable costs**. We show how total labour cost and average labour cost change as output changes in Figure 3.14.

So much for labour costs. But labour is not the only cost of production. If the entrepreneurs have 10 machines costing £100 each, and if the rate of interest is 10 per cent per annum, then they must find £100 per year to pay the supplier of the capital. Whether they use the capital or not, the entrepreneurs must pay their capital costs. Since these capital costs do not vary with the level of output, they are called **fixed costs**.

If they produce just 1 unit of output per year then all capital costs have to be attributed to that 1 unit. Even before labour costs are added, it has already 'cost' £100 to produce.

If 10 units are produced per year then this £100 of capital cost can be spread over 10 units, so that they each bear £10 of the total £100.

If 100 units are produced per year then each unit will bear only £1 of capital costs. It will be clear from this that, as output is increased, the total cost of capital (£100) remains constant, but the average cost of capital (the cost per unit of output) steadily decreases. Average and total fixed cost curves are shown in Figure 3.15.

Entrepreneurs must bear both fixed costs (capital) and variable costs (labour) and so must add *total fixed costs* to *total variable costs* to yield *total cost*. Similarly, we can add average fixed costs to average variable costs to yield average total cost. Total cost and average total cost curves are shown in Figure 3.16.

Capacity output

The average total cost curve shown in Figure 3.16 is the standard U-shaped average total cost curve. This U-shape comes about because the average fixed cost curve is falling and the average variable cost curve is at first flat and then rises. At low levels of output the falling curve dominates, but eventually the rising curve becomes dominant.

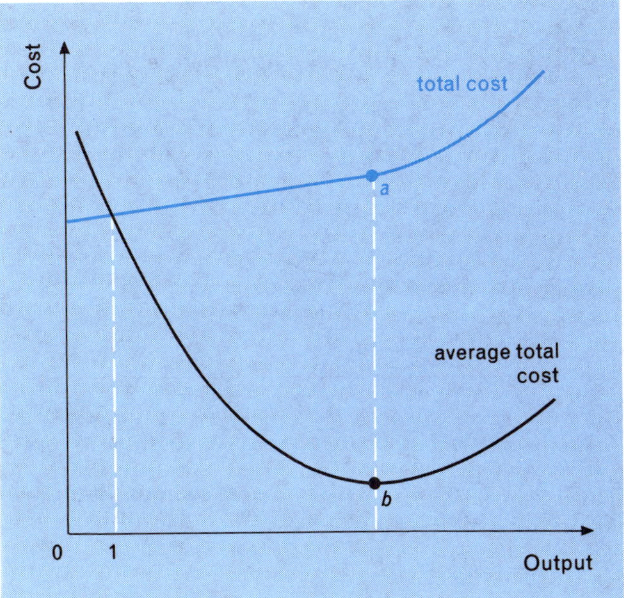

Figure 3.16 **Total cost and average total cost curves.**

Being U-shaped the average total cost curve has a unique minimum at *b* in Figure 3.16 and this minimum average total cost point corresponds to point *a* in Figure 3.13, i.e. where the line *KK* cuts the expansion path. Average total costs in the short run cannot fall below long-run average total costs, but at one level of output the two will be equal. This occurs at the minimum short-run average total cost – point *b*. This minimum-cost point is called the **capacity point**.

Notice the word 'capacity' does not imply that maximum output has been reached. More output can be produced by moving to the right of point *b*. The word 'capacity' is being used here to indicate the most efficient level of output, i.e. that with the lowest average cost.

The particular U-shaped average total cost curve shown in Figure 3.16 is associated with a particular quantity of capital (*KK* in Figure 3.13). Had we chosen a different quantity of capital, we would have obtained a different short-run average total cost curve. All such average total cost curves will have the U-shape, but they will have different capacity points. The capacity point of our original average cost curve (point *b* in Figure 3.16) occurs at that level of output which actually lies on the expansion path (see Figure 3.13). As output grows, the entrepreneurs are constrained to move along the fixed capital line *KK*, i.e. to use more and more labour. At point *a* they have that combination of capital and labour which they would choose if they could vary the quantity of both labour and capital.

Now, if they had a greater amount of capital, say *K′K′*, the entrepreneurs would expand along *K′K′* and achieve their lowest average cost at point *c*. This point has more capital and more labour and hence produces more output. Therefore the capacity point associated with capital *K′K′* will occur at a higher level of output than we obtained for *KK*. Thus the average cost curve for *K′K′* has the same U-shape, but it is centred on a higher level of output, as shown in Figure 3.17.

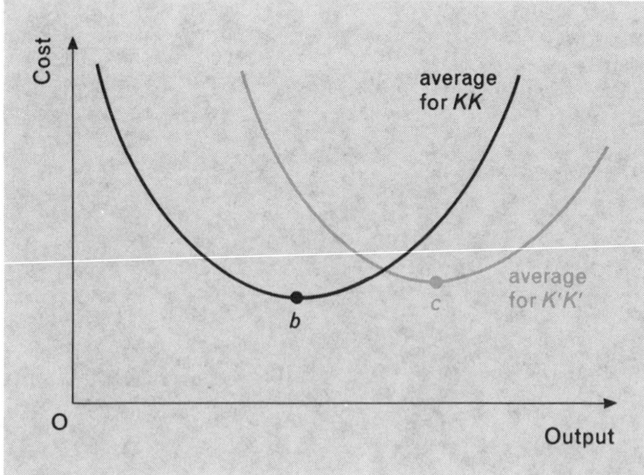

Figure 3.17 The effect of an increase in capital on capacity output.

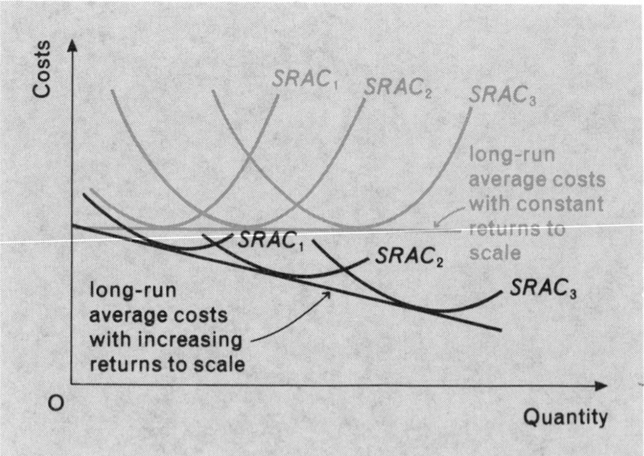

Figure 3.18 Long-run average cost curves with constant and increasing returns to scale.

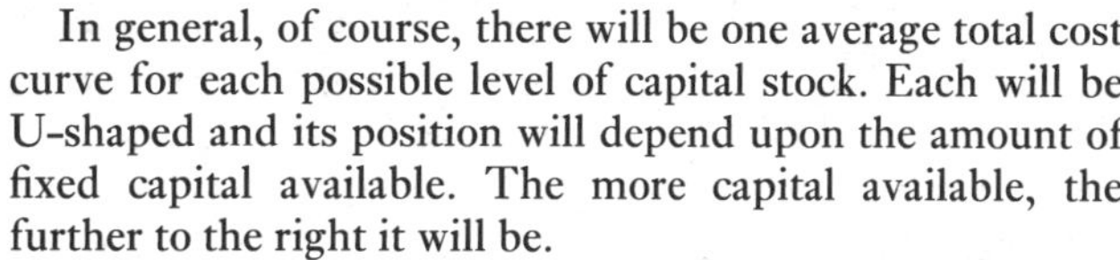

In general, of course, there will be one average total cost curve for each possible level of capital stock. Each will be U-shaped and its position will depend upon the amount of fixed capital available. The more capital available, the further to the right it will be.

Each short-run average total cost curve (SRAC) will touch the long-run average cost curve just once. None will fall below it. In other words, the long-run average cost curve envelopes all the short-run average total cost curves. This is shown in Figure 3.18.

This somewhat detailed analysis of production takes us a long way in our analysis of how an economy works. The costs of production help us to identify and deal with the supply side of scarcity. We have yet to analyse the demand side of scarcity and it is to the demand side that we turn in Chapter 4.

SUMMARY

1. Entrepreneurs' decisions take place either in the long run or in the short run. In the long run all factors are variable and there is a free choice, but in the short run capital is fixed and only the quantity of labour can be changed.
2. This distinction between the long run and the short run may involve a matter of months or a matter of years.
3. When making short-run decisions the entrepreneurs take capital costs as fixed – they do not change with output. Labour costs, however, do vary with output.
4. The law of diminishing return states that as more and more units of a variable factor are applied to some fixed factors then successive increases in output must eventually get smaller and smaller.
5. The average fixed cost (i.e. the cost of capital per unit of output) steadily decreases as output increases.
6. The average variable cost (i.e. the cost of labour per unit of output) is at first constant and then rises.
7. The average total cost (the sum of capital and labour costs per unit of output) will be falling when output is low, will reach a minimum and will then rise and continue to rise.
8. This U-shaped average total cost curve has a point of minimum cost which is called its capacity point.
9. Output can exceed capacity output, but will then raise average cost above its minimum.
10. There will be one U-shaped average cost curve for each quantity of capital. The larger the quantity of capital, the higher will be the capacity output.
11. Each short-run average cost curve will touch the long-run average cost curve just once. The long-run average cost curve is drawn by connecting all of these points.

Exam Preparation and Practice

MULTIPLE-CHOICE QUESTIONS

1. Scarcity exists because:
   A Land is fixed in supply.
   B Capital is fixed in supply.
   C Wants are infinite, but all resources are limited in supply.
   D Wants are limited, but resources are infinite.

2. Diminishing returns occur when:
   A Profit rises as output rises.
   B Profit falls as output rises.
   C Output increases less than proportionately when the amount of all inputs rise.
   D Output rises less than proportionately when the amount of just one input increases.

3. The rewards of a farmer who owns his own farm, provides his own capital and works on the farm are made up of:
   A Rent, wages and interest.
   B Rent, wages, interest and profit.
   C Wages, interest and profit.
   D Rent, interest and profit.

4. An entrepreneur will wish to produce:
   A On the highest attainable isoquant.
   B The lowest possible isocost line.
   C At the point where the lowest possible isocost line touches the desired isoquant.
   D At the point where the highest possible isocost line touches the desired isoquant.

5.

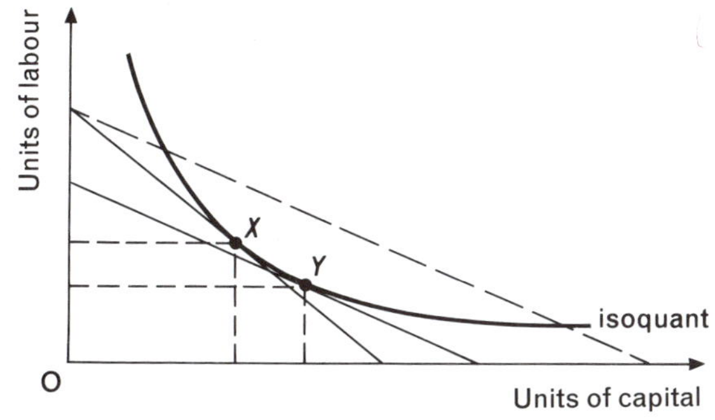

The diagram shows the isoquant facing a firm at the desired level of production. What could cause the firm to change from producing at point *X* to producing at point *Y* on the isoquant?
   A A rise in the desired level of production.
   B A fall in the desired level of production.
   C A rise in the rate of interest.
   D A fall in the rate of interest.

6. The long-run is best defined as:
   A A period when the supply of all factors is fixed.
   B The period when the supply of at least one factor is fixed.
   C The period when the supply of all factors is variable.
   D The period of one generation.

7. A firm experiences increasing returns to scale when:
   A Its long-run average cost curve is falling.
   B Its long-run average cost curve is rising.
   C Its short-run average cost curve is falling.
   D Its short-run average cost curve is rising.

8.

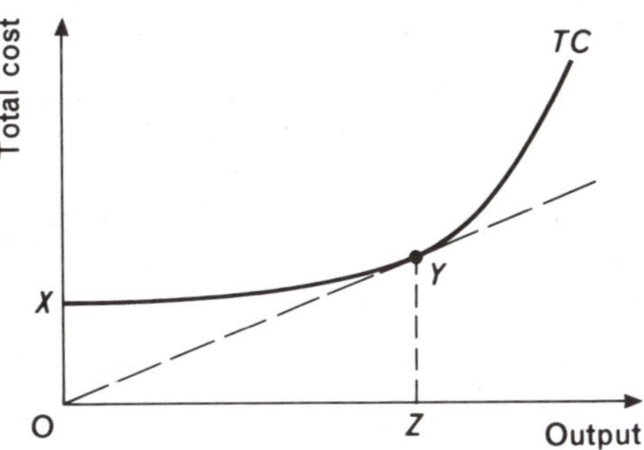

The diagram shows the total cost curve for a manufacturing firm. At output *OZ* short-run average cost is equal to:
   A *OX*
   B *YZ*/*OZ*
   C *OZ*/*OY*
   D *OY*/*OX*
   E *OZ*

Answer key

Where there are three numbered alternatives

A	B	C	D	E
1, 2, 3	1, 2	2, 3	1	3
Correct	Correct	Correct	Correct	Correct

Where there are four numbered alternatives

A	B	C	D	E
1, 2 and 3	1 and 3	2 and 4	4 only	1 and 4
Correct	Correct	Correct	Correct	Correct

9. Which of the following conditions is (are) necessary for the law of diminishing returns to apply?
   1 At least one factor must be in fixed supply.
   2 Demand must be falling.
   3 Total production must be falling.

10.

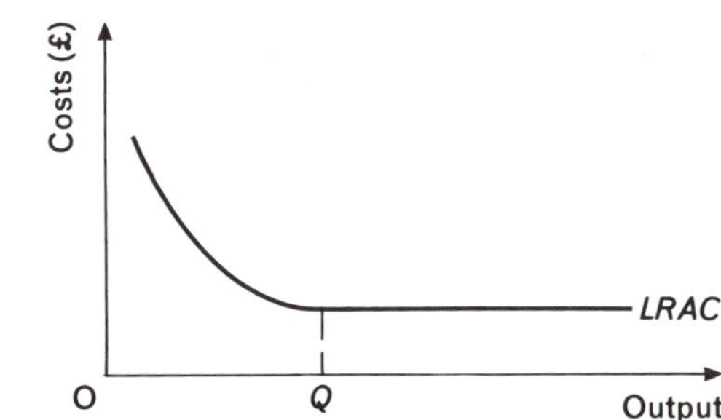

The cost curve in the diagram above shows
   1 Increasing returns to scale and then constant returns to scale.
   2 Decreasing returns to scale and then constant returns to scale.
   3 Decreasing returns to scale throughout.
   4 A firm that will usually have to produce *OQ* units of output to compete with rivals.

11. Which of the following are examples of external economies of scale?
   1 Using a machine for an extra two hours a day because of extra orders.
   2 A fall in the cost of steel to a motor car manufacturer due to the installation of a larger, more efficient blast furnace.
   3 A fall in the price of petrol to a haulage company due to the building of extra capacity at an oil refinery.

EXERCISES

1. Explain what is meant by a 'factor of production'.
2. Briefly define:
   (a) Capital.
   (b) Land.
3. Give one major difference between labour as a factor of production and capital and land as factors of production.
4. What type of payments do the following factors receive?
   (a) Capital.
   (b) Land.
   (c) Enterprise.
5. Why do entrepreneurs receive any payment at all?
6. When deciding how to produce a good, how will a profit-maximizing firm try to organize its factor inputs?
7. A firm faces the following isoquants.

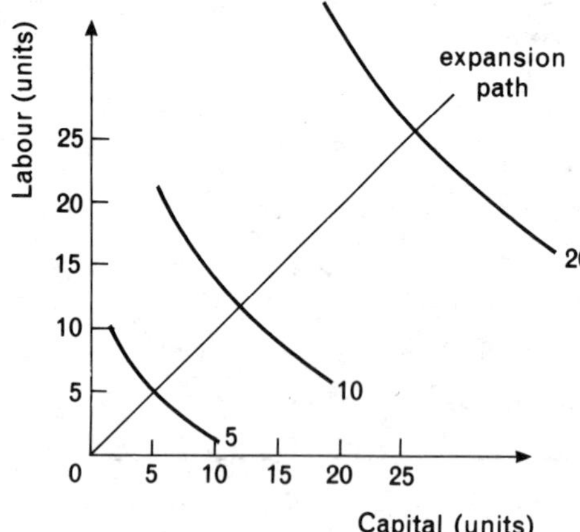

   (a) Draw the total cost curve for a profit-maximizing firm when the cost of both capital and labour is £10 a unit.
   (b) Is the firm experiencing increasing, constant or decreasing returns to scale over the output range shown?
   (c) How might you account for this phenomenon?

8. The diagram below shows the isoquants faced by a firm and the amount of capital (*KK*) the firm employs.
   (a) In the short run, how much labour does the firm employ to produce 60 units of output?
   (b) Will the firm choose a different combination of labour and capital in the long run? If so why?

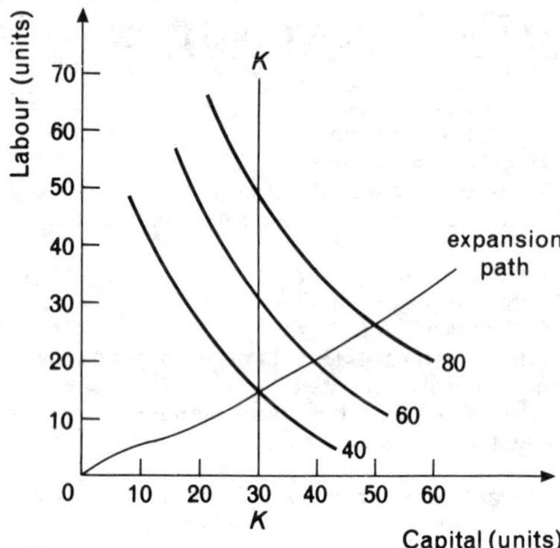

9. The following is a table of costs for a manufacturing firm. Complete the empty columns and draw:
   (a) The firm's total cost curve.
   (b) The firm's average fixed cost curve.
   (c) The firm's average total cost curve.

Output (units)	Fixed cost (£)	Total variable cost (£)	Total cost (£)	Average fixed cost (£)	Average total cost (£)
0	40	0			
1	40	20			
2	40	35			
3	40	50			
4	40	70			
5	40	95			
6	40	125			
7	40	160			
8	40	200			

4 Consumer behaviour

In this chapter we will discuss:

1. How people make decisions about what goods to consume.
2. The way in which people gain satisfaction from consuming goods.
3. Why demand for a good will vary with its price.
4. Why the demand for various goods reacts differently to changes in price.
5. How the consumption of some goods is related to others.

Introduction

We have already seen that exchange is a vital ingredient in the working of the economy: it allows people to specialize in their work. Exchange stands between the two other areas of microeconomics – production and consumption. In Chapter 3 we looked at production; in this chapter we will be concerned with consumption.

Consumption is the 'using up' of goods and services. It may occur in order to produce other goods (coal is 'consumed' in the production of iron), or it may take place simply because we like consuming goods and services (coal is burnt in the fireplace to keep us warm or to give our homes a cosy glow).

In the first example, the consumption takes place in the productive sector, and hence is determined by entrepreneurs. We have already seen how entrepreneurs decide how much to spend on various inputs like capital and labour. In the second example, however, consumption takes place in the home. It is this aspect of consumption with which this chapter deals.

The theory of consumer behaviour

Economists refer to people who are buying goods and services for pleasure as consumers. Consumers may act individually or as a family group, and the term used by economists for both of these is a **household**. Households may contain one or more persons, but members of a household are assumed to make their consumption decisions together. We shall be trying to explain how households make their buying decisions and how those decisions could be changed.

As far as the market is concerned, individuals bring money to market and take away goods. They demand goods, rather than supply goods, and hence households constitute the demand side of the market. Thus the theory of consumer behaviour is also known as demand theory. Explaining demand is therefore a matter of explaining the buying behaviour of economic units called households.

We have said that we are trying to explain the behaviour of households, but obviously households are all very different from one another. What is it then that we seek to explain? It is clearly impossible to explain what one particular household is going to buy in the coming week. Its behaviour would depend on a number of things particular to itself – whether the people in the household liked oranges or not, whether they owned a refrigerator, etc. What we can do is explain the behaviour of an 'average' household. Some will like oranges and some will not, but 'on average' households do like oranges. This 'average' household is called a representative household or a representative consumer. This means that quite a lot of idiosyncratic behaviour is evened out and we no longer need to know the detailed history of each household before we can explain household behaviour.

Consumers (households) buy goods and services because they give pleasure. We will assume that consumers are clever enough to buy those goods and services which give them the most pleasure. That is to say, they know what they like and they know what to do to get it. This ability of consumers to work out how to spend their incomes to their best possible advantage is called *consumer rationality*.

This definition of rationality may seem very straightforward, but it is an important behavioural assumption and it allows economists to make sense of consumers' observed behaviour. Economists do not suggest that all consumers are really rational all the time; we all make mistakes from time to time. Rather economists hope to use the assumption of rationality to explain the behaviour of the representative consumer. Some will make mistakes which lead them to buy too much of something, but others will make mistakes which lead them to buy too little of it. If there are enough consumers (a very large number) then all these mistakes will cancel out and the representative consumer will act rationally.

SUMMARY

1. The theory of consumer behaviour seeks to describe and explain the decisions made by households about what to buy.
2. Consumers do not supply goods to markets, but only demand them from markets in exchange for money. The theory of consumer behaviour is therefore sometimes called demand theory.

3. Different consumers react differently when faced with the same situation. So we cannot explain the behaviour of particular households, but we can explain the behaviour of a representative consumer.
4. To help us explain how representative consumers behave we assume that they act rationally and succeed in maximizing the pleasure they get from their spending.

Utility theory

A very early attempt by economists to explain the behaviour of consumers was to invoke the idea of **utility**.

We have already seen that households buy goods not in order to produce other goods, but simply to get pleasure from them. We like eating good food and wearing good clothes. We like to be warm and comfortable. There are many different sources of pleasure and many different kinds of pleasure. Eating fruit yields a pleasurable sensation, but it is quite different from the pleasure derived from watching television. However, both activities (forms of consumption) are providing utility. An aspirin gives no pleasure yet yields utility by ridding someone of a headache.

Thus utility is gained by the presence of pleasure and/or the absence of pain. Utility is measured in units called utils. No one really knows what a util is, but as we shall see it is useful to be able to say that utility has increased by, for example, 8 utils or 10 utils.

In the materialist world of economics, utility is gained only by consuming goods and services. If you have no goods then you get no utility. The more goods you have, the more utility (and the more utils) you have. This is a materialist view because we rule out the possibility of gaining happiness from religion, abstinence or contemplation of the infinite. Conversely, if a 'good' does not yield utility then it is not a 'good' at all – a key definition then is that *all goods yield utility*.

Now that we have defined the concept of utility, we can use it to explain how a consumer behaves. We can also redefine rational consumers as those who buy that combination of goods which maximizes their utility. The existence of scarcity means that consumers will always want more than they can have. They can have more of one thing only if they give up something else. Rational consumers must therefore choose that combination of goods from among the possible combinations which yields them most utility.

To help us decide how much of each good a rational consumer will buy we need to use the concept of marginal utility. The marginal utility of a good is defined as: the change in the total utility a consumer gets from consuming a little more of that good while maintaining the same level of consumption of all other goods.

To illustrate these concepts we will look at a representative consumer's behaviour in relation to one good, a bar of chocolate. Say our consumer gets 8 utils from the consumption of one bar of chocolate per week and knows it.

Table 4.1 Diminishing marginal utility

Number of chocolate bars	Total utility (in utils)	Change in utility (marginal utility)
1	8	8
2	15	7
3	21	6
4	26	5
5	29	3
6	30	1
7	30	0
8	28	−2

If consumption is increased to two bars per week then total utility goes up to, say, 15 utils. The consumer has gained another 7 utils. The increase in total utility due to an increase in consumption of one bar of chocolate is the marginal utility of chocolate. Thus the marginal utility of the second bar is 7. If the consumer increases consumption to 3 bars a week then total utility will rise to, say, 21 utils. The marginal utility of the third bar is lower than the second, just 6 utils. If the consumer continues to increase weekly consumption of chocolate then total utility will continue to rise but each successive increase will yield less and less utility. This is summarized in Table 4.1. The table shows that each additional bar yields less and less utility. Eventually the gains disappear altogether and no extra utility is derived from the seventh bar, which yields just as much utility as the sixth bar. Since the seventh bar yields no utility, it is technically not a good. When consumers have enough of a good we say they are satiated. The eighth bar is one too many and proves a positive nuisance, so the total utility actually falls if the eighth bar is forced on to the consumer. The marginal utility of this eighth bar is therefore negative.

In economics we confine our analysis only to 'goods', i.e. to those which have not reached satiation point. Thus in this case we are concerned only with the first 6 bars.

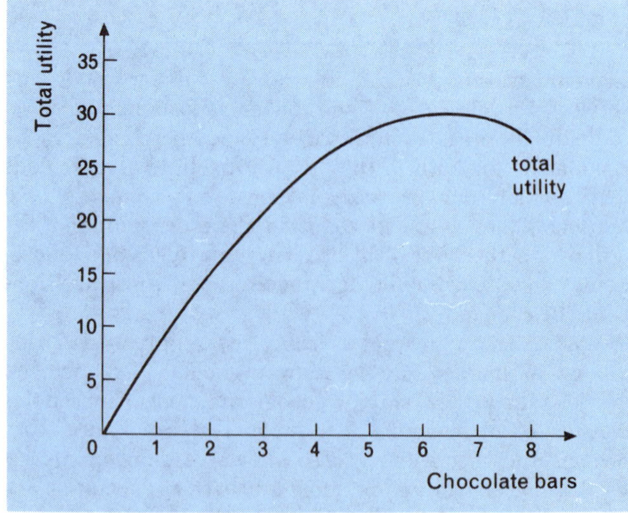

Figure 4.1 Total utility gained by a consumer from chocolate.

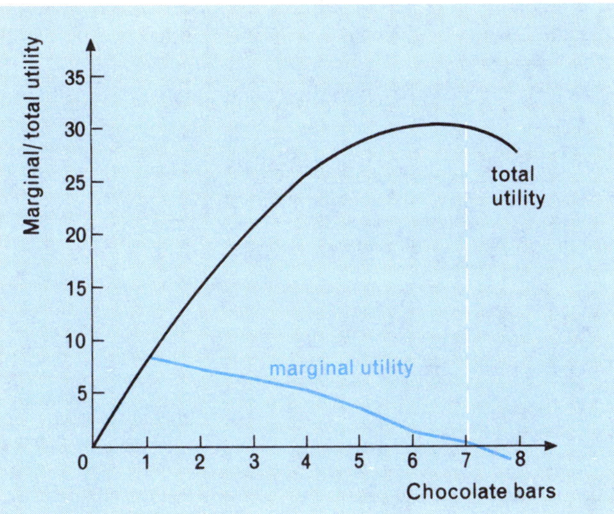

Figure 4.2 Total and marginal utility of a consumer.

The important point is that marginal utility is always declining. This decline in marginal utility is known as the **law of diminishing marginal utility**. Although it is called a law, it is in fact only an assumption. The law of diminishing marginal utility states: successive equal increments of a good consumed by a household yield smaller and smaller increases in total utility, the consumption of all other goods being held constant.

It is important to remember that the consumption of other goods must remain the same for this statement to be true. Imagine that we are discussing the consumption of strawberry jam and that after a few spoonfuls some bread becomes available. The consumer can now enjoy the jam in a quite different way and may well get more utility from the next spoonful.

The concept of total and marginal utility is shown graphically in Figures 4.1 and 4.2. Note the shapes and positions of the two curves. In Figure 4.1 the total utility curve starts from the origin, at first climbs rapidly, then climbs more slowly, reaches a peak and then declines. The way the shape of the total utility curve changes is decided by how the marginal utility curve changes. Initially the consumer gets a lot of utility from the first units of the good consumed, but he or she gets less and less from each subsequent unit. This means that the addition to total utility slows as more is consumed. The total utility curve peaks when marginal utility is zero, showing that the consumption of one extra unit of a good adds nothing to the consumer's enjoyment of the product. As the marginal utility curve moves into the negative region, showing positive displeasure at consuming the product, total utility declines also.

Consumption decisions

We can use a simple example to show that, if consumers get a greater utility from the last pound they spend on one good than from the last pound they spent on another good, then they can increase their total utility by changing their expenditure on the two goods.

Suppose a consumer can buy only two goods – chocolate and crisps. She divides up her income between these two goods and gains 4 utils from the last pound she spends on chocolate and 8 utils from the last pound she spends on crisps.

The consumer has limited income, so if she buys more crisps she has to give up some chocolate. By spending £1 less on chocolate she loses 4 utils. By spending that £1 on crisps she gains 8 utils. This gives her a net gain of 4 utils: 4 utils are lost by not buying the last pound's worth of chocolate and 8 are gained from consuming an extra pound's worth of crisps ($8-4=4$).

The 8 utils gained from £1 of crisps are due to the change in the number of crisps times the marginal utility of crisps. Thus if the marginal utility of crisps is 1 util per packet and there are 8 packets to the pound then the additional £1 would yield $8 \times 1 = 8$ utils. The number of packets to the pound depends upon their price – it is in fact equal to 1/price. Thus 8 packets to the pound means a price of £1/8 = 12.5p per packet.

The change in the total utility due to spending £1 more on crisps is therefore equal to the marginal utility of crisps × (1/the price of crisps). Similarly, the change in total utility due to spending £1 less on chocolate equals the marginal utility of chocolate times the change in the quantity of chocolate. This in turn is equal to the marginal utility of chocolate × (1/the price of chocolate).

As expenditure is switched from chocolate to crisps, less chocolate is being consumed so its marginal utility will have risen due to the law of diminishing marginal utility (see Figure 4.2). Similarly, since more crisps are now being consumed, the marginal utility of crisps will have fallen. If, after the change, another pound's worth of crisps still increases utility by more than the loss of utility from forgoing a pound's worth of chocolate, then consumers will move another £1 from chocolate to crisps.

Since the marginal utility of crisps will be falling as more crisps are consumed and the marginal utility of chocolate will be rising as less chocolate is consumed, eventually the gain in utility from switching another £1 to crisps will equal the loss in utility from switching another £1 away from chocolate.

Switching will continue until this point is reached, i.e. until the last pound spent on chocolate yields exactly the same utility as the last pound spent on crisps. Indeed, it continues until the utility gained from the last penny spent on one good is the same as the utility gained from the last penny spent on any other good.

This suggests that total utility is maximized when:

$$\frac{\text{Marginal utility of good 1}}{\text{Price of good 1}} = \frac{\text{Marginal utility of good 2}}{\text{Price of good 2}}$$

This says that the utility gained from the last penny spent on good 1 is the same as the utility gained from the last penny spent on good 2. This is the point where the consumer maximizes utility and is known as **consumer equilibrium**.

In our example we considered only two goods, but the conclusion holds for any number of goods, so the general

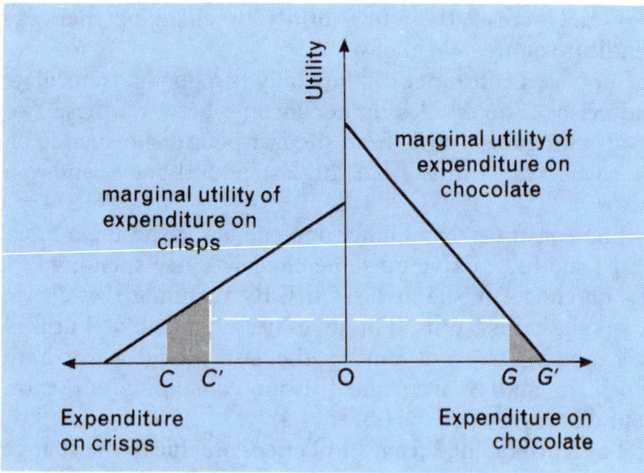

Figure 4.3 Consumer equilibrium.

equilibrium condition is:

$$\frac{\text{Marginal utility of good 1}}{\text{Price of good 1}} = \frac{MU \text{ good 2}}{\text{Price 2}} = \frac{MU \text{ good 3}}{\text{Price 3}} = \ldots = \frac{MU \text{ good } n}{\text{Price } n}$$

Where n is the total number of goods consumed.

Another way often used to express this equilibrium condition is to state that for two goods:

$$\frac{MU \text{ good 1}}{MU \text{ good 2}} = \frac{\text{Price good 1}}{\text{Price good 2}}$$

This condition is derived from and hence equivalent to the two other equilibria stated above.

If you are still unsure about the consumer equilibrium condition, consider Figure 4.3. This shows the marginal utility curves, placed back to back, for a particular consumer who can buy only two goods, crisps and chocolate. Both goods' marginal utilities decline but they do so at different rates. The consumer decides to consume OC of crisps and OG of chocolate. At this point the marginal utility gained from the last penny spent on each good is the same and so the consumer is in equilibrium.

Would it pay the consumer to adjust his spending? The answer is no. Suppose the consumer moved CC' of income away from buying crisps and spent the equivalent amount (GG') on chocolate. The consumer loses the amount of utility represented by the shaded area under the crisps marginal utility curve and gains utility equivalent to only the shaded area under the chocolate marginal utility curve. There is a clear loss of utility as the shaded area gained under the chocolate curve is clearly smaller than the area lost under the crisps marginal utility curve.

Using utility analysis

We can get some general indications from utility analysis about how consumers will behave. If we assume that a consumer starts from an equilibrium condition and that the price of a good falls then we would expect the consumer to buy more of that good. Consider the following example, where the price of crisps falls from 10p to 5p while the price of chocolate remains constant at 20p. Let us say that the marginal utility of crisps is 5 utils and that of chocolate is 10 utils.

Before the price change the consumer is in equilibrium where:

$$\frac{\text{MU of crisps}}{\text{Price of crisps}} = \frac{\text{MU of chocolate}}{\text{Price of chocolate}}$$

which implies in this case:

$$\frac{5}{10} = \frac{10}{20}$$

After the price change:

$$\frac{5}{5} > \frac{10}{20}$$

This is clearly an inequality and cannot be an equilibrium point.

The consumer must now change expenditure to return to an equilibrium position where utility is maximized. A number of changes of expenditure are possible. With the same **money income** as before (the same number of pounds to spend) the consumer can: (a) buy more crisps; (b) buy more chocolate; or (c) buy more of both crisps and chocolate.

Thus the consumer is made better off even when money income remains unchanged if one or more prices fall. The consumer's income in terms of goods rather than pounds has therefore increased. This is called a change in **real income**.

How will this increase in real income be used to regain consumer equilibrium? One possibility would be to buy more crisps (option (a) above). Buying more crisps reduces the marginal utility of crisps until the ratio of marginal utilities again equals the ratio of prices. This will occur when the marginal utility of crisps has fallen to 2.5. Thus:

$$\frac{2.5}{5} = \frac{10}{20}$$

In this case the fall in the price of crisps led to an increase in the consumption of crisps.

In a more complicated world where there is expenditure on crisps, chocolate and other goods there are no such clear-cut results. We are unable to say exactly how much the representative, rational consumer would spend on each good following a change in the price of any one good.

There is a major difficulty when we come to use utility: it is impossible to measure. Every person gains a different amount of utility from every good; some people like certain goods more than others. We are unable to measure a util because utils do not exist, and so it is impossible to ask a consumer, 'how many utils did you get from that packet of crisps?' We therefore cannot say that one person gets more utility than another. We cannot, in other words, make *interpersonal comparisons* of utility.

Even if we stick to one individual, we can apply utility only in a limited way. We can say whether the consumer's utility has risen or fallen, but not by how much. More goods certainly mean more utility, but twice the number never means twice the utility. Utility can be used to *rank* goods for a particular consumer (crisps yield more utility than chocolate), but it cannot be used to say *by how much* crisps are preferred to chocolate. The technical name for measurements of this kind is ordinal measures.

A better understanding of ordinal measures may be had by comparing them with the more usual cardinal measures. An example of a cardinal measure is distance. The unit of measurement is a metre. We can use metres to measure the distance between, say, London and Singapore and between London and Paris. We can rank these distances – we can say that Singapore is further away from London than Paris is. But we can also say *by how much* Singapore is further from London than Paris is (we can express the difference in metres). As we shall see, life for the economist would be much easier if utility were also a cardinal measure.

SUMMARY

1. No doubt there are many reasons for consumers buying particular goods in particular quantities, but we assume that the single aim of the consumer – the aim that embraces all others – is to maximize utility.
2. Utility can be derived from many sources, but whether it comes from eating fruit or watching television it is still utility.
3. Utility may be measured in utils.
4. A consumer gains utility from the consumption of goods, but at a decreasing rate. This is known as the law of diminishing marginal utility.
5. A consumer aims to maximize total utility and does this by trying to get exactly the same amount of extra utility from the last penny spent on each good ($MU_1/P_1 = MU_2/P_2$).
6. If the price of one good falls, we know that the consumer will probably buy more of that good. But we cannot say this with certainty, nor can we say how much more of the good the consumer will buy.
7. Utility is an ordinal rather than a cardinal measure and hence it can only be used to rank goods in the eyes of a particular consumer. It cannot be used for interpersonal comparisons or to say by how much a consumer prefers one good to another.

Indifference analysis

To overcome the difficulties that they encountered with utility theory economists devised another set of tools to analyse consumer behaviour: **indifference analysis**.

The first thing to notice about utility is that we can get it from all kinds of goods. If we are prevented from buying one particular good, we can simply switch to another and get our utility from that instead. Consider the case when a person regularly has bread and apples supplied to her. She derives a certain amount of utility from consuming them: say this amount of utility is 100 utils. Now if some bread is taken away from the consumer, she will have less utility (i.e. fewer than 100 utils). But if at the same time the consumer is given more apples, her utility can be brought back to its original level. Apples can be substituted for bread and can maintain the level of utility.

Since total utility is the same from both combinations of bread and apples, it follows that the consumer cannot choose between them. The consumer does not really mind which combination she has. In other words, she is *indifferent between* them. The word 'indifferent' is used here in the technical economic sense and must not be confused with being indifferent *to* something, i.e. not caring whether you have it or not. Being indifferent *between* two combinations of bread and apples does not mean that you want neither. In fact you want both, but if you had to choose one or the other you simply would not care which.

Now as well as those two combinations there are a whole range of combinations among which the consumer would be indifferent. Slightly more apples will compensate for slightly less bread over a very wide range indeed. It is possible to show all these combinations graphically. In Figure 4.4 the vertical axis represents the amount of apples and the horizontal axis represents the amount of bread.

Let us assume that the consumer originally has 2 apples and 4 loaves of bread (point *A*). If her number of apples is reduced to one and a half, she will only be compensated for this by having 7 loaves (point *B*). She is indifferent between the combination of bread and apples represented by points *A* and *B*. What other combinations of the two goods will give her the same utility?

We know that both bread and apples yield utility. It follows that if the consumer has less of one without more of the other then she will be worse off. The consumer will have lost utility by half an apple and would not have been compensated by an increased amount of bread. This means that any point to the south-west of point *A* in Figure 4.4 (for example, 1 apple and 3 loaves must yield less utility than is obtained from *A*. The points we are looking for (points of equal utility with *A*) cannot therefore lie to the south-west of *A*. Similarly, any point to the north-east of *A* (e.g. 3 apples and 6 loaves) has more of both goods which

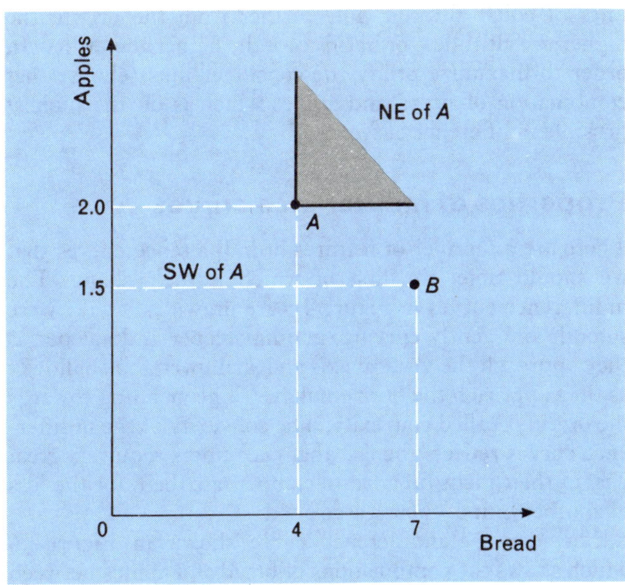

Figure 4.4 Ranking combinations of goods.

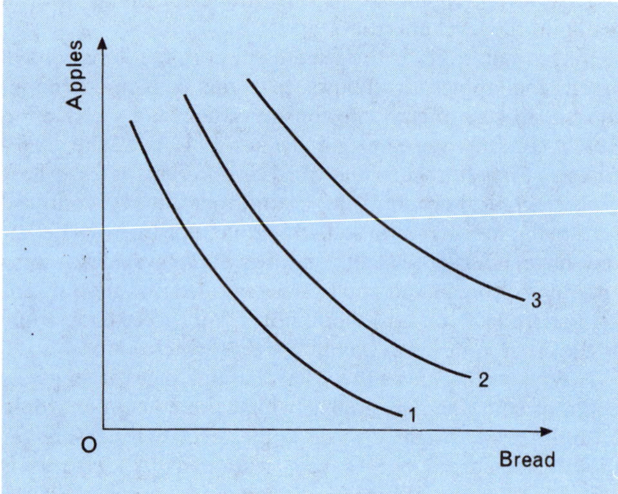

Figure 4.5 An indifference map.

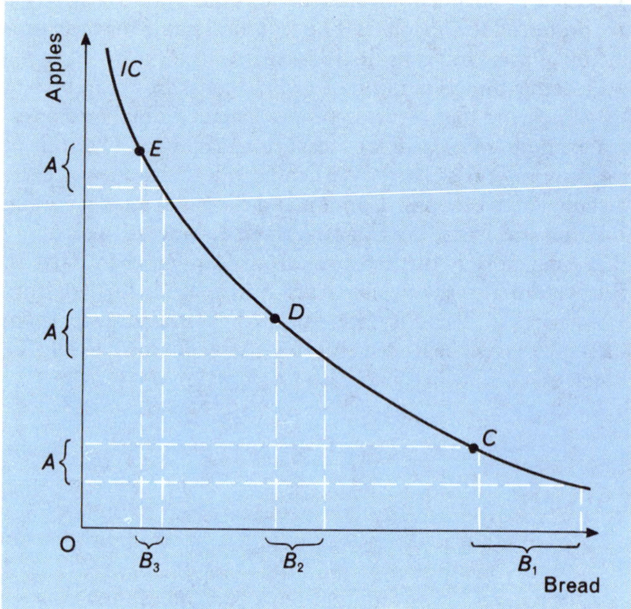

Figure 4.6 Marginal rate of substitution.

must make the consumer better off. This means that the consumer would prefer any point north-east of *A* to *A* itself. It follows that the points we are looking for cannot lie to the north-east of *A* either.

This line of reasoning tells us that points in Figure 4.4 which yield the same amount of utility as combination *A* must lie either to the north-west of *A* or to the south-east of *A*. That is to say, a line connecting all these indifference points must be downward sloping from left to right. Such a line is called an **indifference curve**.

We can draw as many indifference curves as we like provided only that they slope downwards. Each indifference curve will represent a different level of utility. Curves further from the origin, representing higher quantities of both goods, yield higher utility. In Figure 4.5 curve 3 is preferred to curve 2, and curve 2 is preferred to curve 1.

This collection of indifference curves is known as an indifference map and may be thought of as like a geographical map. The indifference curves are like contour lines – lines of equal altitude. The further from the origin, the higher the altitude – or in this case the higher the utility. In order to maximize utility the consumer must choose that combination of bread and apples which is on the highest possible indifference curve.

Properties of indifference curves

There are a number of features of indifference curves that we should note, the first of which is their shape. The indifference curves in Figure 4.5 are drawn as if they were smooth and gently curving, getting steeper and steeper as they approach the vertical axis and shallower and shallower as they approach the horizontal axis. This bending towards the origin is called convexity. The convexity of the indifference curves reflects the fact that consumers require a great deal of their plentiful good to compensate them for the loss of another unit of their scarce good.

Consider the indifference curve shown in Figure 4.6 which shows the combinations of bread and apples between which a consumer is indifferent. When the consumer is at point *C* he has a relatively large amount of bread in relation to apples. He is therefore prepared to swap B_1 units of bread to gain *A* units of apples. As he moves up the curve to point *D* the consumer has more fruit and less bread. At *D* the consumer is therefore prepared to give up only B_2 units of bread to gain an extra *A* units of apples. At point *E*, where the consumer has relatively little bread in comparison to apples, he is only prepared to swap B_3 units of bread to gain *A* units of apples. This behaviour represents the consumer's action in relation to the relative scarcity of the goods he is consuming and reflects the amount of one good that he is prepared to substitute for another while remaining indifferent between the combinations of the two goods.

The amount of one good which the consumer is prepared to give up to gain more of another is therefore reflected in the slope of the indifference curve. It is known as the *marginal rate of substitution*. In Figure 4.6 the marginal rate of substitution (the slope of the indifference curve) at point *C* is measured by the change in the quantity of bread (B_1) divided by the change in the quantity of apples (*A*).

When using indifference curves you should remember a number of features that will help you to draw good diagrams. The first is that they must never cross. In Figure 4.7 two curves are shown that cross. Three points, *A*, *B* and *C*, are shown on curve I_1, and this implies that the consumer is indifferent between them. Point *D* lies to the south-west of point *A* and so, according to our previous analysis, contains less of at least one of the goods. The consumer must therefore prefer *A* to *D*. On curve I_2 three points, *D*, *B* and *E*, are also marked, and the consumer must be indifferent between these points as they lie on the same indifference curve. This provides us with a contradiction as the consumer is indifferent between points *A* and *B* and indifferent between points *D* and *B*. This should imply that the consumer is indifferent between points *A* and *D*, but we have already seen that point *A* must be preferred to point *D*. Thus indifference curves can never cross as this contradicts the logic on which indifference curves are based.

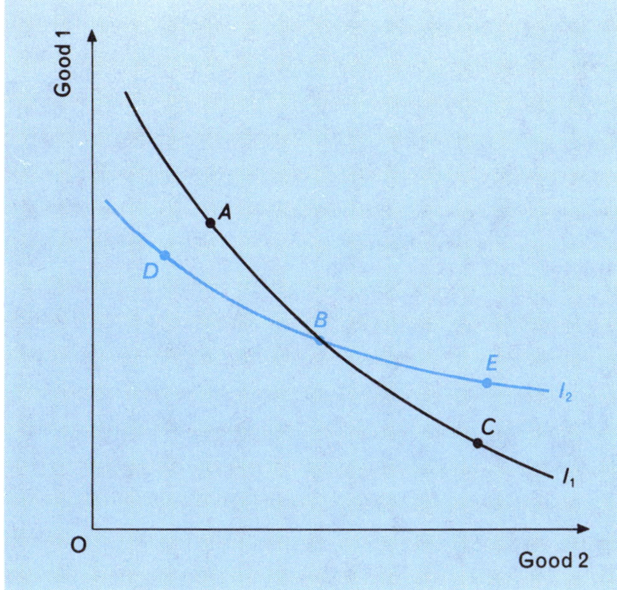

Figure 4.7 Indifference curves can never cross.

The second feature to remember is that indifference curves cannot have any thickness. If we were to draw curves in this way you would not be able to see them, but the consequences of 'thick' indifference curves should be noted and are demonstrated in Figure 4.8.

Figure 4.8 shows an indifference curve that has two points, *A* and *B*. An indifference curve shows all combinations of goods between which a consumer is indifferent, and so the consumer should be indifferent between points *A* and *B*. It is clear from Figure 4.8 that the bundle of goods represented by point *B* must contain at least one more unit of one good than the bundle of goods represented by point *A* because it is further to the north-east, and so the consumer would prefer to consume at point *B*. Thus the consumer cannot be indifferent between point *A* and point *B* and so indifference curves can have no thickness. To avoid this always draw indifference curves with a sharp pencil.

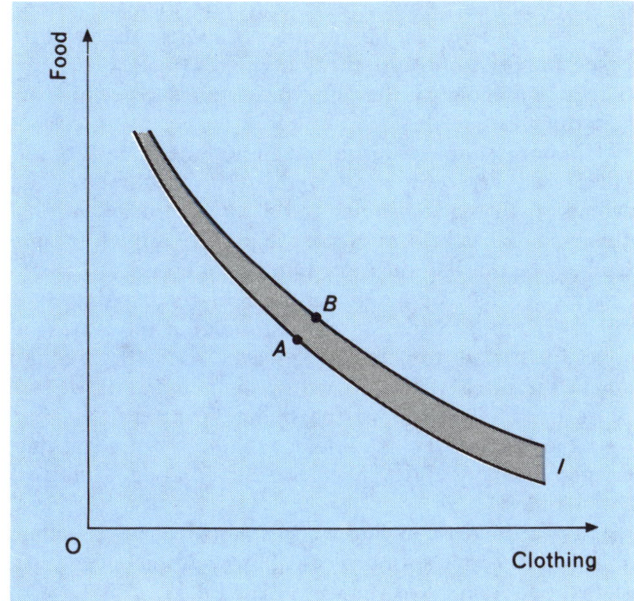

Figure 4.8 Indifference curves have zero thickness.

The last point to make is that indifference curves need not represent a consumer's choice between two goods only. When discussing thick indifference curves we referred to 'bundles' of goods at points *A* and *B* because they could contain many different goods. The axes of Figure 4.8 are labelled 'Food' and 'Clothing', both of which embrace many products. For a consumer to prefer one bundle of food and clothing to another, one bundle might have to contain, say, only one extra pair of socks or one extra humbug.

SUMMARY

1. It is possible to say that a consumer can rank bundles of goods and can rank two bundles equally. When this occurs, the consumer is said to be indifferent between the bundles.
2. When all bundles that have equal ranking in the eye of the consumer are joined together they form an indifference curve.
3. Each indifference curve represents one level of utility to the consumer. The further from the origin an indifference curve lies, the higher the level of utility the curve represents.
4. The slope of an indifference curve is called the marginal rate of substitution (MRS) and represents the consumer's willingness to substitute one good for another while maintaining the same level of utility.
5. The whole set of indifference curves is called an indifference map.
6. Indifference curves are convex, very thin, never touch and never cross.

The budget constraint

The rate at which I am prepared to give up bread for apples may be quite different from the rate that you would agree to. It all depends on our tastes and preferences. If I were particularly fond of apples, I might be reluctant to give up very many, no matter how much bread was offered. If you liked bread, you would be equally reluctant to give it up for apples. The indifference map drawn up for an individual is therefore an attempt to describe his or her particular tastes and preferences. Where these tastes come from, whether we approve of them or not, and whether they can be changed or not, is beyond the scope of this book. We will assume that they are what they are and take them to be fixed. Our indifference maps are in other words taken as 'given' by economists. What we now have to do is to see how a consumer chooses which combination of goods to buy, i.e. where he or she will choose to be on an indifference map. This involves choosing an indifference curve and then choosing a point on it. In order to do this, we have to know something about the consumer's income, the price of bread and the price of apples. It is to this question that we now turn.

We have seen that consumers obtain higher and higher levels of utility as they move from one indifference curve to the next, further and further away from the origin. If consumers wish to maximize their utility (as we assume) then they should get as far away from the origin as possible.

The economic problem arises because the consumer's choice of indifference curve is limited. Consumers cannot have as much as they want of everything. Our next task then is to discover what choices they do have – this is called the choice set – and having done that, we can go on to see which of the many possible choices available is actually chosen.

Since the consumer can obtain goods only by paying for them, the ability to consume depends on the ability to pay. The consumer's ability to pay depends in turn on his or her income. Every week or month most individuals receive a sum of money. This, together with any possible borrowings, limits their ability to buy more and more of all goods.

To fix our minds, let us assume that a consumer receives £10 every week, all of which he spends on bread and apples. Assume further that bread is 50p per loaf and apples are 25p per kg. Since he is assumed to spend all his income, it must be that the amount spent on bread plus the amount spent on apples equals £10. The amount spent on bread is the price of a loaf multiplied by the number of loaves bought. And the amount spent on apples equals the price of apples multiplied by the number bought.

If the consumer spent all his income on bread, he would buy 20 loaves per week. Alternatively, he might spend all his income on apples, in which case he would buy 40 kg of apples per week.

Between these two extremes, there is an infinite number of combinations of apples and loaves which he could buy with his £10 per week. If, instead of spending all his income on bread, he bought only 19 loaves then with the 50p left over he could buy 2 kg of apples; with two fewer loaves, he could buy 4 kg of apples and so on. These combinations of bread and apples which exactly use up his income every week can be represented diagrammatically as in Figure 4.9,

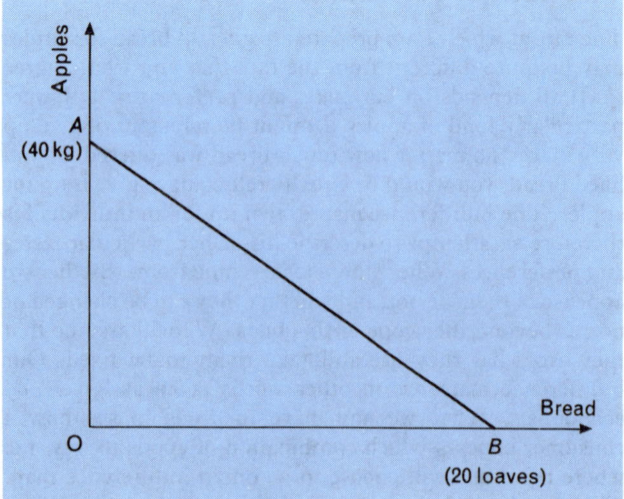

Figure 4.9 Budget constraint.

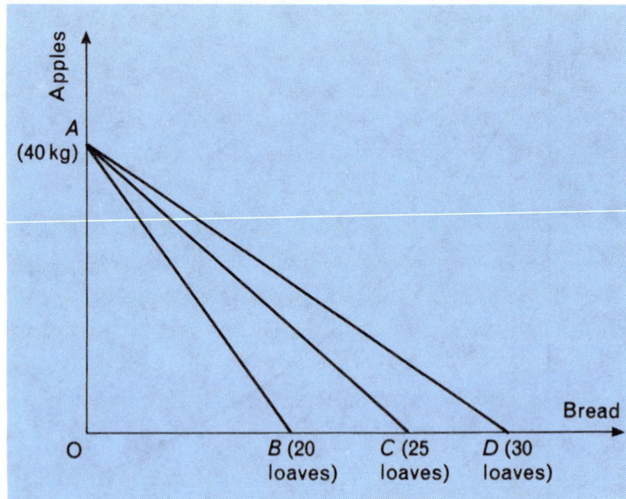

Figure 4.10 Effect of a decrease in the price of bread on the budget constraint.

where the number of loaves is measured on the horizontal axis and the number of kgs of apples on the vertical axis.

From this figure we see that the curve of possible purchases is a straight line joining point A, where all income is spent on apples, to point B, where all income is spent on bread. This tells us that consumers are constrained to choose a point on the line AB. If they try to go above it, they will find that they are unable to afford it. If they go below it then they are not spending all their income and this means that they are sacrificing the utility they would gain from the extra goods they could buy. They are not maximizing their utility and so are not behaving rationally. The line AB is called the consumer's **budget constraint**, and it is this constraint which prevents consumers from buying all the things they would like.

Whereas indifference curves relate quantities of goods to utility, the budget line introduces prices and income into our analysis. So we now have six items under consideration: the quantity of apples, the quantity of loaves, the price of apples, the price of bread, the household's (weekly) income and the household's utility. Our next step is to see how all these things are related.

If, in our example of bread and apples, the price of bread is decreased (say to 40p per loaf) then with the same level of income (£10) our consumer could buy more loaves (25, rather than 20 as before). Since the price of apples has not changed, he can buy the same number of apples as before. This means that the budget line still starts at point A in Figure 4.10, but instead of going to point B (20 loaves) it moves further out to point C (25 loaves). A further reduction in the price of bread (with income and the price of apples fixed) would move the budget constraint further along the horizontal axis to point D. The new budget line therefore contains all the points of the old budget line and more besides.

A similar increase in choice also results from a reduction in the price of apples. In this case, however, the budget line rotates about point B as shown in Figure 4.11.

As a final example of movements of the budget line, Figure 4.12 shows the effect of increasing income while

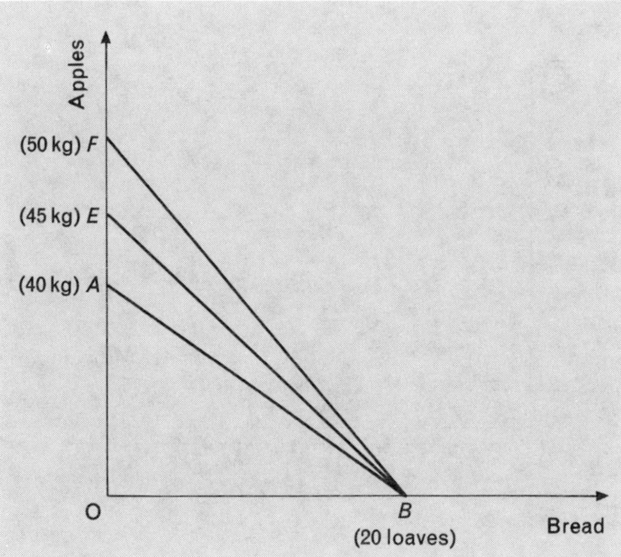

Figure 4.11 Effect of a decrease in the price of apples on the budget constraint.

leaving prices unchanged. Since the consumer can now buy more of both goods, the budget line moves out from the origin. Line *GI* represents a higher income than line *AB* and line *HJ* still higher. All lines are parallel to each other because relative prices are unchanged.

It is interesting to note that, if we change both prices and income by the same proportion, we leave the budget line unchanged. Say our consumer has an income of £10 per week and buys bread at 50p per loaf and apples at 25p per kg. His budget line, as before, is a straight line connecting 20 loaves on the horizontal axis and 40 kg of apples on the vertical axis. Then the consumer can buy either 20 loaves or 40 kg of apples or any combination along this budget line.

Say he now has an income of £20 per week. But bread now costs £1 per loaf and apples cost 50p per lb. Thus income and all prices have doubled. Now he can buy (£20/£1) 20 loaves or (£20/50p) 40 kg of apples, exactly as before. He has doubled his money income, but the increase in prices means that he is no better (or worse) off than before.

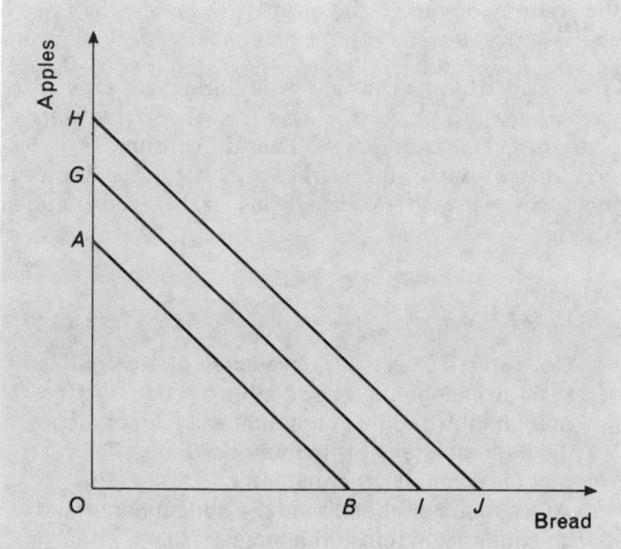

Figure 4.12 Effect of an increase in income on the budget constraint.

This suggests that we should distinguish between income measured in pounds and income measured in goods or utility. The former is called **money income** or **nominal income** and the latter is called **real income**. For nominal or money income to be constant, we must receive the same number of pound notes each week. For real income to be constant, we have to stay on the same indifference curve. It does not matter where on the indifference curve, since by definition we are indifferent among all the points on an indifference curve.

If we wish to increase our consumer's real income, then we must let him move to a higher indifference curve. We could do this either by increasing his nominal income and leaving prices unchanged, or by leaving his nominal income unchanged and reducing prices. Both have the effect of moving the budget line further away from the origin and hence giving him access to higher indifference curves.

SUMMARY

1. In order to maximize utility, consumers should consume the maximum quantity of all goods.
2. Consumption is limited because goods cost money and consumers typically have limited incomes.
3. If the consumer's income is known and the prices of the goods are known then we can work out all the different combinations of goods the consumer could possibly afford.
4. This turns out to be a straight line and is called a budget line of budget constraint.
5. The budget line will change its slope when one of the prices is changed, but if no prices are changed (or all prices are changed by the same proportion, say a 10 per cent rise in *all* prices), there will be no change in the slope of the budget line.
6. When a price is decreased, the budget line swings away from the origin and hence the choice set open to the consumer increases – he or she is made better off.
7. An increase in income, with no change in prices, moves the whole budget line bodily outwards away from the origin with no change of slope. The choice set is again increased and so the consumer is again better off.
8. If all prices and income are changed by the same proportion (say a 10 per cent increase in all prices and a 10 per cent increase in income) then the budget line remains unchanged.
9. Since income has increased but there is no increase in the choice set, it is customary (and useful) to distinguish between money income (or nominal income) and real income. It is the latter which depends upon the size of the choice set and upon nominal income and prices.

Choosing the goods

Consumers will aim to maximize their utility given their income. We have represented the set of choices open to consumers by the budget line. And we previously represented the tastes and preferences of consumers by a map of indifference curves. Both these diagrams have the same axes (quantity of bread and quantity of apples) and hence we can superimpose one on the other to find a consumer equilibrium. This is done in Figure 4.13.

The line AB – the budget line – represents all possible combinations of apples and bread available to a consumer, and she can choose any point along it. If she chose, say, 9 apples and 1 loaf (point L) then she would be on indifference curve IC_1. But if she moved to point K (i.e. 8 apples and 2 loaves) then she would move to a higher indifference curve, IC_2. Since IC_2 is above IC_1, she is better off at K than at L. She would continue to get better off as she moved along the budget line substituting loaves for apples until she reached point M.

At point M she has 6 apples and 4 loaves and is on indifference curve IC_3. Moving below M – say to N – will reduce her utility back to what it was at point K. From this it will be clear that, in order to maximize utility, our consumer will choose point M out of all the possible points on the budget line. She would, of course, prefer to be on indifference curve IC_4, but IC_4 nowhere touches the budget line and hence is beyond her reach.

We can see from Figure 4.13 that the consumer has chosen a point on the highest attainable indifference curve, point M on IC_3. The budget line just touches IC_3 at one point (if it touched more than this there would be two or more possible consumption bundles attainable), and the budget line is therefore tangential to indifference curve IC_3. Thus the slope of the budget line equals the slope of the indifference curve at the chosen point (in this case point M). Point M is a point of consumer equilibrium and providing no circumstances change the consumer will have no desire to change from this consumption pattern.

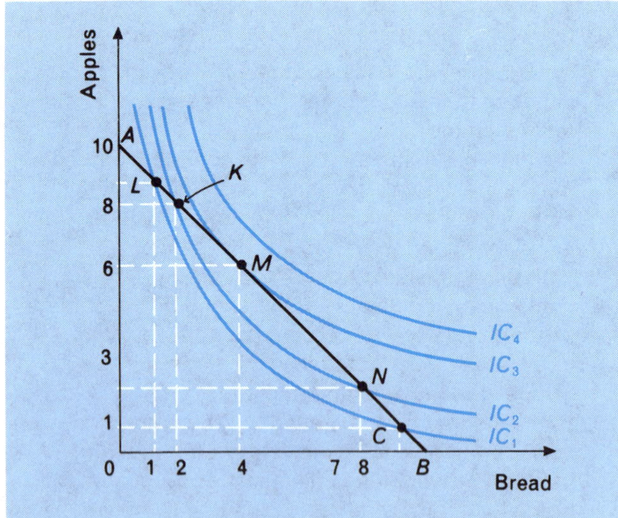

Figure 4.13 Combining budget lines and indifference curves.

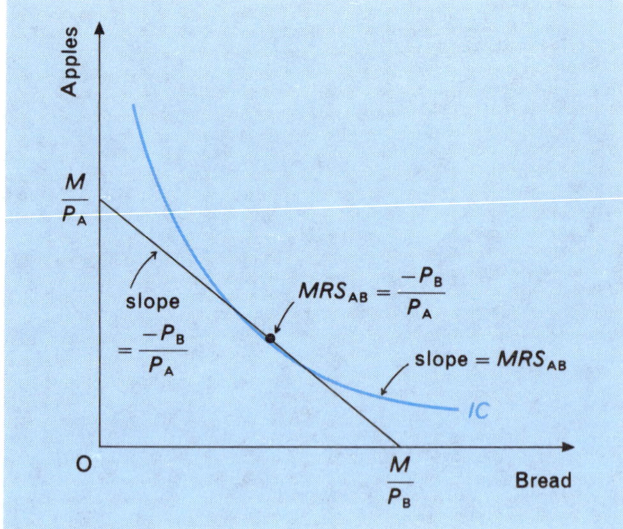

Figure 4.14 Consumer equilibrium.

The budget line in Figure 4.14 is shown to intercept each axis where all of the consumer's money income M is spent on the one good represented on the axis. For example, if all income is spent on bread then the budget line joins the bread axis at $\frac{M}{P_B}$ where P_B is the price of bread. This means that the intercepts of the budget line are $\frac{M}{P_A}$ and $\frac{M}{P_B}$ and that the slope of the budget line is the ratio of the prices of the two goods $\frac{-P_B}{P_A}$.

As we have already explained, consumers are in equilibrium when they consume at a point on the highest attainable indifference curve. At this point the budget line and indifference curve are tangential and their slopes at that point are identical:

$$MRS_{AB} = \frac{-P_B}{P_A}$$

This means that at a consumer equilibrium *the ratio of the prices of the two products is equal to the marginal rate of substitution of the two products.* Thus the consumer's preferences match exactly the market price ratio and the consumer has no wish to change his or her consumption pattern.

SUMMARY

1. Consumers seek to maximize their utility from their given income. They do this by choosing the point on the budget constraint which just touches the highest attainable indifference curve. This point is a consumer equilibrium.
2. At a consumer equilibrium the budget constraint is tangential to the indifference curve.
3. When two lines are tangential their slopes are the same. This means that at the point of consumer

Case Study 4.1 Brewing trouble

Procter & Gamble is so incensed by a boycott of its Folgers coffee that it has staged a counter-boycott. The Cincinnati-based soap and food giant has announced that it will yank all advertising from any TV station that broadcasts a 'highly offensive' anti-Folgers commercial from a political advocacy group called Neighbour to Neighbour. The ad shows a cup of Folgers coffee that turns to blood when poured.

This ultimatum has forced television stations to choose between carrying commercials from Procter & Gamble or from Neighbour to Neighbour, which accuses Procter & Gamble of indirectly financing a brutal war when it buys coffee beans from El Salvador. Most stations have not found it a difficult choice. Procter & Gamble, America's biggest advertiser, spends more than $600m a year on television advertisements for Pampers nappies, Tide detergent, Charmin lavatory paper, Crest toothpaste and scores of other products.

Neighbour to Neighbour has tried without success to get its commercial aired in Washington DC, Cincinnati and two cities with Folgers coffee plants, New Orleans and Kansas City. Only three stations, all of them in the north-east corner of the United States, have defied Procter & Gamble's counter-boycott.

The most defiant is WHDH-TV, the CBS affiliate in Boston whose refusal to stop airing the anti-Folgers commercials has cost it Procter & Gamble advertising worth $1m a year. Mr Seymour Yanoff, WHDH-TV's president, says: 'For me, it was a question of access. What if Procter & Gamble had $1,000 and Neighbour to Neighbour had $1m?'

Despite Procter & Gamble's success in keeping its foe off the airwaves elsewhere, its aggressive counter-boycott has boomeranged. Neighbour to Neighbour is thrilled by the publicity which the controversy surrounding Procter & Gamble's boycott has brought to its own anti-Folgers campaign. Worse, Procter & Gamble is being portrayed as a corporate bully that denies its critics the right of free speech – even when they are willing to pay for it.

1. Does the existence of persuasive advertising and powerful advertisers prevent consumers from getting the proper information from which they can maximize utility?

Source: *The Economist*, 26 May 1990

equilibrium the consumer's marginal rate of substitution of one good for the other equals the price ratio of the two goods.

Changes in consumption behaviour

In order for any change to occur, we must either change the consumer's range of choice (move his or her budget line) or change the consumer's tastes (move his or her indifference map). The second of these might be achieved by advertising but is not usually considered to be part of economics – economists like to think of tastes and preferences as fixed and given. That being so, we are left with movements of the budget line and this is what we concentrate on. We have already seen that we can move the budget line by either changing income or changing relative prices.

We shall look at each of these in turn. First we shall look at the effect of income on consumption.

An income–consumption curve

If we double a consumer's money income and hold prices constant, how will he respond? Will he buy more of both goods? Will he buy a lot more bread and a few more apples? Or will he reduce the amount of fruit? Figure 4.15 offers a possible answer.

The budget line is moved out from *aa* to *dd* in a series of steps (remember that all these budget lines are parallel to each other). At each level of income he will choose that combination of bread and apples which lies at the point of tangency between the budget line and the indifference curve. These points are labelled *k*, *l*, *m* and *n* in the figure. By joining up these points we sketch out how his choice of bread and fruit changes as his income increases. This line is called the *income–consumption curve*.

You may think that, since the indifference curves bend smoothly away from origin, the income–consumption line should be a straight line passing through the origin. This would mean that if we doubled his income then the consumer would simply double the quantity of each good. It is just possible that our consumer would behave like this, but it is not very likely. Fortunately, the assumption of smoothly bending indifference curves does not imply straight-line income–consumption lines.

It turns out that our income–consumption lines can be almost any shape. One condition which must be satisfied, however, is that for any increase in income the consumption

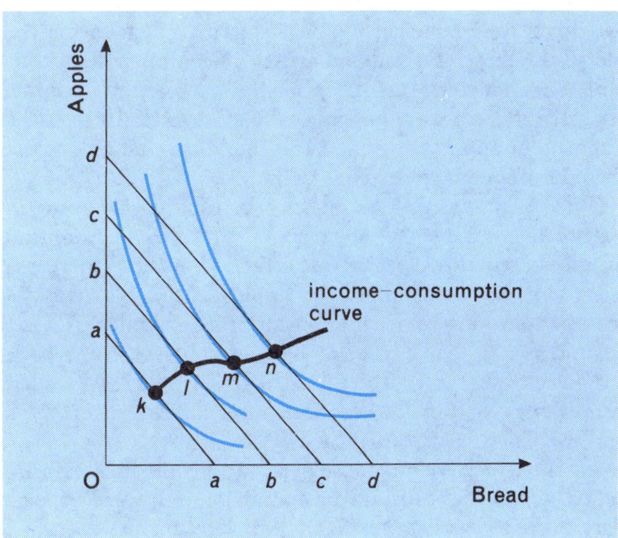

Figure 4.15 Income–consumption curve.

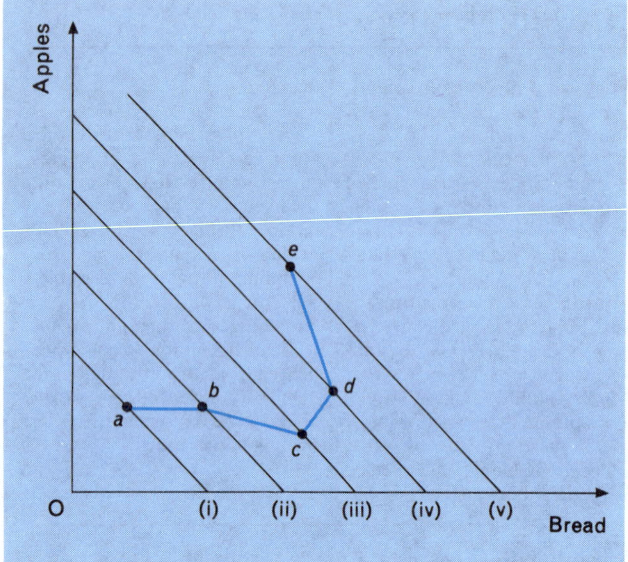

Figure 4.16 Deriving an Engel curve.

of *at least one* good must increase. A possible income–consumption line is shown in Figure 4.16.

As income is increased from (i) to (ii) the consumer moves from combination *a* to combination *b*. This means he leaves his consumption of apples unchanged and spends the entire increase in income on bread. The increase in income from (ii) to (iii) causes him actually to reduce his consumption of fruit and further increase his consumption of bread. The next increase in income from (iii) to (iv) is spent on more bread and more fruit – a bit of both. Finally, the increase in income from (iv) to (v) causes him to reduce his consumption of bread and greatly increase his consumption of fruit.

Engel curves

All these outcomes are possible, although it is very difficult to demonstrate this with our simple diagram. (One reason for using mathematical methods in economics is that we are less likely to be misled by the diagrams.) Let us for the moment take this result on trust. The information contained in an income–consumption line can be conveyed in a slightly different way. In Figure 4.17 the vertical axis is the quantity of apples consumed and the horizontal axis is the amount of income received.

The points *a*, *b*, *c*, *d* and *e* correspond to those in Figure 4.16. As income increases, at first the consumption of apples remains constant (*ab*), then as income increases still further the consumption of apples falls (*bc*). Finally, as income continues to rise the consumption of apples rises too (*cd* and *de*).

Curves such as that depicted in Figure 4.17 are called **Engel curves** after the economist (not the Engels of Marx and Engels) who first used them.

Goods which we buy more of as our income increases are called **normal goods** and are found on an upward or level part of their Engel curve. Goods which we buy less of when we get richer are called **inferior goods** and are found on a downward part of their Engel curve.

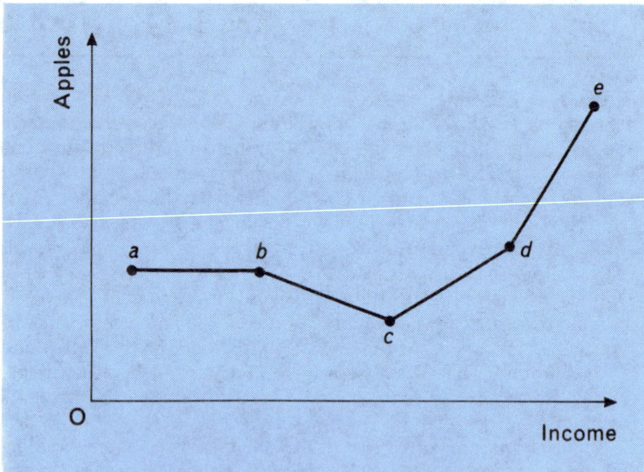

Figure 4.17 Engel curve.

An example

This behaviour can be illustrated by taking an example such as margarine. When people are very poor they eat dry bread, but as their income grows they begin to buy margarine to go with the bread. Their consumption of margarine is therefore growing as their income grows. At this income level margarine is a normal good.

If income is increased still further, people will begin to buy butter instead of margarine and so the consumption of margarine begins to decline as income increases. Over this range margarine is an inferior good.

The next stage occurs when the consumer is rich enough to afford meat, milk, cream etc., all of which are not only fattening but also full of cholesterol. This may cause him to switch out of butter into low-fat margarine again. Over this range of income margarine is again a normal good.

It is not difficult to construct similar examples, but the point is that you cannot say, simply by thinking about the good, whether it is a normal or an inferior good. Whether a good is a normal good or an inferior good is a matter of fact (i.e. our recorded buying habits) not a matter for conjecture.

Summary of consumer theory so far

What we have managed to say so far about the behaviour of a consumer is that his or her choice of goods will depend upon: tastes and preferences (assumed fixed); money income; and the prices of the goods available. Furthermore, any increase in money income may cause the consumer to buy more of a good or less of a good or the same amount of a good. If the consumer buys more (or the same amount) then it is a normal good. If he or she buys less then it is an inferior good.

At least one good must be a normal good. Any good may be a normal good at some income levels and an inferior good at other income levels. These statements are so all-inclusive that they actually convey no information at all. Even without economic theory, we could say that as a consumer gets richer, she will either increase or decrease or leave unaltered her consumption of bread – there is nothing else she could possibly do.

Table 4.2 Demand for food as a proportion of disposable income

	After-tax income at 1980 prices (£m)	Expenditure on food at 1980 prices (£m)
1981	157,683	22,676
1982	157,938	22,587
1983	160,440	22,858
1984	163,996	22,488

Source: *Monthly Digest of Statistics.*

This listing of the set of all possible alternative courses of action is nevertheless useful in that it offers us a language, a kind of shorthand, for analysing a problem. To say we are dealing with a normal good now conveys quite a lot of information briefly and accurately. We shall make much use of this language later. In the meantime we can even use it to show, in Table 4.2, what actually did happen to the demand for food.

We see from Table 4.2 and Figure 4.18 that consumers' expenditure on food fell from £22,676m in 1981 to £22,488m in 1984, even though the disposable income rose from £157,683 to £163,996. Thus, apart from the small leap in 1983, there seems to be a decline in the amount spent on food. We now know that this may signal that 'food' is an inferior good. Knowing this, it is possible to say something about the probable levels of demand for food in the near future.

But these figures are not entirely suitable for drawing up an Engel curve. An Engel curve should show the relationship between income and consumption *with relative prices fixed*. Our data do not satisfy this condition since, although they allow for inflation, they have not taken into account the fact that relative prices have changed between 1981 and 1984.

We have therefore only the beginning of a language and its use. We require something more of our theory than a classification system. We require it to restrict in some way the range of all possible actions so that we can say something definite about how our consumer will behave. To do this we turn to the second method of moving the budget line, i.e. we see what happens when a price changes.

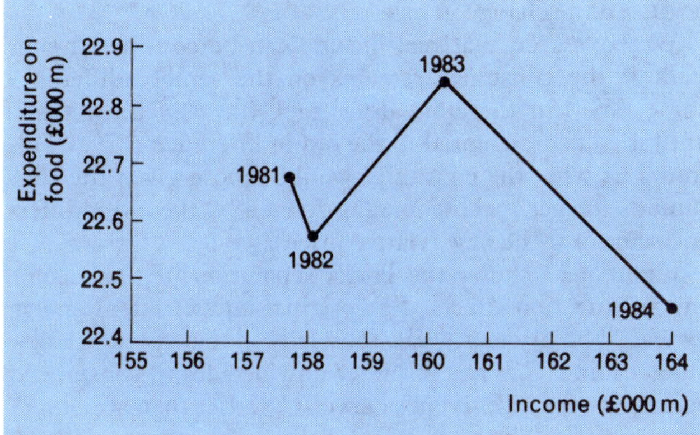

Figure 4.18 Income and expenditure on food, 1981–84.

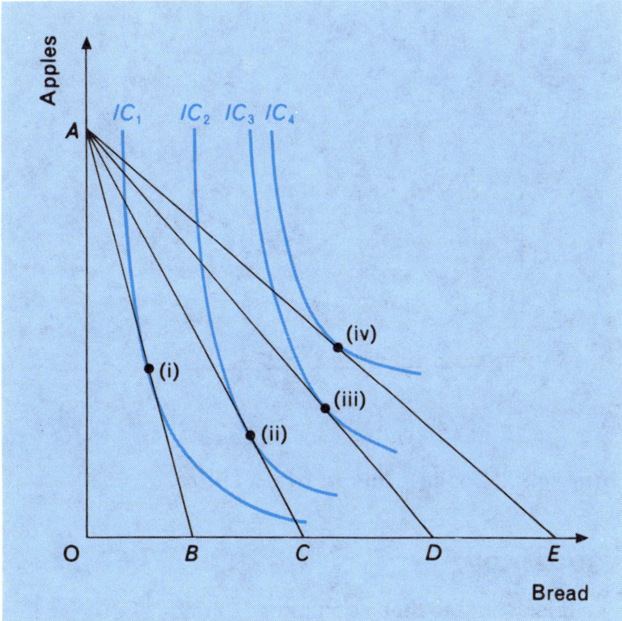

Figure 4.19 Deriving a price–consumption curve.

A price–consumption curve

We have already seen that, if we reduce the price of bread, the budget line swings to the right (see Figure 4.10). Recall that the original budget line *AB* swings out with successive cuts in the price of bread, first to *AC* and then to *AD*.

In order to see how our consumer responds to this price fall, we simply need to superimpose his indifference map on to Figure 4.10 and see where his new point of tangency is. This is done in Figure 4.19.

At the original price we have budget line *AB* and the consumer chooses point (i) where indifference curve IC_1 is just tangential to the budget line.

At a slightly lower price, we have budget line *AC* and the consumer chooses point (ii) where indifference curve IC_2 is just tangential to his new budget line. The same applies to the two further price reductions represented by budget lines *AD* and *AE*.

If we did this for a large number of prices of bread we would generate a large number of points like (i), (ii), (iii) and (iv). Joining these points up we get a *price–consumption curve*. A price–consumption curve is similar to an income–consumption curve and is shown in Figure 4.20.

The price–consumption curve in this diagram shows a case in which a decrease in the price of bread initially increases the consumption of bread and decreases the consumption of apples. As the price of bread continues to fall, the consumption of bread and the consumption of fruit both increase together. Further reduction in price results in a reduction in the consumption of bread and an increase in the consumption of apples. This last point may seem surprising, but it is actually possible.

Thus the effects of changing a price are very similar to the effects of increasing income: anything can happen. There is, however, a way forward. We may not be able entirely to rule out some of these responses to a price fall but we can deduce that some of them are very unlikely indeed.

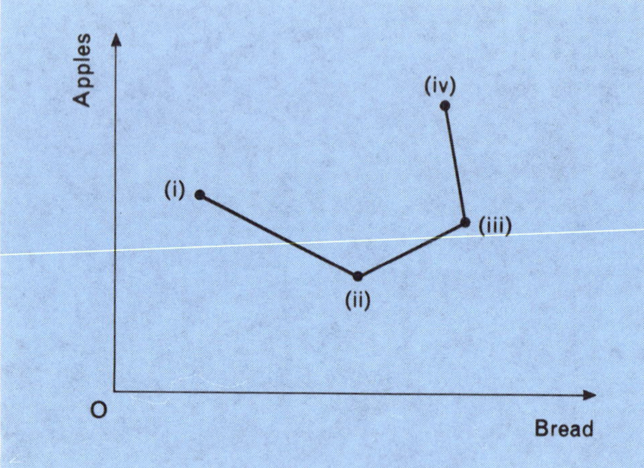

Figure 4.20 Price–consumption curve.

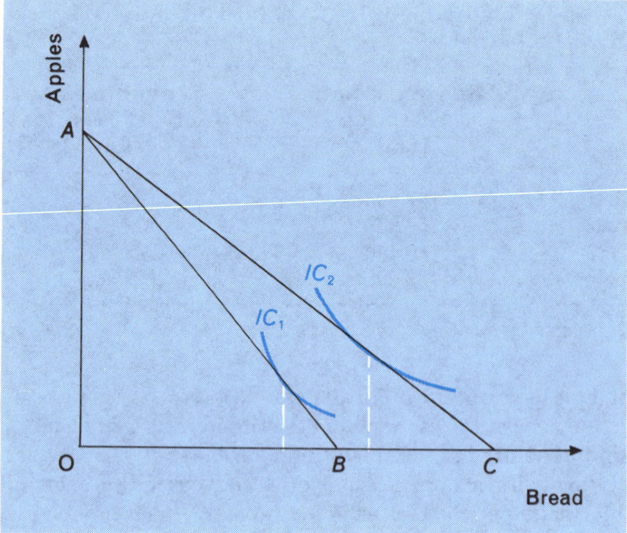

Figure 4.21 Effect of a fall in the price of bread on bread consumption.

SUMMARY

1. It is assumed that a consumer's tastes and preferences are fixed and given.
2. If consumers' incomes increase then their real income rises and they can buy more goods. This is represented by a parallel shift of the budget constraint away from the origin.
3. Tracing all the points of tangency for a consumer at all levels of real income yields the income–consumption curve.
4. Income–consumption curves can be any shape. If a good is a normal good then more of it will be bought as income rises. Less of an inferior good is bought as income rises.
5. An Engel curve maps consumption of a good against income. An Engel curve that slopes upwards from left to right (positively sloped) represents a normal good. An inferior good has a negatively sloped Engel curve.
6. If the price of a good changes then consumers change their consumption. Tracing all of the points of tangency for a consumer as one price changes yields the price–consumption curve. The price–consumption curve can be any shape.

*Income effects and substitution effects

We have seen that when the price of bread falls the budget line swings out and the consumer's choice set is increased. So although money income is unchanged, the consumer's real income has been increased. We have also seen that when real income is increased consumers will buy more of a normal good and less of an inferior good. These effects–the effects due purely to increased real income – are called the **income effects** of a price change and they will depend on whether the good is normal or inferior.

Another effect of a price change must also be considered: the fact that the *relative prices* of goods have also changed. When the price of bread falls it becomes relatively cheaper with regard to apples than it was. If a good becomes cheaper then consumers are inclined to buy more of that good: in other words, when the price of bread falls the consumer may be induced to buy more bread and fewer apples, in effect substituting bread for apples. This is known as the **substitution effect** of a price change.

Consider Figure 4.21, which shows the total effect of a fall in the price of bread. The total consumption of bread has risen, but it is not obvious how much of this change is due to the rise in the consumer's real income (the income effect) and how much is due to the change in the relative prices of bread and apples (the substitution effect). It would be helpful if we could separate these two effects.

One way of separating the income and substitution effects was proposed by an economist called Hicks. He suggested that, in order to decide how much of a total change in consumption was due to the substitution effect, we should try to see how much a consumer would change purchases if *real income* rather than *money income* were held constant. Thus as the price of a good fell the consumer's money income would be reduced so that the consumer was no better off. If this is done there is no change in real income so any change in the consumption of the goods must be due to the change in price.

We have seen that real income can be considered constant if the consumer remains on the same indifference curve. We can therefore draw back the new budget line until it is just tangential to the old indifference curve. This shows us what the consumer would choose given the consumer's former real income (as defined by the old indifference curve) at the new relative prices.

Figure 4.22 shows the Hicks separation of the income and substitution effects. The original budget line is shown by AB. The price of bread then falls so that there is a new budget line AC. The consumer now decides to consume at point Z on the indifference curve IC_2 rather than at point X on curve IC_1. The total effect of the price change is shown by the distance TT' on the bread axis. To separate the income and substitution effect the new budget line AC is

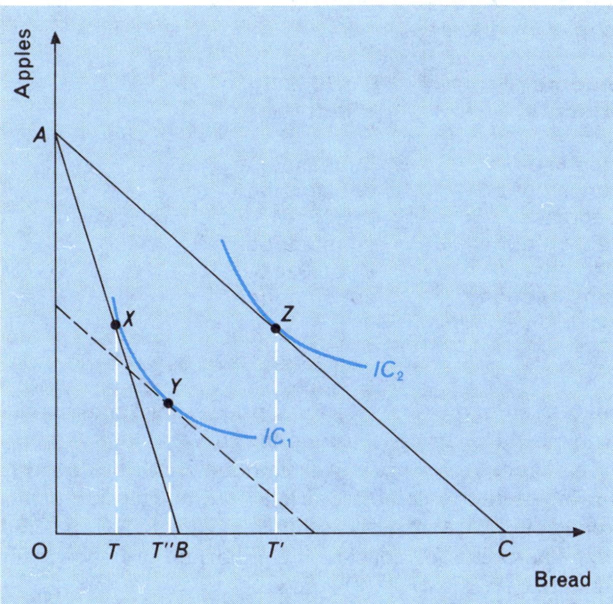

Figure 4.22 Income and substitution effects.

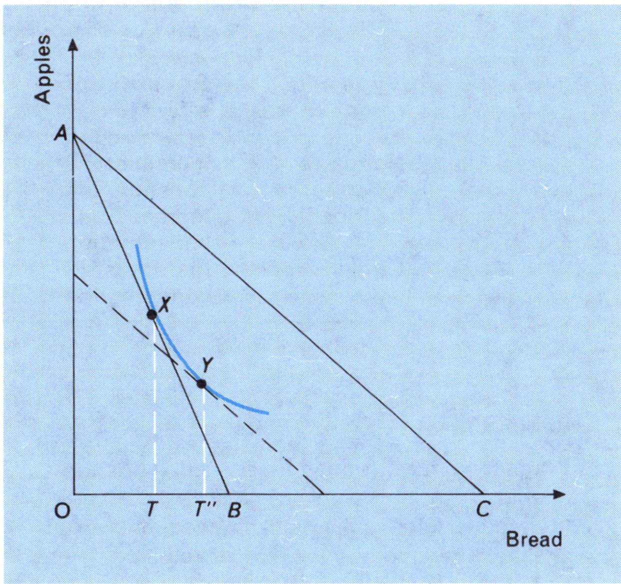

Figure 4.23 Substitution effect.

drawn back parallel to itself towards the origin until it is just tangential to the original indifference curve IC_1 at point Y. This shows that the movement from point X to point Y is due to the change in relative prices – the substitution effect – and that the rest of the increase in the consumption of bread is due to the consumer's increased real income. This is also shown on the bread axis: the distance TT'' is equivalent to the substitution effect, while the distance $T''T'$ is due to the income effect.

The substitution effect alone is shown in Figure 4.23 and is given by the movement from X to Y along the original indifference curve. *The substitution effect is always negative.* If you reduce the price of a good, the quantity demanded will always increase. The substitution effect is therefore unambiguously to increase consumption of that good whose price is reduced: price down – consumption up.

We have seen that income effects can be positive or negative depending on the type of good. For a normal good an increase in real income causes consumption of the good to rise. This reinforces the substitution effect of a price change.

As an inferior good has a negative income effect, this will work *against* the substitution effect. The total change in consumption of the inferior good will therefore not be as great as the change for a normal good. Usually even for inferior goods the substitution effect outweighs the income effect, so there will usually be an increase in the consumption of an inferior good following a price fall. It is possible, however, that the income effect will be so negative as to outweigh the substitution effect. In this case the demand for a good will *rise* as the price rises. Such goods are called **Giffen goods**.

A Giffen good is very unusual but a frequently quoted example is the case of potatoes in Ireland in the eighteenth and nineteenth centuries. Potatoes constituted a very large part of household expenditure because people were very poor and had to buy the relatively cheap potatoes to make up the bulk of their diet. When the price of potatoes rose the peasants had to buy more of them because their real income had fallen so much that they could no longer afford other goods such as meat. They had to buy more potatoes just to survive. In modern times with a great variety of goods being bought, it is unlikely that any one good is a big enough part of a consumer's budget for it to have a dominant income effect. We can therefore conclude that in most cases the demand for a good will fall as its price increases.

The income and substitution effects for a Giffen good are shown in Figure 4.24 where the substitution effect is equivalent to TT' and the income effect is shown by the distance $T'T''$ (see also Table 4.3).

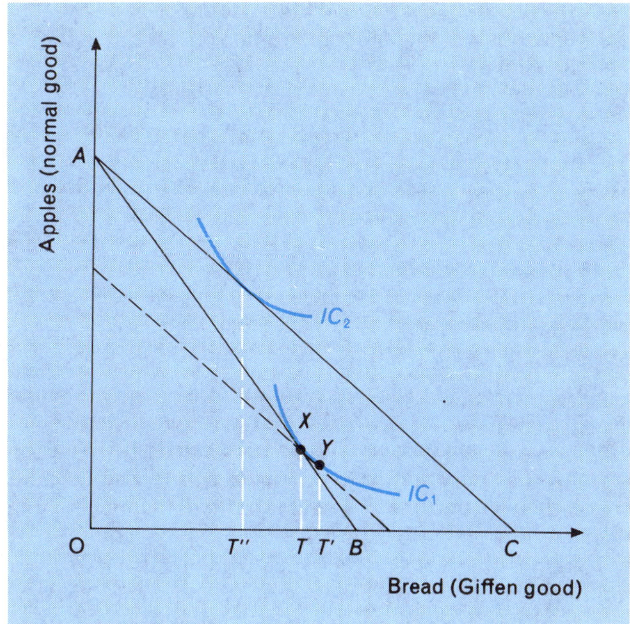

Figure 4.24 Income and substitution effects for a Giffen good.

Table 4.3 Summary of income and substitution effects (effect of a fall in the price of a good on the consumption of that good)

Type of good	Substitution effect	Income effect	Total effect
Normal	Increases consumption	Increases consumption	Increases consumption
Inferior	Increases consumption	Decreases consumption	Increases consumption
Giffen	Increases consumption	Decreases consumption	Decreases consumption

SUMMARY

1. When the price of a good is reduced, it has two effects:
   (a) It makes that good relatively cheaper than all the other goods whose prices remain unchanged.
   (b) It increases the real income of the consumer.
2. The first of these two effects is called the substitution effect and is due to consumers buying more of the now relatively cheaper good. People always choose to substitute a cheaper good for a more expensive one and so the substitution effect always causes an increase in consumption.
3. The second effect is known as the income effect and causes an increase in consumption of normal goods (i.e. as the price falls, real income rises and for normal goods consumption increases) and a decrease in the consumption of inferior goods.
4. Following a price fall only Giffen goods experience an overall fall in consumption.
5. The income and substitution effects can be separated by seeing how much consumption would change if the consumer could choose a new point on the old indifference curve, but at the new relative prices. The movement along the indifference curve shown by this is the substitution effect; the remainder of the overall change is the income effect.

The demand curve

A consumer's demand curve for a good shows the quantity of that good which the consumer is willing and able to buy at various prices of that good when *tastes, all other prices and money income are held constant*. The words in italics are often used in microeconomics and are usually invoked by saying ***ceteris paribus***, or *cet. par.* for short. The demand curve then is the line showing what will happen to the demand for a good when its price changes, *cet. par.*

It is possible to construct such a demand curve from indifference curves. We have already seen that the amount of a good that a consumer buys varies as price changes and that there are two effects on consumer behaviour (the income and substitution effects). The sum of these effects can be seen in the total effect of a price change and this can be mapped by a price–consumption curve.

In Figure 4.25 a price–consumption curve for bread is shown. As the price of bread falls, the budget line pivots around point A, starting at AB then moving to AC, AD and AE. The points of consumer equilibrium are shown for each price level as W, X, Y and Z.

The price–consumption curve for bread is drawn through these points. From the diagram it is possible to read off how much bread is demanded at each price, e.g. 10 loaves are demanded when the price of bread is P_1. We can transfer this information on to a graph to show the consumer's demand curve for bread with respect to price.

The demand curve shown in Figure 4.25 is downward sloping, reflecting the fact that the lower the price of bread, the more a consumer would choose to demand. This is entirely in line with the behaviour we would expect if bread was a normal good, since both the substitution effect and

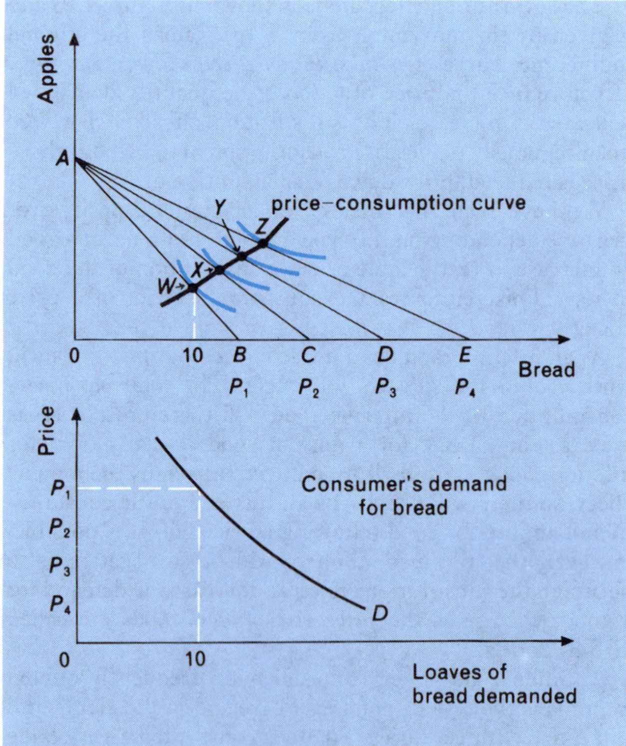

Figure 4.25 Deriving a demand curve from indifference analysis.

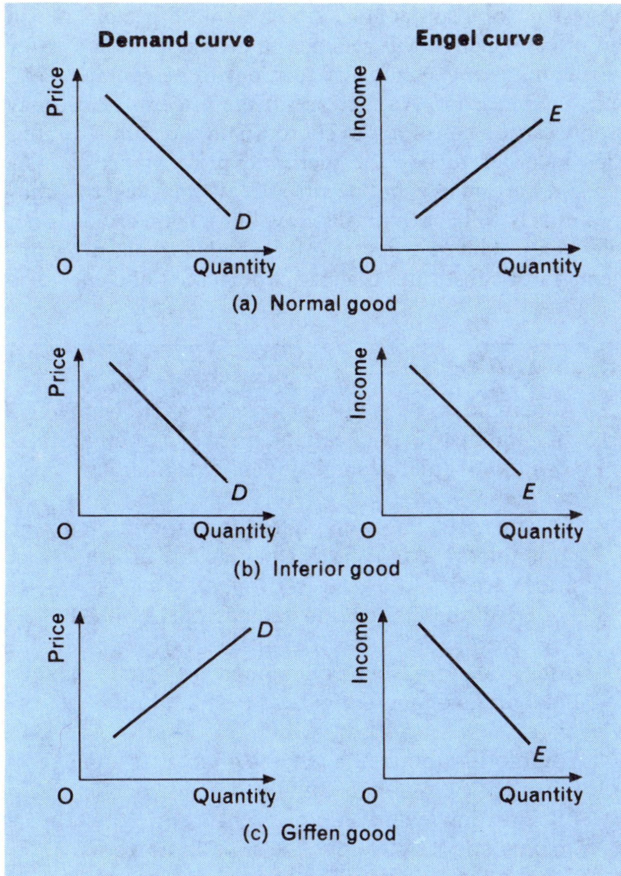

Figure 4.26 Demand and Engel curves for different types of goods.

the income effect suggest that more of a normal good is bought as price falls.

A relevant question is: what does a demand curve for an inferior good look like? We have already seen that no good is likely to be an inferior good at all levels of income and prices, but let us suppose that there is such a good. The demand curve for an inferior good would look very similar to that in Figure 4.25 because the substitution effect usually outweighs the income effect for such a good. The main difference is that the demand curve for an inferior good may be more steeply sloped than that of a normal good. If the inferior good is a Giffen good then part of the demand curve may be positively sloped where the income effect is greater than the substitution effect.

Figure 4.26 summarizes the shapes of the demand and Engel curves for the various types of goods.

Some possible counter-examples

Apart from the Giffen goods case, there are one or two other well-known examples of upward-sloping demand curves. The first is due to the fact that as the price of a good falls more people will buy it. This increase in popularity may have one of two possible effects. It may put some consumers off the good and hence cause them to buy less of it as its price falls. This is the so-called snob effect and will cause demand by some households to fall as a falling price increases the popularity of the good. Packaged holidays may be an example of this.

Alternatively, it might happen that as a good becomes more widespread so more people feel that they should have it too. This is the so-called bandwagon effect. This effect, of course, reinforces the downward slope of the demand curve and, unlike the snob effect, does not tend to produce upward-sloping demand curves. The spread of central heating and double glazing may be examples of this.

Both these effects rely on some interaction between consumers. What one consumer does is often influenced by what others are doing. In our theory this is tantamount to a shift in a consumer's indifference map. In the case of the snob effect, the utility derived by this section of consumers depends on both the good in question *and* its exclusiveness. Altering its exclusiveness therefore shifts the indifference curves. Similarly, the bandwagon good implies that consumers 'learn' about particular goods and feel they should have them by observing that others have them. Their indifference map is therefore also affected by the increasing popularity of the good in question.

These two cases therefore break an assumption on which we based our demand curve, i.e. that tastes are fixed. They can therefore be analysed by our theory only by relaxing this fixed tastes assumption. This complexity is beyond the scope of this book.

Another possible cause of an upward-sloping demand curve is that the price of a good may suggest a particular quality. Thus some consumers will assume that a high price means a high quality. This is the so-called Veblen effect (after the economist Thorsten Veblen). Price therefore carries information other than the cost of a good to the consumer: it contains information about quality too. In this case an increase in price may cause more to be bought rather than less. This again is an induced change in tastes and is beyond our scope.

Complements and substitutes

There are many goods whose consumption is related to other goods. Consider the demand for petrol. This is clearly related to the demand for motor cars. If nobody wanted to buy and drive motor cars then there would be no need to buy petrol. Goods related in this way are called **complements.**

If goods are complements then a rise in the price of one would lead to a fall in demand for the other.

If two goods are perfect complements in the eyes of consumers then they have indifference curves like those shown in Figure 4.27. The indifference curves of complements are right angles and any budget line will be tangential to one of these curves on a right angle. The implication of this is that a change in the price of one good leads to there being no substitution effect as the goods are used in fixed proportions only. (There is, of course, an income effect.)

Another way in which goods might be related is for them to have very similar uses. That is to say, they can be substituted for one another. Examples of such goods are butter and margarine, which consumers use more or less interchangeably. Goods like this are called **substitutes**.

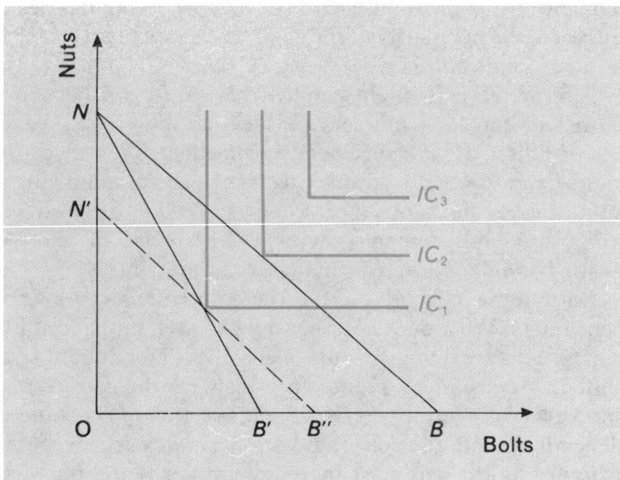

Figure 4.27 Indifference curves for perfect complements.

If goods are substitutes then a rise in the price of one would lead to a rise in demand for the other.

Other examples of substitutes are cars and buses, watching television or videos, and bread and fruit. The last two, bread and fruit, may not appear to be very close substitutes, but both compete for a share of a consumer's income and both fulfil the functions of food. It is possible for goods to be 'weak' or 'close' substitutes. Jaguar cars and BMWs are quite close substitutes, but Jaguars and Austin Metros are not.

If two goods are perfect substitutes so that a decline in the demand for one leads to a corresponding rise in the demand for the other then a consumer's indifference curves for such products are as shown in Figure 4.28.

It should be stressed here that whether a good is a complement or a substitute is a question of fact to be discovered by looking at actual examples. It might be suggested, for example, that since cars need petrol a rise in the price of petrol will reduce the demand for cars. Now petrol and cars may actually turn out to be complements, but they need not. An increase in the price of petrol may simply cause a consumer to cut down on the number of bus trips in order to pay the increased price of petrol. The demand for cars may not be affected. We may feel that they are unlikely to behave in this way, but our theory does not rule it out. The question then of whether goods are complements or substitutes is a matter of fact not of conjecture.

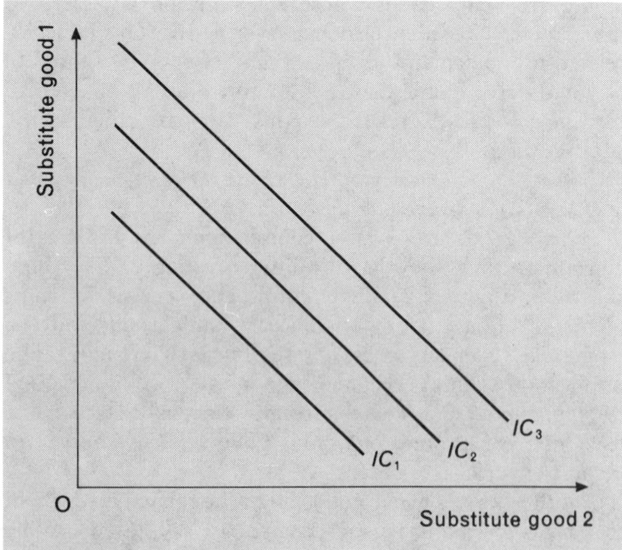

Figure 4.28 Indifference curves for perfect substitutes.

SUMMARY

1. A demand curve is defined as a curve showing the relationship between the price of a good and the quantity of it which a household would consume.
2. This curve is drawn up under the assumption that consumers' tastes, money income and all other prices are fixed (i.e. *ceteris paribus*).
3. For all normal goods, the demand curve will be downward sloping to the right, i.e. the lower the price, the more will be consumed. This is because the income effect reinforces the substitution effect.
4. For inferior goods, the income effect acts against the substitution effect, but the demand curve remains downward sloping to the right. When the income effect outweighs the substitution effect the good is a Giffen good and the demand curve will be upward sloping.
5. Other examples of upward-sloping demand curves rely on changes in consumer tastes. These changes are induced by price changes and give rise to snob effects and Veblen effects.
6. If more of one good is consumed when the price of another good is reduced then the two goods are complements.
7. If less of one good is consumed when the price of another good is reduced then the two goods are substitutes.
8. Indifference curves for perfect complements are right angled; for perfect substitutes they are straight lines.

Movement along and movement of the demand curve

Choosing a price is tantamount to choosing a point on the demand curve and changing the price moves us *along* the demand curve. If, on the other hand, we change income or change other prices, then we actually move the demand curve itself. Figure 4.29 shows this distinction and suggests how changes in income or changes in other prices may affect the position of a demand curve.

The original demand curve is D_1, and as the price of apples falls (*cet. par.*) the consumer moves from (i) to (ii) and then to (iii). Lower prices imply an *expansion in the quantity demanded*. Higher prices would imply a *contraction in the quantity demanded*.

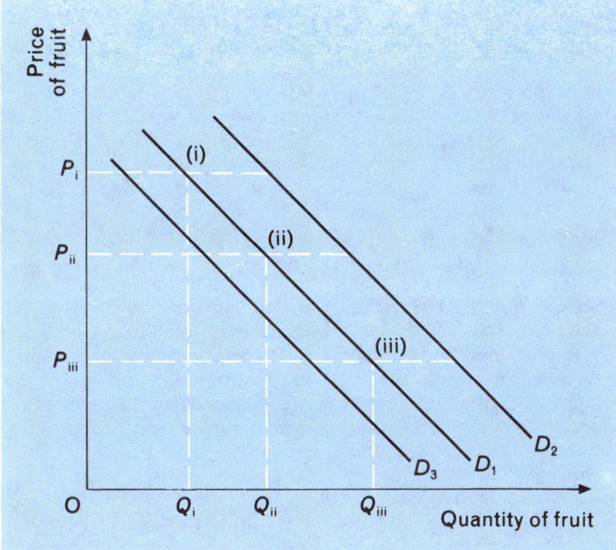

Figure 4.29 Movement along and movement of the demand curve.

Now say we keep the price of apples constant, but increase the consumer's money income. If apples are normal goods then at any given price level the consumer will buy more apples. Thus for normal goods an increase in money income move the demand curve to the right – to D_2 – an *increase in demand*.

If apples are inferior goods then an increase in money income will cause fewer apples to be consumed and hence moves the demand curve for apples to the left – to D_3 – a *decrease in demand*.

Movements of the demand curve can also be induced by changing the price of some other good. Say we kept money income fixed and lowered the price of bread. This would cause us to move *along* the demand curve for bread but would also induce a movement *of* the demand curve for apples.

If bread and apples are complements then raising the price of bread will cause fewer apples to be consumed at any given price of apples. This means that the demand curve for apples moves to the left.

Conversely, if bread and apples are substitutes then raising the price of bread will cause more apples to be consumed at any given price of apples. This means that the demand curve for apples moves to the right.

The distinction between movements *along* and movements *of* the demand curve is important and we will return to it later in the book.

SUMMARY

1. Movements *along* the demand curve have to be sharply distinguished from movements *of* the demand curve.
2. With money income, tastes and all other prices held constant, a change in the price of a good will leave the demand curve for the good unchanged but will move the consumer along that demand curve. This represents an expansion or contraction in demand.
3. An increase in money income will move the demand curves for normal goods to the right. This represents an increase in demand.
4. An increase in money income will move the demand curves for inferior goods to the left. This represents a decrease in demand.
5. An increase in the price of one good will, *ceteris paribus*, move the demand curve for another good to the right if the two goods are substitutes.
6. An increase in the price of one good will, *ceteris paribus*, move the demand curve for another good to the left if the two goods are complements.

Exam Preparation and Practice

MULTIPLE-CHOICE QUESTIONS

1. A consumer will maximize his utility when he spends his income so that:

A The ratio of marginal utility to price is the same for each good consumed.
B The marginal utility gained from each good consumed is zero.
C The ratio of total utility to price is the same for each good consumed.
D The marginal utility gained from each good is at its maximum.

2. A consumer maximizes her utility when she spends her income on two goods X and Y so that:

A $\frac{\text{Marginal utility X}}{\text{Marginal utility Y}} = \frac{\text{Price X}}{\text{Price Y}}$

B $\frac{\text{Marginal utility X}}{\text{Marginal utility Y}} = \frac{\text{Price Y}}{\text{Price X}}$

C Marginal utility X = Marginal utility Y

D Marginal utility X × Price X = Marginal utility Y × Price Y.

3. When the marginal utility obtained from a good is zero:

A All other goods must be yielding zero marginal utility.
B Total utility from the good is also zero.
C Total utility from that good is at a maximum.
D The consumer has no wish to change the combination of goods consumed.

Case Study 4.2 The birth of a broader economic discipline

A group of US academics is trying to launch a new kind of economics: a set of theories more likely to promote a kinder, gentler America than the free market doctrines of the 1980s.

The new economics goes by the ungainly title of 'socio-economics'. The 'socio' indicates that the theories incorporate elements from psychology, sociology and political science. Indeed, a fundamental assertion of socio-economics is that traditional economics is unable to solve many real-world problems because its approach is too narrow.

One of the movement's high priests is Mr Amitai Etzioni, a professor at the George Washington University and a former adviser to President Jimmy Carter. In 1988, he published *The Moral Dimension: Towards a New Economics* (Free Press, New York). The following year he helped launch the Society for the Advancement of Socio-Economics, a group that appears to be flourishing. It has about 800 academic members in 22 countries. Honorary fellows include such respected figures in economics as Amartya Sen and Kenneth Boulding.

Mr Etzioni is also an editor of *The Responsive Community*, a quarterly launched this winter. The opening editorial declares war on 'Me-ism', greed and selfishness in the US, arguing that the rights of the individual must be balanced with responsibilities toward the community. It hopes to appeal to both liberals and conservatives.

At present, socio-economics lacks definition. There is no body of established theorems, no textbooks, no official university courses, no stream of PhDs anxious to change the world. In these early days, enthusiasts mainly share a common approach, a belief that economics must involve 'the whole person and all facets of society'. The fledgling discipline defines itself negatively by rejecting crucial elements in market or 'neoclassical' economics – the only approach taken seriously in most US and UK universities.

A central criticism is that traditional economics exaggerates the autonomy of the individual. It portrays us as 'sovereign' consumers, independently forming preferences for different commodities and activities. Society is dismissed as an empty concept, signifying nothing but an aggregation of individuals.

Socio-economists believe the communities that stand behind individuals warrant closer attention. Individuals do not leap into the world as fully-formed philosopher kings. What we regard as worth having or doing is heavily influenced by the values of our society. Rather than ignoring society as an explanatory variable, the new economics seeks to place equal weight on the individual and the community.

A second objection focuses on the rocky moral foundations of market economics. Originating in 19th century utilitarianism, neoclassical theory regards the maximisation of happiness or 'utility' as man's only goal. By definition, no preference can be regarded as 'better' or 'worse' than another. A taste for peanuts thus occupies the same moral footing as a taste for God.

Mr Etzioni rejects this moral subjectivism, arguing that we have a 'divided self': part of us seeks pleasure; but another part is powerfully moved by ethical considerations – by a need to do what is 'right' even when it is taxing or unpleasant. Socio-economics believes better predictions of human behaviour will be possible if room is found for both pleasure and duty as sources of motivation.

A third objection is that the neoclassical model of decision-taking is unrealistic. It depicts us as perfectly rational beings, relentlessly seeking the most efficient means to our goals. Emotions are allowed to influence ends, but not means. Yet in assuming that human behaviour typically involves 'optimisation subject to constraints', market economics is implicity endowing us with the information-processing powers of a modern computer.

For socio-economists, this rationalist vision of economic man is untenable. In their eyes, everything we do is influenced by emotions and values. Psychological research, moreover, confirms that we lack the intellectual capacity to process information efficiently. People can hold only some seven items (sometimes as low as three) in their immediate mental grasp. In most instances we could not maximise 'utility', even if this were our goal.

If you are doubtful, analyse your own decisions. How often have your choices of where to live or what to buy been based on cold logic? At college, did you thoroughly assess the merits of different career options? Or did you, like me, make an essentially arbitrary decision based on intuition, and only the vaguest understanding of the merits of different options?

1. Does the assumption of rational, utility-maximizing consumers make consumer theory unrealistic or a simplified but useful approach?

Source: Michael Prowse, *Financial Times*, April 1991

4.

Apples

A B X C D

O Bread

If a consumer is initially maximizing utility at point X on the budget constraint and bread is an inferior good, which is the only point of A to D the consumer would choose following a rise in money income?

5.

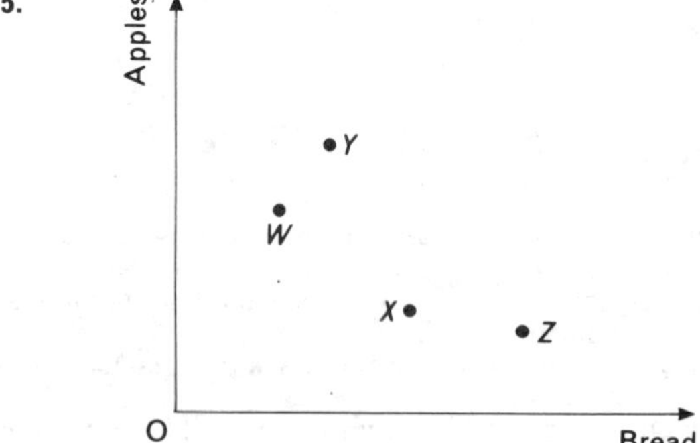

The diagram shows four possible bundles of goods a consumer could choose. According to indifference analysis a consumer will always prefer:

A W to X. **C** W to Y.
B W to Z. **D** Y to W.

6. 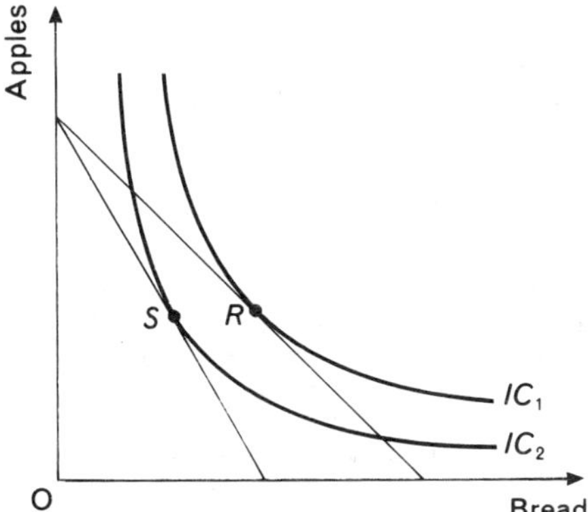

The diagram shows a consumer's indifference curves for apples and bread. The movement from consuming at point *R* to consuming at point *S* must be due to:
A A fall in money income.
B A rise in the price of bread.
C A fall in the price of bread.
D A rise in the price of apples.

7. The diagrams show sets of indifference curves.

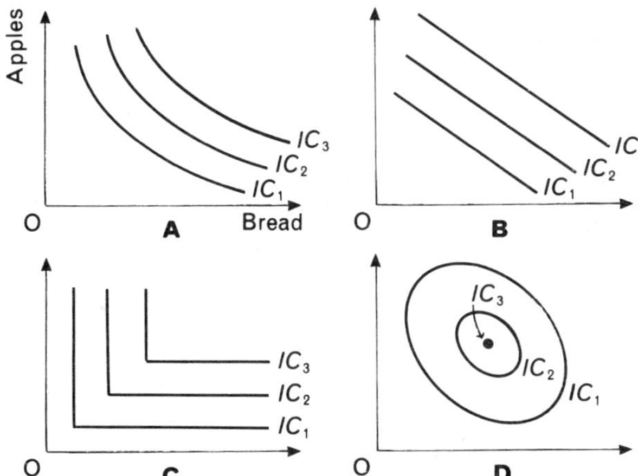

Which diagram shows indifference curves for a consumer who regards apples and bread as perfect substitutes?

Answer key

Where there are three numbered alternatives

A	B	C	D	E
1, 2, 3 Correct	1, 2 Correct	2, 3 Correct	1 Correct	3 Correct

Where there are four numbered alternatives

A	B	C	D	E
1, 2 and 3 Correct	1 and 3 Correct	2 and 4 Correct	4 only Correct	1 and 4 Correct

8. Consumer equilibrium occurs and maximum satisfaction is gained when
1 the same satisfaction is derived from the last penny spent on each commodity consumed.
2 the ratio of marginal utility to price is the same for all commodities consumed.
3 the total utility derived from each product is the same.
(AEB)

9. The prices of goods consumed by a household change. The resulting new expenditure pattern shows that the household's marginal utilities are lower than before, but greater than zero. From this we can say:
1 The total utility derived by the household has risen.
2 The household is worse off than before.
3 The average price of goods consumed by the household has risen.
4 The average price of goods consumed by the household has fallen.

10. A Giffen good is one where:
1 Consumption rises proportionately with income.
2 More of the good will be consumed if the price of a substitute falls.
3 Consumption rises when the price of the good rises.

11. If the price of a good X falls relative to the prices of all other goods:
1 the substitution effect will usually lead to more units of X being consumed.
2 consumers will always devote a higher proportion of their income to the purchase of X.
3 the income effect will always lead to more units of X being consumed.
(LON.)

EXERCISES

1. A consumer has £3.75 to spend. He purchases 6 packets of biscuits and 4 cans of cola. The price of biscuits is 25p a packet and cola is 50p a can. On returning home his wife tells him he should have bought fewer biscuits and more cola.
(a) What does this tell us about the utility gained by these two consumers from the two goods?
(b) Is it possible to say by how much the man's wife prefers cola to biscuits?
(c) Could the man's behaviour be utility maximizing? If so, why?. If not, why not?

2. A consumer gains utility from the consumption of both apples and bread. The table shows the total utility gained by the consumer as she consumes successive units of the two goods (the consumption of all other goods remaining constant).

Bread		Apples	
No. of loaves	Total utility	No. of apples	Total utility
1	12	1	8
2	22	2	15
3	29	3	21
4	35	4	26
5	38	5	30
6	38	6	33
7	36	7	34
		8	34
		9	32

(a) On graph paper sketch the total and marginal utility curves for (i) bread and (ii) apples for this consumer.
(b) (i) When the marginal utility of bread is zero, what is the consumer experiencing in terms of total utility from bread?
(ii) Is this always the case for any good when marginal utility is zero?
(c) If the price of bread is 2 and apples is 1, what amounts of the two goods will the consumer choose to buy when her income is (i) 5 (ii) 14?

In the questions that follow it is advisable to plot all curves on graph paper.

3. **(a)** Plot an indifference curve to show that a consumer is indifferent between consuming a bundle of goods con-

taining 3 oranges and 2 bananas and a bundle containing 2 oranges and 3 bananas.

(b) On the same diagram draw another indifference curve to show that the consumer is indifferent between a bundle of goods containing 4 oranges and 3 bananas and a bundle containing 3 oranges and 4 bananas.

(c) Why is the indifference curve you have drawn for (b) above further away from the origin than the curve you drew for (a)?

4. A consumer has a choice between four bundles of goods:

1 3 oranges and 3 bananas
2 3 oranges and 4 bananas
3 4 oranges and 3 bananas
4 4 oranges and 4 bananas

Suggest a rational preference ordering for these bundles of goods and draw possible indifference curves to represent them.

5. (a) A consumer is indifferent between a bundle containing 3 oranges and 4 bananas and a bundle containing 4 oranges and 3 bananas. Draw an indifference curve to represent this.

(b) The same consumer is indifferent between a bundle containing 3 oranges and 4 bananas and a bundle containing 4 oranges and 4 bananas. Draw a separate indifference curve to represent this.

(c) Is this a logical ordering for one consumer? If not, why not?

6. There is no reason why we must restrict our analysis to just two goods. Can you suggest how the choice between more than two goods might be shown on an indifference map?

7. (a) A consumer has an income of £5. Draw a budget constraint for him when the price of oranges is 10p and bananas are 15p.

(b) Draw a new budget constraint for when the consumer's income doubles to £10.

(c) The price of oranges now rises to 20p. Adjust the budget constraint you drew for (b) accordingly.

8. Suppose a consumer has an income of £2 and the price of oranges is 10p and the price of bananas is 20p.

(a) Draw an indifference curve to show that at these prices and income the consumer prefers to consume 8 oranges and 6 bananas.

(b) Why does the consumer not choose (i) 6 oranges and 4 bananas; (ii) 12 oranges and 4 bananas?

***9.** A consumer buys 15 lutes and 5 barrels of wine when the price of lutes is £5 and the price of wine is £15 a barrel.

(a) What is the consumer's total income?

(b) Sketch the budget constraint for the consumer and mark clearly the amount of lutes and wine the consumer could buy if he devoted his entire income to just one of the products. (Wine should be plotted on the horizontal axis.)

(c) The consumer's income rises so that he can now buy a combination of 18 lutes and 9 barrels of wine. What is the consumer's new income?

(d) Sketch the new budget constraint for the consumer and mark clearly the amount of lutes and wine the consumer could buy if he devoted his entire income to just one of the products.

(e) The consumer's income rises again and he can now buy a combination of 24 lutes and 12 barrels of wine. Suppose the three points 15 lutes, 5 barrels of wine; 18 lutes, 9 barrels of wine; and 24 lutes, 12 barrels of wine; are equilibrium positions for the consumer at each income level. Superimpose indifference curves to show this on your diagram.

(f) Trace the line of the income–consumption curve from the initial equilibrium to the last one.

(g) For each change in income, state if lutes and wine are normal or inferior goods.

***10.** A consumer has an income of £100 and can spend this on two goods, cloth and grain. The consumer could buy 20 rolls of cloth if she spent all of her money on cloth, or 30 bushels of grain if she spent all of her money on grain.

(a) What is the price of cloth per roll and grain per bushel?

(b) Draw the budget constraint represented by this income and these prices, placing cloth on the horizontal axis.

(c) Draw an indifference curve to show that the consumer prefers a combination of 9 bushels of grain and 14 rolls of cloth. Label this curve IC_1.

(d) The price of cloth falls to £4 a roll. Draw the new budget constraint.

(e) The consumer now prefers a combination of 12 bushels of grain and 15 rolls of cloth. Draw an indifference curve to show this and label it IC_2.

(f) The price of cloth falls to £2.50 a roll. Draw the new budget constraint.

(g) The consumer now prefers a combination of 15 bushels of grain and 20 rolls of cloth. Draw an indifference curve to show this and label it IC_3.

(h) Draw the price–consumption curve between the first equilibrium point and the final one.

(i) Derive the demand curve for cloth from your diagram.

11. (a) Draw an indifference curve with the following points:

16 bushels of grain, 9 rolls of cloth
13 bushels of grain, 11 rolls of cloth
9 bushels of grain, 14 rolls of cloth
6 bushels of grain, 18 rolls of cloth
4 bushels of grain, 21 rolls of cloth
3 bushels of grain, 23 rolls of cloth

(b) The budget constraint runs from 22 bushels of grain to 24 rolls of cloth. The equilibrium position is 9 bushels of grain and 14 rolls of cloth. Suppose that the price of cloth now falls so that the consumer could buy 40 rolls of cloth if he devoted his entire income to cloth. The new equilibrium position is 10 bushels of grain and 22 rolls of cloth. On an indifference map show: (i) the total effect of the price change; (ii) the substitution effect of the price change; (iii) the income effect of the price change.

(c) Is cloth a normal or an inferior good?

5 Market supply and market demand

In this chapter we will discuss:

1. How market demand and market supply curves are found.
2. How markets determine the price of a product.
3. Why the market price of a product may change.
4. How firms respond to changes in market price and why.
5. How economists measure the response of demand and supply to changes in price.

Introduction

In Chapter 3 we looked at the way goods are produced. Goods are produced by firms in which profit-maximizing entrepreneurs combine scarce factors of production (land, labour and capital) to produce goods and services. The entrepreneurs decide how much land, labour and capital to use and how much to produce. The scarcity of factors of production is reflected in the costs of production. Typically, the cost of producing a unit of output (average cost) changes as the level of output changes.

Scarcity is more of a problem in the short run, when some factors are fixed in supply, than in the long run when all factors are variable. In the long run the least-cost combinations of factors can be chosen and costs will depend on the scale of production. If there are increasing returns to scale then the firm's long-run average cost curve will decline – average costs fall as output increases. If there are constant returns to scale then the firm's long-run average cost curve is horizontal. If there are decreasing returns to scale then the firm's long-run average cost curve is upward sloping.

In the short run only labour can be varied, so the least-cost combinations are no longer available. There will be one short-run cost curve for each quantity of capital. They will all be U-shaped and just touch the long-run cost curve at their lowest points. These cost curves represent the constraints on the *supply* of goods and services.

In Chapter 4 we looked at the demand for goods. Goods are demanded by households. We have proved that, with very few exceptions, a household's demand for a good will decline as its price increases. Thus an individual household's demand curve for a particular good slopes downwards. Taken together, households' demand represents the 'wants' side of the economy.

Constructing market demand and supply curves

In this chapter we will bring these two aspects – scarcity and wants – together by forming a market. The market should convey to buyers just how difficult it is to supply the goods they want, and should convey to suppliers just how strong is the household demand for certain goods. Having done that, it has to ensure that the quantity of goods supplied just equals the quantity of goods demanded, i.e. the market must *clear*.

Markets are where information on supplies of goods and demands for goods is processed and where the production plans of entrepreneurs and the consumption plans of households are reconciled. Quite a lot of information can be exchanged through markets, but we will concentrate on only four items:

1. The quantity which demanders are willing to buy.
2. The price they are prepared to pay.
3. The quantity which suppliers are willing to sell.
4. The price they will sell at.

Demand

The quantity which households are willing to buy can be found from the demand curves we derived in Chapter 4. We know that each household will demand less of a good as its price goes up – household demand curves are downward sloping. This means that we can say nothing about the quantity which will be demanded in the market until we know what prices are. On the other hand, we can say nothing about the price that households are prepared to pay until we know the quantity being demanded.

The first two pieces of information in our list, quantity demanded and price, are therefore interrelated. We can ask households to choose the quantity they would buy if we first specified the price, or we can ask them how much they would be prepared to pay if we first told them how much they have to buy. But we cannot ask them to determine both quantity and price.

In order to break this deadlock we will assume that the market is organized by an auctioneer. This auctioneer is not quite the same as the type of auctioneer which you will be familiar with – once again economists are guilty of using a word in a slightly different way from everyone else. The usual kind of auctioneer offers a *quantity* for sale (a 'lot') and seeks the highest price from consumers. The economist's auctioneer does the opposite, calling out a *price* for a certain good and seeing how much of it consumers are willing and able to buy at that price.

For our auctioneer, therefore, households are assumed to be price takers. They take the prices as given in the market (by the auctioneer) and have only to decide how much to buy at that price. We further assume that the auctioneer treats all households equally and offers them all the same price.

What the auctioneer (market) can discover from households is not a single price and a single quantity but a *series* of prices and quantities representing what all households together would demand at each and every price called out by the auctioneer.

The market demand curve

The total amount demanded in the market at each price produces a market demand curve. A market demand curve is constructed in Figure 5.1.

There are three households in this market. Household (a) buys 4 oranges at a price of 6p each, household (b) buys 1 at that price and household (c) buys 5. They all face the same price – the market (auctioneer's) price – and so at a price of 6p the total demand will be $4+1+5 = 10$ oranges. This is shown in Figure 5.1(m).

If the market price falls to 4p then household (a) buys 7, (b) buys 2 and (c) buys 11 oranges. The market demand at a price of 4p will therefore be $7+2+11 = 20$ oranges. This can be repeated for any number of prices and so the market demand curve can be constructed.

As can be seen from Figure 5.1, the market demand curve is the *horizontal sum of household demand curves*. The prices are common to all households and the quantities are added together. Since each demand curve slopes downward, so too must the market demand curve. The information contained in the market about demanders is therefore summarized by the market demand curve.

We turn next to consider what information the market has about supply.

Supply

As far as the supply side of the market is concerned, we know about:

1. The long-run total cost curve.
2. The long-run average cost curve.
3. The short-run total cost curve.
4. The short-run average cost curve.

We need to deduce from these how much the entrepreneurs will supply to the market and the price at which they will supply it. We begin by examining the short run only.

Entrepreneurs decide how much to supply to the market and are assumed to behave in ways which maximize their profits. In order to discover how much is supplied it is necessary to see how supply affects profits.

Profits are defined as the difference between revenue and cost:

Profit = Revenue – Costs

We already know something about costs, but what of revenue? The amount received by entrepreneurs for the supply of goods depends on the quantity they sell and the price they get for them:

Revenue = Sales × Price

Having made use of the auctioneer on the demand side of the market, we do so again on the supply side. We assume that the prices called out by the auctioneer apply equally to all buyers and all sellers. Entrepreneurs, like households, are therefore price takers and, in response to each price called out by the auctioneer (market), offer a quantity for sale.

Say the auctioneer calls out a price of £10. The entrepreneurs will receive an additional £10 for every extra unit they sell. Their total revenue will therefore increase by £10 when sales are increased by 1 unit of output. The technical term for this increment in total revenue is **marginal revenue**. Marginal revenue is the increase in total revenue when one additional unit is sold. In the present case it is equal to price.

This tells us that, as the quantity supplied increases, one determinant of profit (revenue) also increases. A 10 per cent increase in sales generates a 10 per cent increase in revenue.

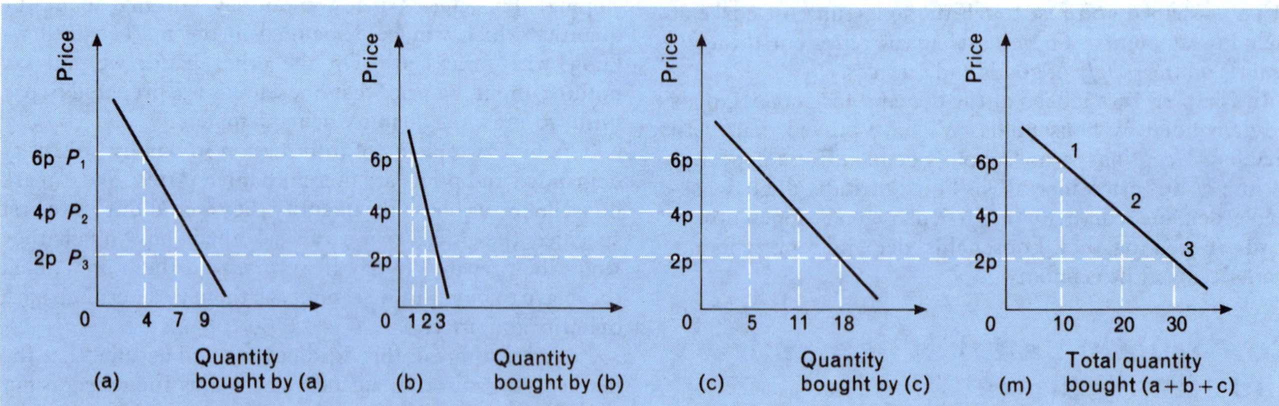

Figure 5.1 Constructing a market demand curve.

Table 5.1 An example of how costs change with production

(a) Quantity produced	(b) Fixed cost	(c) Variable cost	(d) Total cost	(e) Average fixed cost	(f) Average variable cost	(g) Average total cost	(h) Marginal cost
			(b)+(c)	(b)/(a)	(c)/(a)	(d)/(a)	[change in (d)]
q	*FC*	*VC*	*TC*	*AFC*	*AVC*	*AC*	*MC*
0	60	0	60	–	–	–	–
1	60	5	65	60	5	65	5
2	60	8	68	30	4	34	3
3	60	15	75	20	5	25	7
4	60	24	84	15	6	21	9
5	60	35	95	12	7	19	11
6	60	48	108	10	8	18	13
7	60	63	123	8.5	9	17.5	15
8	60	80	140	7.5	10	17.5	17
9	60	99	159	6.6	11	17.6	19
10	60	120	180	6	12	18	21
11	60	143	203	5.5	13	18.5	23
12	60	168	228	5	14	19	25
13	60	195	255	4.5	15	19.5	27
14	60	224	284	4.3	16	20	29
15	60	255	315	4.0	17	21	31

We next look at what happens to costs as more is supplied. As sales are increased (production is increased), the entrepreneur moves along the U-shaped short-run average cost curve. Short-run average costs at first fall, then reach a minimum and then rise. It might seem from this that the entrepreneur would choose to supply that quantity at which average costs were at a minimum (i.e. at the firm's capacity point), but this would be a mistake.

Imagine an entrepreneur supplying that quantity. If sales were increased by one more unit, costs would rise but so would revenue. Revenue would rise by the price (the marginal revenue) and if costs rose by less than this then profits would increase. Thus it would pay the entrepreneur to increase output.

Expanding output would continue to increase profits until the increase in costs exactly equalled the increase in revenue. At that point costs would increase by the same amount as revenue increased, so profit would remain unaltered. To expand output further would increase costs by more than revenue and hence reduce profits.

This means that profits are maximized at that level of output at which the increase in total revenue when sales are increased by 1 unit is exactly equal to the increase in total costs when production is increased by 1 unit.

This can be put more succinctly if we use some technical terms. We know that the increase in total revenue when sales are increased by 1 unit is called marginal revenue. Similarly, the increase in total costs when production is increased by one unit is called **marginal cost**. Thus profits are maximized when:

$$\text{Marginal cost } (MC) = \text{Marginal revenue } (MR)$$

This is a very important result in economics and we shall make much use of it. It is *always* the case that profits are maximized when $MC = MR$.

In the particular case of the auctioneer, marginal revenue equals price. This tells us that when an auctioneer calls out a market price entrepreneurs will supply that level of output at which their marginal cost equals that price. Thus if we know how marginal costs vary with output then we can say how much will be supplied at each price.

The short-run marginal cost curve relates the change in total cost to the quantity produced. Let us see what this means by use of an example. The figures in Table 5.1 show quantities produced and the corresponding costs in columns (a) – (g).

These columns are fairly self-explanatory. Fixed cost (b) remains the same (60) throughout. Variable costs (c) steadily rise and the sum of these two yields the steadily rising total cost column (d). Average fixed cost (e) is fixed cost (b) divided by quantity (a). Average variable cost (f) is variable cost (c) divided by quantity (a). The sum of these two (e and f) yields the average total cost column (g), which can also be derived by dividing total cost (d) by quantity (a). All these columns have the properties we would expect. In particular, average variable cost and average total cost both fall at first, then reach a minimum and then rise and continue to rise as output is increased.

The total cost of producing no output is £60 (fixed cost only). Increasing output by 1 unit will increase total cost to £65. The difference between these two total costs (i.e. the marginal cost) is £5. If production is increased by a further unit from 1 to 2 then total cost is seen to rise from £65 to £68. The marginal cost at output level 2 is therefore £3. The marginal cost at each level of output has been calculated and is shown in column (h) of Table 5.1.

Notice that the marginal cost follows the same pattern as the average variable cost and average total cost. First it falls, then it reaches a minimum and then it rises steadily as output is increased.

Curves representing the first four columns are shown in Figure 5.2 and curves representing the remaining columns are shown in Figure 5.3. Note that the short-run marginal cost curve cuts the short-run average total cost curve at its

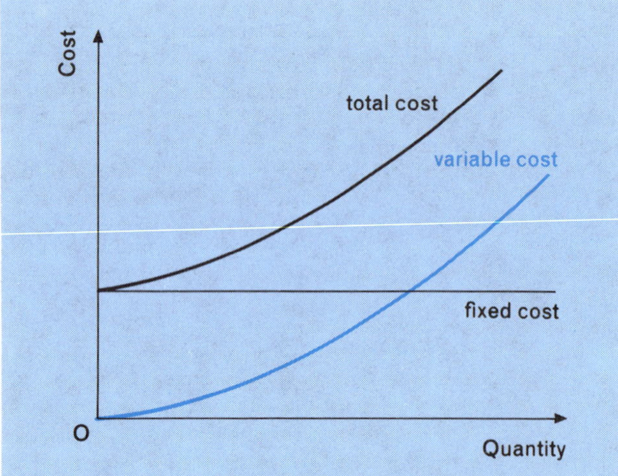

Figure 5.2 Fixed, variable and total cost curves.

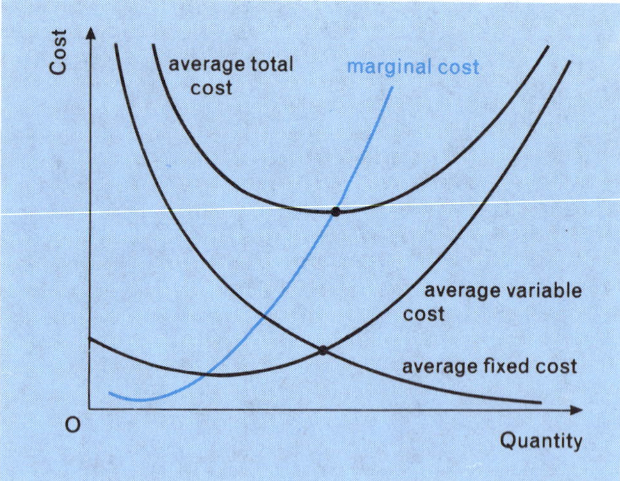

Figure 5.3 Short-run marginal, average fixed, average variable and average total cost curves.

lowest point. And it cuts the short-run average variable cost curve at its lowest point too. These are neither coincidences nor the result of poor draughtsmanship. The marginal cost curve must cut these average curves at their lowest points.

Let us take a simple numerical example. Imagine a producer producing 10 units of output at a total cost of £100 and a variable cost of £50. The average total cost would therefore be £10 and the average variable cost would be £5.

If the marginal cost at this level of output were £20 then increasing output to 11 units would increase total cost to £120 (100+20) and variable cost to £70 (50+20). The average cost now would be £10.91 (120 divided by 11) instead of £10, and the average variable cost would be £6.36 (70 divided by 11) instead of £5. Thus both would increase because the marginal cost (£20) is greater than the average total cost (£10) and greater than the average variable cost (£5).

Now if the marginal cost at output 10 units were not £20 but £8, then the total cost of producing 11 units would be £108 (100+8) and the variable cost would be £58 (50+8). The average total cost would now be £9.82 (108 divided by 11) instead of £10, and the average variable cost would be about £5.27 (58 divided by 11) instead of £5. Thus in this example, average total costs have fallen from £10 to £9.82 and average variable costs have risen from £5 to £5.27. This is because the marginal cost (£8) was above average variable cost (£5) but below average total cost (£10).

Finally, take the case where, at an output of 10 units, the marginal cost is £4. The total cost of producing 11 units would now be £104 (100+4) and the variable cost would be £54 (50+4). Therefore the average total cost would be £9.45 (104 divided by 11) and the average variable cost about £4.91 (54 divided by 11). Both the average total cost and the average variable cost have fallen. The reason again is clear: the marginal cost at this level of output (£4) is below the average total cost (£10) and below average variable cost (£5), so they both fall.

So much for the relationship between the marginal cost curve and the average total cost and average variable cost curves.

There remains only the relationship between the marginal cost curve and the average fixed cost curve. In brief, we can say that there is no relationship! The marginal cost curve is entirely independent of the fixed cost curve. This can be seen fairly readily from the numerical example in Table 5.1. We can enter whatever figure we like in column (b) – fixed costs – and have no effect whatever on column (h) – marginal costs. This is because marginal cost is the change in total cost when production is increased by 1 unit. But by definition the fixed cost cannot change as production changes and hence cannot affect marginal cost. Therefore marginal cost is independent of fixed cost.

SUMMARY

1. In order to do the job efficiently, our auctioneer (the market) needs to know how suppliers will respond to price changes.
2. Supply decisions are taken by entrepreneurs who seek to maximize their profits.
3. Changing the quantity supplied may change the cost of production. We therefore need to look at cost curves.
4. As well as total cost, total variable cost, total fixed cost, average total cost, average variable cost and average fixed cost, we introduce the idea of marginal cost.
5. Marginal cost is the increase in total cost due to the production of one more unit of output.
6. Like the average total cost curve and the average variable cost curve, the marginal cost curve has a U-shape.
7. The marginal cost curve cuts the average total cost curve and the average variable cost curve at their lowest points.
8. Marginal cost is independent of fixed cost.

Marginal costs and supply curves

We have established two important features of this kind of 'auctioneer' market:

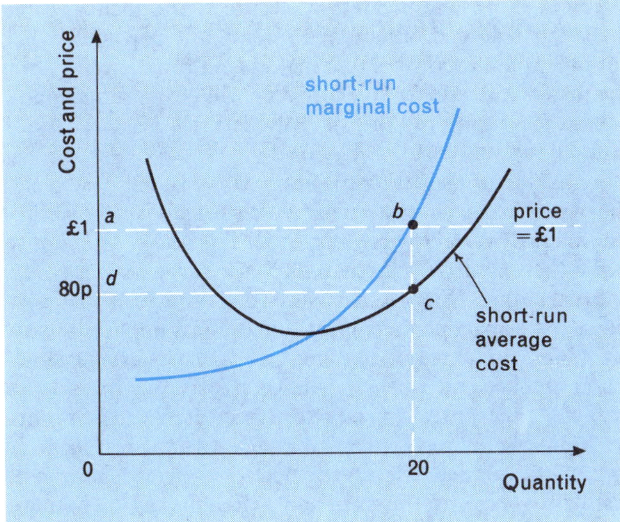

Figure 5.4 Total profit when price is greater than average cost.

1. Production = amount offered for sale.
2. Marginal cost = price.

Wherever we see 'production' we can substitute 'sales' and wherever we see 'marginal cost' we can substitute 'price'. This means that we can immediately convert marginal cost curves (which show how marginal costs are related to production) into supply curves (which show how price is related to the amount offered for sale). The firm's short-run marginal cost curve is its supply curve.

The firm's short-run marginal cost curve and its short-run average cost curve are shown in Figure 5.4. We are going to use this diagram to see how the entrepreneur reacts when the auctioneer calls out a price.

Say the price is announced as £1. We know that the entrepreneur will expand production until marginal cost equals price. This occurs at output 20. At 20 units the entrepreneur is therefore maximizing profits. Above 20 units, costs increase by more than price. Below 20 units costs increase by less than price.

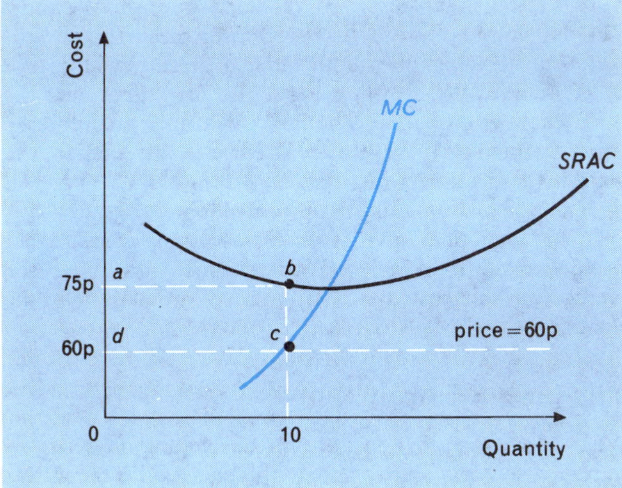

Figure 5.5 Total loss when price is less than average cost.

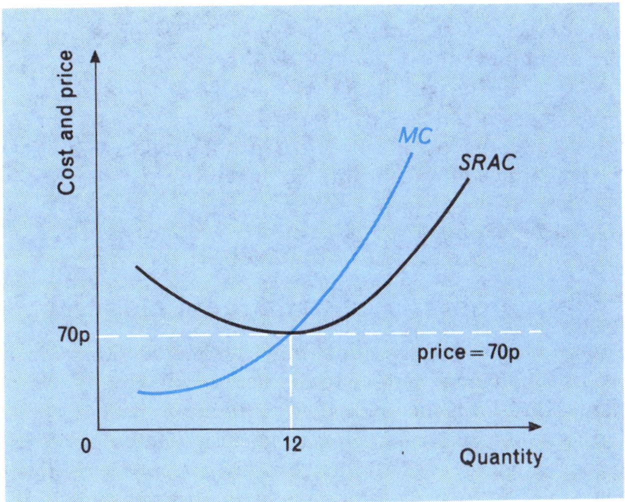

Figure 5.6 Zero (normal) profit when price equals average cost.

Now we note in passing that at 20 units the average total cost of production is 80p. This is the cost of producing each one of the 20 units of output. We note also that the revenue received from each unit is £1. So the profit per unit is 20p. The total profit (profit per unit × number of units) is equal to the area of rectangle *abcd* in Figure 5.4 and is £4.

Now let us repeat this exercise, but with a very much lower price. The same cost curves are retained and reproduced in Figure 5.5. Here we have a price of 60p, and at that price the entrepreneur will expand output until marginal cost equals 60p. This occurs at quantity 10 units. In this case, however, we have an example of loss making. Even though the entrepreneurs are maximizing their profits, they are nonetheless making a loss. Average cost is 75p, which is greater than average revenue (60p). They are therefore making a loss on every unit of 15p and a total loss equal to the area of rectangle *abcd*, which is £1.50. This demonstrates that profit maximization includes loss minimization and does not always imply that profits are actually being made.

Now let us repeat the exercise yet again, but this time with a price which just equals average costs. The cost curves are reproduced in Figure 5.6. If the auctioneer calls out a price of 70p then the entrepreneur will expand output until the marginal cost just equals 70p. This occurs at a quantity of 12 units, which, it will be recalled, is capacity output (see p. 37). At this price the average cost of producing 1 unit exactly equals the revenue gained by selling 1 unit. So at this price, profits are zero.

SUMMARY

1. A profit-maximizing entrepreneur will respond to the prices of the auctioneer (market) by producing that quantity of output which equates marginal cost to price.
2. The short-run marginal cost curve of the firm is therefore the firm's supply curve.

3. Being on this curve ensures profit maximization, but may result in positive profits, zero profits or losses. Zero profits should strictly be called zero excess profits, since the short-run average total cost curve includes 'normal' profits. Quite what is meant by normal profits will be taken up in the next section.

Excess profits, losses and plant closures

You may be tempted to think from the foregoing that when profits fall below zero, entrepreneurs will simply close plants. But this is incorrect. The assumption that entrepreneurs could avoid making losses by closing down plants is, of course, not the case. In the short run, entrepreneurs must meet their fixed costs. The option to close the plant will therefore only be considered if the losses due to running it are greater than the costs that have to be met even when the plant is closed. That is to say, it will be closed when the losses incurred by operating the plant are greater than the fixed costs.

Imagine that the auctioneer calls out a price (65p) which happens to equal the marginal cost just where the marginal cost curve cuts the average variable cost curve, i.e. at the lowest point on that curve (see Figure 5.7). At this output (11 units) profits are maximized and average total costs are 75p. Average fixed costs are the difference between average total costs (75p) and average variable costs (65p), i.e. average fixed costs are 10p.

Since the price is below the average total cost, the entrepreneur will be making losses of 10p on every unit. In total, the losses on 11 units are £1.10. Notice too that, since average fixed cost is 10p, total fixed cost is £1.10, i.e. at this level of output (11 units) the running loss (£1.10) equals the non-running loss (fixed costs). This shows that where the marginal cost curve cuts the average variable cost curve (at its minimum) the losses incurred by production are exactly equal to the losses which would have to be met if production were to cease.

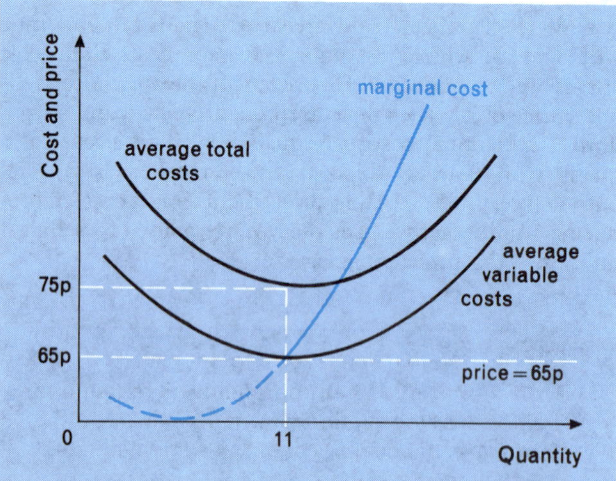

Figure 5.7 Shut-down price and the firm's supply curve.

Prices above 65p mean that closure would incur greater loss than would production. Prices below 65p mean that closure would incur less loss than would production. Thus the profit-maximizing entrepreneur will only produce (and equate marginal cost to price) if the price is in excess of average variable costs.

Thus the firm's short-run supply curve is that part of the short-run marginal cost curve which lies above the short-run average variable cost curve. In Figure 5.7 the supply curve is that part of the marginal cost curve shown by an unbroken line. The broken section of the marginal cost curve is not part of the supply curve. This applies only in the short run, since in the long run all costs are variable. Thus, in the long run, shut-down costs are zero and the firm will only continue producing (in the long run) if profits are sufficient to keep the capital in this particular process. If profits are higher elsewhere then the entrepreneur will gradually run down the plant and switch the capital to more profitable processes.

The level of profit necessary to keep the entrepreneur's capital in a particular process is called **normal profit**. Normal profit is assumed to be included in total costs and hence is also included in average costs.

When profits are below normal (price is below average total costs) capital will be switched out of the process. When profits are above normal (price is above average total costs) capital will tend to be switched into the process. When profits are normal (price equals average total costs) the process remains at a constant size.

The shape of the supply curve

We have drawn the marginal cost curve as if it initially falls, then reaches a minimum and then rises continuously. This shape is based on the fundamental 'law' in economics mentioned in Chapter 3 – the law of diminishing returns. Recall that as successive units of a variable factor are applied to a fixed quantity of another factor, changes in output will eventually diminish. We now know that this means as output increases, with one or more factors fixed, then the marginal costs will eventually rise and thereafter will continue to rise.

This tells us that supply curves slope upwards. We know that the supply curve is that section of the marginal cost (*MC*) curve which lies above the average variable cost (*AVC*) curve. We also know that the *MC* curve cuts the *AVC* curve from below. The *MC* curve must therefore be rising by the time it cuts the *AVC* curve. Any section of the marginal cost curve which lies above the *AVC* curve will therefore be unambiguously upward sloping.

In an 'auctioneer' market the firm's supply curve is that section of the marginal cost curve which lies above the average variable cost curve, and it is upward sloping to the right.

The market supply curve

We have spent a great deal of time developing the relationship between cost curves and supply curves. So far in this chapter we have developed a market demand curve and a firm's supply curve. The next step is to generate a market supply curve.

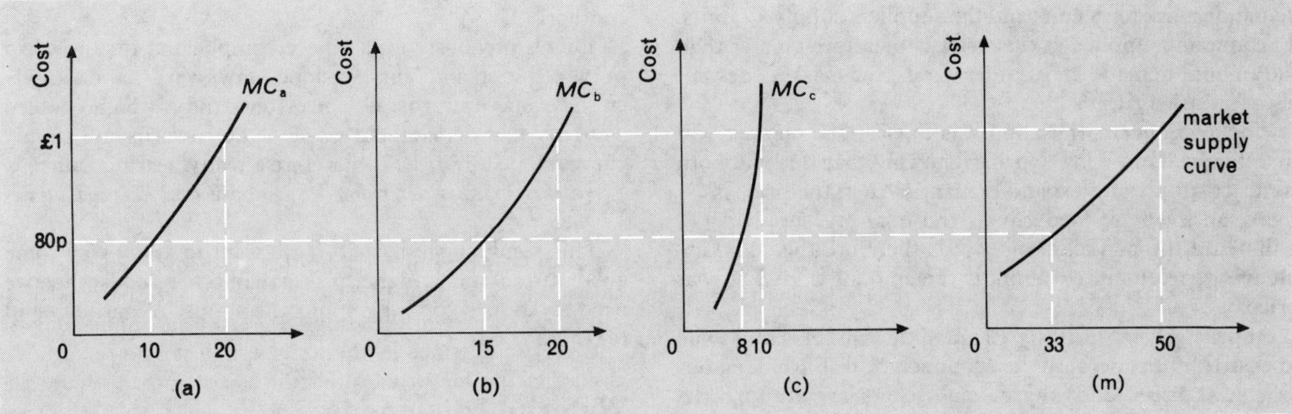

Figure 5.8 Constructing a market supply curve.

There will normally be a large number of firms supplying similar, if not identical, goods to the market. Thus when the auctioneer calls out a price several firms will offer to supply a certain quantity of goods at that price. This is illustrated in Figure 5.8, which shows the supply curves of three firms (a), (b) and (c) and the supply curve for the whole market (m).

When the auctioneer calls out a price of 80p firm (a) supplies 10 units, firm (b) supplies 15 units and firm (c) supplies 8 units. Total or market supply is therefore 33 units. If the auctioneer then calls out a higher price (£1) then the firms offer 20, 20 and 10 units respectively. The market supply at this price is therefore 50 units. By calling out a number of prices, we can construct the whole market supply curve. It will be upward sloping to the right.

We now have both the market demand curve, which is downward sloping, and the market supply curve, which is upward sloping. We shall see in the next section how these two curves are used to describe the operation of markets.

SUMMARY

1. Entrepreneurs will close down plants if, by so doing, they can avoid (or reduce) losses.
2. In the short run, they must meet their fixed costs whether they produce or not.
3. They will not close down when the losses of operating are greater than the losses of not operating (i.e. fixed costs).
4. The supply curve, in the short run, is that part of the marginal cost curve which lies above the short-run average variable cost curve.
5. This will always be upward sloping.
6. In the long run, there are no fixed costs and production will continue only if at least normal profits are being made.
7. Normal profit in that minimum level of profit necessary to justify an entrepreneur remaining in a market.
8. Normal profits are included in average total cost and so, in the long run, production will continue only if price is greater than or equal to average total cost.
9. When price is less than short-run average total cost (*SRATC*) the process will be gradually run down.
10. When price is greater than *SRATC* the process will tend to expand.
11. When price equals *SRATC* the process is in long-run equilibrium.

The determination of prices

The market demand curve shows how the demand for goods by consumers changes with the prices called out by our 'auctioneer'. It is downward sloping to the right. The market supply curve shows how the supply of goods by producers changes with the prices called out by the auctioneer. It is upward sloping to the right.

We can represent these two curves on a single diagram as in Figure 5.9. The price called out by the auctioneer is measured along the vertical axis, and the quantity demanded at that price and the quantity supplied at that price are measured along the horizontal axis.

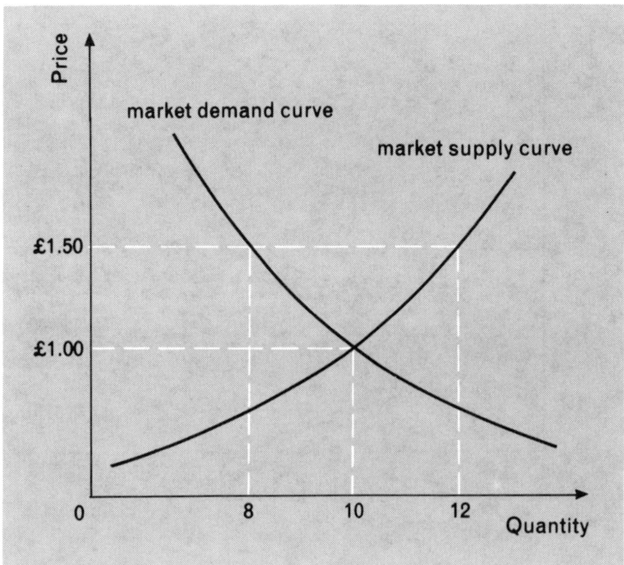

Figure 5.9 Market equilibrium and price.

When the auctioneer calls out a price of £1.50, the demanders ask for 8 units and the suppliers supply 12 units. The amount supplied at this price is therefore greater than the amount demanded. In other words, the market does not 'clear' at price £1.50.

The auctioneer, whose job it is to clear the market, will therefore call out a lower price, knowing that this will both contract supply and expand demand. When the price is £1 the quantity demanded equals the quantity supplied (10 units) and the market clears. £1 is therefore the **market-clearing price** and 10 units is the amount traded at that price.

At price £1 and quantity 10 units, the market is said to be in **equilibrium** because the auctioneer will stop calling out any new prices and buyers and sellers are trading the amounts they wish to trade given the price. It is this price which is called the market price or, alternatively, the value in exchange. As we can see, the price will depend on the shapes and positions of the supply and demand curves. That is what is meant when people say, 'It all depends on supply and demand.'

Uniqueness

We now know how market prices are formed in an auctioneer's market and we can see that there will only be one price which clears the market. This is due to the fact that demand curves slope downwards and supply curves slope upwards. After the intersection, one curve goes on ever upward and the other goes on ever downward and hence they can never meet again. This is a very useful and interesting result. The market determines the price by the interaction of supply and demand curves and it settles down on one and only one price.

As a counter-example imagine a world in which the supply curve *and* the demand curve were both upward sloping (see Figure 5.10). In this example there are four market-clearing prices and economists would need to explain not only what these prices were, but also which one was likely to be in operation on any particular day, and when and how the market moved from one equilibrium to another.

This is obviously much more complicated than a world in which demand curves slope downwards and supply curves slope upwards. Our previous study, which enabled us to say that demand curves slope downwards and supply curves slope upwards, is therefore already bearing fruit.

Market price is determined by supply and demand and is unique.

This result suggests that, if we want to know why some goods attract much higher prices than other goods, then we need to know something about the supply of and demand for those goods.

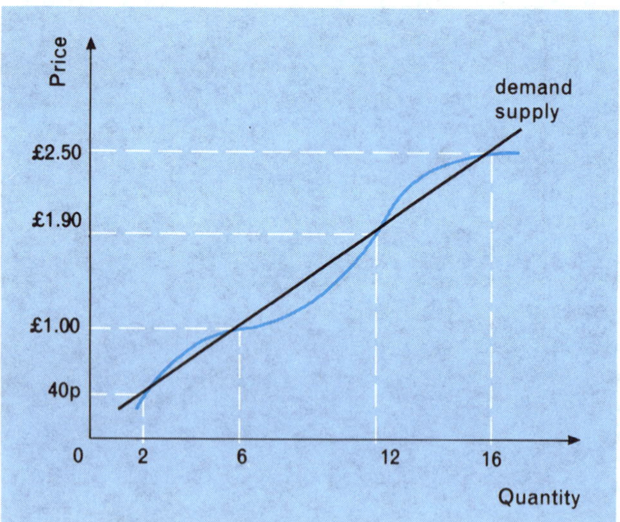

Figure 5.10 Upward-sloping demand and supply curves.

Water and diamonds

As an example, consider the paradox of value expressed earlier in terms of water being essential to life but cheap, and diamonds being almost useless but expensive. We can say that the demand curve for water must begin very high on the price axis, since people would pay enormous sums for that amount of water necessary for life itself. Once those essential needs were satisfied there would be other needs, such as washing, cooking and irrigating. We would therefore expect the demand curve to fall when these needs had been met.

For diamonds, on the other hand, the initial price may not be very high compared with that of water. We do not need diamonds to live. But it is difficult to imagine a situation in which we all have enough diamonds. The demand curve may therefore begin lower than that of water, but may fall less steeply. These curves are shown in Figure 5.11.

We can see from these demand curves that we *could* live in a world in which water was more expensive than diamonds. For example, if the quantity of water available was 1 litre per week then the price of water would be very high (£100 per litre) – much higher than any possible price of diamonds. No matter how few diamonds are available, diamond prices cannot go much above £60.

On the other hand, if the quantities of water and diamonds were 3 litres per week and 4 carats respectively then the prices of water and diamonds would be equal at £50.

If the quantity of water is increased still further (say to 7 litres per week) then water becomes very cheap (£2 per litre) – much cheaper than diamonds, which remain at £50.

What we are saying is that market value depends on both demand *and* supply and we cannot really say anything about market value without knowing both the demand curve and the supply curve. By adding supply curves to Figure 5.11 we get Figure 5.12.

Figure 5.12(a) shows the demand and supply curves for water, and Figure 5.12(b) the demand and supply curves for diamonds. If water can be obtained without much exertion of labour or expenditure of capital then the supply curve for water will be far over to the right. No matter how high the demand curve is initially, the market price will be very low. The production of diamonds, on the other hand, amounts to a rather large mining operation involving much labour and capital. The supply curve will therefore be well over to the left and the price of diamonds is therefore quite high.

This serves to underline a point made earlier: *exchange*

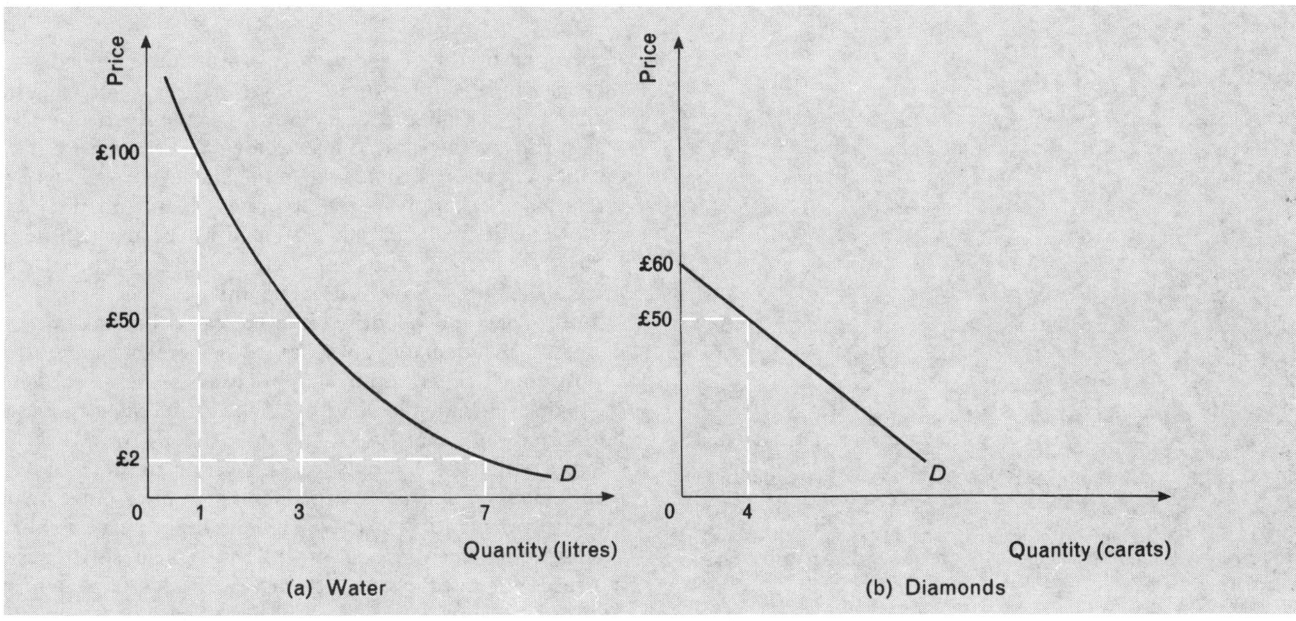

Figure 5.11 Demand curves for water and diamonds.

value (or market value) need not reflect the value to us of particular goods. It measures the value to us *and* the ease of supplying a particular good.

SUMMARY

1. Market price and quantity traded are determined by the intersection of the market demand curve and the market supply curve.
2. Since supply curves always slope upwards and demand curves always slope downwards, they can only intersect once. Market-clearing price and quantity are therefore unique.
3. Market price is also known as the value in exchange and exchange value does not necessarily equal value in use.
4. Exchange value depends partly on value in use but also on the ease of supply. This helps to explain the paradox of value.

Changes in price

To say that a market-clearing price is determined by supply and demand is not, of course, the same thing as saying that

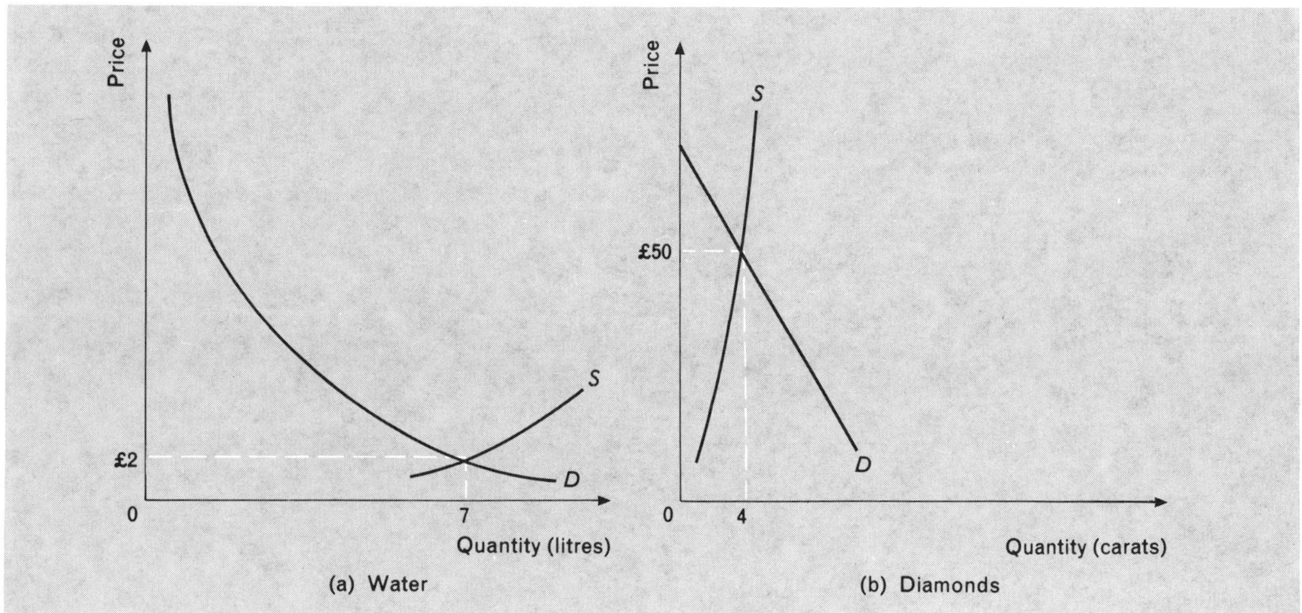

Figure 5.12 A paradox of value.

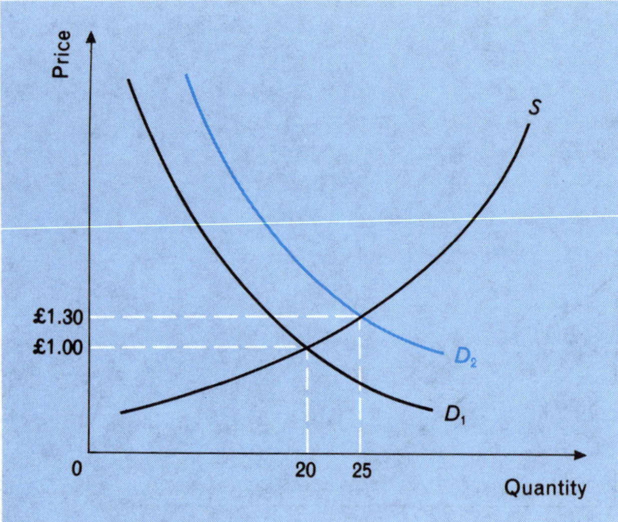

Figure 5.13 Effect of an increase in income on the demand curve.

it never changes. Market prices can, and do, change. We shall see later that price changes are essential to the proper working of a free-market economy.

The most obvious cause of a price change is a change in the position of either the demand curve or the supply curve. Let us consider each in turn.

Movements of the demand curve

We will first consider the demand curve and see how changes in it may result in price changes. Recall that the demand curve is the relation between the quantity of a good demanded and its price when tastes, all other prices and money income are held constant. If any one of these (tastes, prices or income) were to change then the demand curve would move.

Imagine first a *change in income*. For normal goods, an increase in income would mean that more would be demanded at each and every price, i.e. the demand curve would shift to the right. This is shown in Figure 5.13. The demand curve constructed when income level was low (D_1) intersects the supply curve at price £1 and quantity 20 units. The demand curve constructed when income level is high (D_2) intersects the supply curve higher up to yield a price of £1.30 and a quantity of 25 units.

Both price and quantity have increased because movements *of* the demand curve cause movements *along* the supply curve. Since supply curves always slope upwards to the right, movements along it (to the right) must increase both price and quantity.

Notice that if the supply curve is very steep then movement along it will cause a large increase in price but a small increase in quantity. But when the supply curve is very shallow, movement along it will result in a small price increase and a large quantity increase. This is shown in Figure 5.14. In Figure 5.14(a) the supply curve is steep and movement of the demand curve causes price to double and quantity to increase by 20 per cent. In Figure 5.14(b) the supply curve is shallow and so the same movement of the demand curve causes the price to increase by 20 per cent and quantity to double.

Thus the effect on price and quantity of a movement of the demand curve depends on the shape of the supply curve.

The changes in price and quantity shown in Figure 5.14 were induced by an income change. An increase in income moved the demand curve for a normal good *bodily* to the right. There are, however, other ways of moving the demand curve, such as a *change in consumers' tastes*. If, for example, the good in question were cigarettes and it became

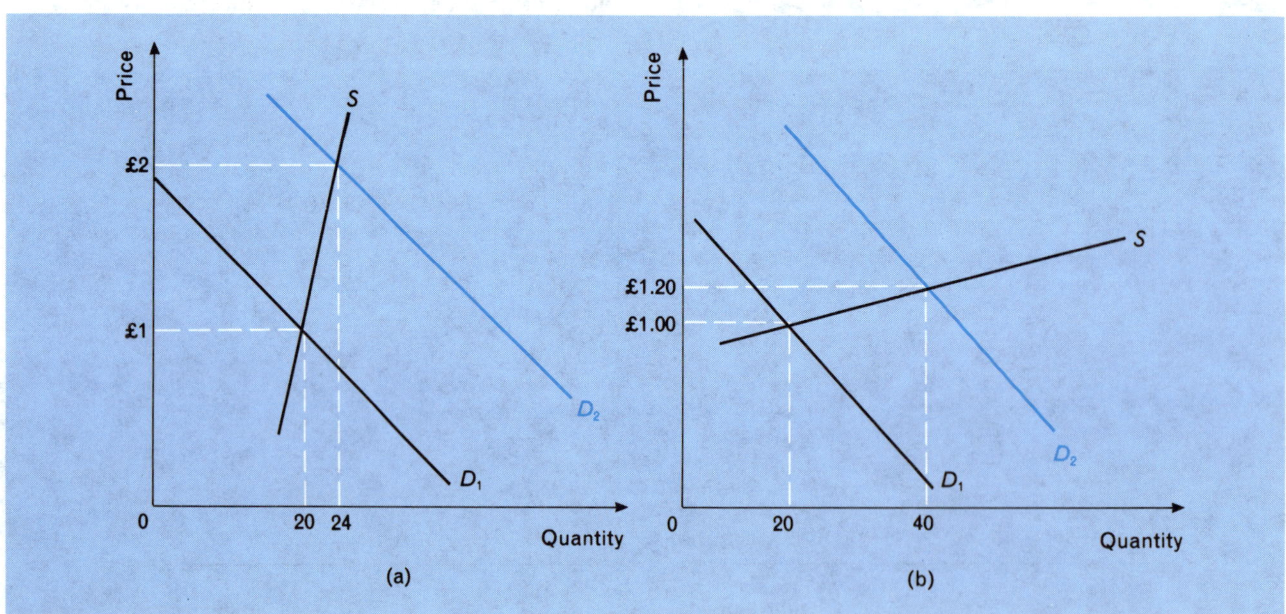

Figure 5.14 Effect of a shift in the demand curve with (a) a steep supply curve, (b) a shallow supply curve.

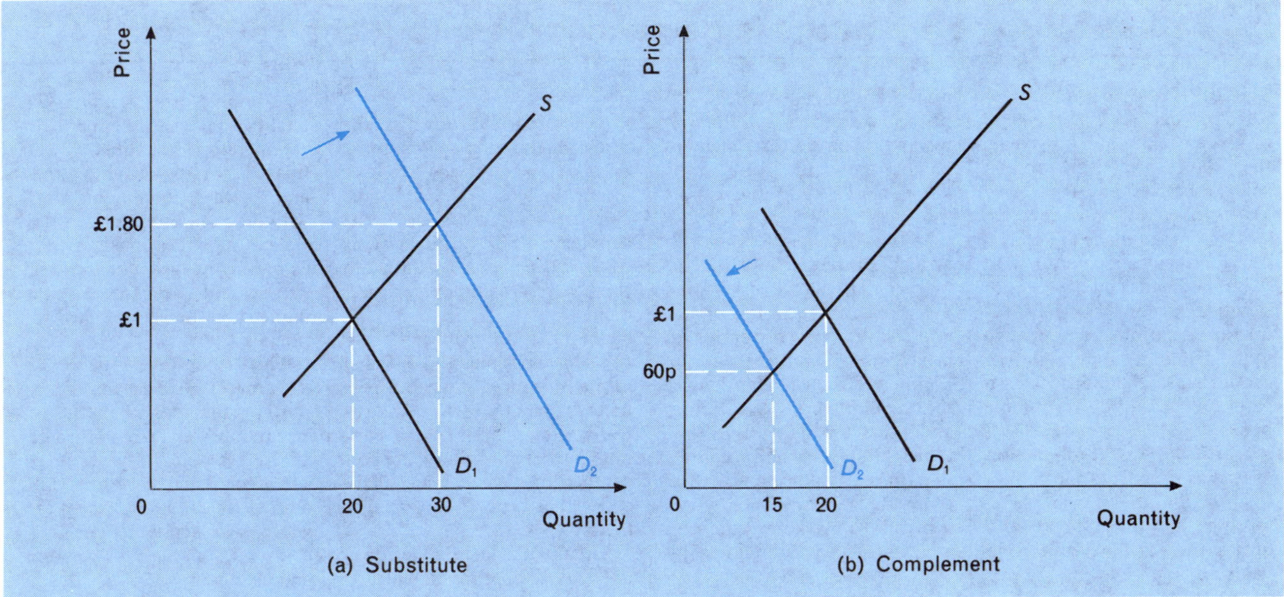

Figure 5.15 Effect of an increase in the price of (a) a substitute, (b) a complement on the demand curve for a good.

widely known that cigarette smoking was *not* harmful to health then the resulting change in tastes would cause the demand curve to move to the right. Once again, price and quantity would rise.

Advertising can have a strong influence on consumer tastes and so affect the position of the demand curve. Other factors that can have an effect are changes in the size of the population, the expectations people have about the future, changes in the distribution of income and seasonal variations.

Alternatively, the demand curve could be moved by *changing the price of another good.* If the good whose price is changed is a *substitute* for cigarettes (say cigars) then an increase in the price of cigars will cause more cigarettes to be bought at any given cigarette price – hence the demand curve for cigarettes moves to the right. If the good whose price is changed is a *complement* for cigarettes (say matches) then an increase in its price would move the demand curve for cigarettes to the left. This is shown in Figure 5.15.

Figure 5.15(a) shows what happens when the price of a substitute is increased. This moves the demand curve to the right, increases price from £1.00 to £1.80 and increases quantity from 20 units to 30 units. Figure 5.15(b) shows what happens when the price of a complement is increased. This moves the demand curve to the left, reduces the price from £1.00 to 60p and reduces quantity from 20 units to 15 units.

One way of changing market price is therefore to move the demand curve. Alternatively, of course, we could move the supply curve. Let us now look at the movement of the supply curve.

Movements of the supply curve

Supply curves are constructed from the marginal cost curves of firms, and hence can be moved if the cost curves are altered This may be due to some *improvement in production technique*, or to a *change in factor prices* (wages, rent or interest). Reductions in factor prices and/or improvements in production techniques would reduce costs and move the supply curve to the right (for any given output costs would be lower). This is shown in Figure 5.16.

As you can see, the movement of the supply curve causes the equilibrium point to move *along* the demand curve. Since demand curves always slope downwards to the right, any rightward shift in the supply curve would cause price to be reduced (from £1.80 to £1.00) and the quantity traded to be increased (from 40 units to 50 units).

As before, the size of the price reduction and the size of the quantity increase will depend on:

1. The distance the supply curve moves.
2. The shape of the demand curve.

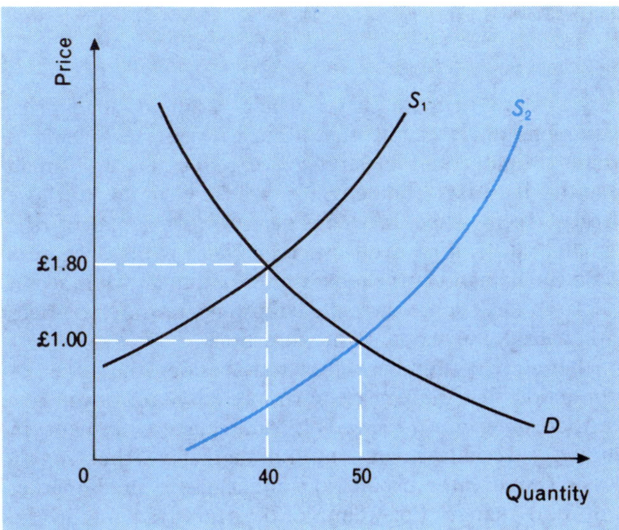

Figure 5.16 Effect of an increase in supply on price and quantity.

Case Study 5.1 Surge in demand is just producers' cup of tea

The 1990s should prove a rewarding decade for the tea-producing nations. For years they have seen their product sold to the world at ludicrously low prices. Even now, the cost of a cup of tea made at home is only a little over a penny.

But demand is on the verge of significantly outstripping production. This impending change in the demand–supply equation should make the industry, as a whole, a healthily profitable one.

Since 1952 world production of tea has risen from 530 million to 1.64 billion kilos in 1988. During that time supply and demand kept more or less in balance.

But through those years the make-up of the market was undergoing dramatic changes. While the UK has remained the single biggest tea-importing country, even though the British taste for a cuppa has declined, other nations, through increasing affluence, have been steadily acquiring a liking.

The demand by India, the Soviet Union, the Middle East and other developing nations has more than offset the decline in the UK. In India, the world's biggest producer, the growth in domestic demand is such – 75 per cent over 10 years – that it is facing a constant struggle to balance the requirements of the home market and the export trade.

It was against the background of these shifts in the market that the London-based Tea Council last month organised the first tea convention to be held in Britain.

Jimmy Hilditch, president of the Tea Buyers' Association and a director of Lyons Tetley, told delegates from 27 countries that on the assumption of 3 per cent annual growth in world demand the market would need an extra 555 million kilos by 1998.

But if the recent growth rate of 5 per cent continued an extra one billion kilos would be required.

So far an increase in efficiency has' kept production mounting. Yields of more than 2,000 kilos a hectare have been registered in some countries compared with 500 to 1,000 in the early 1950s.

But, said Mr Hilditch: 'There must be a limit to how much a bush can produce. Commonsense suggests it will be difficult to match the improvements of the past.'

The recent slowdown in the rate of increase in new planting needed to be reversed.

Fortunately, despite the coming swing in favour of the suppliers, the producing nations shown no sign of succumbing to the lure of a commodity agreement.

Apart from rubber, these pacts have all collapsed or fallen into a moribund state. But perhaps the fact that tea has a relatively short shelf-life and cannot be stockpiled like other soft commodities, such as cocoa and coffee, has been the overriding factor.

Equally, the fact that tea does not stay fresh for long means that prices in future will be subject to a good deal of short-term volatility.

While demand worldwide has been growing the importance, in volume terms, of London as an auction centre has fallen away sharply. In 1952 there were five auction centres compared with 12 today. Yet London's auction share of the market has dropped from 24 to 3 per cent.

But, as Mr Hilditch points out, London has greater all-round expertise than other tea marketing centres, the financial facilities to provide capital for production investment and finance for day-to-day trade and excellent communications with the rest of the world.

That has positioned London as a fully-fledged international market and is regarded by the industry as the benchmark for pricing.

There is, however, one worrying area of concern for the industry, summed up in the inelegant phrase 'share of throat'.

For example, 15 years or so ago tea's share of the UK market for all fluids, except tap water, was nearly 60 per cent. Today it stands at 44 per cent and is under vigorous attack, particularly from the soft drinks sector.

The price of tea is a strong point in its favour. On the Tea Council's reckoning, coffee costs twice as much while soft drinks are 10 times as dear.

But, as the Tea Council's executive director Illtyd Lewis notes, the volume of fluids we drink is finite. The battle for a share of our throats will get fiercer.

1. According to the article, what has happened to the market demand curve for tea in the UK?
2. What has happened to the world market demand and supply curves for tea?
3. What are the implications for the world price of tea of (a) reduced new planting, (b) a slowing in the rate of productivity growth per bush?
4. Can you explain why tea prices are likely to be volatile?

Source: David Green, *Independent* 1990

Very shallow demand curves would result in small price reductions and large quantity increases. Very steep demand curves would result in large price reductions and small quantity increases. These results are very similar to those already seen when we considered movements of the demand curve. The main difference here is that, whereas when the demand curve moves price and quantity move in the same direction, when the supply curve moves, prices and quantity move in opposite directions.

There are a number of factors besides the costs of production that can cause the supply curve to move. The weather or *seasonal variations* can cause movement in supply, especially in agricultural markets. Other *supply shocks* can disrupt production and cause overall market supply to change. For example, the Iran–Iraq war in the 1980s caused a fall in world oil production, effectively moving the supply curve of oil to the left.

What we have shown so far is that changes in price and quantity may come about from movement of either the supply curve or the demand curve. They may also come about through *tax changes*, and we will look now at the effect of taxes on prices.

SUMMARY

1. Market price can be changed by bodily moving the demand curve or the supply curve.
2. The demand curve was drawn up on the assumption that income, tastes and all other prices remain constant.
3. Changes in income, tastes or in the price of other goods will therefore cause the demand curve to move.
4. If income is increased then the demand curve of a normal good will move bodily to the right.

5. If income is increased then the demand curve of an inferior good will move bodily to the left.
6. If the price of a substitute is increased then the demand curve will move to the right.
7. If the price of a complement is increased then the demand curve will move to the left.
8. Movement of the demand curve results in movement along the supply curve.
9. Supply curves always slope upwards to the right. Therefore leftwards movements of the demand curve will decrease both quantity and price. Rightward movements of the demand curve would cause both price and quantity to increase.
10. The shape of the supply curve will determine whether movements of the demand curve result in large price changes and small quantity changes, or in small price changes and large quantity changes.
11. The supply curve can be moved by changing the efficiency of the production process or by changing factor prices.
12. Improvements in efficiency and/or lowering the price of factors of production will move the supply curve to the right.
13. A lowering of efficiency and/or an increase in the price of factors of production will move the supply curve to the left.
14. Movements of the supply curve cause movements along the demand curve. Thus rightward shifts of the supply curve will increase quantity and reduce price whereas leftward movements will cause price to increase and quantity to fall.
15. The shape of the demand curve will determine whether movements of the supply curve will result in large price changes and small quantity changes or in small price changes and large quantity changes.

The imposition of a tax

In the analysis so far we have assumed that the price paid by the demander is the price received by the supplier. This may seem reasonable but is highly unusual. Most goods attract a **tax**. This means that the demander pays more for a good than the supplier receives: the difference goes to the government as a tax. Three questions are suggested by this:

1. What will happen to price when a tax is imposed?
2. What will happen to the quantity traded when a tax is imposed?
3. How much income will the government receive from the tax?

In order to answer these questions we need another diagram (see Figure 5.17). With no tax the market would settle down at price of £1 and a quantity of 20 units. There is only one price and it is common to both suppliers and demanders. Now imagine that each good sold attracts 40p in tax. This means that the price received by sellers (80p) is 40p less than the price paid by demanders (£1.20). The new

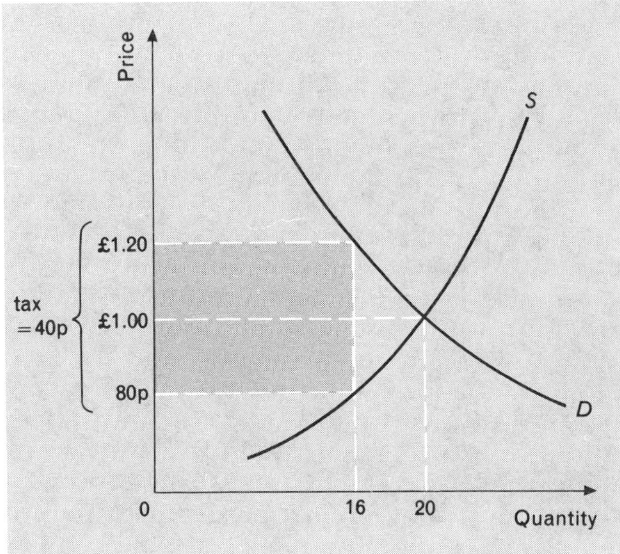

Figure 5.17 Effect of a tax on price and quantity.

equilibrium will therefore occur at quantity 16 and at prices £1.20 and 80p.

In this particular example, the price paid by demanders *rises* from £1.00 to £1.20 and the price received by suppliers is *reduced* from £1.00 to 80p. The quantity traded is reduced from 20 to 16 units.

If the demand curve is shallow and the supply curve steep, then almost all the tax will be borne by the suppliers. This is illustrated in Figure 5.18. Before the introduction of the tax the quantity traded was 20 units and the price paid by demanders equalled the price received by suppliers (£1). After the tax is imposed, the price paid by demanders rises very slightly from £1 to £1.02. The price received by suppliers, however, is reduced by a very large amount from

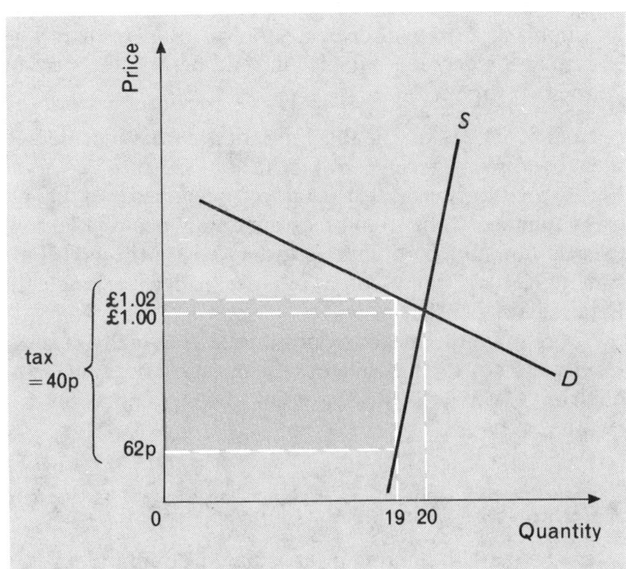

Figure 5.18 Effect of a tax with a steep supply curve and a shallow demand curve.

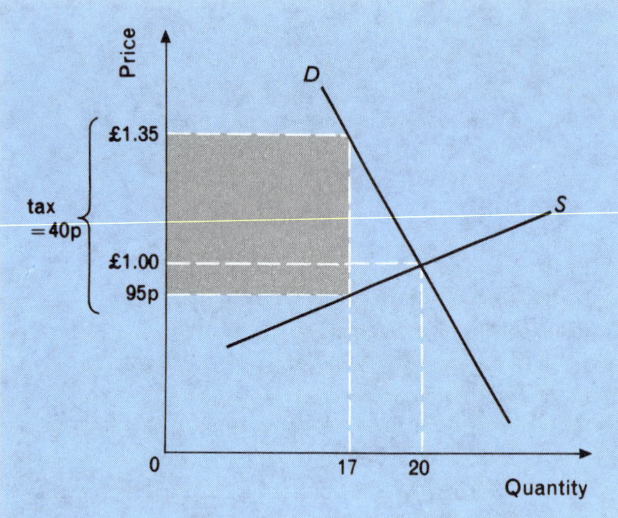

Figure 5.19 Effect of a tax with a steep demand curve and a shallow supply curve.

£1 to 62p. In other words, almost all the tax is paid by the suppliers. Quantity traded is again reduced, but not by as much as in Figure 5.17.

If the demand curve is very steep and the supply curve almost flat, then most of the tax will fall on the demanders. This is illustrated in Figure 5.19. As you can see, the price paid by the demanders rises by almost the full amount of the tax from £1 to £1.35. But the price received by suppliers has fallen only slightly from £1 to 95p. Once again the quantity traded is decreased, this time from 20 to 17 units.

From these examples we can answer the first two questions above:

1. Imposing a tax will increase the price paid by consumers and reduce the price received by suppliers. Who suffers most will depend on the steepness of the two curves: the agent with the steeper curve will bear most of the tax.
2. Imposing a tax will decrease the quantity traded. The size of the decrease will also depend on the steepness of the two curves.

In order to answer the third question – what income will the government receive from this tax? – turn again to Figure 5.19. It is clear that the government receives 40p on every unit sold. Thus 40p times the number sold (17 units) tells us how much revenue is generated by the tax. This sum (£6.80) is represented by the shaded rectangle in Figure 5.19.

There is a rather neat way of summarizing many of these results and our examination of it brings us to the concept of **elasticity** which is discussed in the appendix to this chapter.

SUMMARY

1. The market-clearing price is paid by demanders and received by producers unless there is a tax on the good in question.
2. The imposition of a tax causes the price paid by the demanders to be higher than the price received by the sellers. The difference between these two prices is the amount of the tax and goes to the government.
3. The tax burden is not always shared equally by both buyers and sellers. When the demand curve is shallow and the supply curve is steep, most of the tax will be borne by the supplier. When the demand curve is steep and the supply curve shallow, then the buyer will bear most of the tax.
4. The imposition of a tax generally reduces the quantity traded.

The workings of the price mechanism

So far we have been interested in the way in which the market works to determine exchange value. This is indeed an interesting and important function of a market, but there is more to a market than this.

One of the more remarkable aspects of our economy is the way *it organizes the production and distribution of goods and services*. The shepherd marshalling his flock in Cumbria has to decide how many sheep to have, how long to keep them, what breed to stock, how best to feed them, etc. and yet he cannot know to what use his wool will eventually be put, nor even who will buy it from him.

In some economies, a Central Planning Bureau decides how and what to produce and for what purposes. The central planners issue appropriate instructions and shepherds in such economies are required to follow the instructions.

In our type of mixed economy we do not use the device of a Central Planning Bureau. There is very little detailed economic planning by our government and rarely does it issue instructions to consumers or producers.

How, then, does our shepherd in Cumbria know what to do? The answer, suggested by Adam Smith in *The Wealth of Nations* (1776), is that the price mechanism will co-ordinate the actions of all economic agents. Not only will it co-ordinate their actions and plans, but it will do so by providing each agent with the necessary information *and* the incentives to work for the good of the whole society. Thus the Central Planning Bureau is simply not necessary – the economy will run itself.

This is a very powerful claim indeed, and provides much of the material for modern economics. In this section we look at just how this information and incentive system works at the microeconomic level.

Markets

We have seen the following in this and earlier chapters:

1. Market price is shown as the interaction of the market supply and market demand curves.
2. The market supply curve is the sum of every producer's marginal cost curve.

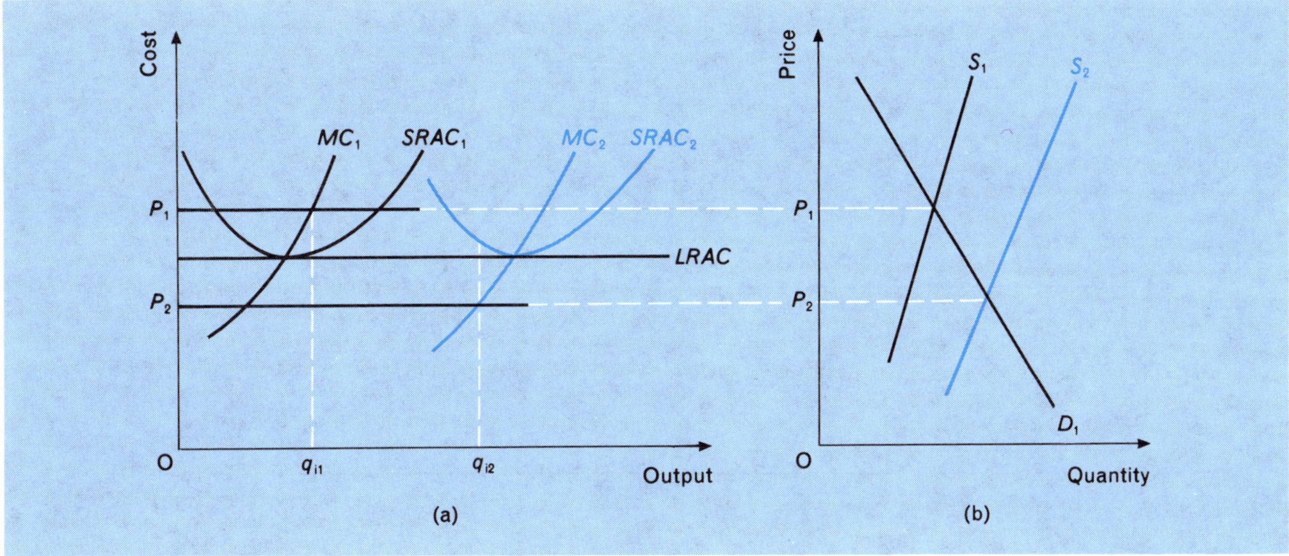

Figure 5.20 Market supply and demand and a firm's cost structure.

3. Marginal cost curves slope upwards when we assume that some factor of production (usually capital) is fixed.
4. Production decisions are made by the entrepreneur with the aim of maximizing profits.
5. In the long run, when capital is allowed to vary, average costs will:
   (a) rise for decreasing returns to scale;
   (b) remain constant for constant returns to scale;
   (c) fall for increasing returns to scale.

We can summarize these points as in Figure 5.20.

Constant returns to scale

Figure 5.20(a) shows the cost structure of a particular firm. Its long-run average cost curve is drawn horizontally, indicating constant returns to scale. And superimposed on this $LRAC$ curve are two short-run average cost curves with their corresponding marginal cost curves. $SRAC_1$ and MC_1 are drawn up to a particular quantity of fixed capital (say K_1). $SRAC_2$ and MC_2 are drawn up for a greater quantity of fixed capital (say K_2). Moving from $SRAC_1$ to $SRAC_2$ involves expanding capital stock from K_1 to K_2.

Figure 5.20(b) shows the market demand curve D_1, which is downward sloping to the right. It also shows two market supply curves. S_1 is the sum of all firms' marginal cost curves when each has K_1 units of capital and hence corresponds to MC_1 and $SRAC_1$ in part (a) of the figure. S_2, on the other hand, is that market supply curve which would emerge if each individual firm in the industry had K_2 units of capital. S_2 is therefore associated with MC_2 and $SRAC_2$.

With K_1 units of capital, S_1 applies and market price is P_1. At this price the profit-maximizing entrepreneur in charge of firm (i) will produce at q_{i1}, i.e. where $MC = P$.

At this price and quantity the entrepreneur will be making profits because P_1 is larger than average cost $SRAC_1$; in other words, the revenue received per unit is greater than the cost per unit.

If, on the other hand, our firm has K_2 units of capital then S_2 applies and market price will be P_2. At this price the profit-maximizing entrepreneur will produce q_{i2} units of output, since doing so will equate market price (P_2) with marginal cost (MC_2). Under these circumstances there are losses since price (P_2) is lower than average costs ($SRAC_2$).

Thus we have two cases: case 1 with capital stock K_1, market price P_1 and excess profits being made; case 2 with capital stock K_2, market price P_2 and losses being made.

Long-term equilibrium

Our hypothesis is that in case 1, the profitable case, the firms would expand capital stock since their current capital yields excess profits. If existing firms do not expand then new firms will be attracted into the industry by the prospect of making high profits. In any event, there will be a tendency for the market supply curve to move to the right.

Conversely, when capital stock is K_2 and firms are making losses, there will be a tendency to take capital out of the industry. This will gradually move the market supply curve to the left.

Thus whenever the firm is making excess profits or losses, there will be a tendency for it to change its capital stock. The market will therefore settle down at that capital stock which yields neither excess profits nor losses. This is shown in Figure 5.21.

In Figure 5.21(b) market price is determined by the intersection of the market supply curve S_1 and the market demand curve D_1. S_1 is the sum of each firm's MC curve (MC_i). In Figure 5.21(a) the firm has capital stock K_3 and has marginal cost curve MC_i and short-run average cost curve $SRAC_i$.

The entrepreneur will maximize profits by equating MC to price and hence produces at q_i. At this level of production average costs are exactly equal to price and hence there are neither losses nor excess profits. There is therefore no incentive to change capital stock. This therefore is a long-run equilibrium configuration towards which an entrepre-

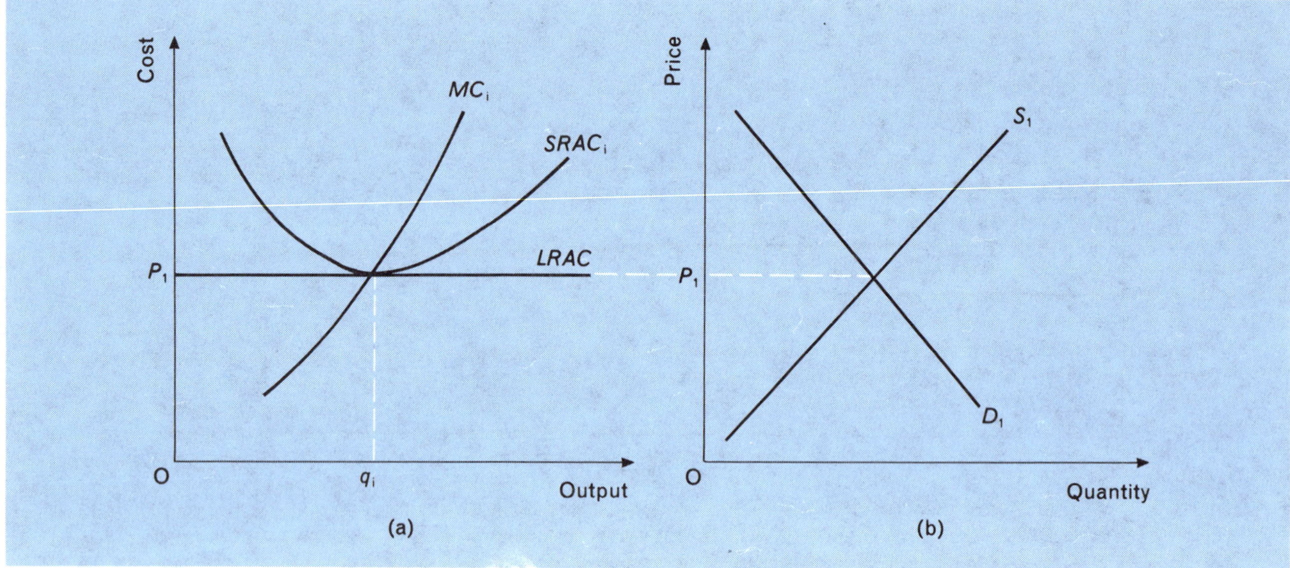

Figure 5.21 Long-term equilibrium.

neur would move simply by maximizing profits and seeking out profitable investments.

Notice that in the long run the firm will tend to produce at the lowest point of the *SRAC* curve, i.e. at the capacity point. Notice too that the price here is exactly equal to the long-run average cost. In this particular case then we can say that market price will tend towards the long-run average cost.

Thus, in the long run, with constant returns to scale, an auctioneer-type market and profit-maximizing entrepreneurs, the market will settle down to produce at the *lowest possible cost*, with no excess profits and price equal to the long-run average cost. This price is called 'natural' or 'just' price and should not be confused with short-run market price, which may be above or below the natural price.

Normal profit

We have said that there is no excess profit or loss in the long-run equilibrium, but this should not be taken to mean that profits are zero. Remember that there must be sufficient profit to keep the entrepreneur in business, not so much profit as would induce expansion, and not little enough profit to force the entrepreneur out of business. This level is called **normal profit**. It is difficult to say what this level of profit will actually be. It will depend partly on the willingness of entrepreneurs to face the risks entailed, and partly on the 'riskiness' of the particular business under consideration.

Responding to change

To explore further how this self-regulating economy works, consider what happens if there is a change in demand. Say tastes changed so that the market demand curve moved to the right. This is shown in Figure 5.22.

With market demand D_1 and supply S_1, price is P_1 and the market is in long- and short-run equilibrium, each firm producing q_1, and, in total, all firms together producing Q_1.

Now let the demand curve move to the right – to D_2. Since there can be no immediate change in scale, the first thing to happen is that market price rises to P_2 as firms move up their short-run marginal cost curves so as to maximize profits. They then each produce q_2 and make excess profits since price (P_2) is now greater than average cost ($SRAC_1$).

These excess profits will eventually induce an increase in capital stock which will move the supply curve to the right and give rise to $SRAC_2$ and $SRMC_2$. Capital stock will continue to change until the new market supply curve (S_2) is such as will yield the original market price (P_1). That is to say, market price will be brought back to the long-run average cost (*LRAC*) or 'natural' price.

The increase in demand will therefore bring about an increase in supply of exactly the amount required, but will not alter the long-run price.

The sequence of events is worth going over once more.

1. People wanted more of the good – demand shifted to the right.
2. Prices rose and caused excess profits to be made by producers of the good.
3. These excess profits encouraged the producers to expand (provided an incentive) and provided the wherewithal (excess profits) necessary for expansion.
4. As new capital was bought, output increased and prices began to fall.
5. Prices fell until no excess profits were being made and hence the incentive to increase capital stock disappeared.

This is the essential operation of the price mechanism. Suppliers, by responding to price signals, will end up doing what consumers want them to do and they will do it in an efficient manner – no one makes excess profits and everyone produces at minimum average cost.

A similar sequence of events will occur if the demand fell, i.e. if the demand curves shifted to the left. Price would fall, producers would move down their short-run marginal cost curves and make losses. Some capital would be shed or moved to other uses and eventually the supply curve would

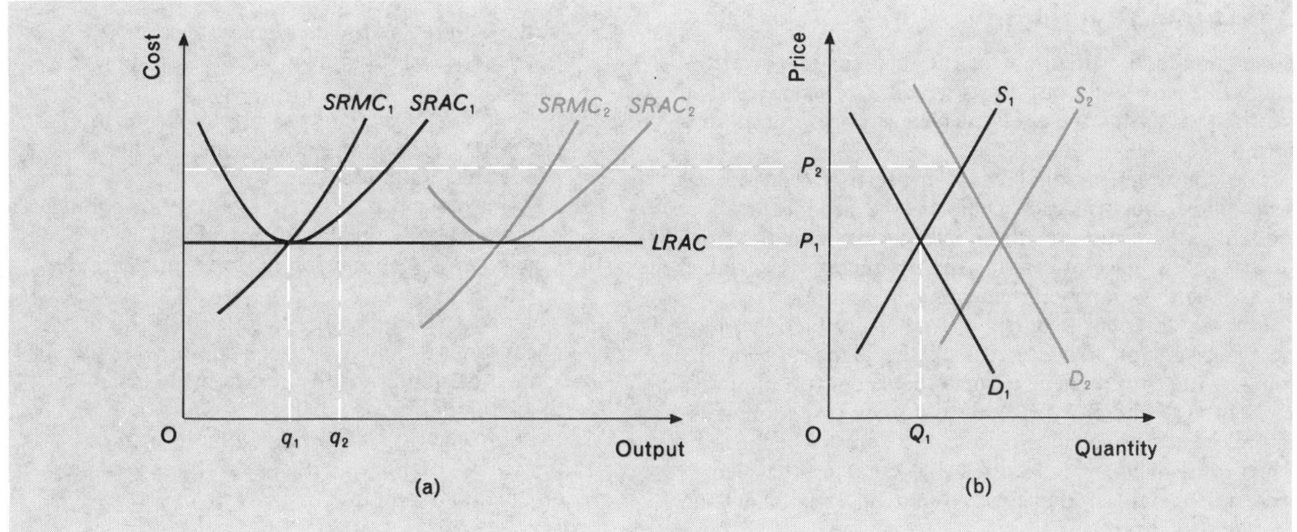

Figure 5.22 Effect of an increase in demand on long-run price and supply (constant returns).

move to the left. This would continue until market price once more equalled long-run average cost.

In this kind of market, quantities are determined (in the long run) solely by demand and price solely by cost. This result springs partly from our assumption of constant returns to scale. It is this assumption which leads to a horizontal long-run average cost curve. We shall now see what happens with increasing returns to scale.

Increasing returns to scale

If increasing returns to scale are obtained then the long-run average cost curve will be downward sloping as shown in Figure 5.23. Since the *LRAC* curve of the firm is downward sloping, the two short-run average cost curves ($SRAC_1$ and $SRAC_2$) are not on the same level.

Imagine the market settles down with supply curve S_1 and demand curve D_1, yielding price P_1 and each firm producing q_1. Now let the demand curve shift to the right to D_2. In the short run the entrepreneurs will move up their short-run marginal cost curves to q_0 at price P_0. At this price and quantity the entrepreneurs are making excess profits since P_0 is greater than $SRAC_1$. This will induce an expansion of capital stock and move the *SRAC* curves along the long-run average cost curve and eventually yield supply curve S_2, made up of all the marginal cost curves ($SRMC_2$). The market will therefore reach equilibrium at a lower price (P_2), where neither profits nor losses will be made since P_2 just equals short-run average costs. *Thus market price, even in the long run, will depend on both the supply curve and the demand curve when there are increasing returns to scale.* There is therefore no single 'natural' or 'just' price when we relax the assumption of constant returns to scale.

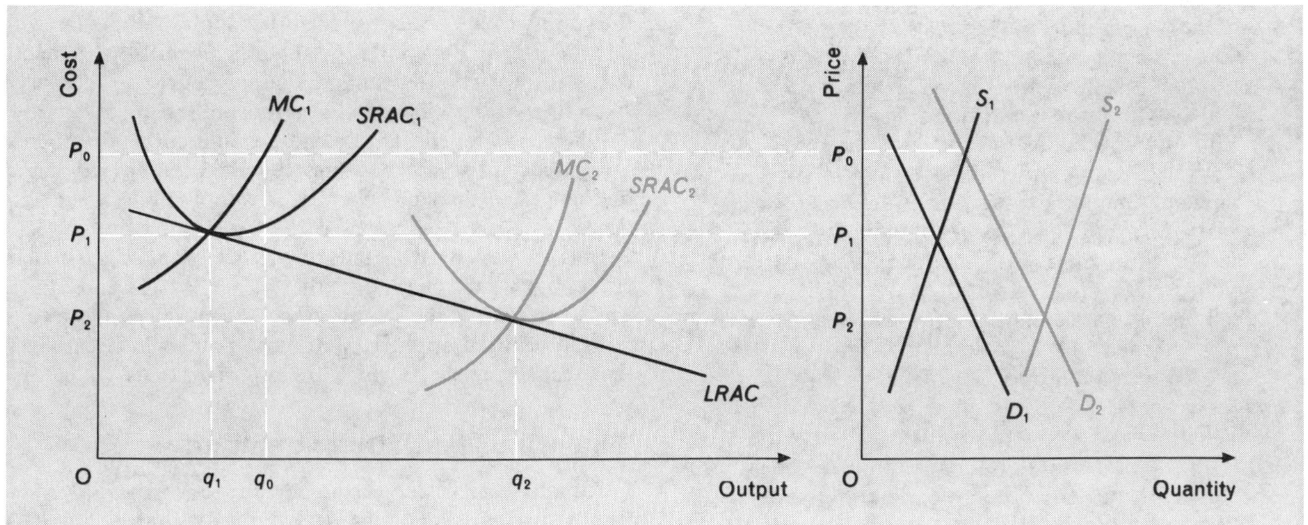

Figure 5.23 Effect of an increase in demand on long-run price and supply (increasing returns).

Consumer sovereignty

If we confine our attention for the moment to a world in which there are constant returns to scale, we see that Adam Smith's claims for the price mechanism are indeed supported.

The consumer is 'king' in the sense that *the consumer decides* how much of each good will be produced. If we suddenly desire more cloth and less wine then the price mechanism will see to it that wine production is curtailed and that cloth production is encouraged.

The entrepreneur is put in charge of production and is merely asked (or allowed) to seek the highest profit. By doing so the entrepreneur ensures that excess profit always tends to zero and that price always tends to its long-run, natural or just price. This price is the lowest which can be achieved. Efficiency is assured by the fact that entrepreneurs operate at the lowest point on their short-run average cost curves.

We therefore seem to have a flexible, efficient and responsive system of economic organization, all provided free without the cost or dangers inherent in the bureaucracy associated with a Central Planning Bureau. It is little wonder that Adam Smith is regarded as the intellectual parent of the free market.

In order to obtain this result we have had to make a number of simplifying assumptions. Not least is our assumption that the market is 'cleared' by the activities of an 'auctioneer'. We have assumed that everyone in the market takes price as given and everyone faces the same price. Now in some markets this assumption may be quite acceptable, but for many goods this assumption is obviously not very realistic.

In Chapter 6 we examine markets which lack the auctioneer and in which prices are formed by agents in the market.

SUMMARY

1. Free-enterprise economies are orchestrated by the price mechanism rather than by central planning bureaux.
2. The price mechanism transmits signals to producers and to consumers via markets.
3. Those signals are costs and prices.
4. Self-interest causes the entrepreneurs to organize production in the economy in an efficient manner. Excess profits are driven to zero and production occurs at the lowest point on the short-run average cost curve (the capacity point).
5. When there are constant returns to scale, market price always returns to equal the long-run average cost of production. This is the natural or just price.
6. When there are constant returns to scale, the long-run price is determined entirely by the long-run cost curve and quantity is determined by the demand curve.
7. When there are increasing returns to scale, there is no longer a natural or just price and both the supply curve and the demand curve are necessary to determine price and quantity traded.
8. In the short run, prices may deviate away from average costs and thereby generate either excess profits or losses.
9. These excess profits provide both the incentive and the wherewithal to expand capital stock.
10. Losses provide the incentive to reduce capital stock.
11. These responses to profits and losses in the short run are what guides the economy to its long-run equilibrium. That is how the price mechanism works.
12. In such a world, the consumer is 'king' and producers respond to the consumer's wishes in an efficient manner.

Appendix: Elasticity

What is elasticity?

We have seen that the price of a good and the quantity traded will be determined by the intersection of its supply and demand curves. We have seen that movements of the demand curve will change the price and the quantity sold by moving the point of intersection along the supply curve.

If the supply curve is relatively flat then the movement of the demand curve will result in a large change in quantity and a small change in price. If, however, the supply curve is relatively steep then the movement of the demand curve will result in a small change in quantity and a large change in price.

We also know that the effect of imposing a tax on a good depends on the relative steepnesses of the supply and demand curves. If the demand curve is relatively steep and the supply curve is relatively flat then almost all the tax will be paid by the buyers. If, on the other hand, the demand curve is relatively flat and the supply curve is relatively steep then the suppliers will bear most of the tax.

The shapes of the supply and demand curves are therefore important when analysing how the economy responds to changes in demand, changes in supply and changes in tax.

It is all very well to talk of the 'shape' of a particular curve, but what exactly does that mean? What we need is a way of measuring the shape – preferably a way of measuring it which can be applied to all curves and which captures those aspects of shape which are important to us.

The price elasticity of demand

Fortunately such a measure already exists and is very widely used in economics. It is rather technical but it is important and must be learned. The measure is called the **elasticity** of a curve and is defined as the responsiveness of quantity demanded to changes in price.

Case Study 5.2 Hotels: A gap in the market

This is the time of the year when it is best to avoid driving on a Friday – or a Saturday, or a Sunday, or a Monday. Just three weeks after the Easter weekend the British are settling into their next three-day break, to commemorate May Day. And another will be round soon: spring fever now arrives with no fewer than four bank holidays in 6½ weeks.

Not surprisingly, the short-break market is booming. One direct result is a resurgence of investment in the hotel industry, which virtually dried up between the mid-1970s and the mid-1980s. The tourist authorities are working hard to make the most of it. Forget that old image of the English hotel as an overpriced, seaside guest-house, they say. But it may take time.

In December 1989 208 English hotels were being built, extended or refurbished, at a cost of £1.2 billion, compared with 42 projects worth £128m in December 1985. At one end of the market, entrepreneurs are turning country homes into luxury hotels charging over £100 a night; at the other, spartan bed-and-breakfasts charging barely £10 are being urged by local tourist boards to provide the minimum of comforts that a fussy traveller (or a foreign visitor) might expect.

The big weakness has always lain between these two extremes: where most of the demand exists, the industry has depressingly little to offer. Compared with other European countries, medium-standard hotels are scarce and over-priced. The escalating cost of hotels in London is a pure function of undersupply – even now the capital has only two new hotel developments in progress. But in the provinces the problem is harder to explain. Why, for example, does it cost £52–80 for a single room in a hotel listed by Michelin as 'comfortable' in Sheffield, but only £19–37 in Bordeaux? Despite differences in land and labour costs, the answer, unsuprisingly, is that comfortable hotels are not common in Sheffield but the demand for their rooms is strong.

For a casual tourist or a salesman on a budget, the problem in Britain is not just affording two-star hotels, but finding them. Britain has two-thirds as many hotels as France, but most of these are generally small and unclassified. Ratings, if they exist at all, tend to be high with prices to match, leaving only one-eighth as many rooms in British one- or two-star hotels as in similar French ones.

But the concept of the 'budget' hotel – providing clearly defined, branded standards at low prices – is now starting to catch on in Britain. The biggest operator, Trusthouse Forte, has opened 55 'Travelodges' attached to its roadside restaurants; it hopes to have 100 by the end of the year. It has proved relatively easy to develop hotels next to out-of-town restaurants: often the land is already owned by the operator, and there is no need to provide food in the hotel. So other companies like Granada and Rank have followed suit.

The ready-owned land suitable for such developments will soon be used up. Other companies, notably French ones like Ibis and Campanile are trying to start budget-hotel chains in Britain from scratch. Campanile already has a dozen hotels, but is finding development harder than in France. The main problem is buying land. Local councils, by law, cannot sell land cheap, and a budget hotel often is not feasible if land must be acquired on the market: often only an office development or four-star hotel will then yield an adequate return.

So genuine budget hotels still account for only 1% of rooms in Britain, against 5% in France and 20% in America. The tourist authorities might do well to make better use of the biggest existing resource: the bed-and-breakfast. To do that, they need a proper classification scheme (building on their new 'crown' ratings) and – far harder – a centralised reservations system.

1. How would the provision of more 'budget' hotel rooms affect the market demand and supply curves?
2. What factors prevent the market from providing more 'budget' hotel rooms as we might expect in a free market?

Source: *The Economist*, 5 May 1990

It is measured as *the percentage change in quantity divided by the percentage change in price*. That is:

$$\frac{\%\ \Delta \text{ quantity demanded}}{\%\ \Delta \text{ price}}$$

where Δ is a small change.

We can perhaps best introduce the idea of elasticity by looking at the elasticity of a particular demand curve. Then, when we have a clearer idea of elasticity, we will show how it can be applied to other curves too.

In Figure 5.24 we have drawn the usual downward-sloping demand curve with price measured in £s per kilogram and quantities measured in kilograms. We have drawn a straight line demand 'curve' for simplicity, but our results can be applied to any curve. We can see from the diagram that:

1. At point *b* the price is £10 per kg and the demand is for 75 kg.
2. By reducing the price to £9 we move to point *c* where demand is for 90 kg.
3. When the price is reduced by £1 the quantity demanded is increased by 15 kg.

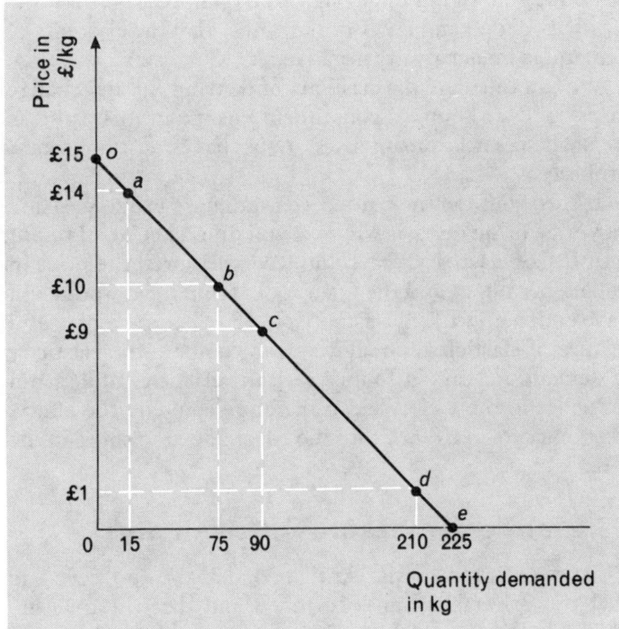

Figure 5.24 Demand curve.

In order to find the elasticity we need to know the *percentage change* in price and the *percentage change* in quantity.

The reduction in the price from £10 to £9 is a reduction of £1 in £10 and the percentage change is therefore 10 per cent (£1 ÷ £10 × 100 = 10%). In other words, it is the *change* in price divided by the *original* price and multiplied by 100. The percentage change in price is therefore 10 per cent.

Strictly speaking this should be −10 per cent since it is a decrease in price from £10 to £9 (the change is a *negative* amount). If we increased the price from £10 to £11 then the percentage change would still be 10 per cent (£1 ÷ £10 × 100) but in this case it would be +10 per cent, denoting a 10 per cent increase in price.

From all this we now know that our price has changed by −10 per cent. What then of the percentage change in the quantity demanded?

We know that the quantity increased by 15 kg from 75 kg to 90 kg. The change (15) divided by the original quantity (75) is equal to 0.2. The percentage change in quantity is therefore 0.2 multiplied by a hundred, which equals 20 per cent ((90−75) ÷ 75 × 100 = 20%). Notice that since we had an increase in quantity the percentage change is +20 per cent.

We now know that the percentage change in price is −10 per cent and the percentage change in quantity is +20 per cent. We also know that the elasticity is the percentage change in quantity divided by the percentage change in price. It is therefore a simple matter to calculate that the elasticity is −2, i.e.:

$$\frac{20\%}{-10\%} = -2$$

The minus sign occurs because the decrease in price caused an increase in the quantity demanded. This is always the case for demand curves so we know that the elasticity of demand will always be negative. Because of this it is customary to ignore the sign and simply say that the elasticity of demand is 2. But remember that the elasticity of demand is in fact always negative .

We can calculate the elasticity of demand for any change in price if we know its consequent change in quantity. As we shall see, it has many uses; it also has a very important property.

It turns out that no matter what units we use to measure our price or quantity it will make no difference at all to our measure of elasticity. We could have measured the price in dollars per ounce and the quantity in tonnes, we would still have ended up with an elasticity of −2. This is a very useful feature of elasticity and allows us to compare the elasticity of demand for cars in France with the elasticity of demand for shoes in the UK. We can therefore compare the effects of taxing cars in France with the effect of taxing shoes in the UK.

The range of measures of elasticity

When we worked out the elasticity of demand above we said that the price fell from £10 to £9 and that the quantity demanded increased from 75 kg to 90 kg. The change in price was £1 and the change in quantity was 15 kg.

Now, for our straight line demand 'curve', a £1 decrease in price will *always* result in an increase in quantity of 15 kg no matter where you are on the demand curve. In Figure 5.24 we could have started at point *a* and decreased the price from £15 to £14 per kg. This would have increased the quantity demanded from nothing (at £15) to 15 kg (at £14). Once again we have cut the price by £1 and once again we have increased the quantity demanded by 15 kg. As we have said, this is true along the entire length of the demand curve.

But what can we say about the elasticity at this new part of the curve? Is this the same as before too? We can find out whether it is the same or not by calculating the *percentage* change in price and the *percentage* change in quantity demanded at this new part of the curve.

The price decreased by £1 from £15 to £14 so the percentage change in price is: −£1 ÷ £15 × 100 = 6.66 per cent. Once again it is negative because we have decreased the price, but notice that although the price has again fallen by £1 the *percentage* fall is now only 6.66 per cent and not the 10 per cent it was before. This is because the decrease of £1 is now expressed as a percentage of £15 rather than of £10 and so is slightly lower.

The next step is to calculate the percentage change in the quantity demanded. We know that the quantity demanded changed from nothing (none was bought when the price was £15 per kg) to 15 kg when the price was reduced to £14.

This presents us with a difficulty. In order to calculate the percentage change in the quantity demanded we must divide the change in quantity (15 kg) by the quantity demanded when the price was £15 per kg. But this quantity is zero – none was bought at that price. To get out of this difficulty it is customary to say that when a number is divided by zero the result is a very, very large number indeed. It is called infinity (∞). The percentage change in the quantity demanded is therefore infinity.

All that remains to be done in order to calculate the elasticity of the demand curve at point *a* is to divide the percentage change in quantity (infinity) by the percentage change in price (−6.66%):

$$\frac{\infty\%}{-6.66\%} = -\infty$$

Since infinity is such a large number, it is again customary to say that dividing it by any number has no effect – it remains at infinity. We can now say that the elasticity of the demand curve where it cuts the vertical axis is −∞. It is always infinity here, for all demand curves, because the starting quantity is always zero. It is always negative because all demand curves slope downwards.

So the elasticity changes as we move along the straight line demand 'curve'. It was −2 between points *b* and *c* and it was −∞ between points *o* and *a*. The next obvious question to ask is: what is the elasticity at the other end of the demand curve?

When the demand curve cuts the horizontal (quantity) axis the price is zero and it is a free good. At zero price the quantity demanded is 225 kg. This is shown as point *e* on the curve.

Say now we increase the price to £1 per kg. Once again we see that a £1 change in price induces a change in the quantity demanded of 15 kg. Demand therefore decreases

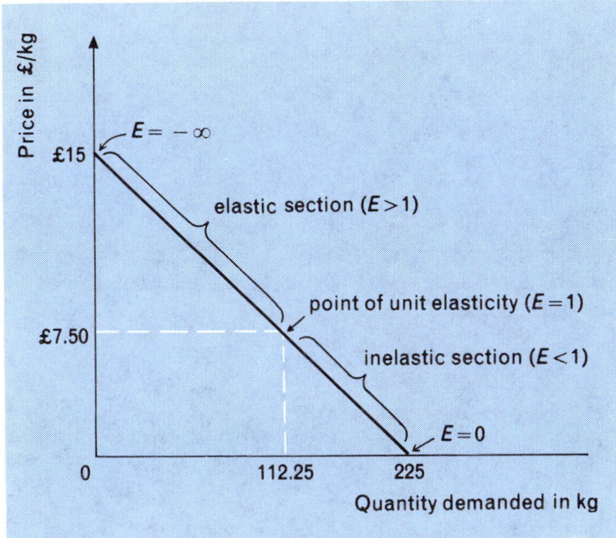

Figure 5.25 Elasticity along the demand curve.

by 15 from 225 to 210 kg. The percentage change in quantity is therefore: $15 \div 225 \times 100 = 6.66$ per cent. Strictly speaking this should again be -6.66 per cent because it is a reduction in quantity.

We now need to calculate the percentage change in price. Once again we face a difficulty. The starting price was zero so we have to divide the change in price (£1) by zero. This we now know is called infinity, so the percentage change in the price is $+\infty$.

All we have to do now to find the elasticity is to divide the percentage change in quantity (-6.66 per cent) by the percentage change in price ($-\infty$). Now since infinity is such a large number, any number divided by it is assumed to give the answer zero. Thus the elasticity of the demand curve where the curve cuts the quantity axis is zero. This is true for all demand curves whatever their shape or position.

The results of this analysis are shown in Figure 5.25.

Now we know quite a lot about the elasticity of demand curves. We know that it is always negative. We know that it changes as we move along the curve even when it is not really a curve at all but a straight line. We know that where it cuts the price axis the elasticity is always $-\infty$. And we know that where it cuts the quantity axis the elasticity is always zero.

At some point in between these two axes the elasticity was calculated as -2 and we can infer from this that there will also be a point where the elasticity is -1. The inference is that, since elasticity changes from zero at one end of the demand curve to $-\infty$ at the other, it must pass through all the numbers in between. One such number is -1.

We take a special interest in this particular value because it has many important properties. It is called the point of unit elasticity and divides the demand curve into two sections.

All the elasticities above the point of unit elasticity have elasticities which lie between -1 and $-\infty$. Ignoring the sign, these elasticities all have values greater than unity.

All the elasticities below the point of unit elasticity lie between -1 and zero and so have elasticities of less than unity.

The upper part of the curve, that lying above the point of unit elasticity, is called the elastic part of the curve. It is called elastic because the percentage change in quantity is greater than the percentage change in price – that is, the elasticity is greater than unity.

The part of the demand curve which lies below the point of unit elasticity is called the inelastic part of the curve. It is called inelastic because the percentage change in quantity is less than the percentage change in price. Again this must be the case otherwise the elasticity would not be less than unity. These sections are illustrated in Figure 5.25.

Point elasticities

There is one thing more we need to know about elasticity before we can go on and apply it to some other curves. We have seen that the elasticity calculated by moving from point *b* to point *c* is -2. The 'shape' of the demand curve between these two points is therefore described as having elasticity of -2.

Now if this really were a good way of measuring shape then we would expect the elasticity measured between points *b* and *c* always to be -2. But unfortunately this is not the case.

To illustrate this point let us measure the elasticity between points *b* and *c* again, only this time we will start from point *b* rather than from point *c*. A true measure of shape would be the same whether we moved from *b* to *c* or from *c* to *b*. Direction should not alter shape.

The price change is still £1, but now it changes from £9 to £10. The percentage change in price is therefore: $£1 \div £9 \times 100 = 11.11$ per cent.

Notice that this time we move from *c* to *b*, so price has increased. This means that the percentage change is *positive* rather than *negative* as it was before. Notice too that it is a little larger than before (11.11 per cent rather than 10 per cent). This is because, although the price has still changed by £1, it is now divided by 9 rather than 10.

What then of the percentage change in quantity? The change in quantity is still 15 kg as before, but this time it decreases from 90 kg to 75 kg. The percentage change in quantity is therefore: $-15\text{ kg} \div 90\text{ kg} \times 100 = -16.66$ per cent.

This differs in two ways from our previous result. First, it is now a negative number. This is because we have a quantity decrease rather than an increase. Secondly, it is slightly smaller than before. This is because, although the change in quantity is the same at 15 kg, it is now divided by 90 rather than by 75.

The elasticity is the percentage change in quantity (-16.66 per cent) divided by the percentage change in price (11.11 per cent) and is equal to -1.5. This is much smaller than we had previously calculated and we now have the somewhat unsatisfactory result that the elasticity between points *b* and *c* is measured as -2 when we move from *b* to *c* and is measured as -1.5 when we move from *c* to *b*.

There are many ways of handling this problem. We could, for example, take the average of the two elasticities. But it turns out that the only really satisfactory way forward is to confine our measures of elasticity to very short sections of the curve.

As the two points *b* and *c* get closer and closer together, so the differences in elasticity due to direction get smaller and smaller too. When the points actually meet to form one point the elasticities are exactly equal.

Technically, we are said to measure the elasticity at a 'point' on the curve rather than over a section of it. Elasticities measured in this way are called point elasticities.

Elasticities which are measured between two separate points are called arc elasticities.

SUMMARY

1. For a number of reasons we need to be able to measure the 'shapes' of the various curves we meet in economics.
2. The standard way of doing this is to use the concept of elasticity.
3. Elasticity is defined as the percentage change in quantity divided by the percentage change in price.
4. The elasticity of demand curves is always negative because they always slope downwards.
5. The elasticity is $-\infty$ where the demand curve cuts the price axis.
6. The elasticity is zero where the demand curve cuts the quantity axis.
7. There is a whole range of elasticities along the curve between these two extremes.
8. It is therefore not possible to say that one curve is more or less elastic than any other – they all have elasticities ranging from $-\infty$ to zero.
9. At some point on the curve the elasticity will be -1. This is the point of unit elasticity.
10. Points above the point of unit elasticity have elasticities greater than 1 and are on the elastic part of the demand curve.
11. Points below the point of unit elasticity have elasticities less than 1 and are on the inelastic part of the demand curve.
12. It makes no difference which units are used to measure prices or quantities – they have no effect on the calculated value for the elasticity.
13. It does, however, matter which direction we choose to measure elasticity in. If we measure it by moving up a section of the curve we get one result, but if we measure it by moving down that same section we get a different elasticity.
14. To overcome this problem it is necessary to measure the elasticity over very small sections indeed. These sections are so short as to be points on the curve and hence we refer to point elasticities rather than to elasticities of whole curves or of long sections of a curve.

Using elasticity

Elasticity and movements of the supply curve

Figure 5.26 shows a market in which the demand curve (D)

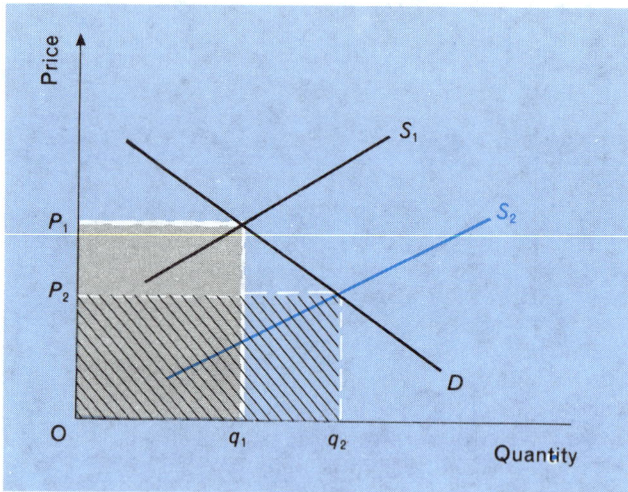

Figure 5.26 Effect of a shift in the supply curve on total expenditure.

remains stationary while the supply curve moves bodily to the right from S_1 to S_2.

We can see that this movement causes the market price to fall from P_1 to P_2. This change in price affects both consumers, who wish to buy more (q_2 instead of q_1 units), and producers, who will find that their sales and revenue change.

Before the supply curve moved, the consumers were buying quantity q_1 at price P_1. This means that they were spending £$(q_1 \times P_1)$ on the good in question. This sum is equal to the area of the grey rectangle in Figure 5.26 and also represents the total revenue of producers at price P_1.

After the supply curve has shifted, the consumers' expenditure on this good is the new quantity (q_2) multiplied by the new price (P_2) and equals £$(q_2 \times P_2)$. The sum is equal to the area of the blue rectangle in Figure 5.26. The question we are going to look at here is whether consumers' expenditure on the good increased, decreased or stayed the same – and hence what the effect of the supply curve shift was for producers' revenues.

From Figure 5.26 we can see that expenditure when the price is P_1 is equal to the area of the grey rectangle. The expenditure when the price is P_2 is equal to the blue rectangle. Thus expenditure will have increased if the area of the blue rectangle is greater than that of the grey. The rectangle with both blue and grey shading is common to both, so blue is greater than grey when the rectangle with blue shading only is larger than the rectangle with grey shading only.

Now the area of the grey rectangle is equal to the change in price ($P_1 - P_2$) multiplied by the original quantity (q_1). The area of the blue rectangle is equal to the change in quantity ($q_2 - q_1$) multiplied by the new price (P_2).

There are three possible outcomes following the move in the supply curve:

1. If the area of the grey rectangle is the same as the area of the blue rectangle then total expenditure on the good remains the same.
2. If the area of the grey rectangle is less than the area of the blue rectangle then total expenditure rises.

3. If the area of the grey rectangle is greater than the area of the blue rectangle then total expenditure falls.

How is this connected with elasticity? We have seen that when demand is unit elastic (equal to 1) then a 10 per cent fall in price leads to a 10 per cent rise in demand. In such a situation total expenditure on the good remains the same (the first of our three possible outcomes).

If the elasticity of demand is between 1 and ∞ (price elastic) then following the movement of the supply curve the percentage change in price is smaller than the percentage change in demand, i.e. for a 10 per cent fall in price quantity demanded rises by more than 10 per cent and total expenditure must rise following the price fall (the second of our possible outcomes).

If the elasticity of demand is between 1 and zero (price inelastic) then following the movement of the supply curve the percentage change in price is greater than the percentage change in quantity, i.e. for a 10 per cent fall in price quantity demanded rises by less than 10 per cent and total expenditure must fall following a price fall (the third of our possible outcomes).

Figure 5.27 summarizes this by showing the total revenue curve underneath the demand curve. Total revenue peaks at unit elasticity; thereafter, reducing price reduces revenue.

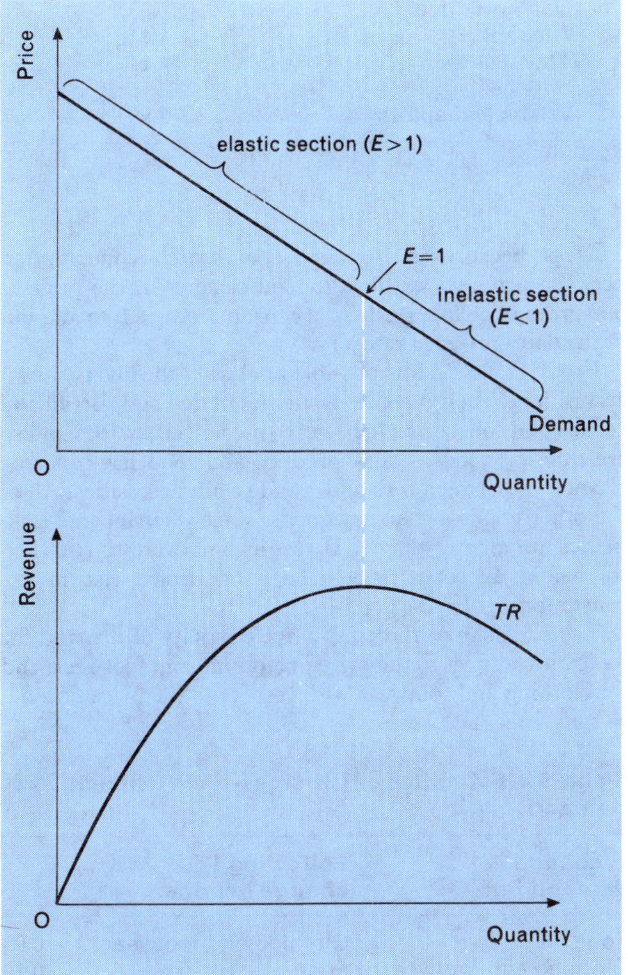

Figure 5.27 The relationship between price elasticity of demand and total revenue.

From this we can say that when the elasticity of demand is greater than unity (i.e. for elastic parts of the demand curve) moving the supply curve to the right will increase expenditure on the good.

When the elasticity of demand is less than unity (i.e. for the inelastic part of the demand curve) moving the supply curve to the right will decrease expenditure on the good.

And finally, when the elasticity of demand is equal to unity (i.e. at the point of unit elasticity) there will be no change in expenditure.

We can now begin to see how useful it is to know something about the elasticity of demand for a product. Simply by knowing the elasticity we can say right away what will happen to expenditure. This is just one of the many ways in which the concept of elasticity is used by economists.

Income elasticity of demand

Now we turn our attention to applying the idea of elasticity to curves other than the demand curve.

We know that an Engel curve traces out what happens to the demand for a good when the real income of the consumer is changed – when all prices are held constant. In other words, the Engel curve shows us how consumption responds to changes in real income. We can measure the degree of this response (the slope of the Engel curve) by using the income elasticity of demand.

The income elasticity of demand for a good is defined as the percentage change in the quantity demanded divided by the percentage change in real income:

$$\frac{\%\ \Delta \text{ quantity demanded}}{\%\ \Delta \text{ real income}}$$

We know that the consumption of normal goods will increase as income increases. Following a rise in real income we therefore expect the consumption of normal goods to rise. In other words, a rise in income leads to a rise in consumption and so the income elasticity of demand for a normal good is positive.

For example, let us assume that when real income rises by 10 per cent, consumption of butter rises by 5 per cent and consumption of beef rises by 15 per cent.

The income elasticity of demand for butter is: $5\% \div 10\% = 0.5$.

The income elasticity of demand for beef is: $15\% \div 10\% = 1.5$.

The response of the demand for butter is quite modest, perhaps because butter is an everyday good for most people, whereas the response in the demand for beef is larger than the change in income. The nature of the two goods is the reason for the different responses: both are normal goods, but beef is an expensive item and as people become better off they substitute beef into their diets in place of cheaper foods. In this sense, beef is a luxury good.

Economists can use the income elasticity of demand to classify goods. If the income elasticity of demand for a good lies between zero and 1 it is said to be a necessity whereas if the income elasticity of demand for a good is greater than 1 it is said to be a luxury good.

For some goods we find that a rise in income produces a fall in consumption as consumers switch to other goods that they can afford with their greater income. In this case the income elasticity of demand is negative and such goods are called **inferior goods**.

Thus we have a nice shorthand way of describing normal and inferior goods. Normal goods have positive income elasticities and inferior goods have negative income elasticities.

Cross elasticities

So far we have looked at how the demand for a good changes with its price and with income. We also know that the demand for one good depends on the prices of other goods too. We know, for example, that if the price of a good is increased then the demand for its complements will fall and the demand for its substitutes will rise.

We can measure the extent of the response of demand for one good following a change in the price of another by using the cross-price elasticity of demand. This is defined as

$$\frac{\%\ \Delta \text{ quantity demanded of good 1}}{\%\ \Delta \text{ price of good 2}}$$

For example, suppose the price of tea rises by 20 per cent. This induces some people to drink more coffee and the demand for coffee rises, say, by 15 per cent. The cross-price elasticity in this case is: $15\% \div 20\% = 0.75$.

Of course, coffee and tea are substitutes and we would expect a reaction in the consumption of one following a change in the price of the other. The cross-price elasticity measures the degree of this response. It is also possible to classify two goods by their cross-price elasticities. For substitutes the cross-price elasticity is always positive, as with tea and coffee; for complements it is always negative, as in the case of nuts and bolts.

In practical terms, elasticity is an important source of information for firms. If firms know how their customers will respond to a change in price, or how their markets are likely to change with the growth of real incomes or a change in competitors' prices then they can plan more effectively.

Estimates of elasticity

Table 5.2 reports some estimates for the price elasticity of demand for particular goods. Goods which are in everyday use, such as dairy produce, have very low elasticities, reflecting the fact that they are necessities. Should their price rise there will be only a small change in demand: in the case of dairy produce a 10 per cent rise in price will lead to only a 0.5 per cent fall in demand. Expenditure abroad has and estimated elasticity of −1.63. This suggests that, unlike dairy produce, a change in the price of goods in this category will lead to a larger change in demand. A 10 per cent rise in the price of foreign holidays, for example, would lead to a 16.3 per cent fall in demand.

It has also been observed that for broad categories of goods the estimate of elasticity is much closer to 1. For example, the estimate for 'food' is −0.52 as compared to −0.05 for dairy produce and −0.22 for bread and cereals.

Table 5.2 Estimates of UK price elasticity of demand

Good	Demand elasticity
Dairy produce[2]	−0.05
Bread and cereals[2]	−0.22
Food[1]	−0.52
Alcohol[1]	−0.83
Services[1]	−1.02
Expenditure abroad[2]	−1.63
Catering[2]	−2.61

Sources:
1. Muellbauer, 'Testing the Barten model of household composition effects and the cost of children', *Economic Journal*, Sept. 1977.
2. Deaton, 'The measurement of income and price elasticities', *European Economic Review*, vol. 6, 1975.

Table 5.3 Estimates of UK income elasticity of demand

Good	Income elasticity
Tobacco[1]	−0.50
Bread and cereals[2]	−0.50
Food[1]	0.45
Dairy produce[2]	0.53
Alcohol[1]	1.14
Travel abroad[2]	1.14
Services[1]	1.75
Wines and spirits[2]	2.60

Sources: As Table 5.2.

This is because it is possible to switch consumption between products within the food category if the price of one product changes, whereas consumers switch in and out of the dairy produce category.

From Table 5.3 it is possible to classify the goods shown according to their income elasticities of demand. Bread and cereals and tobacco have negative income elasticities and so are inferior goods. Dairy produce and food have income elasticities between zero and 1 and so are necessities. All of the other goods are luxury goods, since their income elasticities are greater than 1. If real income were to rise then we would expect a more than proportional rise in the consumption of these goods.

Table 5.4 shows the cross-price elasticity of demand for food with respect to the price of clothing and footwear, and for clothing and footwear with respect to the price of food.

Table 5.4 Estimates of UK cross-price elasticities of demand

% change in demand for:	Following 1% change in price:	
Food	Clothing and footwear	−0.03
Clothing and footwear	Food	0.19

Source: Deaton, 'The analysis of consumer demand in the UK 1900–1970', *Econometrica*, March 1974.

For a given rise in the price of clothing and footwear, food consumption will fall (by 0.3 per cent for a 10 per cent rise in the price of clothing and footwear), indicating that the two goods are complements. However, for a rise in the price of food there will be a rise in the consumption of clothing and footwear (by 1.9 per cent for a 10 per cent rise in the price of food), in this case indicating that the two goods are substitutes! This shows that estimating these effects in isolation is quite difficult.

Elasticity of supply

The elasticity of supply measures the slope of the supply curve, or how supply responds to changes in price. It is defined as the percentage change in quantity supplied divided by the percentage change in price:

$$\frac{\%\ \Delta \text{ quantity supplied}}{\%\ \Delta \text{ price}}$$

For example, if the price of a good rises by 10 per cent (say because of a rightward shift in the demand curve) and this causes firms to increase their supply by 20 per cent then the elasticity of supply is $20\% \div 10\% = 2$.

We have seen that supply curves normally slope upwards from left to right and so have a positive slope. This reflects the fact that most suppliers will wish to supply more as the price of a good rises.

The long run and the short run

All of the measures of elasticity we have examined will vary according to the period of time under consideration.

For example, if there is a change in the price of petrol then the immediate effect on the demand for petrol will be small – the price elasticity of demand in the very short run will be inelastic. This is because only some journeys can be curtailed or cut out altogether, and other forms of transport will still involve fuel consumption. In the longer term people can buy more fuel-efficient cars and so reduce petrol consumption. Thus the price elasticity of demand for petrol will be more elastic in the long run than in the short run. This is illustrated in Figure 5.28.

The same case can be made for the elasticity of supply. Firms can change their capital stock in the long run, but not the short run. Thus the response of supply to a change in price will be greater (supply will be more elastic) in the long run.

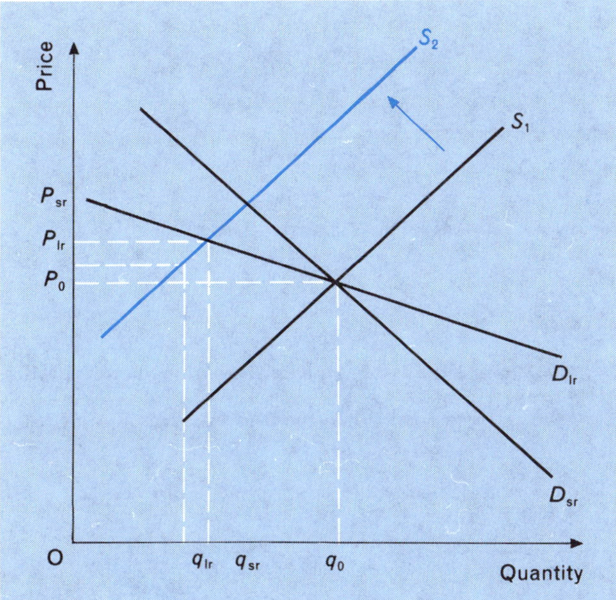

Figure 5.28 Effect of a decrease in supply on short- and long-run price and quantity.

SUMMARY

1. As we move down a demand curve so the price falls and the quantity sold increases. There is likely to be a change in the amount of money spent on the good.
2. Expenditure will increase if we are on an elastic section of the demand curve, i.e. where the elasticity is greater than unity.
3. Expenditure will decrease if we are on an inelastic section of the demand curve, i.e. where the elasticity is less than unity.
4. Expenditure will remain unchanged at the point of unit elasticity, i.e. where the elasticity is unity.
5. The concept of elasticity can be applied to any curve and need not be confined to the demand curve.
6. Income elasticity of demand is defined as the percentage change in quantity demanded divided by the percentage change in real income.
7. Income elasticity of demand will be positive for normal goods and negative for inferior goods.
8. It is possible to measure how the demand for one good changes in response to changing the price of another good. This is called cross-price elasticity.
9. Cross-price elasticity is defined as the percentage change in the quantity demanded of one good divided by the percentage change in the price of another good.
10. If the cross-price elasticity is positive then the two goods are substitutes.
11. If the cross-price elasticity is negative then the two goods are complements.
12. When estimating the price elasticity of demand the range of estimates will be greater when using narrow categories of goods than when using broad categories.
13. The degree of responsiveness of supply to a change in price is known as the elasticity of supply and is defined as the percentage change in quantity supplied divided by the percentage change in price.
14. The elasticity of both demand and supply will differ between the long run and the short run because in the long run there is greater scope for making adjustments.

Case Study 5.3 Cardiff sets a price on footballers' success

The spirit of John Major's citizen's charter is filtering down to the fans on the windswept terraces of Ninian Park, home of Cardiff City football club. When the season opens on Saturday poor performance from the team will be compensated by reduced prices for supporters.

The reasoning is straightforward business economics in the Thatcherite tradition. Only if the Bluebirds – as the team is known – reach the top three in the fourth division will fans be expected to pay the full entrance fee.

In the Bob Bank stand, popular with many fans, they will pay £3 if the team is eighth or lower. Prices will increase to £4 if it rises between seventh and fourth position; and a first, second or third place will lift prices to £5. Tickets for juniors and pensioners will be £2 regardless.

The scheme has been dreamed up by Rick Wright, chairman of the Barry Island holiday resort, who bought the club in April and is its financial controller. The ground has a 20,000 capacity, but last year crowds averaged only 3,000 to 3,500. 'I'd rather have 8,000 people paying half price than 4,000 paying the full amount,' Mr Wright said. 'For £5 you expect to see a promotion-winning side. Unless the fans are watching such a side, they won't be paying £5.'

The idea is a twist on the citizen's charter. 'In this case, though, we start out from the bottom price. If the team makes it to the top eight and the play-offs, then people pay for the added value,' Mr Wright said. 'Cardiff City finished last season in its lowest position for 100 years. When the season starts we'll be giving people value for money. Once we start giving them quality, we'll expect them to pay the full price.'

The Football League has seen nothing like it. 'We are not aware of this happening anywhere else, but they are certainly at liberty to do it,' a spokesman said. 'Lets hope the fans respond accordingly.'

Eddie May, club manager, said the players were also likely to benefit. If there are a lot of people here, it creates a nice atmosphere and the team plays better. If we have some success, then prices go up. But by then people will want to watch us anyway.'

Mike Lambert, who is chairman of the supporters' club, agreed. 'This is very refreshing. The club are considering the needs of the supporters, and the value for money, which supporters usually don't get.'

1. Does economic theory support Mr Wright's pricing strategy?

Source: Peter Victor, *The Times*, 15 August 1991

Exam Preparation and Practice

MULTIPLE-CHOICE QUESTIONS

Costs and supply

1. A firm is operating at an output where its average cost curve is falling. This implies that its marginal cost curve must be:
   A rising.
   B equal to average cost.
   C greater than average cost.
   D less than average cost.
   E falling.

2. For a firm to remain in production in the short run the minimum price a firm requires must cover the firm's:
   A total cost of production.
   B average variable cost of production.
   C average fixed costs of production.
   D average total costs of production.
   E marginal cost of production.

3. A firm has fixed costs of £40,000, average variable costs of 60p and average total costs of £1.85 per unit. What is the firm's output?
   A 21,621
   B 29,500
   C 32,000
   D 66,666

4. A firm has fixed costs of £2,000 and variable costs of 80p a unit. If, in the short run, it can sell 2,500 units at £1 each, it should:
   A close down because it is not covering fixed costs.
   B continue because it is covering its fixed costs.
   C close down because it is not covering its variable costs.
   D continue because it is covering its variable costs.

Study the diagram and answer questions 5, 6 and 7.

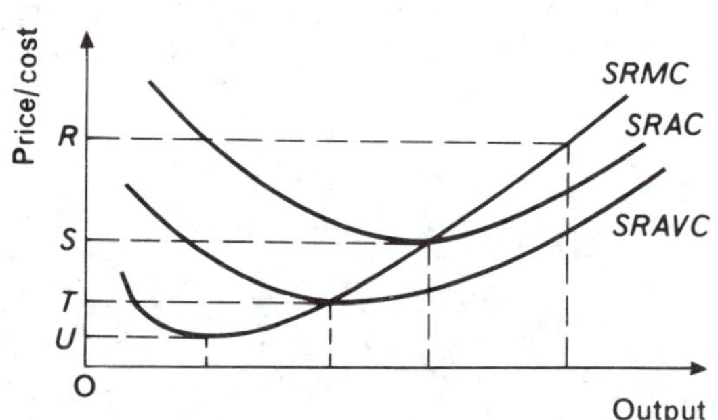

Select your answers for questions 5 to 7 from:
A *OU*
B *OT*
C *OS*
D *OR*

5. At which price level would the firm be earning normal profit?

6. At which price level would the firm be covering only fixed costs?

7. Below which price would the firm close down in the short run?

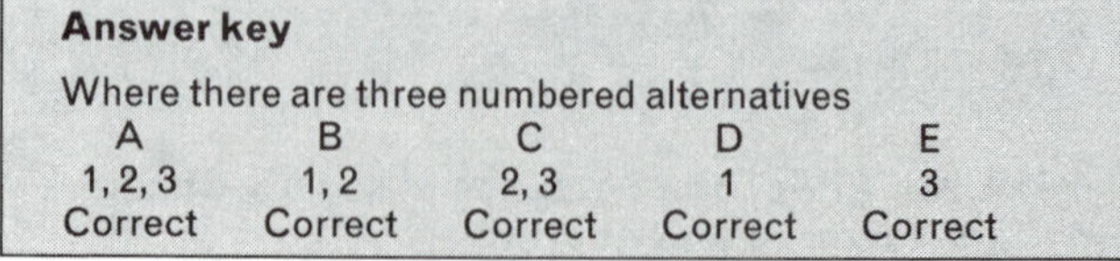

Answer key

Where there are three numbered alternatives

A	B	C	D	E
1, 2, 3 Correct	1, 2 Correct	2, 3 Correct	1 Correct	3 Correct

8. A firm's costs are given by:
Total costs (£) $= 100+2x$
where x is the level of output. Which of the following is (are) true?
1 Marginal cost is £2.
2 Fixed costs are £100.
3 The firm requires a price of £50 per unit to continue in production in the short run.

Market demand and supply

The diagrams show the demand and supply curves for a number of different industries. For each diagram P_1 and Q_1 represent the initial price and quantity, and P_2 and Q_2 the price and quantity following a change.

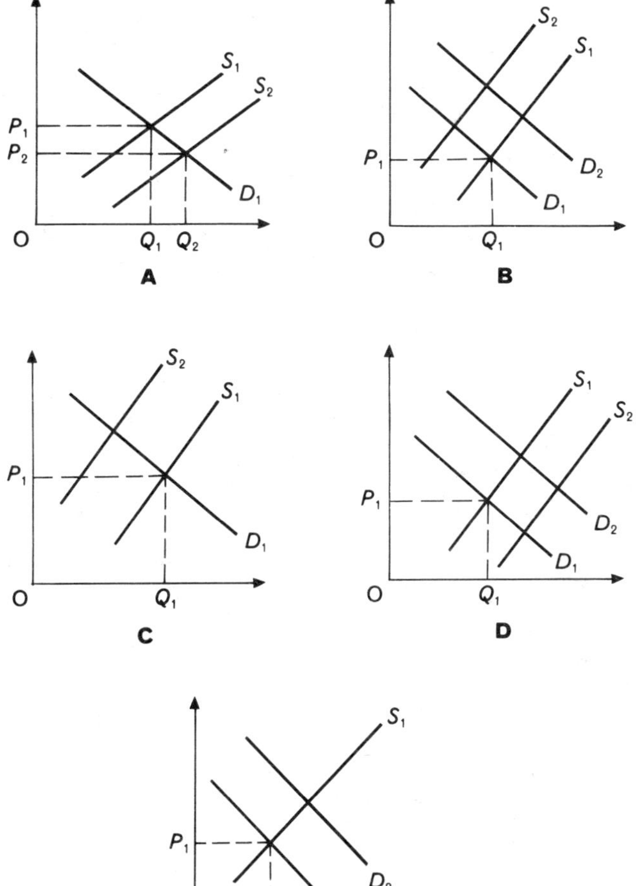

For questions 9 to 11 select the diagram which most accurately represents the events described.

9. The introduction of a new, more efficient method of production for a manufacturing industry.

10. The effect of a rise in real income coupled with an increase in wage costs.

11. The effect of an advertising campaign and the lifting of restrictions on importing the good.

12. An industry is initially in equilibrium at P_1, Q_1. What set of events could cause the market to move to P_2, Q_3?

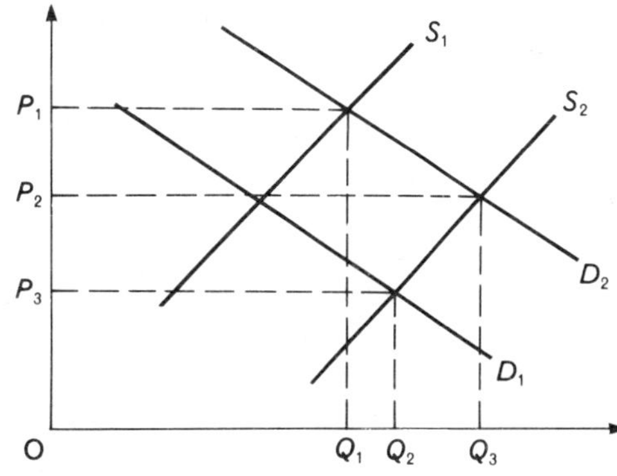

A A fall in the price of a substitute good for the industry's product.
B A fall in the price of a complementary good for the industry's product.
C A fall in the unit costs of production of the industry's product.
D A rise in the price of a substitute good for the industry's product and a fall in the unit costs of production for the product.
E A fall in the price of a complementary good for the industry's product and a fall in the unit costs of production of the product.

13. The diagram shows the demand and supply curves for a good which has a close substitute.

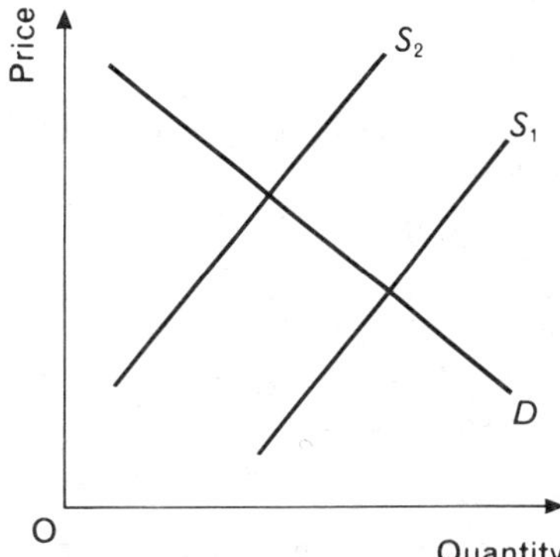

The movement in the supply curve from S_1 to S_2 is due to factors that have no influence on the substitute good. *Ceteris paribus* the effect on the substitute good will be:
A To increase demand and raise price.
B To increase demand and lower price.
C To reduce demand and raise price.
D To reduce demand and lower price.

14. The government decides to limit the range that the price of wheat may vary between. If the price rises above OP_2, the government releases wheat from its stock at that price. If the price falls below OP_1, it buys up wheat at that price. This is shown in the diagram.

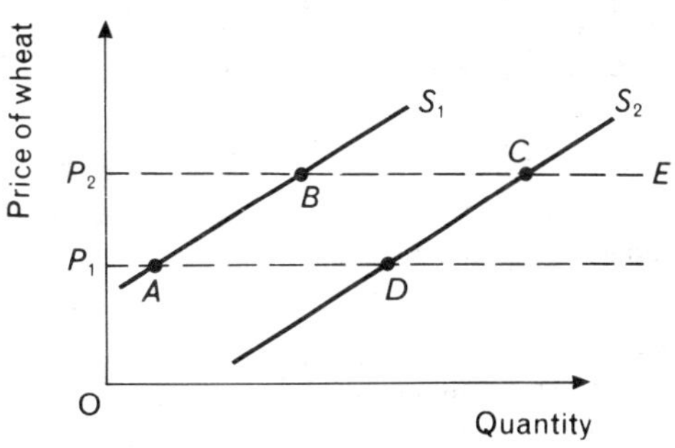

If the ruling market supply curve is S_2, what is the effective supply curve given government intervention?

A P_1ABCE
B P_1DCS_2
C P_1ADCE
D P_1ADCS_2
E P_2BCE

15. In the diagram *SS* is the supply curve for petrol before tax. S_1S_1 is the supply curve after a specific tax has been placed on each gallon of petrol.

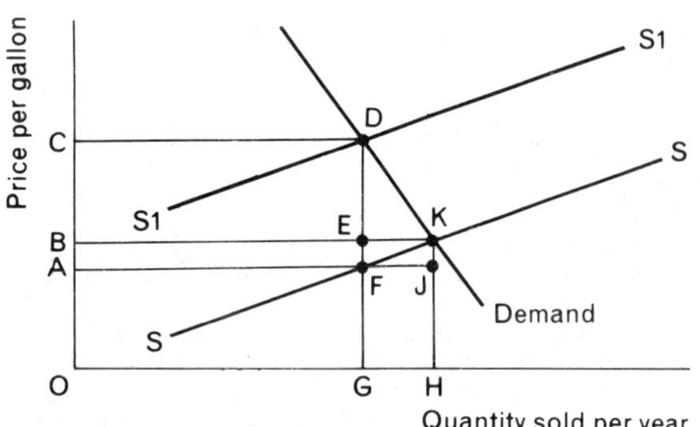

The annual revenue collected by the government in taxation is:

A CDKB
B ACDF
C ABKJ
D BCDE

(AEB)

16. From the diagram for question 15, what is the total amount of tax paid by consumers?

A *OCDG* **C** *ACDF*
B *OAFG* **D** *BCDE*

Answer key

Where there are three numbered alternatives

A	B	C	D	E
1, 2, 3 Correct	1, 2 Correct	2, 3 Correct	1 Correct	3 Correct

Where there are four numbered alternatives

A	B	C	D	E
1, 2 and 3 Correct	1 and 3 Correct	2 and 4 Correct	4 only Correct	1 and 4 Correct

17. Which of the following could cause the demand curve for a product to shift to the right?

1 A fall in the price of a substitute.
2 A fall in the price of a complement.
3 A rise in interest rates.
4 A loss of popularity of a substitute.

18. If the government set a minimum price for a product that was above the free-market price, which of the following would occur?

1 Market demand will exceed supply
2 Rationing may have to be imposed.
3 Market supply will exceed demand.

Elasticity

19. The price elasticity of demand for a downward-sloping straight-line demand curve is:

A −1
B 0
C Between 0 and −1
D Between 0 and infinity
E Between −1 and infinity

20. Price elasticity of demand is best described as a measure of:

A The responsiveness of demand for a good to a change in its own price.
B The responsiveness of demand for a good to a change in the price of a substitute.
C The responsiveness of demand for a good to a change in supply.
D The responsiveness of demand for a good to a change in the price of a complement.

21. Which of the following would you expect to have the most price inelastic demand for travel via the Channel Tunnel?

A Non-drivers.
B Businessmen with offices in both London and Paris.
C Residents in North-East France who commute to work in South-East England.
D British wine merchants.

22. The demand for tea is known to be price inelastic. In a free market what is the most likely effect of a failure of the tea crop?

A A fall in the price of tea.
B A rise in the income of tea producers.
C A fall in consumers' expenditure on tea.
D A rise in the demand for tea.

23. Following a 1% rise in price, consumer spending on a good rises by 1%. This implies that, *ceteris paribus*, the price elasticity of demand for the product is:

A Between −1 and −infinity
B Between 0 and −1
C Between −1 and −2
D −1

24. A firm knows that the price elasticity of demand for its product is −1.8. The firm decides to raise its price from 80p to 88p. If the firm presently sells 4,000 units a month, how many could it expect to sell after the price rise?

A 3,280 **C** 4,320
B 3,680 **D** 4,400

25. Tea and coffee have a cross-elasticity of demand of 3. If the price of coffee rises from 60p per kilo to 90p per kilo, *ceteris paribus*, the percentage rise in the demand for tea will be:

A 50%
B 75%
C 100%
D 125%
E 150%

26. The income elasticity of demand for beef is estimated to be 1.2. From this we can say that:

A When the price of beef rises by 10% consumer spending on beef will rise by 12%
B When the price of beef rises by 10% consumer spending on beef will fall by 12%
C When incomes rise by 10% expenditure on beef will rise by 12%.
D When incomes rise by 10% expenditure on beef will fall by 12%.

27. If the elasticity of demand is price inelastic and the elasticity of supply is price elastic, the imposition of a lump-sum tax on a good will:

A Fall mostly on consumers.
B Fall mostly on producers.
C Fall equally on consumers and producers.
D Fall entirely on consumers.

28. The industry output of a good is 2,000 units a week at the present market price of £10. If the output of the industry's product rises to 2,600 units a week following a rise in price to £12, what is the elasticity of supply?

A 1 **D** 2
B 1.5 **E** 2.6
C 1.6

Answer key

Where there are three numbered alternatives

A	B	C	D	E
1, 2, 3	1, 2	2, 3	1	3
Correct	Correct	Correct	Correct	Correct

Where there are four numbered alternatives

A	B	C[1]	D[2]	E[3]
1, 2 and 3	1 and 3	2 and 4	4 only	1 and 4
Correct	Correct	Correct	Correct	Correct

29.

	Elasticity of demand for commodity			
	Bread	Butter	Meat	Fish
With respect to price of:				
Bread	−0.2	−1.1	+2.4	+0.2
Butter	−0.8	−0.8	+0.7	+0.2
Meat	+1.4	+0.4	−1.2	+4.8
Fish	+0.9	+0.1	+3.1	−1.6

From the table, which of the following statements are true?
1 Bread and butter are complements.
2 Meat and fish are substitutes.
3 Butter and fish are substitutes.
4 Bread and fish are complements

30. In the diagram, line OZ represents the income/consumption curve for a particular good.

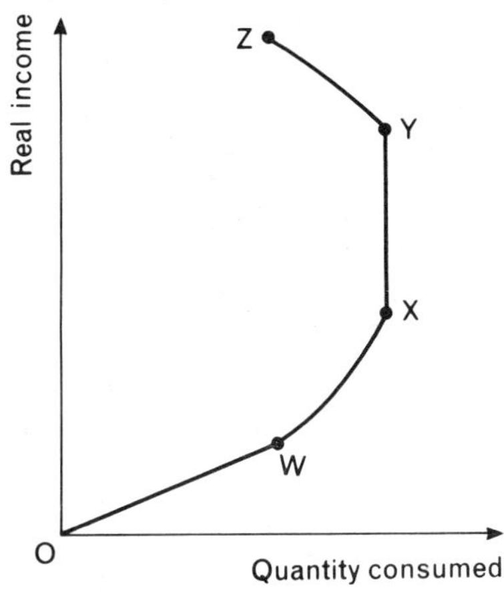

Income-elasticity of demand for the good is:
1 negative from Y to Z
2 positive from O to W
3 unity from X to Y

(AEB)

EXERCISES

1. (a) Draw a demand curve for a normal good.
(b) Show how the demand curve will move in response to the following events:
(i) An increase in real income.
(ii) A fall in the price of a good that is a substitute for the good shown.
(iii) A change in consumer tastes away from this type of good.
(iv) A fall in the price of a good that is a complement for the good shown.

2. (a) Draw a supply curve for a normal good.
(b) Show how the supply curve will move in response to the following events:
(i) The discovery of a more efficient method of production.
(ii) The effect of a dramatic rise in the cost of energy.
(iii) The sudden rise in popularity of a good made from similar raw materials.

3. A firm faces the following demand and supply functions:
Demand $= 18 - 2P$
Supply $= -6 + 6P$ where P = price.
Either by drawing or by mathematics find the equilibrium price and output where demand equals supply.

4.

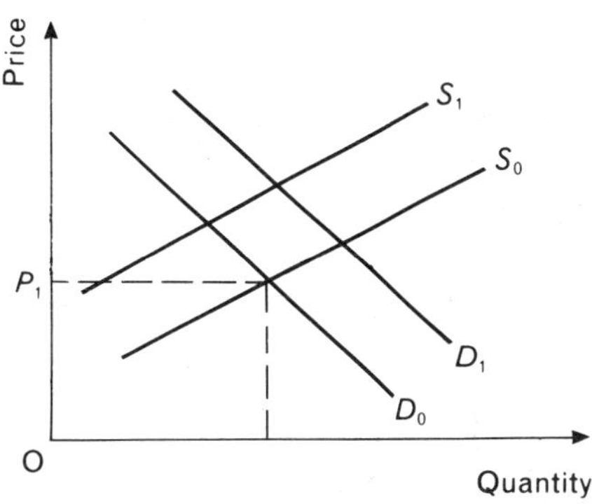

The diagram shows the market for product X. The market is initially in equilibrium at price OP_1. Good Y is a substitute for good X. Draw a demand and supply diagram for good Y and show how it would react to the following changes in the market for good X:
(a) A shift in the supply curve of X from S_0 to S_1.
(b) A subsequent shift in the demand curve for X from D_0 to D_1.
(c) If good Y was a complement for good X, how would the events in (a) and (b) affect the market for good Y?

5. Which of the following will affect the market for bicycles and how?
(a) A rise in real income.
(b) A general warming and drying of the British climate.
(c) A fall in the price of petrol.
(d) A shift in the opinion of society towards improved levels of fitness.
(e) A fall in the price of bus travel.

6. If the price of a good is £5 and 2,000 units of the good are sold, what is the value of total consumer expenditure?

7. Calculate from the graph the own-price elasticity of demand for the product shown when price falls from:
(a) 30p to 29p a kilo.
(b) 20p to 19p a kilo.
(c) 10p to 9p a kilo.

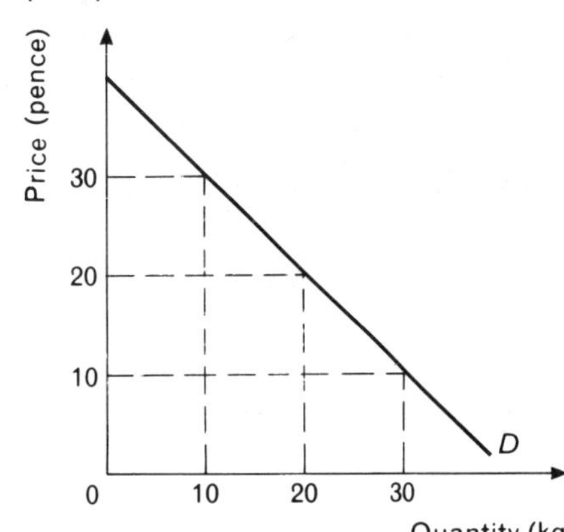

8. From the data in the following diagram, calculate the total revenue curve for the product. At what price elasticity of demand does the total revenue curve peak?

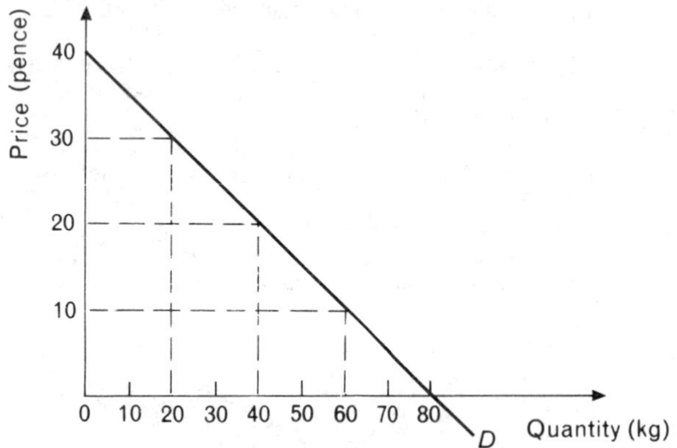

9. A firm calculates the own-price elasticity of demand for its product to be (−)3. At present the firm sells 12,000 units of its product at £2 each. What will be the effect on the company's sales if the price is raised to £2.40 per unit?

10. The figures on the left are estimates of the own-price elasticity of demand for the goods on the right. Match the goods on the right to the correct elasticities.

(−)0.05	Alcohol
(−)0.8	Holidays in Australia
(−)1.2	Salt
(−)2.6	Catering
(−)6	Wine

11. The own-price elasticity of demand for 'food' as a category of goods is estimated to be (−)0.5. The own-price elasticity of demand for 'dairy produce' is estimated at (−)0.05 and for pâté de foie gras at (−)2.9. How would you account for the wide range of own-price elasticities for specific food items in comparison to the generally inelastic demand for food overall?

12. If the price of electricity were to double, what would you expect the effect on the demand for electricity to be (a) immediately, (b) in one year and (c) in five years? Explain your answer.

13. The real income of consumers rises by 10 per cent.
(a) Calculate the income elasticity of demand for the following goods.

	Demand (units)	
	Before	After
Bread (loaves)	10,000	9,000
Beer (barrels)	7,000	7,630
Video recorders	6,000	7,200

(b) Classify each of the goods on the basis of their income elasticities of demand.

14. The price of aviation fuel rises, causing a rise in the price of foreign holidays by 5 per cent. Calculate the cross-price elasticity of demand with respect to foreign holidays for the following products.

	Demand (units)	
	Before	After
Domestic holidays	12,000	15,000
Summer clothing	7,000	6,000

Are these goods complementary to or substitutes for foreign holidays?

15. The manager of a firm of travel agents receives the following information:

- Mortgage rates are expected to rise by 2 per cent over the next year.
- Real incomes are expected to remain constant.

What use could she make of this information?

DATA-RESPONSE QUESTIONS

1.

High tax weapon in smoking battle

Higher taxation on cigarettes is likely to reduce smoking, Mrs Joy Townsend, a research scientist at Northwick Park Hospital, Harrow, told the association.

Mrs Townsend argued that the effect of public education about smoking and health had changed the pattern of smoking. The difference between men's and women's smoking habits had narrowed. Most importantly, by 1964, 49% of unskilled workers, the lowest social class, smoked cigarettes, while only 17% of the professional class did so.

In 1981, the then Chancellor, Sir Geoffrey Howe, imposed one of the largest post-war increases in tobacco tax, putting the price up by 20%. Since then the tax has been increased in line with inflation.

An important aspect of taxation was that it impinged differently on different income groups. Tobacco tax rises did not fall more heavily on the poor, because low income earners reduced their smoking in response to tax increases. The downward drift in real cigarette prices over twenty years had effectively increased smoking levels of the lower socio-economic groups and had been an important factor in the divergent habits of the social classes.

In the past four years, cigarette prices had risen by 26% in real terms and consumption had fallen by 20%. Government revenue had increased by 10% providing an extra £435 million.

Tax was therefore working as an ally of preventive medicine and health education costing less than £200 per life per year compared with some £800 per life per year for bypass surgery or £5000 for heart transplant programmes.

Source: adapted from *The Guardian* 4th September, 1986

(a) Explain what is meant by the phrase "The downward drift in real cigarette prices" (line 19). *(2 marks)*

(b) (i) Use the figures in the article to calculate the price elasticity of demand during the "past four years" (line 23). *(1 mark)*
(ii) Why might this figure not provide a correct measure of the responsiveness of the demand for cigarettes to a change in price? *(2 marks)*
(iii) According to the article, how does the price elasticity of demand for cigarettes for people in the higher socio-economic groups differ from the price elasticity of demand for those people in the lower socio-economic group? *(2 marks)*

(c) Explain and illustrate, using a demand and supply diagram, the likely effect of the change in cigarette prices in 1981 upon the market for cigarettes and government tax revenues. *(5 marks)*

(d) Outline the **economic** arguments in favour of high levels of taxation on tobacco. *(8 marks)*

(AEB)

2. **Pensioners' incomes and expenditure 1970–1985**

Ten million people – one in four adults – in the United Kingdom are over state pension age (60 for women and 65 for men). As the number of pensioners has grown – there are three million more pensioners than in the early 1950s – so has interest in their incomes.

Income is taken to include social security benefits[1], as well as pensions from employers (occupational pensions), income from savings and investments, and earnings. Except where noted otherwise, it is net of income tax and national insurance contributions, and refers to the income of the 'pensioner unit', defined as single people over state pension age and married couples whose husbands are aged 65 or over. All values for income and spending are in terms of 1985 prices.

Source: *Employment Gazette,* May 1987, article by A. Dawson and G. Evans)

(a) Describe the main changes in pensioners' incomes since 1970.

(b) Are the changes in the pattern and levels of pensioners' expenditure since 1970 consistent with what might be predicted by economic theory?

(c) How, if at all, is the increasing number of pensioners likely to influence future average living standards in the UK?

(JMB)

[1]The main benefits received by pensioners are NI retirement pensions, supplementary pensions, housing benefit and benefits for disability.

Table 1 Pensioners and the working population 1970–1985 (000s)

	1970	1975	1980	1985
Total working population	25,308	25,877	26,839	27,624
of which:				
(a) employed	24,753	25,039	25,326	24,445
(b) unemployed	555	838	1,513	3,179
Pensioners	7,649	8,422	9,164	9,771

Table 2 Average net weekly incomes at 1985 prices (£ per week)

					Increase 1970–85	
	1970	1975	1980	1985	£	per cent
All pensioner income units	59.70	68.10	71.90	83.00	23.30	39
Married pensioner income units	84.60	96.20	99.70	115.30	30.70	36
Single female pensioners	43.10	52.50	54.00	62.30	19.20	45
Single male pensioners	60.20	57.80	59.80	70.70	10.50	17
National personal disposable income per head	61.05	71.11	77.72	81.44	20.39	33

Table 3 Sources of pensioners' incomes (£ per week at 1985 prices)

					Increase 1970–85	
Income sources	1970	1975	1980	1985	£	per cent
Retirement pension and income-related benefits	32.70	40.80	45.30	50.80	18.10	55
Other benefits	1.60	2.30	2.40	3.10	1.50	94
Total social security benefits	34.30	43.00	47.60	53.90	19.60	57
Occupational pensions	10.60	10.40	12.20	18.60	8.00	75
Investment income	11.20	11.00	8.80	12.80	1.60	14
Employment earnings	11.30	11.20	8.70	5.80	−5.50	−49
Total private income	33.10	32.60	29.80	37.20	4.10	12
Total gross income	67.40	75.70	77.40	91.10	23.70	35
Income tax and NI contributions	−7.70	−7.50	−5.50	−8.10	0.40	5
Total net income	59.70	68.10	71.90	83.00	23.30	39

Note: Income sources are shown to the nearest 10 pence and totals may not add owing to rounding.

Table 4 Percentage of pensioner income units in each quintile of equivalent income for the whole population

Year	Bottom	Second	Third	Fourth	Top	All
1970	50	28	11	6	5	100
1975	42	34	12	7	5	100
1980	38	39	12	6	5	100
1985	25	40	18	9	7	100

Quintile: each fifth of total income units.

Table 5 Pensioners' expenditure patterns

Commodity group	Per cent expenditure 1970	1975	1980	1985	Per cent change in prices 1970–85
Housing (gross costs)†	15	16	18	21	581
Fuel, light and power	11	10	10	10	613
Food	29	29	26	23	453
Alcoholic drink	3	3	3	3	421
Tobacco	4	3	3	2	546
Clothing and footwear	7	7	6	5	227
Durable household goods	5	5	6	6	258
Transport and vehicles	7	8	9	9	477
Services	12	11	12	14	462
Miscellaneous and other goods	8	8	8	7	458
Total*	**100**	**100**	**100**	**100**	—

† Gross housing costs in this table are the sum of gross rates, rents and mortgage interest plus house maintenance expenditures: they do not include imputed rent for owner occupiers. Note that prices relating to housing are net of housing benefit.

* Totals do not always sum to 100 owing to rounding.

6 Types of market

In this chapter we will discuss:

1. How firms maximize profits.
2. Some of the models economists have put forward to explain the behaviour of firms.
3. The results suggested by these models.
4. How realistic the assumption of profit maximization is.
5. How firms are prevented from becoming too powerful in the UK.
6. The way in which state-owned industries are managed.

Introduction

In the earlier chapters on markets we introduced the idea that an auctioneer called out prices to find a market clearing price. Trade only took place when the auctioneer had found the price at which consumer demand equalled the amount producers wished to supply.

Of course, the auctioneer does not really exist, nor is there any institution which does the job of the auctioneer. Markets must therefore work without the guidance the auctioneer provides.

In fact there are many alternatives to the auctioneer but only one of these alternatives behaves in exactly the same way as the auctioneer-type of market. In this chapter we shall look at some of the various forms which markets can take.

Profit maximization

The logic of profit maximization is that firms will expand (or contract) output until the last unit produced adds nothing to profit, but also takes nothing away from profit. This would be where the cost of producing this last unit (its marginal cost) was equal to its **marginal revenue**. We shall now look at marginal costs and marginal revenue in a little more detail.

Total costs

We know that an entrepreneur can change total cost by changing production levels. As output grows, the firm moves along the total cost curve. Cost will therefore be increasing as output expands (see Chapter 3). You will recall that the increase in total cost due to an increase in output of 1 unit is called marginal cost, and that with every increase in production a firm's total cost will rise by its marginal cost. We also know that marginal cost itself will vary with output. The relationship between total cost and marginal cost is shown in Figure 6.1.

From Figure 6.1 we can see that the total cost curve (*TC*) starts from the point *FC* on the vertical axis. This is because in the short run the firm must pay its fixed costs whether it produces or not. Marginal cost (*MC*) at first declines as more efficient use is made of capital equipment and then slowly increases due to diminishing returns. This rise and fall in *MC* is reflected in the shape of the total cost curve. The marginal cost is equal to the slope of the total cost curve. The total cost curve is always rising, steeply at first then becoming shallower and then turning up more steeply again.

Total revenue

Total revenue (*TR*) is equal to the total number of units of output sold multiplied by the selling price ($TR = P \times Q$ where P is price and Q is quantity). The change in total revenue due to the sale of one more good is called marginal revenue (*MR*). As yet we know little about marginal revenue or how it is related to the demand curve. The relationship between total revenue and marginal revenue is shown in Figure 6.2.

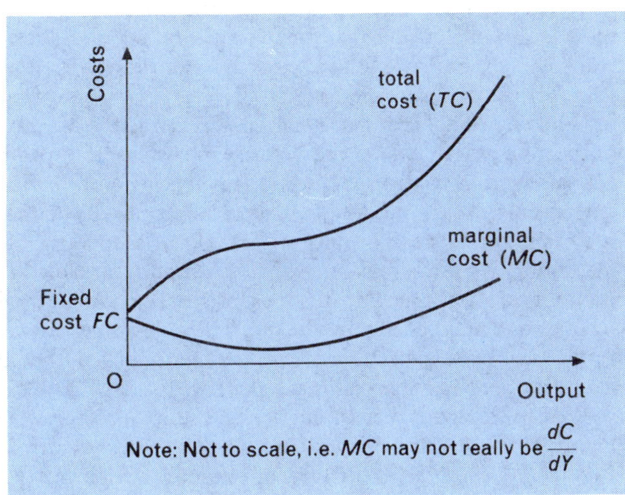

Figure 6.1 Total cost and marginal cost.

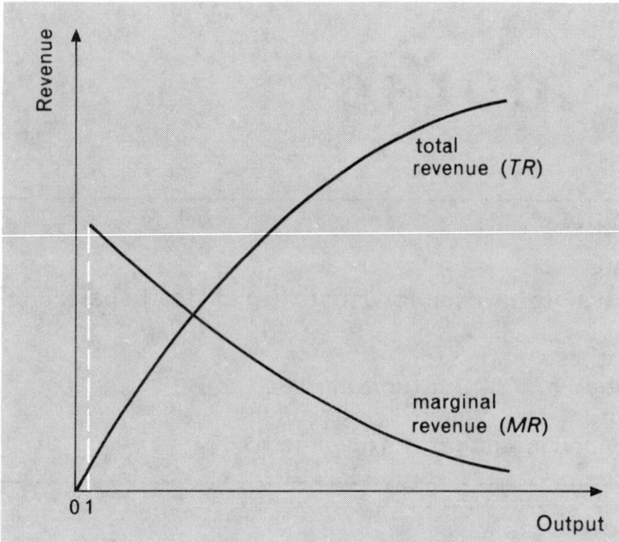

Figure 6.2 Total revenue and marginal revenue.

The total revenue curve starts from the origin, since when sales are zero revenue is also zero. As sales rise, so does revenue. Revenue is increased by the fact that the number of units sold increases. But as output grows, so the price of the output falls. This is because the demand curve for the good is downward sloping – thus to sell more the firm must reduce price. Thus as output increases there are two conflicting influences on revenue – price is falling but quantity is increasing. The result of this is that the marginal revenue curve will slope downwards.

Profit-maximizing output

Now that we know the shape of the cost and revenue curves and that entrepreneurs aim to maximize profit, we can say something about the behaviour of firms. If marginal revenue is greater than marginal cost then it will pay the entrepreneur to expand output. The firm's revenue will go up by more than it costs so profit will rise.

If, on the other hand, marginal cost is greater than marginal revenue then it will pay the entrepreneur to reduce output. By doing so the firm will reduce both costs and revenue, but will reduce costs by more than revenue. Profits must therefore increase.

When marginal cost *equals* marginal revenue the increase in revenue exactly offsets the increase in costs so that profit is unaffected by changes in output. It is at this point that the entrepreneur can no longer increase profits by either increasing or decreasing output – the firm is operating at maximum profit. This is a very important rule in economics. It applies to all types of market and is used throughout microeconomic theory. The rule is: *the profit-maximizing entrepreneur always chooses that level of output at which marginal revenue equals marginal cost.*

We can show this diagrammatically. Figure 6.3 shows the marginal cost and marginal revenue curves from Figures 6.1 and 6.2. At the level of output at which the two lines cross the firm is making maximum profits. If the firm were producing output *Oa* then it would benefit from

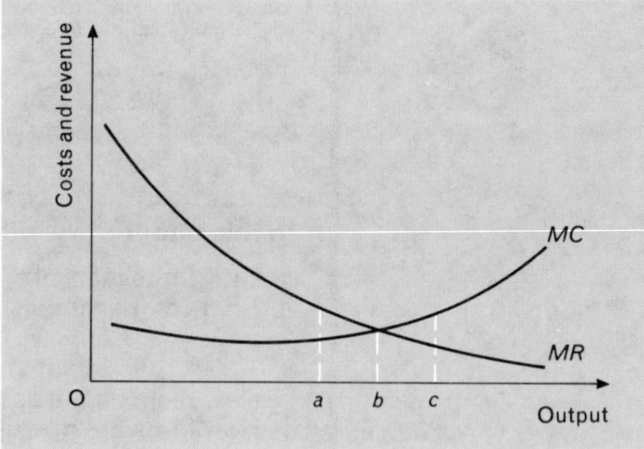

Figure 6.3 Marginal cost and marginal revenue.

increasing production, since at output *Oa* marginal cost is less than marginal revenue. Producing a little more will add to profit because marginal cost to the right of *a* is still less than marginal revenue. This situation persists until output *Ob* is reached. If the firm were producing output *Oc* then it would pay it to reduce production because costs would fall faster than revenue.

We can show the same case using total costs and total revenue and this is done in Figure 6.4. Points *a* and *c* are shown to be the points at which profit is zero, while point *b*

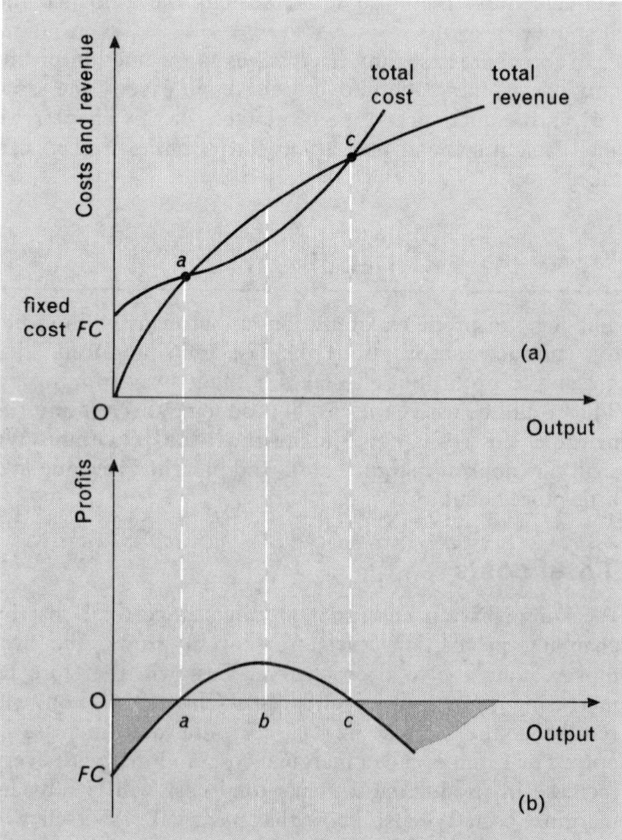

Figure 6.4 Total cost, total revenue and the level of profit.

is the profit-maximizing output. Outside the range of output $a - c$ the firm makes a loss. The extent of the loss at each level of output is shown by the shaded areas in Figure 6.4(b). Profits are greatest when the vertical distance between the total cost curve and the total revenue curve is greatest. This is where marginal cost equals marginal revenue, as shown in Figure 6.3.

The slopes of the total revenue and total cost curves are important. From output *Oa* to output *Ob* the total revenue curve is becoming less and less steep, while the total cost curve is becoming steeper. At output *Ob* the slopes of the two lines are identical, and this reflects the fact that the two curves are changing at the same rate. The rates of change (slopes) of the two curves are, of course, marginal cost and marginal revenue, confirming our earlier result that at point *b* the two are equal. Above output *Ob* the slopes of the total cost and total revenue curves change so that they are never the same again. There is only one profit-maximizing position.

Average revenue

So far we have concentrated on the variables that affect the entrepreneur's decisions about output and have yet to consider average revenue. Average revenue plays no role in determining the profit-maximizing level of output, but it plays an important part in determining the level of profits. Average revenue is price, so the average revenue curve which relates average revenue to output also relates price to output. The average revenue curve is therefore also the demand curve.

Figure 6.5 shows a demand curve to illustrate this point. The demand curve (*D*) shows that when 15 units are produced they can be sold for £20 each. Total revenue is £20 × 15 = £300. The average revenue is the revenue per unit of output and is found by dividing total revenue (£300) by output (15). This gives an answer of £20, the price of the product. If output expands to 20 units then each can be sold for £15. The same calculation reveals that average revenue

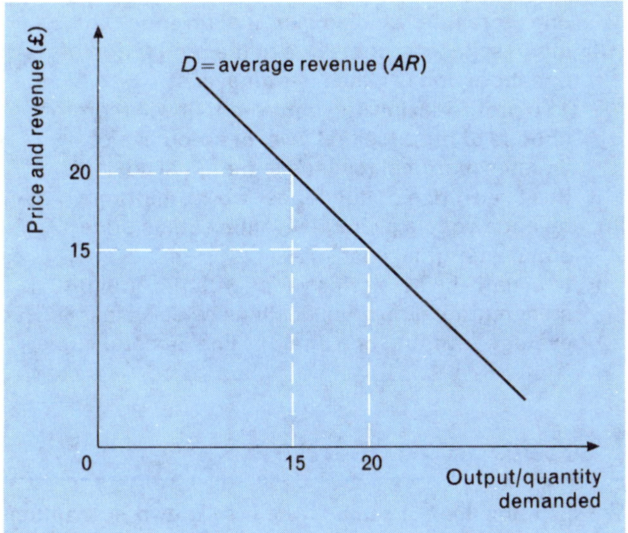

Figure 6.5 The demand curve and average revenue.

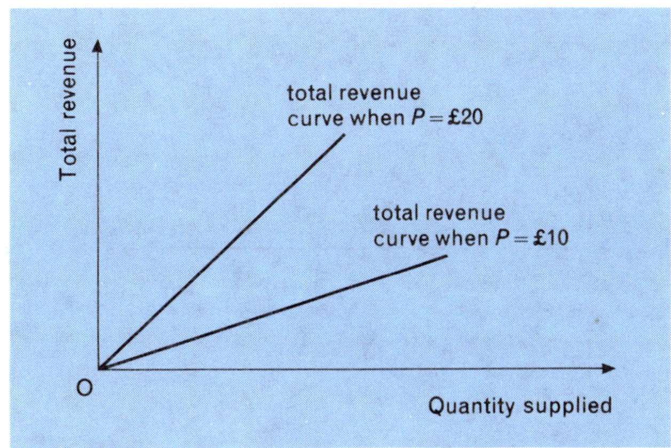

Figure 6.6 Total revenue with fixed prices.

is again equal to price. Thus the average revenue curve of a firm is its demand curve.

Average revenue and marginal revenue

The fixed-price case

Say we have a market where the price of goods is fixed. An auctioneer has called out a price and consumers can purchase all they wish at that price and suppliers can supply what they wish. This implies that the total revenue curve will not be 'curved' at all, but will be a straight line going through the origin, as shown in Figure 6.6. If the price is fixed at £10 then the lower of the two total revenue curves applies. If the price called out is £20 then each unit can be sold at £20 and so the total revenue curve is a steeper straight line.

The total revenue curves will be straight lines only when the price is fixed. If price changes as sales increase then we will see the more general shape shown in Figures 6.2 and 6.4. The important feature of the straight-line total revenue curve is that, for each additional unit sold, the total revenue increases by the price. Since the increase in total revenue due to the sale of one additional unit is marginal revenue, we can say that in the fixed-price market, and only in the fixed-price market, *marginal revenue equals price*.

Furthermore, since every unit is sold for the same price, no matter how many are sold the *average revenue also equals price*. Thus *marginal revenue equals price equals average revenue*.

This is illustrated in Figure 6.7. The demand curve (*D*) = average revenue (*AR*) = marginal revenue (*MR*) = price (*P*) and is a horizontal straight line. In this case the market is said to have an infinitely elastic demand curve.

We have assumed that entrepreneurs are profit maximizers and that they will always equate marginal revenue to marginal costs. Therefore, for the fixed-price case we can say production occurs such that:

price = average revenue = marginal revenue = marginal cost

The variable-price case

Generally, markets do not work with fixed prices and the marginal and average revenue curves diverge. Consider

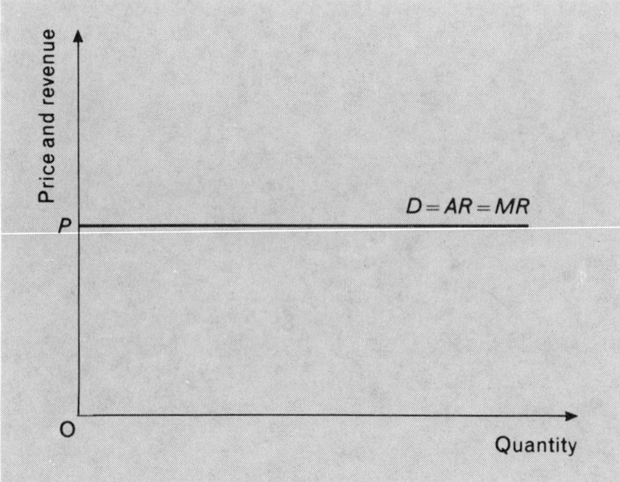

Figure 6.7 Average and marginal revenue with a fixed price.

again the demand curve shown in Figure 6.5. As the price of the goods falls from £20 to £19, the quantity sold rises from 15 to 16. The average revenue falls from £20 to £19. What about marginal revenue?

Total revenue at a price of £20 is £300 (£20 × 15). As price falls to £19 total revenue rises to £304 (£19 × 16). Thus the change in total revenue is £4 (marginal revenue is £4). Repeating the same operation for a further fall in price to £18 causes total revenue to rise to £306 (marginal revenue is £2). Thus marginal revenue (*MR*) is below average revenue (*AR*) and declining *twice* as fast. This is shown in Figure 6.8.

When the demand curve is a straight line (linear) the marginal revenue curve is also a straight line. The marginal revenue curve will start at the same point on the vertical axis as the average revenue curve (when sales equal zero, marginal revenue equals average revenue) and decline at twice the rate as average revenue. That is, the marginal revenue curve is twice as steep as the average revenue curve.

The marginal revenue curve crosses the horizontal axis in Figure 6.8 when output is 18 units. This reflects the fact that above 18 units of output total revenue will start to fall as output grows. Thus total revenue increases as price falls (as output rises to 18 units) and falls as price falls further.

Recall that when we looked at the elasticity of demand in Chapter 5 we saw that if the elasticity of demand was greater than unity (price elastic) then as price fell expenditure (total revenue) rose. If the elasticity of demand was less than unity (price inelastic) then as price fell expenditure (total revenue) also fell. Thus when the marginal revenue curve is above the horizontal axis the elasticity of the average revenue curve (the demand curve) is greater than unity. When the marginal revenue curve is below the horizontal axis the elasticity of the demand curve is less than unity. We can therefore deduce that the level of output at which the marginal revenue curve crosses the quantity axis is the output at which the price elasticity of demand is unity.

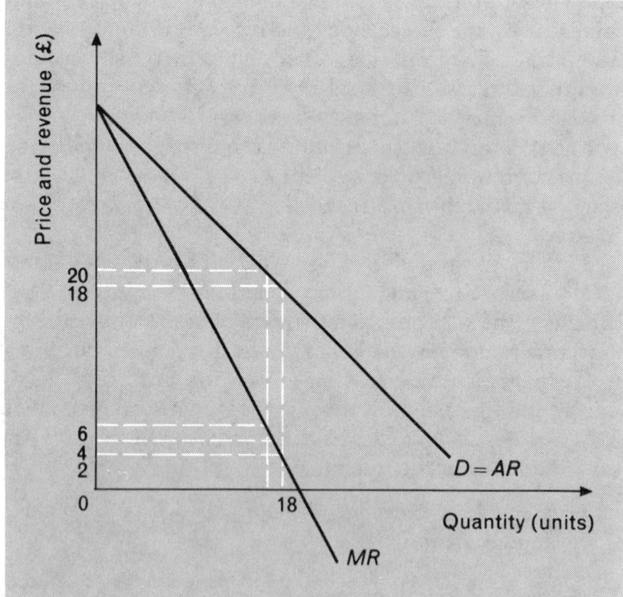

Figure 6.8 Average and marginal revenue with a downward-sloping demand curve.

SUMMARY

1. Production is organized by the profit-maximizing entrepreneur.
2. Profits are the difference between total revenue and total cost.
3. If, by increasing output, total revenue is increased by more than total cost then the entrepreneur will expand production.
4. If, by decreasing output, total cost decreases by more than total revenue then the entrepreneur will reduce production.
5. When the change in total revenue, due to a change in output, exactly equals the change in total cost, the entrepreneur will neither expand nor reduce output.
6. The increase in revenue due to the production of one more unit is called marginal revenue. The increase in total costs due to the production of one more unit is called marginal cost.
7. The profit-maximizing entrepreneur will therefore choose to produce that level of output which equates marginal revenue to marginal cost.
8. In a fixed-price or auctioneer world, marginal revenue equals average revenue equals price equals marginal cost.
9. In a market where price varies with the amount sold, marginal revenue declines twice as fast as average revenue for a straight-line demand curve.

Perfect competition

We shall now look at some of the best-known descriptions of how firms behave in various forms of market. Each type of market assumes a different elasticity of demand facing the entrepreneur.

Market demand curves always slope downwards, but an individual firm's demand curve need not. Even when it does, it need not have the same elasticity as the market demand curve. The different ways of deriving a firm's demand curve from the market demand curve give rise to the different market forms.

One of the earliest descriptions of how firms and markets behaved was **perfect competition**. In this approach each firm is imagined to be such a small part of the entire market that it can have no influence on the market price.

Suppose that the market is supplied by a great many firms. Say, for example, that the market absorbed 10 million units of output and there were a million firms each producing 10 units. This would mean that any one of these firms could double its output and yet increase the market supply by only one millionth. This is such a small increase in market supply that it is highly unlikely to have any effect on the market price at all, i.e. market price will remain unchanged even if one firm doubles its output.

A firm operating in such a market would behave as if it could sell as much as it wanted at the going market price. The firm would effectively face a horizontal, perfectly elastic demand curve at the ruling market price. It would therefore seek to produce an output that maximized profits at this given market price. Such a firm is known as a *price taker*.

In the economist's model of perfect competition it is assumed that there is *freedom of entry into and exit from the industry*. Firms are free to enter or leave the industry at zero cost. This implies that when firms are making high (low) profits others will come in (leave) the industry and so swell (reduce) supply so that market price will fall (rise) and profits will return to normal. This tendency to earn only normal profits works only in the long run when capital and labour can be changed. In the short run abnormal profits can be earned.

The products of all firms in the industry are assumed to be homogeneous. That is, the product of one of the firms is indistinguishable from the product of any other firm. This means that customers are unable to distinguish one firm's product from any other and so no firm could raise its price above the market price and still retain any sales.

Firms and customers are assumed to have perfect knowledge. All producers and consumers are aware of market changes and of each other's actions. Thus any price change or technological development is immediately signalled to all producers and consumers.

Market equilibrium

How will such a market behave? There are no real-world examples of perfectly competitive markets, although agricultural products with their very many farmers and customers come close to perfect competition.

As we have stated earlier, the perfectly competitive firm will be a price taker and so must face a horizontal demand curve for its produce. The level of the market price will be determined by the market demand and supply.

The firm will aim to maximize profits and so will produce where marginal cost equals marginal revenue. This is shown in Figure 6.9. Remember that the average revenue is also the marginal revenue curve in the fixed-price case and so profit is maximized where the firm's marginal cost curve crosses the demand curve.

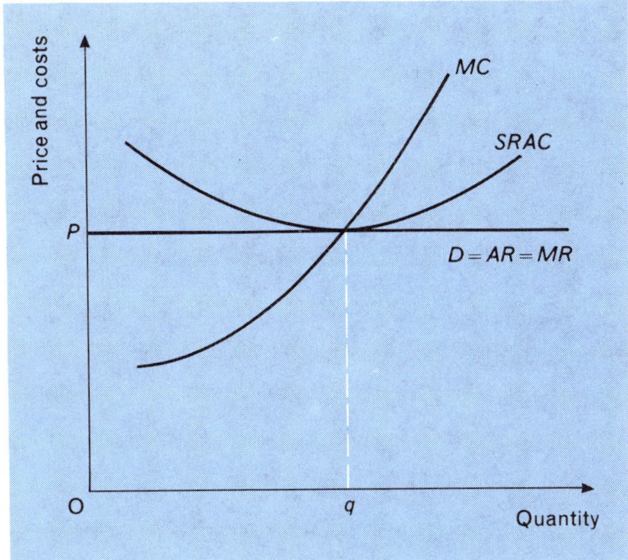

Figure 6.9 Short-run equilibrium under perfect competition.

The short-run marginal cost (*SRMC*) and short-run average cost (*SRAC*) curves have the usual U-shapes with the marginal cost curve crossing the average cost curve at its minimum point. In Figure 6.9 the average cost curve is just tangential to the demand curve and this implies that at output Oq the average cost of production is OP. As the average cost curve includes normal profit, this implies that the firm is earning normal profits.

Apart from in the short run it is not possible for the perfectly competitive firm to earn anything other than normal profit. This follows from the assumptions of perfect knowledge and the perfect mobility of factors of production. If the industry is faced with a price higher than OP in Figure 6.9 then all firms will expand production, moving along their marginal cost (supply) curves. The firms will then earn excess profits until firms outside the industry which are only earning normal profit are attracted to the industry by the greater returns available. As factors of production are perfectly mobile, they can be adapted for use in the industry that is earning higher profits. Figure 6.10 shows the market adjustment process.

Figure 6.10 shows an individual perfectly competitive firm on the left and the market demand and supply curves on the right. The initial position is shown by the market demand curve D_1 and the market supply curve S_1. This leads to a market price of OP_1. The individual firm maximizes profit by equating marginal cost to marginal revenue and producing Oq_1 units of output. By doing this the firm earns excess profits equal to the shaded area in the diagram.

This situation cannot persist because firms outside the industry will enter the market in an attempt to share the excess profits. This will cause the market supply curve to move to the right and so reduce the market price. (Recall that the market supply curve is the sum of all firms' marginal cost curves, and so firms entering the industry cause the curve to move.) Firms will continue to enter the

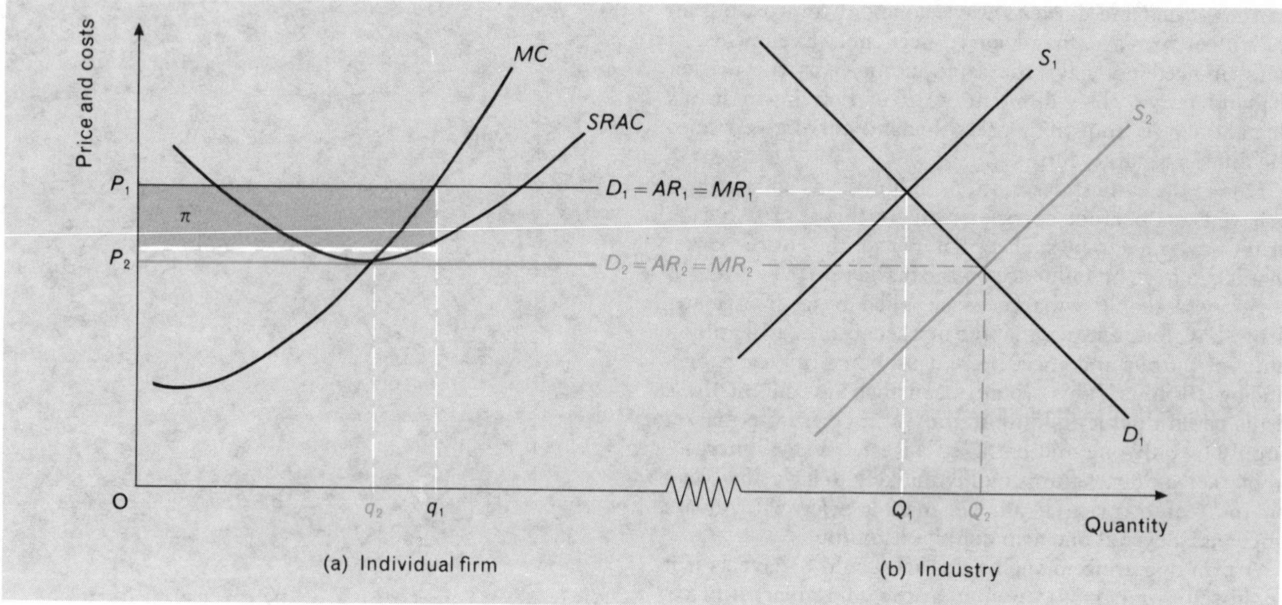

Figure 6.10 The relationship between the perfectly competitive firm and the market.

industry until the supply curve has reached S_2 and the market price is OP_2. Here only normal profits are earned and so there is no more incentive to enter the industry.

In addition to new firms entering the industry when excess profits are being earned, existing firms will also wish to expand their productive capacity. This will contribute to the movement of the market supply curve and will mean that part of the extra market output is due to existing firms expanding. This process was discussed in Chapter 5.

The market will settle down to a new level of output OQ_2 at a new market price of OP_2. The individual firms in the industry will produce less, Oq_2 instead of Oq_1, and will earn less profit (normal profit). The assumptions of the model mean that whenever profits deviate from normal there will be a tendency for prices and output to move to restore normal profit to the industry. This is the 'perfect competition' that gives the model its name. A firm cannot gain any advantage over its rivals because any such advantage is competed away. Any firm that allows its costs to rise above those of its competitors will find that it cannot stay in business by raising price. Inefficiency is not tolerated. All firms operate at their capacity points and consumers can buy all they want at this lowest possible price.

SUMMARY

1. If the demand conditions facing firms in an industry vary then different market situations will arise.
2. In all situations the market demand curve will slope downwards, but a firm that is part of that market need not face a demand curve of the same elasticity.
3. If no single firm can influence market price then it accepts the market price, is a price taker and faces a horizontal (infinitely elastic) demand curve.
4. In such a market there are many sellers and many buyers. The market is said to be perfectly competitive with each firm supplying identical products.
5. In perfectly competitive markets marginal cost equals average cost equals price.
6. Free entry and exit of firms ensures that only normal profit is earned.
7. This is the only market form that behaves in the same way as the auctioneer's market.

Monopoly

An alternative to the perfectly competitive market (in which there are a very large number of sellers) is to move to the other extreme and have only one seller. Markets in which there is only one seller are called **pure monopolies**. The demand curve facing a monopolist is the whole market demand curve.

A monopolist will be aware that the market demand curve slopes downwards and that any change in output will lead to a change in price. The question is: will this affect the firm's behaviour? Will market price and quantity be the same as in perfectly competitive markets or different?

Entry of new firms into the market is not possible. The monopolist need not consider the possibility of new firms entering its industry in search of excess profits.

Market equilibrium

We know that, no matter what the market form, a profit-maximizing firm will equate marginal revenue to marginal cost. For a monopolist we also know that the marginal and average revenue curves diverge. This means that the equi-

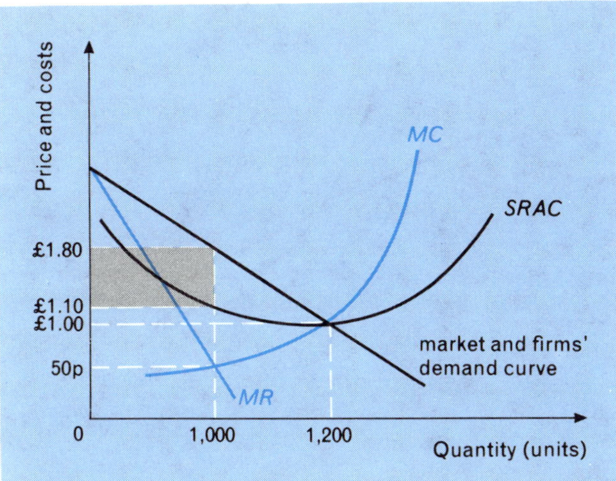

Figure 6.11 Short-run equilibrium monopoly.

librium price and output of a monopolist will be different from those in a perfectly competitive industry.

In order to construct the monopolist's cost curves imagine for the moment that the monopoly is formed not by one gigantic firm, but simply by someone buying up all of the little firms and co-ordinating their production and pricing decisions. As in the perfectly competitive case, the marginal cost curve for the whole market will be the sum of all the individual firms' marginal cost curves. Similarly, the market average cost curve will the the sum of all the individual firms' average cost curves.

Thus the market demand curve and the aggregate cost curve are the same for both a monopoly and a perfectly competitive market. This is shown in Figure 6.11.

We know that the perfectly competitive market will settle down where the market demand curve cuts the market supply curve. The market supply curve is the industry marginal cost curve (*MC*). So the perfectly competitive industry settles down to produce 1,200 units at £1 each and makes only normal profits. Notice also that it produces at minimum average cost.

In a monopoly industry, however, the monopolist knows that the demand curve is downward sloping. This implies a downward-sloping marginal revenue curve which lies below the average revenue curve. In equating marginal revenue (*MR*) to marginal cost (*MC*) a level of output is chosen which is lower than in the perfectly competitive case.

In Figure 6.11 marginal revenue equals marginal cost at an output of 1,000 units. At this level of output marginal cost and marginal revenue equal 50p. The average cost of producing 1,000 units can be read off the *SRAC* curve and is £1.10. The price at which each unit can be sold is read off the demand curve and is £1.80.

In equilibrium then the monopolist produces 1,000 units of output and sells them at £1.80 each. It is sometimes said that the monopolist may therefore choose either output or price, but not both, i.e. if the monopolist chooses to charge £1.80 then 1,000 units must be produced. This is true, but it is more helpful to remember that the monopolist is driven by profit maximization and chooses price and output to achieve that goal.

The price and output decision of the monopolist differs from that of the firm in a perfectly competitive market in two important respects. First, note that the monopolist is earning **excess profit**. When producing 1,000 units the monopolist's average cost is £1.10 per unit and this covers normal profit. The monopolist sells each unit at £1.80, thus making 70p per unit over and above normal profit. This excess profit is £700 and is shown by the shaded rectangle in Figure 6.11.

As entry into the industry is not possible there is no force for change in this market and the monopolist can continue to earn excess profits indefinitely.

The second thing to note is that the monopolist does not produce at the minimum short-run average cost, i.e. *the monopolist does not produce at the capacity point*. In Figure 6.11 the monopolist produces less output at a higher cost and at a higher price than would a firm in a perfectly competitive industry. This has caused some economists to argue that monopolies should be discouraged and has led to the establishment of the Monopolies and Mergers Commission in the UK and antitrust legislation in the USA. (The Monopolies and Mergers Commission is dealt with later in this chapter.)

Monopolist behaviour in the long run

In the perfectly competitive case the long-run equilibrium is very similar to the short-run equilibrium. Here we show how the long-run situation of the monopolist differs from the situation under perfect competition.

In the long run the monopolist is free to change capital stock as well as other factors of production, and consequently long-run cost curves depend upon returns to scale rather than on diminishing returns to one factor. For constant returns to scale the long-run average cost curve is a horizontal straight line, i.e. average costs do not vary with output.

The long-run average cost curve (*LRAC*) and the market demand curve are shown in Figure 6.12. In order to maximize profits in the long run the monopolist would choose to produce Oq_1 units of output. The monopolist's costs are the long-run average costs (OP_0), which equal long-run mar-

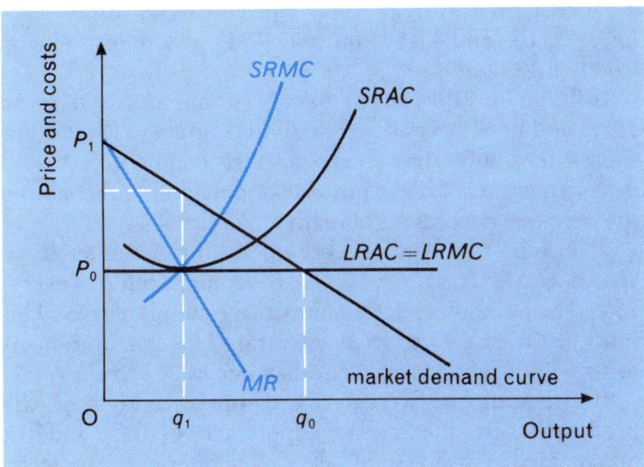

Figure 6.12 Long-run equilibrium under monopoly.

ginal costs ($LRMC$). Average revenue is OP_1, i.e. the price which Oq_1 units would attract on the market.

For the monopolist to be in both short-run and long-run equilibrium it is necessary for both $LRMC$ and $SRMC$ to equal MR. This implies that for constant returns to scale, in the long run the monopolist will produce at minimum long-run and hence minimum short-run average cost.

The monopolist will continue to produce at Oq_1 units of output since here profits are maximized. In the perfect competition model these excess profits would be competed away and output would expand as new entrants began production. The expansion would continue until no more excess profits were earned (output Oq_0) when average long-run cost equals price.

Thus, being the only firm in a market where there are barriers to the entry of other firms, the monopolist will again be *producing less* than would be produced in a perfectly competitive market and *charging a higher price* (Oq_1 rather than Oq_0 and OP_1 rather than OP_0 in Figure 6.12). Even in the long-run then there are reasons for claiming that monopoly should be discouraged.

Are monopolies always bad?

These conclusions about monopoly rely partly on the assumption of constant returns to scale. If we relax the assumption and allow increasing returns to scale then we arrive at a different conclusion about the comparison between monopoly and perfect competition (see also Table 6.1).

Increasing returns to scale are often associated with monopolies since one reason for their market dominance is that very large firms are more efficient (have lower average costs) than small firms when there are increasing returns to scale. They can therefore force competitors out of business by reducing price and expanding output. In order to benefit from increasing returns to scale the monopoly must be one very large firm rather than a single ownership of many small firms.

What happens when there are increasing returns to scale? The long-run average cost curve will be downward sloping, so the average cost facing a small firm will be higher than the average cost facing a very large firm. Therefore even if the monopolist does equate the marginal revenue to marginal cost the firm may well be producing at lower costs, lower prices and higher output. This is demonstrated in Figure 6.13.

In Figure 6.13 we have a market (or monopoly) demand curve and its associated marginal revenue curve (MR). The short-run supply curve for the perfectly competitive market is shown as SC. This is upward sloping and is the sum of the marginal cost curves of many small firms.

The short-run marginal cost curve for the monopolist is shown as $SRMC$. It too is upward sloping, but lies everywhere below the perfectly competitive supply curve. This must be the case with increasing returns to scale since many firms will each be less efficient than one large firm.

If the industry is perfectly competitive then it will produce where the market supply curve (SC) and the market demand curve intercept. Therefore the perfectly competitive industry will produce Oq_c units at a price of OP_c.

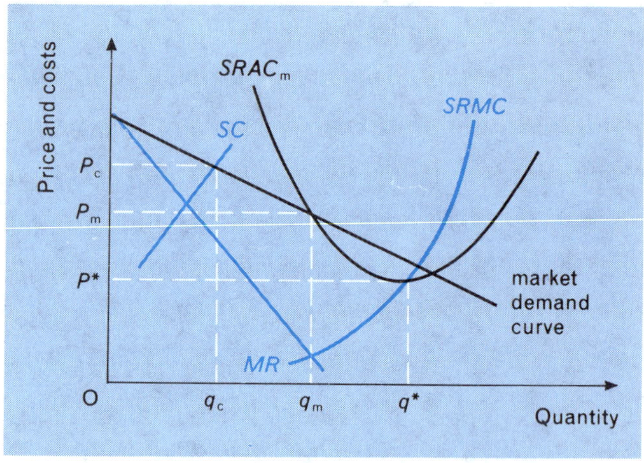

Figure 6.13 Higher output and lower prices under monopoly with increasing returns to scale.

If the industry is a monopoly then the amount produced will be determined by the profit-maximizing position. This is where the $SRMC$ cuts the marginal revenue curve. The monopolist will produce Oq_m units at price OP_m. Thus, although for the monopolist the marginal cost does not equal the price, it is producing more output at a lower price and a lower cost than would be produced if the industry were perfectly competitive.

Ideally we would like to have the economies of scale and produce at the lowest possible average cost. This means producing Oq^* units of output at price OP^*. Some economists have therefore argued for the imposition of marginal cost pricing. They would allow monopolies to form, but would oblige them to operate at that level of output at which $MC =$ price, rather than at $MC = MR$. We shall come across this again when we look at the Monopolies and Mergers Commission.

Do monopolies exist?

This is a question that can have several answers. In the UK firms can be investigated as monopolies when they have as little as 25 per cent of market share. This definition of monopoly differs sharply from our definition of pure monopoly where a firm has 100 per cent of the market.

Here we are concerned with pure monopoly. Do any pure monopolies exist? It is possible to think of many industries where one firm controls the entire industry. For

Table 6.1 Perfect competition and monopoly compared

Perfect competition	Monopoly
Many sellers	One seller
Many buyers	Many buyers
Firms profit maximize	Firms profit maximize
Homogeneous product	One product only
Price taker	Can choose price
Price = marginal cost	Price > marginal cost
No barriers to entry	Barriers to entry
Earns normal profits in equilibrium	Earns excess profits in equilibrium

example, British Gas has a monopoly on domestic gas supply in the UK – no other firm can supply homes with this type of energy. British Gas is not a pure monopoly, however, because there are many other forms of energy. Households could decide to use electricity, wood, coal and so on. British Gas is not a pure monopoly because its product has close substitutes.

The same applies to other so-called monopolies – in every case the goods they are producing have some form of substitute. Thus the pure monopoly, like the perfectly competitive market, does not exist in the real world. Nevertheless the behaviour and structure of some markets may approach these theoretical models.

Barriers to entry

We have stated that there is no possibility of new firms entering the monopolist's market. Such **barriers to entry** can arise in any form of imperfect market structure (we shall be looking at other forms in the following sections) and it is worthwhile to ask ourselves how this happens.

The most common forms of barrier arise out of being the only firm that knows how, or is allowed, to produce a given product. A patent or copyright allows a firm exclusive rights to make a product, and keeping a process secret also allows exclusive production rights. Patents do run out, however, and secrets can be discovered. It is also possible to produce a similar product, or one that performs a similar function, without breaking patents. Thus these barriers tend to be short term only.

Another type of barrier to entry occurs when the scale of production of the firms in the industry is already so vast that the capital required for a new firm to set up in the industry is prohibitive. This will arise when there are economies of scale in an industry and to compete a new entrant must reach a certain size. This is shown in Figure 6.14.

The **minimum efficient scale (MES)** is the lowest output a firm must achieve in order to compete. In Figure 6.14 there are economies of scale up to output *OQ* and constant returns to scale thereafter. If the MES is a very considerable proportion of the market then new firms will not be able to afford to enter the market. Firms will either not be able to afford the set-up costs for their plant to reach MES or not be able to capture enough of the market to make a profit.

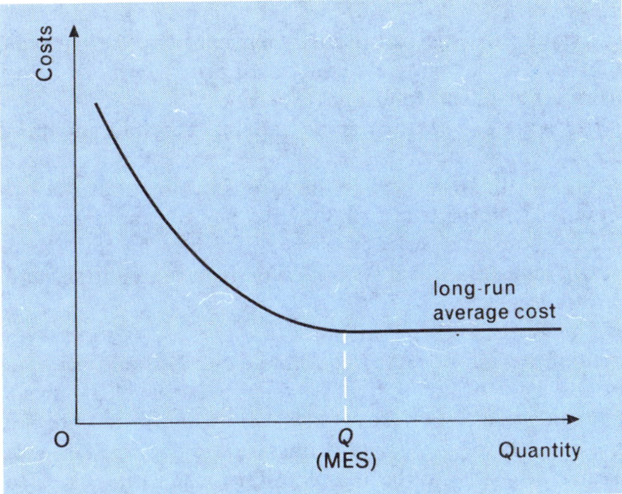

Figure 6.14 Minimum efficient scale.

Existing firms can put up other barriers such as advertising. Building up brand loyalty among customers is an important weapon for a firm in maintaining market share. A new firm entering the market must compete against products with years of familiarity among consumers. The cost of a campaign to challenge the existing brands may be too great to make it worth entering the market.

Finally, existing firms may decide not to exploit fully their market positions and not charge the full profit-maximizing price. This leads to a short-term loss of profit, but makes it very difficult for new firms to recover their costs. This tactic, known as entry forestalling, means that the firm sacrifices current excess profits to earn long-run excess profits.

SUMMARY

1. A monopolist is the sole supplier of a good in a market.
2. The demand curve facing a monopolist is therefore the market demand curve.
3. Monopolists are aware that if they wish to sell more then they must lower their price.
4. Monopolists seek to maximize profits by producing where marginal revenue equals marginal cost.
5. A monopolist will charge a price higher than its marginal cost of production and produce at an output lower than its capacity point.
6. The monopolist can charge a price higher than its average cost of production and can maintain this because no other firm can enter the market. The monopolist can therefore earn excess profits in the long run.
7. If there are economies of scale then a monopolist *may* charge a lower price and produce more than a perfectly competitive industry. If there are constant or decreasing returns to scale then the monopolist will charge a higher price and produce less than a perfectly competitive industry.
8. There are few, if any, pure monopolies in the real world because most goods have substitutes of some form.
9. Monopolies can only be maintained if no other firms can enter the market. New entrants to the market are kept at bay by barriers to entry.

Monopolistic competition

The two theories of the firm that we have so far considered are at the extremes of the range of possible market forms. There are many intermediate possibilities.

Monopolistic competition is a mixture of the theory of perfect competition and the theory of monopoly. There are many firms, but each faces a downward-sloping demand curve and produces a slightly different product. There is freedom of entry to the market and firms earn normal profit in long-run equilibrium but do not operate at capacity output.

Product differentiation results when the products of each firm are close substitutes but are distinguishable by consumers who develop a preference for one product over another. Unlike in perfect competition, raising price does not lose the firm its entire market share – some customers remain 'loyal'.

Firms are free to enter and leave the industry at will, so that if firms see that they can earn a greater (excess) profit by entering the industry then they will do so in the long run.

Market equilibrium

Let us start with a situation where a representative firm is making excess profits. This is shown in Figure 6.15. The firm faces the usual marginal cost and short-run average cost curves *MC* and *SRAC*. The firm faces a downward-sloping demand curve D_1, which is the demand curve for its particular product only given the present market conditions. The firm maximizes profits by producing Oq_1 units of output (20) where $MC = MR_1$. The firm charges price OP_1 and has average costs AC_1.

The firm is able to charge a higher price (£10) for its product than the average cost of production (£8). This means that the firm is making excess profits of £2 per item, or £40 overall.

These excess profits would induce two responses:

1. The existing firms in the industry could increase their capital stock and expand output.
2. New firms could enter the market and produce similar goods.

Let us suppose that it is the second possibility that

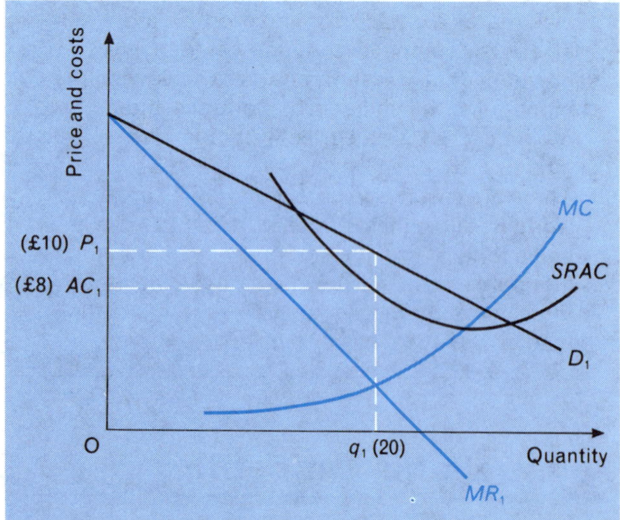

Figure 6.15 Short-run equilibrium under monopolistic competition.

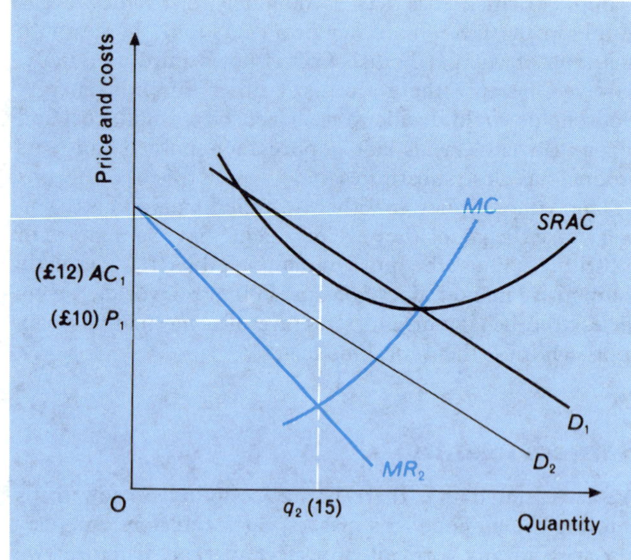

Figure 6.16 Monopolistic competition as new firms enter the industry.

occurs. New firms begin to enter the market attracted by the possibility of earning higher profits. This will cause overall market supply to rise and price to fall, and the new firms will entice customers of existing firms away. Thus the market share of the original firms in the market will fall.

This has the effect of moving the original firm's demand curve D_1 to the left. At each and every price the firm can sell fewer of its products. This effect is shown in Figure 6.16.

The firm shown in Figure 6.16 will continue to maximize profits but must now do so under new market conditions. The firm now faces the demand curve D_2 and the ruling marginal revenue curve is MR_2. The new profit-maximizing output is Oq_2, 15 units (where MR_2 crosses *MC*). From the demand curve D_2 we can see that the firm can charge only £10 for this output. The average cost of producing 15 units is £12 and so the firm makes a loss of £2 a unit, or £30 overall.

Given the case shown in Figure 6.16, some firms will leave the industry in search of higher (normal) profits elsewhere. Eventually, the number of firms in the industry will stabilize. This will occur when neither excess profits nor losses are being made and yet all firms are maximizing profits. This is shown in Figure 6.17.

In Figure 6.17 the firm is maximizing its profits at output Oq_3 (17 units) when $MC = MR_3$. At this output average cost is equal to price and so the firm is earning only normal profits. However, the firm is not operating at minimum average cost as a perfectly competitive firm would. Prices are therefore higher than under perfect competition, and output is lower.

The key element of monopolistic markets is the movement of the individual firm's demand curve. Equilibrium in the market is brought about by the movement of the firm's demand curve, which is caused either by new firms entering the industry or by existing ones leaving it in search of greater profit. Note that the equilibrium position can also be altered by the expansion of existing firms and this affects the *supply* curve.

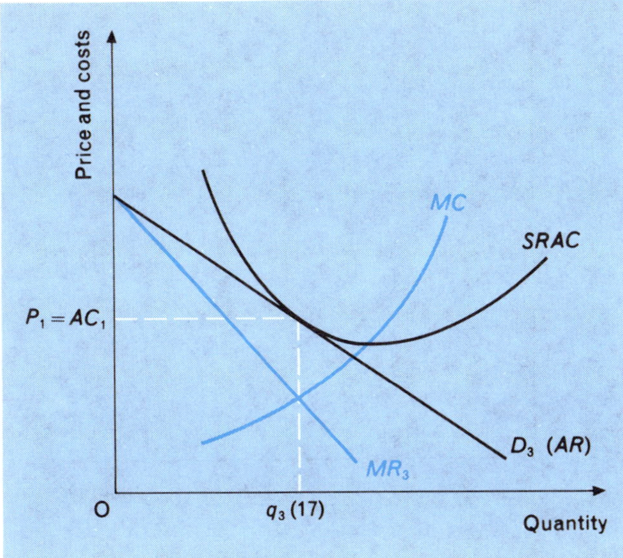

Figure 6.17 Long-run equilibrium under monopolistic competition.

Monopolistically competitive markets are similar to perfectly competitive markets in the sense that free entry and exit leads to only normal profits being earned in equilibrium. They are also similar to monopoly markets in that production does not take place at the lowest possible cost. Overall prices are higher and output lower than in perfect competition without firms earning excess profits.

SUMMARY

1. Monopolistic competition is similar to perfect competition except that the products of the firms are differentiated.
2. This means that each firm faces a downward-sloping demand curve.
3. Any excess profits will be bid away in the long run by profit-seeking entrants.
4. In long-run equilibrium the demand curve facing each firm will take up a position such that excess (abnormal) profits are zero.
5. Price and cost remain above those of a perfectly competitive market.
6. Output is below that which yields the lowest average costs, i.e. below 'capacity'.

Oligopoly

The most common form of market structure is **oligopoly**. *Oligos* is Greek meaning few – this is a market with few firms. However, unlike the previous three models there are no hard and fast rules about how many or what size the firms should all be. Indeed, there is no reason for one firm in the market to resemble another in any way other than its product being a substitute for all of the other firms' products.

In the real world most markets are dominated by a few firms. For example, Procter & Gamble and Lever Brothers dominate the washing powder market, and there are some other smaller firms as well. Another example is the motor car industry, which has sixteen major firms and many minor ones. Oligopoly theory is therefore more realistic and more difficult to characterize than the previous models.

The kinked demand curve model

One of the early attempts to model the oligopoly market has become known as the **kinked demand curve model**. The aim of the model is to explain the behaviour of firms in a market dominated by a few large firms, none of which can take control of the market.

The industry is dominated by a few (three or so) firms. The exact number is not of great relevance. Usually it is not envisaged that more than seven or eight firms can dominate an industry, but as we have seen the motor industry has sixteen major firms.

The firms in the industry are interdependent. This means that the actions of one firm will affect the activities of another. There being so few firms, each will face a downward-sloping demand curve and any attempt by one firm to get a higher market share will induce a response from the others.

The market has settled down to an accepted price level for each firm's product. This is a model of a mature market. The firms have already established their positions and their products. This leads to an accepted price for each firm's product and any attempt to deviate from this price causes competitors to react.

Market equilibrium

The implications of having an accepted market price and a situation where the actions of one firm affect the other firms in the market leads to there being a 'kink' in the firm's demand curve. This is shown for an individual firm in Figure 6.18.

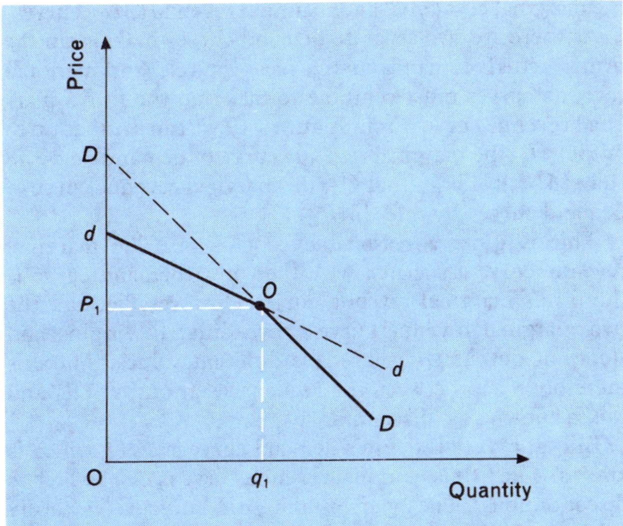

Figure 6.18 The oligopolist's 'kinked' demand curve.

The ruling market price is OP_1 and the firm produces Oq_1. The firm believes its demand curve to be *dOD*. The kink, at *O*, in the demand curve is caused by the firm's attitude towards the other firms in the industry. Any action on its part to alter its price would cause its competitors to react, and the firm believes that its competitors would react differently to a price rise than to a price cut.

Suppose the oligopolist were to raise its price. The firm believes that its competitors would leave their own prices unchanged since the original firm would now be selling its goods at a higher price than its competitors and would lose market share. Hence the demand curve *dd* is the firm's demand curve when it tries to move above its current price.

The oligopolist believes that if it were to reduce price from OP_1 then its competitors would match its actions and reduce their prices too, otherwise they would lose market share. All the firms in the industry will gain a share in the extra sales due to consumers buying more at a lower price, but each will retain its own 'share' of the market. The gain will be so widely spread that the firm's demand curve below the ruling price will be more inelastic than that above the ruling price.

As far as the firms in the industry are concerned this is a most pessimistic view of the future. The worst possible outcome always follows the action of the oligopolist firm. However, pessimism is an assumption of *this* oligopoly model only, and need not occur in other models with the same basic assumptions.

The oligopolist firm therefore faces the demand curve *dOD*. This does not in itself mean that the firm will not change its price if it can earn a higher profit by doing so. In a moment, however, we shall see that the ruling market price and the kink give the profit-maximizing price and output for quite large changes in costs.

Marginal cost and marginal revenue

As the oligopolist is operating at the price and output dictated by the kink in the demand curve and is assumed to be a profit maximizer, this must be the profit-maximizing output. To be sure of this we need to know the position of the marginal cost (*MC*) and marginal revenue (*MR*) curves.

As there are two separate demand curves making up the firm's actual demand curve, the two relevant marginal revenue curves must combine to make up the firm's marginal revenue curve. From Figure 6.19 we can see that up to output Oq_1 the marginal revenue curve of demand curve *dd* rules (MR_d); after output Oq_1 the marginal revenue curve of demand curve *DD* rules (MR_D).

This is quite a reasonable conclusion. The marginal revenue curve associated with the ruling demand curve is the firm's marginal revenue curve. However, because the two marginal revenue curves have different origins and slopes at output Oq_1 they have different values. There is therefore a gap between the two curves at output Oq_1 and this is known as a 'discontinuity'.

In Figure 6.19 the firm's demand curve is *dOD*, which is kinked. The firm's marginal revenue curve is *drsn*, which is discontinuous. The 'gap' in the *MR* curve is vertically below the kink in the demand curve.

As the firm is a profit maximizer producing at output Oq_1, the marginal cost curve (*MC*) must cross the *MR* curve between points *r* and *s*. This is shown in Figure 6.20. The curve MC_1 passes through the discontinuity of the *MR* curve and so the firm does indeed maximize profits by producing Oq_1 and charging the accepted market price P_1.

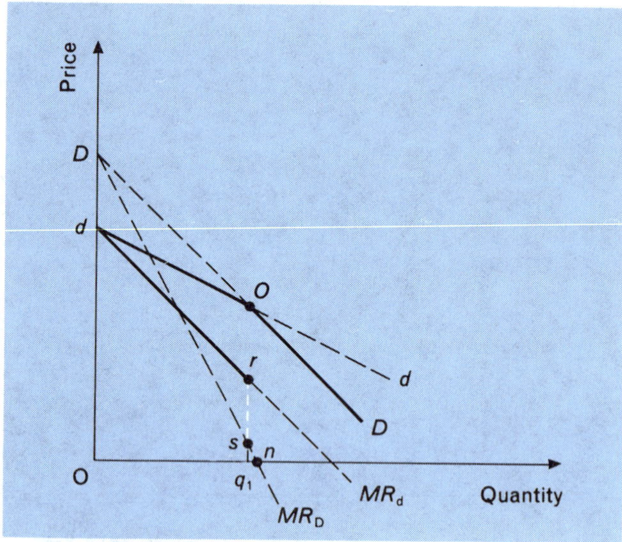

Figure 6.19 Marginal revenue under a kinked demand curve.

A feature of this oligopoly model is that firms are reluctant to change their price for fear of causing an adverse reaction by their competitors. The model allows firms this stability because of the *MR* discontinuity. If costs were to rise, say to MC_2 in Figure 6.20, then the new profit-maximizing position would be the same as the old. This model therefore predicts stability in both prices and output for an oligopolistic industry.

If costs were to rise outside the range *r* to *s* then some change in price and output would occur. This would lead to a new position for the kink and so a new accepted market price for the firm.

The oligopolist earns excess profits equal to the shaded area of Figure 6.21. The firm charges OP_1 per unit, but it costs the firm only *OAC* to make each unit. The firm is also

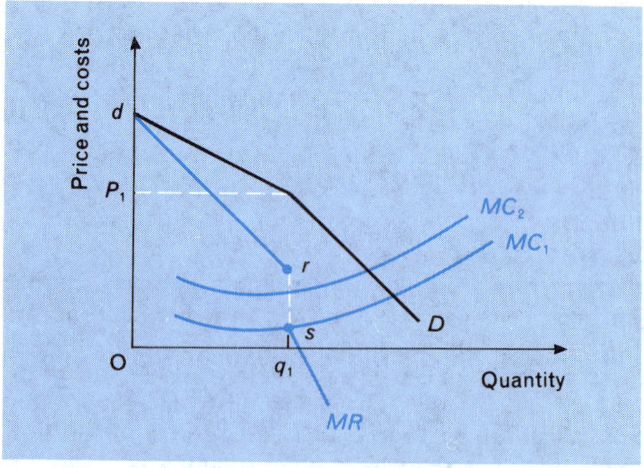

Figure 6.20 Profit-maximizing output under oligopoly.

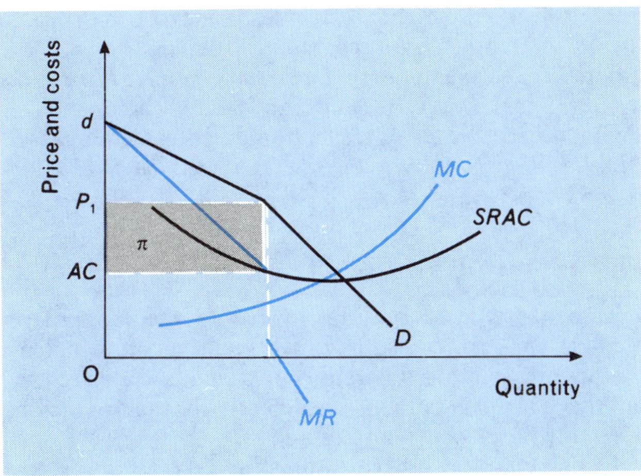

Figure 6.21 Equilibrium under oligopoly.

operating at above minimum average cost, and so price is higher and output is lower than in a perfectly competitive industry.

Collusion

The kinked demand curve model is just one theory of oligopoly. There can be as many theories as there are industries because no two industries are exactly alike.

One of the distinct possibilities in a market where the actions of one firm are likely to affect another is for the firms to try to work together. If they do this they can maximize their joint profits and avoid much of the expense of competing with one another. There are a number of options.

Cartels

A **cartel** is a formal agreement between firms to work together for mutual profit. In this way the firms of the industry can set prices and output as though they were a monopoly, and so reach maximum joint profits. Such action would clearly lead to higher profits, higher prices and lower output. Most governments see this as a clear disadvantage to the consumer and have outlawed cartels.

The best-known example of a cartel still operating is OPEC, the Organization of Petroleum Exporting Countries. The members of OPEC, which control a sizeable proportion of the world's oil output, meet together to decide on the prices they will charge and therefore how much they can afford to offer for sale. Once this has been agreed each country is given a quota and may not produce more than this. As a cartel OPEC had spectacular success in 1973 and 1979 in forcing up the price of oil and so raising the revenues of its members. In recent years many members have cheated and overproduced, making the agreed price difficult to maintain. Cheating is always a potential danger to cartels.

Consultation

As cartels are usually outlawed, another option is to consult informally with competitors. This too is usually illegal, but it is more difficult to prove. Many industrialists talk to each other, and industries have trade associations for this very purpose. Who can say that when discussing a union pay claim employers did not discuss, quite legitimately, the implied price rises to cover the claim?

Price leadership

A system may arise where no collusion takes place, but where the member firms of an industry look to one firm to lead the way. The difference between this and the kinked demand curve model is one of different behaviour assumptions.

Thus one firm may emerge as the market leader and all of the other firms may price their products according to that one firm. If Firm A is the market leader then Firm B may price its goods at 5 per cent less. If Firm A charges £1, Firm B charges 95p. Should Firm A raise its price to £1.20, Firm B raises its price to £1.14 (95 per cent of £1.20). All other firms in the industry make a similar adjustment. This is known as dominant-firm price leadership.

Table 6.2 Market forms compared

Perfect competition	Monopoly	Monopolistic competition	Oligopoly
Many sellers	One seller	Many sellers	A few dominant sellers
Many buyers	Many buyers	Many buyers	Many buyers
Firms profit maximize	Firms profit maximize	Firms profit maximize	Firms profit maximize
Homogeneous product	One product only	Differentiated product	Differentiated product
Price takers	Can choose price	Some ability to set price	Some ability to set price
Price = *MC*	Price > *MC*	Price > *MC*	Price > *MC*
No barriers to entry	Barriers to entry	No barriers to entry	Barriers to entry
Earns normal profits in equilibrium	Earns excess profits in equilibrium	Earns normal profits in equilibrium	Earns excess profits in equilibrium

Other industries have no need of a leader – different firms initiate price movements at different times. For example, following a change in costs Firm A may raise its price and all of the others may follow. On the next occasion, say following a change in demand, Firm C may change its price first and all the others follow. An example of this might be the retail petrol market where any of the major firms, e.g. Esso, Shell, Texaco or BP, might announce a price change which is followed by the others. In this sense one firm is acting like a barometer, signalling changing market conditions. Hence this is known as barometric price leadership.

This small selection of market forms is designed to illustrate the effects on market prices and quantities traded of the structure of the market (see Table 6.2 on p. 107). Exactly the same set of demanders and exactly the same cost curves do not always give rise to exactly the same price. Much depends on whether the market is *competitive* or *monopolistic*, and whether there is *freedom of entry*.

SUMMARY

1. Many industries contain only a few dominant firms and the actions of any one of these firms affect the sales and revenues of all of the other firms in the industry. This market structure is known as an oligopoly and in it firms are interdependent.
2. In the kinked demand curve model, firms take a pessimistic view of the reactions of their competitors and so try not to deviate from the accepted market price.
3. If the firms in the industry believe their demand curve to be kinked then prices will be stable in the face of changing costs. This is because of a gap (discontinuity) in the marginal revenue curve.
4. Oligopolists will earn excess profits in the long run due to barriers to entry.
5. When firms within a market realize that their actions are interdependent they may wish to co-operate to maximize joint profits. They may form a formal organization, a cartel, or consult informally. Such co-operation may be against the law.

Discriminating monopoly

So far we have assumed that all buyers are charged the same price. However, if a firm has a monopoly then it may also be able to divide the market up and charge different consumers different prices.

If a monopolist can split the market up then it can maximize profits in both markets separately, rather than accepting a compromise price for both. This will lead to higher profits for the firm.

In **discriminating monopoly** we assume that *the market is controlled by one firm – a monopoly*. No other firm sells goods that can be substitutes for the monopolist's goods in any market. In addition, *the market can be divided into separate sectors*. For example, it may be possible to divide the market into geographical regions, or into age groups. We then assume that *no trade is possible between the separate market sectors*. Thus goods sold in one sector cannot be transported or resold to another by the purchaser. And finally, *each sector of the market has a different elasticity of demand for the product*.

Market equilibrium

Imagine that a market can be divided up into two separate sectors. The firm can supply each sector at the same cost (i.e. we are ignoring different transport and supply costs), but the demand conditions are different for the two sectors. This situation is shown in Figure 6.22.

For simplicity we have assumed constant costs, so the marginal cost curve is MC in both markets. The left side of Figure 6.22 shows the demand and marginal revenue curves for sector 1 (D_1 and MR_1), and the right shows the demand and marginal revenue curves for sector 2 (D_2 and MR_2). The firm maximizes profits in both markets and so equates MC to MR_1 in sector 1 and MC to MR_2 in sector 2. This leads to a different price being charged in each sector, OP_1 in sector 1 and OP_2 in sector 2.

As long as people in sector 1 cannot buy the good and resell it in sector 2 then the monopolist will be able to discriminate between the two markets. You may notice that the firm has equalized the marginal revenue obtained in both markets, i.e. the firm gains as much from the sale of the last unit in sector 1 as it does from the sale of the last unit in sector 2.

The example we have used has only two sectors. In fact there may be many sectors, providing that each is quite separate from the others. Whenever trade is possible between two sectors a monopolist will find it impossible to discriminate between them for very long. For example, if a firm were to sell its goods in one part of the country for a lower price than in another, someone would eventually buy in one area and resell in the other.

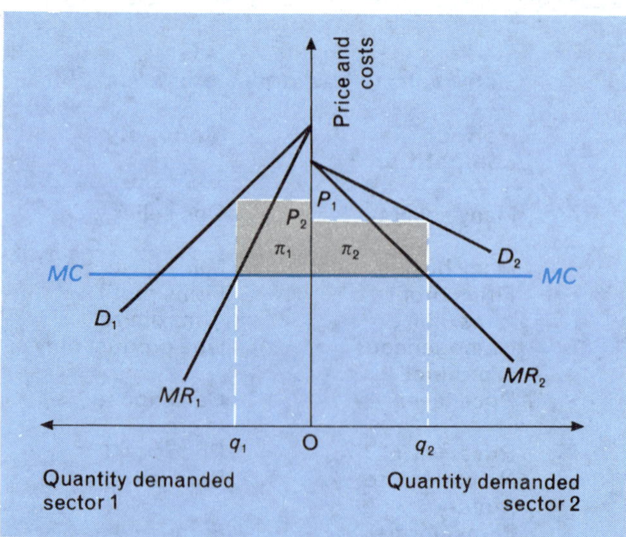

Figure 6.22 Equilibrium under discriminating monopoly.

Case Study 6.1 BA faces turbulent summer in fight for transatlantic seats

British Airways flies into the start of its most important money-making summer season next week, amid slower passenger growth, more seats competing for custom and analysts issuing warnings of a fresh round of cut-price fares.

Avmark, the international aviation consultant of Washington and London, estimates there will be at least 58 more return flights a week into London's Heathrow and Gatwick airports this summer, creating 16,350 more weekly seats, with eight American carriers accounting for 57 per cent of the 838 flights and because some are using smaller planes, about 52 per cent of the 118,152 seats.

Analysts say this is the first summer that BA has faced any real competition, from Virgin Atlantic, a British rival, and from the two new powerful American carriers – United Airlines, which bought Pan Am's routes, and American Airlines, which paid $445 million for three Heathrow routes from Trans World Airlines.

Paul Turk, senior executive of Avmark, said: 'It looks like there will be a 7 per cent rise in the number of US departures to London and a rise of between 3 and 4 per cent in the number of seats. There is already a price war on transatlantic fares and I expect it will intensify once American starts operating on July 1.

'To establish market share, the fight is likely to be hardest fought between United and American for US passengers this summer, and that may mean much cheaper fares being sold this side of the Atlantic than the other. But it is bound to spill over on the kind of prices BA can charge.'

Lee Howard, chief executive of Airline Economics, the Washington consultant, said: 'I would not be surprised if American Airlines ran that North Atlantic service at a loss this year, just to establish their market.'

Weekly return flights from US to London Heathrow and Gatwick (summer 1991)

Carrier	Flights	Seats
BA	278	83,400
Virgin	84	30,000
American	168	35,900
United	122	30,500
TWA	42	11,000
Delta	42	9,700
Continental	36	13,500
Northwest	24	11,200
Pan Am	24	7,728
USAir	14	2,900

1. What does the article suggest about the structure of the transatlantic air passenger market prior to 1991?
2. What would you expect the structure of the market to be in the future, and what would be the consequence for the price of airline tickets?

Source: Philip Robinson, *The Times*, 28 May 1991

An example

There are examples of price discrimination in the real world. Discriminating firms tend to divide the market not by area, but by customer characteristics. For example, British Rail allows young people and old-age pensioners to travel at a lower cost than other people even though they are occupying seats on the same train.

British Rail must make more profit by discriminating in this way or it would not do it. But why should the middle-aged (25 to 60 or 65 as defined by British Rail) have to pay more? Is this not unfair? The argument in defence of discrimination is that if everyone were to pay the same price then cost would exceed revenue and the firm would have to close down. In this case no one could have the good. But if the producer is allowed to charge different prices to different buyers then profits can be made and the firm survives. Thus the middle-aged may complain that they are being discriminated against, but they are met with the argument that they either pay more than other customers do or they do without the good completely.

Some goods are sold at different prices at different times of the day or on different days of the week. Thus night storage heaters consume electricity at night and at a much lower cost per unit than electricity sold during the day. Train fares for non-peak travelling hours are often less than those for peak times. This is discrimination in a way, but it is not due to the segmentation of the market into groups of consumers. Anyone can buy low-cost electricity at night and anyone can travel at the cheaper rate at the cheaper times. What is being reflected here is not so much differences in demand but differences in supply. In other words, the lower prices are being used to reschedule demand to take advantage of excess capacity.

SUMMARY

1. When a producer can charge different prices to different sets of customers there is no single market price.
2. Such producers must be monopolists and be capable of preventing trade between customers.
3. These 'discriminating monopolists' maximize profits in each market, as would a pure monopolist, by equating marginal revenue to marginal cost in each market section.
4. This price discrimination may seem unfair, but it may be the only way of keeping the producer in business.

Alternatives to profit maximization

In all of the market structures that we have considered so far we have assumed that the entrepreneur's motive is to maximize profit. In this section we question the assumption of profit maximization and look at some alternative goals for a firm.

Do firms want to maximize profits?

When economists first began to formulate theories about how firms might work most were small, owner-managed businesses. It was therefore reasonable to assume that the owners were interested in the firm making as much profit as possible, since they then received a higher income. Today firms are much larger and are usually run by managers and directors and owned by very many shareholders who take no part in the business.

The owners of firms have become different from those who manage them. This is known as the *divorce between ownership and control*. Employed managers will have a different set of motives to those of the eighteenth- and nineteenth-century owner/manager. To the manager a higher dividend due to higher profits brings only a little reward and recognition. A higher salary, a larger company car or being head of the largest firm in an industry are likely to be more important to the modern manager than shareholders' profits.

It is further argued that firms today do not need to maximize profit to survive. The harsh world of perfect competition, in which any firm that does not keep costs to a minimum goes bankrupt, does not exist. Most firms can get by in today's complex business world as long as they can hold on to their market share by following the lead of other firms in the industry. Thus we have reason to doubt profit maximization as the prime motive of modern business.

Another doubt that has been raised is the ability of managers to maximize profits even if they wanted to. Few firms know how to calculate their marginal costs. Fewer still have a good idea about the position and shape of their demand curve and of their marginal revenue curve. How then can they find $MC = MR$?

This criticism has been rejected by some economists. Professor Milton Friedman has written that it is not necessary for business people to understand economic theory to profit maximize – they will do so by instinct. Professor Friedman points to a pool (snooker) player who pots balls *as if* he knew the complicated mathematics needed to calculate the angles and impact speeds for a perfect pot. It is argued that business people maximize profit *as if* they understood economic theory.

Even with Professor Friedman's defence there is reasonable cause to suspect that firms sometimes act with motives other than profit maximization. We shall look at some possibilities.

Sales revenue maximization

One suggestion is that firms will try to maximize their total revenue. The firm's aim would be to produce that level of output where the total revenue curve was at its height, i.e. output Oq_1 in Figure 6.23.

At output Oq_1 the firm is sacrificing profit for turnover, since profit is maximized at output Oq^*. The main reason for pursuing this strategy is that executive salaries tend to rise with turnover rather than profit. The managers may also wish to follow this course for the prestige of having the highest turnover of any firm in the industry, i.e. the 'biggest' firm.

Output maximization

A closely related alternative motive is the maximization of output. This could not be pursued to its limit because after output Oq_3 in Figure 6.23 the firm makes a loss. It is doubtful if shareholders would accept operating at Oq_3 for

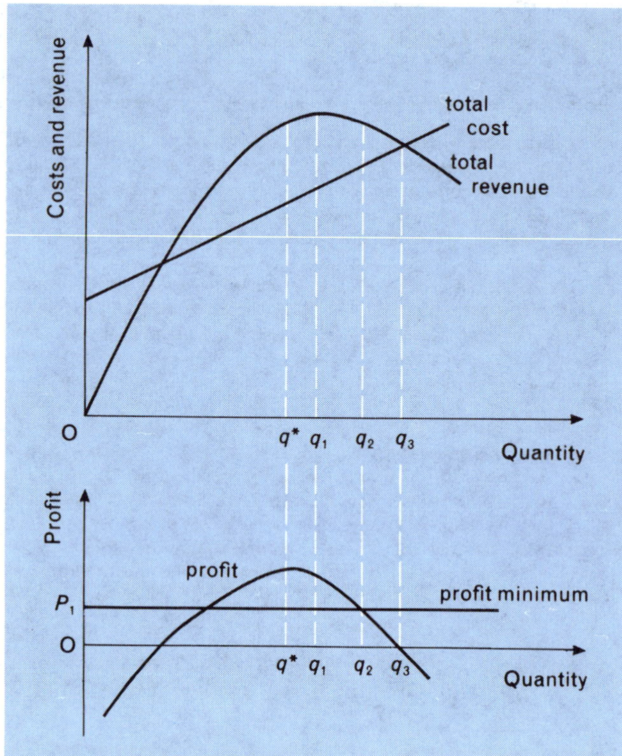

Figure 6.23 Sales revenue and output maximization.

long because they would receive no dividends when profits were zero.

The output-maximizing firm must accept that it must earn at least a certain level of profit that will satisfy the shareholders. If that level is OP_1 in Figure 6.23 then the output-maximizing firm will produce Oq_2 units, the maximum given its profit constraint.

The reasons for following this course would again be the prestige of size, the margin of safety or the possibility of larger salaries in a larger firm.

Utility maximization

The utility maximization model suggests that managers aim to satisfy their own needs rather than those of the firm. The model's proposers suggest that managers will have a preference for 'managerial slack'.

Managerial slack may be in the form of having more employees than is strictly necessary, avoiding high-risk or high-stress strategies, or granting generous executive allowances such as expense accounts and large company cars. In such a company profit is therefore sacrificed in favour of managerial comfort.

X-inefficiency

The managerial slack described above is an example of **X-inefficiency**. Profit maximization implies keeping costs, at any level of output, to a minimum. Allowing costs to rise above this level is, by definition, inefficient.

X-inefficiency is certainly a fact of managerial life. For example, people make non-urgent telephone calls during peak-rate times. The loss due to X-inefficiency is, however, difficult to assess. This aside, if firms did want to profit maximize then they would ruthlessly hunt down these inefficiencies to gain the extra profit. That firms do not do this suggests that they have other goals in addition to profit maximization.

Profit maximization

Does all of this mean our profit maximization models are false and useless? Luckily it does not. We can still use the models to predict the behaviour of firms in a given situation, and groups of firms often act *as if* conforming to one of our profit maximization theories. Moreover, economists are aware of the different motives of firms and are developing theories to account for them.

SUMMARY

1. Many models that seek to explain the behaviour of firms assume that they aim to maximize profits.
2. There are doubts about whether firms would aim to do this – or could even if they wanted to.
3. Defenders of the profit maximization assumption claim that firms act *as if* they were profit maximizers even if they are not.
4. Other goals of a firm may be to maximize company size (by output or revenue) or to maximize managerial salary or comfort.

Monopolies and Mergers Commission

We have seen that the free working of the price mechanism brings about an efficient allocation of resources, provided there are no monopolistic tendencies. We can remind ourselves of the principal results by considering the cost and revenue curves for a firm in a perfectly competitive market. These are shown in Figure 6.24. Figure 6.24(b) shows the market demand curve (D_m) and the market supply curve (S_m). Recall that this market supply curve is the sum of each firm's marginal cost curve – at least when the market is perfectly competitive.

The market demand and market supply curves determine the market price (P_m) and the quantity traded (q_m). From Figure 6.24(a) we see that this market price is taken as 'given' by each firm, so that the demand curve facing each firm in the industry is a horizontal line (D_i). In order to maximize profits each firm equates its marginal revenue to its marginal cost. This occurs at q_i, which is also the point of minimum average cost. Thus the market settles down to a point of lowest average cost and zero excess profits.

But if the market is supplied by a single firm (a monopoly) then the firm's demand curve is the market demand curve (D_m). As this is downward sloping, we know that it will have a more steeply sloped marginal revenue curve associated with it (MR_m in Figure 6.24(b)). If we assume that the marginal cost curve of the monopolist is simply the aggregate of many small firms then S_m is the monopolist's marginal cost curve. This marginal cost curve is associated with the monopolist's average cost curve of AC_m.

In order to maximize profits the monopolist equates marginal revenue (MR_m) with marginal cost (S_m). From Figure 6.24(b) we see that this results in a market price of P_{mm}, an average cost of production of AC_m and a quantity traded of q_{mm}. We therefore have higher prices, higher costs and less output.

The fact that under monopoly less is supplied and at a higher cost obviously represents a loss to the economy – a social loss. This has led to the belief that monopolies should be discouraged and/or controlled by legislation.

It is also clear from Figure 6.24(b) that the monopolist earns excess profits equal to $£(P_{mm} - AC_m) \times q_m$. This excess profit is of concern if we bothered about income distribution, but of itself it does not represent a social loss.

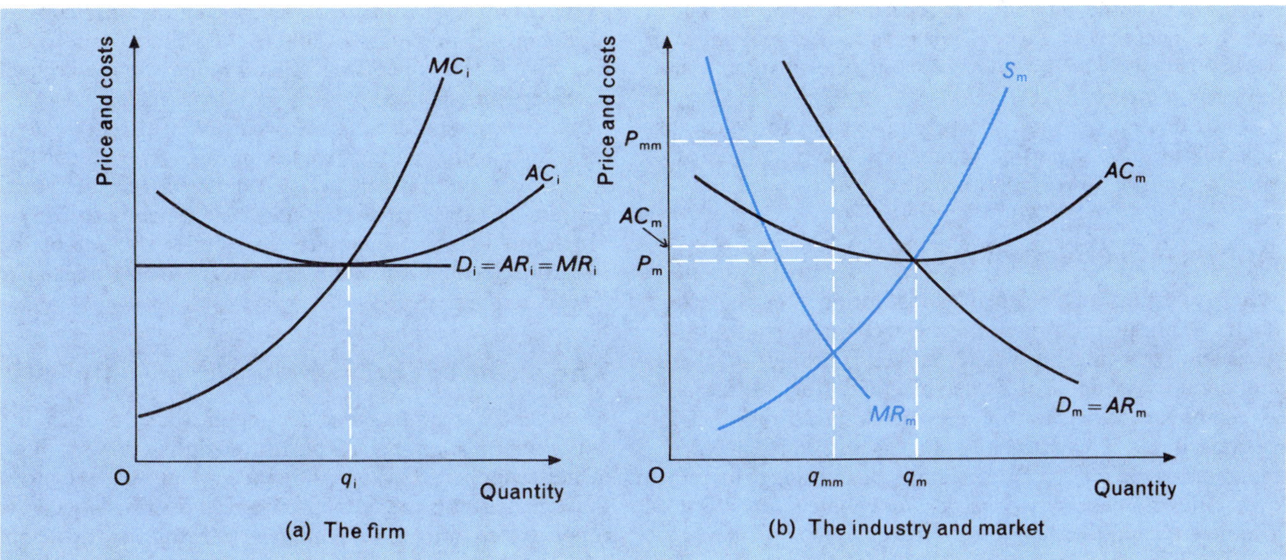

Figure 6.24 Equilibrium under perfect competition and monopoly.

The consumers pay more, but the producer receives more and hence it is a straightforward transfer from one group (consumers) to another (producers).

Monopoly power

It is not necessary for an industry to contain only one firm for there to be excess profits and monopoly power. The assumption makes the exposition of the basic arguments somewhat simpler, but we have seen the cases of monopolistic competition and oligopoly where firms also have market power. In general, any firm which faces a downward-sloping demand curve has a degree of monopoly power. The downward slope causes the marginal revenue curve to fall below the average revenue (demand) curve, and hence price no longer equals marginal cost.

Where more than one firm can exist in the market, it is possible to have monopoly losses without there being any excess profits. This is the case in monopolistic competition where we saw that, because free entry was possible, all excess profits were competed away, but prices were higher and output lower than in perfect competition.

It is also possible that, due to increasing returns to scale, the costs of an industry that is run by a monopoly are lower than the costs of a perfectly competitive industry, and this was demonstrated in our discussion of monopolies earlier. The possibility of there being increasing returns to scale weakens the case against monopoly power. This is not a complete argument, however, as a firm can gain market dominance by exploiting increasing returns to scale, and this then acts as a barrier to the entry of other firms.

Monopsony

Apart from imperfect competition on the sales side, there is also the possibility of imperfect competition on the buying side of the industry. When one firm is the sole buyer of a factor it is known as a **monopsonist** and it has the power to influence the market in which it buys, just as a monopolist can influence the market in which it sells. An example is where a firm is the only buyer of a particular type of labour and so can act in such a way that it pays a lower real wage to workers than they would receive if the market were perfectly competitive.

Thus monopolists and monopsonists can cause a social loss, the former by causing higher product prices and the latter by causing lower factor prices.

Actual and effectual monopolies

When we speak of one 'firm' constituting the whole industry we mean one owner or one entrepreneur controls the decisions regarding the whole market. Technically, then, monopoly is to do with ownership, and (for the reasons given above) a concentration of ownership into a few hands is undesirable. Government policy is therefore aimed at maintaining diversity of ownership. But although diverse ownership is a necessary condition for competition, it is not a sufficient condition.

As we have seen, there are several ways that owners could get together and act in unison. Collusion will allow firms to earn excess profits and share them out among themselves. Practices such as these are specifically designed to restrict competition and are called 'restrictive trade practices'. They have the same consequences as monopolies and/or monopsonies, and so are considered undesirable by advocates of the free market.

Other disadvantages of monopolies and restrictive practices

As well as producing distortions of prices and quantities in the short run, it has also been claimed that monopolies and restrictive trade practices distort long-run cost curves. The main argument here is that by protecting themselves from competition firms have no incentive to adopt new techniques or to pursue new ideas by research and development expenditure. Indeed, if a new invention does appear on the scene, an invention which could render existing capital obsolete, then collusive (co-operating) producers could agree among themselves not to take it up. Possible improvements in productive efficiency are therefore stifled in order to protect the vested interests of the owners of existing capital.

Thus long- and short-run efficiency may suffer when producers are shielded from the cold wind of competition.

Conversely, however, it may be argued that it is only the very large monopolists who can afford to mount research programmes. This is partly because research and development (R & D) cannot be conducted on a very small scale.

There is some evidence to suggest that small firms do not engage in such R & D, but that there is no difference in R & D expenditure between medium and very large firms. This is an argument in favour of medium-sized firms rather than monopolies.

But there is a second, stronger argument. The expense of R & D can only be recouped if its benefits are kept by the company funding the research. Drug companies, for example, argue that because they spend so much money on research they should be allowed to have a monopoly of the production of a new drug. This recompenses them for their initial expenditure and provides funds for their new projects. If other firms in the industry could simply copy the products and processes of others then there would be no incentive for any one firm to spend money on research and development.

This argument leads to the provision of patents. Patents confer ownership on the inventor or discoverer of a product or process. Thus it can be used only with the patentee's permission. If a patent is used in a manner likely to constitute a public disservice then under the Patents Act 1949 the Secretary of State can intervene and weaken the powers of the patentee.

The extent of monopoly power in the UK

Arguments for and against monopolies would be of little importance if monopolies constituted only a very small part of the economy. There is, however, plenty of evidence to show that in the UK and elsewhere industry is becoming concentrated into fewer and fewer 'firms' or 'ownership units'.

Table 6.3 shows what percentage of UK national manufacturing output is produced by the 100 largest firms. From

Table 6.3 Manufacturing concentration in the UK: % of output produced by 100 largest firms, 1949–85

Year	1949	1953	1958	1963	1968	1970	1985
% output	22	27	32	37	41	41	38

this table it is clear not only that the percentage of output produced by the top 100 firms has almost doubled since 1949, but that at 38 per cent the degree of concentration is very high indeed.

It is possible to look at the **concentration ratio** for an individual industry. This is calculated by dividing the market share of the largest firms (by sales value or output) by that of the total industry.

The most commonly used industry measure is the five-firm concentration ratio. The output of the five largest firms is divided by the industry output. In 1986 the average five-firm concentration ratio for the UK was 42.1 per cent by sales and 39.5 per cent by output.

This growth of concentration may be explained either in terms of a few particular firms growing faster than others or in terms of mergers and takeovers between existing firms. A **merger** is the bringing together of two existing firms under common ownership by mutual agreement. A **takeover**, on the other hand, implies that one firm buys the shares of another possibly without the consent of those who control the bought-out firm.

Mergers and takeovers may be aimed at reducing competition among firms of similar kinds. Thus, for example, one manufacturer of textiles may take over or merge with a competing manufacturer of textiles. There is, however, another way in which mergers and takeovers may reduce competition. This is where a firm takes over or merges with one of its suppliers (or one of its buyers). This kind of merger or takeover gives the firm a captive customer and hence it need not compete with other suppliers for this customer's business. To use a textile manufacturing example, textile spinners compete among themselves to sell their yarns to weavers. But if one spinning firm merges with or takes over a weaver then it could insist on that weaver buying yarn only from its parent company.

These two types of merger or takeover are called **horizontal integration** and **vertical integration**: horizontal when firms at the same stage of production merge (mergers between spinners) and vertical when firms at different stages of production merge (mergers between spinners and weavers).

As in the case of monopoly power, it is possible again to dispense with considerations of who formally owns the companies. We need instead to concern ourselves with collusion (among different owners) to buy only from particular sources or to sell to particular customers at lower prices than others. This is another example of restrictive trade practices. They aim at restricting competition by encouraging several 'independent' firms to agree mutually on common purchasing and selling policies.

Legislation

There can be little doubt that over the years there has been a steady erosion of competition in UK manufacturing industries. It is also clear from our economic theory that this erosion of competition may bring some benefits in the form of returns to scale and better research and development efforts. On the other hand, competition does make for efficient production and 'fair' pricing of outputs and inputs. Ideally we would like to be able to reap the benefits of large-scale production without having to bear the possible costs.

One way of doing this is simply to replace the entrepreneur with a government appointee and instruct him or her to manage the industry or company so as to maximize social benefits and minimize social costs. This is the *nationalization* route. As we will see, nationalized industries and their boards are charged with considering the widest social issues when making decisions.

A second way of proceeding is to leave the company in private ownership but to *constrain its commercial freedom* so as to make its behaviour conform more closely with the national interest. This could mean limiting the rate of profit or insisting that prices equal marginal costs. The problems with this kind of control are to do with policing and enforcement. Privately owned companies with a strong incentive to behave in a particular way will spend a great deal of time and effort in trying to circumvent legally any restrictions imposed on them. In these cases it becomes necessary to form a judgement about whether the control is worthwhile. The costs of enforcement could possibly exceed any savings or any increased efficiency.

The third approach to the problem is one of trying to *preserve competition*. Attempts to this in the UK have always been moderated by the recognition that competition may cause more social losses than would monopoly.

There seem in practice to have been three aims in UK competition policy:

1. The control of monopolies which already exist.
2. The prevention of new monopolies through mergers.
3. The prevention of restrictive trade practices.

The Monopolies and Restrictive Practices Act of 1948 set up the Monopolies and Restrictive Practices Commission. The Commission originally comprised between four and ten members but was subsequently increased to 25 in 1953. It was charged with inquiring into any firm which supplied more than one-third of the UK market for a particular good, or where there was evidence to suggest that some firms were colluding in a manner deemed to be detrimental to competition.

It was up to the appropriate minister, rather than up to the firms concerned, to initiate any inquiry. Furthermore, it was for the Commission to show that any practice was, on balance, against the public interest: the onus of proof was on the accuser rather than the accused.

Having investigated the pros and cons of the case, the Commission made a recommendation to the appropriate minister who, in Parliament, had the final say in whether the practice should be allowed or not.

One difficulty with this procedure is that, whereas monopolies and mergers are open to public inspection, many restrictive practices are not. The minister therefore could reasonably be expected to identify monopolies and mergers which were suitable for reference to the Commission, but how could he or she reasonably be expected to be aware of collusion?

The 1956 Restrictive Trades Practices Act therefore altered the earlier requirements. It was now the responsibility of colluding firms to register their restrictive practices. Furthermore, it was up to the firms, rather than the minister, to show that these practices were not against the public interest, i.e. *the onus of proof shifted.*

The case had to be made before the newly formed Restrictive Practices Court. The Act provided seven 'gateways' through which restrictive practices could be justified. They are as follows:

1. Protecting the public against injury in connection with the installation, use, or consumption of goods.
2. Making available other 'specific and substantial' benefits to the public.
3. Counteracting restrictive measures taken by any one person who is not party to the agreement.
4. Permitting the negotiation of fair terms for the purchase or sale of goods with buyers and sellers who represent a preponderant part of the trade.
5. Preventing the occurrence of serious and persistent unemployment in an area.
6. Maintaining the volume of earnings of the export trade in a commodity where this is substantial in relation to the trade of the United Kingdom as a whole or to the total trade in that commodity.
7. Maintaining some other restriction which the Court holds to be justified under one of the other gateways.

Satisfying one of these gateways is a necessary, though not a sufficient, condition for exemption. The 'tailpiece' of the gateways requires that the benefits accruing from the restriction outweigh the costs. It requires that the Court must be satisfied that the restriction is *not unreasonable*, having regard to the balance between the benefits resulting or likely to result and any detriment to the public or persons who are not party to the agreements.

It is, of course, arguable that this legislation has simply caused formal agreements to be replaced with 'informal' agreements.

Resale price maintenance

In 1964 the Resale Prices Act addressed the problem of resale price maintenance. This was not a matter of collusion between several suppliers to restrict competition by charging the same price for their products. It was the practice for some companies to insist that all retail outlets sold their products at prices set by the manufacturer. This meant that very low-cost distributors could not compete with other distributors on the basis of lower prices.

The 1964 Act presumed that this practice was *against the public interest* but allowed manufacturers to appeal to the Restrictive Practices Court on any of five criteria:

1. That abolishing price maintenance would reduce the quality or variety of goods available.
2. That abolition would reduce the number of shops.
3. That abolition would lead to higher prices in the long run.
4. That abolition would create a danger to health.
5. That abolition would interfere with the proper pre-sales or post-sales services.

Again there was a tailpiece. It is necessary to satisfy at least one of these criteria but it is not sufficient. It must still be shown that the benefits of RPM outweigh the social costs.

Case Study 6.2 Wet-shave market probe

The Monopolies and Mergers Commission has been asked to investigate whether a monopoly exists in the market for blades and razors for wet shaving.

In a separate mergers reference by the Secretary of State for Trade and Industry, the Commission was also asked to look into the recent financial arrangements between the US-based company, Gillette, and Swedish Match NV.

Swedish Match has taken over the consumer products business of Stora, which includes the Wilkinson Sword brand. The Office of Fair Trading says Gillette has about 60 per cent of the UK market for wet shaving products, and the combined businesses would have 80 per cent of the market. The reference, however, is unique in that the Gillette involvement in Swedish Match is a minority stake which gives it no voting rights.

But OFT sources maintain the Director General, Sir Gordon Borrie, believes it gives Gillette the ability to materially influence the policies of Swedish Match.

The OFT has also concluded that Gillette and Wilkinson Sword will not have the same incentive to compete as they would if they were at arms length. It feels that the relationship constitutes a merger. However, it says that the MMC may not agree and therefore it has decided that a monopoly reference should also be made.

This refers to the effects of the relationship between the two companies on competition in the UK.

OFT sources said a merger had never previously been found to exist where one company had taken a non-voting stake and become a creditor.

Although the companies involved are not British, Nicholas Ridley, the Trade Secretary, has jurisdiction as long as they remain distinct and continue to do business in the UK.

Depending on the outcome of the MMC's reports, he may take action, including ordering that agreements be unwound and that the business be divided.

Gillette said yesterday that it was 'surprised' at the reference decisions. It pointed out that its 21.9 per cent equity stake involved neither board level representation nor voting rights.

1. To what extent should authorities (in either the UK or the EC) be prepared to set off gains in economies of scale against reduced competition?
2. Does the Gillette–Wilkinson Sword case suggest that companies are likely to collude secretly rather than merge when government competition policy exists?

Source: Mary Fagan, *Independent*, 15 June 1990

Mergers

The original Monopolies and Restrictive Practices 1948 Act was further augmented and modified by the Monopolies and Mergers Act of 1965. The addition of the word 'merger' in the title hints at the Act's significance. Working on the assumption that prevention is better than cure, the Act seeks to prevent the formation of monopolies through mergers. The prevention, of course, operates only if the resulting monopoly is deemed to be against the public interest.

The 1965 Act therefore charges the Monopolies Commission to investigate proposed and completed mergers in which: 1. More than £5m (now £15m) worth of gross assets are involved or 2. When the resultant merged companies would control more than 25 per cent of a UK market. Notice that this is a lower percentage than the one-third required to constitute a monopoly.

Again it is very difficult to assess the impact on the UK economy of these attempts at controlling mergers. Many mergers are abandoned before they get off the ground simply because it is felt that the Commission would not approve of them. Even if approval were more or less certain, there remains the question of how worthwhile it is to embark on such time-consuming argument.

It is known, however, that some 50 major proposed mergers were abandoned between 1965 and 1975 following informal advice from the Commission.

The attempt to avoid the formation of monopolies by way of mergers has therefore had some effect.

Fair trading

The Monopolies and Restrictive Practices Commission was renamed the **Monopolies and Mergers Commission** in 1973. The 1973 Fair Trading Act also brought the criterion for identifying a 'monopolistic merger' in line with that for identifying a monopoly. Both are now required to control 25 per cent of a UK market. This Act also set up the Office of the Director General of Fair Trading in place of the Registration of Restrictive Practices.

Section 84 of the 1973 Fair Trading Act states:

> when considering whether any particular matter operates against the public interest the Commission shall take into account among other things, the desirability of:
>
> (1) maintaining and promoting effective competition between persons supplying goods and services in the UK.
> (2) promoting the interests of consumers, purchasers and other users of goods and services in the UK in respect of prices charged for them and in respect of their quality and the variety of goods and services supplied.
> (3) promoting, through competition, the reduction of costs and the development and use of new techniques and new products and of facilitating the entry of new competitors into existing markets.
> (4) maintaining and promoting the balanced distribution of industry and employment in the UK.
> (5) maintaining and promoting competitive activity in markets outside the UK on the part of producers of goods, and suppliers of goods and services in the UK.

In order to see how these guidelines are applied let us look at one particular case.

The Monopolies and Mergers Commission publishes as a Command Paper its findings on each case referred to it. One such concerns the proposed takeover of A.E. plc by Guest, Keen and Nettlefolds plc. In this case the Commission concluded:

> Accordingly we conclude that the proposed acquisition of A.E. plc by GKN plc may be expected to operate against public interest; the particular effects adverse to the public interest being the loss of competition in the supply of what we have called overlap products, especially in plain bearings and cylinder liners . . . and the likely consequent increase in imports of these products . . . resulting in a loss of added value and employment in the industry in the UK. We are unable to recommend any remedy to remove the public interest detriments which could be expected to arise from this merger and we therefore recommend that it should not be permitted. (Cmnd 9199, HMSO, 1984)

This makes it clear that the Commission was invoking guideline 4, 'promoting the balanced distribution of industry and employment in the UK'.

It also makes clear how detailed the Commission's considerations are. It actually considers quite specific products like cylinder liners and does not deal simply in broad sweeps of general economic policy.

The nationalized industries

All this legislation was aimed at the private sector of the economy, but the Competition Act of 1980 extended the power of the Director General of Fair Trading to cover the nationalized industries too. As we shall see, the nationalized industries are themselves charged with considering the wider social costs and social benefits of what they do. But increasingly the purely commercial criteria have emerged as dominant. In such cases it seems right to bring the nationalized industries under the same control as operates for the private sector.

The EC

Legislation of this kind extends also to the EC. No doubt as harmonization proceeds, the EC guidelines will take over from the UK's own. What is clear is that the EC deems certain business activity to be incompatible with the Treaty of Rome. Specifically, therefore, any agreement which is likely to affect trade between member states and which restricts within the Common Market offends against the EC rules.

SUMMARY

1. Economic theory suggests that monopoly power is likely to act against the public interest by producing less at a higher cost than would a perfectly competitive system.
2. This case is weakened if there are increasing returns to scale or if it can be shown that monopolies are more innovative than small firms.
3. Increasing returns to scale can be used not only

to justify monopolies but also as an explanation as to how they come about and continue in existence.

4. Among other things increasing returns to scale provide a barrier to entry behind which the monopolist shelters from potential competitors.
5. When buyers act in unison, or where there is only one buyer, they too can distort the market in their favour. This is called a monopsony.
6. Legislation in the UK is aimed at preventing and/or controlling monopoly and monopsony power, but figures show an ever-increasing level of concentration in the UK manufacturing industry.
7. This can come about by one company growing, by mergers between existing companies, or by takeovers.
8. The 1973 Fair Trading Act regards a company with 25 per cent of the UK market as having monopoly power, and set up the Office of the Director General of Fair Trading to investigate whether particular cases operate against the public interest.
9. The Director General then makes recommendations to the appropriate minister.
10. The 1980 Competition Act brought the nationalized industries under the same scrutiny.
11. The EC will extend these attempts at maintaining competition throughout the EC.

The nationalized industries

The nationalized industries are corporations which are owned by the state – they are public corporations. Public corporations include not only the nationalized industries, but also the Bank of England, the British Broadcasting Corporation, the National Film Finance Corporation and the National Enterprise Board.

In 1979 the nationalized industries accounted for about 9.5 per cent of GDP and 11.5 per cent of investment. Privatization has reduced the size of the state-owned sector, but in 1989 nationalized industries still accounted for 5 per cent of GDP and 6 per cent of investment, and employed 750,000 people. By any standard public corporations constitute an important part of our economy.

Public corporations should not be confused with public companies. Public companies are in fact privately owned and are public only in the sense that their shares are quoted on the Stock Exchange.

Nor should public corporations be confused with other government departments such as the Department of Social Security or the Department of Education and Science. Departments such as these are part of the public sector and they do produce and distribute goods and services. They are not, however, public corporations since they do not *market* their goods and services. Health is provided (almost) free on the basis of need and education is actually compulsory for those between the ages of five and sixteen years.

Nationalized industries are therefore publicly owned

Table 6.4 The nationalized industries

Industry	Group
Central Electricity Generating Board British Coal British National Oil Corporation	Fuel and power
Post Office	Communications
British Rail National Bus Company Scottish Transport Group British Transport Docks Board British Waterways Board	Transport
British Steel Corporation British Shipbuilders British Aerospace	Manufacturing

corporations which produce goods and services and sell them on the open market.

The actual number of nationalized industries changes from time to time as some industries are returned to private ownership and as some erstwhile private corporations are taken into public ownership. Table 6.4 shows twelve industries which are, or have been, nationalized. They are divided into four groups: fuel and power, communications, transport and manufacturing. Nationalization of the first three of these is sometimes explained in terms of their being 'strategic' industries. That is to say, they are industries which would be essential to the supply and deployment of the armed forces in time of war. Whatever the merits of this 'strategic' view, it does not lead inevitably to the conclusion that these sectors should be nationalized. Indeed since 1979 many industries have been passed from public to private ownership (privatized), these are shown in Table 6.5.

Natural monopolies

A somewhat stronger case for nationalization can be made on the grounds that some of the industries listed are **natural monopolies**.

Natural monopolies occur when the existence of competitors leads to a massive waste of resources. For example, the distribution of gas and electricity, and the railways both have monopolistic power simply because it would be prohibitively inefficient to have more than one of each operating in the same area. To run several gas mains and electricity mains to each consumer or to provide several railways between two towns would be wasteful duplication leading to a reduced level of efficiency. In such cases, where the most efficient solution involves a high level of monopoly power, it is customary to exercise fairly rigid control over the monopolist and one way of doing this is to nationalize the enterprise. This is the solution that has been used in the UK, but in many countries such enterprises remain in private ownership and operate under close regulation. This is true even for those **public utilities** which provide 'essential' services such as gas, electricity and water. When in private ownership they are legally required to moderate normal commercial practice by taking account of wider issues.

Nationalized industries that have been privatized in recent years have conditions written into their articles. For example, British Telecom has an enforced pricing policy.

Table 6.5 UK privatization, 1979–91

Year	Company	Business	Proceeds (£m)
1979	British Petroleum (1st part)[1]	Oil	276
	ICL[1]	Computers	37
1980	Fairey	Construction	22
	Ferranti[1,2]	Hi-tech industrial	55
	Motorway service stations (Dept of Transport)[2]	Motorway services	28
1981	British Aerospace (1st part)	Aerospace	43
	British Petroleum (2nd part)	Oil	200
	British Sugar Corporation[1]	Sugar refining	44
	Cable and Wireless (1st part)	Telecommunications systems	182
1982	Amersham International	Radio-chemicals	64
	National Freight Corporation[3]	Road haulage	7
	Britoil (1st part)	Oil	627
1983	Associated British Ports (1st part)[1,2]	Seaports	–34
	International Aeradio[2]	Aviation communications	60
	British Rail Hotels[2]	Hotels	51
	British Petroleum (3rd part)[1]	Oil	543
	Cable and Wireless (2nd part)	Telecommunications systems	263
1984	British Gas (onshore)[2]	Oil	82
	Associated British Ports (2nd part)[1,2]	Seaports	48
	Enterprise Oil	Oil	380
	Sealink[2]	Ferries	66
	Jaguar	Cars	297
	British Telecom (govt. retains 49.8% of shares)	Telecommunications	3,916
	Inmos[2]	Computer systems	95
1985	British Aerospace (2nd part)	Aerospace	350
	British Shipbuilders (1st part)[2,3]	Various shipyards	220
	Britoil (2nd part)	Oil	449
	Cable and Wireless (3rd part)	Telecommunications systems	900
1986	British Shipbuilders (2nd part)[3]	Various shipyards	67
	Royal Ordnance (1st part)[2]	Weapons manufacture	11
	National Bus Company	Bus and coach carriers	260
	BA Helicopters[2]	Helicopter carriers	135
	British Gas	Gas	5,600
1987	Unipart[3]	Car parts	30
	Leyland Bus[3]	Bus manufacture	4
	British Airways	Airline	900
	Royal Ordnance (2nd part)[2]	Weapons manufacture	190
	British Rail Doncaster Wagon Works[3]	Rolling stock manufacture	7
	Rolls-Royce	Aero engines	1,100
	British Airports Authority (BAA)	Airports	600
	British Petroleum (4th part)[1]	Oil	7,200
1988	British Steel	Steel	2,400
	Rover Group (sold to British Aerospace)[2]	Car manufacture	–435
1989	Water companies (10)	Water supply and sewage treatment	5,240
1990	Electricity distributors (12)	Area supply of electricity	
1991	National Power, PowerGen	Electricity generation	

Notes: 1. In these cases the companies were only partly government owned in the first place.
2. These were private sales to other companies.
3. These were management and/or worker buyouts.

Source: J. Sloman, *Economics*, Harvester Wheatsheaf, 1991.

Non-commercial considerations

The idea that, by satisfying the normal commercial criteria for success, a corporation may be going against some wider interest is a theme running through the justification for nationalization.

British National Oil Corporation (BNOC) is a case in point. Formed in 1976, it was originally given the task of exploration, production and distribution of oil, before exploration and production were transferred to Britoil in 1982. The chairman of BNOC said, 'The Corporation's objectives in its new role continue to be commercially and profit orientated within broad national interest considerations'. However, these broader considerations are not specified.

The same is true of a much older industry – the railways. For the first 100 years they were in private hands, strictly regulated and not very profitable. They were taken into public ownership in 1948 in a very run-down condition from which private capital could not redeem them. Even after modernization some lines are still 'uneconomic', by which we mean that on the usual commercial criteria they would be closed.

However, the Minister of Transport may decide on *broad social and economic grounds* that certain unprofitable services should continue. In this case the minister and the Railways Board agree a cost and the loss is made up in the accounts of BR so that the company does appear to be acting commercially. These *public service obligation payments* currently stand at about £1,300 million per year. The cost of overriding purely commercial considerations is therefore appreciable. But again, quite what is meant by 'broad social and economic grounds' is unclear.

Protecting jobs

There can be little doubt that for some industries 'the broad social grounds' for nationalization are largely to do with maintaining employment.

British Steel, for example, was first nationalized in 1951 by the Labour Party, denationalized in 1953 by the Conservatives, renationalized in 1967 by Labour and finally privatized by Mrs Thatcher's Conservative government. Even after large cutbacks in employment and output, British Steel lost £869m in 1982/3. The government, however, continued to provide financial support, since the loss of the industry and its 81,000 jobs were considered politically and socially unacceptable.

Government sensitivity to the employment consequences of the failure of 'commercially' run corporations was starkly illustrated by the public takeover of BL and Rolls Royce Aero Engines Ltd. This was done through the National Enterprise Board (itself a public corporation), which subsequently 'sold' the two companies to the Department of Industry. These two firms were taken into public ownership (although they were not actually called nationalized industries) in order to save the jobs they provided.

In 1974 the government announced that 'because of [BL's] position in the economy as a leading exporter and its importance to employment' it would receive financial support.

Nationalization therefore enables some social control to be exercised over the *rate* of decline of declining industries. By offering these industries some protection from competitive commercial forces the government can slow down the rate of decline. This eases the problems of adjustment, particularly the reallocation of the labour force.

The government has therefore to strike a balance between the social cost of unemployment and the financial costs of maintaining uneconomic industries.

If the maintenance of uneconomic industries were the only reason for nationalization, however, the nationalized industries would all be loss-making and declining. This was certainly not the intention of those who supported the nationalization of industries. According to Labour politician Tony Crosland:

> Nationalization was to encourage expansion where risks were too high for private producers; where monopolies existed and where industry requires structural change. Such firms were to act as highly competitive price leaders and pace setters, provide a yardstick for efficiency, support government investment plans and, above all, produce a better product or service.

Job generation

This view, that the public sector should give a lead to the private sector, is reflected in the work of the National Enterprise Board. This public corporation was set up in 1975 with the aims of *promoting industrial efficiency and worker participation*. Little has been done about worker participation, but efficiency was promoted by investment in new high-technology areas such as information technology. Once again the Board took a rather wider view of what constitutes a good investment than is implied by commercial viability. The NEB is now combined with the National Research and Development Corporation under the joint title of British Technology Group (BTG). In his 1983 BTG chairman's address Sir Frederick Wood claimed:

> My colleagues and I firmly believe that the justification for a state-backed body to be involved in supporting the development and growth of high-technology ventures lies in the very fact that its activities as a whole may not necessarily be a success in purely commercial terms.

Once again we have a rather vague appeal to something beyond the commercial criteria of success. Employment is again a consideration since, although the activity is not aimed at perpetuating an existing (possibly declining) industry, it is aimed at starting up new industries which will provide the jobs of the future. It is therefore employment generation rather than employment protection which is the hallmark of this public-sector activity.

Private versus social cost

The promotion of employment prospects by state intervention in the economy does make economic sense. For the private firm the level of unemployment is not a consideration when making investment or output decisions on commercial grounds. The costs of supporting the unemployed does not fall directly on the private sector. But for the government the level of unemployment constitutes a drain on the public purse. The cost to the private sector of closing a plant is therefore less than the cost imposed on the public sector – *private and social costs diverge*. Getting people into employment is a major aim of government economic policy and it may pay the government to keep a firm producing beyond the point where private commercial criteria would have closed it down.

Cost–benefit analysis

The most widely known attempt at making this concept of 'the wider public interest' operational, particularly for major investment projects, is a branch of applied economics called **cost–benefit analysis**. This is an effort by economists to identify and quantify the social costs and social benefits of various investment projects in order to rank them or to decide whether to pursue them or not. A fuller account of cost – benefit analysis is provided in Chapter 7.

Exercising public control

Even without the problems of assessing 'the wider public

interest', there remains the problem of specifying the commercial guidelines for the various nationalized industry boards. These guidelines fall into four broad categories:

1. Pricing decisions.
2. Investment decisions.
3. Measuring efficiency.
4. Controlling external finance.

We will consider each of these in turn.

Pricing decisions

The pricing decisions of nationalized industries are complicated by the fact that in almost every case they have monopoly power. We saw earlier that monopolistic industries produce less output at higher prices than do competitive industries. Figure 6.25 will serve as a reminder here.

MC is the marginal cost curve for the industry and *MR* is the marginal revenue associated with the market demand curve *AR*. Were the market to be made up of a large number of perfectly competitive sellers then the *MC* curve would be the supply curve and the *AR* curve would be the demand curve. Thus the market would settle down at quantity q_c and price P_c. If, however, the industry is monopolistic, the *MC* curve is not the firm's supply curve. The sole supplier will equate *MC* to *MR* and produce q_m units of output at price P_m.

If the nationalized industries pursued the usual commercial criteria they would therefore be producing too little at too high a price. It would seem reasonable in these circumstances for the government to instruct the nationalized industries to ignore 'narrow commercial interest' and behave as if they were perfectly competitive. The shorthand way of doing this is to tell them to equate price to marginal cost. The only point at which price equals *MC* and supply equals demand is at P_c, q_c – the perfect competitive outcome. This is so-called **marginal cost pricing rule** for public corporations. The rule has been applied not only to nationalized industries but also to public utilities in private ownership.

The marginal cost pricing rule is remarkably simple and provides a good example of how economic theory can be applied to a pratical economic problem. There are, however, two exceptions.

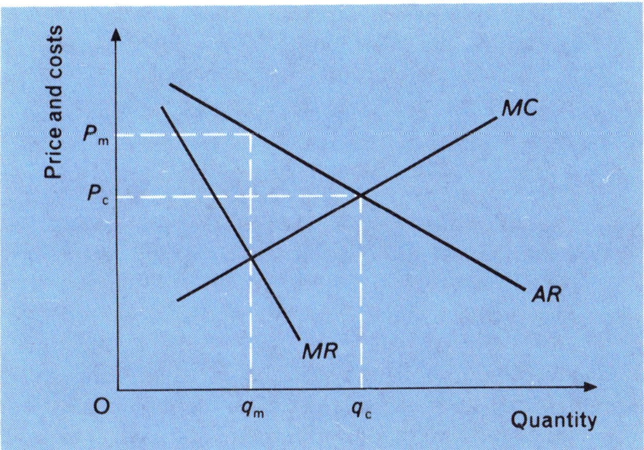

Figure 6.25 Equilibrium under perfect competition and monopoly.

1. *The theory of the second best.* The marginal cost pricing rule is based on the argument that perfect competition gives rise to a more efficient allocation of resources than does monopoly. This argument, however, is not as straightforward as it seems. It has been shown that if some industries remain monopolistic then forcing the nationalized industries to follow competitive rules may not improve the efficiency of resources allocation. In a first best world (i.e. where there are no remaining pockets of monopoly), the marginal cost pricing rule will give rise to an efficient allocation of resources. But in a second best world (i.e. one in which some monopoly remains), imposing marginal cost pricing elsewhere is not unambiguously a good thing.

This second best problem arises because the various sectors of the economy are all mutually interdependent. The behaviour of one sector influences the price faced by other sectors. It will influence labour costs and raw material costs as well as the prices of goods which flow from one sector to another. In this kind of world, one sector's monopolistic behaviour will therefore be transmitted throughout the economy to other sectors.

The theory of the second best argues that these distortions may best be counteracted by everywhere departing from perfectly competitive decision rules.

It no longer therefore follows that we should impose marginal cost pricing rules on nationalized industries, unless of course we consider that the rest of the economy is perfectly competitive. If we are not prepared to make this assumption then we lose this very simple pricing rule.

2. *Profitability.* The second problem with marginal cost pricing is that it may not lead to a profit. In Figure 6.25 there is no average cost curve and so we do not know whether average costs exceed average revenues or not. All we know about the average cost curve is that it will be at a minimum where it crosses the marginal cost curve. We cannot therefore infer from the *MC* curve anything about the position of the average cost curve.

The marginal cost pricing rule may yield positive, zero or negative profits. Under normal circumstances these profit levels would signal to the industry whether it should be growing, contracting or remaining the same size.

When profits are above normal the industry expands and moves the supply curve to the right. This reduces prices and restores normal profits. When profits are below normal the industry contracts and moves the supply curve to the left. This increases prices and again restores normal profits.

The question for the nationalized industries is what constitutes 'normal' profits.

Investment decisions

The government issues guidelines for the various industries. These guidelines are in terms of the rate of return expected on capital invested and tend to reflect what the industry has earned in the past. Coal and railways are asked to try to break even, i.e. they are not required to make profit, but must avoid making a loss. The Post Office aims at 3.25 per cent. Thus for existing industries the rates of return are targets rather than investment criteria.

For new industries or new investments the criteria used by the National Enterprise Board, for example, were: (a) the Financial Times Share Index; (b) the cost of government borrowing. By aiming at a rate of return which exceeds the cost of government borrowing, the government ensures some profit and the comparison with the performance of the private sector ensures that the first criterion is a realistic one in terms of general economic performance. It would be somewhat hard on the nationalized industries if they were required to do better than the firms quoted on the Stock Exchange.

Measuring efficiency

Whether these rates of return are used as targets for existing investments or as criteria for new investment, they make sense only in the presence of a sensible pricing policy. Clearly, an industry which has a great deal of monopoly power (as in the case of the Post Office) can set its prices at whatever level is necessary to meet its target rate of return. In 1983 the chairman of British Telecom reported that 'our tariff policy was of course geared to meet the financial targets set by the government'. Meeting a target rate of return by exploiting monopoly power is to remove that target's usefulness as an indicator of efficiency.

Because of this difficulty most nationalized industries provide information on their real performance: output per man-shift; changes in prices compared with the retail price index; utilization rates, etc. Some of these are suitable criteria for judging efficiency either in terms of the industry's own track record (e.g. improvements in output per man-shift) or by comparison with the performance of other sectors (e.g. the retail prices index). Information of this kind is useful for external checks on efficiency by the Monopolies and Mergers Commission.

Controlling external financing

The fourth and final kind of guideline concerns a nationalized industry's ability to raise external finance. Although the 'equity' in nationalized industries is owned by the public sector, there is nothing to prevent them from raising private loan capital. This loan capital is called external financing and it is under the control of the boards of the nationalized industries.

Those who lend money to such industries are likely to feel that their capital is safe since, to all intents and purposes, it has been lent to the government. They are likely to believe that the government would not let nationalized industries go into bankruptcy.

In order to control this liability the government imposes external financing limits (EFLs). Each industry is given an upper limit to the amount it can raise as loans. The total (over all nationalized industries) in 1981/2 was about £2.25 billion, most of which went to the National Coal Board (£886m), the British Steel Corporation (£730m) and British Rail (£920m). Some sectors (e.g. British Gas until privatized in 1986) have negative EFLs, which means that they are actually paying money into the government rather than borrowing under its aegis.

Doubts have been expressed about the rigidity of EFLs. In many instances they have been exceeded, only for them then to be revised upwards at no penalty to the offender. EFLs then, like so much else in the public sector, are targets rather than constraints.

In order to impose strict limits it would be necessary to have some sanctions. But if the activation of the sanctions brings about the socially harmful failures of large employers then the sanctions cannot be activated and the discipline cannot be imposed.

SUMMARY

1. Nationalized industries are public corporations which sell their products on the open market.
2. The number of nationalized industries is ever changing as some are 'privatized' and sold back to the public.
3. The reasons for nationalization are many and varied. They derive from strategic arguments, natural monopolies and political ideology.
4. Since these industries are controlled by the state, rather than by profit-maximizing entrepreneurs, we need some guidelines to determine pricing, production, investment and employment.
5. These guidelines are couched in only the most general terms but seem to hint at a more social role for these industries than for those in the private sector.
6. The most significant aspect in their deliberations seems to be the effect of their actions on employment. Governments are reluctant to apply 'commercial' criteria to these industries if closure means a massive loss of jobs.
7. This can be justified in that the costs of unemployment fall on the government, which has to provide unemployment benefit, and not on the private-sector employer. Thus the government may continue to finance a 'commercially' unviable industry simply because it is cheaper to subsidize employment than to pay benefit.
8. The monopoly position of many nationalized industries is moderated by the suggestion that they follow the marginal cost pricing rule. This ensures that they produce at lowest average costs.
9. In order to guide investment decisions the government decrees that certain rates of return should be earned on new capital projects. For existing industries this is based on their past performance. For new industries the Financial Times Share Index and the cost of government borrowing are used.
10. Investment funds may also be attracted from external sources and the government places fixed limits on these. They are called external financing limits (EFLs) and in 1980/81 totalled £2.25 billion.

Exam Preparation and Practice

MULTIPLE-CHOICE QUESTIONS

1.

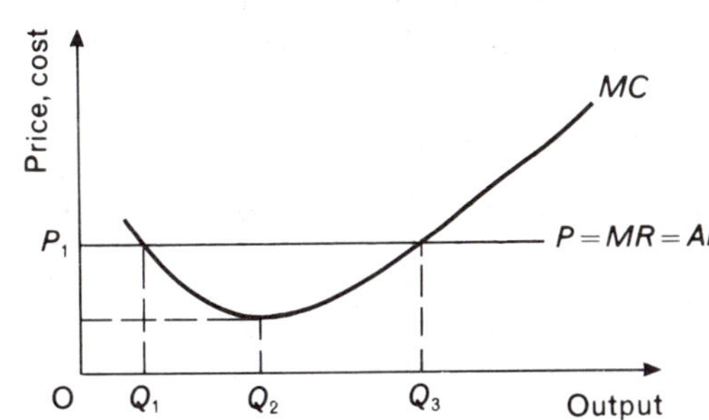

The diagram represents the cost and revenue curves for a profit-maximizing firm in a perfectly competitive industry. The firm will:

A Produce OQ_3 units.
B Produce OQ_2 units.
C Produce OQ_1 units.
D Leave the industry.

2. Which of the following does *not* occur under conditions of perfect competition?
A Many firms participate in the industry.
B No firm can influence the behaviour of others.
C All firms produce the same product.
D Barriers to entry exist for new firms.

3.

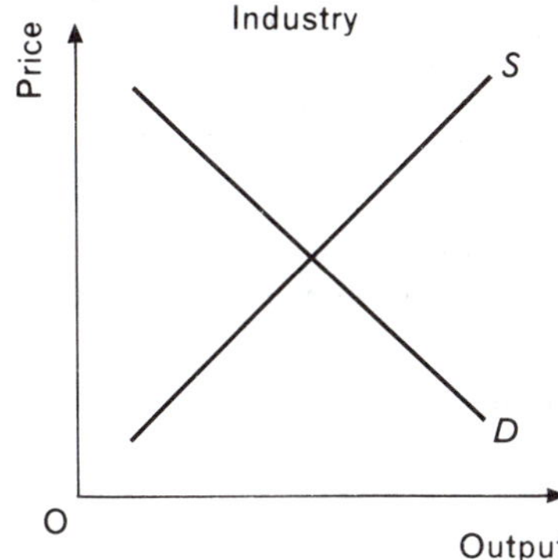

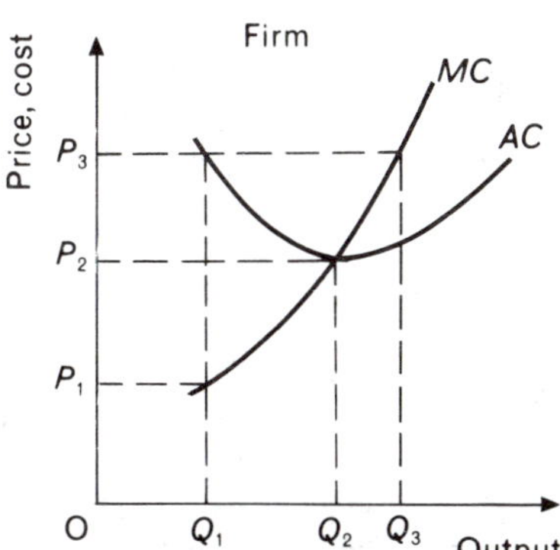

The diagram shows the market demand and supply curves for a perfectly competitive industry and the cost curves for a single firm in that industry. Which combination of price and output will the profit-maximizing firm choose?

A OP_1, OQ_1 **C** OP_2, OQ_2
B OP_3, OQ_1 **D** OP_3, OQ_3

4. Which of the following statements is **not** true of a profit-maximizing monopolist?
A It produces where marginal revenue = marginal cost.
B It produces where marginal cost = price.
C It can choose the price or output it produces at, but not both.
D It does not face competition from firms with similar products.

5.

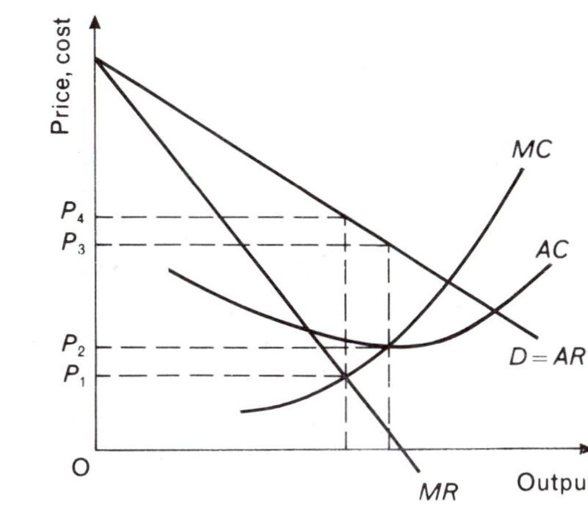

The diagram shows the cost and revenue curves for a profit-maximizing monopolist. Which price would the firm charge?

A OP_1
B OP_2
C OP_3
D OP_4

6. Which of the following statements most accurately describes a situation of monopolistic competition?
A There are many buyers and few sellers with no barriers to entry.
B There are many buyers and many sellers with no barriers to entry.
C There are many buyers and many sellers with barriers to entry.
D There are many buyers and one seller with no barriers to entry.

7. The diagram represents a firm operating under conditions of stable oligopoly. The equilibrium output is OQ.

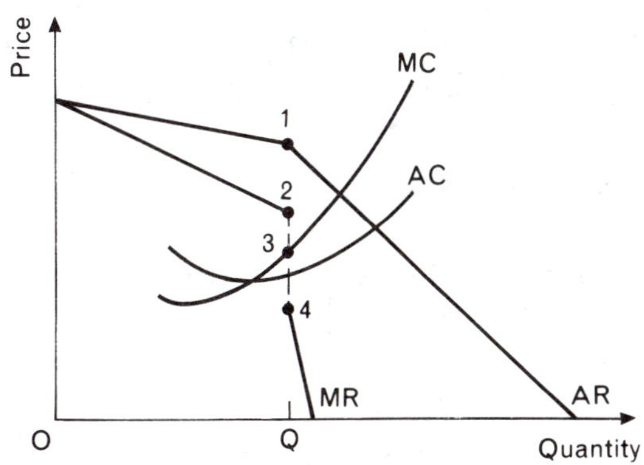

The equilibrium output will remain at OQ, as long as the marginal cost at OQ lies between points

A 1 and 3 **C** 2 and 3
B 1 and 4 **D** 2 and 4

(AEB)

8. A firm may charge different prices to consumers when:
   A Different consumers gain different amounts of utility from a product.
   B The costs of supplying each consumer is different.
   C The consumers are divided into quite unconnected markets.
   D Consumers are free to choose between the products of different firms.

9.

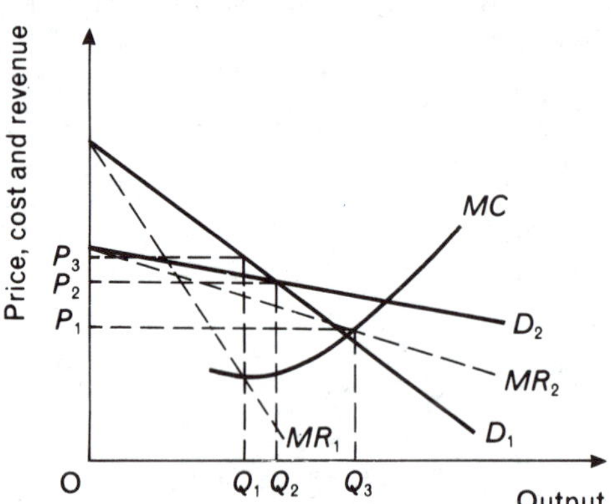

The diagram shows the demand curves facing a discriminating monopolist. D_1 and MR_1 represents the demand and marginal revenue curves for market 1; D_2 and MR_2 for market 2. The firm will:
   A Sell OQ_2 units at price OP_2 in each market.
   B Sell OQ_1 units at price OP_3 in market 1 only.
   C Sell OQ_1 units at price OP_3 in market 1 and OQ_3 units at OP_1 in market 2.
   D Sell OQ_1 units at price OP_3 in both markets.

Answer key

Where there are three numbered alternatives

A	B	C	D	E
1, 2, 3 Correct	1, 2 Correct	2, 3 Correct	1 Correct	3 Correct

Where there are four numbered alternatives

A	B	C	D	E
1, 2 and 3 Correct	1 and 3 Correct	2 and 4 Correct	4 only Correct	1 and 4 Correct

10. A profit-maximizing firm under conditions of perfect competition will:
   1 Equate marginal cost to marginal revenue.
   2 Earn normal profit in equilibrium.
   3 Face a horizontal demand curve.

11. An oligopolist facing a kinked demand curve is likely to:
   1 Prefer non-price competition.
   2 Expect demand in response to price increases to be elastic.
   3 Expect demand in response to price decreases to be inelastic.

(LON.)

12. Which of the following earn normal profit in the long-run?
   1 Discriminating monopolists.
   2 Perfectly competitive firms.
   3 Oligopolists.
   4 Firms in monopolistic competition.

13. Which of the following is/are examples of vertical integration?
   1 A brewer taking over a chain of public houses.
   2 Marks and Spencers taking over a clothing retailer.
   3 Two firms of accountants merging.
   4 A baker buying a farm that grows wheat.

14. The purpose of the Monopolies and Mergers Commission is to:
   1 Regulate nationalized industries.
   2 Prevent the creation of harmful monopolies.
   3 Supervise newly privatized industries.
   4 Scrutinize proposed mergers.

EXERCISES

1. From the following cost and revenue schedules draw the total cost, total revenue and profit curves for the firm.

Output	Total costs (£)	Total revenue (£)	Profit
10	70	50	
20	100	100	
30	130	150	
40	160	200	
50	200	250	
60	245	300	
70	300	350	
80	370	400	
90	460	450	
100	560	500	

   (a) At what range of output is profit maximized?
   (b) At what range does the firm begin to experience diminishing returns?
   (c) Construct marginal revenue and marginal cost curves from the table and confirm your answer to (a).

2. (a) Show that, for a profit maximum, marginal cost must equal marginal revenue.
   (b) A firm faces the following cost and revenue functions:
   Total revenue $= 100Q - Q^2$
   Total cost $= 5 - 12Q + Q^2$
   where $Q =$ output.
   What is the profit-maximizing output?
   (NB Only A-level mathematicians should attempt part (b).)

3. Why does a perfectly competitive firm face a horizontal (perfectly elastic) demand curve when the industry faces a downward-sloping demand curve?

4. The diagram depicts a firm's cost and revenue curves under perfect competition.

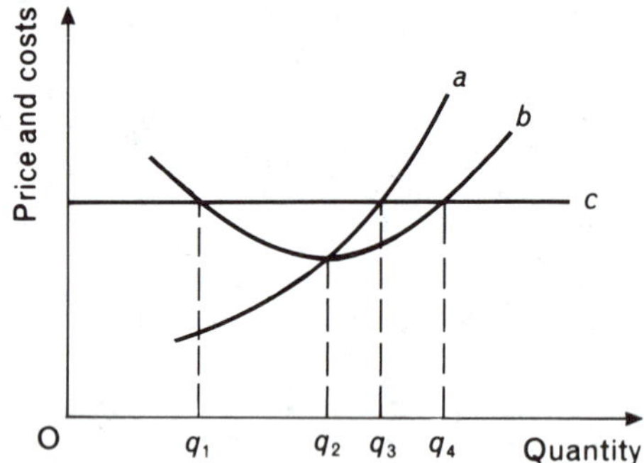

   (a) What are the curves labelled *a*, *b* and *c*?
   (b) If the situation shown is an equilibrium:
      (i) How much is produced?
      (ii) Mark on the diagram any area of excess profit.
      (iii) Would you expect this equilibrium to last for long? Explain your answer.

5. The diagram shows a firm in a perfectly competitive industry and the industry demand and supply curves.

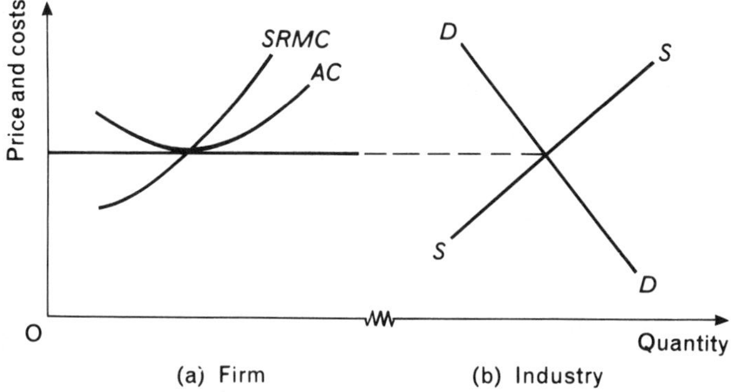

(a) When the industry demand curve is *DD* and the industry supply curve is *SS*:
   (i) Will firms want to enter or leave the market?
   (ii) What is the level of profit earned by the firm?
(b) (i) By drawing a new demand curve, show that the firm will earn excess profits if the market demand increases.
   (ii) How will firms react to this change in demand in the short run? Mark on the diagram how much profit they earn.
   (iii) Show on the diagram how supply will react in the long run.
(c) Draw a possible average variable cost curve for the firm and show the price level at which the firm will shut down. Draw a new industry demand curve to represent this price using either supply curve you have drawn.

6. A monopolist faces the following demand, revenue and cost curves.

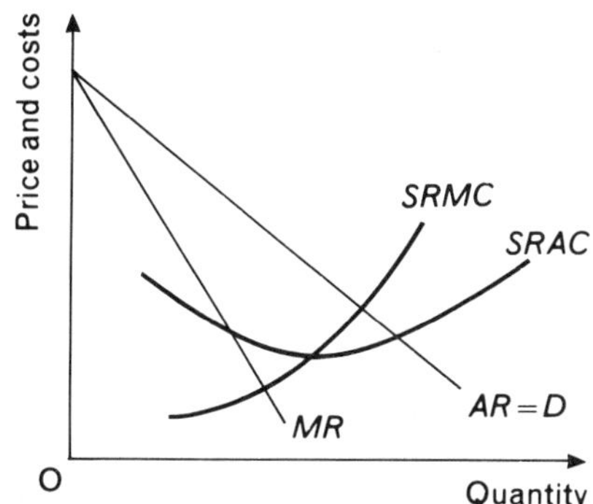

On the diagram mark the following:
(a) The profit-maximizing level of output.
(b) The price associated with this level of output.
(c) The area of the diagram that marks the monopolist's profit.

7. Which of the following features do monopolists and perfectly competitive firms share?
(a) They aim to maximize profit.
(b) Profit is maximized where marginal cost = marginal revenue.
(c) Price equals marginal cost in the long run.
(d) In the long run average cost is minimized.
(e) Excess profits can be earned in the short run.
(f) Excess profits are earned in the long run.

8. An industry's cost and revenue curves can be drawn as shown in the following diagram.

(a) If the industry is perfectly competitive, what is:
   (i) the market price;
   (ii) the industry output?
(b) If the industry is run by a monopolist, what is:
   (i) the market price;
   (ii) the industry output?

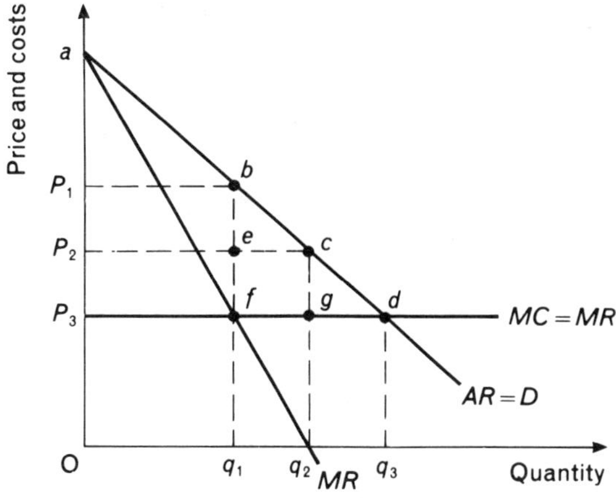

(c) From your answer to (b)(i) is this the price you would expect a firm to charge if it feared long-term entry by other firms?

9. Which of the following features do firms operating in monopolistic competition and firms in perfect competition share?
(a) Firms aim to maximize profit.
(b) Profit is maximized where marginal cost equals marginal revenue.
(c) Price equals marginal cost.
(d) The firm operates at capacity output in long-run equilibrium.
(e) Excess profits can be earned in the short run.
(f) Long-run profits are normal.
(g) All firms offer homogeneous products.
(h) There is free entry and exit into the industry.

10. The following diagram depicts a firm operating under conditions of monopolistic competition.

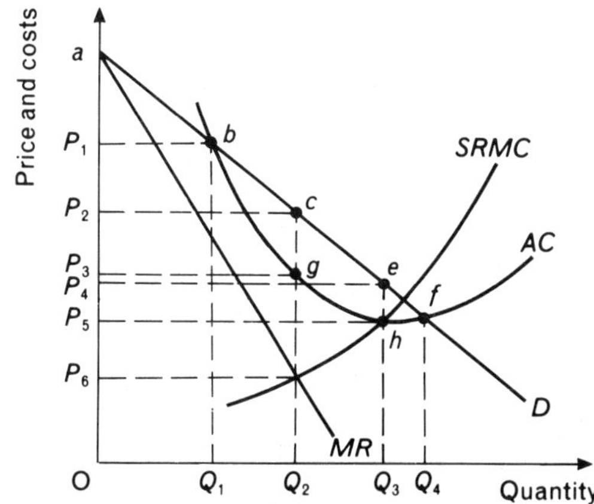

(a) What is the firm's profit-maximizing price and output?
(b) What area of the diagram represents excess profit?
(c) If the firm is earning excess profits, what is the likely behaviour of:
   (i) firms within the industry;
   (ii) firms outside the industry?
(d) What will be the effect of (i) and (ii) on the firm's demand curve?

11. Which of the following are features of an oligopoly market?
(a) Many small firms.
(b) Differentiated products.
(c) One firm's actions influence other firms in the industry.
(d) The industry is dominated by the actions of a few firms.
(e) Firms engage in advertising.

12. Which of the following features do oligopolists (who face a kinked demand curve) share with perfectly competitive firms?

(a) Firms aim to maximize profit.
(b) Profit is maximized where marginal cost equals marginal revenue.
(c) Price equals marginal cost.
(d) The firms operate at capacity output.
(e) Profits are normal in the long run.
(f) The products of each firm are differentiated.
(g) There is free entry and exit to the industry.

13. The following diagram depicts a firm operating in an oligopoly market.

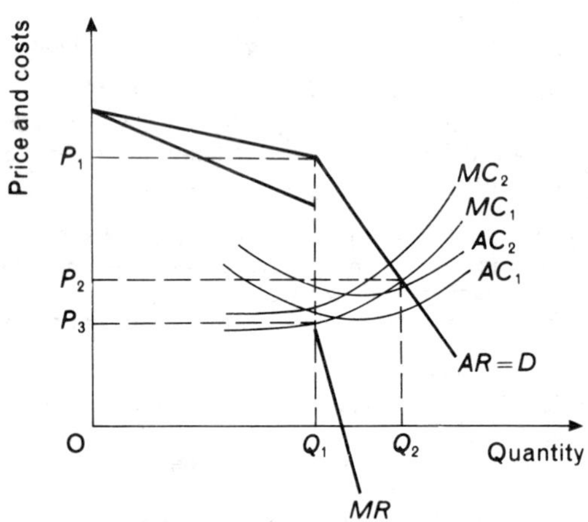

(a) What is the profit-maximizing output and price for the oligopolist when the ruling cost curves are MC_1 and AC_1?
(b) If costs rise to MC_2 and AC_2, what effect does this have on the price charged by the firm and the quantity of output produced?

14. The following diagram depicts the demand, cost, revenue and profit functions for an industry with constant costs.

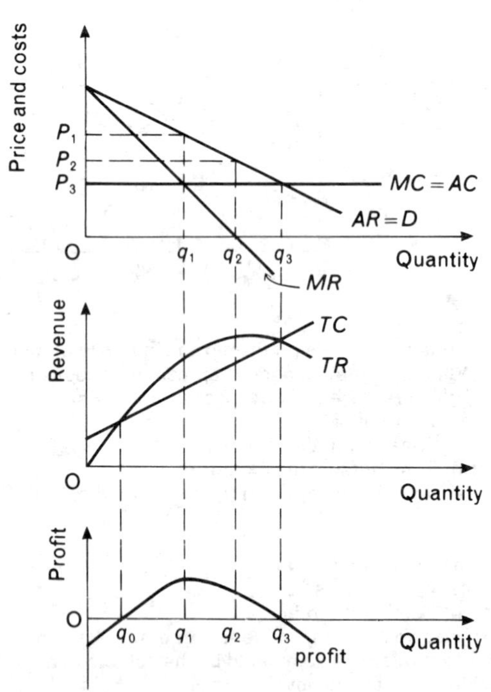

(a) What price would a profit-maximizing firm operating under monopoly conditions charge and how much would the industry produce?
(b) How much would a revenue-maximizing monopolist charge and how much would the industry produce?
(c) How much would a perfectly competitive firm charge and how much would the industry produce?

DATA-RESPONSE QUESTIONS

1. A monopolist has separated its customers into two markets, A and B. The prices and quantities in these two markets are as follows:

MARKET A		MARKET B	
Price (£)	Quantity	Price (£)	Quantity
10	10	5	10
9	20	4.50	20
8	30	4	30
7	40	3.50	40
6	50	3	50
5	60	2.50	60
4	70	2	70
3	80	1.50	80
2	90	1	90
1	100	0.50	100

(a) What conditions are necessary for the monopolist to be able to separate the two markets in this case? **(2 marks)**

(b) (i) On the graph paper provided plot the monopolist's demand and marginal revenue curves in markets A and B. **(4 marks)**

(ii) Assuming that the marginal cost of production is constant at £1.90, what quantity will the monopolist sell in each market if it is a profit maximizer? **(2 marks)**

(iii) What price will the monopolist charge in each market? **(2 marks)**

(c) Comment on the relationship between the price elasticity of demand and marginal revenue in market B. **(4 marks)**

(d) Assume that the monopolist now cuts its price in market A by £0.50. What is the price elasticity of demand at the new price charged? **(3 marks)**

(e) Assume that the monopolist now faces an increase in the rates payable on its premises. How will the profit maximizing monopolist adjust the prices charged in each market? **(3 marks)**

(LON.)

2. Read the passage below and then answer the questions which follow.

An important part of the case for big business rests on the claim that across a wide range of industries modern technology requires plants of a very large absolute size and this means that they can supply a relatively large fraction of the domestic market. Anything less would mean that unit production costs are higher than they need be and are therefore certainly above those of foreign competitors.

But an efficient allocation of a given set of resources is one which yields both a maximum and 'correct' (in the sense of best meeting consumers demands) output. The central result from monopoly theory is that resource allocation will be distorted by the ability of monopolists to restrict output below a level that would best accord with consumer demand (that is price would be greater than marginal cost). Hence from a given bundle of resources economic welfare is likely to be lower in the presence of monopoly. To the extent, therefore, that large size is correlated with monopoly (itself a subject of some dispute) allocative inefficiency will result.

However, this may still strike an uncommitted bystander as not getting to the heart of the matter. Increasingly high on the list of problems associated with very large firms is their alleged effect on the environment. What is the point of these firms ensuring, for example, that they are both technically and economically efficient in a *private* sense if, in their achievement, they are simultaneously generating very high social costs which do not enter their accounts but which nevertheless impose enormous burdens on the community?

Michael Utton, *The Political Economy of Big Business*, Blackwell

(a) Explain in your own words the economic argument lying behind the first paragraph. **[5]**

(b) Why, under monopoly, is price normally greater than marginal cost? **[6]**

(c) Why might the correlation of large size with monopoly be 'a subject of some dispute' (line 20)? **[7]**

(d) Discuss the implications for the community of large firms 'generating very high social costs which do not enter their accounts' (lines 29–30). **[7]**

(OXFORD LOCAL)

3. **The Nationalised Industries**

In 1979, the nationalised industries accounted for about 9 per cent of GDP and 11.5 per cent of investment. They employed over 1.7 million people. Since then, the privatisation programme has substantially reduced the state-owned sector of industry. Nonetheless, those industries still in public ownership remain a major presence in the economy, accounting for 5 per cent of GDP and 6 per cent of investment, and employing just over 750,000 people. The industries' performance is thus of considerable importance for the country as a whole.

The following tables show the changes in productivity (output per person employed) and the operating profits of those industries which were in the public sector at the 31st March 1989.

Table 1 Nationalised industries' productivity

	Annual percentage changes		
	Nationalised industries	All manufacturing industries	Whole economy
1978–79	3.5	1.8	1.8
1979–80	0.9	0.9	0.8
1980–81	−1.8	−5.3	−3.7
1981–82	2.2	6.8	3.5
1982–83	2.4	6.3	4.0
1983–84	4.7	8.6	3.9
1984–85	5.5	4.7	1.2
1985–86	8.1	1.8	2.8
1986–87	8.3	4.7	3.6
1987–88	6.8	7.5	4.4

Table 2 The current cost operating profit of the nationalised industries

	£ million
1983–84	− 183
1984–85	−4030*
1985–86	444
1986–87	318
1987–88	243
1988–89 (estimate)	1837

* Note: this figure was affected by the miners' strike

The financial controls on the nationalised industries have been built on the arrangements which were set out in the 1978 White Paper "The Nationalised Industries". The control framework operates at a number of levels:

- **Strategic objectives** are agreed with each individual industry.
- **Financial targets and performance aims.** Financial targets, usually set for three year periods, are the primary control on the industries.
- **External financing limits (EFL's)** were introduced in 1976 as a short term control on the amount of finance, whether grant or borrowing, which an industry may raise during the financial year to supplement the income from its trading activities.
- **Investment appraisal and pricing principles.** Most nationalised industries are required to aim at a rate of return on their new investment programmes of 5% in real terms. This is intended to ensure a proper return on investment in the industries and, at the same time, that the industries do not divert resources away from areas where they could be used more effectively. It is set taking into account the pre-tax rates of return achieved by private companies.
- **Monitoring** plays an important part in stimulating and controlling the industries' performance in the interests of the taxpayer and consumer.

Source: *The Government's Expenditure Plans* 1989–90 to 1991–92

(a) (i) What conclusions, if any, is it possible to derive from the productivity figures in Table 1 about the performance of the nationalised industries between 1978–79 and 1987–88? *(5 marks)*

(ii) Do the figures in Table 2, showing the operating profit of the nationalised industries, provide evidence of an improvement in the performance of these industries? *(5 marks)*

(iii) What other information might be useful in assessing the performance of the nationalised industries? *(5 marks)*

(b) How does the size of its "External financing limit" (line 26) affect a nationalised industry? *(4 marks)*

(c) To what extent does the data support the view that nationalised industries should **not** be privatised? *(6 marks)*

(AEB)

7 Cost–benefit analysis

In this chapter we will discuss:

1. Why markets sometimes fail to work.
2. How the consumption of a good by one consumer can affect the utility of others.
3. How economists try to measure the effects of this consumption – the costs and benefits of consuming a particular good.

Introduction

The **free-enterprise economy** works by developing economic decisions down to the level of individual consumers and individual entrepreneurs. This myriad of decisions is orchestrated by the price mechanism. Every pound a consumer spends on a good is a 'vote' for its production. Every pound the entrepreneur has to pay out for the production of a good is a 'vote' against its production.

If, for example, many consumers wanted to buy coal, but very few workers wanted to work as miners then the price of coal would be high. The high price signals to consumers that they are asking rather a lot of the labour force by giving them dangerous and unpleasant work to do (i.e. causing them great disutility). The high price further signals that consumers should be sparing in their use of coal so as to minimize the percentage of the labour force engaged in mining. Conversely, of course, the high price of coal signals to the workforce that consumers really do want the coal rather badly. The high price results in high wages and so enough labourers are persuaded to go into coal mining.

In a Robinson Crusoe economy, Robinson knows whether the utility he gets from a coal fire exceeds the disutility of his mining the coal. He can therefore decide for himself whether to dig coal or not. In our community we do not know how much utility others will derive from coal fires, or how much disutility others will experience in going down mines. For all we know some people might actually like working in dusty darkness.

It is the price mechanism that does for a community what Robinson Crusoe does in his own mind. It signals to consumers the disutility attached to coal mining and signals to labourers the utility derived from coal fires. When working perfectly, then, the price mechanism brings about a pattern of production which maximizes the utility we get from consumption while minimizing the disutility of engaging in certain forms of production.

In order to cast 'votes' in the market, consumers must have something to spend, i.e. some purchasing power.

Apart from gifts, purchasing power is usually bestowed on consumers as income – as wages, interest, profit or rent. In order to receive an income it is necessary to make some contribution to production – labour, capital, risk bearing or land.

Miners, for example, agree to dig coal and after a week's work each receives, say, £150 in wages. After work they switch from being producers to being consumers, and as consumers they each have 150 votes to cast each week. Had they worked only half the time, they would have produced only half as much coal and received only £75 in wages. They would then have cast only 75 votes. The votes they cast as consumers therefore reflect their contributions to production. Those who contribute most get most votes, and those who contribute only a little get a few votes.

Thus, when the system is working perfectly, every pound's worth of production generates a pound's worth of voting. The pattern of what is produced then reflects the preferences of those who do most of the producing.

Reasons for government intervention

This method of economic organization (the market) sometimes fails to work in a way which Robinson Crusoe would wish. In so far as we have a 'Robinson Crusoe' to express a view it is the government – our elected representatives. There are many reasons why the government may take a different view from that of the market. We will look at some of them.

The distribution of votes

The most obvious is that in the market place votes are unequally distributed (some people have high incomes and lots of votes, while others have low incomes and very few votes), whereas in the political ballot each voter has only one vote. A representative, elected government would therefore reflect the preferences of an economy in which everyone made an equal contribution to production. It is most unlikely that this would resemble the preferences of the actual economy and so the government might decide to override the market.

The government can step in to reallocate votes. If, for example, it imposes an income tax, it would be taking a lot of votes away from those who contribute a lot to output, a few votes away from those who make small contributions and no votes away from those who contribute nothing. If these tax revenues were distributed equally among all citizens then the pattern of production would be moved away from that preferred by the high-income group towards that preferred by the lower-income groups.

The fact that the government does put different tax rates on different goods and does impose income taxes suggests that the patterns of production and consumption which would be thrown up by the free-market mechanism do not always meet with political approval.

Merit and demerit goods

Alternatively, the government may feel that it has more information on certain goods than the typical consumer does. The government may take the view that the value of some goods is underestimated by consumers (these are called **merit goods**) and that some goods are overvalued by consumers (these are called **demerit goods**). The government could simply try to share this information more widely – and indeed it does this through advertising and by public service announcements on radio and television. In many cases, however, this fails to have much effect and so the government steps in to 'correct' the market.

If, for example, it is decided that cigarette smoking is 'bad', but that milk drinking is 'good', then the government can put a tax on cigarettes and subsidize milk. The effect of the tax is to put up the price of cigarettes to consumers, thereby falsely signalling to consumers a high production cost of cigarettes. The effect of the subsidy on milk is, of course, the exact opposite of this – consumers are encouraged to consume more milk than they would in a free market.

We have been warned at length about the ill (fatal) effects of tobacco, but many people continue to smoke it. The government therefore puts a very high tax on tobacco further to discourage its use. This kind of state intervention is said to be 'for the consumer's own good' and gives rise to taunts of the 'nanny' state.

The 'wider' view

In some cases market prices correctly reflect the cost to private individuals decisions, but not the costs to society as a whole. In the case of an entrepreneur deciding whether to lay off or retain workers the appropriate information would be the value of what they produce and their wage bill. If the value of what they produce exceeds the wage bill then they will be retained, otherwise they will be laid off.

As far as the government is concerned, the costs are slightly different. The government has to pay unemployment benefit, so it would like workers to be kept on the pay roll even when they produce less than their wage bill. It might cost the entrepreneur £10 per worker per week to retain 'unprofitable' workers. By firing them might impose a cost on the state of £50 per week per worker by way of unemployment benefit. The government might therefore take a rather different view of the desirability of sacking the workers and might try to reduce the number of people laid off.

We saw in Chapter 6 that the boards of nationalized industries are charged with taking a wider view of their function than that implied by purely commercial considerations. The purely commercial considerations are those such as profit maximization which dominate the free-market system. As part of their wider view, boards are asked to consider the employment consequences of their decisions.

For some goods (and bads) there are no markets and so markets cannot send the correct signals to producers and consumers. This is the case when ownership cannot be established – as, for example, when industries discharge waste material into the sea or smoke into the atmosphere. Since no one owns the seas or the air, there is no charge for using them as sinks. But it is becoming increasingly obvious that there are costs associated with pollution and that we should find some way of moderating it.

Some wish simply to outlaw such activities completely, but this is to put an infinite price on them. Complete prohibition would cause some products to disappear from the market altogether, and others would become extremely expensive. There would then be underuse of the sea and the air as resources. Ideally we should find ways of imposing the real costs of pollution on those who do the discharging. Market prices would then truly reflect costs and benefits and we would neither overuse nor underuse our resources. This is the basis of the proposed green tax.

Apart from having a different constituency, a different information set and different costs from the market, the government also has a longer time perspective than individuals. We each have a finite life and make our decisions accordingly. The state, however, is immortal and must consider 'tomorrow' as well as 'today'. Thus if, as individuals, we have no interest in what happens after we die then we may wish to use up all the oil on earth in our own lifetimes and price it accordingly. Those not yet born do have an interest in how much oil we use up, but they have no vote in the current market. The government may feel that it should protect the interests of future generations and cast votes on their behalf. One way of doing this is to impose a tax on oil so as to discourage the present generation from consuming it all.

Another, perhaps less obvious, reason for markets to fail is that market value reflects true value *only at the margin*. If we are deciding whether to dispense with one cup of water or one diamond then we could base our decision on market price and throw away the water. But if we are considering whether to do away with our only well or our only diamond mine then we would not wish to be guided by market prices. The true costs and benefits of various options are therefore reflected by market value only for fairly small (marginal) changes.

If, as we have suggested, the wider view is the one taken by our elected representatives then one solution to the economic problem would be to consign all 'big' economic decisions to Parliament. Members of Parliament are not charged with maximizing their own utility, or with maximizing profits, or with concerning themselves only with market values. They are charged with maximizing social benefits and minimizing social costs. They are clearly well placed to decide whether to build a new road or a new airport, or whether to generate electricity through nuclear

Case Study 7.1 Taxes are key to motoring habits

Changes in the tax burden borne by motorists would be the most direct way the Government could persuade the public to opt for more ecologically sound cars.

At present, to put a new car on the road, a driver can expect to pay an additional 25 per cent of the retail price in taxes.

Added to that would be the cost of insurance, road tax and duty on petrol to keep the car running, plus the cost of regular MoTs to ensure the car stays on the road.

All these financial penalties on the driver offer the Government considerable scope to manage motoring tastes and encourage car buyers to opt for more environmentally friendly vehicles.

Industry, too, through tax incentives, could be persuaded to develop new technology that would cut CO_2 emissions.

A new car attracts a basic car tax of 10 per cent of five-sixths of the manufacturer's recommended retail price. That effectively adds 8.3 per cent to its value. On top of that is VAT on the invoice price, including the car tax. Together, they represent a total tax bill on the new car of 24.6 per cent of its retail value.

Such tax bills could be varied in relation to the size and efficiency of the car's engine, big 'gas guzzling' cars attracting far higher basic car tax.

The current road fund licence of £100 for all UK cars could also be modified to reward those going for smaller vehicles. There are precedents for this on the Continent. In Italy, France and Germany, for example, the level of road tax, although much lower than here, is related to engine size.

Also the Germans operate incentives to fit catalytic converters. Although the initial outlay for the driver is high, he receives in return long-term road-tax benefits.

Insurance already takes account of car size as well as the age and experience of the driver but additional tax liability could be introduced on the insurance for larger and inefficient cars.

Encouragement to industry could take the form of tax relief on research and development into smaller but more powerful car engines, say the Society of Motor Manufacturers and Traders.

As well as simply pricing leaded petrol out of the market by imposing heavy tax duties, the Government could also make diesel fuel and diesel-powered cars more attractive.

Tax incentives to manufacturers to design and build, and to motorists to drive, diesel cars could be introduced. However, this would probably have to be introduced in conjunction with an educational programme. 'For some reason, diesel is erroneously perceived as a dirty and inefficient fuel. It certainly isn't and would help to cut CO_2 emissions from motor cars,' an SMMT spokesman said.

MoT charges could also be linked to whether a car's engine met stringent efficiency standards.

There has already been much debate on the imposition of major tax burdens on companies who offer cars – especially big cars – as incentives to their employees. Serious penalties, instead of tax benefits, could be introduced.

1. The article suggests ways of reallocating consumer 'votes'. What will be the effect on the car market in the short term if the proposals are adopted?
2. How would you expect the proposals to affect the market in the long term? Are the benefits concentrated on the present or future generations?

Source: David Black, *Independent*, 9 June 1990

power stations. In making these decisions, ministers and their civil servants have sought guidance from economists, and this is where **cost–benefit analysis** (CBA) comes in.

CBA is a branch of applied economics aimed at helping the political arm of our economy reach decisions on whether or not to embark on or permit the private sector to embark on particular 'large' projects, such as airports or motorways. CBA is therefore essentially a method of project appraisal and is relevant when the project under consideration is very large and one for which the wisdom of the market is inadequate.

SUMMARY

1. In free-enterprise economies all economic decisions are co-ordinated by the price mechanism.
2. When working well this system should require no interference by the government.
3. The government does in fact interfere for the following reasons:
   (a) Not all goods produced under the free-enterprise system are approved of by the government.
   (b) The 'votes' we cast in the market place depend on how much we earn. The votes cast in the ballot box are on a one citizen, one vote basis. The preferences expressed through the market may therefore differ from those expressed through the ballot box.
   (c) The free-enterprise system only takes account of narrow commercial considerations, but the government takes account of wider social considerations.
4. When the government does interfere in the economy it seeks the guidance of economists, and the appropriate economic theory is called cost–benefit analysis.

Problems with costs and benefits

Comparability and units of measurement

The first problem to be faced by anyone seeking to augment or modify purely commercial criteria in project appraisal is that of comparability. Commercial profits and losses are all expressed in monetary units (£s) and hence are easily compared. But how, for example, can the benefits of clean air be compared with the intrusive ugliness of very tall chimneys? We have no units in which to measure these things (no units of utility) and even if we had such units (say utils) how could we assess the 'utils' derived from having clean air?

The economist's response to this kind of problem is to

attempt to construct a monetary value of the non-commercial costs and benefits. They can at least then be added, subtracted and compared.

Of course, no one would want to pretend that all relevant considerations can be reduced to marks on a financial balance sheet. The claim is that some apparently non-commercial criteria can be translated into money terms, and it may be useful to take this approach as far as we can before attempting the subjective assessment of unlike things.

Timing

Even with a money measure of some costs and benefits, the problem of comparing them is complicated by the fact that the costs and benefits (however measured) often arise at different times and for different durations.

If the costs and benefits have different time profiles then we need some way of comparing, say, the cost of disrupting the traffic for two years with the benefits of having an extra lane on a motorway for the next 40 years. The appropriate techniques here are those of investment appraisal. They pose some interesting problems for those considering the 'social' rather than the 'profit-maximizing' view of long-term investments. We shall shortly see how CBA handles such problems.

Interpersonal comparisons

Finally we shall look at the thorny problem of who gains and who loses. Many projects will yield benefits to one group (group A, say motorway users) and impose costs on another group (group B, say those living within earshot of the motorway). This unequal distribution gives rise to the problems of interpersonal comparisons – does the benefit to A exceed the loss to B? We shall examine some ways of overcoming this problem.

SUMMARY

1. Economists seek to express costs and benefits in monetary terms.
2. Market prices are not adequate for assessing the monetary values since they do not reflect total utility.
3. Market prices are not always available since there is no market for some costs and some benefits.
4. Costs and benefits are not always coincident in time. Costs often occur first and the benefits flow afterwards.
5. Costs and benefits are not always borne by the same group of people. The costs are sometimes borne by one group as benefits accrue to another group.

Money measure of value

We spent some time in the earlier chapters of this book investigating prices. We saw that a 'price' is the amount of money which has to be exchanged for a good in a market. Price is therefore 'exchange' value or 'market' value expressed in money units.

This would seem to be exactly what is wanted for cost–benefit analysis, since price is a money measure of market (or social) benefits balanced against market (or social) costs. There are, however, two questions to be answered. First, we need to know when and under what circumstances exchange value is an appropriate measure of social benefit and social cost. Second, we need to know what to do when there is no market in which prices can be formed.

The first of these problems can perhaps best be illustrated by reconsidering the water and diamond paradox. We know that water is essential to life and yet it commands a very low price, whereas diamonds, which are practically useless, have a very high price. Now, say we are considering a project which would use up all the fresh water but which would enormously increase the quantity of diamonds. If we used only current exchange values to assess costs and benefits then we would conclude that the loss of water is a trivial cost but that the gains from diamond production would be very great. We would therefore decide to go ahead and would end up with no water and lots of diamonds.

Clearly this is a very naive approach to decision making, but it serves to illustrate that by using current exchange values (market prices) as indicators of costs and benefits we would make some grave errors.

Of course, for very small changes in the quantity of water and very small changes in the quantity of diamonds, exchange values do serve as reasonable indicators of value. But the kind of very large projects being considered in this chapter require something more than exchange values. We can introduce these problems by considering the demand and supply curves shown in Figure 7.1.

Figure 7.1(a) depicts the market demand curve for diamonds (D_d), which is downward sloping to the right and the market supply curve for diamonds (S_d), which is upward sloping to the right.

The intercept of the demand curve and the vertical axis (a) indicates the price at which no diamonds would be bought. The intercept of the horizontal axis and the supply curve (c) shows how many diamonds would be simply 'picked up' by people going about their normal business. In order to get more than this quantity it is necessary to engage in the 'production' of diamonds (by mining, for example), and beyond this point the marginal cost curve (supply curve) rises very sharply.

In Figure 7.1(b) the amount of fresh water supplied 'free' by rainfall to one's garden is given by e. If we want more than that we have to bring it from rivers or reservoirs, and costs began to rise. The marginal cost curve (supply curve) is thereafter upward sloping.

The demand curve for water indicates that there is a price (g) at which we would not be able to afford even one cup of water.

Now the total expenditure on diamonds is price (P_d) × quantity (q_d), which is equal to the area of rectangle OP_dbq_d. The market value of the water is again price (P_w) × quantity (q_w), which is the area of rectangle OP_wfq_w. From this it is clear that the total value of water is far less than the total value of diamonds and, judging by those values, it would be far better to deprive consumers of water than to deprive them of diamonds.

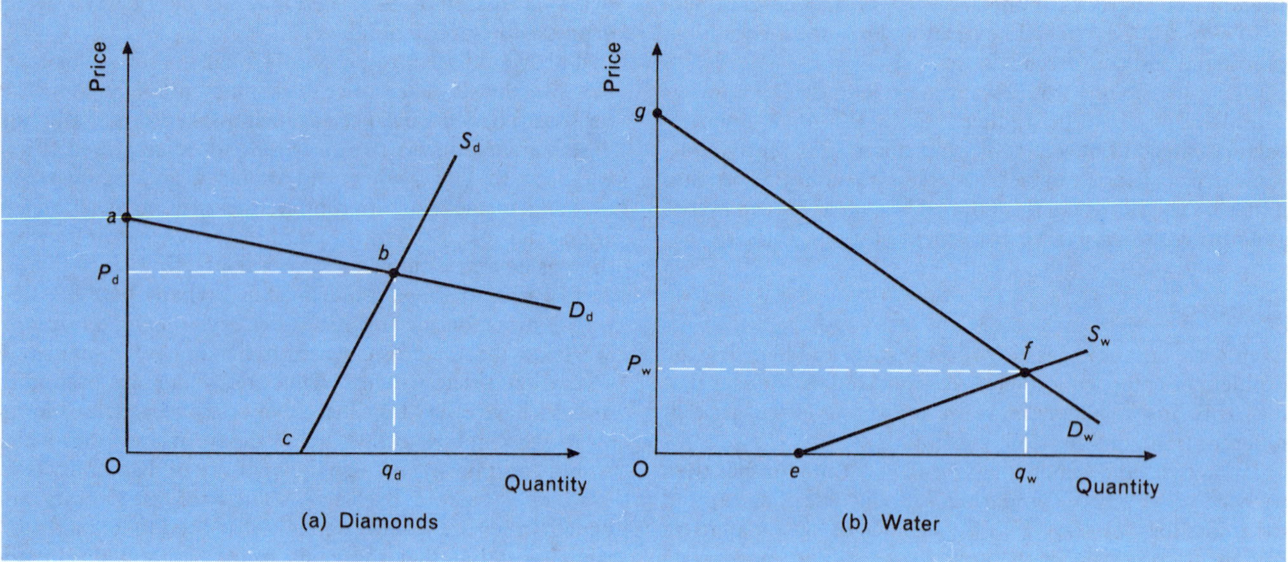

Figure 7.1 The water and diamonds paradox.

We already know, however, that just because the marginal utility derived from a good is low, it does not mean that the total utility derived from a good is low. Hence the fact that consumers pay P_w for water and P_d for diamonds does not mean that the total utility they get from diamonds is greater than the utility they get from water.

Consumer surplus

The difference between what consumers give up for a good and the benefit they derive from a good is called **consumer surplus**.

A good way of illustrating and measuring consumer surplus is by looking at the demand for a particular good. Consider the demand curve for oranges in Figure 7.2. At a price of 3p the consumer buys 3 oranges and hence in total spends 9p on oranges (point *g* on the curve). At a price of 6p none are bought (point *d*) and when oranges are free then the consumer would like 6 of them (point *m*).

Imagine now that the sellers of oranges pretend to have only one for sale. At that level of supply they could get 5p for the orange (point *e* on the curve). Having sold that orange for 5p they then 'discover' that they have another orange. This second orange sells for 4p (point *f*). Finally they 'find' a third and final orange which they sell for 3p. Their total income from the sale of 3 oranges is now $5+4+3 = 12$p compared with the 9p they would have received if all the oranges had sold for 3p. The sellers could therefore, by judicious use of their market power, squeeze 3p more out of the consumer. When this power is used, the total sum paid equals the area of the three rectangles. *Ojec*, *jifk* and *ihgl*. Only the last orange is sold for its 'market' price.

If we divide up oranges into very small pieces and sell each piece separately then the number of rectangles increases and their total area approximates to the area under the demand curve (*Ohgd*). Thus the maximum amount of money which suppliers could get from the consumer for 3 oranges is $Ohgd = (3 \times 3) + \frac{1}{2}(3 \times 3) = 13\frac{1}{2}$p. This is the maximum amount the consumer is willing to pay for the 3 oranges. In a market, of course, only 3p is paid for each orange and so the consumer spends *Ohga* ($3 \times 3 = 9$p) on oranges. The difference between the two is called consumer surplus and takes a monetary value ($4\frac{1}{2}$p) equal to the area of the triangle *agd*. More generally, consumer surplus is measured as the area under the demand curve and above the price line.

If the consumer is totally deprived of oranges, the utility lost is equal to the value £(*Ohgd*). There remains the unspent income £(*Ohga*) which can now be spent on other goods. Thus the net loss of utility by the consumer on being deprived of oranges is the difference between the two (*Ohgd* – *Ohga*), which again is consumer surplus *agd*.

If the consumer is deprived of, say, only one of the 3

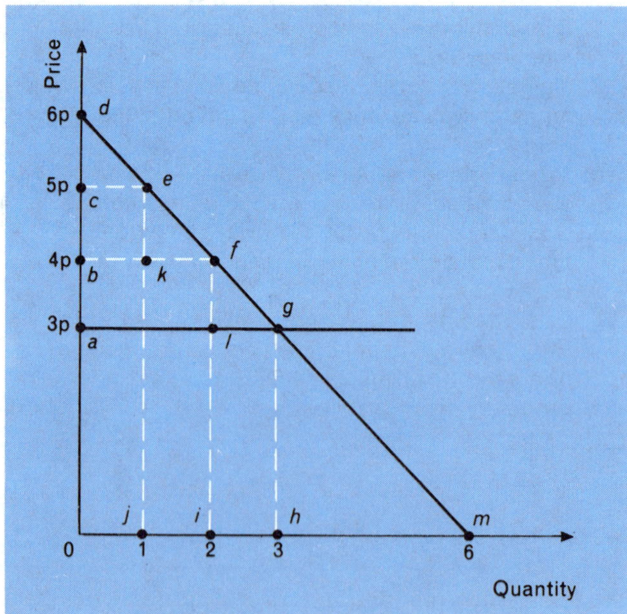

Figure 7.2 Consumer surplus.

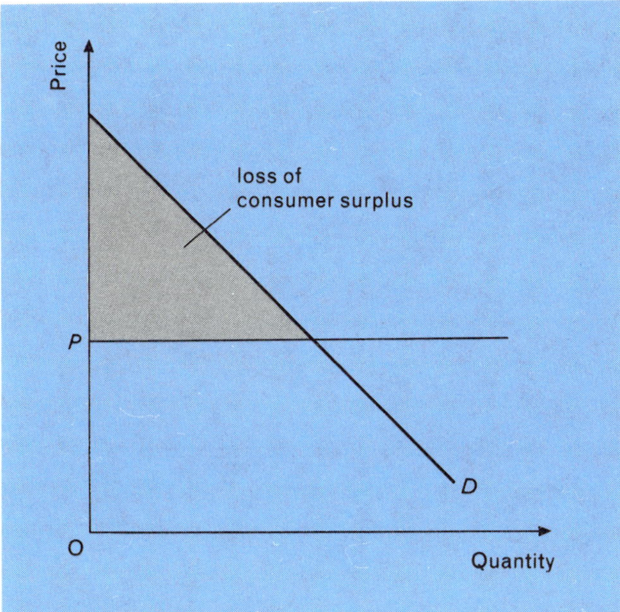

Figure 7.3 Loss of consumer surplus when consumers are prevented from buying any of the good.

oranges, consumer surplus changes from *agd* to *bfd*. The loss of consumer surplus is therefore the area *abfg*. But notice that if the removal of one orange from the market does not result in a change of price (and this could be done by simply leaving some demand unsatisfied) then the change in consumer surplus is much less.

Compare the three cases. Under the original conditions ($P = 3$p and $q = 3$) the consumer surplus is *agd*. With P still held at 3p, but q reduced to 2, the new consumer surplus is area *alfd*. The change in consumer surplus is in

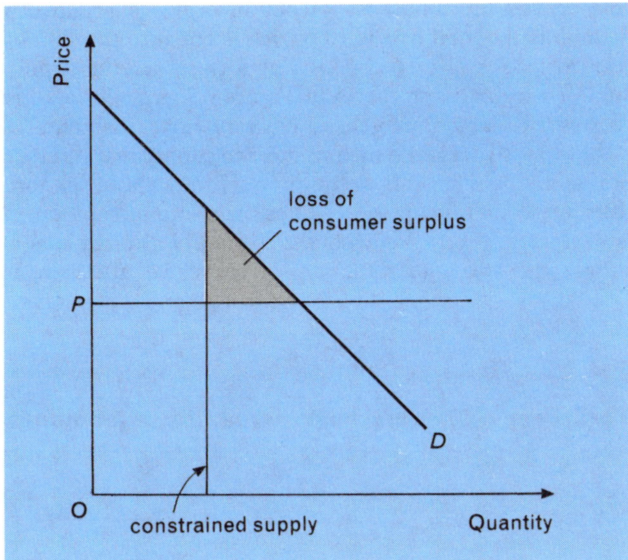

Figure 7.4 Loss of consumer surplus when consumers are constrained to buy fewer goods than they would wish.

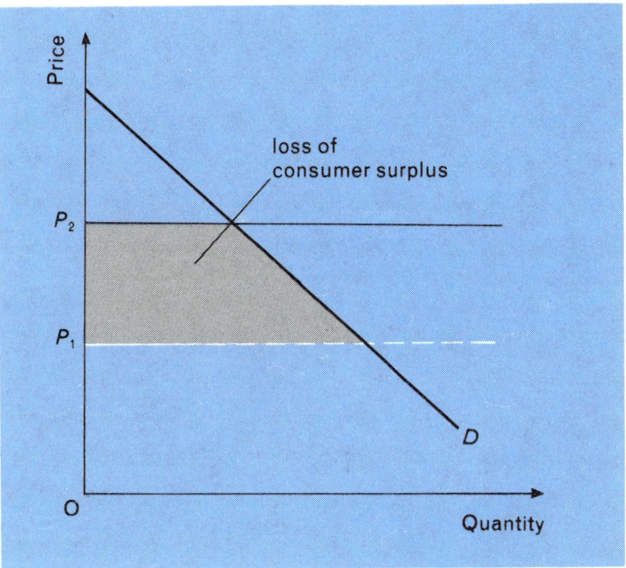

Figure 7.5 Loss of consumer surplus when consumers are faced with a higher price.

this case the small triangle *lfg*. Finally, if P is increased to 4p and q is reduced to 2 then the consumer surplus changes from *agd* to *bfd* and the loss is *abfg*.

The difference arises because in one case the consumer is not only prevented from buying the third orange (involving a loss of consumer surplus of *lfg*), but is also obliged to pay the higher price for the 2 oranges which are bought. The consumer therefore loses the utility equal to the sum (*abfg*).

We therefore have three cases for assessing consumer surplus:

1. Where consumers are prevented from buying any of the good in question. The loss of consumer surplus is then the area bounded by the price line the demand curve and the vertical axis (Figure 7.3).
2. Where consumers are constrained to buy fewer goods than they would wish to at the going price. The loss of consumer surplus here is the area bounded by the price line, the demand curve and the constrained supply line (Figure 7.4).
3. Where consumers are faced with a higher price (P_2) which causes them (a) to consume less of the good and (b) to pay more for what they continue to consume (Figure 7.5).

We can use these ideas of consumer surplus to look again at our water and diamonds paradox. The demand and supply curves for these two goods are shown in Figure 7.6.

From the figure it is clear that depriving consumers of diamonds deprives them of consumer surplus measured by the area of triangle $P_d ba$. However, depriving them of water deprives them of consumer surplus measured by the area of triangle $P_w fg$.

The same kind of comparison can be drawn when consumers are deprived of some diamonds and some water. Say the quantity of diamonds is reduced from q_d to q_{d1}. The loss of consumer surplus is equal to area *ibh*, which is small. Depriving consumers of some water – say a reduction from

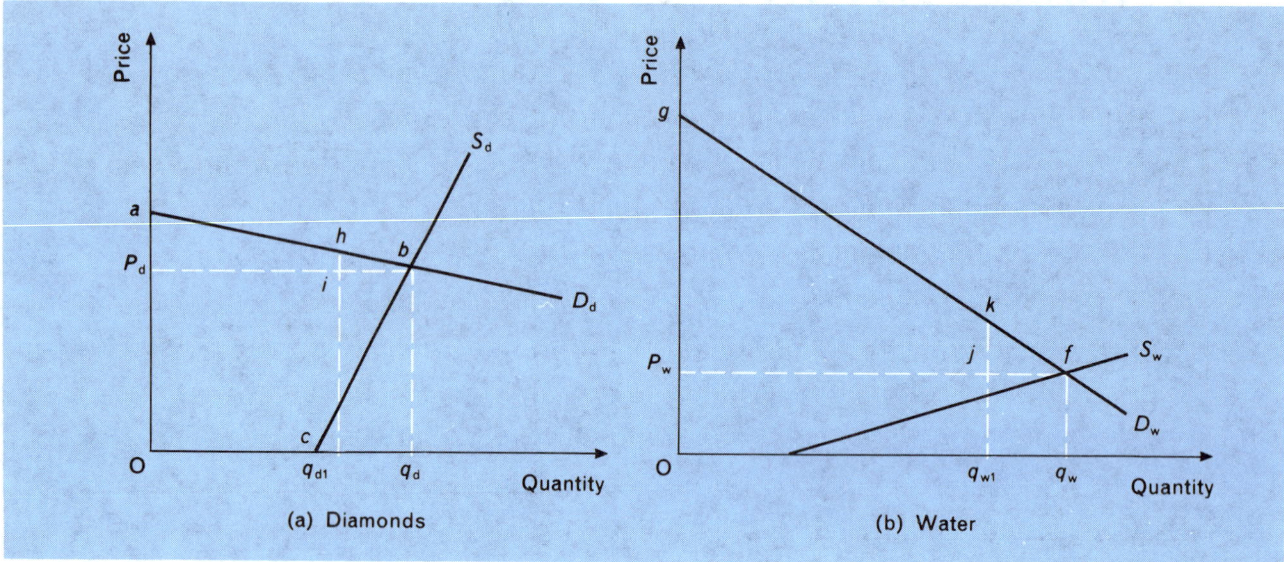

Figure 7.6 Consumer surplus for diamonds and water [for cartoon 1]. What would he be prepared to pay for a glass of water?

q_w to q_{w1} – would deprive them of consumer surplus measured by the area of triangle *kfj*, which is large.

What is important then is not the current exchange values (prices), but the consumer surpluses.

We should not choose to sacrifice the good with the lower price; we should choose to sacrifice that which yields the lower consumer surplus. That is to say, we should be concerned less with value in exchange and more with value in use.

Cost–benefit analysis attempts to get behind exchange values and bases its decisions instead on consumer surplus. In order to do so it must have some idea of the shapes and positions of demand curves – mere knowledge of current market price is not enough.

Producer surplus

We have seen that, in perfectly competitive markets, consumers are obliged to pay only the market price, but that they could be forced to pay a much higher price if the seller could find some way of expropriating the consumer surplus. The same kind of argument can be advanced about the seller. In this case the difference between what producers receive and what they would actually be prepared to accept is called **producer surplus**.

The question is: what is the minimum amount that producers would accept for their output?

Recall that the supply curve is the marginal cost curve (in auctioneer-type markets) and that the area under the marginal cost curve is equal to total cost. This latter can be seen from the numerical example in Table 7.1. Here, total cost is originally zero. This is the case when diamonds are being picked up rather than mined. As more diamonds are supplied, it is necessary to mine them and costs are incurred. Total costs rise from 0 to 1, then from 1 to 3, then from 3 to 6 and finally from 6 to 10. The increments in total cost (1, 2, 3 and 4) are marginal costs and it is this sequence of numbers which gives rise to the marginal cost curve in Figure 7.7.

It is clear from Table 7.1 that summing the marginal costs yields the total cost. Hence in order to produce 6 diamonds the total cost is 10, which is equal to the sum of marginal costs $(1+2+3+4)$. The area under the supply curve (marginal cost curve) in Figure 7.7, triangle cq_db, is therefore equal to the total cost of supplying q_d diamonds.

In order to persuade the producer to supply that number of diamonds, then, it is necessary only to pay a little more than it cost to produce them. Thus the minimum amount it is necessary to pay the producer to supply q_d diamonds is simply the area under the supply curve, i.e. the area of

Table 7.1 Costs of diamonds

Total cost	Marginal cost	Quantity of diamonds
0	0	0
0	0	1
0	0	2
1	1	3
3	2	4
6	3	5
10	4	6

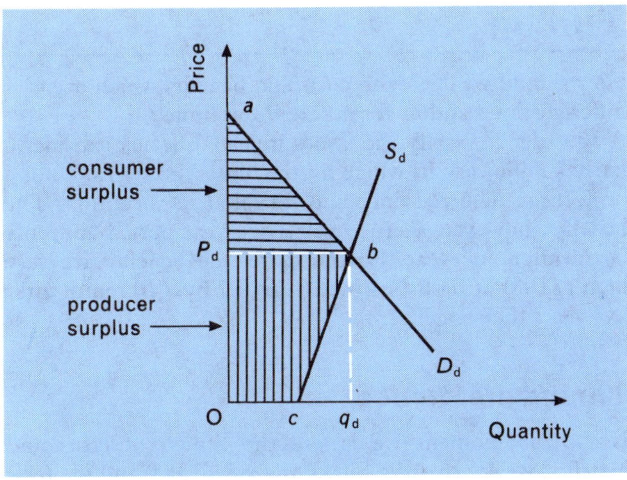

Figure 7.7 Producer and consumer surplus.

triangle cq_db. Hence producer surplus is the difference between this and total revenue (OP_dbq_d) – and is equal to the area $OcbP_d$.

Total surplus

If we reduce the number of diamonds being traded to zero, we not only deprive the consumers of consumer surplus (P_dba), but we also deprive the producers of producer surplus ($OcbP_d$). The total surplus is therefore the sum of these two and is equal to the area bounded by the two axes, the demand curve and the supply curve. This is shown in the shaded area of Figure 7.7.

We can use a similar figure to examine what the loss of surplus – both consumer and producer – will be if the quantity of diamonds is restricted to, say, q_{d1}. This is shown in Figure 7.8. By reducing the quantity of diamonds from q_d to q_{d1} and maintaining price at P_d, we can see that the consumer loses surplus to the value of the horizontally shaded area. Producers, on the other hand, lose surplus to the value of the vertically shaded area. The total loss of surplus is therefore the sum of these two – the total shaded area – and this is known as a 'deadweight' loss.

The allocation of this loss of total surplus between producers and consumers depends upon our assumptions about the change in price. We have assumed above that the original price remains unchanged. But if the price rises to match demand exactly with the restricted supply (P_{d1}) then the consumer loses not only the surplus represented by the vertically shaded triangle, but also the surplus represented by the area P_dabP_{d1}. This loss of consumer surplus, however, represents a gain in producer surplus – simply a transfer of surplus from consumers to producers.

If the government is interested only in total loss of surplus rather than in any redistribution of surplus then the shaded area is the appropriate measure and assumptions about whether prices rise, fall or remain the same are irrelevant.

The net outcome of all this is that for large projects the government must try to estimate the effect they will have on both consumer surplus and producer surplus. These surpluses are not reflected in market prices. Thus, even when a market exists and exchange values can be established, we still need to know something about demand and supply curves before we can make an assessment of alternative projects.

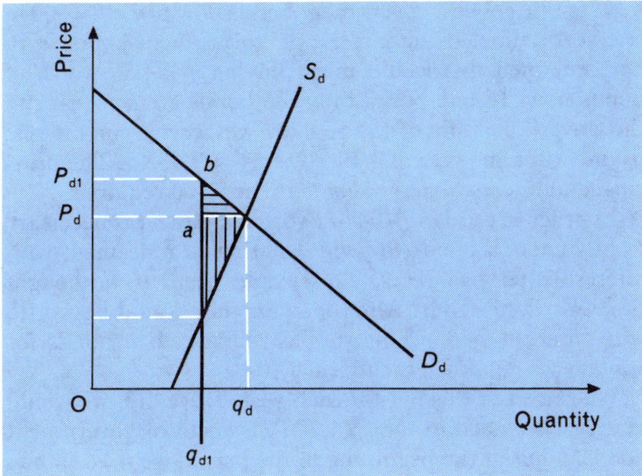

Figure 7.8 Loss of surplus with constrained supply.

When no market exists

The problem of assessing costs and benefits becomes rather more difficult when there is no market. Take the case in which a new motorway is expected to reduce the number of road deaths as well as to improve the efficiency of transport. In order to take this reduced death rate into our calculations, we need some idea of the 'value' we place on human life. There is, of course, no market for human lives and hence no objective market price for them.

A second example might be a project which destroys a place of outstanding natural beauty. There is no market for such beauty spots – people simply go and visit them – and hence there is no market price for beauty spots either.

However, with a little imagination it is possible to infer an implicit valuation of lives and beauty spots. We know, for example, that some jobs are much more dangerous than others. Steel erectors stand a much higher chance of being killed at work than (some) school teachers. Because of this they get extra wages. This extra payment is sometimes actually called 'danger money'. By knowing the increased risk and the increased wage, we can infer an implicit value which the market places on human life.

Similarly, although there is no market for beauty spots there is a market for hotel rooms, and hotels with good views will attract higher prices than those overlooking the gasworks. Again, then, by comparing the prices charged by two hotels which differ only in their locations we can infer an implicit market price for beauty spots.

Cost–benefit analysis makes much use of this kind of reasoning. There are no hard and fast rules for the application of this methodology. What is required is an imaginative search for markets which implicitly value the 'goods' or 'bads' which are not explicitly marketed. It is something of an art rather than a science.

SUMMARY

1. It has long been understood that market prices do not always represent the 'true' value of things. This has often been illustrated by the water and diamond paradox, which gives a very high price to comparatively useless diamonds and a very low price to something as essential as water.
2. Economic decisions based on market value could therefore cause a valuable commodity (water) to be sacrificed for the increased production of a relatively useless commodity (diamonds).
3. When advising governments and other decision-making bodies, the cost–benefit analyst has therefore to find a way of assessing this 'true' value. This value is often called 'value in use' so as to distinguish it from market value, which is 'value in exchange'.
4. The first important step towards a solution to this problem was the recognition of consumer surplus.
5. Consumer surplus is the difference between the maximum amount that a consumer would be prepared to pay for a good, rather than go without it completely, and the amount actually paid in the market place.
6. Consumer surplus can be measured as the area under the demand curve and above the price line.
7. Fortunately this measure of consumer surplus can be expressed in money terms (e.g. £s) and hence can be compared directly with other costs and benefits.
8. The amount of consumer surplus actually lost when someone is prevented from buying a good will depend on how the purchase is limited. If it is limited by raising the price of the good then the loss of consumer surplus is higher than if the price remains the same and a physical quota is put on the amount purchased.
9. Like the consumer, the producer also enjoys a surplus – a producer surplus.
10. Producer surplus is the difference between the minimum amount a producer would be prepared to accept for its goods and the amount it actually receives for them at market prices.
11. Producer surplus is measured as the area above the supply curve (i.e. the marginal cost curve) and below the price line.
12. The total amount of surplus lost when the sales of a good are restricted is therefore the sum of the lost consumer surplus and the lost producer surplus.
13. Some restrictions on sales cause a redistribution of surplus away from consumers to producers as well as causing a net ('deadweight') loss of surplus.
14. Where no market exists for a good it is necessary to infer its value . This involves a degree of value judgement in the analysis.

Timing

How should we deal with costs and benefits which occur at different times and/or for different durations?

In order to clarify the issues involved, let us consider a fairly simple case in which all the 'costs' (say £1,000) of a project are incurred once and for all at its inception. The benefits, however, accrue over a five-year period and only begin after one year. Furthermore, the benefits are very high (£500) at first, but each year fall by £100 until after five years they reach zero.

Timing preference

If for the moment we ignore the timing of costs and benefits, we see that the total costs are £1,000 and the total benefits are £1,500 (500 + 400 + 300 + 200 + 100). Thus the benefits outweigh the costs. But what if we have a preference for early payments and hence we attach great importance to the early cost of £1,000, but very little importance to the distant benefit of £100?

Individuals tend to have positive time preference – that is, they prefer payment today rather than payment tomorrow – and in order to persuade them to accept payment tomorrow we have to pay them something extra. This additional payment is the interest payment.

The rate of interest will be high if we really dislike postponing our income and low if we do not mind very much. In this way the interest rate reflects our time preference. It also provides the solution to our problem of comparing costs and benefits when they differ in their timing.

Net present value

The investment illustrated in Figure 7.9 offers a particular income stream (£500 after one year, £400 after two years, etc.) in return for an immediate downpayment of £1,000. Now it would be possible to obtain exactly the same income stream (£500, £400, £300, etc.) not by investing in this project, but by lending the money to the government, i.e. by investing in government bonds.

In order to receive £500 in one year's time, we would need to buy enough government bonds now to yield £500 in one year's time. If the interest on government bonds is 10 per cent then this would mean buying £454.55 worth of bonds now. In one year's time the bonds are sold back to the government for £454.55 and we receive an interest payment for one year of $0.10 \times 454.54 = £45.45$. The principal and interest together come to the £500 required.

In order to receive £400 in two years' time it is necessary to buy enough bonds to yield £400 when redeemed, with interest, after two years. This would occur if we bought £330 worth of bonds. After one year they would be worth, with interest, £363. This sum is reinvested in bonds for another year and will then yield £400.

We can work this out for each year. If we did, we would find that we need in total £1,209.21 worth of government bonds. Thus at the beginning of the period we need to buy all £1,209.21 worth of these bonds and, by selling them off at the rate of £454.54 after one year, £330 after two years,

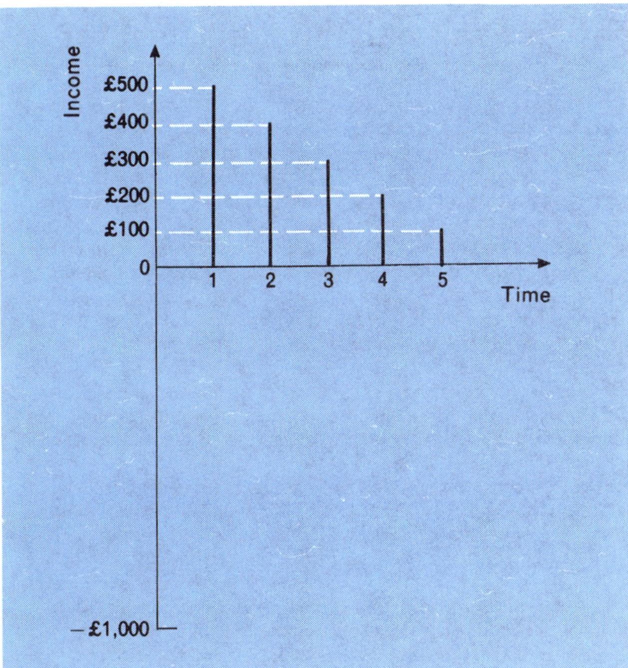

Figure 7.9 Investment income over time.

etc., we can reproduce exactly the same income stream as is generated by the proposed project.

The total amount to be spent on government bonds at the start of the period (£1,209.21) is called the **net present value (NPV)** of the income stream. By this technique we can work out the net present value of any income stream for any rate of interest.

The purpose of converting the streams of income into these net present values is that we can now compare them directly. We know, for example, that the net present value of the project outlined above (£1,209.21) is greater than its cost (£1,000). Hence if we had to choose between investing in the project or investing in government bonds it would be best to invest in the project. By investing in the project we obtain the income stream (£500, £400, £300, etc.) for £1,000, whereas to obtain it through government bonds would cost £1,209.21.

If we had a number of projects, each with its own income stream, we could work out their respective NPVs. These NPVs can then be divided by their respective costs and if the ratio is greater than unity then the project is acceptable, i.e. its benefits exceed its costs. This type of analysis is further explored in Chapter 9 (pp. 182–3).

SUMMARY

1. Typically we prefer to receive benefits early rather than late. This is called our time preference.
2. This means that in comparing costs and benefits it is necessary to allow for the timing of those costs and benefits.
3. One way of doing this is to assume that our time preference is represented by the rate of interest. The higher the rate of interest, the more we prefer benefits now rather than later.
4. Any particular time profile of benefits with any given interest rate can be expressed as its net present value.
5. Different projects can therefore be compared by comparing their net present values.
6. The higher the net present value, the better. But in any case the net present value should exceed costs if the project is to be undertaken.

Interpersonal comparisons

The final problem to be dealt with in this chapter is that which arises when the costs are borne by one group of people and the benefits accrue to another group. We have already seen how this could happen when the costs fall on the current population and the benefits accrue to some future population. But the same kind of problem also occurs between contemporaries.

If, for example, we are considering a new airport, there will be many residents of the proposed site who strongly object to having parts of their environment sacrificed. Buildings and countryside may have to be bulldozed flat. Furthermore, even those whose houses are spared will have to live with the noise of aircraft landing and taking off.

The local community will therefore bear a great cost if the new airport is built. The local people may themselves never fly, but even if they did the benefits they enjoy from flying will certainly not exceed the cost to them of the airport. On the other hand, many people do benefit from air transport. If they happen to live away from the proposed airport site then they bear none of these costs. What then can an economist say about such projects?

If we could say that person A has lost 100 'utils' through the airport and person B has gained 500 'utils' then we could say that the benefits exceed the costs. But unfortunately utils are not cardinal measures of utility. They do not measure utility like kilometres measure distances. We can use kilometres both to measure whether someone is moving away from or towards the airport and to measure who is furthest from the airport. Kilometres are a cardinal measure, but utility is measured only on an ordinal scale.

We can say whether someone's utility is increasing or decreasing in the same way as we can say whether they are moving nearer to or further away from the airport. But we cannot say which of the two has the higher utility, nor can we say which has gained or lost most utility. In this way, then measuring utility differs from measuring distances, and because of it we cannot make interpersonal comparisons of costs and benefits.

This difficulty has led economists to take a very restricted view of what constitutes an improvement in social welfare. If we cannot compare individuals' utility then we can unambiguously say only that a project improves social welfare if it brings benefits to at least one person while making no one any worse off. This is little enough, but it is something.

This definition of an improvement in social welfare is due to the Italian economist Vilfredo Pareto (1848–1923) and hence is called a Pareto improvement.

Case Study 7.2 Free market philosophies railroad the public sector

The Cabinet is today due to reject requests for the injection of public funds into the high-speed rail link from the Channel tunnel to London.

It will use arguments based on the promotion of free markets and fair competition and the elimination of government subsidies. But although these are fine in principle, there is a growing file of evidence that where major projects are concerned the Government regularly changes the economic ground rules to suit itself.

Mrs Thatcher and her Transport Secretary, Cecil Parkinson have ruled out public funding ostensibly because the promoter of the venture, European Rail Link, is demanding 'colossal subsidies' for a project which would then be able to compete unfairly with the ferries and airlines and which cannot in any case be supported by the taxpayer under the terms of the Channel Tunnel Act.

The likely demise of the high-speed link contrasts with policy in France and other European nations, where governments have formulated a national transport infrastructure strategy and are helping to fund it.

But it also raises wider questions. First, in what circumstances is public as opposed to private funding appropriate? Second, why are some subsidies more acceptable than others?

The economic argument against funding the link goes something like this: the taxpayer is being asked to subsidise relatively well-off commuters in Kent (who would be offered 50 per cent of the line's capacity) and wealthy businessmen journeying by rail from London to the Continent. The general body of taxpayers receives nothing in return, apart perhaps from a reduction in government subsidy to British Rail if the project proves profitable.

Moreover, why should the high-speed link need any public funding when the Channel tunnel itself is being financed entirely with private money? Because of its privately-funded status the tunnel was not subject to the cost-benefit analysis that every public sector project such as a new motorway must pass to gain approval. Originally, the City was willing to finance the project on a straightforward calculation of revenues to be paid by customers.

That does of course provide a wonderfully clear bottom line. There is no need to ask further questions because the project is viable on the strictest of tests.

But this is a narrow basis for judging infrastructural developments. Many projects which fail the City financing test would pass it on a wider analysis, for example on the benefits to a large number of taxpayers of relieving congestion elsewhere, or on the benefits of promoting economic growth. Private investors cannot realistically pay for that element of a project.

Because of the request for government support, the rail link was in fact subjected to the cost benefit test which the tunnel project ducked, but it failed.

There are several issues entangled here. Roads may be 100 per cent publicly funded but the costs of building a motorway are in theory more than offset by the income raised from road fund licences and petrol duty. In contrast, the tax taken from a new railway line is nil, and in strict profit and loss terms it must rely on passengers to pay its way.

In the case of railways, critics claim the dice are loaded when the Government does the cost benefit analysis. Little effort is made to measure the exceptionally wide benefits to the economy from an improved railway infrastructure, whereas for a road every last penny of benefit is thrown in.

True or not, it is difficult to deliver a neutral economic analysis when there is evidence that overriding emotional responses and political expediency are at work. To her critics, Mrs Thatcher's reluctance to stump up for the high-speed link is less to do with subsidies and more to do with her antipathy towards Europe on the one hand and railways as a mode of transport on the other.

There is certainly anecdotal evidence that when it comes to judging infrastructure projects, the playing field is far from level and neutral economic judgments are rarely made. It may seem strange that whilst the Prime Minister is closing the public purse on the European Rail Link, she is busily seeking ways in which the Government can formulate a package of subsidies to entice MCA, the US entertainments group, to locate a planned £2bn theme park at Rainham Marshes in Essex rather than on the outskirts of Paris.

Why are both the second Dartford crossing and the second bridge over the Severn being privately-financed whilst the Government is funding 90 per cent of the capital cost of the Manchester Metrolink light railway?

On a more general level, there are plenty of examples of public spending and taxation decisions in which the Government's attachment to market disciplines is inconsistent. For example, it fought fiercely to retain the nuclear programme, in the face of a clear judgment from the City that it was not economically viable.

Even at the level of general taxation, anomalies abound. For example, the Government has set its face against large scale intervention in industry. Yet it announced an £800m a year stamp duty cut in the Budget explicitly to encourage the development of a computer settlement system by the stock exchange, part of the securities industry. Manufacturing's request for a similar tax boost was ignored.

In theory the cheapest way of funding infrastructure projects is through the public sector, where the money is raised through taxation or bond issues and the rate of return is set at a much less onerous level than would be demanded by private investors.

The downside is that without private sector involvement there is less pressure to keep costs down. The Humber bridge and the Channel tunnel are classic cases in point. So there is a powerful argument for joint public-private projects.

In reality, however, private investors are finding economic rules are invariably bent to suit political circumstances. But disillusion is setting in. The high speed link decision, which may actually be based on the political risks of piloting a private bill offensive to Kent voters through the Commons before an election, is likely to deter private sector investment in the road programme.

The director of one merchant bank closely involved in a number of schemes said: 'I think it is inevitable that the private sector will be put off. There is a general air of disenchantment.'

1. What factors should be taken into account when deciding if the Channel tunnel rail link should be built?
2. Can cost–benefit analysis explain why the government chose to subsidize the Manchester Metro link, but not the Channel link? If so, what are the differing factors involved?

Source: Michael Harrison and Peter Rodgers, *Independent*, 14 June 1990

When the economy settles down in such a way that no Pareto improvement is possible (i.e. any change would cause someone to be worse off), it is said to be Pareto optimal. The economy is at a **Pareto optimum**.

At minimum, then, we would expect CBA to lead to decisions which were at least Pareto optimal. It would be regarded as unsatisfactory if CBA rejected projects which could bring benefits to some without making anyone worse off.

So far so good, but satisfying this criterion provides no help with the problem of making interpersonal comparisons – it simply restricts us to considering only those projects which involve no losers. Obviously for many of the projects which are referred to the cost–benefit analyst there will be losers as well as gainers.

Motorways, airports, housing estates, bridges, etc. all cause some members of the community to suffer losses while bringing benefits to many others. The restriction imposed by the Pareto criterion is therefore unacceptable – we must find some way of deciding whether the benefits enjoyed by one group exceed the costs suffered by the other group.

One way forward has been suggested by two twentieth-century economists, Kaldor and Hicks. They suggest that the test should be whether or not the gainers could afford to 'compensate' the losers and still want to go ahead with the project. This is called the Kaldor–Hicks compensation test. Thus even when considering projects which do make some people worse off, it is possible to use the Pareto criterion by 'adding' some compensating redistribution of income to the project. In this way the project is modified so that there are no 'losers', any potential loser having been compensated just enough to leave him or her indifferent as to whether the project goes ahead or not.

Say, for example, we were planning to build a new airport. Everyone would like this to be done except a few local residents who dislike the noise of aircraft. Do we go ahead or not? The Kaldor–Hicks compensation test would say yes, if the rest of us could club together and pay the protesters just enough to make them withdraw their objections. Thus, with this technique of compensation, even projects which would of themselves be unsuitable candidates for Pareto assessment can be treated.

Notice that the compensation may not actually be paid. There are cases, of course, where losers do actually receive sums of money by way of compensation, but from the point of view of the cost–benefit analyst all that is required is the principle of compensation. If in principle it is possible to compensate losers and still have a Pareto improvement, then the project should be approved. Arguments about the distributional effects of projects (or any other form of government economic activity for that matter) require us to know what else is happening in the economy. Other projects and other policies may have reinforcing or moderating effects on the redistribution brought about by the project under consideration, and hence some overall (economy-wide) view must be taken.

SUMMARY

1. This chapter on cost–benefit analysis seeks to show how the free-enterprise system of resource allocation can be helped when dealing with large projects involving appreciable 'social' costs and 'social' benefits.
2. Demand analysis is used to demonstrate the importance of consumer surplus.
3. Supply analysis is used to draw attention to the existence of producer surplus.
4. There are difficulties in making interpersonal comparisons of utility when all we have are ordinal measures.
5. The solution offered by Pareto appears at first sight to be highly restrictive, but when augmented by the compensation test of Kaldor and Hicks becomes much more generally applicable.
6. Economic theory is thus being used here in two ways:
   (a) It is used to demonstrate the shortcomings of the free-enterprise system for a certain type of decision.
   (b) It is used to construct an alternative method of making these decisions – namely, cost–benefit analysis (CBA).
7. It is stressed, however, that CBA, like so much of applied economics, does not provide a clear set of rules for all occasions. It is simply a rough and ready way of offering guidance to decision makers. It raises issues which might otherwise be overlooked and suggests what needs to be done. In the final analysis the decision maker has to use his or her own judgement and subjective assessment of the issues raised.

Exam Preparation and Practice

MULTIPLE-CHOICE QUESTIONS

1. Which of the following is not a difficulty encountered when attempting a cost–benefit analysis of a project?
   A Current commodity prices.
   B Future commodity prices.
   C Timing of payments.
   D Interpersonal comparisons.

2. The diagram shows the supply and demand conditions for a car park run by a district council.

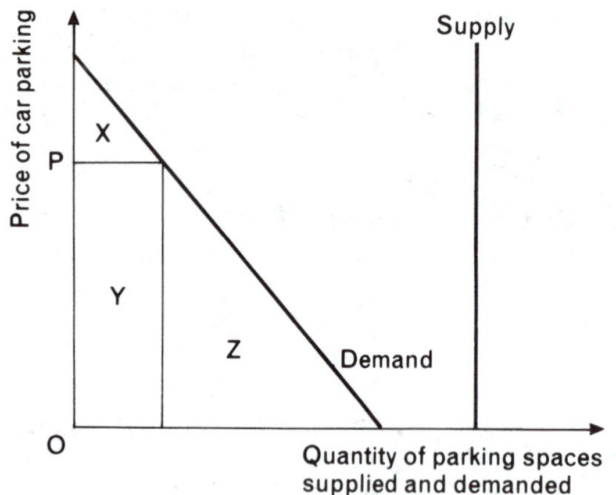

The council originally allows free parking, but then decides to charge the price of OP. Motorists' consumer surplus is reduced by an amount represented by area.
   A X
   B X+Y
   C Y+Z
   D X+Y+Z

(AEB)

3.

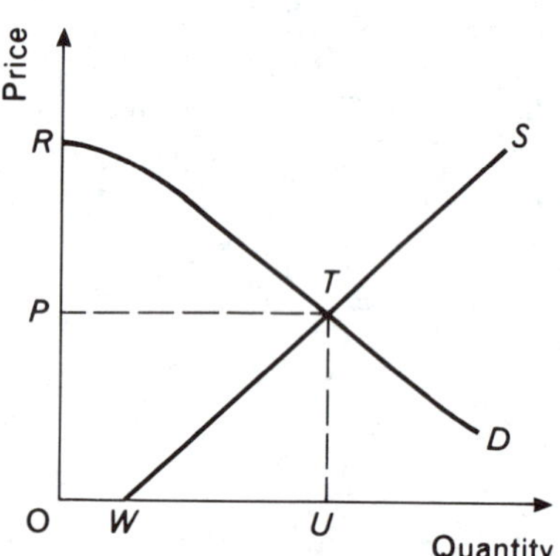

The diagram shows the market demand and supply curves for a good. When price *OP* is charged, total consumer *and* producer surplus is:
   A *OPTW*
   B *OPTU*
   C *PRT*
   D *ORTW*

4. The present value of £100 payable in one year's time when the rate of interest is 10% is:
   A £110.00 **C** £90.90
   B £99.00 **D** £90.00

5. The Kaldor–Hicks compensation principle states that a project should be allowed to proceed if:
   A The government will compensate all losers from the project.
   B The benefits from the project are sufficient to ignore objections.
   C The value of benefits if paid to the losers would more than compensate them for their loss.
   D Those who benefit from the project make annual payments to the losers.

EXERCISES

1. The diagram shows the market demand curve for apples. Find the value of the consumer surplus when the price of apples is (a) 10p/kg, (b) 8p/kg and (c) 5p/kg.

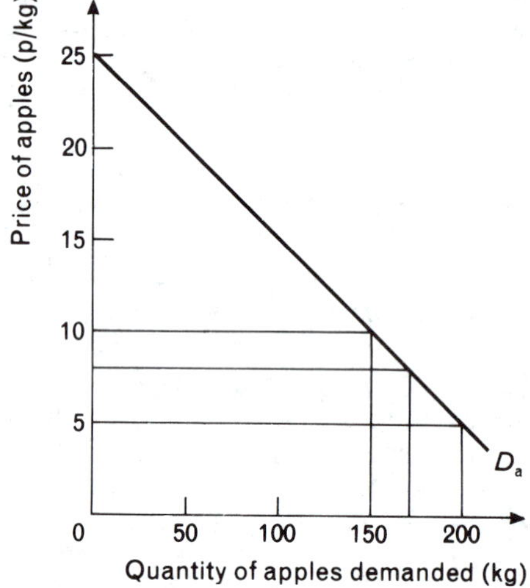

2. Suppose that the price of apples in the market in Exercise 1 is 5p. A firm acquires a monopoly in the market for apples and raises the price to 9p. What is the value of consumer surplus lost?

3. Suppose the monopoly seller of apples decides to restrict sales of apples to 100 kg. What is the loss of consumer surplus when the original price is again 5p.

4. The following diagram shows the demand for and supply of apples in a competitive market. The market price is 7p. What

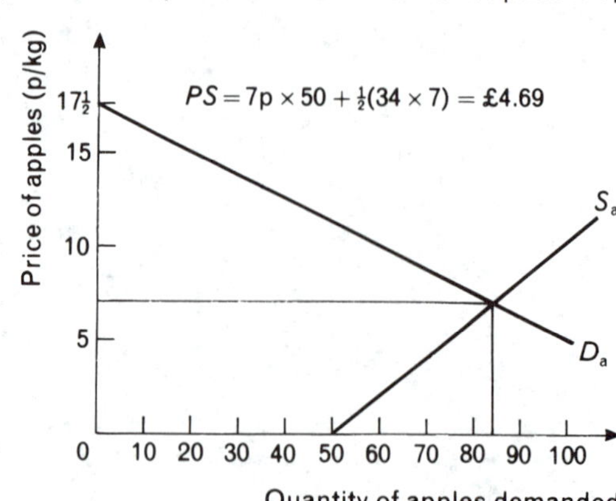

is the value of the producer surplus in this market? Why does producer surplus arise?

5. The government is considering building a nuclear power station on a coastal site 6 miles from the nearest houses.
   (a) What costs and benefits would the government want to consider?
   (b) How would the advisers to the government overcome:
      (i) the fact that costs such as pollution, noise and dirt and spoiling of countryside have no markets and so have no market price;
      (ii) the fact that the power station will have a life of over 30 years and must then be expensively 'decommissioned'.
   (c) Will using the market prices of electricity give a true picture of the power station's value in use?

6. When the government's advisers have completed their study of the power station project they find that there is a net benefit to society equivalent to £1,000,000, most of which goes to the company operating the power station and its customers. How might it be possible to judge if this is sufficient for the project to be undertaken?

7. Below we reproduce the results of an investigation into two alternative treatments for varicose veins. One treatment involves only out-patient treatment (injection–compression), the other a stay in hospital that averages 3.7 days per patient (surgical).

   To assess fully the costs and benefits of both treatments, what other factors than those listed need to be taken into account?

Average cost per patient of alternative treatments for varicose veins, 1967–68

	Injection–compression £	Surgical £
Medical staff	2.88	2.02
Nursing staff	1.12	2.02
Secretarial staff and medical records	1.04	2.76
Cost of rooms	0.03	13.71
Materials for treatment	4.70	1.34
Pathology	–	1.19
X-rays	–	5.80
'Shared costs'*	–	15.38
Total	£9.77	£44.22

* Shared costs covers domestic staff, catering, heat and light, maintenance, etc.
Source: Piachaud and Weddell, 'The economics of treating varicose veins', *International Journal of Epidemiology*', vol. 3, no. 1, 1972.

8 Comparative economic systems

In this chapter we will discuss:

1. The nature of the economic problem which each type of economic system is attempting to solve.
2. The nature and problems of capitalist, centrally planned and mixed economies.
3. Attempts to improve the forward planning of market economies.
4. The concept of the social market.

Introduction

In this chapter we will look at the different types of economy that are found in the world. Each type of economy is a different answer to the basic economic problem: *what, how and for whom to produce*.

Describing each type of economy is becoming more difficult. In the West a system based on the market is used, but with varying degrees of state intervention. In the Eastern bloc, which was characterized as a purely state-directed system for so many years, we now find a confused system which may or may not be moving towards a type of limited market. The term 'mixed economy' might be applied to all present world economies, but this is neither informative nor helpful.

We will look first at the characteristics of the three types of economy that students are traditionally taught about, how they are supposed to work and some reasons why they fail. We shall then consider recent developments in the thinking of both East and West.

Capitalist economies

These are economies that try to allocate resources through the use of markets and they are the type of economy that Adam Smith was examining prior to 1776. Such economies are also referred to as free-market economies or just market economies or **free-enterprise economies**. Free markets are also sometimes described as *laissez-faire*, which means they have total freedom to operate without any government intervention whatever. Completely free-market economies do not exist and have not done so for many years.

In Adam Smith's day there was very little state intervention in the economy, and very little industry too by today's standards. What fascinated Smith was how the economic system worked without anyone issuing instructions. He showed that it was the interaction of market forces which determined what would be produced, how it would be produced and who would benefit from this production. The market did all this, avoided systematic overproduction and largely satisfied the wants of the consumers – there were few shortages and few queues.

Modern market economies likewise work with little or no direction from above. We can usually find what goods and services we require without even having to give prior notice. This is an example of what Smith called the 'invisible hand' guiding the economy. He showed that if everybody acted in their own best interests, and, if markets worked properly (perfectly), then the economy would work well.

It is self-interest and competition which makes market economies work. The constant pressure to make a profit results in all firms trying to produce goods in the most efficient manner. Consumers have the right to buy from any firm and to choose the firm with the best product and fairest price. Thus any firm that produces a product that does not meet consumers' expectations will rapidly lose custom and go out of business.

From this we can say that market economies deal with the scarcity problem by allowing the market (which is the interaction of demanders and suppliers) to determine what is produced, how it will be produced and for whom the benefits of production are destined. Because of competition it is consumers who dictate what will be produced by allocating their incomes to the goods they most prefer. Firms then compete to supply these goods in the most efficient way possible. This system is known as **consumer sovereignty** because it is the customers who dictate the nature of production through their demand.

Features of a capitalist economy

In a capitalist economy any individual is free to own, buy and sell any property or resource to which he or she has legal title. In other words, it is possible for people to own things and natural resources. Thus in such an economy someone may own a house, a factory or even a mountain, and may dispose of these as he or she sees fit. One characteristic of a capitalist economy, therefore, is the institution of private property.

Market economies further rely on the ability of some people to organize others into productive units. Thus one person sets up a mill, borrowing funds, buying a building, machines (capital) and raw cotton (land) and employing people (labour). All of these resources are put to work and the final product is sold in the market place. Part of the return from the sale of the garments goes to pay labour, part goes to pay interest on borrowed funds and part goes to the suppliers of the raw cotton, but some goes to the organizer of production, the entrepreneur, in return for bearing risks. The entrepreneur who took the risk is rewarded with profit.

In a capitalist economy the entrepreneur is free to own, borrow, buy, hire, rent and sell. Free choice and free enterprise are essential features of market economies and are strongly defended by believers in the system as being fundamental rights.

Those who support central planning (particularly communist countries) tend to emphasize the role of capitalists rather than entrepreneurs in free-enterprise systems. They argue that the economy is controlled by the capitalist class, who use (or rather misuse) their political power to oppress and exploit the working class.

The government's role in a market economy, however, is not necessarily zero. At the very least there must be a government with the authority to impose law and order. Without a framework of laws and sanctions to enforce them the institution of private property and indeed of any contract is meaningless. It would simply not be possible to organize markets and firms. The role of the government is therefore to provide and maintain the *economic climate in which free enterprise can flourish*. It is not to direct or control the economic decisions of its citizens.

To summarize, in a market economy citizens are allowed to decide on the distribution of resources by their free interaction in markets. There will usually be some functions for government to perform, but these will be only those most necessary to allow the economy to operate.

Criticisms of capitalist economies

The best-known criticism of capitalist economies was made by Karl Marx (1818–83), who claimed that they were dominated by a capitalist class which exploited the working class. Marx has influenced many societies to change their economic systems to conform to his ideas and the ideas of his followers. In particular, the class struggle is resolved in some countries by outlawing private property, profits and private enterprise. All factors and functions apart from those of labour are vested in the state. The state represents the workers and so performs those functions to serve the interests of labour rather than those of capitalists.

There is a sound economic criticism of capitalist economies that can be levelled from the point of view of 'fairness'. It is claimed that a market economy results in an optimal allocation of resources and that, from any given starting point (i.e. any initial allocation of resources), a competitive market economy will reallocate resources through trading in markets until the most efficient allocation is reached. But the crucial point is that the final allocation depends on the initial allocation – on the starting point. If the initial allocation is such that most resources are concentrated in a few hands and most of the population is living at just above subsistence level, the final allocation, although 'efficient', may still make the poor no better off. In other words, market economies have no tendency to solve social problems.

Markets are also incapable of dealing properly with some goods such as **public goods** and **merit goods**. Public goods are those which, if provided for one, are perforce provided for all, and where the consumption of the good by one person in no way affects the consumption by another. An example of a public good is defence, which once provided protects everyone (much to the annoyance of some). No matter how much protection I get it makes no difference to the defence available to you. When benefits or costs are imposed on outsiders in this way they are known as **externalites**. The market cannot provide defence because few individuals will voluntarily pay their share – it is too easy to let someone else pay, but still to enjoy the benefit.

A merit good is one that can be provided by the market, but not in sufficient quantities. For example, if the state did not provide education then only a small percentage of the population would be able to afford (or even want to afford) to go to school. Thus the state bypasses the market and provides education free of charge to all.

The market is unable to pass on what are known as **social costs**. These are costs which arise out of a productive process, but which are not directly charged to the producer and hence are not passed on to the consumer. The market therefore underestimates the costs. An example of this is smoke from a factory chimney, which rises into the atmosphere and descends as acid rain many hundreds of miles away. The forests of Norway are being destroyed by acid rain caused partly by sulphur emissions from the UK. The firms that have caused these emissions are not at present called upon to pay for the costs of replanting forests and deacidifying lakes. This cost is borne by the Norwegian taxpayer, but it should be borne by the consumer of the firm's product. Thus if the firm had to pay the social costs as well as the private costs of production (wages, rent, etc.) then the final price would be much higher.

In a similar way there may be social benefits which people get free from a productive process as a by-product. In both cases the market needs the assistance of government. The prospect of a polluter's tax is a real possibility in the UK as awareness of environmental issues grows.

It is possible to illustrate this using a firm's cost curves. A firm faces private costs of production which are reflected in its marginal cost curve. In a perfectly competitive market this is the firm's supply curve. Let us suppose that the product which the firm produces causes pollution, which must be cleaned up. It is reasonable to suppose that the amount of pollution released will increase with the amount of output the firm produces. Hence the cost of cleaning up the pollution will rise with output. If the social costs are added to the firm's private costs then we find that we can draw a new marginal cost curve that reflects both costs. This lies above the firm's private marginal cost curve as shown in Figure 8.1.

The situation in Figure 8.1 can help us to decide what action might be taken. Perhaps the most obvious solution is to ask consumers of the product instead of the public as a

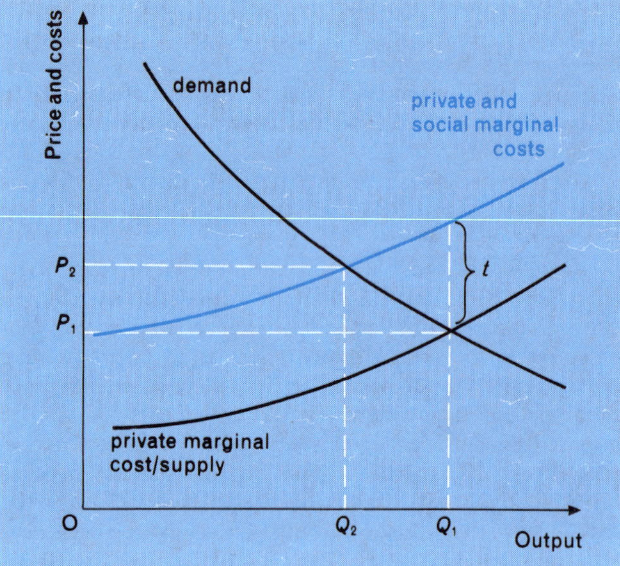

Figure 8.1 Private and social marginal costs.

whole to pay the clean-up costs of the product. This can be achieved by imposing a tax on the product equal to t. As we have already seen, only a proportion of this tax is passed on to the consumer since the rest is paid by the firm, but it has the effect of reducing consumption of the good (from Q_1 to Q_2) and so reducing overall pollution. It also provides a fund to pay the clean-up costs. The 'polluters pay' under this system, providing that the true social costs can be indentified and that governments have the political will to impose the tax. (Cigarettes could be dealt with in this way, but the excise duty on them does not cover the National Health Service costs of treating smokers.)

The existence of **monopolies** in a market economy can prevent the optimal allocation of resources because such firms are able to prevent other firms from entering the industry. When this occurs the consumer is charged a higher price than he or she would be charged under competitive conditions (since price is greater than marginal cost) and far less is then bought and sold (see Chapter 6). To prevent this government legislation may be necessary to reduce a firm's power in a particular market and to allow competitors to exist. There is a counter-argument that large firms produce more cheaply than many small firms. This possibility was considered in Chapter 6.

There is a class of monopolies that can be tolerated in a capitalist economy: these are known as **natural monopolies**. Industries such as gas, water and electricity supply fall into this category even though all are now privately owned limited companies in the UK. No home has the choice of buying mains water from more than one company. This is not because it would be impossible, but because it would be prohibitively expensive to build more than one water main per street. Imagine a world where every house had six water pipes, five electricity cables and several gas pipes running to the door. Most would lie unused and traffic would never move for the constant road works! In fact few companies can survive in such a world due to the large set-up costs associated with laying down the mains network for the industry. Unless everybody uses the one mains system the cost per customer is prohibitively high. In a competitive situation only one company would survive and would pick up the customers of the bankrupt companies.

When there are such high set-up costs any firm in the industry is faced with very large fixed costs. This causes the average total cost curve of the firm to fall over a significant proportion of the industry output. This is because the fixed costs of the firm are so large when compared to the variable costs (such as labour) that they dominate the average. When the firm does increase output its costs rise only fractionally. This makes it very difficult for small firms to compete because they will face higher average costs than any firm with a larger output.

Consider the example of a railway system. To develop the system, lay the track, provide the rolling stock and build the stations would be very expensive. Should the railway company decide to put an extra carriage on a train the cost involved will be very small. The company will use an otherwise idle carriage and the train will use a little more fuel to pull the extra weight of the train and passengers. The marginal cost of this operation is dwarfed by the fixed costs of the whole system. In such natural monopolies the average cost curve of the firm falls constantly and the marginal cost curve will therefore always lie below the average cost curve. (This is always the case when the average cost curve is falling.) This situation is shown in Figure 8.2.

As the diagram shows, if the firm tries to price 'efficiently' where marginal cost equals price then it will always make a loss. Competition will cause all firms to make losses until there is only one left. That firm can then equate average cost to price. As there is no allocatively efficient solution in this case, and it may take a long time for one firm to emerge, or firms may collude, many governments prefer to nationalize such industries.

Finally, there is the argument that markets have no

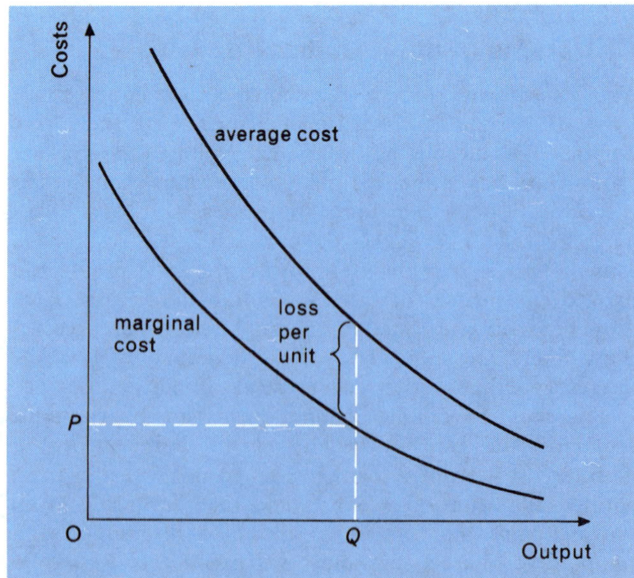

Figure 8.2 Average and marginal costs under natural monopoly.

representatives of future generations and therefore fail to make proper provision for future needs. Consider a competitive economy that works very well without government. Then the problem of global warming due to industrial activity and the use of fossil fuels is discovered. There is no mechanism to prevent the continued use of harmful products because the market is allocating resources 'efficiently' according to current prices and costs. Firms will not individually switch to alternative energy sources because if they are more expensive they will force up costs and cause the firm to lose custom or profit. In such a case there is a role for government.

The fact that markets are unable to provide public goods at all, provide merit goods in insufficient quantities and produce vast differences in the incomes of people has led many to doubt the economist's definition of efficiency. How can an allocation of resources that leaves such vast room for improvement be efficient?

The answer lies in the fact that economists are describing what is known as allocative efficiency. Allocative efficiency occurs where every factor of production earns the best return it can and where no amount of swapping around of factors will cause greater production at an equal or lower cost. The statement of allocative efficiency makes no claim about fairness and we must remind ourselves again that politics and economics often tread a similar course, but for different objectives. Many economists, however, do say that a situation should be changed – they make **normative** statements about what should happen.

SUMMARY

1. All economic systems have to address the economic problem of scarcity. Each system must find ways of deciding what will be produced, how it is to be produced and to whom the benefits of production will be distributed.
2. Capitalist economies allow the free interaction of economic agents to make all decisions via the market. There is only limited government activity aimed at enabling rather than controlling nature.
3. It is claimed that in a free market where everyone acts in their own best interests the final output of the economy is that desired by consumers and the prices are the lowest possible.
4. Capitalist economies can only exist where people are able to own property and are free to direct other resources in a productive process.
5. There are numerous criticisms of the capitalist system:
   (a) The system is divisive with entrepreneurs and those with inherited wealth living a life different from those who only have their labour to sell.
   (b) There is no automatic process for dealing with poverty, and the continued operation of capitalism need not improve the position of the poor.
   (c) The market cannot provide public goods, such as defence, at all and undersupplies merit goods, such as education.
   (d) Firms consider only their own costs when making price and output decisions and so ignore social costs, such as the effect of pollution caused by the product or its manufacture.
   (e) The existence of monopolies causes a deviation from the best market solution and there is no process to correct this. Some industries can only be operated as monopolies due to their cost structure (natural monopolies).
   (f) The market has no method of forward planning.

Command economies

These are economies which allocate resources through central planning by state-run organizations. Such economies are usually associated with socialist and communist countries, although they are not the only types of society that could adopt planning. In the rapidly changing politics of Eastern Europe it is difficult to tell how many countries will operate command economies in the future. We can say that most East European countries have operated such economies and that at present even the post-*perestroika* Soviet Union does so, along with China, Romania and Albania.

Command economies owe much to the thinking of Karl Marx. The Marxian system does not start with the assumption of placing the individual at the centre as market economies do. Rather, individual interests are seen as being subservient to the greater needs of society as a whole. Marx wished to see a system where resources are allocated 'From each according to his ability, to each according to his needs.' In other words, each member of the community gives of his or her best and receives the goods and services he or she needs. Such a system has no need for competition or markets or capitalists or private profit. Allocative efficiency and social justice are both dealt with by the central planners, and the poor and the less able are provided for by society via the state.

The basic problem facing a command economy is, however, exactly the same as the problem facing a market economy, that of scarcity. Most command economies tackle this by constructing detailed plans on what to produce and how to produce it given the nation's resources. When making these decisions the **central planning bureau (CPB)**, as it is known, also decides for whom the output of the economy is destined. By deciding that the economy is going to produce so many tractors, for example, it has answered the 'for whom?' question and has, because of scarcity, also made a decision not to produce domestic washing machines. The decisions of the CPB are guided by social priorities and are made on behalf of the people it is elected to represent.

Thus the command economy is quite different from the market economy. There is but one decision maker (the CPB) and resources are allocated according to its wishes. There is only a limited role for prices and this may vary between different command economies.

Features of a command economy

To help outline the essential features of a command economy it is useful to use an example. The best known of these is the former Soviet Union. The Soviet economy was run from 1929 to 1991 on the basis of plans lasting five years or more. The economy was declining rather than growing, and the government wanted to plan Soviet industrialization along lines that would maximize economic growth.

The aim was to eliminate the use of markets and to direct production as the government wished. Without planning it was felt the industry would produce too many consumer goods at the expense of investment goods and that agriculture would not give up its surplus labour to the new industries that the government wanted to create. Indeed the matter of capital accumulation was crucial to the thinking of the planners.

Most economies have the choice between producing goods that will be consumed now and producing goods that will help produce more goods (capital goods). If capital goods are produced then this means – because of scarce resources – that less can be consumed now. But in later years growth will be much faster due to the greater amount of machines, factories, etc. available to make goods.

This can be illustrated on a production possibility frontier as shown in Figure 8.3. If PPF_1 represents the economy's current production possibility frontier then a choice of where to produce can be made anywhere along it. The choice of point A produces rather more consumer goods than capital goods when compared to point B. The citizens of a country that chose point A would enjoy a higher standard of living during the current year than those in a country that chose point B. The next year, however, the production possibility frontier of the country that chose mix A expands to only PPF_2, whereas the country that chose mix B now has many more capital goods and is able to produce far more of both types of good, as represented by PPF_3.

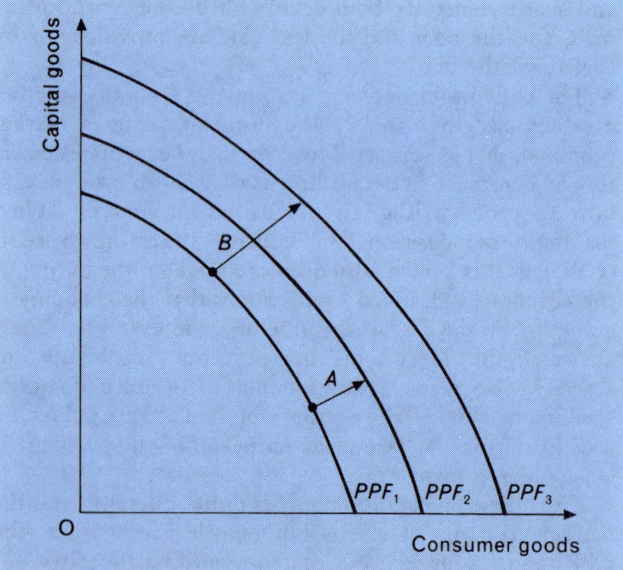

Figure 8.3 Present and future consumption.

This is the logic which underlines the concept of planning: an economy can plan to expand its productive capacity and, if the plan works, can enjoy a higher future standard of living.

The Soviet Union has issued plans to guide its economy ever since 1929 and we can look at its modern planning process in detail.

The best-known feature of Soviet planning is the industrial goods planning process, which is shown in Figure 8.4. This process decides what and how much each industrial unit will produce. The decision of the planning committee, Gosplan, is designed to be in line with the current five-year plan, but this is by no means a simple operation.

Suppose the plan calls for the production of an extra 20,000 motor cars. The factories that will make the cars are given their quotas and report back that they need not only an extra amount of steel, but also an extra 10,000 square metres of factory space and accompanying machinery. This must cause a change in the provisional allocations made by Gosplan. To meet the quota Gosplan must provide the extra steel, the factory extension and the extra machinery. This means revising the steel output plan, which means that there will be a need for extra coking coal and other raw materials and that these plans must also be revised. Various enterprises are now given their revised quotas and they make similar requests for more resources – thus the revision process starts again.

It is quite possible for the planners to find that they cannot provide the resources necessary to meet the plan. It is also not uncommon for the plan to fail to add up properly due to poor information, i.e. outputs may not equal inputs. This is hardly surprising when you consider that over 20 million individual commodities are produced in the Soviet Union.

Once the decision on what to produce has been made and the plan issued, the next question is how to allocate labour to the various enterprises. In this case the Soviet Union does behave quite like a market economy as it too faces shortages of workers in certain industries or areas. Soviet workers are largely free to choose the job they do from those on offer, and to fill shortage areas the Soviets offer various incentives. Wage rates for workers with skills in short supply, or for those who are prepared to work in unpopular regions (e.g. Siberia), are higher than for other workers. Often such workers are 'promoted' to higher-paid positions, but continue to do the same job. Finally, the workers are offered training schemes and incentives to learn to fill vacancies.

This process would seem very similar to that of a market economy, but in fact the rates of pay are decided centrally, not by markets which reflect the relative scarcity of labour. Thus the process of wage adjustment to fill skill or regional shortages is much slower than in a market economy.

It would be quite impossible, given present technology, to decide which consumer goods each family could have from the current round of production. The Soviet Union does allow consumers to spend their incomes freely, but of course the goods available are determined by the current plan and the prices are set centrally. Thus prices do have a limited role to play here, but there is no reason to suppose that prices will change in response to shortages or surpluses of goods.

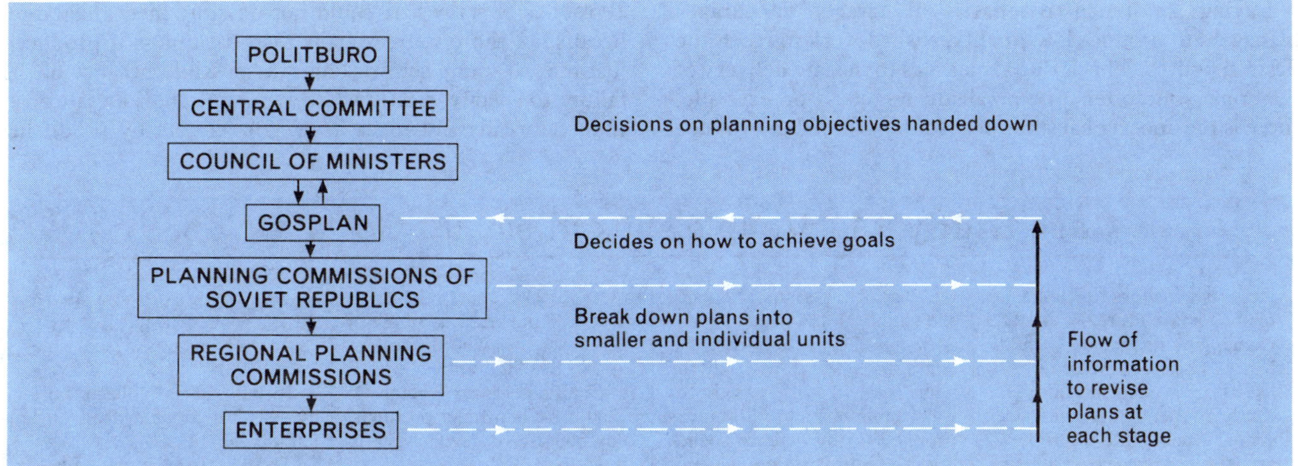

Figure 8.4 Soviet industrial goods planning process.

In fact some prices in the Soviet Union have remained unchanged for many years and attempts to change them are bitterly resisted by consumers. This means that when the price of a good is relatively low there is excess demand for it and the only way to obtain the good is to join a queue. Long queues rather than higher prices are the indicators of shortages, and literally hours and hours are spent queuing up for basic goods. Russian consumers complain about shortages of essential goods such as bread and meat, but the planners have been slow to respond. Even when things go well shortages occur. In 1989 there was an excellent grain harvest, yet by December there was a bread shortage.

The Soviet Union has experienced particular difficulty in agriculture, partly because it is still very sensitive to price changes. Farms are organized as co-operatives and so a low price for agricultural products leads to low farm incomes. This in turns leads to farm workers offering to work fewer hours or working less hard; instead they concentrate on the small plots of land they are allowed to farm for themselves. The introduction of limited free agricultural markets – where the produce of the private plots may be sold – has led to a rise in overall production. The authorities have steadily raised the prices paid to collectives and this has led to a rise in their production. This is exactly the response that we would expect in a market economy, but once again it has been a slow and cumbersome process.

One area where the Soviet Union finds it impossible to plan is in foreign trade. The Eastern bloc countries have a particular problem with trade because their currencies are not freely convertible into the Western currencies necessary to buy the technologically more advanced goods of the capitalist world. This aside the planners cannot plan how much foreign countries wish to buy of their output in a given year. In the realms of exports then the Soviet Union is in the hands of the market and the demand for Soviet goods varies with price. This is not as serious a problem as it appears: only a small proportion of the USSR's output is traded and most of this is trade with other Eastern bloc countries, which is organized and controlled through Comecon. Even so the Soviet Union would like to trade more, but at present does not have the foreign currency or quality of goods to do so.

From this it can be seen that planning the output of an economy is not easy, and even the oldest of the planned economies requires the help of prices in allocating goods. These prices are not the same as those in market economies because they need not change in response to shortages; nor do they determine producers' incomes as they do in the West.

Criticisms of command economies

Communist command economies have not been highly thought of in the West. There is a widespread belief that command economies are not as efficient as market economies and that, despite the weakness of pure markets in coping with 'the poor', the poor in the Eastern bloc have a significantly worse lot than those in the West. It is a significant fact that, although they aim to accelerate growth through planned investment, the planned economies have never caught up with the unplanned Western economies in the European Community or the USA. Indeed the gap between them has widened.

The greatest difficulty in planning seems to be a lack of information. Even a small economy has thousands of firms and millions of workers and consumers producing and consuming several million goods. The market allocates resources, decides on remuneration to each type of worker and comes up with prices so that (in perfect markets) all goods that are produced are sold. If this were not true then we would observe long queues or piles of unwanted goods in the streets. In the command economies such problems are supposed to be eliminated by careful planning. Yet in the former Soviet Union queues are an everyday fact of life and the state warehouses are full of unsold (perhaps unsaleable) goods.

Since rewards are not linked to economic performance but are calculated by the central planning bureau according to need, there is an acute lack of incentives to work hard or be efficient. Managers are charged with meeting their targets or providing reasons for not doing so. The strategies adopted by the managers are consequently defensive and secretive. Managers who fail to meet their targets may claim that a lack of materials was the cause, despite the fact that they hold large stockpiles.

Laying so much emphasis on targets encourages managers to produce low-quality, rushed work to reach the desired figures. This is due sometimes to the late delivery of materials, but often to unrealistic targets. For example, there is the apocryphal story of a factory ordered to produce 20 tonnes of screws. It could not possibly meet this target because of the resources at its disposal unless it produced just one 20-tonne screw! This was possible because of the failure to specify exactly what was required. The saucepan industry really did meet its weight targets by producing

Case Study 8.1 Rouble and strife in the Soviet Union

First-time visitors to Russia are ready for a culture shock. The vague, grey image one formerly had of cities like Moscow may have been transformed more recently by perestroika and television access. But the reports, and those newsreel pictures of scrambles for scarce, unappetising-looking meat, have prepared you for the worst – or so you think.

In fact they have not, and the tales you hear on arrival from expatriates and Russians alike are soon borne out by your own experience: you witness the corruption, you experience the inefficiency and you encounter a citizenry whose economic system has made the wasting of time into an art form.

The voters, as they now are, are fed up, but the problem is that, after five years of glasnost and perestroika, things are going from bad to worse. Soviet bureaucrats and independent economists talk openly about how dreadful everything is; and even the optimists believe that, although things may get better, they will get a lot worse first.

What good are potential improvements in the economic situation from 1992 onwards to a President Gorbachov with whom public patience has already run out, and who has the increasingly popular Russian president, Boris Yeltsin, at his heels?

One way of appreciating the enormous task facing the USSR is to look back to the arguments advanced by Western Marxists for decades after the Second World War. Not only was central planning necessary in wartime; it also delivered the goods in peacetime. Just look at the production targets achieved by the Soviet Union, they argued, and consider the waste of capitalism.

Capitalism, they insisted, was only propped up by the 'military/industrial complex', and by 'imperialist defence spending'.

In this they were hardly discouraged by Moscow, yet all the while the real truth was that it was Communism itself that was propped up by defence spending. The Soviet system was not delivering the consumer goods, and many Moscow experts thought the game was up by the 1970s – until the oil price rise bailed out the USSR for another decade.

Despite all the derision he received at the time, it was probably President Reagan's Star War plans that convinced the Kremlin they had lost the economic war. The Soviet economic system could not withstand a further escalation in defence spending.

We now know that Western experts had persistently overestimated Russia's economic strength.

My favourite economic news of this year has been the revelation by Soviet experts to the CIA that Soviet defence spending was much higher as a proportion of gross domestic product (GDP) than the CIA had calculated (the Americans had thought it was only twice the US rate) and that the USSR's GDP was itself much lower than the CIA estimate.

The fact of the matter is that this is a desperately poor people, despite the economy's endowment of natural resources; statistics now widely quoted by the Russians suggest that Soviet GDP is in the region of 1,000 billion roubles, compared to the $5,000 billion US economy.

It is anybody's guess how many roubles there will be to the dollar when the market is eventually allowed to decide, but it would be a generous estimate to suggest that Soviet GDP amounted, realistically, to $500 billion.

The anachronism of the tower blocks apart, the standard of living and way of life of the Muscovites who do not belong to the elite reminds one of immediate post-war Britain. Of 1,200 basic consumer products, only 150 are on regular sale in the shops.

From the point of view of the consumer, this economy has been mismanaged on a colossal scale. One of Gorbachov's many problems is that the often promised radical economic reforms have not even begun. There is much talk about the prospect of a proper banking system, a stock market, a system of property rights – indeed, a system of property ownership.

Capitalism is about ownership of land and capital, and market economics are about the efficient use and movement of capital and labour in a way that maximises the satisfaction of a society of consumers.

Moscow's new breed of economist recognises the price mechanism as a better means of signalling consumer needs than State-ordained production targets. Realistic rates of interest – to reward those who part with liquidity rather than produce more goods that nobody wants – are enthusiastically urged by members of ministries and government agencies that still happen to be practising the old ways.

But Prime Minister Ryzhkov's highly unpopular package of price increases – including more than doubling the price of food – threatened a drastic reduction in real incomes (one estimate is 16 per cent of real income per capita) and was announced without any detailed and concrete explanation of how the much-discussed move towards a market economy would be achieved.

It looked, and felt like another administered price rise without much element of 'market' in it. And it threatened to hurt when people were impatient for results which benefited *them*.

It has officially been postponed, but looks a dead duck politically.

Thus there is much talk of abandoning the old ways, but not much progress. Since it took the capitalist West the best part of 100 years to civilise what some refer to here as 'jungle capitalism', one should perhaps not complain about slow progress since 1985.

But Gorbachov's problem is that in five years he is seen to have delivered less than nothing.

Gorbachov's political cycle is hopelessly out of synchronisation with his economic reforms. Nobody believes this economy can be 'restructured' from domination by the arms industry and extreme inefficiency in the civilian sector without massive unemployment and civil unrest.

The very first whiff of decentralisation has produced a payments crisis as Soviet enterprises have, in the words of one official, 'readily and willingly fulfilled the import side of their obligations', while exports – not least oil revenues – have been falling.

Helping the USSR over its overseas payments crisis, and possibly over the horrendous period ahead – when it faces the worst effects of reform without any immediate benefits – is becoming an issue for the impending World Economic Summit. The Germans and the French, at least, say they want to help.

The terrible thing is that it is not just officials in the US who say things like: 'In the absence of fundamental macroeconomic reforms in the Soviet Union … assistance can be just like water in a sieve.' The same fear haunts Moscow.

1. Does the experience of the Soviet Union mean that all planned economies must fail?

Source: William Keegan, *Observer*, 24 June 1990

Case Study 8.2 Thankless task of trying to right 40 years of communist misrule

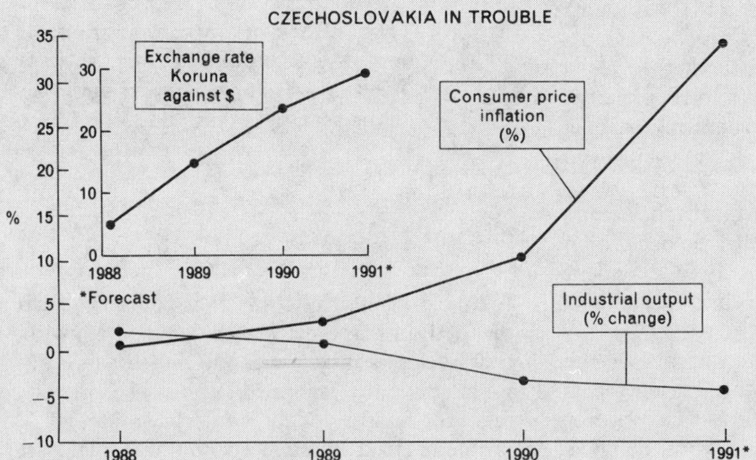

THE West is preparing to pour substantial amounts of aid, advice, private sector investment and economic assistance into the economies of eastern Europe. Yet no one seems clear what path of development they can follow to prosperity. All that can be said with certainty is that the developing country model, on which western policy seems to be based, is inappropriate.

The uniqueness of east Europe's economy and the required policy responses are a theme frequently heard from Vaclav Klaus, the Czechoslovak finance minister, who expresses dissatisfaction with what he sees is a paternalistic western approach.

Mr Klaus says Czechoslovakia cannot follow the path of Spain or Portugal 15 years ago, by attracting a capital inflow to compensate for a trade deficit while the country imports equipment. He also rejects British-style privatisation via the stock market, or eastern German *Treuhand* sales.

The difference between Czechoslovakia and other economies in trouble goes beyond the overt symptoms of reduced industrial production, rising unemployment and inflation, says Mr Klaus. More fundamentally, countries such as Czechoslovakia are not undeveloped in the conventional sense, as evidenced not least by the unseemly sights of the chimneys in Saxony, northern Bohemia and Bratislava. They have just become inefficient.

Before the second world war Bohemia had the highest per capita gross national product in Europe. Nor does Czechoslovakia as a whole suffer from outright poverty or squalor despite 40 years of communist mismanagement.

The problem is lack of the most fundamental economic freedom, taken for granted in the West: the right to private ownership. If the problems are so vastly different, then surely so must be the solutions.

The traditional model for ailing developing economies involves a squeeze on domestic consumption through combined fiscal and monetary policies, to coincide with increased imports of capital goods. The result is still a short-term current account deficit, but this is balanced by a capital account surplus.

The increase in the capital surplus is usually achieved through net foreign capital inflows, a combination of aid and direct private-sector investments in domestic assets, which do not raise the government's foreign debt.

Economic growth would really accelerate once domestic savings are sufficient to create domestic investments. The reward is increased industrial production, employment and exports. This is roughly what happened in South Korea, the most recent example of successfully applied development economics.

The difficulties of attracting a capital account surplus to Czechoslovakia lie in the lack of a legal framework for enterprise and an investment environment. This is something no western assistance could provide.

Czechoslovakia differs in this respect from Hungary, where the transition to a more liberal regime of trade has taken place over a longer period. East Europe is, for the same reason, different from the authoritarian regimes of South America. As Warren Oliver, chief economist at UBS-Phillips & Drew, said: 'Fascist corporate style leaves more of a free market economy in place than communist corporate style.' The difference is mainly that Chile, for instance, allowed some private ownership, while Czechoslovakia did not, and still does not to any large degree.

Merchant bankers and others argue that a stronger capital account could be achieved via sales to foreign companies or investors. But Czechoslovakia's industry, with a few exceptions, is worth little. The 1,300 joint ventures and takeovers in Czechoslovakia to last year had a capital of only 3.8 billion korunas ($130 million).

The most notable exception is Volkswagen's takeover of Skoda, the long-established carmaker, but the expected inflow of DM10 billion did not occur at the takeover. It will happen over 10 years as VW upgrades Skoda plants.

In the short and medium term the effect of foreign investment, even if it was to increase exponentially over time, will be marginal in terms of capital inflows, apart from usually being unpopular.

At the same time, Czechoslovakia's trade account is coming under strain. Foreign trade between east European countries has all but collapsed after the switch to hard currency trading. The cost of energy, now settled in dollars rather than transfer-roubles or barter deals, has soared. This now represents the trade balance's main negative.

Zdenek Lukas, economist at the Vienna Institute for Comparative Economic Studies, estimates Czechoslovakia's foreign debt will rise from $8.1 billion last year to about $12 billion to pay for imports.

While privatisations or direct investment will not do much for the country's accounts, they may still be worthwhile in improving the competitive environment. This is the idea behind Czechoslovakia's programme to privatise large companies, which will start next year. Though some will be sold directly to foreign investors, most will go to Czechoslovakians via 'investment vouchers', at a price of 2,000 korunas, just over one half of the average monthly wage.

These can be used to acquire shares in selected companies. Many westerners find great difficulty in comprehending this. It involves no valuation of companies, no effective increase in the companies' capital, only a transfer of ownership from the state to the private sector.

The government admits that even this transfer will be made under highly imperfect conditions. People would have to use their coupons in exchange for shares in companies about which there is little financial information.

The voucher system was created amid a recognition that private ownership of land and assets is necessary for further development. There can be little more than a hope that simply giving away free shares will fundamentally change attitudes. But these are essentially internal processes, which could not be achieved by western benevolence.

1. What is the significance of buying energy 'in dollars rather than [in] transfer-roubles or barter deals'? (Transfer roubles implies a paper transaction only in Russian currency.)
2. What is the significance of the lack of private ownership in the transformation of Czechoslovakia to a mixed economy?

Source: Wolfgang Münchau, *The Times*, May 1991

mainly heavy catering saucepans, while consumers were unable to buy saucepans for domestic use.

Many argue that greater reliance on the price mechanism would allow economies to allocate resources much more efficiently. In recent years areas such as Estonia, Lithuania and Latvia have been allowed to develop a private business sector, but only in small businesses. In a further development factory managers have been allowed to take responsibility for their plants and to reap a personal reward if a profit is made. In such cases targets have even been exceeded. However, the experiment was for the outer reaches of the Soviet Union only, and Mr Gorbachev made it clear that the future even for a reformed Soviet Union was a socialist not a capitalist one. The newly independent republics such as Russia now appear to be charting a course towards a market economy.

While we have listed a number of criticisms of the command system in general, there is another reason for its apparent failure which is specific to the Soviet Union. For many years the USSR was preoccupied with defence. Following the 1917 revolution the Soviets were invaded by the allied powers and for a number of years fought a civil war. As the only communist power, the Soviet Union felt threatened and devoted a great deal of its resources to defence. Following the Second World War the Soviet Union and the Eastern bloc were in a permanent state of readiness as the 'cold war' was fought out with the United States. All this military effort produced no more consumer and investment goods, and seriously hampered the Soviet economy and those of its allies. However, the objective of security was achieved, together with a degree of economic growth and a successful space programme. As expenditure on defence declines and workers enjoy a greater share of the goods produced, their enthusiasm may be reawakened and the efficiency of their economy increased.

SUMMARY

1. A command economy makes decisions centrally about what, how and for whom to produce. The role of consumers and individual firms in the decision-making process is minimal.
2. The central planning bureau makes decisions based upon social priorities decided by the state. It is common for there to be a national plan setting out both broad and specific targets.
3. By taking decisions out of the hands of individuals it is claimed that long-term plans can be made, such as the decision to invest a greater proportion of national output and so allow the country to grow faster in the future.
4. Planning is a complex process even for a small economy. It is common for plans to be incomplete or, due to poor information, inaccurate.
5. Prices do have a role in command economies, but they are set centrally and do not adjust to excess demand or supply as they do in market economies.
6. Criticisms of command economies include:
   (a) There is little incentive to work hard as the rewards of improved output do not go directly to those who make the extra effort.
   (b) Managers of state enterprises have a vested interest in not telling the truth to the planners to avoid difficult output targets.
   (c) The task of planning any economy is too complex to be done satisfactorily.
   (d) The system is not able to respond as quickly as the market to changing conditions.

Mixed economies

A mixed economy is one that combines features of both planned and free-market economies. It is not possible to characterize a mixed economy in the same way as the ones we have already examined because each mixed economy is a different mixture of the two other systems. The economic problem faced by such economies remains the same, i.e. scarcity, and decisions must still be made about what to produce, how to do so and to whom the produce will be distributed.

There are now two types of mixed economy. One originates from the gradual evolution of market economies where governments have taken a larger and larger role. The other originates from command economies that have adopted more aspects of the market approach. The latter have developed only very recently (although we saw in the previous section that command economies do use some aspects of markets) and so we will confine our attention to the former.

Since the turn of the century there has been a gradually increasing role of government in economies such as the UK. The Great Depression of 1929–39 spurred politicians to find ways of reducing the most socially damaging aspects of markets, such as mass unemployment. Since 1945 most 'free market' governments have tried to help markets find full employment and to help industries develop and grow. These governments have also tried to provide for the less well-off and to see that the public and merit goods which the market cannot provide have been available. They have done all of this while allowing the rest of the economy to continue to operate as a market economy. Thus governments direct the allocation of some resources, while allowing the rest to be allocated by the market.

The problems of capitalist economies were outlined earlier. It is these that mixed economies are trying to resolve without abandoning the parts of the market mechanism that they see as good. When looking at mixed economies it is impossible to ignore the political views of the society concerned. Even within such countries there will be disagreement as to the extent of government intervention that is desirable. We can list the issues involved and leave it to the individual to decide on their importance. This is done in Table 8.1.

During the nineteenth century the industrialized countries experienced regular cycles in economic activity. A period of high employment and output (a boom) would be followed by a period of slower growth or even negative growth and increasing unemployment (a slump or depression). In the UK the cycle followed a roughly seven-

Table 8.1 Issues in market economies

Failings of market economies	Solutions of a mixed economy
Monopolies	Regulation of firms holding more than a certain percentage of the market. (See Chapter 6.)
Social costs and benefits	Legislation to control harmful effects, e.g. Environmental Protection Act 1990.
Income distribution	Social security payments to worst-off, Pensions, Taxation of wealthy.
Lack of public and merit goods	Provision of goods paid for by taxation.
Cyclical nature of market economies	Intervention to direct resources in a counter-cyclical way.
Lack of long-term planning	Issuing of forecasts. Encouraging investment in certain areas of the country or in particular industries.

year pattern up to the early years of this century. After this cycles became more irregular and the depression of the 1930s lasted almost the whole decade.

The incentive for politicians to try to mitigate the worst effects of recession were very strong, and today politicians are sometimes blamed for unemployment as much as for any other failings. Thus governments try to influence the level of economic activity by their own spending and by the issue of money. This is the fundamental difference between a mixed economy and a market economy: in the former, the government feels responsible for the management of the economy.

Features of a mixed economy

As the mixed economies do vary so much, we can only make generalizations about them. Clearly each has an element of government control and an element of market allocation. In what follows it must be understood that every mixed economy takes a slightly different view.

The government deals with poverty by attempting to redistribute income from the better-off to the worse-off. It does this by allowing labour to continue to find its own employment at the going wage rate, but taxing those in employment and making transfers to the unemployed, old and low-paid. The most usual method is to tax incomes in such a way as to make the best-paid contribute most. Thus most income tax systems have a range of income where no tax is paid and thereafter the percentage paid rises as the workers' income does. The poorest are given pensions or allowances to bring their income up to some socially acceptable level. It is possible for those in work to receive benefits, often in kind, such as free school meals for their children.

Associated with the relief of poverty most mixed economies try to provide public and merit goods at a price that most can afford. This may range from free education to subsidized train services. This is an area of great diversity and few general rules apply even in such areas as health care which the UK provides almost free of charge while others charge according to income.

When dealing with industry all mixed economies have built up a maze of rules, regulations, incentives and disincentives. They fall into the broad categories of maintaining competition, preventing the decline of important industries, encouraging investment both generally and in certain areas, and controlling industry via planning and safety measures. In some cases it is felt that the state must take control of the industries concerned (nationalization), whereas other countries prefer to regulate an industry while leaving it in private hands.

Allied to the assistance of industry is a general concern for the well-being of the economy. No government wishes to see its population out of work and so the encouragement of employment is important. Government can help remove uncertainty for business: for example, it might guarantee export earnings once a sale is confirmed, or it might issue forecasts of future trends in an effort to help firms make plans in an atmosphere of greater certainty. In addition the

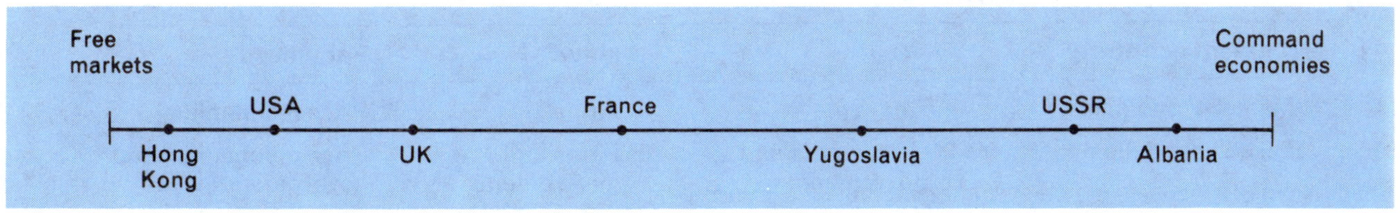

Figure 8.5 The free market/command economy spectrum.

government can, according to some economists, intervene in an economy by spending more or less itself and so influence the overall level of demand, employment and output.

There are therefore many areas where governments can be active. Not all mixed economies have all of the features outlined here and the reader is encouraged to look at her own economy to decide where on the spectrum it lies. Figure 8.5 (p. 149) places some economies on such a spectrum, but as in the former Soviet Union political events may change their positions.

A comparison of competing economic systems

Without going into a blow-by-blow account of each system it is possible to make some general observations.

Firstly, each system that we have examined is trying to solve the same basic economic problem: scarcity. Secondly, each system is making a decision on what to produce, how to produce it and to whom the benefits of production should be distributed (see Table 8.2). It is not surprising that each system comes up with different answers, for each reflects different preferences as to how an economy should be run. The failings of a system from an outside point of view may be deemed a success from within the system.

It is often argued that one system is superior to another. This is certainly a pointless exercise, since each of the two 'pure' systems has its good and bad points. The mixed economy tries to distil out the good points of both market and command economies, but as we have seen no two countries have as yet distilled out exactly the same solutions.

In conclusion, all societies are left to solve the same economic problem and it is usually a political decision as to which solution is used. In this book we are generally concerned with the workings of a mixed economy based on competition, such as the economies of the European Community, the USA and Australasia.

SUMMARY

1. Mixed economies are those where there are both markets and government intervention in the economy.
2. Most western economies are mixed economies, having moved from being market economies. In Eastern Europe many of the former command economies are now adopting some elements of the market to also become mixed economies.
3. Mixed economies seek to avoid the worst aspects of capitalist and command economies, while keeping the good aspects of both.
4. The problems that a western mixed economy tries to tackle by intervention are: income distribution and poverty; unemployment; social costs; monopolies; the provision of public and merit goods; cyclical disturbances; and the lack of long-term planning.
5. The range of mixed economies is very wide and each country has chosen its own particular mix of market and command economies. Whatever the mix chosen, all economies try to answer the questions of what to produce, how to produce it and to whom the benefits of production will go.

Helping markets along – indicative planning

Various attempts have been made in mixed economies to help the market to perform better and more efficiently. We have seen examples of direct intervention by the state, but there are other options. Indicative planning does not require the government to interfere with firms, but none the less attempts to guide the economy along a smoother path.

One of the most frustrating aspects of market and mixed economies as far as governments are concerned is their unpredictability. The cyclical nature of most economies means that if an economy grows by 3 per cent this year there is no reason whatever for it to do the same next year. For both firms and governments this leads to great uncertainty. Firms must make investment decisions and employ resources on the basis of their expectations. Governments construct expenditure plans and social programmes on the basis of expected tax revenue. The uncertainty attached to the future means that the wrong decision is often made, which means both an inefficient allocation of resources and also losses (or lost opportunities).

The aim of indicative planning is to provide a clearer picture of the future via a 'national plan', and so to remove much of the uncertainty. That is, it aims to *indicate the nature of the future*. In this way it is hoped to promote faster and more stable growth, and thus to encourage more efficient investment.

The theory of indicative planning

As we have seen, the aim of indicative planning is to promote faster growth in a more certain environment. The basic problem in a market economy is that overall investment (aggregate investment) decisions, and indeed all other

Table 8.2 How each economic system allocates resources

Type of economy	What?	How?	For whom?
Market economies	Consumers	Firms	Price mechanism
Mixed economies	Consumers and government	Firms and government	Price mechanism and government
Command economies	Central planning bureau (CPB)	CPB	CPB

decisions, are made by a wide variety of people. Not surprisingly, different people have different views of the future and so the decisions of these people are not necessarily consistent. This is of particular concern when we consider investment, which is vital to the growth and success of any country.

Imagine a situation where every firm had a slightly different view of the future. The investment decisions made in this economy would almost certainly be incompatible. One firm's investment could stand idle because another's was insufficient to process the semi-finished goods that are the inputs of the former's plants. In other words, bottlenecks and underutilization would occur. How much easier life would become if all firms had a similar view of the future.

Indicative planning seeks to provide firms with this common view of the future by producing a national plan that sets out forecasts or targets for a number of years ahead. In addition, a set of microeconomic plans are produced to guide various sectors or industries. These plans aim for a high level of growth and expect to achieve this by removing uncertainty and raising expectations.

Thus the situation where all firms have different views of the future is replaced by one where they all have the same view. Not only are their decisions now consistent, but they are influenced by the plan to be more efficient in their use of resources and to achieve a higher rate of growth. In some ways the plan hopes to be self-fulfilling. The very existence of the plan encourages firms to follow it, and so the plan is fulfilled.

The need for planning is seen to be more urgent in the modern world with its rapid technical progress. A nation that does not invest early in the newest technology can be left out of the development of a product. In recent years many countries have bemoaned their poor performance in the area of computer technology and so their dependence upon imported equipment. It is precisely such opportunities and needs that indicative planning seeks to highlight, and for which it seeks to mobilize domestic investment.

Problems of indicative planning

The possibility of successful indicative planning has been the subject of considerable scepticism. Only the French have used it for a substantial period; other countries, including the United Kingdom, have flirted with the process but rejected it. In the UK the National Economic Development Office (NEDO) was to be the focus of the indicative planning exercise and one of its functions was to co-ordinate the work of the 'little Neddies', each of which brought together interested parties in a particular industry.

The most common criticism has been that the process used to compile the national plan does not actually produce a realistic plan at all. The practice is to find out from the various industrial sectors what their plans are and to aggregate them. Once this considerable amount of information has been collected, an estimate of exports, imports, growth and government activity can be added in, and from this a forecast can be made for the whole economy.

The obvious result from the information gathered will be that most sectors have inconsistent plans and that these must be reconciled. A national plan is published which presents forecasts or targets for overall growth, and similar plans are produced for the various sectors of the economy. There is no process by which industries' plans can be brought in line with the national plan except for the industries concerned to abandon their original (submitted) plans and to adopt a revised plan based on the one issued by the planning authority.

The plan is therefore relying on the plan itself to reconcile the intentions of the various sectors. The whole process relies on everybody 'playing the game' and taking notice of the plan.

We have seen how difficult planning is in a command economy where all economic agents are, at least nominally, controlled by the state. What hope is there of getting the necessary information in a mixed economy, where there is no compulsion to co-operate or provide accurate information? Furthermore, once all of the data are collected, how can they be put together? The task is truly enormous.

Much of the criticism is about the practicality of indicative planning, not the benefits of successful planning. It would be easy to forget that much in life is a matter of confidence and therefore that expectations play a crucial role. If people expect growth then they will be stirred to greater efforts and this may actually achieve the growth. We can conclude that indicative planning could help a mixed economy to greater efficiency.

France has long used indicative planning. We shall now look at the French experience to see how indicative planning can be used in practice.

The process of French planning

The French began producing plans after the Second World War, partly to aid recovery from the war and the depression of the 1930s and partly to convince the United States that its financial aid would be well used. From 1954 to 1980 a series of four- or five-year plans were produced (the second plan ran from 1952 but was extended to 1957) to guide the French economy to greater heights.

Some of the French plans have been staggeringly optimistic. For example, the seventh plan forecast that between 1976 and 1980 there would be an annualized rate of growth of 5.5 to 6 per cent, the creation of 1.1 million new jobs, the reduction of inflation to below 6 per cent and the removal of the balance of payments deficit. Such goals proved impossible in the setting of the late 1970s, although the plan was much admired and the British Conservative Party borrowed ideas from it for its 1979 election manifesto. This said, the idea of planning is partly to raise and lead expectations and such optimism was therefore necessary.

The actual process of French planning emerged from practice rather than from theory, since in the early days the French were breaking completely new ground. This means that each plan was constructed in a different way. For our purposes we will try to characterize the general planning formula of the second to seventh plans. The second plan began in 1952; the seventh in 1976.

The planning process was overseen by the General Planning Commissariat (CGP). Under the CGP were Planning Commissions which were of two types, vertical and horizontal. A Planning Commission was the place where 'the planners met the planned', and between them they would produce an agreed plan for their particular area of the economy or interest.

The vertical commissions would correspond to particular areas of the economy – for example, agriculture or electronics. Membership of the commissions was open – anybody could be appointed so that as wide an input as possible was available. Each commission contained representatives of employers, employees and civil servants.

The horizontal commissions were responsible for matters that crossed sectoral divides, such as social policy. The most important of the horizontal commissions was the General Economic and Financing Commission, which was the forum to which the other commissions reported. The horizontal commissions were necessary to iron out inconsistencies in the sector plans and to take a more general perspective.

The later plans had three distinct planning stages. What follows is based on the sixth plan.

1. A review of the previous plan takes place.
   A forecast is made for the planning period.
   Long-term studies are made beyond the planning period.

In this stage the planners hoped to learn from previous experience and to build a picture of what might happen if no plan is made. The long-term forecasts were intended to prevent conflict between medium-term plans and long-term trends.

2. The Planning Commissions are set up.
   The commissions review options and attempt to find solutions to problems highlighted in the first stage.

Thus the second stage had the Planning Commissions reviewing various options for the plans and assessing the likely impact of each. The options were then put to the government, which chose the option it preferred. The third stage involved working out a plan for the specific option chosen.

3. Vertical commissions produce detailed plans for implementation.
   Plans are brought together by horizontal commissions.
   The CGP reports.

The French Parliament accepted the plan as a guide to economic policy and a framework for public investment. The plans were never law, however, and this means that no French government has ever been compelled to follow them.

The published plan allowed the whole of France to know where the planners expected to be in four or five years' time. Because of the wide consultation process, the plan had credibility in the eyes of most business people and so was more likely to be acted upon.

The aim of indicative planning is to remove uncertainty and to raise expectations in order to achieve a more efficient allocation of resources and faster growth. The question of whether the French achieved this is an open one.

The impact of French planning

Unfortunately it is not possible to say that French planning was either a success or a failure. The earlier plans (second to fourth) were considered triumphs; those that followed were not. The eighth plan was abandoned in 1981, although this was due as much to a change in government as to the failure of the plan.

It is perhaps unfair to judge the French planners by the later plans, since these were of a character quite different from the earlier ones. Until the fifth plan the emphasis was on the vertical or sector plans and on the attempt to encourage industry to invest and grow. The sixth to eighth plans included sector plans, but there was much more emphasis on economic aggregates. The ninth plan (1984–8) moved away from sector plans and specific targets, although it did contain 'special programmes' for areas such as telecommunications and nuclear power.

Confining ourselves to the earlier plans, it is not at all clear how much these helped. We have no way of knowing how France would have performed without the plans, and so we can only resort to comparisons.

As Table 8.3 shows, France grew at a respectable rate from 1968 to 1973, but from then on it tended to grow more slowly than the other six major industrial western powers. In fact the governments of France were losing the will to follow the plans by the mid-1970s, and the plans were relegated to reference points only following the 1973 oil crisis. Indeed, the seventh plan was not even implemented on time.

There is no doubt, however, that the earlier plans did contribute something to French economic performance. As Tables 8.4 and 8.5 show, French growth compared most favourably with that of France's European neighbours. In Table 8.6 we can see that the growth of labour productivity (a possible measure of the efficiency of investment) in France was also higher than in most European countries throughout the period 1960 to 1986.

Table 8.3 Growth of real GNP/GDP in the OECD area (% changes from previous period)

	1968	1969	1970	1971	1972	1973	1974	1975	1976	1977	1978	1979	1980	1981	1982	1983	1984	1985	1986	1987
United States	4.2	2.4	−0.3	2.8	5.0	5.2	−0.5	−1.3	4.9	4.7	5.3	2.5	−0.2	1.9	−2.5	3.6	6.8	3.0	2.9	2.9
Japan	12.5	12.1	9.5	4.3	8.5	7.9	−1.4	2.7	4.8	5.3	5.2	5.3	4.3	3.7	3.1	3.2	5.1	4.9	2.4	4.2
Germany	5.8	7.5	5.0	3.0	4.2	4.7	0.2	−1.4	5.6	2.7	3.3	4.0	1.5	0.0	−1.0	1.9	3.3	2.0	2.5	1.7
France	4.3	7.0	5.7	8.2	4.4	5.4	3.1	−0.3	4.2	3.2	3.4	3.2	1.6	1.2	2.5	0.7	1.4	1.7	2.1	1.9
United Kingdom	4.0	1.8	2.2	1.7	3.2	7.1	−1.8	−1.1	2.9	2.2	3.6	2.7	−2.4	−1.2	1.6	3.3	2.6	3.6	3.3	4.5
Italy	6.5	6.1	5.3	1.6	3.2	7.0	4.1	−3.6	5.8	1.9	2.7	4.9	3.9	1.1	0.2	1.0	3.2	2.9	2.9	3.1
Canada	5.4	5.4	2.6	5.8	5.7	7.7	4.4	2.6	6.2	3.6	4.6	3.9	1.5	3.7	−3.2	3.2	6.3	4.3	3.3	3.9
Total of above countries	5.4	4.7	2.6	3.4	5.1	5.9	0.1	−0.6	4.9	4.0	4.6	3.3	0.9	1.7	−0.7	2.9	5.2	3.2	2.8	3.1

Source: OECD.

Table 8.4 Average annual rate of growth of total output (%)

	1950–60	1960–70	1970–77
France	4.4	5.7	3.8
West Germany	7.6	4.6	2.4
Italy	5.9	5.3	3.0
Netherlands	4.8	5.5	3.2
Denmark	3.3	4.7	2.8
Belgium	3.1	4.7	3.7
United Kingdom	2.8	2.9	1.8

Source: *United Nations Statistical Year Book.*

Table 8.5 Average annual rate of growth of per capita GDP at constant prices

	1950–60	1960–70	1970–75
France	3.6	4.6	3.2
West Germany	6.7	3.5	2.3
Netherlands	3.4	4.1	2.3
United Kingdom	2.4	2.3	1.7

Source: *United Nations Statistical Year Book.*

French statistics compare well in the fields of growth and productivity. France has not done so well in terms of inflation or international trade. It has had continual balance of payments problems, and this has hampered the implementation of many of the plans. However, since efficiency was a major goal of the plans, a crucial test could be said to be France's ability to remain competitive in international markets. Here we see that France avoided the considerable loss of foreign markets that the UK suffered up to 1983, as Figure 8.6 shows.

If we look at the impact that planning has had on the French themselves there is a less favourable picture. A survey of firms in 1967 suggested that only 24 per cent were influenced by the plan when making investment decisions, although 51 per cent of large firms claimed to be influenced. On production decisions only 20 per cent of firms claimed to be influenced by the plan, with again large firms claiming to be influenced most. Perhaps the most disappointing response for the planners has been from French public institutions, which are thought to have paid least attention to official plans.

The evidence about the value of indicative planning in France is inconclusive. The detailed sector plans are no longer produced, although the French government claims to favour planning to guide the economy. Without doubt the greatest difficulty in implementing the plans has been the government itself, which has frequently ignored or acted in direct contravention of the plans when faced with changing economic and political circumstances.

The overall effect of indicative planning has probably been small, but 'the indirect effect on confidence and its role as a forum for interest groups ... [has been] extremely valuable' (Hare, 1985).

SUMMARY

1. One of the main problems of market economies is their unpredictability.
2. One way of overcoming the uncertainty that this creates is to issue forecasts of the medium-term future – an indicative plan.
3. Only the French have used indicative planning for a long period. The UK developed one national planning organization, NEDO, in the 1960s, but this was abandoned.
4. Indicative plans are not enforceable – firms may ignore them if they wish. Thus it is important to make the plan credible.
5. The greatest difficulties encountered by the French have been in the process of planning, a problem which is also encountered in command economies.
6. Early French plans appear to have improved the performance of the French economy. Since 1973 it is not possible to say if planning has helped or not.

The social market

The 'social market' is a term that has been much used in the UK by a variety of sources in recent years. It is difficult to pin down an exact meaning because it appears that many people use the term to mean different things.

The social market is certainly a form of mixed economy, but with the emphasis much more on markets to solve problems such as the provision of public goods than on direct state intervention. The problem in trying to discuss this subject in a textbook is that the degree of state intervention envisaged by its various proponents varies greatly.

Its supporters range from those who believe that welfare departments (such as the National Health Service in the UK) should be provided directly by the state via taxation,

Table 8.6 Average annual real value added in manufacturing per person employed (%)

	1960–68	1968–73	1973–79	1960–86
France	6.8	5.8	3.9	5.0
West Germany	4.7	4.5	3.1	3.5
Italy	7.2	5.6	2.9	4.9
United Kingdom	3.4	3.9	0.6	3.0

Source: *OECD Historical Statistics.*

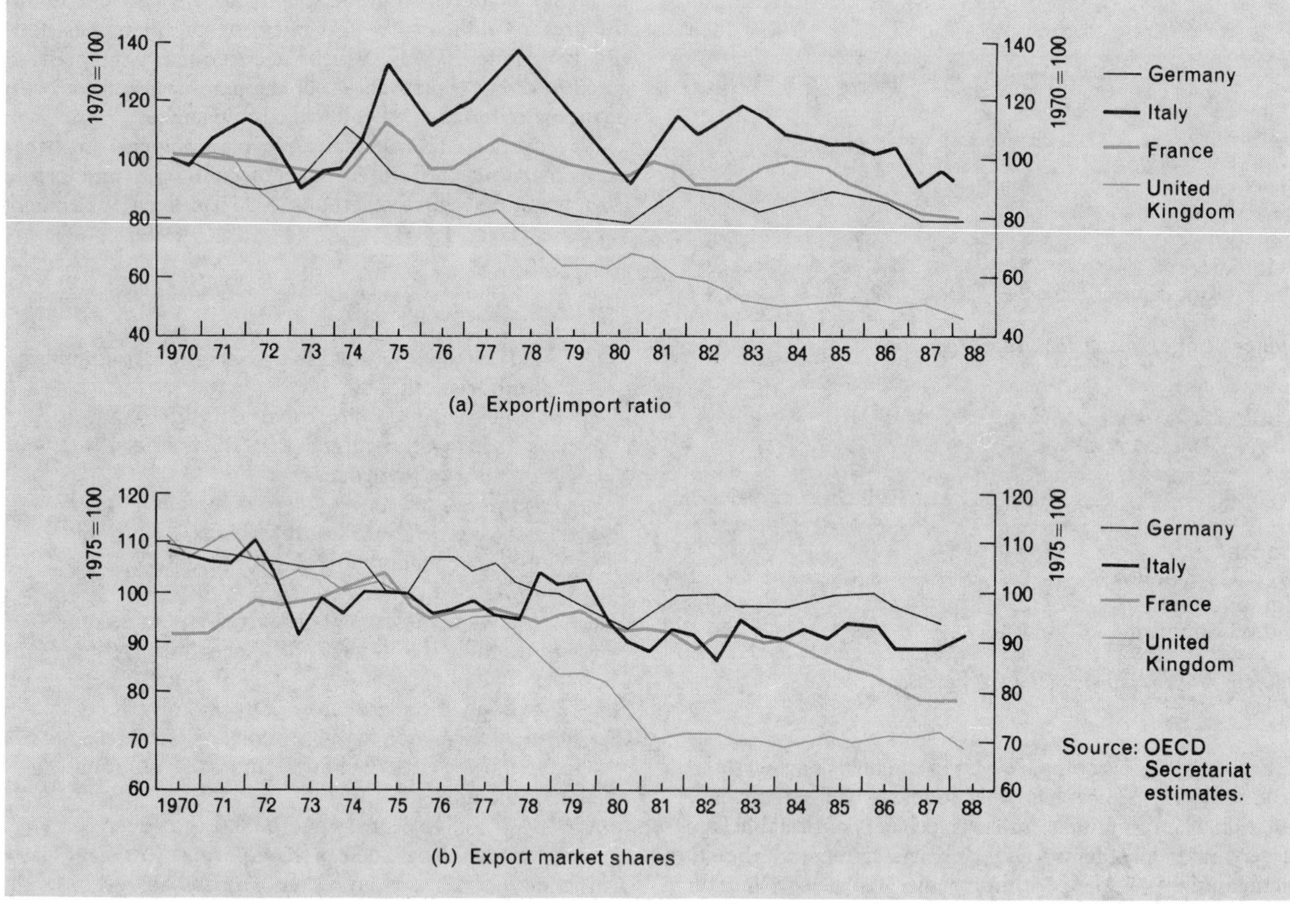

Figure 8.6 Export/import ratio and market shares for manufactures, 1970–88.

to those who believe that the state should only provide the means for people to acquire the benefits of welfare services. For our purposes it is useful to examine the same origin of the term 'social market' and then examine some of the contributions made in its name to the ongoing discussion of the degree of state involvement in the economy.

Post-war German origins

Following the collapse of Germany in 1945 there was a need to find a system of economic management for the new nation of West Germany. (East Germany, being the Soviet-controlled area of occupation, chose central planning until reunification.) In the years before the war there had been a large degree of planning in Germany, which had been most successful in achieving the goals it set itself.

Among many Germans there was a wish to move away from the pre-war system. There was no wish to abandon the welfare provision that free markets find difficult to provide, but there was a fear that government regulation would once again lead to intolerable state interference and direction. The aim was to integrate markets and social elements into one system so that the interventions of government would work with market forces and not against them. This was the concept of the social market.

Molsberger, a German economist, has written that 'In a social market economy the state shapes the economic order – the legal and institutional framework for private economic activity – but (normally) does not interfere with the market process.' The German economy was run along these lines for 30 years, although it is a matter of dispute as to how far Germany can be called a social market today.

The social market is therefore a mixed economy system which emphasizes the role of the market in solving social problems. For example, rather than having the government provide health care the social market approach looks to find a way of helping the market to provide this merit good. It is only in the area of public goods, such as defence, that the social market would opt for purely state provision.

The social market in the UK

In the United Kingdom the provision of welfare services has been by state welfare departments, such as the National Health Service and local authority social services and education departments. These welfare departments are paid for from general taxation and those who wish to consume them do so on demand. For example, there is no theoretical restriction on the amount of health care a person may receive, no matter how ill he or she may be (although queuing has proved to be a practical restraint with long 'waiting lists' for the treatment of non-urgent cases).

After 1979 the government of Margaret Thatcher looked to move the state away from direct involvement in the running of the economy. To this end it enacted various measures to allow markets to work more freely. These measures, known as **supply-side** measures, removed legal restrictions particularly in the labour market, in transport and in the provision of financial services. There is now a suggestion that such measures could be applied to the provision of welfare services.

Mrs Thatcher's government did not have a monopoly on such ideas. The Social Democratic Party (SDP) under Dr David Owen proposed the idea of the social market in the mid-1980s. The SDP clearly rejected many of the old ideas of the 'planned economy in which the private sector has to be fitted somehow into the Government's plans' (Dick Taverne, SDP National Committee 'Economic Affairs,' 1985). The Owen/SDP view, however, while accepting the greater choice markets gave, never envisaged the withdrawal of the state from welfare provision. Exactly how far they wished to go along the road to free markets is uncertain. We must therefore look at the more clear-cut view of the right wing in order to define the limits of the change proposed.

The 'right-wing' approach to the social market is to propose the withdrawal of the state from the provision of welfare services. Under such a system the NHS would therefore cease to exist and the government would encourage the market to fill the gap.

So how would people get access to the health care they need? The intention of proponents of this type of social market is that the state would ensure that the infrastructure of a health service remained, but the market would pay for the service. At present the government both maintains the infrastructure and pays for the service, and many opt out of the system to provide their own care via organizations such as BUPA.

The argument advanced against the present system is that it is wasteful. The NHS has little incentive to be efficient, due to its vast size and apparently limitless central funding. Furthermore, the double provision of public and private services could be rationalized. The social market in this case will help eliminate waste and allow the market to provide a merit good, but without the loss of allocative efficiency that non-market solutions often lead to.

It is not for us to describe the final outcome of this move to freer markets. The process, after all, has only just started. However, the 1990 reforms of the NHS may give us a clue. General practitioners are given a budget to spend on their patients as they feel necessary. The aim is to encourage them to economize on the use of hospital services, drugs and so on. A similar system will operate for administrative 'health districts' where each will be allowed to 'buy in' services from another area. If one district cannot provide an operation then it can transfer the patient to another area and transfer funds from its budget to cover the cost. One advantage of this will be that hospitals will specialize in areas of medicine they do best, leading to cheaper, more effective care.

Eventually, patients would have their own 'health budgets' to spend where they wished. They could go to the GP or hospital of their choice when they required treatment and 'pay' from their budget. The government would provide the minimum budget as a credit, and if people wished to they could add to their budget from their own funds or via insurance policies.

This system would allow a market to evolve in health care with each patient being a consumer and spending his or her income (budget) in whatever way the patient wished. There would be an incentive for providers of health care to compete for the business of patients. This would involve offering the best services and ensuring that, like firms, they operated on a cost-efficient basis.

The proposals outlined here are somewhat speculative. Moreover, we have taken health only as an example – education could just as easily have been used. This account is intended only to give an insight into the views of influential thinkers on the right and one perspective on what a mixed economy could be like.

SUMMARY

1. The social market is a term used to describe a variety of views all of which have as their aim the improvement of the market economy.
2. Rather than direct intervention supporters of the social market believe in assisting markets to find a solution to a problem such as the provision of merit goods.
3. Political views on the future of a social market vary, but most people now accept that markets have a greater role in the provision of services in the future.
4. The National Health Service internal market may be an example of the Social market provisions of the future.

Exam Preparation and Practice

MULTIPLE-CHOICE QUESTIONS

1. Which of the following must always be true in a free-market economy?
   A There is no advertising.
   B Monopolies do not exist.
   C Resources are allocated according to consumer demand.
   D All industries are perfectly competitive.

2. Which of the following goods would the market find it most difficult to supply unaided?
   A Defence.
   B Education.
   C Postal services.
   D Long-range transport.
   E Health services.

3. Which of the following statements most accurately describes a mixed economy?
   A Goods are produced for export and domestic use.
   B What is produced is determined partly by the market and partly by government.
   C What is produced is determined by firms.
   D All types of goods are produced.

Answer key

Where there are three numbered alternatives

A	B	C	D	E
1, 2, 3 Correct	1, 2 Correct	2, 3 Correct	1 Correct	3 Correct

Where there are four numbered alternatives

A	B	C	D	E
1, 2 and 3 Correct	1 and 3 Correct	2 and 4 Correct	4 only Correct	1 and 4 Correct

4. The market economy is criticized as a method of resource allocation because:
   1 The wishes of entrepreneurs are ignored.
   2 Social costs are not fully reflected in market prices.
   3 Government activity is too great.
   4 Firms can gain an unfair monopoly market position.

5. Which of the following statements are true of a purely centrally planned economy?
   1 Consumers have no influence on production decisions.
   2 Workers receive a money wage which they may spend as they wish.
   3 Black markets occur for goods in short supply.
   4 The central planning bureau adjusts prices so that demand equals supply for all goods.

6. Which of the following has (have) a role in a pure command economy?
   1 The profit motive.
   2 Forward planning.
   3 Prices.

7. Mixed economies must have which of the following features?
   1 A government sector.
   2 A price system.
   3 Entrepreneurs.
   4 An economic planning authority.

EXERCISES

1. The concept of consumer sovereignty is often criticized by opponents of totally free markets as leading to 'producer sovereignty', where firms dictate what is to be produced and ensure that their products will sell by advertising. Why might this criticism be true? Is this the only criticism that can be levelled at totally uncontrolled economies?

2. Distinguish between public and merit goods and give two examples of each.

3. Excessive noise from aircraft is disturbing the residents of an island nation. Is there a market solution to the problem of noise?

4. Under what circumstances would a monopoly aid the efficient allocation of resources in an otherwise free-market economy?

5. In a command economy does the central planning bureau have any use for 'prices'?

6. The task of planning an entire economy has proved to be difficult, if not impossible. What lessons might command economies learn from market economies?

9 Factor markets

In this chapter we will discuss:

1. What determines how many workers a firm will wish to employ.
2. How much time people will want to give up to work.
3. The wage that workers will be paid to work.
4. How workers or firms can group together to influence wages and employment levels.
5. Why some people and groups are paid more than others.
6. How much of the other factors of production (land and capital) firms will employ.
7. How much land and capital will be paid.

Introduction

As we have seen, the principal characteristic of a free-enterprise economy is the central role of the entrepreneur in making production decisions. It is the entrepreneur who decides what to produce, how much to produce and how to produce it.

In the earlier chapters we looked at the way entrepreneurs make price and output decisions. In this chapter we shall look at the way the entrepreneur makes decisions about how much of each factor of production to employ. The factors of production employed are labour, capital and land. Each of these was described in Chapter 3 and you may like to look at that chapter again to remind yourself about them.

Labour

In this section we shall look at how an entrepreneur decides how much labour to employ and how much to pay it. To do this we shall assume that all other inputs are fixed, i.e. our analysis will be for the **short run**.

We will then look at the supply of labour, particularly as it is affected by the existence of trade unions. We will also deal with the subject of economic rent and the various non-economic factors that affect labour earnings.

In the second section we will apply this analysis to the other factors of production (capital and land).

Demand for labour

We will start our investigation by assuming that the market for labour is a *perfectly competitive market* – both buyers and sellers of labour are price takers. (This is the auctioneer type of market we referred to earlier.) Labour is bought (employed) by profit-maximizing entrepreneurs and, as in the theory of production, the entrepreneur will maximize profits by equating marginal cost (MC) to marginal revenue (MR).

The marginal cost of labour is the cost of hiring one more worker, which in this case is the given wage rate. The marginal revenue of one more worker will be the extra revenue gained from selling the addition to output resulting from the increased employment.

Since all markets are perfectly competitive, the revenue gained will equal the increased output times the price of output. The price is 'given', so we need only to discover how much additional output will result if one more worker is hired.

Marginal product of labour

The additional revenue due to employing one more unit of labour is called the **marginal revenue product of labour** and depends on two things: firstly, the additional amount of output produced when labour input is increased by one man-hour; secondly, the price which that additional output will sell for. We can illustrate this point by a simple example.

Table 9.1 shows how a firm's output changes as more labour is employed. To simplify things we assume that this firm can only employ the services of a worker for a whole day rather that an hour at a time.

Column 2 shows how much is produced when the number of workers shown in column 1 are employed. This is the firm's total product (*TP*). As we saw in Chapter 3, the more labour that is employed, the more the firm produces. But, as column 3 shows, the law of diminishing returns applies. This means that each successive worker will have less and less effect on output. The addition to total product due to employing an additional worker is known as the **marginal physical product of labour** (*MPP*) and is given in column 3.

We can show this relationship on a graph, as shown in Figure 9.1.

We are, of course, interested in the *value* of the additional contribution of labour. Column 4 shows this as the marginal revenue product (*MRP*) of labour, the value of the extra output produced by adding an extra worker. This is found

Table 9.1 Employment, output and marginal revenue product

Number employed (1)	Units of output (TP) (2)	Marginal physical product (MPP) (3)	Marginal revenue product (MRP) (£) (4)	Wage rate (W) (£) (5)	Total profit (π) (£) (6)
1	5	5	75	60	15
2	12	7	105	60	60
3	22	10	150	60	150
4	33	11	165	60	255
5	43	10	150	60	345
6	50	7	105	60	400
7	55	5	75	60	415
8	59	4	60	60	415
9	62	3	45	60	400
10	64	2	30	60	370
11	64	0	0	60	310
12	62	−2	−30	60	220

by multiplying *MPP* (column 3) by the price of the good produced, in this case £15. We can represent the marginal revenue product of labour for each level of employment by a graph (see Figure 9.2).

We can now apply the profit-maximizing conditions stated earlier. The entrepreneur will equate the marginal cost of employing labour to the marginal revenue product of labour. The marginal revenue product curve shows us the marginal revenue gained from employing additional units of labour as employment expands, and the marginal cost of labour is the wage rate. This is constant and hence is a horizontal line.

In Figure 9.3 the wage rate is £60 per week (shown by the line *W*) and equals the *MRP* of labour when 8 workers are employed.

The sense of this argument can be seen from Figure 9.4, which shows a firm's *MRP* curve and the going wage rate. The firm should employ labour up to point L^* as this is where $MC = MR$. But what happens if the firm employs L_1? Clearly, at L_1 the cost of employing an extra unit of labour (*W* or L_1c) is less than the extra revenue that the firm would gain by the distance *bc*. If the firm increases labour employed from L_1 to L^* then the whole of the area under the *MRP* curve (L_1baL^*) is received by the firm, but only L_1caL^* is paid out in wages. The firm should therefore hire more labour.

If employment is increased beyond L^* to, say, L_2 then it costs the firm L^*adL_2 in wages, but it gets only L^*aeL_2 in return. Total profit declines by the value of triangle *ade* and

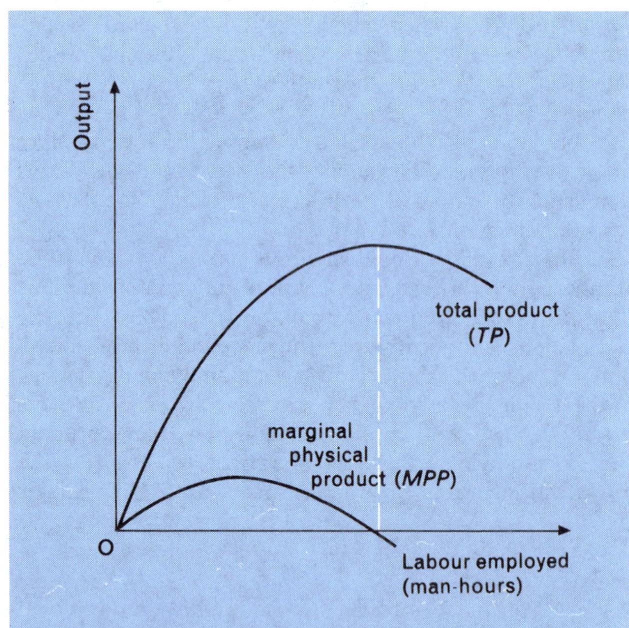

Figure 9.1 Total product and marginal physical product of labour.

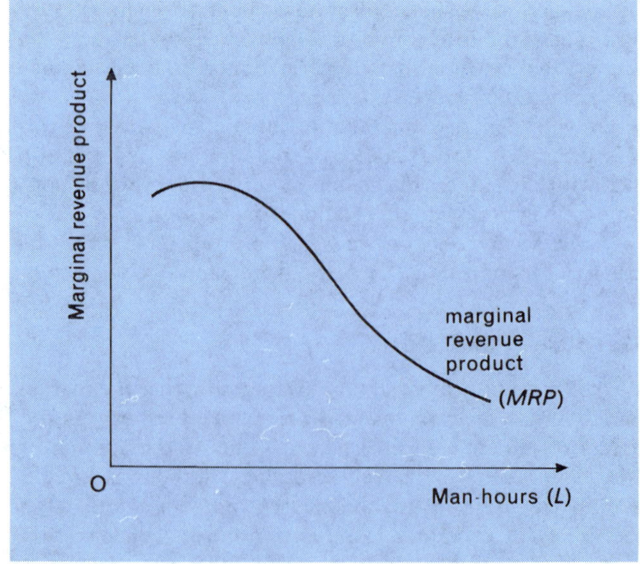

Figure 9.2 Marginal revenue product of labour.

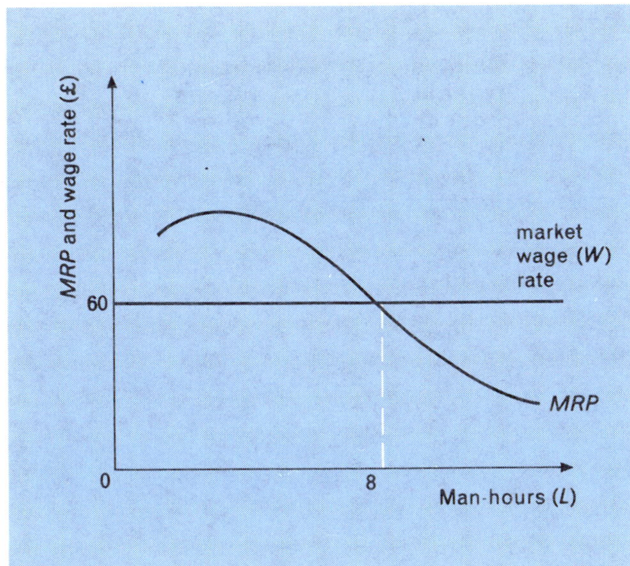

Figure 9.3 Labour market equilibrium.

so the firm should employ less labour. This can also be seen in Table 9.1 when total profit declines on the employment of the ninth worker.

We can therefore conclude that the profit-maximizing output is where the marginal revenue product of labour (MRP_L) is equal to the wage rate. In the case of Table 9.1, 8 workers are employed. From this analysis it can be seen that the last worker employed is paid exactly the value of his or her contribution to production (the value of the worker's marginal product). This is often pointed to as a sign of the 'fairness' of the market system as no employer could be expected to pay any worker more than he or she contributed to production.

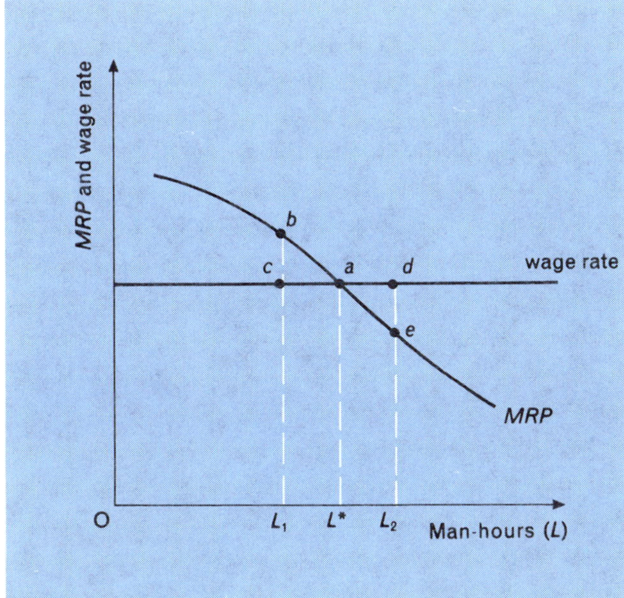

Figure 9.4 Reaching equilibrium in the labour market.

SUMMARY

1. Factors of production are demanded by firms in order to produce for a profit. The profit-maximizing firm equates marginal cost to marginal revenue.
2. In the short run the amount of capital is fixed and the firm must equate the marginal cost of labour to the marginal revenue gained from employing labour.
3. When employing labour the firm's marginal revenue is the price of the product multiplied by the increase in output due to employing one more worker. This is known as the marginal revenue product of labour.
4. The increase in output due to employing one more worker is called the marginal physical product of labour.
5. The law of diminishing returns says that as the quantity of labour increases then (in the short run) the marginal physical product of labour decreases. Thus the marginal revenue product of labour curve is also downward sloping.
6. The marginal cost of labour in a perfectly competitive labour market is the wage rate.
7. The profit-maximizing level of output occurs where the marginal revenue product equals the wage rate.
8. This implies that workers are paid the value of their marginal product.

Demand curve for labour

The marginal revenue product curve is the demand curve for labour as it tells us the amount of labour a firm will hire at each wage rate.

The position and slope of the curve will depend on a number of factors. In the previous section we saw that the marginal revenue product curve is made up of two components, the marginal physical product and the price of the product ($MRP = MPP \times P$). If either should change then the demand curve for labour will move.

Suppose the price of the good in our example falls from £15 to £10. The new marginal revenue figures are shown in Table 9.2. The new and old marginal revenue product curves are shown in Figure 9.5.

The fall in the price means that the new *MRP* curve lies below the old one and this will mean that, at any given wage rate, less labour will be employed. This is shown in Figure 9.6. If the price of the good rises then the curve moves to the right in a similar manner.

If the productivity of labour changes for any reason then it is the marginal physical product which is affected. If labour productivity increases, the *MRP* curve will move to the right – for example, from D_{L1} to D_{L2} in Figure 9.6. You can prove this for yourself by increasing the *MPP* figures in Table 9.2 by 50 per cent and finding the new *MRP* figures. It can then be seen that at any given wage rate more labour will be demanded.

The curve on its own is clearly incapable of determining the wage rate and the employment rate. Given a wage rate it

Table 9.2 The effect of a price change on marginal revenue product

Number employed	Units of output	Marginal physical product	Marginal revenue product 1 Price = £15 (£)	Marginal revenue product 2 Price = £10 (£)
1	5	5	75	50
2	12	7	105	70
3	22	10	150	100
4	33	11	165	110
5	43	10	150	100
6	50	7	105	70
7	55	5	75	50
8	59	4	60	40
9	62	3	45	30
10	64	2	30	20
11	64	0	0	0
12	62	−2	−30	−20

will tell us how many workers would be employed by this entrepreneur. Conversely, if we know how many workers are employed then we can find out what the wage rate is.

Elasticity of demand for labour

The exact shape of the demand curve for labour will determine how responsive the employment of labour is to a change in the wage rate. This is the same phenomenon we met when discussing the responsiveness of the demand for a good to a change in its price. In both cases the shape can be summarized by the curve's elasticity.

The elasticity of the labour demand curve will obviously depend upon the *MRP* of labour, i.e. the *MPP* of labour and the product price. There are other relevant factors, however, such as the elasticity of demand for the final product in markets that are not perfectly competitive. Suppose the demand for the final product is very price elastic and the wage rate of labour rises. The firm will pass on at least some of this cost increase in the form of higher prices. This will lead to a more than proportionate fall in demand for the product and so the firm will find that it no longer needs to employ as much labour. Hence the elasticity of demand for labour is also very price elastic (price in this case being the wage rate). If demand for the product is price inelastic then the wage rate can rise without causing a large fall in employment.

The elasticity of demand for labour will also depend upon the proportion of costs accounted for by labour. If labour costs are a very high proportion of total costs and the wage rate rises, this will have a significant effect on total costs. This will have to be passed on to the consumer, causing a fall in demand. So in this case demand for labour

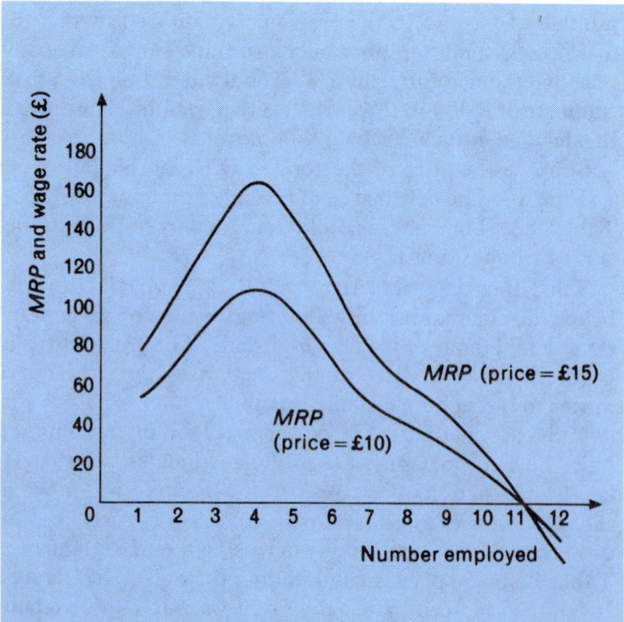

Figure 9.5 Marginal revenue product curves at different product prices.

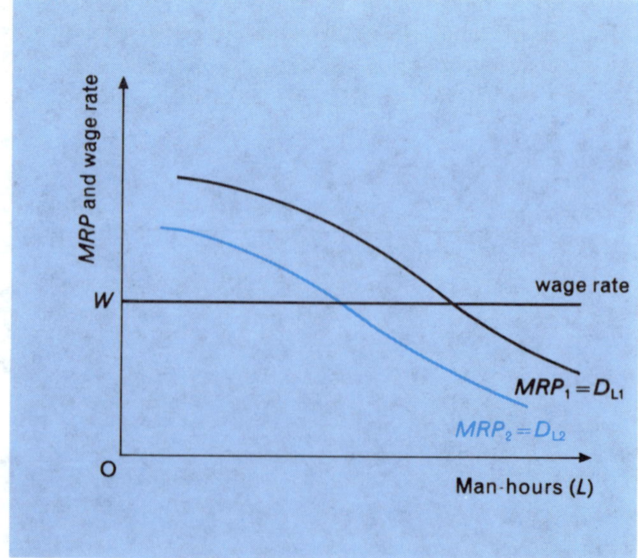

Figure 9.6 How the price level and productivity affects the labour demand curve.

will be price elastic. If labour accounts for only a small proportion of costs then a wage rise may be absorbed or may add only a little to costs and so affect employment little.

In the long run another factor affecting the elasticity of demand for labour will be how easy it is to substitute capital for labour. If capital can be brought into the productive process easily then when the wage rate rises entrepreneurs will opt for the now cheaper factor combination and will shed labour. If it is difficult to bring in capital (and this is likely in the short run) then labour demand will again be relatively unaffected. Clearly, the longer the time scale, the easier it is to switch from labour-intensive to capital intensive techniques.

The labour demand curve we actually observe will reflect all of these factors and it is possible for them to work against one another, but each makes a contribution.

So far we have concentrated on the demand for labour by individual firms, but we are actually interested in the market as a whole. To move from individuals to markets we have to sum all the individual demand curves to obtain the market demand curve for labour.

If we can then go on to say something about the market *supply* curve for labour, we can use them both to determine the market-clearing wage rate and the total level of employment for this or any other labour market.

Market demand curve for labour

So far we have derived the labour demand curve for each firm or entrepreneur. To find the market demand curve for labour we need to assume that each entrepreneur faces the same wage rate (the market wage rate) and then we can add together the demands of all entrepreneurs at each wage rate.

If there were three entrepreneurs in the market then, by calling out a wage rate, we could work out what each would demand at that rate, and summing them would yield the market demand at that wage rate. This is shown in Figure 9.7.

At wage rate 4, firm 1 demands 40 workers, firm 2 demands 35 and firm 3 demands 20. The total market demand at wage rate 4 is therefore $40+35+20 = 95$.

We can conduct a similar exercise for all other wage rates, such as wage rate 2, and so construct the downward-sloping market demand curve for labour shown in Figure 9.7(d).

All we now need is the market labour supply curve, and it is to this that we now turn.

SUMMARY

1. The marginal revenue product (*MRP*) curve for labour is the demand curve for labour.
2. The *MRP* curve can shift position, moving to the right (left) when either the price of the product or productivity increases (decreases).
3. The elasticity of demand for labour depends upon the elasticity of demand for the good produced, the proportion of costs accounted for by labour and how easily capital can be substituted for labour.
4. The market demand curve for labour is found by adding up all firms' individual demand curves for labour.

*The individual's decision to supply labour

We saw in Chapter 3 that we have to pay people to work because in order to work they have to give up leisure. Leisure being a good thing, we have to compensate them for having less leisure by giving them wages.

One way of looking at the individual's decision on how much time to spend working and how much time to spend on leisure is to use indifference curves. As workers give up leisure to work they gain income (wages) and with this income they can buy goods. The utility they derive from the goods must offset the utility they lose by giving up leisure. Thus we can say that workers are faced with an income–leisure trade-off.

There is a limit to how much time any worker can give to either work or leisure, and ultimately this is restricted to the number of hours in the day or week. The horizontal axis in Figure 9.8 defines the maximum number of hours available

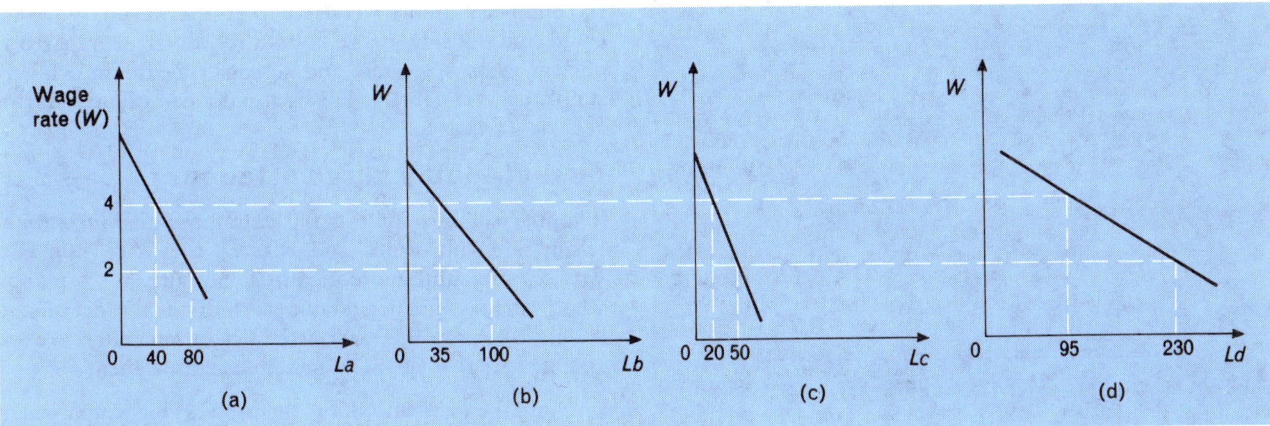

Figure 9.7 Constructing the market demand curve for labour.

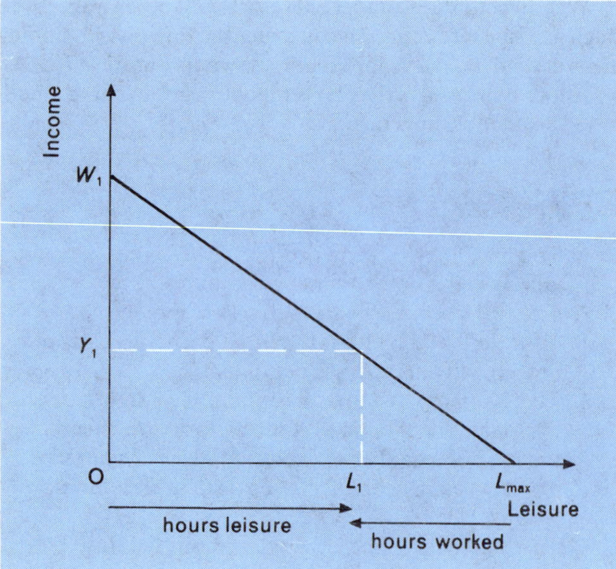

Figure 9.8 Income–leisure trade-off.

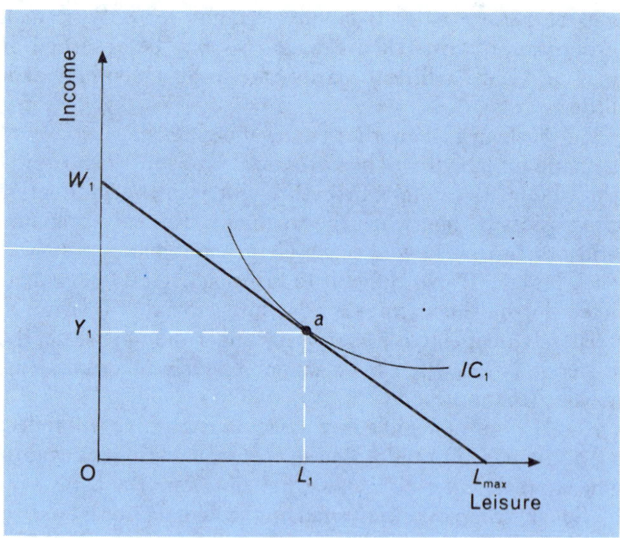

Figure 9.10 Indifference map of work and leisure.

in a week as L_{max}. If workers do no work then they get no income. As workers offer to work more hours per week their incomes will rise. For example, if workers offer $L_{max} - L_1$ hours per week then they will earn an income equal to OY_1.

The value of income OY_1 is determined by the wage rate, since it is equal to the number of hours worked multiplied by the wage rate. The line $L_{max}W_1$ is known as the worker's **budget constraint** as it defines all the combinations of goods and leisure open to workers.

There will be a different budget constraint for each wage rate. The higher the wage rate, the more goods can be had for a given number of hours worked. In Figure 9.9 the wage rate increases from £2 to £4 an hour. Assuming that

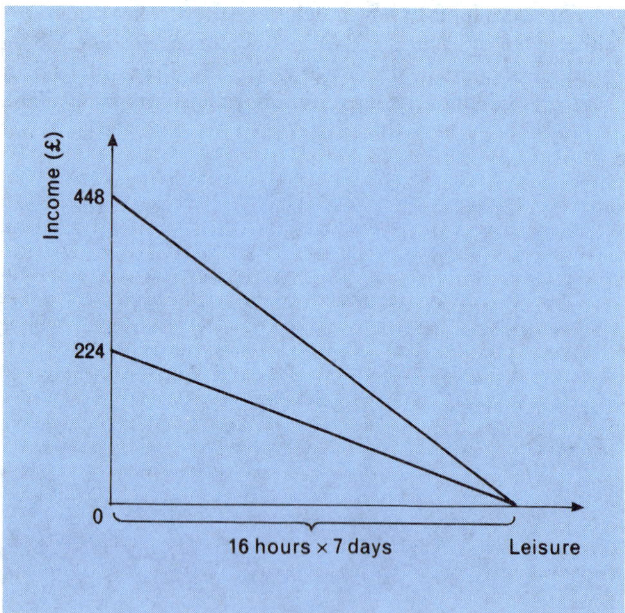

Figure 9.9 Budget constraints and the wage rate.

workers could work for 16 hours a day, 7 days a week (they have to sleep!), their maximum income rises from £224 to £448 each week.

We can use indifference curves to represent workers' tastes between leisure and income. Just as we used them in Chapter 4 to show how a consumer chooses between two goods, we can use them here to show how workers will choose between work and leisure. Such an indifference map is shown in Figure 9.10.

The worker will choose the combination of leisure and income that yields the greatest satisfaction (or utility), shown by the highest attainable indifference curve, in this case IC_1. At point *a* the worker offers $L_{max} - L_1$ hours of work at the going wage rate as defined by the budget constraint.

As the wage rate rises, we would expect workers to change their decisions about the number of hours they will work. It is usually assumed that the higher the wage rate, the more leisure they will give up.

This is shown in Figure 9.11(a) when the wage rate rises to give a new budget constraint $L_{max}W_2$. The new equilibrium point is at *b*, where the worker has decided to increase the number of hours work from $L_{max} - L_1$ to $L_{max} - L_2$. We could find out how many hours the worker is prepared to offer at every wage rate and so construct the individual's supply curve of labour. This is also done in Figure 9.11(b).

Market supply curve of labour

The analysis above reflects the assumption that income and leisure are substitutes and that as the wage rate rises workers substitute more income for leisure. We can apply what we have learned about an individual's decision to supply labour to the market for labour generally. We will assume here that, as the wage rate increases, then:

1. More people will offer themselves for employment; and/or
2. Those currently in work will offer to work more hours per day or for more days per week.

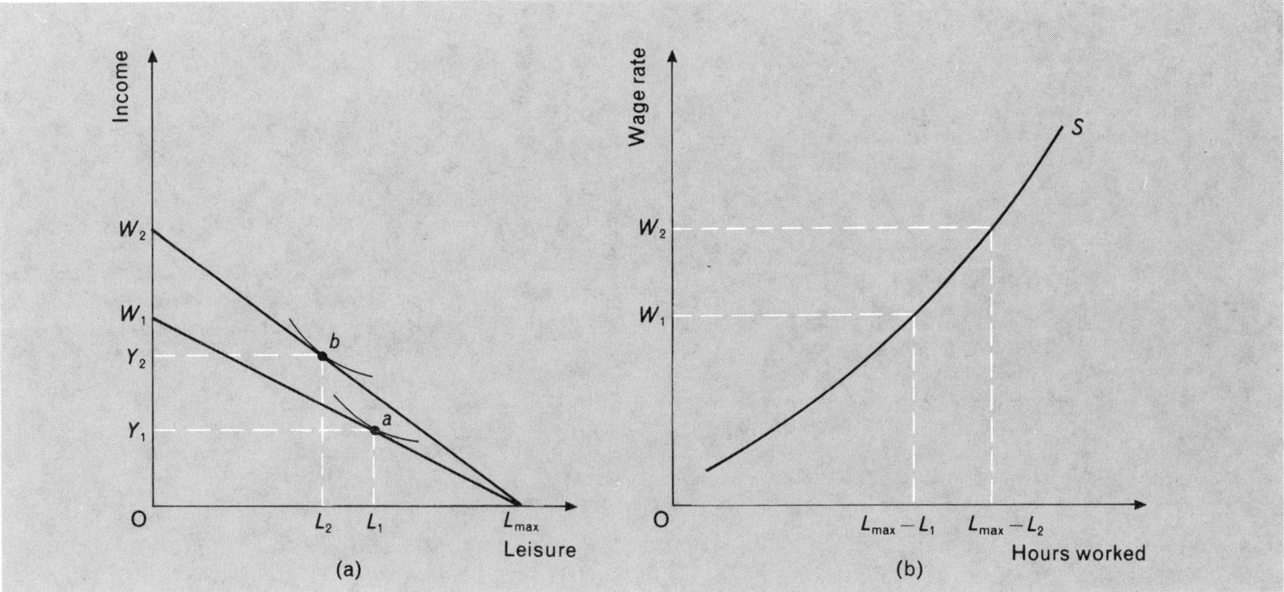

Figure 9.11 Constructing the individual's supply curve of labour.

In any event the supply curve of labour is upward sloping to the right so that, as the wage rate rises, the supply of labour offered on the market increases. This is shown in Figure 9.12.

This part of the theory is rather questionable. First, workers often cannot choose how many hours to work and might have to work a set number of hours per day. Secondly, different hours often attract different wages so that overtime hours yield more than normal hours. Thirdly, different wages are paid to different types of labour, and we should not talk of *the* labour market as if all labour were the same. Finally, there are reasons to believe that sometimes an increase in the wage rate will reduce the number of hours offered for work.

We will look at some of these refinements later. For now we can say that labour supply is a function of the wage rate because we believe that workers get utility from goods they can buy with the income they receive from working. Thus offering workers more money for giving up a certain period of leisure gives them the chance to buy more goods and induces them to give up more of their leisure time.

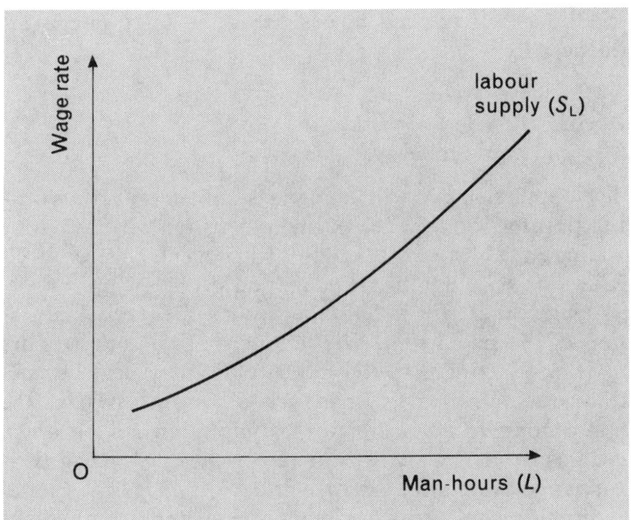

Figure 9.12 Market supply curve of labour.

For ease of explanation we have referred throughout to the 'wage rate'. By this we mean the number of goods which can be had for an extra hour's labour. This is called the real wage rate and depends on the money wage rate – how many £s workers get per hour – and on the price of goods. All this analysis is therefore in terms of real wages not money wages.

SUMMARY

1. Individuals choose between income and leisure. They like both income and leisure, but must work in order to buy goods.
2. The amount a worker can earn is limited by the time available and the wage rate.
3. Workers will choose the combination of work and leisure that maximizes their utility.
4. Raising the wage rate induces workers to supply more labour.
5. Adding up the amount of labour offered by individuals at each wage rate yields the Market Supply Curve of Labour.

The labour market

Bringing the market supply curve and the market demand curve together yields the market-clearing wage rate and the level of employment, as shown in Figure 9.13. If wages were to rise above W^*, say to W_1, then the labour being demanded by entrepreneurs, L_{D1}, would be less than the amount being offered, L_{S1}. Workers would compete among themselves for work and gradually bid wages down to W^*.

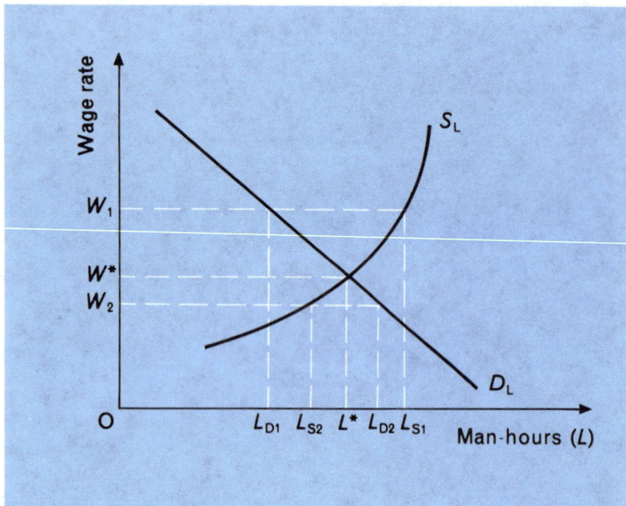

Figure 9.13 Market-clearing wage rate and level of employment.

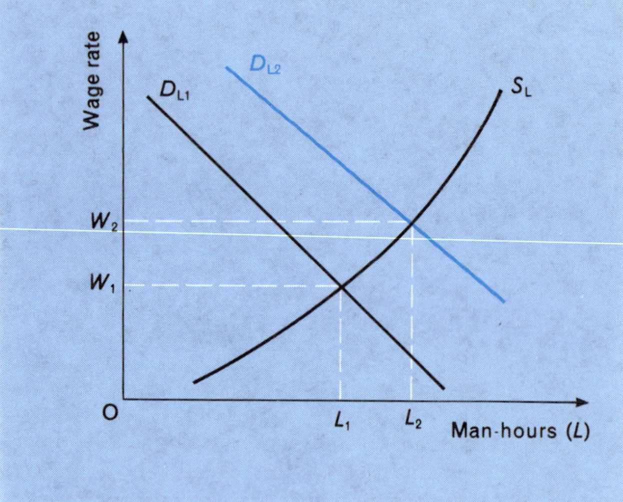

Figure 9.14 Effect of increased demand for labour on the wage rate and level of employment.

If wages were too low, say W_2, then entrepreneurs would be seeking L_{D2} workers but only L_{S2} would be available. Entrepreneurs would therefore bid among themselves for the available labour and force wages up to W^*.

This model, though rather simple, is much used in economics. We shall encounter it again and again, especially when we come to look at macroeconomics, which is concerned to explain the behaviour of the economy as a whole. Meanwhile we can make a number of rather interesting observations from a microeconomic point of view.

The first thing to notice is that wages in this particular model are determined by the market. Neither labourers nor entrepreneurs decide on wages: there is no suggestion here of an exploitive class of capitalists grinding workers down and offering the lowest possible wages. Competition among employers ensures that the wage rate does not fall below W^* and competition among labourers ensures that the wage rate does not rise above W^*. The determination of the wage rate is not then a matter of competition between entrepreneurs and labourers, but a matter of competition *among* entrepreneurs on the one hand and *among* labourers on the other.

If labour wishes to increase its wage rate, within the framework of perfectly competitive markets and the free-enterprise system, then it must bring about a shift in the demand curve for labour. If, for example, labour became more skilled, or worked harder or more efficiently, then the marginal physical product of labour curve would move to the right. Thus the demand curve (the *MPP* curve multiplied by the price of the product) would move to the right. The result is shown in Figure 9.14.

With the original level of labour skill the demand curve for labour is D_{L1}. This, together with the supply curve S_L, yields a wage rate of W_1 and a level of employment L_1. With extra training, etc. the new demand curve for labour is D_{L2} and this not only improves the real wage to W_2, but also increases employment from L_1 to L_2.

Another way of increasing the marginal revenue product of labour is to increase the amount of capital stock available. When there is a lot of capital available, the marginal physical product curve will move to the right because each labourer will have more tools, machines and other equipment and so will be able to produce more in a given time – hence wages and employment will be high. In some countries with very little capital stock (e.g. India), the demand curve for labour will be well over to the left. At the same time the very large population will mean that the supply of labour curve is well over to the right. These two facts combine to yield very low wage rates, which are characteristic of a poor country.

In other countries (e.g. the USA) there is an abundance of capital compared to the population size, and hence the demand curve for labour is well over to the right and the supply curve more to the left. It would also be true to say that the capital equipment available to workers in the United States embodies the most modern technology and will be generally more efficient than the capital equipment available in India. This yields a high wage rate and is characteristic of a rich country.

Some of these issues were explored in Chapter 2, but it will be clear from this analysis that the wage rate is influenced by:

1. Population size.
2. Skill and effort of workers.
3. Amount of capital available.

The population size that has greatest influence is the **working population**. By the working population we mean those willing and able to work, and this will depend on a country's education system, retirement age and so on.

The level of skill will also depend on the level of education of the population. Workers in western countries are more productive than those in the Third World because they are compelled to attend school, and many have the opportunity to go on to further education, all of which enables them to cope with more complex tasks than their contemporaries in the Third World.

In this model, the provision of capital is an unambiguous benefit to labour, raising both wage rate and employment. The picture which emerges is one of class harmony. Labour and capital co-operate to their mutual advantage and neither class can impose its will on the other. This lack of class power springs from the existence of a perfectly competitive labour market.

In the real world we see capital as a class negotiating through its legal agents (factory managers, etc.), and labour as a class represented by trade unions. This form of group activity arises because, as we have seen in Chapter 6, market price depends not only on supply and demand, but also on the structure of the market. Employers' federations and trade unions can therefore be understood (at least in part) as attempts to manipulate market structure to the benefit of one group or another.

In what follows we shall first see what happens if the sellers (labourers in this case) combine to act as a monopolist supplier of labour. Next we shall see what happens if buyers (firms in this case) combine to act as a single buyer of labour (a monopsony). Finally, we shall see what happens when monopoly labour meets monopoly capital.

SUMMARY

1. The market-clearing wage rate is set by the interaction of the market demand for labour and the market supply of labour.
2. In the market it is the competition among entrepreneurs and among workers that determines wages, not competition between workers and entrepreneurs.
3. When labour supply is very high (low) compared with labour demand, wages will be very low (high).
4. The demand for labour can be increased by improving productivity (shifting the demand curve for labour to the right) and this will cause an increase in wages and employment.
5. In addition to the level of effort, the amount of capital, state of technology and the level of training will influence productivity.

Monopoly labour

We begin with the assumption that the labourer cannot force the employer to employ a certain number of men *and* pay them a certain wage rate. In other words, the trade union is unable to force the entrepreneur off the entrepreneur's labour demand curve. This can be seen in Figure 9.15, where the union may choose any point on the labour demand curve (D_L). It could insist on a wage rate W_1, but would have to accept a level of employment of L_1. Conversely, it could insist on L_2 man-hours being bought, but would have to put up with a wage rate of W_2. It cannot specify a wage rate W_1 *and* a level of employment L_{S1}.

We can see from Figure 9.15 that the wage rate W_2 that is associated with the level of employment L_2 is actually below the equilibrium wage rate W^*. This means that, despite the union's best efforts to increase employment, the resulting wage rate would attract only L_0 workers to this particular industry.

It is clear then that, although the workers (as a union) can

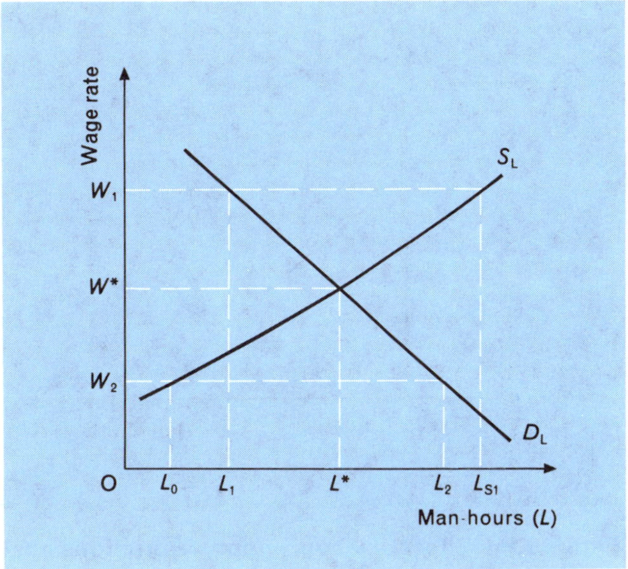

Figure 9.15 Wage rate and employment level trade-off.

specify any point on the entrepreneur's demand curve, they will never actually be interested in points *below* the equilibrium wage rate.

By insisting on a higher wage, say W_1, the workers will reduce employment from the equilibrium level L^* to L_1. This means that some workers, $L^* - L_1$, who could otherwise be employed are deprived of work. These workers will find themselves unemployed if the new wage rate W_1 is suddenly imposed on the market.

There is another change to take into account. There are now many more people offering to work at the new wage rate than there were at the equilibrium wage rate W^*. Thus by forcing wage rates above market-clearing rates, unions will give rise to $L^* - L_1$ actual unemployment and $L_{S1} - L_1$ registered unemployment, because L_{S1} people desire to work at this wage rate.

The beneficiaries of this agreement will be those who remain in employment. In this model, then, workers' associations may be looked upon as acting in the interests of the employed labourers. These kinds of model are used to justify the accusation that trade unions cause unemployment. By forcing up wages, they price some workers out of employment. We shall see in a moment whether this argument holds up when the firms themselves also form themselves into associations.

Unions have other options open to them to raise the incomes of their members. One of the most common methods is to try and restrict the number of labourers offering to work. This can be done by insisting that only particular groups be allowed to do certain jobs. For example, only members of Equity can perform in theatres, only members of GPMU can operate certain machines in the printing industry, only barristers can address the higher courts of law. By controlling the size of the membership of these bodies, they can force up their wage rate (or fees). This is shown in Figure 9.16.

In the figure the union succeeds in restricting supply to

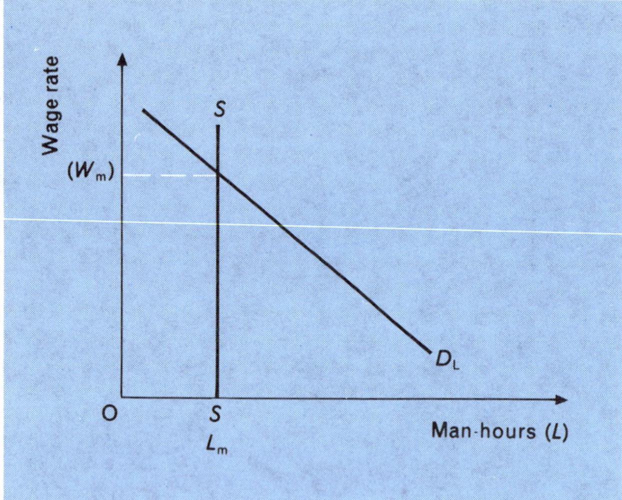

Figure 9.16 Effect of labour supply restrictions on the wage rate and level of employment.

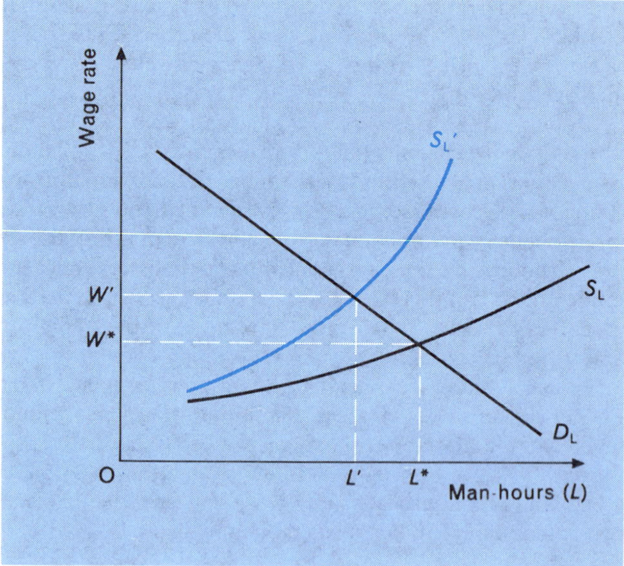

Figure 9.17 Effect of reduced supply of labour on the wage rate and level of employment.

L_m, perhaps by issuing only so many union cards. The effect is to produce a market wage rate of W_m. It is difficult in this case to get any idea of the loss of jobs being caused since there is no indication of free-market equilibrium, and no one who is not in the association can apply for any of the work being done.

It would be a very strong union indeed that could maintain the situation shown in Figure 9.16 indefinitely when the wage rate W_m was substantially above the free-market equilibrium. While SOGAT was able to maintain very high earnings for its members in Fleet Street for many years, eventually newspaper proprietors found it possible to make a complete break with them. The new newspaper printing presses now located in the London docklands employ many non-SOGAT workers, using new methods at more competitive wage rates.

Another way of looking at the behaviour of trade unions is to imagine that they have some control, but not absolute control, over the supply of labour. This is shown in Figure 9.17.

Here the labour association can restrict the entry of workers into the industry, but can only do so to a limited extent. If the wage rate rises then labourers will be attracted to the industry, but not so many as in the free market. In Figure 9.17 the labour supply curve S_L is the free-market supply curve and S_L' is the restricted supply curve. The curve S_L' may be brought about by union membership or professional exams, such as barristers' examinations, which limit the number of people who can work. The curve will not be vertical as in Figure 9.16 because there are always people prepared to work at less than the union rate and people who are prepared to take the time and trouble to work for their professional exams.

It can also be argued that the shape of the labour supply curve (the elasticity of supply) changes over time. In the short term the labour supply curve looks like the one in Figure 9.16, but in the longer term, as people react to the higher wages, undertake training and so on, the labour supply curve becomes more like curve S_L' in Figure 9.17. In other words, the elasticity of supply of labour changes with time and so do the rewards to labour as a result.

Finally, a method of raising wage rates and reducing employment is minimum wage legislation. In some industries (Wages Council industries) the minimum wage is set by law, although this practice is not particularly widespread. The payment of unemployment benefit, on the other hand, is perfectly general, and in a sense the level of unemployment benefit is a national minimum wage, since few would accept a job if it paid less than no job at all. If unemployment benefit or minimum wage rates are set too high then there will be unemployment, as shown in Figure 9.18.

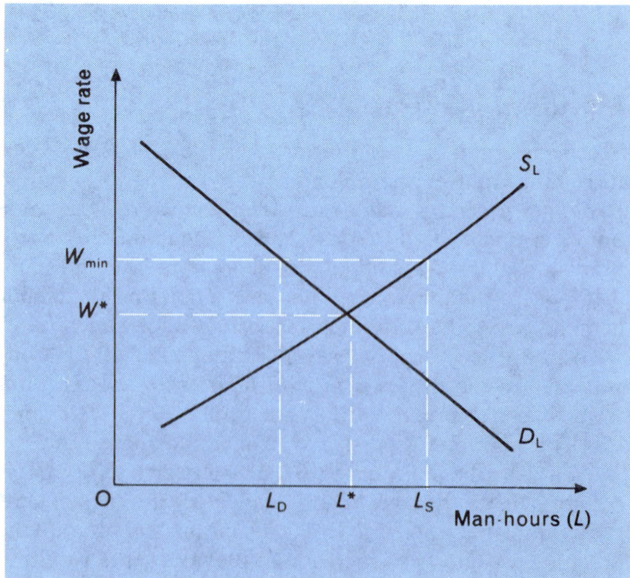

Figure 9.18 Effect of minimum wage legislation on the level of employment.

Here the free-market equilibrium would be a wage rate of W^* and an employment level of L^*. If a minimum wage rate is imposed at W_{min} (or if this represents the unemployment benefit) then employment will fall from L^* to L_D, and L_S workers will be seeking jobs in this minimum-wage sector.

Arguments of this kind have led some to suggest that, when there is a lot of unemployment, minimum wages should be done away with and unemployment benefit cut. Others argue that in any humane society there are minimum standards below which no one should be forced to live. The 'market' may be amoral and realistic, but it is not appropriate for deciding all aspects of life.

SUMMARY

1. By forming associations (trade unions), labour can turn itself into a monopoly seller of labour. In such circumstances it is possible to increase the wages of labour, but only at the expense of employment.
2. If the wage rate is set above the market equilibrium then the registered level of unemployment will rise.
3. Trade unions or professional organizations may try to limit the supply of labour by imposing strict membership conditions. In doing so they raise the wage rate.
4. The short-run elasticity of supply of labour is lower than the long-run elasticity.

Monopsony

We have seen that the demand for labour is determined by entrepreneurs who maximize their profits by equating the marginal revenue product of labour to the marginal cost of labour.

In perfectly competitive markets each entrepreneur behaves as if his or her demand for labour will have no effect on wage rates. They can double their demand, but because each is so small a part of the labour market no single entrepreneur will have any significant effect on the market demand for labour and hence any influence on the market price of labour (wage rate). This means that the marginal cost of labour is the wage rate.

Now if all the employers get together and act as a single buyer in the market, they will see that wage rates do rise as they demand more labour – we saw this effect when we looked at labour supply earlier in the chapter.

When the wage rate is seen to depend on how much labour is demanded, the marginal cost of labour is *not* the wage rate. We can show this in Figure 9.19.

Figure 9.19(a) shows the position of a particular firm in a perfectly competitive labour market – firm i. The firm's marginal revenue product curve of labour is shown as its demand for labour curve (D_{Li}). The firm takes the wage rate as given since it cannot influence it, and hence faces the labour supply curve (WW). It therefore employs L_{i1} people.

Figure 9.19(b) shows the market configuration. The market demand curve D_{Lm} is the sum of all firms' demand curves. If the market were perfectly competitive then it would settle down at W^* and L_m^*. How will it settle down if, instead of there being many small firms, the market comprises just one firm – one single buyer of labour?

Markets in which buyers exercise power over price are called **monopsonies** and differ from perfectly competitive markets in that the buyer knows that in order to buy more labour it is necessary to pay a higher wage rate.

The firm will soon discover that having to pay more to attract extra workers brings with it the problem of keeping its existing workers. They too will demand the higher rewards offered to the new employees. This means that the additional cost of employing one more worker will equal not only that worker's wages, but also the cost of paying existing employees the same wage. This can be illustrated with a numerical example.

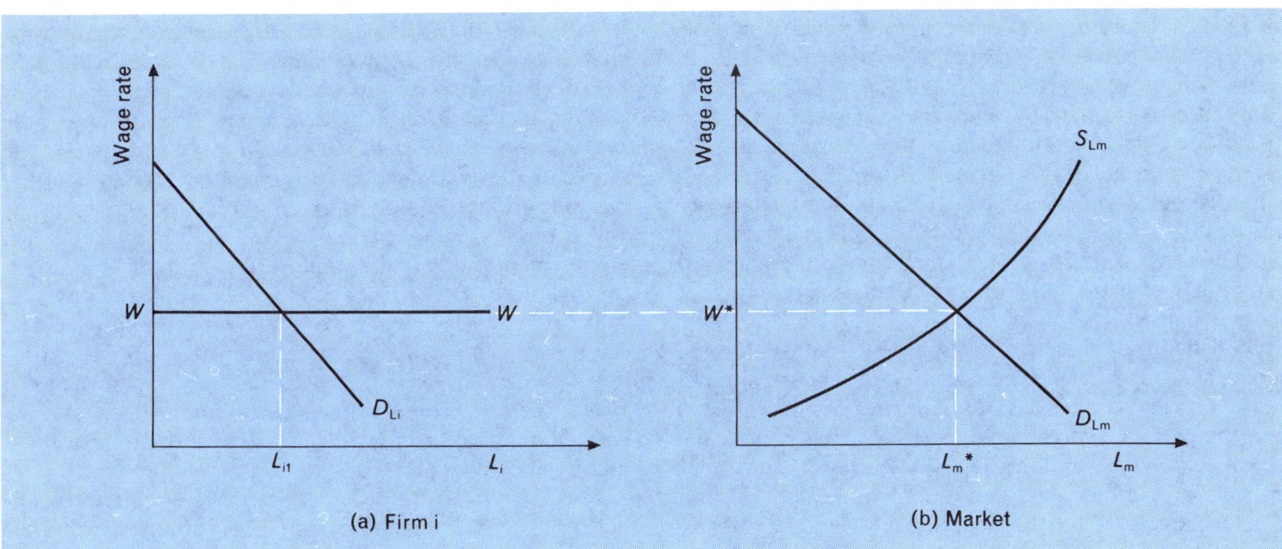

Figure 9.19 Labour market equilibrium for the firm and market.

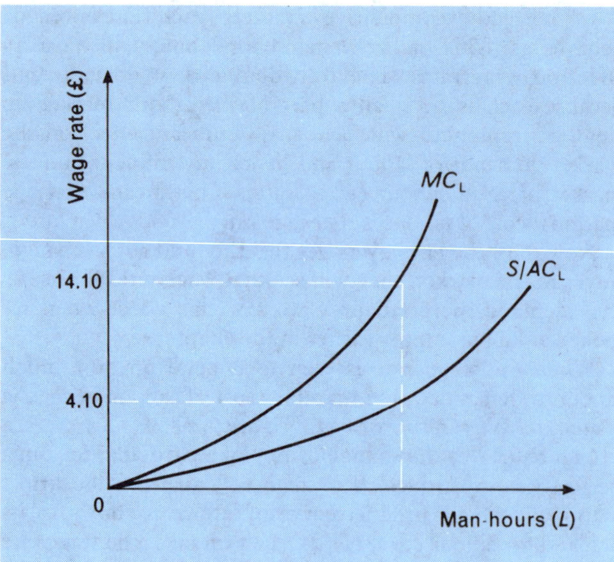

Figure 9.20 Marginal and average cost of labour under monopsony.

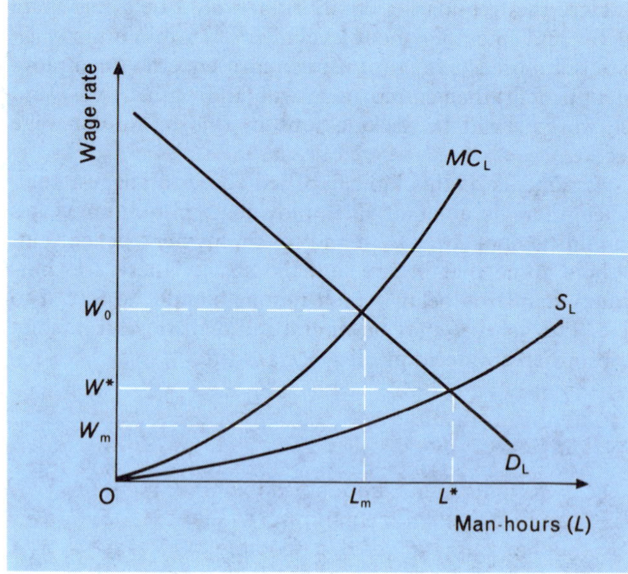

Figure 9.21 Wage rate and employment level under monopsony.

Suppose a firm employs 100 people and pays them all the same wage rate of £4 an hour. The firm requires an extra worker and because it is a monopsonist must pay more to attract the extra labour it needs. Let us say the firm must pay its 101st worker £4.10 an hour. The marginal cost of employing the extra worker is not £4.10, but £14.10 an hour:

Direct cost of 101st worker	= £4.10
Extra wages for existing workers	= (100 × 10p)
	= £10
Marginal cost of employing 101st worker	= £14.10 per hour

The additional cost of hiring one more worker is therefore greater than the wage rate. Thus for the monopsonist the marginal cost of labour is greater than the wage rate, and thus the marginal cost curve of labour lies above the average cost curve of labour. This is illustrated in Figure 9.20.

In order to maximize profits the entrepreneur has to equate the marginal cost of labour with its marginal revenue product. The result of this is shown in Figure 9.21.

The labour supply curve and marginal cost curve are similar shapes to those in Figure 9.20. The monopsonist will therefore maximize profits at L_m where the marginal cost of labour equals the marginal revenue product of labour ($MC_L = MRP_L$).

The labour supply curve in Figure 9.21 shows that the monopsonist can obtain the quantity of labour required (L_m) at a wage rate of W_m. This differs in a number of ways from the perfectly competitive situation. Firstly, both the level of employment and the wage rate are lower than under perfect competition (when they would be equal to L^* and W^* respectively). This would seem to be one reason why employers may form themselves into confederations when negotiating wage contracts.

Secondly, under perfect competition labour is paid the value of its marginal revenue product (wage rate = MRP). In the monopsony case the MRP of labour is greater than the wage rate. Thus the argument that a free-market solution to income determination is fair because workers are paid the value of their contribution to output does not hold in this case.

So far we have seen that not only do the physical productivity of workers and the market price of the product they make influence the income of labour, but so does the structure of the market for labour. Let us now see the effect of trade unions and employers' federations existing together.

Monopoly labour and monopsony

Whenever a workforce is faced with monopsony it will be in its interests to form into an association too. In a similar way, an industry faced with an organized labour force will find it beneficial to form an employers' federation.

This market does not yield a simple solution as the previous ones have done because the point at which the market settles will depend on the relative strengths of the two sides. If the labourers have the most power then they will force the wage rate up to W_0 in Figure 9.21 when employment is L_m. If the employers have most power then they will force wages down to W_m when employment is L_m.

In fact any wage rate between W_m and W_0 is possible, and the level of employment can be negotiated up to L^* provided the unions accept a wage rate that does not exceed W^*. Thus when competition is taken out of the market the co-operative aspect of labour and capital disappears and a picture of conflict emerges.

Furthermore, in this market there is no reason for supposing that when workers bid up wage rates they will price themselves out of jobs. They have already been excluded from employment by the behaviour of the profit-maximizing monopsonist.

SUMMARY

1. It is possible for employers to join together so that they act as a single buyer of labour and attempt to reduce wage rates.
2. A single buyer of labour, a monopsonist, faces an upward-sloping supply curve for labour and the marginal cost of labour is greater than the wage rate.
3. The marginal cost curve of labour lies above the average cost curve and so less labour is employed and at a lower wage rate than under perfect competition.
4. If the industry contains a monopoly seller of labour and a monopsonist then the eventual wage rate depends on the relative bargaining strengths of the two sides.

*More on the supply of labour

We mentioned previously some reservations as to the realism of a constantly upward-sloping labour supply curve (Figure 9.12). We can now examine some of the more technical aspects of labour supply.

Let us look first at the reactions of workers who face the prospect of higher and higher earnings. Earlier we stated that they would offer to give up more and more leisure as the wage rate increased.

They may indeed decide to work more hours and earn more money. On the other hand, they may decide to continue working the same number of hours as before since they will still be earning more than they did before. They may even decide to work fewer hours than before and still receive a higher income. This behaviour is quite rational because they have decided that the marginal benefit that they gain from one more hour worked is less than the benefit gained from one more hour with their family.

We saw in Chapter 4 that when a person has a lot of one good and only a little of another that person will require a very great deal of the good they have in abundance to compensate them for giving up a small amount of the good they have only a little of. (This was shown to be the marginal rate of substitution of one good for another.) In the case of the workers above they have reached the point where, with the pay rise, they can earn more than previously by working less. They therefore decide to swap some of the goods that could be bought with the extra income for extra leisure. We would not expect this reaction when somebody has a lower income, but we might not be surprised to see top executives deciding to take extra holiday rather than working long hours at their city desks when their earnings potential rises.

Indifference curve analysis can be used to explain this reaction. Consider Figure 9.22, which shows an individual's labour supply reaction. As the wage rate rises to W_2 from W_1 more hours of labour are offered per week. We can see that between points A and B on the labour supply curve the reaction of the worker is as we would have previously expected.

When the wage rate rises from W_2 to W_3 the worker decides to take some as income and some as leisure, since at the higher wage rate more income can be earned while working fewer hours. The worker has a new income of Y_3, which is greater than Y_2, and works $L_{max}-L_3$ hours, which is fewer than previously ($L_{max}-L_2$). This has the effect of causing the labour supply curve to bend backwards between points B and C, as shown in Figure 9.22.

This analysis is for the individual worker. There is no reason to suppose that all workers behave in the same way at the same income levels. Some people seem unable to stop working; others have a strong preference for leisure and so very quickly reach the point where they substitute extra income for extra leisure. When looking at the aggregate supply of labour we cannot predict the exact shape of the labour supply curve. For example, as one person decides to

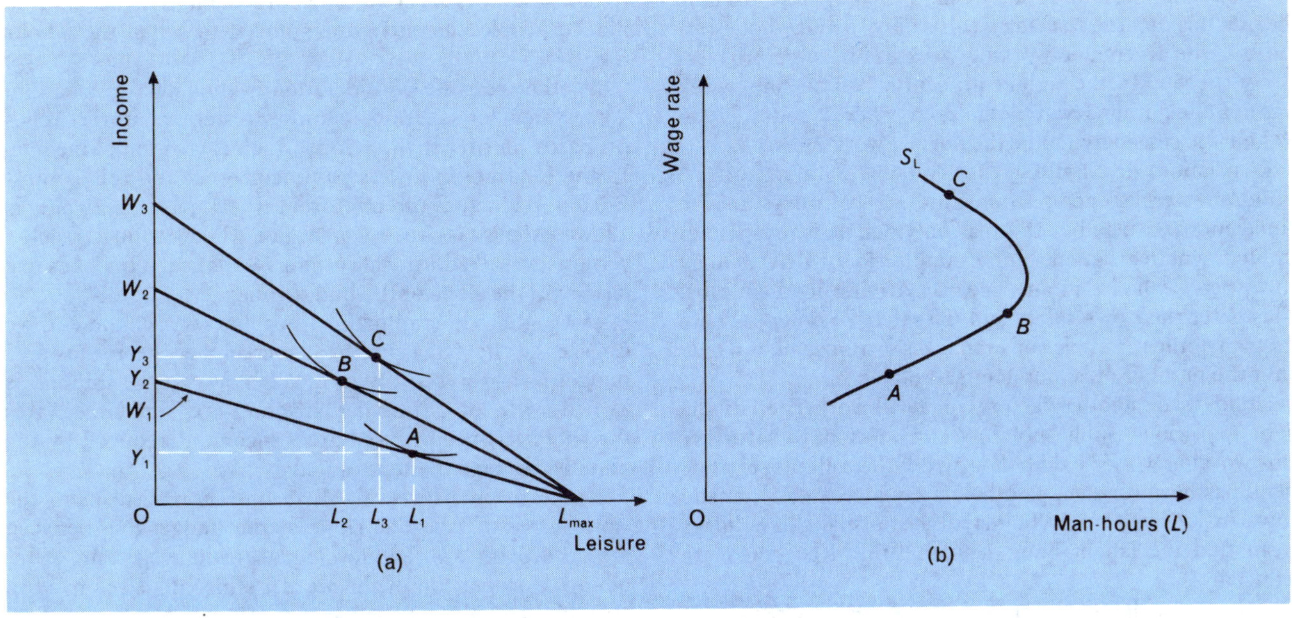

Figure 9.22 Backward-sloping curve of labour.

work less, another may be willing to take on his or her work and so a firm or industry may still have the labour it needs.

Although we have only an imprecise answer to how much labour will be supplied in aggregate, we are able to make assumptions about how workers might behave with regard to incentives and we will make use of this later.

Other determinants of labour supply

We have looked at the way an individual decides between income and leisure. We stated earlier that the higher the wage rate, the more people will decide to enter the active workforce. There are a number of demographic considerations to take into account in total labour supply.

On the simplest level the available labour force is equal to the size of the population. We have been using man-hours as our measure of labour supply, since these reflect a number of considerations which we shall look at more closely here.

It is easy to see that no one can work every hour of the day, every day. The labour-hours available from the entire population are therefore limited. In modern societies there are usually other constraints on the number of hours that people can work in a given period. Young people are compelled to attend school until 16 years of age in the UK, and when they work part time they can work only a certain number of hours. We can say that more generally the **working population** does not contain those in full-time education. It therefore excludes many over the age of 16 in sixth forms, universities and so on.

Neither will the working population include all those who are beyond the retiring age (65 for men, 60 for women) or those incapable of work, such as the chronically ill and disabled. We can therefore say that the working population is all those between 16 and 65 (60 for women) not in full-time education. However, there are some other considerations.

Custom and legislation also limit the number of hours that can be worked. It may be traditional that people do not work on a certain day of the week, or it may have become the practice that the working week is only so many hours. In the UK the acceptable working week has become progressively shorter. In the eighteenth century an 80-hour week was not uncommon, even for children, whereas today $37\frac{1}{2}$ to 39 hours is considered to be the normal working week.

Legislation has limited the available labour supply. Children were stopped from climbing chimneys in the nineteenth century, but this was only one of many Acts of employment legislation. For example, lorry drivers may only spend 8 hours in any one day driving in their cabs. This is for their own safety and the safety of others. There are many other examples of similar restrictions, all of which limit the number of labour-hours available.

Holidays are another factor. Today all workers enjoy the right to various public holidays and most have a further four working weeks' paid holiday from their employer. The trend has been for such paid holiday to increase, and many now consider five weeks' holiday to be normal. All holidays mean that the labour-hours available to an economy are reduced.

A final consideration is the quality of the labour force. Is the labour of 100 adult members of a newly discovered Amazon tribe worth the same as that of 100 adult members of the UK workforce? The answer, of course, is no. Their capabilities are quite different and we would not expect any of the Amazon tribesmen to be able to work a lathe for a considerable time. Thus we must also bear in mind the acquired skills and education of the workforce when looking at labour supply.

*Further considerations of the budget constraint

The budget constraint we have drawn so far has been a simple straight line equal to the sum of the wage rate multiplied by the number of hours worked. The real world is not as simple as that, and it is worth considering some modifications.

Figure 9.23(a) shows a budget line as previously defined. Let us ask the question: what happens when someone has no work? This occurs when a person is unemployed. According to Figure 9.23(a) the unemployed person has no income, but this is not realistic. In all western countries most unemployed people receive some income from the state. This takes many forms, but for simplicity we will refer to it all as unemployment benefit. The implication of this is that a person's income is never zero, and so the individual's budget constraint must look more like that shown in Figure 9.23(b).

Figure 9.23(b) shows that people get an income of Y_1 regardless of whether they work or not. It is unlikely then that a person will choose to work when his or her income is less than Y_1, and it would be a strange set of preferences indeed that allowed an indifference curve to be tangential to a point between L_{max} and a.

A point made most strongly by some economists is that unemployment benefit prevents people taking jobs at wages below Y_1. They say that this is a major cause of unemployment as many jobs exist at these lower wage rates. This is a point of some controversy, but some recent measures by Mrs Thatcher's UK government can be seen as attempts to reduce the real level of unemployment benefits and so induce people currently unemployed to rejoin the labour force.

Another real-life consideration is the effect of taxation. The system of taxation in most western countries relies primarily on **direct taxation**, which is taxation of income. In the UK most workers pay income tax and this is most usually deducted directly from their pay. Everyone is allowed some tax-free income, but when earnings reach a certain level all additional earnings are taxed. This leads to a change in the slope of the budget line.

If we ignore unemployment benefits for the moment, we can see the effect of a single-rate percentage income tax on a budget constraint in Figure 9.24. A certain amount is earned without attracting income tax, but once this threshold has been passed gross income is reduced by the same percentage as the tax rate.

Up to income level Y_1 all income is passed on to the worker free of tax. The slope of the budget line between L_{max} and point t is therefore equal to the wage rate. After point t a proportion of the worker's income is removed in tax and this leads to a change in the slope of the budget line, which then equals the wage rate less the tax rate.

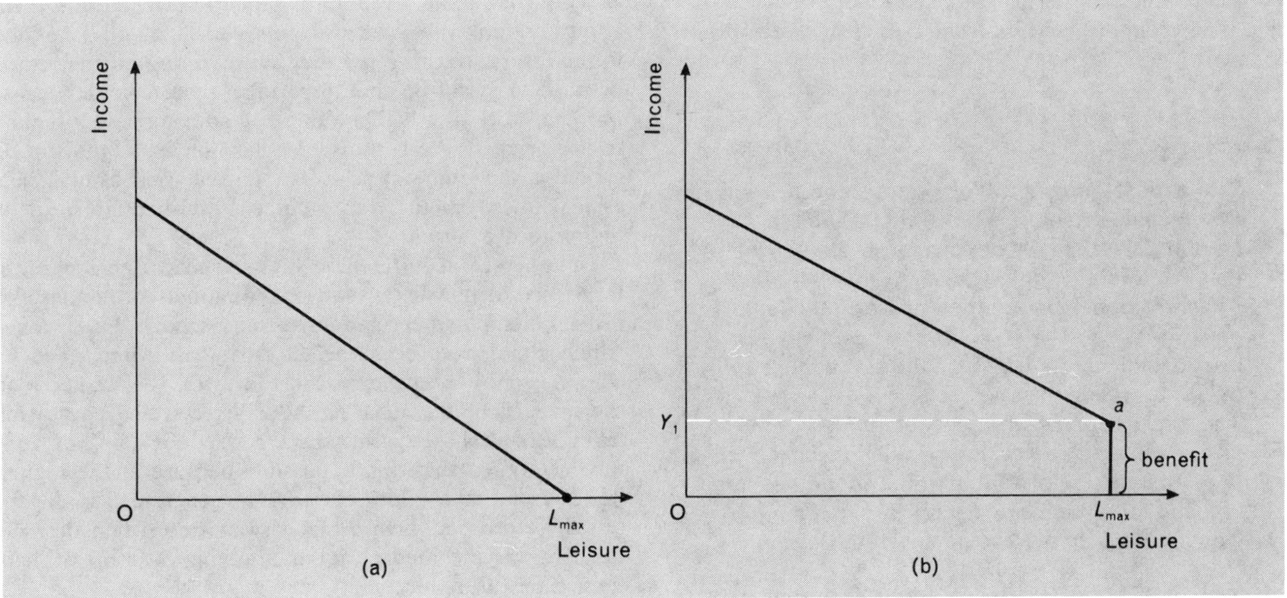

Figure 9.23 Effect of unemployment benefit on the budget constraint.

It is sensible for workers to make their decisions about how many hours to work on the basis of the income they will receive, not on gross income. Income net of tax and all other deductions at source is known as **disposable income**.

We can combine the effects of paying unemployment benefit and levying an income tax on one diagram. If we examine Figure 9.25 we can see that the higher the rate of tax, the more pronounced the change in the slope of the budget constraint.

In the figure the effects of two possible tax rates are shown. It should be clear that the higher the tax rate, the more likely the worker is to choose a mix of income and leisure between points *a* and *t*. This is due to the shape of the worker's indifference curves. The choice of point *t* would not be unusual as beyond this the reward for working diminishes.

In the UK there have been many tax rate bands, producing many kinks in the budget constraint. It is the view of some economists that this has been a major disincentive to work beyond a certain point and that reducing the rate of tax will induce people to work more. This is one explanation for Chancellor Lawson's abolition of all but one of the higher rates of income tax, and his reduction of the top rate to 40 per cent in the 1988 budget. Supporters of this move argue that lower tax rates will lead to people working more

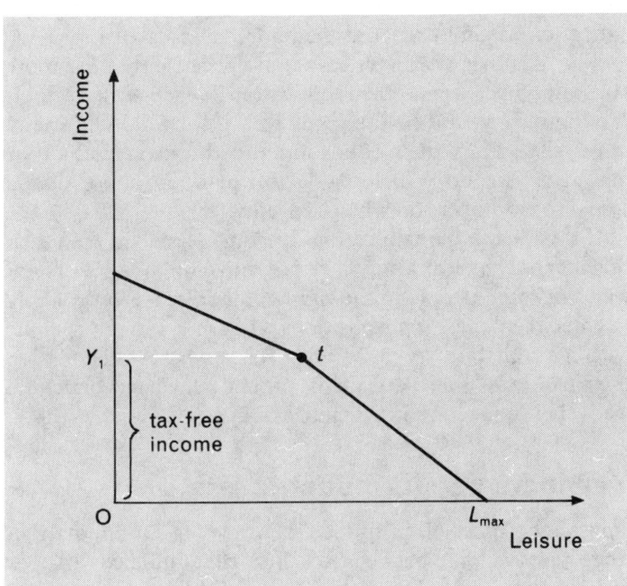

Figure 9.24 Effect of unemployment benefit and direct taxation on the budget constraint.

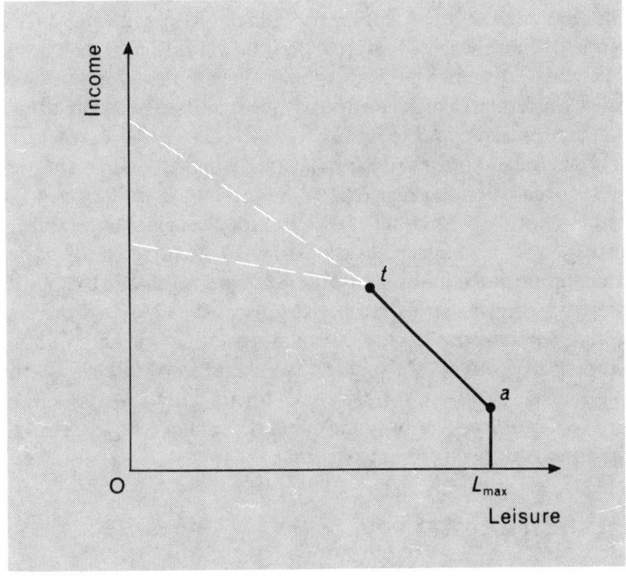

Figure 9.25 Effect of different tax rates on the budget constraint.

hours and much harder as they keep more of what they earn. The economy benefits from greater output and employment.

SUMMARY

1. While most workers will offer more labour when the wage rate rises, it is possible that after a certain point they will choose more leisure when they are offered higher wages.
2. The individual labour supply curve could bend backwards on itself at high wage rates, but it is not possible to predict when the aggregate supply of labour will do this.
3. The total supply of labour is determined by the size of a country's working population, which will depend upon factors such as: the school-leaving age; the retirement age; customs (e.g. not working on Sunday); the quality of the labour force.
4. The consumer's income will depend upon state benefits and the tax rate imposed, as well as the wage rate and the number of hours worked. This means that the budget constraint is rarely a straight line.

Differences in the wages of labour

So far our theory suggests that, in perfectly competitive labour markets, labour will be paid a wage equal or related to its marginal revenue product. When we look at the real world we see that there are vast differences in rewards for very similar workers.

The types of difference we have in mind are the differentials between the salary of a City executive and a school teacher, between a man and a woman doing the same job, and between white people and black people in the UK. None of these wage differences can be completely explained away by differences in marginal revenue product and we must therefore take account of other factors when considering the rewards paid to labour.

The most common explanation using the analysis we have already encountered is to suggest that differences in wages can be explained by the steepness of the labour supply curve. Workers take time to acquire skills (the training period), and if some workers are reluctant to spend their time in this way then the supply curve of such workers is steeper than the supply curve of unskilled workers. Thus the supply curve for skilled workers looks like L_S' in Figure 9.17, and the supply curve for unskilled workers like L_S. This, of course, only explains differences *between* professions and not differences *within* them.

Human capital

Human capital is the term economists use to describe the education and experience a person builds up over his or her lifetime. For example, people who spend an extra two years at school are doing it to improve their knowledge and their ability to think and solve problems, skills that will be of use in the future. In this sense they are investing for the future because they will be able to perform more complex tasks, produce work of a higher value and so command a higher future wage. We can think of education as a build-up of capital in the same way as investing in physical capital such as machines – both require current sacrifice and lead to higher future output.

In order to acquire these higher skills a person must forgo income now because he or she cannot both undertake full-time employment and also attend school. The income which could have been earned during the time taken to complete an A-level course is lost for ever. It is argued that the extra income that he or she will receive as a result of taking exams is the incentive and reward for doing so. It is further argued that this is possible because of the higher *MRP* that better-educated workers generate. Employers can therefore pay them a higher wage rate when they do qualify. The income lost due to studying is an investment for greater future income.

If we look at the income profiles of workers with various qualifications, we find that those with A levels earn more than those without and that people who invest even more of their time in taking a degree earn more than those with just A levels. This would seem to be clear evidence that forgoing income now to gain extra qualifications is worthwhile, but a question we must ask is whether or not this extra income is due to a real rise in a worker's *MRP*.

The evidence is quite clear that it pays people to attend a university in terms of the extra income that they receive in later life. It is also clear that graduates' earnings rise in real terms as they get older, perhaps reflecting their increasing competence and responsibility.

But an alternative explanation of these increased earnings is that the graduates are just more able than their peers and so are able to undertake more complex jobs. In other words, graduates are only using their God-given talents and this leads them to the better-paid jobs. If this is not so, why do sociology graduates make successful bankers when their education has not prepared them for such a career?

The idea that graduates earn more because they are more able, not because of their education, suggests that their productivity would be the same even if they did not attend university. Thus their education and the investment they make in it in terms of lost salary provide no more than a signal to employers on who to employ.

If the idea that qualifications are only signals is true then this means that education does not move the *MRP* curve of well-educated people to the right at all. The truth probably lies between these two positions. There are many people with natural ability who would succeed whatever education they had, and there are many others who have benefited from their education in a practical way.

Teachers versus industrialists

One of the most often quoted examples of an anomaly in wage rates is that between teachers and industrialists, or university lecturers and city executives. Most of them have degrees and yet teachers and dons earn, on average, much less than their former fellow students.

Case Study 9.1 Recruitment and racism

An Asian graduate arrived at the reception desk of a big company for a job interview. 'You're not on my list,' said the receptionist. 'But I haven't told you my name yet,' replied the graduate.

I heard this story from Marie Stewart, an Afro-Caribbean woman with a PhD, who has 'lost count of the number of times I turned up for interviews and got looks which said: No, you can't be Dr Stewart.'

She now works for project Fullemploy, advising companies on how to avoid discriminating against ethnic minorities in recruitment. Research published this year by the Commission for Racial Equality shows that graduates who are members of ethnic minorities have a harder time getting jobs than their white counterparts, and often settle for inferior posts.

The CRE researchers matched an ethnic-minority sample of students with a white sample. Nearly three-quarters of the former received no job offers in their final year; only half of white graduates did not. Soon after graduation, one in three of the ethnic-minority graduates still had no job offers: the figures for whites was less than one in four.

Graduates from ethnic minorities are much more likely than other graduates to be employed in the often denigrated public sector. Graduates of Caribbean and African origin are much less likely to work in industry, while Afro-Asians and Asians are more likely to be self-employed.

A separate CRE study on pharmacy graduates, many of whom are Asian, confirmed earlier findings that Asian pharmacists were taking lower-status jobs in less prestigious organisations.

One graduate who wanted a career in pharmacological research eventually became a sub-postmaster. He told the CRE researchers: 'I had one interview in that whole period. Letters? I must have written 100 at least.'

Ramesh, an Asian with three A-levels, applied for a job in his local DHSS office that required only O-levels. He was asked whether he was 'serious about a career in the civil service' or if he 'planned to run a corner shop'. He did not get the job.

But racial stereotyping is not the whole story. The graduate recruitment process is still bedevilled with secrecy, ill-defined criteria, snobbery and amateurism. Employers still talk about wanting to attract the 'top 5 per cent' of graduates without having any clear criteria.

Interviewees are not given a clear idea of what criteria are being used for selection. Ethnic-minority graduates often believe that a good academic performance will see them all right. 'Unfortunately the graduate labour market in Britain does not operate in this way,' say the CRE researchers.

'In most employment areas, recruiters appear to be looking for sets of personal attributes and skills which are difficult to operationalise and difficult to counter.'

Students who have followed conventional career paths tend to be favoured. Employers prefer young graduates who took all their O-levels together, their A-levels at the same time, then went straight to university. They dislike career breaks.

This excludes a great many people whose experience could be valuable. Many ethnic-minority graduates leave school with no qualifications and return to education later in life. Others arrive in Britain in their teens, and their school qualifications do not come in neat bunches.

The 'milkround' goes mostly to universities, rather than to the polytechnics which have a much higher proportion of ethnic-minority graduates.

Tariq Madood of the CRE is working with the Association of Graduate Recruiters and the Association of Graduate Careers Advisers to change the situation. 'The engine of change is the economic situation,' he says. 'It is bad business to be indifferent to the 5 per cent of graduates who are from ethnic minorities.'

1. Does the article help to explain why members of ethnic minorities receive a lower average wage than white Britons?

2. To what extent does the article confirm the view that academic qualifications are a 'signal' to employers on whom to employ?

Source: Francis Beckett, *Independent*, 14 June 1990

These observations do not mean that the marginal productivity theory of wage determination is wrong, just that there are other factors to be considered which we have previously held to be constant. In this case teachers and lecturers have usually chosen to enter their particular professions because they like their jobs more than the extra income they could have earned elsewhere. Most academics find the desire to pursue the finer aspects of their subjects more attractive than the extra goods they could buy with the higher income they could earn, say, by working for BP. If this is the case then we must conclude that academics get greater utility from their work and research than they would from their alternative incomes.

Discrimination

If we look at data for the wages of men and women, we find that as a rule men get paid more than women, even when they work in the same industry having joined at the same time with the same qualifications. We also find that, on average, white people are paid more than non-whites, and that the average wage of a black person with a degree, for example, is lower than the average wage of a white graduate.

Such differences may be due to different *MRP*s, but this argument seems difficult to justify. It will be useful to look in detail at the rewards paid both to women and to non-white people. We shall see that differences in wage rates may not have strictly economic causes.

Pay differences between men and women

When considering average earnings in no section of the adult workforce do women earn more than men. For example, in 1985 in the sector of 'Clerical and selling'* the average weekly wage of a man was £165 while the woman's average was £105. There must be some reason for this other than the simple idea that the *MRP* of all women is lower than men's. It has, of course, been proved that men are not inherently more intelligent than women.

It should not be assumed from the evidence presented that all women earn less than men – there are women who hold top jobs and head companies. However, there are very few of them. It appears that women generally occupy the lower-ranking jobs and fail to get or take promotion. There may be economic reasons for this.

Consider a firm taking on young recruits at least some of

* As defined by the Department of Employment *New Earnings Survey*.

whom will be expected to go on to senior management. All senior managers require a significant degree of training over many years, and a company will have to spend a significant sum in addition to an employee's salary to provide this training. A manager must choose new staff members with this in mind, and it is possible that, no matter what assurances are given at the interview, a female candidate may be expensively trained and then leave to have a family. A similar argument can be advanced when selecting candidates for promotion. The result of this process is that men find themselves in the higher-paid jobs even though their female counterparts may be just as able or more so, and we therefore observe a higher average wage rate for men.

Another factor is the extent to which women go on to higher education. We have already seen that graduates get paid more than non-graduates. So if fewer women as a percentage of the population go on to higher education then there will always be more male applicants for the higher-paid jobs. In fact while more people do go on to further education today than ever before, a lower percentage of women do so than men.

There are a number of possible explanations for this. It might be that the education system fails to encourage girls to aim for a place in higher education to the same extent as boys. Even in mixed schools it has been shown that teachers give more attention to boys. Moreover, the division of subjects promotes the home-keeping skills of girls and the academic and practical skills of boys. The latter problem is compounded when boys and girls attend separate schools.

Sometimes girls are not even expected to have a career. 'A woman's place is in the home' is a sentiment that has been found at all levels of society. Girls may be encouraged to see their future role as supporting a husband in his career rather than having one of their own.

It has also been suggested that the lower potential returns for women with higher education puts them off trying to get one. If a woman sees that the rewards of women are not much higher following the sacrifice of three years' income while studying then she may well decide that she would prefer to enter the labour market immediately.

All of these factors are less prevalent today than they were 20 years ago and the gap between the wages of men and women is not as wide as it was. The law has now forbidden the practice of paying women less than men for doing the same job in the same workplace. But the law cannot change attitudes and these will only change over a long period of time.

Racial discrimination

In the same way that women get paid less than men, non-whites are paid less than whites. The differences may have many of the same causes. Non-whites tend not to go on to higher education, and there is no good reason for this in terms of ability. It has been suggested that it is not the amount, but the quality of education offered to non-whites that is the problem. Non-whites tend to go to inner-city schools where discipline and attendance is poor, and where better teachers move away to other less difficult schools. Due to low expectations inner-city schools do not encourage their students to go on to college or university and leaving school early becomes an accepted way of life.

There is also the problem of gaining a job in the first place. Employers see the inner-city schools as being of poor quality and assume that those who attended them are poor candidates for a job. Promotion from the jobs that non-whites do get is also difficult. Whites appear to get steady promotion and training and so reach higher-paid jobs.

It is almost impossible to give a reasoned answer to the question of why non-whites fare badly in the labour market. As with women it is likely that there is still an element of discrimination for no reason whatever. However, it is impossible to quantify the degree of this discrimination.

SUMMARY

1. Some workers are paid far more or less than others and much of this difference cannot be accounted for by differences in the marginal revenue product of labour.
2. The supply of skilled workers is more inelastic than that of unskilled workers and so they are able to command higher wages.
3. Highly educated workers are said to have invested in human capital and so are more productive than other workers.
4. Some economists claim that higher education is only a signal to employers and that well-educated workers would perform well in any case.
5. There is evidence of some wage differences being due to discrimination, but some of the differences are due to the decisions of workers who like their lower-paid jobs or firms who regard one class of worker as a bad risk.

Economic rent and labour

We saw in Chapter 3 that, although land is provided free by nature and hence has no supply cost, it nevertheless attracts a rent (or **economic rent**). In general, rent is any payment over and above supply cost and is occasionally paid to factors other than land.

In particular, we could think of a worker who is willing to supply labour at £2 an hour. That would be the supply cost of an hour's labour from this worker. In order to attract more workers the employers raise the wage rate to £2.50 an hour, which is the supply cost of the additional labour. But in a perfectly competitive market the original worker will have to be paid £2.50 too, although he or she will have worked for£2 an hour. The £2 an hour is the supply cost and the extra 50p an hour is economic rent.

Another term for the supply cost of a factor of production is its **transfer earnings**. If earnings fall below supply costs then the labourer will not work, i.e. will *transfer* to some other activity. In the above example the worker's transfer earnings were £2 and the economic rent was 50p.

Thus transfer earnings are defined as *the amount that a factor of production must be paid to stop it transferring to another use*, i.e. the minimum a factor will accept. Economic rent can be defined as *any excess over transfer earnings that is paid to a factor of production*, i.e. that portion of income above the minimum necessary to keep the factor from moving to another use.

It is possible for situations to arise where rewards are all rent. This occurs when the supply curve of labour is completely vertical, so that a fixed quantity is supplied whatever the wage (see Figure 9.16). In this case the wage actually paid could be very low or very high depending on where the labour demand curve crosses the vertical supply curve.

It is also possible for all of earnings to be transfer earnings. This occurs when the supply curve of labour is horizontal. In such a case a firm can hire as much labour as it wants at a given wage rate. Both of these cases are discussed in the next section when considering the employment of land and capital (pp. 178–80).

It is much more usual for labour to be paid a combination of transfer earnings and economic rent. This is always the case when the labour supply is represented by the normal upward-sloping curve, as shown in Figure 9.26.

The market wage rate is W^* and this is paid to all labourers employed in this industry. Let us suppose we can pick out the services of one worker at the point L_1. This worker would be prepared to work for the wage of W_1, as we can see by reading the wage rate from the labour supply curve at this point. Despite the fact that the worker would work for the wage W_1, the wage actually paid is W^*. This sum of $W^* - W_1$ is over and above transfer earnings and hence is rent.

The wage W_1 is the worker's transfer earnings, and the difference between this and what the worker is paid is economic rent. We can imagine many such workers all entering the market at different wage rates, as shown by the labour supply curve. It follows that the shaded area above the labour supply curve is all economic rent, and the area below it, up to the amount of labour employed L^*, is transfer earnings. Only the very last worker employed is earning all transfer earnings as it is only this worker who has been just induced to join the labour force by the wage W^*.

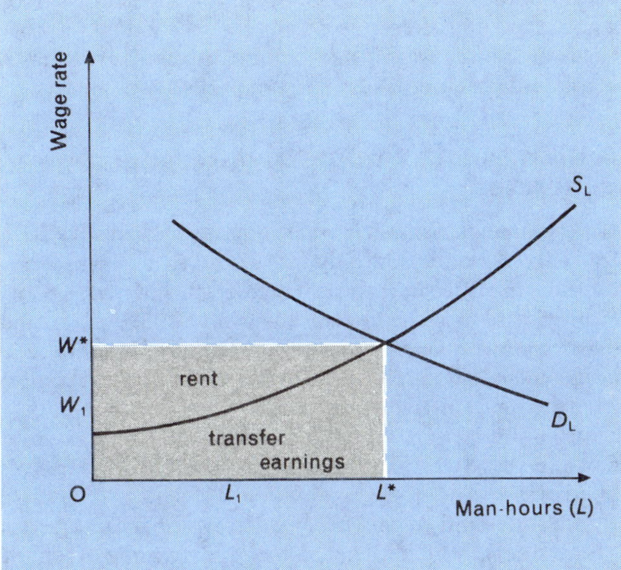

Figure 9.26 Transfer earnings and economic rent in the labour market.

We can see that, as a firm or industry raises the wage rate to attract extra workers, it pays an increasing amount of economic rent. The next question to ask is: can the rewards of labour be all economic rent?

The chances of one person earning all economic rent are remote, but pop stars and famous sports people do earn a sizeable amount of rent. Consider the earnings of Jason Donovan (or Queen, for the older readers among you). The supply of Jason Donovans is strictly limited to one and so the supply curve of this factor looks like the one in Figure 9.16, a vertical line. Jason Donovan earns many thousands of pounds for singing and performing, and yet if he did not sing he would pursue some other career, say being a postman at £140 a week.

The transfer earnings of Jason Donovan as a pop star are therefore £140 a week, and since he clearly gets more than this, the difference is economic rent. If the fickle public turn away from *Neighbours* and Jason Donovan then his earnings will fall. When they fall to £139.99 a week he will transfer to being a postman.

SUMMARY

1. The earnings of any worker can be made up of two elements, transfer earnings and economic rent, in variable proportions.
2. Transfer earnings are the amount that a factor must be paid to keep it in its present employment. Economic rent is all earnings greater than transfer earnings.
3. If a worker is paid less than his or her transfer earnings, i.e. less than could be earned elsewhere, then the worker will change employment.
4. If the supply of labour is absolutely fixed then all income earned is economic rent.
5. If the supply of labour is perfectly elastic then all income is transfer earnings.
6. Most workers earn a mixture of economic rent and transfer earnings as most people would supply labour at a wage rate lower than the one they actually receive.

Land

We have already seen in Chapter 3 what constitutes land and capital. We now look at both of these factors in more detail, at how much of each will be employed and how much they will be paid.

First, though, we must emphasize the interdependence of all the factors of production. There is no possibility of carrying out business without some contribution from land, labour, capital and enterprise.

Land and economic rent

In everyday language the word 'rent' is used to describe payments made for the use of someone else's property: most familiar is 'the rent' paid for a house, a farm or a television set. As we saw earlier, economists can use the word 'rent' to refer to that part of a payment made to labour which is over and above supply costs or transfer earnings. Most labourers earn very little rent, but for a few particular individuals rent forms the major part of their earnings.

In the case of land, however, there is no supply cost and hence all returns to land are rent. Moreover, as we saw in Chapter 3, rent can be used to refer to a payment made for the use of any natural endowment.

In what follows we will investigate the concept of rent more fully, and in particular how rent relates to the payments made to those who own land.

Why pay rent?

Since land is, by definition, provided at zero cost by nature (no one has done anything to bring about oil fields in the North Sea or coal underground in Wales), it would seem that land has a zero supply cost. How then can it attract any payment at all?

Obviously not all land receives a rent. Sunlight and rainwater descend at no charge. Whale fishers pay nothing to hunt. We are therefore confining our discussion of rent to those goods for which there is a market, i.e. for which *ownership* and *exchange* are possible.

Perhaps the easiest way forward is to take the case of farmland. Farmland is 'owned', is sometimes used by its 'owner', is sometimes used by others, earns rent and is a natural endowment. It therefore covers most of the cases we will meet.

Imagine a valley of very fertile land surrounded by mountains, the tops of which are completely barren. Between the floor of the valley and the tops of the mountains there is a whole range of fertility, beginning at a maximum, gradually diminishing as we move up the hillside, further diminishing as we reach the mountain slopes and eventually diminishing to zero.

The first farmers to settle on the land would use the best land and enjoy very high yields per acre and per worker.

The next wave of farmers to arrive would be obliged to make use of slightly worse land and hence would produce less per acre and less per worker. As successive waves of farmers arrived, so worse and worse land would be brought under cultivation.

We have here something which looks very much like the law of diminishing marginal productivity which we encountered earlier. Each additional farmer increases output, but the increments diminish as more farmers join in. There is, however, an important distinction to be drawn between the example of the valley being gradually brought more and more under cultivation and the earlier example of more and more workers being used to operate the same fixed quantity of capital.

Extensive and intensive margins

In the case of the valley, the addition of another farmer further up the slopes has no effect whatever on the productivity of other farmers. Those who were there before still have good land and still produce large quantities of crops per acre. The new farmer will produce less than they do, but they will produce the same as before.

Conversely, in the case of workers being applied to machines, each additional worker reduces the productivity of *all* the workers previously employed. It is for this reason that we carefully defined the marginal physical product of labour as the change in *total* output when one more person is employed rather than the increased output due to the last person employed. Since we had homogeneous labour, the last worker produces no more nor less than anyone else; it is just that everyone's productivity is slightly less with the additional worker than it would be without.

Thus we have two notions of marginal physical product: the first (the valley example) where productivity decreases at the margin but is unchanged within the margin; and the second (the worker/machine case) where productivity declines everywhere as labour input is increased. In order to distinguish between them, the first is called the extensive margin and the latter is called the intensive margin. It is the existence of the extensive margin which gives rise to rent.

We could also apply the idea of an extensive margin to land which is used for commercial rather than for agricultural purposes. There is a high demand for office space, theatres and shops in the centre of London. This is because offices, theatres and shops in the centre of a large city attract a lot more business than they would if they were in the middle of an agricultural, rural community. Those few square yards at the centre of the city command very high 'rents' indeed. Those square yards of land slightly further away from the centre attract slightly less business and hence command a slightly lower rent. It is nevertheless very high in comparison with most rents in the UK.

Just like in the case of the farmland in the valley, the land in the centre has the highest rent and as we move out from this centre the rent becomes progressively less and less. The rents in the urban case are determined not by the innate properties of the land (as is the case for rural land), but simply by its location. Land within a certain distance of a city centre is by definition limited and, being expensive, is typically used very intensively. This means getting the most commercial use out of each square metre and so we see very tall buildings with each bit of land supporting a large amount of commerce. We do not see very tall (skyscraper) barns or farmhouses in the country because land is not so scarce and need not be used economically.

A numerical example of how rent is generated

If we assume for simplicity that all farms in the valley are of equal acreage and grow only wheat, and that all wheat sells for the same price in the wheat market, then we can say that farmers who hold the lower lands will have higher incomes than those who farm higher up the slopes. This difference in income is called rent. It arises not from better labour, or from better capital or from better farming know-how. It arises purely from natural endowment. Farmers lower down have better land provided, at no cost to themselves, by nature.

If all the land in the valley were owned by one person (the rentier), who did not do all the farming, then the rentier could charge farmers rents for their farms. Rents on lower farms would be much higher than rents on higher farms. And, if the market worked perfectly, these differen-

Table 9.3 An example of rent varying with income

Farm	A		B		C	
Costs (labour and capital)	£1,200		£1,200		£1,200	
Output (tonnes)	500		200		100	
Price of wheat	Income	Rent	Income	Rent	Income	Rent
£2.40	£1,200	0	£480	0	£240	0
£6	£3,000	£1,800	£1,200	0	£600	0
£12	£6,000	£4,800	£2,400	£1,200	£1,200	0

tial rents would be such as to equate the incomes of the tenant farmers, i.e. any difference in income due to the land would be absorbed as rent by the rentier.

In order to see how this would come about and how the amount of rent is determined, let us consider a simple numerical example. Let there be three farms (A, B and C) of equal size (50 acres) with equal quantities of labour (10) and equal quantities of capital (£100). Labour cost is £20 and capital cost £10 per unit. The amounts of wheat produced on the three farms are 500, 200 and 100 tonnes respectively.

When the price of wheat is £2.4 per tonne, farm A can earn 500 × £2.4 = £1,200. This amount would just meet the cost of labour and capital (10 × 20) + (100 × 10). Thus when wheat fetches a very low price there is no possibility of paying rent and only the best land is used. Farms B and C would fall into disuse.

If the demand for wheat increases such that its price rises to £6 per tonne, the first farm will make a surplus of income over expenditure as follows:

$$(500 \times £6) - (10 \times £20) - (100 \times £10) = £1,800$$

Farm B now can just break even since its income would be 200 × £6 = £1,200, which exactly matches its expenditure on labour and capital.

However, there is now a surplus of £1,800 being earned by farm A. The rentier could ask farmer A to pay some rent for the use of the land. If farmer A refused then the rentier could invite farmer B to take over farm A. Farmer B would be willing to pay anything up to £1,800 rent, since even at £1,800 rent the farmer is no worse off than would be the case by staying on farm B. Thus competition between tenants and the existence of a surplus gives rise to an income for the rentier – an income exactly equal to the 'rent'.

Imagine next that there is a further increase in demand for wheat and as a consequence its price rises to £12 per tonne. At this price farm A now makes a surplus of £4,800 and farm B makes a surplus of £1,200. Furthermore, at this price farm C becomes operative since it can now just meet its costs. Its income would be £12 × 100 = £1,200 and its expenditure would be £1,200. Total rent from the valley would now amount to £6,000 (£4,800 from farm A and £1,200 from farm B).

Once again this amount could be extracted from tenant farmers by the landowner or rentier. This analysis is summarized in Table 9.3.

What we have seen is that an increasing demand for wheat will increase the wheat price and thereby render profitable farms which once were derelict. As the extensive margin is increased, so farms within it yield higher and higher rents – innermost farms yielding the highest rents and those at the margin yielding zero rent.

Thus the demand for wheat will determine both the area cultivated and the rent of land, even though land is a 'free' good.

Supply and demand curves

We can make this model more general by imagining a very large number of farms spreading up the hillsides. Each farm has the same acreage, labour force and capital stock, but the amount produced falls as we move up the hillsides. The 'cost', in terms of labour and capital, per tonne will therefore rise as more wheat is grown and more farms are activated. We can represent this increasing cost on the vertical axis of Figure 9.27.

As can be seen from the figure, the cost curve rises and point *a* is where farm A meets its labour and capital costs, i.e. its non-rent costs; point *b* is where farm B meets its non-rent costs; and point *c* is where farm C meets its non-rent costs.

The curves D_1, D_2 and D_3 are three possible demand curves. When demand is low, i.e. at level D_1, price P_1 obtains and only farm A (and any farms of higher productivity) will operate.

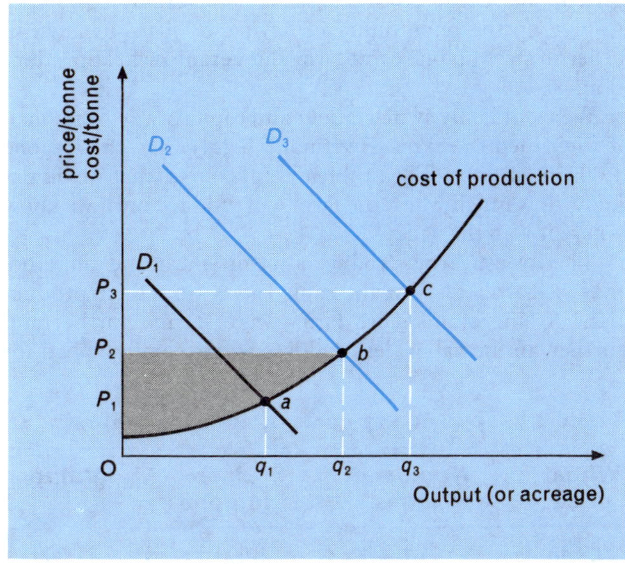

Figure 9.27 Rent or producer surplus at different levels of demand.

When demand moves to D_2, all farms up to and including farm B are operational. At point *b*, for example, farm B has costs equal to P_2 and hence makes no surplus. But all farms below farm B have lower costs (represented by the cost curve). They will therefore be making surpluses equal in sum to the shaded area between the revenue curve P_2b and the cost curve *Oab*.

This area is rent or producer surplus. In this model, moving the demand curve affects neither the amount produced by a farm nor its costs until the farm itself is at the margin. At the margin the farm either closes or opens – there are no intermediate phases. Thus farm A will continue to produce 500 tonnes at a cost of £1,200 no matter how far the demand curve moves. Thus any price increase beyond P_1 represents a surplus over and above the amount necessary to keep that farm in production.

All farms inside the margin receive rent (or producer surplus). Farms at the margin (by definition of the margin) just meet their costs. Any fall in price and they would go out of business.

Opportunity costs

Since, by assumption, each farm uses the same amount of labour (10) and the same amount of capital (£100), in order to set up a new farm we have to withdraw labour and capital from some other use. This labour and capital may previously have been used to produce cloth, in which case creating a new farm reduces the amount of cloth available. Say 10 workers and 100 units of capital could be used to produce 1,000 square metres of linen. Setting up one farm would then deprive us of 1,000 m^2 of linen. This amount of linen would have to be given up for each and every farm created. So in obtaining more wheat we lose linen, i.e. the **opportunity cost** of wheat from a new farm is 1,000 m^2 of linen.

This notion of opportunity cost is both interesting and important. When we are deciding what to produce with our limited resources, it is useful to know what goods we have to give up in order to produce others. In the example, we have to give up the opportunity of having 1,000 m^2 of linen in order to start up one extra farm and get into wheat production.

We would only switch labour and capital away from linen if we valued the extra wheat more highly than the forgone 1,000 m^2 of linen. The problem is, of course, that we do not know how much wheat the farm will produce until we know where it is in the valley.

The lowest farms produce a lot of wheat and therefore may well attract labour and capital away from linen production. As more and more farms were started further and further up the valley, less and less wheat would be had for each additional sacrifice of linen. Eventually we would reach a point at which the value of wheat produced by an additional farm would exactly equal the value of linen forgone. This would occur at the marginal farm, where rent was zero and the value of its wheat was equal to the value of forgone linen, i.e. the value of wheat produced by the marginal farm exactly equals its opportunity cost.

This means that: (a) only at the margin do the relative values of wheat and linen reflect their opportunity costs; and (b) even though farm A gets paid more and more for its wheat as demand grows, its opportunity cost (in terms of linen) remains the same.

This is shown in Table 9.4, with a numerical example. When only one farm is operating (wheat is £2.4 per tonne) the value of the wheat produced (£1,200) exactly equals the value of the linen forgone (£1,200). There is no rent being paid and the opportunity cost of wheat (1,000 m^2 of linen) exactly equals in value the wheat gained (500 tonnes).

Now switch more labour and capital from linen production to open up farm B. The price of wheat rises to £6 in order to make this switch possible, since the value of corn produced on farm B (200 tonnes at £6 a tonne) exactly equals the value of forgone linen. Thus for farm B, which is paying no rent, the opportunity cost exactly equals the value of wheat gained. But, at this price, the value of the wheat produced on farm A is 500 tonnes × £6 per tonne = £3,000, which is much more than the opportunity cost of operating farm A. The difference between the opportunity cost of farm A and the value of its wheat is the rent it pays (£3,000 – £1,800 = £1,200). Thus the difference between the opportunity cost of producing the wheat (1,000 m^2 worth £1,200) and the value of the wheat (£3,000) is rent.

This means that rent is no part of the *true* cost of producing anything. The payment of rent does not reflect a cost because there is no cost associated with the use of land. Rent reflects nothing more than a shortage. In our example, it reflects a shortage of 'good' land. If all the land in the valley were equally productive and there was plenty of it then no rent would be yielded at all.

Pure rent

This idea, that rent is a payment for pure scarcity rather than a true supply cost, may perhaps best be illustrated with a more extreme example of scarcity. Consider the case of an old master – say the *Mona Lisa*. There is clearly only one such painting and there is no possibility of obtaining any more. How can an economist try to explain its market value in terms of the usual supply and demand curves?

The supply curve is simply a vertical straight line – there is one and only one, and only one will remain no matter what price the 'auctioneer' calls out.

Table 9.4 Opportunity costs of linen and wheat

Wheat price	Number of farms	Linen forgone	Value	Wheat received	Value	Rent	Value minus rent
£2.40	1	1,000 m^2	£1,200	500 tonnes	£1,200	0	£1,200
£6	2	2,000 m^2	£2,400	700 tonnes	£4,200	£1,800	£2,400
£12	3	3,000 m^2	£3,600	800 tonnes	£9,600	£6,000	£3,600

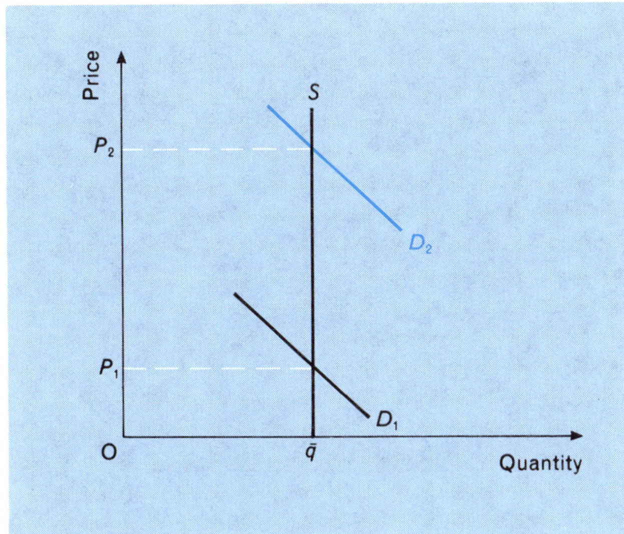

Figure 9.28 Pure rent.

The demand curve, on the other hand, will be price sensitive. Increasing the price will elicit fewer offers to buy, so the demand curve will slope downwards to the right.

This supply and demand configuration is shown in Figure 9.28. If demand were low (D_1) then price too would be low (P_1). If demand is high (D_2) then price too will be high (P_2). Price is completely unaffected by supply costs and depends entirely on demand.

The opportunity cost of supplying the picture is very small. If it were not used as a work of art then it could possibly be used as firewood. The opportunity cost of having the *Mona Lisa* is therefore the heat forgone by not burning it. Since this is very very small, we can say that the entire value of the picture is rent, i.e. the difference between its exchange value and its opportunity cost is rent and its opportunity cost is zero.

This result is the exact opposite to that obtained when dealing with goods which can increase in supply. When returns to scale are constant the long-run supply curve is not vertical but horizontal. Price is then purely supply (cost) determined and is independent of demand.

The two cases are shown in Figure 9.29. Figure 9.29(a) shows a horizontal supply curve of a produced good. This ensures that P is purely supply (cost) determined no matter what the level of demand. As demand increases from D_1 to D_2, price remains constant and the quantity traded increases.

In Figure 9.29(b) the supply is fixed and hence the quantity traded cannot change. As demand increases from D_1 to D_2, all that happens is that the price increases from P_1 to P_2. Now no change in production or supply has occurred, and hence costs have not changed. Thus price has risen above costs, and rent results.

We can use these figures to make a number of observations.

First, if a tax is imposed on the good then in Figure 9.30(a) the whole amount is paid by the demander – market price increases by the amount of the tax and less is traded. But in Figure 9.30(b) all the tax is borne by the seller and exactly the same quantity is traded at the same market price. The amount of tax imposed per unit traded is T.

So in Figure 9.30(a) the demander pays T more per unit than the supplier receives. This decreases the amount traded from q^* to q_T by moving it along the demand curve until it lies T above the supply curve. Conversely, in Figure 9.30(b) the demand price remains unaltered at P_D and the supply price falls to $P_D - T$.

The fact that we can impose a tax on 'rent' without decreasing the quantity produced has led some economists to argue that tax should be applied only to rents. Any other

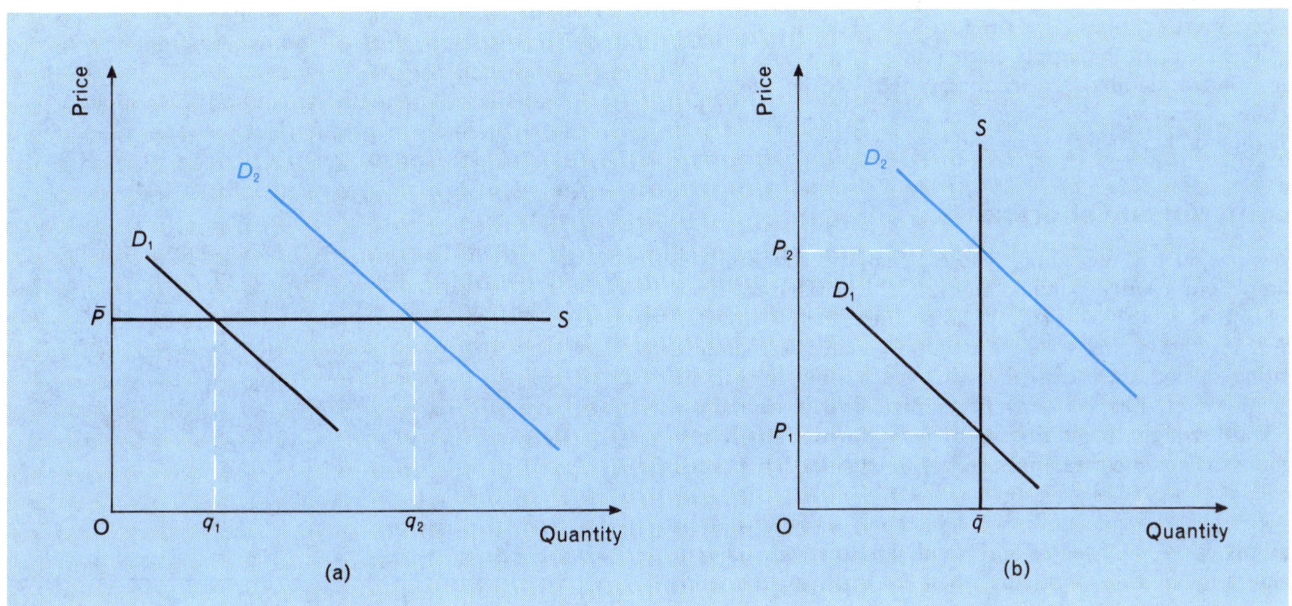

Figure 9.29 Price determination under constant returns to scale and fixed supply.

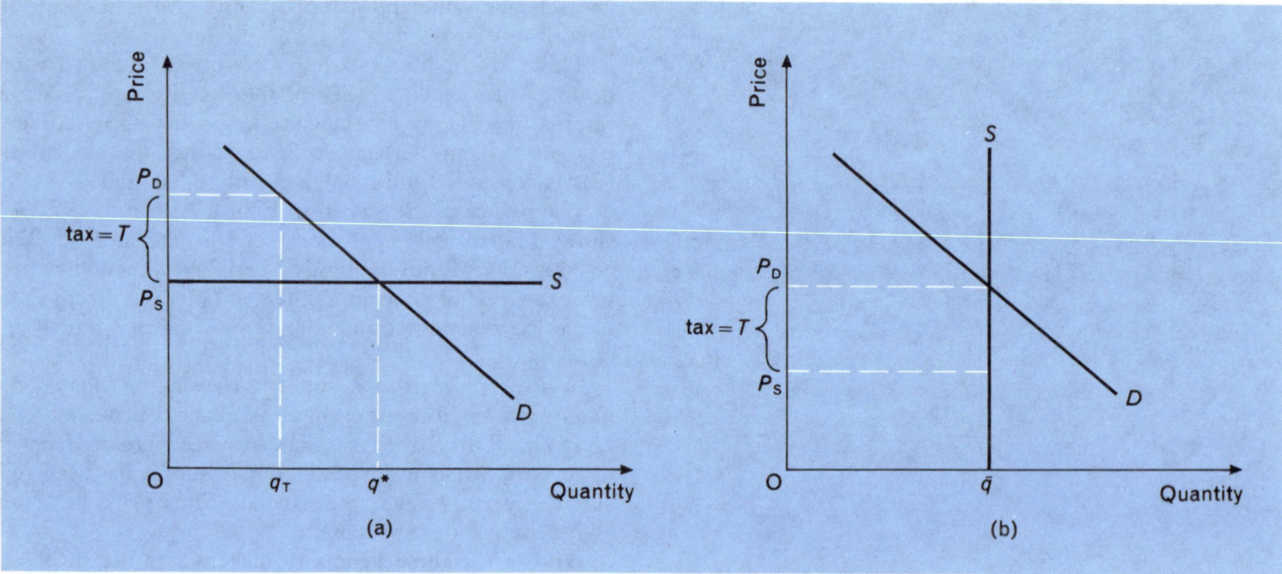

Figure 9.30 Effect of a tax on price and quantity traded under different supply conditions.

form of taxation will cause us to produce (and consume) less than we otherwise would.

Secondly, we can say of a good which is produced under constant returns to scale that if its price is very high, it is because the price of labour and/or the price of capital is high. As price is cost determined, any increase in the wage rate will raise the long-run supply curve and hence raise the market price. But, for a good in fixed supply, the market price is independent of supply costs. Increasing wage rates and/or capital costs will have no effect on its price.

A more general model than those in Figure 9.30 is one in which both supply *and* demand influence market price. Upward-sloping supply curves tell us the cost of production at every level of output, and the demand curve tells us where on the supply curve production will occur.

The shape of the supply curve (whether it is flat, vertical or upward sloping) is therefore central to the theory of value. This leads us to the final part of this section: the distinction between the long and the short run.

Long run and short run

We saw in the preceding chapters that the shape of the supply curve will depend on how long the firm has to adjust its factors. In the short run the labour force can be adjusted but not the capital stock. The supply curve is therefore rather steep. Since capital is in fixed supply, it will be earning rent. That is to say, the supply curve for capital is a vertical straight line in the short run, and hence any return going to capital corresponds exactly to what we have called rent.

In the long run, however, capital will expand and its supply curve will become horizontal. Thus capital will earn rent only in the short run when its quantity does not respond to its return. In the long run, when it does respond by supplying more and hence sending its reward down, it will earn zero rent.

In the short run capital is said to earn **quasi rents** – 'quasi' because it will be earned only in the short run.

However, in the case of land there can be no question of altering supply in response to price (at least not to any appreciable extent), so land will earn rent even in the long run. The same is true of works of art or vintage wines. For most goods and for some factors of production the supply is price sensitive only in the long run, and hence the factor will typically earn only quasi rents.

SUMMARY

1. If the price of anything rises above its opportunity cost (which equals its transfer earnings) then it is said to earn rent.
2. This rent may be permanent or temporary. In the latter case it is called quasi rent.
3. The extent to which anything earns rent depends entirely on demand.
4. Transfer earnings depend entirely on supply.
5. If the price of wheat is high, it is not because the rent of farmland is high, but rather the rent of farmland is high because the price of wheat is high.
6. Taxing rent has no real effect on the quantities produced or the market prices of anything – it merely takes some rent away from rentiers and gives it to the government to spend. This has led some political economists to argue that only land should be taxed, since any other tax distorts market prices and causes less to be produced.

Capital

In Chapter 3 we saw that capital was made as an aid to making other things. We also saw that capital is rewarded for its use in the production process with the payment of interest and that exactly how much capital is employed will depend upon the rate of interest relative to the wage rate. We will now investigate these issues further.

Types of capital

We can distinguish between two broad types of capital, **fixed capital** and **circulating capital**. Fixed capital refers to such things as buildings, machines, lorries and other durable goods. Circulating capital is made up of such things as stocks of raw materials and semi-finished goods. The essential distinction between the two is that fixed capital remains in one form until it wears out. For example, a lathe remains a lathe until it breaks down beyond repair and is scrapped. Circulating capital, on the other hand, changes its form as it passes through the productive process.

To take an example, consider a steel manufacturer. The firm buys coal, iron ore and limestone as its raw materials. To do this it must tie up some of its resources – that is, it spends money which it could have invested elsewhere. The raw materials are then transformed first into pig iron and then into steel by the application of labour and fixed capital such as a blast furnace. Finally, the firm ends up with a stock of finished steel ready to sell. In order to continue production the firm must always have a stock of raw materials, some work in progress and some finished goods ready to sell. If at any time the firm runs out of, say, pig iron then it must shut down the productive process.

Although circulating and fixed capital have some quite different features, they also have things in common. Firstly, they are both necessary for production – without either nothing could be produced. Secondly, the existence of both requires a sacrifice – the forgoing of present consumption.

If people so choose they can consume all of the output of a given period of time and have a very high standard of living now. If this is done it means that there is no investment and in time the machinery and other capital used in production will wear out and will not be replaced. Production in the future will fall and people will not be able to enjoy such a high standard of living.

If, however, people are prepared to give up some consumption now then they can replace the machines and other parts of the capital stock which have worn out. If people choose to forgo a little more consumption then they can invest in more capital and increase future production, but there is a cost – a higher standard of living in the future requires a lower standard of living now. Putting it another way, if people save something now rather than consume everything now then they can invest in the capital stock.

Table 9.5 UK physical capital, 1987 (£ billion at 1987 prices)

Dwellings	524.7
Other buildings and works	546.8
Plant and machinery	455.1
Inventories	84.3
Road vehicles	48.7
Trains, ships and aircraft	15.9
	£1,675.5 billion

Source: UK National Accounts.

This is a very simplified picture of capital, but note that the common use of the word 'capital' in everyday conversation does not appear in it. People commonly talk of their 'capital' as their wealth, whether it be old masters, money or deposits in their building society. Economists, however, use the word to mean a stock of real things, such as machinery, which enhance production.

Measurement of capital

The importance of capital to production is enormous and so it is natural that both governments and economists should want to measure it. To do this it is broken up into various categories, as shown in Table 9.5.

The table shows what is known as physical capital – that is, the actual capital equipment in use. Dwellings are clearly a stock of past production, but they are not usually part of the productive process. It is therefore usual to ignore dwellings when looking at the amount of capital engaged in production.

A feature of industrial economies is that since the Industrial Revolution there has been a steady increase in both the total amount of capital and the amount of capital per worker. This enables today's economies to produce more by using capital to make labour more productive.

The capital stock of the country grows by the process of **investment**. Some investment is necessary to replace worn-out capital (**depreciation**) and so will serve only to maintain rather than to increase capital stock. This is called replacement investment.

When depreciation is deducted from total or gross investment we get a figure known as **net investment**.

It is, of course, possible for gross investment to be less than depreciation. In this case net investment is negative, we fail to invest enough even to make up our losses and capital stock decreases.

If net investment is positive then it means that the economy is investing more than is necessary to maintain the present level of capital. We would therefore expect a higher future level of capital, and hence higher production.

SUMMARY

1. Capital is a stock of past products used to aid current production.
2. Capital can be in the form of fixed capital (e.g. factories), or circulating capital (e.g. raw materials).
3. The greater the economy's stock of capital, the more an economy can produce.
4. Investment in capital is divided into net and gross investment: Net investment = Gross investment – Depreciation

*Investment decisions by a firm

A firm must decide how much capital to combine with the other factors of production. As we have already seen, a firm aims to maximize profits and once the firm has made a decision on the amount of capital to employ it is stuck with it. Capital stock can be changed only in the long run, thus it is important that the firm gets investment decisions right.

The question a firm must address when considering investment decisions is: will the investment bring in a return greater than the cost of investing?

Net present value

This is a method of assessing if an investment project is worth undertaking. It tells us if the future return from a project is worth more or less than the initial investment.

A typical investment decision could be characterized as follows. A firm can buy a new machine that costs £2,000, and this machine would provide the firm with an income of £2,200 in the next year. At the end of the year the machine would wear out and would have to be replaced. (There is no scrap value.) The firm must decide if £2,200 in a year's time is worth £2,000 now. That is, it must work out the value today (the *present* value) of £2,200 to be delivered in one year's time.

The basis of the **net present value (NPV)** method is that a pound today is worth more than a pound tomorrow. If you are offered £100 now or £100 in a year's time then it would be strange if you took the option of waiting a year. If you took the money now and deposited it in a bank then in a year's time you would have £100 plus interest. The difference between the value of £100 now and £100 in a year's time is the interest payable on £100.

If we return to the example of the machine, we can suppose that the firm also has the alternative of putting the £2,000 in a bank and receiving interest. Let us suppose that the rate of interest is 10 per cent. The firm would receive £200 interest in the year and so would end up with £2,200. This is exactly the same as would have been received from buying the machine and so there is no advantage in buying the machine.

This example shows that when the interest rate is 10 per cent, £2,200 in a year's time is worth £2,000 today. In general we can say that the net present value (NPV) of £X in one year's time when the interest rate is r per cent will be:

$$NPV = X/(1+r)$$

In the example given above we have:

$$NPV = \frac{2{,}200}{(1+r)} = \frac{2{,}200}{(1+0.1)} = \frac{2{,}200}{(1.1)} = £2{,}000$$

Suppose that the rate of interest fell from 10 per cent to 5 per cent. The present value of machine will then be:

$$NPV = \frac{2{,}200}{(1+r)} = \frac{2{,}200}{(1.05)} = £2{,}095$$

In this case the net present value of the machine (£2,095) is greater than its price (£2,000) and so it pays to buy it.

Suppose next that the rate of interest rose to 15 per cent. The present value will then be:

$$NPV = \frac{2{,}200}{(1+r)} = \frac{2{,}200}{(1.15)} = £1{,}913$$

In this case the present value of the machine (£1,913) is less than the price of the machine and so it should not be bought.

The dependence of present value on the rate of interest is shown in Figure 9.31. It can be seen that in this case the machine is not worth buying if the interest rate is more than 10 per cent. At rates below this the present value of the future returns is positive. In other words, the firm gets more back than it invests. In general, the decision rule is to *buy machines which have a greater net present value than their price*.

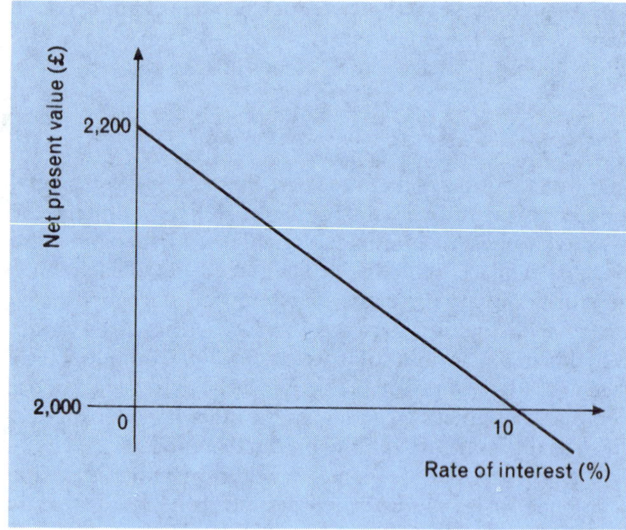

Figure 9.31 Relationship between net present value and the interest rate.

Real rate of interest

The examples we have used so far have not distinguished between returns in today's prices and returns in future or past prices. For example, the machine that yields £2,200 of revenue in a year's time for an investment of £2,000 now makes no reference to inflation. In a year's time the purchasing power of money may have declined so that £2,200 buys much less than today. We must take account of this.

The solution is to use *nominal* rates of interest when we use figures for future returns that are also in nominal terms, and to use *real* rates of interest when we use figures that are in real terms. Nominal terms mean figures that have not been adjusted for inflation; real terms mean figures adjusted for the effects of inflation.

Thus if we looked at the nominal rate of interest of an investment, it would tell us how much would be earned in actual money (pounds or dollars). For example, £1 invested at a nominal rate of 10 per cent yields 10p in one year, leaving the investor with £1.10. If we adjust these figures for inflation then we try to see not how much money the investor gets, but how much more (or less) he or she can buy. If the nominal rate of interest is 10 per cent, but inflation is 5 per cent, then the £1 invested yields £1.10, but this will buy less in a year's time than today. In fact to buy the same amount of goods with £1 in a year's time the investor requires £1.05 and so the real gain is only 5p. From this it can be seen that the real rate of interest is 5 per cent, i.e. the nominal rate of interest minus the rate of inflation.

Real rates of interest can be positive or negative. There have been periods of negative real interest rates, which imply that borrowers are repaying less in real terms than they borrowed – a very good deal for borrowers! This is one reason why interest rates rise when inflation rises. Lenders require a greater return for the risk of lending money and giving up current consumption.

An example of negative real interest rates occurred in 1976 when inflation reached 25 per cent during the year. The average rate of inflation for the year was 16.5 per cent and the average nominal interest rate was only 14.4 per cent, giving a real rate of interest of −2.1 per cent. In 1989 the real rate of interest was around 7 per cent, which is historically very high.

Net present value over a number of years

So far we have only considered a situation where a firm is thinking one year ahead. This is unrealistic, of course, as most machines last for many years.

As we saw previously, if £100 is deposited in a bank for one year at 10 per cent interest then it will earn £10. The deposit will then be worth £110. If this sum is left where it is for a second year then it will earn £11 interest (£110 × 0.1). The deposit would then be worth £121. If the £121 were left in the bank for a third year then it would earn £12.10 interest during that year (£121 × 0.1) and so on.

When interest is being earned on money in this way it is called compound interest.

We can use almost the same formula to calculate NPV over a number of years as we used for one year. The main difference is that we must use the compound interest rate rather than the annual interest rate. The compound interest rate is $(1+r)^n$. The annual rate raised to the power n, where n is the number of years compounded.

What, for example, is the net present value of £133 to be paid in three years' time? Assuming an interest rate of 10 per cent, our modified formula is simply:

$$NPV = \frac{133}{(1+r)^3} = \frac{133}{(1.1)^3} = \frac{133}{1.33} = £100$$

Demand for capital

We know that a machine will be bought if its net present value exceeds its price, so capital will be demanded up to the point where the net present value just equals the price. To buy less capital than this is to forgo profits and to buy more is to make losses on the additional capital. We know that net present value depends on the income generated by the machine in a few years' time and on the interest rate. As more and more capital is bought, it will generate smaller and smaller increments in future output – this is due to the law of diminishing marginal productivity.

Thus as investment grows, the income it generates will fall and so will its net present value. Therefore, for a constant interest rate, the NPV of capital will fall as more investment is undertaken. This is shown in Figure 9.32.

In the figure we can read off the quantity of capital that the firm will want to employ by equating the NPV to the price of a machine. In this case, with the rate of interest fixed at R_1 the firm will most profitably employ K_1 units of capital.

The industry demand curve for capital is found by adding up all of the firms' demand curves for capital as we

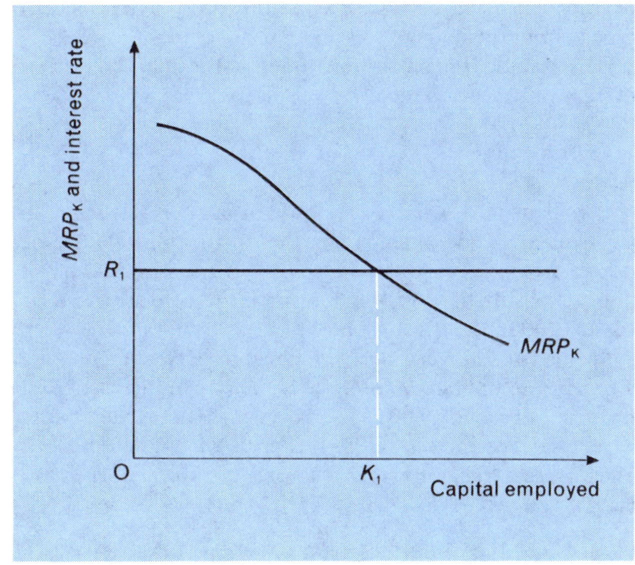

Figure 9.32 Equilibrium in the capital market.

did when finding the industry demand for labour curve earlier in this chapter.

There are various imperfections in the capital market, but these are similar to those for labour which we looked at earlier, and so we shall not pursue them here.

Valuing bonds and assets

The NPV method allows firms to place a value on the worth of an investment now if the value of the future income stream is known. Clearly this value is going to depend very much on the interest rate. The higher the rate, the less a future income is worth. This provides us with an important reason why firms cut back on investment if they think that interest rates are going to be high.

One of the decisions many financial institutions have to make every day is what price to pay for a financial asset or bond. The bond may be a government security or a piece of commercial debt, but whatever the source the institution must be sure that the price it pays gives it at least a competitive return.

Let us suppose that an institution must decide how much to offer for a new issue of £100 government bonds that will never be redeemed, but pay £5 a year interest for ever (such a bond is known as a consol). If the market rate of interest is 10 per cent, how much should the institution pay? An alternative investment paying the market rate would give the institution £10 a year interest if it invested £100. Clearly, then, £100 is too much to pay. The institution should pay an amount that will return it 10 per cent on its investment and this (maximum offer price) can be found by the following formula:

$$\text{Present value of a consol} = \frac{\text{Value of annual payment}}{\text{Market rate of interest}}$$

$$= \frac{£5}{10\%} = \frac{£5}{0.1} = £50$$

In this case the institution should offer no more than £50

for the consol as otherwise it could get a better return elsewhere in the market.

What would the institution offer if the market rate of interest were 7 per cent?

$$\text{Present value} = \frac{£5}{0.07} = £71.43$$

This tells us that if the market rate of interest fell from 10 per cent to 7 per cent then the institution would be prepared to pay more for the consol. If the market rate of interest fell further to 5 per cent then the consol would be worth £100 to the institution.

This gives us a very clear relationship between the price of bonds and the rate of interest. If the rate of interest rises, the price of bonds falls. The reverse is also true: if the market rate of interest falls, the price of bonds rises. In other words, *the price of bonds and the interest rate are inversely related*.

SUMMARY

1. Firms invest in capital to gain a flow of future revenues.
2. A firm will invest in a project if the present value of those future revenues is greater than the cost of the investment.
3. The net present value of a machine depends on the rate of interest, future revenues and the number of years before returns become available.
4. Future revenues decline as investment grows, so *NPV* decreases as the level of investment increases.
5. *NPV* declines as the interest rate rises, so an increase in the interest rate will discourage investment.

Exam Preparation and Practice

MULTIPLE-CHOICE QUESTIONS

1.

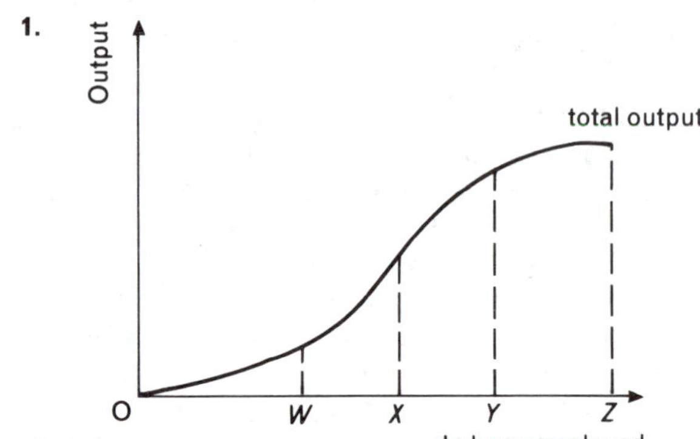

The diagram shows how the output of a firm varies with the amount of labour employed. At which point does the marginal productivity of labour begin to decline?

A When *OW* workers are employed.
B When *OX* workers are employed.
C When *OY* workers are employed.
D When *OZ* workers are employed.

2.

Number of workers employed per week	Marginal physical product (units)
10	30
20	25
30	18
40	10
50	2

The table shows, *ceteris paribus*, the marginal physical product of labour for given levels of workers employed. If 40 workers are employed and the price of the product made is £1.20, what is the weekly wage rate?

A £10
B £12
C £24
D £40

3. The following diagram shows a supply curve for labour.

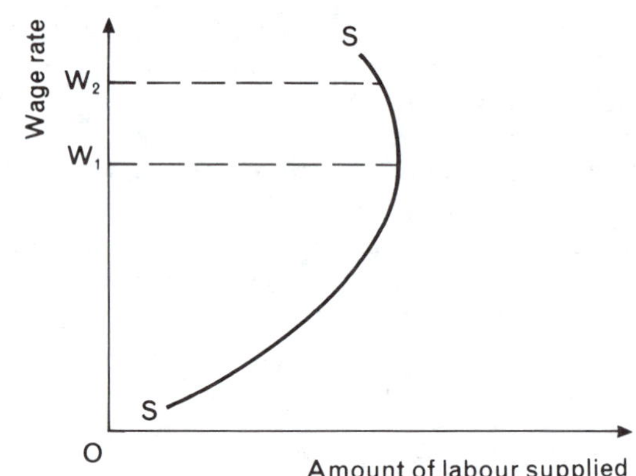

The supply curve shows that, as wage rates increase from W_1 to W_2,

A the occupational mobility of labour increases.
B capital is substituted for labour.
C hours of leisure become more highly valued.
D the supply of the market product becomes price inelastic.

(AEB)

4.

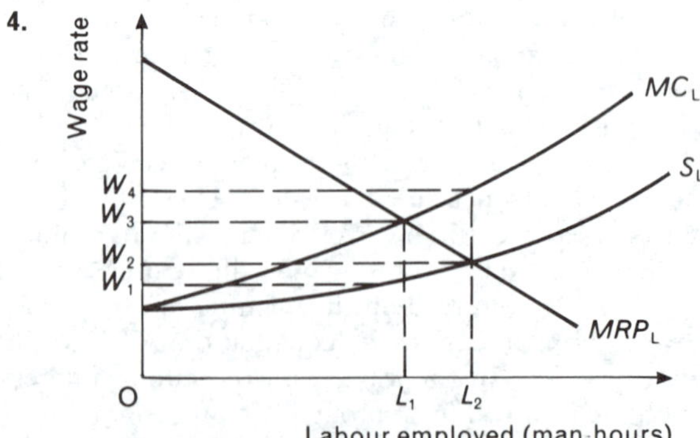

In the diagram MRP_L represents a firm's marginal revenue product curve for labour. S_L is the supply curve of labour and

MC_L the marginal cost of employing labour. A profit-maximizing firm will:

A Employ OL_1 units of labour at a wage rate of OW_1.
B Employ OL_1 units of labour at a wage rate of OW_3.
C Employ OL_2 units of labour at a wage rate of OW_2.
D Employ OL_2 units of labour at a wage rate of OW_4.

5. A firm is a monopsonist and at present employs 30 workers at £3 an hour. To hire an extra worker the firm finds it must pay £3.10 an hour. What is the marginal cost of employing the 31st worker?
A £3
B £3.10
C £5.70
D £6.10

6. The diagram below illustrates the demand and supply curves for labour in a particular industry.

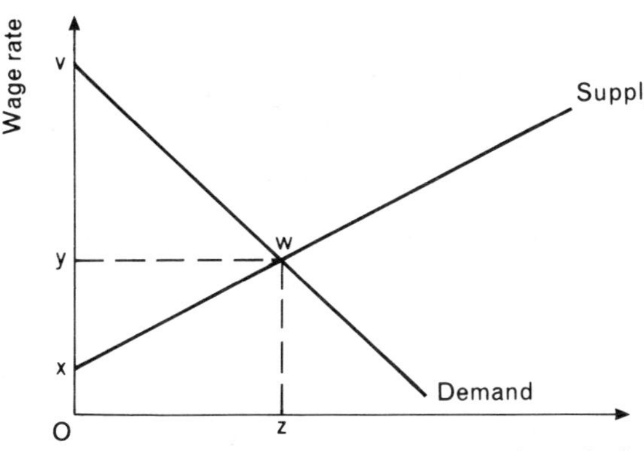

If Oz men are employed at wage Oy, the total economic rent earned by labour is:
A ywv
B Oywz
C Oxwz
D xwy

(AEB)

7. A footballer is paid £8,000 per week. If the man was not a footballer he would be an accountant earning £700 a week. His present weekly earnings are:
A All economic rent.
B £7,300 economic rent and £700 transfer earnings.
C £7,300 transfer earnings and £700 economic rent.
D All transfer earnings.

8.

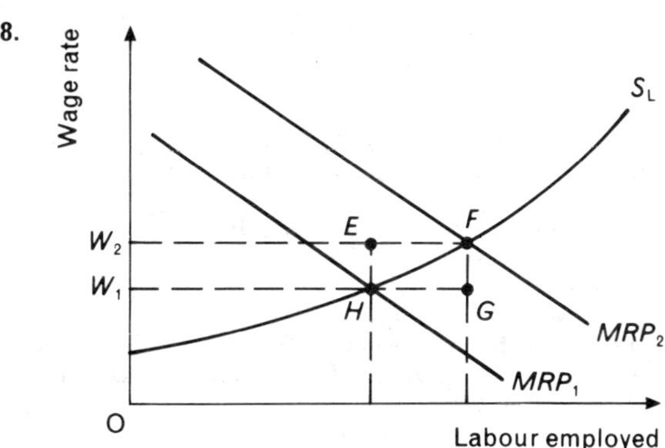

In the diagram MRP_1 and MRP_2 are marginal revenue product of labour curves. S_L is the supply curve of labour. Following a shift of the *MRP* curve from MRP_1 to MRP_2, the increase in economic rent paid to labour is:
A W_2FHW_1
B W_2EHW_1
C *EFH*
D L_1HFL_2

Answer key

Where there are three numbered alternatives

A	B	C	D	E
1, 2, 3 Correct	1, 2 Correct	2, 3 Correct	1 Correct	3 Correct

Where there are four numbered alternatives

A	B	C	D	E
1, 2 and 3 Correct	1 and 3 Correct	2 and 4 Correct	4 only Correct	1 and 4 Correct

9.

Number of workers employed	Total output per week
1	20
2	45
3	75
4	95
5	110
6	115

The table shows how a firm's output varies with the amount of labour employed by the firm in the short run. For this firm:
1 Marginal physical product is at its greatest for the third worker employed.
2 Diminishing returns set in from the employment of two workers.
3 It is always most profitable to employ six workers.

10.

Wage rate
S_L
MRP_2
MRP_1
O
Labour employed

The diagram shows two marginal revenue product of labour curves for an industry. What could have caused the movement from MRP_1 to MRP_2?
1 An increase in labour productivity.
2 A rise in the wage rate.
3 A rise in the cost of capital.
4 The establishment of a trade union.

11. A factor of production may not earn economic rent if:
A It is fixed in supply.
B Its supply curve is perfectly elastic.
C It has an elasticity of supply greater than 1.
D Demand for the factor is fixed.

12. A factor of production will earn more economic rent if, *ceteris paribus*:
A Its supply increases.
B The supply curve becomes more inelastic.
C The supply curve becomes more elastic.
D The demand curve becomes more inelastic.

13. When discounting the purchase price of an asset against its prospective yield, the present value of £100 receivable in one year's time, at an interest rate of 7 per cent is:
A £107.00
B £106.55
C £93.46
D £93.00

14. Which of the following is not an item of circulating capital for a manufacturing firm?
A A bank deposit.
B Machinery.
C Raw material stocks.
D Stocks of finished goods.

EXERCISES

Labour

1. A firm produces Wim-wams using a fixed amount of capital (i.e. this is the short run), and total production varies with labour as shown below.

Labour employed	Total output (Wim-wams per week)
1	4
2	9
3	15
4	20
5	24
6	27
7	29
8	30

(a) Calculate the marginal physical product of labour for each level of employment.
(b) Calculate the average product of labour and state when it reaches a maximum.
(c) If Wim-wams sell for £8 each and the firm is a profit maximizer in a perfectly competitive market for both factors and goods, calculate the marginal revenue product of labour.
(d) On graph paper draw the marginal revenue product of labour curve that you have calculated.
(e) If the wage rate is £40 a week, how many people will the firm employ?
(f) If the wage rate falls to £20 a week, how many people will the firm employ?
(g) The demand for Wim-wams suddenly rises and the new market price is £12. What is the new equilibrium level of employment? (Find this by drawing the new *MRP* curve.)
(h) The firm invests in some new machinery that results in a 50 per cent increase in labour productivity. Calculate the new marginal physical product figures and the new marginal revenue product curve assuming that the price of Wim-wams remains at £12.
(i) What is the new level of employment when the wage rate is £40 a week?

2. (a) A worker can choose to work or stay at home. Suppose that the worker could earn £4 an hour if he chose to work. Draw the worker's budget constraint assuming that he could work for a maximum of 80 hours a week.
(b) The government legislates to restrict the working week to 42 hours. How does this affect the worker's budget constraint?
(c) The wage rate rises to £5 an hour. Draw the new budget constraint.
(d) The worker has a strong preference to work. Add indifference curves to the new budget constraint to show that he would work for as many hours as he is permitted to do by law.

3. The diagram below shows an industry labour demand curve D_2 and labour supply curve *S* when both sides of the market are perfectly competitive.
(a) What is the equilibrium wage rate and how much labour is employed?
(b) Workers organize themselves into a union in order to raise wages by restricting the supply of labour. The new

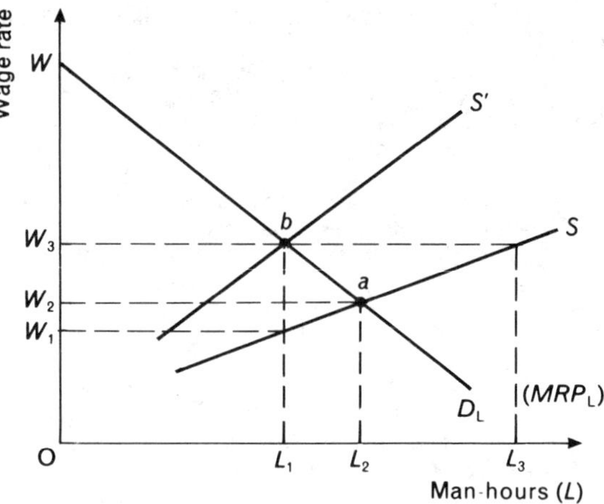

labour supply curve is shown by *S'*. What is the new equilibrium wage rate and level of employment?
(c) Who gains and who loses from the formation of the union?
(d) Suppose that the industry only employs labour and capital.
(i) When there is no union what is the industry wage bill?
(ii) How much is available to pay capital?
(iii) When the union is formed how does this affect the total wage bill and the amount available to pay capital?

4. The diagram below shows an industry labour demand curve and labour supply curve.

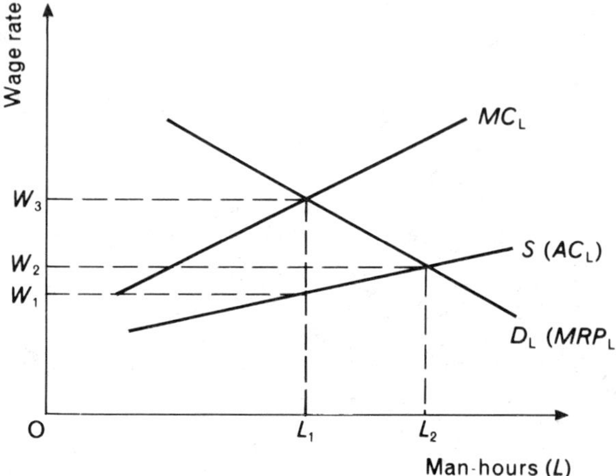

(a) When all markets are perfectly competitive what is the equilibrium wage rate and how much labour is employed?
(b) The firms in the industry join together to form an association that becomes a monopoly buyer of labour (a monopsony).
(i) What is the new level of employment?
(ii) What is the new wage rate?
(c) Why does the marginal cost of labour differ from the average cost in the monopsony situation?
(d) If the workers joined together to form a union, what would be the wage rate if:
(i) The firms in the industry acted as independent hirers of labour?
(ii) The firms in the industry acted as a monopsonist?
(e) Could the union maintain the wage rate of W_3 indefinitely?

5. The diagram below shows the reaction of a worker to various wage rates offered to her.

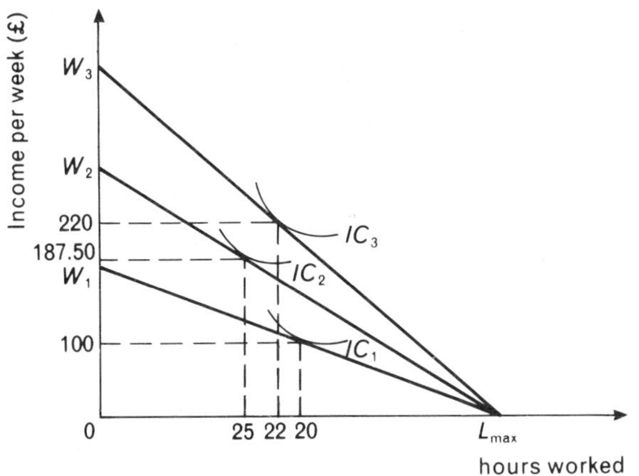

(a) Draw the labour supply curve implied for this particular worker.
(b) Is the behaviour of this individual rational? Explain a possible reason for this behaviour.
(c) What are the values of the wage rates represented by the lines $L_{max}W_1$, $L_{max}W_2$ and $L_{max}W_3$?
(d) Suppose the government imposes an income tax of 25 per cent on all wages over £200. What effect is this likely to have on the consumer?

6. The graph below shows three possible age/earnings profiles for a 16-year old who has just completed public examinations. The teenager could go on to study until the age of 18 or go to work directly. If the teenager chooses to stay at school and is successful then there is the opportunity to go to university.

Profile A represents the income of a person who leaves school at 16, B is the income profile of a person who continues to study until the age of 18, and C is the profile of someone who goes on to university.

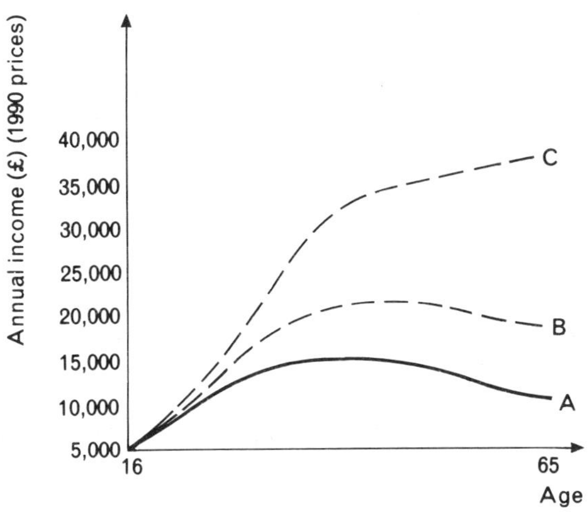

(a) Why are employers prepared to pay people more if they have gone on to higher education?
(b) How would you answer the charge that qualifications mean nothing – that if people are well motivated and able then they will succeed in their chosen profession whatever their qualifications?
(c) Why do you suppose profile *C* continues on an upward trend while *A* and *B* turn down?
(d) What must the teenager give up in order to gain the higher future income offered by a university education? Are there any non-financial benefits to set against the immediate cost of prolonged education?
(e) Suppose the income profiles in the graph have been drawn for a man. Draw another set for a woman from the point of view of (i) an employer and (ii) a career-minded woman. Why might the two views differ?

7. A man is employed as a builder's labourer at £160 a week. Due to a boom in the construction industry another builder offers him £200 a week to work for him. If the worker accepts this offer, how much of his wages will be rent and how much transfer earnings?

Land and capital

8. A farmer can rent a piece of land for £50 a year. The land could produce 10 bushels of wheat a year or 12 bushels of barley.
(a) If the price of wheat is £3 a bushel and barley is £4.20 a bushel and there are no labour costs, should the farmer rent the land? If so, what crop should he grow?
(b) Labour costs are now assumed to be £50 a year and the landowner asks the farmer to 'offer him' a rent in return for the use of the land. In each of the following cases what is the *maximum* the farmer would be prepared to offer?

	Price of wheat (per bushel)	Price of barley (per bushel)
(i)	£5	£4
(ii)	£7.50	£6.50
(iii)	£11.25	£9.25

(c) Another piece of land further up the valley can produce 8 bushels of wheat or 8 bushels of barley a year and also costs £50 in labour to farm. At what price of wheat would the farmer consider renting the second piece of land?

9. (a) Why does the level of rent vary with the price of the crop produced in question 8?
(b) Is the concept of rent applicable to any form of land or any other factor of production?

10. An American millionaire offers to hire a Royal Palace in London for his holiday. Due to a cold political climate he is given the chance to hire the palace at £100,000 a month (exclusive of bills). Explain why most of this price is rent.

11. Classify the following as either fixed or circulating capital:
(a) A firm's delivery van.
(b) The stock of paper held by a printer.
(c) The same firm's printing press.
(d) The pile of coal held for an emergency generator at a chemical plant.
(e) Money in a firm's bank account that will be used to pay debtors.

12. A firm has a stock of 10 machines, each of which has a life of 10 years and is then scrapped. At present the firm needs to replace 1 machine a year. State the amount of gross investment and net investment in each of the following years:

	Machines scrapped	Machines purchased
(a) 1990	1	1
(b) 1991	1	2
(c) 1992	1	0

13. State which of the following are a stock of capital and which are a flow of capital services:
(a) A lathe.
(b) The use of a workshop.
(c) A company car used by a firm's representative.
(d) A hire car used by the representative while her car is repaired.
(e) Building land in central London.
(f) A car parking space as viewed by a car owner.

14. A firm has the chance to invest in a project which will yield the following returns at the end of each year shown:

Year 1	Year 2	Year 3
£400	£400	£400

The initial investment required is £1,000. What information does the firm require before deciding if it should invest or not?

15. The market rate of interest is assumed to be 10 per cent. Calculate the net present valve of the following future cash flows:

	Year 1	Year 2	Year 3
(a)	£200	nil	nil
(b)	nil	£200	nil
(c)	nil	nil	£200
(d)	£200	£200	£200

16. A government consol pays £15 a year in interest and was originally sold on to the market at £100. The present market value of the consol is £187.50.

(a) What was the market rate of interest when the consol was issued?

(b) What is the present market rate of interest?

(c) What would the market price of the consol be if the rate of interest were 10 per cent?

DATA-RESPONSE QUESTION

1. The diagram below illustrates the framework which economists use to analyse an individual's decision to supply labour time. An individual is assumed to choose between leisure and income; to obtain income he must give up leisure i.e. work for a certain number of hours.

The hypothetical individual whose situation is illustrated can obtain employment at an hourly wage rate of £4 an hour and can choose freely the number of hours he wants to work. Thus his opportunity line is represented by the line **AB** indicating the daily combinations of leisure and income he can choose; his tastes for leisure and income are represented by indifference curves, three of which are illustrated. Given his tastes, the individual chooses a combination where he enjoys 14 hours leisure and obtains a daily income of £40; he thus supplies 10 hours of labour time.

Using this framework consider whether the individual's supply of labour time is likely to increase or decrease in response to **each** of the following hypothetical changes in the opportunities open to him for substituting leisure for income.

(Opportunity line can be read as budget constraint.)

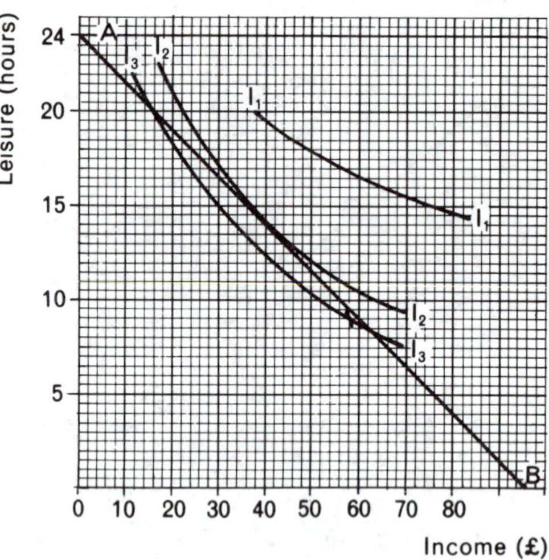

(a) The individual is offered an overtime rate of £8 an hour **after** he has worked 10 hours (note the opportunity line is now no longer a continuous straight line but will kink at the point corresponding to 10 hours). [7]

(b) The individual obtains alternative employment at an increased hourly rate of £8. [6]

(c) The government imposes an annual poll tax equal to a daily lump sum tax of £10 on each individual (so that, for example, the individual earning £40 now receives £30 net of the poll tax for the same number of hours worked). [6]

(d) The government introduces an income support scheme whereby anyone earning less than £40 a week receives 50 pence cash grant for each £ that income falls below the threshold level. (An individual with no income from work thus gets £20.)

Give a brief explanation of your answer in **each** case by drawing a sketch of the change in the individual's opportunity line and his new preferred position. [6]

(WJEC)

10 The distribution of income

In this chapter we will discuss:

1. How economists measure the degree of inequality in the distribution of income.
2. Why income might not be distributed evenly.
3. The distribution of wealth.
4. How income and wealth might be redistributed.
5. The nature of poverty in the UK.

Introduction

In this chapter we shall be looking at how the fruits of our productive efforts (incomes) are *distributed* among us, i.e. who gets what and why.

Interest in this question arises from two considerations. First, we have already seen in Chapter 5 that redistributing income from the high- to low-income groups brings about changes in the pattern of demand for goods and services.

The second reason for taking an interest in income distribution is much less technical. Most people take the view that income distribution should be 'just', and 'justice' usually means that income inequality should be reduced. Many social commentators therefore take an interest in how national income is distributed among its recipients, why it is so distributed and what, if anything, could and should be done about this distribution.

Measuring income distribution

We have seen above that by 'income distribution' we mean the distribution of income among its recipients. Unfortunately, the number of recipients is very large indeed and it would be impossible to match each and every income stream to each and every recipient. In order to make the problem manageable, we need some form of aggregation. By dealing with groups of recipients we can analyse the distribution of income among a few groups rather than the many individuals.

Table 10.1 UK functional distribution of income, 1950–90

	Total domestic income (£m)	Income from employment (£m)	%
1950	12,177	7,627	62.63
1960	23,028	15,160	65.57
1970	45,362	30,550	67.35
1975	99,642	68,390	68.64
1980	205,014	135,909	66.29
1985	309,461	195,570	63.20
1990	478,804	314,857	65.76

There are a number of ways in which we could form the recipients into groups. We could group them according to age, sex or region, or in many other ways. Our choice depends partly on the purpose of our study and partly on the theory and data available to us. If, for example, we were investigating the claim that racial prejudice existed at work then one piece of relevant information would be whether income distribution among racial groups showed any unexplained bias. But this information would tell us very little about discrimination against female workers, for example.

Functional distribution of income

Another possible grouping which immediately suggests itself is that which accords with the economic function of the recipient: that is, according to whether he or she is a labourer, a capitalist, a rentier or an entrepreneur. This is called the functional distribution of income and would yield four groups. Information of this kind would be of interest to those investigating the comparative reward going to the social classes. High profits may, for example, lead to labour increasing its wage demands in order to restore compatability.

The distribution of income between wage earners and 'others' is shown in Table 10.1. This table seems to suggest that the proportion of output going to labour has remained fairly constant for the last 40 years at about two-thirds of the national income. We shall have more to say about this later.

The functional distribution of income is of great interest to economists, partly because it is something about which economic theory has plenty to say. We shall investigate this further below.

Table 10.2 UK household distribution of income, 1979/80

Income £/week	Percentage of all households	Household cumulative %	Income cumulative %
0–30	5.5	5.5	1.25
30–39	7.6	13.1	4.52
40–49	6.0	19.1	6.57
50–59	5.2	24.3	8.74
60–69	4.2	28.5	10.81
70–79	3.7	32.2	12.91
80–89	8.5	40.7	18.39
100–119	8.9	49.6	25.82
120–139	9.3	58.9	34.99
140–159	9.0	67.9	45.23
160–179	7.2	75.1	54.51
180–199	5.8	80.9	62.87
200–249	9.5	90.4	79.08
250–299	4.9	95.3	89.30
300–	4.7	100.0	100.00

Household distribution of income

In so far as our interest in income distribution derives from ideas of social justice, we are not so interested in grouping recipients into productive classes. Rather we are interested in them as households – as consuming units. This kind of income distribution usually involves specifying the number of households within particular income bands. Table 10.2 offers an example of such a distribution for the UK for the fiscal year 1979/80.

From the first two columns of this table we can see that there are almost as many households receiving more than £300 per week (4.7 per cent) as there are households receiving less than £30 per week (5.5 per cent). It is also clear that more than 50 per cent of all households receive less than the national average of £134.

Lorenz curves

The last two columns in Table 10.2 show the cumulative percentage of households and the corresponding cumulative percentage of income. If income were perfectly equally distributed then the first 10 per cent of households would receive 10 per cent of national income, the first 20 per cent of households would receive 20 per cent of national income, 50 per cent of households would receive 50 per cent of national income and so on. The most common way of illustrating this and thereby demonstrating inequality in income distribution is by way of a Lorenz curve (see Figure 10.1). The vertical axis measures the proportion of income and the horizontal axis measures the proportion of households. Each axis therefore spans the range 0–100 per cent.

The line *OA* is a 45° straight line and if income were perfectly equally distributed then all our observations would lie on that line. From Table 10.2, however, we see that the first 5.5 per cent of households receive not 5.5 per cent of national income, but only 1.25 per cent. Next we see that 13.1 per cent of households receive not 13.1 per cent of national income, but only 4.52 per cent. This yields point *B*. The points for 49.6 per cent and 75.1 per cent of

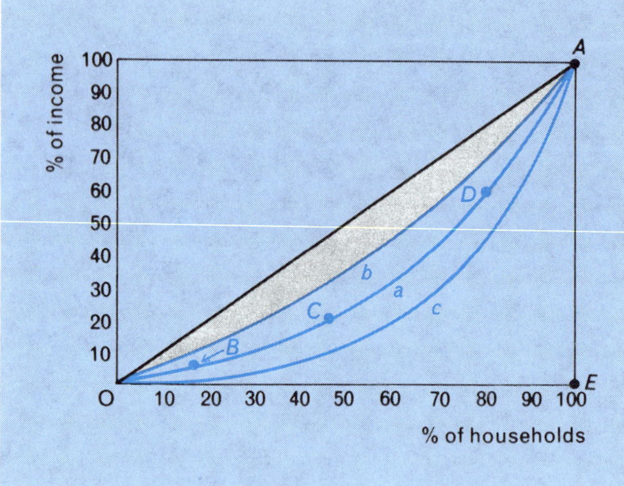

Figure 10.1 Lorenz curve.

households are marked as *C* and *D*. Eventually, of course, the two lines must join up since 100 per cent of the population must take 100 per cent of the income (*A*). Drawing a line through all these points yields curve *a*, which is called the Lorenz curve.

The degree of inequality can be judged by the extent to which the Lorenz curve deviates from the 45° line. Thus the distribution represented by Lorenz curve *b* is more equal than that represented by Lorenz curve *a*, which in turn is more equal than that represented by Lorenz curve *c*. The extreme case of inequality would be where the Lorenz curve followed the horizontal axis up to 99.99 per cent and then rose vertically. This would imply that 99.99 per cent of the households had no income and the further 0.01 per cent of households had 100 per cent of the income.

Gini coefficients

This pictorial representation of inequality is useful as far as it goes, but it is difficult to say whether the change in inequality between *b* and *a* is greater, equal to or less than the change between *a* and *c*. Furthermore, it is often necessary to have a clear numerical measure of inequality – a summary statistic. This would enable us, for example, to measure the rate of change of inequality or compare the effects on inequality of various economic policies.

Such a measure is given by the Gini coefficient, which derives directly from the Lorenz curve. We have already seen that for perfect equality the Lorenz curve lies on the 45° line *OA*, and that for perfect inequality the Lorenz curve practically follows the axes *OEA*. As the Lorenz curve moves away from perfect equality, the area between it and the 45° line grows bigger. The Gini coefficient is the area between a Lorenz curve and the 45° line (the shaded area in Figure 10.1) divided by the area under the 45° line (the area corresponding to perfect inequality). The Gini coefficient therefore has the range of zero, when there is no inequality, to 1, when there is perfect inequality. Thus we have a single figure which summarizes the extent of inequality and which is independent of the units of measurement of income, the size of the income and the size of the population.

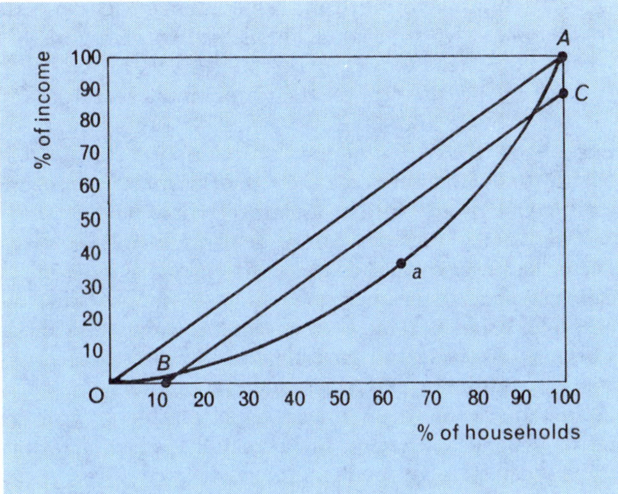

Figure 10.2 Two income distributions.

This particular way of summarizing inequality (a single number) is obviously more convenient than having to reproduce the Lorenz curve. But this simplification is not achieved at zero cost. The information contained in the Lorenz curve diagram is greater than that contained in the Gini coefficient.

This point is perhaps best illustrated by the fact that two different Lorenz curves could give rise to identical Gini coefficients. This would matter less if the differences in the Lorenz curve were irrelevant when considering income distribution, but they are not. Figure 10.2 provides an example of this.

The straight line OA again represents the perfect equality case. Lorenz curve a shows that the lowest-paid groups fall below that perfect equality, but nevertheless do receive some income. Lorenz curve $OBCA$, however, shows that the first 10 per cent of households receive nothing. The next 89.99 per cent of households receive exactly equal incomes (the Lorenz curve rises at 45°). The last 0.01 per cent of households ($C-A$) receive 10 per cent of national income. Thus this second Lorenz curve arises from an economy in which income is perfectly equally distributed except that the top 1 per cent of households receive 10 per cent of the national income and the bottom 10 per cent of households have no income at all.

A policy maker may well feel quite differently about these two income distributions: distributions which would give rise to two quite different communities. And although these differences are clear from the Lorenz curve, it is quite possible for the area under OA and above curve a to be exactly the same as the area under OA and above curve $OBCA$. Thus there is the possibility that the Lorenz curves have identical Gini coefficients and that relevant information has been lost by using such summary statistics.

SUMMARY

1. Economists are interested not only in the level of national income but also in who gets it, i.e. in how national income is distributed.
2. Income distribution influences economic behaviour such as saving, but is also of interest in that income inequality and poverty are seen as undesirable, divisive elements in our society.
3. The functional distribution of income shows how income is divided up among the four factors of production: labour, capital, land and entrepreneurs.
4. The household distribution of income shows how income is divided up among households.
5. Inequality can be represented by tables, by Lorenz curves or by Gini coefficients.
6. Gini coefficients are calculated from the areas bounded by Lorenz curves, but although they provide useful summaries of various distributions, they convey less information than do Lorenz curves. Two quite different curves could give rise to the same Gini coefficient.

Functional distributions of income

So far we have dealt only with describing and measuring inequality. Our next task is to try to explain how it comes about.

We have already suggested that income is generated by engaging in productive activity. 'Income' received from other sources may be in the form of grants (supplementary benefits, gifts, charity payouts) or speculations (gambling). No doubt there are many ways of receiving income other than by engaging in production, but for the moment we will consider non-production sources of income as being merely transfers between economic agents. These transfers will clearly affect the distribution of income and we will need to look at them, but the first cause – the initial distribution of income – is that which arises from production.

Income is received in return for supplying a factor of production – land, labour, capital or risk-bearing. And we have seen in Chapter 9 that the amount received is determined by the usual supply and demand conditions. These together determine the quantity of a factor and its price. Thus if, for example, we know how much labour is supplied and its wage rate then we know how much income is received by labour.

Marginal productivity theory

The main result to emerge from Chapter 9 was that each factor is paid its marginal revenue product. A typical case is illustrated in Figure 10.3.

In a perfectly competitive market the supply of and demand for this factor are equated at price PF_1 and quantity F_1. The total income of this factor is therefore $PF_1 \times F_1$, the shaded area in Figure 10.3. Being on the demand curve means that each factor receives its marginal revenue product (MRP). Hence this is called the marginal productivity theory of income distribution.

For labour and land this is quite straightforward. Labour

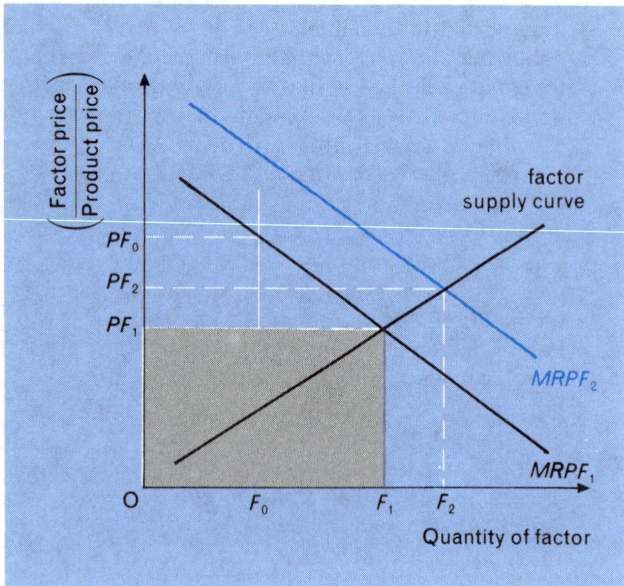

Figure 10.3 Marginal productivity theory of income distribution.

receives a wage rate (in £s per man-hour) which exactly equals the *MRP* of labour. Each man-hour earns the amount by which output is increased when one more man-hour is worked. Similarly, land receives a rent (in £s/unit) which exactly equals the *MRP* of land.

But for capital the picture is slightly more complicated. The use of capital involves both postponement of consumption and exposure to risk. In return for the former it receives interest and in return for the latter it receives profit. Profit, being the return for bearing risk, is highly variable, sometimes very low – even negative – and sometimes very high. On balance, however, it must be enough to persuade entrepreneurs to continue to put capital at risk, and this level of profit is called **normal profit**.

Thus the marginal revenue product of capital must be sufficient to yield interest payments to capitalists (per cent per annum) and normal profits to entrepreneurs (per cent per annum). We will therefore combine these two factors and simply call them capital.

It seems from this, then, that income distribution among labour, capital and land is technologically determined. The marginal productivity curve of these factors depends only on the technological relation between factor inputs and output.

This theory has been used to justify free-market income distribution on the grounds that each factor gets what it contributes. If one more man-hour results in an increase in output of £20 then labour is paid £20 per man-hour. If it results in an increase in output of only £2 then labour is paid £2 per man-hour.

Improving marginal physical productivity

Any factor wishing to improve its rate of remuneration must therefore find ways of increasing its marginal revenue product.

There are two ways in which this may be done. The first is by attempting to move the whole demand curve – the *MRP* curve – to the right. This is shown in Figure 10.3 where the demand curve moves from $MRPF_1$ to $MRPF_2$. If this were done, the price of the factor would rise from PF_1 to PF_2. This would either leave the supply of the factor unchanged (the pure rent case) or increase its supply (as in Figure 10.3). In either case the rate of payment (price) and total payment price (price × quantity) would increase.

This strategy (of moving the demand curve) is a viable one if the factor concerned can engineer such a move or if it can persuade the government to do so. Labour, for example, could become better trained or more efficient at work, or persuade the government to bring these things about by retraining and education programmes.

Sometimes, however, the marginal productivity of one factor depends largely on the availability of other factors. Labour can be made much more productive if it is supplied with plenty of up-to-date capital. Land requires labour and capital if it is to be abundantly productive, and without materials and labour, capital would produce very little.

Thus the first way of improving a factor's *MRP* (by moving the whole demand curve) is either a long-run process (education) or beyond the control of the factor (depending on other factors) or both.

Monopoly power

A second and somewhat more direct way of increasing a factor's *MRP* is by moving along the demand curve. This is shown in Figure 10.3, in which the supply of the factor is restricted from F_1 to F_0. This restriction raises the *MRP* of the factor from PF_1 to PF_0. Such a restriction, of course, implies some monopoly power on the part of the seller of that factor. The most obvious examples of this come from the labour market, in which professional associations and trade unions restrict the number of labourers who can offer themselves in particular markets.

In order to explore the consequences of such monopolies it is necessary to disaggregate the factors of production further by classifying them as either 'in' or 'out' of the monopoly. Thus we have cartel labour and non-cartel labour; cartel capital and non-cartel capital; and cartel land and non-cartel land.

Labour cartels are easily imagined – trade unions and so on. Land cartels arise when planning permission must be sought for certain uses. Thus, for example, anyone with building land inside a green belt will obtain a far higher price than if there were no green belt. What is not so easy to imagine is a capital cartel. One possibility might be capitalists within the UK prevailing upon the government to prevent foreign capital from coming into the UK.

Whatever arguments may be offered in support of such cartels, the effect of them is to drive up the price of the factor inside the cartel.

Notice that, although the price of the factor rises when it is restricted in supply, the income going to the factor may fall, rise or remain unchanged. The rise in price is brought about by a fall in supply, hence the total income of the factor ($PF \times F$) may not rise. We have already seen in Chapter 5 that if the elasticity of the demand curve is unity then reducing the quantity by 10 per cent increases the price by 10 per cent, thus leaving income unchanged. When the elasticity of demand is between zero and unity, the quantity restriction will result in an increase in price and income. When the elasticity of demand is between unity and infinity, the restriction on quantity will result in an increase in price but a decrease in income.

The main conclusion to be drawn from this is that in perfectly competitive markets factors receive their marginal revenue products as determined by market clearing. In this case the functional distribution of income is technologically determined – each factor gets its marginal revenue product. If there is too much of a factor then it will have a low *MRP* and hence a low price.

This market outcome can be changed by some factors forming themselves into cartels. For any particular factor, say labour, anyone within the cartel will receive a higher price than the free-market price, but the remaining labour (that outside the cartel) will either have no work at all or be obliged to accept lower than the free-market price for its labour. In this way the monopolization of a factor can increase the inequality in incomes. It has been estimated that, for the UK labour market, trade union members receive on average 8 per cent more than do their non-unionized counterparts. However, it is also the case that in some ways they reduce income inequality by pursuing a policy of equal pay for equal work for union members. Thus, for example, a policy of equal pay for women will reduce pay inequality.

This functional income distribution is, however, of secondary interest, since it is the inequality of income among consuming units (households) which is at the root of most concerns with inequality.

In order to move from factor incomes to household incomes, it is obviously necessary to know which factors are supplied by which households. In the case of labour, for example, a single, unskilled, non-union person will have a much lower household income from work than would a household comprising two skilled union members.

Wealth

Inequalities which arise from this unequal wage earning are, however, small compared with inequalities which arise from the ownership of capital or land.

No matter how highly paid a labourer is, there are only so many working hours per week and only one pair of hands per worker. Contrast this with a landowner or a capitalist, who can own virtually limitless amounts of land and capital. Thus even if the interest on capital were very low indeed, it would still be possible for some citizens who own a very large amount of capital to receive an income hundreds of times higher than any member of the labour force. Similarly for land: low rents do not imply low incomes for landowners.

This raises the distinction between income and wealth. It is possible to be very wealthy and yet have no income. This would arise, for example, if someone owned the Mona Lisa. He or she would have great wealth, but if that was all the person did own and if the person happened also to be unemployed then he or she would have no income.

It is also possible to have a very high income and no wealth. Some entertainers apparently earn enormous incomes and fritter them away so that they never actually accrue a stock of wealth.

Table 10.3 UK distribution of marketable wealth, 1971 and 1981

Percentage of wealth owned by	1971 (%)	1981 (%)
Most wealthy 1%	31	23
Most wealthy 2%	39	31
Most wealthy 5%	52	45
Most wealthy 10%	65	60
Most wealthy 25%	86	84
Most wealthy 50%	97	94
Total wealthy (£ billion)	140	535

Source: *Social Trends*, 1985.

These two cases are, however, extremes. Usually a wealthy person can put wealth to productive use and hence receive an income from it. Income distribution among households therefore depends not only on the prices of the factors of production, but on the distribution of the ownership of them among households, i.e. the wealth distribution.

The distribution of marketable wealth in the UK for the years 1971 and 1981 is shown in Table 10.3. From this we can see that the top 5 per cent of wealth owners owned between them over half (52 per cent) of the wealth of the whole population in 1971. Furthermore, the top 50 per cent of wealth owners owned almost all the wealth (97 per cent). This leaves 50 per cent of the population with virtually no wealth at all.

Since the distribution of wealth provides an important part of the explanation of the distribution of income, it is necessary to get some idea of how wealth distribution came to be what it is.

Some of the explanation of wealth distribution is lost in the mists of time. Some landowners came into possession of it by way of gifts from the sovereign in return for services rendered. Others obtained it by straightforward purchase financed through savings. Fortunes can be built up by successive generations of one family saving out of income. In order to save, of course, it is necessary to have some 'spare' income. Those who receive very low incomes will therefore find it very difficult to build up a stock of wealth.

To the extent that wealth has been derived from past income, its distribution can be explained in the same way as we explained income distribution. A particular distribution of income, together with a propensity to save, will give rise to a particular wealth distribution. Those who begin with the highest incomes will save more and hence will build up more wealth. This wealth will further increase their income and they will save more and accrue even more wealth. This leads to more income and more saving, and the accumulation of wealth accelerates. Thus any inequality in a fresh-start income distribution would tend to be accentuated over time until a very great degree of inequality resulted.

The same result would, of course, occur if the fresh-start income distribution were perfectly equal but if income receivers had different propensities to save. Those with high propensities to save will accrue wealth and hence will boost their income above that of the low savers. This leads to even more saving and greater wealth.

Inequalities in income and wealth are therefore intertwined and, in a perfect free-market system, inevitable.

SUMMARY

1. The functional distribution of income can be explained in terms of marginal productivity theory.
2. Each factor receives its marginal revenue product, and hence its reward depends directly on its contribution to output.
3. Marginal productivity can be improved by improving the factor itself or by adding more of the other factors to it.
4. Factor prices can also be forced up by forming a cartel or a union.
5. Factor earnings may or may not rise as factor prices are forced up in this way. If the elasticity of demand for them is inelastic then earnings will rise with factor price; if the elasticity is equal to unity then earnings will remain unchanged as factor price rises; if the elasticity is greater than unity (elastic demand) then earnings will fall as factor price increases.
6. Income depends in part on wealth, and wealth too is unequally owned.
7. The reasons for wealth inequality are not easily discovered but depend in part on differences in propensities to save and differences in incomes.
8. Wealth and income therefore interact and tend to reinforce inequality rather than moderate it.

Income redistribution

One of the impressions left by this analysis of income and wealth distribution is that whatever inequality there is has come about because some households are more productive than others and/or have a higher propensity to save. There is, it seems, no 'injustice' here. There is a view, however, that wide divergencies of income and wealth are inherently a bad thing for a society. Such inequality gives rise to envy and resentment. These are divisive forces and weaken those cohesive forces which make us a community.

There is also the view that some very low levels of income are intolerable in any humane society. This is the problem of poverty rather than income distribution and will be taken up again later in the chapter. However, poverty is relevant to income distribution in two ways.

Firstly, the definition of poverty depends on the income received by other members of the community. Thus the level of income which is regarded as a poverty level in the UK will be far higher than that for, say, India. Poverty therefore implies that the low income receivers are at the bottom end of a fairly wide distributional inequality.

Secondly, the remedy for poverty often lies in the redistribution of income. Hence curing poverty means depriving other income groups of their original allocation of income. This raises two questions: who pays, and how much do they pay?

Apart from the view that inequality is of itself socially unacceptable, there is also the view that the bulk of inequality came about not through saving but through quite unjustifiable land grabbing or 'theft'. Feelings of this kind have given rise to a fairly widespread conviction that we should try to moderate the income and wealth inequalities thrown up by the untrammelled operation of the free-market system. We should, in other words, try to make income distribution more equal.

Income tax

Perhaps the best-known method by which the state attempts to moderate income distribution is through a **progressive** income tax system. The state has to collect tax revenue in order to finance its activities. The economists' debate about how to raise this public finance has led them to suggest a progressive income tax – a direct tax on income. Their reasoning had nothing to do with making income distribution more equal. They argued that, in order to spread the cost of public finance evenly over the population, the poor should pay less than the rich. Furthermore, they should pay proportionately less. Someone with an income of £1,000 per year may be asked to contribute, say, £10, whereas someone with an income of £10,000 per year would be asked to contribute, say, £200. This being proportionately more (2 per cent rather than 1 per cent), the income tax is said to be progressive. Were the poor required to pay proportionately more than the rich then the tax system would be **regressive**.

Thus the progressive income tax recommended by public finance analysts went some way to correcting the initial inequality in income. Arguments for a more equal distribution would, of course, reinforce the public finance arguments for progressive income tax.

Table 10.4 shows the distribution of income in the UK both before and after tax for the year 1980/81. We can see from this table that income tax is progressive, with higher income groups paying higher proportionate tax rates. This

Table 10.4 UK distribution of income before and after tax, 1980/81

Income group (%)	Average income (£)		Percentage of income paid in tax
	Before tax	After tax	
Top 1	31,200	20,000	35.9
2–5	15,100	11,700	23.0
6–10	11,300	9,010	20.3
Top 10	14,800	11,200	24.6
11–20	8,700	7,080	18.6
21–30	6,970	5,720	17.9
31–40	5,700	4,710	17.3
41–50	4,520	3,800	16.0
51–60	3,480	3,010	13.5
61–70	2,480	2,260	8.8
71–75	1,660	1,600	3.4

ranges from 3.4 per cent for that group of income receivers within the 71–75 per cent range to 35.9 per cent for the top 1 per cent of income receivers.

The range of income before tax (1,660–£31,200) is much greater than the range after tax (1,600–£20,000), the bottom end having remained about the same and the top end falling by about one-third.

It would seem then that progressive income tax has a big effect on the distribution of incomes. Economic theory, however, sugests that this may not be quite what it seems. Recall that if factor prices are determined in the market then they are influenced by both demand and supply. This is illustrated in Figure 10.4.

We can see from this figure that the imposition of tax on the factor of production will raise its price to the entrepreneur from P_1 to P_2+T. Thus the imposition of a tax actually increases the pre-tax income. Post-tax income received by the factor has fallen to P_2. This is £T less than the amount paid by the entrepreneur, but the actual reduction is that represented by P_1-P_2 and not that represented by P_2+T-P_2, i.e. T.

The point can be illustrated further by referring to the justification offered for paying very high salaries to company chairmen and top civil servants. The justification is that, although earning £30,000 per year, they only receive £20,000. This is tantamount to saying that any attempt to redistribute income by way of income tax will simply raise pre-tax incomes rather than lower post-tax incomes.

Unfortunately for economists, it is rather difficult to gather information about what pre-tax income would have been in the absence of a tax. The main point, however, remains – imposing a tax will lower post-tax incomes even if by somewhat less than Table 10.4 would have us believe.

Figure 10.4 also reminds us that the imposition of a tax actually reduces the quantity of the factor employed. In our diagram the quantity of the factor falls from q_1 to q_2. Thus there is a loss in terms of national output due to what is called the disincentive effect of income tax. In the language of economics we have suffered a Pareto loss (see Chapter 7),

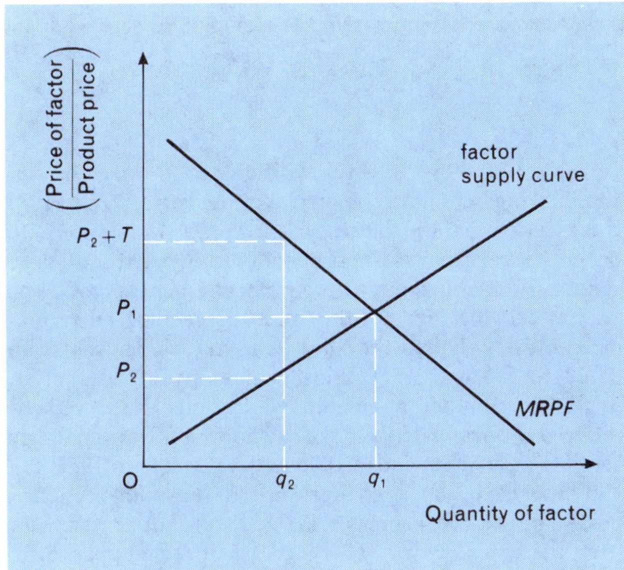

Figure 10.4 Effect of a tax on income distribution.

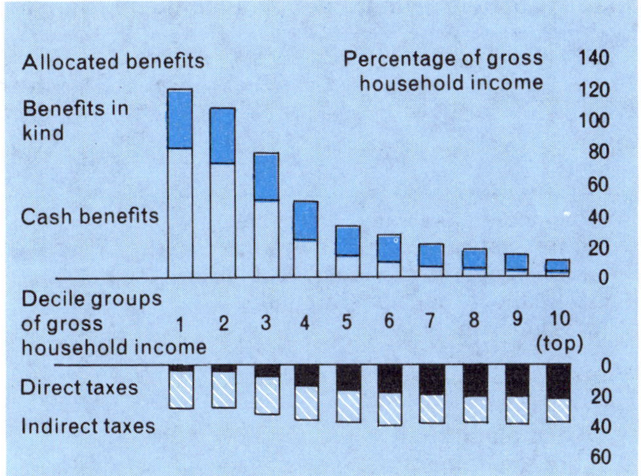

Figure 10.5 Average UK taxes paid and benefits received as a percentage of gross household income, 1981.

but do so because we would prefer more equal income distribution even with the loss of output.

One problem with this way of equalizing incomes is that the very poor who pay no tax remain very poor. There are two ways in which the real income of this group can be raised. Firstly, indirect taxes can also be made progressive. Indirect taxes are those paid when income is spent rather than when it is earned. Thus, for example, VAT and Customs and Excise duties are indirect taxes. They are, of course, the same for everyone, but can be made effectually progressive by being kept to zero on goods bought by the poor (e.g. bread and sugar), and being high on goods bought by the rich (luxuries). Thus the disposable income of the poor is worth proportionately more in terms of goods than is that of the rich.

A second method of augmenting the income of the poor is by way of direct subsidies and benefits. These can take the form of money payments made by the state to those who are in need – those whose incomes have fallen below some minimum level – or the provision of some free goods and services. Health and education constitute two of the largest.

Thus the distribution of income thrown up by the free market is moderated by progressive direct and indirect tax and the provision of direct and indirect benefits. The effects of all direct and indirect taxes and benefits on income distribution are shown in Figure 10.5.

From the bar chart we can see that the lowest 10 per cent of income earners (bar 1) are allocated benefits in kind and cash which account for more than 120 per cent of gross family income. That is to say, they get more from benefits than from earnings. Direct tax is tiny for this group, but indirect tax accounts for 30 per cent of its income. This indirect tax burden becomes proportionately less as income increases, so that it accounts for only 8 per cent of the income of the top 10 per cent of income receivers.

Benefits and income taxes are, however, progressive. A more detailed breakdown is offered in Table 10.5. One conclusion is immediately apparent. Judging by the size of benefits in cash, there is a far higher proportion of retired people in the lowest one-fifth income group than in any

Table 10.5 Redistribution of UK income through taxes and benefits, 1987[1]

	Quintile groups of households ranked by equivalized disposable income[2]					All households
	Bottom fifth	Next fifth	Middle fifth	Next fifth	Top fifth	
Average per household (£ per year)[3]						
Earnings of main earner	780	2,650	6,630	9,380	16,900	7,270
Earnings of others in the household	100	430	1,700	3,540	5,380	2,230
Occupational pensions, annuities	140	410	620	780	1,140	620
Investment income	140	260	400	630	1,810	650
Other income	80	110	120	180	240	140
Total original income	1,220	3,850	9,470	14,510	25,470	10,900
+Benefits in cash						
Contributory	1,480	1,560	990	630	430	1,020
Non-contributory	1,690	1,220	880	440	240	900
Gross income	4,400	6,630	11,340	15,580	26,140	12,820
−Income tax[4] and NIC[5]	150	620	1,760	2,920	5,770	2,250
−Domestic rates (gross)	430	440	480	510	620	500
Disposable income	3,810	5,570	9,100	12,150	19,740	10,070
Equivalized disposable income[2]	3,730	5,370	7,450	10,230	18,540	9,060
−Indirect taxes	1,040	1,300	2,120	2,590	3,180	2,050
+Benefits in kind						
Education	800	660	840	630	360	660
National Health Service	1,030	980	920	790	630	870
Housing subsidy	100	100	60	30	20	60
Travel subsidies	40	50	50	60	80	60
School meals and welfare milk	80	30	20	10	10	30
Final income	4,820	6,080	8,870	11,070	17,660	9,700
Average per household (numbers)						
Adults	1.7	1.7	2.1	2.1	2.0	1.9
Children	0.7	0.6	0.8	0.6	0.4	0.6
Economically active people[6]	0.3	0.7	1.4	1.7	1.7	1.2
Retired people	0.7	0.7	0.4	0.2	0.2	0.4
Number of households in sample	1,479	1,479	1,480	1,479	1,479	7,396

Notes:

1. These estimates are based on the *Family Expenditure Survey*. These 1987 figures incorporate major changes to the methodology and should not be compared with figures from earlier editions of *Social Trends*
2. Equivalized disposable income has been used for ranking to construct the quintile groups. The average equivalized disposable income for each group is shown below disposable income, but all other income values are unequivalized.
3. Rounded to the nearest £10.
4. After tax relief at source on mortgage interest and life assurance premiums.
5. Employees' national insurance contributions.
6. Comprising employees, the self-employed and others not in employment but who were seeking or intending to seek work, but excluding those away from work for more than 1 year.

Source: *Social Trends*, 1991.

other. It seems that those who rely on a retirement pension are among the worst-off of our citizens. They make more use of the Health Service and housing subsidy and pay very little income tax, but a high proportion of their income goes in indirect taxes.

It is also clear from this table that the distribution of income before taxes and benefits (original income) is much less equal than that after tax and benefits (final income). The former ranges from £1,220 per year to £25,470 per year, while the latter ranges from £4,820 to £17,660. Thus it moves from a factor of about 21 to 1 to a factor of about 4 to 1. The bottom two-fifths of income groups are net receivers in the sense that their final incomes are greater than their original incomes. The remaining three-fifths are all net contributors to the state, but the middle fifth makes only a small contribution.

Table 10.6 shows how these differences between original and final incomes have changed over the years 1976 to 1981. It is clear from these figures that, although the bottom fifth benefits most from tax and benefits (moving from 0.8 per cent of national income before taxes and benefits to 7.4 per cent after), they received a lower percentage of national income in 1981 than they did in 1976 (7.1 per cent compared to 7.4 per cent). This is possibly because of the increasing number of unemployed, which had markedly reduced the original income of the bottom fifth from 0.8 per cent of national income in 1976 to 0.6 per cent in 1981.

These fairly small changes apart, it would seem that post- and pre-tax incomes remained substantially the same over these five years. The increase in the upper fifth's income came more from its increased original income than from any taxation change aimed at rewarding enterprise.

Table 10.6 UK distribution of original and final income, 1976–81

	Quintile groups of households					Total
	Bottom fifth	Next fifth	Middle fifth	Next fifth	Top fifth	
Original percentage of national income[1]						
1976	0.8	9.4	18.8	26.6	44.4	100.0
1978	0.7	9.2	18.8	26.8	44.5	100.0
1980	0.5	8.5	18.6	26.9	45.5	100.0
1981	0.6	8.1	18.0	26.9	46.4	100.0
Final percentage of national income[2]						
1976	7.4	12.7	18.0	24.0	37.9	100.0
1978	7.3	12.7	18.1	24.1	37.8	100.0
1980	6.9	12.3	18.0	24.1	38.7	100.0
1981	7.1	12.4	17.9	24.0	38.6	100.0

Notes:
1. Households ranked by original income.
2. Households ranked by final income.
Source: *Family Expenditure Survey*, 1981.

Wealth taxes

Attempts at redistributing income have been augmented by taxes aimed at redistributing wealth. The main thrust of these attempts has been towards the intergenerational transfer of wealth. The argument seems to be that, although wealth built up out of savings is somehow 'legitimate', wealth which is inherited is not. Wealth owners are therefore free to do as they wish with their own wealth in their own lifetime, but on their death they become liable for a tax on wealth (death duties).

According to Table 10.3 there was some redistribution of wealth between 1971 and 1981. In 1971 the most wealthy 1 per cent owned 31 per cent of the nation's wealth, whereas in 1980 they owned 23 per cent.

To some extent taxes can be avoided, and it clearly pays the very rich to put some effort into finding legal ways of avoiding their income and wealth tax liabilities. Some of these tax avoidance methods result in the data on income and wealth distribution appearing slightly more equal than they actually are.

SUMMARY

1. Distribution of both wealth and income can be related to production by way of the functional distribution of income and marginal productivity theory. This seems to suggest that whatever income distribution arises is somehow justifiable in the sense that it was 'earned'.
2. Most people feel that too much inequality is socially divisive and in any event that low-income groups may fall below some minimum accepted standard of living.
3. Most governments have attempted to produce a distribution of income and wealth which is more equal than that thrown up by the free-market system. This has been done by way of progressive income taxes, benefits for low-income groups and wealth transfer taxes.
4. These have resulted in a more equal distribution of income and, to a lesser extent, of wealth, but these results are somewhat obscured by the tendency of taxes to influence not only post-tax income and wealth but also pre-tax income and wealth.

Appendix: Poverty in the UK

'For ye have the poor always with you; . . .' (Matt, 26:11)

Introduction

In this appendix we will first look at two possible views of the nature of poverty – one view involves income distribution, the other does not. We then look at 'official' views of poverty and see what the minimum income levels are for the UK. Alternative policies are then briefly outlined, and the arguments both for and against state involvement in poverty issues are sketched. Finally, we see what the tax–benefit system has done to income distribution in the UK in recent years and what if anything charities can do to help.

Absolute poverty

As the quotation above suggests, the problem of poverty is both ancient and unsolved. Indeed, we have yet even to find a generally agreed definition of poverty.

One view is that poverty exists when there are people who are unable to satisfy even their basic biological needs. In order to survive and to reproduce we need a certain minimum amount of protein, energy, shelter, etc. and this minimum can presumably be calculated by scientists. Since it can be calculated scientifically, it is an absolute, *objective* measure of poverty and hence is independent of personal judgement, public opinion or social context.

Most social scientists would argue, however, that this biological minimum is an inadequate indicator of poverty since people are not merely animals seeking to survive but social beings wanting to 'live'. To 'live' is not merely to stay alive. In order to 'live' we have to be capable of engaging in our society, and that is an altogether different matter from merely staying alive.

The minimum income necessary to permit social activity obviously includes, but equally obviously exceeds, the minimum income necessary for physical activity. The word 'necessity' therefore takes on a wider and vaguer meaning. As Adam Smith points out in his *Wealth of Nations* (1776):

> By necessities I understand not only the commodities which are indispensably necessary for the support of life, but whatever the custom of the country renders it indecent for creditable people, even the lowest order, to be without ... Custom ... has rendered leather shoes a necessary of life in England. The poorest creditable person of either sex would be ashamed to appear in public without them.

Relative poverty

Once we accept the idea that there are some minimum standards of living which are socially and not biologically determined then we have to abandon the idea of an absolute definition of poverty. Socially determined minimum standards depend, in part, on the general level of income in a society. Rich societies have a higher minimum level than poor societies. Thus being poor in England in 1992 is not the same as being poor in England in 1892, nor in India in 1992.

People clearly do care about their relative incomes – though not always for the noblest of reasons. Their concern may arise out of some rather base sense of envy, those at the bottom of the heap being unhappy not so much because they have little, but because others have more. If this were the case then those who 'suffered' from poverty would be victims of their own deadly sin (envy) and need not detain us here.

It could, however, be argued that even those without sin could suffer from being relatively poor. This is because the quality of their lives in some respects depends on their relative income more than on their absolute income. If, for example, most people in your society have cars and you do not then the shopping and social arrangements – being made for the convenience of the majority – will disbar you from some normal social activities. It is difficult to get to out-of-town shopping centres, and to carry the amount of shopping which would justify a visit, without a car. It is also difficult to visit friends if the public transport system gives way to private motor cars.

By moving from a biological to a social minimum we move from an absolute, objective notion of poverty to a relative, subjective one. Poverty is a relative thing because whether or not you are poor depends not so much on the level of your income, but on where you are in the income distribution of your society. It is therefore your *relative* rather than your *absolute* income which is relevant. The notion of poverty is subjective because there is no objective way of determining the minimum level of participation necessary in order to belong to a society. This type of decision is based on value judgements and different people will have different ideas as to what is an acceptable minimum. What is clear is that your welfare depends not only on your income level, but also on the income level elsewhere in your society, i.e. on your relative income.

The official view

Our somewhat glib reference to 'your society' rather begs the question: how do we define 'your society'? Is it your street, your town, your county, your country – or where do we draw the line? No doubt we each have our own ideas on this and some of us would take a very broad definition indeed. Overseas aid reflects this wider concern. For our present purpose we will take it that your society is the United Kingdom.

This view of society, and the belief that poverty is a relative, rather than an absolute, notion is reflected in the definition of poverty adopted by the Council of Europe: 'Persons beset by poverty: individuals or families whose resources are so small as to exclude them from the minimum acceptable way of life of the Member State in which they live.'

What constitutes a 'minimum acceptable way of life' depends, as we have said, on personal judgement and public opinion, and is hence *subjective* rather than *objective*. We do, however, have some indicators of what officially constitutes poverty.

In the UK the 'official' poverty level (the minimum acceptable income level) is the level of Income Support. In 1991 this stood at £39.65 per week for a single person over 25; about £83.55 for a family with children under five and about £113.60 for a family with one child aged 14 and another child aged 16. Income Support includes child benefit, water rates and 20 per cent of community charge, but is not intended to cover other housing costs.

As far as earnings are concerned, the Council of Europe's 'decency level' is set at 68 per cent of the average earnings of men and women. This gives a figure for the decency level of earnings in the UK of £155 per week in 1989.

These are only indicators of what are currently regarded as poverty levels and decency levels. They are constantly subject to revision and hedged around with rules and regulations designed to deter the undeserving and the cheat. Access to this minimum level of financial support is not therefore always a straightforward matter, and it is quite possible for citizens of the UK to fall below even the Income Support level of income.

Policy matters

This distinction between being absolutely poor and being relatively poor is not just a nice debating point for academic economists. It has quite important policy implications. By way of illustration consider two alternative policies aimed at reducing poverty.

Policy 1 is designed to make the poor absolutely better off and calls for a reduction in the higher rates of income tax. Cutting the higher rates of income tax is said to encourage hard work and enterprise. This stimulates economic growth and makes everyone (including the poor) better off. In absolute terms the poor are better off but the rich benefit more than the poor because of the high-rate tax cuts. In other words, it increases everyones' income (including, of course, that of the poor), but makes income distribution more unequal.

Policy 2 is also designed to make the poor absolutely better off, but calls for an increase in the level of Income Support. This will not, of course, stimulate people to greater and greater effort or encourage enterprise. If anything it might weaken the resolve of the unemployed to find work. The policy therefore has no positive effect on incentives or on economic growth. Thus there is no increase in total income. The income of the poor does rise, however, and has to be paid for by a decrease in the post-tax income of the rich. Thus economic growth is not stimulated, but income is more equally distributed.

Which policy should the government pursue? Would the 'poor' prefer to be more equal in a lower-income country or less equal in a higher-income country?

These are not easy questions to answer. As we have seen, people do care about their relative income as well as their absolute income, and the one is often achieved only at the expense of the other – there is a trade-off between growth and distribution. For those, like the current government, who favour the absolute measure of poverty, this trade-off is irrelevant. The simple aim is to increase the absolute income of the poor and this means going for growth and ignoring the effects on income distribution.

But if one takes the relative income view of poverty, as did earlier, Labour governments, then the trade-off is a significant factor in policy choice. Clearly, if the emphasis is put on making income distribution more equal, it is necessary also to be aware of the costs in terms of growth forgone.

Efficiency and growth

According to economic theory, income distribution is determined by the supply of, and demand for, factors of production – i.e. the functional distribution of income. Scarce labour will earn high wages, successful entrepreneurs will earn high profits and savers will receive interest. These wages, profits and interest payments are the 'prices' which signal scarcities and surpluses, and we should respond by changing our skills, our location etc. in order better to serve the needs of the market. Thus some disparity of incomes is what makes for the efficient and dynamic allocation of resources. This 'dynamic' aspect of the market means that our economy can quickly respond to new opportunities, and this in turn leads to economic growth. Economic growth means that we can all be better off and we do not need to rob Peter in order to pay Paul.

Any attempt to moderate this market-determined income distribution (by progressive taxation, for example) will weaken market forces and lead to economic stagnation and a general lowering of welfare. Thus there are efficiency arguments against redistribution through taxation.

Rights and coercion

As well as these economic arguments there are also moral issues to consider. Some argue that the income distribution thrown up by the market is, in some sense, just – or at minimum is not unjust. This 'market' income distribution was not the intended outcome of purposeful action. It was not designed by man or by a particular group. It is therefore impossible to say that it is unjust in the same way that it is impossible to say that the unequal distribution of intelligence is unjust. It is what it is and that is that.

To go further one could argue that, as far as the market is concerned, the more you put in the more you get out. Those who work hard and long and those who take risks and build up businesses put a lot into the economy and by doing so earn the right to take a lot out. On this view it is not for the state to legislate for a more equal income distribution. Care for the poor should not be a matter for state coercion, but rather a matter for voluntary giving through charities.

Others, however, take a somewhat less individualistic view of society and see the relief of poverty as a proper function of the state. This may be on the grounds that the state can do the job better than charities or on moral and political grounds.

In terms of the former, for example, it could be argued that:

1. The government is the most efficient collector and redistributor of our charitable obligations, i.e. it does the work of charities more effectively than do privately run organizations.
2. The task of providing for the poor is too great for any institution other than the state.

As regards the moral or political argument it could be said that:

1. Citizens have certain basic rights and can demand from the state (their fellow citizens) a minimum level of material support.
2. Too much income disparity leads to the breakdown of society and the outbreak of crime and violence and even revolution.
3. Income distribution is only partly determined by the free operation of the market and is heavily influenced by custom and by politics. The incomes of archbishops, for example, can hardly be said to be determined by supply and demand in the market for archbishops; nor is the distribution of royalties from North Sea oil and gas, or the income from various privatization exercises. The government decides how to distribute its royalties, etc. and cannot simply withdraw and leave things to the market. It therefore needs a policy to guide it in its disbursement and in its collection of revenues. Both disbursement and collection affect the poor.

Case Study 10.1 Poverty 'rose faster in Britain than in any other EC state'

The number of Britain's poorest people, those living on less than half the average wage, increased more rapidly between 1980 and 1985 than in any other EC country, according to a new analysis of a study from the European Commission.

The figures issued today by Michael Meacher, Labour's social security spokesman, also show that the European research gives a higher percentage of British poor than the Government's figures.

The commission's study found that in 1980, 9.2 per cent of the UK population (5,032,400 people) had less than half the average wage, but by 1985 this had risen to 12 per cent (6,636,000 people).

However, in the data on UK households below average incomes for 1985, only 9.2 per cent of the population were in this category, compared with 8.3 in 1981. The Rotterdam UK work used published government statistics.

Using the European figures, which were completed 10 months ago, Mr Meacher's researchers worked out percentage increases and decreases to show trends. The UK ranks highest for poverty in this list, with a 30.4 per cent increase, between 1980 and 1985, in the number of people living on less than 50 per cent of average wage. That was marginally worse than the Irish Republic, which had an increase of 30.18 per cent.

West Germany ranked third; its poor increased by 26.87 per cent. Belgium showed the greatest improvement, with the highest decrease in its numbers of poor in the five years reviewed.

The analyses follow exposure last month by the Social Services Select Committee of a statistical error which showed that the Government had got its poverty figures wrong. Contrary to ministerial claims that Britain's poorest people had benefited from rising living standards, corrected statistics showed that the incomes of the poorest 10 per cent of the population had risen by only half the national average. Last night Mr Meacher called on Tony Newton, Secretary of State for Social Security, to explain why publication of the latest Households Below Average Incomes figures for 1987 were delayed by six months.

The Department of Social Security said last night that the figures had been widely discredited and that the EC accepted that they were a definition of inequality, not poverty. 'The Government view is that the concept of a poverty line set a particular variable of income per member state is patently absurd. By that standard, people with incomes below this line in one country could be considerably better off than people above the line in another.'

Relative levels of poverty in the EC: individuals living below 50% of average earnings

Country	Year	%	1985 poverty level (1 = highest)	1980–85 % increase or decrease	Highest % rise in poverty (1 = highest)
Belgium	1980	7.6	12	−5.25	12
	1985	7.2			
Denmark	1980	13.0	6	+13.08	5
	1985	14.7			
France	1979	17.7	5	−1.13	10
	1985	17.5			
Germany	1978	6.7	9	+26.87	3
	1985	8.5			
Greece	1981	24.2	2	−0.03	9
	1985	24.0			
Ireland	1980	16.9	3	+30.18	2
	1985	22.0			
Italy	1980	9.4	8	+24.47	4
	1984	11.7			
Luxembourg	1980	7.9	10	No change	8
	1985	7.9			
Netherlands	1981	7.0	11	+5.71	6
	1985	7.4			
Portugal	1981	27.8	1	+0.72	7
	1985	28.0			
Spain	1980	20.5	4	−2.47	11
	1985	20.0			
UK	1980	9.2	7	+30.43	1
	1985	12.0			

1. The figures show how many people live on below 50 per cent of average earnings. Would you be surprised if nobody lived on below 50 per cent of average earnings?
2. Can you suggest an alternative definition of poverty that would be more appropriate for comparing the UK with other EC States?

Source: Celia Hall, *Independent*, 6 June 1990

State intervention: taxes and benefits

The effect of state intervention through the tax and benefit system on the distribution of income is immense. Table 10.7 shows that the distribution of income thrown up by market forces (original income) is very unequal indeed. In 1976 the poorest fifth of households received only 0.8 per cent of total income. To see what this means imagine that there are 100 householders and their total income is £100. The poorest 20 households would receive 80p between them, i.e. they would get 4p each. The richest 20 would receive £44.40 between them, i.e. £2.22 each. The richest get more than 50 times as much as the poorest.

In 1985 the inequality had increased and, to continue our illustration, the bottom fifth then received only 30p between them, i.e. 1.5p each. The richest received almost

Table 10.7 UK distribution of original and disposable income, 1976–85

	Quintile groups of households		
	Bottom fifth	**Middle fifth**	**Top fifth**
Original income			
1976	0.8	18.8	44.4
1981	0.6	18.0	46.4
1985	0.3	17.2	49.2
Disposable income			
1976	7.0	18.2	38.1
1981	6.7	17.7	39.4
1985	6.5	17.3	40.6

Source: *Social Trends* (1988).

Table 10.8 UK homelessness, 1983–86

	1983	**1984**	**1985**	**1986**
Homeless households in priority need	84,000	89,000	102,000	109,000
Households in temporary accommodation	11,000	14,000	17,000	22,000

£2.50 each. This is partly because there were more retired persons and partly because there were more unemployed, but that is what market forces brought about.

After the government has collected income tax and paid unemployment benefit, etc. the inequality is much less marked. In 1976 the poorest fifth got 7 per cent of total disposable income. In our illustration they would get £7 between them, or 35p each. The richest 20 received £38.10 between them, or about £1.90 each. This disparity too became wider in 1985 with the poorest fifth then receiving only £6.50 between them.

Thus income distribution, both before and after direct taxes and benefits, has become steadily more unequal. There has, however, been an appreciable rate of economic growth so that the level of income of the poorest fifth has risen. GDP at constant factor cost was £191,871m in 1976 and by 1985 this had risen to £218,622m. Since 6.5 per cent of £218,622m is £14,213m and 7.0 per cent of £191,871m is £13,430m, the fall in percentage from 7.0 to 6.5 per cent is more than made up for by the increase in the level of real income. (We cannot be sure, of course, that the growth rate would have been the same under a different tax structure.)

These income figures are relevant to any study of poverty, but statistics alone cannot tell the whole story. There is more to poverty than simply minimum income levels and income distribution. There are many direct indicators of poverty which augment the official income distribution figures. The incidence of certain diseases, the height and weight of children and the numbers who appeal for charitable assistance are just some examples of direct indicators of poverty.

We have been getting richer and richer, but homelessness, for example shows a steadily rising trend (see Table 10.8).

Charity

What then can be said about charitable giving? Is it possible to shift the burden of welfare support from the state to the private sector? A look at the figures shows just what a hard task that would be. Charitable giving by the largest 200 charities in the UK in 1985 amounted to about £850 million, which is slightly more than the state spends on arts and libraries alone (£787m) and comes nowhere near the amount needed for high-spending social services (housing, for example, accounts for £3,672m). Thus if the market is to be left to determine income distribution and charities left to look after those people and services which are not considered to be adequately catered for then we shall have to get used to the idea of giving away a very large part of our income indeed.

Conclusion

We have tried to show that 'poverty', like most familiar words, is by no means a simple concept. It can be associated with a particular *level* of income or with a particular point on a community's income *distribution.* There are no clear guidelines as to where to draw either line, but what is clear is that one's view of poverty has significant implications for policy choice. Essentially the choice is between equality and growth. The old left put the emphasis on equality and the new right put it on growth.

Equally there are disagreements about the role of the state in all this. Some argue that the state does not have the need, the duty or the right to impose a redistribution of income. Others maintain either that the state is a more efficient agent for organizing income redistribution than are private charities, or that the state has political and moral duties which involve income redistribution.

It is evident from the data available that our tax and benefit system does involve a massive redistribution of income, and that without it the poor would be very poor indeed. It is also evident that private charities have to grow at an astonishing rate if they are even to begin replacing the state as the major redistributor of income.

Exam Preparation and Practice

MULTIPLE-CHOICE QUESTIONS

1. The Lorenz curve, drawn for any economy, shows:
   A The ideal distribution of income.
   B The distribution of income needed for maximum economic growth.
   C The cumulative proportion of income earned by a given percentage of households.
   D How much each household in an economy earns.

2. The diagram shows a number of Lorenz curves. Which shows the most equal distribution of income?

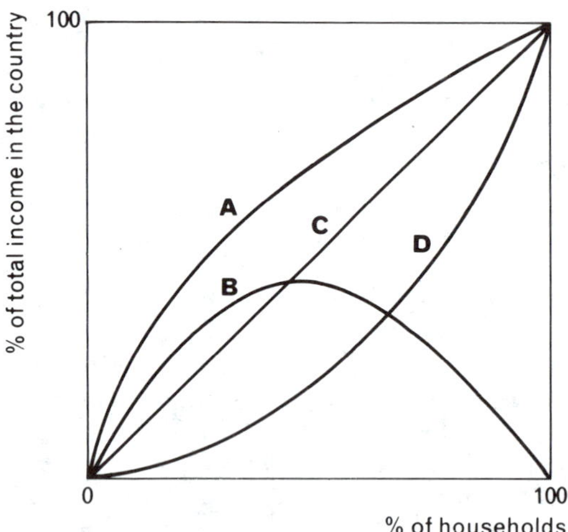

3. A progressive tax is one which requires:
   A All taxpayers to pay the same sum.
   B The least well paid to pay a higher proportion of their income in tax than the most well paid.
   C The most well paid only to pay tax.
   D The most well paid to pay a higher proportion of their income in tax than the least well paid.

4. The diagram below represents the percentage of an individual's income taken in tax under a particular system.

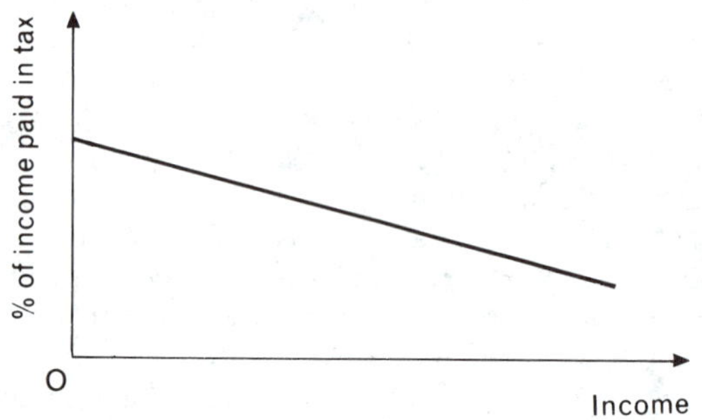

The diagram shows that the tax is:
A Flat rate. **C** Progressive.
B Negative. **D** Proportional.

Answer key

A	B	C	D	E
1, 2, 3 Correct	1, 2 Correct	2, 3 Correct	1 Correct	3 Correct

5. Which of the following will necessarily lead to an uneven distribution of income from a starting point of equality?
   1 Differing marginal and average propensities to save among individuals.
   2 The ability to bequeath wealth.
   3 Different marginal physical productivities of labour.

EXERCISES

1. The table gives the household distribution of income for two countries.

Household cumulative (%)	Income cumulative (%)	
	Country 1	Country 2
10	5	3
20	10	7
30	16	11
40	23	16
50	29	25
60	36	35
70	40	46
80	48	57
90	58	68
100	100	100

   (a) Draw the Lorenz curve for each country on the same graph.
   (b) Is it possible to say which country has the most equal distribution of income?

2. In a mature society, such as the UK, would redistributing income to a situation of perfect equality necessarily lead to a permanently equal distribution of income?

3. To what extent do you agree that redistributing income by taxation and state benefits is a 'good' thing? How might a redistribution from the rich to the poor affect the pattern of consumption in the economy?

DATA-RESPONSE QUESTION

1. Look again at Tables 10.5, 10.6 and 10.7 and answer the questions below. All questions carry equal marks.
   (a) How does the distribution of total original income compare with the distribution of final income?
   (b) Account for the differing levels and differing sources of income for each group of households in the tables.
   (c) What policies might be pursued to reduce the inequalities in income distribution?
   (d) How might the policies you suggest affect:
      (i) the motivation of the most well off;
      (ii) the motivation of the least well off;
      (iii) economic growth?

PART III

MACROECONOMICS

11 An introduction to macroeconomics

In this chapter we will discuss:

1. The nature of macroeconomics.
2. How macroeconomics continues to be an area of debate within economics.

Macroeconomics

So far in this book we have taken the economic problem to be one of scarcity. We have only so much land, labour and capital and we must find out how to make best use of them. The problem therefore is to allocate these scarce resources to the production of all the many goods we want so as to get the most out of them. When all our resources have been so allocated our economy is said to be working at **capacity**. If we manage to achieve capacity working and then wish to produce more of any one good (say bread), we have to reallocate some resources away from the production of some other good (say milk).

The amount of milk we have to give up in order to produce another loaf is called the **opportunity cost** of the loaf and we have represented this trade-off between milk and bread as a production possibility frontier (*PPF*). Figure 11.1 shows such a frontier. We can choose to be anywhere on the frontier but cannot stray beyond it. Our study of microeconomics demonstrates how it is the job of the price mechanism to ensure that we choose the best point on our *PPF*. That is to say, the price mechanism ensures that the combination of bread and milk actually produced is that which reflects our preferences.

It would clearly be unsatisfactory if the economy settled down at some point *inside* the *PPF*, since this would mean that we could have more of everything simply by moving up to the frontier. Despite this there is plenty of evidence to suggest that we do indeed spend long periods of time well within the *PPF*.

In the macroeconomic part of this book we are concerned not with choosing the best point on our *PPF*, but with why we are not always on our *PPF*.

If we look over our past economic performance (see Figure 11.2) then we see that from the beginning of the century our national output and employment have fluctuated a great deal. These fluctuations take three forms.

Firstly, there is clearly an underlying upward trend in output. We have been getting better and better off as time has gone by. This means that we have been experiencing **economic growth**.

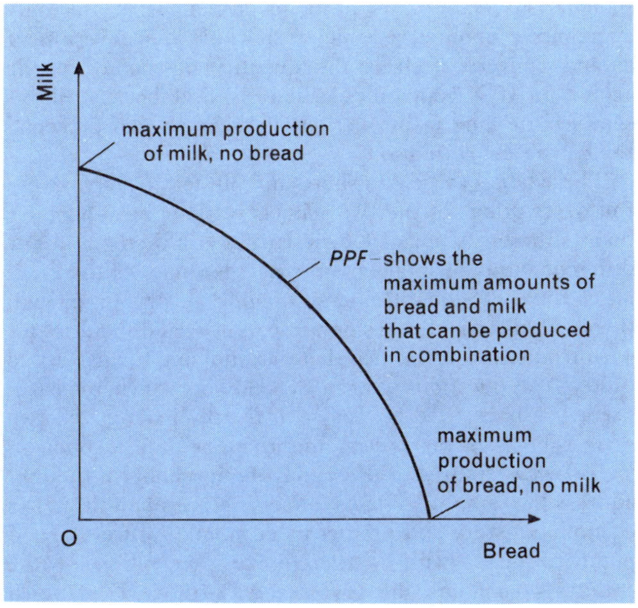

Milk
maximum production of milk, no bread
PPF – shows the maximum amounts of bread and milk that can be produced in combination
maximum production of bread, no milk
O
Bread

Figure 11.1 Production possibility frontier.

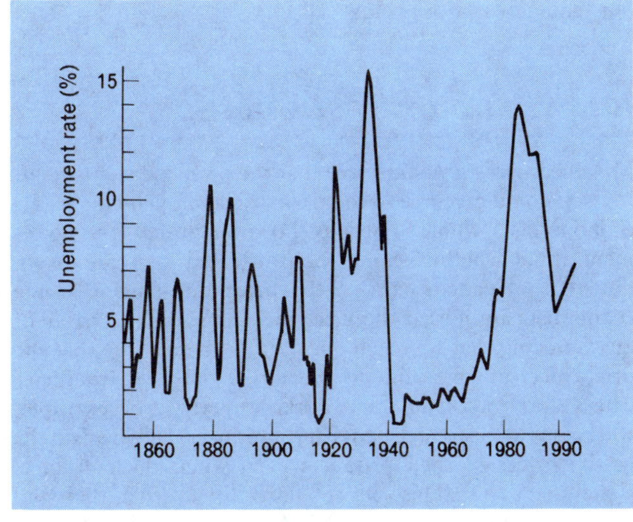

Figure 11.2 Unemployment in the UK, 1851–1990.

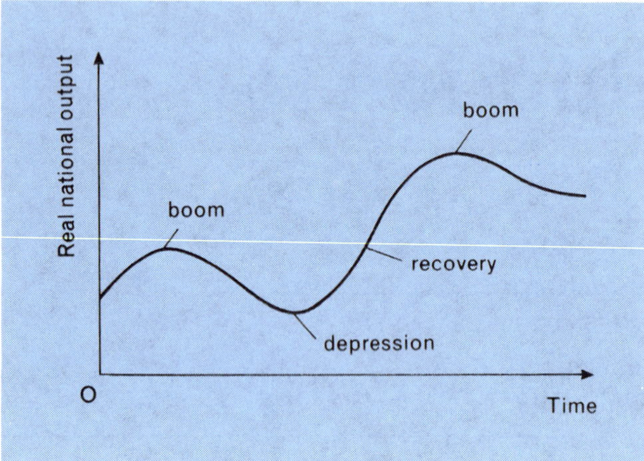

Figure 11.3 A business cycle.

Secondly, there are regular swings around this upward trend. Every 4 or 5 years or so output reaches a peak, then falls away to reach a minimum before rising again to another peak. These are called **business cycles** and a stylized diagram of a business cycle is shown in Figure 11.3.

Thirdly, there are periods during which output remained below capacity for protracted periods of time. These are called **depressions**. The worst depression was between the wars when there was very high unemployment, very low output and many idle factories. This was a world-wide phenomenon and was obviously a huge waste of resources – the UK economy was clearly not on its *PPF* but well within it. This clear demonstration of waste caused some economists to question the ability of the price mechanism always to work well – always to guide us to the best of the possible alternatives open.

This questioning did not extend beyond the immediate concern about under-capacity working and did not therefore look into the performance of particular industries or markets. It concerned itself only with the aggregate performance of the economy and gave rise to what came to be called **macroeconomics**. Macroeconomics is concerned with describing, explaining and working out policies to cure our tendency to work below capacity.

Macroeconomic debates

Most economists would agree that the price mechanism left to itself could give rise to regular cyclical movements in the economy as a whole. There is, however, much less agreement about whether or not the protracted depressions are due to the inadequacies of the price mechanism. Some economists argue that the price mechanism is incapable of guaranteeing that we reach our *PPF*. Others argue that the price mechanism could do the job if only we would let prices and wages do their work properly. For example, workers may resist wage cuts and producers may resist falls in the prices of their products even when the market is signalling them. This lack of flexibility, rather than the price mechanism as such, is the root cause of the problem.

Those economists who believe that the price mechanism needs help if it is to perform well at the aggregate level base their case on a theory which was advanced in the 1930s to explain the high unemployment being experienced during the Great Depression. This new theory led to a revolution in economic thought, a revolution which resulted in the government accepting responsibility for managing the economy in aggregate. It was not to be responsible for determining a point on the *PPF* – that was to be left to the free market – but it was to be responsible for ensuring that the economy was on or near its *PPF*. In other words, the government became responsible for the management of the economy in aggregate. Macroeconomics grew out of this revolution.

For many years this revolutionary macroeconomics ruled the world. All western governments took responsibility for managing their aggregate economic performance and were increasingly elected on their ability to manage it well. But in recent years there has been a swing away from this view and macroeconomics is reverting to the study of business cycles again. The tendency to work below capacity for long periods of time is increasingly laid once more at the door of those who refuse to bow to the signals of the price mechanism. Now it is argued that underemployment results from capital and/or labour pricing themselves out of the market. If they choose to ignore the market signals and find themselves underemployed then they have no one to blame but themselves. The government should do no more than is necessary to allow the price mechanism to work – it certainly should not accept responsibility for managing the economy.

In what follows we shall see what these two views are and on what theories they rest. The revolutionary macroeconomics sprang from a book called *The General Theory of Output, Employment and Interest*, which was published by John Maynard Keynes in 1936. This type of macroeconomics is therefore called **Keynesian economics** (pronounced cain-sain). The alternative is known as either **monetarism** or classical economics. It is sometimes called monetarism because its proponents claim that the only aggregate economic variable with which the government should concern itself is the quantity of money in the economy. It is sometimes called classical because it resembles the kind of business cycle theory which preceded the Keynesian revolution.

These labels are useful shorthand but fail to convey very full descriptions of the two schools of thought. There are many different kinds of Keynesianism and there are many different kinds of monetarism. Macroeconomics therefore lacks the cohesion of microeconomic theory or growth theory. This lack of cohesion presents special difficulties for an introductory text since there are no simple answers to quite basic questions – it all depends on which theory is used. We have tried to deal with this by making the two main schools of macroeconomic thought quite explicit in the issues we address. Fortunately, both schools of thought address the same set of facts – they try to explain the UK's economic history and predict its economic future. A good point to begin with is therefore a description of the country's economic history, i.e. with the UK national accounts.

SUMMARY

1. Macroeconomics is concerned with why the economy might not produce on its production possibility frontier.
2. The UK economy has shown long-run economic growth, but this has fluctuated, giving rise to business cycles.
3. The regular depressions of business cycles have led some economists to doubt the ability of the price mechanism to allocate resources for the economy as a whole.
4. Macroeconomics is therefore concerned with describing, explaining and working out policies to cure our tendency to work below capacity.
5. Economists who believe that the government should act to even out inevitable business cycles are influenced by the work of J.M. Keynes and are often called Keynesians.
6. Those economists who believe that the price mechanism, if left to itself, will allocate resources efficiently are called classical or monetarist economists.

12 National accounts

In this chapter we will discuss:

1. The way in which we 'add up' what we have produced.
2. The problems encountered in this process.
3. The use of index numbers.
4. The components of aggregate supply and demand.
5. Government budgets.

Introduction

Many people have need of information in order to make decisions, and statistics are one possible source. Economists and government are particularly interested in those statistics that relate to production, prices and financial flows.

The economist requires statistics to be able to test and refine economic theory. Governments require statistics to guide their policy decisions. In this chapter we look at how the principal UK national accounts are compiled and some limitations on their use.

Published accounts

National accounts are rather like a company's accounts or a household's accounts. They record UK national income and expenditure, the amount we consume and the amount we save and invest. They also record how much of UK national income comes from overseas and how much of UK national expenditure is spent on goods produced overseas. The UK national accounts therefore record our national income and expenditure flows.

Annual accounts are presented on a calendar year basis (January–January) rather than on a financial year basis (April–April). They are prepared by the Central Statistical Office (CSO) and are available from Her Majesty's Stationery Office (HMSO), which publishes them.

The official title of these annual accounts is *National Income and Expenditure Accounts*. They appear once a year in a book with blue covers, which is therefore usually referred to as the Blue Book. Although there is only one issue per year, each issue contains a great deal of information about the economy. The information given refers not only to the current year but also to many past years. Thus we can see at a glance whether, for example, national income is rising or falling, and by how much.

There are other sources of information too. *Economic Trends*, which is also prepared by the CSO and published by HMSO, appears monthly and contains not only annual but also quarterly statistics. That is to say, they record what happened in each of the three-month periods. January, February and March; April, May and June; July, August and September; and October, November and December. Each three-month period has its own set of accounts. These enable us to see how national income and other items in the national accounts vary with the 'seasons', and since they are published every month, they offer slightly more up-to-date information than does the annual Blue Book.

An example of the sort of data given in such publications is shown in Table 12.1. This shows national income in millions of pounds for the years 1983 to 1990, with the quarterly figures given for 1990 and 1991. So we can see that national income has been increasing. In the first year it rose by £20,536 million, in the second by £24,750 million and so on. It seems that the UK has been enjoying economic growth, at least according to these figures.

The table also shows that there is some seasonal pattern in national income. It grows steadily in the first two quarters, but this growth slows and there is a fall in national income after the fourth quarter in 1990. This variation in quarterly data is normal, and it is not unusual for the second quarter to show a fall on the first quarter, although national income for the year is usually higher than the previous year. Thus national income does not grow or decline uniformly, but fluctuates around a trend. The last two quarters' data show the beginning of a recession.

As well as these annual and quarterly accounts there is

Table 12.1 UK national income, 1983–91 (£ million)

1983	264,070	
1984	284,606	
1985	309,356	
1986	331,107	
1987	361,616	
1988	402,515	
1989	439,546	
1990	476,943 – quarters	I 115,320
		II 118,114
		III 121,431
		IV 122,078
1991		I 120,149
		II 122,099

Source: *Economic Trends*.

another publication (again by HMSO for the CSO) which uses each calendar month as an accounting period. It is called the *Monthly Digest of Statistics.* As well as reporting annual and quarterly figures, it contains (when possible) monthly figures too.

In addition to these general statements of accounts, there are some specialist publications, such as *Financial Statistics* and *Trade Accounts.* There are also some sources of information outside the CSO and other government agencies. The National Institute of Economic and Social Research (NIESR) is an independent body which every month publishes a set of national accounts. They are quarterly accounts and appear in the *National Institute Review.*

There is, it seems, no shortage of information as to how the economy has performed. It is not our intention here to delve too deeply into national accounting, but we do need to know something of what national accounts contain and how they are constructed.

SUMMARY

1. National accounts record the national economic activity.
2. Accounts are published annually, quarterly and monthly by HMSO for the CSO.
3. Some non-government bodies also publish national accounts.

The circular flow

Imagine an extremely simple economy comprising only firms and households. It has no government and no international trade. Firms buy factors of production from households and use these factors of production to produce goods and services. These goods and services are then either sold to households as consumer goods or sold to firms as investment goods. This is shown in Figure 12.1.

In return for supplying the firms with factors of production the households receive factor incomes (wages, interest, profits and rent), which in aggregate constitute national income. Having received this income, the households save some and spend some on goods and services (consumer expenditure). The amount they spend on goods and services accrues to the firms, which, together with investment expenditure, constitutes the total revenue of the firms. All this revenue is then paid out on factors of production as national income and households spend some and save some and the process starts all over again. This is shown in Figure 12.2.

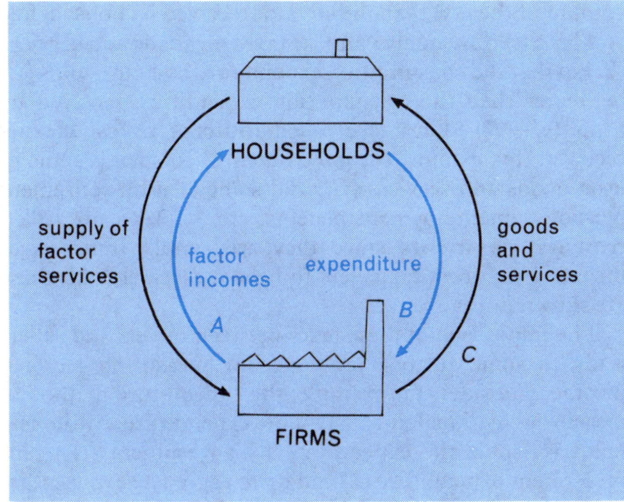

Figure 12.1 Circular flow of income.

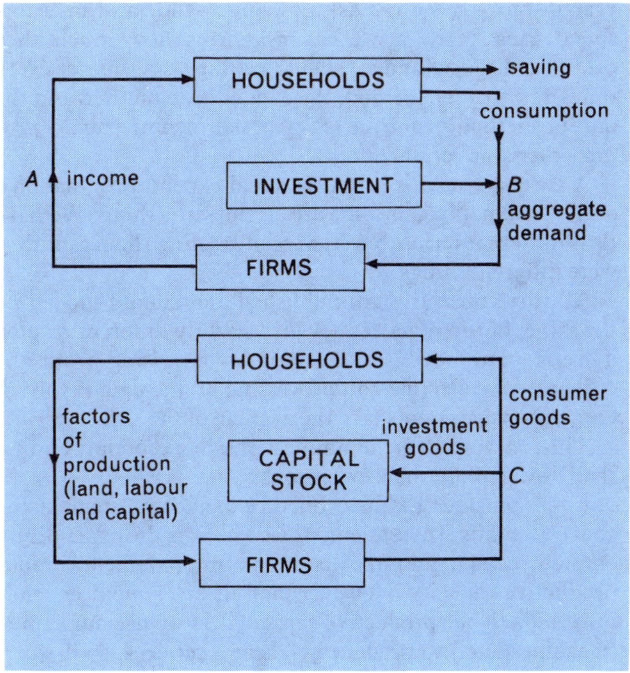

Figure 12.2 Consumption, saving and investment in the circular flow.

From these figures it should be clear that the counterclockwise flow of factors from households to firms and of goods and services from firms to households is matched by the clockwise flow of incomes and expenditures. The real things (goods and factors) flow counterclockwise and the money to pay for them flows clockwise. This is the **circular flow of income.**

UK national accounts contain information on each of these flows – national income, consumption expenditure and investment expenditure.

One important and interesting feature of the circular flow is that there are three separate ways of measuring national income. We can measure how much income the households receive each year (flow *A* in Figure 12.2). This is called the income-based measure. Secondly, we can measure the total expenditure in the economy, flow *B* (consumers' expenditure plus investment expenditure). This expenditure constitutes the revenue of the firms which is then paid out to factors and so must equal flow *A* (national income). The third method is to measure the output produced by firms. Their total output equals consumption plus investment, flow *C*, and so equals total expenditure, which in turn equals national income.

Thus we can ask households how much they receive each

year in income, we can ask how much they and investors spend each year, or we can ask firms how much they produce each year and we should get the same answer every time. The income method, the expenditure method and the output method of measuring national income should produce the same result.

A corollary of this is that national expenditure, national output and national income are all the same thing. We have three different terms, but beware of treating them as if they were different things.

All three measures are published and should indeed be the same, but in practice they give slightly different results. This is partly due to statistical error arising from the difficulty of collecting and processing all the data involved. Our national accounts take the average of the three.

This, as we said, is the simplest possible economy and we shall now explore some extensions.

First, consider the investment expenditure item in the above accounts. Investment, as we know, is the expenditure on new capital and results in an improvement in our productive capacity. However, not all investment expenditure adds to our productive capacity. As we use our capital (machines, etc.) to produce goods and services, so it wears out and eventually has to be replaced. This is called **depreciation**.

Some of the new investment therefore goes on replacing worn-out capital (replacement investment). We therefore have to distinguish between gross investment and net investment. Gross investment is the total expenditure on new capital. Net investment is that which adds to our capital stock. The difference between gross and net investment is depreciation. Thus:

Gross investment − Depreciation = Net investment

This distinction between gross and net investment poses a problem when measuring national income. Recall that the expenditure method of measuring national income is based on the sum of consumption expenditure and investment expenditure. The question therefore is: which investment expenditure should we use? We could use either gross investment or net investment. The convention is to publish both. The measure of national income based on net investment is called net national income and that based on gross investment is called gross national income.

Gross national income is the value of all goods and services produced in the UK before allowing for the fact that we have used up some of our machines in producing those goods and services.

Net national income is the value of all goods and services produced in the UK minus the amount we need to put aside to keep our capital stock intact. This latter measure is the truer indication of our performance, since depreciation of capital is a drain on our resources and should be allowed for when calculating how well off we are as a result of our economic activity.

SUMMARY

1. In a simple, closed economy without a government, national income equals national output which equals national expenditure.
2. These three terms all refer to the same thing and offer three ways of measuring national income – the income method, the output method and the expenditure method.
3. Although in theory these three measures should be identical, they are in practice different because the collection and processing of the data are not perfect.
4. All three measures are published together with an average measure.
5. In producing goods and services we use up some of our capital stock and this is called depreciation.
6. Gross investment expenditure is partly to make up this depreciation and partly to increase our capital stock.
7. That part of gross investment which goes to making good depreciation is called replacement investment.
8. That part of gross investment which goes to increasing our capital stock is called net investment:
   Gross investment = Net investment + Depreciation
9. Gross national income is measured before allowing for depreciation.
10. Net national income is measured after allowing for depreciation:
    Gross national income = Net national income + Depreciation

Introducing government

The main effect of introducing the government into our simple model is to introduce an intermediary between households and firms. Households receive income from firms (Y) but then pay some of this to the government in the form of income taxes (T_d). These are called **direct taxes** since they are imposed directly on incomes. This means that the amount paid out by firms is greater (by the amount of the tax) than the amount received by households.

The government also impose taxes on goods and services (T_i) so that the consumption expenditure by households (C) is greater than the consumption expenditure received by firms ($C-T_i$). These are called **indirect taxes**. Having received this income, the government then spends some of it on goods and services (G_f) and some of it on retirement pensions, unemployment benefits, etc. (G_h). G_h are called **transfer payments** since they are simply transfers of income away from taxpayers to benefit receivers. All these are shown in Figure 12.3

The imposition of these taxes between buyers and sellers leads to some further problems for measuring national income. Consider, for example, the expenditure method of measuring national income. The expenditure by households (C) plus the expenditure by government (G_f) plus investment expenditure (I) add up to aggregate expenditure from the point of view of the buyers. But, from the point of view of the firms, total expenditure is what they receive

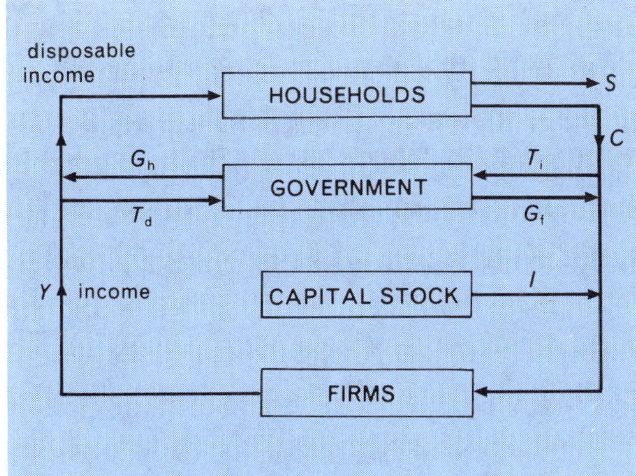

Figure 12.3 Circular flow including government.

from their customers not what their customers spend. The difference between the two is of course indirect taxes (T_i).

So, from the buyers' point of view expenditure is £$(C+G_f+I)$ but from the point of view of the sellers expenditure is £$(C+G_f+I-T_i)$. This is because the government has removed £T_i from the circular flow of income in the form of indirect taxes imposed between the buyers and the sellers.

The amount given out by firms (national income) is the amount they receive, so the expenditure method of measuring national income should measure expenditure from the point of view of the sellers (firms). Therefore total expenditure has to be adjusted for indirect taxes. This adjustment is called the adjustment to factor cost. Thus:

National income at factor cost = National expenditure − Indirect taxes

The introduction of the government into our simple model has therefore introduced a new source of demand for goods and services (G_f) and a new source of income for households (G_h). It has also caused the value of national income provided by firms (Y) to differ from the national income received by households ($Y-T_d$) and the value of expenditure by households, government and investors ($C+G_f+I$) to differ from that received by firms ($C+G_f+I-T_i$).

In order to be consistent then we have to decide whether to measure things from the point of view of firms (producers) or from the point of view of demanders. The convention is to measure things from the point of view of the firms, so consumers' expenditure is adjusted to factor cost by taking off the taxes paid on goods and services. This leaves the income received by firms and paid out by them in the next period as national income.

SUMMARY

1. Governments impose taxes on goods and services so that firms get less from the sale of their goods than their customers pay for them.
2. The difference goes to the government as indirect taxes.
3. When using the expenditure method to calculate national income this difference has to be allowed for, since not all the expenditure by households reaches the firms.
4. The convention is to measure expenditure as seen by the firms, so indirect taxes are subtracted from household expenditure and this is called the adjustment to factor cost.
5. Governments impose taxes on the incomes received so that households receive less than the firms pay out.
6. The difference goes to the government and is called direct taxes.
7. The income which the government receives from taxes is typically either given back to households directly (as pensions, supplementary benefits, etc.) or spent on goods and services like schools, hospitals and armaments.
8. The amounts given back to households directly are called transfer payments.

Introducing international trade

When a country does not trade with any others it is known as a 'closed' economy. We now consider an 'open' or trading economy.

In our closed economy model we quite rightly assumed that all the revenue generated by UK firms would be passed on to UK households as national income. But in an open economy some factors of production will be supplied to UK firms by foreigners, e.g. Japanese capitalists own shares in some UK factories and some Spaniards work as waiters in UK hotels. This means that some of the revenue generated by UK firms is sent abroad – e.g. as dividend payments to Japanese capitalists – and this is called property income paid abroad ($PIPA$).

Conversely, of course, UK nationals own land and capital abroad too, so they will receive income from abroad to augment that received from UK firms. This is called property income from abroad ($PIFA$).

The difference between the revenue generated by UK firms and the income of UK residents is therefore the difference between the property income sent abroad and the property income received from abroad. This is called net property income from abroad ($NPIFA$).

$$\text{National income} = \text{Domestic income} + PIFA - PIPA$$
$$\text{National income} = \text{Domestic income} + NPIFA$$

This is shown down the left-hand side of Figures 12.4 and 12.5.

This distinction between national income and domestic income (i.e. between nationality and domicile) carries over to national output (national product) too. National product is that part of the output of UK and foreign firms which is due to UK nationals. Domestic output is the total output of firms in the UK whoever owns them.

Recall that this output can be measured either gross or

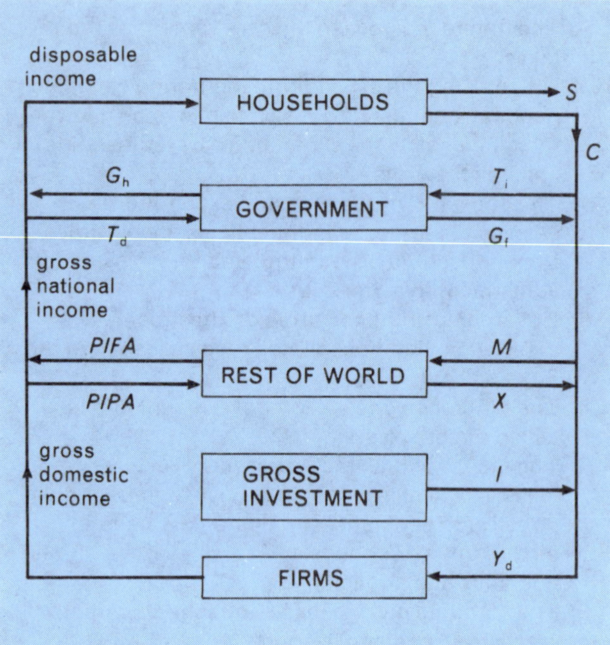

Figure 12.4 Circular flow including government and international trade.

net of depreciation. We therefore have net domestic product, gross domestic product, net national product and gross national product.

Two further complications arise when we move from a closed to an open economy. The first is that not all expenditure in the UK is on UK-produced goods and services. Some of the goods and services bought in the UK are supplied from overseas (i.e. they are imported) and so some of UK national expenditure flows abroad to foreign firms rather than accruing to UK firms. This is shown as flow M (for *im*ports) on the right-hand side of Figures 12.4 and 12.5.

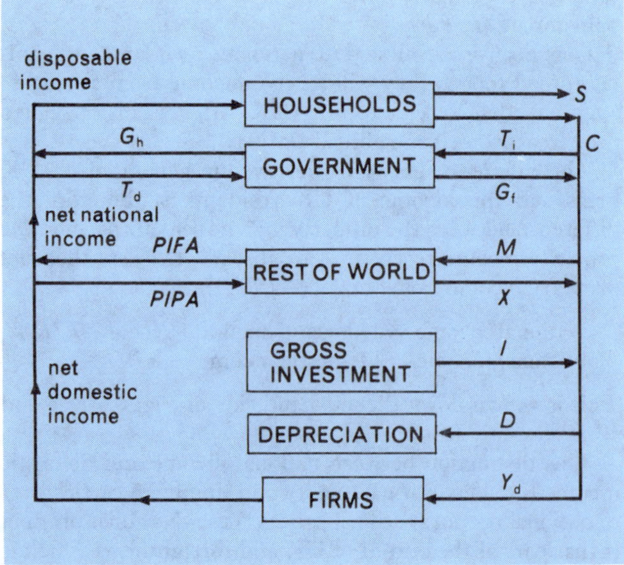

Figure 12.5 Circular flow including government, trade and depreciation.

The second is that some of the output of UK firms is sold overseas (exports), so that only part of the revenue of UK firms comes from UK sources. This is shown as flow X (for *ex*ports) on the right-hand side of Figures 12.4 and 12.5.

Aggregate demand (Y_d) for UK products is therefore consumer expenditure (C) less indirect taxes (T_i) plus government expenditure on goods and services (G_f) less imports (M) plus exports (X) plus investment expenditure (I), i.e.:

$$Y_d = C - T_i + G_f - M + X + I$$

SUMMARY

1. In an open economy UK firms pay some of their dividends to foreigners and this outflow of income is called property income paid abroad (*PIPA*).
2. Households receive some income from foreign firms and this is called property income from abroad (*PIFA*).
3. The difference between what is paid abroad (*PIPA*) and what is received from abroad (*PIFA*) is called net property income from abroad (*NPIFA*).
4. Some of the UK demand for goods and services is satisfied by foreign firms. The inflow of goods and services from abroad is called imports.
5. Some of the goods and services produced by UK firms are bought by foreigners. This flow of goods and services overseas is called exports.
6. Domestic income is calculated without allowing for net property income from abroad.
7. National income is calculated after allowing for net property income from abroad.

Measuring economic activity

So far, then, we have the following 'aggregate' variables:

UK household supply of factors of production
UK household demand for goods and services
UK household saving
UK firms' supply of goods and services
UK firms' demand for labour
UK investors' demand for investment goods
Indirect taxes
Direct taxes
Government demand for goods and services
Government transfer payments
Imports of goods and services
Exports of goods and services

This is an impressive list and we will be meeting some items very often in what follows. Indeed macroeconomics seeks to explain the behaviour of many of these items. But even before we begin the macroeconomic analysis, there is quite a lot to say about the ways in which these items are measured and interrelated.

Let us look first at just one of these items: UK firms' aggregate supply of goods and services.

Producers supply apples, oranges, shoes, telephones, haircuts, etc. So how can we sensibly talk of aggregate supply by all firms of all goods and services taken together? This is an ancient and as yet unsolved problem in economics, but the most obvious way forward is to discover how much money was spent on the goods and services, i.e. what value of goods and services was produced. We simply add up the money value of apples, oranges, shoes, telephones, haircuts, etc. to yield the aggregate value of domestic output (aggregate home production).

There are at least two consequences of this. First, we exclude from aggregate production all goods which have no market price or of which we have no record.

This means that we take no account of voluntary (unpaid) work. This includes the work done by homemakers, the home repairs and improvements done by DIY enthusiasts, and the clubs, associations and charities run by volunteers. Since none of this work has a 'market' price, it cannot be valued in money terms and hence cannot be included in our measure of aggregate production. No one can doubt that this is a very significant omission.

Another type of omission is 'unrecorded' work, often referred to as the **black economy**. This may be illegal production (e.g. the growing and distribution of hard drugs) or perfectly legal production (e.g. motor car repairs). The reason for not reporting the former to the CSO is obvious – no one wants to be arrested! The reason for not reporting the latter (legal production) is that by failing to report such work the 'firm' and the 'customer' avoid taxes or other penalties – such as a reduction in supplementary benefits. It is difficult to assess the size of the black economy, but it has recently been estimated at between £3 billion and £4 billion. Thus its omission from national accounts estimates of output is important.

The second consequence of using the monetary value of output as a measure of aggregate production is that, simply by doubling all prices, we can double our measure of aggregate production. This doubling occurs even though there is no change in the quantities of goods and services actually produced.

This increase in the aggregate price level, if it persists, is called **inflation**. We have to find some way of correcting our measure of domestic output for inflation.

This is easy to deal with if we know for sure that *all* prices have doubled. We can clearly allow for that by halving our measure of aggregate production. But usually not all prices double – price changes are not uniform. Some goods may increase in price by 300 per cent, while others actually fall in price. In such cases it is by no means simple to correct our 'money measure' of aggregate production for changes in prices.

The set of tools for addressing this problem comes under the general heading of index numbers (see pp. 219–20 and the description of the ECU in Chapter 23). These are methods of generating an index of the general price level so that if the index doubles then, despite the fact that not all prices have doubled, it remains legitimate to halve the money measure of aggregate production. If the prices under consideration are producers' prices then the price index is called the wholesale price index. This measures by how much the producers' money income increases due simply to price changes.

If the prices under consideration are the prices paid by consumers then the index is the retail price index (the RPI). It is the RPI which is usually taken as the indicator of inflation. When the retail price index remains steady, there is zero inflation; when the index is going up at 10 per cent per year, there is a 10 per cent rate of inflation; and so on.

Apart from this method of explicitly calculating the price index and making allowance for any changes in it when measuring the value of domestic output there is a simpler way forward.

The prices of all the individual items which make up aggregate domestic output do change over time, but instead of using the 1990 prices to value output in 1990 and the 1991 prices to measure the value output in 1991 we can always use 1990 prices. Thus we can use the prices which ruled in 1990 to value the output produced in 1991, 1992 and 1993. By fixing the prices in this way there can be no change in the value of aggregate output without there being a change in the actual (real) level of output.

Output measured in this way is published in the UK national accounts and is called constant priced output. However, although this seems to solve the inflation problem, there are some difficulties. Our measure of aggregate output will depend on which year's prices are chosen, and the rate at which it grows will also depend on our choice of base-year prices.

Consider, for example, an economy which produces only three goods – bread, milk and cloth. In 1985 it produced 4 loaves at 50p each, 5 litres of milk at £1 per litre and $3m^2$ of cloth at £2 per m^2. In 1990 it produced 6 loaves at £1 each, 6 litres of milk at £1 per litre and $6m^2$ of cloth at £6 per m^2.

The value of output in 1985 at 1985 prices was:

$$4 \times £0.50 + 5 \times £1 + 3 \times £2 = £13$$

The value of output in 1990 at 1985 prices was:

$$6 \times £0.50 + 6 \times £1 + 6 \times £2 = £21$$

Thus when using 1985 prices we see that output has risen from £13 to £21, which is an increase of 8/13 = 61.5 per cent.

If we now use 1990 prices to value output then the value of output in 1985 valued at 1990 prices was:

$$4 \times £1 + 5 \times £1 + 3 \times £6 = £27$$

The value of output in 1990 valued at 1990 prices was:

$$6 \times £1 + 6 \times £1 + 6 \times £6 = £48$$

Thus when using 1990 prices we see that output has risen from £27 to £48, which is an increase of 21/27 = 78 per cent.

It should be clear from this example that both the level and the growth rate of national output depend crucially on which year's prices are used to provide the constant priced value of output. In one case the growth rate was about 60 per cent and in the other it was about 80 per cent – an appreciable difference.

The CSO changes the base year every five years or so. It has recently changed from using 1980 prices to using 1985 prices.

Before leaving this issue one further point should be made. If the value of output in 1990 at 1985 prices differs from its value in current (1990) prices then it must be the case that the difference is due only to price differences between the two years. The actual quantities produced are the same in both cases (i.e. the 1990 quantities), so changes in value can only be due to price changes.

Thus if we divide the value of output at 1990 prices by the value of output at 1985 prices the result is an indication of how prices have moved *in aggregate*. Using the example given above, we see that the 1990 output valued at 1985 prices was £21 and the 1990 output valued at 1990 prices was £48. We can therefore conclude that prices have in aggregate gone up by 48/21 = 229 per cent. This index of aggregate price level is called the gross domestic product (GDP) price deflator. It is usually reported in the UK national accounts and turns out to be similar to, but not identical with, the wholesale price index.

SUMMARY

1. Despite the fact that macroeconomics deals only with national 'aggregates', it turns out that there are a great many aggregates to record.
2. One of the difficulties of dealing with aggregates is how to aggregate dissimilar things.
3. This problem has yet to be solved but is dealt with by aggregating (adding together) the *values* of all the dissimilar things to give their 'aggregate value' or the 'value of the aggregate'.
4. This is unsatisfactory for two reasons:
   (a) Only items which have a market value can be included in our national accounts.
   (b) A general rise in prices results in a rise in the value of the aggregate even though the 'true' aggregate remains unchanged.
5. There is no way of correcting our national accounts for (a), but some guesses have been made as to the size of 'non-market' items which should perhaps ideally appear in our national accounts.
6. There are two solutions to (b). The first makes use of index numbers to work out how the aggregate price level has changed. This index is then used to correct the value of the aggregate for any changes in the general price level. The second solution is always to value output in terms of one year's prices. Since the same prices are being used to value each year's output, any change in value over time must be due to changing quantities and not to changing prices.
7. The problem with this solution is that our measure of output and its rate of change are heavily dependent on which year's prices are chosen.
8. By valuing output at constant and current prices we can calculate how prices have in aggregate changed between the base year and the current year. Dividing the current value by the constant priced value yields an implicit price deflator known as the GDP price deflator. This is not quite the same thing as the price index referred to earlier, but it is similar to it and is regularly published by the CSO.

A closer look at the expenditure method

We can now examine this method of national income accounting in more detail. Our starting point must be to consider the various forms which expenditure can take in an economy like the UK where there is a government and foreign trade.

From our circular flow model we can identify consumers' expenditure on goods and services. In addition, firms will want to invest in such things as buildings and machinery (fixed capital), and to increase their holdings of stocks. The government will also consume resources and its expenditure must be included. An open economy like the UK must also take account of foreign trade – expenditure by foreigners on UK goods adds to total expenditure, while spending on imports reduces it. Further adjustments must be made for taxes and subsidies and for income from abroad.

Table 12.2 shows the 1989 estimates of UK national income by the expenditure method. The table reflects the new Central Statistical Office reporting of national income accounts. This method differs from the old in that the 'statistical discrepancy' item is introduced and the adjustment to factor costs is made at the end of the calculation. You may find the old method reported elsewhere and this is shown in Table 12.3.

The first item in Table 12.2 shows the value of consumers' expenditure. This is expenditure on such things as food, haircuts and washing machines. This item does not include spending on property by households, since houses are regarded as productive assets. Thus the purchase of new houses is included in domestic fixed capital formation.

General government final consumption includes all central and local government current spending on final goods and services, such as education, the NHS and the salaries of public servants. The important point here is that this item only includes current spending. Investment by nationalized industries and capital expenditure by the public authorities are included in gross domestic fixed capital formation. A further item of government spending excluded from the accounts is transfer payments, which we earlier called G_h in our circular flow model, e.g. social security benefits and pensions. Such payments are not made in return for productive services, but are transfers from one part of society to another.

Gross domestic fixed capital formation, in addition to recording investment in new dwellings and government capital expenditure, contains all private fixed capital investment, such as new machines and factories. This is distinguished from capital tied up in stocks of raw materials, finished goods and work in progress (working capital), which is listed as a separate item.

The sum of these first four items gives us total domestic expenditure at market prices: that is, spending by UK residents on goods and services in the UK. Adding foreign residents' spending on goods and services produced in the UK gives us total final expenditure, but from this the cost of buying goods from abroad must be subtracted. This gives gross domestic product (GDP) at market prices.

It is at this point that the CSO has changed its account-

Table 12.2 UK gross national product, 1989: expenditure method (£ million, current prices)

Consumers' expenditure	328,453
General government final consumption	99,426
Gross domestic fixed capital formation	100,472
Value of physical increase in stocks and work in progress	3,102
Total domestic expenditure (at market prices)	531,453
Exports of goods and services	123,396
Total final expenditure	654,849
less Imports of goods and services	−142,527
Gross domestic product (at market prices)	512,322
Statistical discrepancy	920
Gross domestic product (average estimate)	513,242
Net property income from abroad	4,582
Gross national product (average estimate)	517,824
less Taxes on expenditure	−80,136
plus Subsidies	5,668
Gross national product (at factor cost)	443,356
less Capital consumption	−56,186
National income (net national product at factor cost)	387,170

Source: *Annual Abstract of Statistics*, 1991.

ing procedure. In the past it was felt that the expenditure method was the most reliable of the three, and the income and output estimates included a residual error to bring all three estimates into line. Now the estimate of expenditure also contains an allowance for error and poor reporting of transactions. This is known as the 'statistical discrepancy'. In 1989 the figures underestimated GDP by £920 million. Adding this to the estimate brings the expenditure estimate into line with the average estimate of the three methods.

Adding net property income from abroad gives us gross national product (GNP) at market prices. This is done because the income from abroad is not the result of the labours of people within the UK during the accounting period. It may, for example, be the proceeds of rent from a factory owned by a UK resident in the West Indies.

The final two items in the account are the factor cost adjustment. In addition to taking into account indirect taxes (T_i) there is the further complication of some goods being subsidized, which lowers their price in the shops. Therefore the value of taxes on expenditure is removed and the value of subsidies is added to the estimate to yield GNP at factor cost.

To find national income from the GNP figure it is necessary to subtract depreciation (capital consumption).

Table 12.3 The former CSO expenditure method

Consumers' expenditure +
General government final consumption +
Gross domestic fixed capital formation +
Value of physical increase in stocks and work in progress =
Total domestic expenditure +
Exports of goods and services −
Imports of goods and services =
Gross domestic product at market prices −
Taxes on expenditure +
Subsidies =
Gross domestic product at factor cost +
Net property income from abroad =
Gross national product at factor cost −
Capital consumption =
National income

The income and output methods

These two methods should provide the same answer as the expenditure method. Both follow the theoretical framework set out in the circular flow model.

The income method adds up all sources of income within the country. Table 12.4 shows the income method of compiling the national income accounts. The first items correspond to the broad classifications of wages and salaries, interest, rent and profit. There is also an *imputed*, that is to say estimated, charge for the consumption of non-trading capital. This is an estimate of 'income in kind' from owner-occupied non-trading capital. A similar estimate is made for owner occupation in the rent category. Following this item, additions and deductions are made to turn GDP into national income, as we saw in the expenditure method. The item 'stock appreciation' takes account of rises in the value of stocks held when no extra physical stock is held, i.e. it removes the effect of inflation.

Table 12.4 The income and output approaches to national income accounting

Income approach	Output approach
Income from employment	Agriculture, forestry and fishing
Income from self-employment	Energy and water supply
Gross trading profits of companies	Manufacturing
Gross trading surplus of public corporations	Construction
Gross trading surplus of general government enterprises	Distribution; hotels and catering; repairs
Rent	Transport
Imputed charge for consumption of non-trading capital	Communication
= **Total domestic income**	Banking, finance, insurance, business services and leasing
—Stock appreciation	Ownership of dwellings
	Public administration, national defence and compulsory social security
	Education and health services
	Other services
= GDP (income-based)	Adjustment for financial services
Statistical discrepancy	Statistical discrepancy
= **GDP at factor cost**	= **GDP at factor cost**
+Net property income from abroad	
= GNP (average estimate)	
– Capital consumption	
= Net national product ('**national income**')	

The output method is found by aggregating the value of outputs of all firms. A possible scheme is shown in Table 12.4, but any method of classifying output, say into smaller or larger industry groups, is possible. For sectors such as education and defence the 'value of output' is counted as the cost of providing the service, e.g. teachers' salaries.

The output method is regarded as the least reliable of the three methods, relying as it does on incomplete surveys. Everybody in the country who earns money is subject to scrutiny by the Inland Revenue, and all businesses must file accounts. Estimating income and expenditure is therefore much easier than following output. The high cost of a full survey means that it is not even carried out every year. The output estimate therefore relies heavily on the other two and on partial surveys.

The main problem to be avoided when calculating national income by the output method is double counting. The products of many industries are the inputs of another. Thus if we were simply to count the output of all firms, we would end up counting some production two, three or more times. Consider the example of the production of bread (Table 12.5).

If we were to add up the value of the production from each stage, we would arrive at a figure of £600. This is misleading, however, because only £300 worth of bread has been produced. Thus simply adding up the output of each firm will overstate the level of national output. The solution is either to add up the 'value added' at each stage of production, or to take the value of the *final* product only. Both methods should give the same answer. In our example the final sales of the baker, who sells to the ultimate consumer, are the same as the total value added at each stage of production.

SUMMARY

1. The expenditure method of national income accounting adds up consumers' spending, government expenditure, investment and net exports to find GDP at market prices.
2. It is necessary to make an allowance for errors in the collection of data. This is shown as a statistical discrepancy.

Table 12.5 Calculating the value added

	Sales (£)	Purchases of inputs (£)	Value added (£)
Farmer grows wheat	100	0	100
Miller mills wheat to flour	200	100	100
Baker produces bread from flour	300	200	100
			300

3. GNP (average estimate) is found by adding net property income from abroad to GDP at market prices adjusted for statistical discrepancies.
4. To find GNP at factor cost, taxes are subtracted and subsidies are added to GNP (average estimate).
5. National income equals GNP at factor cost minus depreciation (capital consumption).
6. Only payments made for productive services are included in the accounts. Transfers, such as old-age pension expenditure by the government, are excluded.
7. The income method of collecting national accounts adds up all wages and salaries, interest, rent and profits. Estimates are made for 'income in kind'.
8. The output method adds up all of the production of the various sectors of the economy. It is regarded as the least accurate of the three methods.

Comparing national accounts across countries

One possible use of national accounts is to compare the living standards of different countries. This is not as simple as it sounds. While many countries construct their accounts along similar lines (the United Nations standardized system) not all do so and each country has different characteristics which mean that the figures are not directly comparable.

The old command economies do not use the standardized system. The former Soviet Union, for example, did not include government services in its accounts. Other discrepancies arise, such as varying sizes of the black economy. If a good, such as alcohol, is prohibited in a country then we would expect a large illegal, and so unreported, market in the good. In a country where no such prohibition exists the national accounts will appear to suggest greater output than in the country with the larger black economy.

A further difficulty arises from making comparisons in a common currency. Say we wanted to compare the living standards of the UK and France. The UK national accounts are expressed in £ sterling, the French accounts in French francs. To make a comparison one of the sets of accounts must be converted into the other currency. The question is: at what exchange rate is this done? Exchange rates vary from day to day, and so converting a whole year's figures at one rate is clearly unsatisfactory.

Another problem with exchange rates is that converting national accounts from one currency to another does not reflect the true purchasing power of the currency within its own country. For example, converting a foreign sum of money into £ sterling may give us the answer of £4.50, a sum of only little spending power in the UK. However, this £4.50 in the country's own low-price economy may buy a month's groceries and so is of great significance there. This importance is lost in the comparison.

The use of national accounts for comparing living standards is also suspect for other reasons. The most obvious adjustment that must be made is to allow for the population of a country. If two nations have the same national income, but one has twice the population of the other, then on average people in one are twice as well off as people in the other. This will not follow exactly, however, because the distribution of income in the country with the lower population may be heavily biased towards a few inhabitants. Thus the bulk of the population of the more populous country may still be the better off. The question of income distribution was taken up in Chapter 10.

These reservations aside, a common measure of welfare is *real disposable income per head*. The measure uses real income to adjust for inflation and disposable income to take account of different taxation schemes. Dividing real disposable income by the population gives us real disposable income per head and allows for different population sizes.

Finally, some people dispute the whole basis of measuring welfare in money terms at all. A measure such as national income can count only material wealth and ignores the 'quality of life'. How can one account for a clean environment, freedom of speech and other basic human rights? There is no easy answer, but the quality of life does count for much and so any money measure of welfare is not completely adequate.

SUMMARY

1. Not all countries use the same method of national income accounting, so nations' accounts are not directly comparable.
2. In addition it is difficult to use national accounts to compare living standards in different countries because of the following:
   (a) Different national currencies – at what exchange rate are the accounts converted?
   (b) The variation in purchasing powers of currencies in different countries.
   (c) Monetary values for output cannot measure the 'quality of life'.
   (d) The sizes of population and taxation schemes of countries are all different.
3. Perhaps the most satisfactory measure to use when comparing material living standards is real disposable income per head.

The public sector

We have seen how national accounts reflect the consistency of flows between sectors of the economy (households, firms, government and overseas). It is also possible to draw up accounts for any one sector.

Consider, for example, the government sector. What the government spends on goods and services and welfare payments ($G = G_h + G_f$) less the amount it receives in the form of taxes ($T = T_i + T_d$) must equal the amount to be borrowed by the government. This new borrowing is called the central government borrowing requirement (CGBR). Therefore:

$$G - T = CGBR$$

The government can 'borrow' in two ways:

1. It can issue government bonds. These are sold to households and/or foreigners to whom the government pays some form of interest in return for the loan.
2. It can issue cash. This too is technically known as government debt. The differences between issuing cash and issuing bonds are twofold:
   (a) Cash can be issued without the consent of any other agent. In order to issue bonds, for example, the government must first persuade someone to buy them. But if the government simply prints pound notes then it can buy what it wants directly without first persuading savers to part with their savings.
   (b) In order to persuade savers to part with their savings the government has to offer them some inducement for doing so: that is, the government has to pay interest on the debt it issues as bonds. It does not pay interest on the debt it issues as cash.

Thus the difference between government income (*T*) and government expenditure (*G*) is the amount of government debt and may be covered by issuing either interest-bearing debt (bonds) or non-interest bearing debt (cash).

Fiscal policy and monetary policy

Decisions about government income and expenditure are called **fiscal policy** and are announced each year in the budget. An excess of expenditure over income is called a budget deficit. An excess of income over expenditure, on the other hand, is called a budget surplus. When income equals expenditure we have a balanced budget. Some economists argue that fiscal policy should always aim to balance the budget. We shall see later why others hold different views.

Over the years, UK governments have tended to run more deficits than surpluses. Table 12.6 shows that between 1964 and 1990 there were only five surplus years. The UK has therefore built up a great backlog of debt called the **national debt**. Recall that this is not a debt owed by the citizens of this country to citizens of other countries. Typically, it is a debt owed by all UK citizens (via the government) to some UK citizens (those who lent the government their savings).

The government, as we have seen, has the option of issuing either interest-bearing debt (bonds) or non-interest bearing debt (cash). In deciding the composition of its debt the government is pursuing **monetary policy**. Thus the size of the national debt is determined by the history of fiscal policy, and the composition of the debt is determined by the history of monetary policy. Some economists hold the view that the government should not meet its borrowing requirement by issuing cash, but should issue only bonds. We shall see later why other economists hold different views.

All this activity by central government is recorded in the UK national accounts. These allow UK citizens to see what the government is up to and how it is handling those aspects of their economic lives which they leave in the government's hands.

SUMMARY

1. Each sector of the national accounts has its own accounting identity.
2. They are called identities rather than equations because they must necessarily (by definition of their items) always hold.
3. The government may finance its expenditure by raising tax revenue.
4. Decisions on how much the government will spend, and how much it will raise as taxes, are called fiscal policy and are announced in the annual budget.
5. When expenditure exceeds tax revenue there is a budget deficit.
6. When tax revenue exceeds expenditure there is a budget surplus.
7. When expenditure equals tax revenue there is a balanced budget.
8. Budget deficits are financed by the government issuing interest-bearing debt (bonds) or non-interest bearing debt (cash).
9. Decisions about whether to issue cash or bonds are called monetary policy.
10. There is a strong tendency to have budget deficits rather than budget surpluses. Thus there has been a gradual build-up of government bonds and cash. Together they constitute the national debt.

Table 12.6 UK central government borrowing requirement, 1964–90 (£ million, before allowing for inflation)

1964	434	1973	2,331	1982	7,855
1965	610	1974	3,323	1983	14,493
1966	543	1975	8,372	1984	10,137
1967	1,155	1976	6,791	1985	11,804
1968	759	1977	4,410	1986	8,461
1969	−897	1978	8,308	1987	4,059
1970	−670	1979	10,375	1988	−4,933
1971	638	1980	10,806	1989	−5,135
1972	1,600	1981	10,398	1990	−4,605

Note: Minuses indicate surpluses.
Source: *Monthly Digest of Statistics*.

Price indexes

It is easy to trace out how the price of a particular good changes over time. If its price rises then we can say that consumers are made worse off; conversely, if it falls then consumers are made better off. But what if there are two or more goods under consideration? If their prices change at different rates, can we say anything about how they have moved 'on average'? If one of the prices has fallen and the other has risen, can we say whether 'on average' the price has risen (consumers are worse off) or fallen (consumers are better off)?

The problem being addressed is how best to represent changes in the average price of a number of goods whose individual prices are behaving differently. A price index is a method of measuring how, on average, many different prices have changed over a period of time.

The most common price index in use in the UK is the retail price index (RPI). The RPI seeks to measure how the prices of consumer goods have changed, on average, over time. It is a measure of the changes in the cost of buying consumer goods, i.e. a measure of the cost of living.

Constructing a price index

Consider a simple example of constructing an index for only two goods, say bread and apples. The index is to measure a change in average price over a particular period. The start of that period is called the base period. Let us say that we will start our index in 1990. In 1990 the cost of bread and apples was as follows:

Bread 50p per loaf Apples 20p per kg

Let us further assume that in 1990 the following quantities were bought:

	Cost
200 loaves	£100
100 kg of apples	£ 20
Total	£120

This combination of goods (200 loaves and 100 kg of apples) is called a 'basket' of goods, and the price index is based on changes in the price of that basket.

The price index is calculated by:

$$\text{Price index} = \frac{\text{Cost of basket now}}{\text{Cost of basket in base year (£120)}} \times 100$$

In 1990 the price index is therefore:

$$\frac{£120}{£120} \times 100 = 100$$

Since 120/120 = 1, and 1 × 100 = 100.

To construct the index for 1991, the 1990 quantities of bread and apples are used with the 1991 prices. Let us suppose that in 1991 the price of bread rises by 10 per cent to 55p a loaf and the price of apples by 25 per cent to 25p a kilo.

1991	Price per unit	Quantity in basket	Cost of basket
Bread	55p	200	£110
Apples	25p	100	£ 25
		Cost of basket in 1991	£135

The price index for 1991 will be $\frac{135}{120} \times 100 = 112.5$.

This says that between 1990 and 1991 the average price level rose by 12.5 per cent, i.e. the rise in the index from 100 to 112.5 represents a 12.5 per cent rise in the index. Notice that the answer we obtained was not 17.5 per cent, the mid-point of the two price increases (10 per cent and 25 per cent). This was because consumers spent much more on bread than on apples and so the change in the price of bread was given more weight in our index than the change in the price of apples.

Let us examine this index a little more closely. The index is:

$$\frac{200 \times £0.55 + 100 \times £0.25}{200 \times £0.50 + 100 \times £0.20} \times 100$$

The bottom line is the value of the basket in the base year (£120) and so the index can be written as:

$$\left[\frac{200 \times £0.55}{£120} + \frac{100 \times £0.25}{£120}\right] \times 100$$

It can also be written as:

$$\left[\frac{200 \times £0.50}{£120} \times \frac{£0.55}{£0.50} + \frac{£100 \times £0.20}{£120} \times \frac{£0.25}{£0.20}\right] \times 100$$

$$= \left[\frac{£100}{£120} \times \frac{£0.55}{£0.50} + \frac{£20}{£120} \times \frac{£0.25}{£0.20}\right] \times 100$$

The first term is the expenditure on bread in the base year (£100) divided by the total expenditure in the base year (£120) = $0.8\dot{3}\dot{3}$.

The second term is the increase in bread price (£0.55/£0.50 = 110%, a 10% rise).

The third term is the expenditure on apples in the base year (£20) divided by the total expenditure in the base year (£120) = $0.1\dot{6}\dot{6}$.

The fourth term is the increase in the price of apples (£0.25/£0.20 = 125%, a 25% rise).

Thus the index is [$0.8\dot{3}\dot{3} \times 110\% + 0.1\dot{6}\dot{6} \times 125\%$].

In other words, the index is the sum of each individual price change when each change is multiplied by (*weighted by*) its proportion of the base period basket.

A more complicated example

We will suppose that there are three goods in the representative basket and will first construct a price index for each good (as in the previous example) and then combine them into the average index – the RPI.

Let the three goods be bread, apples and potatoes and let them account for 50, 20 and 30 per cent respectively of the base period expenditure. Thus bread has the greatest weight in the index (0.5) and apples the lowest weight of only 0.2. If the price of bread rises by 10 per cent it will affect consumers to a greater extent than a 10 per cent rise in the price of apples, since bread accounts for half of household expenditure, whereas apples are only 20 per cent. The weights in this example are therefore:

Bread	0.5
Apples	0.2
Potatoes	0.3

Suppose the price of bread rises by 10 per cent, the price of apples remains the same and the price of potatoes rises by 25 per cent. The price index for each good will be:

Bread	110
Apples	100
Potatoes	125

The new overall price index will be:

$$(0.5 \times 110) + (0.2 \times 100) + (0.3 \times 125) = 55 + 20 + 37.5 = 112.5$$

Accordingly, the aggregate price index has risen by 12.5 per cent.

As the index is based on the proportion of income spent on each good, this index accurately reflects the rise in the cost of living in this example. At the end of the year £1 will indeed buy $12\frac{1}{2}$ per cent less than it would have done at the beginning of the year, given this pattern of expenditure.

Retail price index

The second of our two examples of how to construct a price index conforms more accurately to how the retail price index is constructed in the UK. There are some 600 goods in the retail price index, and prices are collected for these goods from all over the country to get a national picture of price movements rather than a regional one.

Table 12.7 RPI weightings, January 1990.

Item category	Weight
Food	0.154
Alcoholic drink	0.083
Housing	0.175
Fuel and light	0.054
Clothing and footwear	0.073
Motoring expenditure	0.128
Leisure goods	0.047
All weights sum to	1.000

The index is constructed in two stages. First an index for each of the main categories of goods is constructed. Within each of these categories the weight given to each item reflects the relative importance of the item to the representative household budget. Each of these indexes is then given a weight within the RPI and the final index is constructed. The figures in Table 12.7 reflect the weights given to some groups of commodities as at January 1990.

It is the aim of the index to reflect changes in the cost of living for a representative household. This representative household is difficult to track down, however, and so the index must be only a guide to the average change in the cost of living.

There has been some dissatisfaction with the retail price index as a measure, and you can see this in Case Study 12.1. An illustration of the problem with indexes is given by mortgage repayments, which alone had a weighting of 0.06 in the RPI in 1990. When mortgage repayments rise due to

Case Study 12.1 Indices that fail to measure up

The Government's attempt to manipulate the market's views of inflation is backfiring. The new 'underlying underlying' index released for the first time last month and again yesterday has at a stroke redefined the meaning of inflation, but irritated a lot of people.

There are many measures of rising prices, of which the Retail Price Index is one of the least satisfactory. The Bank of England has recently offered us the 'retailed (*sic*) price index', based on those goods which are actually traded; there is the producer price index, which measures factory gate inflation; other indices include the GDP deflator, which although accurate is delayed, and a variety of specially constructed measures, of which the latest emerged this week from brokers James Capel.

But the fact is that for a long time the Government has pointed to the RPI excluding mortgages as the underlying rate. Since the introduction of the poll tax sent that rate soaring, statisticians have produced the new 'underlying underlying rate' which eliminates both distortions.

It does in fact have a use, in that when trends become complex it is better to look at them in as many ways as possible. But in May, this one actually signals the opposite of what the Treasury intended: it shows how firmly inflationary forces have taken hold.

The official explanation that two fifths of the jump is down to the delayed effects of excise duty increases on alcohol and tobacco is unconvincing. As Keith Skeoch of James Capel points out, the index for dutiable items has risen 0.9 per cent, whereas the anticipated effect was 0.55 per cent.

This is clear evidence that brewers and tobacco companies are using the Budget as an excuse to push up prices, which is also a more general problem. Even retailers seem to be pretty successful in passing on costs. Manufacturers are managing the same feat, as the last producer price index showed.

Ten per cent RPI inflation is now of course certain. If it happens in August, the headlines will appear in September, just before the Conservative Party conference. From then on, the RPI may begin to fall (so expect the underlying underlying index to disappear, because it will go on rising).

Whether this means anything for the timing of ERM entry is, however, open to doubt: the last week has shown that the date of entry has been divorced from the inflation rate and is now a political decision. Expectations about early entry have been raised so high, in order to support sterling, that they can no longer be disappointed without serious market risks.

1. How is it possible for different measures to give different figures for 'inflation'?

Source: Ian Griffiths, *Independent*, 16 June 1990

interest rate changes, the RPI also rises. The change in the RPI therefore overstates the change in the cost of living for a non-mortgage payer (which is unchanged) and understates it for the mortgage payer (for whom mortgages may take a third of disposable income). A similar problem arises for tax changes.

SUMMARY

1. A price index shows how the prices of a certain set of commodities have moved, on average, over a period of time.
2. A common way of constructing a price index is to give each commodity the influence on the index that reflects the share of expenditure it commands. This provides a weighted average.
3. The retail price index (RPI) is the most common measure of price changes, and this uses a weighted average of 600 commodities.

Exam Preparation and Practice

MULTIPLE-CHOICE QUESTIONS

1.

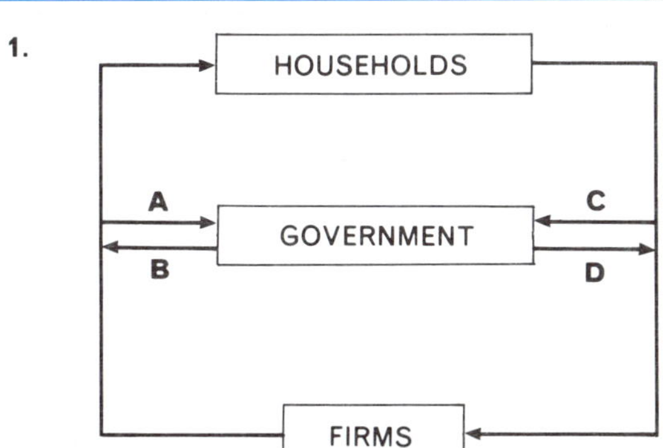

Which of the flows represents indirect taxation?

Questions 2 and 3 relate to the table below, which is taken from a country's national accounts for 1992.

	£ million
Consumers' expenditure	40
General government final consumption	10
Gross domestic fixed capital formation	8
Value of physical increase in stocks and work in progress	2
Exports of goods and services	6
Imports of goods and services	4
Net property income from abroad	2
Taxes on expenditure	6
Subsidies	1
Capital consumption	4

2. What is the value of gross domestic product?

3. What is the value of gross national product?
 A £55m
 B £59m
 C £62m
 D £64m
 E £66m

Questions 4 and 5 relate to the figures below, which show the data used by a country to calculate national income for a given year.

Wages and salaries	£20,000 million
Profits and rents	£ 5,000 million
Net property income from abroad	£ 2,000 million
Depreciation	£ 3,000 million

4. The country's gross national product is:
 A £22,000m
 B £25,000m
 C £27,000m
 D £30,000m

(AEB)

5. The country's net national product is:
 A £20,000m
 B £24,000m
 C £27,000m
 D £30,000m

(AEB)

6. Which of the following items would not be recorded in a country's national income accounts?
 A The purchase of a second-hand car.
 B The purchase of a new car.
 C The purchase of new books by a school.
 D The purchase of new books by a private individual.

7. Which of the following measures most accurately reflects the standard of living of a nation's population?
 A National income.
 B Gross national product.
 C Real national income.
 D Real national income per capita.

8. The data in the following table give details of the value of output of all stages of production for two industries.

	Industry 1 (£ million)	Industry 2 (£ million)
Extraction	100	30
Manufacturing	200	70
Retail sales	400	140

There are no materials brought in to the process except those obtained at the extraction stage. What is the combined value added of the industries?
 A £360m
 B £410m
 C £540m
 D £940m

9. Which of the following is a transfer payment?
 A Family Credit payments.
 B The salaries of firemen.
 C Government purchases for the Royal Air Force.
 D Rent collected from council house tenants.

10. The retail price index of a small country contains only three goods. Below the share of expenditure on each good and the price index for each good is given for two years.

Good	1990 price index	Weight in base year	1992 price index
Bread	100	40	140
Apples	100	25	150
Milk	100	35	120

The retail price index for 1992 is:
A 130
B 133.5
C 135.5
D 136.6

11. If the retail price index (RPI) for August stands at 265.4 and in the next month prices rise by 1 per cent then the RPI for September will be:
A 266.4
B 268.05
C 271.4
D 274.05

Answer key

Where there are four numbered alternatives

A	B	C	D	E
1, 2 and 3 Correct	1 and 3 Correct	2 and 4 Correct	4 only Correct	1 and 4 Correct

12. The data in the following table show figures for a country's national income and retail price index.

	1990	1991	1992
National income	£1,000m	£1,100m	£1,210m
Retail price index	100	105	115.5

From this we can say that:
1 Real national income rose over the three years.
2 Inflation fell between 1990 and 1991 and rose from 1991 to 1992.
3 Real national income remained the same between 1991 and 1992.
4 Real national income per capita rose between 1990 and 1991.

EXERCISES

1. The following figures are taken from the national accounts of Little Trivilvania for 1990.

	£ million
Consumers' expenditure	6,684
Exports	2,900
Imports	3,479
Gross domestic fixed capital formation	2,000
Taxes on expenditure	1,400
Subsidies	340
Capital consumption	1,200
General government final expenditure	1,845
Net property income from abroad	180

(a) Calculate GDP at market prices.
(b) If the average estimate for GDP at market prices is £10,160 million, what is the statistical discrepancy?
(c) What might cause this statistical discrepancy?
(d) Calculate GNP (average estimate).
(e) Calculate GNP at factor cost.
(f) Calculate national income.

2. The table shows the inputs and output of the industries of Little Trivilvania.

	Inputs		Total sales	Exports
	Domestic	Imported		
Primary sector	0	0	1,500	400
Manufacturing sector	1,100	300	1,900	300
Tertiary sector	1,600	100	2,400	200

Calculate national income by the output method by value added.

3. The table shows the national accounts (expenditure method) from two countries. Country A uses £ sterling, country B the dollar. Country A is a market economy using the UN standardized system of national accounts. Country B is a command economy and does not report spending on defence. In country B the consumption of alcohol is banned and none is legally produced within the country. The exchange rate is fixed at £1:$4.

	Country A (£)	Country B ($)
Consumers' expenditure	1,000	400
Government final consumption	400	400
Gross domestic fixed capital formation	200	100
Exports	250	40
Imports	200	30
Net property income from abroad	25	10
Taxes on expenditure	180	–
Subsidies	10	100
Capital consumption	120	10

(a) Calculate the reported national income of each country.
(b) Does converting the national income of country A into dollars give a fair comparison of the standard of living in both countries? What factors would you want to consider before making a comparison?

4. Which of the following would not be included in the national accounts of the UK?
(a) Old-age pensions paid by the government.
(b) The salary of a police officer.
(c) The value of goods sold at post offices.
(d) The value of home improvements carried out by a homeowner.
(e) The value of mushrooms picked wild from a meadow.

5. The table shows various indexes for Little Trivilvania over three years.

	Index of GNP	Index of RPI	Index of population
Year 1	100	100	100
Year 2	110	105	100
Year 3	121	110.25	100

(a) By how much did real GNP change between
(i) Years 1 and 2.
(ii) Years 2 and 3?
(b) Given your answer to (a), is it possible to say that the standard of living rose over this period of time?

6. The RPI of a country is calculated using the following weights for the commodity groups shown:

Food	0.2
Housing	0.35
Transport	0.15
Consumer durables	0.2
Entertainment	0.1.

If the RPI = 100 at the start of year 1:

(a) What will be the RPI at the end of the year following these price rises?

Food	12%
Housing	22%
Transport	5%
Consumer durables	−2%
Entertainment	16%

(b) The large rise in housing costs is attributable to a rise in the cost of home loan repayments. To what extent is your answer to (a) a fair reflection of the change in the standard of living of a person who rents his or her house?

DATA-RESPONSE QUESTIONS

1.

(a) (i) Using the table below on Economic Growth and Inflation Rates which of the 'Big Seven' OECD member countries achieved the best economic performance in terms of the criteria included in the table throughout the period 1980–83? [1]

(ii) Explain why you draw this conclusion. [1]

(b) (i) Which country achieved the greatest percentage *improvement* in growth rate over the four year period? [1]

(ii) Suggest **two** economic reasons for this improvement. [2]

(c) Compare the pattern of growth rates in the economies of Japan and West Germany. [2]

(d) (i) Which **one** of the countries listed suffered the highest rates of inflation during the period? [1]

(ii) State **two** major economic consequences of such inflation. [2]

(e) Consider the change in annual inflation rates in the period 1980–83 for total OECD economies. Suggest how government economic strategies are likely to have produced this change. [4]

[Total 14 *marks*]

(CAMBRIDGE LOCAL)

2.

(a) Using the bottom table on the General Index of Retail Prices explain briefly:

(i) the principle of weighting.

(ii) the principle of index numbers.

(iii) how the general index of retail prices is constructed. [9]

(b) The Price Indexes for Alcoholic drink and for Housing show the same increase from 15th January 1974 to 1983. However, this statement obscures significant differences between the items during the period. Explain these differences and suggest why they occurred. [8]

(c) Identify the significant trends evident from examining the table. [8]

(OXFORD AND CAMBRIDGE)

Economic Growth and Inflation Rates in Big Seven OECD economies 1980–83

Country	GNP/GDP growth (%)				Inflation (%)			
	1980	1981	1982	1983	1980	1981	1982	1983
United States	−0.2	2.0	−1.9	3.3	13.5	10.4	6.2	3.2
United Kingdom	−1.6	−1.9	2.3	3.5	18.0	11.9	8.6	4.6
Japan	4.2	3.5	2.9	3.0	8.0	4.9	2.6	1.9
West Germany	1.8	−0.4	−1.1	1.2	5.5	5.9	5.3	3.0
France	1.3	0.1	1.8	0.9	13.5	13.4	11.9	9.5
Italy	4.0	−0.5	−0.3	−1.5	19.0	19.3	16.5	13.0
Canada	0.0	2.8	−4.4	3.0	12.2	12.5	10.8	5.6
Average for 'Big Seven'	1.2	1.2	−0.4	2.5	11.9	10.0	7.0	4.3
Total OECD	1.3	1.1	−0.2	2.3	12.6	10.4	7.6	5.1

Source: *Barclay's Bank*

General Index of Retail Prices (15th January 1974 = 100)

	1974		1978		1983	
	Weights	Index	Weights	Index	Weights	Index
All items	1000	108	1000	197	1000	335
Food	248	106	233	204	203	309
Alcoholic drink	73	110	85	196	78	367
Tobacco	49	116	48	226	39	441
Housing	126	106	113	173	137	367
Fuel and light	58	111	60	228	69	465
Durable household goods	58	108	64	182	64	250
Clothing and footwear	89	109	80	171	74	215
Transport and vehicles	135	111	140	207	159	366
Miscellaneous goods	65	111	70	206	75	346
Services	53	107	56	192	63	343
Meals bought out	46	108	51	208	39	364

Source: *Monthly Digest of Statistics*

13 Money

In this chapter we will discuss:

1. What is money?
2. How banks can create money.
3. Monetary motorways – the definitions of money.
4. Money and the price level.
5. Why people choose to hold money.
6. The nature of government debt.

Introduction

Recall that in Part I of this book we saw that productivity depends on the division of labour, and that the division of labour leads to specialization of production. Specialization in production, together with a need for variety in consumption, means that goods must be exchanged. Exchange takes time and effort. The gains which accrue from the division of labour will therefore be increasingly offset by the time and trouble spent in exchanging what one produces for what one wants to consume. Improving the efficiency of exchange therefore not only saves time and effort spent in exchanging, but has the further advantage of permitting a greater division of labour and hence more production per worker.

As we have seen, the two main devices for improving the efficiency of exchange are **markets**, which centralize information on supplies and demands, and **money** (a 'medium of exchange'), which enables the efficient processing of information.

Almost any good could be used as a medium of exchange – we could, for example, use pins. The essential thing is that every buyer and seller must deal in the chosen good whatever that chosen good might be. But although any good is eligible as a medium of exchange, it would be wise when choosing one to bear in mind certain properties which an ideal medium of exchange would have.

Properties of money

The ideal properties of a medium of exchange can be deduced from a consideration of the functions it is to serve.

First, recall that the medium of exchange is to be traded for each and every other good in the market. If someone comes to market in order to exchange some bread for some cloth, it is first necessary to exchange the bread for money. The money is then held until it in turn is exchanged for cloth. There will be a period of time between having bread and having cloth during which the trader must hold money. This may be an appreciable period. It would be unfortunate, to say the least, if money lost value during that period. If, for example, we chose butter as our money and the butter deteriorated (became rancid) while we were holding it then we would get far less cloth for our bread than we had originally expected. People would therefore be reluctant to accept butter as money. It is desirable then for the good we choose as our medium of exchange to be durable. We want it to be durable in the sense that its value does not change over time. *Durability* then is the first property of a medium of exchange.

Second, recall that the medium of exchange must be capable of being used in exchange for something as valuable as a house and also for something as cheap as a box of matches. The good we choose must therefore have sufficient value to exchange for high-valued things like houses, and yet must be capable of being supplied in pieces of low enough value to exchange for boxes of matches. This is to say, the good must be divisible.

Clearly, all goods are divisible in the sense that they can be broken up into pieces or divided into parts, but the divisibility sought here is a special kind of divisibility. The good chosen as our medium of exchange must be divisible in a *value-preserving way*. Diamonds, for example, satisfy the durability condition mentioned above, have sufficient value to exchange for houses, and can no doubt be broken up into bits of very little value. But this divisibility is not a value-preserving kind. One large diamond weighing 10 grammes is worth a great deal more than the same weight made up of lots of tiny diamonds. So no one would want to break up a diamond in order to exchange parts of it for low-valued goods. A diamond could therefore be used as a medium of exchange only for deals involving goods of equal or greater value. Rather than impose these restrictions on the size of deals which our medium of exchange can be used for, it would be far better to choose a divisible good – a good which comes in high-valued sizes, but which can be divided up into many small pieces with each piece retaining its share of the original value. The second property of our medium of exchange is therefore *divisibility*.

This kind of value-preserving divisibility would be possible with wine. We could have a vat of wine equal in value to, say, either one suit of clothes or 10,000 boxes of matches. In exchange for the suit the whole vat is given up. But for a box of matches only 1/10,000th part of the vat need be given up. That 1/10,000th part of the vat is worth exactly 1/10,000th of the value of the whole vat. Furthermore, if that 1/10,000th part of wine were mixed back with the rest of the vat again, the value of the vat would return to its original value. Thus the wine can be divided into low-valued parts and recombined into high-valued quantities, and the value of the parts and of the whole is preserved. Wine is therefore divisible in a value preserving way and a possible candidate for the role of medium of exchange.

The trouble with using wine as our medium of exchange is that, although it is durable and divisible, it comes in different qualities. There are good wines and poor wines, and the quantity we have to give up in exchange for, say, a loaf of bread will depend on the quality of wine being offered. A small amount of a high-quality wine would be equivalent to a large quantity of poor-quality wine. Hence different-quality wines become different media of exchange. We would have not one medium of exchange but many media of exchange, and this rather defeats the original aim of simplifying things. It would be so much easier if we chose a good of uniform, invariate quality. Goods which have the same quality throughout are called homogeneous goods and this property is called homogeneity. If we want a single medium of exchange, we must therefore choose a homogeneous good.

There is another advantage of choosing such a good. In order to know the value of the wine being exchanged it is necessary to know both how much wine is on offer and its quality. Measuring quality is extremely difficult. A homogeneous good can be valued simply by measuring its quantity, and we have no need to go into the difficulties of judging its quality. Issues of quality are not easily resolved and are often matters of opinion. If we can avoid questions of quality and stick to valuing a good simply by measuring its quantity then we can be objective in our measurements. For example, the quantity of a good can be measured by weighing it, and weight is not a matter of opinion – it is a matter of fact. Thus homogeneity is a valuable attribute for any good which is to be used as a medium of exchange since it ensures that there is only one medium of exchange and that it can be measured by purely physical, objective methods. The third property of our medium of exchange is therefore *homogeneity*.

There is one further property which our chosen medium of exchange should possess. It is perhaps the least obvious of them all. We have been referring throughout this section to the 'exchange' of goods, but we have not yet spelled out what this means. The word 'exchange' can be used in two ways. In the first use of the word, a good is said to be exchanged when one person gives up possession of it and another person takes possession of it – the good is physically handed over. In the second use of the word a good is said to be exchanged when one person gives up the ownership of a good to someone else.

Buying and selling is about exchanging ownership and need not necessarily involve exchanging possession. You can own something without possessing it and you can possess something without owning it. A car hire firm, for example, owns its cars but does not possess them. Typically, the cars are in the possession of the firm's customers. Conversely, of course, the customers possess the cars but do not own them.

To continue the example, two customers could agree to swap cars. In this case there has been a change of possession – cars are exchanged – but there has been no change of ownership – both cars are still owned by the firm. Similarly, if the firm sold a car to the customer who had been hiring it then there would be a change of ownership with no change of possession. A change in ownership is therefore not always the same thing as a change in possession.

This distinction between ownership and possession turns out to be quite important because changes in possession are much more obvious than changes in ownership. It is fairly easy to find out who possesses a good – you can simply look and see who has it. What is not so obvious or easily demonstrated is ownership. Ownership is a legal matter and proof of ownership often involves producing a legal document, like a deed, and demonstrating its authenticity. This can be a lengthy and expensive business.

Since ownership is difficult to demonstrate, it follows that it is equally difficult to demonstrate a change of ownership. And since markets are there to facilitate changes of ownership, any difficulty about establishing who owns what would affect the working of the market.

In order to reap the maximum rewards from the market and from the consequent specialization of production it is therefore essential to solve the proof of ownership problem. The obvious answer is to say that ownership will be implied by possession. As far as the medium of exchange is concerned, if you possess it you are deemed to own it. This is what is meant by 'possession being nine points of the law'. We have already seen that possession and changes of possession can be easily demonstrated. Thus ownership of the medium of exchange can also be easily demonstrated.

Thus buyers come to market with their money. When they buy something they hand over some money. When the money has changed hands it immediately becomes the property of the seller and the deal is complete. There is no need for time-consuming legal wrangles or to produce proof of ownership. This identification of ownership with possession is therefore a neat and effective way of solving the proof of ownership problem.

The point is that traders must possess the medium of exchange and must take it with them when they go to market. In order to be taken to market the medium of exchange must be *portable*. There is little point in choosing, say, land as our medium of exchange. We may own several acres of land and land is clearly divisible, but we cannot take it with us to market. We cannot therefore possess it when we trade. In order to use it as a medium of exchange we would have to produce deeds and proof of authenticity. The good we choose as a medium of exchange should ideally be a good we can take around with us – a portable good.

All this means that when choosing our medium of exchange we should look for something which is durable, divisible, homogeneous and portable.

It is of course, impossible to find a good which satisfies all these requirements perfectly, but we can find goods which come fairly close to meeting them. The desired four properties are most obviously found in metals, and the most popular of the early media of exchange was gold. Gold does not rust or corrode (durability), it is soft and can be cut up and reconstituted (divisibility), it is more or less of uniform quality (homogeneity) and, though heavy, it can certainly be carried around (portability).

Metal can also be improved as a medium of exchange if, instead of having to be weighed every time it is exchanged, each piece of metal is pre-weighed and stamped with its weight. The weighing and stamping is done by the state (by the Royal Mint) and is called coining. The costs and difficulties associated with exchange are greatly reduced by this simple device of a coin and by equating possession to ownership. The exchange of possession of these pre-weighed pieces of metal is all that is needed to settle an account.

Functions of money

Having established the properties that money must possess, we now consider the functions that money must be able to perform.

We have already referred to the need for money to be a medium of exchange. Any medium of exchange must be generally acceptable in settlement of a debt. If this is so, workers are able to specialize in production and then exchange their produce for that of others.

The second function that money must be able to perform is that of a store of value. We have already discussed the need for money to be durable, but it is important that money does not lose value when held for long periods, even if it remains in the same physical state. In this sense cash has proved a poor store of value in recent years, since inflation has reduced the purchasing power of notes and coins of a given face value.

Some assets are very good stores of value – houses and shares, for example, tend to rise in value, protecting the owner against inflation. Unfortunately, houses and shares are not good at fulfilling the role of a medium of exchange and so do not count as money. There is therefore a trade-off between an asset being a medium of exchange and a store of value. This trade-off is summarized in the term 'liquidity', houses being one of the least liquid and cash being the most liquid asset. Liquidity is discussed further on page 233.

If an asset can fulfil both functions, those of a medium of exchange and a store of value, then it can be used as money. In addition, there are two further functions that it is desirable for money to fulfil: those of a unit of account and a standard of deferred payment.

A unit of account allows us to place a value on a good. Thus we can say one thing is worth £10 while another is worth £5, or we can say that last year we earned £5,000. In this way, we can measure different stocks and flows by the same unit of account.

When money is a standard of deferred payment it can be used for transactions that will take place in the future. When negotiating the contract to build a power station, for example, it is necessary to specify payments that will be made long into the future. If money cannot be used to specify such payments then the contract may never be undertaken as those who are giving their services will not know what it is they are to receive in payment. An economy that cannot embark on long-term capital projects will be a very poor society indeed.

Banks and money creation

As we have seen, one of the properties required of the good chosen as a medium of exchange is that it should be portable. We recall that portability is necessary since ownership is inferred from possession. If you possess the coin then you are deemed to own the coin. This clearly makes for swift and easy exchanges. The problem is, of course, that it is possible to gain possession of coins by theft. If a thief steals a car or a painting then it is possible to show that the car or painting actually belongs to someone else. But there is no way of identifying particular coins as belonging to a particular individual. Coins therefore present their owner with a security problem.

The solution to this problem led to a very important development in economics. The coins were deposited in safes and the depositors were issued with notes proving that they had the deposits of coins. The note would say something like '50 lbs of silver is held by A. B. Smith for B. T. Brown'. These notes bore the depositor's name, B. T. Brown, so that if the note was stolen the thief would have to prove that he or she was the person named on the note before being able to cash or exchange the note.

Depositors could use their coins by taking them out of the deposit and spending them. Whoever received them would usually redeposit them in the safe again until they were next wanted to buy something. Coins would therefore be moving into and out of the safes or deposits as their owners traded among themselves.

If owners of coins had no immediate plans to spend them, they could either leave them in the deposit or lend them to someone who wanted to buy something, but who was short of immediate funds. We have already seen that this lending attracts a reward called interest. Rather than let their coins lie idle for an appreciable time, owners of coins would therefore lend out at interest. The loan would, of course, eventually be repaid, but while it was in operation the lender would receive interest payments from the borrower. Some buyers were therefore buying goods with their own coins, while others were buying goods with borrowed coins (credit). Credit means that coins which otherwise would be idle are put to active use. Credit therefore helps to keep money circulating.

The credit multiplier

Now the story by no means ends here. It soon became clear to depositors that they need not actually withdraw coins from the deposit. They had a note promising that they held a deposit of so many coins. The note was proof of ownership and when they wanted to trade they could simply sign a note over to someone else in exchange for goods. Thus the ownership of coins could be changed by exchanging the note (appropriately signed over to the new owner) without the coins having to leave the deposit. This is clearly much more secure than drawing out coins, taking them to the market and then redepositing them. But it has other, far more important, ramifications.

The owners of the safes were banks. As it became more and more the custom to exchange notes rather than coins, the banks realized that the coins rarely left their safes. As far

Table 13.1 The credit multiplier

Round	New deposits (1)	Total deposits (2)	Active coins (3) = (2) × 0.1	Idle coins (4) = (1) − (3)
1	100	100	10	90
2	90	190	19	81
3	81	271	27	73
4	73	344	34	66
5	66	410	41	59
6	59	469	47	53
7	53	522	52	48
8	48	570	57	43
9	43	613	61	39
10	39	652	65	35
11	35	687	69	31
12	31	718	72	28
13	28	736	74	26
14	26	762	76	24
15	24	786	79	21
16	21	807	81	19
.	.	.	.	.
.	.	.	.	.
.	.	.	.	.
.	1	1,000	100	0
.	0	1,000	100	0

as the bankers were concerned, then, there were hoards of idle coins lying in their safes. Thus they could lend these coins out at interest. The owners of the coins were unaware of this activity so they did not complain; the borrowers received a loan so they were happy; and of course the bankers received interest on other people's deposits so they too were happy.

To see what this means, consider a numerical example. First, imagine that someone deposits 100 coins in a bank. When engaging in exchanges this person sometimes signs over notes and sometimes withdraws coin: 9 times out of 10 notes are signed over and 1 in 10 times coins are withdrawn. Therefore, of the 100 coins deposited only 10 are 'active' – only 10 of them are withdrawn, exchanged and then re-deposited by their new owner. Thus as far as the banker is concerned there are 90 coins which are permanently 'idle'. The bank therefore lends out 90 coins to borrowers. The borrower behaves in the same way as the original depositor: 90 coins are deposited with the bank and coins are withdrawn only for one in ten transactions. The bank therefore now has 81 idle coins. These 81 coins can be lent out to someone else, who can then again deposit the 81 coins at the bank.

This process continues with the amounts being loaned out decreasing by 10 per cent at every 'round'. This continuing reduction will eventually bring the process to a halt. When this is all complete the total amount of loans made will add up to the value of 900 coins, which together with the original deposit of 100 coins means that the medium of exchange has effectively been increased to 1,000 coins. And all this is because of an original deposit of 100 coins. The original deposit has been 'multiplied' tenfold simply because we choose to change ownership of our medium of exchange by note rather than by changing possession, and this is the operation of the **credit multiplier**.

The process is demonstrated in Table 13.1. In the beginning there is a deposit of 100 new coins from the mint. This is shown in column 1. Of these 100 coins, 10 are kept as liquid assets and 90 coins are lent out. These 90 coins are then redeposited in the bank and so in round 2 they turn up as new deposits. This is shown in column 2, row (round) 2. Of these 90 coins, 9 are retained as liquid assets and 81 are lent out. These 81 are then deposited in the bank and turn up in column 2. This process continues in an ever-decreasing manner until there are deposits of 1,000 coins. These deposits are used as a medium of exchange by drawing cheques on them. All of the newly issued 100 coins are in continuous use as a medium of exchange.

The central bank

Since notes were being used as a medium of exchange, it became wearisome to keep signing them over to other new owners. Notes therefore became depersonalized and were deemed to be owned by the person who possessed them – their bearer. Thus notes became as coins had been before them. They were printed in fixed denominations (£1, £5, £10, etc.) and the printing of them became the exclusive right of one bank – the central bank.

In the case of the UK the Bank of England is the central bank and issues notes for England and Wales. The Bank of Scotland prints its own notes for Scotland. Since the Bank of England is a creature of the state, it follows that its notes and coins are directly under state control.

Legal tender

Notes and coins are together called cash. These notes and coins carry face values which differ greatly from their intrinsic value. The value of the paper and ink contained in a £20 note is clearly far less that its £20 face value. Thus this kind of money, unlike the gold coins which preceded it, has no appreciable value in use; it only has value in exchange.

All citizens are prepared to accept the note, not because it has intrinsic value – it does not – but because they can be sure that they can exchange it for £20 worth of goods. They can be sure of this because cash (provided it is not in too bulky a form) is **legal tender**.

It is legal tender because citizens are required by law to accept cash in full and final payment of debt. A shopkeeper may in law refuse to take your watch in exchange for goods, but he or she cannot refuse to accept cash.

Cash is therefore a medium of exchange which has little or no intrinsic value but is accepted because it has the force of law behind it: it is therefore sometimes called **fiat money**.

Cheques

So cash is deemed to be owned by its possessor, its bearer. Thus the Bank of England £5 notes have the phrase 'I promise to pay the bearer on demand the sum of £5' printed on them.

This raises the same security problem as using gold, so notes and coins tend to be deposited in banks – the **commercial banks**, such as Barclays, Lloyds, Midland and Nat West. Again ownership can be changed either by writing a note to the bank or by withdrawing the notes and coins and giving them to someone else. By far the largest proportion of our exchanges are carried out by written instructions to the bank. We simply ask our bank to switch funds from one account (the buyer's) to another account (the seller's). This is done by cheques.

The net result again is that bankers see that they have a lot of idle notes in their vaults and they begin lending them out. This leads to deposit creation.

Deposit creation

Banks lend money by allowing some customers to draw cheques even before they have deposited any notes or coins in the bank. The bank has 'created a deposit'. It has allowed customers to act as if they had made deposits. The outcome of this is that not only is cash being used as a medium of exchange, but so are chequing accounts. The value of these chequing accounts is determined by the actual deposits of cash plus those deposits created by the banks. If one-tenth of our transactions are cash transactions and nine-tenths are by cheque then the banks can create 10 times as many deposits as the initial cash deposit. Thus the previous situation is almost exactly replicated with banks now holding cash, which is created by the central bank, and creating deposits (or chequing accounts) with its idle cash.

Chequing accounts are now part of our medium of exchange, and are therefore properly regarded as part of our money stock. But cheques are not cash, and nor are they legal tender: no shopkeeper is obliged by law to accept cheques.

Cash is controlled by the state and banks can create chequing accounts only up to some multiple of their cash holdings. So the state can effectively put an upper limit on the quantity of money in the economy (cash + the value of chequing accounts).

Definitions of money

The reason for having different definitions of money arises because of the very great difficulty we have in deciding what should count as money in our economy.

For example, there are deposit accounts and current accounts available at all banks. A current account is that account which is affected by cheques. In other words, cheques switch ownership in current accounts not in deposit accounts. Strictly, then, if cash is put into a deposit account it should not count as part of money stock since it is not available immediately as a medium of exchange. It can quickly be switched from a deposit to a current account (this takes a month at most) so it is *potentially* part of money stock. The same is true of building society deposits. People may or may not be able to write a cheque on their building society accounts, but they can get the cash out and use it quite quickly. The question is then: what do we count as money?

Should we count only cash and current accounts? Or cash, current accounts and deposit accounts? Or cash, current accounts, deposit accounts and building society accounts? Or all these plus national savings accounts, plus our holding of premium bonds, etc? To help overcome this problem, various definitions of money supply are allowed.

The narrowest definition in use is M0, described as the 'wide monetary base'. M0 includes all notes and coins in circulation outside the Bank of England plus banker's operational deposits at the Bank of England. The latter arise because on occasions the Bank of England may require banks to deposit money with them for the purposes of monetary control, presently 0.45 per cent of the banks' eligible liabilities (see Chapter 17).

In 1987 a series of measures of the money supply (see Table 13.2), apart from M0 which gradually include more and more financial assets, was introduced.

M1 is: notes and coins in circulation with the public plus private-sector sterling sight bank deposits (current accounts).

M2 is: notes and coins in circulation with the public plus private-sector non-interest-bearing sterling sight bank deposits; plus private-sector interest-bearing retail sterling bank deposits; plus private-sector holdings of retail building society shares and deposits and national savings bank ordinary accounts.

M3 is: M1 plus private-sector sterling time deposits; plus private-sector holdings of sterling certificates of deposit. (This measure was formerly called Sterling M3 (£M3) and has been an important indicator for monetary policy in the UK.)

M4 is: M3 plus private-sector holdings of building society shares and deposits and sterling certificates of deposit; minus building society holdings of bank deposits and bank certificates of deposit and notes and coins.

M4c is: M4 plus bank and building society deposits in foreign currencies.

M5 is: M4 plus holdings by the private sector (excluding building societies) of money market instruments (bank bills, Treasury bills, local authority deposits), certificates of tax deposit and national savings instruments (excluding Save As You Earn and other long-term deposits).

M0, M1 and M2 are 'narrow' measures of the money supply; M3, M4 and M5 are 'broad' measures. The number of measures of the money supply reflects uncertainty over exactly what constitutes money. The measures of the money supply reported here were introduced in 1987. The main change then was the recognition of the two wider measures M4 and M5. This was probably because in today's sophisticated financial markets what passes as a medium of exchange is growing.

However, the Bank of England has had great difficulty distinguishing between the data now that most current accounts attract interest and many building societies act like banks with cheque accounts. Thus the M1 and M3 measures were abandoned in June 1989 and M4c and M5 in February 1991. Because government monetary policy has previously placed great importance on some of these measures, you will find them still reported in a historical sense and discussed further in this book. However, only M0, M2 and M4 data will be published in the future.

Liquidity

There is no clear cut-off point between those of our assets which we regard as money or near money and those which are not money. Generally, a piece of land or a house would

Table 13.2 UK monetary aggregates, 1989

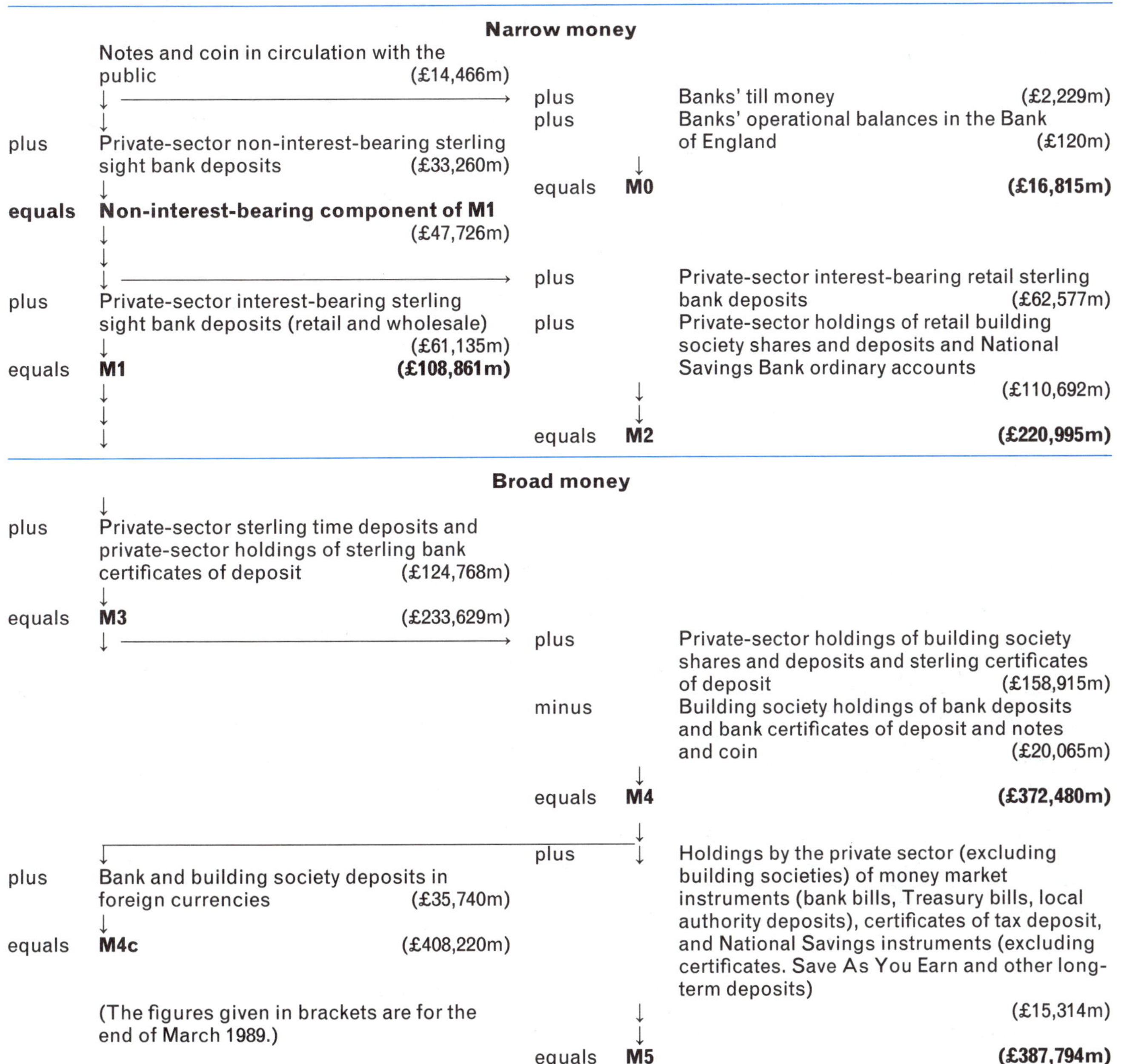

	Narrow money				
	Notes and coin in circulation with the public	(£14,466m)	plus	Banks' till money	(£2,229m)
			plus	Banks' operational balances in the Bank of England	(£120m)
plus	Private-sector non-interest-bearing sterling sight bank deposits	(£33,260m)	equals	**M0**	**(£16,815m)**
equals	**Non-interest-bearing component of M1**	(£47,726m)			
			plus	Private-sector interest-bearing retail sterling bank deposits	(£62,577m)
plus	Private-sector interest-bearing sterling sight bank deposits (retail and wholesale)	(£61,135m)	plus	Private-sector holdings of retail building society shares and deposits and National Savings Bank ordinary accounts	(£110,692m)
equals	**M1**	**(£108,861m)**	equals	**M2**	**(£220,995m)**
	Broad money				
plus	Private-sector sterling time deposits and private-sector holdings of sterling bank certificates of deposit	(£124,768m)			
equals	**M3**	(£233,629m)	plus	Private-sector holdings of building society shares and deposits and sterling certificates of deposit	(£158,915m)
			minus	Building society holdings of bank deposits and bank certificates of deposit and notes and coin	(£20,065m)
			equals	**M4**	**(£372,480m)**
plus	Bank and building society deposits in foreign currencies	(£35,740m)	plus	Holdings by the private sector (excluding building societies) of money market instruments (bank bills, Treasury bills, local authority deposits), certificates of tax deposit, and National Savings instruments (excluding certificates. Save As You Earn and other long-term deposits)	(£15,314m)
equals	**M4c**	(£408,220m)			
	(The figures given in brackets are for the end of March 1989.)		equals	**M5**	**(£387,794m)**

Sources: *Economic Progress Report* (August 1988); *Bank of England Quarterly Bulletin*.

not be regarded as 'money'. The property of being money is sometimes called **liquidity**. Liquidity has two distinct characteristics: firstly, the ease with which an asset can be converted into cash; secondly the certainty with which its cash value is realized.

Since notes and coins are already 'cash', they are perfectly liquid assets. Demand deposits (current accounts) are not cash but can be converted to cash fairly easily. Furthermore, the amount of cash which the account will yield is known with certainty. Demand deposits are therefore a very liquid asset. Time deposits (deposit accounts) are a little more difficult to convert into cash, but again there is absolute certainty about the amount of cash available. Time deposits are therefore quite liquid but not as liquid as demand deposits.

A house can be converted into cash, in the sense that it can be sold, but this is done only with great difficulty and the cash to be raised by the sale of the house is by no means certain. A house is therefore an asset, but a very illiquid asset, and hence would not usually be included in anyone's definition of money stock.

What we can say about money is that is comprises all those assets which are deemed to be actual or potential media of exchange. These are liquid assets and are created either by the state (cash) or by commercial banks and other financial institutions. The state can control the money supply either by controlling the amount of cash or by controlling the behaviour of the commercial banks and the financial institutions.

SUMMARY

1. Money is a 'medium of exchange' – its existence allows exchange to take place more easily.
2. The good chosen as money should be durable, divisible, homogeneous and portable.
3. Money must also fulfil the functions of a store of value, a unit of account and a standard of deferred payment.
4. Money can act as a medium of exchange either by being physically exchanged for goods, or by having its ownership registered to the supplier of goods.
5. This ability to register changes of ownership leads to a multiplication of the amount of money available to act as a medium of exchange.
6. If one-tenth of transactions use a physical exchange of money then the multiplication factor is ten.
7. The Bank of England (the UK central bank) now has the monopoly of supplying cash in the UK.
8. Cash has no intrinsic value, but it is accepted in return for goods because it is legal tender and has the force of law behind it. It is fiat money.
9. Cash is deposited in commercial banks (Barclays, Lloyds, Midland, Nat West, etc.)
10. These cash deposits plus those deposits 'created' by the commercial banks (loans) may be switched to other owners by issuing cheques.
11. There are many definitions of the money supply in use because many assets may be used as 'money'. The narrowest definition is M0; the widest is M5.
12. Many assets can be readily turned into cash, or into chequing accounts. Liquidity is the ability to be converted easily and quickly into a known amount of cash.
13. Each definition of the money supply has a slightly different level of liquidity.

Money supply and the price level

Attempts by the state to control money supply are the results of **monetary policy**, and we shall see later how such policy is conducted.

For the moment we shall assume that the quantity of money is perfectly controllable by the state and that we know precisely what it is. These may seem rather strong assumptions, but they will enable us to see the significance of money supply for the economy as a whole.

We should, however, keep in the back of our minds the knowledge that money supply is a somewhat vague concept and capable of only imprecise measurement. Our national accounts do of course attempt to measure it and report their estimates in the Blue Book, *Economic Trends* and *Monthly Digest of Statistics*.

To give some idea of the size and variation of the money supply consider Table 13.3. The quantity of money is a 'stock' concept rather than a 'flow' concept. Thus it is necessary to specify at which *point* in time the stock was measured. This is quite different from, say, income or expenditure which are flow concepts. For flows it is necessary to specify a time *period*, e.g. how much is spent in a week or a year.

The point in time referred to in Table 13.3 is a particular day in December. We can see that money supply at that time of year in 1990 was about £19 billion for the M0 definition and £490 billion for the M5 definition. Both measures have been rising steadily, but at different rates.

The quantity theory of money

The economic significance of the quantity of money in the economy extends beyond its role as an aid to exchange. Imagine an economy in which there are only firms and

Table 13.3 Size of the UK money supply, 1982–90 (£ million)

	M0	M5
December 1982	12,049	166,141
December 1983	12,766	187,779
December 1984	13,472	212,580
December 1985	14,095	239,365
December 1986	14,665	276,203
December 1987	15,338	319,207
December 1988	16,402	372,466
December 1989	17,334	439,787
December 1990	19,484	492,561

Source: *Economic Trends*.

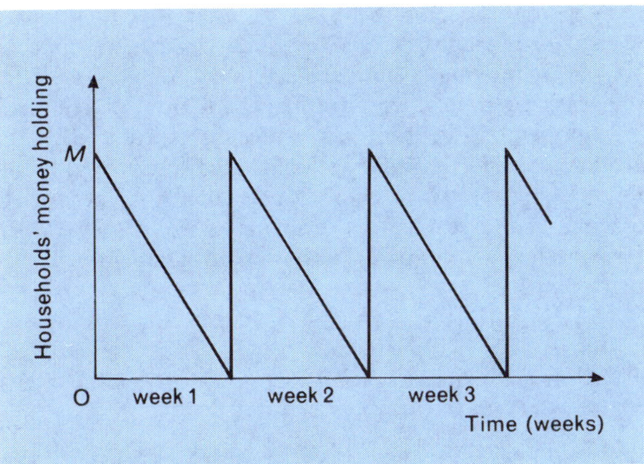

Figure 13.1 Households' money holding over time.

households. The firms hire workers and pay them every Friday. Over the following seven days the households buy goods from the firms so that all the money they received on Friday gradually finds its way back into the hands of the firms. The following Friday the firms then give all the money out again as wages. This process continues every week of the year (see Figure 13.1).

The total amount paid out on Friday is equal to the quantity of money in the economy (M_s). It is paid out 52 times every year, i.e. the money stock goes around the system 52 times every year. This is called the **income velocity of circulation** of money (V).

If the household receives £M_s, V times every year, then the annual income of households is £$M_s \times V$ per annum. Say, for example, that there are 100 million £1 notes in circulation. The weekly income of households would be £100 million, since they receive the notes every Friday from the firms. The annual income of households is therefore 52 × £100 million = £5,200 million i.e. $M_s \times V$.

This is the total income received by households and so it is **national income** (Y).

This national income is spent on the goods produced by the firms. Say the quantity of goods produced is Y_o. This is total production by all firms and hence is **national product**. Now let the average price of these goods be £P per unit. This means that the total *value* of goods produced (and sold) (**national expenditure**) will be $P \times Y_o$, i.e. the quantity of goods times their price.

Thus we have national income as being equal to money supply times the velocity of circulation ($M_s \times V$) and national expenditure as being equal to national output times price ($P \times Y_o$). Furthermore, since in the example all the income is spent, our national income equals national expenditure. Therefore:

$$M_s \times V = P \times Y_o$$

This is the quantity equation and is an important element in much modern economic policy, in particular the **quantity theory of money**. It simply says that the quantity of money (M_s) times its velocity of circulation (V) is equal to national output (Y_o) times the average level of prices (P).

Note that Y is sometimes replaced by T for transactions in the quantity equation, which then reads:

$$M_s \times V = P \times T$$

This is the form of the equation used by its original exponents, but for our purposes it does not alter the implications of the equation.

Inflation

Now M_s is, by assumption, precisely controlled by the state. V is not controlled by the state but is governed by custom. It is customary in this country to pay some workers weekly, other workers fortnightly and yet others monthly. If this pattern of payments remains fairly constant then we can say that V will remain fairly constant too.

This means that if money supply (M_s) is increased then either national product (Y_o) or average price level (P) must increase.

If we can show that national product is fixed by activity elsewhere in the economy, then the increase in M_s can only result in an increase in the average level of prices (P). Money supply would therefore be directly related to price level and doubling money supply would double all prices.

This is a very fundamental result: it says that the general (average) level of prices is a function of money supply. A continuing rise in the level of prices is called **inflation**, and control of inflation is one of the major economic objectives of the present government. This in turn means that the government will seek to control money supply. Thus inflation policy becomes monetary policy.

This all turns on the assumption that national output is fixed elsewhere in the economic system, and that the price level passively follows money supply, i.e. the price level is free to rise or fall in line with the quantity of money.

Cost-push inflation

An alternative approach would be to say that the price level is determined elsewhere in the economy. If wages are increased, or if oil prices increase, then industry's costs are increased. This will lead to an increase in prices whether or not money supply has increased.

If this is what happens then when $M_s \times V$ remains constant and P increases, Y_o must fall. National output and the level of employment will therefore decrease as prices are forced up by increased costs.

One reaction to this would be to say that any increase in costs should be matched by an equal increase in money supply. This would enable the economy to continue producing its existing level of output while meeting the higher costs and prices.

However, one way of discouraging these increases in costs would be to keep the money supply constant. This means for example, that any increase in wages which increased costs would result in higher unemployment. Thus workers are discouraged from pushing up wages by the threat of unemployment.

Two views

This gives rise to two seemingly diametrically opposed interpretations of economic policy. Those who see the need to control inflation as being paramount would argue that unemployment is being *caused* by unjustifiable money wage increases. It is therefore the responsibility of those who control money wage rates and lies outside the remit of the government.

On the other hand, those who see the maintenance of employment as paramount would argue that the government should match price increases in money supply. In other words, they should 'validate' these price increases. If unemployment occurs it is therefore as a direct result of restrictive monetary policy. This is within the control of the government and hence it is the government which must bear the responsibility for unemployment.

It is therefore possible for two economists to agree on the appropriate economic theory (the quantity theory of money) and to observe the same facts (costs, prices and employment levels), yet offer quite different interpretations and ascribe responsibility on the one hand to the labour force and on the other hand to the government.

What is clear from this is that there is some reason to suppose that the government can control, or at least influence, money supply. Furthermore, its attitute to money supply will influence the economy either by way of price level (inflation) or by way of national output, or perhaps by some mixture of the two. In a system in which the price level is perfectly flexible, changes in the money supply will affect only price level. These will have no effect whatever on output or employment. In a system in which price level does not respond to changes in money supply, changes in the money supply and/or changes in the price level will bring about changes in output and employment.

SUMMARY

1. The quantity equation says that the quantity of money (money supply) multiplied by the velocity of circulation (the number of times each year each pound is exchanged) must equal the value of national output.
2. The value of national output is equal to the real output multiplied by the aggregate price level.
3. The quantity equation is therefore: $M_s \times V = P \times Y_o$
4. If the velocity of circulation (V) is fairly constant then any change in the quantity of money (M) must result in either a change in price (P) or a change in output (Y) or some mixture of the two.
5. Some economists regard price as being much more flexible than output so that changes in money supply result in changes in price level. Inflation is therefore a result of having too much money in the economy.
6. Other economists argue that price level is determined largely by costs and not by money supply. This means that as prices rise, output will fall unless more money is supplied.

The demand for money

We have seen that money is a medium of exchange, and in the quantity theory of money it was assumed that all the money in the economy would be used as a medium of exchange. It would be 'active' money in that it would be constantly moving around the economy. The rationale for this was that anyone who had inactive money – idle money – would lend it out at interest rather than leave it idle. The economy's need for money (the demand for money) therefore depends only on how much money is needed to facilitate market exchanges. The quantity of money needed for this purpose is given by the quantity equation. Recall that:

$$MV = PY$$

where M is the quantity of money in circulation (i.e. active money)
V is its velocity of circulation
P is aggregate (average) price level
and Y is the level of national output.

Since this is the only demand for money it follows that any increase in money supply must change one of V, P or Y. With V and Y held constant, this upholds the monetarists' claim that increasing money supply increases the average price level. In other words *inflation is a monetary phenomenon*. It is caused by there being too much money.

There are, however, other views. In his *General Theory of Employment, Interest and Money* (1936), John Maynard Keynes offered two reasons why a rational person would hold idle money despite the loss of interest. The possibility that some money will be held in idle balances means that the strong link between money supply and price level no longer holds. An increase in money supply could simply be absorbed into idle balances. This would leave active balances, and hence price level, unchanged. It is therefore important to have some understanding of these other demands for money – the demands for idle balances.

The two types of idle balance described by Keynes were:

1. Precautionary balances.
2. Speculative balances

We will consider them in turn.

Precautionary balances

In a way these are the simplest to understand. In the quantity theory it was implicitly assumed that some time before they received their pay on Friday the households ran completely out of money. Casual observation suggests that this is rarely the case. There are unexpected calls on our funds and we have learned to keep 'a bit by', 'just in case'. Thus not all the money in the economy will be in circulation – a small amount will be held on to continuously as a precautionary balance. It is usually assumed that the amount actually held will depend on one's income. Those who regularly spend £100 per week may always have £1 in their wallets, whereas those who spend £200 would hold £2 in reserve.

Since this form of idle balance changes with income, it will not break the strong monetarist link between money supply and the price level. If money supply is doubled then it must be absorbed either into active, **transactions** balances or into **precautionary** balances. This means that price level must double since, by doubling, it will double both the active and the precautionary balances.

This result does not, however, carry over to the other form of idle balances.

Speculative balances

The monetarist argument against idle balances was that no rational person would allow his or her money to lie idle when it could be lent out at interest. To simplify matters assume for the moment that the only borrower of money is the government. Assume further that it borrows by issuing a particular type of bond. This bond is simply a piece of paper which entitles the bearer to receive a fixed sum of money each year from the government. By buying such a bond the holder of idle money would transfer the idle balance to the government and receive this annual payment (interest payment).

If the bond holder wished to stop lending money to the government then the bond could be sold. The government might or might not buy it back – it is under no obligation to do so. Were the government not to buy it back, the bond would have to be sold to someone else. Exchanges of this kind take place in the bond market.

Bonds such as we have described here are government consolidated stock (**consols**) and have a market price which is determined by the supply of and demand for them.

Say a consol carries the guarantee of £10 per year to the owner, and can be had on the market for £100. This means that a consol would yield a return of 10 per cent per annum (£10 for every £100 spent on bonds). In other words, the rate of interest is 10 per cent and it is this 10 per cent which would be forgone by holding idle balances.

But there is a problem with this. Say the government decides to issue a lot more consols. Each will yield £10 per annum and is 'sold' on the bond market. This is equivalent to increasing the supply of bonds and will, according to the usual laws of supply and demand, cause the market price of consols to fall. Say the price fell from £100 to £50. This would mean that a return of £10 per year can now be had for £50 rather than £100. The interest rate has therefore doubled to 20 per cent. In general, *as the bond price falls the interest rate rises in exact proportion*. If, for example, the bond price rose to £200 then the interest rate would be 5 per cent per annum.

It should be clear from this that as far as consols are concerned fluctuations in price are nothing more than the reciprocal of the fluctuations in interest rate. The market price of bonds is determined by supply and demand and hence so is the interest rate. What has this to do with idle balances? Well, if someone expects the price of bonds to fall (interest rates to rise) that person would be wise to sell the bonds he or she owns and to hold idle money until the bond price has fallen. The bonds can then be bought back at the lower price. Otherwise the person's £100 worth of consols could be reduced to £50 overnight by a doubling of interest rates.

This means that because interest rates (and hence bond prices) are liable to sudden changes it will sometimes pay to 'speculate' in the bond market. This is done by moving out of bonds and holding speculative balances of idle money when interest rates are expected to rise.

If many people expect interest rates to rise then there will be a large holding of idle money, but if no one thinks interest rates are going to rise then there will be no speculative holding of idle balances.

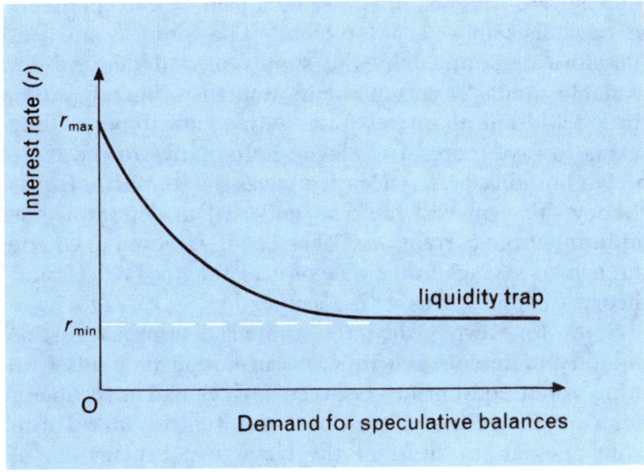

Figure 13.2 Demand curve for speculative balances.

Now Keynes argued that if interest rates were very low then quite a lot of people would expect them to rise so there would be a large demand for speculative balances of idle money. As interest rates increased then gradually more and more people would come to believe that further rises were unlikely. They would then switch back out of idle balances into bonds. Eventually the interest rate would be so high that no one would believe it could rise any higher. No one would demand speculative idle balances.

This relationship between the rate of interest and the demand for speculative balances is shown in Figure 13.2. The minimum interest rate (r_{min}) occurs where *everyone* expects the interest rate to rise, so everyone holds only idle money and no one holds bonds. The curve here is horizontal and is called the liquidity trap.

As the interest rate rises, the demand for speculative balances falls until finally, at r_{max}, everyone is holding bonds and no one is holding speculative idle balances.

This means that if there is an increase in the money supply *and* a fall in the interest rate, then some, or perhaps all, of that increased money supply could be absorbed into idle balances. It would have no effect on the active balance and hence no effect on price level.

Liquidity preference theory

We can combine the demand for idle balances with the demand for active balances to yield the total demand for money. This Keynesian approach to the demand for money is called **liquid preference theory**.

Notice that, according to this (Keynesian) view, the interest rate determines what proportion of our current assets we wish to hold as money and what proportion we wish to hold as bonds. As the interest rate falls, we switch out of bonds into money. We know that money is more liquid than bonds, so another way of expressing the Keynesian view is to say that the interest rate determines the level of liquidity we choose. This is a liquidity preference theory of the interest rate.

This is quite different from the classical account of the

interest rate. Interest, it was said, is paid by entrepreneurs to capitalists in return for loans. The interest rate was therefore determined by the supply of and demand for loanable funds. If entrepreneurs wanted to borrow more, they would bid up interest rates with a view to persuading savers to save more. The classical alternative to the Keynesian liquidity preference theory was the **loanable funds theory**. The interest rate was not used to determine the liquidity of the current *stock* of assets; it was used to equate the *flow* of savings to the *flow* of investment. The classical theory is explored further in Chapter 14.

Since, for Keynes, the interest rate is determined by this liquidity preference schedule, it can no longer be used to bring about equilibrium between savings and investment. Some other mechanism must be found. It is this mechanism which lies at the heart of the Keynesian explanation of output and employment. This will be dealt with in Chapter 14.

SUMMARY

1. The monetarist view is that money is used solely as a medium of exchange.
2. This means that any increase in the supply of money must be absorbed into the demand for active balances – the transactions balances.
3. In order to do this either output or price level must change. Output is unlikely to change and so price level changes. Therefore money supply affects price level and only price level.
4. The interest rate is determined by the supply of loanable funds (saving) and the demand for loanable funds (investment) and is the mechanism for matching saving to investment.
5. The Keynesian view is that money is used not only as a medium of exchange, but also as a store of value – a way of holding wealth.
6. When used as a store of value it is idle rather than active.
7. Idle money balances are held principally for speculative reasons.
8. Their riskiness robs bonds of some of their liquidity, and it is this which has to be compensated for by the interest payment. In order to persuade people to give up the liquidity of money it is necessary to pay them interest. The more liquidity they give up, the higher will be the interest rate.
9. If money supply is increased then some of it will be used as a medium of exchange (active money) but some will be used as a store of value (idle money).
10. The division between these two uses is rather complicated, but essentially the price level is unlikely to increase since the money will be absorbed into idle balances and the interest rate will take whatever value is necessary to achieve this absorption.
11. In the liquidity trap, any amount of money can be absorbed with no change in the interest rate.
12. The interest rate is determined by the liquidity preference schedule, so it can no longer be used to bring about the equilibrium between savings and investment. A different mechanism exists, which is at the heart of Keynesian output and employment analysis.

Appendix: Public debt

In this appendix we shall look at how public debt is made up. As we have seen the government can decide how to hold its debt and one of the choices it has is to issue more cash. Even if the government decides to issue bonds this will affect the rate of interest and therefore also decisions on money holding.

The composition and size of public debt therefore have a significant effect on the money supply and the demand for money.

Central government debt

Recall that, in the past, governments have tended to spend more than their income, i.e. they have conducted their fiscal policy in such a way that they have had budget deficits. Over the years these deficits have accumulated and now constitute the national debt. The size of the debt clearly depends on what the government does in its annual budget. If it decides to overspend some more then the national debt will continue to grow. If, however, the budget is in surplus (income exceeds revenue) then the debt will be reduced.

The size of the central government debt therefore depends on past and present fiscal policies. In 1987 it stood at about a quarter of UK gross domestic product: central government debt was about £106,000 million and the interest paid on it was about £11,000 million.

Table 13.4 gives the recent figures for the central government borrowing requirement.

Rules versus discretion

We should bear in mind that reliable data are not quickly available. It takes some time to collect, collate and publish data, and those which are published quickly are still out of date (being at least 3 months old) and are also the least accurate because they have been assembled quickly.

Control of the economy is made difficult (some would say impossible) by this lack of accurate up-to-date information. This has led some monetarists (Milton Friedman in particular) to argue against the government attempting to control the economy through monetary policy at all.

Monetary policy is discretionary action taken by the authorities to control the quantity of money in the economy, and it is against the word 'discretionary' that Milton Friedman is reacting. The authorities, Friedman claims, have insufficient information to exercise such dis-

Table 13.4 UK central government borrowing requirement, 1984–90 (£ million)

1984	10,160
1985	11,804
1986	8,461
1987	4,059
1988	−4,933
1989	−5,135
1990	−4,605

Source: *Monthly Digest of Statistics.*

cretion beneficially, and should instead be obliged to follow certain simple rules.

This is the 'rule versus discretion' debate. The simple rule suggested by Friedman is that money supply should be increased at a steady, predetermined, annual rate and should not be open to any interference by the authorities. The annual rate would be in line with the rate of real economic growth, so that the money supply would just match the increasing demand for transactions balances. These objections notwithstanding, the government still has to finance its expenditure and decide how best to do so.

Public-sector borrowing requirement

The central government borrowing requirement (CGBR) is not the same thing as the **public-sector borrowing requirement (PSBR)**. The public sector includes not only central government but also the local authorities (LAs) and the public corporations (PCs). Local authorities, such as Hampshire County Council, and public corporations, such as British Rail, also run budget deficits and surpluses. These too are part of the PSBR.

Table 13.5 shows values for these three elements of the PSBR over the past few years.

It is clear that there have been significant changes with central government moving from current deficit to surplus since 1988. The PSBR has generally followed the CGBR, but local authority borrowing has had a significant influence, as have privatization proceeds which are included in the calculation as negative debt (i.e. a repayment).

A boom in tax receipts and the large privatization proceeds led the government to spend far less than it received between 1988 and 1991. When this causes the PSBR to become negative the government is repaying debt and the PSBR then becomes the public-sector debt repayment (PSDR).

Public-sector debt

These PSBR figures show the additions to the public-sector debt each year. Rather confusingly, this accumulated debt (like the central government debt) is also sometimes referred to as **national debt**.

In 1987 the total public-sector debt was about £172,000 million, which is about 42 per cent of UK GDP in that year. This public-sector debt has to be held by someone in some form or another. There are many possible types of holder and many possible forms of debt. Public authorities borrow from different sources (banks, private citizens and foreigners, for example) and issue several different types of security (Treasury bills, consols, etc.), so the debt is composed of different securities (assets) held by different lenders. It is the intentional changing of the composition of this debt which constitutes monetary policy.

Cash

Part of this borrowing is financed by the issue of notes and coin. The public sector pays for its overspending by simply printing new notes and minting new coin and spending them. Notes and coin are therefore part of government debt. But they are special in that they can be issued without having to pay interest and without having first to persuade investors to accept them. This non-interest-bearing government debt is called cash.

Non-marketable debt

A second part of public-sector borrowing is the issue of National Savings Certificates. These are issued to particular individuals who have been persuaded to buy them because of the return offered (e.g. they yield interest and, on occasion, are indexed to keep pace with inflation). Once

Table 13.5 UK public-sector borrowing requirement, 1984–90 (£ million)

	CGBR	*LABR*	*PCBR*	*PSBR*
1984	10,160	470	550	10,240
1985	11,804	3,379	905	7,520
1986	8,461	5,192	995	2,273
1987	4,059	4,664	831	−1,436
1988	−4,933	4,223	2,712	−11,868
1989	−5,135	1,994	2,181	−9,310
1990	−4,605	−3,152	609	−2,062

Note: Minus signs denote a surplus of income over expenditure. Privatization proceeds mean figures do not sum.
Source: *Monthly Digest of Statistics.*

issued, however, they are not transferable – there is no market for National Savings Certificates. Hence this part of government debt is called non-marketable debt. The distinction between marketable debt and non-marketable debt is important since, as we have said, it is by entering the market for government debt and changing its composition that the authorities seek to conduct monetary policy.

Bills and bonds

A third part of public-sector borrowing is the issue of marketable debt like **Treasury bills** and **consols** (consolidated stock).

Treasury bills are sold on the open market at whatever price they will fetch. They are commitments by the government to give the owner of the bill a fixed sum of money (£10,000) on a particular day. The bills have a life of 91 days, so that 90 days after the day they were issued they are redeemed for their promised face value. During those 90 days they can be bought and sold on the open market and can be bought back by the government if it so wished. (Some Treasury bills have a life of only 63 days, but 91 days is more normal.)

Consols, on the other hand, have infinite lives: that is to say, the government is not obliged to buy them back at all. They are not commitments to pay one fixed sum on a particular day, but rather are commitments to pay a fixed sum once a year for as long as the consol is held. The government raises money by selling consols on the open market, again at whatever price they will fetch. They could, of course, be bought back by the government if the government so wished, but the government is not obliged to buy them.

Budgets

Thus the government has to finance the public-sector borrowing requirement and it may do so by issuing cash, non-marketable debt like National Savings Certificates, and marketable debt like Treasury bills and consols.

In the case of a public-sector surplus some of this debt has to be withdrawn – either the quantity of cash or the quantity of marketable debt has to be reduced.

In the case of a balanced budget there is still scope for monetary policy since the composition of debt still outstanding may be changed. The government could, for example, buy some consols with some newly printed cash, thereby moving from illiquid to liquid debt, or it could sell some Treasury bills and use the proceeds to buy some consols, thereby moving from liquid to illiquid debt – 'funding'. Neither change would alter the total level of public-sector debt.

The trend towards surpluses in the public sector is in part a reflection of the view that good housekeeping requires expenditure not to exceed income. It is also a result of the increased importance attached to monetary policy. If the public sector runs a deficit then new debt must be issued and this rather ties the hands of the policy makers. If it is issued as liquid debt then it will increase money supply and is, according to the monetarists, inflationary. If it is issued as illiquid debt then it will push up interest rates; this pushes up costs and is again inflationary.

It is not only the inflationary aspect which disturbs many modern politicians. As government expenditure rises, the government becomes a bigger and bigger influence on the economy. This 'big government' is thought by many to be politically dangerous in that it gives too much power to the state. Moreover, the higher interest rates discourage private investment and so 'crowd out' private investment to make room for government spending. They therefore argue for a small public sector and a balanced budget.

SUMMARY

1. Data available to the government are unreliable and refer to the past rather than to the present.
2. Some economists therefore argue that monetary policy involving the exercise of discretion by the authorities should not be attempted.
3. The public-sector borrowing requirement (PSBR) is made up of borrowing by the central government, local authorities and public corporations. When these three together have more than enough revenue to meet their expenditures they pay off some of their accumulated debt and the PSBR becomes the PSDR – the public sector debt repayment.
4. The PSBR is financed by a combination of:
   (a) Cash – printing the extra money required.
   (b) Non-marketable debt, such as National Savings Certificates.
   (c) Bills and bonds, such as Treasury bills and consols, that may be bought and sold on the open market.
5. Running a balanced budget does not mean that there is no scope for monetary policy: the composition of existing outstanding debt can be altered from more liquid to less, or vice versa.

Exam Preparation and Practice

MULTIPLE-CHOICE QUESTIONS

1. The table shows details of the money stock for a country for a particular year.

	£ million
Notes and coins in circulation	12,000
Bankers' operational deposits at the Bank of England	2,500
Commercial bank current accounts in sterling	47,000
Commercial bank deposit accounts in sterling	63,000

Assuming the data in the table to be complete, what is the value of the M1 definition of the money stock?
A £14,500m **C** £61,000m
B £59,000m **D** £124,000m

2. Commercial banks ensure they keep at least 5% of their deposits as cash. On receipt of a new cash deposit of £100 the maximum additional deposits a bank will feel able to create will be:
A £105 **C** £2,000
B £1,000 **D** £20,000

3. All banks use a cash ratio of 10%. A customer of Bank X writes a cheque for £1,000 payable to a customer of Bank Y. When the cheque is paid into Bank Y the effect on the banking system will be to
A increase assets by £1,000.
B increase loans by £9,000.
C reduce assets and liabilities by £10,000.
D leave assets and liabilities unchanged.

(AEB)

4. If expectations about the future level of interest rates change so that rates are generally expected to fall, the demand for money will:
A Rise as people hold greater speculative balances.
B Fall as people hold lower speculative balances.
C Fall as people hold lower transactions balances.
D Rise as people hold greater precautionary balances.

5. The income velocity of the circulation of money is constant at 5. If the money stock rises from £200 million to £300 million and the level of output remains static at £1,000 million, the average price level must rise to:
A £1 **C** £2
B £1.50 **D** £2.50

6. Of the following, which will necessarily cause the PSBR to rise?
A An increase in the borrowing of British Rail.
B A balance of trade deficit.
C A fall in the rate of interest.
D An increase in bank lending.

Answer key

Where there are three numbered alternatives

A	B	C	D	E
1, 2, 3 Correct	1, 2 Correct	2, 3 Correct	1 Correct	3 Correct

Where there are four numbered alternatives

A	B	C	D	E
1, 2 and 3 Correct	1 and 3 Correct	2 and 4 Correct	4 only Correct	1 and 4 Correct

7. Which of the following features must money possess?
1 Easily carried to the point of transaction.
2 Made from precious metal.
3 Acceptable in all countries.
4 Acceptable in settlement of debt.

8. Which of the following can fulfil the functions of money?
1 Gold.
2 Cheques drawn on a commercial bank.
3 Shares in ICI.

9. Which of the following are included in the money supply definition M4?
1 Notes and coins.
2 Private-sector sterling time deposits.
3 Private-sector holdings in building society share accounts.
4 Private-sector holdings of bank deposits in foreign currencies.

10.

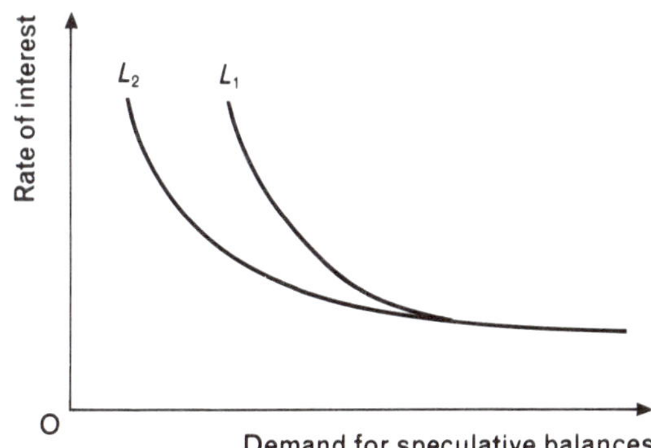

Where wealth can be held only as money or bonds, the movement of the liquidity preference schedule from L_1 to L_2 will, *ceteris paribus*, cause:
1 A rise in the rate of interest.
2 An increase in the holding of idle balances.
3 A larger liquidity trap.
4 A greater holding of bonds.

EXERCISES

1. For each of the following items state if it has all of the necessary properties to be a medium of exchange:
(a) Blackcurrant jam.
(b) Cows.
(c) Walnuts.
(d) Sea shells.
(e) Iron.

2. If commercial banks are required to keep 10 per cent of their assets in the form of cash, what would be the effect on the money supply of each of the following?
(a) A new deposit of £100 cash with a commercial bank.
(b) The imposition of a fine, payable in cash, on a commercial bank by the Bank of England of £10,000.
(c) A change in the law so that commercial banks are required to keep $12\frac{1}{2}$ per cent of their assets as cash.

3. From the data provided calculate:
(a) M0.
(b) M1.
(c) M3.

	£m
(i) Bankers' operational deposits at the Bank of England	4
(ii) Private-sector time deposits	412
(iii) Private-sector sterling sight deposits (non-interest bearing)	120
(iv) Notes and coin in circulation with the public	25
(v) Private-sector holdings of sterling certificates of deposit	100
(vi) Private-sector sterling sight deposits (interest bearing)	90

4. Arrange the following assets in order of liquidity, placing the most liquid first:
A Ford Fiesta.
£500 in a current account at Lloyds bank.
£500 in £10 notes.
A local authority bond with 90 days to run.
Shares in Eurotunnel plc.
£500 in National Savings Certificates.
A loan to your brother and his wife for their house deposit.

5. The quantity theory of money states that $MV = PY$. If $M = 100$, $V = 2$ and $Y = 50$:
(a) What is the average price level?
(b) If V and Y are fixed, what is the consequence of allowing the money supply to double?
(c) If V is not fixed, what are the consequences of a doubling of the money supply for the price level?

6. How would you expect each of the following events to affect: (i) transactions demand for money, (ii) precautionary demand for money and (iii) speculative demand for money?
(a) A rise in the level of money income.
(b) A fall in the rate of interest.
(c) A rise in the rate of interest, but to a level still below the liquidity trap.
(d) A change in expectations so that a fall in the rate of interest is now expected.

14 The determination of national output

In this chapter we will discuss:

1. What determines the level of income, output and employment.
2. The view that governments can manipulate the level of prices and output.
3. The conflicting view that the market decides on the level of prices and output.
4. The cause of business cycles.

Introduction

National output is the sum of the outputs of all the firms in the economy. The determination of national output might then be thought of as involving no more than adding up the outputs already determined at the microeconomic level, i.e. at the level of individual firms. However, there is more to it than that. Many factors bearing on the determination of national output become apparent only when the whole economy is considered as a unit. Nevertheless a good starting point is the kind of explanation offered by microeconomics.

At the microeconomic level, decisions on how much to produce are taken by entrepreneurs. These decisions are therefore governed by the need to maximize profits. In the short run, capital stock is assumed to be fixed and the entrepreneur has to decide how much to produce with a particular level of capital stock. This is tantamount to deciding how much labour to employ, since with fixed capital stock the only way to increase output is to employ more labour. In other words, *there is a direct relationship between output and employment*. As output increases so will employment, but because of the law of diminishing returns each successive increase in employment leads to smaller and smaller increments in output.

This relationship between employment and output is carried over from microeconomics to macroeconomics – to the aggregate of all firms. It is called an *aggregate short-run production function*. Figure 14.1 shows such a function.

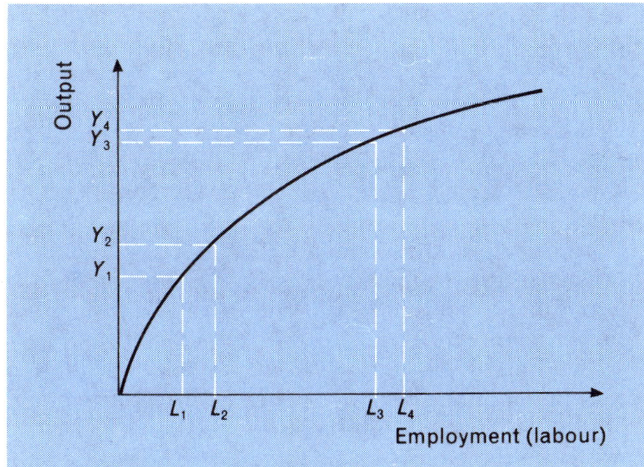

Figure 14.1 Aggregate short-run production function.

At each level of employment (L_1, L_2, L_3 and L_4) there is only one level of output (Y_1, Y_2, Y_3 and Y_4). Therefore deciding output is the same thing as deciding employment in the short run. Notice that, because of diminishing returns, increasing employment from L_1 to L_2 causes a larger increase in output than does increasing employment from L_3 to L_4. This will be important to the models of national income determination that we will examine in this chapter. You should remember that when a change in 'national income' or 'national output' is referred to, this will imply a corresponding change in aggregate employment.

The Keynesian view of the determination of national output

Aggregate demand

In his book *The General Theory of Employment, Interest and Money*, Keynes argued that the most important determinant of national output was how much could be sold. In other words, the quantity of output will be *demand determined*. The level of demand in the economy as a whole is known as **aggregate demand**. To determine the level of output it is first necessary to calculate the level of aggregate demand. This will determine how much is produced and this in turn will determine the level of employment (see the aggregate short-run production function in the previous section.) To investigate this concept further we need a simple model of the economy and we shall return to the one proposed in Chapter 12.

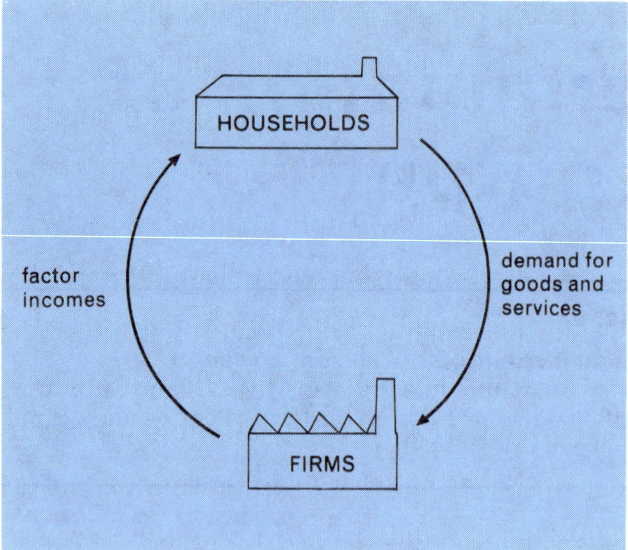

Figure 14.2 Circular flow of income.

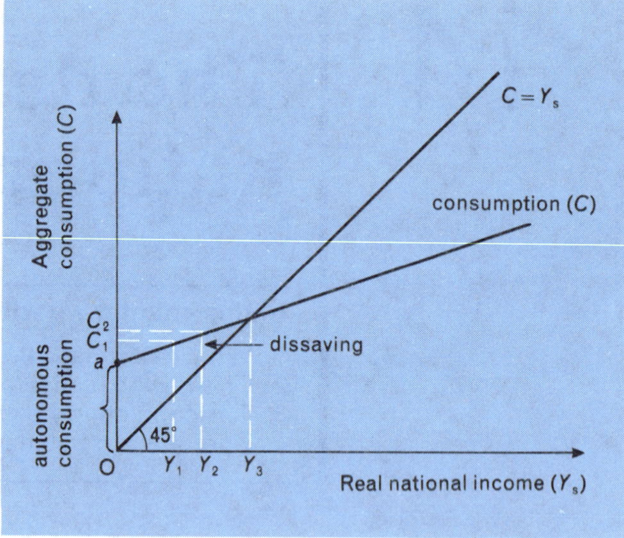

Figure 14.3 Consumption function.

A two-sector model of the economy

In Chapter 12 we saw how we could characterize the economy as having just two sectors, households and firms. (For now we are assuming away governments and overseas trade, but we will bring them in later.) Households own all the factors of production and firms produce all the goods and services. Households therefore supply firms with factor services and buy goods and services from them.

As goods and services flow from firms to households there is an equal and opposite flow of payments from households to firms. Similarly, the flow of factor services from households to firms attracts an equal and opposite flow of payments from firms to households. These flows of payments between households and firms constitute the circular flow of income and this is shown in Figure 14.2.

In this simple model there are two possible sources of demand and together they make up aggregate demand. They are the demand by households for consumer goods (C) and the demand by firms for investment goods (I). In this model, the total (aggregate) demand in the economy Y_d is therefore the sum of consumption demand (C) and investment demand (I). We can write this in a shorthand manner as:

$$Y_d = C + I \tag{14.1}$$

Our next task is to discover what determines C and what determines I, and thereby to discover the level of aggregate demand in the economy.

Consumption

According to Keynes, the demand for consumer goods will depend primarily upon consumers' income. National income, in this simple model, is equal to national output, which in a closed economy is equal to aggregate supply (Y_s) (see Chapter 12). So we can use the term Y_s to mean national income or national output.

Keynes argued that as income (Y_s) increased then so would expenditure on consumer goods, i.e. the more people earned, the more goods they would demand. But the increase in consumption spending would not be as great as the increase in income because some of the extra income would be saved. This relationship between C and Y_s is shown in Figure 14.3.

You will note that the line C, which is called the **consumption function**, does not begin at the origin, but at point a on the consumption axis. This is because when income is zero households will still demand goods in order to live. The consumption that takes place when income is zero is called **autonomous consumption** and will be financed by using up savings (dissaving) or current borrowing.

As income (Y_s) rises, so does consumption (C), but not at the same rate. If consumption did rise at the same rate as income then the consumption function would run parallel to the 45° line from point a, implying that for every extra £1 earned £1 is consumed. In fact the slope of the consumption function is shallower than the 45° line, reflecting the fact that for each extra £1 of income consumers spend only part of it. In Figure 14.3, as income rises from Y_1 to Y_2 then consumption rises from C_1 to C_2. At income Y_2 consumers are still consuming more than they are earning – they are still dissaving. Consumers continue to dissave until income reaches Y_3, at which point consumption equals income. Beyond Y_3 income exceeds consumption so consumers are saving.

The slope of the consumption function is of interest to us. The steeper the line, the larger the proportion of extra income that is consumed. Consider the two consumption functions in Figure 14.4.

When income rises by £100 the shallower of the two consumption functions (C_1) indicates that consumption rises by £60. As the consumption function (C_1) has the same slope throughout its length, every time income rises by £100, £60 will be consumed and £40 saved. In other words, 60 per cent of any increase in income is consumed and the rest is saved. If the steeper consumption function

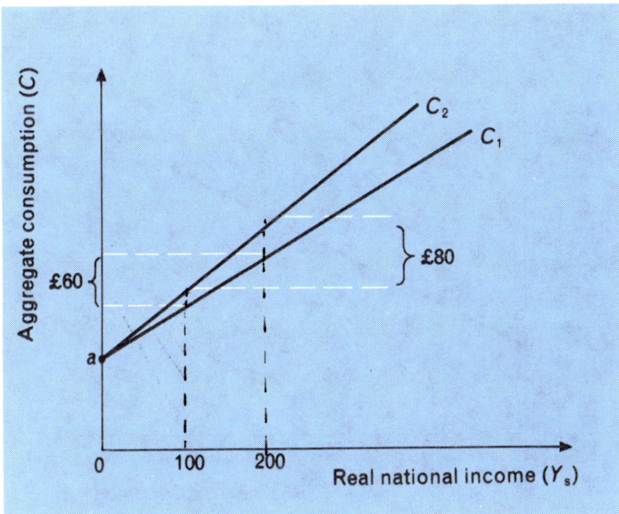

Figure 14.4 The slope of the consumption function and the marginal propensity to consume.

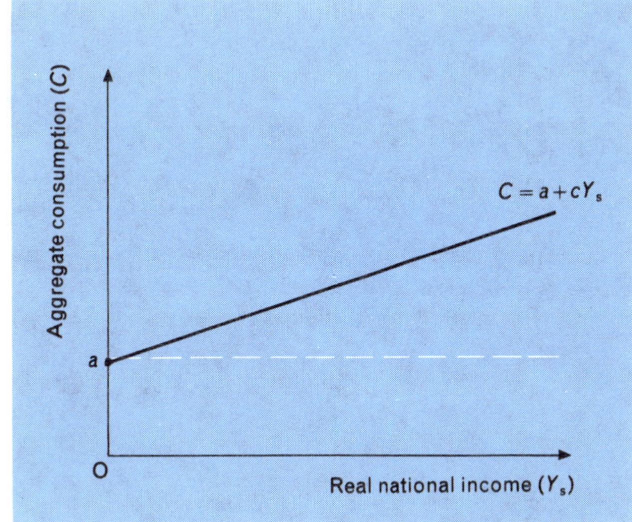

Figure 14.5 Effect of autonomous consumption on average and marginal propensities to consume.

(C_2) rules then a rise in income by £100 leads to a rise in consumption of £80. Thus when income rises, 80 per cent of the increase is consumed and 20 per cent is saved.

The slope of the consumption function therefore determines how much of extra income is consumed and how much is saved. The technical term for the increase in consumption per extra £1 of income is the **marginal propensity to consume (MPC)**.

In Figure 14.5 we show a consumption function which indicates that autonomous consumption is a and that the slope of the consumption function (the MPC) is c. For a given level of income, then, consumption is the sum of a and c per cent of income. Thus:

$$C = a + cY_s$$

Thus if a = £200 and $c = 0.5$, then when income (Y_s) is £500 consumption is:

$$C = 200 + 0.5(500) = 200 + 250 = £450$$

You will note from this that only £50 is saved, not £250. This is because of the autonomous consumption a. So the average amount of income consumed, the **average propensity to consume (APC)**, is not the same as the marginal propensity to consume in this case.

Marginal propensity to consume can be defined as:

$$\frac{\text{Change in consumption}}{\text{Change in income}} \quad \text{or} \quad \frac{\Delta C}{\Delta Y_s}$$

whereas the average propensity to consume is:

$$\frac{\text{Total consumption}}{\text{Total income}} \quad \text{or} \quad \frac{C}{Y_s} = \frac{a + cY_s}{Y_s} = \frac{a}{Y_s} + c$$

So in the case of the example above, if Y_s rises by £100, from £500 to £600, then the change in total consumption is equal to £50, i.e. £100 × 0.5.

The marginal propensity to consume is:

$$\frac{\Delta C}{\Delta Y_s} = \frac{50}{100} = 0.5$$

The average propensity to consume is:

$$\frac{C}{Y_s} = \frac{500}{600} = 0.83$$

You will notice that the MPC has remained unchanged at 0.5, but this is not true of the APC. When income was £500 the APC was much higher:

$$\frac{450}{500} = 0.9$$

That is to say, when income is £500, 90 per cent of income is consumed on average, but as income rises to £600 only 83 per cent of income is consumed on average. Thus the average propensity to consume falls as income rises, but the marginal propensity to consume remains the same.

The UK consumption function

We can look at the data on consumption and saving for an economy. Some data for the UK are shown in Table 14.1. The data used for income are disposable income: that is, income which households are free to spend as they wish. The taxes and other deductions they must pay have been excluded from this figure. This is more accurate than using

Table 14.1 UK disposable income, 1950–1990 (£ million)

Year	1950	1955	1960	1965	1970	1975	1980	1985	1990
Disposable income	69,838	79,585	94,239	110,359	122,123	142,629	160,620	241,362	378,854
Consumption	68,629	76,743	87,675	100,389	111,168	124,824	136,890	217,941	345,958

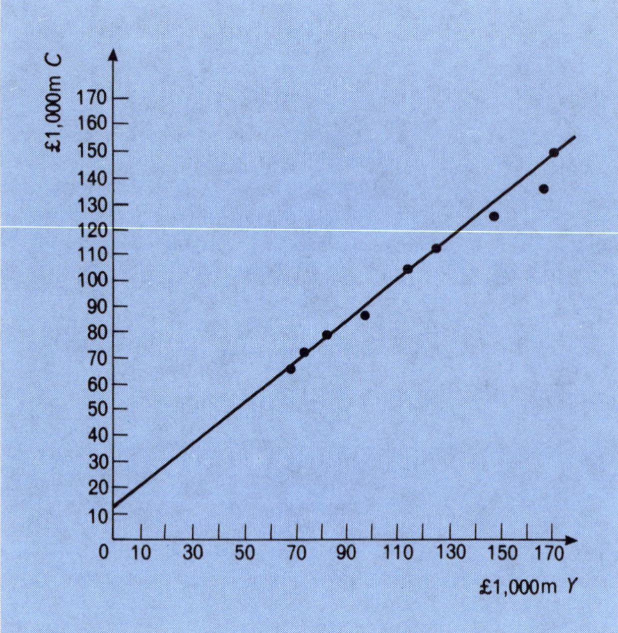

Figure 14.6 UK consumption function.

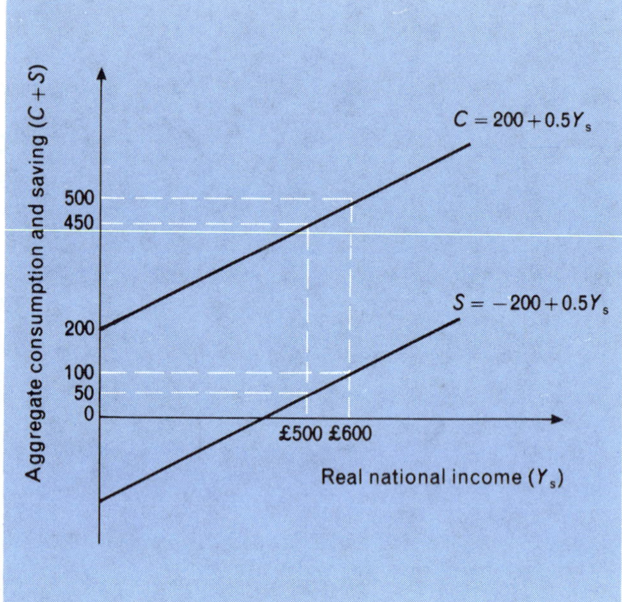

Figure 14.7 Consumption and savings functions.

data for gross income because people make consumption decisions on the basis of the income they actually have available to spend. The figures shown are in millions of pounds, but corrected for inflation so that they are 'as if' the price level had remained constant at its 1980 level.

The data from 1950 to 1980 in Table 14.1 are also represented in Figure 14.6. (After 1980 there is a slight change in the relationship and so we have left this out of Figure 14.6. This is not unusual – we would expect a slight change over a period of 40 years, especially at a time of high inflation.) From the diagram the level of autonomous consumption (a) is equal to £11,000 million and the marginal propensity to consume (c) is 0.82. Not all of the observations fall precisely on the line, but there is some strong evidence here for the Keynesian proposition that consumption does indeed depend on income and increases as income increases, but not by as much.

Saving

If income is not consumed then it is saved (S). The amount of saving can be found from the consumption function. You will recall that when income is zero households will still consume some goods (autonomous consumption) and that this will be financed out of savings or from borrowing (from other people's savings). Thus we know that when national income is zero saving is equal to $-a$.

As income rises then a proportion, c, is consumed. The rest is saved and we can call this proportion s, the marginal propensity to save (*MPS*). As income is either consumed or saved, the *MPC* plus the *MPS* account for all of income. Therefore:

$$MPC + MPS = 1 \quad \text{or} \quad c + s = 1\ (MPS = \Delta s / \Delta Y)$$

If we consider our earlier example, when *MPC* is 0.5, income is £500 and autonomous consumption is £200 then a rise in income of £100 leads to a rise in consumption of £50. This implies that the other £50 of extra income is saved and so the *MPS* (s) is equal to 0.5:

$$0.5 + 0.5 = 1$$

The consumption function and savings function for this example are shown in Figure 14.7.

In the same way as the *MPC* plus the *MPS* = 1, so the average propensity to save (*APS*) plus the average propensity to consume (*APC*) sum to 1. Also as income rises the average propensity to consume falls and so the average propensity to save rises. Thus in our earlier example when income was £500 total saving was £50 and the *APS* was:

$$\frac{s}{Y_s} = \frac{50}{500} = 0.1$$

When income rises to £600 then savings rise to £100, so the *APS* is then:

$$\frac{100}{600} = 0.17$$

Note that the *APC* and *APS* will alter with the level of national income only in the situation where there is autonomous consumption. If the consumption function is $C = cY$ then $MPC = APC$ and $MPS = APS$. You will find that many examination questions ignore autonomous consumption. In much of the following we shall do the same for the sake of simplicity.

Having now established that all disposable income is either consumed or saved, we can write that:

$$Y_d = C + S \tag{14.2}$$

This compares with 14.1 which stated:

$$Y_d = C + I$$

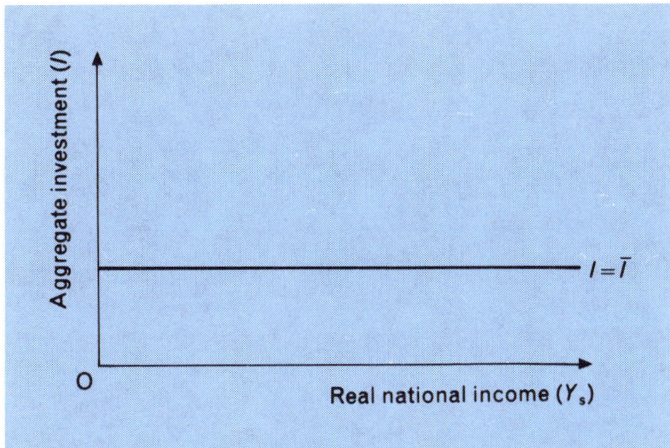

Figure 14.8 Relationship between national income and investment.

which implies that, since C is the same in both cases, then $S = I$. That is, savings equal investment. This brings us back to investment, so we will now turn our attention to what determines investment.

Investment

Investment is the other element of aggregate demand that we identified earlier. Decisions on the volume of investment are made by firms, and we shall assume that these decisions are independent of the level of income Y_s. That is, investment is fixed at some constant level, so $I = \bar{I}$ and is the level of investment which firms have long planned to make. The relationship between income and investment is shown in Figure 14.8.

Equilibrium national output

Recall that the purpose of our investigation is to determine the level of national output. We now know that aggregate demand is made up of consumption and investment demand, and we have seen what determines these two components. Thus $Y = C + I$, which we now know can be written $Y = a + cY + I$.

We have also seen that investment must equal savings because of the two ways of explaining aggregate demand (equations 14.1 and 14.2). The problem here is that we also know that investment is fixed at $\bar{I}$, and so there is only one level of output at which $S = I$ as savers need not plan to save the same as firms plan to invest. This level of output is known as the equilibrium level of output/income and it is the level of income at which the economy will settle down.

To explain this point let us return to the circular flow of income which is illustrated in Figure 14.9. The diagram shows the flow of income to households in the form of factor payments. Some of this income is consumed and some is saved. That income which is saved is not passed on to firms in the form of consumption spending. Thus the flow from households to firms is diminished by the amount that households save. Savings are therefore a withdrawal from the circular flow.

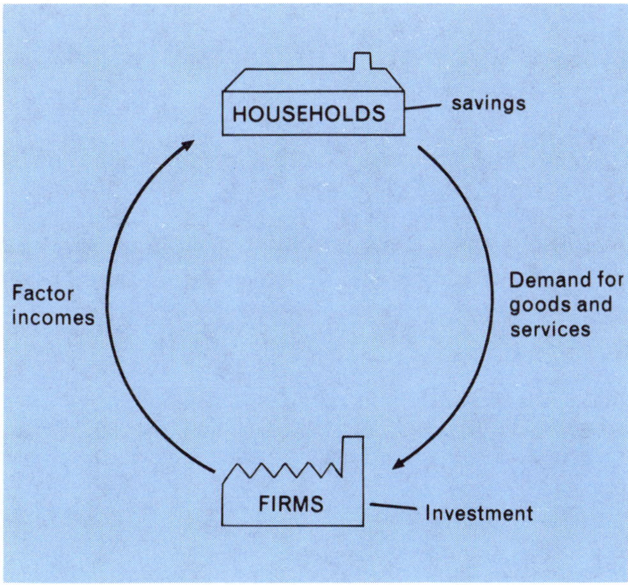

Figure 14.9 Circular flow of income with savings and investment.

If the situation where households saved a proportion of their income continued without adjustment then with each spending round the size of the flows between households and firms would get progressively smaller until they reached zero. Fortunately there is a compensating flow, investment. Investment demand is fixed and decided by firms and so is not dependent on the circular flow. It is therefore an addition to the circular flow and is known as an injection into the circular flow.

It should be clear that the size of the circular flow will remain the same whenever savings equal investment. If this is not the case – if, say, investment is greater than savings – then at each spending round the volume of the circular flow will get larger. As savings are a function of income, they too will rise as income rises until savings again equal investment. The flow stabilizes where withdrawals (savings) balance injections (investment). An example of this process is shown in Table 14.2.

The table shows that when $I =$ £200 and the MPC is 0.6 (for the moment we assume there is no autonomous consumption) then equilibrium national income is £500. At that level of national income, output (aggregate supply Y_s) equals aggregate demand (Y_d) and savings equal investment. We can therefore say that there are two ways of defining the equilibrium level of national output: where $S = I$ and where $Y_d = Y_s$.

If income Y_s were to fall to £300 in Table 14.2 then we would find that aggregate demand would exceed aggregate supply and savings would be less than investment. This means that injections into the circular flow (£200) are greater than withdrawals (£120) and so the circular flow will expand. This process will continue until saving again equals £200 and national output reaches £500. The reverse would be true for any situation where Y_s is greater than £500. Saving would then be greater than investment and so Y_s would fall back to £500.

There is therefore a tendency for the economy in aggregate to move towards this position of equilibrium.

Table 14.2 Calculating equilibrium national output

$Y = C + I$
$C = cY$
$I = \bar{I}$
$C = 0.6Y$
$I = 200$
so $Y = 0.6Y + 200 = 200 + 0.6Y$

National income Y_s (£)	Consumption (£)	Savings (£)	Investment (£)	Aggregate expenditure Y_d (£)		
300	180	120	200	380	$Y_d > Y_s$	$S < I$
400	240	160	200	440	$Y_d > Y_s$	$S < I$
500	300	200	200	500	$Y_d = Y_s$	$S = I$
600	360	240	200	560	$Y_d < Y_s$	$S > I$
700	420	280	200	620	$Y_d < Y_s$	$S > I$

We have now discovered all of the elements needed to determine national output. These are:

1. The components of aggregate demand: consumption and investment.
2. How these components are determined.
3. The conditions in which the economy will be at equilibrium national output.

We can now transfer this information on to a graph.

Figure 14.10 shows the consumption function and the investment function combined into an aggregate expenditure function. We know that equilibrium occurs when either $S = I$ or $Y_d = Y_s$, and the later condition occurs on the 45° line marked in the diagram. Y_d is the sum of expenditures $C + I$ and is shown by the expenditure function E which is equal to the level of investment ($\bar{I}$) when national income is zero. Where the expenditure function E crosses the 45° line the economy is in equilibrium.

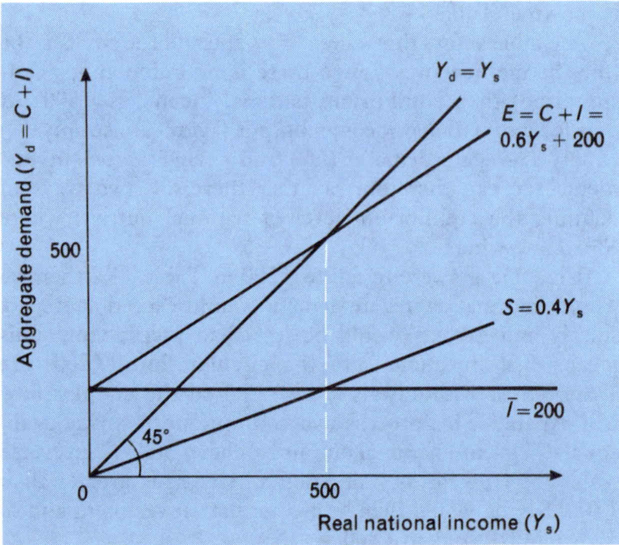

Figure 14.10 Equilibrium national output.

Figure 14.10 uses the same figures as Table 14.2 as an example. Note that the lower half of the diagram shows that at the equilibrium level of output the savings function (S) crosses the investment function (I), which is the other equilibrium condition.

SUMMARY

1. Macroeconomics is the study of economic aggregates and is confined to the short run.
2. In the short run, capital stock is fixed and so national output is related to employment.
3. Keynes believed that the level of output is demand determined.
4. Aggregate demand is made up of consumers' demand and investment demand by firms in a two-sector model ($Y_d = C + I$).
5. Consumption is a function of income. The rate at which extra income is consumed is known as the marginal propensity to consume. Income that is not consumed is saved.
6. When income is zero households must still consume some goods in order to live. This is known as autonomous consumption.
7. The marginal propensity to consume plus the marginal propensity to save equals 1.
8. The average propensity to consume will fall and the average propensity to save will rise as income rises, when there is an element of autonomous expenditure.
9. Investment is determined by firms and is assumed to be independent of national income.
10. Aggregate demand is therefore $Y_d = a + cY + I$.
11. Savings are a withdrawal from the circular flow and investment is an injection into the circular flow.
12. Equilibrium national output occurs where $S = I$ and $Y_d = Y_s$. It is shown where the expenditure function crosses the 45° line.

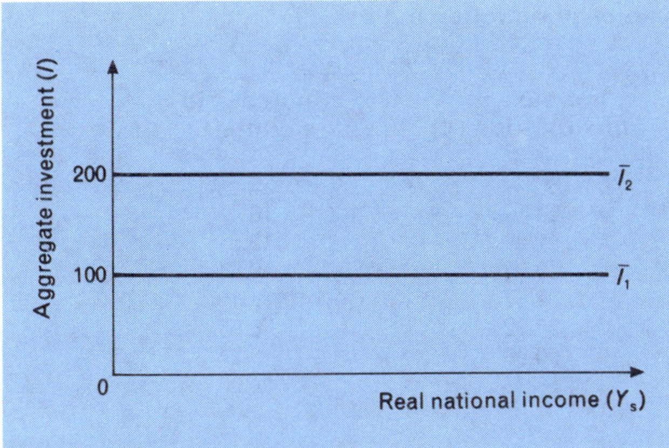

Figure 14.11 Effect of an increase in investment on the investment function.

The multiplier

When discussing investment we stated earlier that it would be decided by firms and would be independent of national income: we stated that $I = \bar{I}$. We can now consider what happens if the level of investment should change.

We will not alter the assumption that investment is independent of the level of income; rather we shall examine what happens if the level of investment changes so that the investment function makes a parallel shift, as shown in Figure 14.11. In the diagram investment rises from £100 to £200 (I_1 to I_2), causing an upward shift of the investment function. Investment is now £200 at all levels of national income.

This movement of the investment function means that the level of aggregate demand also changes. This causes the expenditure function to shift vertically upwards by the same amount as the increase in investment, from E_1 to E_2 in Figure 14.12. Thus following the rise in investment there is a new equilibrium level of national income, which rises from Y_1 to Y_2.

There is an unusual feature in this diagram. The increase in national income (Y_1 to Y_2) is greater than the increase in investment (I_1 to I_2, or £100). This is due to a process known as the **multiplier**. The multiplier in this case is equal to the change in income divided by the change in investment:

$$\text{Multiplier} = \frac{\text{Change in income}}{\text{Change in investment}} = \frac{\Delta Y}{\Delta I}$$

This outcome is not an accident, but is the result of the continual movement of the transactions process around the circular flow. We can illustrate this with an example.

Say firms decide to increase their expenditure on investment by £100 and this generates £100 worth of new output and so generates £100 of new income. It is an injection into the circular flow. The effect of this new income does not stop there. This £100 increase in income brings about an increase in consumption. If the *MPC* is 0.8 then the increase in consumption will be £80. The original increase in demand of £100 will therefore give a secondary boost to demand of £80. The process continues, since this £80

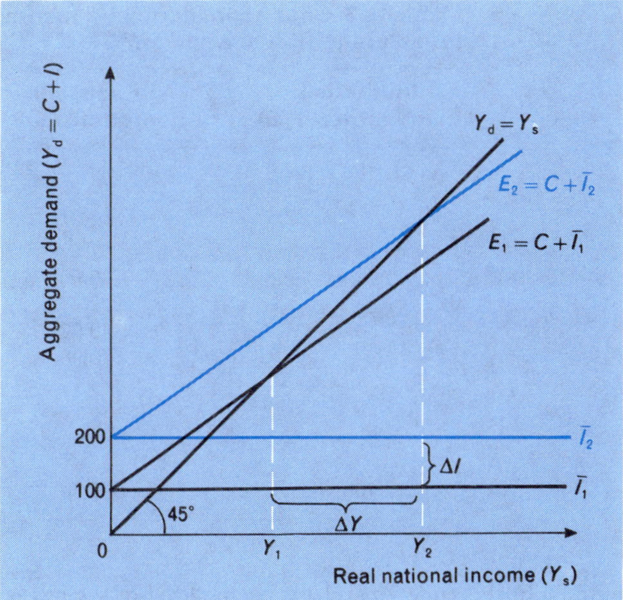

Figure 14.12 Effect of an increase in investment on national income: the multiplier.

increase in demand will cause income to increase by £80 and so induce a further increase in consumption of £64 (80 per cent of £80). This £64 turns up as demand, thus output increases and income increases yet again. This cycle continues with the increases getting smaller and smaller with each 'round'. Eventually it will come to rest when saving has increased by the initial increase in investment so that once again $S = I$. This occurs at a level of national income £500 higher, and with savings and investment both £100 higher. Table 14.3 summarizes this example.

Luckily there is no need to go to all the trouble of working out a table like Table 14.3 every time we wish to calculate the value of the increase in income following a new injection. The multiplier will be equal to 1 over the marginal propensity to save:

$$\text{Multiplier} = \frac{1}{MPS} = \frac{1}{1 - MPC}$$

As the *MPC* and *MPS* sum to 1, the multiplier can be expressed by either of the two formulas shown. In the case of our numerical example the *MPS* is 0.2 and the *MPC* is 0.8. Thus by either formula the multiplier is equal to 5, which is the answer we found in Table 14.3:

$$\frac{1}{0.2} = \frac{1}{1 - 0.8} = 5$$

The multiplier has important implications for Keynesian theory. Clearly investment is a very significant factor in the determination of national output and we have now seen that any change in investment is magnified by the multiplier.

The paradox of thrift

We have seen that increasing investment causes a rise in national income. We have also seen that the consumption function has an important influence on the level of national

Table 14.3 Change in income, consumption and saving following a rise in investment of £100 when *MPC* = 0.8

Initial rise in investment (£)	Increase in income (£)	Increase in consumption (£)	Increase in saving (£)
100	100	80	20
	80	64	16
	64	51.2	12.8
	51.2	40.96	10.24
	40.96	32.77	8.19
	32.77	26.22	6.55
	26.22	20.98	5.24
	20.98	16.78	4.20
	.	.	.
	.	.	.
	.	.	.
100	500.00	400.00	100.00

output. In the same way, changing the level of savings or the marginal propensity to save also affects the level of national output.

It is usually supposed that saving is a virtue. Young people are often urged by their elders to save some of their income – to be 'thrifty'. The classical economists believed that these extra savings would lead to extra investment. This is not the case in the Keynesian model, where saving is an evil in that it causes a reduction in national income and so a rise in unemployment.

Let us examine the effect of a change in the marginal propensity to save, so that households consume a higher percentage of their income. This is shown in Figure 14.13, where the *MPS* rises from 0.2 to 0.3. Notice also that this causes the *MPC* to fall from 0.8 to 0.7, since $MPC + MPS = 1$.

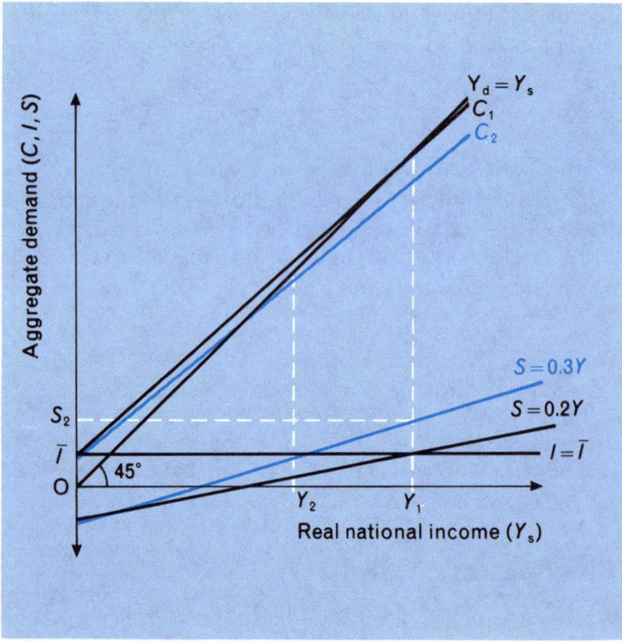

Figure 14.13 The paradox of thrift.

The situation at the old level of national income Y_1 is that investment remains at I, but savings are S_2. This cannot be an equilibrium level of output because S does not equal I. In fact the level of withdrawals from the circular flow (savings) have risen, and this will lead to a contraction of aggregate demand and a fall in national income. The contraction of national income will continue until $S = I$ again, which occurs at Y_2 in Figure 14.13.

A similar result occurs if there is a shift in the savings function due, say, to a fall in autonomous consumption.

We can therefore see that in the Keynesian model increasing the level of savings leads to a lower level of national output and not an increase in the level of investment as predicted by classical economists.

Government

Our model has so far been unrealistic in the sense that there are no developed societies without government involvement in the economy. Governments have a number of functions, most of which involve expenditure, and such expenditure must be financed either by taxation or by borrowing.

In fact introducing government adds two new elements to our simple model. Firstly, we must add government expenditure (G) to aggregate demand so that it now becomes:

$$Y = C + I + G$$

The second effect arises from the way governments raise their revenue – typically in the form of taxes (t). A tax on household income will reduce the amount that consumers have available to spend on goods and services. So consumption will depend on income after tax. Thus:

$$C = a + cY(1-t)$$

We can now look at the effect of both of these additions to the model.

Government spending

We will assume to start with that government spending is

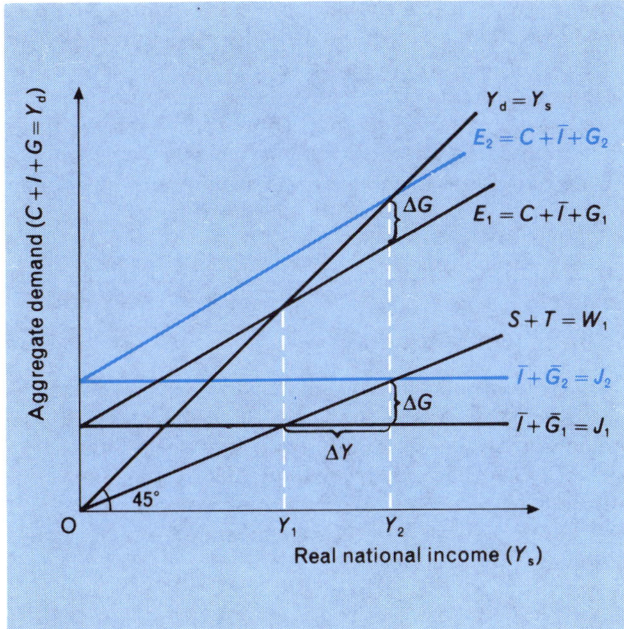

Figure 14.14 Effect of an increase in government spending on national income.

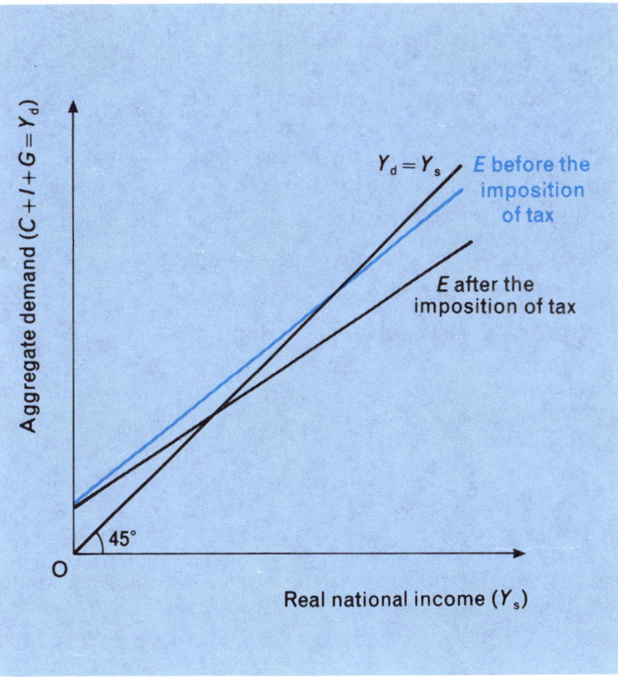

Figure 14.15 Effect of an income tax on the consumption function.

decided by the government and is not dependent on the level of national income. Let it be fixed at $G = \bar{G}$. Like investment, G is an injection into the circular flow, and it is therefore treated as investment was treated. Figure 14.14 shows the effect of an increase in government spending. You will notice that the rise in government spending from G_1 to G_2 has caused a multiplied rise in the level of national income, as would a rise in investment.

Taxation

Taxation in this model is a simple proportion of income: for every £1 we earn, we pay £t to the government. Like savings, tax is a withdrawal from the circular flow of income. The tax rate, t, represents the fixed percentage of income that is claimed from households by the government (t is therefore the marginal propensity to tax).

Let us suppose that the *MPC* remains at 0.8, autonomous expenditure is 100 and the government imposes a tax rate of 10 per cent. The consumption function therefore changes from:

$$C = 100 + 0.8(Y)$$

to:

$$C = 100 + 0.8(0.9Y)$$

Consumption expenditure therefore falls.

For example, say income is £1,000. In the no-tax case consumption would be $100 + 0.8 \times 1{,}000 =$ £900. With taxes, consumption would be $100 + 0.8 \times (0.9 \times 1{,}000) =$ £820. Thus imposing an income tax of 10 per cent reduces consumption from £900 to £820.

The effect of imposing an income tax can also be shown on a diagram. Taxing incomes in this way reduces the slope of the consumption function as shown in Figure 14.15.

Equilibrium with a government sector

Equilibrium still requires aggregate demand to equal aggregate supply ($Y_d = Y_s$), but we now have an additional injection and an additional leakage (G and t). The equilibrium point is no longer where $S = I$, therefore, but where total withdrawals (W) equal total injections (J). Writing T for total tax revenue, equilibrium occurs when:

$$W = J$$

or:

$$S + T = I + G$$

This can be seen in Figure 14.14. The savings function now becomes the withdrawals function, and the investment function becomes the injections function.

The multiplier with a government sector

In the two-sector model without government the only withdrawal is saving and the multiplier is equal to 1 over the marginal rate of withdrawals, which is identically equal to 1 over the marginal propensity to save. Thus:

$$\text{Multiplier} = \frac{1}{\text{Marginal rate of withdrawals}} = \frac{1}{\text{Marginal propensity to save}}$$

In our more realistic model there are two withdrawals – savings and tax – and the multiplier has to be redefined to include the effects of the tax.

It might seem that all we have to do is add the marginal rate of taxation to the marginal propensity to save and we will have the new marginal rate of withdrawals. This would be a mistake. Remember that these withdrawals occur in sequence. First the tax is withdrawn and then the savings are withdrawn. This means that the amount withdrawn as a tax is $t \times Y$ and the amount withdrawn as savings is not sY but $s(Y-tY)$. Saving is out of disposable income $(Y-tY)$ rather than out of pre-tax income (Y). Thus the total withdrawals are found by:

$$\text{Withdrawals} = tY+s(Y-tY) = Y(t+s-st)$$
$$= Y(s+t[1-s]) = Y(s+tc)$$

Therefore the marginal rate of withdrawals is *not*:

$$\frac{1}{s+t}$$

but:

$$\frac{1}{s+ct}$$

In the case of our two-sector model without taxes the multiplier was:

$$\frac{1}{s} = \frac{1}{0.2} = 5$$

With taxes it is now:

$$\frac{1}{s+ct} = \frac{1}{0.2+0.10\times0.80} = 3.57$$

The multiplier has fallen from 5 to 3.57 after the introduction of a 10 per cent income tax. Of course, the size of the reduction in the multiplier will depend upon the rate of taxation chosen by the government, but the multiplier will always be less where there is an income tax than where there is none. Other things being equal, this reduction in the multiplier should reduce national income. However, other things need not be equal and this effect could be offset by an increase in injections.

Important note on A-level examinations

We have had considerable difficulty in deciding how we should present the multiplier in this book. This has arisen because the examination of the multiplier on the multiple-choice paper of *all* UK A-level boards adopts the formula:

$$\text{Multiplier} = \frac{1}{s+t}$$

As you have seen, we have chosen to define the multiplier as:

$$\frac{1}{s+ct}$$

which is the correct definition because of the sequence in which direct tax is paid on income and then consumption decisions are made on disposable income.

In multiple-choice papers the correct answer to questions appears always to require the first of the two definitions. You should be aware of this, although we shall continue to use the formally correct version of the multiplier in the text.

We regret this confusion, but wish to stress that it is our belief that any candidate with elementary skill in algebra, or seeking to develop his or her knowledge further, would find the incorrect presentation confusing. This has sometimes led candidates to assume that they do not understand the multiplier! We have taken the advice of a Chief Examiner on this point and have been told that his board would be delighted to see the multiplier defined correctly in essays.

Economic policy

One of the primary motivations of the Keynesian economists after 1936 was to show that there was no need for a prolonged period of low output and high unemployment (a depression) as there had been in the 1930s. From our three-sector model we can deduce that, since national income and ouput are equal to $C+I+G$, equilibrium output is found by solving the equation:

$$Y = \frac{a+I+G}{s+ct} \tag{14.3}$$

(This is derived formally in the appendix to this chapter.)

We already know that if I or G is increased then national output rises by that amount multiplied by the value of the multiplier. We have also seen that changing the level of taxation will affect the value of the multiplier, and from equation 14.3 we can see that increasing the rate of tax t will cause the level of national output Y to fall.

The implication of this is that if the government wishes to alter the level of national output (Y) then it can do so by altering G or t or both, and both are within its control. Suppose the economy is in the situation shown in Figure 14.16, where the level of national output is Y_1. Let us further suppose that the full-employment level of output is Y_f. In this model it is possible for the government to push the economy towards full employment by raising its own spending (G) from G_1 to G_2. This causes a rise in national output which is equal to the change in G, ΔG, times the multiplier. *The government can therefore spend its way out of a depression.*

A similar result could be achieved by lowering the rate of taxation, which would pivot the expenditure function upwards and so lead to a higher level of national output.

As we saw in Chapter 12, manipulating government revenue (T) and government expenditure (G) is known as fiscal policy.

Inflationary and deflationary gaps

In Figure 14.16 the actual level of national output is below the full-employment level of output. There is insufficient aggregate demand to employ all labour. If the economy operated like the markets we discussed in Chapter 5 then prices (in this case wages) would fall until the market cleared. One of the points put forward by Keynes is that labour markets do not in fact clear in this way. Nevertheless there is a downward pressure on wages and prices, and this is called deflationary pressure.

In Figure 14.16 the distance D is known as the **deflationary gap** – the amount by which aggregate demand

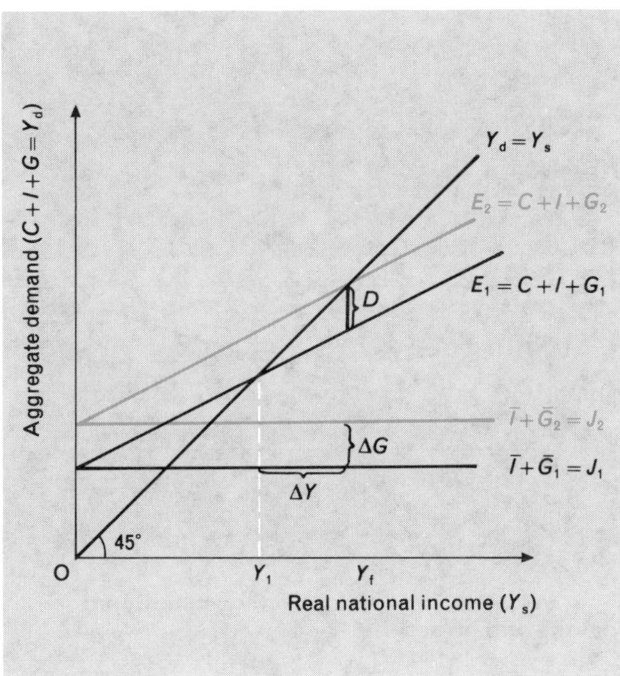

Figure 14.16 Fiscal policy and the deflationary gap.

must rise for the economy to reach the full-employment level.

Figure 14.17 shows a situation where the level of aggregate demand exceeds the full-employment level of national income. In this situation there is more aggregate demand than the economy can satisfy. The excess demand will tend to bid up the prices of goods and the wages of labour. The distance *P*, which measures the excess demand, is known as an **inflationary gap**.

From our previous analysis it should be clear that by

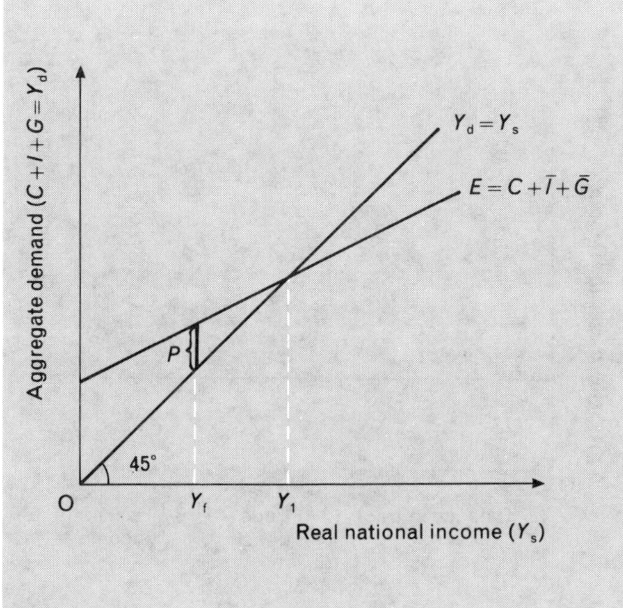

Figure 14.17 The inflationary gap.

fiscal policy governments are able to close both of these gaps to maintain national output at a level around the full-employment equilibrium.

SUMMARY

1. For a given change in the level of investment, national output will rise by a multiple of this change. The value of the multiplier in the two-sector model is $1/MPS$ or $(1-MPC)$.
2. National income rises following an injection, thereby raising withdrawals until they equal the injection. Thus injections raise the level of national output.
3. If the marginal propensity to save rises, or the savings function shifts upwards, then the extra leakages from the circular flow will cause national income to fall.
4. When there is government activity in an economy its expenditure is an injection into the circular flow and its taxation is a withdrawal.
5. Government spending affects national income in the same manner as investment. Government taxation affects the economy in the same way as savings.
6. The multiplier in an economy with a government is equal to 1 over the marginal rate of withdrawals. When the withdrawals are savings and taxation the multiplier is $1/(s+ct)$.
7. The value of the multiplier falls with each additional withdrawal from the circular flow.
8. In the Keynesian model the government can use fiscal policy (the manipulation of government spending and taxation) to influence the level of national output and so prevent excessive unemployment or inflation.
9. When national output is below the economy's full-employment level there is said to be a deflationary gap. When the level of aggregate demand is above the economy's full-employment level there is said to be an inflationary gap.

An economy with international trade

So far we have dealt with a **closed economy**, but as we saw in Chapter 12 the UK is an **open economy** with a high level of imports and exports. (See Chapter 20 for a fuller discussion of UK trade.) Including international trade in our model adds two more items to the determination of aggregate demand and supply. This now becomes:

$$Y = C+I+G+(X-M)$$

Thus aggregate demand (Y) equals consumption by households (C) plus investment by firms (I) plus expenditure by the government (G) plus expenditure by foreigners on UK goods (exports, X), less expenditure by UK residents on foreign goods (imports, M).

The term $(X-M)$ gives net exports. If the country

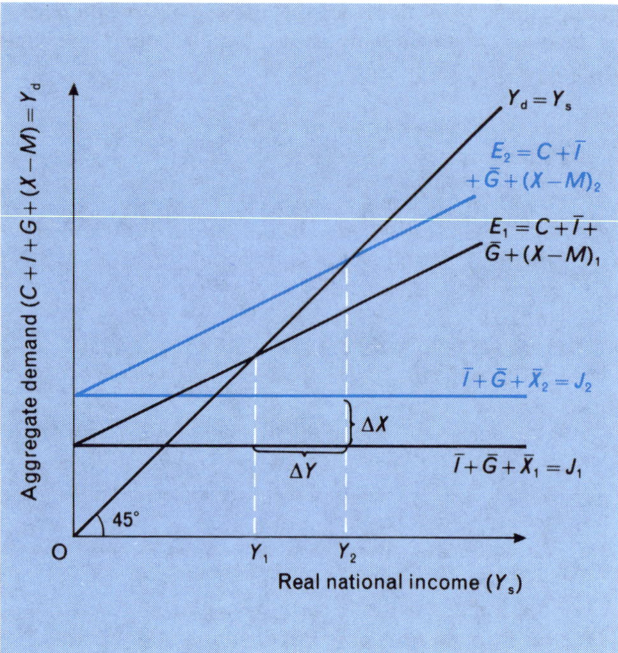

Figure 14.18 Effect of an increase in exports on national income.

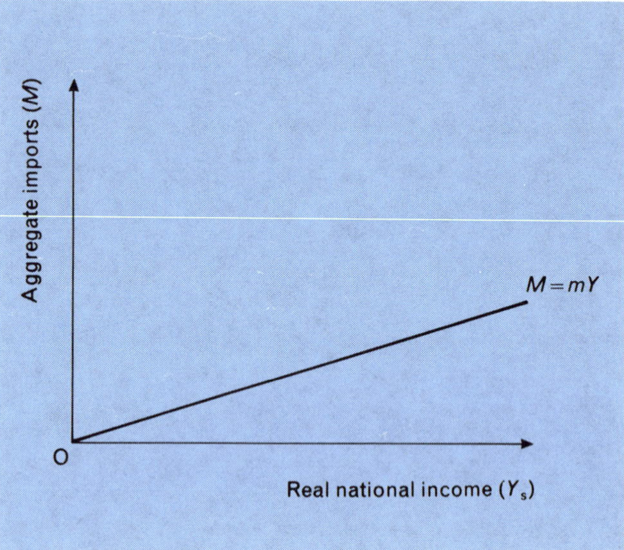

Figure 14.19 Relationships between national income and imports.

exports more than it imports this will be a positive figure and this will add to aggregate demand. If the country imports more than it exports then its net exports are negative and aggregate demand is reduced.

These two items X and M, affect the model in different ways and we will now look at each in turn.

Exports

Exports are assumed to be determined independently of national income, as were investment and government spending earlier. This is because the level of exports depends upon the decisions of foreigners to buy UK products, and this will largely depend on the level of national income in their own countries. Thus as far as the UK is concerned, the level of exports is fixed at a given level, $X = \bar{X}$.

Exports constitute an additional demand for UK goods and services and are an injection into the circular flow to be treated in the same way as investment and government expenditure. Figure 14.18 shows the effect of an increase in exports. Notice that the rise in exports from X_1 to X_2 has caused a multiplied rise in the level of national income from Y_1 to Y_2.

Imports

In this model demand for imports is seen as a simple function of income, as was the demand for domestically produced consumer goods. This is written as:

$$M = mY$$

Imports will be a percentage (m) of national income (Y), and so m is the marginal propensity to import (MPM). Thus as national income rises so will imports. This is shown in Figure 14.19.

Spending on imports is, of course, passed on to foreigners who are outside the circular flow. Therefore imports are another withdrawal from the economy.

Balance of trade

When there is a 'balance of trade' exports equal imports. As exports are assumed to be fixed at $\bar{X}$ and as imports vary with income ($M = mY$), balanced trade will only occur when $\bar{X} = mY$, i.e. when $Y = X/m$. This is shown in Figure 14.20, where exports equal imports at the level of national income Y_1. To the left of Y_1 exports exceed

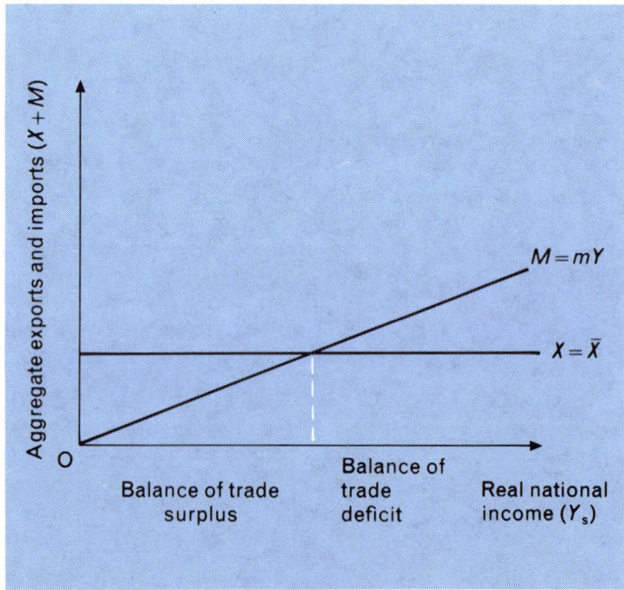

Figure 14.20 Balance of trade.

imports and there is a trade surplus. To the right of Y_1 imports exceed exports and there is a balance of trade deficit.

Equilibrium in the open-economy model

Equilibrium still occurs where aggregate demand equals aggregate supply, $Y_d = Y_s$, but there is now an additional injection and an additional withdrawal from the circular flow. Thus the new equilibrium condition will be where total withdrawals equal total injections, i.e.:

$$S+T+M = I+G+X$$

or

$$W = J$$

This is shown in Figure 14.21.

We saw earlier that in a closed economy, with government, equilibrium national income can be found by solving the equation:

$$Y = \frac{a+I+G}{s+ct} \qquad (14.3)$$

In an open economy this becomes:

$$Y = \frac{a+I+G+X}{s+ct+m} \qquad (14.4)$$

Exports (X) are added to the injections I and G and autonomous expenditure a, and the marginal propensity to import (m) is added to the other marginal propensities to withdraw. It may be helpful to work through a numerical example.

An example

Aggregate demand is given by:

$$Y = C+I+G+(X-M)$$

where

$$C = a+cY(1-t)$$
$$I = \bar{I}$$
$$G = \bar{G}$$
$$X = \bar{X}$$
$$M = mY$$

Therefore:

$$Y = a+cY(1-t)+I+G+(X-mY)$$

Equilibrium occurs when:

$$S+T+M = a+I+G+X \qquad (1)$$

or:

$$Y = \frac{a+I+G+X}{s+ct+m} \qquad (2)$$

Suppose that the variables have the following values:

$a = 50$, $\bar{I} = 100$, $\bar{G} = 120$ and $\bar{X} = 90$
$c = 0.8$, $t = 0.1$ and $m = 0.15$

By method 1 we have $S = 0.2(Y-T)$ $[= 0.2Y-0.02Y]$, $T = 0.1Y$ and $M = 0.15Y$, so:

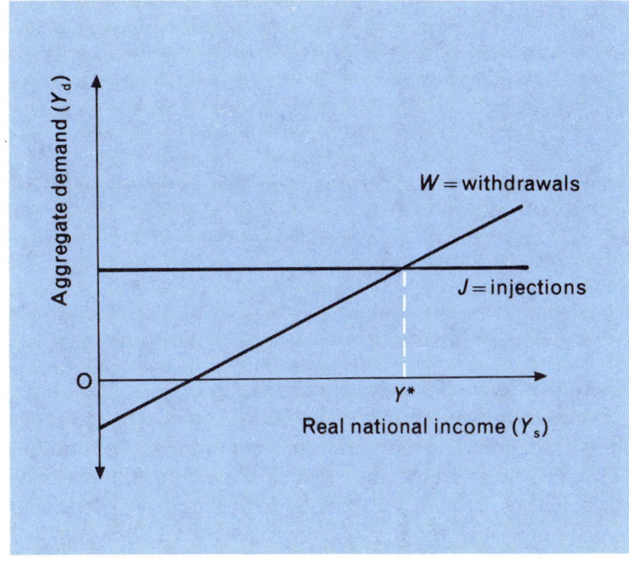

Figure 14.21 Equilibrium in the open economy.

$$0.2Y-0.02Y+0.1Y+0.15Y = 50+100+120+90$$
$$0.43Y = 360$$

therefore:

$$Y = 837$$

We can confirm this result by plugging in the values to the equation of method 2.

$$Y = \frac{a+I+G+X}{s+ct+m}$$

$$Y = \frac{50+100+120+90}{0.2+(0.1\times 0.8)+0.15} = \frac{360}{0.43} = 837$$

Suppose the government perceived a deflationary gap and wished to raise the level of national income. It could raise government spending to 200 ($G = 200$), and this would cause national income to change in the following way.

By method 1:

$$0.2Y-0.02Y+0.1Y+0.15Y = 50+100+\mathbf{200}+90$$
$$0.43Y = 440$$
$$Y = 1{,}023$$

By method 2:

$$Y = \frac{50+100+\mathbf{200}+90}{0.2+(0.1\times 0.8)+0.15} = \frac{440}{0.43} = 1{,}023$$

Notice that the level of national output has risen by £186 due to an increase in government expenditure of £80, implying a multiplier of 2.3. This is confirmed by calculation:

$$\frac{1}{0.2+(0.1\times 0.8)+0.15} = \frac{1}{0.43} = 2.326$$

It is also possible to calculate the government's budget deficit or surplus following the rise in spending and the state of the balance of payments:

Government budget $= G - T$
$G = 200$
$t = 0.1Y$
$Y = 800$

Therefore $T = 80$ and the government's budget deficit will be $200 - 80 = 120$.

Balance of trade $= X - M$
$X = 100$
$M = 0.2Y$
$Y = 800$

Therefore $M = 160$ and the trade deficit is $160 - 100 = 60$.

This example is provided to show you that there is an alternative to the graphical representation of this model. Some people are reluctant to use it because of their fear of mathematics. In fact little mathematical ability is required to use the model and if you can master the algebra you will save yourself a lot of time in examinations. The appendix to this chapter outlines the full algebraic version of the model.

The multiplier in an open economy

The multiplier is again altered by the introduction of an additional withdrawal, imports. The multiplier remains:

$$\frac{1}{\text{Marginal rate of withdrawals}}$$

but in an open economy it is now:

$$\frac{1}{s + ct + m}$$

which will have a smaller value than the multiplier in the closed economy.

Continuing the example from our previous discussion of the multiplier, suppose that $MPS = 0.2$, $MPT = 0.1$ and now $MPM = 0.2$. The value of the multiplier was $1/s$ in the closed economy without government and $1/(s + ct)$ in the closed economy with government, and fell from 5 to 3.57 with the introduction of a government sector. Now, when international trade is introduced, the multiplier is:

$$\frac{1}{0.2 + (0.1 \times 0.8) + 0.2} = 2.08$$

Thus the value of the multiplier declines as we add more withdrawals to the economy. This implies that government fiscal policy has less effect in an open economy than in a closed economy.

SUMMARY

1. Countries that trade with others are open economies.
2. Exports are goods produced domestically and sold abroad. The demand for exports is assumed to be fixed at $\bar{X}$.
3. Imports are goods demanded domestically and produced by foreigners. The demand for imports is assumed to depend upon domestic national income, i.e. $M = mY$.
4. There is a 'balance of trade' when exports equal imports ($\bar{X} = M$).
5. Exports are an injection into the circular flow; imports are a withdrawal.
6. Equilibrium national output in an open economy is where total withdrawals ($S + T + M$) equal total injections ($I + G + X$).
7. The multiplier is equal to 1 over the marginal rate of withdrawals, but will have a lower value in an open economy than in a closed economy due to the extra withdrawals of import spending.

Some policy implications of the Keynesian model

Stop–go

In order to see how Keynesian policies might be operated – and to see their limitations – consider an economy which has settled down in a deflationary gap. We mean by this that the output is neither growing nor contracting but that there are workers unable to find work.

The government decides to increase aggregate demand by increasing government expenditure (G), i.e. its fiscal policy is to run a budget deficit. This, via the Keynesian multiplier, will increase national output and hence increase employment. Unfortunately this increase in output will induce an increase in imports. (The import function tells us that a £1 increase in income will cause imports to increase by £m.) As output and hence imports increase we will eventually run into a balance of trade problem. Exports, which are supposed to earn us enough to pay for our imports, have not been increasing, but imports have. Imports must therefore eventually exceed exports.

This imbalance of international trade can continue only as long as we can pay for the additional imports out of our reserves of gold, dollars and other foreign currency or as long as we can borrow more gold and dollars, etc. (foreign exchange reserves) from foreigners. Neither of these options can be pursued indefinitely as sooner or later (generally sooner) the government is forced to reduce aggregate demand so as to reduce national income and hence reduce imports.

This led to the notorious **stop–go** era of Keynesianism during which a series of expansions were followed by deflations. The problem essentially arose from the fact that the UK is open economy.

One solution to this balance of payments problem would be to engineer an increase in exports (X) rather than an increase in government expenditure (G). An increase in exports should have as big an impact on national output (and hence employment) as would a similar increase in government expenditure (G). The difference is, of course, that the increase in exports means that as imports subsequently increased they would not cause a balance of payments crisis – exports have already been increased.

This is called an export-led boom and may be engineered

by giving awards and honours to exporters, by making credit available to exporters on favourable terms and by using government offices abroad to promote trade.

Another possible solution to the balance of trade problem would be to allow the price mechanism to operate. This means allowing the price paid by foreigners for UK goods to fall when the country wishes to export more. Simultaneously, of course, the price paid in the UK for foreign goods (imports) should increase and thereby reduce UK demand for imports.

Between 1974 and 1990, when it joined the exchange rate mechanism of the European monetary system, the UK tried to get the price mechanism to work in this way. Before 1974 successive UK governments tried to override this aspect of the price mechanism and ran into balance of trade crises.

A third possible solution to the increase in imports is to try to control them by putting on **tariffs** (taxing imports) or applying physical **quotas**. The latter has been attempted in the case of Japanese cars. The Japanese were asked to keep the exports of cars to the UK down to some 'reasonable' level.

There are a number of reasons why some economists think that such controls should be avoided. Partly they risk retaliation – other countries could impose tariffs and quotas on UK exports. Partly they argue that UK households should be free to buy what they want from where they want. And partly, of course, they argue that international competition encourages greater efficiency.

What does emerge is the idea that the government can affect imports and the balance of trade by pursuing a Keynesian full-employment policy. This implies that the government is responsible for trade balance as well as employment.

Crowding out

The next problem with the implementation of Keynesian economic policies arises from an internal conflict rather than an external balance. If we imagine that the price mechanism is capable of maintaining trade balance, and is permitted to do so, then the government will be free to pursue an expansionist fiscal policy when unemployment occurs, without fear of precipitating an imbalance of trade.

If it does so, however, it might discover that its expansion of government expenditure (G) is offset by a decrease in private-sector investment (I). The argument is that, in order to finance its expenditure, the government borrows. The increased government borrowing means that there is less available for private investors. Private investment is thereby **crowded out** by government expenditure. The shortage of funds is reflected in an increased interest rate.

Thus the expansionary effect of a budget deficit may be much less than the Keynesian multiplier would suggest. It might even be the case that the increase in government expenditure is *exactly* offset by an equal and opposite change in private investment. Crowding out is in this case 100 per cent and fiscal policy is totally ineffective – except, of course, that it increases interest rates and switches expenditure away from the private to the public sector.

Monetarists argue that crowding out is in fact 100 per cent and furthermore that the decline in private investment will prevent economic growth from occurring. This is because many of the improvements in production rely on investment in new machines and processes. Reducing investment will therefore reduce the ability to introduce these new things. They also argue that switching from private to public expenditure leads to inefficiency since the public sector is protected from the competitive forces to which the private sector is exposed.

The net effect, once again, is to increase the economic role of government. It is now responsible for employment, trade, investment and economic growth.

Inflation

Finally there is yet another possible outcome of an expansionary fiscal policy. If the government succeeds in running a budget deficit without running into a balance of trade deficit or seriously reducing investment, it is still possible that producers will respond to the increased aggregate demand simply by increasing prices rather than output. Thus an additional £100 million in aggregate demand may simply bid up prices and leave output and unemployment unchanged.

This leads us to the question: to what extent are *prices* rather than *quantities* responsive to economic changes?

Herein lies an important distinction between monetarists and Keynesians. Monetarists, as we have seen, explain output in terms of full employment in the labour market and explain price level by the quantity theory of money (see Chapter 13). Doubling money supply simply doubles price level and leaves output unchanged. On the other hand, Keynesians explain output in terms of aggregate demand and have a much more complicated view of the demand for money. The introduction of idle balances means that there is no clear connection between money supply and the amount of money being used for transactions. Thus Keynesians have neither the fixed output nor the fixed transactions balances which are necessary to use the quantity theory as the theory of price level. To Keynesians the quantity theory is merely one part of their demand for money function.

This means that Keynesians have to look elsewhere for an explanation of price level. Typically, Keynesians explain price level in terms of costs. Thus whether or not an expansion of aggregate demand will lead to an increase in output or an increase in price level will depend on how costs respond to aggregate demand.

What we have learned here is that the implementation of Keynesian policies has extended still further the role of the government in our economic lives. Since the expansion may lead to increased costs and prices, it follows that the government is now at least partially responsible for output, unemployment, imports, exports, investment, growth, costs and prices.

The gradual extension of government into economics which came with Keynesianism was viewed by some with great misgivings. Economic 'freedom' was seen as an essential part of political freedom and hence something that should be protected. Other observers felt that Keynesian policies were not working as they were originally expected to work and that some other macroeconomic theory should be sought.

Not everyone, of course, has such misgivings about

Keynesian economics. Many point to the full employment and rapid growth rates achieved by most western economies between 1944 and 1964 as evidence that Keynesian policy has worked in the past and can work again today. They argue that the intrusion of government into our economic lives is benign rather than sinister and anyway is a price well worth paying for a fully employed economy.

SUMMARY

1. The use of Keynesian policies in an open economy is more problematic than in a closed economy.
2. The Keynesian multiplier is changed and there is now the risk of causing a balance of trade deficit as output expands.
3. This has led to stop–go policies, export-led booms and exchange rate policy.
4. Even in a closed economy, there are problems with implementing Keynesian policies.
5. The expansion in government expenditure may simply crowd out private investment and leave output and employment unchanged.
6. The expansion in government expenditure may also simply cause prices to rise rather than output.
7. These difficulties have led to a gradual extension of government control over the economy and caused misgivings among some economists.

The classical view

According to the classical school, the actual level of employment, and hence the level of national output will be determined by the demand curve for labour (Figure 14.22) together with the labour supply curve. If we assume that the households supply more labour when the real wage increases, we have an upward-sloping supply curve of labour. Adding this to Figure 14.22 gives us Figure 14.23.

Now that we have both supply and demand curves we can find the equilibrium or market clearing level of employment (L^*) and the real wage $(W/P)^*$. Having determined employment we have also determined national output.

Essentially we are saying that national output is determined by what happens in the labour market. L^* is called **full employment** and is that level of employment at which anyone who wishes to work *at the going wage rate* can find a job.

There will still be unemployed workers, as is shown by that part of the labour supply curve which lies above $(W/P)^*$ and to the right of L^*. These workers, however, require a higher wage than $(W/P)^*$ if they are to be attracted into the workforce. They have, in other words, chosen unemployment. They are 'voluntarily' unemployed. Short of moving the demand curve, there is very little which can be done about this unemployment. It is the **natural rate of unemployment**.

Note that the 'natural rate of unemployment' need not be the same as the level existing under what the Keynesian model regards as 'full employment'. The natural rate might

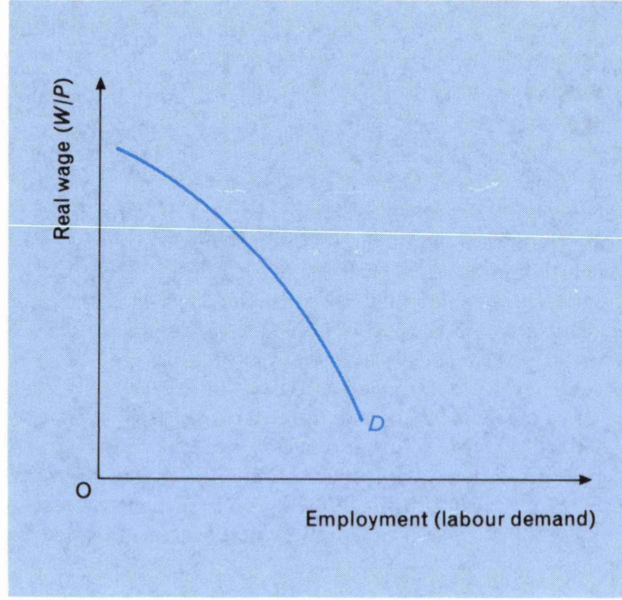

Figure 14.22 Demand curve for labour.

be as high as 10 per cent of the workforce; the Keynesian view is that it is around 3 per cent of the workforce. This is both confusing and a source of controversy.

Other sources of unemployment are taken up in more detail in Chapter 17. The first essential thing to note here is that full employment does not mean that every person is in work. *Full employment is the level of employment which clears the labour market* (i.e. L^*).

The second essential thing to note is that doubling money wages (W) and doubling price level (P) has absolutely no effect on either real wage or employment (or output). All that matters here is real wage (W/P), and provided real wage is free to find its equilibrium level then

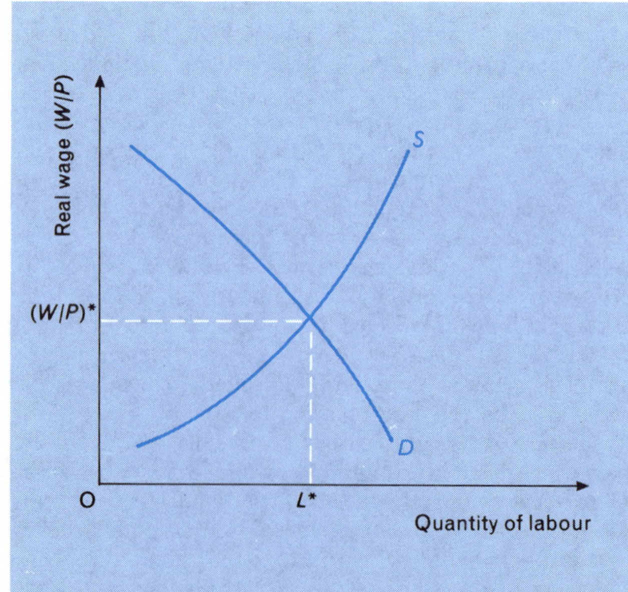

Figure 14.23 Equilibrium in the labour market.

full employment and full-employment levels of output will be achieved.

The monetarist view

Monetarists take the classical view that real variables are determined independent of the price level and hence the quantity of money.

All that the quantity of money can do is determine price level (P). By doing so, it also determines the nominal value of wages (W) and the nominal value of national output.

Thus there is a dichotomy between *real* variables, which are unaffected by money supply, and *nominal* variables which are affected by money supply. Since money supply cannot affect real variables it is said to be *neutral*.

This is the nub of monetarist economic theory: if markets are allowed to work freely, they will clear and by clearing will determine all the real variables – the variables which are of economic interest. These market-clearing conditions will be completely unaffected by money supply. All that money will do is to change nominal variables, in particular the rate of inflation.

If unemployment occurs here it will be 'voluntary', and hence those who are unemployed have no justifiable claim on the state for financial support. They are either too lazy to work for the going wage or too greedy to settle for what everyone else is receiving. The unemployed, according to this view, are therefore the undeserving poor.

There are some other 'real' variables of interest here too – apart, that is, from employment, real wage and national ouput. The three we shall consider are savings, investment and interest rates. These, like most aspects of the monetarist theory, are determined by market forces.

Saving is done by households, and the amount put by out of current income (saving) will be influenced by the rate of interest which is being offered. High interest rates are likely to encourage more saving and so there will be an upward-sloping relationship between saving (the supply of loanable funds) and interest rate. This is shown by line S in Figure 14.24. We also need a demand for loanable funds schedule if we are to say anything about the behaviour of the market for loanable funds. Typically the savings of households are borrowed by the producers (firms) to finance their activity. In other words, the demand for loanable funds comes from entrepreneurs who wish to invest.

Entrepreneurs will be keen to borrow when interest rates are low because there will be lots of projects capable of covering the low interest charges *and* yielding profits. As the interest rate goes up, some projects will become unprofitable and so the demand for loanable funds by firms will fall. The demand schedule will therefore be downward sloping from left to right, as shown by line I in Figure 14.24.

The market for loanable funds clears when investment and saving are equal at I^* and S^* respectively, and when interest rate is r^* per cent per annum. If saving exceeds investment, there will be a surplus of loanable funds looking for borrowers. This will compete down the rate of interest, which in turn will increase investment and decrease saving. This will continue until the supply of loanable funds exactly equals the demand for them.

These saving and investment decisions are in real variables and the interest rate is also a real interest rate. By doubling the level of prices we would double the nominal value of saving and double the nominal value of investment, but their intersect would stay at r^* so the real interest rate, real investment and real saving are unchanged.

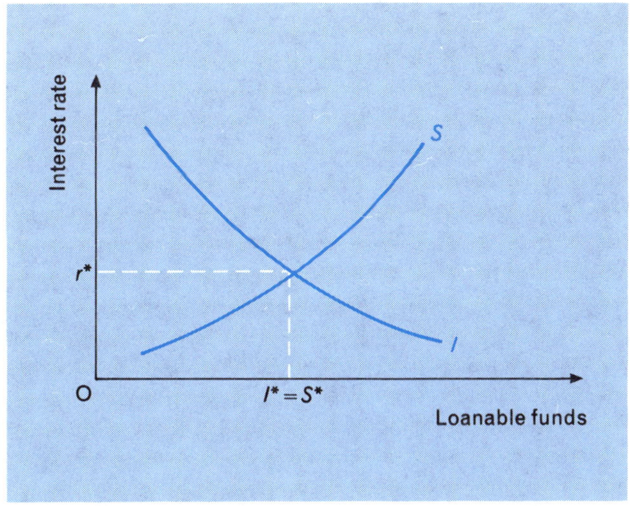

Figure 14.24 Equilibrium in the market for loanable funds.

Thus the market for loanable funds clears and by clearing determines savings, investment and interest rate. Markets are therefore pervasive in monetarist explanations of macroeconomic activity in more or less the same way as they were used in our microeconomic theory. The price mechanism is deemed to work everywhere.

SUMMARY

1. There will be an upward-sloping supply curve of labour which, together with the demand curve, determines market-clearing employment and the real wage rate.
2. This market-clearing level of employment is full employment.
3. Those who remain unemployed when full employment is reached are voluntarily unemployed. This unemployment rate is the natural rate.
4. In classical economics the labour market is assumed to clear, and the market-clearing level of employment determines the level of national output.
5. Money supply affects only nominal values and leaves real values unchanged. Money is neutral.
6. Investment is equated to savings by changing the interest rate.

Determination of aggregate investment

In the Keynesian model we have assumed that investment

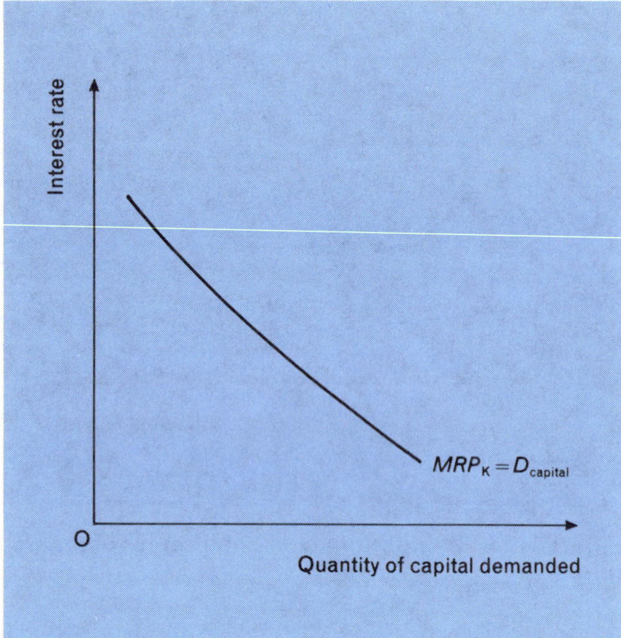

Figure 14.25 A firm's demand curve for capital.

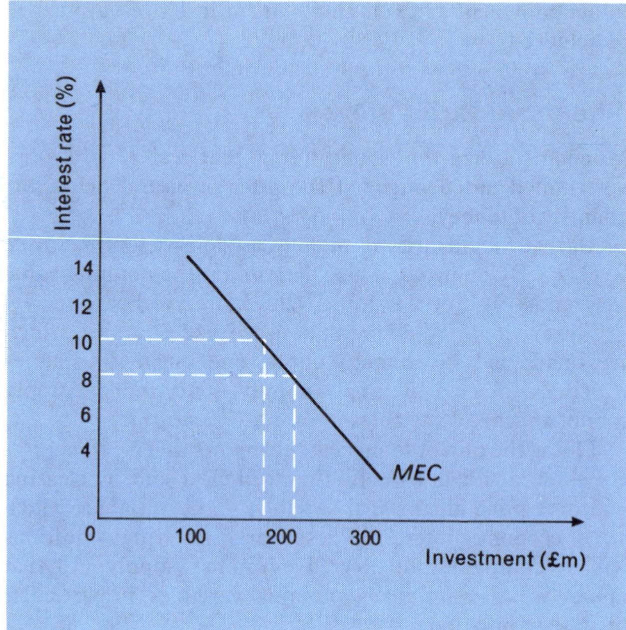

Figure 14.26 Marginal efficiency of capital schedule.

demand is fixed at some given level. We have allowed the level of investment to alter, but not with respect to the level of national income. We will now investigate what might cause these changes in investment.

In Chapter 9 we saw that firms will make investment decisions based upon the net present value of a project, given the rate of interest. This led to the conclusion that the higher the rate of interest, the less capital a firm would demand. The firm's demand curve for capital was said to be the marginal revenue product curve for capital. This is shown in Figure 14.25.

We are now concerned with the investment demand for the economy as a whole, and we can use the conclusions from Chapter 9 to draw an investment demand curve for the whole economy. We can rank all possible investment projects by their rate of return, i.e. how much will be invested when the rate of interest is 10 per cent, how much will be invested when it is 8 per cent, and so on. Table 14.4 does this for a hypothetical economy. The data in Table 14.4 can be translated into a graph as in Figure 14.26, which is the aggregate demand curve for capital and is known as the **marginal efficiency of capital** (MEC) curve.

Table 14.4 Aggregate investment demand schedule

Interest rate (%)	Aggregate investment demand (£m)
14	115
12	150
10	185
8	220
6	255
4	290

The implication of the *MEC* is that a change in the rate of interest will lead to a change in the level of investment. For example, suppose the rate of interest falls from 10 per cent to 8 per cent. Many projects that were unprofitable at 10 per cent will now be profitable. Firms will realize that they can now make higher profits by increasing investment, so there will be an overall rise in investment.

This is shown in Figure 14.27(a), where the fall in the rate of interest leads to a rise in investment from I_1 to I_2. This leads to a rise in investment from I_1 to I_2 in Figure 14.27(b), and so to a rise in national income. Notice that there is a multiplier effect on national income which rises from Y_1 to Y_2.

It is worth noting that this gives the government an extra tool with which to influence the economy in addition to fiscal policy (the manipulation of government spending (G) and taxation (t)). If the government can influence the rate of interest then it can influence the level of investment and so national income. In fact, the government can influence the rate of interest via monetary policy.

Business cycles

In Chapter 11 we stated that macroeconomics was concerned with deviations from capacity output. In fact the UK economy has rarely been at its capacity output, although the trend in capacity output is clearly upward, indicating economic growth (see Figure 14.28). What is not as clear from Figure 14.28 is that these deviations from capacity also take a cyclical form, on occasions the economy operating much closer to capacity than at others. A typical cycle is shown in Figure 14.29, where actual output is seen to deviate around a trend.

Cycles have been observed in market economies since the industrial revolution. When output is falling this is known

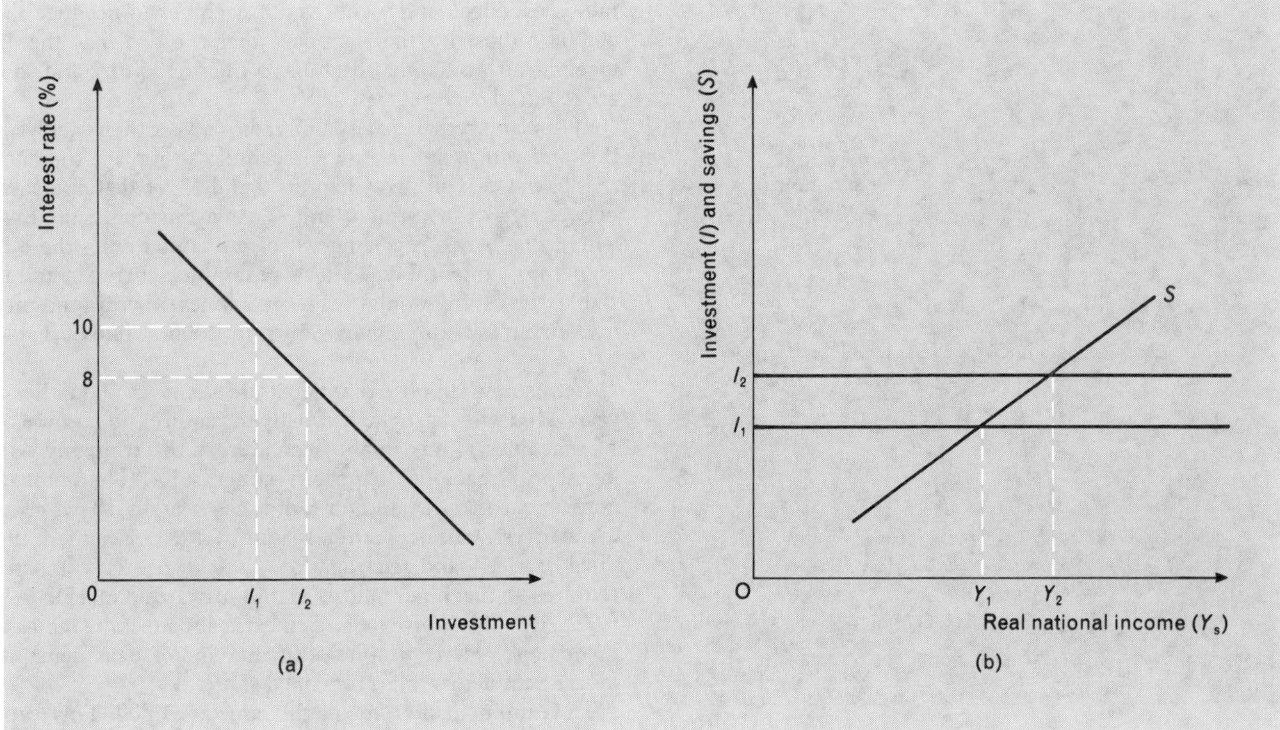

Figure 14.27 Effect of a fall in the interest rate on investment and national income.

as a depression or a recession and at its lowest point there is a trough. Following a depression output turns upwards and this is known as the recovery phase. Then, as output continues to rise, the economy moves into a boom. Typically, in a depression there is a high unemployment as national income falls and in a boom (as capacity output is approached) inflation becomes evident. Figure 14.30 shows how UK output has moved around its growth trend between 1965 and 1990. The next question is: what causes these fluctuations in output?

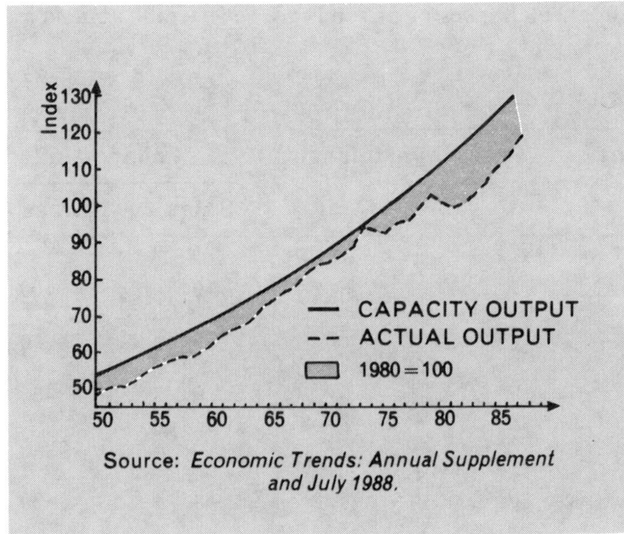

Figure 14.28 Actual and capacity output of the UK economy, 1950–87.

The accelerator theory of the business cycle

The **accelerator** theory takes the view that a business's decisions on investment depend on the change in the level of its sales rather than the rate of interest. This is not an unreasonable assumption from the point of view of business managers, who will base their decisions about how much plant and machinery they require on the amount they must

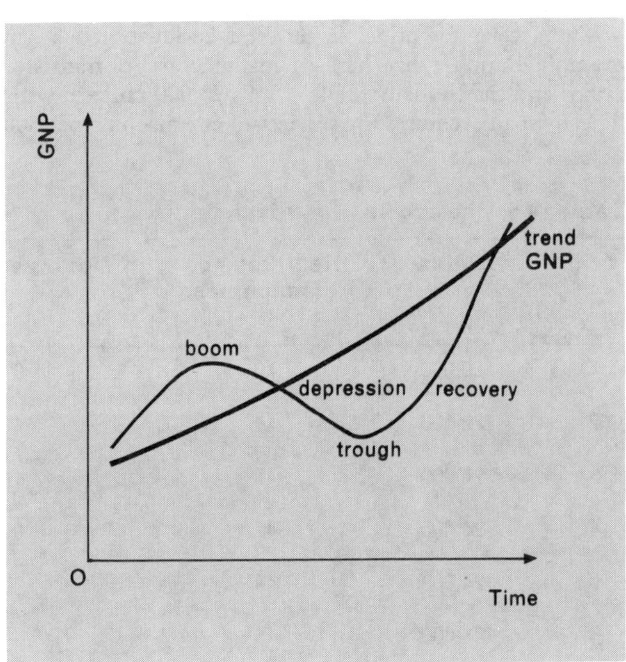

Figure 14.29 A business cycle.

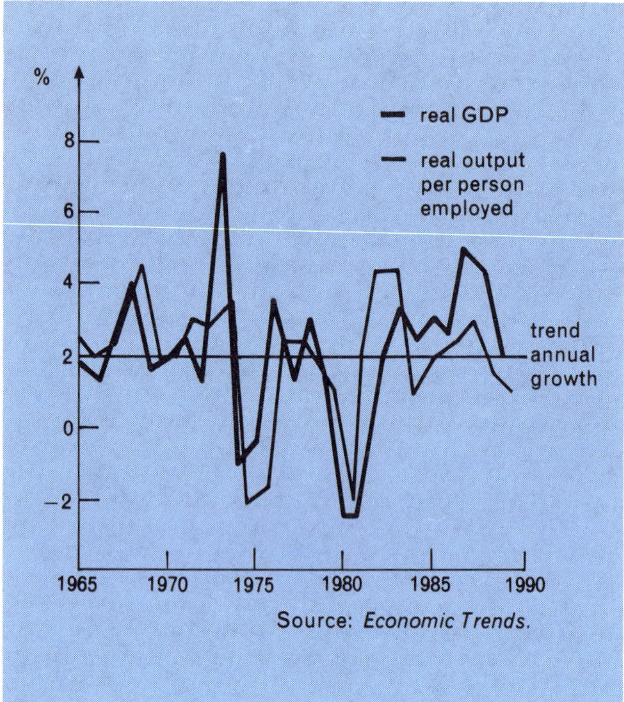

Figure 14.30 Growth of output and labour productivity in the UK, 1965–89 (% per annum).

produce to meet demand. As sales expand, more capital is required to meet the demand; but if sales fall, there will be no investment even if interest rates fall.

The accelerator theory takes the view that the main source of information that firms have on their likely sales for next year is the change in sales this year. Thus if firms experience rising sales this year, other things being equal, they will expect a further rise next year and plan their investment accordingly.

The accelerator principle can best be illustrated by an example. Suppose that there is a manufacturer of transistor radios and that initially the firm sells 20,000 radios a year. The company requires the services of one machine per 500 radios produced and so needs 40 machines to produce the 20,000 radios. Further, suppose that the firm has the 40 machines it needs, that each has a life of 10 years and so 4 are replaced each year.

If demand remains at 20,000 radios a year then each year the firm will invest in 4 new machines to replace the ones that have worn out. In Chapters 9 and 12 we distinguished between gross investment and net investment. In the case where the firm is replacing worn-out capital only, there is no net investment. Hence in this example, when demand is stable, gross investment is 4 machines a year and net investment is zero. This is shown in the first line of Table 14.5.

Let us now suppose that demand rises to 22,000 radios a year. This will cause the company to require the services of 44 machines. Thus in the second year the company will invest in 8 machines, a net investment of 4. The point to note here is that demand for radios has risen by 10 per cent, while investment demand has risen by 100 per cent. In the third year demand rises again to 24,000. So the company requires 48 machines and so again purchases 8 machines, 4 to replace those worn out and an extra 4 to meet the increase in demand. Here, despite a further increase in demand, investment demand has remained static.

In year 4 demand remains the same at 24,000. This leads to the firm replacing only the 4 machines that have worn out. Here there is no net investment and the demand for investment goods has fallen by 50 per cent. If demand remains the same in year 5 then again there is only gross investment.

In year 6 sales turn down and the firm only has to produce 23,000 radios. For this it needs 46 machines. It has 44 (48 less the 4 that have worn out) and so buys only 2. Demand has fallen by just over 4 per cent, but investment demand has fallen by 50 per cent. If in year 7 demand falls again, to 21,000, then the firm needs only 42 machines. It has these without purchasing any new ones and so gross investment in year 7 is zero.

From our example we can see that investment demand is likely to vary considerably following only a modest change in the level of consumer demand. The implications for the suppliers of investment goods are considerable, but so are

Table 14.5 The accelerator principle

Year	Sales	Required no. of machines	Net investment	Gross investment	% change in	
					Sales	Gross *I*
1	20,000	40	0	4		
					10	100
2	22,000	44	4	8		
					9	0
3	24,000	48	4	8		
					0	−50
4	24,000	48	0	4		
					0	0
5	24,000	48	0	4		
					−4	−50
6	23,000	46	0	2		
					−9.5	−100
7	21,000	42	0	0		

Table 14.6 Effect of the accelerator on national output

Year	*a*	*I*	*Y*	*C*	*K*
1	50	0	100	100	60
2	50	0	100	100	60
3	75	0	150	150	60
4	75	30	210	180	60
5	75	36	222	186	90
6	75	7	164	157	126
7	75	−35	81	115	133
8	75	−50	50	100	99
9	75	−19	113	131	49
10	75	38	225	188	30
11	75	68	285	218	68
12	75	36	222	186	135

Note: a = autonomous consumption; I = investment; Y = national output; C = consumption; K = capital stock at beginning of period.
Source: R. C. O. Matthews, *The Trade Cycle*, Nisbet and Cambridge (1959).

the implications for national output. We can now translate what we have observed in this one firm to the level of the economy.

If the economy behaves as the accelerator model predicts then investment will vary with *changes* in the overall level of sales. If we ignore the effect of stock changes, we can assume that sales equal national output (Y). This means that investment demand for next year will depend on changes in output last year, because firms *expect* the new level of demand to continue.

The effect of the accelerator on overall investment will be similar to that shown in the example. Investment will rise and fall in a cycle. As we have already seen in the section on the multiplier, investment is an important part of aggregate demand and so we must also consider the effect of such changes on the whole economy.

When investment rises the increase in aggregate demand is greater than the initial change as a result of the multiplier effect. In this way, modest changes in investment can have profound effects on national output. Thus if investment is cyclical then there will be a magnified cyclical influence on national output. Another numerical example will demonstrate this point.

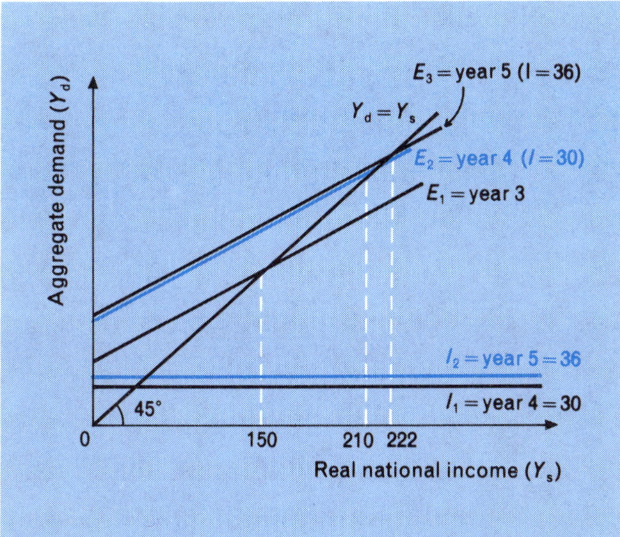

Figure 14.31 Effect of the rise in investment due to the accelerator in years 3, 4 and 5.

Let us assume that the multiplier is equal to 2 and that the capital/output ratio of the economy is fixed at 3:5. (That is to say, the amount of capital required is always equal to three-fifths of the level of national output.) Table 14.6 shows a closed economy with no government. The consumption function is $C = a + cY$ and $c = 0.5$.

Investment in the current year is determined by the change in output last year: that is, output last year minus the output of two years ago. So:

Investment 1991 = 3/5 (Output 1990 − Output 1989)

or:

$$I_{1991} = 3/5\,(Y_{1990} - Y_{1989})$$

The fraction 3/5 (or 60 per cent) comes from the need to maintain the capital/output ratio at 3:5.

In 1992, then, the demand for investment will be given by:

$$I_{1992} = 3/5\,(Y_{1991} - Y_{1990})$$

and so on.

Table 14.6 shows an example based on these figures and worked through for 12 years, starting with no changes at all in years 1 and 2. Then in year 3 autonomous consumption rises to £75 and because of the multiplier effect (which is equal to 2) output and consumption rise to £150. In year 4 there is a need to increase the capital stock by £30 because of the rise in output:

$$I_4 = 3/5\,(Y_3 - Y_2)$$
$$I_4 = 3/5\,(£150 - £100) = 3/5\,(£50) = £30$$

The rise in investment has a further multiplied effect on output and this rises by £60 (£30 × 2) and so in year 5 there is a further need to raise the capital stock. The necessary investment in year 5 is £36, and of course this also causes output in year 5 to rise, but only by £12 (£210 to £222). This is because the *rise* in investment is only £6 (£30 to £36). This is shown in Figure 14.31.

In year 6 there is only a need to add £7 to the capital stock and so investment falls despite the rise in output in the previous year. The fall of £29 in investment has a multiplied effect on output which falls to £164. The economy finds that in year 7 it has a surplus of capital and so does not replace all of the capital that wears out. There is negative net investment, causing a further multiplied fall in output. This is shown in Figure 14.32.

Case Study 14.1 Topping the business cycle

America's economy has now been expanding for 91 months. It still has some way to go before it tops the 106-month boom of 1961–69 during the Vietnam war, but this is already the longest-ever expansion in peace time. Indeed, excluding the Vietnam war, the past six American upswings lasted an average of only 35 months before the economy switched back into recession. Doomsters fear that the next recession will also be longer and deeper; optimists argue that the business cycle has been broken.

If the OECD's latest projections turn out to be correct, then the world expansion has some way to run. Its forecasters have pencilled in steady GNP growth of 3% this year and next for the 24 rich economies. But just because the world avoids outright recession (defined as two or more quarters of negative growth), it does not mean that the business cycle is dead. A downturn does not have to be a full-blown recession with a collapse in output; it might instead take the form of a slowdown in the rate of growth.

The output of the industrial economies seems to have become less bumpy since the second world war, with fewer declines in output. The chart shows the ratio of the level of real GNP to its trend level since 1960. Greater stability is particularly marked in West Germany and Japan. Research suggests that the length of the business cycle has not changed, but that expansions have become longer and downswings shorter and shallower. Mr Victor Zarnowitz, of the University of Chicago, has calculated that since 1945 the average downswing in America has lasted only 11 months, compared with 21 months during the six previous cycles.

Scholars have come up with numerous theories to explain the business cycle, from the mundane (the interaction of consumption and investment) to the insane (planetary alignments). Is the muting of the business cycle something to do with global warming? Perhaps, but economists prefer other reasons why economic activity has become steadier.

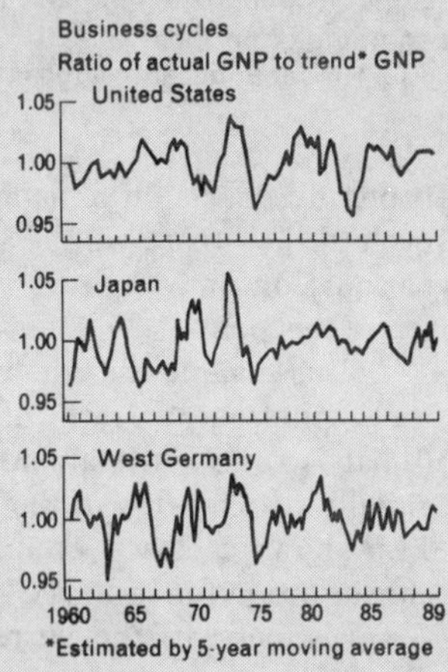

- *The shift in output from manufacturing to services.* The demand for most services is much less sensitive to changes in income than the demand for goods, partly because services, unlike goods, cannot be stored. Also, most services are less capital-intensive, and investment tends to be the first thing to be chopped when the going gets tough. In America employment in government and private 'non-cyclical' services (i.e. excluding capital-intensive services such as transport, communications and utilities) has jumped from 28% of all jobs in 1899 to 64% now.
- *The surge in government spending*, from an average of 28% of GNP in OECD countries in 1960 to 41% today, has had a cushioning effect because the public sector does not shrink during recessions. 'Automatic stabilisers' have also played a bigger role. Taxes automatically shrink and social-security benefits rise as the economy goes into recession, which helps to prop up household income.
- *Better methods of stock control.* Computers now give retailers and manufacturers up-to-the-minute information, allowing them to match production more closely to orders and so avoid an involuntary build-up of stocks. In the past, unwanted stocks of products would pile up rapidly as demand slowed, forcing firms to close factories and sack workers to trim stocks back. The slashing of stocks often turned a soft landing into a hard recession. Destocking in Britain in 1980 accounted for more than the whole of the slump in GDP, while underlying demand continued to expand.
- *Financial reform.* Some of the worst recessions before the war were aggravated by financial crashes and consequent credit crunches. Today, prompt intervention and co-operation by central banks can avert such panics. The October 1987 crash hardly touched the real economy.

These four changes will continue to smooth the business cycle in future years, and so ward off the feared depression. But other factors have also played a part in prolonging the current expansion. These could yet be reversed.

- *Lower inflation.* Previous expansions were typically brought to a halt by rising inflation, which forced governments to slam on the monetary brakes. That is why eternal vigilance on inflation is the best way to prolong an expansion. Central banks tend to understand this, governments not. In America, for instance, the White House is trying to bully the Fed into easing up in its fight against inflation. Moreover, the Fed is worried about the build-up of America's corporate debt, and the evident fragility of its domestic financial system. The result is a reluctance to raise interest rates. A gradual upward drift in inflation – with an old-fashioned crunch to follow – is not implausible.
- *The oil-price collapse* in 1986 was nicely timed, giving a boost to growth just as the economies of America and Japan had started to slow. Doomsters still fret about a renewed surge in oil and other commodity prices.

Perhaps the biggest reason for hoping that a world recession can be avoided is that the big economies are currently less synchronised than for many years. In the 1970s, countries' business cycles were closely aligned: they boomed and went bust in step. Today, the lack of synchronisation is reflected in the huge external imbalances between the big three economies. In the early 1980s America was the locomotive for the world economy, giving Japan and West Germany export-led growth. Today, domestic demand is sagging in America and Britain, but it remains buoyant in Japan and West Germany (which grew at an annual rate of 10% in the first quarter of this year).

Strong overseas demand for their exports should help to keep America and Britain out of recession. At the same time, the shrinking external surpluses of Japan and West Germany, as they meet more of the rise in domestic demand with imports, will help to keep inflation at bay.

Even so, it is too soon to pop the champagne. Perhaps the biggest risk to expansion is always the external shock – a sudden trade war, oil-price rise, debt default, what have you. In early 1979, just before OPEC doubled the price of oil and pushed the world into recession, most forecasters looked forward to continued brisk growth.

1. Does experience since the article was written suggest that business cycles are still a feature of western economies?
2. How important do you believe the accelerator model to be in the light of the article?

Source: *The Economist*, 9 June 1990

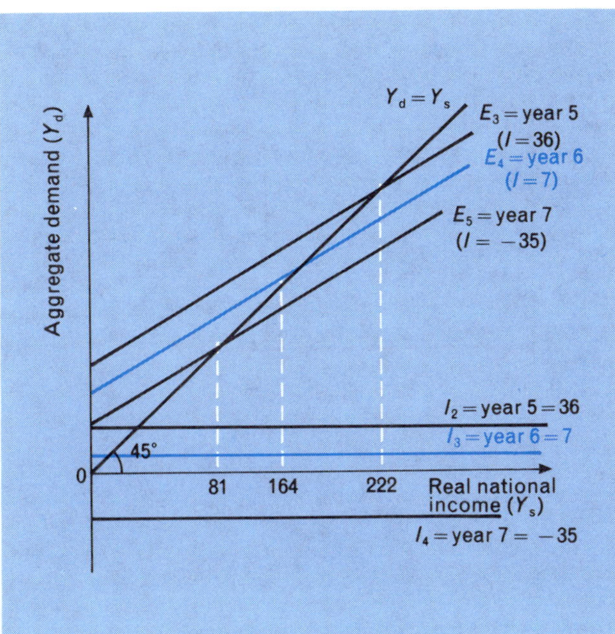

Figure 14.32 Effect of the fall in investment due to the accelerator in years 5, 6 and 7.

Thus a cyclical motion has been set up by one change in aggregate demand. (Here we changed autonomous consumption, but a change in any component of aggregate demand will have the same effect.) As you can see from Table 14.6, the downward cycle continues until year 9 when there is a rise in output and consumption which is followed by a rise in investment in year 10 and another 'boom' period. The multiplier amplifies the effect of the accelerator and so makes changes in investment very significant for the economy as a whole.

It is important to remember that this model relies primarily on the expectations of firms, not on the numbers we choose for the multiplier and the capital/output ratio. If businesses *expect* a change in output and sales to be maintained then they will invest or disinvest accordingly. An important lesson to be drawn from this model is that business confidence is crucial. If a generally optimistic mood prevails then the economy can be expected to grow as businesses invest and the accelerator and multiplier do their work. A generally pessimistic mood may lead to a fall in investment and an overall decline in output. It is possible for such moods to become self-fulfilling prophecies.

SUMMARY

1. The level of investment undertaken by firms will vary with the level of interest rates.
2. The level of investment for the whole economy is shown by the marginal efficiency of capital schedule. The lower the rate of interest, the greater the level of aggregate investment.
3. A fall in the rate of interest will cause a rise in investment which has a multiplied effect on national income.
4. The accelerator theory suggests that changes in investment due to changes in the level of demand (sales) will lead to a cyclical pattern for national income.
5. The level of business confidence (expectations) is vital to the level of investment and so is an important factor in business cycles.

Aggregate demand and supply – an alternative method of national income determination

So far our analysis has been concerned with 'aggregate expenditure' ($C+I+G+X-M$). Here we introduce the concept of an aggregate demand curve and an aggregate supply curve. We do this so that we can also discuss the relationship between the price level and national output.

To avoid confusion we should point out that the aggregate demand schedule (*AD*) is not the same as the aggregate expenditure function (*E*) of the previous section. This mistake is sometimes made by students because the vertical axis in income–expenditure models is frequently labelled 'aggregate demand' (Y_d). This is to allow us to see the level of aggregate demand in the model. The diagram does not trace out the aggregate demand curve itself.

Aggregate demand is the amount of goods and services required at a given price level. An aggregate demand curve therefore traces out the level of aggregate demand at various price levels. We are therefore introducing the price level, which was previously missing, into our analysis. (An inflationary gap is assumed to lead rising prices – if you examine Figure 14.17 you will find that price does not appear on either axis.)

From product markets to economies

It is tempting to assume that aggregate demand and aggregate supply curves behave as if they were demand and supply curves of a particular product (as we discussed in Chapter 5). This is not a valid assumption and you should avoid this way of thinking.

The classical (pre-Keynes) economists believed that the whole economy did work like one large product market. Equilibrium occurred where the demand curve crossed the supply curve. If there was unemployment then wages and prices would fall until full employment was reached (see Figure 14.23).

In the *General Theory*, Keynes denied that you could treat the economy in aggregate like a single market. According to Keynes, people would not accept the lower wages implied by the classical model, so the aggregate (average) price level was 'sticky' downwards. When faced with high unemployment (a depression), prices and wages would not fall to restore full employment. We have already seen the policy ideas that followed from Keynes's analysis.

Having made the distinction between individual markets and the aggregate economy we can now look at how aggregate demand and supply curves are constructed.

Aggregate demand curve

Aggregate demand is the total amount of goods and services that consumers plan to purchase at a given price level. The **aggregate demand curve (AD)** shows the relationship between aggregate demand and the price level. For a given price level we can read off the level of real national income (Y_s) from the aggregate demand curve.

The aggregate demand curve in Figure 14.33 is shown as downward sloping, just like the demand curve for a product. The differences here are firstly that the price level is the average price level, and secondly that movements along the curve are not explained in the same way as for a single product.

In the case of a single product, if the price changes then people will buy more due to their utility-maximizing behaviour (see Chapter 4). But if the average price level changes, there are a number of other effects.

When the price level rises, interest rates usually follow as lenders try to protect the real value of the loans they have made and of the repayments they receive. Rising interest rates cause a fall in demand for goods such as houses, cars and investment goods because many of these goods are purchased with loans. By this means, aggregate demand will fall following a rise in the average price level.

Price rises also cause a fall in the real value of assets denominated in money terms – cash and bonds, for example. Such assets will have a lower purchasing power than previously and so this will lead to a lower level of purchases, i.e. a lower level of aggregate demand. This is known as a wealth effect.

When the price level rises at a faster rate in the UK than in other countries then UK goods will become relatively more expensive in comparison with foreign goods. UK residents and foreigners will buy fewer UK-produced goods and more foreign goods. Overall the demand for goods produced in the UK will fall, i.e. aggregate demand will fall.

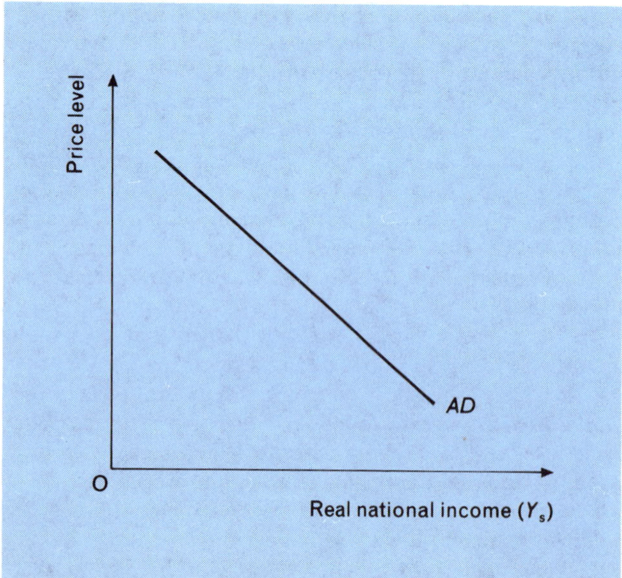

Figure 14.33 Aggregate demand curve.

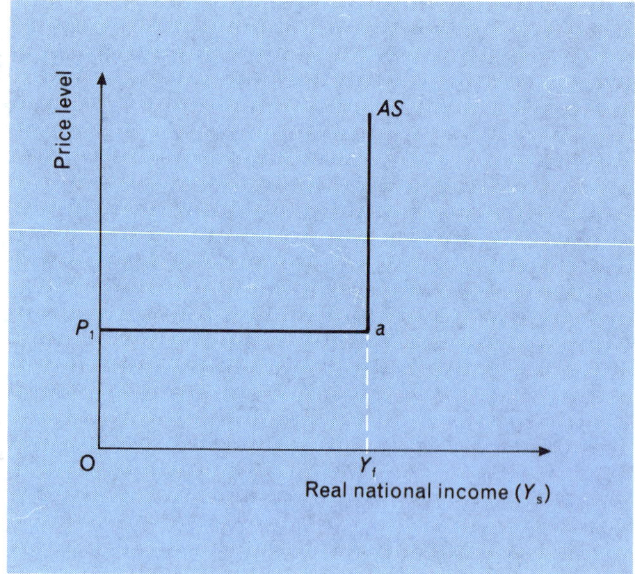

Figure 14.34 Aggregate supply curve.

Aggregate supply curve

Aggregate supply is the total amount of goods and services that producers plan to supply at a given price level. The **aggregate supply curve** (*AS*) shows the relationship between aggregate supply and the price level. For a given price level we can read off the level of real national income (Y_s) from the aggregate supply curve.

It is not possible simply to draw an upward-sloping curve for aggregate supply. This is because we are dealing with the average price level and overall supply. It is necessary to take into account the capacity of the economy to produce (supply).

If the economy has excess capacity then it is possible to produce more without raising prices – that is to say, unit costs remain the same. Eventually the capacity of the economy to produce will be reached (the full-employment level of output) and then it will no longer be possible to increase output. This, admittedly very simple, case suggests that the aggregate supply curve is a reverse L-shape (see Figure 14.34).

As output expands from 0 to Y_f (the full-employment level), the average price level remains the same at P_1. When point *a* is reached the economy is working at full capacity and so no further output is possible. Any attempt to expand production causes costs to rise as factor prices are bid up. There is no rise in production, but there is a rise in the price level.

An alternative aggregate supply curve

We can adjust the aggregate supply curve to make it more realistic. The economy does not suddenly reach its capacity point: different industries reach capacity at different times. Often the constraint on production is a 'bottleneck', a part of the productive process that has reached its capacity before other parts of the process, and which then prevents the full use of these other parts.

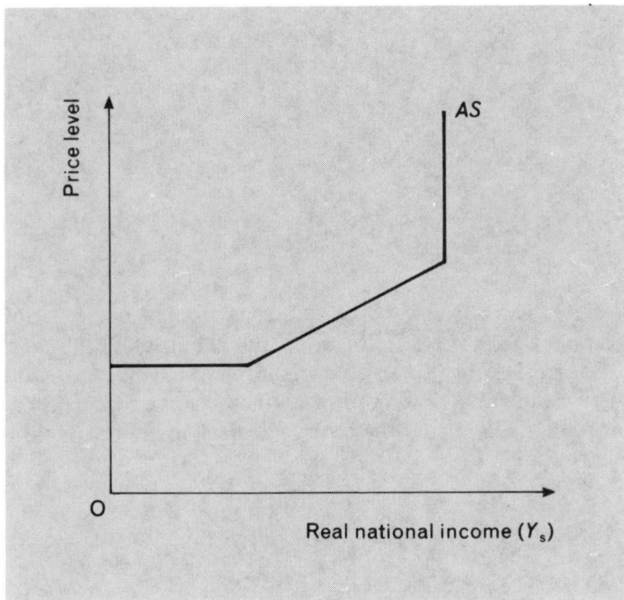

Figure 14.35 Modified aggregate supply curve.

Overcoming bottlenecks involves hiring more factors of production. This will cause their prices to be bid up. As more firms reach capacity constraints, competition for the services of factors of production will become greater and their prices will rise more quickly. Eventually full employment will be reached. This implies that the aggregate supply curve has an upward-sloping section, as in Figure 14.35.

Determination of national output and the price level

Equilibrium national income occurs where the *AD* curve crosses the *AS* curve. In Figure 14.36 *AD* crosses *AS* at a level of national income Y_1 and an average price level P_1.

This gives us a way of analysing how the level of national output and the price level are related. We will be able to use it when discussing inflation, which can be caused by movements of either of the curves.

The causes of inflation are fully discussed in Chapter 16, but it should be clear that as *AD* shifts to the right (say because of an increase in the supply of money) then the average level of prices will rise. How far prices rise will depend upon where the initial *AD* curve cuts the *AS* curve. For example, a shift from AD_1 to AD_2 in Figure 14.37

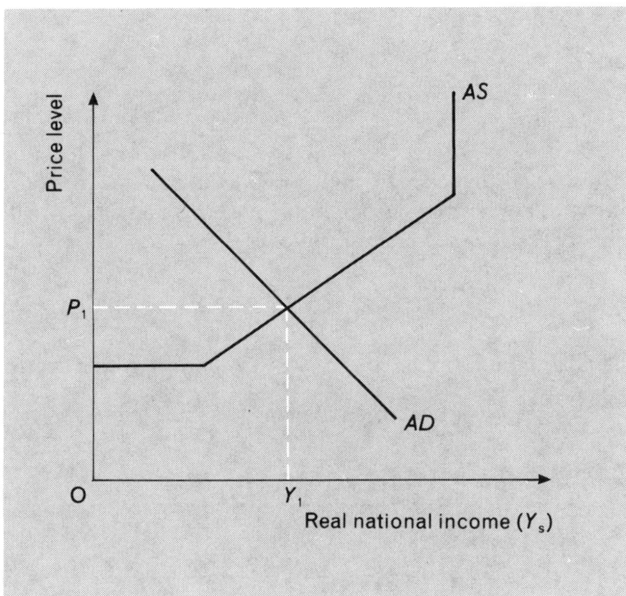

Figure 14.36 Equilibrium national output and price level.

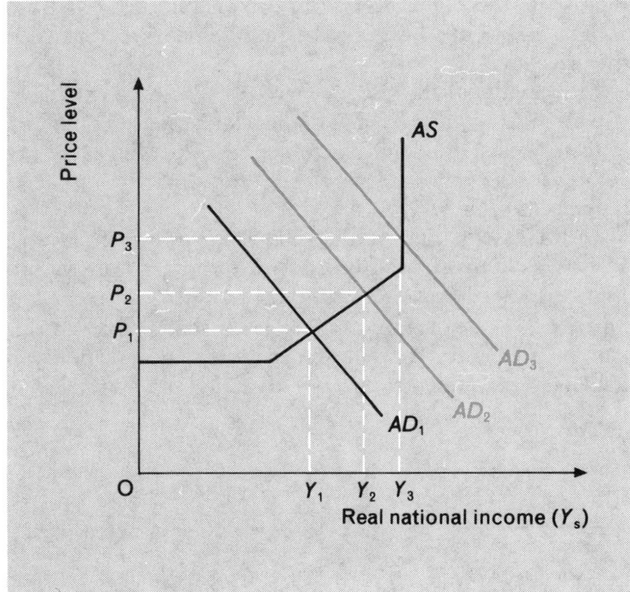

Figure 14.37 Effect of an increase in aggregate demand on national output and price level: demand-pull inflation.

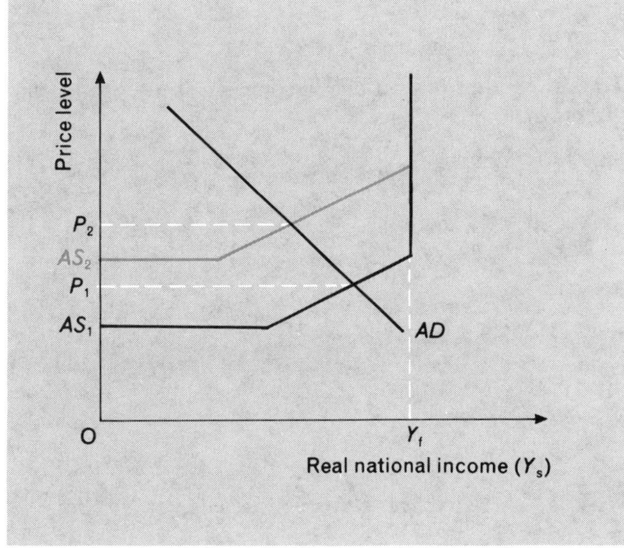

Figure 14.38 Effect of a decrease in aggregate supply on national output and price level: cost-push inflation.

represents the same increase in demand as the shift from AD_2 to AD_3, but a lower rise in output and a greater rise in the price level.

Movements of the supply curve can also cause prices to rise by shifting the AS curve to the left (say because of a rise in factor costs). The movement from AS_1 to AS_2 in Figure 14.38 causes the price level to rise, but capacity output to remain the same at Y_f.

In the case of Figure 14.37 the rise in the price level is known as **demand-pull inflation**, and in the case of Figure 14.38 it is called **cost-push inflation**, due to the initial causes of the rise in prices. We shall return to this matter in Chapter 16 when the analysis of this section will help us to examine the causes of inflation in the UK.

*Appendix: The algebraic determination of national income

We have seen that in the Keynesian model of national output determination the critical factor is aggregate demand. In this appendix we show how national output is determined in each of the three models we developed earlier using algebra only. All of the relevent diagrams and explanations can be found in the text of the chapter.

Two-sector model

Aggregate demand is:

$$Y_d = C + I \quad (1)$$
$$C = a + cY \quad (2)$$
$$I = \bar{I} \quad (3)$$

To find equilibrium national income substitute for (2) and (3) into (1):

$$Y = a + cY + \bar{I} \quad (4)$$

so:

$$Y - cY = a + \bar{I}$$

so:

$$Y(1-c) = a + \bar{I}$$

so:

$$Y = \frac{a+\bar{I}}{1-c} \quad (5)$$

We know that income is either consumed or saved. So:

$$Y = C + S \quad (6)$$

This implies that:

$$s = sY \quad (7)$$

and:

$$s = 1 - c$$

Therefore:

$$Y = \frac{a+\bar{I}}{s} \quad (8)$$

From (1) and (6) we have that $Y = C + I = C + S$. Thus:

$$S = I \quad (9)$$

When I is fixed at $\bar{I}$, S will equal I at only one level of output. This is the equilibrium national output.

From (5) and (8) we can see that any change in I will increase national income. For a given change in I national income Y will rise by the change in $I \times 1/s$, where $1/s$ is the multiplier.

Closed economy with government

Aggregate demand is now:

$$Y = C + I + G \quad (12)$$
$$C = a + cY(1-t) \quad (13)$$
$$I = \bar{I} \quad (3)$$
$$G = \bar{G} \quad (14)$$
$$S = Y - C = Y - a - cY(1-t) \quad (7)$$
$$T = tY \quad (15)$$

Therefore to find equilibrium national output solve (12) for (13), (3) and (14):

$$Y = a + cY(1-t) + \bar{I} + \bar{G}$$

so:

$$Y - cY(1-t) = a + \bar{I} + \bar{G}$$
$$Y[1 - c(1-t)] = a + \bar{I} + \bar{G}$$

$$Y = \frac{a+\bar{I}+\bar{G}}{1-c(1-t)} \quad (16)$$

or:

$$Y = \frac{a+\bar{I}+\bar{G}}{s+ct} \quad (17)$$

From (17) any change in I or G will increase national income. For a given change in G (or I) national income will rise by the change in G multiplied by:

$$\frac{1}{s+ct} \quad (18)$$

This is the multiplier in the closed economy with government.

Open economy

Aggregate demand is:

$$Y = C + I + G + (X - M) \quad (19)$$

Equations (13), (3), (14), (7) and (15) hold:

$$X = \bar{X} \quad (20)$$

$$M = mY \qquad (21)$$

Therefore to find equilibrium national output solve (18) for (13), (3), (14), (19) and (20):

$$Y = \frac{a+\bar{I}+\bar{G}+\bar{X}}{s+ct+m} \qquad (22)$$

For a given change in I, G or X national output will rise by the change multiplied by:

$$\frac{1}{s+ct+m} \qquad (23)$$

This is the multiplier in an open economy.

Exam Preparation and Practice

MULTIPLE-CHOICE QUESTIONS

1.

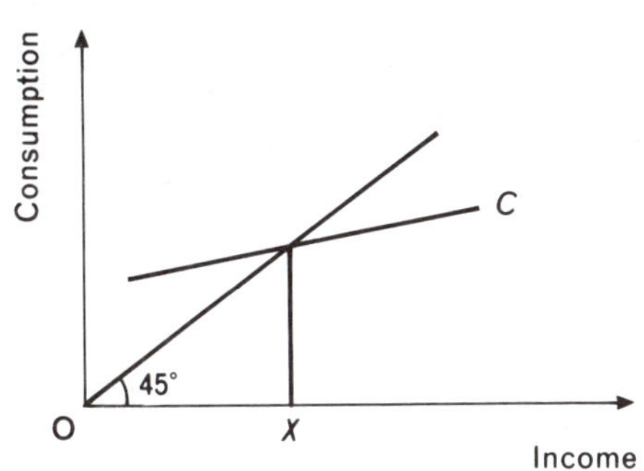

The diagram above indicates a situation in which, with National Income at OX, average propensity to consume is

A 0
B 0.5
C less than 1.0 but greater than 0.5
D 1.0
E greater than 1.0

(LON.)

2.

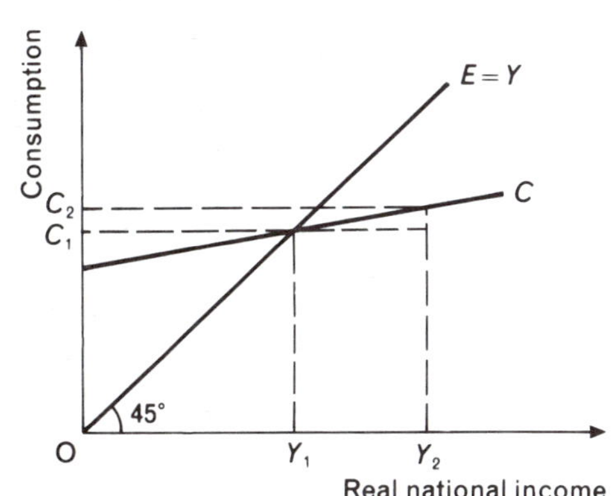

The diagram shows the consumption function for an economy. When national income rises from OY_1 to OY_2 the marginal propensity to consume is shown by:

A OC_1/OY_1
B OC_2/OY_2
C $(C_2-C_1)/(OY_2-OY_1)$
D C_2-C_1

3. If the marginal propensity to consume in a closed economy with no government is 0.75, the marginal propensity to save will be:

A 0.2
B 0.25
C 0.3
D 0.75 − 0.25

4. In a Keynesian model of the economy, which of the following statements implies a closed national economy with no government sector in equilibrium?

A The economy has reached the point of full employment.
B Planned savings and investment are equal.
C Aggregate consumption expenditure equals aggregate income from producing consumer goods and services.
D The level of investment is static.

(AEB)

5.

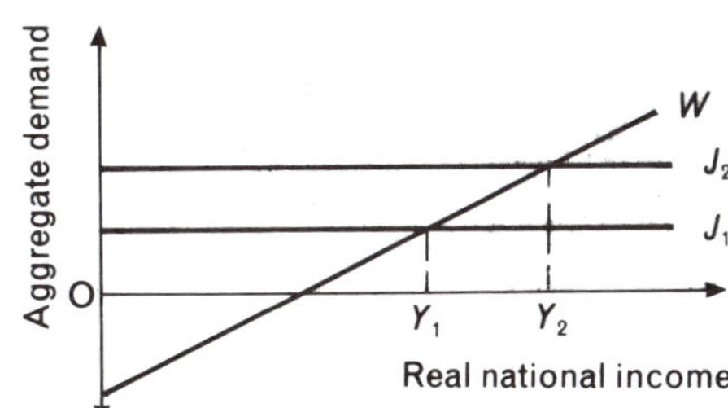

The diagram shows the injections functions (J) and withdrawals function (W) for an economy. What could cause the equilibrium level of national income to rise from OY_1 to OY_2?

A A rise in the level of exports.
B A fall in the level of investment.
C A rise in the marginal propensity to consume.
D A rise in the marginal propensity to save.

6. The multiplier in a closed economy with a government sector is equal to:

A 1 − marginal propensity to consume.
B 1 − (marginal propensity to save + marginal propensity to tax).
C 1/marginal propensity to save + marginal propensity to tax.
D 1/marginal propensity to consume.

7.

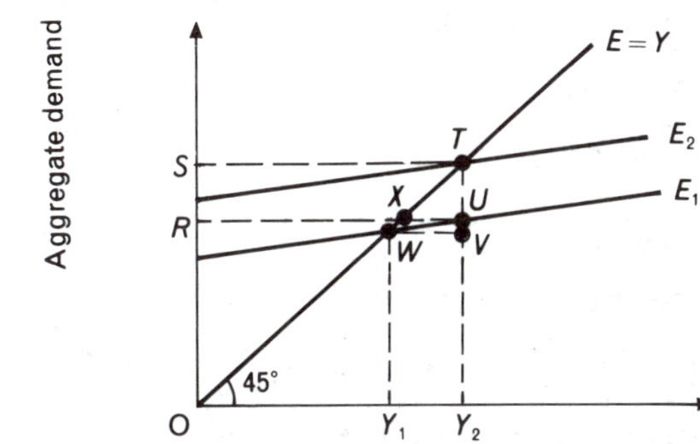

The diagram shows how equilibrium national income changes following a new injection into the circular flow. Which of the following represents the value of the multiplier?

A RS/WV
B RS/XU
C UT/XU
D WV/UT

Questions 8 and 9 relate to the following information.

A closed economy with no government is presently in equilibrium. The marginal propensity to save is 0.2. Following a new injection of £1,000, the economy moves to a new equilibrium.

8. By how much does national income rise?

9. By how much do savings rise?
A £1,000
B £2,000
C £3,000
D £4,000
E £5,000

10. An open economy with no government has a consumption function of $C = £100 + 0.6Y$. Exports are £200 and investment is £100; the marginal propensity to import is 0.1. What is the equilibrium level of national income?
A £640
B £666
C £800
D £920

11.

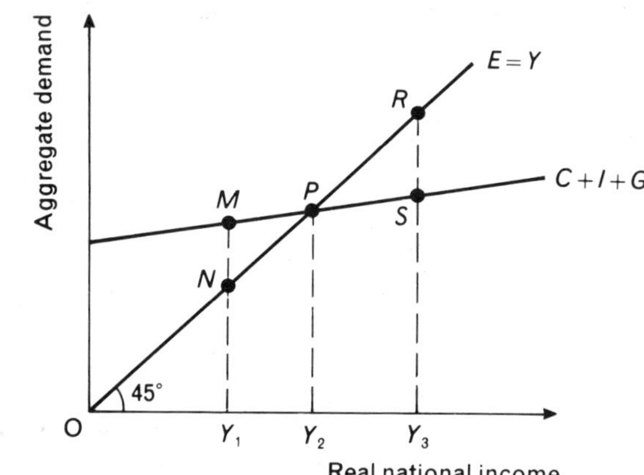

The diagram shows an economy in equilibrium at income OY_2. If the full-employment level of income is OY_1, which of the following represents the inflationary gap?
A *MP* **C** *RS*
B *MN* **D** *SP*

12. Manipulating aggregate demand will be least effective when:
A There is no government sector.
B The economy is open with a high marginal propensity to import.
C There is high unemployment.
D Planned investment is zero.

13. Which theory states that net investment is a function of changes in national income?
A Accelerator.
B Multiplier.
C Crowding out.
D Fiscal policy.

Answer key

Where there are three numbered alternatives

A	B	C	D	E
1, 2, 3 Correct	1, 2 Correct	2, 3 Correct	1 Correct	3 Correct

Where there are four numbered alternatives

A	B	C	D	E
1, 2 and 3 Correct	1 and 3 Correct	2 and 4 Correct	4 only Correct	1 and 4 Correct

14. As real output increases in an economy where the consumption function is $C = 500 + 0.7Y$:
1 Consumption expenditure will rise.
2 Savings will rise.
3 The average propensity to consume will fall.
4 The marginal propensity to consume will fall.

15. If an economy is at a full-employment equilibrium, which of the following will cause an inflationary gap to arise?
1 A rise in the marginal propensity to save.
2 A rise in the rate of direct taxation.
3 An increase in the level of exports.

16. The accelerator theory suggests that the level of net investment depends on changes in the level of national income. These changes may *not* occur in practice because
1 business expectations of profit may be very pessimistic.
2 firms may have considerable spare capacity.
3 the rate of interest may be too low.

(AEB)

17. The diagram shows a simple Keynesian model with no international or government sectors. M represents the supply of money, LP the liquidity preference schedule, MEI the marginal efficiency of investment, and SS the savings function. The broken line represents an initial equilibrium. [*MEC* = *MEI*.]

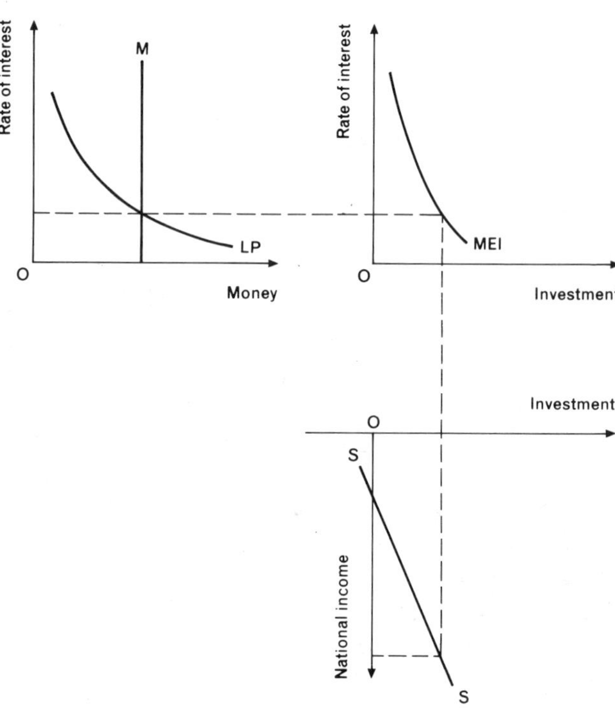

If the authorities increase the supply of money, then
1 investment will decrease.
2 national income will increase.
3 bond prices will increase.

(LON.)

18. What could cause the marginal efficiency of capital schedule to shift to the right?
1 A fall in the cost of capital equipment.
2 An increase in government tax relief on new investment.
3 A fall in the rate of interest.

EXERCISES

1. If the consumption function is $C = a + cY$:
   (a) What is the marginal propensity to consume?
   (b) What is the average propensity to consume?
   (c) If $Y =$ £200, $a =$ £50 and $c = 0.8$, what is the total level of consumption?
   (d) If income rises to £300, by how much will consumption rise?
   (e) What is the average propensity to consume at the new level of income?
   (f) Given the consumption above, what is the savings function?
   (g) Draw a graph of the consumption function, showing the level of consumption when income is £200 and £300.

   NB The answer to this question is provided for both formulations of the multiplier discussed in the text.

2. Aggregate demand for an economy is given by $Y = C + I$, where $C = a + cY$ and $I = \bar{I}$.
   (a) When $a =$ £100m, $c = 0.7$ and $I =$ £200m, what is the equilibrium level of national output?
   (b) If a government is established and it decides to impose an income tax of 15 per cent and spend £100m a year, what is the new level of national income?
   (c) What is the government's budget deficit/surplus?
   (d) What is the value of the multiplier?
   (e) If the government raised income tax to 20 per cent, what would be the new value of the multiplier?

3. (a) On graph paper draw a diagram to show an economy represented by $Y = C + I + G$.
   $C = cY$, $S = sY$, $I = \bar{I}$ and $G = \bar{G}$. Presently there is no income tax. $c = 0.8$, $\bar{I} =$ £200m and $\bar{G} =$ £200m.
   Label the expenditure function, total withdrawals function and total injections function.
   (b) On the diagram show the effect of a rise in the marginal propensity to save to 0.4.
   (c) Show the effect of the imposition of a 10 per cent income tax.
   (d) Using the final withdrawal and expenditure functions from (c) show, on a separate diagram, the size of the deflationary gap if the full-employment level of national income is £1,000m, and the effect of increasing government spending by £100m in an attempt to reduce this gap.

   NB The answer to this question is provided for both formulations of the multiplier discussed in the text.

4. Little Trivilvania is an open economy with a government. From the national accounts we know that the *MPC* is 0.7, income tax is 20 per cent, government spending is £400m, gross domestic fixed capital formation is £300m and exports are £200m. There is a strong import demand with 30 per cent of income being spent on foreign goods. (You may take the consumption function to be $C = cY$.)
   (a) What is the level of Little Trivilvania's national income?
   (b) What is the government budget deficit/surplus?
   (c) Should the government be worried about Little Trivilvania's balance of payments?
   (d) The full-employment level in Little Trivilvania is £900m. Would the government wish to alter its fiscal policy? If so, what course of action might it take?

5. How would the following events affect the level of UK national income?
   (a) An increased desire by foreigners to buy British goods.
   (b) A 'Buy British' campaign.
   (c) A general loss of confidence by firms in the level of future sales.
   (d) A government campaign to promote sales of National Savings bonds.

6. The following table is a multiplier–accelerator model. The table shows the levels of consumption, available capital and net investment for an economy. Capital is required in fixed proportion to output (1 unit of capital: 10 units of output) and capital has a life of 5 years. The value of the multiplier is 2 and there are no other influences on consumer spending.

Year	Sales (£m)	Capital stock (£m)	Capital required (£m)	Net investment (£m)	Gross investment (£m)	Change in investment (£m)
1	1,000	80	100	0	20	0
2	1,000	80	100	0	20	
3	1,200	80	120			

   (a) Complete the table to year 8.
   (b) If the multiplier is 5 instead of 2, how will this affect the business cycle?

DATA-RESPONSE QUESTIONS

1. Study the data below, then answer the questions which follow.

   The following is data for a hypothetical closed economy which initially is in short run macroeconomic equilibrium.

   (i) The consumption function is given by the equation

   $$C = 100 + 0.8\,Y_D$$

   where C denotes consumption in £ billion and Y_D denotes disposable after-tax income in £ billion.

   (ii) All government revenue is raised by a 25% proportional income tax. Hence

   $$Y_D = 0.75\,Y$$

   where Y denotes national income in £ billion.

   (iii) Private investment spending = £1,400 billion.

   (iv) Government expenditure on goods and services = £2,500 billion.

   (v) National income (Y) = £10,000 billion.

(a) What are the initial values of consumption, savings and government tax revenue? [5]

(b) What is the relationship between the average propensity to consume and the marginal propensity to consume in this economy? How does the average propensity to consume vary as disposable income increases? [5]

(c) Suppose that private investment spending subsequently decreases to £1,000 billion. What, other things being equal, is the change in national income that is predicted by the Keynesian income-expenditure model? [5]

(d) If government expenditure and the tax rate remain unchanged, what is the government budget deficit or surplus at the equilibrium level of national income **following** the decrease in private investment? [5]

(e) Suppose the government wishes to achieve a return to the original national income of £10,000 billion via increasing after-tax disposable incomes by means of non-taxable cash benefits paid to households. If the consumption function is unchanged, by how much must government expenditure on cash benefits increase? [5]

(WJEC)

2. The following data refers to the UK economy.

	Real consumers' expenditure (£ million, 1980 prices) C	Real personal disposable income (£ million, 1980 prices) Y
1973	127,669	143,961
1974	125,810	142,828
1975	125,113	143,310
1976	125,504	142,514
1977	124,868	140,606
1978	131,742	150,624
1979	137,612	158,743
1980	137,234	161,572
1981	136,936	157,742
1982	138,201	158,554
1983	143,791	162,677
1984	146,888	166,664
1985	152,038	170,965
1986	159,165	178,849

Source: *Data Supplement, The Economic Review*, September 1987, Philip Allan.

(*a*) What is meant by the term 'real personal disposable income'? **(3 marks)**

(*b*) What factors might have caused 'real personal disposable income' to change between 1973 and 1986? **(4 marks)**

(*c*) From the data, calculate the marginal propensity to consume between 1985 and 1986. **(3 marks)**

(*d*) To what extent does the data support the Keynesian hypothesis that consumption is a function of income? **(5 marks)**

(*e*) What factors other than current disposable income may affect consumption? **(5 marks)**

(LON.)

15 *The *IS*/*LM* diagram

In this chapter we will discuss:

1. A Keynesian model of the economy that includes the money market and the goods market.
2. How the views of both the Keynesians and the monetarists may be represented in one diagram.

Introduction

When Keynes first published his *General Theory of Employment, Interest and Money* in 1936 it was met with blank incomprehension by some and with hostility by others. The incomprehension sprang partly from the revolutionary nature of his ideas. It is not easy for those brought up in one school of thought readily to grasp alien ideas. But part of the difficulty with the book was the writing style. It is long and involved and gives the impression that the author was trying to obscure rather than reveal his thoughts to his readers.

What was wanted was an interpreter who could give a simple, accessible account of the new ideas in terms understandable to those schooled in the doctrines of classical economics. This service was provided by John Hicks (who was later knighted and was a Nobel laureate), who wrote *Mr Keynes and the Classics: A suggested interpretation* in 1937. This paper simplified the economy by considering just three kinds of market: the market for all goods and services taken together (the goods market); the market for financial assets and money (the money market); and finally the labour market, where all those seeking employment met all those offering it.

The essence of the Keynesian point of view is that these markets are interdependent and that all three of them cannot be in equilibrium simultaneously. If the supply of goods equalled the demand for goods and if the supply of money equalled the demand for money then the demand for labour would typically be less than the supply of labour, and unemployment would result. Briefly, if the goods market cleared and if the money market cleared then the labour market would not clear. We will begin by looking at the goods market and the money market separately, and then consider the ways in which they are interrelated. Finally, we show how this interrelation leads to protracted unemployment.

The goods market

According to Keynes, the supply of goods and services will always be limited by lack of demand. That is to say, firms would produce the amount demanded and would like to produce more, but if they did they would not be able to sell it. If you want the economy to produce more than it is currently producing then you simply increase demand. If you reduce demand then output will be similarly reduced. Output then is demand determined, and the goods market clears by allowing supply (output) to follow passively where demand leads. All that is needed is to predict demand – we need know nothing further about supply.

We have already seen that, in a closed economy, there are three sources of demand for goods and services: households, firms and the government. Aggregate demand is therefore made up of households' expenditure (consumption), business expenditure (investment) and government expenditure.

Consumption rises as income rises, as shown in Figure 15.1. Investment is decided by businesses, which base their decision on the cost of borrowing investment funds, i.e. the rate of interest. As interest rates rise, businesses are less inclined to borrow and hence are less inclined to invest in new capital. Investment demand therefore falls as interest rates rise. This is shown in Figure 15.2. Government expenditure (G) is determined by political considerations, and we shall take this element of aggregate demand as 'given' ($G = \bar{G}$).

In sum then we have three elements of aggregate demand: consumption, which rises with income; investment, which falls as interest rates rise; and government

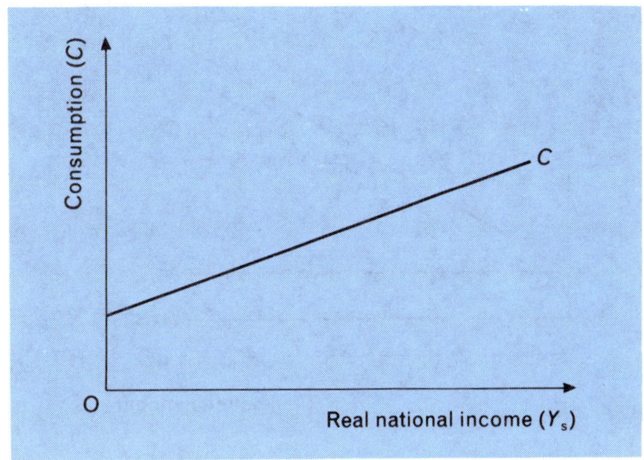

Figure 15.1 Consumption function.

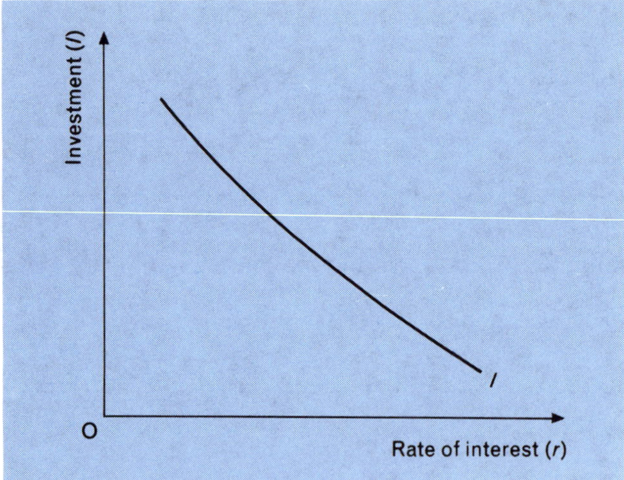

Figure 15.2 Investment function.

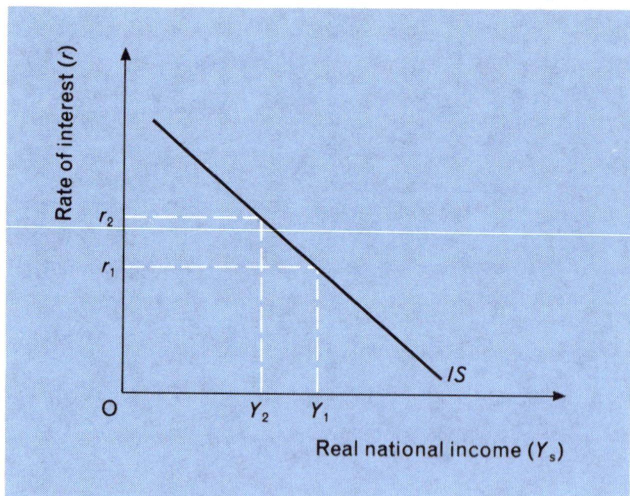

Figure 15.4 *IS* curve.

expenditure, which is determined outside the system (see Chapter 14). These three are represented in Figure 15.3.

Aggregate supply (Y_s) is measured along the horizontal axis. Aggregate demand is measured up the vertical axis. The first element, government expenditure (G), does not vary as output (supply) varies, so is a horizontal straight line. The second element, investment, is also independent of supply (but remember it does decrease as interest rates rise), so this too is a horizontal straight line (but we can change its position by changing interest rates). The third element, consumption, rises as income (supply) rises, so this is shown by an upward-sloping line.

When all these three are taken together they must add up to aggregate supply. The 45° line shows all points at which aggregate demand equals aggregate supply, and the economy will go to that level of output at which the expenditure line (E_1) crosses the 45° line. This is shown as Y_1 in Figure 15.3.

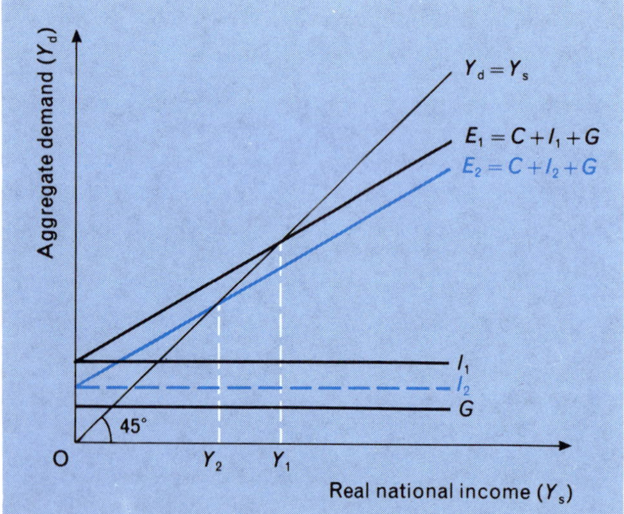

Figure 15.3 Aggregate demand and aggregate supply.

If we now imagine that interest rates rise then we know that investment will fall – say from I_1 to I_2. This moves the expenditure function down from E_1 to E_2. The new point of intersection occurs at Y_2, which lies below the original level of output (Y_1). If we took a higher level of interest rates still then investment would fall again, aggregate demand would fall again and we would have an even lower level of output.

The net result of all this is that as interest rates rise output will fall. This is shown in Figure 15.4. At the original rate of interest (r_1) the level of output is Y_1, at the higher rate of interest (r_2) the level of output is Y_2, and so on for all levels of interest rate. The *IS* curve shows all combinations of interest rate and output at which the supply of goods equals the aggregate demand for goods. In other words, the *IS* curve represents those combinations of interest rate and income for which the goods market clears. The curve is downward sloping.

The money market

The market we have just been looking at is in equilibrium when the annual *flow* of goods and services demanded is equal to the annual *flow* of goods and services supplied. The market we are now going to look at is to do with *stock* rather than flows. The stock referred to is the stock of wealth. Every year we receive a quantity of income, spend some and save the rest. Over time these savings build up into a stock of wealth.

When we talk of someone's income we say £2,000 *per year*, which is quite different from £2,000 *per month*. In other words, when specifying flow variables we have to specify the time period over which that flow is measured. If, on the other hand, we speak of someone's wealth we simply say that they had £2,000 on 1 January 1992. There is no need to specify a time dimension – only a date when the measurement was made.

The question here is how that wealth will be held. It could be held as stocks and shares, paintings, government bonds or even money. As a simplification let us assume that there are only two assets – government bonds and money. It is possible to extend our results to include many other assets too, but the explanation of the problem is easier to see if we confine ourselves to considering only these two assets.

As a further assumption let us say that the amount of wealth remains constant. Of course, our savings will add continually to our wealth, but we can say that in the short run these changes are too small to have any appreciable effect on our stock of wealth for a year or two. Our stock of wealth is fixed (at, say, £W) and there are only two assets – bonds (B) and money (M) – so that our stock of bonds (B) plus our stock of money (M) must equal our stock of wealth (W). That is:

$$W = B + M$$

There will be a supply of bonds by the government and a demand for bonds by wealth holders. There will also be a supply of money by the government and the banks, and a demand for money by the wealth holders. The money market will be in equilibrium when the supply of bonds equals the demand for bonds, and when the supply of money equals the demand for money. Notice that we only have to explain one of these. Since wealth is given, any excess demand for bonds must imply a deficient demand for money. Similarly, any deficient demand for bonds must imply an excess demand for money. Thus if the supply of bonds equals the demand for bonds then it follows that the supply of money must equal the demand for money.

Keynesians concentrate on explaining the supply of and demand for money and allow the bond market to be the residual.

Demand for money

We have already seen in Chapter 13 that there are two kinds of demand for money. One kind of demand is for 'active' money and is called the transactions demand for money. The second kind of demand is for 'idle' money, which consists partly of speculative and partly of precautionary balances.

Active money is money being exchanged for goods and services, and this demand goes up as income goes up:

$$M \times V = P \times Y$$

where M is the demand for transactions balances
V is the velocity of circulation
P is the aggregate price level
and Y is the real GDP

This demand for active money is shown diagrammatically in Figure 15.5. The demand curve is an upward-sloping straight line. In this case a 10 per cent increase in income results in a 10 per cent increase in the demand for active balances.

Idle balances are held not to facilitate exchanges, but to avoid loss (speculative demand) or inconvenience (precautionary demand). Both these demands are influenced by interest rates, as we have seen in Chapter 13.

The relationship between the demand for idle balances and the interest rate is shown in Figure 15.6. As interest rates fall, the demand for idle balances increases. Eventually it reaches the point of minimum interest rate, i.e. the liquidity trap.

The total demand for money therefore depends on income (active demand) and on interest rates (idle demand) and, for the money market to clear, must equal the supply of money.

Let us assume that the supply of money is fixed and that income is increasing. As income increases, so the demand for active balances increases. Since the supply of money is fixed, this increased demand for active balances can only be satisfied if there is a corresponding decrease in idle balances. This decrease in idle balances will cause an increase in the interest rate. Thus, in order for the money demand to equal the money supply, any increase in income must be matched by an increase in the interest rate. This relationship between income and interest rates is called an LM curve and is shown in Figure 15.7.

The figure shows that at very low incomes nearly all the money supply has to be held as idle balances. This means being in or near the liquidity trap, so at first the LM curve is flat. As income increases, more and more money is absorbed in active balances and so less and less is available for idle

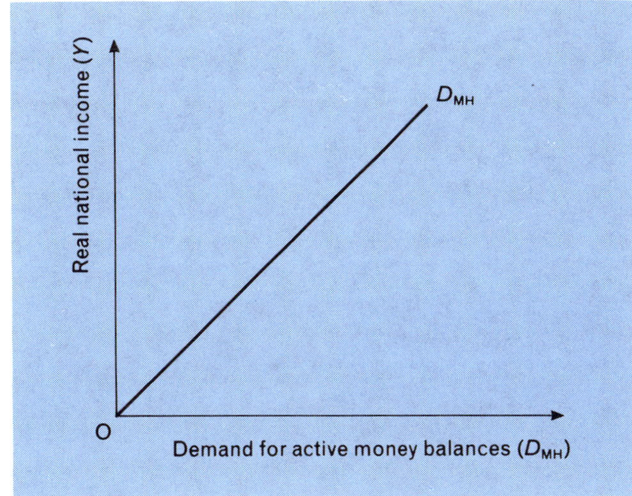

Figure 15.5 Demand for active money balances.

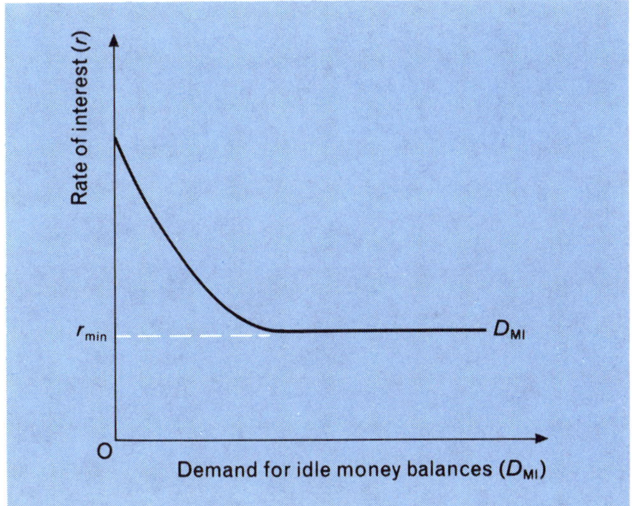

Figure 15.6 Demand for idle money balances.

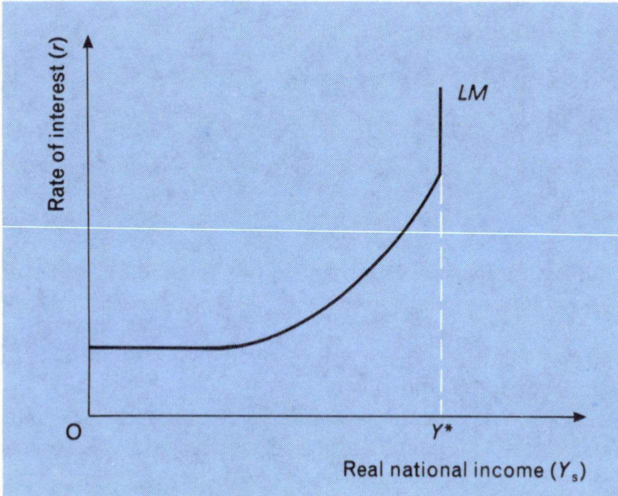

Figure 15.7 *LM* **curve.**

balances. Therefore the interest rate rises. Eventually all the money is being used for active balances and there are no idle balances. This occurs at income level Y^*. Once all the money is being used for active balances it is impossible to increase income still further and so the *LM* curve becomes vertical. (NB This level of output represents the maximum that can be transacted with the available money supply; it does *not* represent the full-employment level of output.)

The *IS*/*LM* diagram

We now have two curves: the *IS* curve, representing all those combinations of income and interest rate at which the supply of goods and services equals the demand for goods and services; and the *LM* curve, representing all those combinations of income and interest rate at which the supply of money equals the demand for money. Both curves have the same axes and hence can be drawn on the same diagram. This is shown in Figure 15.8 and is called the *IS*/*LM* diagram.

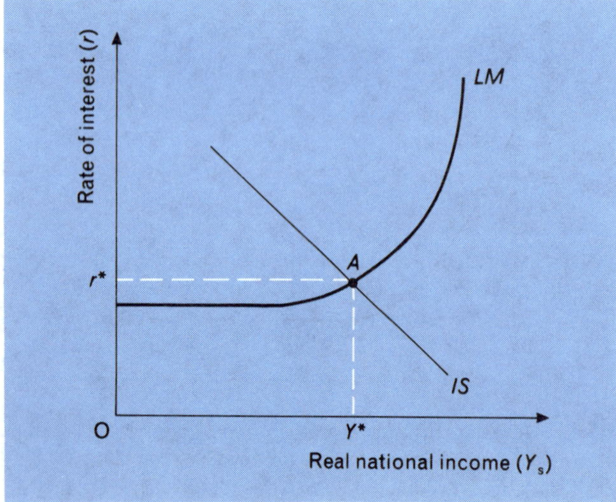

Figure 15.8 *IS*/*LM* **diagram.**

For the goods market to be in equilibrium we must be on the *IS* curve. For the money market to be in equilibrium we must be on the *LM* curve. In order for both markets to be in equilibrium we must therefore be on both curves simultaneously. There is only one combination of income and interest rate which is common to both curves and that is where they cross – point *A*. The economy therefore settles down at an interest rate of r^* and an income level of Y^*.

It seems then that the level of output is determined by the goods market and the money market rather than the labour market. There can be no reason to suppose that this level of output will be sufficient to employ all those seeking work at the existing wage rate, and hence there will be involuntary unemployment.

This result is very similar to the result we obtained in Chapter 14, where we looked only at the goods market. We have, however, gained a great deal by extending our analysis to include the money market. First, recall that in our previous analysis aggregate demand depended on government expenditure, investment expenditure and the multiplier. Any increase in investment or government expenditure had a multiplied effect on income and yet we had to assume that investment demand was fixed. We have now allowed investment to be determined by the interest rate and have shown that even so there is no tendency for investment to go to the level required for full employment of labour.

Secondly, in our previous model there was a role for the government in attaining full employment via fiscal policy, but there was no role for monetary policy. In this improved model we have both government expenditure (fiscal policy) and the supply of money (monetary policy).

To see just how all this fits in let us consider how fiscal policy works in terms of the *IS*/*LM* framework.

SUMMARY

1. The *IS*/*LM* diagram is a summary of the Keynesian system. It brings together the goods market, the money market and the labour market.
2. Supply in the goods market is determined by aggregate demand, which in a closed economy is made up of demand from consumers, firms and government.
3. Equilibrium in the goods market can be achieved with various combinations of interest rate and income, and all these combinations are represented as an *IS* curve.
4. Wealth may be held as either bonds or money. There are therefore two markets: the market for bonds and the market for money. For one of these markets to be in equilibrium so must the other.
5. Money can be either 'active', held in transactions balances, or 'idle', held in precautionary or speculative balances. The higher the level of income, the greater the demand for active balances.
6. Equilibrium in the money market requires certain combinations of interest rate and income, and all these combinations are represented as an *LM* curve.

7. The *LM* curve is at first horizontal (the liquidity trap) then upward sloping and then vertical, when all money is held in active balances.
8. The economy will be in equilibrium where the *IS* curve intersects the *LM* curve. The level of employment will be determined by the level of national income, so there may be involuntary unemployment.

Fiscal policy

Recall that we constructed the *IS* curve by adding up three elements of aggregate demand: consumption, investment and government expenditure. Consumption was explained by income (the consumption function), investment was determined by interest rates (the investment function) and government expenditure was determined politically.

Any increase in government expenditure will increase demand by the amount of the increase times the multiplier. In terms of the *IS/LM* diagram, an increase in government expenditure moves the *IS* curve to the right by the amount of the increase times the multiplier. This is shown in Figure 15.9.

This *IS* curve moves from IS_1 to IS_2, and the distance between them (measured horizontally) is the change in government expenditure ($G_2 - G_1$) times the multiplier. However, it is clear from the figure that, although output rises, it rises by less than this amount. According to the pure multiplier theory, output should rise from Y_1 to Y_2. But in order for the economy to stay in equilibrium it must be on both the *IS* and the *LM* curves. The new intersection point is at Y_3, so some of the expansion is lost. Let us now see why this is so.

The effect of government expenditure on aggregate demand was calculated by allowing government expenditure to be increased *while holding investment expenditure constant*. Consider an increase in government expenditure of £100 million and a marginal propensity to consume of 0.8 (there is no taxation). This government expenditure will generate £100 million worth of income in the first round. This increase in income will lead to an increase in consumption of £80 million (£100m × 0.8), which in turn will generate a further increase in income of £80 million. This £80 million income will generate £64 million more consumption, which generates more income and so on until the full multiplier has run its course and income has increased by £500 million, or £100m × 1/(1 − 0.8). According to this calculation, consumption and income are rising but investment remains constant. It turns out that this assumption can only rarely by justified.

The *LM* curve tells us that as income rises it will cause an increase in the interest rate. This increase in the interest rate will reduce investment. Thus as one element of aggregate demand (government expenditure) increases, another element of aggregate demand (investment) falls. The final effect of the increase in government expenditure will therefore be moderated. Income first increases by the full amount of the multiplier to Y_2. This induces an increase in the interest rate and a reduction in investment so that income falls back to Y_3.

The technical term for this secondary effect is **crowding out**. The idea is that as the government increases its expenditure it leaves less room for private expenditure and so private investment is 'crowded out' by government expenditure. It is obviously important to allow for this effect when deciding fiscal policy. If crowding out is very severe then the government will have to increase its expenditure by much more than the simple multiplier would suggest if it is to have the desired effect.

Unfortunately, it is hard to know how much crowding out there will be. Consider first the positions of the *IS* and *LM* curves in Figure 15.10.

This figure shows the *IS* curve intersecting the *LM* curve in its vertical section. In this case, movements of the *IS* curve (say from IS_1 to IS_2) will have no effect at all on

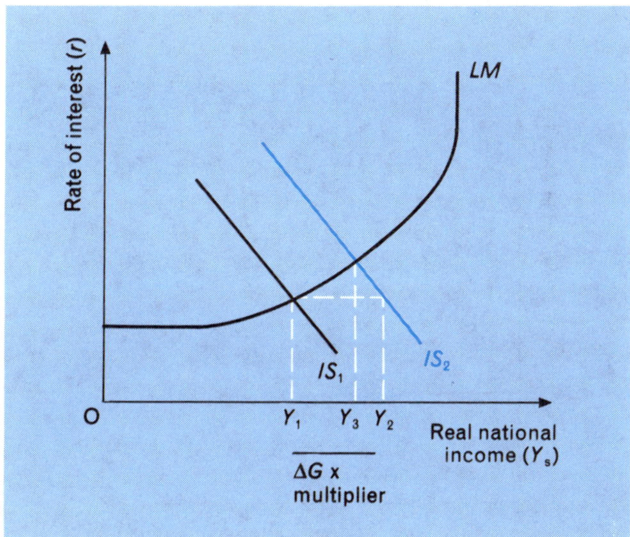

Figure 15.9 Movement of the *IS* curve following a change in fiscal policy.

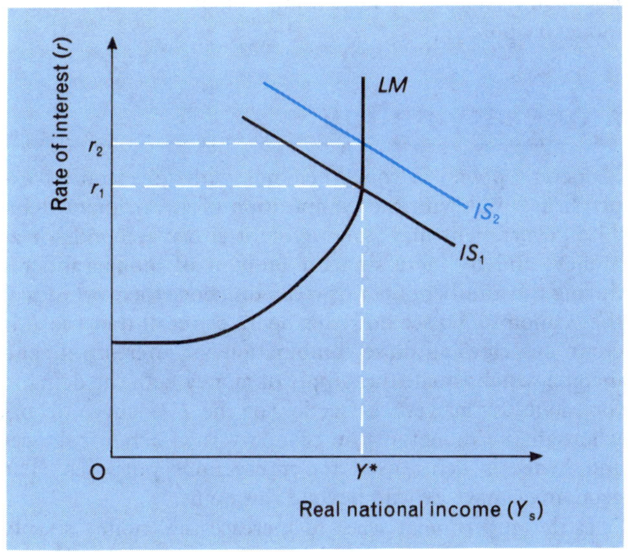

Figure 15.10 100 per cent crowding out of fiscal policy.

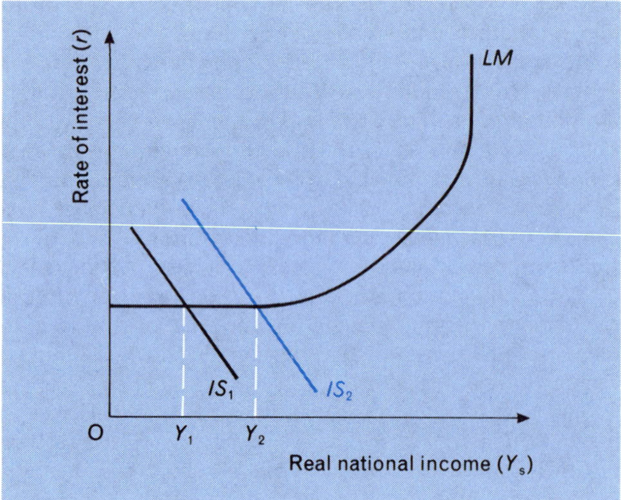

Figure 15.11 No crowding out of fiscal policy.

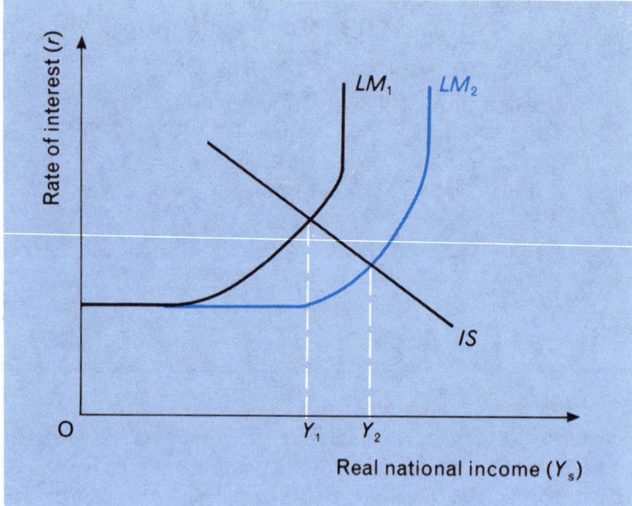

Figure 15.12 Movement of the *LM* curve following a change in the money supply.

income, which remains at Y^*. But the interest rate rises substantially – in fact it rises enough to crowd out completely the increase in government expenditure. This is called 100 per cent crowding out. Therefore if the economy is on the vertical part of the *LM* curve, fiscal policy will affect only the interest rate and will have no effect on income. If investment falls by as much as government expenditure rises, the net effect will be zero.

Consider next the position of the *IS* curve in Figure 15.11. In this case the *IS* curve intersects the *LM* curve in its horizontal section, so that there is no increase in the interest rate as income increases from Y_1 to Y_2. Since the interest rate remains constant, investment also remains constant. There will be no crowding out and the multiplier will have its full effect. This is the only case in which the full simple multiplier works and our assumption of constant investment is correct.

Between these two extremes there is some increase in the interest rate and some crowding out, but fiscal policy will have some effect. The next thing to look at is the effect of monetary policy.

Monetary policy

Monetary policy is concerned not with government expenditure, but with the composition of government debt. The government may issue its debt either as bonds or as money, and by increasing the amount of money and reducing the number of bonds it can influence the workings of the economy. To see how this operates recall that the *LM* curve describes all those combinations of interest rate and income which equate the supply of money with the demand for money. The vertical section of the *LM* curve occurs when all the money in the economy is in active balances and hence is being used for transactions purposes. The economy cannot expand beyond this point.

If the government were to increase the money supply then this vertical section would move to the right. This is because with the increased money supply more transactions (and hence more output) can be supported. Increasing the money supply will therefore move the whole *LM* curve to the right, as shown in Figure 15.12. It will be immediately apparent from the figure that this rightward movement of the *LM* curve has two effects: first, it lowers the interest rate; second, it increases income. Thus expansionary monetary policy increases income, as does expansionary fiscal policy; but in the case of monetary policy there is a decrease in the interest rate rather than the increase that results from fiscal policy.

Notice again that the increase in output is less than the horizontal movement of the *LM* curve. Once again we have to ask: by how much will this original movement be abated? Consider first the arrangement shown in Figure 15.13. In this case the *IS* curve intersects the *LM* curve in its horizontal section (the liquidity trap) and any increase in money supply will have absolutely no effect on either the interest rate or income. This is because in the liquidity trap the economy has an insatiable desire for idle balances, so the new money is simply absorbed in idle balances with no

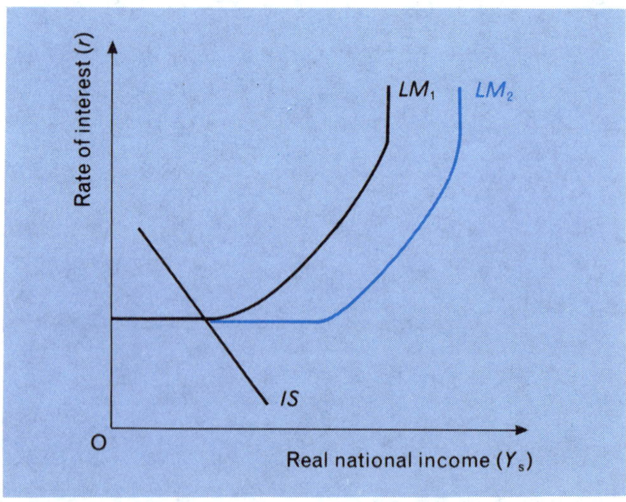

Figure 15.13 Monetary policy ineffective.

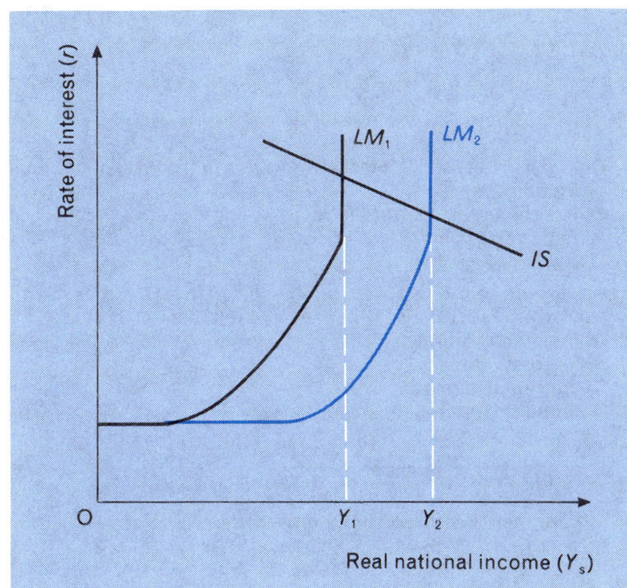

Figure 15.14 Monetary policy fully effective.

other effect. Monetary policy is therefore ineffective in the liquidity trap.

Consider next the situation shown in Figure 15.14. The *IS* curve cuts the *LM* curve in its vertical section and the increase in income is exactly the same as the horizontal movement of the *LM* curve. There is no abatement and monetary policy is at its most effective.

Keynes argued that during a depression output is low and so the economy will be in the liquidity trap. In such circumstances monetary policy is totally ineffective – any increase in money supply is absorbed into idle balances and any decrease in money supply simply reduces idle balances. The only way out of a depression is therefore to conduct fiscal policy, which is at its most effective in the liquidity trap. Expansionary fiscal policy means increasing government expenditure, i.e. running a budget deficit. The Keynesian prescription is therefore to spend your way out of a depression. This was quite revolutionary: the received wisdom held that in hard times the government should cut its expenditure, and that ideally the aim should always be to balance its budget.

Monetarists argue that the economy is always in or near the vertical part of the *LM* curve, so fiscal policy will be ineffective. If the government increases its expenditure then it crowds out private investment and interest rates (and hence costs and prices) will rise. Monetarists therefore argue against fiscal policy and deny the Keynesian case for spending one's way out of a depression.

The *IS/LM* diagram therefore encompasses both the Keynesian and the monetarist models. On the horizontal section of the *LM* curve the Keynesian prescription works. On the vertical section of the *LM* curve the monetarist prescription holds. On the upward-sloping part of the *LM* curve Keynesian prescriptions will work, but with less and less effect as the curve becomes steeper. The two schools of thought are therefore no longer to be considered as mutually exclusive alternatives, but rather different emphases within a common framework. The *IS/LM* diagram therefore represents what is called the 'neo-classical synthesis'.

SUMMARY

1. Fiscal policy moves the *IS* curve. It moves it to the right when government expenditure is increased and to the left when government expenditure is decreased.
2. The effectiveness of fiscal policy depends on where the *IS* curve intersects the *LM* curve.
   (a) If it crosses the *LM* curve in the liquidity trap, income increases by the full amount of the multiplier and the interest rate remains the same.
   (b) If it crosses the *LM* curve in the upward-sloping section, there will be an increase in both income and the interest rate. The increase in income will be less than that of the full multiplier – this is known as partial crowding out.
   (c) If it crosses the *LM* curve in the vertical section, there will be an increase in the interest rate but no increase in income – crowding out will be 100 per cent.
3. Monetary policy moves the *LM* curve. Increasing the money supply moves the *LM* curve to the right and decreasing the money supply moves the *LM* curve to the left.
4. The effectiveness of monetary policy depends on where the *LM* curve intersects the *IS* curve.
   (a) If it crosses the *IS* curve in the liquidity trap, neither increases nor decreases in the money supply will have an effect on income or the interest rate.
   (b) If it crosses the *IS* curve in the upward-sloping section, an increase in the money supply will increase income and decrease the interest rate.
   (c) If it crosses the *IS* curve in the vertical section, an increase in the money supply will cause a greater increase in income and a decrease in the interest rate. Monetary policy is most effective here.
5. The *IS/LM* diagram therefore encompasses both the Keynesian and the monetarist theories. Which view holds at any given time depends on where the *IS* and *LM* curves intersect.

Exam Preparation and Practice

MULTIPLE-CHOICE QUESTIONS

1. The *IS* curve represents:

A The combinations of national income and the rate of interest where the money market is in equilibrium.
B The combinations of national income and the rate of interest where the government budget is balanced.
C The combinations of national income and the rate of interest where the goods market is in equilibrium.
D How national income will react to a change in monetary policy.

2. In the diagram below what will be the effect of an increase in the money supply?

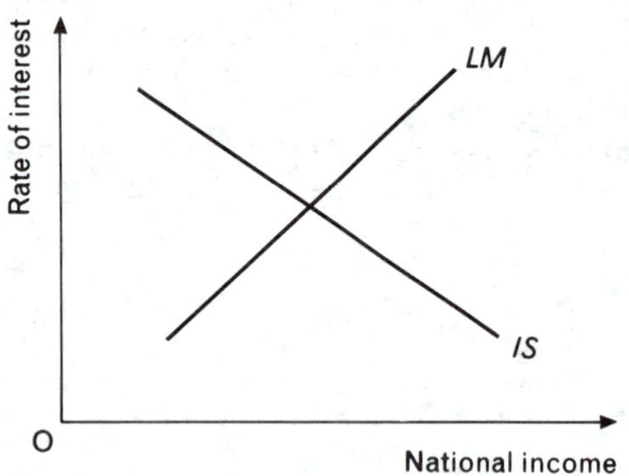

A A rise in the rate of interest and a fall in the level of national income.
B A rise in the rate of interest and a rise in the level of national income.
C A fall in the rate of interest and a fall in the level of national output.
D A fall in the rate of interest and a rise in the level of national income.
E No change in the rate of interest and a rise in the level of national income.

3. In the diagram below what will be the effect of an expansionary fiscal policy?

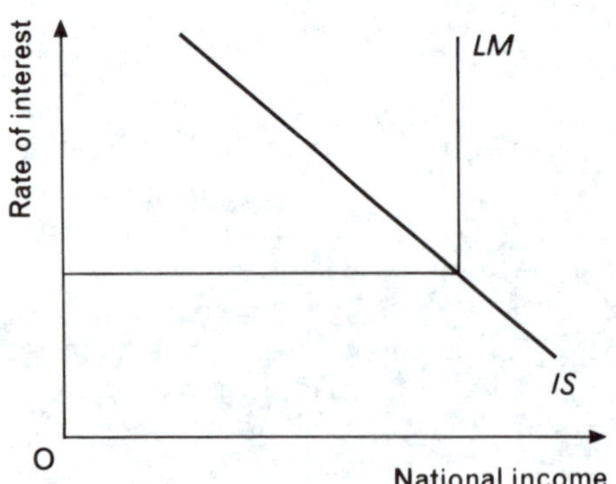

A A rise in the rate of interest and a fall in the level of national income.
B A rise in the rate of interest and a rise in the level of national income.
C A rise in the rate of interest and no change in the level of national income.
D A fall in the rate of interest and a rise in the level of national income.
E No change in the rate of interest and a rise in the level of national income.

4. According to monetarists, public-sector investment 'crowds out' private-sector investment as a result of a rise in

A the money supply.
B interest rates.
C aggregate demand.
D liquidity preference. (AEB)

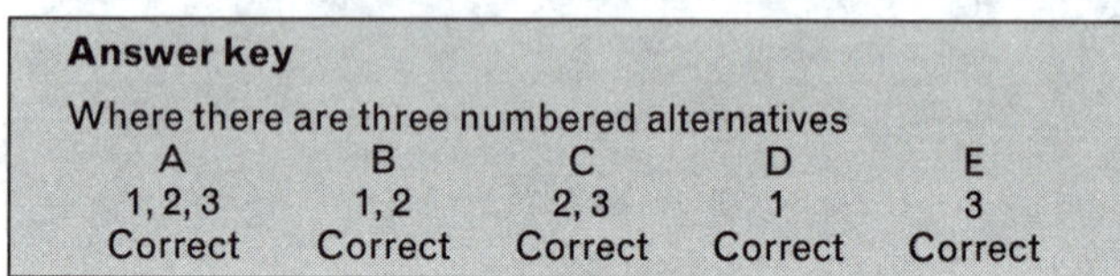

Answer key

Where there are three numbered alternatives

A	B	C	D	E
1, 2, 3	1, 2	2, 3	1	3
Correct	Correct	Correct	Correct	Correct

5. With the economy in the liquidity trap:

1 Fiscal policy will have the full multiplier effect.
2 Monetary policy will be ineffective.
3 The rate of interest will rise following a shift of the *IS* curve to the left.

EXERCISES

1. The diagram below shows *IS* and *LM* curves.

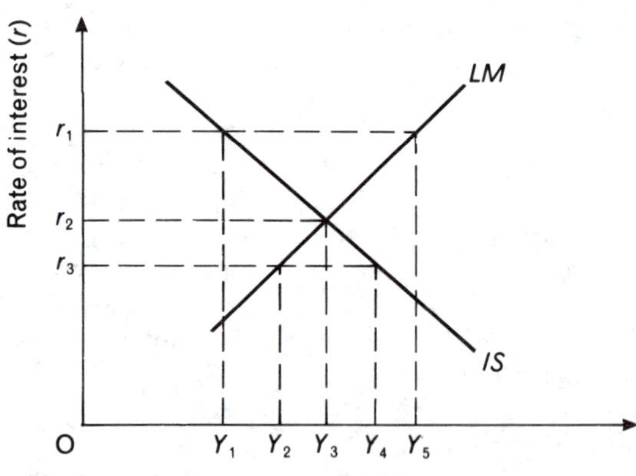

(a) At what rate of interest and level of income will the goods market and the money market be in equilibrium?
For questions (b) and (c) answer: (i) equilibrium, (ii) excess demand or (iii) excess supply.

(b) If the rate of interest is r_1 and the level of income is Y_1, what will be the prevailing conditions in each of the goods market and the money market?

(c) If the rate of interest is r_3 and the level of income is Y_4, what will be the prevailing conditions in each of the goods market and the money market?

2. In the diagram below the prevailing *IS* curve is IS_1 and the prevailing *LM* curve is LM_1. What will be the effects of each of the following actions? (State the movement of the relevant curve and the effect on income and the rate of interest.)

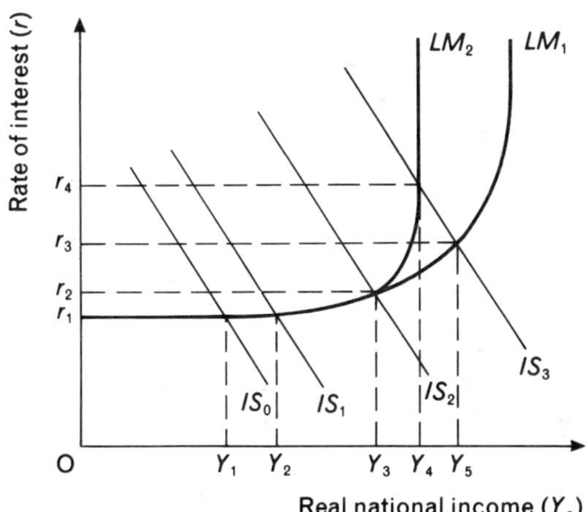

(a) An increase in the government budget deficit.
(b) Following (a), a contraction of the money supply.
(c) A further increase in government spending.

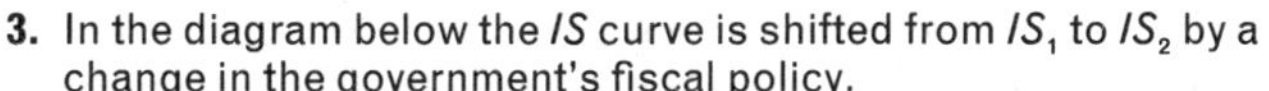
3. In the diagram below the *IS* curve is shifted from IS_1 to IS_2 by a change in the government's fiscal policy.

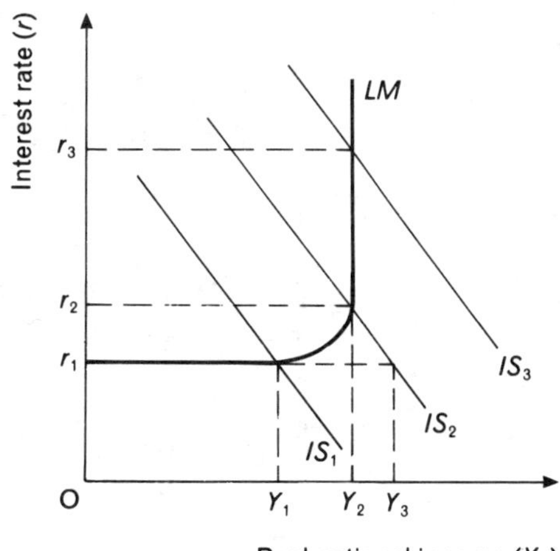

(a) What is the full multiplier effect of this change?
(b) Why is the actual effect on income not the same as the full multiplier effect?
(c) If the ruling *IS* curve moved to IS_3, why would there be no effect on income?
(d) Under what circumstances would there be a full multiplier effect following a change in fiscal policy?

16 Inflation

In this chapter we will discuss:

1. What causes the general price level to rise.
2. The monetarist view – the quantity theory of money.
3. The Keynesian view – excess aggregate demand and cost-push.
4. The relationship between inflation and unemployment.
5. The costs of inflation.

Introduction

This chapter is about the determination of the aggregate price level – that is to say, if we imagined our national output as one enormous aggregate 'good', what would its price be? We have seen that the prices of individual goods are determined by the intersection and supply and demand curves for individual goods. But we know that if we were to double all prices and incomes then there would be no change in the quantities of the various goods traded; nor would their relative prices change.

If, before doubling prices and incomes, we produced and sold 100 units of food and 50 units of drink then we would still produce 100 units of food and 50 units of drink after we had doubled all incomes and prices. Furthermore, if a unit of food were worth ten times a unit of drink before the doubling (say £10 for a unit of food and £1 for a unit of drink) then a unit of food would still be worth ten times a unit of drink after the doubling (£20 for food and £2 for drink).

Strictly, then, microeconomic theory explains only the ratios of prices rather than their absolute levels.

Obviously the same ratio would occur at any absolute level. In other words, the *aggregate* price level can move independently of relative prices, while our theory so far explains only relative prices. The obvious questions are: what determines the aggregate price level; and does the price level matter?

It is clear from Figure 16.1 that there have been periods in history when the UK aggregate price level has been steadily rising. Any persistent rise in the aggregate price level is called **inflation**.

In what follows we shall look at the two most popular explanations of inflation and see how closely they conform to the evidence. The first type of explanation arises from monetarist theory and connects aggregate price level to the quantity of money in circulation. The second arises from Keynesian theory and connects inflation to the level of aggregate demand in the economy. Both are called **demand-pull inflation,** since they operate via the demand side of the whole economy.

Yet another explanation of aggregate price level is based on the idea that price level is pushed up by costs – **cost-push inflation** – rather than pulled up by demand. Supporters of this explanation argue that production costs can increase independently of demand. This might be due to OPEC forcing up the price of oil, or trade unions forcing up the wage rates of labour. These costs have to be met and so will result in increased price irrespective of the level of aggregate demand.

Demand-pull inflation – the monetarist view

According to monetarist theory the rate of inflation is 'always and everywhere a monetary phenomenon' and we should look to money supply to explain it. It is the purpose of this section to examine this theory, to look at the relevant data and to see if there is any empirical support for the monetarist claim.

The data shown in Table 16.1 are annual and relate to the period 1981–90 (columns 2, 3, 6, 7 and 8 are relevant here).

It is immediately apparent from column 2 that the retail price index has been increasing and has more than doubled over the period, so there has indeed been some inflation. It is the rate of change of this index which is usually taken as a measure of inflation, and year-on-year changes are shown in column 3. This column shows that the annual rates of inflation were in double figures for many of the early years, but fell below 6 per cent later on.

Columns 6, 7 and 8 show the three most common measures of money supply – M1, M3 and M4. M1 is a narrow definition of money and rose from about £35.8 billion in 1981 to about £104 billion in 1988, which is an increase of 291 per cent. M3 is a rather broader definition of money and rose from £84 billion to £223 billion, which is an increase of 265 per cent. M4, the only broad measure still reported, rose from £138 billion in 1981 to £473 billion in 1990 – a rise of 343 per cent. The RPI, on the other hand, rose by only 142 per cent between 1981 and 1988 and by 168 per cent between 1981 and 1990. The question for monetarists then is: why has the RPI not risen as fast as the money supply?

In order to address this quesion we need to remind ourselves of the theoretical connection between money and

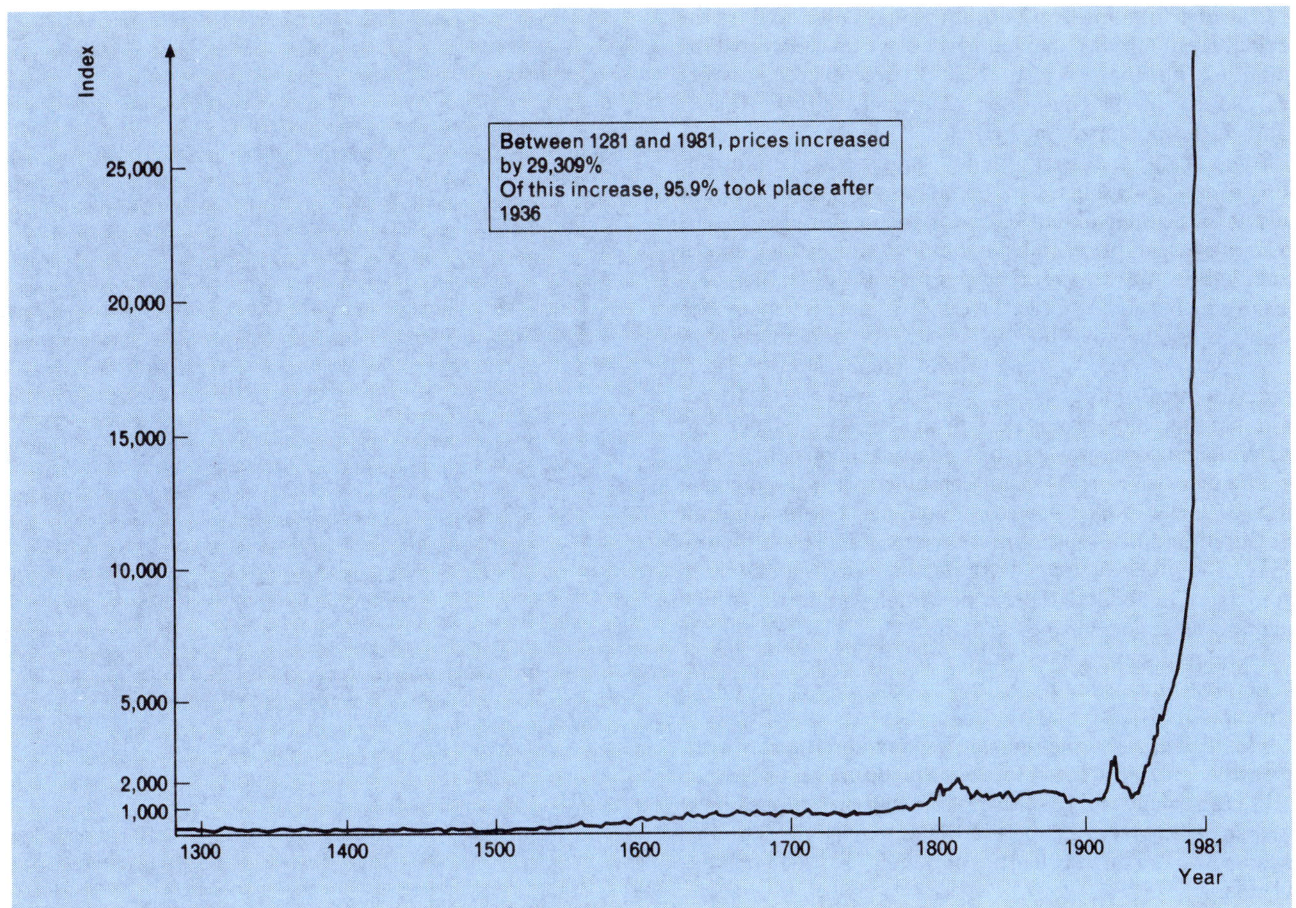

Figure 16.1 Inflation before and after Keynes, 1281–1981: price index for S. England (1281 = 100).

price level. Recall that, according to the quantity theory of money, the money supply is related to price level as follows:

$$M \times V = P \times Y$$

where M = the quantity of money in the economy (M1, M3 or M4 seem equally acceptable)
V = the velocity of circulation
P = the aggregate price level (the RPI)
Y = the level of real GDP.

This equation suggests that in order for money supply (M) and price level (P) to move together (as suggested by the monetarists) both the velocity of circulation and the level of real output must either remain constant or move together.

Table 16.1 UK economic data, 1978–87

Year	GDP (£m, 1985) (1)	RPI (1985 = 100) (2)	IFL (3)	PSBR (£m) (4)	TBR (%) (5)	M1 (£bn) (6)	M3 (£bn) (7)	M4 (£bn) (8)
1981	319,301	79.1	11.9	10,590	14.62	35.8	84.0	137.8
1982	324,727	85.9	8.6	4,954	9.72	39.9	90.8	154.7
1983	336,769	89.8	4.6	11,636	8.84	44.4	100.8	175.3
1984	343,945	94.3	5.0	10,240	9.12	51.3	110.5	199.3
1985	356,851	100.0	6.1	7,521	11.17	60.8	125.1	225.2
1986	369,851	103.4	3.4	2,275	10.65	74.2	150.7	261.4
1987	386,975	107.7	4.2	−1,436	8.38	91.1	185.0	302.9
1988	403,645	113.0	4.9	−11,868	12.91	104.3	222.9	355.0
1989	411,541	121.8	7.8	−9,283	15.02	N/A	N/A	422.3
1990	413,873	133.4	9.5	−1,932	13.50	N/A	N/A	473.4

Notes: GDP = gross domestic product valued at 1985 prices; RPI = retail price index based on 1985 = 100; IFL = approximate inflation rate (first differences of RPI); PSBR = public-sector borrowing requirement at current prices, in billions; TBR = Treasury bill rate; MI = notes and coin in circulation plus sight deposits, in billions; M3 = M1 plus time deposits, in billions.
Sources: *Economic Trends* and *Financial Trends*, various issues, Bank of England.

Consider first how real output (Y) has behaved over the period. Real output remained fairly constant between 1981 and 1982, but then grew at about 3 percentage points per year, so that in 1990 output was 27 per cent greater than it had been at the start of the period.

Some of the increase in money supply will therefore be absorbed in providing the transactions balances for this new output, so that not all the increase in money supply will lead to an increase in price. Indeed, if money supply increases at exactly the same rate as real output increases then there will be no change in the price level. Any increase in money supply must therefore turn up as either a price increase or an output increase. In other words, money supply determines nominal output ($P \times Y$) and an increase of 10 per cent in money supply must lead to an increase of 10 per cent in nominal income (velocity being assumed constant).

The increase in real output combined with the increase in the price level mean that nominal output (output measured in current prices) rose from £254,934 million to £552,058 million between 1981 and 1990. This amounts to an increase of about 216 per cent, which compares with an increase of about 343 per cent in M4. Thus not all the increase in money supply can be accounted for by increases in nominal income and we have to look elsewhere for an explanation.

This brings us to the remaining unexplored term in the quantity equation – the **velocity of circulation** (V).

We can calculate the velocity of circulation and see how it was changed over the period by dividing the nominal income ($P \times Y$) by the quantity of money (M1, M3 or M4). That is:

$$V = (P \times Y)/M$$

The velocities calculated by using M1 and by using M3 are shown in Table 16.2 and Figure 16.2.

Measures V1 and V2 show that the velocity of circulation has been falling in recent years, and these falls have been very large indeed. V1 fell from about 6.0 to about 4.0 between 1978 and 1987, which is a fall of 33 per cent. V2 fell from about 3.0 to about 2.0, which again is a fall of about 33 per cent.

This fall in the velocity of circulation means that a greater quantity of money is required even to finance a constant level of nominal income. Hence some of the increase in money supply has been mopped up by the reduction in velocity and will not turn up as a price increase. A 33 per cent fall in velocity would allow money supply to rise by 33 per cent without affecting price level.

Thus the measured rise in money supply (which is about 350 per cent for both M1 and for M3 between 1978 and 1987) is absorbed partly by an increase in real output (about 17 per cent over the whole period), partly by a reduction in velocity (about 33 per cent) and partly by an increase in the aggregate price level (about 100 per cent). This analysis is confirmed for the present main monetary aggregate, M4. In Table 16.2 V3 represents the velocity of circulation of M4. The monetarist idea that there is a strong link between the money supply and the price level is not therefore quite as straightforward as is sometimes claimed. The link is weakened because the velocity of circulation and real output do not either remain constant or move in unison.

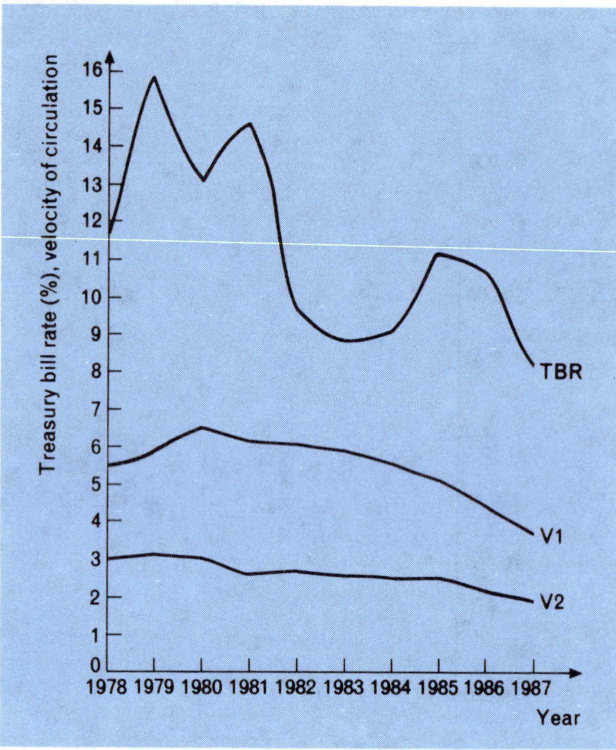

Figure 16.2 UK velocity of circulation and Treasury bill rate, 1979–87.

Of course, sophisticated monetarists do not assume that other things are constant or even that they move in self-cancelling ways. They do, however, claim that changes in velocity can be predicted and controlled. Thus it will still be possible to predict the effects on the price level of changes in the money supply once changes in velocity are accounted for.

These monetarists argue that the velocity of circulation depends on (is a stable function of) interest rates. If interest

Table 16.2 UK velocity of circulation and Treasury bill rate, 1978–87

Year	1978	1979	1980	1981	1982	1983	1984	1985	1986	1987	1988	1989	1990
V1	5.5	5.9	6.5	6.2	6.1	5.9	5.5	5.1	4.4	3.9	N/A	N/A	N/A
V2	3.0	3.1	3.0	2.6	2.7	2.6	2.5	2.5	2.2	1.9	N/A	N/A	N/A
V3	N/A	2.04	2.03	1.85	1.8	1.74	1.63	1.58	1.47	1.39	1.32	1.22	1.17
TBR	11.6	15.8	13.1	14.6	9.7	8.8	9.1	11.2	10.6	8.2	12.9	15.0	13.5

Notes: V1 = velocity of circulation based on M1 as money supply; V2 = velocity of circulation based on M3 as money supply; V3 = velocity of circulation based on M4 money supply; TBR = Treasury bill rate (from Table 16.1).

rates are held constant then velocity should be constant; if interest rates increase then so will the velocity of circulation. (This is because people are much less willing to hold money if doing so loses them high interest payments.)

If this is true then we would expect the increases in velocity shown above to occur at times of high interest rates. It is to test this contention that we have included the Treasury bill rate in Table 16.2. Casual inspection of these figures does not support the view that velocity varies systematically with the interest rate in the short run – not every increase in the Treasury bill rate corresponds to decreases in V1 and V2. On the other hand, the secular (long-run) decline in velocity is associated with a secular decline in the Treasury bill rate. Between 1979 and 1987 the TBR fell from 15.8 to 8.2, V1 fell from 5.9 to 3.9 and V2 fell from 3.1 to 1.9 with most of the decrease occurring later in the period.

In summary we can say that the simple monetarist view of inflation is that it is always and everywhere a monetary phenomenon. This is usually interpreted as meaning that any increase in inflation is associated with an increase in the money supply. Control money and you control inflation.

We have looked at the relevant data since 1978 and find no simple relation either between M1 and inflation or between M3 and inflation. This caused us to look again at the theory and to introduce two other considerations. First we found that real output had not remained constant, so that some increase in the money supply would have been absorbed in financing the increased real output.

Changes in real output do not, however, explain all the differences between money and inflation. This implies that the velocity of circulation has changed. We calculated the velocity based on M1 and that based on M3 and neither was constant. Simple monetarism is therefore inappropriate for the period under consideration.

A slightly more sophisticated view of monetarism states that velocity is known to change, but that its change is predictable. It is a function of the interest rate. A casual look at the figures suggests that no systematic relationship between interest and velocity exists in the short run, but there does seem to be a secular relationship.

SUMMARY

1. Inflation is a general and persistent rise in the aggregate price level.
2. Monetarists claim that inflation is 'always and everywhere a monetary phenomenon'.
3. Monetarists use the quantity theory of money to explain inflation: $MV = PY$. If V and Y are constant then a rise in the money supply leads to a higher price level – inflation.
4. Neither output, Y, nor the velocity of circulation, V, appears to have been consistent in recent years.
5. Monetarists also claim that V will be a stable function of interest rates. The evidence does not support this view.
6. Monetarists suggest that if governments can control the money supply then they can control inflation.

Demand-pull inflation – the Keynesian view

In Chapter 14 we encountered the Keynesian model of national output determination. In that model we saw that when aggregate demand exceeded the full-employment level of output an **inflationary gap** developed. Not being able to hire enough labour to meet the demand for their products, firms compete among themselves for labour and so bid up wage rates. This increases their costs and in turn causes prices to increase.

The cause of the inflationary gap is that demand is too high, possibly due to the government running an expansionary fiscal policy – there is no assumption that money supply has been increased. According to Keynesian theory, therefore, excess demand – from whatever source – bids up costs and this in turn causes prices to rise. To explore this further we need to refresh our memories as to how costs and prices are related in our mixed economy.

We saw in the microeconomics part of this book that price equals marginal cost in perfectly competitive markets with profit-maximizing entrepreneurs. Thus in order to say something about the connection between prices and costs it is necessary to know something about marginal costs.

In macroeconomics we confine ourselves to short-run considerations only. In the short run the entrepreneur can change labour input but has to take capital stock as 'given'. Thus in macroeconomic models the only costs which vary with output are labour costs. In other words, marginal costs are associated only with labour costs and not at all with capital costs.

Thus an increase in output of 1 unit will require an increase in labour input of, say, 10 man-hours. If labour was paid £2 per man-hour then this additional unit of output would increase costs by $2 \times 10 = £20$. The marginal cost (the change in total cost associated with an increased production of 1 unit) is therefore £20. And, according to our theory, this equals price.

If output is increased by yet another unit then the labour input will again increase, this time by 12 man-hours. (This is more than the previous increase because of the law of diminishing returns.) If the wage rate has remained unchanged the additional cost of this labour will be $12 \times £2 = £24$. The marginal cost has increased from £20 to £24 and so the price will also increase from £20 to £24.

Thus if we know the level of output, we can find the marginal cost of producing one extra unit of output and that will tell us the price. We also know that, since marginal cost increases with output, so will the price.

All this, however, is based on the assumption that the wage rate remains unchanged as output (and employment) rises. But there are good reasons to suppose that wage rates do change as employment increases.

The argument is that, as aggregate employment increases, some skills become scarce, and in regions which are more active than others there will be a general labour shortage. Where shortages of labour occur the employers will compete among themselves for the scarce labour and will bid up wage rates.

It should be stressed here that the shortages will result in continuing wage increases. A labour shortage, if maintained, may produce, say, a 5 per cent increase in wages every year. It is not a once and for all increase in costs, such as occurs when employment and output increase. Increased costs which occur through wages being bid up will continue at the rate of 5 per cent every year.

Not all skills in all regions will be fully employed. Some regions – and some skills – will still be underemployed, so in aggregate there will still be some unemployment. It is likely, however, that as aggregate unemployment falls, more and more shortages will be experienced and more and more wages rates will be bid up faster and faster. We would therefore expect that high levels of unemployment would be associated with low annual wage increases (there may even be decreases at very high unemployment rates). Conversely, when unemployment rates are very low the annual wage increases should be very large.

The economist A.W. Phillips gathered some data on unemployment rates and wage increases for the UK for the years 1861–1913 and 1923–1958. It was on these data that the famous **Phillips curve** was founded. By plotting unemployment against annual wage increases he found the relationship shown in Figure 16.3.

This diagram really does seem to conform to our belief about what happens to wages when unemployment falls. At high levels of unemployment annual wage increases are small or even negative and at low levels of unemployment annual wage increases are high. At about 4.5 per cent unemployment, wage rates remain unchanged. Increasing employment slightly – so that unemployment falls to 4 per cent – brings about an increase in wage rates of 0.5 per cent each and every year.

We have already seen that price depends on marginal costs and that marginal costs depend on wage rates and labour productivity. Thus if unemployment is maintained (held) at 4 per cent then wages will be increasing by 0.5 per cent every year. With no change in productivity this would lead to an annual increase in marginal cost – and hence prices – of 0.5 per cent.

Thus we have a theory of inflation based on excess demand leading to rising costs and hence to a rising price level. This new theory is based on costs of production and says that as output expands the demand for labour expands. This reduces the level of unemployment and causes labour shortages in some markets. These labour shortages induce annual increases in marginal costs and hence lead to annual increases in prices, i.e. inflation.

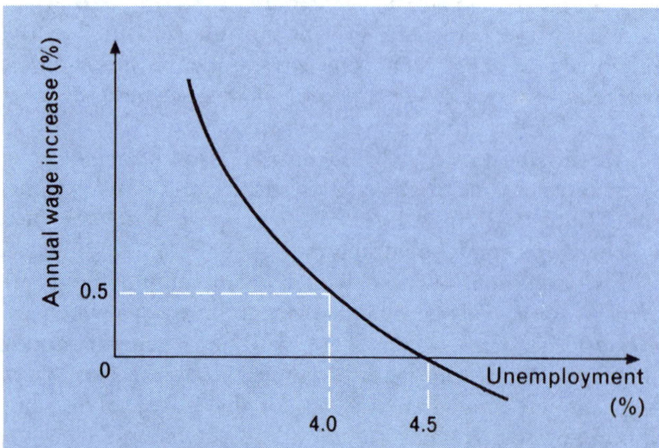

Figure 16.3 Phillips curve.

This poses something of a problem. The government would clearly like to have low unemployment and low inflation rates. Unfortunately, the Phillips curve seems to suggest that we can have either one or the other but not both – there is a trade-off between unemployment and inflation.

When this trade-off is incorporated into the Keynesian model we have the result that a fiscal expansion will be shared between output increases and price increases depending on where we are on the Phillips curve. If there is a great deal of unemployment then a fiscal expansion will result in large output increases and small price changes. If there is a low unemployment rate then a fiscal expansion will have a greater effect on prices and a much smaller effect on output.

Thus when expansionary policies are wanted – i.e. in times of high unemployment – the fiscal policy will work. If, however, the government tries to expand the economy when it is already fully employed then the result will be large price increases and small output increases.

Productivity change

The version of the Phillips curve given above is based on the assumption that, although labour productivity falls as output expands, it does not otherwise change. Thus if demand is held at a level which results in 4 per cent unemployment then all the annual wage increase (0.5 per cent) turns up as additional labour cost.

In fact, of course, there is plenty of evidence to suggest that labour productivity does change over time. It has steadily increased and continues to do so. This is due partly to the greater use of capital, partly to improved production techniques and partly to better labour.

Now if labour productivity (output per man-hour) increases by 0.5 per cent every year then a 0.5 per cent annual increase in wage rates will leave the labour cost per unit of output unchanged. Thus marginal costs remain unchanged and so will prices. If productivity increases by less than wage increases then costs will rise, but by not as much as wages. If productivity rises are larger than wage increases then costs will fall.

Productivity therefore stands between wage rates and labour costs per unit of output. It therefore stands between wage rates and prices. This can be illustrated by redrawing our original Phillips curve, but this time we will plot the percentage change in wage rates and the percentage change in prices on the vertical axis.

This is shown in Figure 16.4. Here the line *WW* is our original Phillips curve. It shows that wage rates remain constant when unemployment is 4.5 per cent and rise by 0.5 per cent per annum when unemployment is 4.0 per cent.

Prices will not increase by as much as wage rate increases because some of the wage increase will be absorbed by productivity increases. The line showing how prices change with unemployment will therefore lie below the line showing how wage rates change with unemployment.

In Figure 16.4 a 'price' line is drawn below the 'wage' line and labelled *PP*. This line shows that when wage rates

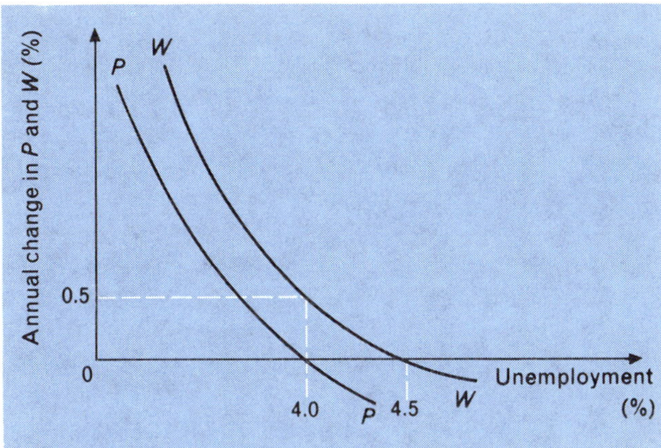

Figure 16.4 Effect of a productivity increase on price level and wage rates.

are increasing by 0.5 per cent per year there is no increase in price level. This implies a productivity change of 0.5 per cent per year.

Therefore productivity change means that the trade-off between inflation and unemployment is not quite as harsh as our original Phillips curve suggested. We can have unemployment rates below 4.5 per cent without inflation. The key is to keep wage increases equal to or below productivity increases. Even so the trade-off remains and has led to a number of attempts to circumvent it. These are taken up in the next section.

Cost-push inflation

The third possible explanation for inflation is that it is caused by a rise in costs. This differs from the Keynesian explanation in that the cost increase is not precipitated by excess demand. Such a rise in costs can be caused by factors outside the control of the domestic economy. For example, in 1973/4 and again in 1979 OPEC raised the price of crude oil, which led to an increase in costs in oil-importing countries. This increase in price level will cause the standard of living to fall.

If workers and capitalists try to maintain their real incomes by bidding up their wages and profits then prices will rise again and we enter an inflationary spiral. Events such as the OPEC price increase are known as 'supply shocks', and it is a matter of debate as to how long the inflationary effects from such shocks (the upward spiral) will last.

Prices and incomes policy

Recall that part of the reasoning underlying the Phillips curve trade-off was the idea that, as a labour market tightens up, some skills in some regions become scarce. These shortages cause wage rates to be bid up by employers competing against each other for the scarce labour. Wage rates can also be bid up by workers taking advantage of the sellers' market to force up their wage rates.

Thus the increase in wages comes about because employers and workers react in particular ways to labour shortages. This suggests that one solution to the trade-off problem would be to reach some agreement between government, employers and workers. The government would offer to increase aggregate demand so as to reduce unemployment below 4 per cent. But this offer would be conditional on the employers and the workers agreeing not to take advantage of this level of demand to put up either prices or wages.

This could be done voluntarily as was tried by Harold Wilson's Labour administration of 1974, which called it the Social Contract. Alternatively, it could have the force of law. This is the so-called **prices and incomes policy**. This kind of policy still finds favour in some circles and is still very much on the political agenda. One way of enforcing such a policy is to fine or tax any company which awarded wage increases greater than the increase in productivity.

Once again, however, the government is led to play a greater role in our economic lives. With a prices and incomes policy it is now responsible for the distribution of national product as well as controlling output, employment, imports, exports, investment and growth.

This theory of inflation and its policy implications did not meet with universal approval. Furthermore, in the late 1970s and early 1980s many free-enterprise economies were experiencing high inflation rates and high unemployment rates together. We seemed to have moved off the Phillips curve and the time was ripe for a counter-attack.

SUMMARY

1. If, as Keynesians suggest, price level is determined by costs rather than by money supply then Keynesians need some explanation of how costs change.
2. The most popular explanation of costs was that based on the Phillips curve.
3. The Phillips curve shows how, in the distant past, the level of wage rates changed as the level of unemployment changed.
4. There is a trade-off between the rate at which wage rates increase and the level of unemployment.
5. These wage increases would result in price increases if they were greater than productivity increases.
6. There is also cost-push inflation. This is due to rises in costs independent of aggregate demand, e.g. a rise in the world price of oil.
7. Inflation can be eased by agreeing a prices and incomes policy.

Inflation and unemployment

The counter-argument to the Phillips curve came from the monetarists. It led to the demise of the Phillips curve and its reinterpretation in line with monetarist views. Recall that monetarists argued that labour supply and labour demand are both determined by the real wage rate and not by the money wage rate, and that where the labour market clears is known as the natural rate of (un)employment.

According to this view, a 10 per cent increase in money wages and a concomitant 10 per cent increase in prices would leave the real wage rate unchanged. This should leave labour supply and labour demand unchanged. There can therefore be no increase in employment when money wage rates and prices go up together. This clearly does not fit in very well with the original Phillips curve, which suggested that employment did increase even though real wages had not changed.

The expectations-augmented Phillips curve

The monetarist response to this was to suggest that workers agree a money wage and employment contract at the start of each year and stick to it for the coming year. They try to negotiate a real wage rate but are unable to do so because they do not yet know what the price level will be in the coming year. They therefore guess what the price level will be. This, together with their contracted money wage rate, determines the real wage rate and so their supply of man-hours.

Thus the relationship between money wage rates and (un)employment depends on what workers expect price levels to be in the coming year. If they underestimate next year's price level then they will think their real wage rate is higher than it actually turns out to be. Their original offer to supply labour will therefore be too high. But it will only be high because they made a mistake.

Thus, in our example, if the level of the wage rate this year is 10 per cent above last year's and prices are not expected to rise then more workers will offer themselves for employment. This 10 per cent increase in the wage rate must, however, cause prices to increase. The price increase will be the wage increase (10 per cent) less the productivity increase (0.5 per cent). Thus prices will go up by 9.5 per cent. At the end of the year the workers are therefore only 0.5 per cent better off than before. If they persist in believing that prices will not increase in the coming year then every year the additional 10 per cent wage rate increase will induce the additional workers to remain in the labour force. Unemployment will therefore be held permanently below the natural rate of unemployment (i.e. the rate at which no mistakes are made).

This seems to have been the case when Phillips' data were being generated. During those years workers may well have believed that the price level would not go up the following year. Thus the Phillips curve is based on a zero price change expectation.

Obviously, if prices do continue to rise then eventually workers will come to expect prices to rise. They will no longer offer more labour when money wage rates rise by 10 per cent. Indeed, if they expect prices to go up by 10 per cent over the coming year then they will offer no more labour than before.

If they expect prices to go up by 10 per cent, they will require a 10 per cent wage rise to stay at 4.5 per cent unemployment (the natural rate). To persuade them to

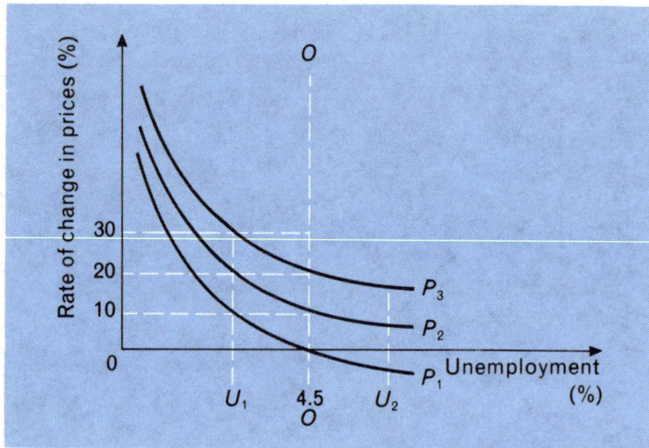

Figure 16.5 Expectations-augmented Phillips curve.

offer more labour than that (say to reduce unemployment to 3 per cent) they must be paid 10 per cent to compensate them for the expected price rise, plus 10 per cent to give them the required increase in real wage rate. The original Phillips curve has therefore shifted upwards by 10 per cent – by the expected rate of inflation.

This 20 per cent increase in the wage rate will cause prices to rise by more than the expected 10 per cent, so the workers have again made a mistake. They therefore revise their expectations of inflation upwards, say to 20 per cent. They now require a 20 per cent wage rate increase simply in order to keep unemployment at 4.5 per cent. The Phillips curve has moved upwards yet again. The curve is being augmented by inflationary expectations: it is the **expectations-augmented Phillips curve**. This is shown in Figure 16.5.

In the figure P_1 is the original Phillips curve, where the expected inflation rate is zero. A 10 per cent increase in wages induces a fall in unemployment to U_1. This, however, causes a 10 per cent price increase, which is then expected to occur again next year. Thus all points on the previous line (P_1) are increased by 10 per cent to compensate for expected inflation. This yields a new Phillips curve, P_2. When this is in place, a price increase of 20 per cent is necessary to bring unemployment down to U_1. This inevitably causes prices to rise by 20 per cent (10 per cent more than expected). Thus workers again revise their expectations upwards to 20 per cent. The Phillips curve then shifts upwards again to P_3.

This process will continue for as long as unemployment is kept below 4.5 per cent. Inflation will be going up and up without end.

NAIRU

If unemployment were allowed to return to 4.5 per cent along P_3 then the expected inflation rate (of 20 per cent) would actually prove correct and hence would no longer be revised upwards. Therefore any point to the left of 4.5 per cent unemployment will yield steadily increasing (accelerating) inflation. Any point on the 4.5 per cent unemployment rate will leave inflation constant. This unemployment

Table 16.3 UK unemployment and price level, 1978–90

Year	Unemployment (% of total labour force)	Consumer price index (1978 = 100)
1978	6.0	100.0
1979	5.1	106.1
1980	6.6	123.2
1981	9.9	140.4
1982	7.4	162.3
1983	12.6	170.7
1984	13.0	177.9
1985	13.2	184.7
1986	11.8[1]	192.9
1987	10.6[1]	200.9
1988	8.4[2]	210.7
1989	6.3[2]	227.1
1990	5.9[2]	248.3[3]

Notes:
1. Not directly comparable with previous figures due to a change in the counting method (count reduced by approx. 50,000 people).
2. As 1, count reduced by approx. 90,000 people.
3. Estimate.

Sources: *National Institute Economic Review*, no. 115, February 1986; *Annual Abstract of Statistics*; *Employment Gazette*.

rate is therefore called the **non-accelerating inflation rate of unemployment** (NAIRU) or long-run Phillips curve.

It is this 'jacking up' of the Phillips curve by workers' expectations of inflation which has generated the recent observations of high unemployment and high inflation. The problem now becomes: how do we get back down to zero inflation rates?

One solution would be to reduce workers' expectations of inflation. If these expectations are revised downwards then the economy simply moves down line *OO* (NAIRU). Unfortunately, it seems that people often base their expectations of inflation on what has actually happened in the recent past. Thus in order to reduce people's expectations of inflation it is necessary actually to reduce inflation.

According to Figure 16.5, the only way to do this is to move to the right of line *OO*. If aggregate demand is reduced to give a level of unemployment of, say, U_2 then wage rises will be less than the rate of inflation. This will bring the rate of inflation down, which in turn will reduce expectations and hence shift the Phillips curve down. As long as we stay to the right of line *OO* this process will continue until we reach Phillips curve P_1. Then we can go back to line *OO* and have 'full employment' with zero inflation.

The observant student will have noticed that the curves are much shallower to the right of *OO* than to the left. Therefore much higher levels of unemployment are necessary if the expectations are to be revised downwards as quickly as they were revised upwards during the period of expansion. The downward adjustment is therefore much more painful and time consuming.

Thus the monetarist argument is that Keynesianism was and is a mistake. It bought short-run gains in employment at the expense of gradually accelerating inflation. It led to increasing government involvement in our economic affairs and switched resources from the private to the public sector. The current distress is a result of these mistaken policies, and their undoing will take time and patience.

The Keynesians argue that there is very little evidence to show that the monetarist solution is working. There seems to be little or no improvement in unemployment even though inflation and inflationary expectations have been moderated over the period 1982 to 1989, and since 1989 both inflation and unemployment have risen (see Table 16.3). Moreover, the free-market system has broken down in the past and no doubt will do so again.

SUMMARY

1. The Phillips curve seems not to have retained its earlier shape in more recent times. We have had high inflation and high unemployment.
2. One explanation is that the Phillips curve moves around depending on what we expect the rate of inflation to be. It is an expectations-augmented Phillips curve.
3. Non-Keynesians argue that, when we hold correct expectations, the Phillips curve is vertical and unemployment does not move away from its natural rate.
4. This unemployment rate is sometimes called the non-accelerating inflation rate of unemployment (NAIRU).

A note on testing economic theories

The monetarist response to the empirical testing and rejection of their 'positive' theory has been to argue that there will be a time lag between an increase in the money supply and the consequent increase in the aggregate price level.

The retail price index is plotted against money supply

Case Study 16.1 The long-run (natural) rate of unemployment

Estimates of the long-run rate of unemployment are given in Table 16.4. In their recent book, *The Causes of Unemployment*, Greenhalgh, Layard and Oswald (1983, p. ii) say 'the natural rate of unemployment (sometimes called the NAIRU, or non-accelerating inflation rate of unemployment) . . . is probably best defined as the long-run rate of unemployment: it is the unemployment that prevails if price expectations are fulfilled'. I have followed their lead and have simply called the natural rate, the equilibrium rate or the NAIRU the long-run rate of unemployment.

[Methods of estimating the natural rate differ.] Nickell estimated what he called the equilibrium rate of unemployment from underlying equations explaining the inflow to unemployment and outflow from unemployment . . . Minford's estimated long-run rate of unemployment [is based on an equation system] . . . explaining unemployment, real wages, output and the real exchange rate. [Estimates by] Sumner and Ward and Layard *et al.* are derived essentially from an augmented Phillips curve and can accurately be described as NAIRUs.

The first striking feature of these estimates is the way that long-run rate of unemployment seems to rise almost hand-in-hand with actual unemployment, even over short periods . . . It is convenient to focus on the successive estimates of Layard *et al* . . . because they all derive from a similar augmented Phillips curve method. The actual rate of UK unemployment (on OECD definitions) and estimated NAIRUs are as shown in Table 16.5.

Although the NAIRU rose over the period it was above actual unemployment in the decade 1966–75 but below it in the 1980s. The authors attribute the rise in the NAIRU over the whole period to:

(i) the fall in sustainable productivity growth since the early 1970s, which means more unemployment is needed to make workers willing to accept the feasible rate of real wage growth;
(ii) an unfavourable change in wage setting behaviour (i.e. on top of the lower productivity effect) in which the unions have had a role to play;
(iii) greater choosiness about jobs among unemployed people; . . .

The second feature of the estimates of the long-run rate of unemployment is that current unemployment [i.e. in 1984] is substantially above the long-run rate . . .

In discussing the 1980 estimate of the long-run unemployment rate, 7.25%, Minford states that it 'can be lowered substantially by measures to reduce real benefits, labour tax rates and union monopoly power'.

1. Following the measures of the 1980s designed to reduce union power and free the working of the labour market, and the increase in productivity growth in the 1980s, would you expect the NAIRU to have fallen or will the 1990s necessarily be characterized by high unemployment?

2. Do you agree with Samuel Brittan that 'NAIRU is neither an economic constant, nor even a useful parameter' as it appears that it just follows the actual rate of unemployment around and there is no agreed way of measuring it?

Source: D. Metcalf, 'On the measurement of employment and unemployment' *NIESR Review*, no. 109.

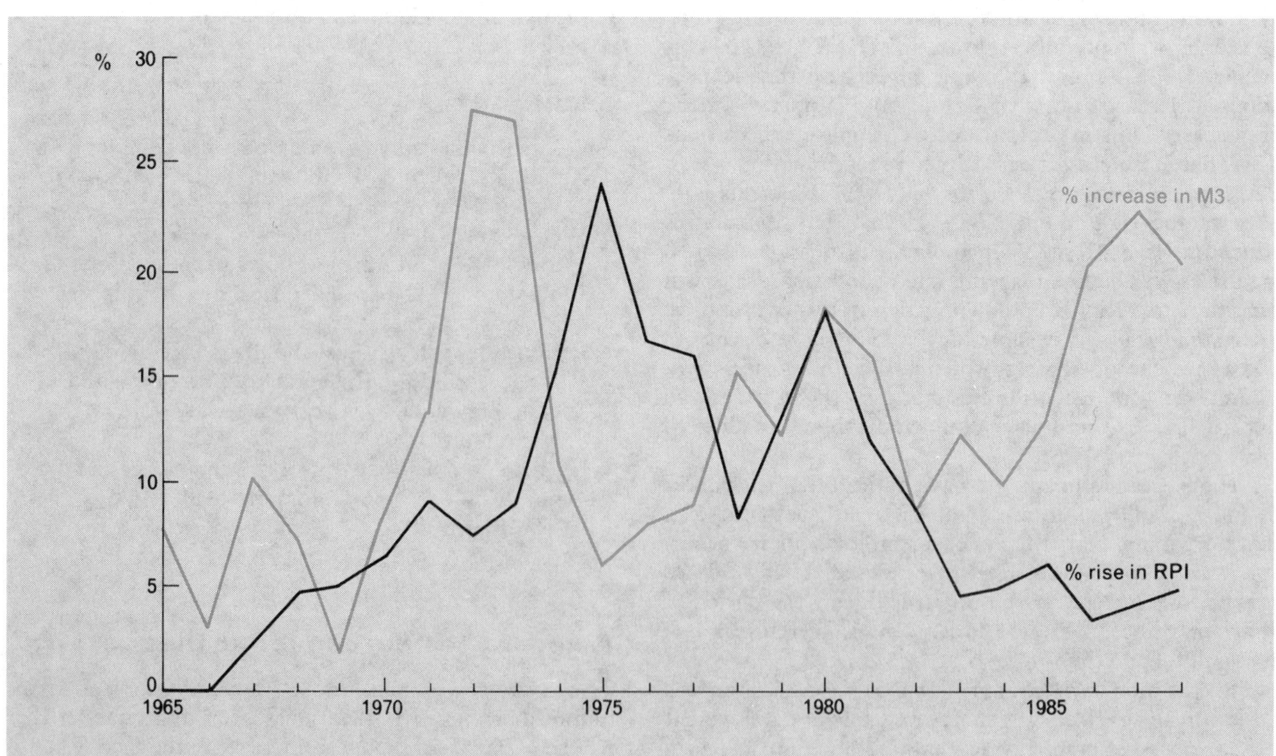

Figure 16.6 Changes in M3 and retail price index, 1965–88.

Table 16.4 Estimates of the long-run rate of unemployment

Author	Year(s)	Long-run rate of unemployment (per cent)	Corresponding actual rate of unemployment	Definitions and estimation methods
Sumner and Ward (1983)	1970s average	4.00	4.0	GB wholly unemployed. NAIRU calculated from Phillips curve augmented by price and tax expectations.
Nickell (1982)	1979	5.80	6.6	GB male unemployment, excluding school leavers. Equilibrium rate calculated from inflow to and outflow from unemployment equations.
Minford (1983)	1980	7.25	7.4	UK unemployed. Calculated from four equation system to explain unemployment, real wages, output, real exchange rate.
Layard *et al.* (1984)	1981–83 average	9.00	10.8	UK unemployment as per cent of civilian labour force. NAIRU calculated from a wage equation containing real wages, unemployment and trend. The 9 per cent is the average of four alternative estimates given.

(M3) in Figure 16.6 and with a two-year lag in Figure 16.7. The fit is now somewhat better than with no lag, but it is still not particularly good. The figures suggest that the fit is quite good in the early period but worsens towards the end of the period. Thus the lag itself seems to vary over time!

The breakdown of the Phillips curve which was used to reject Keynesian policies has also come in for some rescue work.

The Keynesians make use of the distinction drawn between the short-term unemployed and the long-term unemployed. The long-term unemployed are those who have been without employment for more than a year. The level of long-term UK unemployment is higher now than it has ever been. During the Great Depression the peak for long-term unemployment was less than 500,000. In the 1950s it was as low as 20,000. In 1986 it was 1,350,000.

The percentage of all unemployed who are long-term unemployed varies across age groups and across countries. In the UK in 1986, 26 per cent of unemployed 18- and 19-year-old males were long-term unemployed. But between the ages of 55 and 59 years, 63 per cent of those unemployed were long-term unemployed. Thus the older the age group, the higher the proportion of the unemployed who are long-term unemployed. For an international comparison consider the figures for 1984. The percentage of all unemployed who were long-term unemployed was 68 per cent for Belgium; about 40 per cent for France, Ireland, Italy and the UK; and about 12 per cent for Austria, Norway, Sweden and the USA.

The extent of the variation among age groups and among

Table 16.5 Estimated NAIRU vs. actual unemployment.

	Estimated NAIRU per cent[1]	Actual unemployment per cent
1966–70	2.2	1.9
1971–75	4.0	2.8
1976–80	5.5	5.5
1981–83	9.0	10.8

Note: 1. Average of four estimates.

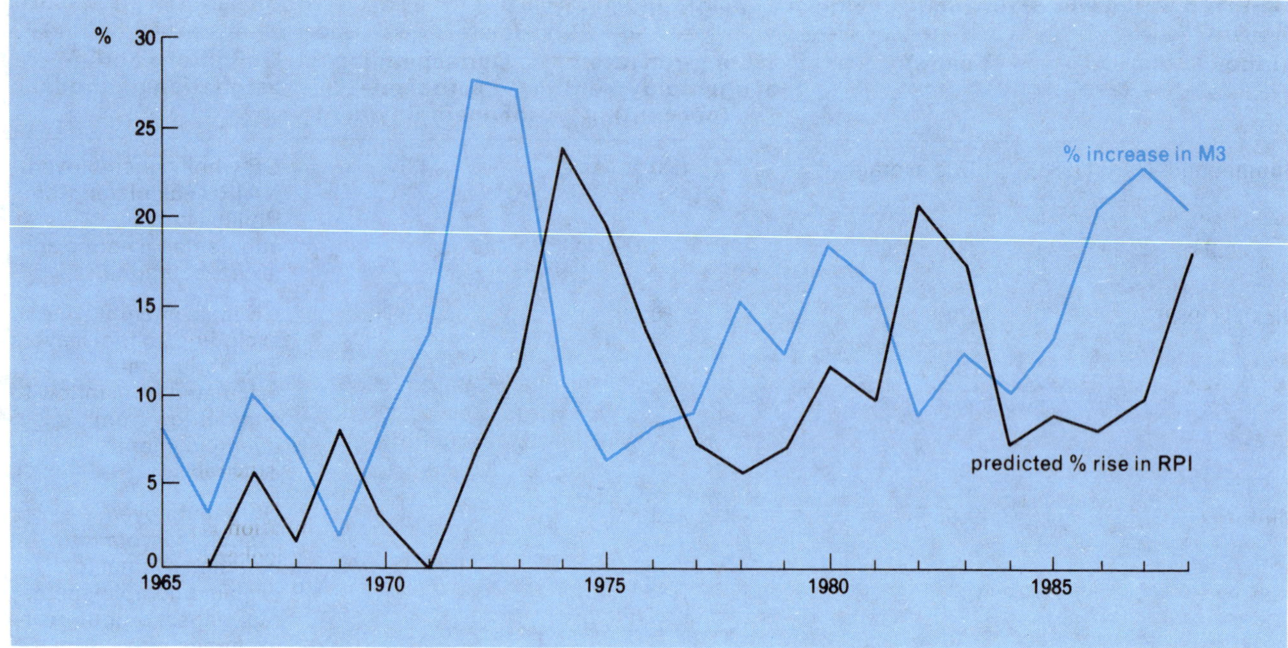

Figure 16.7 Changes in M3 and retail price index with two-year lag, 1965–88.

countries is therefore very marked. In what follows we shall be less concerned with the distribution of the long-term unemployed than with the fact that they are a new and large phenomenon.

The essential point is that these long-term unemployed become 'detached' from the labour market. The unemployed themselves become deskilled by not being able to practise what skills they once had and by not being able to keep up to date with all the new developments in their trade or profession. Employers come to think that anyone who has been unemployed for that long must in some way be suspect. And anyway, since there are so many newly unemployed, there is no need to take a chance on employing a long-term unemployed person.

A number of interesting points follow from this. First, if the long-term unemployed really are detached from the labour market then they should be excluded from the labour supply side of the labour market. Thus any Keynesian expansion of aggregate demand would run into labour shortages long before full employment was reached. As soon as the market had used up most of the short-term unemployed, it would experience labour shortage and hence inflation would begin again. Since the long-term unemployed are registered as unemployed and are far more numerous than ever before, we would expect high inflation and high registered unemployment to appear together in the 1980s. Thus we have another explanation of the famous breakdown of the Phillips curve.

The point of this note is that those who wish to hold on to their favourite theories in the face of contradictory evidence can usually come up with some defensive reinterpretation of the theory or its application. Thus two theories can persist for many years even though they are being contínously subjected to empirical testing.

Does inflation matter?

We have looked at the causes of inflation and some possible solutions to the problem. But why is inflation a problem?

From the 1930s to the early 1970s unemployment was seen as the most serious and distressing problem facing western economies. Since then almost every western government has moved the control of inflation to the top of its priority list. This is because of a combination of factors: the rapidly rising inflation rates experienced in the early 1970s; the existence of high inflation and unemployment, contrary to standard Keynesian theory; and the increasing belief that the costs of inflation were greater than the costs of policies designed to reduce inflation.

The argument over exactly how great are the costs of inflation, and if the costs of reducing inflation outweigh the benefits, continues among economists. In the following sections we shall outline some of the costs of inflation to society.

The costs of anticipated inflation

We can distinguish between the costs of anticipated (expected) inflation and the costs of unanticipated (unexpected) inflation. This is because if inflation is fully anticipated then consumers can react to reduce the impact of inflation on them. If this is the case then prices, wages, interest rates, etc. will all be adjusted to take account of the expected level of inflation. There will then be only two types of inflation cost to society: 'menu costs' and 'shoe leather costs'.

Menu costs arise from the need to alter prices during the inflation, e.g. altering the prices on menus. Such costs will be modest during periods of moderate inflation, but the faster prices rise, the more frequently price tags must be changed. At the height of the hyperinflation in Germany in 1923 (the rate of inflation reached over 29,000 per cent per month!) prices could be changed every few hours. Obviously it is easier for a restaurateur to change prices than it is for a manufacturer of industrial machinery, so the extent of menu costs will vary with the rate of inflation and from industry to industry.

Shoe leather costs arise from the desire of people to protect the value of their money holdings during inflation. Cash attracts no interest, so if people keep their money at home, in cash, during a period of inflation then its purchasing power will diminish. This can be at least partly offset by depositing the money in an interest-bearing bank or building society account, with the investor withdrawing the money as it is needed for transactions.

The higher the rate of inflation, the higher the rate at which cash loses purchasing power. If inflation is low then people may be prepared to draw out sufficient cash for one month's transactions at a time, making 12 visits to the bank a year. As the rate of inflation gets higher, people may feel that they will lose too much by holding a whole month's spending money in cash. So they will draw out only two weeks' money at a time, leaving the rest of the cash to gain more interest (26 visits a year).

The higher the rate of inflation, therefore, the greater is the incentive to leave cash in an interest-bearing account for as long as possible, requiring more and more frequent visits to the bank. The more visits made to the bank, the more people wear out their shoes – hence the term shoe leather costs. The term is intended to sum up all of the extra time and effort required to manage with smaller cash balances.

The costs of unanticipated inflation

The costs of anticipated inflation are believed to be relatively small. However, the costs of unanticipated inflation can be significant. These costs range from the redistribution of wealth to the loss of output and employment.

One cost is known as fiscal drag. This occurs when, due to inflation, the government finds that its tax revenues rise. During inflation money incomes and profits rise and this leads to higher receipts from income tax and corporation tax (taxes on profits). The way income tax systems usually work is to allow people to earn a certain amount tax free and then pay a certain rate on all income over that amount up to another present level where the rate of tax increases. The levels at which tax rates change (tax thresholds) are usually set once a year, so if there is unanticipated inflation during the year then the tax thresholds will not take account of this.

Thus as money incomes rise with inflation, people will have to pay more tax, and may even find themselves paying a higher rate of tax, because their money has risen above a tax threshold even though their real income is unaltered or falling. Even if income does not cross a tax threshold, the tax-free element of income is worth less in real terms and so people are worse off.

The redistribution effect of inflation is also worrying and occurs in a number of ways. Firstly, there is a redistribution of wealth from lenders to borrowers. Imagine that someone makes a loan expecting no inflation and requires a return of 4 per cent in real terms. If the loan is for £1,000 they ask for 4 per cent interest and expect the repayment of £1,040 at the end of the year. If during the year inflation is 10 per cent then to maintain the purchasing power of the original loan a repayment of £1,100 is required, but only the agreed sum of £1,040 is returned. The lender returns to the borrower a lower amount of money in real terms than was borrowed. (The borrower has paid a real rate of interest of −6 per cent.) The highly volatile rate of inflation has led to many lenders insisting on variable rates of interest in their loan agreements.

Another redistribution occurs between the young and the old. Older people tend to hold more assets denominated in money terms (building society accounts, for example) and these are devalued during inflation. The young, on the other hand, tend to be net borrowers (holding mortgages, etc.) and so benefit from inflation. As retired people tend to have fixed incomes (pensions) and the young have wages and salaries which generally keep pace with or ahead of inflation, there is a further change in the relative purchasing abilities of the two groups. Thus the old lose out and the young gain.

A most important effect of inflation is on the working of the price mechanism. When we looked at microeconomics we saw that prices are signals to consumers and producers. The efficient working of the price mechanism leads to an efficient allocation of resources. During inflation, however, the price mechanism can become unreliable as an indicator to both consumers and producers and leads to a fall in output and employment.

During inflation producers will not be able to tell if price rises are due to increased demand (a change in relative prices) or inflation (a change in the general level of prices). When the price mechanism works properly firms respond to a price rise by increasing supply, but during inflation they are uncertain and may not increase supply. When the price rise is due to a rise in demand there is a clear loss of output and employment – the loss of output and employment that would have followed had the price mechanism been working properly.

The behaviour of consumers during periods of inflation also has implications for output and employment. During inflation people often suffer from 'money illusion'. Even though their incomes have risen sufficiently to maintain their real incomes, they believe that the price rises they observe in the shops have made them worse off. The reaction to this observation is to consume less, leading to a fall in the level of demand. Another possible reaction is to save more because of greater uncertainty about future real incomes. Both reactions can lead to a fall in output and so employment.

Finally, there is the problem of international competitiveness. If the inflation rate of the UK is higher than that of a competitor then UK producers will find that they become less competitive in world markets. UK exports will fall and imports will rise, and the overall level of employment and output will fall. This effect can be offset by allowing the exchange rate to devalue, thus maintaining the price of UK exports and imports. However, there may be competing pressures on the exchange rate, as we shall see later.

There are serious costs associated with inflation. Exactly how high these costs are is difficult to estimate, but they are potentially considerable. The control of inflation therefore occupies the minds of policy makers throughout the market economies.

Case study 16.2 Monetary policy in the second half of the 1980s

An extract of a speech by the Governor of the Bank of England to Tyne and Wear Chamber of Commerce at Durham Castle, 5 April 1990.

Inflation matters

The key problem with inflation is the uncertainty it creates. In theory, if the level of inflation could be foreseen, it could be discounted – that is to say, we could modify our behaviour to take account of it. But . . . it is impossible in practice to forecast inflation accurately.

The higher the inflation rate, the less stable it is likely to be; and the less stable the inflation rate, the greater the uncertainty . . . The upshot is that contracts are written, and behaviour is modified, to minimize the effects of the uncertainty. In other words, we find ourselves worrying about how to protect wealth, rather than how to create it.

Uncertainty about inflation . . . is very damaging to the proper functioning of the economy. With a steadier general price level, individual price signals can be read more clearly. More rational decisions can be taken about whether to save or whether to borrow . . . to invest . . . or to consume, and what or when to produce. In short, it provides the necessary context for resources to be effectively deployed. This is the very basis of a market economy . . .

[I]t is [not] necessary to rest the counter-inflationary case on sophisticated theoretical arguments . . . In the 1970s inflation was consistently high, averaging 12% . . . and company profitability was squeezed . . . This contributed to progressively rising unemployment.

But from 1981 to 1987 – when underlying inflation was falling – profitability rose; net investment in the whole economy more than doubled; and following the initial shake-out, unemployment has recently almost halved despite a very rapid increase in the size of the labour force . . . inflation was brought under control by a firm non-accommodating policy stance . . .

Criticisms of current policy

Agreement on [the need to control inflation] does, of course, leave plenty of room for argument about how it is reached. You will be familiar with the complaint that excessive reliance has been placed on interest rates, with the result that . . . they are simply too high . . .

[I]t is the real rate [of interest] that bites. The net real rate *is* still higher than we have experienced for much of our recent history. But . . . it is not outrageous. Indeed, it remains modest compared to measures of industrial profitability.

In any case, there can be *no* doubt that lower interest rates would add to the inflationary pressures in the economy in a number of ways. They would increase debt-financed spending, and thus domestic demand. And by weakening sterling, they would also directly increase the prices of imported goods . . . The lower exchange rate would, in the short run, improve British competitiveness . . . but with a high level of overall demand, this would tend to reduce employers' ability to resist wage pressures and thus undermine the cost base of industry in the longer term.

By fuelling higher inflation, lower interest rates would not be sustainable, since nominal rates would sooner or later have to rise to compensate for the deterioration in the value of money.

Roots of current inflation

I want first to argue that the roots of the recent resurgence of inflation have been essentially financial and substantially monetary, and have therefore called for a corresponding monetary response.

[The recent rise in inflation was not fully appreciated earlier] because over the past three or four years there have been significant discrepancies in the official statistics and material revisions to them, which has made interpretation difficult.

In particular, the output and domestic demand statistics for 1987 and 1988 have been consistently revised upwards . . . This is one reason why policy has not seemed impressively effective . . . we put the brakes on when the speedometer indicated we were doing 60 m.p.h. Some time later it said we were doing 55. When the tachograph was opened . . . it revealed that we had actually been doing 70. Thus the problem was *not* that the brakes were ineffective, but . . . the speedometer had been misleading . . . more brake pressure was . . . appropriate.

So there was excessive demand and [so] inflationary potential. Attempts to meet [excess demand] from domestic sources eventually encounter bottlenecks and competitive bidding for scarce skills, which are liable to spill over into pay and costs.

The inflationary damage emerges only after some delay . . . William McChesney Martin, Chairman of the Federal Reserve Board in the 1950s and 1960s, said that it was the duty of a central banker to take away the punch bowl just as the party was hotting up. So it is; and he cannot expect to be thanked for it. But any criticism of his attempts to clear heads the next day should take the form of a remonstration that he was not firmer the night before.

The root of the problem was a consumer boom, which coincided with strong – and very necessary – growth in investment spending.

But why did consumer spending grow so much faster than disposable income?

The starting point may have been the rebuilding of consumer confidence as we recovered from the 1981–1982 recession. This . . . involved increased optimism about *long-term* growth prospects. Once people were confident that earnings were likely to rise year by year, they were prepared to borrow and spend larger amounts, even though the higher incomes . . . were not immediately available . . . Moreover, the extra demand and the confidence itself . . . was likely to lead to an investment boom, so that domestic demand outstripped output, pushing the current account into deficit and putting upward pressure on prices.

But the other key ingredient was that the increased spending was so easily financed, on account of a massive increase in the availability of credit, whose roots can be traced back to the lifting of a series of restrictions on lending institutions in the early 1980s.

The immediate impact of this liberalization was rapid credit growth . . . forecasts as to how far the borrowing would go were decisively proved wrong.

The personal sector collectively went into deficit on a considerable scale, depressing the savings ratio – by which I mean the net ratio, or gross savings less borrowings and investment, divided by personal income – to levels not seen since the 1950s.

Furthermore, house prices had been bid up to *unprecedented* multiples of earnings, especially in the South East.

This in turn had the effect of releasing equity withdrawal . . . [some] spent not on building . . . but on cars, video recorders and other durables, many of which were imported or would otherwise have been exported . . .

[T]he developing credit boom of the 1980s owed more to increased confidence and general decontrol than to low interest rates, but of course this is by no means the whole story. First, the controls which remained in place during the early 1980s rationed some people's access to credit . . . Relaxing the controls lowered this 'shadow price', and was therefore analogous to a reduction in interest rates.

Moreover, actual interest rates were reduced over a period during which we now see they clearly should not have been.

The fact of the matter is that, in the net real terms . . . rates became very low, although unlike the 1970s, they were still positive. To those who complain that rates have risen too much, I would reply that it was absolutely necessary to get away from such unrealistically – and ultimately damaging – low real rates.

---

1. If all incomes were fully indexed, i.e. rose in line with inflation automatically, would inflation matter?

2. The Governor does not mention the role of wage rises or trade unions in inflation. What does this tell you about his views on economic theory?

Source: Robin Leigh Pemberton, *Bank of England Quarterly Review*, May 1990

SUMMARY

1. Inflation is considered to be an important problem by economists and politicians, although the extent of the costs of inflation is unclear.
2. The costs of inflation depend upon whether inflation is anticipated or not.
3. The costs of anticipated inflation are menu costs and shoe leather costs.
4. Costs of unanticipated inflation are as follows:
   (a) Fiscal drag.
   (b) Redistribution of wealth from lenders to borrowers and from the old to the young.
   (c) Disruption of the efficient working of the price mechanism, leading to uncertainty.
   (d) Consumers can suffer from 'money illusion' and change their behaviour.
   (e) Reduced competitiveness of domestic goods if domestic inflation is greater than foreign inflation.
   (f) Lower output and employment due to (c), (d) and (e).

Exam Preparation and Practice

MULTIPLE-CHOICE QUESTIONS

1. A rise in inflation as defined by the retail price index will mean that:
A The cost of living has fallen.
B The standard of living has risen.
C The money supply has risen.
D The purchasing power of money has fallen.

2. The effect of an annual pay settlement on the wages of three workers in a year when retail prices rose generally by 15% is illustrated in the table below.

Worker	*Initial weekly wage*	*Pay increase (per week)*
Mr X	£50	£8
Mr Y	£80	£10
Mr Z	£100	£12

From this data it may be inferred that
A money wages have fallen for all three workers.
B real wages have fallen for all three workers.
C real wages rose for Mr X but not for Mr Y.
D Mr Y experienced a greater fall in real wages than Mr Z.
E Mr Z experienced a greater proportionate rise in money wages than Mr X. (LON.)

3. According to monetarist economists, inflation is mainly caused by:
A Rising wage costs due to labour shortages.
B The expansion of the money supply at a faster rate than real output.
C A rise in the average cost of imported raw materials.
D Excessive wage demands by trade unions.

4.

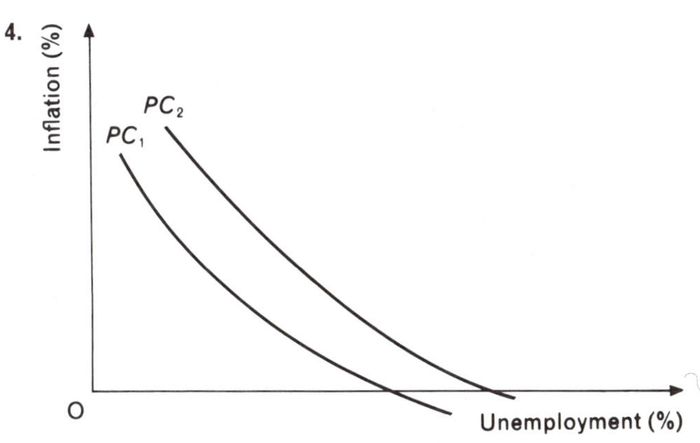

The diagram shows two possible Phillips curves. If the ruling Phillips curve shifts from PC_1 to PC_2, the cause is likely to be:
A A lower rate of inflation.
B A higher rate of unemployment.
C A general upward revision of inflationary expectations.
D The imposition of a prices and incomes policy.

5. If the rise in prices in an economy is known to be due to excess demand, which of the following policies is likely to be most effective in reducing the rate of inflation?
A An increase in direct taxation.
B A prices and incomes policy.
C An increase in government spending.
D The purchase of bonds by the government on the open market.

6. Which of the following is **not** likely to be a consequence of a period of high inflation?
A A rise in the percentage of real income paid in direct taxation.
B An increase in the proportion of income held in interest-bearing accounts.
C An improvement in the relative incomes of old-age pensioners.
D An improvement in the international competitiveness of exports.

Answer key

Where there are three numbered alternatives

A	B	C	D	E
1, 2, 3	1, 2	2, 3	1	3
Correct	Correct	Correct	Correct	Correct

7. If personal income tax allowances are not increased by the same percentage rate as the annual rate of inflation then the
1 money yield from income tax will rise.
2 real yield from income tax will fall.
3 number of income tax payers will fall. (AEB)

8. Cost-push inflation may be caused by
1 increased prices of imported raw materials,
2 exchange rate depreciation,
3 wage increases unrelated to rises in productivity. (AEB)

9. Inflationary expectations will be fulfilled when:
1 Inflation next year exceeds inflation this year.
2 There is no excess demand.
3 The level of unemployment is at its natural rate.

EXERCISES

1. The data in the following table are taken from the national accounts of Little Trivilvania.

Year	% change in		
	M3	RPI	Real GDP
1985	5	2	2
1986	6	3	0
1987	10	6	2
1988	12	8	2
1989	14	10	3
1990	9	7	2
1991	9	4	2

(a) Plot a graph of the rate of growth of GDP, the RPI and M3 for Little Trivilvania for the period shown.
(b) To what extent do the data support the monetarist view that inflation is 'always and everywhere a monetary phenomenon'?
(c) Can you account for the apparent change in the relationship between M3 and the RPI in 1990/91?

2. The date in the following table are for the UK between 1971 and 1989.

Year	Rate of change of RPI(%)	Unemployment (%)
1971	9.5	3.4
1972	6.8	3.7
1973	8.3	2.6
1974	15.9	2.6
1975	24.2	4.6
1976	16.5	6.0
1977	15.8	6.1
1978	8.3	5.9
1979	13.4	5.0
1980	18.0	6.4
1981	11.9	9.8
1982	8.6	11.3
1983	4.6	12.5
1984	5.0	11.7
1985	6.1	11.3
1986	3.4	11.5
1987	4.0	10.4
1988	3.1	8.5
1989	7.5	6.8

(a) Plot a graph of unemployment (horizontal axis) against inflation.
(b) Is there any evidence of a Phillips curve relationship in the graph you have drawn?
(c) Does the expectations-augmented Phillips curve provide a better explanation of events in the UK?
(d) Is there any evidence that there is a 'natural rate' of unemployment for the UK?

3. The diagram below shows a set of short-run Phillips curves. PC_1 is the ruling Phillips curve when inflation is expected to be zero. The economy is initially at the level of unemployment U_1.
(a) If the government were to pursue an expansionary fiscal policy and unemployment fell to U_2, what would be the immediate consequence for inflation?
(b) What would be the level of inflation in the following year if unemployment remained at U_1?
(c) If in year 3 the government changed its fiscal policy and unemployment rose to U_3, what would be the effect on the inflationary expectations of the population?
(d) At what rate of unemployment would inflation become stable?

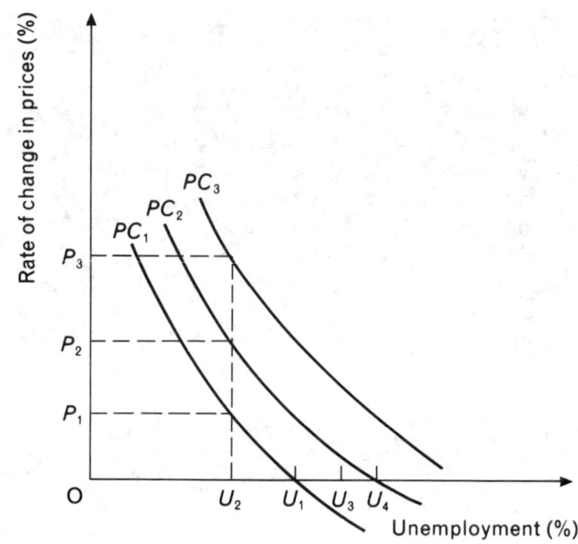

4. Which of the following are possible consequences of unanticipated inflation?
(a) A rise in output.
(b) A redistribution of wealth from lenders to borrowers.
(c) A fall in investment.
(d) A rise in the inflationary expectations of consumers.
(e) A rise in government tax revenues.
(f) A fall in export earnings.

5. Classify each of the following events as causes of (i) demand-pull monetarist inflation, (ii) demand-pull Keynesian inflation, (iii) cost-push inflation.
(a) A rise in the price of imported foodstuffs.
(b) A union demand for increased wages due to a shortage of labour.
(c) A rise in the money supply due to government borrowing.
(d) A reduction in the marginal rate of taxation.

DATA-RESPONSE QUESTION

1. Explain and interpret the diagram below.

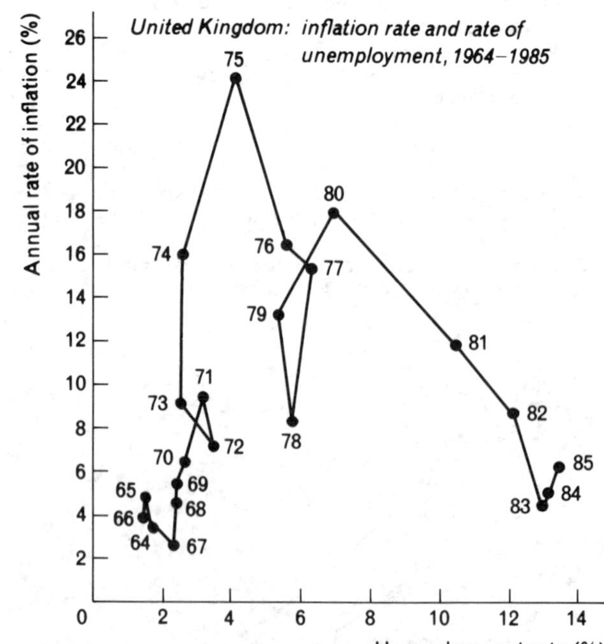

Sources: *Economic Trends*, 1975–87, CSO.
Annual Abstract of Statistics, 1987, CSO.
(LON.)

17 Unemployment

In this chapter we will discuss:

1. The nature of unemployment.
2. Reasons for unemployment and measures that might reduce it.
3. How unemployment is measured.
4. Who is unemployed.

Introduction

Unemployment is a recurring and important issue in economics. Views have changed as to its nature and its causes. And these changes of view are, as we shall see, closely associated with developments in economic theory.

It is clear from Figure 17.1 that in this century there have been two periods of high and sustained unemployment – 1922–39 and 1974 to date. There have been peaks of high unemployment at other times too (1908 and 1909). And there have been times of very low unemployment – 1914–18 and 1942–5. Both these periods of very low unemployment occurred during major wars when maximum demands are made on the economy and when manpower is already depleted by recruitment into the armed forces.

Despite the evidence that it is possible to achieve extremely low levels of unemployment, we find that typically it fluctuated between 0.5 and 1.5 million before the First World War and between 0.5 and 0.7 million after the Second World War, until the current spate of very high unemployment was set off.

In this chapter we shall be looking into these figures to see what they appear to represent and what they actually represent. The former question requires us to make use of some of our economic theory; for the latter question we must look at the sources of government statistics. It is to the economic theory which we turn first.

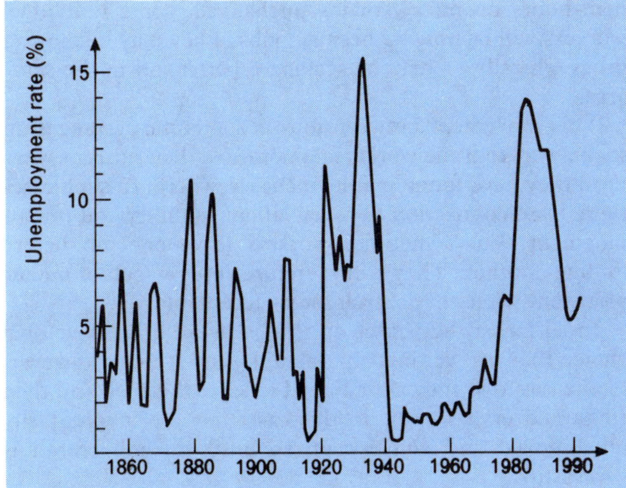

Figure 17.1 Unemployment in the United Kingdom, 1851–1990.

The nature of unemployment

Unemployment is a subject which raises very strong feelings and is a positive minefield for the unwary. In order to clear up some of the misapprehensions we will begin with a very simple model indeed. Though simple, the model does convey the essentials of an economist's approach to unemployment. It is also a model which is easily extended to cover more 'realistic' assumptions.

Robinson Crusoe

The model is one in which a single isolated economic agent (Robinson Crusoe before the arrival of Man Friday) is faced with the problems of staying alive on a desert (i.e. deserted) island. He will no doubt find some fruit and perhaps nuts on the island, and there may be fish in the sea and a fresh water spring. In these circumstances he may decide simply to live off nature (this is what we have elsewhere called living off the 'land') and spend all his time at leisure. By 'leisure' is meant doing exactly what he wants to do. In our language he would be totally unemployed.

On the other hand, he may decide that the bounty of nature is not quite what he wants. He may build a hut, collect and store nuts, cultivate certain kinds of fruit, etc. These things involve him expending his effort and intelligence in ways distasteful to him. He would be working rather than playing, and would do so only in order to reap the product of his labour.

He would work one more hour per day if and only if the benefit he derived from working that extra hour exceeded the 'cost' to him of losing another hour's leisure. In economic language: when the marginal physical product of an hour's labour yielded an increase in utility greater than the marginal utility of leisure.

He may reach this point after only one hour's work or after 10 hours or even after 20 hours. In any event, he will be at full employment when he is working the number of hours he wishes to work.

This suggests that there is no definite set number of hours which we can say represents full employment. If Robinson is a very energetic person with a strong taste for physical comforts, he may work for 20 hours a day. If, however, he is rather lazy and quite content with living off the land he might work only one hour a day. *The number of man-hours for full employment is therefore a variable.* It is likely to change over time and differ between persons and places.

Of course, Robinson is self-employed and works only for himself. He can do whatever work he wishes. But in our modern economy the vast majority of workers are employees. They may seek work but will they, like Robinson, find the amount of work they want?

A slightly more general model

In a free-enterprise economy, offers of employment are made by profit-maximizing entrepreneurs. We have seen in Chapter 9 that such entrepreneurs will employ labourers up to the point at which their marginal physical product just equals their real wage. Thus workers will receive, for each hour of labour, an hourly real wage equal to their marginal physical product. When the utility gained from that hour's wage exactly equals their marginal utility of leisure then they will be fully employed.

This outcome is shown in Figure 17.2. Recall from earlier chapters that:

1. The upward-sloping supply curve suggests that as real wage is increased then workers will want more hours of work. This implies that as their leisure time grows less and less, i.e. more and more hours are given over to work, the marginal utility of leisure increases, hence they need a higher real wage to persuade them to give up any more leisure time.
2. The downward-sloping demand curve is derived from the law of diminishing returns – as employment increases then the marginal physical product (*MPP*) of labour falls. The profit-maximizing entrepreneur equates *MPP* with real wage and hence, at any point on the demand curve, the real wage equals the *MPP* of labour. (Or, *MRP* equals the money wage rate.)

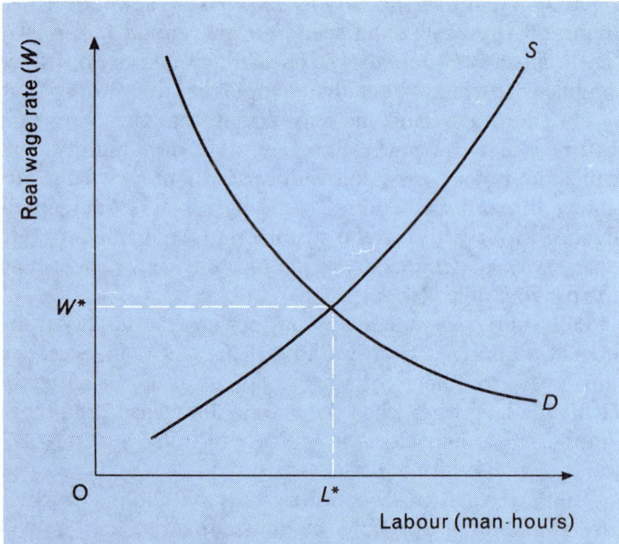

Figure 17.2 Equilibrium in the labour market.

If markets clear then the marginal physical product of labour yields just the amount of utility lost through a marginal reduction in leisure.

Thus our economy, as modelled here, exactly replicates the Robinson Crusoe island. On the island he works for himself and works for L^* hours per day; in the UK he works for an entrepreneur and is employed for L^* hours per day.

This suggests that there is nothing intrinsic in the free-enterprise system which prevents agents from working as they would if they were the controllers of employment. Full employment means the same thing under both systems and is equally achievable under both systems.

The natural rate of unemployment

If our economy really were like this model then unemployment would never occur. The economy would settle down to a level of employment L^* and remain there for ever. There may well be people who never work, but they are the *voluntarily* unemployed. They may be very rich and not need to work. They may have claims on the state (retirement pensions, for example) and hence prefer no longer to work. They may prefer to have leisure and unemployment benefit. In any event, the economy is fully employed in that employment is at its natural rate L^* and any unemployment is voluntary and hence at its **natural rate**.

The data contained in Figure 17.1, however, suggest that there is something wrong here. If unemployment fluctuates very widely then either the model is wrong or something is happening to the supply and demand curves in Figure 17.2. That is to say, our assumption of a stationary economy is hardly tenable.

Frictional unemployment

As a first step to making the model 'dynamic' we can introduce the idea that, although the aggregate number of man-hours on offer remains unchanged, some individual workers will be moving between jobs. They may be moving geographically or may be seeking a better job in the same area.

This movement between jobs is sometimes arranged in such a way that the workers do not leave their current work until they have found employment elsewhere. In such cases there is no connection between labour mobility and unemployment. But sometimes workers leave one job before finding another. They will therefore enter a spell of unemployment while they search for an acceptable job.

In so far as they enter on this job search by their own choice they are voluntarily unemployed. It may, however, be the case that they were forced to leave their job and then embarked on a search. In this case they are involuntarily unemployed and will remain so until the job search is successful.

This kind of movement between jobs is inevitable in all but the most rigidly ossified economy. The unemployment which results is called **frictional unemployment**: 'frictional' because it is a loss of employment caused by movement of labour.

The size of this problem depends partly on the number of workers moving between jobs and partly on the time they take to find something suitable. If 10 per cent of the labour force is on the move and spend 6 months searching then the loss of employment will be equivalent to 5 per cent of the labour force per year (i.e. 10 per cent × 1/2 a year). If, however, they find work in one week then the loss will be much smaller. In this case it will be 0.2 per cent (i.e. 10 per cent × 1/50 of a year).

In an attempt to improve the job search the government set up employment exchanges. The aim was simply to provide a centre into which those seeking work and those offering work could feed their requirements. The centre would then speedily match up the two and the worker would be back in employment. The same idea lies behind the much less formal job centres which have sprung up in recent times.

No doubt these centres have brought about some reduction in frictional unemployment, but some will remain. Some of the unemployment represented in Figure 17.1 will therefore be frictional unemployment. It will grow as the working population becomes more mobile professionally and geographically.

Seasonal unemployment

Some of the movement between jobs has a strong seasonal pattern. Some jobs (deck chair attendants, ice-cream sellers and ski instructors, for example) will only be available at certain times of the year. We may find that some workers are frictionally unemployed between their seasonal working times. Others may simply not look for alternative employment and may remain unemployed until their season for work comes round again. These seasonal jobs have to be done and will impose a seasonal shift on to the demand curve for labour. When in season the demand curve moves to the right and a lot of the otherwise voluntarily unemployed are attracted into the labour market (see D_1 in Figure 17.3).

When in season the natural rate is L_1 and wages are bid up to W_1, but when out of season the natural rate falls to L_2 and the wage rate falls to W_2.

This regular movement of the demand curve for labour will therefore be responsible for some unemployment and its pattern will be regular and repeating, usually with the seasons of the year - hence **seasonal unemployment**.

Structural unemployment

Not all changes in the demand for labour are seasonal or even regular. By 'changes in demand' we mean movements of the whole demand curve for labour. Why should this happen? Labour demand, like that for all factors of production, is a **derived demand**. Labour is demanded because it is an aid to the production of goods and services. Thus the demand for labour is *derived* from the demand for goods and services. One obvious reason for movements of the labour demand curve is therefore changes in the demand for goods.

The demand for goods may change due to (a) changing

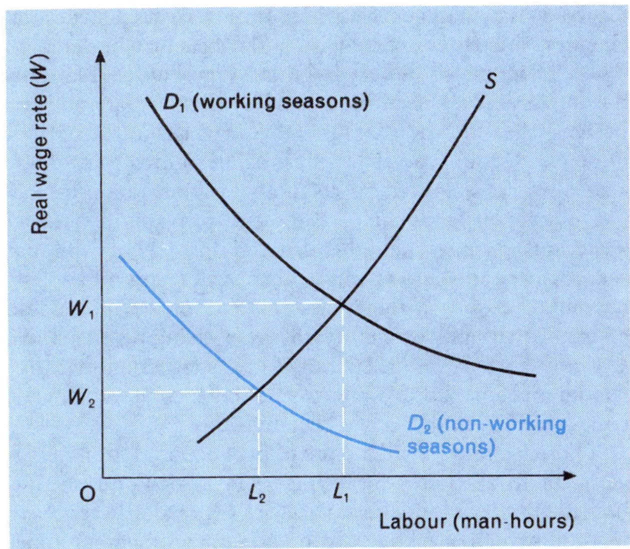

Figure 17.3 Seasonal unemployment.

tastes, (b) changing patterns of trade or (c) changes brought about through product innovation. All these changes may produce **structural unemployment**.

Changing tastes

Changing tastes may be illustrated by the growing realization that cigarette smoking endangers lives; or that some dairy products contain high levels of cholesterol; or simply by a fashion change, as in the case of hair cream which was once widely used by men but is no longer deemed acceptable. In cases such as these the industries concerned face a protracted decline in the demand for their products.

Changing trade

Changes in trade patterns pose the same problem for those industries which once supplied manufactured goods to many non-industrialized parts of the world. With the spread of technology and capital, more and more countries are producing manufactured goods and hence are displacing some long-established UK industries. Shipbuilding is a good example of a once thriving export industry which lost the competition with emerging industrial nations.

Product innovation

Product innovation is an even more dramatic cause of demand failure. Product innovation is a form of technical progress that results in new products becoming available. This is distinct from *process* innovation (which we shall deal with later), in which technical progress results in new ways of making existing products.

There are many examples of product innovation, each of which led to a decline somewhere in the economy. Television led to the demise of cinemas; nylon and rayon decreased the demand for wool and cotton; aircraft travel across the Atlantic virtually wiped out passenger liners and the ports which serviced them.

Changes in demand such as these three are called structural changes, since they are changes in the structure of demand. These changes can be very large and very sudden, and they do not *necessarily* result in unemployment. If labour were perfectly flexible and adaptable then changes in the pattern of demand would merely result in labour moving from one type of work (shepherding) to another (nylon spinning).

However, if labour finds it difficult to respond to rapid structural change then the demand for labour will not match the supply and unemployment will result. Obviously it would be quite a remarkable labour force which could adapt swiftly and efficiently to these changing demands. Coal miners may not take kindly to the suggestion that they should become hotel waiters, and hotel waiters may be equally reluctant to work in coal mines.

There is inertia in all factors of production, but labour is additionally restricted by feelings – loyalty to one's neighbourhood, for example. This leads to regional differences in unemployment. Where structural unemployment does occur it often takes many years to fall, while in other areas there are labour shortages.

There are, however, ways of moderating this kind of unemployment. The government offers retraining schemes and in some cases slows down the rate of decline by offering the industry some protection from declining demand (as is sometimes the case with nationalized industries).

So there are quite understandable reasons for there to be some permanent and some fluctuating levels of unemployment even in a perfectly competitive free enterprise economy. Seasonal and structural unemployment arises from movements of the demand curve for labour, movements which the supply of labour curve cannot keep up with.

Labour supply

There are, however, some reasons for supposing that the supply curve of labour will also move about.

We can delineate three possible reasons for shifts in the labour supply curve: (1) population size, (2) participation rates and (3) replacement ratios.

Population

It is fairly obvious that the larger the population, the more man-hours will be offered at any given wage rate. Population can change through changes in births and deaths or through immigration and emigration. Some of these changes can be quite rapid. The post-war baby boom, for example, caused a sharp increase in the labour force some 16 years later.

Participation rates

Even without a change in population size it is still possible to increase the supply of labour by increasing the proportion of the population seeking work – that is, increasing the participation rate. Typically, those under 16 and those above retirement age do not actively seek work. Furthermore, many married women work in their homes rather than seek work in the market-place. However, the number of married women seeking work can change over time, as can the school-leaving age and the retirement age. Thus the participation rate can change, sometimes quite quickly.

Table 17.1 Growth in UK working population, 1841–1990

Year	Working population employed and unemployed (000s)
1841	6,908
1851	9,473
1861	10,523
1871	11,752
1881	12,731
1891	14,499
1901	16,280
1911	18,286
1921	19,354
1931	21,055
1951	23,809
1961	24,744
1971	25,207
1981	26,565
1982	26,556
1983	26,548
1984	27,265
1985	27,714
1986	27,791
1987	28,337
1988	28,225
1989	28,556
1990	28,591

Changes in the participation rate shift the supply curve and should bring about shifts in the wage rate, the natural employment rate and the natural rate of unemployment. But over and above this change in the natural rate of unemployment there will also be some unemployment due to the inability of employers to respond rapidly to sudden increases in the supply of labour. The economy cannot find employment for large numbers of new workers at the drop of a hat.

Table 17.1 shows the estimated working population (employed and unemployed) in the UK. This shows an increase from 9,473m to 23,809m between 1851 and 1951. There followed a slow rise to 1981, then a slight fall to 1983 when the slow rise begins again. Had the labour force remained at its 1951 level there would be 5 million fewer workers seeking jobs today. (This does not, of course, mean that population control would cure unemployment: population decline may, for example, result in a fall in the demand for labour too.)

Replacement ratios

The third and final reason for a shift in the supply of labour curve is change in the **replacement ratio**. This is the ratio of the disposable income obtainable while out of work to the disposable income obtainable while in work. Say, for example, a worker receives a take-home pay of £180 per week. The worker is then made redundant and receives a benefit payment of £90 per week. The worker's replacement ratio is 90/180 = 50 per cent.

Thus if benefit is high compared with take-home pay then more people would opt for leisure and withdraw from the labour force. This is a particularly acute problem when the replacement ratio is greater than unity. In this case unemployment (and other) benefits *exceed* take-home pay. For some low-paid workers with large families this is indeed the case.

The replacement ratio can be changed simply by the government enacting the appropriate legislation. Some economists are currently arguing that the replacement ratio is too high and attracts too many workers into unemployment. These would, of course, be classed as voluntarily unemployed since they have chosen unemployment.

Objections to this kind of unemployment benefit are posited on the argument that those in work should not be expected to support the unemployed at a standard of living above what is necessary to induce them to find work, i.e. it is a concern for the over-taxed employed rather than for the unemployed.

In so far as unemployment is voluntary it should not perhaps give too much cause for concern. In so far as it is involuntary it derives from the inability of some parts of the economy to respond quickly enough to changes induced elsewhere. In the nature of things these changes are inevitable, but adjustments should not persist for too long – eventually the market should respond and regain the natural rate of unemployment.

Unfortunately, as we have seen, sometimes very high levels of unemployment do persist – sometimes for many years. The question is: why?

SUMMARY

1. There are a number of reasons for expecting some unemployment.
2. Some people will be between jobs and still searching for something suitable – they are voluntarily unemployed only if they have chosen to search.
3. Some people will be in seasonal jobs and either choose or are obliged to be unemployed in between times.
4. There will be those who find themselves deprived of their traditional employment and who are either unwilling or unable to move into new jobs and new areas which are expanding.
5. Finally, some people will prefer leisure and benefits – they are voluntarily unemployed.

Causes of unemployment

Neo-classical view

The neo-classical explanation for persistently high unemployment is that a failure in the labour market prevents market clearing.

Wage rigidity

The most obvious cause of such a failure is wage rigidity. If wage rate fails to fall when supply exceeds demand then

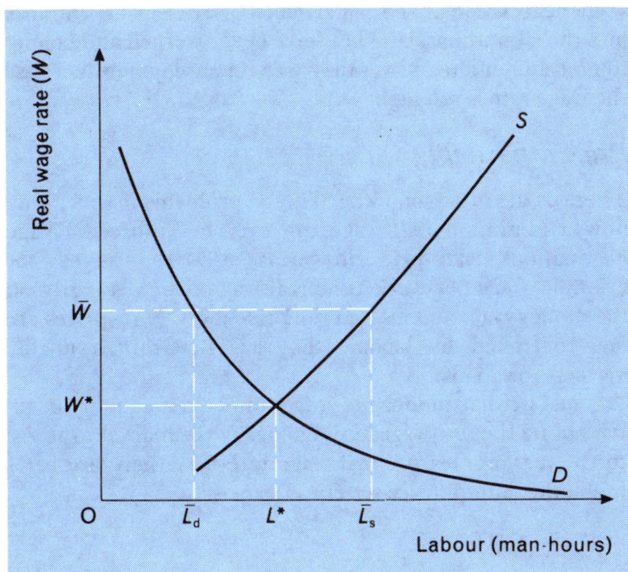

Figure 17.4 Effect of a minimum wage on employment.

there will be persistent excess supply, i.e. persistent unemployment. A simple way of looking at this would be to imagine a minimum wage. This could be set by wages councils or by trade unions (see Figure 17.4).

For market clearing the real wage must be W^* and the natural level of employment will be L^*. If a minimum wage of $\bar{W}$ is set then $\bar{L}_d$ labour will be demanded and $\bar{L}_s$ labour will be supplied.

In such a market there will be $\bar{L}_s - \bar{L}_d$ people actively seeking work at the going wage rate $\bar{W}$ and unable to find it. They will clearly be involuntarily unemployed in the sense that they are currently wanting to join the workforce at the current wage rate.

This kind of model lies behind calls to cut wages. The excess labour ($\bar{L}_s - \bar{L}_d$) is said to have *priced itself out of the market*. This may or may not be the case. Minimum wage legislation can hardly be blamed on the labour force – they were priced out of the market by forces beyond their control.

Trade unions

There is a stronger case for arguing that trade unions price people out of work. Many trade unions are interested more in the wages of their members than in the wages of the whole labour force.

Imagine, for example, that a free market for labour existed and settled down at W^*, L^* in Figure 17.4. A trade union is then formed. There are L^* members of the union and they have to decide on a wage claim. They are assumed to be aware of the fact that if they push wages up to $\bar{W}$ then they will lose $L^* - L_d$ jobs. If they decide to go ahead anyway then the consequent unemployment is said to be voluntary. This leads to the conclusion that labour brings unemployment upon itself and consequently should not expect sympathetic support from government.

This is, of course, rather simplistic. Many of those who lose jobs because wages are too high have no influence over wage negotiations. This is particularly true of new entrants into the labour market. They have never worked and belong to no trade union and yet may face unemployment because the wage rate is too high.

Price inflexibility

There is also the somewhat knotty problem of specifying how a minimum *real* wage can ever be enforced. Wage negotiations take place in terms of *money* wages, for example £120 per week. The real wage depends partly on the money wage but also on the price level. Now prices are not controlled by labour; they are determined in the markets for goods.

Thus neither unions nor government can actually negotiate or fix the real wage rate. Failure of the market to adjust to the market-clearing real wage rate may therefore be as much the fault of price setters as wage setters.

Expectations

In fact, of course, the wage negotiators try to make some allowance for future price changes. If they expect prices to rise by 10 per cent over the contract period they will add 10 per cent to their wage claim. They may be mistaken in their estimates of future inflation and hence offer too much or too little labour should actual price increases turn out to be greater or less than expected.

This expectations problem has been dealt with at length in Chapter 16. There it was pointed out that employment may depart from its natural rate if expectations turn out to be false. However, agents are expected eventually to get their expectations right and the economy then returns to its natural (full-employment) rate. Once again it is a question of waiting until the adjustment has taken place. Full employment will then be restored by market forces.

Policy

Most of the policy prescriptions which flow from these views of unemployment are to do with 'getting the market to work'. Wage flexibility stands high on the list of recommendations, together with exhortations to seek work wherever and whatever it is. If this still results in an unacceptably high level of unemployment then the replacement ratio should be cut – usually this means cutting welfare payments rather than raising wages. In this model 'too much unemployment' means an unacceptably high burden of welfare support rather than an unacceptably high level of unemployment *per se*. This is because unemployment is largely voluntary and hence presents no problem other than the need to provide welfare support.

Keynesian view

A somewhat different interpretation of market failure is offered by Keynes. Briefly recapitulating Chapter 14, we may say that output and hence employment are determined by effective demand. When effective demand is low there will be unsold goods in stock and workers will be laid off. In these circumstances it is not clear what would happen to unemployment if wages fell. If a fall in wages increased effective demand then employment would increase. But if, as is often argued, a fall in the wage rate leads to a further reduction in effective demand then a wage cut would reduce employment still further.

In this kind of model, unemployment is clearly beyond the control of the labour force. Many willing and able workers would be unsuccessfully seeking work at the going wage rate. There may well be wage flexibility, perfect expectations of future prices and no unemployment benefits at all, and yet there would still be very high levels of unemployment. Without the appropriate level of aggregate demand there can be no decrease in unemployment.

The Keynesian prescriptions are therefore directed not at making the labour market work, but rather at restoring effective demand to its full-employment level. This type of unemployment is known as demand-deficient or **cyclical unemployment**.

Policy

Unemployment in this model is a problem because many families are made much worse off than they need be (or would choose to be). Unemployment is involuntary and, with proper government policies, unnecessary. The unemployed are not victims of their own greed or rigidity or lack of foresight; they are victims of an economic system in which there has been a failure in effective demand. They therefore deserve and claim sympathetic and generous support from the state.

This Keynesian argument won worldwide support and had the effect of altering public attitudes to the unemployed. It also resulted in the widespread adoption of **demand management policies** which ensured full employment in the three decades following the Second World War. This may help explain the low and stable unemployment figures of the Keynesian years compared with the unemployment figures for the years before the 1929 slump, which were higher and more variable.

Stagflation

Keynesian analysis came under fire when in the late 1970s unemployment began to rise at the same time as prices. The fact that prices were going up suggested that demand was too high. But at the same time the high level of unemployment suggested that demand was too low. There was therefore an unexplained coexistence of stagnation of output an inflation of prices: **stagflation**.

Contradictions of this kind leave a policy vacuum. To fill it economists and politicians alike have tended to return to the pre-Keynesian approach. They have looked again at the labour market and sought to show that the fault lies there rather than in any demand deficiency.

The political consequence of this is that once again the unemployed are increasingly regarded as victims of their own (and their fellow workers') inflexibility. By being so inflexible they put themselves beyond government concern and thus the Keynesian case for government liability is denied.

Technical change

Over and above these political arguments about the role of governments in unemployment, there is growing concern about the influence of technical change on unemployment. We have already touched upon this under the heading of structural unemployment.

The technical change referred to there was that of product innovation. The advent of new products alters the structure of employment and this, together with the inability of some parts of the labour force to respond, results in structural unemployment.

There is, however, another form of technical progress which results in *new ways of producing existing goods* rather than the production of new goods – that is process innovation rather than product innovation.

Process innovation occurs continually but is sometimes marked by sudden spurts which precipitate fears of labour being replaced by machines. There have been two such spurts in our economic development. The first was the replacement of human muscle power by steam engines, internal combustion engines and electrical motors. One mechanical digger did the work of 50 men with shovels. The introduction of these new sources of power combined with the organization of workers in the workplace constituted the Industrial Revolution.

Many labourers feared that the introduction of these new methods would cause unemployment, and so they tried to wreck the machines. These were called Luddites after Ned Ludd, who smashed up new machines in Nottingham in the early nineteenth century.

Their fears proved unfounded. Despite the enormous increases in productivity of workers and machines, there was no obvious decline in employment. Hours of work fell, work became less strenuous and much more was produced. There were clearly some who suffered by finding their skills no longer marketable. But this inability to respond to demand changes is structural unemployment and should not therefore be persistent. Unemployed workers do take up new work eventually, and each year new workers enter the labour force and other workers retire.

These lessons of history have not, however, prevented the re-emergence of fears consequent upon the introduction of the so-called new technology. This is the second spurt in economic development and consists in the replacement of human *intellectual* effort by machines – the earlier spurt was the replacement of human muscular effort.

The ability of these new devices to do the work of machine minders, process controllers and information processors gives rise to fresh doubts about future demand for labour. The Trades Union Congress, however, welcomes the new technology as, by improving efficiency, it will actually create new jobs to replace those jobs being taken over by the new technology.

The fallacy of the Luddite argument, both then and now, is the assumption that there is a fixed amount of work to be done, and that if it is done by a machine then it cannot be done by workers. In fact, as history shows, the amount of work expands, as does the amount of leisure, and everyone is better off. There is no evidence that fluctuations in unemployment are correlated with the adoption of new technology.

What is involved, of course, is the restructuring of the labour force. There will be lower demand for machine minders but higher demand for computer programmers and leisure services. Some workers, particularly those with a large investment in their current jobs, will lose out. It will appear to them that jobs are being destroyed. Individual trade unions will therefore have rather different views from those of the TUC.

SUMMARY

1. The economic theory used so far in this chapter suggests that unemployment may be either voluntary or involuntary.
2. Of these two, the latter is much more a cause for concern than the former. Unfortunately there is no clear way of deciding what is voluntary and what is involuntary.
3. One group of economists (neo-classicals) believes that the main causes of unemployment lie in the imperfections of the labour markets.
4. These may be induced by the exercise of union power, by lack of foresight of workers and employers, by too high unemployment benefit or by an unwillingness of labour to respond to frictional, seasonal and structural job loss.
5. This school of thought holds that all unemployment is voluntary and is therefore a cause for concern only in so far as it imposes a tax burden on the employed.
6. A second group of economists (Keynesians) believes that the bulk of unemployment is due to deficient effective demand.
7. This is beyond the control of workers but is amenable to government fiscal policy. Thus, this group holds that unemployment is involuntary and as such does give cause for concern. There are people who can work, who want to work and who could produce enough to cover the cost of employing them. They are, however, prevented from working and are denied the goods they could produce.
8. Keynesians are faced with the task of explaining why, if there is deficient demand, prices continue to rise (stagflation).
9. Technical change is a continuing source of structural unemployment, but overall has led to greater employment, output and leisure time.

Measuring unemployment

At the start of this chapter we referred to the statistics published on unemployment. It is necessary now to look briefly at what these figures actually mean.

We can discover how many people are employed because their tax and national insurance payments are recorded. We also know how many people there are between school-leaving and retirement ages. If we used these figures to measure unemployment we would find that in, say, 1982 there was a 66 per cent employment rate. This implies an unemployment rate of 34 per cent, which is very much higher than the recorded unemployment that year (12.3 per

Case Study 17.1 On the measurement of employment and unemployment

In May 1984 unemployment was, officially, 3.1 million. Critics of the count put the true figure at between 1.7 million and 4.4 million . . .

The long standing controversy on how to measure unemployment has been given a new twist by recent changes in coverage and the method of counting unemployed people . . . Lipsey . . . estimated that with an official total of 3.1 million (October 1983) it was a straightforward matter to boost the total to 4.4 million or cut it to 1.7 million depending on your point of view.

I present some illustrative numbers in Tables 17.2 and 17.3. Table 17.2 attempts to calculate the number of people seeking work. Row 1 gives the official May 1984 UK unemployment unadjusted including school leavers. The corresponding figure for UK unemployment seasonally adjusted excluding school leavers is 56,000 lower. Row 2 grosses up the new count figures on the old count basis. The old count, pre-October 1982, differs both in coverage and method of counting from the post-October 1982 count (the details are set out in Table 17.3) . . . the May 1984 new count figure of 3.085 million is equivalent to 3.459 million on the old count. In row 3 I control for the fact that the new computer count is more accurate than the old manual count . . . there is now less delay between the unemployed person finding a job and this being reflected in the figures. The Department of Employment (DE) indicated that the . . . figure should be reduced by 2.5% because of this.

Those people who would have been registered unemployed on the old count basis, but were not actively seeking work, must also be deducted (row 4). [The DE] puts this figure at 'between 10 and 20 per cent' of the registrant count . . . I have deducted the absolute 1981 figure of 400,000, because it is not self evident that a constant proportion is justified . . . It should be noted that this figure embraces one very important group who are now no longer included in the count – men aged over 60 . . . (see Table 17.3). Finally, I add the unregistered unemployed, i.e. 'those identified in surveys as unemployed who did not register as unemployed . . . and were not therefore covered by the monthly count', (DE *Gazette*, June 1983 . . .) . . . the official DE estimate for unregistered unemployment in 1981 is also 400,000 . . . These data suggest that the numbers seeking work in May 1984 were around 3.4 million.

The major omissions from Table 17.2 are the groups covered by the special employment and training measures. In April 1984 these were as follows:

Adults	
Job release scheme	94,000
Temporary short time working compensation scheme	12,000
Enterprise Allowance	29,000
Community programme	113,000
Other	1,000
Youths	
Youth training scheme	270,000
Young workers scheme	92,000
Other	12,000
TOTAL	622,000

The DE state that the numbers claiming unemployment benefit are reduced by 440,000 as a consequence of these special measures. Clearly, it would be absurd to add all the 440,000 to the numbers seeking work . . . [some of the schemes would continue even if unemployment fell, e.g. YTS, and some on these schemes would prefer 'proper jobs', e.g. Community programme] . . . perhaps we might add between 0.1 million and 0.2 million to the seeking-work total in Table 17.2.

The changes in coverage and counting between the old and new methods of measuring unemployment are set out in Table 17.3. The coverage has changed independently of the new counting method: the unemployment rate of men aged 60+ is now meaningless consequent on two . . . measures . . . First . . . men aged 60+ [can] secure national insurance credits without signing on at an unemployment benefit office . . . Secondly, providing the man of 60+ drops out of the labour force he is now eligible for the higher (long term) rate of supplementary benefit.

The switch to counting claimants at Unemployment Benefit offices rather than . . . Job Centres has also affected the figures. They are more accurate for two reasons. First they now include the severely disabled (row 3). Second, the computer count . . . [is more accurate – see earlier discussion] (row 4). However, some people previously registered for work but did not claim benefit and such people can no longer be counted (row 5). This makes the new figures less accurate. The net effect of these three elements for school leavers (row 6) is to cause unemployment to be some 26,000 lower than it would otherwise have been (in June, July and August the equivalent figure is 100,000 to 200,000). Therefore, ignoring unregistered unemployment and those registered but not seeking work, which roughly balance out, the new count understates 'true' unemployment by around 200,000.

[Does rising registered unemployment equal rising actual unemployment?]

. . . [I]t is possible that more of those seeking work register as unemployed (old count) or claim benefit (new count). The National Institute (1983) recently presented some evidence on this from the Population Censuses of 1971 and 1981:

	Between 1971 and 1981 unemployment grew by	
Total Census	1.31 million,	127 per cent
Total registered	1.68 million,	245 per cent
Women Census	0.3 million,	194 per cent
Women registered	0.6 million,	645 per cent

The National Institute concludes that 'the implication is that the rise in registered unemployment, especially female unemployment, between 1971 and 1981 may be due in part to an increase in the proportion of the unemployed who register as well as an increase in the numbers seeking work.'

We should not be surprised that the proportion registering rose between 1971 and 1981. Among women changes in national insurance contributions and benefit entitlement play a part. In addition we must remember that unemployment rises primarily because spell durations lengthen rather than because the inflow to the register rises. Presumably longer spell durations result in the individual registering at some point, implying a growing fraction of the unemployed stock will be registered.

1. Do you consider the new (post-October 1982) unemployment count to measure employment (a) More accurately than before? (b) More in line with economic theory?

2. Does rising registered unemployment necessarily mean a rise in the number of people unemployed and seeking work?

Source: D. Metcalf, *NIESR*, no. 107

Table 17.2 Number of people seeking work

Component	Adjustment (m)	Total (m)
1. New count, UK unemployment unadjusted including school leavers May 1984	–	3.085
2. Gross up to old count figure	+0.374	3.459
3. Adjust 2 for greater accuracy of computer count, multiply by 0.975	−0.087	3.372
4. Deduct registered unemployed on old count basis but not actively seeking work	−0.400	2.972
5. Add unregistered unemployed on old count basis	+0.400	3.372
Total		3.372

Notes and sources:

Row 1 DE Press Notice 1/6/84.

Row 2 Gross-up method based on coefficients from regression equation over 1971–82 (monthly observations) when data are available on both old and new count definitions. DE *Gazette*, December 1982, table 2.1; Unemployment Unit *Bulletin*, 11 January 1984, and Press Release 1/6/84.

Row 3 DE *Gazette*, December 1982, p. S20.

Row 4 DE *Gazette*, June 1983, p. 266. Figure refers to GB 1981. Note that this figure includes the men aged 60+ who, from April 1983, no longer have to register to claim NI credits.

Row 5 DE *Gazette*, June 1983, p. 267. Figure refers to GB 1981. Based on weighted average of evidence from Population Census, EC Labour Force Survey, General Household Survey.

Table 17.3 Recent changes in the coverage and counting of unemployment

Component	Effect (000)	New count gives better estimate of 'true' unemployment than old count
COVERAGE. All refers to men aged 60+		
1. Secure NI credits without signing at UB office (effective April 83)	−107 (by June 83)	Yes
2. Qualify for higher rate of SB, providing leave labour force		
(i) after 1 year on SB (Nov. 81)	−37 (by Feb. 82)	No
(ii) immediately come on to SB (June 83)	−54 (by Aug. 83)	No
COUNTING: Adults		
3. Include severely disabled (Oct. 82)	+23 (ave. 82)	Yes
4. Switch from manual to computer count (Oct. 82)	−78 (ave. 82)	Yes
5. Exclude people previously registered but not claiming benefit, who can no longer be counted	−135 (ave. 82)	No
COUNTING: School leavers		
6. Net effect of 3–5 (Oct. 82)	−26 (all months except June, July, Aug.)	–

Sources: Rows 1 and 2 DE Press Notice 1/6/84, note 9 and Unemployment Unit *Bulletin*, 11 January 1984; rows 3–5 DE *Gazette*, December 1982 S20; row 6 Unemployment Unit *Bulletin*, 11 January 1984 (during June, July and August the corresponding figure is between 100,000 and 200,000).

cent). The difference arises because, as we pointed out earlier, not everyone of working age is a member of the workforce. Many women work at home and full-time students can continue to study long after their school-leaving age.

How, then, can we discover the number of persons who would want to work if offered a job?

Registered unemployed

The unemployment figures actually reported are derived from those unemployed who actually register as seeking work.

At one time it was necessary only to register as being available for work in order to claim unemployment benefit. It is now necessary to be actively seeking work. There are government statistics on those unemployed who seek unemployment benefits and these figures form the basis of most estimates of the actual number of unemployed.

The figures are not entirely satisfactory. Some people who register do so simply in order to claim benefit, and they do not in fact wish to find work. On the other hand, some of the unemployed are not entitled to benefit even if they have registered. They are therefore not included in the figures, even though they are seeking work. These are typically married women who wish to work, but who are normally supported by their husbands and who did not contribute to the National Insurance Fund when they worked. They are therefore not entitled to unemployment benefits.

Since 1973 the functions of finding work for the unemployed and of paying out unemployment benefit have been separated. Job centres exist to find jobs, but have nothing to do with registration for unemployment benefit.

There have also been a number of changes in the circumstances governing the payment of this benefit. It is no longer necessary for the unemployed over the age of 60 to show that they are available for work before they can qualify for benefit. Also more and more women workers are qualifying for benefit and so tend to register more now than they did before.

Some of the variations in the unemployment figures are therefore the result of these administrative changes rather than reflections of any underlying reality. Of course, as far as the neo-classical economists are concerned, the problem of unemployment is no more than the burden of benefits, and hence measuring the number applying for benefit is all that is required.

If, however, we are concerned to reduce unemployment in order to improve the welfare of the unemployed (the Keynesian view), then the number applying for benefit is not appropriate since it measures both the voluntarily and involuntarily unemployed.

Underemployment versus unemployment

There are other ways in which the unemployment figures conceal rather than reveal relevant facts. For example, there will be many people in work who want to work more hours, either by doing overtime work for their current employer or by 'moonlighting' for another employer at night or at weekends. We have no way of deducing the amount of this **underemployment**. We concentrate exclusively on those who are wholly unemployed.

The distribution of unemployment

The figures as published give no idea of how unemployment is shared out among the whole workforce. There is evidence to suggest that the level of unemployment is borne largely by one group only. If a level of unemployment of 13 per cent were shared equally among all labourers, then each of us would be unemployed for 13 per cent of our working lives, i.e. about seven weeks every year. In fact the data show that in April 1983 25 per cent of female unemployed and 40 per cent of male unemployed had been out of work for more than a year. Thus long-term unemployment falls mainly on males and the same group bears almost all the unemployment. Indeed, some workers *never* experience unemployment.

Age structure

The aggregate unemployment figures also mask the unequal distribution of unemployment among the various age groups. The young (under 19 years) have an unemployment rate twice that of the average, and those over 55 years of age are much more likely to suffer prolonged periods of unemployment. Thus it seems that those newly entering the labour force have great difficulty in getting started. Once started they face fairly good employment prospects. They may enter unemployment but quickly find a new job. This lasts until the age of 55 years. Thereafter if they become unemployed they face a long period of unemployment.

Those at either end of the age spectrum therefore bear a disproportionate share of unemployment. Indeed, there is some evidence to suggest that the increased levels of unemployment are the results of (a) the failure of new workers to enter the workforce; and (b) the fact that those who become unemployed after their 55th year face prolonged periods of unemployment. This opposes the popular view that unemployment increases because more people are *becoming* unemployed in each period rather than remaining unemployed for more time periods.

Of these two age groups, the young tend to attract more sympathy than do the old. This is partly because it is felt that they have not been given a chance, partly because, if allowed to continue, youth unemployment 'breeds' unemployable adults, and partly because disillusioned youth is thought to be prone to anti-social activities.

This has led even extremely market-oriented economists to advocate state schemes to encourage youth employment. The Youth Training Scheme (YTS) is aimed at subsidizing the employers of under-18 year olds to offer some work experience and training to teenagers who would otherwise have no work.

There have been a number of such schemes. Some are seen as ways of exploiting very low-paid labour. Some are seen as purely cosmetic attempts at reducing the number of *registered* unemployed no matter how pointless the work they do. Some are seen as genuine attempts to provide work experience, and possibly some training.

Less attention is paid to the over-50s. The view seems to be that they are almost retired anyway and hence can be regarded as 'nearly' retired. There is, however, plenty of evidence to suggest that the unemployed, at any age, suffer feelings of worthlessness and inadequacy. These feelings are over and above those caused by the economic deprivation resulting from being unemployed.

Feelings of this kind lie at the heart of many of the strong views held by economists and politicians about the whole subject of unemployment.

Regional differences

There are two other ways in which the distribution of unemployment is unequal. The first is geographical, and the second, closely related, is among industries.

Table 17.4 Regional distribution of UK unemployment, 1981, 1989 and May 1991 (%)

	1981	1989	May 1991
North	13.9	8.9	10.2
Yorkshire and Humberside	11.1	7.0	8.5
East Midlands	9.6	5.1	7.2
East Anglia	8.7	3.5	5.7
South East	7.6	3.7	6.6
South West	9.3	4.1	7.0
West Midlands	12.8	6.0	8.3
North West	13.0	7.8	9.3
Wales	13.7	6.9	8.7
Scotland	12.8	8.6	8.9
Northern Ireland	17.0	14.3	13.7
UK total	10.7	6.5	7.7

Table 17.4 shows that in some regions (the South East and East Anglia) unemployment is below average, whereas in others (the North) it is well above average. There are a number of reasons why this distribution of unemployment may occur. One is that some industries are declining and are largely located in particular areas. Thus the decline of an industry (and its consequent unemployment) will affect some regions much more than others.

Table 17.5 shows the industrial distribution of unemployment. Once again it is apparent that some industries (e.g. construction) have very high unemployment, whereas others (mining, etc.) have (comparatively) very low levels of unemployment.

If the price mechanism worked perfectly then the regions of high unemployment would have lower wage rates and hence would be very attractive to employers. Industry would therefore move into the region and eventually the level of unemployment would even out. This seems not to happen, at least without extra efforts by way of advertising the region's advantages and by way of government regional investment grants.

These investment grants are further augmented by the creation of enterprise zones and free ports. The former are aimed at reducing state involvement to a minimum for industries setting up in particular regions. The latter is a device for simplifying the Customs and Excise rules when goods are brought to these shores purely with the intention of exporting them again when they have been worked on.

So there are a number of ways in which the unequal distribution of unemployment among regions may be caused, and possibly cured. However, these market and non-market forces may not be capable of taking employment to the unemployed. Firms may simply wish to stay where things look successful and go-ahead.

Table 17.5 Industrial distribution of UK unemployment, 1981 (%)

	1981
Agriculture, forestry and fishing	11.3
Manufacturing	13.6
Construction	33.6
Mining, quarrying, gas, water and electricity	6.8
Distribution	10.0
Professional and other services	13.4

In this case it becomes necessary for the unemployed to move to where the work is. Labour should follow market forces. It should see that wages in one region are low compared with those of other regions, and those seeking work in a region of high unemployment should see that the opportunity to work is higher in other regions. Forces such as these, it is argued, should cause labour to move from regions of high unemployment to regions of low unemployment.

There are, of course, many reasons why labour is reluctant to move: family, friends, countryside, societies and many of the qualities which go to make up a 'life' cannot simply be replaced with a new set whenever the job prospects of a region change. Once again, then, there is cause for disagreement between economists.

Those economists who support the idea that market forces lead to efficiency argue that the unemployed should be prepared to move to find work. If they are not prepared to move then they are *voluntarily* unemployed: they have chosen not to get a job. The way forward is to cut unemployment benefit so as to get them to move.

On the other hand, those economists who suspect that market forces may need some help in producing a tolerably humane society will argue that the unemployed cannot be expected to 'get on their bikes', to tear up their roots and move whenever market forces dictate. They are justified in waiting for suitable work to appear in their 'travel-to-work area'. Thus they are involuntarily unemployed and should be supported and nurtured.

The costs of unemployment

Unemployment has a profound effect upon a society and imposes costs upon it. The costs of unemployment can be split up into two sets, the costs to the individual unemployed and the costs to society as a whole. Such a division does ignore the uneven costs placed on certain age groups and regions, but these have already been discussed.

The costs borne by the unemployed

The most obvious cost to the person (or family) is the financial hardship unemployment imposes. All people who have been employed find that their income is lower when unemployed. (This is not the same as saying that the earnings of the unemployed will rise if they take a job because that job may not compensate them fully for the loss of benefit.) The unemployed receive a state benefit from one of two sources, National Insurance Unemployment Benefit or Income Support. Unemployment benefit is a flat rate payment made for up to 52 weeks, while Income Support is designed to maintain a minimum level of income and is payable regardless of the period of unemployment although it is only payable to those without a certain level of savings.

Families have been shown to suffer the greatest financial hardship from unemployment, despite being eligible for the greatest benefits. In recent years the real value of unemployment benefit has fallen and the earnings related supplement of unemployment benefit (paid to compensate those on higher earnings) has been abolished. This has made the prospect of being and staying unemployed less acceptable, and has contributed to the incidence of poverty in the UK.

A further important, but unmeasurable, cost of unemployment is the psychological effect it has on the individual. People who are unemployed feel varying degrees of frustration, boredom, depression and shame. There is also a perceived loss of social standing and status and an accompanying loss of self-respect, self-confidence and motivation. While such feelings do vary between individuals, the duration of unemployment is critical. The longer the period of unemployment the greater the financial pressure and the strain of repeated rejection mounts up. Added to this, the long term unemployed find it even more difficult to gain employment because they have been unemployed for so long; employers appear to view the duration of unemployment as a signal not to employ.

The costs borne by society as a whole

The costs of unemployment to society can be split into three categories: the financial cost to the government, the loss of output and growth, and the social and political consequences.

The financial cost to the government, and so the taxpayers, is represented by increased government spending and reduced revenue to the Exchequer. All unemployed people are entitled to some form of benefit (providing their savings are not too high) and so each unemployed person causes greater benefit payments by the government. In 1988–89 there were 755,000 people receiving unemployment benefit at the cost of £1,481 million to the Exchequer, a further 4,925,000 people were claiming income support, although nearly 75 per cent of these were not registered as unemployed. Unemployed people cannot pay income tax or national insurance; they also spend less than if they were in employment, and so the tax yield from direct taxation and from VAT and other duties is lower than it would be in a full employment situation. It is difficult to gauge the exact cost to the Exchequer of each unemployed person due to the combined effect of lost revenue and increased spending. The Treasury estimated the cost at £3,400 extra per person unemployed in 1981 while the House of Lords Select Committee calculated the figure to be £5,000 per person. At today's prices the figures can certainly be doubled.

The loss of output due to unemployment is very difficult to measure. There is the immediate loss of output which can be estimated as the difference between capacity output and current output. This leaves aside two important questions. Firstly, is there a natural rate of output and if so what is it? This is crucial to any estimate of lost output and as we have seen a matter of some dispute. Secondly, it ignores the lost economic growth that would have occurred had there been full employment. This is a matter of lost future output and its measurement is a matter of pure speculation. There is no doubt that unemployment does have an opportunity cost and this is considerable – it also lasts forever, because lost output today can never be recovered.

The social and political consequences of unemployment are the most difficult to measure. There is little doubt that unemployment can lead to increased crime, delinquency, drug abuse, ill health and political extremism. There is also little doubt that areas of high unemployment see the most intense manifestations of these effects. There is, however, no way of measuring the contribution of unemployment to these phenomena. In other words, while many suspect unemployment to be a cause of them, many dispute the extent of unemployment's influence and there is no way of proving the case one way or the other. For example, in 1981 there were riots in Brixton and Toxteth, both areas of high unemployment, but there is genuine confusion as to the actual cause of the riots. In 1991 there were riots in Oxford which is not an area of high unemployment. The case is difficult to prove, but the fact remains that unemployment has profound social implications and is certainly a contributing factor to discontent.

SUMMARY

1. Economists who support the free market as a way of organizing our economic affairs feel that much of the recorded unemployment is voluntary. Their policies to deal with it therefore tend to be aimed at encouraging the unemployed actively to seek work, whatever and wherever it may be. They couple this with moves to free the market from monopolistic (trade union) imperfections. These two types of policy should reduce both voluntary and involuntary unemployment.
2. On the other hand, Keynesian economists argue that markets sometimes fail through lack of aggregate demand. Thus the unemployed have no means of increasing the demand for their services – they are largely involuntarily unemployed. Their policy prescriptions are (a) to increase aggregate demand by way of government expenditure; and (b) to increase unemployment benefit to help cushion the economic consequences of unemployment. The unemployed are, after all, victims of the government's inability to maintain aggregate demand.
3. Whatever policy we may prefer, it is important to have some idea of the size of the unemployment problem. Unfortunately, the published statistics do not reflect the true level of underemployment of labour, nor do they distinguish between voluntary and involuntary unemployment.
4. Finally, it seems that the unemployment which is currently registered is by no means equally distributed. Some age groups suffer more unemployment than others. Some workers remain unemployed for very long periods, whereas others are never unemployed. Regions of the North and North West have much higher levels of unemployment than those of the South and South East. It also seems that some industries have much higher levels of unemployment than others.
5. These maldistributions of unemployment call for, and are given, quite separate policy prescriptions ranging through job creation, job protection, regional policies and enterprise zones.
6. Unemployment imposes costs upon both the unemployed and society as a whole.
7. The unemployed suffer a loss of financial and

social status and can become demoralized and de-skilled.

8. Society as a whole must bear the costs of higher public spending on benefits and lower output. Society may also suffer a higher level of crime and other anti-social activities.

Case Study 17.2 Jobless rate rises above EC average

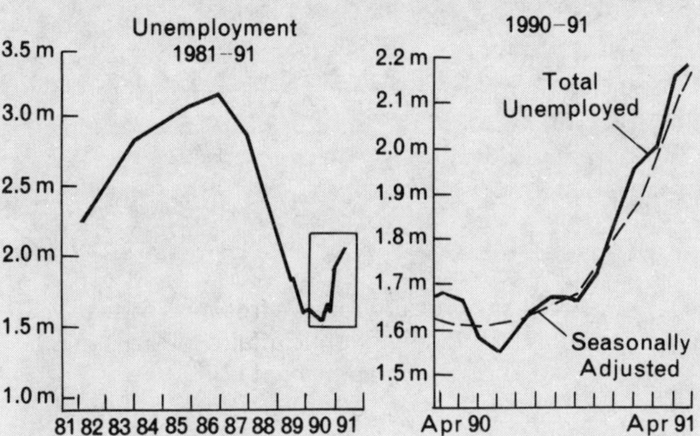

The number of people out of work increased by 84,100 to 2,175,100 last month, taking Britain above the European average, according to figures published yesterday.

The seasonally-adjusted total, regarded by experts as the most accurate guide, grew for the 13th consecutive month and is now 568,100 higher than March last year when a record-breaking run of 44 falls came to a halt.

Labour said the April increase was the biggest for that month since the Second World War.

The climb above the EC average is a blow for Mr Howard, Employment Secretary who pointed out during earlier rises that Britain was still doing better than the rest of the Community.

Of the 20 countries used by the Department of Employment to compare jobless rates, only six are above Britain, including Ireland, Italy and France.

Yesterday Mr Howard said the rise was lower than in the previous two months and there was 'unmistakable evidence' the battle against inflation was being won.

The Government, he said, was providing more practical assistance than ever before to help people to find work.

The increase in average earnings dropped 0.25 per cent to nine per cent in March and is 1.25 per cent below its peak last July, although further falls were needed, he said.

'The Government is laying the foundations for future economic growth but the prospects for employment and for unemployment in the coming months depend crucially on the level of wage settlements,' he said.

'A recovery in business confidence will not be translated into more jobs unless we remain competitive in international markets.'

Last month's jobless total represents 7.6 per cent of the workforce and took unemployment to its highest level since August, 1988.

With future rises of around 80,000 likely during the coming months, the total could be near three million by the end of the year.

The actual April increase was 56,382 to 2,198,455, or 7.7 per cent. The adjusted rise was greater because unemployment would normally be expected to fall in the month by 27,900 due to seasonal factors recorded over the past 10 years.

The West Midlands and North recorded the largest jumps in their jobless rates for a year.

This is a sign that the recession is spreading from the South-East, which to date has borne the brunt of the downturn in the economy.

The increases in Yorkshire and Humberside and Scotland were the biggest in those regions since national dole queues started lengthening 13 months ago.

Between March and April, 359,200 (up 89,400 on a year ago) people joined the unemployment count and 298,100 (up 10,800) left.

The controversial scaling-down of the main adult training scheme while unemployment is rising resulted in a 25,000 fall last month to 172,000 in the number on Employment Training.

The Youth Training programme, at 350,000, is down 9,500 on last year and other schemes have declined by 20,632 to 57,368 in 12 months.

Job hunters also face an increasingly tough time after the number of vacancies at JobCentres – one-third of those in the economy – were down 18,400 in April and 37 per cent over 12 months to an eight-year low of 125,000.

Manufacturing employment continued its decline with a 45,000 April drop to 4,872,000.

Short-time working grew by 280,000 hours a week in March to 1,020,000. Department of Employment officials believe that may be responsible for the fall in average earnings.

Regional unemployment totals

	Total (adjusted)	Monthly change	Rate (%)
South-East	590,600	+28,800	6.3
East Anglia	55,600	+ 2,100	5.5
South-West	150,400	+ 6,400	6.8
West Midlands	206,700	+10,900	8.0
East Midlands	133,900	+ 5,200	6.9
Yorks and Humber	199,800	+ 8,000	8.3
North-West	275,300	+ 8,000	9.0
North	140,100	+ 5,100	10.0
Wales	108,900	+ 4,000	8.4
Scotland	214,500	+ 5,200	8.6
Northern Ireland	99,200	+ 400	13.7

Overtime increased marginally by 330,000 hours to 10,360,000 a week.

The total is still well below the 12.8 million of March last year.

Output declined 5.1 per cent in the three months to March.

A 3.2 per cent drop in employment resulted in a 1.9 per cent fall in productivity.

Unit wage costs rose 11 per cent in March, down 0.3 per cent and the first fall since April last year.

The number of working days lost due to industrial disputes went up 23,000 in March to 54,000 – the highest level since August last year – because of a spurt in public administration and education disputes.

However, the total lost in the year to March, at 800,000 days is still well below the previous 12 month's 5.1 million and substantially lower than the annual average of 6.4 million over the past 10 years.

The total of 43 stoppages in March, up nine on February, is the lowest for that month since 1932.

1. Why does Mr Howard discuss inflation and wage claims when commenting on the unemployment figures?
2. Why is the seasonally adjusted total 'regarded by experts as the most accurate guide'?
3. What is the significance of the number of vacancies at job centres?

Source: Kevin Maguire, *Daily Telegraph*, 17 May 1991

Exam Preparation and Practice

MULTIPLE-CHOICE QUESTIONS

From the list below select the response that is the best example of:

1. Frictional unemployment.
2. Seasonal unemployment.
  A A person who has recently left one firm and has negotiated a job with another.
  B A telephone operator made redundant due to the installation of new high-technology exchanges.
  C A worker made redundant due to a fall in demand following a contraction in government expenditure.
  D An unemployed shipbuilder from Tyne and Wear.
  E A farm worker laid off during February because of snow.

3. Which of the following is an inappropriate policy for reducing regional unemployment?
  A Retraining schemes.
  B Free ports.
  C Fiscal policy.
  D Varying regional taxation.

4. Which of the following is most likely to reduce the level of cyclical unemployment?
  A An increase in the standard rate of income tax.
  B A rise in government spending.
  C The introduction of retraining schemes.
  D A rise in the level of interest rates.

Answer key

Where there are three numbered alternatives

A	B	C	D	E
1, 2, 3 Correct	1, 2 Correct	2, 3 Correct	1 Correct	3 Correct

Where there are four numbered alternatives

A	B	C	D	E
1, 2 and 3 Correct	1 and 3 Correct	2 and 4 Correct	4 only Correct	1 and 4 Correct

5. Which of the following are included in 'registered' unemployment in the UK?
  1 A 40-year-old former school teacher.
  2 A married housewife whose husband works.
  3 A university student on Christmas holiday.
  4 A 17-year-old school leaver who has never worked.

6. Regional unemployment can arise because of:
  1 Import penetration in a particular industry.
  2 Labour immobility.
  3 Technological progress.

EXERCISES

1. The following diagram shows supply and demand in the labour market.
  (a) If the wage rate is fixed at £10/hour, what is:
    (i) the level of employment?
    (ii) the level of unemployment?
  (b) To what level would the wage rate have to fall for there to be no involuntary unemployment?
  (c) If the wage rate does fall to the level suggested in your answer to (b), what do the people who previously wanted to work do now?

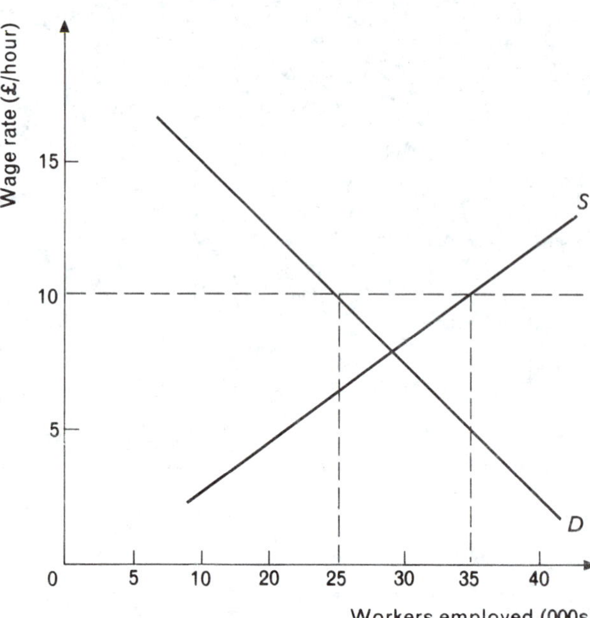

2. A worker who previously took home £180 a week is unemployed and receives £112 a week in unemployment benefit. The family also gets a further £32 a week in benefits from the Department of Social Security, and the children receive free school meals worth £8 a week.
  (a) What is the worker's replacement ratio as represented by (i) unemployment benefit and (ii) total benefits?
  (b) The worker is offered a job at a take-home pay of £160 a week. Would the worker take the job?
  (c) If the worker's children lost the right to free school meals and the families other benefits were reduced by £10 as a result of taking the job, would this alter the worker's decision?

3. Which of the following policies could be used to relieve heavy local unemployment. Which is likely to be the most effective?
  (a) Expansionary fiscal policy.
  (b) The establishment of a regional development agency.
  (c) A government training programme for unemployed workers.
  (d) A grant for 16 to 18 year olds who stay in full-time education.
  (e) A scheme to pay removal expenses for those seeking work in other regions.

4. The employment figures for Little Trivilvania are shown in the following table.

Year	Workforce	Employed workers	Distribution of employment: Manufacturing	Services	Agriculture
1988	10,000	9,600	6,000	2,600	1,000
1989	10,400	9,776	5,400	3,476	900
1990	11,000	10,175	4,900	4,425	840

  (a) What is the percentage rate of unemployment in each year?
  (b) From the data what are the most likely causes of the rise in unemployment?

DATA-RESPONSE QUESTIONS

1. **£20bn – the cost of Britain's dole queue**

What are the costs of unemployment? There are many different components in the total cost to the unemployed and to society including the social costs of increased ill-health and wasted lives. Here we concentrate on measuring the direct costs to the Exchequer – the costs of benefits to the unemployed and the loss of revenue from the loss of jobs.

In reply to Parliamentary questions Ministers defend their refusal to estimate the loss of government revenue through unemployment by saying, for example, that it "depends on the causes of unemployment" (Mr Rees, December 13, 1984).

The argument is rather obscure. It seems to mean that, if unemployment is due to unsustainable earnings levels, it would be wrong to use those earnings levels in calculating lost taxes. But scaled-down earnings assumptions for the unemployed can be made. One should also recognise that deflationary policies do play a major role in explaining unemployment.

The table summarises our results for direct Exchequer costs of unemployment in 1984–85. The benefits total, the more straightforward to estimate, includes National Insurance Unemployment Benefit, Supplementary Benefit, Housing Benefit, benefits to those aged 60 to 65 who no longer register, and the Government's contribution to redundancy payments.

The revenue loss arises not only for the registered unemployed but also for those who would work were more jobs available (especially housewives and early retirees). Another difficult assumption is the choice of earnings level had they been in work.

We tried to follow the procedures of government economists in the past – when they were allowed to make these estimates – in deriving a figure for this (we came up with £110 per week as average for all unemployed) and for the average tax rate.

Our estimate of the total cost is therefore around £20 billion, or £6,600 per registered unemployed person.

We are not arguing that unemployment could be reduced to zero or that this would save £20 billion. We would rather use our figure in estimating the cost of the increase in unemployment from a particular date or in comparison with performance elsewhere. For example, the unemployment rate in 1979 was 5.4 per cent. The Exchequer cost of unemployment at that level now would be some £12.5 billion less than the present total. And if unemployment in Britain had increased no faster than in France or Germany, the Exchequer would have saved some £7.5 billion and employment would have been 1.5 million higher.

We have also attempted to calculate for a hard-pressed local authority the spending and revenue losses attributable to unemployment. With Cleveland County Council's help, we estimated some of these costs for that authority at £490 per year for each extra registered unemployed. This included extra spending on free school meals, staying on in sixth form and further education, services for the unemployed, and losses in revenue and rates. However, we have not added these to the Exchequer costs because we do not know how typical these are.

The loss of income to the unemployed themselves can also be calculated. This is the difference between their net pay in work (using the same assumptions about earnings levels as in the Exchequer cost calculations) and their benefit income out of work. The total loss of income by all registered unemployed comes out at £6.786 billion for the year 1984–85 or £2,120 per person per year. These costs are higher, and the Exchequer costs lower, because the Government have cut, abolished and taxed benefits.

Direct Exchequer costs of unemployment, 1984–85

	£ billion
Benefits	7.44
Lost income tax	5.69
Lost NI contributions	5.20
Lost indirect taxes	1.58
	19.91

The full economic cost of unemployment to the nation is the lost output now and (because of lost investment) in the future. This lost output constitutes lost incomes – to the Government and to the unemployed, with a residual in lost profits, lost self-employed income etc. And this loss of income, by reducing spending, has exacerbated the loss of jobs.

What is the significance of our estimates? First, the calculations bring out the scale of the Government's deflationary fiscal policies. The Public Sector Borrowing Requirement target is set so low that it does not even cover the cost of unemployment's rise relative to our European neighbours.

Secondly, the cost of job creation is much reduced by the savings in the Exchequer costs of unemployment. The gross costs of projects employing people at the earnings level in our calculations should be reduced by around £6,300 per person removed from the unemployment count. Estimates obtained by Christopher Huhne gave the net cost of removing one person from the register by public investment at £14,000, using the National Institute model, and £20,500, using the Treasury model (Guardian, December 13, 1984). These figures would be lower the more labour intensive the project. Paul Ormerod of the Henley Centre, for Forecasting, for instance, has argued that the labour content of public infrastructure spending would reduce the net cost per person removed from the unemployment count to only £7,000 (The Times, April 11). Given these figures, some expansion of public borrowing to finance needed public investment would have economic and social benefits and cut the appalling costs of unemployment.

We are not arguing that paying people in state jobs costs no more than the dole. As Samuel Brittan has pointed out "basically all that the Government can pay someone on a public payroll at no net cost, is the saving in benefit grossed up for tax" (Financial Times, January 15, 1981). The net cost of the Community Programme is very low (around £2,000 per person) because the pay level on the programme is not much more than that. But it is a very negative approach to minimise the net cost in job creation. Attention should also be paid to the value of output. It is the need for renewed infrastructure and restored services which strengthens the argument for a revival in regular public spending as well as special programmes.

Source: *Financial Guardian*, 6 June 1985

(a) According to the article, what factors should be taken into account in calculating the financial costs of unemployment to the exchequer, local authorities and the individual?

(b) With the aid of diagrams explain the economic logic behind the statements that "this loss of income by reducing spending has exacerbated the loss of jobs" (underlined in paragraph 11) and that "some expansion of public borrowing" would "cut the appalling costs of unemployment" (underlined in paragraph 13).

(c) Explain how the social costs of unemployment differ from the economic costs and discuss how changes in the way unemployment is measured may affect estimates of the social costs of unemployment.

Note: Use your own words. Phrases copied directly from the article should be indicated by quotation marks.

(JMB)

---

2. It is often asserted that real wages are "too high". When thinking about such an assertion it is important to recognise at the outset that real wages are not set as the consequence of activity in any particular market. Thus, real wages do not emerge from the labour market, for example. Wage bargaining and related activities which do take place in the labour market serve to generate a nominal wage which is set for some limited period, typically about a year. The resulting real wage which finally emerges then depends on a series of complex interactions in the remainder of the economy and will be influenced by, among other things, shifts in the exchange rate, the level of world activity and government fiscal and monetary policy. These factors will, in their turn, also determine the level of employment and unemployment. To state that the real wage is "too high" is presumably to state that "the economy could magically be shifted to a situation with lower unemployment". Then real wages would also have to be lower. It tells us nothing about what could be done to bring about the desired shift. Furthermore, it is theoretically possible for this statement to be false and it is, in any event, of little value in understanding what is going on in the British economy.

(Source: *Midland Bank Review*, Spring 1985, Midland Bank plc.)

(a) Distinguish between nominal and real wages. **(2 marks)**

(b) How might real wages be affected by:

(i) 'shifts in the exchange rate' (line 12); **(3 marks)**

(ii) 'the level of world activity' (line 13); **(3marks)**

(iii) 'government fiscal and monetary policy' (lines 13–14)? **(3 marks)**

(c) (i) Explain the reasoning in the passage suggesting that a cut in real wages could reduce unemployment. **((6 marks)**

(ii) Explain why 'it is theoretically possible for this statement to be false' (lines 21–22). **(3 marks)**

(LON.)

18 Macroeconomic policy

In this chapter we will discuss:

1. The nature of taxation.
2. Monetary policy – controlling the money supply.
3. Recent developments in money and credit.
4. The role of expectations in economics.
5. Supply-side economics.

Introduction

We have seen in the earlier chapters of Part III of the book that macroeconomic policy consists of fiscal policy and monetary policy. It was shown earlier that they are connected through the government income and expenditure identity: if the government's fiscal policy leads it to spend more than its income (i.e. it runs a **budget deficit**) then it must raise the difference by issuing new debt. Deciding on the composition of government debt, whether to issue interest-bearing bonds or non-interest bearing cash, is monetary policy.

There are a number of considerations which bear on these decisions. Some of these considerations are not strictly to do with 'controlling' or 'managing' the economy as such, but nevertheless should be dealt with briefly before proceeding to the economic management issues.

Public finance

It is fairly clear that in one way or another the government has to meet the cost of running Parliament, the Civil Service, the law courts, the police force, the armed forces, the motorways, etc. Thus whether it wishes to become involved in the economy or not, it is inevitably faced with the problem of how to raise the income necessary to meet all these needs. There are three possibilities here:

(1) One possibility would be to raise all the income from *taxes*. This is the balanced budget approach. If all government expenditure is met out of taxes then all the roads which are built today (for the benefit largely of future generations) are paid for entirely by the current crop of taxpayers. Furthermore, if the country were engaged in a war to defend itself from invasion then the current population would have to bear the entire cost of preserving the country's freedom for future generations.

It is well known that taxes are unpopular. Taxpayers are acutely aware of their loss of income to the government, and any tendency to increase it is not welcome. This results in a number of arguments about who should pay what. The general view is that the rich should pay proportionately more than the poor. Thus a citizen with an income of, say, £45,000 per year may be expected to pay £15,000 in tax, whereas a citizen with an income of only £10,000 per year may be asked to pay £1,000 a year in tax. The rich citizen pays more in absolute terms (£15,000 as compared with £1,000) and more proportionately (one-third of income rather than one-tenth).

Tax systems such as this are called **progressive** because the proportion of income which goes in taxation increases with income. The converse of this is a **regressive** tax system, in which the proportion of income which goes in taxation decreases as income increases. This would be the case, for example, where every citizen paid the same amount of tax irrespective of income. If the citizen with an income of £45,000 paid £2,250 and the citizen with an income of £10,000 also paid £2,250 in tax, then £4,500 would have been raised in total. In this case the rich person pays only 5 per cent of income in tax, whereas the poor person pays 22.5 per cent of income. This tax system is therefore regressive.

There is a great deal of economic theory dealing with this subject. It suggests that the pattern of taxation should reflect not only the pattern of benefits, but also the hardship caused by the payment of tax. Thus a rich citizen may be felt to have more to gain from the defence of the country than would a poor citizen. If this is so, then the rich should pay a higher amount of tax. Furthermore, it may also be argued that a tax bill of £2,250 would not cause the rich citizen very much hardship, but would cause immense hardship to the poorer citizen. In order to try to equate the hardship it may be necessary to ask the rich to pay even more than the proportion of public expenditure which benefits them. It is this second argument which leads to the advocacy of progressive taxation.

(2) Expenditure may also be financed out of *borrowing* rather than taxes. This would, of course, mean that we would have to pay interest on the borrowings. The interest would be paid every year by the taxpayers active each year. Thus debt issued now to finance today's expenditure would gradually be paid off by a succession of taxpayers over the

Case Study 18.1 The UK taxation system

There are four main forms of taxation:

Direct taxation	Income tax
	National insurance contributions
Taxation of companies	Corporation tax
	National insurance
Indirect taxation of final consumption	Value added tax
	Excise duties
Local taxation	Community charge/council tax
	Business rates

Income tax

A person can earn up to £3,295 (1991/92) before having to pay income tax. This sum is known as a personal allowance. A married couple can earn a further £1,720 before paying income tax (the married allowance). In addition, further expenses and allowances may be claimed depending on status.

After all allowances a person's taxable income is calculated and 25 per cent of taxable income up to £23,700 is paid as income tax. Any additional income is taxed at 40 per cent. Tax thresholds (allowances) are usually raised by at least the rate of inflation each year in the budget.

Income tax is most commonly collected at source by the employer and passed on to the Inland Revenue (see Table 18.2).

National insurance

This is paid by both employers and employees. Employees earning more than £52 a week pay 9 per cent of their earnings over this sum, but only 2% on the first £52. Employees who are in an occupational pension scheme get a further discount. This is again usually collected at source by the employer and passed on to the Inland Revenue.

Employers have a graduated scale which rises with an employee's weekly earnings (see Table 18.3).

Corporation tax

Levied on company profits, this has again been graduated, this time in order to assist small businesses. In 1990/91 firms with profits of less than £200,000 paid 25 per cent, with the rate rising to 35 per cent for firms making profits over £1 million. To encourage investment capital expenditure can be offset against corporation tax. The tax is again collected by the Inland Revenue.

Value added tax (VAT)

This is an indirect tax, i.e. it is paid by consumers in the final price of the good and the seller passes on the revenue to the Customs and Excise. VAT is paid on the value added to a product at each stage of production, but this is equivalent to a tax on the total value added by all processes. This leads to a confusing situation where some EC countries claim it is a tax on final consumers while for others it is a tax paid by users at each stage of production.

In the UK the rate of VAT is 17.5 per cent (increased from 15 per cent in April 1991) on the value added to all non-zero-rated goods. A zero-rated good is defined by the Customs and Excise and is usually a necessity good. Examples include food, books and children's clothes. Approximately 55 per cent of all goods sold by value are zero rated.

Excise duties

These are specific duties on goods, and rather than being a percentage of the value of the goods they are a fixed sum per unit. Examples of goods that attract excise duties are alcohol, tobacco and petrol. The levels of excise duties are usually raised in the budget in line with inflation, but have sometimes been increased to discourage the consumption of some demerit goods such as tobacco.

Community charge

This is a poll tax, i.e. it is a tax per head of the population. The proceeds go to pay for local council services and so the level varies for each local authority. The tax proved so unpopular that it is to be replaced in 1993 by the council tax, which will be calculated on the value of property, although there are discounts for properties with few occupants (see Table 18.4).

In 1990/91 the UK government raised about £220 billion via taxation. Table 18.4 shows the percentage of total tax revenue collected by each type of tax.

When the Chancellor makes decisions about tax rates he or she must take into account a number of factors, not least of which is the extra revenue that the change will raise. Table 18.5 shows the revenue implications for the changes in the taxes shown. The sums relate to Treasury estimates in 1989 and can be taken as an indication of the effect of an increase or decrease (see Table 18.5).

1. Adam Smith proposed four canons of taxation that good taxes should follow:

   Equality – people should pay in proportion to their respective abilities.

   Certainty – the time, manner of payment and quantity to be paid should be clear to all.

   Convenience – tax should be easy to pay.

   Economy of collection – The cost of collection should be only a small percentage of the revenue raised.

   To what extent do you believe the UK tax system meets Adam Smith's canons of taxation?

next 100 years or so. The timing of the debt repayments and the interest payments should, it is argued, reflect the timing of the benefits which accrue from the expenditure rather than allowing all the costs to fall on taxpayers active in the year when the expenditure was actually made.

Of course, some expenditure, like that on health and education, does largely benefit the current population and could properly be raised out of current taxation. But other forms of expenditure, such as that on infrastructure and wars, cannot reasonably be laid solely at the door of current taxpayers. Thus by issuing interest-bearing bonds of various lengths the government can spread the costs of its activities among current and future taxpayers.

(3) The third possibility is for the government to finance its expenditure by simply *printing money*. To see the advantages and disadvantages of this, imagine a country which produces only corn and uses only labour in its production. Assume that there are 10 workers, that together they produce 100 tonnes of corn and that each worker receives £10 in income. When the 10 workers come to spend their income (on corn) there will be £100 chasing

Table 18.1 Percentage of revenue gained from various sources of taxation (latest figures available, 1982–88)

Country	Corporate	Individual (direct)	Property	Consumption (including excise duty)	Customs	Other	Non-tax
Belgium	6.4	64.3	2.0	22.2		1.3	3.8
Denmark	6.3	45.3	4.3	29.2		1.0	13.3
France[1]	5.9	53.9	1.9	29.4		1.2	8.0
Germany[2]	7.3	56.1	2.1	20.9		0.7	12.9
Greece	5.6	45.5	2.4	32.5		9.3	12.8
Ireland	3.1	42.8	3.8	35.5		2.1	12.5
Italy[1]	6.6	67.8	1.9	24.2		1.8	2.3
Luxembourg	17.0	47.4	6.4	23.0		0.5	9.6
Netherlands	6.7	57.7	2.1	21.3		2.1	10.9
Portugal[1]	12.2	30.5	1.7	37.6	1.0	8.5	8.5
Spain	5.2	51.3	2.6	27.9		4.9	17.7
UK[3]	9.6	38.8	11.7	27.2		1.2	11.4
USA	7.0	50.7	8.7	13.3		1.0	19.3

Notes:
1. Central government figures as opposed to general government.
2. Former West Germany only.
3. Property tax figure due to domestic rates, now abolished.
Source: *Book of Vital World Statistics*, Economist Publications, 1990.

Table 18.2 Summary of UK income tax, 1991/92 (single person)

Income (£ per year)	Taxable income (£ per year)	Marginal tax rate (%)
0–3,295	0	0
3,295–26,995	1–23,700	25
26,996+	23,700+	40

Table 18.3 Summary of national insurance, 1991/92

Employees' income per week (£)	Employers' marginal national insurance rate (%)	Weekly wage (£)	Marginal national insurance rate (%)
0–52	2	0–52	0
52+	9	52–84.99	4.6
		85–129.99	6.6
		130–184.99	8.6
		185+	10.4

Table 18.4 Percentage of total UK tax revenue collected by various types of tax, 1990/91

Tax	% of total revenue
Income tax	25.1
National insurance	16.4
VAT	15.8
Other indirect taxes (excise duties)	13.7
Corporation tax	9.5
Community charge	5.6
Other	13.8

100 tonnes. The market clears at a price of £1 per tonne and each worker gets 10 tonnes.

Now imagine that after the workers have done their work and received their wages (£10 each), but before they spend their income, the government prints 20 new £5 notes (i.e. doubles the money supply). The government then enters the market for corn in competition with the workers. There are now £200 chasing 100 tonnes of corn, so the price of corn doubles to £2 per tonne. Workers can now only afford 5 tonnes each and the remaining 50 tonnes are bought by the government.

Thus the effect of the government printing money to finance its expenditure is to reduce the real wage of each worker by 50 per cent. This is exactly equivalent to imposing a tax on them. Notice too that the tax falls entirely on the current workforce and is neither progressive nor regressive – each worker pays the same proportion of income as tax.

Table 18.5 Revenue implications of a change in taxation levels, 1989

Tax	Change	Yield (£ million)
Income tax		
Basic rate	1p (1%)	1,500
Higher rate	1p (1%)	130
Allowances	1%	205
Corporation tax	1%	390
Value added tax	1%	1,515
Excise duties		
Beer	1p per pint	90
Wine	1p per bottle	40
Spirits	10p per bottle	20
Cigarettes	1p per packet	35
Petrol	1p per gallon	60

Source: *Autumn statement*, 1989.

One advantage, to the government, of paying its bills in this way is that the citizens are unaware of this 'tax'. They do not receive tax demands from the Inland Revenue or from VAT officials. The government is not therefore seen as a voracious predator. Secondly, it is an extremely cheap way of raising revenue. There is no need for the Inland Revenue to be involved, and no one need fill in tax returns.

The disadvantages are that it causes price levels to go up, it imposes all the burden on current citizens and it fails to distinguish between the acute hardship experienced by the poor and the trivial hardship experienced by the very rich.

Monetary policy

These public finance considerations are aimed exclusively at how best to finance public-sector expenditure. We have seen that this sometimes gives rise to the issuing of new interest-bearing bonds and/or the issuing of new money. This public financing has over the years resulted in an accumulation of public debt (the national debt). The debt comprises the stocks of bonds outstanding and the amount of cash in circulation.

Monetary policy is not merely concerned with the financing of this year's expenditure; it is more concerned with altering the composition of all outstanding debt. Thus even if this year's budget is balanced so that it is not necessary to issue new bonds and/or cash, the government could still engage in monetary policy by converting some existing bonds into money (buying bonds from the public) or by converting some money into bonds (selling some new bonds to the public).

Say, for example, that over the years the stock of bonds issued by the government has accumulated to £100 and the stock of notes and coins has accumulated to £50. The government could issue 10 more bonds at £1 each to bring the stock of outstanding bonds up to £110. This must, at the same time, reduce the notes and coin in circulation from £50 to £40, since the public pays the government for the bonds with notes and coin.

This buying (or selling) of bonds on the open bond market is called **open-market operations** and constitutes one way in which the government can affect the amount of money in circulation. Switching out of notes and coin into bonds is called **funding**. Funding government debt is the action of rendering it less liquid. Moving from highly liquid notes and coin to highly illiquid consols is therefore funding.

There are, of course, more than these two forms of government debt, but consols and cash represent the two extremes of liquidity of government debt. Between these two extremes is a whole spectrum of assets.

Recall that **consols** (consolidated stock) are undated so that the government need never redeem them (buy them back). The government can buy them back if it so wishes, but it is not obliged to do so. As long as the consol is held by a member of the public the government must, each year, pay its owner the fixed sum of money promised on the consol. Consols can be sold by one member of the public to another on the open market and these supplies and demands will determine the market price of consols. Because no one knows, in advance, what the price of consols will be when they come to be sold (converted into cash), they are of uncertain value and are therefore illiquid.

This is not true of all forms of interest-bearing government debt and we shall look at just one more type of asset which is issued by the government.

Treasury bills

A **Treasury bill** is, like a consol, a piece of paper issued by the government. Unlike the consol, however, the Treasury bill does not promise to pay the owner a fixed sum of money each year. Instead it promises to pay the owner a fixed sum just once – 90 days from the date of issue. Treasury bills are therefore '90-day' or '3-month' bills.

To see how they work, consider a Treasury bill being issued on 1 January 1992. Whoever buys the bill knows that in 90 days' time the bill can be presented to the government broker and £10,000 will be paid for it. If it was originally bought for £9,500 then the reward for holding it for 90 days (one-quarter of a year) is £500. Thus the 'interest' received for these Bills is £500/£9,500 per quarter. This is equivalent to about 5.25 per cent per quarter or about 21 per cent per year.

If, however, the bill was originally bought for £9,750 then the reward for holding it for 3 months would be £250. This is equivalent to an annual interest rate of about 10 per cent.

Thus the government broker goes to the bond market and sells the Treasury bills for what they will fetch, the market price. This market price, together with the prestated, certain redemption value (£10,000) will determine the effective rate of interest on Treasury bills – the Treasury bill rate.

In this respect Treasury bills are rather like consols: as their price rises, the implicit interest rate on them falls. Where they differ from consols is that they have a certain value at a particular date – 90 days from the date of issue. This means that, as time passes, the Treasury bill matures and becomes more and more liquid.

If, for example, the buyer intended to sell the bill within 10 days of its issue then the market value would be uncertain – it would be illiquid. But if it was intended to sell it 88 days after the date of issue, then its price would be fairly certain – it cannot be very different from its redemption value of £10,000. Thus mature Treasury bills are very liquid and very young Treasury bills are illiquid.

At any one time then there will be a whole range of Treasury bills outstanding, so that lenders can choose the level of liquidity they prefer. The government broker, of course, is faced with the problem of finding sufficient funds to buy back the Treasury bill after 90 days. This can be done by issuing new Treasury bills to raise the necessary funds. This is called 'rolling over' the debt and requires constant activity by the government broker in the bond market. One advantage of funding the debt – moving it into consols – is that consols need never be 'rolled over' since they need never be redeemed.

There are then three main forms of government debt: (1) consols, (2) Treasury bills and (3) notes and coin. Government monetary policy consists of the movement of government debt among these three assets.

SUMMARY

1. Government expenditure can be met by:
   (a) Imposing taxes.
   (b) Issuing notes and coin.
   (c) Issuing Treasury bills.
   (d) Issuing consols.
2. Imposing taxes or issuing notes and coin mean that the present population meets all the costs of government.
3. When the benefits of this kind of expenditure are likely to be reaped by future generations, it may seem more just to issue Treasury bills or consols.
4. When taxes are raised, they may be either progressive or regressive. 'Progressive' means that the rich pay a higher proportion of their income in tax. 'Regressive' means that the poor pay a higher proportion of their income in tax.
5. The proportions of consols, Treasury bills and cash in government debt are determined by monetary policy.

Controlling the money supply

Monetary policy and interest rates

If the government tries to issue large quantities of consols then the consol price will fall. This, of course, means that the interest rate on consols – the long rate – will rise. This will tend to bid up all interest rates and so make it less attractive to borrow money for investment. Private-sector investment plans will therefore be revised downwards (See Chapters 9 and 14).

A similar result occurs if the government increases the supply of Treasury bills. Their price falls and hence the Treasury bill rate – the short rate – rises. This too will have an effect on other interest rates and make borrowing more expensive.

In both these cases there will be a change in the structure of interest rates. In the first case the long rate will increase by more than the short rate. In the second case the short rate will increase by more than the long rate.

In both cases private-sector investment is discouraged by the higher cost of borrowing. And in both cases the government has to pay more for the same overall level of national debt. All new debt (and the rolled-over Treasury bills) will attract the higher interest rate and this has to be paid by the borrower (the government).

This has led some commentators to argue that government debt should not be manipulated as a means of macroeconomic management. They argue that monetary policy should be conducted in such a way as to maintain an orderly market for government debt which is conducive to the lowest possible cost to the government of servicing its debt.

Money supply

Even so monetary policy does play a part in economic management. The main macroeconomic effects of altering the structure of debt derive partly from the interest rate effects we have just described, but also from its effects on money supply.

We saw earlier that one definition of money (M4) comprised not only notes and coins issued by the state, but also current and time deposits created by the commercial banks and some deposits held by the public in other financial institutions, such as building societies. We also saw that the creation of deposits by the commercial banks depends upon the amount of cash they hold and their cash reserve ratio. With a cash reserve ratio of 1:10 the commercial banks can create 10 times as much 'money' as they have 'cash'. This is called the commercial banks' credit multiplier.

Funding

All this was spelled out in a very simple model with only cash and consols as assets, but it is clear from the foregoing that there is a wider range of assets – some liquid and some less liquid – which the commercial banks may hold. In brief we need only know that, as government debt becomes more liquid, the commercial banks can create more in the way of chequing accounts.

This means that 'funding' government debt – moving from liquid debt into illiquid debt – will have the effect of reducing the reserves of the commercial banks and hence cause them to reduce their chequing accounts. The reduction in chequing accounts will be greater than the original reduction in reserves because of the commercial banks credit multiplier.

Imagine that we have a government which follows monetarist policies and wishes to control inflation by controlling the money supply. To do this it instructs the Bank of England to 'fund' its debt.

This funding would certainly reduce money supply, but it would also increase interest rates as we have seen. This increase in interest rates would increase costs and hence push up prices. If the government wishes to avoid this cost-push inflation then it can make its debt more liquid. Unfortunately this leads to an increase in the money supply, which pulls up prices and again causes inflation.

The government is therefore in something of a cleft stick: to reduce the quantity of money it must 'fund' its debt; this increases interest rates and pushes up costs and prices. It therefore causes the very inflation it was designed to prevent. On the other hand, if the government wishes to reduce interest rates then it must issue more cash. This, via the commercial banks credit multiplier, increases money supply and pulls up prices.

All this springs from our assumption that the government's monetary policy is nothing more than open-market operations – buying and selling various forms of government debt on the open market. Fortunately, there are other ways of pursuing monetary policy.

We have assumed that the reserve ratio of the commercial banks (which determines the commercial banks' credit multiplier) is decided by the commercial banks themselves. This is not strictly true – the government can ask the commercial banks to increase their reserve ratio. This will reduce the commercial banks credit multiplier and, with no change in government debt, bring about a reduction in money supply (M3). The advantage of this way of reducing money supply is that, since it does not involve any change in the quantity or composition of government debt, there will be no direct change in interest rates (although the Governor of the Bank of England argues in Case Study 18.3 that interest rates *will* be affected).

Special deposits

This is also true of another way of reducing M4. The Bank of England is, among other things, the bankers' bank – commercial banks actually bank with the Bank of England. Thus some of the reserve assets of the commercial banks are held as cash deposits in the Bank of England.

From time to time the Bank of England decrees that part of these deposits may no longer be regarded as being liquid. They are called **special deposits**. In one fell swoop the government can reduce the liquid assets (reserves) of the commercial banks by simply declaring that some of their deposits at the Bank of England are 'frozen'. In order to maintain their reserve ratios (liquid asset ratios) the commercial banks have to reduce their chequing accounts. Thus M4 is reduced with no change in the size or composition of government debt. There will therefore again be no direct change in interest rates.

Changing the reserve ratios and calling for special deposits impose costs on the commercial banks. These banks make their profit by lending to customers – creating overdrafts on which the customer pays interest to the bank. When they are prevented from making full use of their lending power they are prevented from making some profits. The commercial banks are therefore critical of this type of monetary policy. They argue that they among all financial institutions are being singled out and used (or abused) as an instrument of the government's monetary policy.

Debt reduction

One way out of this impasse would be for the government actually to reduce the quantity of its outstanding debt. If it could do this then it could reduce the number of consols and Treasury bills in the hands of the public, thereby reducing interest rates, and it could reduce the amount of cash in circulation too.

In order to reduce its outstanding debt it must either decrease its expenditure or increase its income (or both). The problem of controlling its expenditure is that it is determined largely by commitments made by previous governments. If, for example, unemployment benefit rates are fixed then the cost to the Exchequer of unemployment will rise or fall with the level of unemployment and there is very little the government can do about it. As unemployment increases, so will the government's expenditure on unemployment benefit.

Similar reasoning can be applied to the cost of state retirement pensions. The number of persons retiring will depend on the age structure of the population and thus too is largely outside the control of the government. As more people retire, the government must find the wherewithal to pay them pensions.

There are several large items of government expenditure of a similar kind, and the room left for the government to cut expenditure is therefore quite small. This throws most of the weight on to attempts to raise more revenue. Increasing taxes is frowned upon, partly because taxes add to costs and thus fuel inflation and partly because they are alleged to discourage people from working hard, since workers now get less for their efforts (see Chapter 9).

Thus economic analysis of macroeconomic policy must be conducted within the fairly restrictive limits imposed by political practicalities and in full recognition of the interrelation of interest rates and money supply. The government simply does not have a free hand in either fiscal or monetary policy – there are always constraints and unpleasant side effects to be considered.

Automatic stabilizers

Not all economic theories find these political practicalities a barrier to macroeconomic management. Indeed, Keynesians argue that they are positively helpful in maintaining full employment.

Their argument is not difficult to follow. Recall that Keynesians blame deficient aggregate demand for the bulk of unemployment. Now as unemployment increases, the number of persons claiming benefit goes up – this increases government expenditure. At the same time, the number paying income tax falls, thus decreasing government income. If the government does nothing about this then it will obviously be faced with a growing budget deficit – tax revenue falling and expenditure rising. But this is precisely what Keynesians want. The budget deficit will augment aggregate demand and hence will bring employment back to the full-employment level.

Thus there is an automatic tendency for the economy to return to full employment provided the government does not step in and reduce benefit rates or raise taxes.

Macroeconomic policy in an open economy

So far in this chapter we have treated the economy as if it were a self-contained entity, but clearly it is not. We have already seen that the UK is an open economy, exporting about one-third of its GDP and importing about one-third of all it consumes. We also know that it can borrow from and lend to the rest of the world. The UK is therefore an open economy and must acknowledge this in its conduct of macroeconomic policy.

If the UK is a relatively small economy in a large world thenwe can assume that what happens in the UK will have a negligible effect on the rest of the world. But since it is an open economy, what happens in the rest of the world will affect the UK.

This is particularly true for international finance – international lending and borrowing. If the UK government issues some consols or some Treasury bills and thereby forces up UK interest rates then foreign lenders will be attracted to buy UK government debt. This is because the interest rate on UK government debt becomes slightly higher than that on the debt issued elsewhere.

This inflow of lending from foreign investors looking for the highest interest rates is called **hot money**. It comes swiftly into the UK when UK interest rates rise, but is equally quickly bid away to other countries when interest rates fall again.

If this hot money comes from the USA then it will be in dollars. In order for it to buy UK government debt it must first be converted into pounds. The foreign lenders therefore go first to the international money market and change their dollars for pounds. This increases the demands for pounds on the foreign exchange market and is therefore likely to push up the price of pounds in terms of dollars, i.e. it will increase the exchange rate. This will, of course, affect the UK balance of trade.

Since pounds are now more expensive in terms of dollars, the pound price of imports will fall, making them relatively cheaper in the UK; the dollar price of UK exports will rise, making them relatively more expensive. Thus the UK will be decreasing its exports and increasing its imports. This will result in a contraction of the UK economy (an export-led deflation) and a balance of trade deficit. Also, since UK imports have increased in price, there will be an increase in UK costs and prices.

If the government wishes to prevent the exchange rate from changing, it will have to supply pounds on the international exchange market. The sequence of events would be as follows:

1. The UK government decides to cut the money supply.
2. To do this it issues some new consols.
3. This attracts foreign investors.
4. To buy UK consols they need pounds rather than dollars.
5. The foreigners therefore try to buy pounds on the international money market.
6. The UK exchange rate rises.
7. To remedy this the UK government prints pounds and uses them to buy dollars on the international money market.
8. These pounds are taken by the foreigners and given to the UK government in return for consols.
9. The net result is that the government is providing the pounds to buy its own consols.
10. The newly issued consols will reduce the quantity of pounds in the UK only if at least some of these consols are bought by UK citizens. In this case the consols will have been bought with pounds taken out of circulation rather than with pounds newly printed to satisfy foreigners' demand for pounds.

The net result of all this is that, if the government tries to cut the money supply by funding its debt, it is likely to induce a slight rise in UK interest rates, an inflow of hot money from abroad and upward pressure on the exchange rate. In so far as this hot money is converted into sterling by the government (bought with newly printed pounds), there is no change in the UK money supply.

SUMMARY

1. Consols are less liquid than Treasury bills, and Treasury bills are less liquid than cash.
2. By selling consols on the open market (in return for cash) the government makes its debt less liquid.
3. These are called open-market operations and rendering the debt less liquid is called funding.
4. Funding tends to increase interest rates and reduce the money supply.
5. Reducing the money supply by funding therefore has the side effects of reducing private investment and increasing production costs (interest payments).
6. In an open economy, the increased interest rate will induce an inflow of hot money from abroad.
7. This disturbs the exchange rate, disrupts the balance of trade and renders monetary policy less effective.
8. Many elements of government expenditure and income are largely beyond the control of the government. This results in less control than may be expected, but also yields some automatic Keynesian stabilizers.

Recent developments in credit and money

In the heyday of Keynesian economics attention was focused on deciding the level of the budget deficit rather than how it was to be financed. Theorists and politicians alike tended to ignore financing problems on the grounds that the composition of public-sector debt had implications only for the money supply, and that any increase in the money supply would be quickly absorbed into speculative balances with no effect on price level or interest rates. This was because the economy was in, or near, the 'liquidity trap' in which the speculative demand for money was infinitely elastic (see Chapter 13). None of the extra money supply would find its way into transactions and so prices need not rise.

In those Keynesian days the aim of monetary policy was to maintain an orderly market for government debt and to keep the cost of servicing that debt to a minimum. Thus interest rates were to be kept low while retaining public confidence in government bonds. The immediate post-war Labour government tried to get the interest rate on government debt down to 2.5 per cent! This was rarely achieved, but interest rates were very low in those days (see Table 18.6).

Table 18.6 Treasury bill rate, 1950–90

Year	1950	1952	1954	1956	1958	1960	1970	1980	1985	1990
Treasury bill yield	0.514	2.41	1.78	4.92	3.17	4.40	6.93	13.6	11.2	13.5

Sources: *Economic Trends*; *Annual Abstract of Statistics*.

All this has changed and the recent trend towards budget surpluses is in part a reflection of the view that good housekeeping in the public sector requires that expenditure should not exceed income – a return to 'Victorian values'. It is also a result of the increased importance attached to monetary policy.

If the public sector runs a deficit then new debt must be issued and this rather ties the hands of the policy makers. If it is issued as liquid debt then it will increase money supply and is, according to the monetarists, inflationary. If, on the other hand, the new debt is issued as illiquid debt it will (again according to monetarists) push up interest rates; these push up costs and are again inflationary. Nor is that all: the increased interest rates discourage private investment and so 'crowd out' private investment to make room for government spending.

It is not only the inflation and investment aspects which disturb many modern politicians. As government expenditure rises, the government becomes a bigger and bigger influence on the economy. 'Big government' is thought by many to be politically dangerous in that it gives too much power to the state. Thus they argue for a small public sector and a balanced budget.

Keynesian credit controls

During the Keynesian years of the sovereignty of fiscal policy, the authorities (by which we mean the Bank of England and the Treasury) paid scant attention to monetary policy but did, however, try to control the expansion of credit. The aim, as always, was to manipulate aggregate demand rather than to engage in monetary policy.

One fairly volatile element of aggregate demand was that for consumer durables, such as cars and washing machines. These consumer durables were usually bought on credit via hire-purchase arrangements. The authorities interfered in this credit market by imposing constraints on it. Typically, they increased the size of the minimum downpayment or lowered the maximum repayment period. Thus to buy something for £6,000 it is possible to borrow, say, £5,000 if the borrower has first saved up £1,000 (the downpayment). The £5,000 and interest must be repaid in, say, 2 years. These 'Keynesian'-type credit controls were aimed exclusively at consumer spending and affected only a very narrow aspect of credit creation.

Control of money supply

As the concern for inflation replaced the concern for unemployment, the authorities switched attention away from controlling aggregate demand and concentrated instead on controlling money supply. At first this meant controlling the credit created by the commercial banks. The maximum they can create depends on their stock of liquid assets and on the commercial banks' credit multiplier. Their liquid assets include cash, deposits at the Bank of England, money-at-call (which is money they have lent, but which must be repaid by the borrowers on the banks' demand), and Treasury bills. By freezing some of these assets and/or by altering the credit multiplier, the authorities sought to control the credit created by the commercial banks.

The banks objected on the grounds that there were other credit-creating institutions with whom the banks had to compete for both depositors and borrowers. These other financial intermediaries were free from the controls put on the banks and therefore had an unfair competitive advantage. It was also the case that, by setting up subsidiaries outside the controlled sector, the banks themselves could avoid the impact of the controls. Thus the controls were seen as unfair and avoidable.

Disintermediation

The banks' attempts to avoid the effects of controls had the effect of casting them as credit arrangers rather than credit extenders. In other words, when their ability to extend credit was constrained they tried to satisfy frustrated customers by putting those who wished to lend in touch with those who wished to borrow. This change in the role of the banks was called 'disintermediation'. It meant that banks were acting less as financial intermediaries and more as brokers.

Banks also started offering this go-between service elsewhere so that previously direct arrangements now went through a bank. In this case it was called 'reintermediation'. This term later came to mean any activity which caused the re-routing of flows of funds through the banks.

Competition and credit control

General dissatisfaction with controlling the money supply in this way gave rise to *Competition and Credit Control* in 1971. This was a document issued by the Bank of England which indicated how control was to be exercised thereafter.

Under these new arrangements the rules were to apply to all financial intermediaries not just to the London clearing banks. All were now required to hold liquid assets and all were subject to special deposits, so there could be no accusation of unfairness. That was the credit control part.

The competition part came about by the banks (and the **discount houses**) acting more independently and not setting interest rates together. The government no longer set a 'Bank rate', but instead tied it to market rates and called it the 'minimum lending rate'.

The institutions included in this revised scheme were the commercial banks and the so-called licensed deposit takers (LDTs). These latter accept deposits and create deposits in much the same way that the banks do, and are therefore influential in determining money supply. Their ability to create deposits depends on their reserve assets and their deposit/reserve asset ratio. Reserve assets (or 'eligible assets', or 'high-powered money') include Treasury bills, commercial bills, money-at-call and gilt-edged securities with less than a year to maturity.

Commercial bills are 3-month bills very like Treasury bills – they are in fact the forerunners of Treasury bills – but they are issued by the private sector rather than the Treasury to finance commerce rather than public-sector borrowing. Thus not all high-powered money is supplied by the authorities since some commercial bills are also acceptable.

Essentially, high-powered money consists of all those assets which the Bank of England is prepared to accept in return for providing funds as 'lender of last resort'. Thus should a bank run into liquidity problems it can appeal to the Bank of England and convert its high-powered money into cash.

The deposit/reserve asset ratio of the banks was 12.5 per cent and that for the licensed deposit takers was 10 per cent. Thus if they could control the amount of eligible assets, the authorities could control the money supply.

Supplementary special deposits

This new arrangement (competition and credit control) seems to have been no more effective than its predecessor. It proved not to be up to the task of controlling money supply and in 1973 'supplementary special deposits' were introduced. These were deposits by intermediaries at the Bank on which no interest was paid. This loss of interest in effect represents a fine which was imposed when an intermediary (a commercial bank, for example) allowed certain of its liabilities to grow too fast. That is, if it increased its lending to consumers too much then it had to make the supplementary special deposit. This was supposed to keep lending within certain bounds and became known as the 'corset'. It was abandoned in 1980 partly because once again it was thought that the financial intermediaries had found ways around the control.

Apart from supplementary special deposits there were also changes in the way the minimum lending rate was fixed. It once again came to be fixed by the authorities. Later still the minimum lending rate was suspended indefinitely. There is now no announcement of the rate at which the Bank will act as lender of last resort.

Monetary base control

As we shall see in the next section, controls on banks' ability to create credit were relaxed in 1981, but this has not prevented some commentators from calling for another form of control.

Monetary base control aims to reduce the banks' ability to create money by closely controlling the availability of liquid assets, in this case the monetary base. Exactly what comprises the monetary base is debatable, but any definition would include all notes and coins held either by the public or in bank vaults, and bankers' deposits with the Bank of England (which can easily be converted into cash). This is now often described as 'high-powered money'.

As we have seen, the banks will want to keep some proportion of their deposits as cash even if they are not legally obliged to do so. Those who advocate monetary base control suggest that limiting the supply of high-powered money will limit the supply of funds available for banks' liquid assets and so will limit their ability to expand their balance sheets.

The monetary base is theoretically in the control of the Bank of England, since only the Bank can issue new cash. So if the total money supply is equal to the cash held by the non-bank private sector plus bank deposits (equation 18.1) and high-powered money is equal to all cash held either by banks (a fraction of total deposits) or by the non-bank public (also a fraction of total deposits) (equation 18.2) then there is a direct relationship between the monetary base and the total money supply (equation 18.3).

$$M = cD + D = (c+1)D \qquad (18.1)$$

where M = the stock of money
D = the deposit liabilities of the banks
cD = the fraction of bank deposits held by the non-bank public as cash.

$$H = cD + rD = (c+r)D \qquad (18.2)$$

where H = the high-powered monetary base
rD = the fraction of bank deposits held by the banks as cash.

The ratio of the money supply to the monetary base is therefore:

$$\frac{M}{H} = \frac{(c+1)D}{(c+r)D}$$

Cancelling the Ds and multiplying both sides by H gives:

$$M = \left[\frac{(c+1)}{(c+r)}\right]H \qquad (18.3)$$

From this it should be clear that if the authorities can influence H, the monetary base, they can influence the total money supply.

There has been considerable scepticism expressed about the effectiveness of monetary base control (see Case Study 18.3), but as it has yet to be tried, there can be no proof either way.

Evidence that is available suggests that if banks kept a higher ratio of very liquid assets (r in the equation) to deposits than was strictly necessary then, as with special deposits, reducing the growth of high-powered money would have little effect. Even so the money supply measure M0 does conform quite closely with the definition of the monetary base used here and has been targeted for some years. The experience of 1987 to 1990 suggests that there are practical problems attached to this approach – for instance, deciding when the monetary base should be controlled (again see Case Study 18.3).

Controlling the demand for money

In 1981 banks and licensed deposit takers were allowed to decide their own 'prudent' level of reserves, but were required to hold 0.5 per cent of their liabilities as deposits in the Bank of England (0.45 per cent since October 1986). This means that the commercial banks' credit multiplier is very large indeed (1/0.5 = 200) and so they can create a very great deal of money.

The quantity of money in the system is partly cash (notes and coin), but mostly it is credit created by the commercial banks, etc. The government can introduce more cash into the economy by simply printing notes and spending them. But banks can only increase the amount of bank credit if they can find customers to borrow from them. That is, banks can only be 'loaned up' (up against their lending limits) if they can find enough borrowers.

The demand for credit is assumed to be a stable, decreasing function of the interest rate. As the interest rate increases, the demand for bank deposits falls. So although the banks have plenty to lend and want to lend it, there is no demand for it – there are too few bank customers. Therefore by keeping interest rates high, the government can prevent the growth of bank credit.

Targets and the Medium-Term Financial Strategy

There has been a tendency in recent years to announce in advance what the money supply growth will be in the coming year. These announcements have not always been very accurate – between April 1976 and April 1979 the announced targets (in terms of £M3) were rarely hit (see Table 18.7).

The concern over the growth of M3 (formerly sterling M3) has also led to concern over the size of the **public-sector borrowing requirement (PSBR)**. The Conservative government elected in 1979 was concerned about borrowing in its own right. It believed that over the course of a business cycle the government should balance its budget. But there was a further consideration.

There is a relationship between the growth of the money supply and the PSBR, and this can be seen by examining the following equation:

Increase in M3 = *PSBR* – Purchases of public-sector debt by the private (non-bank) sector + Increase in bank lending + Increase in international reserves

The equation shows that bank lending is an important element in the growth of the money supply, but not the only one. Bank lending to the public could be strictly under control and yet the money supply could continue to rise due to the need of the government to borrow. Thus government borrowing from banks must be limited as well if the anti-inflationary policy is to succeed. Note that government borrowing from the private sector reduces the money supply.

M3 data are no longer collected by the Bank of England, but the equation also holds for M4, where the third term becomes 'Increase in' bank and building society lending.

The government has been very concerned to limit the PSBR in recent years. As we saw in Chapter 13, in the late 1980s there was a public-sector debt repayment. According to the equation above this will reduce the growth of M3. In recent years the economy has experienced a recession and in 1991/92 a PSBR of £8 billion is planned. This is an example of the sort of automatic stabilizer discussed earlier and reflects the view of Chancellors Lawson, Major and Lamont that the government budget should be balanced over the business cycle.

The equation linking changes in M3 with the PSBR and bank lending has received much attention during the 1980s. It is important to remember, however, that the equation tells us nothing about causation. It is an *ex-post* relationship: that is, looking back it must be true. Attempts to control the money supply by manipulating one element of it, say the PSBR, ignore the effect this will have on the other components of the identity. The equation is a useful description of the relationship but would not necessarily survive if used for economic policy (see the earlier section on disintermediation for the sort of problem that can arise).

The series of annual targets was succeeded in 1980 by the **Medium-Term Financial Strategy (MTFS)**, in which the growth of sterling M3 (M3 since 1987) and the PSBR are targeted for each of the next four years. However, these medium-term (four-year) targets, like the annual target, have not always been met. So why should such targets be publicly announced when they invariably turn out to be wrong?

One argument for announcing targets is that they commit the government to a particular sequence of policies. Hence we will know with some confidence what the government is intending to happen. We can then form our expectations accordingly. If the Chancellor tells us that he intends to keep the growth of, say, sterling M3 to not more than 6 per cent in the coming year then we are unlikely to form expectations of inflation of much more than 6 per cent.

We know from the expectations-augmented Phillips curve that the expected rate of inflation can affect both the actual rate of inflation and/or the level of unemployment. Expectations then are very important and if we can affect them by making an announcement then it makes sense to spell out government intentions. The 'Announcement' becomes a weapon in the government's armoury.

Table 18.7 Money supply targets and the MTFS

Period	Sterling M3	
	Target (%)	Outturn (%)
April 1976–April 1977	9–13	7.5
April 1977–April 1978	9–13	15.6
April 1978–April 1979	8–12	11.3

Medium-Term Financial Strategy

	1980/81	1981/82	1982/83	1983/84
Sterling M3				
Target growth (%)	7–11	6–10	5–9	4–8
Outturn (%)	19.4	12.8	11.2	9.4
PSBR				
Target (as % of GDP)	3.75	3.0	2.25	1.5
Outturn	5.6	3.4	3.2	3.2

Sources: Thompson, Brown and Levačic, *Managing the UK Economy*, Polity Press, 1987; various financial statements and budget reports.

Exchange rates

Another new aspect of monetary policy is the increasing concern with exchange rates. Until 1972/73 the UK operated a system of fixed exchange rates (the Bretton Woods Agreements), and under fixed exchange rates fiscal policy is much more effective than monetary policy. Between 1972/73 and 1990 the pound was allowed to float, and under floating exchange rates monetary policy is more effective than fiscal policy. This switch of effectiveness was yet another reason to change from fiscal to monetary controls.

As far as the implementation of monetary policy goes there is a major side effect when the exchange rate is floating. Imagine that the demand for money is reduced by raising interest rates. As interest rates in the UK rise, international investors will be attracted to buy UK assets. As we saw before in order to buy UK assets the foreign investor must first change dollars into pounds. Thus the demand for pounds on the foreign exchange market will increase and the price of pounds will rise in terms of dollars. In other words, the pound appreciates against the dollar.

This reduces the pound price of UK imports and increases the dollar price of UK exports. The cheaper imports help to keep inflation down, but the dearer exports put UK exporters at a disadvantage in international markets. Thus attempts at controlling the demand for money by increasing the rate on interest lead to an adverse movement of the exchange rate.

As an aside we might note that it is precisely this adverse side effect which reinforces the deflationary effect of an interest rate rise. Not only is the demand for money cut, but so is the demand for UK exports. Thus the level of aggregate demand is cut too.

Monetary policy can therefore be said to be of central importance to the government. It is the main weapon in the attempt to control inflation and is also being used to influence exchange rates. Since 1990 the UK has been a member of the exchange rate mechanism (ERM) of the **European Monetary System (EMS)**, which commits the UK to keeping the exchange rate within certain limits relative to other EMS currencies. This puts a second role on monetary policy, since interest rates also affect the exchange value of the pound. Although it is argued that ERM membership will help to control inflation, it has yet to be seen if monetary policy can perform both tasks simultaneously. (See Chapter 23 for a discussion of the EMS and ERM.)

SUMMARY

1. During the 'Keynesian era' governments ran budget deficits to cure unemployment and ignored the implications of the change in debt on the money supply.
2. Since the mid-1970s monetary policy has become more important as monetarist views have held greater sway.
3. During the Keynesian era governments attempted to control consumer credit in order to influence aggregate demand.
4. Attempts to control the money supply by restricting the liquid asset holdings of commercial banks were largely unsuccessful due to disintermediation.
5. Since 1979 the emphasis of UK policy has been to control the demand for money by the use of interest rates.
6. Some people have suggested that controlling the supply of high-powered money would be a better alternative.
7. Targets have been set for the growth of the money supply since 1976. The targets have not always been met, but their announcement affects expectations and expectations influence inflation rates.
8. Control of the public-sector borrowing requirement (PSBR) has also been important because of the contribution this makes to the change in the money supply.

Case Study 18.2 Defining the problem of credit

The chancellor is in danger of sounding like a cracked record. Again yesterday, he was bewailing the growing volume of credit; as if it were a phenomenon over which he has no control; as if the government is merely a distressed bystander; as if it is not much to do with him. He blames the lending institutions for doing no more than they are required by their shareholders: lending money and making profits.

There is no doubt credit is continuing to roll up at a much faster rate than is desirable, and the figures for May released earlier this week showed the highest level of advances for three months. Where they should have been falling, they were still rising. The response from the government, consistent even if ineffective, is to make a lot of noise and keep interest rates high. Nobody seems to mention money supply any more.

There are two threads to the rise in credit, one economic and the other social, and it is far from certain which one Mr Major is hoping to unravel with his exhortations. The economic thread is that too much credit, regardless of to whom it is advanced, is stoking an economy that he is trying to dampen down, so contributing to inflation. The social thread is that the wrong people are being encouraged to borrow amounts which they cannot afford to buy goods they do not need.

On several occasions, he has referred to the distaste which many people feel for indiscriminate marketing of credit through mailshots, which suggests a concern for the social consequences of over-borrowing. If that is his main worry, then steps need to be taken to control the methods used to market credit. Controls are strict on the selling of investments, are being tightened for timeshare, and could be seen as draconian in the case of insurance. In credit, so long as the lender quotes the proper APR in the right size typeface, few further questions are asked.

On the other hand, if our chancellor is primarily concerned that growth of credit is upsetting his dead-reckoning on the economy, the steps he needs to take are towards the Bank of England. The volume of lending, at least through the banking system, could be regulated through deposit requirements, without necessarily getting into the difficulties posed by the imposition of the notorious 'corset' a decade or so ago. Monetary base control, I believe, is the technical term for such mechanisms.

The government's theological objections to direct controls on credit agreements, on repayment terms and so on, are easily understood and in general wholly defensible. Credit must be kept above ground and as far as possible in the hands of responsible lenders. But that does not mean that there is nothing that can be done, and the first objective should be to define whether the problem is genuinely economic, social, or merely one of taste.

1. Does the rise in the number and types of credit available make it inevitable that traditional monetary policy will be ineffective?

Source: David Brewerton, *The Times*, 6 July 1990

9. Under a system of floating exchange rates, when monetary policy is tightened to reduce inflation the policy is aided by the appreciation of the exchange rate. The price of imports falls and the demand for exports falls also, reducing aggregate demand.

Case Study 18.3 Monetary policy in the second half of the 1980s (part 2)

This is the second part of the speech made by the Governor of the Bank of England to Tyne and Wear Chamber of Commerce on 5 April 1990 (see p. 290). Here the Governor discusses possible alternative methods of monetary control.

Possible alternative policy responses

[S]ome ... argue for lower interest rates [and] claim that alternative measures are available [to reduce inflation].

(a) Credit controls

I have suggested the relaxation of controls had similar effects to reducing interest rates. Would it not be possible to reverse the process by reimposing controls? There are three answers to this – all, I am afraid, discouraging.

The clock simply cannot be turned back. Exchange controls have gone, and [cannot be reimposed] *vis-à-vis* European Community countries. Any credit restrictions could therefore be circumvented by going offshore ... one could buy a car in, say, Düsseldorf on credit, even if HP controls applied in Durham.

Credit controls would discriminate unfairly between borrowers ... [and would be] equivalent to differential interest rates. Some would have access to relatively cheap credit, while the rest would have limited access, if any at all. This is likely to be socially unjust and is certainly economically inefficient.

Even if one allows that credit controls *would* have some temporary effect, ... the promise they hold ... can be illusory, since it would be extremely difficult to judge when to lift any controls, and indeed to have the courage to do so ... in practice, I suspect the clouds rarely lift enough [to remove controls] ... The point is this: such addictive drugs *do not* represent a good bargain for anyone.

(b) Reserve ratios

[There is] the occasional suggestion that the central bank has another magic wand available: reserve ratios ... there seems to be some confusion here, . . . such requirements, which we *have* used in this country ... are *not* credit controls . . . They work through their effect on money market interest rates, and would not therefore provide an alternative to interest rates.

(c) Funding policy

Another suggestion . . . is to load more of the burden of adjustment on to *long-term* rates. This proposal looks back to the period when the government was a heavy borrower in the gilt-edged market and indeed to the phase of *overfunding* when the government borrowed substantially more long term than it needed to finance its deficit.

The effect ... was to push up long-term yields and to hold down the growth of broad money, so that ... the growth of demand was restrained.

More recently ... the government has had no deficit to finance. In these circumstances, the equivalent of old-style overfunding would be to buy back less stock than the value of the surplus.

Policy has ... [been] guided by the 'full-fund' rule, with government debt being brought back on a scale equivalent to the surplus. Would it not have been a good idea, we are sometimes asked, to employ the surplus in another way?

There are a number of points that can be made against this. First, the case for overfunding depends on there being a robust and predictable relationship between the behaviour of broad money and the level of demand. There was indeed a time when we thought that this relationship was such that managing broad money *did* provide a reliable indirect means of managing demand and thus inflation. But developments in the first half of the 1980s ... led us to abandon that view ...

The second difficulty is that ... overfunding has in any case become a less than effective means of managing broad money. While there are various accounting relationships that suggest that this might be straightforward, in fact in the real world we have to take account of the behaviour of other users of the capital markets ... the private sector [has] exploited the opportunity to tap the market for funds since the government ceased to be the dominant borrower; indeed 'crowding out' has been replaced by 'crowding in' ... the absence of government funding has arguably had less of an effect than might be expected on the growth of broad money.

(d) Fiscal policy

Some critics ... maintain that the burden of [macroeconomic policy] ... has fallen too much on monetary policy – and particularly interest rates. Could the 'one club' of interest rates usefully be supplemented by fiscal measures?

The answer is unequivocally 'yes'. But, let me stress that fiscal policy *has* supported monetary policy. The allegedly exclusive dependence on monetary policy has been greatly exaggerated.

Fiscal policy has been consistently tight over recent years ... in 1989 the PSDR was getting on for 2 per cent of GDP. Efforts to do more via fiscal policy would take us down the road of fine tuning, whereas this part of government policy has ... been directed towards medium- and long-term goals.

There is ... the more specific accusation that taxes were reduced inappropriately in the 1988 Budget ... the injection was totally overshadowed by the expansion of credit ... [and the tax cuts] would not account for the whole [of the expansion of credit].

There is a further problem affecting all [four alternative measures discussed] on account of the role played by interest rates in relation to the exchange rate, which is of course important to the control of inflation. Even supposing domestic demand management *could* satisfactorily be achieved at a lower level of interest rates, it might not be possible to reduce them if there were a risk that the exchange market would be unsettled. In other words, the employment of other measures would not *necessarily* result in lower interest rates.

(e) ERM membership*

If [ERM] membership is to mean anything, realignments would have to be regarded as a last and not a first resort. It is possible but by no means certain that, within the ERM, lower interest rates would not immediately depress the currency, in which case inflationary pressures would not make themselves felt immediately. Any excess of the growth of sterling unit labour costs over deutschmark or French franc unit labour costs would represent a loss of competitiveness.

Thus, while the ERM could constitute an alternative discipline, it would not be a soft option. The plain fact is that nominal wage increases have to come down ... if the knowledge that the exchange rate would not be allowed to depreciate helped focus the attention of both sides of industry on the fundamental determinants of competitiveness, then ERM membership could be beneficial.

* The speech was made before Britain's ERM entry.

1. Does the Governor's argument rule out an EC-wide credit control policy?
2. To what extent does this speech show that fiscal and monetary policy must work together?

Source: Robin Leigh Pemberton, *Bank of England Quarterly Review*, May, 1990

*Rational expectations

One of the more influential developments in economics over recent years is the 'new' treatment of expectations. This new treatment is called **Rational expectations** (for reasons which will become clear later) and has had an enormous impact on macro-economics. This impact has been on both the theoretical and the policy side. First we will discuss the role of expectations in economics, and this will involve a brief excursion into microeconomics. Then we will offer an account of the birth of rational expectations. Finally, we will demonstrate how the concept of rational expectations is used in modern macroeconomics.

Expectations in economics

Quite a lot of microeconomics seeks to explain how the price mechanism operates – how the 'invisible hand' co-ordinates the actions of individual agents. In doing so, of course, it offers an account of the behaviour of economic agents. For example, it explains how demanders of goods and services decide what to buy and how much to buy.

The result of this microeconomic theorizing is to show how these choices change when the income of the demanders is changed and/or when the prices of the goods and services are changed. It shows that the market clears at one and only one price, and at one and only one quantity. We can also show that, in perfectly competitive markets, this price/output combination is Pareto optimal (see Chapter 7).

These are powerful results and should not be under-played, but this whole analysis is cast entirely in a timeless world in which all decisions are made in one period and in which no account is offered of how the market gets to its equilibrium. Let us consider these two points in turn.

The timelessness of our analysis is a major difficulty, since most consumers are motivated not only by their current incomes and current prices, but also by their future incomes and future prices. If the future were known with absolute certainty then all these decisions could be made together. If we know our future income and future prices then we can make our lifetime plans now and stick to them. Our timeless model would then be appropriate.

It is obvious, however, that no one can know the future with anything like the certainty required for this 'once-and-for-all' decision. But neither can we ignore the future. In deciding what to buy today it is natural to think about the future. Would we buy a car this year if we thought that car prices were about to fall?

In the absence of certainty it is necessary to make guesses about the future. If we guess that the price of a particular good is going to rise in the near future then we may well buy it now rather than stick to a plan to buy it much later. Furthermore, if we guess that our income will be much higher in the future then we may decide to spend more than we earn at the moment by taking out a loan. We will pay the loan back later when our income increases.

The point is that our current behaviour depends not only on our current aims, tastes and income, but also on what we expect them to be in the future. The influence of these expectations is rarely negligible and in some instances is very significant indeed. Expectations have therefore to be incorporated in our model of consumer behaviour.

Expectations affect the behaviour not only of consumers, but also of producers. Recall that in our investigations of various types of market (Chapter 6) the 'kinked demand curve' was constructed by letting a producer form expectations about how the firm's competitors would react to the firm increasing or decreasing its prices. Each individual firm expected that its competitors would react to an increase in price by leaving their prices unchanged, but would react to a decrease in price by reducing theirs too. It was this asymmetry of competitors' expected responses which gave rise to the kink in the demand curve.

Expectations also entered the modern version of the Phillips curve. Recall that the original Phillips curve was drawn up with data from a period when price level was not expected to change. The breakdown of the Phillips curve was ascribed to the growing realization that the price level was going to change – that it was rising and would continue to do so. The **expectations-augmented Phillips curve** is described in Chapter 16 and is really a sequence of Phillips curves arising from the upward movement of the basic Phillips curve as expectations of inflation increase.

It was argued in Chapter 16 that the Phillips curve shape is due to mistaken expectations. The labour force form their expectations about future prices and then agree a money wage rate. The real wage thus being settled, the labour force decides how much labour to supply. If they expect inflation to be 10 per cent next year and get a money wage rate rise of 20 per cent then they will expect an increased real wage of 10 per cent. This high real wage will result in their offering a lot of labour. In the event, the rate of inflation may turn out to be 20 per cent and result in no increase in real wages. In retrospect their offer of more labour was a mistake.

What we observe, then, is more employment when expectations of inflation are too low. Similarly, when expectations are too high (when prices do not rise by as much as expected) the supply of labour will be reduced and employment will be low. When expectations are correct there will be no increase or decrease in employment. Employment and unemployment will be at their **natural rate**. This natural rate is also called the **non-accelerating inflation rate of unemployment (NAIRU).**

The combination of unemployment and inflation which actually occurs in the economy will therefore depend upon the natural rate of unemployment, the expected rate of inflation and the actual rate of inflation. Determining the natural rate is not our purpose here. We are offering just one account of how expectations may be formed, and how those expectations influence actual behaviour.

This is a somewhat lengthy tour of the expectations parts of this book and is intended to demonstrate how current behaviour is influenced by expectations. We now turn to the second issue raised about the timelessness of our analysis. How do markets find their equilibrium prices and quantities?

In Chapter 5 we investigated the consequences for price and output when there was a movement of either the demand curve or the supply curve. In that chapter we simply assumed that the market would move to its new equilibrium. In Figure 18.1 the market is originally at P_1, q_1 when the demand curve is at D_1. When the demand curve

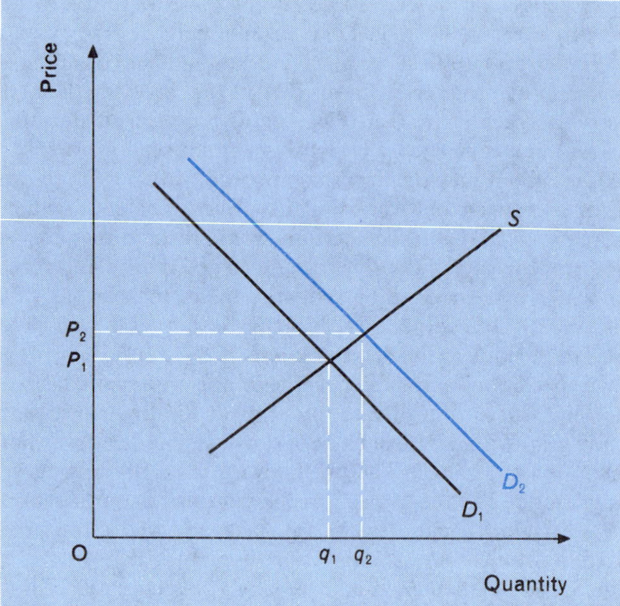

Figure 18.1 Simple model of equilibrium in the goods market.

moves to D_2 the new market-clearing price is P_2 and the quantity is q_2. The question for us here is: how does the market move from 1 to 2?

We could imagine that the shift in the demand curve caught the suppliers entirely by surprise, so that, instantaneously, the quantity supplied remained unchanged at q_1. If this were so then the price would rise to P_3, as shown in Figure 18.2. The next thing to happen would be that suppliers would see this high price and would respond to it by producing q_3. However, in order to sell that quantity (q_3) the price would have to fall to P_4. At this lower price the supply would be cut back to q_4, but on bringing this quantity (q_4) to market the suppliers would find that the price had risen to P_5.

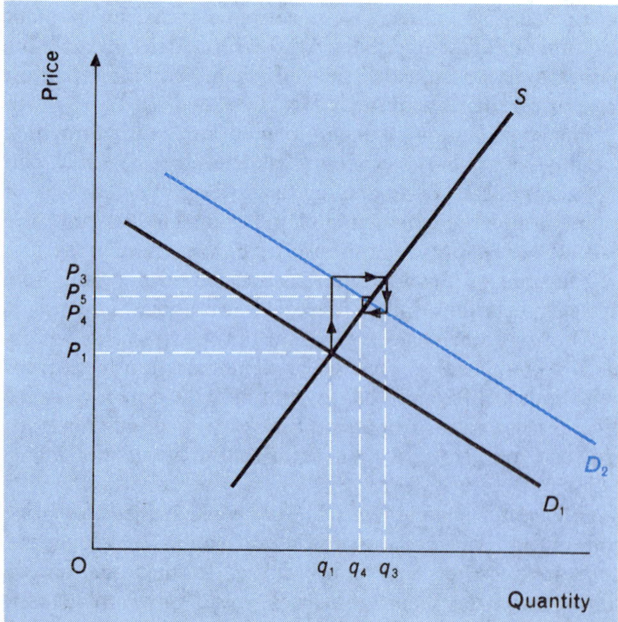

Figure 18.2 Convergent cobweb.

By successive changes in quantity and price, the market converges on to the new equilibrium price and quantity. This process is called the 'cobweb' for obvious reasons, and may take some time to work through. And, as we shall see, it may not always work quite as well as this account would suggest.

Notice that the producers simply followed the market. When the market price was P_1 they reacted to that price, and when it was P_2 they reacted to that. At no time did they think ahead and form expectations about what the price would be in the next period. We could say that, in so far as they did form expectations, they simply expected the current price to persist into the future.

This account of expectations formation is the simplest possible – producers simply assume that next year's price will be the same as this year's price. This is the so-called regressive expectations formation. Expectations about the future depend solely on the past. However, this is a rather naive way of behaving. If the cost of making mistakes about the future is high then producers will surely try to find a more scientific or reliable way of forming expectations.

Rational expectations

This was the problem addressed by the economist John F. Muth in 1961. From his work a great literature grew which continues to dominate many aspects of economics. The Muth model is like our market-clearing cobweb model and addresses a well-known problem which arises in markets when suppliers cannot respond immediately to price changes.

Consider a standard supply and demand curve model, as shown in Figure 18.3. Let us assume that it takes a year to produce more output. Suppliers decide what the price will be next year and then put in hand a production plan for next year. Next year's output (supply) will therefore depend on what next year's price is expected to be. The market we have in mind might be that of an agricultural product like pigs or, as the Americans might say, hogs.

If the hog farmers form their expectations about prices regressively then they will assume that next year's price of hogs is going to be the same as this year's price. So when supply is low (at q_1) the price will be high (P_2) and so farmers will plan to supply q_2 next year. When next year comes they will put q_2 on to the market and the price will fall to P_1. At price P_1 they will then decide to supply q_1 next year and so will cut production. In the following year they supply q_1 and price goes up to P_2 again. They then increase production back to q_2 and the whole cycle starts over again.

This is a form of market failure in that the quantity and price never manage to get to their equilibrium, market-clearing levels. In the cobweb example shown in Figure 18.2 the market eventually settles down at its equilibrium point – it is said to 'converge' on its new equilibrium. But markets need not converge and we need to look at how the market reacts when out of equilibrium.

In the hog market case Muth shows how the participants in a market follow the rules which should take the market to its equilibrium, but instead the prices and quantities con-

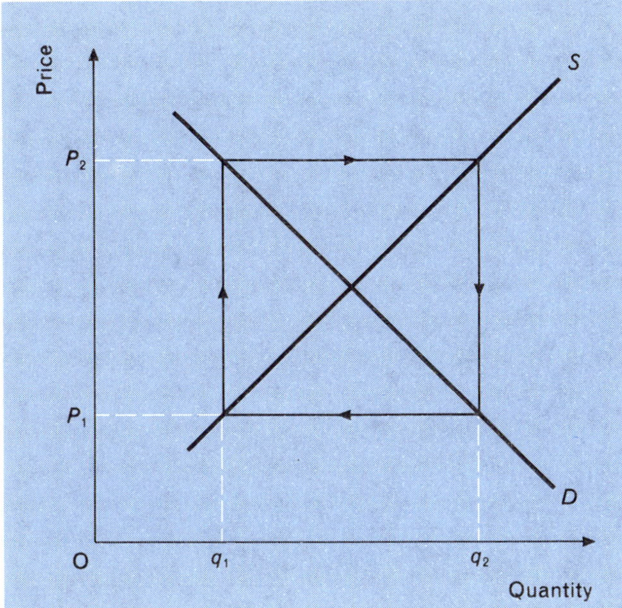

Figure 18.3 Non-convergent cobweb.

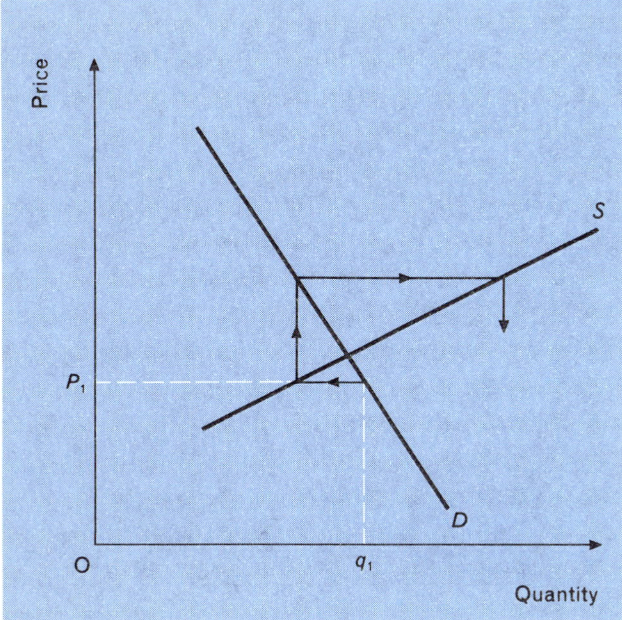

Figure 18.4 Divergent cobweb.

tinue to follow each other round and round the equilibrium. This example is rather rare in that the slopes of the supply and demand curves are such that the market neither converges on the equilibrium (as in Figure 18.2) nor moves away from it.

In Figure 18.4, however, the cycles of quantity and price are again apparent, but this time prices get further and further away from equilibrium with each successive round. The market therefore 'diverges' away from equilibrium and self-destructs. Dynamics are therefore an important aspect of market systems, and it is clearly necessary to show not only that they converge on to an equilibrium, but also that they do so swiftly enough to prevent the waste of successive over and underproduction.

When Muth looked at these models he argued that no rational hog breeder would continue year after year first to overproduce and then to underproduce. Eventually it would dawn on producers that price moved in a regular way and that they could do better than simply assume that next year's price would be this year's price. According to Muth, rational breeders (or any other rational agent forming expectations about the future) would use economic theory, which explains how markets in general work, and their observations of past prices in their own market to see how the price might behave in the future.

Expectations which are based on the relevant economic theory and which make use of the available data are called **rational expectations**. Of course, people who form expectations in this way will not always get them right – mistakes will be made and some expectations will lead to disappointments – but on balance, it is held, the mistakes will be random. That is to say, people will not make regular mistakes year after year. There will be no markets in which prices rise and fall around the equilibrium value in the manner suggested above. Such regularities would be predictable and hence avoidable.

For rational expectations models, then, there is no protracted search for a new equilibrium – no period in which agents continue making systematic mistakes. They will go immediately to the equilibrium. The long-run market solution becomes the short-run solution too because there is now no need to work through the short-run cobweb.

These then are rational expectations, and from such unremarkable beginnings grew the whole rational expectations approach to economics.

An application of rational expectations

To see the power of this rational expectations approach let us return to the expectations-augmented Phillips curve. In our original account we assumed that workers form their expectations about future prices regressively, i.e. they base their expectations for the coming period on their experience in the previous period. This causes mistakes to be made, which lead to levels of unemployment higher than the natural rate when expectations are too low and unemployment lower than the natural rate when expectations are too high.

Now if the agents form their expectations rationally they will know that a given increase in the money supply will eventually lead to a given rate of inflation. They will not therefore be fooled by the government announcing an increase in aggregate demand or the consequent increase in money wage rates. They will know that this will lead to inflation and hence they will not alter the labour supply. The natural rate of unemployment will be maintained and the short-run Phillips curve (like the long-run Phillips curve – the NAIRU) will be vertical. The government cannot therefore reduce the level of unemployment below its natural rate simply by expanding aggregate demand.

In the original version of the Phillips curve the government faces a trade-off between unemployment and inflation and can reduce unemployment by expanding aggregate demand. This increase in demand will cause shortages in

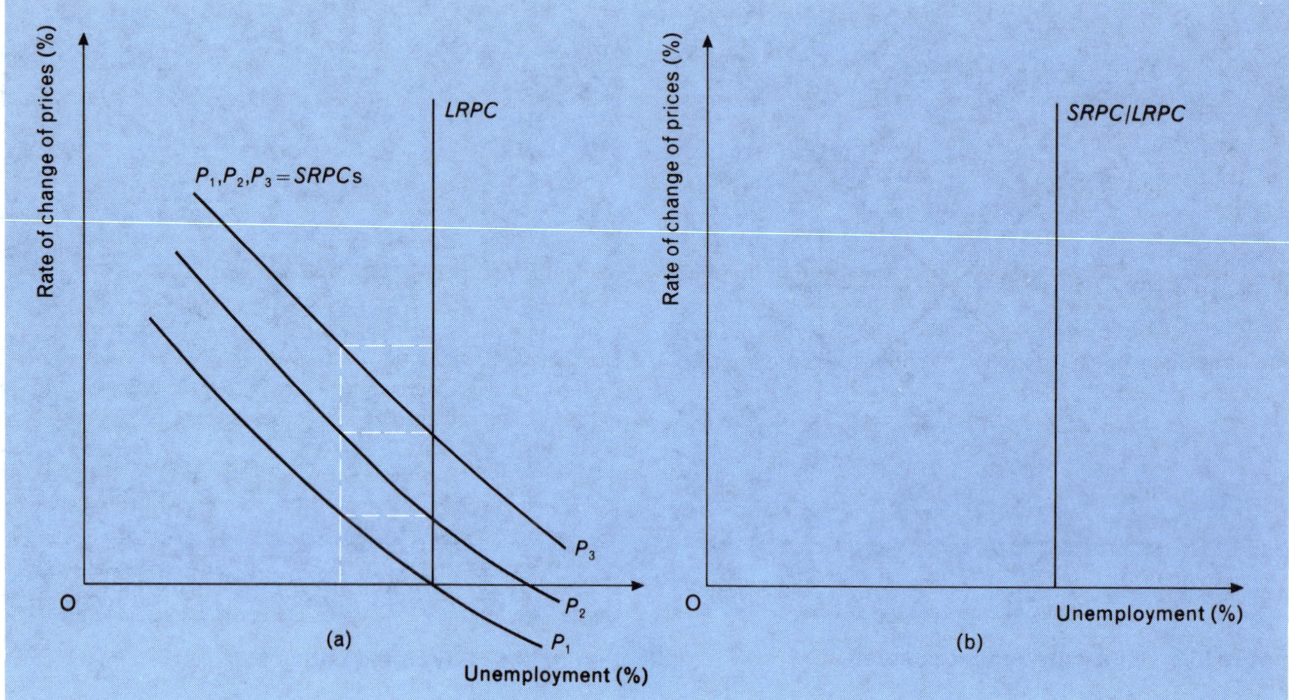

Figure 18.5 Expectations-augmented Phillips curve with (a) regressive expectations and (b) rational expectations.

some labour markets and so push up costs and prices. Inflation is the 'price' we have to pay for low levels of unemployment. Aggregate demand can be increased through either fiscal or monetary policy, but Keynesians typically prefer fiscal policy.

In the second version of the Phillips curve (the expectations-augmented version) this trade-off between inflation and output is short-lived and relies on the workforce forming erroneous expectations about next period's price level. The effect nevertheless exists in this model, and hence it is still possible to argue a case for government intervention in the economy. It is still possible for the government to reduce unemployment below the natural rate in the short run. Figure 18.5 compares this with rational expectations.

The point of the rational expectations argument is to demonstrate that government intervention will not work even in the short run. Workers now form their expectations rationally and therefore will not systematically underestimate the level of inflation. They will not offer too much labour, but will offer what they offered before. Unemployment remains at the natural rate and no longer wanders around the natural rate like the hog breeders wandered around the equilibrium hog price. It goes to the market-clearing equilibrium (natural rate) right away. The introduction of rational expectations has therefore had the effect of reinforcing the political stance that argues against intervention by government.

Conclusions

In economics it is usual to compare one market equilibrium with another (comparative statics). It is simply assumed that markets find their equilibrium values and do so swiftly enough to avoid any costs of being out of equilibrium. Sometimes, however, it is necessary to examine just how a market moves from one equilibrium to another – how long it takes and whether it will ever reach there. In these cases we have to look at the dynamics of the market.

In many cases it is possible to show that the market will converge on to an equilibrium, but it is not always possible to show that this will happen speedily. In other cases the market may not converge, but may continually oscillate around the equilibrium and never actually get there. Still worse is the case where the market diverges further and further away from equilibrium and the market self-destructs.

These various outcomes depend upon the shapes of the supply and demand curves and on the way in which agents form their expectations about future prices. Simple regressive expectations, which assume that the future will be the same as the past, lead to some unsatisfactory outcomes. This in turn suggests that the government (or some other central planning bureau) could usefully intervene to get the market to its equilibrium or to exploit the fact that it is not clearing in order to get high levels of employment.

Alternatively, it could be argued that rational agents will not continue to make mistakes, but that they will eventually become aware of systematic errors and change the way they form their expectations. This is the basis of Muth's argument that agents will use their knowledge of economics and of their own markets to form better expectations of the future price level. With these rational expectations, markets have no difficulty in finding their equilibria and spend no time in getting there. The distinction between the long run and the short run is no longer relevant. If this is indeed what happens then the case for intervention disappears.

In general, then, it may be said that some knowledge of the dynamics of markets is necessary if we are to assess their efficacy. We have to show that markets are capable of getting swiftly to equilibrium in order to make a case against government intervention. These dynamics often entail some account of how economic agents form expectations. Simple regressive expectations lead to short-run Phillips curves which do admit to a trade-off between unemployment and inflation. Rational expectations, on the other hand, lead to a vertical Phillips curve even in the short run. The introduction of rational expectations therefore greatly weakens the already weak case for governments pursuing expansionary policies to reduce unemployment.

SUMMARY

1. An influential recent development in macroeconomics is the rational expectations hypothesis.
2. In elementary demand and supply models, markets move swiftly from one equilibrium position to another. In reality these adjustments take time and agents have to anticipate future prices.
3. Expectations of future prices are formed in a variety of ways.
4. If agents assume that tomorrow will be the same as today then markets may never find equilibrium.
5. Many economic models are based on economic agents having these backward-looking (regressive) expectations.
6. If economic agents use economic theory and their own knowledge of markets to form rational expectations then they will learn from experience and will not make systematic mistakes. They will know where market equilibrium is and will act so that it is actually reached.
7. One implication of rational expectations is that governments are unable to influence the economy in the way Keynesian economic theory suggests.

Supply-side economics

We have seen that the focus of Keynesian economics is aggregate demand. According to Keynesian theory, output and hence employment is determined solely by the level of demand. Aggregate supply plays no role in all this. It is simply assumed that supply will follow wherever demand leads, and so that by modelling demand we model supply too.

This Keynesian assumption that supply depends upon demand is quite different from the assumptions of the pre-Keynesian or classical economists, who argued the reverse, i.e. they thought that demand was dependent upon and determined by supply. Say's Law states that supply creates its own demand. No one supplies goods to market without subsequently demanding goods of equal value. No one can demand goods without first supplying goods of equal value. Thus the value of goods supplied to the market must always equal the value of goods demanded in the market, and since supply precedes demand it must be the case that demand is determined by supply and not the other way around.

In brief: Keynesians look to demand to explain national output; classical economists look to supply to determine national output.

The Keynesian view prevailed from the 1940s to the mid-1970s. Much work was done on explaining aggregate demand, and macroeconomic policies were all to do with managing aggregate demand. However, since the mid-1970s Keynesianism has fallen in popularity and macroeconomics has returned to the view that it is supply rather than demand which drives the economy – and that we need to look at what determines supply and generate policies aimed at improving it. This is the essence of **supply-side** economics.

Like the Keynesian approach, the new supply-side macroeconomics is a short-run theory. Population size and capital stock are fixed and there is assumed to be no technological progress. (Recall that when changes in these three elements are allowed for we are moving into theories of economic growth rather than macroeconomics.) We therefore confine ourselves to the short run and in the short run only labour is variable. As the amount of labour employed increases, so does output. However, due to the law of diminishing returns, each successive increment in employment yields smaller and smaller increments of output. The relationship between output and employment is called the aggregate production function and is shown in Figure 18.6(a).

Since output is directly related to employment, we need only explain one of them – if we know output then we can find employment, or if we know employment then we can find output. Typically, we seek first to determine employment and so we begin our account of supply-side economics by looking at the aggregate labour market.

Much of our analysis has already been covered in Chapter 9. It was shown there that employers' demand for labour decreases as the real wage rate rises, and that employees' supply of labour increases as the real wage rate increases. Thus we have a downward-sloping demand curve for labour and an upward-sloping supply curve of labour. These are shown in Figure 18.6(b).

In equilibrium the labour market clears where these two curves intersect (at N^*), and this market-clearing level of employment is called the full-employment or the natural rate of employment.

Of course, not everyone is employed at N^*. There will be those who are unwilling to work for the going rate (W^*), and they are the voluntarily unemployed. Full employment occurs when all those who want to work (at the market-clearing wage rate) are in work, i.e. when there is no involuntary unemployment.

The **working population** is composed of all able-bodied, sane persons between school leaving age and retirement age. This is shown as line WP in Figure 18.6(b). The difference between the working population (WP) and the employed labour force (N^*) is called either **voluntary unemployment** or the **natural rate of unemployment** (U_n^*). It is made up of those who prefer to live on private income or on state benefits rather than to work at the going wage rate.

If the labour market worked perfectly all the time, the only unemployment would be this voluntary unemployment, and the level of employment would remain at N^*. This level of employment would give rise to output Y^*. Thus national output is determined by where the labour market is cleared (N) with no reference to aggregate demand at all.

In the Keynesian model the only way to change national output was to change aggregate demand. In the supply-side model the only way to change national output is to change something in the labour market. Thus Keynesians concentrate on demand management and supply-siders concentrate on policies affecting the labour market.

SUMMARY

1. Keynesian economists assume that supply is determined by demand. Classical economists believed that demand is determined by supply – Say's Law.
2. In recent years there has been a return to the classical view, and this has given rise to modern supply-side macroeconomics.
3. Supply-side macroeconomics is a short-run theory. The only factor of production which is variable is labour. Thus if the level of employment is explained, so is the level of output.
4. Where the labour market clears, some members of the working population are unemployed. This is the natural rate of unemployment, at which all unemployment is voluntary.
5. In the supply-side model the only way to increase output is to act to change the labour market.

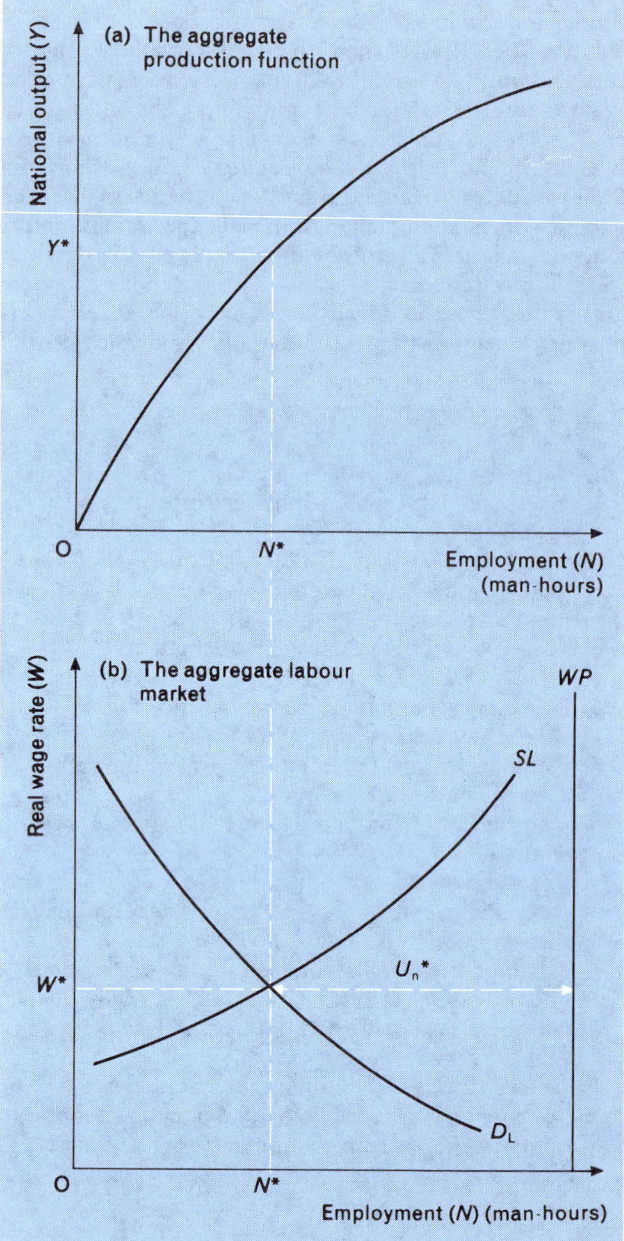

Figure 18.6 Aggregate production function and aggregate labour market.

Supply-side policies

The reason for the Keynesian policies is quite clear – there are those who can work and want to work but are prevented by lack of aggregate demand. The Keynesian solution is therefore to raise aggregate demand until all who can and want to work are in employment. The supply-siders face no such problem. All the unemployed are voluntarily unemployed and hence in their preferred condition. Furthermore, since aggregate demand plays no part in their condition, it is neither necessary nor desirable to play about with aggregate demand.

Their policies derive from rather different considerations. First, the more people there are unemployed, the lower is our national output, i.e. there is less to go around. Secondly, the more unemployed there are, the more the rest of us have to pay out in benefits. Supply-siders therefore look to policies which reduce the number of unemployed so as to make the rest of us, rather than the unemployed, better off.

Their policies take a number of forms and we shall look at the most significant.

Tax distortions

The first thing to notice about the labour market as depicted in Figure 18.6(b) is that the real wage paid out by the employers is the same as the real wage received by the employees. In other words, there is no tax on labour. In fact, of course, there are heavy taxes on labour so that there is a tax wedge between the cost of labour to the employer and the proceeds of labouring enjoyed by the employees. These taxes take three forms.

The first is the national insurance contributions (NICs) paid by employers. These are paid for all employees, even for the lowest earners. They rise with income so that high earners cost their employers more in NICs.

The second tax is the national insurance contributions paid by the employees. These too are paid by all employees, even by the lowest earners, and they rise with income, but

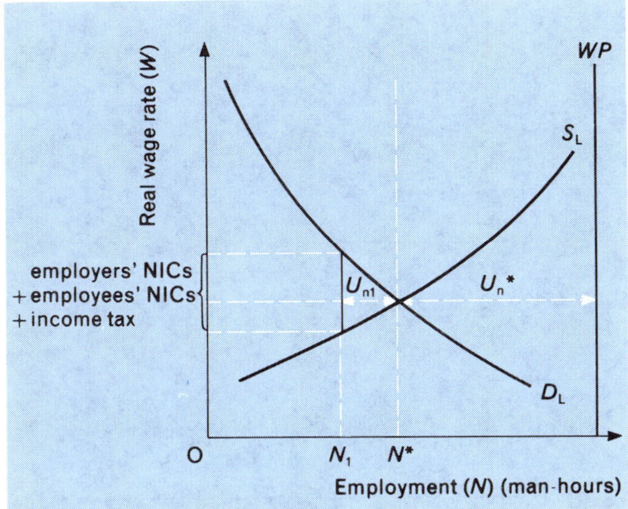

Figure 18.7 Effect of taxes on labour.

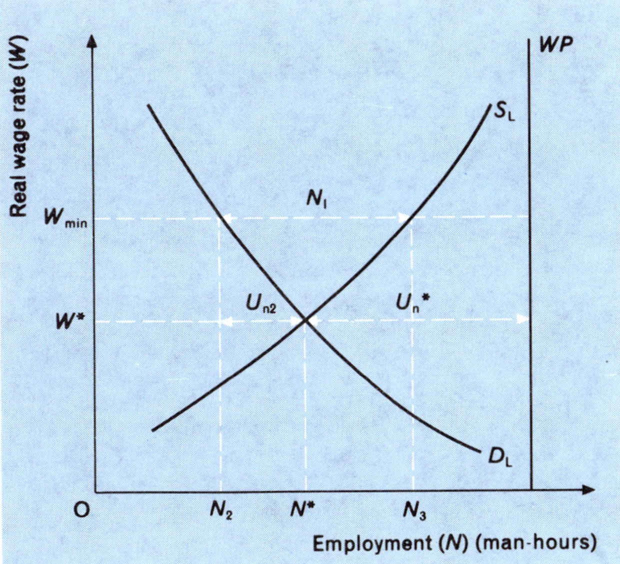

Figure 18.8 Effect of a minimum wage above the market-clearing rate.

they remain fixed above a certain income level. This is therefore a regressive tax on labour (see page 309).

The third tax is the income tax paid by the employee. This is not paid by the lowest earners, but as earnings rise the tax is first imposed at a rate of 25 per cent and then at 40 per cent when earnings reach the highest levels.

Given these taxes, it is clear that the amount paid by the employers is much higher than the amount received by the employees. This reduces the level of employment as shown in Figure 18.7. With no taxes, the market would clear at N^* and unemployment would be U_n^*. With taxes, only N_1 are employed and unemployment rises by U_{n1}. Since none of the unemployed is prepared to work for the going wage rate (after tax), all these unemployed are still voluntarily unemployed.

Even so, national output is below what it could be and there are U_{n1} more people unemployed than there need be. The supply-siders' policy recommendation here would be to cut these taxes and allow the market to move towards N^*. This has indeed been the stated aim, and to some extent the achievement, of successive Conservative governments in the UK.

Market imperfections

The second thing to notice about the labour market is that wage rates are not always free to vary and take up their market-clearing levels. The imposition of minimum wage rates by statutory authorities (**Wages Councils**) and the reluctance of trade unions to allow cuts in wages may prevent wage rates from falling low enough to clear the labour market. This is shown in Figure 18.8.

The imposition of a minimum wage (W_{min}) means that only N_2 can be employed, which increases unemployment by U_{n2}. At this wage rate there are N_3 workers looking for work, but employers are prepared to employ only N_2 of them. Thus it could be argued that N_I workers are involuntarily unemployed – they are looking for work at the going wage rate and are unable to find any. However, this is quite different from the Keynesian case – this level of involuntary unemployment is not to be cured by increasing aggregate demand.

The supply-siders aim instead at freeing the labour market from these imperfections by doing away with Wages Councils and weakening the power of the trade unions to resist wage cuts. Various Acts of Parliament over the last 13 years have been aimed at just these problems.

Benefit cuts

Both the preceding policies are aimed at enabling the labour market to reach its natural rate of unemployment. Other policies are aimed at changing the natural rate of unemployment. The first way of doing this is to make unemployment less attractive by cutting benefits.

The labour supply curves in Figures 18.6 to 18.8 are all drawn up on the assumption that those who choose not to work will be eligible for state benefits. Thus when deciding whether or not to work at the going wage rate, the level of benefits plays an important part. The higher the benefit, the less the incentive to work. Supply-siders argue that cutting the benefit rate will move the whole labour supply curve to the right. This is shown in Figure 18.9.

With high benefits the labour supply curve is S_1, with many workers preferring leisure to work. With low benefit rates the labour supply curve moves to S_2. The result of this benefit cut is threefold. First, the level of employment increases from N^*_1 to N^*_2. Secondly, the natural rate of unemployment falls from U^*_{n1} to U^*_{n2}. Thirdly, the equilibrium real wage falls from W^*_1 to W^*_2.

Notice then that this policy of reducing benefits will succeed in reducing unemployment only if wage rates are flexible enough to fall, thereby absorbing the increased number of workers seeking work. Thus policies tend to be interrelated and depend for their individual efficacy on the implementation of other policies.

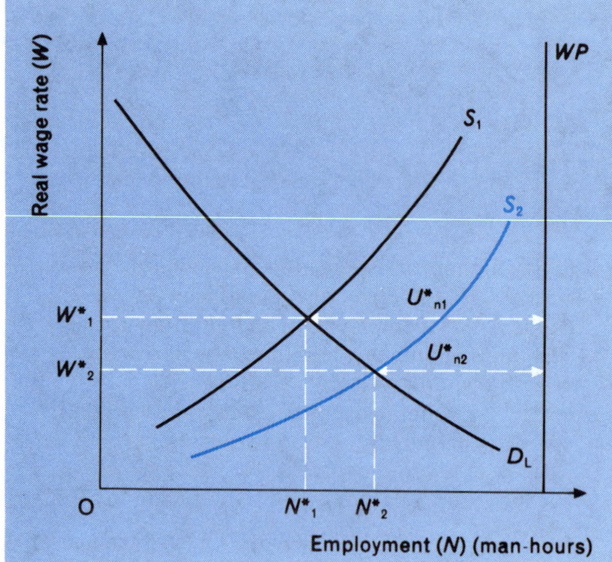

Figure 18.9 Effect of cutting unemployment benefit.

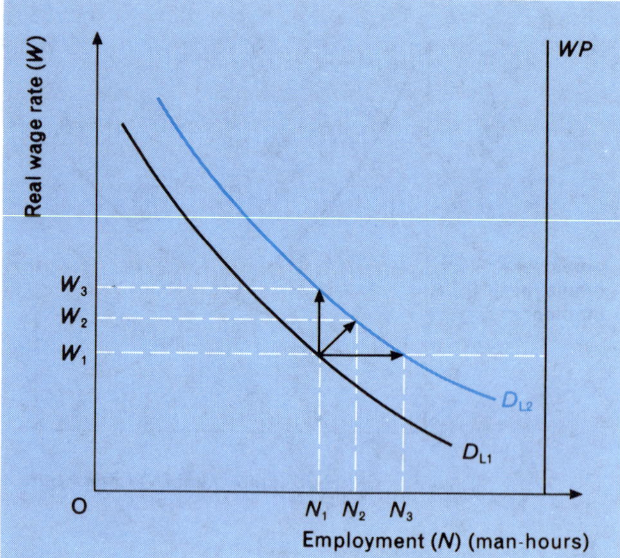

Figure 18.10 A rise in labour productivity causes the labour demand curve to move upwards and to the right.

The policy of cutting benefits, or at least targeting them to those who have good reason for remaining unemployed, has been progressively pursued by successive Conservative governments in the UK.

Training and investment

Apart from moving the labour supply curve, the only other way of influencing the natural rate of unemployment is to move the labour demand curve. The position of the demand for labour curve depends on the marginal product of labour, and hence to move the labour demand curve it is necessary to alter the marginal product of labour. This requires labour to be better trained and/or better equipped with capital.

Thus the policy emphasis is in part placed on training programmes both for the unemployed and for employed workers. The Training and Enterprise Councils (TECs) are the latest in a long line of such schemes, which have included Restart and the Youth Training Scheme (YTS). By improving the training of workers their marginal productivity is increased and it becomes profitable to employ them even when wage rates are high. The demand for labour curve moves to the right.

To say that a downward-sloping curve moves to the right is the same as saying that it moves upwards, so we can either think in terms of increasing the wage rate and keeping the level of employment constant or increasing the level of employment and keeping the wage rate constant. Or we could increase both the wage rate and the level of employment. These possibilities are shown in Figure 18.10. Improving the quality of the workers is one way of increasing productivity, but providing them with more and/or better equipment will also do the trick. Some of the productivity difference between British and German workers has been attributed to differences in per capita capital, and the three main political parties in Britain are increasingly seeking ways of encouraging new investment.

Whether by training workers or by investing in machines, the aim of supply-siders is to shift the labour demand curve to the right. This, like the shift in the labour supply curve, reduces the natural rate of unemployment. But in this case the wage rate is increased as employment increases, rather than decreased as before. This is shown in Figure 18.11.

The original labour demand curve D_{L1} yields a wage rate of W_1 and a natural rate of unemployment of U^*_{n1}. The rightward shift of the demand curve to D_{L2} leads to an increase in wage rate to W_2 and a decrease in the natural rate of unemployment to U^*_{n2}.

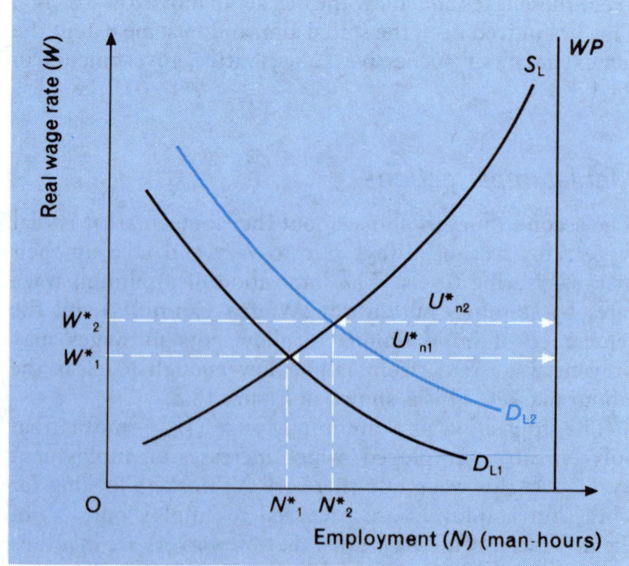

Figure 18.11 Effect of training and investment.

The policy of cutting benefits requires a downward adjustment in real wages, which may be difficult to achieve. The policy of improving labour productivity, however, requires only an increase in wage rates, and it is therefore easier to implement.

A mixture of both policies – moving both curves – could result in wage rates increasing, decreasing or remaining the same depending on the size of the movements. Equal movements lead to no change in wage rates. If demand moves more than supply then wage rates will rise. If supply moves more than demand then wage rates will fall. In any event, unemployment will fall and national output will rise.

Policy differences

We have seen above that cutting benefits is deemed by supply-siders to increase employment and national output by encouraging more people to seek employment. In the Keynesian model this reduction in benefits would be seen as a reduction in aggregate demand, since those in receipt of benefits have less to spend. This reduction in aggregate demand would work through the multiplier to reduce demand still further. This reduction in aggregate demand would cause output and hence employment to fall!

The same policy – cutting benefits – therefore has expansionary effects according to supply-siders and contractionary effects according to Keynesians. Little wonder then that economists sometimes disagree on policies. It all depends on which model you accept.

SUMMARY

1. Supply-side policies look to reduce the level of unemployment and so raise the level of national output.
2. The level of employment may be artificially low due to distortions of the labour market which prevent it from clearing.
3. Taxes on employees' earnings cause employers to pay higher real wages and so to employ fewer workers. Reducing employment taxes would cause a rise in employment and national output.
4. The imposition of a minimum wage above the market-clearing wage rate will give rise to involuntary unemployment. Supply-side policy advocates removing all wage controls.
5. Paying high unemployment benefits causes fewer people to offer themselves for work at the going wage rate. Supply-siders advocate reducing unemployment benefits and so widening the gap between work and unemployment.
6. Improving workers' productivity by training or better capital equipment causes the labour demand curve to move to the right and so reduces the natural rate of unemployment.
7. Supply-side economics is based on the use of microeconomic incentives to affect aggregate supply. Keynesian economics is based on the use of macroeconomic policy to affect aggregate demand.

Case Study 18.4 Supply-side measures in the UK, 1979–1991

Income tax

Reduced from 33% to 25% (basic rate) and 83% to 40% (top rate).

Number of tax bands reduced to two (25% and 40%) in 1988.

Income tax thresholds increased in real terms, allowing workers to keep more of their income.

Benefits

Unemployment benefit reduced in real terms.

All benefits index linked rather than 'earnings related', widening the gap between benefits and earnings.

Earnings-related unemployment benefit abolished.

Taxation of unemployment benefit introduced.

Employers' taxation

Abolition of national insurance surcharge.

Reduction of national insurance contributions for lower paid.

Reduction in rate of corporation tax to 25%.

Introduction of lower rates of corporation tax for 'small' firms and higher profit thresholds for small firms before corporation tax is payable.

Measures for self-employed

Enterprise allowance scheme – unemployed paid £40 per week for one year to set up their own business.

Loan guarantee scheme – bank loans to self-employed partly guaranteed.

Training measures

Youth Training Scheme.

Training and Enterprise Councils.

Measures to increase labour market flexibility

Reduced trade union power in various Employment Acts. Closed shop reduced, ballots for strikes compulsory, employers given right to take court action.

Wages Councils reformed and many abolished.

Legislation on unfair dismissal eased.

Incentives to encourage geographical mobility, e.g. Tenants Exchange Scheme.

Legal right to transfer old occupational pension schemes to new employer. Personal pension schemes for employees allowed.

Other measures

Privatization and deregulation of many industries, e.g. buses, airlines, City of London.

Exam Preparation and Practice

MULTIPLE-CHOICE QUESTIONS

1. Which of the following does not form part of government debt?
   A Premium bonds.
   B Commercial bills.
   C Treasury bills.
   D Notes and coins.

2. A person is awarded a pay rise of £80 a month and finds that at the end of the month her take-home pay has risen by £48. Assuming no other deductions, the marginal rate of direct taxation is:
   A 20%
   B 25%
   C 30%
   D 40%

3. Central government funding operations
   A reduce the national debt.
   B add to the foreign exchange reserves.
   C convert short term debt into long term debt.
   D compound a budget surplus. (AEB)

4. If the Bank of England buys gilt-edged stocks on the open market, all other things being equal, it will
   A increase the money supply and increase the national debt.
   B increase the money supply and tend to lower interest rates.
   C leave the money supply unaffected but raise interest rates.
   D decrease the money supply and tend to raise interest rates. (AEB)

5. Assuming commercial banks to be fully loaned up, when required to hold 1% of deposits in cash the call for £100m of special deposits by the Bank of England will cause the commercial banks to:
   A Reduce loans by £100m.
   B Reduce loans by £1,000m.
   C Reduce loans by £10,000m.
   D Increase lending by £1,000m.

6. Which of the following would indicate an expansionary monetary policy?
   A Open-market purchases of government bonds by the Bank of England.
   B A call for special deposits by the Bank of England.
   C A cut in the standard rate of income tax.
   D The imposition of credit limits on hire purchase agreements.

7. Which of the following is most likely to indicate the working of the automatic stabilizer?
   A Pensions.
   B Changes in the rate of taxation.
   C Unemployment benefit.
   D Investment.
   E Interest on the national debt. (LON.)

8. The return to a fixed exchange rate system reduces the scope for the use of domestic monetary policy because:
   A Monetary policy affects domestic interest rates, which in turn influence exchange rates.
   B Monetary policy is the responsibility of the IMF.
   C The money supply is fixed also.
   D Monetary policy is fully anticipated and discounted.

9. According to the rational expectations hypothesis:
   A There is a short-run trade-off between inflation and unemployment.
   B There is a long-run trade-off between inflation and unemployment.
   C Unemployment is fixed.
   D There is neither a long-run or short-run trade-off between inflation and unemployment.

Answer key

Where there are three numbered alternatives

A	B	C	D	E
1, 2, 3	1, 2	2, 3	1	3
Correct	Correct	Correct	Correct	Correct

10. Bank of England purchases of government securities on the open market would:
    1 Reduce interest rates.
    2 Reduce the supply of money.
    3 Help to meet the government borrowing requirement.

11. Which of the following are supply-side policies?
    1 The establishment of Training and Enterprise Councils.
    2 The abolition of Wages Councils.
    3 Raising public spending on road building.

12. The 'natural' rate of unemployment can be reduced by
    1 expansionist fiscal policies.
    2 retraining schemes.
    3 measures designed to reduce imperfections in the housing market. (AEB)

EXERCISES

1. The following table gives details of gross earnings and after-tax earnings of five people, all of whom receive the same tax allowances and live in a country where income tax is the only direct deduction from income.

Person	Gross earnings(£)	After-tax earnings (£)
A	73,000	41,200
B	48,000	35,800
C	26,500	20,100
D	10,000	8,250
E	3,200	3,150

   (a) Calculate the percentage of income paid in tax by each person.
   (b) Is the tax system in operation progressive or regressive?
   (c) If the tax-free element of income is £3,000 and the thresholds after this are £23,000, £42,000 and £50,000, find the marginal tax rates presently in force.

2. Suppose that the banking system maintains the following cash and liquid asset ratios: cash ½%, liquid assets 10%. The only eligible liquid assets are Treasury bills and cash. The initial combined balance sheet of the commercial bank is:

Cash	£50m
Treasury bills	£950m
Consols	£30m
Loans	£8,970m
	£10,000m

What will be the effects of the following open-market operations on the money supply (assume that the original balance sheet is the starting point for each operation)?

(a) An open-market purchase by the Bank of England of £5m of consols.
(b) An open-market sale by the Bank of England of £5m of consols.
(c) An open-market sale by the Bank of England of £10m of Treasury bills.

3. The government decides that it wants to control the growth of the money supply. Four possible policies are suggested:

(a) An open-market sale of £200m of consols.
(b) An open-market sale of £200m of Treasury bills.
(c) A reduction in the proportion of liquid debt to illiquid debt.
(d) A call for special deposits.

Comment on the consequences and likely effectiveness of each. You should not confine your analysis to the effect on the money supply.

4. Given the annual market rates of interest shown, what is the most that will be paid for (i) a 90-day £100 Treasury bill on the date of issue and (ii) a £100 consol paying £4 a year?

(a) 12½%
(b) 6%
(c) 3%

5. A country has been operating a system of strict capital controls, but is forced to abandon them due to a new international agreement. How will this affect the operation of monetary policy?

6. The government raises interest rates. How does this affect:

(a) The demand for money.
(b) The price of bonds.
(c) The level of investment.
(d) The price level.
(e) The exchange rate.

Do any of your answers depend on the economic viewpoint you take?

7. The market for pigs is shown in the diagram below. The initial quantity supplied is q_1.

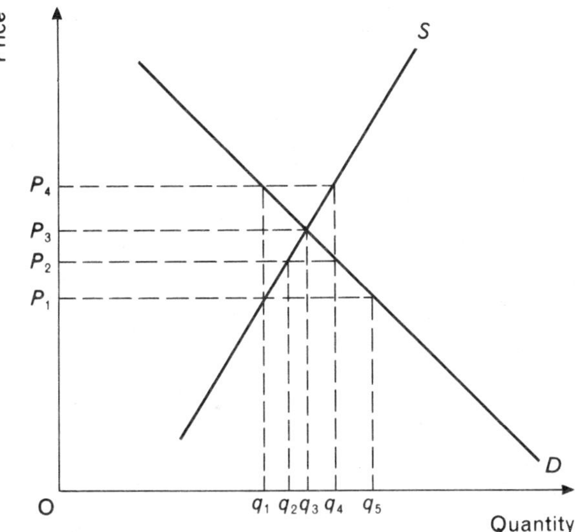

(a) What is the market price when q_1 pigs are offered for sale?
(b) If producers hold 'regressive expectations', what will be the quantity supplied and the market price in the next period?
(c) Will the market price converge on or diverge from equilibrium when producers have regressive expectations?
(d) What will be the market price and quantity in the next period if producers have 'rational expectations'?

DATA-RESPONSE QUESTIONS

1. The following passage is adapted from *Controlling The Money Supply* by David Cobham, Open University Press 1985.

> There are two separate ideas involved in 'control' of the public sector borrowing requirement (PSBR): one is accuracy, that is whether the government can hit its PSBR target; the other is reduction, that is whether the government can reduce the PSBR below some allegedly 'excessive' level.
>
> As regards accuracy there are three major problems for the government. First, the size of the PSBR depends partly on the level of economic activity and employment in the economy. Second, the size of the PSBR will be affected by inflation, which the government may not be able to forecast accurately. A third problem affecting whether the government can hit its PSBR target results from the fact that the coordination of the whole range of public expenditure is a vast bureaucratic undertaking, and it may be impossible precisely to control the total, especially in the short run, without unacceptable disruption in particular areas of expenditure.
>
> These three problems also impinge on the question of controlling the PSBR in the sense of reduction rather than accuracy. But here there is an obvious political problems as well, resulting from political infighting between government ministries and departments as well as between political factions in the Cabinet. Public expenditure cuts as a method of reducing the PSBR will necessarily offend, and therefore face obstruction from, some vested interests within as well as outside the administrative system.
>
> Controlling the PSBR is thus far from straightforward and large errors have occurred in both directions at different times in the past. PSBR control is therefore an inefficient and inflexible instrument for controlling monetary growth.

(a) What is the public sector borrowing requirement (PSBR)? *(2 marks)*
(b) Explain and discuss the difficulties, noted in the passage, which face a government when attempting to control and to reduce the PSBR. *(12 marks)*
(c) Explain briefly why governments might wish to control the PSBR. *(6 marks)*

(AEB)

---

2. Study carefully the passage below, and then answer the questions which follow.

> "Policy makers in Britain never anticipated that putting greater reliance on control of the money supply would be easy. As one advising Mrs Thatcher on this kind of issue in the 1970s, I certainly never supposed that the relationship between any chosen measure of money and g.d.p. would be stable or easy to predict. What did seem to me important was to move away from the situation in the early mid-1970s. It had become all too tempting to finance large Budget

deficits by the creation of money rather than a more balanced portfolio of government debt. I still believe the change in policy was right.

The movement towards a greater emphasis on monetary control which began under Mr Dennis Healey and continued under Mrs Thatcher was also right and was based on detailed statistical work. For example, analysis suggested that there was a *reasonably* stable relationship between changes in one particular monetary aggregate and later changes in g.d.p. This aggregate was the now well known M_3 .... It seemed if the authorities could exert control over M_3 this would give them a reasonable control over g.d.p.

Things have not proved so easy. Indeed Charles Goodhart, a senior adviser to the Bank of England, was led to propound Goodhart's Law. This holds that any economic variable which one seeks to control becomes uncontrollable. With monetary policy, the difficulty has been that the financial system has turned out to be both flexible and creative. Borrowers and lenders responded to attempts to reduce the growth rate for a given measure of money by various changes which enabled them to economise in its use .... Monetary policy has, therefore, proved difficult to operate. But not impossible. It cannot be emphasised too strongly that control over the money supply is not an end in itself .... Control over the money supply is an intermediate stage in an attempt to prevent g.d.p. (total national expenditure) rising so much more quickly than output as to cause an unacceptable degree of inflation. The key question is, therefore, what has actually happened to money g.d.p?

On this, three facts emerge. First, despite the difficulties, its rate of growth has been slowed from about 17 per cent in 1979 to 8 per cent or 9 per cent today.

Second, the rate at which that deceleration took place has been similar to the deceleration after the earlier peak in 1975 .... There has been more similarity than is commonly acknowledged in the behaviour of g.d.p. after 1975 and after 1979.

Third, there is a difference. Instead of picking up again to 17 per cent as in 1979 the rate of growth of money g.d.p. has been brought down below 10 per cent. With inflation of about 5 per cent demand is picking up."

Source: (Extracts from an article by Professor Sir Douglas Hague entitled "Why money is still a four-letter equation", published in *The Times*, 11 April 1984)

(a) What is meant by the "M_3" measure of money supply (l. 20)? [3]

(b) Explain why persistently large Budget deficits, if not financed by a "more balanced portfolio of government debt", could result in the creation of money (ls. 10–11). [5]

(c) The article argues that "control of the growth of money g.d.p." is important. Discuss this view. [5]

(d) What theory underlies the proposition that "if the authorities could exert control over M_3 this would give them a reasonable control over g.d.p." (ls. 21–23). For what reasons has such theory been disputed? [5]

(e) Consider the significance of "Goodhart's Law" (ls. 26–28) for the strategy of controlling M_3. [4]

(f) What is meant by the statement that "with inflation of about 5% demand is picking up" (ls. 55–56)? [3]

(WJEC)

PART IV

THE OPEN ECONOMY

19 The pure theory of international trade

In this chapter we will discuss:

1. The nature of the open economy.
2. The development of international trade theory.
3. The gains countries can make through specializing their production and free trade.
4. How even small, backward countries can gain from trade.
5. How some countries attempt to improve their trading position by restricting trade.

Introduction

An **open economy** is one which is open to influences from abroad – influences which arise beyond its national boundaries. The most obvious way of being 'open' is by way of international trade.

International trade is the exchange of goods and services between the citizens of one country and those of another. The larger the proportion of our production (or consumption) we sell (or buy) abroad, the more 'open' we become.

The UK has long been described as a nation which must trade in order to survive. This is perhaps a slight exaggeration but suggests that it is indeed an 'open' economy. In this part of the book we take a look at the causes and consequences of being an 'open' economy.

The open economy

Before setting out the theory it is worth asking ourselves why we should have a separate strand of economics to deal with international trade. We spent some time in Part II studying exchanges: we know how prices are determined; we know how the quantities exchanged are determined; we know why agents exchange. How does it come about then that we need to distinguish exchanges which take place between two Britons from exchanges which take place between Britons and Indians? In other words, what is the economic significance of the agent's nationality?

Transport costs?

One possible answer may be that it is not so much nationality as distance that matters. It would be possible to argue, for example, that when we are studying exchanges within our national boundaries we can ignore transport costs. But when studying international trade we have to take account of such costs. That is a possible answer, but it is neither theoretically nor factually correct.

Trade theory does not concern itself very much with transport costs. Nor, as a matter of fact, do transport costs between countries always exceed the transport costs within a country. Trade between Dover and Calais is international trade, whereas trade between Dover and Belfast is not.

Language differences?

A second possible answer might be that trade between countries is hampered not so much by transport costs as by language problems. It is easier to arrange an exchange with someone who speaks one's own language.

This again turns out to be a false trail. Trade between Milan and Naples is not international trade, but trade between Milan and an 'Italian' canton of Switzerland is. Trade between a Flemish Belgian and a French-speaking Belgian (a Walloon) is not international trade, whereas trade between a Walloon and a Frenchman is.

Why, then, is there a separate theory of international trade? There are two answers which do withstand scrutiny and lead to two branches of economic theory about international trade.

Who gains

The first reason is frankly chauvinistic. A large part of the theory of international trade is to do with the assessment of the benefit of trade and of the division of that benefit between the trading nations. Is it possible for the British, acting as a political unit, to grab more of the benefits of trade than do the French or Indians? This is a very old theme of economic theory and gave rise to a whole range of policies, stretching from strong protectionism to completely free trade.

This part of the theory is called the *pure theory of international trade* and deals with the generation and allocation of the gains from trade. We will examine the pure theory of international trade shortly.

Whose currency?

The second reason for having a separate theory of international trade arises from the existence of different national currencies.

The fact that Britons require pounds for their goods means that a buyer from India must first change rupees into pounds, and then deal with the British. The exchange of rupees for pounds will take place in the international money market. The workings of this additional market, the international money market, provide the reason for the second part of trade theory – the *monetary theory of international trade*. We deal with this in Chapter 21. But first we have to establish the pure theory of this trade.

SUMMARY

1. International trade theory deals with the exchange of goods and services between countries.
2. Exchanges between countries are worthy of separate study because, unlike exchanges between British nationals, we may be interested to find ways of distributing the benefits of trade more in favour of Britain.
3. A second reason for having a separate theory of trade between countries is that most countries have their own currencies. This means that foreigners wishing to buy British goods must first obtain British currency. The study of currency exchanges therefore separates the theory of trade from our previous study of exchange.
4. These two features of international trade (an interest in the distribution of the benefits of exchange and the need to exchange currencies) give rise to the pure theory of international trade and the monetary theory of international trade respectively.

Mercantilism

One of the oldest trade theories, **mercantilism**, was posited on the belief that international trade was a competition between countries to see who could get the greatest share of a fixed amount of world 'wealth'. It was as if there were just so much wealth available and we should try to import as much of this wealth as possible so that we would be rich and others would be poor.

The clearest way of understanding this rather crude view of the world is to imagine that a country's wealth is measured by the amount of gold it possesses. A rich country – rather like a rich person – is a country which possesses a large quantity of gold. Imagine too that there is only so much gold in the world. The aim of each country is then to gain the maximum amount of the world's gold supply. The only way to obtain gold, apart from piracy, is to sell goods and services in exchange for it.

It follows from this that exporting goods and services results in more gold flowing into Britain to pay for the exports, whereas importing goods and services into Britain causes an outflow of gold from Britain. Importing goods is therefore a *bad* thing and exporting goods is a *good* thing. Importing impoverishes and exporting enriches.

The policies which flow from this are therefore designed to discourage imports and encourage exports. Certainly there is nothing here to support the view that trade should be as unhindered as possible.

This mercantilist view has a certain intuitive appeal and is clearly reflected in much that is said and done even today about international trade. Japan is said to be 'strong' because it enjoys consistent balance of trade surpluses, i.e. the value of its exports exceeds the value of its imports. Britain is 'weak' because it suffers recurring balance of trade deficits, i.e. the value of exports is less than the value of imports. There is a Queen's Award for exporting, but not for importing. The mercantilist view would seem therefore to be still quite widely held. There is, however, quite a lot of economic theory which suggests that the mercantilists have got it all wrong. Let us now look at some alternative views.

Adam Smith and absolute advantage

As long ago as 1776, in *An Enquiry into the Nature and Causes of the Wealth of Nations*, Adam Smith launched a convincing denial of the mercantilist doctrine. He first argued that it simply does not make sense to equate a nation's wealth with the amount of gold it possesses. He went on to argue that trade is concerned not so much with allocating a fixed amount of wealth, but with actually *increasing* the amount of wealth to the benefit of all.

In what follows we look first at Smith's view of what constitutes wealth. We then look at his case for free trade.

Wealth

Adam Smith thought of the wealth of a nation not as the amount of gold it has, but as the *annual flow of goods and services available to its inhabitants*. A rich country is a country with a high national income, not necessarily one with large quantities of gold. The possession of gold, of itself, is not particularly productive. Gold is practically incapable of adding to the flow of goods and services produced. It is useful as a medium of exchange and as a store of value, but not as a productive agent.

Corn, on the other hand, is capable of adding to our production. Corn can be planted and will, next season, yield a much larger quantity of corn. If then the choice is between importing corn (exporting gold) and importing gold (exporting corn), Adam Smith would argue for importing corn and exporting gold. But the mercantilist wants the gold.

The country which imported gold would hold the gold for a year with no increase in its quantity and would forgo the possibility of planting or eating its exported corn. According to the mercantilist view, this country would be 'rich' because it possessed gold. On the other hand, the country which imported corn and increased its production would, according to mercantilists, be 'poor' because it possessed no gold.

SUMMARY

1. The pure theory of international trade has changed and developed over the centuries and many different theories currently coexist.
2. One ancient and persistent view is called the mercantilist view. Mercantilists argue that a country should encourage the export of goods and the import of gold.
3. This mercantilist view was countered by Adam Smith who advocated free trade and argued that the importation of gold is not something we should direct our trade policy towards.
4. Adam Smith argued that we would do better to export gold and import productive goods and services.

Trade increases wealth

The second thrust of Adam Smith's argument was that trade is capable of increasing the quantity of wealth available and hence trade is not *solely* a matter of allocating a fixed quantity of wealth among the various countries. In other words, trade is not entirely a competitive exercise; it is also, at least in part, co-operative.

Smith argued that some countries can produce some goods more efficiently than other countries can. This being so, we could all produce more if we each concentrated our productive efforts on the production of those goods we are best at producing.

As a simple example, we could consider the UK as capable of producing metal goods because it has the coal and the foundries. India, on the other hand, has the climate and land to produce rice.

This means that instead of the UK going to extreme lengths to produce its own rice and India trying to build up its metal-manufacturing sector, the UK should specialize in the production of metals and India should specialize in the production of rice. Having produced as much of both as we can, we then trade with each other so that we each 'consume' both metals and rice.

International trade therefore encourages efficient production and permits a varied 'diet'.

Absolute advantage

Smith's argument therefore was this. Some countries can produce certain goods quite cheaply. We should therefore arrange production so that each country produces only those goods which it can produce more cheaply than any other country can, i.e. each country specializes in the production of those goods in which it has an **absolute advantage**. This can perhaps best be illustrated by a numerical example.

Imagine two countries, say the UK and India, two goods, say metals and rice, and one factor of production, say labour. Then assume that the UK can produce a tonne of metal with 20 men, whereas India would require 40 men. On the other hand, India can produce a tonne of rice with 20 men, whereas in the UK it would require 40 men. These figures are shown in Table 19.1.

Table 19.1

	Labour requirements (workers/tonne)	
	India	**UK**
Rice	20	40
Metal	40	20

Production possibility frontiers

We can now use these figures to see how much metal and rice can be produced by each country. If we assume for the moment that there are 800 people available for this work in each country, we can see that the UK could produce either 40 tonnes of metal or 20 tonnes of rice, or some mixture of the two. India, however, can produce 20 tonnes of metal or 40 tonnes of rice, or again some mixture of the two. If we represent the quantity of rice on the vertical axis and the quantity of metal on the horizontal axis, we can show these production possibilities for each country in Figure 19.1.

When the UK devotes all its 800 workers to the production of rice it can produce 20 tonnes. If all 800 were switched to the production of metal they could make 40 tonnes. If, however, only 400 are set to grow rice and the remaining 400 are set to produce metal, they would produce at point *a* on the production possibility frontier, i.e. 10 tonnes of rice and 20 tonnes of metal.

Similarly, if India devotes 400 of its workers to producing rice they would produce 20 tonnes. The remaining 400 workers would then produce 10 tonnes of metal – point *b* on its production possibility frontier.

Autarky

Production possibility frontiers represent the range of production possibilities in each country. If there were no trade between countries then the production possibility frontiers would also represent the consumption possibility frontier. Our range of choices as to what we can consume is exactly the same as what we produce. If India devotes 400 workers to rice and 400 to metal then it produces and consumes 20 tonnes of rice and 10 tonnes of metal. This state, the state of self-sufficiency, is called **autarky**. In autarky there is no trade and no distinction between what is produced and what is consumed.

Table 19.2(a) summarizes the production and consumption occurring in the UK and in India in autarky and with equal distribution of workers between the production of rice and metal.

The last column denotes the total production of rice by both India and the UK (20 tonnes by India, 10 by the UK). Similarly for metal. India produces 10 tonnes of metal and the UK produces 20 tonnes of metal, hence total production is 30 tonnes.

The next step is to see what happens to total production when we allow trade to take place.

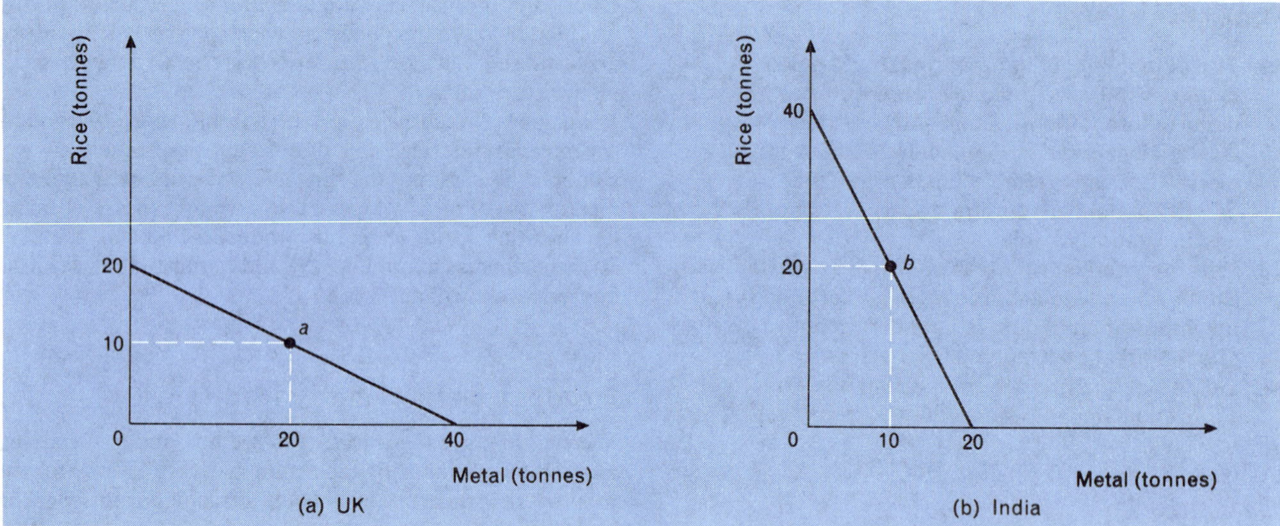

Figure 19.1 Production possibility frontiers for the UK and India.

Trade

According to Adam Smith's theory, each country should specialize in the production of that good which it produces most efficiently. We can see from the labour requirements in both countries that metal requires only 20 workers per tonne in the UK but requires 40 workers per tonne in India. In terms of the labour costs, which are the only costs in this model, we see that India produces rice cheaply and the UK produces metal cheaply.

If India specializes in rice, it can produce 40 tonnes, and if the UK specializes in metal it can produce 40 tonnes. These figures are given in Table 19.2(b). It is clear that the total production has risen from 30 tonnes of rice to 40 tonnes of rice. Metal too has risen from 30 tonnes to 40 tonnes. It seems that, as far as production is concerned, Adam Smith was right: specialize and prosper!

What remains to be done is to investigate how the 10 extra tonnes of rice and the 10 extra tonnes of metal will be distributed between India and the UK. But before turning to the 'consumption' side of trade, we have two more points to make about the 'production' side of trade. The first concerns the extension of Adam Smith's theory by David Ricardo. The second concerns the possibility that complete specialization will not always occur.

Ricardo and comparative advantage

David Ricardo, some 50 years after Adam Smith, showed that even if the UK could produce both rice and metals more efficiently than India, it would still pay both countries to specialize and trade.

Labour requirements

Let us suppose that the UK now has an absolute advantage in the production of both rice and metal. Leaving the Indian requirements unchanged, let the UK now require only 8 workers to produce a tonne of metal and 16 workers to produce a tonne of rice. The new requirements are shown in Table 19.3.

Table 19.3

	Labour requirements (workers/tonne)	
	India	UK
Rice	20	16
Metal	40	8

Table 19.2

	India production (tonnes)	UK production (tonnes)	Total production (tonnes)
(a) Before specialization			
Rice	20	10	30
Metal	10	20	30
(b) Following specialization			
Rice	40	0	40
Metal	0	40	40

Table 19.4

	India production (tonnes)	UK production (tonnes)	Total production (tonnes)	Net gain (tonnes)
(a) Before specialization				
Rice	20	25	45	–
Metal	10	50	60	–
(b) After switching 40 Indian metal workers to rice and 16 UK rice workers to metal				
Rice	22	24	46	1
Metal	9	52	61	1
(c) Final outcome				
Rice	40	15	55	10
Metal	0	70	70	10

In the UK it still takes twice as much labour to produce a tonne of rice as it would to produce a tonne of metal. But now the UK requires less labour in the production of both goods than is required in India.

Autarky

If, as before, India and the UK each devote 400 workers to the production of rice and 400 workers to the production of metals, we will have the production pattern shown in Table 19.4. With the improved efficiency of the UK's production it is now possible for the two countries to produce a total of 45 tonnes of rice and 60 tonnes of metal between them.

The scope for trade

If India and the UK do not trade then world production remains at 45 tonnes of rice and 60 tonnes of metal. With the UK's advantage in the production of both goods it would appear at first sight that India would not relish the prospect of free trade.

At present India must use up the labour of 20 workers to produce 1 tonne of rice. If trade occurs then the UK can offer rice at the cost of just 16 workers per tonne. Similarly, India must use up the labour of 40 workers per tonne of metal in comparison to the UK's cost of 20 workers per tonne.

There is scope for specialization, however. India has an absolute disadvantage in the production of both goods, but the degree of its disadvantage in rice is not so great as its disadvantage in metal. It costs India five times as much labour to produce 1 tonne of metal as it costs the UK (40 workers per tonne as compared to 8 workers per tonne). It costs India only 25 per cent more in workers per tonne to produce rice (20 workers per tonne as compared to 16 workers per tonne).

When this situation occurs India is comparatively better at producing rice than metal. India is said to have a **comparative advantage** in the production of rice. It would make sense for India to concentrate on what it is best at and so specialize in rice production.

To show the advantage of specialization in this case imagine that India transfers 40 workers from producing metal (just enough to make 1 tonne) to producing rice. Indian production of metal falls by 1 tonne, but Indian rice production rises by 2 tonnes. In the UK 16 workers are transferred from rice production (just enough to produce 1 tonne) to metal production. The UK sacrifices the production of 1 tonne of rice, but gain 2 tonnes of metal. The overall result is that there is a net world gain of 1 tonne of rice and 1 tonne of metal, just from the act of specializing. This action is summarized in Table 19.4(b).

If the process of specialization continues, with India transferring workers from metal production and the UK workers from rice production in groups equivalent to 1 tonne's production of each, then the world production of both goods rises. The process will stop when the last 40 Indian workers are transferred from metal to rice production, leaving the UK with 560 metal workers and 240 rice workers. If the UK wishes to switch more workers from rice to metal work it can, but there can be no compensating change in India because its whole workforce is already specializing in rice production. The final outcome is shown in Table 19.4(c). There has been a net gain to world production of 10 tonnes of rice and 10 tonnes of metal.

Competition and trade

The UK still produces both goods more cheaply than India, but it is still possible for trade to take place and for both sides to benefit from the process.

India could offer to buy 10 tonnes of metal from the UK in exchange for 16 tonnes of rice. To get 16 tonnes of rice the UK would need to divert 256 workers to rice production and to sacrifice 32 tonnes of metal production. Buying the Indian rice for 10 tonnes of metal is therefore a very attractive and worthwhile proposition.

For India to acquire 10 tonnes of metal it would have to transfer 400 workers from rice production to metal production. This would require India to sacrifice 20 tonnes of rice production. India therefore gains the equivalent of 4 tonnes of rice by the trade, while the UK gains the equivalent of 22 tonnes of metal.

This is just one possible trade that the two countries could make. India would be prepared to offer up to 20 tonnes of rice for 10 tonnes of metal, as this represents their internal trade-off or opportunity cost of production. The UK would offer up to 32 tonnes of metal for 16 tonnes of rice as this represents their internal opportunity cost of production. Exactly which 'price' is finally struck depends

Table 19.5

	India production (tonnes)	UK production (tonnes)	Total production (tonnes)
Rice	40	0	40
Metal	0	100	100

on the two countries' relative bargaining strengths, and if a country does not specialize completely, such as the UK in this case, then its internal price must be the world price.

The Indians are always likely to be in a difficult position because of their cost disadvantage. However, this does not mean that India will lose out in trade. As the UK does not completely specialize, it continues to buy at its internal prices. India gets all of the advantage of buying at UK prices, whereas the UK still produces some rice, in which it has a comparative disadvantage.

Trade made possible

One way that India can cause trade to occur is to value its labour at a different level to the UK. If Indian wage rates were lower than the wage rates in the UK then Indian goods could be produced at 'competitive prices'. This is the argument used by the advocates of free trade. If Indian workers produce much less than UK workers then they should receive much less. This may seem harsh, but as we see it is to the Indian workers' advantage to be able to trade internationally – the prices of what they buy will fall by more than their money income falls.

Say Indian workers received only 80 per cent of the wage of UK workers. The Indian rice would sell for 20×0.8 workers/tonne (16 workers/tonne) and UK rice would sell for 16 workers/tonne. Indian rice would therefore be capable of competing with UK rice. As for metal, Indian metal would cost 40×0.8 workers/tonne (32 workers/tonne), whereas UK metal would cost 16 workers/tonne. The UK can therefore produce metal cheaper than India. Thus when the wage rate in India is 80 per cent of that in the UK, the price of Indian rice equals the price of UK rice and so India can sell rice on the international market. It cannot, however, sell metal. It will therefore produce only rice and sell some of its rice to buy the metal it needs.

Factor immobility

As an aside we should note that, although India has a lower real income than the UK, there is no assumption that Indian workers will move to the UK. This inability of labour to move from a low-paid country to a high-paid country is another reason for studying international trade separately. There may be cultural or linguistic reasons for Indians not wanting to come to the UK, but more importantly there are political constraints on immigration.

Any wage differences within the UK would, we have learned, be signals to some workers to move out of their current employment (and/or district) into the more highly paid sector. That is what the price mechanism is about. But when these signals cross national boundaries other factors come into play. International trade recognizes these additional factors and develops its own way of handling them.

Partial specialization

Two things are immediately apparent from Table 19.4. First, the total production of rice has increased from 45 to 55 tonnes and the production of metal has increased from 60 to 70 tonnes. Second, whereas India is specializing completely in the production of rice, the UK continues to produce rice and metal. This comes about because complete specialization by both countries would leave them short of rice. We can show this by working out what would happen if both countries did specialize completely. India would produce 40 tonnes of rice and the UK would produce 100 tonnes of metal. This is shown in Table 19.5.

From Tables 19.4 and 19.5 it is clear that total rice production has fallen from 45 to 40 tonnes, and total metal production has risen from 60 to 100 tonnes. Thus, although much more metal is produced, there is insufficient rice to meet requirements. Thus, the UK cannot specialize to the full extent. It must continue to produce some rice.

Having demonstrated that specialization increases production, can we also make good our contention that Indian workers would be better off by reducing wage rates to 80 per cent of the UK wage rate?

Autarky again

Let us just consider the case of equal wages and autarky. Both Indian and UK workers receive 1 gold coin (say a 'royal') each. There are 800 workers, so the total income of India is therefore $800 \times 1 = 800$ royals. And the total income of the UK is also 800 royals. In autarky Indian workers can buy only Indian goods and so pay 20 royals for a tonne of rice and 40 royals for a tonne of metals. Each Indian worker can therefore consume 1/40 of a tonne of rice and 1/80 of a tonne of metal (which is exactly what they produce).

UK workers can buy only UK products and so pay 16 royals per tonne of rice and 8 royals per tonne of metal. Each UK worker can therefore consume 1/32 of a tonne of rice and 1/16 of a tonne of metal (again exactly what they produce). The UK workers are unambiguously better off than Indian workers.

Trade again

Now let us assume that Indian workers receive only 0.8 royals per worker and that both economies are open to trade. The national income of India is now $800 \times 0.8 = 640$ royals.

India can now acquire metal at the cheapest 'world' price of 8 royals per tonne from the UK. To buy in the same amount of metal that it had previously produced under autarky (10 tonnes), it would spend $10 \times 8 = 80$ royals on metal. This would leave the Indians 560 royals to spend on rice $(640 - 80)$.

Table 19.6

	India production (tonnes)	UK production (tonnes)
(a) Before trade		
Rice	40	20
Metal	0	60
	India consumption (tonnes)	**UK consumption (tonnes)**
(b) After trade		
Rice	35	25
Metal	10	50

Because the Indians now pay themselves 0.8 royals per worker, a tonne of rice costs 16 royals in both India and the UK. India can buy the quantity of rice it produced under autarky (20 tonnes) for 320 royals (20×16). Thus even though the Indian workers are being paid less, they can afford to buy exactly what they could before and have some money left over!

To buy 20 tonnes of rice and 10 tonnes of metal costs 400 royals ($80 + 320$) and this leaves another 240 royals of Indian national income to be allocated. We learned in Part II that markets allocate resources according to consumer 'votes'. We can see that if Indian workers decided to buy only extra rice with their spare money they would purchase 15 more tonnes of rice ($15 \times 16 = 240$) and the production–consumption pattern shown in Table 19.6 would emerge.

Thus by allowing their money wage rate to fall from 1 royal per worker to 0.8 royals per worker the Indian workers can compete with the UK in the market for rice. Thereafter they specialize in the production of rice and gain all the advantages of specialization, i.e. 15 extra tonnes of rice. In this example the dominant trading partner (the UK) gets none of the benefits from trade – all the benefits go to India.

Thus, given our numerical example, it is possible to show that the free-trade argument has something to it. 'Protection' or constraint on trade does not unambiguously benefit the weaker trading nations – in fact they may simply deprive the weak from reaping the gains from trade.

SUMMARY

1. International trade increases world production by allowing countries to specialize in the production of those goods which they most efficiently produce.
2. Even when one country is more efficient in producing both goods, trade can still be beneficial.
3. To make trade possible, the less efficient country must accept a lower money wage rate than the efficient country.
4. Even though the money wage rate falls, the real wage increases because the fall in the prices of products is greater than the fall in the money wage.
5. The gains in production, due to specialization, do not necessarily go to the more efficient producers. In our example, all the benefits go to the inefficient producer whose wage rate has fallen.
6. Complete specialization is not always the necessary outcome of free trade. Complete specialization may lead to a reduction in the production of one good – production of the other good would, of course, be greatly increased.

Comparative advantage and opportunity cost

We now try to establish more rigorously the causes of these gains in production for the case when one country is more efficient in the production of both goods.

We have seen that under the new labour requirements the UK produces both goods with less labour than India. The new production possibility frontiers for the UK and India are shown in Figure 19.2.

The UK's production possibility frontier (PPF) shows that it can produce 50 tonnes of rice or 100 tonnes of metal, or any combination along the line joining those two points. For India the maximum production of rice is 40 tonnes and of metal 20 tonnes (both countries have 800 workers).

These PPFs show that, in autarky, India can produce an additional tonne of rice only by giving up 1/2 tonne of metal (20 workers have to be switched from metals to rice production). Thus, in India, the 'cost' of producing an extra tonne of rice is the metal forgone. This we know to be the **opportunity cost** of producing rice (see Chapter 2).

By symmetry the opportunity cost of producing metal in India is 2 tonnes of rice per tonne of metal. *The slope of the PPF therefore reflects the opportunity costs for India.* They are:

1 tonne of rice per 1/2 tonne of metal
1 tonne of metal per 2 tonnes of rice

In the UK, in order to produce an extra tonne of rice, it is necessary to give up 2 tonnes of metal. This would be achieved by switching 16 workers from metal to rice production. The opportunity costs for the UK are therefore:

1 tonne of rice per 2 tonnes of metal
1 tonne of metal per 1/2 tonne of rice

All that is needed for trade to take place is that the opportunity cost of one country is different from the opportunity cost of another country. That is what is meant by **comparative advantage.** India need give up only 1/2 tonne of metal to produce a tonne of rice, whereas the UK has to give up 2 tonnes of metal to produce a tonne of rice. It follows, therefore, that India has a comparative advantage in the production of rice. The converse is also true – the UK has a comparative advantage in the production of metals.

The result of this is very simple. If the UK wants an extra tonne of rice it can either produce it itself (autarky) at the 'cost' of 2 tonnes of metal, or it can ask India to produce the rice at a cost of 1/2 tonne of metal. If India produces the

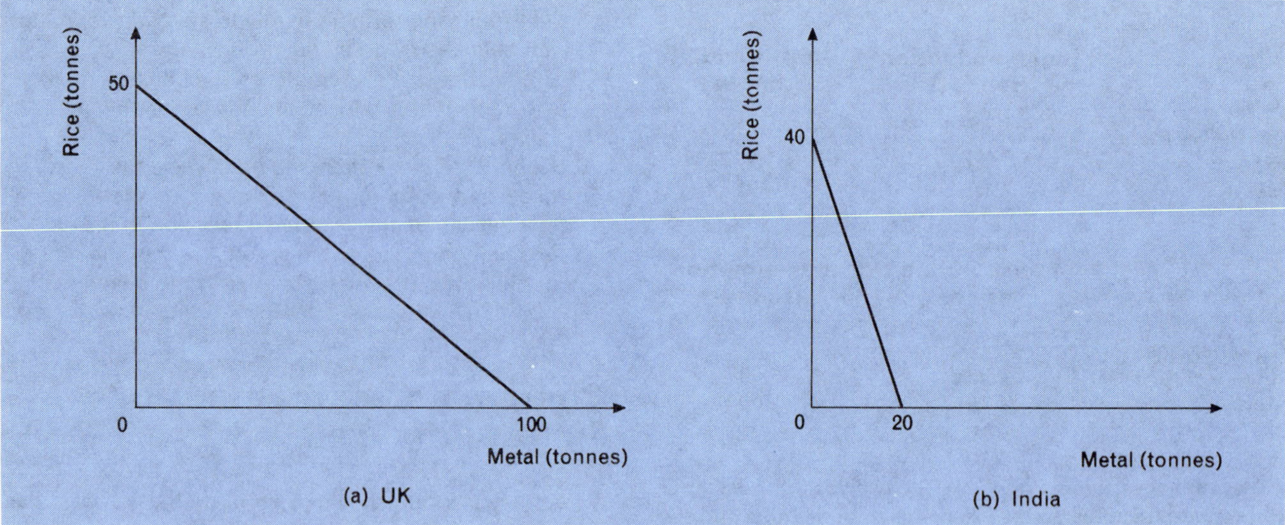

Figure 19.2 Production possibility frontiers where the UK has an absolute advantage in both goods.

additional rice, the UK must produce the metal it has lost (1/2 tonne). Both countries can therefore benefit from trade.

If India and the UK had the same opportunity costs (i.e. their PPFs had the same slopes) then they could not benefit from trade. India would have to give up just as much metal to produce a tonne of rice as the UK would. The UK might as well produce the rice itself. Trade therefore becomes irrelevant.

SUMMARY

1. Trade can result in increased world production, provided each country has a comparative advantage in the production of one good.
2. A comparative advantage can occur even when a country is less efficient at producing both goods.
3. Being less efficient in the production of both goods means having no absolute advantage.
4. A comparative advantage simply means having a differently sloped production possibility frontier.
5. The production possibility frontier represents the opportunity cost of producing each good. It shows how much of one good a country must give up if it is to produce more of another good.
6. When the opportunity costs in India are the same as in the UK, there is no benefit from specializing and hence nothing to be gained from international trade.

The costs of trade – protecting domestic industries

If this theory of comparative advantage is correct then all that is necessary for both countries to benefit from trade is that they have different opportunity costs. What then can it mean to say of a country that it cannot compete in international markets? It could mean that it has the same opportunity cost as everyone else. This is tantamount to saying that it cannot co-operate – that there is no benefit to be gained by trade. This is obviously a highly unlikely event. The chances that a country is incapable of finding anyone with different opportunity costs are not very high.

Alternatively, the claim that we cannot compete might mean that we are incapable or unwilling to reduce our labour costs sufficiently. This means that we are forgoing the possible gains from trade in order to maintain too high a money wage rate.

Declining industries

Although we have shown that specialization can improve total production, we have rather glibly assumed that 'Indian labour will switch from metal production to grow rice and UK labour will give up producing so much rice and switch to producing more metal'.

Such adjustments as this are not made costlessly, and before the Indian labour 'released' from the production of metal can be found work in the rice fields, it will face a considerable spell of unemployment. In these circumstances world production will actually fall when previously 'closed' economies are opened up to trade. Some protection for 'home' industries is therefore sometimes asked for on the grounds that it needs time to adjust. This is the declining industry argument.

Infant industries

At the other end of the scale is the infant industry argument. Some industries argue that they are too young and/or too small to produce efficiently and hence cannot yet compete internationally. If they are afforded some measure of temporary protection they will become competitive and will eventually be able to stand on their own two feet.

Both these arguments against free trade (declining industries and infant industries) are advocating only temporary protection, but we are not told what is meant by temporary. Some declining industries seem to take decades to adjust and some 'infants' remain for many years in their nurseries.

Strategic protection

An argument sometimes offered in support of a more permanent trade barrier is that it is strategically unsound to rely entirely on some other country for food or armaments, for example. Some argue that we should maintain our own nuclear power industry in order that we can produce our own nuclear deterrent. These arguments are, however, much more to do with politics than economics. As far as economic theory is concerned, the conclusions seem to favour free trade rather than protectionism.

SUMMARY

1. The mercantilists' view of wealth led them to conclude that the only good thing about trade was the possibility of importing gold. Exporting goods should therefore be encouraged and importing goods should be discouraged.
2. Adam Smith's view of wealth led him to argue that trade can be mutually beneficial by allowing each country to specialize in the production of those goods in which it has an absolute advantage.
3. David Ricardo went further and demonstrated that trade would be beneficial even when one country was more efficient in the production of all goods. All that is needed is the existence of different opportunity costs within each country, i.e. each country should specialize in the production of those goods in which it has a comparative advantage.
4. In order to benefit from trade it may be necessary for wage rates to differ between trading countries. These wage differences persist because of political barriers to the free movement of labour between countries. Lowering the money wage rate does not, however, lead to a reduced standard of living – in fact it increases living standards.
5. Specialization may not be complete if:
   (a) one country produces very much more efficiently than another;
   (b) some industries are being protected while they die;
   (c) some industries are being protected while they are young;
   (d) some industries have 'strategic' significance.
   Of these (a) is economic and long run, (b) and (c) are short run and (d) is political and long run.
6. All these arguments are aimed at demonstrating that output can be increased through trade. In the next section we shall examine the subsequent problem of 'who gets the increase?'.

Distribution of the gains from trade

In order to get an idea of what determines who gets the increased output generated by trade we will return to our numerical example used earlier in this chapter.

Under 'autarky' we had the production pattern shown in Table 19.7. This pattern output (and consumption) was achieved by each country allocating 400 workers to the production of each good.

Under 'trade' we had the pattern shown in Table 19.8. This was achieved by each country allocating all its 800 workers to the production of the good in which it had an absolute advantage. This determines who produces what (under trade), but we do not yet know who consumes what.

International prices

Imagine first that on international markets metal is exchanged for rice at a ratio of 2 tonnes of metal for every tonne of rice. (In other words, metal price is half that of rice.)

India, which produces only rice, could exchange 10 tonnes of rice for 20 tonnes of metal. The UK, of course, provides the other side of this exchange and supplies 20 tonnes of metal in return for 10 tonnes of rice. The resulting consumption by India and the UK is shown in Table 19.9.

Table 19.7

	India production (tonnes)	UK production (tonnes)	Total production (tonnes)
Rice	20	10	30
Metal	10	20	30

Table 19.8

	India production (tonnes)	UK production (tonnes)	Total production (tonnes)
Rice	40	0	40
Metal	0	40	40

Table 19.9

	India		UK		Total production (tonnes)
	Production (tonnes)	Consumption (tonnes)	Production (tonnes)	Consumption (tonnes)	
Rice	40	30	0	10	40
Metal	0	20	40	20	40

India began with 40 tonnes of rice and no metal. It traded 10 tonnes of rice for 20 tonnes of metal and so ended up consuming 30 tonnes of rice and 20 tonnes of metal. The UK, on the other hand, began with 40 tonnes of metal and no rice. It traded 20 tonnes of metal for 10 tonnes of rice and hence ended up consuming 10 tonnes of rice and 20 tonnes of metal.

Comparing Table 19.9 with the autarky in Table 19.7, we see that UK consumption is the same under trade as it was under autarky. The UK therefore has none of the benefits of trade. India, on the other hand, has increased its consumption of rice from 20 tonnes to 30 tonnes and increased its consumption of metal from 10 tonnes to 20 tonnes. Thus all the benefits of trade (10 tonnes of metal and 10 tonnes of rice) accrue to India. Let us now see what happens if we call out a different international price ratio.

A different price

Taking the same model as before, we will now assume that on the international market 1 tonne of metal will exchange for 2 tonnes of rice (i.e. metal price is now twice that of rice).

Under these prices let India offer to exchange 20 tonnes of rice for 10 tonnes of metal. The UK again provides the 10 tonnes of metal for 20 tonnes of rice. The production and consumption patterns would then be as shown in Table 19.10.

Comparing this table with that for autarky, we see that now it is the UK which has all the benefits of trade. India consumes 20 tonnes of rice and 10 tonnes of metal whether in autarky or trading. (India's *production* does, however, change as it moves from autarky to trade.) The UK consumes 20 tonnes of rice with trade, compared with 10 tonnes under autarky, and 30 tonnes of metal, compared with 20 tonnes under autarky.

Terms of trade

What we have demonstrated is that at one international price ratio (2 tonnes of metal to 1 tonne of rice) India gets all the benefits, whereas at another international price ratio (2 tonnes of rice to 1 tonne of metal) the UK gets all the benefits. This international price ratio is the price of our exports divided by the price of our imports and is called our **terms of trade**.

In our model India's terms of trade would be the price of rice divided by the price of metal. And the UK's terms of trade would be the price of metal divided by the price of rice.

Although production can be increased by specialization, therefore, this increase has to be divided up. The first part of the specialization exercise is co-operative. Countries can agree where their comparative advantages lie and, by specializing in the production of the goods in which they have a comparative advantage, can between them increase total production.

But the second part of the exercise (determining the terms of trade) is not a co-operative but a competitive exercise. When the terms of trade give us the benefits of trade they are said to be in our favour. It is the terms of trade which determine how the production gains from trade are distributed among countries.

Terms of trade and opportunity cost

You may have noticed that the two terms of trade chosen for our example (2 of metal for 1 of rice and then 2 of rice for 1 of metal) happen to be the opportunity cost of producing in the UK and in India respectively.

In the UK (under autarky) 2 tonnes of metal exchange for 1 tonne of rice. On the other hand, in India (under autarky) 1 tonne of metal exchanges for 2 tonnes of rice.

Our choice of these two terms of trade was not arbitrary. The fact is that *if a country's terms of trade are the same as its autarky price ratio (opportunity cost) then that country cannot benefit from trade.* It could either produce both goods in the quantities it needed or it could specialize in the production of only one good and exchange it for the other good required. In either case it would be exactly as well off as the other.

Our examples show that when the terms of trade were

Table 19.10

	India		UK		Total production (tonnes)
	Production (tonnes)	Consumption (tonnes)	Production (tonnes)	Consumption (tonnes)	
Rice	40	20	0	20	40
Metal	0	10	40	30	40

Table 19.11

	India		UK		Total production (tonnes)
	Production (tonnes)	Consumption (tonnes)	Production (tonnes)	Consumption (tonnes)	
Rice	40	25	0	15	40
Metal	0	15	40	25	40

identical with the UK's autarky price ratio then the UK received no benefit from trade and India got it all. When the terms of trade were identical with India's autarky price ratio, India failed to benefit from trade and all the benefits went to the UK.

We conclude from this that, in order for both countries to gain from trade, the terms of trade must lie somewhere between the autarky price ratios.

Let us examine the case where the terms of trade are 1 tonne of rice for 1 tonne of metal. With this international price ratio let India offer 15 tonnes of rice for 15 tonnes of metal. (Conversely, of course, the UK supplies 15 tonnes of metal for 15 tonnes of rice.) The new production–consumption patterns would be as shown in Table 19.11.

Comparing the figures in Table 19.11 with those in Table 19.7 (the autarky case), it is clear that the consumption of rice has gone up in both India and the UK by 5 tonnes each. The consumption of metals has also risen by 5 tonnes in each country.

Thus *when the terms of trade lie exactly between the autarky price ratios of India and the UK, the gains from trade are shared equally between them.*

The UK's terms of trade

The terms of trade are calculated for the UK and published by the Central Statistical Office. If the terms of trade stay more or less constant over time then they are unlikely to attract much attention from economists or policy makers. If they do show signs of being variable then we may well direct some effort at influencing them.

The terms of trade are usually expressed as an index number, as in Table 19.12. In this case the terms of trade are found by the formula:

$$\frac{\text{Index of average price of exports}}{\text{Index of average price of imports}} \times 100$$

We can see that the UK terms of trade do fluctuate but between 1981 and 1990 they remained remarkably steady.

To see what this means we could consider a case in which UK visible trade was in balance. This means that the value of UK exports of goods equalled the value of UK imports of goods. We can write this as:

$$\text{Quantity of exports} \times \text{Price of exports} = \text{Quantity of imports} \times \text{Price of imports}$$

This can be rewritten as:

$$\frac{\text{Price of exports}}{\text{Price of imports}} = \frac{\text{Quantity of imports}}{\text{Quantity of exports}}$$

The left-hand side of this equation is the 'terms of trade' and when they move in our favour the left-hand side of the equation increases. If the left-hand side of the equation increases then, in order to maintain our visible trade balance, we have to increase the right-hand side of the equation too. This means that we can increase our imports and/or decrease our exports. In either case we will be better off. In the first case we have more imports to consume without having to pay any more for them in terms of exports. And in the second case we can keep more of our own production for our own use.

An increase in the terms of trade therefore means an increase in the ratio of real imports to real exports, with no worsening in the visible trade balance. It is somewhat strange then that more is not made of this influence on our welfare in economic and political debates.

SUMMARY

1. Comparative advantage determines who produces what when trade is permitted.
2. The benefits of trade accrue from increased consumption rather than increased production.
3. To see who benefits most from trade, it is therefore necessary to see who consumes the extra goods.
4. This is determined by the relative prices of the two goods on the international market.
5. The price of our exports divided by the price of our imports is called our terms of trade.
6. When our terms of trade equal our opportunity costs, we gain nothing from international trade.
7. Our terms of trade equal our opportunity costs when the prices under trade equal the prices under autarky.
8. When our terms of trade move away from our opportunity cost, they are said to move in our favour and against our trading partners.
9. The determination of our terms of trade is therefore a competitive rather than a co-operative exercise.

Table 19.12 UK terms of trade, 1981–90 (1985 = 100)

Year	1981	1982	1983	1984	1985	1986	1987	1988	1989	1990
Terms of trade	103.4	101.9	100.8	99.7	100.0	94.6	95.9	97.2	97.9	99.5

Source: *Economic Trends.*

Protection

As we have seen, there are a number of reasons why countries wish to protect their home industries. Some of the reasons for protection are political, but there are economic arguments too. One economic reason for restricting trade is to push the terms of trade in one's own favour by imposing a tax on imports. A tax on imports is called a **tariff**.

Tariffs

A tariff is a tax imposed on a specific good that is imported into a country. The tariff will make the imported goods more expensive so that domestically produced brands of the good are more competitive. This will protect domestic industry. The tariff will also affect the terms of trade by causing import prices to rise.

Suppose that the UK has an absolute disadvantage in the production of rice. The UK market for rice is shown in Figure 19.3. If there is autarky then the market price for rice is £20 per tonne and UK production is 100 tonnes. If trade occurs then UK consumers will be able to buy Indian rice. We will assume that India is prepared to supply rice at £10 per tonne. The Indian price is the 'world' market price, and UK consumers may buy as much as they wish at this price.

Figure 19.3 shows that UK consumers will wish to buy 150 tonnes of rice when the price is £10 per tonne. UK growers will supply only a portion of this, 50 tonnes, because they are unable profitably to supply any more. This is shown where the world price line crosses the domestic market supply curve. In effect, trade has caused the market supply curve to become *SAB*.

When trade occurs UK production falls to 50 tonnes and UK consumption rises to 150 tonnes with the difference, 100 tonnes, being imported. This will inevitably involve job losses in the UK rice industry. The government may therefore feel that it would like to limit India's price advantage.

A possible solution is to impose a tariff, say of £5 per tonne, on rice imported into the UK. The effect of such a tax is shown in Figure 19.4 The new supply curve is *SCD* because the world price plus the tariff is £15. Overall UK demand will fall to 125 tonnes and UK firms will be able to supply 75 tonnes of this profitably. Imports are therefore cut to 50 tonnes, and instead of being halved the UK rice industry can remain at three-quarters of its original size.

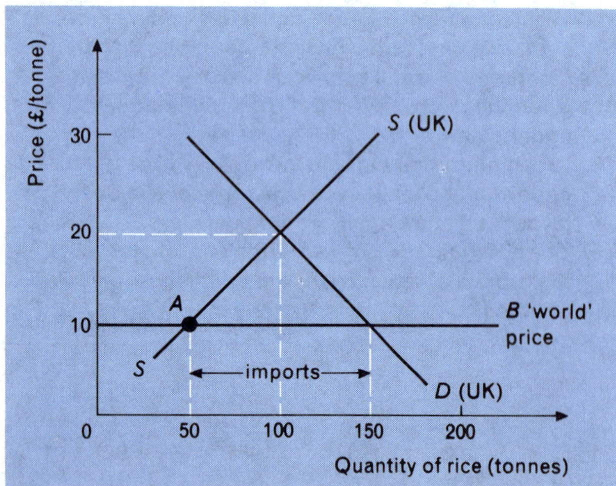

Figure 19.3 UK rice market.

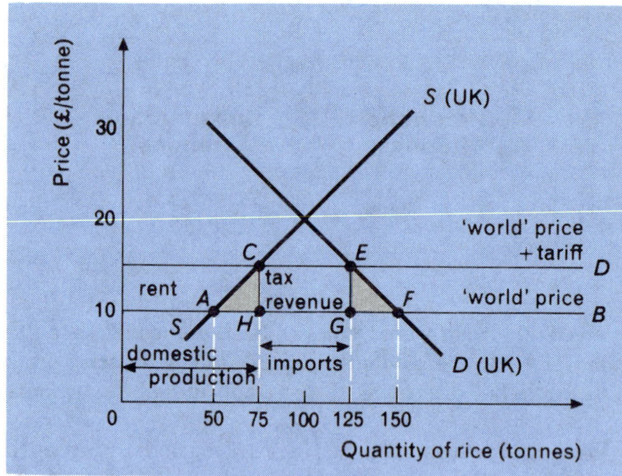

Figure 19.4 Effect of a tariff on the UK rice market.

Effect of imposing a tariff

The most obvious effect of a tariff is to reduce trade between India and the UK. As we have seen earlier in the chapter, trade allows specialization and benefits at least one trading partner, but usually both. Imposing a tariff causes some of these gains to be lost because it reduces the scope for specialization.

We can show the extent of the loss in Figure 19.4. The raising of the market price to £15 causes a direct loss of consumer surplus. Before consumers could purchase rice at £10 a tonne, but they must now pay £15 per tonne. The area marked 'rent' in Figure 19.4 goes directly to firms in the form of extra profits or economic rent. The area *CEGH* is equivalent to the amount of tax collected by the government from the tariff. This is transferred to government funds. The government may use the revenue from the tariff for the benefit of the population and so it may not be totally lost. The areas *CHA* and *EFG* are transferred to nobody and are lost to society. These losses are called **deadweight losses**.

One problem with using tariffs is that they may invite retaliation. If the UK can use tariffs to move the terms of trade in its own favour then India may well impose a tariff on its imports. This will push the terms of trade back to the original level.

The net result of this double imposition of tariffs would be to leave the terms of trade unaltered but to reduce the amounts traded. It is therefore disadvantageous to both countries. It is possible that in the complexity of the real world the tariffs continue to be imposed by one country on another until world trade is dramatically reduced (a trade war) and all of the benefits of specialization are lost.

Other methods of protection

Tariffs are but one of the methods employed by countries to try and favour domestic industries. Other methods range from the simple prohibition of a product (an embargo) to the infinitely cunning 'health restriction' or 'safety measure' that prevents the entry of foreign goods without causing the conflict that other measures involve.

Let us now look briefly at some other methods of protection.

Export subsidies

These work in the reverse way to a tariff. Firms are paid a subsidy or exempted from a tax in order to encourage them to produce more and to export. The effect of an export subsidy is shown in Figure 19.5.

Figure 19.5 shows the UK market for metal. The world price is £30 per tonne, and so the UK sells 70 tonnes of metal in the UK and exports 20 tonnes to India. The government then offers a subsidy of £5 per tonne on all metal exported. This raises the price the firms receive to £35 on all exports, but means they will receive only £30 per tonne for domestic sales.

As no firm wishes to sell to one customer at a lower price than it could get elsewhere, UK firms raise the UK price to £35 and sell only 50 tonnes of metal in the UK. At the price of £35 per tonne firms wish to supply 100 tonnes of metal and so 50 tonnes are exported

There is a loss of consumer welfare equivalent to triangles *ABC* and *DEF*. *ABC* represents the loss of consumer surplus; *DEF* the extra costs of production over the world price.

Exchange controls

One way to prevent people from buying foreign goods is to deny them the foreign currency they need to pay foreign firms. A firm in India will require payment in rupees, and to obtain rupees a UK firm would have to exchange pounds for rupees. If the government controls these foreign exchange dealings, it can prevent imports from India by stopping UK firms from converting pounds into rupees. Of course, this policy could also be operated by India and so overall world trade would be lower. Many countries do impose exchange controls, particularly Third World countries such as Nigeria. Within the European Community all such controls should have been abolished by the end of 1991.

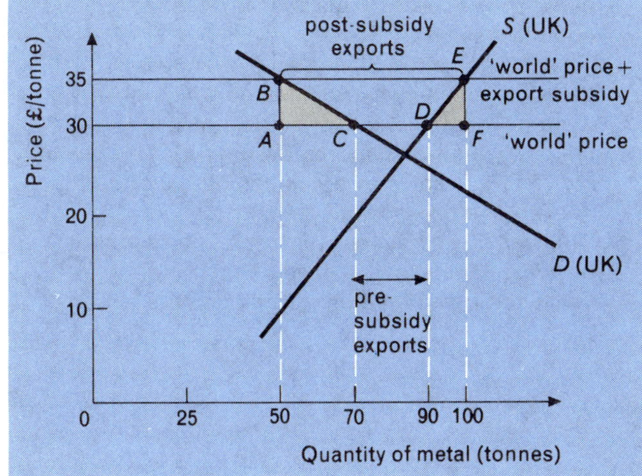

Figure 19.5 Effect of a export subsidy on the UK metal market.

Quotas

A **quota** sets a maximum volume or value on a particular class of imports rather than controlling its price. An example might be the UK setting a limit on Indian rice imports of 50 tonnes a year.

Quotas can be imposed or sometimes negotiated. The UK and European Community have negotiated import quotas with the Japanese on the number of cars they may export to Europe. The Japanese response has been to build cars in Europe, which is a very satisfactory solution for Europe. This need not be the case, however, and may again lead to retaliation and a general reduction in world trade.

Embargoes

An embargo is a complete ban on the import of a product. It could be placed, for example, on Indian metal, and it would then be illegal to import this good into the UK. Embargoes are difficult to maintain as there is often an incentive to break the law – for example, in the importing of drugs.

Embargoes are fairly drastic and rarely occur in modern times except on health grounds, e.g. if food is believed to be contaminated. More common is an export embargo, on such goods as nuclear fuel or weapons.

Non-tariff barriers

Under this heading we can group health and safety restrictions, customs procedures, red tape and 'national standards'. To those not involved in trade such matters may seem trivial, but they represent the single largest obstacle to trade between industrialized countries.

Non-tariff barriers raise the costs of importing firms considerably, and so prevent foreign firms competing with domestic firms. For example, altering the design of only a small proportion of a production run so that they conform to local safety standards adds a great deal to costs. Similarly, waiting at customs posts for several hours or even days adds to transport costs sufficiently to destroy many firms' cost advantage.

Non-tariff barriers are discussed more fully in Chapter 24, but their effect is to reduce the opportunity for trade and so the extent of specialization.

Attempts to trade freely

In order to control and moderate this tendency towards mutually damaging trade restrictions some countries make agreements not to impose penalties on each other's goods.

The **General Agreement on Tariffs and Trade (GATT)** is such a pact and the **Economic Community (EC)** is another. In the latter case the countries within the community agree not to impose tariffs on each other, but jointly impose tariffs on non-members. This is virtually a

Case Study 19.1 A tangled web

As part of the Uruguay round of trade talks due to end in December, officials of the General Agreement on Tariffs and Trade (GATT) hope to abolish the western world's 16-year-old controls on third-world textile and clothing imports, known as the Multi-fibre Arrangement (MFA). But this network of bilateral quotas is turning into one of the most contentious subjects on the Uruguay agenda. And, as so often, America is the cause of the trouble.

When the MFA was set up in 1974 (as a broader successor to previous deals dating back to 1961), it was supposed to be a temporary affair. GATT then decided that developed countries should be allowed time to adjust to the surge of cheap imports. Now after three extensions, the MFA is more restrictive than ever.

According to a study sponsored by the World Bank and published in March, the abolition of the MFA could allow developing countries to increase their yearly exports by $8 billion, though they might lose some $2 billion in 'quota rents', the revenue gained through the higher prices available in protected markets. Countries such as Bangladesh that are trying to build up their textile industries and have small quotas, should benefit most.

Rich countries' consumers would clearly gain. So too would overall employment in rich countries, claims a recent study (conducted in Britain) by Professor Aubrey Silberston, of Imperial College, London, despite a drop in textile jobs. And though the American and European textile-makers loudly dispute such claims, even they are ready to see the MFA fade away, largely because automation and moves up-market have made them more competitive.

What is hotly disputed is how to make the change. The many proposals put forward have now been whittled down to two:

- A slow phase-out of the MFA through agreed annual percentage increases in quotas, until they become so large as to be redundant. This has the backing of the EC and most developing countries.
- The Americans in December 1989 proposed the replacement of the MFA with a system of 'global quotas': importers in the rich countries would each be allocated a quota, which they could use as they chose.

The phase-out would be simple, and at the end of it textiles and clothing would come under GATT rules. But the Americans argue – correctly – that a phase-out would continue the discrimination against those third-world countries that now have small export quotas. The American scheme would be more complicated, but it would be fairer and allow the immediate introduction of competition. What the Americans fail to say is that their scheme would be more restrictive than the MFA because it would apply to all the textile imports of rich countries, including those from other rich countries. In other words, quota walls all round.

The negotiators are nowhere near a settlement. The Americans have been touting their protectionist scheme around the third world; with little success, it seems. The risk is that, if they continue to push it, irritated third-world countries will dig their heels on other pressing issues in the Uruguay round.

1. What type of protection does the MFA represent, and who does it 'protect'?

Source: *The Economist*, 5 May 1990

customs union (a Zollverein) and may be regarded as a club of some countries acting in its own interests and against the interests of 'outsiders'. Alternatively it could be thought of as a step on the road to completely free trade. This would happen by the formation of a number of 'common markets', all of which would eventually merge together.

The principle purpose of GATT is to bring about successive reductions of tariffs worldwide. It is a 'general' agreement rather than one between a few countries. By working towards reductions in tariffs it too will eventually result in a tariff-free world market. International organizations of this type are dealt with in rather more detail in Chapter 23.

SUMMARY

1. In this chapter we have developed the arguments in favour of free trade and contrasted them with the mercantilist arguments for trade restrictions. Once again, we see that fairly simple economic theory yields useful insights into attitudes and policy arguments surrounding international trade.
2. All that is needed for trade to increase production is that the countries concerned have different opportunity costs. This is the law of comparative advantage.
3. The gains from trade are distributed between partners according to the terms of trade. This is the ratio of export prices to import prices, and the larger the difference between the terms of trade and a country's autarky price ratio, the more it benefits from trade. Autarky is the case of complete self-sufficiency.
4. The determination of the terms of trade is therefore an allocative and hence competitive matter. One way of influencing them is by imposing a tax on imports (i.e. a tariff). This will restrict trade and may precipitate tit-for-tat tariffs to everyone's disadvantage.
5. This has given rise to a number of international organizations aimed at developing trade co-operation and reducing impediments to trade.

Exam Preparation and Practice

MULTIPLE-CHOICE QUESTIONS

1.

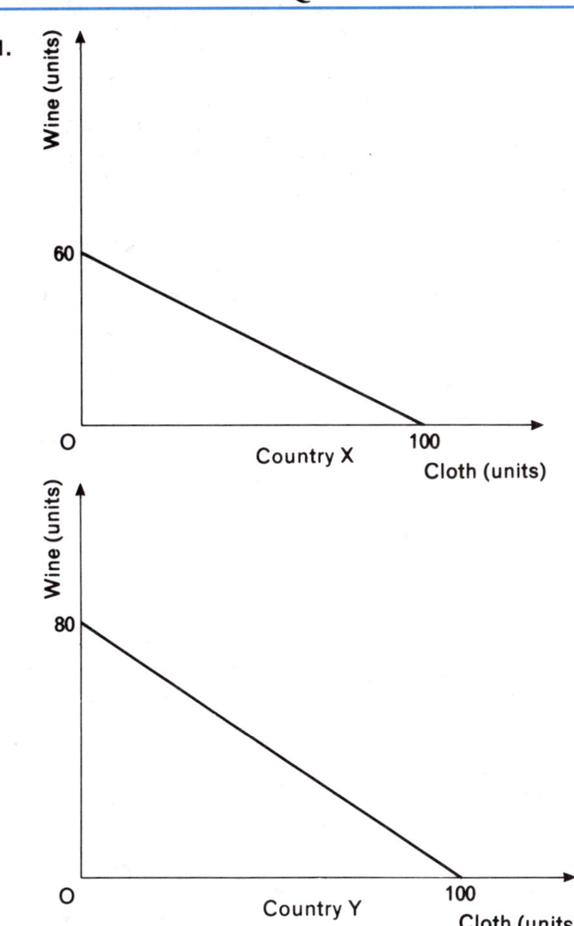

The diagrams show the production possibility frontiers for two countries X and Y. According to the theories of comparative advantage:

A Country X has an absolute advantage in the production of both goods.
B Country Y has a comparative advantage in both goods.
C Country X cannot gain from trade.
D Country X should specialize in cloth production.

2. According to the theory of comparative advantage, no international trade will take place when:
A One country has an absolute advantage in the production of all goods.
B The terms of trade exactly match domestic production costs.
C Transport costs are taken into account.
D One country has a comparative advantage in the production of all goods.

3. The gains from international trade will be divided equally between two countries when:
A The terms of trade lie directly between the two countries' domestic opportunity cost of production.
B The terms of trade are identical to the domestic opportunity cost of production.
C The two countries produce the same goods.
D The two countries have identical workforces and wage packets.

4. The table shows the domestic prices of two products X and Y produced in the United Kingdom and United States of America.

	Good X	Good Y
United Kingdom	£1	£2
United States of America	$2	$5

If transport costs are zero and there are constant returns to scale in both countries, which exchange rate would result in an exchange of goods?
A £1 = $1.00
B £1 = $2.00
C £1 = $2.25
D £1 = $5.00 (AEB)

5. In 1991 a country's index of average price of exports stands at 110 and its index of average price of imports stands at 100. In 1992 the index of import prices rises by 25%. The country's terms of trade index moves from:
A 100 to 125
B 110 to 114
C 110 to 125
D 110 to 88

6. A 'favourable' movement in the terms of trade means that average export prices must have:
A Risen relative to average import prices.
B Risen.
C Fallen.
D Fallen relative to import prices.

Questions 7 and 8 refer to the diagram below.

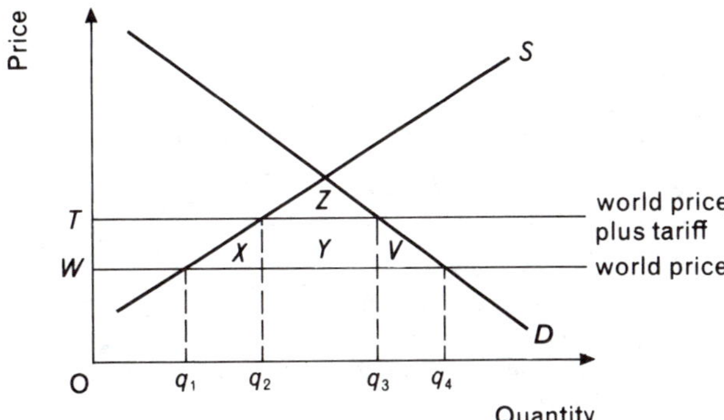

The curve *D* represents domestic demand for the product, the curve *S* domestic supply.

7. On the imposition of an import tariff on the good equal to *WT*, which level of output represents domestic demand?
A $0q_1$
B $0q_2$
C $0q_3$
D $0q_4$

8. Which area of the diagram represents government tax revenue?
A *Y*
B *X*+*Y*
C *X*+*Y*+*Z*
D *Z*+*Y*
E *X*+*Y*+*Z*

Answer key

Where there are three numbered alternatives

A	B	C	D	E
1, 2, 3 Correct	1, 2 Correct	2, 3 Correct	1 Correct	3 Correct

Where there are four numbered alternatives

A	B	C	D	E
1, 2 and 3 Correct	1 and 3 Correct	2 and 4 Correct	4 only Correct	1 and 4 Correct

9.

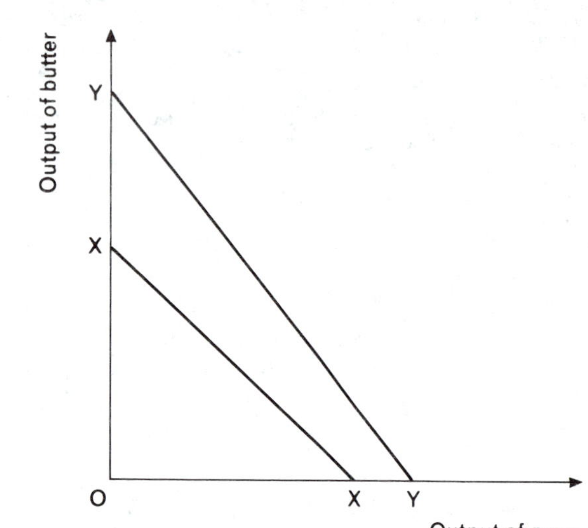

In the diagram XX and YY represent the production possibility boundaries of two countries, X and Y respectively. Each country produces only two goods, guns and butter. From the information provided it can be deduced that

1 country X has comparative advantage in the production of guns.

2 country Y has absolute advantage in the production of both guns and butter.

3 in the absence of international trade, country Y will have a higher real income per head than country X. (LON.)

10. The following table relates to the output per worker in two countries A and B for two products, coal and wheat.

	Coal	Wheat
Country A	20	30
Country B	10	20

Which of the following statements is (are) true?

1 Country A has a comparative advantage in the production of coal and will export it to country B.

2 Country A has a comparative advantage in the production of wheat and will export it to country B.

3 Country A has a comparative advantage in the production of both coal and wheat and will export both to country B.

11. Which of the following policies would move the terms of trade in the favour of a country imposing them?

1 Export subsidies.

2 Quotas.

3 Exchange controls.

4 Tariffs.

EXERCISES

1. Imagine that the world consists of just two countries, Southland and Northway. Each country can produce two goods, cloth and wine. The labour requirements for each country are as shown in the table.

	Southland	Northway
Wine	2 workers/barrel	4 workers/barrel
Cloth	8 workers/bolt	10 workers/bolt

Each country has an available labour force of 800 workers.

(a) If there is no trade (autarky) and each country splits its workforce equally between the two products how much wine and cloth is produced (i) in each country, (ii) in the 'world'?

(b) Does Northway have a comparative advantage in the production of either good. If yes, which?

(c) Trade now occurs. An exchange rate of 3 barrels of wine to 1 bolt of cloth is established. Northway produces only cloth and exports 40 bolts to Southland. Southland produces 360 barrels of wine. How much cloth does Southland produce?

(d) Has world output risen as a result of specialization?

(e) How much wine does Northway import?

(f) Can it be said that both countries have benefited from trade?

2. Below are details of the labour requirements and working populations of three pairs of trading nations.

	Eastplace	Westbottom
Oranges	20 workers/tonne	30 workers/tonne
Bicycles	5 workers/bicycle	3 workers/bicycle

Each country has a workforce of 300 workers.

	Noplace	Elsewhere
Chocolate	60 workers/tonne	30 workers/tonne
Umbrellas	20 workers/gross	15 workers/gross

Each country has a workforce of 600 workers.

	Byway	Highway
Cars	120 workers/car	60 workers/car
Coffee	24 workers/tonne	20 workers/tonne

Byway has a workforce of 240. Highway has a workforce of 720.

(a) Draw the production possibility frontiers for each trading pair.

(b) Would trade be possible in all three cases?

(c) What would be the most in terms of oranges that Westbottom would pay for bicycles?

(d) In which good would Noplace specialize if trade occurred?

(e) Will Byway always be dominated by Highway?

(f) What is the opportunity cost of:

(i) oranges in terms of bicycles in Westbottom?

(ii) oranges in terms of bicycles in Eastplace?

(iii) cars in terms of coffee in Highway?

(iv) coffee in terms of cars in Highway?

3. (a) Calculate the terms of trade for each of the following countries:

(i) Westbottom – Index price of exported bicycles 100
Index price of imported oranges 120

(ii) Elsewhere – Index price of exported chocolate 125
Index price of imported umbrellas 95

(b) Calculate the terms of trade for Westbottom following a 10 per cent rise in the average export price of bicycles when the price of oranges remains the same. Have the terms of trade 'improved' or worsened for Westbottom? Explain your answer.

4. The diagram below shows the market for cars in a country that trades with the rest of the world. The curves D_c and S_c are the

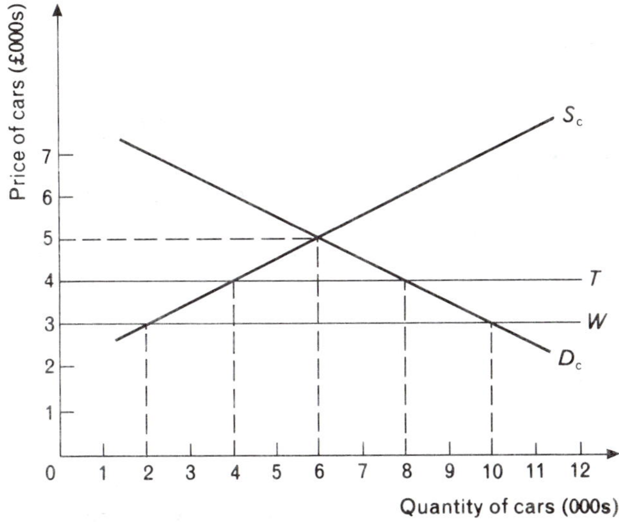

country's domestic demand and supply curves respectively. The world price for cars is *OW*.

(a) If there were no trade, how many cars would be produced domestically and at what price would they each be sold?

(b) If trade takes place, what will be:
   (i) the price at which cars will be offered for sale?
   (ii) the domestic production of cars?
   (iii) the total domestic consumption of cars?
   (iv) the quantity of cars imported?

(c) The country imposes a tariff on cars equivalent to *WT*. What is:
   (i) the new price of cars within the country?
   (ii) the new level of domestic car production?
   (iii) the new domestic consumption of cars?
   (iv) the new quantity of cars imported?

(d) Imposing a tariff brings both costs and benefits.
   (i) What is the value and type of gain made by domestic car producers?
   (ii) What is the value of the gain made for government revenue?
   (iii) What is the value and type of loss to domestic consumers?

DATA-RESPONSE QUESTION

1. The following are extracts from an article by G. Searjeant published in *The Times* on April 7th, 1987. Read it carefully, then answer the questions which follow. **N.B.** Reference is made to the words underlined in questions *(b)–(e)* below.

Dangerous Fallacies in Bilateral Trade

The phoney trade war with Japan is ultimately neither about Japanese telephone utilities nor financial services, the battleground to hand, but the deficit in visible trade. Sanctions face tiresome arguments over international law and self interest. But there has been little challenge to the justice of this complaint. It is based on two assumptions:

1. It must be bad for Britain to have a continuing trade deficit with Japan (or any other country for that matter).
2. Bilateral imbalances are unnatural and must therefore be caused by unfair practices or unequal treatment by the country with the surplus.

Both assumptions are as old as trade itself and both are completely false. Adam Smith in his eighteenth century attack on mercantilism reserved particular anger for the "absurd" doctrine that trade between individual countries should balance. David Hume attacked the "jealousy of trade" denouncing the tendency of nations "to look on the progress of their neighbours with a suspicious eye, to consider all trading states as their rivals and to suppose that it is impossible for any of them to flourish but at their expense".

Smith and Hume have always carried the argument: they have rarely carried the people for long. The present US Congress revels in "the jealousy of trade". In Britain the Sun newspaper for instance, claims that Japan has made "a £3.7 billion profit" from trade with Britain and that the threat this poses to the country "is every bit as deadly as the invasion of the Falklands".

For bilateral trade to balance except by coincidence, is quite unnatural. We should expect it only where trade is arranged by government deals, such as with Communist countries. Britain has had a positive overall balance on its current account in seven of the past ten years and a net balance of £20 billion over the decade. Over the same period Britain has had a large deficit with Japan rising to £3.7 billion in 1986, but as it happens that is not Britain's biggest deficit; last year we had a deficit of £5.5 billion with West Germany. Fortunately there is presently little clamour for a trade war with Germany – though there was when Germany was the fastest rising economic power before the 1914–18 war.

This tells us much about the current clamour against Japan. Admittedly British exports to Japan are proportionately much lower than to Germany. Yet there is little evidence to show that Japan's trade policies although protectionist in general are specifically unfair to Britain.

To the protectionist coalition any trade benefits to other countries are suspicious. Japan's huge trade surpluses certainly present problems. But trade is good for all. Arguments about bilateral balances are merely pretexts to hide the somewhat differing interests of consumers and producers. Consumers should not allow producers to fox them with fallacies.

(a) On the basis of the evidence cited in the article, why is it illogical for Britain to complain about a bilateral trade deficit with Japan? [5]

(b) Do you agree that "for bilateral trade to balance except by coincidence, is quite unnatural"? [5]

(c) Do you agree with the author that "trade is good for all" or with the doctrine (attacked by Hume) that a country can flourish by trade only at the expense of other countries? [5]

(d) What do you consider is meant by the statement that "arguments about bilateral balances are merely pretexts to hide the somewhat differing interests of consumers and producers"? [5]

(e) Why do you think it is that although "Smith and Hume have always carried the argument: they have rarely carried the people for long"? [5]

(WJEC)

20 The balance of payments

In this chapter we will discuss:

1. How international trade transactions are recorded.
2. How the pattern of UK trade has changed over recent times.

Introduction

So far, in this part of the book, we have dealt with 'real' trade – that is, the flow of goods and services between countries. In this chapter we shall be looking not at the flow of goods and services, but at the monetary value of these flows.

The statistics on international trade are drawn together to produce the **balance of payments** accounts, a complete record of the exports and imports of goods and services and capital flows. Because of the nature of trade in goods and services and the flows of capital it is traditional to look at them separately.

Measuring international trade transactions

Balance of trade

If we think of the Indian–UK trade example we used in Chapter 19, we can identify two types of flow. The first is the flow of physical goods: rice leaves India for the UK, and metal leaves the UK for India. The second flow is the monetary payments made by citizens of the UK to Indian farmers for the rice they import, and the payment of Indian nationals to UK firms for the metal products they import.

If we assume that there is only one medium of exchange, say gold, then gold acts as the medium of exchange both within and between countries. This means that when India buys metal from the UK it pays for the metal in gold. The amount of gold flowing from India to the UK will be equal to the quantity of metal (Q_m) imported from India multiplied by its price in gold (P_m).

Similarly, when the UK buys rice from India it too will pay in gold. The quantity of gold flowing to India from the UK will be the quantity of rice imported multiplied by its price in gold ($Q_r \times P_r$).

Clearly, then, some gold will flow out of India to the UK ($Q_m \times P_m$) and some gold will flow out of the UK to India ($Q_r \times P_r$). If these two amounts are equal (i.e. if the value of imports equals the value of exports) then neither country actually loses or gains any gold – inflows equal outflows. This is called a balance of trade.

It is, however, possible for India to export more than it imports. By this we mean that the gold value of India's exports is greater than the gold value of its imports. If the UK and India trade only between themselves, the UK must import more goods than it exports (valued in gold). In this case India is said to have a trade surplus (exports greater than imports) and the UK has a trade deficit (imports greater than exports).

Balance of payments

Since the outflow of gold from the UK now exceeds the inflow of gold, the UK is losing gold to India. In other words, the UK's trade deficit is paid for by exporting gold from the UK. Thus the gold exported to India plus the value of metals exported to India will always equal the value of rice imported into the UK. Payments in must always equal payments out. This is why it is said that the *balance of payments must always balance*. Any deficit (or surplus) on the balance of trade must be exactly offset by a payment of gold. The trade part of the balance of payments is called the current account. The gold part of the balance of payments is called the capital account. Thus a deficit on the trade account (current account) is always offset by a surplus on the capital account and vice versa.

UK balance of payments

The model we have used is deliberately simple, but it does reflect the more complicated picture of UK trade very well. The UK trades in many different goods with many different countries, but each trade can be accounted for individually as in the two-country, two-good model. Adding up all of the international trades would give us the aggregate inflows and outflows and so the balance of trade and balance of payments.

A further complication is that there is not just one medium of exchange. The UK uses the pound sterling for its internal trade, but India uses rupees, France francs and so on. The UK balance of payments is a record of the UK's international transactions in any one year; therefore we value all transactions in sterling. (How foreign currency values are translated into sterling is discussed in Chapters 21 and 22.)

The UK balance of payments is presented in a similar

Table 20.1 Structure of the UK balance of payments accounts

Current account
1. Visible balance (visible exports – visible imports) the **balance of trade**
plus
2. Invisible balance (invisible exports – invisible imports) (services; interest, profits and dividends; and transfers)
equals
3. **Current balance** (visible balance + invisible balance)

Capital account
4. Transactions in UK assets and liabilities
4a. UK external assets
plus
4b. UK external liabilities
equals
Net transactions

Current account
plus
Capital account
plus
5. Balancing item (an allowance for errors and omissions)
equals
Zero: 'the balance of payments always balances'

way to that described in the two-country example above. There is a current account which records the value of the flows of goods and services, and a capital account which records the financial transactions. In Table 20.1 the method of compiling the UK balance of payments is shown.

SUMMARY

1. The balance of payments records the monetary value of the flow of internationally traded goods and services.
2. For each international transaction of goods and services there is a compensating monetary flow to pay for the goods.
3. If a country exports (imports) more goods and services than it imports (exports) then it is said to have a balance of trade surplus (deficit).
4. The balance of payments accounts are made up of two parts:
   (a) The current account – the record of the flow of goods and services.
   (b) The capital account – the record of the flow of financial assets.

The structure of UK balance of payments accounts

Current account

The current account is the record of all transactions of current purchases of goods and services. A division is made between **visible trade** and **invisible trade**.

Table 20.2 UK current account, 1988 (£ million)

Visible trade		
Exports	80,602	
Imports	101,428	
Visible balance		−20,826
Invisible trade		
Services (balance)		4,186
Interest, profits and dividends		5,513
Transfers		−3,545
Current balance		−14,672

Source: *Monthly Digest of Statistics.*

The visible balance (item 1 in Table 20.1) is the difference between the value of tangible goods exported and the value of tangible goods imported. This then is a record of the trade in goods such as metal and rice, although in reality many thousands of goods are traded by the UK. The Central Statistical Office (CSO) groups these goods into 90 separate headings in the UK balance of payments.

The invisible account can be divided into three subsections: trade in services; the flow of interest, profits and dividends between nations; and transfers. 'Services' include expenditure on, for example, tourism, banking services, insurance, shipping and aviation. 'Interest, profits and dividends' are incomes received by UK residents from the ownership of assets abroad and payments to foreigners who own assets in the UK. 'Transfers' are expenditure by the government on embassies, military bases, EC contributions and overseas aid.

Table 20.2 shows the current account for the UK in 1988.

Capital account

The capital account is a record of international transactions in assets. This part of the balance of payments has grown in importance as the flow of funds between countries is no longer restricted to the financing of trade.

The items on the capital account reflect changes in the holding of foreign assets by UK residents, and changes in the holdings of UK assets by foreigners. As was stated earlier, some of the capital flows are necessary to offset any current account surplus or deficit. Other flows reflect investments overseas.

Until recently, the CSO presented the capital account in two parts, 'investment and other capital transactions' and 'official financing'. The official financing section recorded all transactions by the UK monetary authorities (the Bank of England) for, say, financing the current account surplus or deficit. This section has lost much of its significance since the UK authorities use of reserves for balance of payments purposes has declined significantly. The CSO therefore now uses the format of Table 20.1. (Many textbooks and some past exam questions continue to use the old format, although there should be no overall difference in the annual totals.)

The capital account now has two sections, 'transactions in external assets of the UK' and 'transactions in UK

Table 20.3 UK capital account, 1988 (£ million)

Transactions in external assets of the UK (increase in assets shown as a negative flow)	
Direct investment overseas by UK residents	−15,236
Portfolio investment in overseas securities by UK residents	−9,899
Lending, etc. to overseas by UK banks	−19,257
Deposits and lending overseas by UK residents, other than banks and general government	−3,037
Official reserves	−2,761
Other external assets of central government	−891
Total transactions in assets	−51,081
Transactions in UK liabilities to overseas residents (increase in liabilities shown as positive)	
Direct investment in the UK by overseas residents	7,617
Portfolio investment in the UK by overseas residents	6,903
Borrowing, etc. from overseas residents by UK banks	33,844
Borrowing from overseas by UK residents other than banks and general government	5,969
Other external liabilities of general government	904
Total transactions in liabilities	55,238
Net transactions	4,155

Source: *Monthly Digest of Statistics*, December 1989.

liabilities to overseas residents'. The first of these records such items as investments and loans by UK residents and institutions overseas and contains changes in official reserves. As there may be net disinvestment or loan repayment, these flows may be negative or positive. Transactions in UK liabilities records such items as loans to and investments in the UK by foreigners.

The capital account for 1988 is shown in Table 20.3. The table shows that in 1988 UK residents increased their net holdings or foreign assets (such as property in Spain) by £15,236 million. This is shown as a negative figure because it is a flow of funds out of the country. The second part of the table shows that foreigners increased their net holdings of assets in the UK, such as holiday homes, by £7,617 million. In this case we can see that there has been a flow of funds into and out of the country for the purpose of purchasing assets. If we sum these and all of the other capital flows, a figure for net transactions can be arrived at. For 1988 this was £4,155 million pounds, a net inflow of funds to the UK.

The balance of payments always balances

In our simple two-country, two-good model we stated that the current account recorded the movement of goods and the capital account the corresponding financial flows. As the flows are in opposite directions (i.e. goods in – money out and vice versa), the corresponding flows will have opposite signs. Any balance of trade deficit or surplus will be balanced by borrowing or lending from abroad, or by changes in the official reserves. These flows are included in the capital account. The implication of this is that if the current account and capital account are added together they should cancel each other out – that is, they should equal zero.

A quick look at Tables 20.2 and 20.3 shows us that this is not the case. A −£14,672 million current account balance plus a £4,155 million capital account balance equals −£10,517 million not zero. This is a significant difference, but it is not due to a mistake in the accounting theory. It is due to mistakes in actually compiling the accounts. The flow of goods and services and capital flows are very large and complex. Many items go unrecorded or are recorded only after many months or even years. The CSO must estimate these many flows and their value, such as the sales of financial services by the City of London. This leads to many items in the account being incomplete records.

Table 20.4 UK balance of payments, 1988 (£ million)

Current account balance	−14,672
Capital account balance	4,155
Balancing item	10,517
Total	0

Source: *Monthly Digest of Statistics.*

To solve this problem a further item is included in the accounts, the 'balancing item'. The balancing item ensures that the balance of payments balances, as shown in Table 20.4, and should take account of any missed items. The large balancing item for 1988 was due to a large amount of unrecorded net exports and unrecorded net capital inflows.

Problems with statistics

The balance of payments always balances: that is, the current account, capital account and balancing item always sum to zero. The significance of the accounts lies not in the final answer, but in their composition. Economists are interested in individual items within the accounts – how

Table 20.5 UK current account, 1978 (£ million)

	Reported in			% variation
	1979	**1984**	**1989**	
Visible balance	−1,593	−1,542	−1,175	26.2
Invisible balance	2,529	2,704	2,207	18.3
Current balance	936	1,162	1,032	19.4

Source: *Annual Abstract of Statistics*, 1979, 1984, 1989.

many manufactured goods were exported, the destination of UK exports, etc. Economists are also concerned with the size and direction of any trade imbalance – does the country persistently import more than it exports?

This final question attracts a great deal of attention in the press and on television. 'Britain in the red again' has become a common headline. By this statement the press usually mean that the current balance is in deficit: that is, the UK has imported more goods than it has exported. If this is true then there may be a cause for concern, but we must be careful when using published statistics.

Our reason for using the 1988 statistics is that they are reasonably reliable (but still subject to revision). The 1989 statistics are available, but at the time of writing are unreliable. The existence of the large balancing item in the 1988 accounts reveals that there is still much to be discovered even about trade in 1988.

Table 20.5 gives the current account balance of payments figures for 1978 reported in three different years. The wide variation in the figures shows how unreliable recently published figures can be. It is clear that the revision of the 1978 figures cannot be put down to simple allocation of the balancing item to various categories as omissions were discovered. As a matter of interest, look up the 1988 figures in the most recent source you can find. See how much they differ from those reported here.

SUMMARY

1. The current account records transactions of visible trade, such as motor cars, and invisible trade, such as dividend payments.
2. The capital account records transactions in external assets, such as property in Spain, and transactions in UK liabilities, such as foreign purchases on the UK Stock Exchange.
3. The balance of payments should always balance, i.e. the current account and capital account should sum to zero.

Case Study 20.1 Invisibles show up

Hey, presto! The latest rabbit from the Central Statistical Office's hat clocks in at £1.8bn, in the shape of revised invisible earnings for last year. It is standard practice for the CSO to find the odd extra billion of invisible earnings, but usually we have to wait for the Pink Book, which publishes the detailed balance of payments accounts in August, to learn that our invisible exporters did rather better than was thought.

The bigger issue, though, is not that our invisible earnings have been undercounted yet again: they are extraordinarily difficult to count. Rather it is that the dire warnings about the country running an invisible deficit for the first time since the Napoleonic Wars have so far proved unfounded. In all logic, if we continue to run a current account deficit of the present magnitude, the interest on the funds imported to finance that deficit will eventually push invisibles into the red. But it has not happened yet.

This good news, however, does not affect the competitiveness of Britain as an exporter of services, a crucial issue in assessing our comparative advantage within a liberalised EC. Our interest, profit and dividend earnings were higher than first thought, which is helpful. But it says nothing about the efficiency of our exporters in the main categories of internationally traded services: in finance and related services, in travel and tourism, and in transport. For the 1989 figures we will have to wait for the Pink Book.

There are, however, some other benchmarks about. The City is probably doing rather better now than it has for two or three years. Earnings from financial services should be recovering, with insurance earnings doing better than was first thought in that last quarter of 1989. It is small in relation to the insurance business, but the international securities business of the City has been performing increasingly strongly through last year and into this. The Baltic will be benefiting from the recovery in the shipping market. And, smaller still, Liffe [the London futures market] seems to have been increasing its market share of the global futures business.

The tourist account is extremely sensitive to swings in exchange rates, and the devaluation last year (now being reversed) will have given some marginal help. We also know from the tour operators that present demand for foreign holidays is slack. So some improvement is likely there. Transport, on the other hand, is difficult to call.

All in all, though, our position in invisible services should be improving slightly at the moment – and not before time, given the scale of the problem on the rest of the current account.

1. If official figures are so unreliable, is there any point in reporting them at all?
2. What does a surplus in the invisible account tell us about the comparative advantage of that sector of the UK economy?

Source: Hamish McRae, *Independent*, 14 June 1990

4. Due to measurement difficulties a 'balancing item' is added to the accounts to allow for errors and omissions. The current account, capital account and balancing item always sum to zero.

The structure of UK trade

The UK was the first 'industrial nation' in that it was the place where the Industrial Revolution occurred. Because of this Britain dominated world trade for much of the nineteenth century, although from the 1850s the growing industrial base of other European countries and the USA eroded the UK's position. A further significant factor in UK trade was the British Empire, which stretched across the world. The Empire provided the UK with a large market for its manufactured goods and a source of raw materials.

The history of the UK made it a trading nation which concentrated on trade outside Europe. Its lack of natural raw materials also made the UK dependent on importing them from the Empire, working on them, and then exporting many of the finished goods back to the Empire.

As the economies of the world continued to develop and the British Empire declined, the UK found that its old markets also declined. The developing countries of the Empire and now Commonwealth wished to produce their own goods from their own raw materials and to trade with other developed countries as well. Thus since the 1950s Britain has found that many of its traditional industries have declined and the pattern of its trade has altered. In 1973 the UK entered the European Community (EC) and committed itself to trading mainly with its nearest neighbours for the first time since the nineteenth century.

The changing structure of UK exports and imports

As we have seen, the UK traditionally imported raw materials and exported finished manufactured goods. By 1973 the UK was coming to accept that its role had to change. The manufacturing base of the country has declined and has now been largely replaced by service industries. This process, which has often been at the cost of high unemployment, is reflected in the components of UK trade.

Figure 20.1 shows the changing pattern of UK exports and imports. In 1973 73 per cent of UK exports by value were manufactured or semi-manufactured goods. By 1988 this had fallen by 67 per cent. This trend is due partly to the

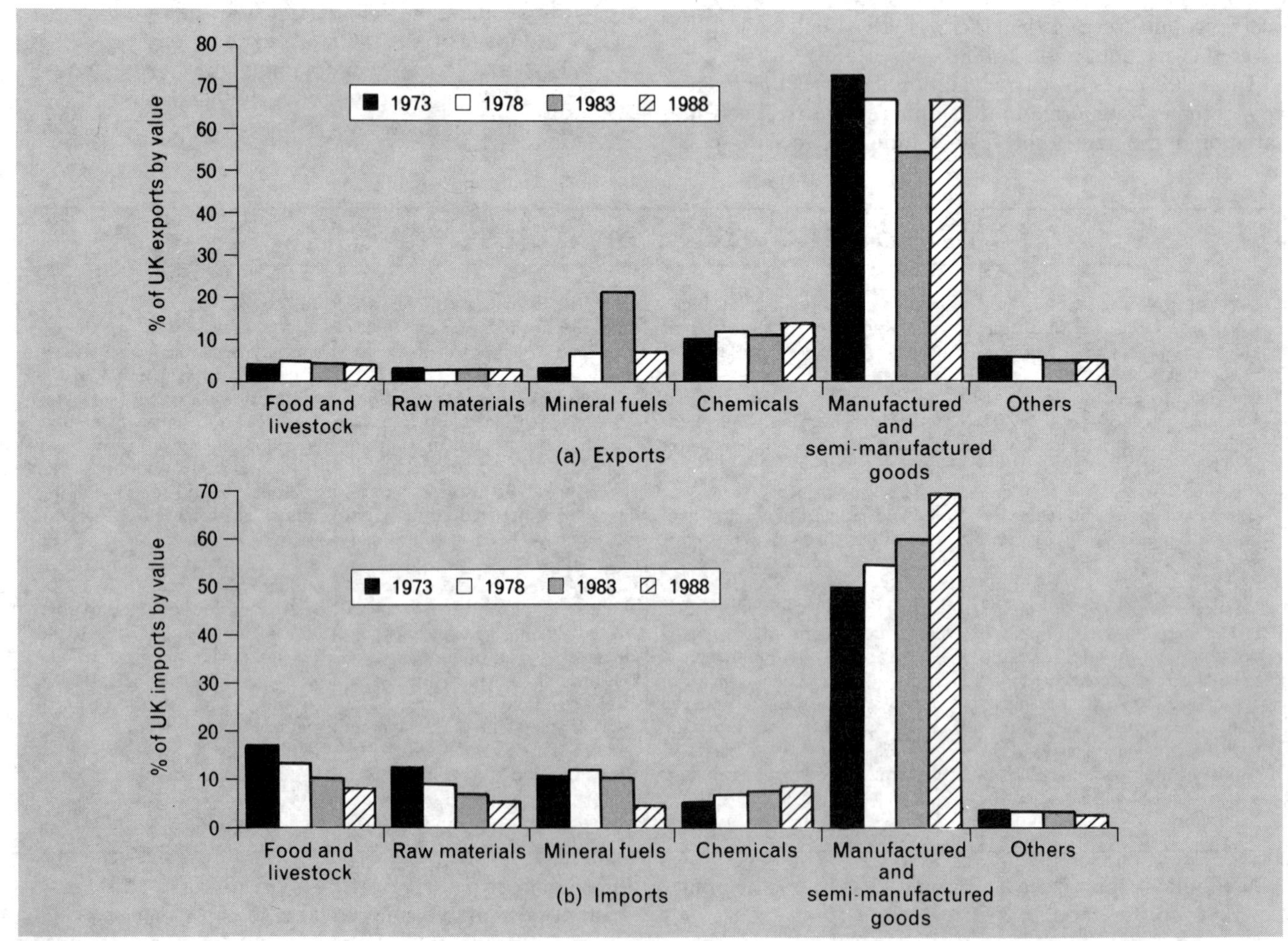

Figure 20.1 Structure of UK imports and exports, 1973–88.

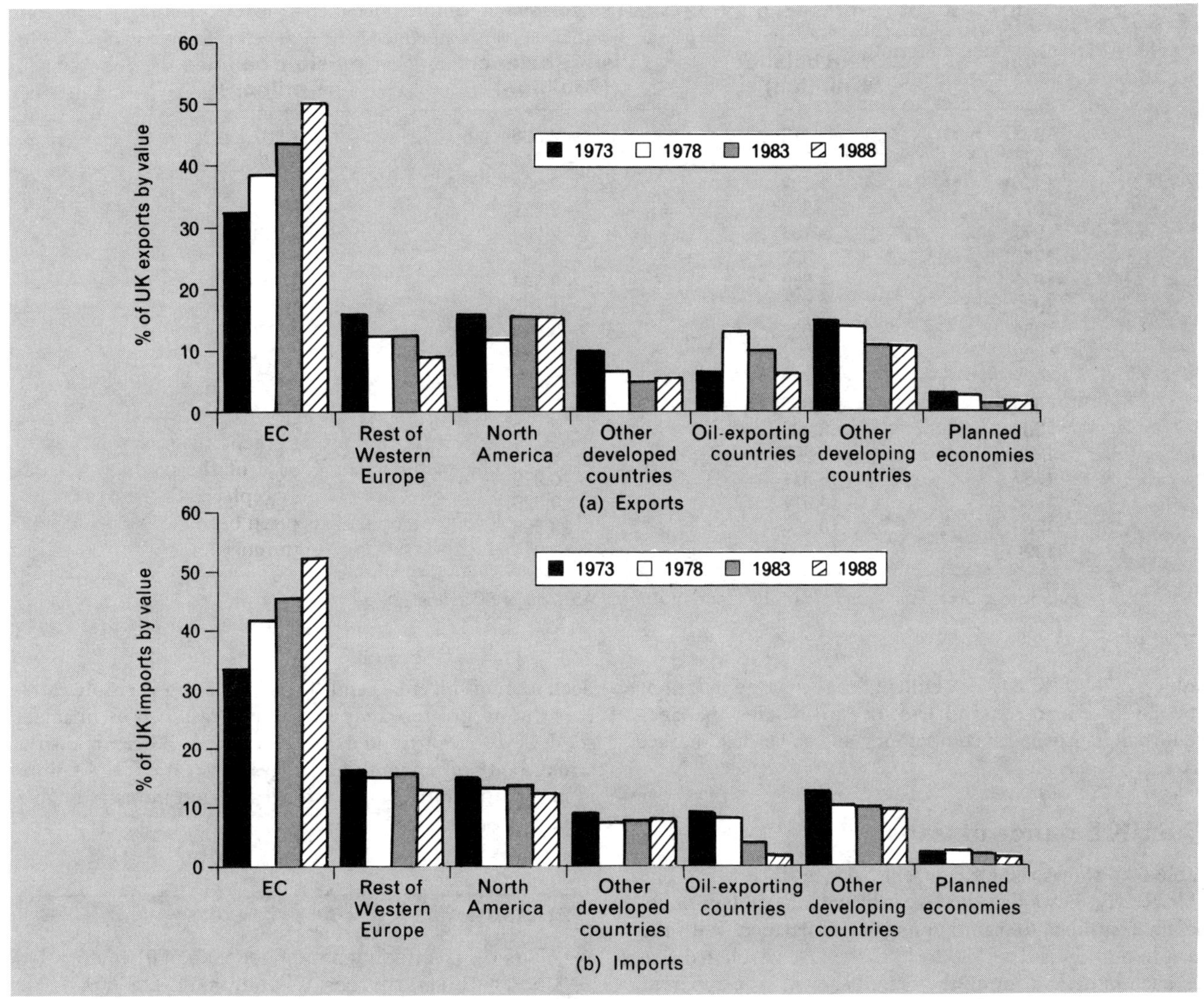

Figure 20.2 Destination of UK exports and origin of UK imports, 1973–88.

rise of other industrialized states and reflects the fact that manufacturing output was lower in 1988 than in 1979. The dip in the percentage share of exports due to manufactures in 1983 reflects the rapid rise and fall in the value of oil exports.

Figure 20.1(b) shows the changing pattern of imports, and the trend here is very clear. In 1973 half of UK imports were finished or semi-finished manufactured goods. By 1988 70 per cent of imports by value fell into this classification. The UK is no longer the 'workshop of the world'. The falling share of raw material imports is due to the declining manufacturing base of the UK. Another interesting point to note is the decline in food and livestock imports. This is due to the quite incredible improvements in farm yields, encouraged by successive governments.

The UK's changing trading partners

The most significant change in UK trade has been in its direction – those with whom the UK deals. Figure 20.2 shows how Europe has become the UK's most important customer and supplier since 1973.

Even allowing for the changing membership of the EC, which was bound to cause an apparent increase in trade with member countries, the extent to which the UK has come to depend on Community trade is remarkable. Europe as a whole now takes approximately 60 per cent of UK exports and supplies nearly 66 per cent of UK imports by value. The traditional markets of the UK have declined in importance as Europe has risen.

The changing trade pattern can be used to explain the rising proportion of manufactured goods in UK imports. These are the products of industrialized Europe. It is not as obvious why this change in the importance of various trading partners should have led to a decline in the share of exports attributed to the manufacturing sector. This is an important question for the UK and is yet to be fully understood.

Among the reasons put forward is competition in traditional markets from domestic industries, e.g. the steel and cotton industries of India. There have also been some new players in the world market such as the Korean ship-

Table 20.6 UK current account, 1973–90 (£ million)

Year	Current balance (£ million)	Visible balance (£ million)	Invisible balance (£ million)
1973	−979	−2,586	1,607
1974	−3,278	−5,351	2,073
1975	−1,582	−3,333	1,751
1976	−920	−3,929	3,009
1977	−136	−2,284	2,148
1978	936	−1,593	2,529
1979	−550	−3,344	2,794
1980	2,820	1,355	1,465
1981	6,628	3,250	3,378
1982	4,587	1,908	2,679
1983	3,758	−1,509	5,267
1984	1,885	−5,169	7,054
1985	3,203	−3,132	6,335
1986	66	−9,364	9,430
1987	−3,671	−10,929	7,258
1988	−14,617	−20,826	6,209
1989	−19,904	−23,998	4,094
1990	−12,792	−17,911	5,119

Source: *Economic Trends* (various issues); *Annual Abstract of Statistics*.

builders. The UK has also suffered higher wage inflation, more industrial unrest and less forward-looking management than its European competitors, and so has lost market share.

The UK balance of trade

Table 20.6 shows the UK current balance since 1973. The table clearly shows that the UK is heavily dependent on its invisible earnings to maintain its current balance. With the exception of the years 1980 to 1982 the UK visible balance has been in deficit during the period shown. The apparent improvement of the late 1970s and early 1980s has been largely due to the influence of North Sea oil, which reduced imports and boosted exports of visible goods (see Figure 20.1).

Since 1986 the invisible balance of the UK has been declining and this, coupled with falling oil prices and lower North Sea oil production, has caused an overall decline in the UK balance of trade. 1990 seemed set to see a record balance of trade deficit, following a £19,126 million deficit in 1989. The cause of this huge imbalance can be said to be too rapid expansion of domestic demand, due to easy credit during 1986–8, which caused a rapid rise in imports. The decline in oil revenues and the reduction in invisible earnings due to greater competition in areas such as financial services also contributed to the decline. There is also a strong body of opinion that suggests that the UK's failure to invest in manufacturing industry has left industry unable to fill the gap left by North Sea oil.

SUMMARY

1. The UK is a trading nation because of its history and natural resources. Its pattern of trade has changed greatly since the days of the British Empire and especially since the UK joined the European Community.
2. The share of UK exports that are manufactured goods has declined and the share of UK imports that are manufactured goods has risen since 1973.
3. The UK's most important trading partners are now the EC countries.
4. The UK has often run a balance of trade deficit, although it has usually maintained a surplus on the invisible trade account.

Exam Preparation and Practice

MULTIPLE-CHOICE QUESTIONS

1. In 1987 the payment of interest, profits and dividends to the UK private sector and public corporations was £46,856 million while similar payments made from the UK abroad were £41,444 million. The net effect on the balance of payments would be recorded as:

A A credit item on the visible trade account.
B A debit item on the visible trade account.
C A credit item on the invisible trade account.
D A debit item on the invisible trade account.

Questions 2 and 3 relate to the data in the table, which shows items on a country's balance of payment account.

	£ million
Exports	1,200
Imports	1,350
Invisible balance	530
Net transactions on the capital account	66

2. What is the value of the visible balance?

3. What is the value of the balancing item?
A −£314m
B −£150m
C £150m
D £314m
E £380m

4. The following table gives information about the visible trade of a country.

	Exports		Imports	
	Price per unit	Number of units	Price per unit	Number of units
Year 1	£100	1000	£500	400
Year 2	£200	600	£800	300

What changes have taken place in the balance of trade and the terms of trade?

	Balance of Trade	Terms of Trade
A	Improved	Improved
B	Improved	Worsened
C	Worsened	Improved
D	Worsened	Worsened

(AEB)

5. The current balance of the balance of payments account was reported as being −£1,243m. Since then the following revisions have been announced:
Increase on visible imports £23m
Increase on import of services £14m
Reduction of transfers abroad £38m
The revised balance is:
A −£1,206m
B −£1,243m
C −£1,244m
D −£1,318m

Answer key

Where there are three numbered alternatives

A	B	C	D	E
1, 2, 3 Correct	1, 2 Correct	2, 3 Correct	1 Correct	3 Correct

Where there are four numbered alternatives

A	B	C	D	E
1, 2 and 3 Correct	1 and 3 Correct	2 and 4 Correct	4 only Correct	1 and 4 Correct

6. Which of the following would be included in the calculation of the UK current account?
1 The expenditure of US tourists in the UK.
2 The sale of insurance services to a Spanish firm by a London insurer.
3 The purchase of shares in a Belgian firm by UK residents.

7. Which of the following are included in the 'invisibles balance'?
1 Loans by a UK bank to a French firm.
2 The purchase of a Spanish-made car.
3 A change in the official reserves.
4 UK contributions to the EC.

EXERCISES

1. Southland and Northway are engaged in international trade. Both countries use the £ sterling as their legal tender and neither trades with any other country. The following trade has taken place:

	Southland	Northway
Visible exports	135 barrels of wine	40 bolts of cloth
Visible imports	40 bolts of cloth	135 barrels of wine

There is no invisible trade or other international activity. If wine is traded at £10 a barrel and cloth at £15 a bolt:
(a) What is the balance of trade for each country?
(b) State the surplus or deficit for each country on its capital account.

2. The following details are taken from the balance of payments accounts of a country.

	£ million
Exports	100
Imports	110
Net financial services	20
Interest, profit and dividends (balance)	15
Transfers (balance)	−5
Transactions in external assets	25
Transactions in external liabilities	10

(a) Construct a balance of payments table from the data.
(b) (i) What is the current balance for this country?
(ii) What is the level of net transactions on the capital account?
(iii) What is the balancing item for these accounts?

3. The following is a summary of the balance of payments accounts for a country. Find the values of the letters.

	£ million
Current account	
Visible trade	
Exports	14,622
Imports	17,966
Visible balance	*a*
Invisible trade	
Services balance	3,799
Interest, profit and dividends balance	1,205
Transfers balance	*b*
Invisible balance	2,794
Current balance	*c*
Capital account	
Transactions in domestic assets and liabilities	
External assets	−40,189
External liabilities	*d*
Net transactions	−742
Balancing item	*e*

4. Under which heading in the UK balance of payments would the following transactions appear, and what sign would they be given (+ or −)?

(a) The repayment of a loan by a UK business to a foreign bank.
(b) The purchase of a lathe by a UK firm from a German manufacturer.
(c) The payment to a UK resident of dividends from a US company.
(d) The maintenance costs of the British Embassy in Paris.
(e) The purchase of a holiday home in Wales by a Belgian resident.
(f) The purchase of two weeks' holiday at the Savoy by a Belgian resident.
(g) The purchase of shares in an Indian company by a UK resident.

DATA-RESPONSE QUESTIONS

1.

(a) With reference to both of the tables below, account for the changing structure of the United Kingdom's Balance of Payments during the period 1981 to 1986. **(10 marks)**

(b) Comment upon the likely future economic consequences for the United Kingdom of the present trends in the Balance of Payments indicated by the statistics. **(10 marks)**

(LON.)

United Kingdom Balance of Payments, 1981–1986
(figures in £ million)

	1981	1982	1983	1984	1985	1986
CURRENT ACCOUNT						
Visible balance	3,360	2,331	−835	−4,384	−2,178	−8,463
Invisible balance	2,952	1,704	4,173	5,858	5,097	7,483
CURRENT BALANCE	6,312	4,035	3,338	1,474	2,919	−980
NET TRANSACTIONS IN UK ASSETS AND LIABILITIES	−6,404	−2,262	−4,742	−6,916	−7,421	−10,747
Allocation of special Drawing Rights	158					
Balancing Item	−66	−1,773	1,404	5,442	4,502	11,727

United Kingdom Visible Balance, 1981–1986
(figures in £ million)

	1981	1982	1983	1984	1985	1986
VISIBLE BALANCE						
Food, beverages & tobacco	−2,356	−2,637	−2,962	−3,524	−3,591	−3,792
Basic materials	−2,024	−1,989	−2,494	−2,850	−2,651	−2,359
Oil	3,112	4,643	6,976	6,937	8,104	4,056
Other mineral fuels & lubricants	−372	−521	−658	−1,546	−1,542	−1,366
Semi-manufactured goods	1,500	1,085	234	−144	102	−578
Finished manufactured goods	3,083	1,286	−2,501	−3,735	−3,103	−4,914
Commodities & transactions not classified according to kind	417	463	568	479	503	487

(Source: *United Kingdom Balance of Payments*, 1987, CSO Pink Book, CSO.)

21 The monetary theory of trade

In this chapter we will discuss:

1. How the balance of trade can be altered by changing the exchange value of a currency.
2. How foreign exchange markets determine the exchange value of a currency.

Introduction

Having finished our survey of the UK balance of payments, we can now turn our attention to the difficult question of international trade policy. The balance of payments records the monetary flows, but as we have seen there may not be a balance of trade. If a trade deficit or surplus occurs and it does not correct itself then the country must do something about it.

Restoring a trade balance

We have seen that any deficit on the balance of trade requires us to export gold or foreign currency. Now we simply could not continue exporting gold or currency for ever, and so a persistent trade deficit is seen as a problem. The UK is importing more than it is exporting and hence must find the gold or foreign currency to make up the difference.

We can return to our example of trade between the UK and India to see how nations can deal with a trade imbalance. The classical economists argue that if we export gold then we will have less gold to use as a medium of exchange in the UK. In other words, the **money supply** in the UK will fall. We will continue producing (and exchanging) the same quantity of goods, but will have less money to exchange for them. This will cause all prices in the UK to fall. Conversely, if India is importing gold, its money supply will be increasing. India will still be producing the same quantity of goods, but will have more money to exchange for them. The price level in India will therefore increase.

This theory of price level is called the **quantity theory of money** and was dealt with more fully in Chapters 13 and 16.

The argument goes on to suggest that, UK goods being cheaper, more will be sold on international markets. Conversely, since Indian goods are dearer, fewer of them will be sold on international markets. This is supposed to correct the imbalance of trade by encouraging UK exports and discouraging Indian exports. This is not as straightforward as it may seem.

Marshall–Lerner conditions

We can examine this argument further by considering the demand curves for UK imports and for Indian imports. The usual conditions apply, in that both demand curves slope downwards, as in Figure 21.1.

Figure 21.1(b) shows that at the original price of rice (P_{r1}) the UK imported q_{r1} of rice. When the price of Indian goods rises to P_{r2} the quantity imported by the UK falls to q_{r2}.

Conversely, in Figure 21.1(a) we can see that at the original price level of imports to India (P_{m1}), q_{m1} is the quantity of imports bought by India. As the price level of UK goods falls to P_{m2} the amount imported by India rises to q_{m2}.

It is clear from this that the price changes, induced by the trade imbalance, cause the quantity exported by the UK to rise and the quantity imported by the UK to fall. But as far as our balance of trade is concerned, it is the *value* of imports and exports rather than the *quantities* which matters. And what is not so clear is that the value of exports by the UK will rise or that the value of the Indian exports will fall.

We have already seen in Chapter 5 that the relationship between the value of sales and the price charged depends upon the elasticity of the demand curve. Recall that the elasticity measures the responsiveness of the quantities demanded to a change in price. When the elasticity of demand is unity then a 10 per cent fall in price will induce a 10 per cent rise in sales. The 10 per cent fall in price is therefore exactly offset by the 10 per cent rise in sales and the revenue received remains unchanged. Thus, if the demand curves for exports had unit elasticities then the reduction in price would not correct the imbalance of trade.

If the elasticity is less than unity then a 10 per cent price reduction would increase the quantity sold by less than 10 per cent. Total revenue would therefore fall and actually worsen the trade deficit.

What is required is that the elasticities are greater than unity. In this case, the increase in quantity sold when the price is reduced will more than make up for the price reduction, and total revenue (the values of sales) will increase.

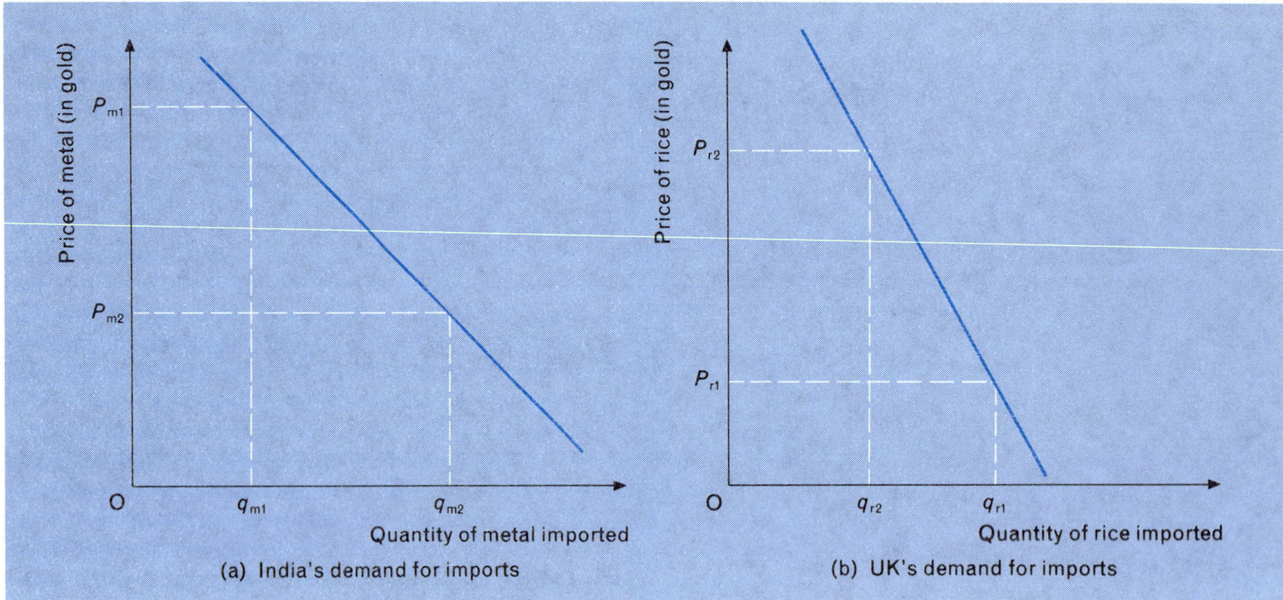

Figure 21.1 Demand curves for Indian and UK imports.

The self-correcting mechanism of this system therefore depends crucially upon the elasticity of the demand curves. Provided the elasticity is greater than unity, the automatic rebalancing of a trade deficit will work. This is known as the **Marshall–Lerner condition**.

We shall see later that this condition applies to models which have more than one currency as well as to models in which there is only one currency. For the moment, though, we will retain our assumption that there is only one currency.

Gold-backed currencies

We may note in passing that even if each country printed its own currency then the automatic correction mechanism would still apply, provided only that the amount of currency in circulation was tied to the amount of gold in the country.

In this case the currency is said to be gold backed, so that if the UK loses gold to India then the UK must reduce the number of pound notes in circulation. This reduction in the UK (pound note) money supply will have the same effect as a reduction in the UK gold money supply, i.e. provided full employment is maintained then UK prices will fall.

Having a gold backed currency is therefore tantamount to using gold itself as a medium of exchange.

The gold standard

The government or banks could go even further than gold backing, and undertake always to exchange a pound note for a fixed amount of gold. This is called making one's currency convertible, i.e. convertible into gold at a known certain rate. When one's currency is tied to gold in this way, one is said to be on the **gold standard**. The UK was on the gold standard until 1914, returned to it in 1925 and finally left it in 1932.

The case for coming off the gold standard rests on an objection to the efficacy of the automatic adjustment process discussed above. It is worth looking into this case a little further.

Price rigidity

So far we have argued that if the amount of gold in the UK were to decrease then the price level in the UK would fall. But it is not always painless or easy to reduce prices. There is, for example, a strong resistance in this country to cuts in money wage rates. Without such cuts, it is difficult to see how price levels can be reduced. The automatic adjustment process which relies on prices (and hence money wage rates) being flexible downwards may not therefore be allowed to work, at least not without some delay and a certain amount of industrial unrest.

We will not here take up the question of inducing downward price flexibility. Sufficient to say it is fraught with institutional and political difficulties. Instead we shall consider an alternative solution. If we do not want the UK price level to change when there is a balance of trade deficit then we have to find a way of charging lower prices in India while keeping the same price in the UK. To do this, we have (a) to maintain the money supply in the UK even when in balance of trade deficit; and (b) to divorce the price charged in India from the price charged in the UK.

What is being suggested is that, even when the UK is losing gold to India, we should not reduce the UK money supply. The UK currency can therefore no longer be gold or 'gold backed'. We must be able to print as many pound notes as we wish, irrespective of our gold stocks. Since we can then maintain our money stock, our price level will not have to respond to trade deficits or surplus.

But this extra degree of freedom gives rise to two further problems. First, now we are free to decide how much money to circulate, we will need a policy about how much money we should put into circulation – the choice is now ours. This is a problem of monetary policy and was dealt with in Chapter 18. It is the second problem we shall take up here.

By insulating our price level from our balance of trade we have abandoned the automatic self-correcting mechanism of a trade deficit (or surplus). Thus we need a replacement for automatic stabilization via the price level. We have such a system and it is a system of **floating exchange rates.**

SUMMARY

1. The exchange of goods between countries is mirrored by an exchange of medium of exchange (money), i.e. countries do not barter.
2. If the value of our imports is greater than the value of our exports then we have a balance of trade deficit.
3. If the value of our imports is less than the value of our exports then we have a balance of trade surplus.
4. Another way of saying we have a balance of trade deficit (or surplus) is to say we have a current account deficit (or surplus).
5. A current account deficit means that we import a greater value of goods than we export. Therefore we spend more gold on imports than we receive for our exports.
6. A current account deficit is therefore 'made up for' by 'exporting' gold, i.e. losing gold overseas. This loss of gold is recorded on our capital account.
7. Accounts which include both current account and capital account are called the balance of payments account.
8. Unlike the current account, the balance of payments account must always balance.
9. A current account deficit can be sustained only by exporting gold. This cannot go on for long, so we require some way of correcting a trade (current account) deficit.
10. According to classical economists, this is done automatically by the price mechanism.
11. As we lose gold, we lose our money supply and our price level falls. This means we export more goods.
12. Exporting more goods will improve our balance of trade if the demand for our exports lies between −1 and −infinity. This elasticity restriction is called the Marshall–Lerner condition.
13. Reducing the price level in the UK means reducing production costs and this is often painful and costly.
14. To avoid this, we can make our money supply independent of the amount of gold we have (come off the gold standard).

Foreign exchange markets

In order to see how the new system works we will assume that UK producers are prepared to accept only pounds for their goods and that Indian producers are prepared to accept only rupees for their goods. Thus in order for a UK importer to buy rice from India it must first obtain rupees. Meanwhile, the Indian importer is seeking pounds in order that it can buy metal from the UK.

A market for currencies is therefore formed and it is called the **foreign exchange market**. The dealers in this market buy and sell national currencies. Pounds are sold for rupees and rupees are sold for pounds. There will be a 'price' for each currency and the 'price' of pounds will be quoted in rupees (say 2 rupees per pound). Conversely, the 'price' of rupees will be quoted in pounds (50p per rupee). These prices are called **exchange rates**. If £1 sells for 2 rupees, then the rupee exchange rate for the pound is 2.

Note that the exchange rate must not be confused with the terms of trade. The exchange rate is the price of one currency in terms of another currency. The terms of trade is the ratio of imported goods prices to exported goods prices. Thus, although the terms of trade will be affected by the exchange rate, they are not the same thing.

There are a number of questions here:

1. What determines our exchange rate?
2. How is it related to our imbalance of trade?
3. Can it be used to correct any imbalance of trade?

We will take these in turn.

Determination of exchange rates

It is clear that, in our simple model, the only reason for a UK resident to buy rupees is to use them to buy Indian goods. Similarly, Indians would buy pounds only in order to use them to buy UK goods.

Let us illustrate what happens with a numerical example, taking it stage by stage.

1. The UK wishes to buy 200 rupees worth of goods from India. It therefore demands 200 rupees from the foreign exchange dealer.
2. India wishes to buy £100 worth of goods from the UK. It therefore demands £100 from the foreign exchange dealer.
3. The dealer stands ready to supply £1 at an exchange rate of 1 rupee per pound. It therefore sells 100 pound notes to India and receives 100 rupees.
4. The dealer also sells 200 rupees to the UK and receives 200 pound notes as payment.
5. At the close of trading, the dealer finds it has run down its stock of rupees (receipts = 100 rupees, disbursements = 200 rupees). It is also building up its stock of pounds (receipts = £200, disbursements = £100).
6. Clearly this state of affairs cannot continue for long. The dealer would soon run out of rupees altogether and have to cease trading. But before it does so, it will of course realize that they are becoming more and more scarce, and that pounds are becoming more and more plentiful. It would therefore increase the price of rupees in terms of pounds, i.e. the UK exchange rate would fall. Instead of getting 1 rupee for £1, the dealer would now get say 1/2 a rupee for £1. The UK exchange rate would have fallen from 1 to 1/2.

This answers the first of our questions: what determines

our exchange rate? Our exchange rate is determined in the foreign exchange market. It will fall when there is an excess supply of pounds and will rise when there is an excess demand for pounds. That is, *it is determined by the supply of and demand for pounds.*

Trade balance and exchange rates

The answer to our second question – how is our exchange rate related to our balance of trade? – follows directly from this. We know that the demand for pounds on the foreign exchange market will equal the value of UK exports measured in pounds. And the supply of pounds on to the foreign exchange market will equal the value of UK imports measured in pounds. Thus when the UK has a trade deficit – its imports (valued in pounds) are greater than its exports (valued in pounds) – there will be a surplus of pounds on the foreign exchange market and this, as we have seen, will have a depressing effect on the UK exchange rate. Conversely, when the UK has a trade surplus there will be a shortage of pounds on the foreign exchange market and there will be upward pressure on the exchange rate.

The connection therefore between our trade balance and our exchange rate is simple and direct. *Our exchange rate falls when we are in deficit and rises when we are in surplus.*

What is slightly more complicated is the answer to our third question – can the exchange rate be used to correct a trade deficit or trade surplus?

Exchange rates and trade imbalance

We now know that a trade deficit will tend to lower our exchange rate and a trade surplus will force it up. What we need to know next is whether the exchange rate has any effect on the surplus or deficit. If we can show that lowering our exchange rate reduces our trade deficit (and raising our exchange rate reduces our trade surplus) then any trade imbalance will be automatically corrected.

It works like this. The UK has a trade deficit. This will cause the supply of pounds on the foreign exchange market to exceed the demand for them. This will lead to a reduction in the UK exchange rate and this in turn will reduce the trade deficit. The adjustment of the exchange rate will continue until the trade deficit falls to zero, and the supply of and demand for pounds on the foreign exchange market will equate.

Demand curves again

What we have to show, then, is that a reduction in our exchange rate actually reduces our trade deficit. It is this somewhat difficult question which we now look at.

We begin by redrawing the demand curves for UK and Indian exports. Once again the UK exports metal and India exports rice, but for these curves the prices are measured not in gold, but in pounds and rupees. The UK's demand curve for rice will relate the quantity demanded and the price in pounds. This is because the UK deals only in pounds. Likewise the Indian demand curve for metal will be expressed in rupee prices because Indians deal only in rupees. These demand curves are shown in Figure 21.2.

Figure 21.2(a) shows how India's demand for metal changes as the rupee price of metal changes. Since the metal is produced by the UK, this demand curve is India's demand for imports curve.

Figure 21.2(b) shows the UK's demand for rice against the price of rice in pounds. Since rice is produced by India, this demand curve is the UK demand for imports curve.

In our two-country world, the imports of India are the exports of the UK, and the imports of the UK are India's exports.

Consider first only Figure 21.2(a). Assume that metals

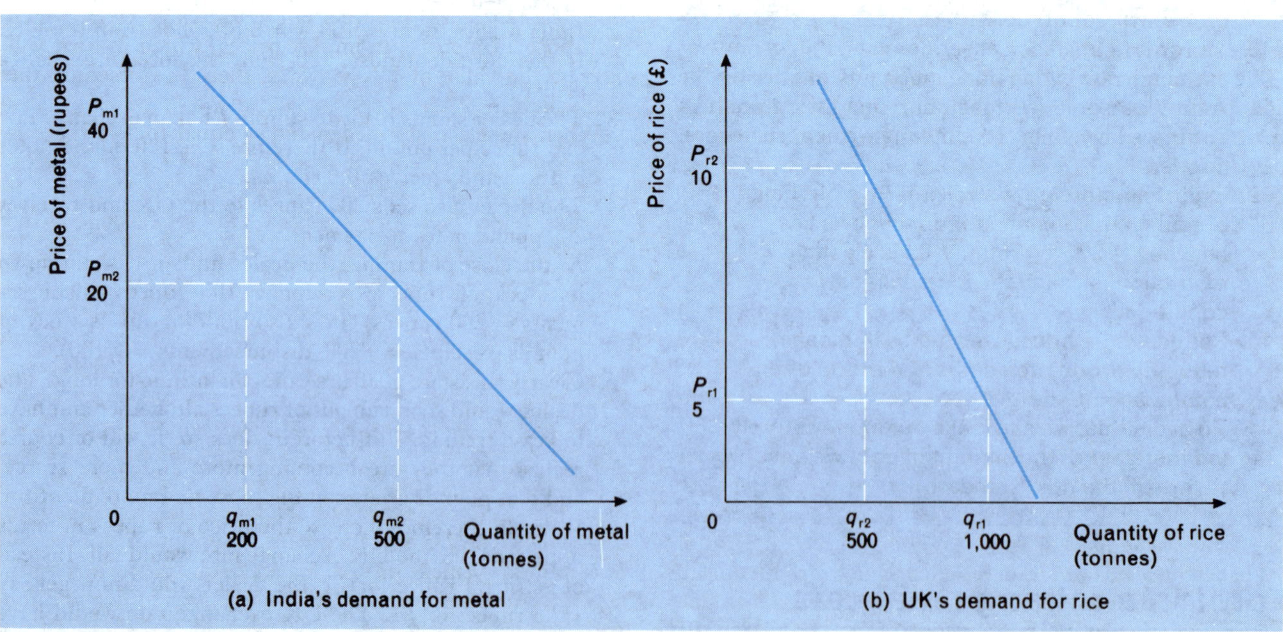

Figure 21.2 Effect of a change in the exchange rate on demand for Indian and UK imports.

Table 21.1 Effect of devaluing the rupee exchange rate on the balance of trade

	Exchange rate	
	1 rupee: £1	**1/2 rupee: £1**
Indian demand for imports	8,000 rupees = £8,000	10,000 rupees = £20,000
UK demand for imports	5,000 rupees = £5,000	2,500 rupees = £5,000
Indian trade balance	−3,000 rupees	−7,500 rupees
UK trade balance	+£3,000	+£15,000

are produced in the UK at a cost of £40 per tonne. If the exchange rate, between pounds and rupees is 1 rupee per pound then the price of metals to an Indian would be 40 rupees. At this price, our figure tells us that India buys (imports) 200 tonnes of metal.

Now let the exchange rate fall, so that there is only 1/2 a rupee per pound. India can now buy metal for only 20 rupees per tonne. At this price, the demand for imports by India increases to 500 tonnes.

This is just what would happen if the cost of producing metal in the UK fell by 50 per cent (to £20 per tonne) and the exchange rate remained at 1 rupee per pound.

Therefore, having an alterable exchange rate allows us to change the price (in rupees) which India pays for UK exports (metal) without lowering the UK price (in pounds). Thus we do not need price flexibility in the UK, only flexibility of exchange rates.

Now consider Figure 21.2(b). We see that, if rice is produced in India at 5 rupees per tonne and if the exchange rate is 1 rupee per pound, then the price of rice to the UK is £5 per tonne. At this price the UK buys (imports) 1,000 tonnes of rice. If the exchange rate falls to 1/2 a rupee per pound then the price of rice to the UK will rise to £10 per tonne. At this price the UK buys only 500 tonnes. Halving the exchange rate therefore increases the price of UK imports (in pounds) without affecting the rupee price in the producing country (India). The balance of trade results for this are shown in Table 21.1.

The exchange rate is therefore a neat way of altering the prices paid by consumers (in their currency) without altering the prices received by producers (in their currency). Thus the need for painful adjustment of production costs (downwards) is avoided.

Marshall–Lerner again

So far we have shown that a UK balance of trade deficit will lead to an excess supply of pounds on foreign exchange markets. This in turn will lead to a fall in the exchange rate, and this decreases the rupee price of UK exports and increases the pound price of UK imports.

We can see from this that the quantity of UK imports falls and the quantity of UK exports rises when the UK exchange rate falls. But is this sufficient to correct the balance of payments deficit?

What is needed to correct a deficit is not a reduction in the quantity of UK imports and/or an increase in the quantity of UK exports. What we need is a reduction in the supply of pounds and an increase in the demand for pounds on the foreign exchange market. This requires a reduction in the pound *value* of UK imports and/or an increase in the pound *value* of UK exports.

The demand for pounds, on the foreign exchange market, is equal to the pound value of UK exports (India demands pounds to buy UK exports). We can see from Figure 21.2(a) that the quantity of goods exported increases as the UK devalues. Since the value of these goods in pounds remains unchanged, the pound value of UK exports will increase as the UK devalues. Thus the demand for pounds on the foreign exchange market will undoubtedly increase as the UK lowers its exchange rate. This part of the adjustment mechanism therefore works well.

The other part of the adjustment mechanism is more problematical. We know that the supply of pounds on the foreign exchange market is equal to the pound value of UK imports. The UK supplies pounds to the market, receives rupees in return and then spends the rupees on rice. We can see from Figure 21.2(b) that, when the UK devalues (reduces its exchange rate) the pound price of UK imports rises and the quantity of UK imports falls. Will the pound value of UK imports rise or fall?

We have already seen from our gold standard model that the pound value of UK imports will rise as price rises when the elasticity of the UK demand curve lies between 0 and −1. As under the gold standard, this will lead to a worsening of the deficit rather than a correction of it. In other words, a deficit will induce a fall in exchange rates, which will cause an increase in import prices, which in turn will *increase* the value of UK imports, thereby worsening the UK deficit!

When the elasticity of demand is equal to −1 there is absolutely no change in the pound value of UK imports no matter what happens to exchange rates.

Thus, under these two conditions the import side of the automatic correcting mechanism for an imbalance of trade fails to work.

The automatic correcting mechanism will work, however, if the elasticity of demand for imports lies between −1 and (−)infinity. In this case a trade deficit induces a fall in the exchange rate and a consequent increase in import prices. This brings about a *decrease* in the value of UK imports and a decrease in the supply of pounds, and the trade deficit is corrected.

In practice when there is a change in the exchange rate the demand- and supply-side effects combine. For there to be an improvement in the balance of trade it is only necessary for the combined price elasticities of demand for both imports and exports to lie between −1 and (−)infinity. It is then rather less difficult for the Marshall–Lerner conditions to be satisfied.

Exchange rate movements and time

If the Marshall–Lerner conditions hold then allowing the exchange value of one country's currency to fall in relation to another will cause its balance of trade to improve. The question we address here is: how quickly does this improvement come about?

The effect of a change in the exchange rate on the price of traded goods is immediate. However, the final effect shown in Figure 21.2 may be achieved only slowly.

Consider the effect of changing the exchange rate from 1 rupee per pound to 1/2 a rupee per pound. The pound has fallen in value and UK exports are now available in India at a lower price. The immediate effect on UK exports will be zero because it takes time for demand to adjust. Thus in the short term the volume of exports remains the same. UK firms receive the same pound value for their goods, but Indians pay fewer rupees.

The immediate effect on imports is for their pound price to rise. Again demand will be slow to respond and the UK will continue to import the same volume of imports in the short term. Thus the pound value of imports will rise initially due to the change in the exchange rate. With no compensating change in exports the initial effect on the balance of trade is that it gets worse.

In time the demand in both the UK and India will respond to the change in prices due to the new level of the exchange rate. In the UK consumers will begin to substitute domestically produced goods for the now more expensive foreign ones. In India the lower price of imports will encourage their greater consumption. Eventually the final position shown in Figure 21.2 will be reached.

In this way, the balance of trade will initially worsen and then improve following a fall in the exchange rate. This has been called the 'J-curve effect' because a graph of the level of the balance of trade against time following a fall in the exchange rate looks like a letter J. This is shown in Figure 21.3. The time scale of the effect will vary from country to country and will depend on the type of goods traded. For the UK it is thought that the time between *O* and point *A* would be about 18 months.

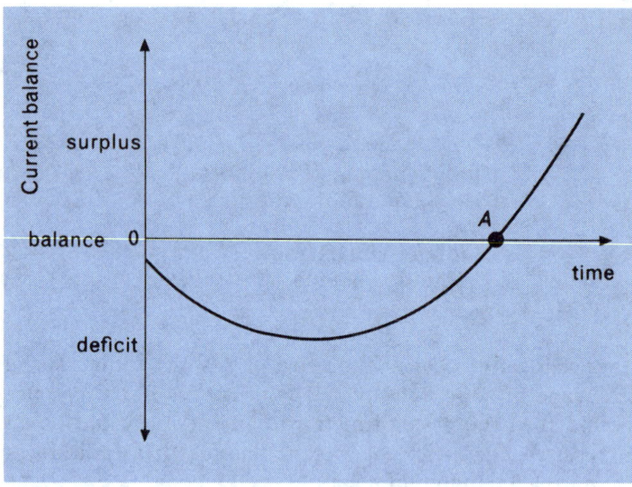

Figure 21.3 The J-curve effect following devaluation.

SUMMARY

1. When each country comes off the gold standard we have two different currencies being used.
2. In order to trade, it is necessary first to exchange currencies in the foreign exchange market.
3. The relative price of the two currencies is called the exchange rate.
4. When we are running a current account deficit, our exchange rate will fall and cause the price of our exports abroad to fall, even though our home price level remains unchanged.
5. This will also cause the price of our imports to rise.
6. The fall in the price of our exports will encourage foreigners to spend more on them.
7. The rise in the price of our imports will discourage us from importing goods, but need not necessarily cause us to spend less on them.
8. If the elasticity of demand for our imports lies between −1 and (−)infinity then we will spend less on imports as their price rises.
9. This automatic correction mechanism will therefore work if the Marshall–Lerner conditions are satisfied.
10. The immediate effect of a devaluation is to worsen the trade balance as demand takes time to respond to the new relative prices. This leads to the J-curve effect as the trade balance improves.

Exam Preparation and Practice

MULTIPLE-CHOICE QUESTIONS

1. A country that is running a trade deficit while operating on the gold standard will find:
   A The domestic supply of gold is rising.
   B Domestic prices rising.
   C The trade deficit automatically worsening.
   D The domestic supply of gold falling.

2. The Marshall–Lerner conditions state that a devaluation will:
   A Only be effective if the elasticity of demand for both exports and imports sum to more than (−)1.
   B Only be effective if the demand for exports is greater than (−)1.
   C Only be effective if the elasticity of demand for both exports and imports sum to be less than (−)1.
   D Only be effective if supported by tariffs.

3. Under which of the following circumstances would a country obtain the greatest benefit in its visible balance from a fall in the value of its currency?

	Demand for Imports	Demand for Exports
A	Price elastic	Price inelastic
B	Price inelastic	Price elastic
C	Price elastic	Price elastic
D	Price inelastic	Price inelastic

(AEB)

4. The domestic price level can be allowed to vary independently of the effects of the balance of trade only when:
   A There are fixed exchange rates.
   B There are floating exchange rates.
   C The country is a member of the EMS.
   D The quantity of gold in the country is fixed.

Answer key

Where there are four numbered alternatives

A	B	C	D	E
1, 2 and 3 Correct	1 and 3 Correct	2 and 4 Correct	4 only Correct	1 and 4 Correct

5. Following a devaluation of the currency, *ceteris paribus*, the current balance initially in deficit would:
   1 Worsen initially.
   2 Continue to worsen.
   3 Improve over time.
   4 Improve immediately.

EXERCISES

1. The classical economists claimed that trade imbalances would solve themselves due to domestic price changes. This belief is based on the quantity theory of money and operating fixed exchange rates based on the gold standard.

   The quantity theory of money is $MV = PY$, where $M =$ money supply, $V =$ velocity of circulation and is fixed, $P =$ the average price level and $Y =$ output and is fixed.

   Suppose the UK is running a balance of trade deficit of £100 million with India and operating on the gold standard. At the start of the year the following values held: $M = £800$, $V = 3$, $P = £16$.
   (a) What is the present level of output?
   (b) Assuming that there have been no other forces for change, what will the effect of the trade deficit be on the average price level?
   (c) If the elasticity of demand for UK exports is (−)2, will the UK balance of trade improve or worsen following the change in price indicated in (b)?
   (d) If the elasticity of demand for UK exports is (−)1/2, will the UK balance of trade improve or worsen following the same price change?
   (e) If workers refused to accept lower wages in order to allow the fall in average prices, what could be the effect on output and employment?

2. Southland and Northway trade with each other in wine and cloth. Southland has the 'South' as its currency, Northway the 'North'. Both countries operate floating exchange rates. The present rate is 1 North for 4 Souths. Southland exports wine, which costs 48 Souths a barrel. Northway exports cloth at 5 Norths a bolt. The demand curve for imports in both countries is shown in the following diagram.
   (a) What is the present balance of trade for each country expressed in their own currencies?
   (b) What would you expect to happen to the North:South exchange rate if the existing situation persists?

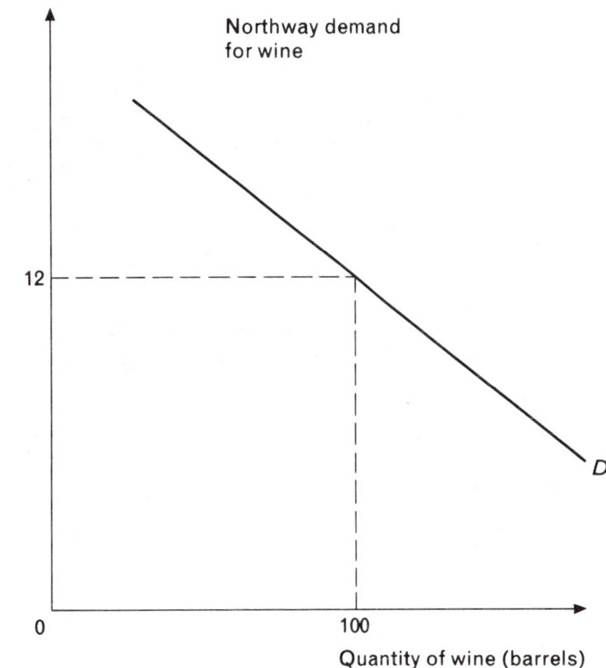

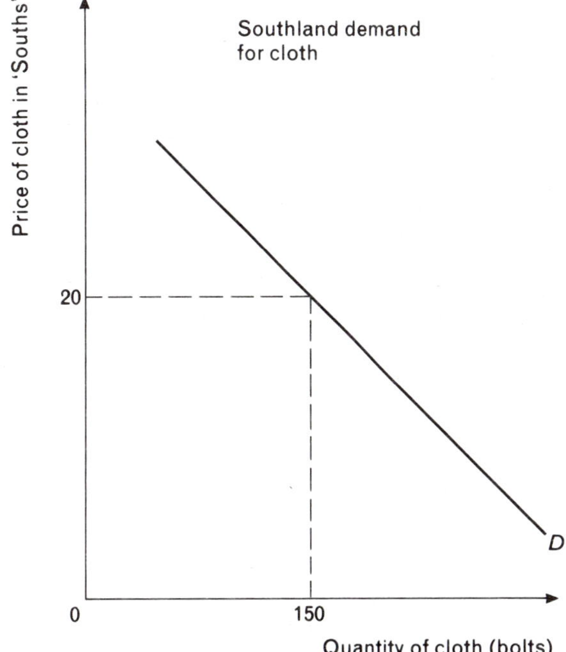

   (c) If the North depreciates against the South so that it is now worth just 3 Souths, what will be the effect on:
      (i) the price of wine in Northway?
      (ii) the price of cloth in Southland?
      (iii) the balance of trade for each country?
   (d) What does your answer to (c)(iii) imply about the elasticity of demand for imports in the two countries?

DATA-RESPONSE QUESTION

1. The following extract refers to a hypothetical economy, Ruritania.

   Ruritania has been faced with a dual problem: firstly, that of falling oil prices which have seriously undermined confidence in the prospects of Ruritanian economic recovery; secondly, that of a serious and seemingly intractable deficit on the current account of the Balance of Payments. It has been estimated that the price elasticity of demand for Ruritanian exports is approximately −0.8 and the price elasticity of demand for its imports is approximately −0.5.

The problem facing the Ruritanian Government is how it should react. Should it defend the value of the currency or allow market forces to significantly depreciate the currency? If it allows the currency to fall, critics argue that the immediate effect would be a worsening of the current account balance. In the longer term they suggest that inflationary expectations stemming from the depreciation will ultimately eliminate any of the price competitive advantages gained.

(a) Given the above situation, would you recommend Ruritania to defend its exchange rate? Justify your answer. **(5 marks)**

(b) How is it possible that the current account balance might deteriorate in the period immediately following the depreciation of the exchange rate. **(5 marks)**

(c) Explain how a depreciation may stimulate inflationary expectations and how this may eliminate any competitive advantage gained. **(5 marks)**

(d) What macro-economic policies could be introduced to prevent inflationary expectations occurring? **(5 marks)**

(LON.)

22 More on the determination of exchange rates

In this chapter we will discuss:

1. How exchange rates are determined.
2. How the risks of exchange rate movements can be avoided.
3. Post-war movements of the sterling exchange rate.

Introduction

So far we have assumed the following:

1. The exchange rate of one currency for another is determined by the supply and demand for the two currencies on the international money market. If the demand for pounds increases and the demand for rupees decreases then the price of pounds, in terms of rupees, will rise. The pound is said to **appreciate** – there will be more rupees to the pound.
2. The demand for pounds by India, say, will be determined by India's desire to import UK goods. The demand for rupees by the UK will likewise be determined by Britain's desire to import Indian goods.
3. India's demand for UK goods will fall as the exchange rate appreciates, i.e. as India has to pay more rupees for each pound it buys.

In what follows we look again at 1 and 3. We explore other ways of determining exchange rates and at other sources of demand for our currency than simply that of overseas buyers of our goods and services.

We have dealt so far with only two currencies at a time. In the real world, there are many different currencies and we will have an exchange rate for each of them. We will have a dollar exchange rate, a rupee exchange rate, a franc exchange rate, etc. By the same token, of course, there will be exchange rates between dollars and rupees, between rupees and francs, etc. The next point to make in this chapter is that these exchange rates are closely related.

Consider the following three exchange rates:

1. 4 rupees per pound.
2. $2 per pound.
3. 1 rupee per dollar.

Anyone with £1 could exchange it for 4 rupees, by exchange rate 1. These 4 rupees could then be exchanged for $4, by exchange rate 3. Finally, these $4 could be exchanged for £2, by exchange rate 2. Thus, simply by exchanging currencies, it is possible to double the number of pounds from 1 to 2. This is called **arbitrage.** By continuing to exchange pounds for rupees, rupees for dollars, and dollars for pounds, one could soon build up a fortune.

To prevent this from happening, the three exchange rates must have a certain relation to each other. If 4 rupees exchange for £1 and if £1 exchanges for 50 cents (1/2 dollar) then it must be the case that 4 rupees exchange for 50 cents. The exchange rate between rupees and dollars is determined once the exchange rates of rupees to pounds and of dollars to pounds are known.

Thus we know that the whole set of exchange rates between pairs of various currencies must exhibit this kind of interrelation.

Floating exchange rates

When the value of an exchange rate is free to fluctuate with demand and supply it is known as a **floating exchange rate.**

We saw in Chapter 21 that as the exchange rate falls, the demand for pounds on the foreign exchange market will certainly rise. We can therefore draw a graph of the demand for pounds against the exchange rate. It will be downward sloping. This is shown in Figure 22.1.

We also saw that the fall in the exchange rate would decrease the supply of pounds only if the elasticity of demand for UK imports were elastic. This being so, we can draw a graph of the supply of pounds against the exchange rate. It will be upward sloping. This too is shown in Figure 22.1.

From the figure, it is apparent that there will be one and only one exchange rate which equates the supply of pounds to the demand for pounds on the foreign exchange markets. This is shown as e^* and the amount of pounds exchanged is shown as q^*.

We next consider changes in the exchange rate. Say, for example, that India has been buying heavily from the UK but for some reason began buying elsewhere (say from

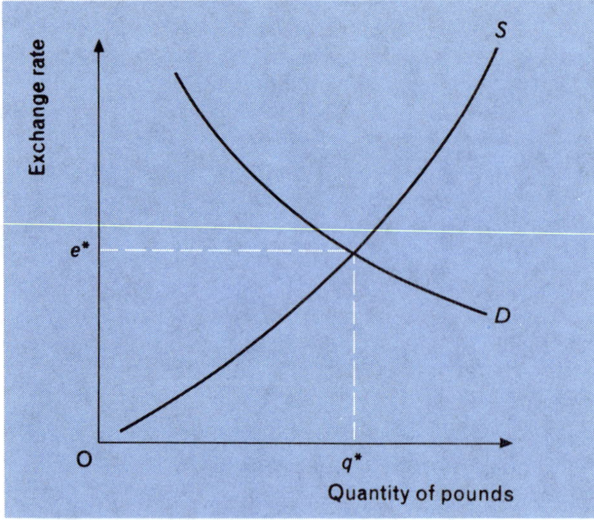

Figure 22.1 Equilibrium in the foreign exchange market.

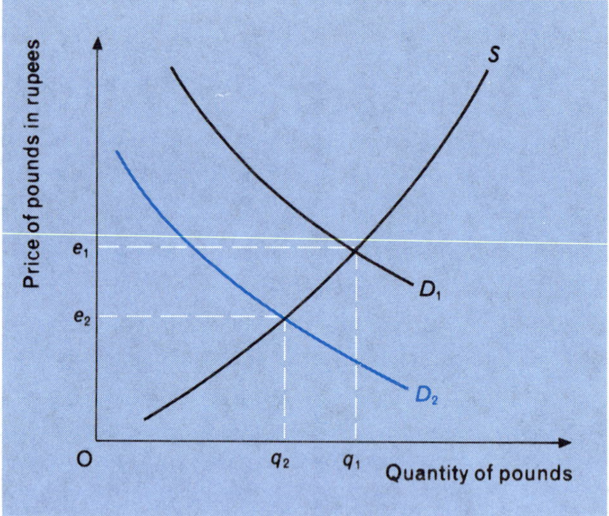

Figure 22.2 Effect of a fall in the demand for pounds on the exchange rate and quantity of pounds traded.

Japan). This would mean a decrease in the demand for pounds, i.e. that the Indian demand curve for pounds would move towards the origin. At every exchange rate India's demand for pounds would be lower than previously. This is shown in Figure 22.2.

As can be seen, the shift of the demand curve has caused a reduction in the exchange rate (a depreciation of sterling against the rupee) from e_1 to e_2 and has caused fewer pounds to be traded (q_1 to q_2).

An increase in demand for UK goods in India has the reverse effect to that shown in Figure 22.2. The supply curve of pounds can also move as UK residents increase or decrease their demand for Indian goods. In the case of an increase in demand for Indian goods in the UK, the supply curve of pounds would shift to the right, indicating that at all exchange rates the UK would supply more pounds. This would cause a depreciation of sterling against the rupee.

In a later section we shall see that the movements of money across the foreign exchange markets can shift the demand and supply curves for pounds. Such movements can be caused by a rise or fall in confidence in a country, or by the interest rate policy of the country attracting, or failing to attract, funds.

There are in fact many influences on the positions of these supply and demand curves and hence the exchange rate can fluctuate quite a lot and quite quickly. Table 22.1 shows how the exchange rate of the pound against the US dollar behaved over the first 8 months of 1985.

Risk and uncertainty

From this table it can be seen that the exchange rate fluctuated from 1.075 in February to 1.416 in July. This is a huge percentage change – around 30 per cent – and these fluctuations affect the prices we pay for our imports and the prices foreigners pay for our exports. It was once argued that UK exporters would be put off exporting by these fluctuations in the exchange rate, simply because they would be so uncertain about the revenue they would receive.

Say, for example, that a British car producer sells cars at £10,000. Thus in February (when the exchange rate is \$1.075 per pound) it agrees to sell its cars to America for \$10,750 each. If the Americans then pay for the cars in July (when the exchange rate is \$1.416 per pound) then the UK producer will receive \$10,750 but only get about £7,600 for each car (10,750/1.416).

Thus those traders who strike bargains in foreign currencies rather than in pounds face great uncertainties and risk making losses if the UK exchange rate fluctuates too much. This uncertainty may make them reluctant to export. There are two ways around this.

Forward markets

In February, when it strikes its bargain in dollars, the UK producer could sign a contract to sell dollars in six months' time (in July). In this contract, it agrees to supply a certain quantity of dollars *and* it agrees an exchange rate for them. This is called a forward contract, and these deals are made in **forward markets**. (The exchange rate which actually rules today for today is called the **spot rate**.)

By agreeing an exchange rate now (for a deal in the future) the car producer is certain of how many pounds it will receive in, say, six months' time. It may, for example,

Table 22.1 $:£ exchange rate, January–August 1985

Month	Jan.	Feb.	Mar.	April	May	June	July	Aug.
Exchange rate ($:£)	1.114	1.075	1.23	1.216	1.286	1.312	1.416	1.396

Source: *Financial Statistics.*

agree to exchange dollars for pounds in six months' time at an exchange rate of \$1.4 per pound. For a £10,000 car it will therefore want \$14,000. If it turns out that in six months' time the actual exchange rate is only \$1.20 per pound then the producer will have 'lost' some pounds. It could have received \$14,000/\$1.20 = £11,700 for its \$14,000, but has agreed to receive only £10,000.

On the other hand, if the exchange rate turned out to be \$1.6 per pound then without the forward contract the UK manufacturer would have made only £8,750 from its \$14,000. The manufacturer therefore gives up the possibility of making a greater profit, and also the possibility of making a loss, in return for certainty.

In order for the UK producer to sign a forward contract, it must find someone who is willing to agree to buy its dollars at a predetermined exchange rate. This person (or institution) does not know what the future exchange rate will be. By agreeing to buy the dollars at a predetermined exchange rate, it therefore risks making a loss if actual rates turn out to be higher than the predetermined rate. (It might agree to buy dollars at, say, \$2 to the pound, but it might turn out that it could have bought them at the market rate of \$2.5 to the pound.) If, on the other hand, the exchange rate turned out to be lower than the predetermined rate (say, \$1 to the pound), then it would make a profit on the deal.

In this way, the risks of making a loss when the currencies are exchanged can be transferred from the UK producer to the foreign exchange dealer who has signed the forward contract with the producer. The dealer is bearing risk and does so because on balance it hopes that exchange rates turn out to be lower than the forward rates, in which case it would make a profit.

Thus the forward markets are markets in risk. Producers who prefer certainty and know they will have dollars to convert into pounds will arrange the deal now at a known exchange rate (the forward rate). Those who prefer uncertainty (the dealers) will agree to buy those dollars at that forward rate in six months' time and hope then to be able to buy the necessary pounds on the foreign exchange market for less than the price they have agreed to supply them at.

By using the forward exchange market, the UK producer can get rid of the uncertainty associated with how much revenue it will receive. This, it is hoped, will encourage producers to export. It should be noticed, though, that we have not removed the uncertainty altogether – we have simply transferred it from the producers to the dealers.

The first method of dealing with uncertainty is therefore aimed at *redistributing* it away from those who do not like it towards those who do like it, those who prefer a gamble to a certainty. The second method of dealing with uncertainty is not to redistribute it but actually to *reduce* it. This is done by using a system of fixed exchange rates, as we shall see in the next section.

SUMMARY

1. When there are many currencies, there will be many exchange rates.
2. Arbitrage ensures that these exchange rates bear a certain relationship to each other.
3. The demand for pounds on the foreign exchange market will increase as the pound is devalued.
4. The supply of pounds on the foreign exchange market will decrease as the pound is devalued, if the Marshall–Lerner condition is satisfied.
5. The exchange rate is determined by the intersection of the supply and demand curves for the currency.
6. When the market is allowed to work freely, we have a floating exchange rate system.
7. Under these circumstances, the exchange rate fluctuates quite widely and imposes risks on our exporters.
8. One way around this is to introduce a forward exchange market. This enables our exporters to be certain of their future income.

Fixed exchange rates

Consider the supply and demand curves for pounds shown in Figure 22.3. The movement of the demand curve from D_1 to D_2 would induce a fall in the exchange rate from e_1 to e_2. If this shift in the demand curve was considered to be temporary – say, due to seasonal or unusual factors – then the exchange rate would eventually go back to e_1 and its excursion to e_2 would have done little more than disrupt foreign exchange dealings and induce uncertainties into the minds of exporters and importers alike.

In these circumstances the UK government may decide to maintain the exchange rate at e_1 even when the demand curve moves (temporarily) down to D_2. In order to do this it must enter the foreign exchange market and 'buy' $q_1 - q_3$ pounds. By doing this it raises the exchange rate to e_1, reduces the market demand for pounds from q_2 to q_3 and buys the difference between that demand (q_3) and the supply at that exchange rate (q_1).

In order to 'buy' these pounds it has to provide dollars,

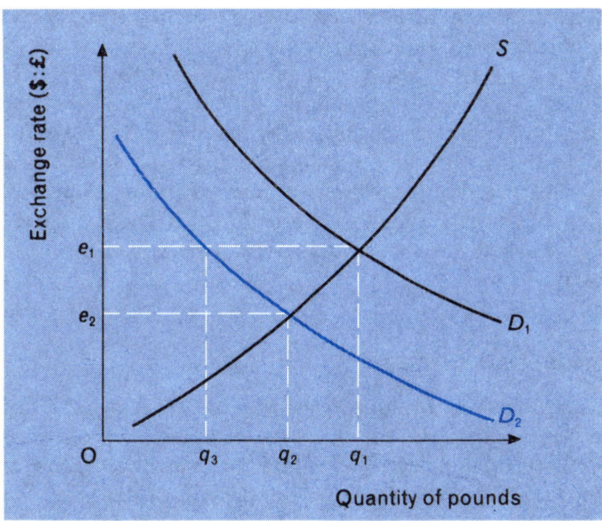

Figure 22.3 Government intervention to maintain a fixed exchange rate.

i.e. it has to act 'as if' it were an American buying pounds for dollars on the open market. By intervening in this way the government can augment the supply of pounds when demand is too high and augment the demand for pounds when demand is too low. This will keep the exchange rate more or less 'fixed'. This is therefore called the **fixed exchange rate policy**.

In order to operate this policy the UK government has to have a store of dollars (or gold and other foreign currencies) so that it can 'buy' pounds when necessary. This store of other currencies is called the **foreign exchange reserves**, or reserves for short.

Devaluation and revaluation

It is hoped that over time the government's purchase of pounds equals its sale of pounds, so that on balance the reserves remain more or less constant. Of course, if the government tries to keep the exchange rate too high it will find itself more often buying pounds than selling them. In this case it will eventually run out of foreign exchange reserves and have to borrow some. This cannot continue for long and so eventually the government will be forced to recognize that it is trying to keep the exchange rate too high. It will then 'announce' its intention to allow the exchange rate to fall to a lower level, a level at which it will in future be maintained by government intervention in the foreign exchange markets. This is known as **devaluation**. Devaluations are the means by which fixed exchange rate policies adjust to the inexorable power of the market.

It could, of course, be the case that the exchange rate is set too low, in which case there will be a **revaluation** as the new, higher maintained exchange rate is announced.

The gold standard

For almost 50 years before the First World War, the exchange values of most trading nations were fixed in terms of the value of gold. This meant that the values of currencies relative to one another were also fixed. This system was known as the **gold standard**. In this period of rapid industrialization, nations were able to trade in certainty and world trade expanded rapidly.

Following the First World War, trade did not recover from the severe disruptions of 1914–18. This was due partly to protectionism by many nations, partly to the failure to establish a new gold standard and partly to the Great Depression. Lessons were learned from this period, however, so at the end of the Second World War steps were taken to establish an internationally agreed exchange rate system.

Bretton Woods

A conference at Bretton Woods in the USA agreed that from the end of the war a system of fixed exchange rates should be established. The aim was to restore confidence to world trade so that it might re-establish itself and grow in a way that was to the advantage of all trading nations. The solution was to link currencies not to gold, but to the US dollar, which in its turn was linked to gold. The initial 1946/47 $:£ exchange rate was $4.03:£1, with the dollar fixed at $35 per ounce of gold.

The direct advantage of this system was to allow countries to operate fixed exchange rates without the need for vast reserves of gold if intervention in the currency markets became necessary. The system was more flexible because, while gold supply is fixed by nature, dollars can be manufactured. Thus central banks need only have a reserve of US dollars which they could borrow in times of crisis from the **International Monetary Fund (IMF)**. The IMF was also established at the Bretton Woods Conference (see Chapter 23 for a full discussion of the IMF).

A further advantage was that there was greater flexibility in the system than previously. Currencies were allowed to vary within a 1 per cent band of their agreed value against the dollar. Devaluations were also permitted when it was clear that the market exchange value of a currency had moved well outside the agreed limits. If a country wished to devalue, due to a persistent trade deficit, then it was obliged to consult the IMF to agree a new rate. This is necessary in any agreed system to avoid 'cheating' – when a country attempts to adopt an exchange rate that is too low relative to its trading partners' currencies. A 'low' or undervalued exchange rate affects a country's terms of trade and may allow the price of the country's exports to be relatively cheap and the domestic price of imports to be expensive, therefore favouring the country's own industries.

The Bretton Woods system is sometimes referred to as an 'adjustable peg' system. The exchange rate might be 'pegged' at a certain level, but the 'peg' could 'crawl' up and down in response to persistent drains on reserves or persistent increases in reserves.

Of course, it is neither possible nor desirable to iron out *all* short-run fluctuations in exchange rates, but the aim was to keep fluctuations within limits. Thus an exchange rate might crawl upwards at 5 per cent per annum, but the fluctuations around that long-term trend should be kept within the 1 per cent variation allowed. This is illustrated in Figure 22.4. This 'bracketing' of the exchange rate has, for obvious reasons, become known as the 'snake in the tube' or the 'tunnel'.

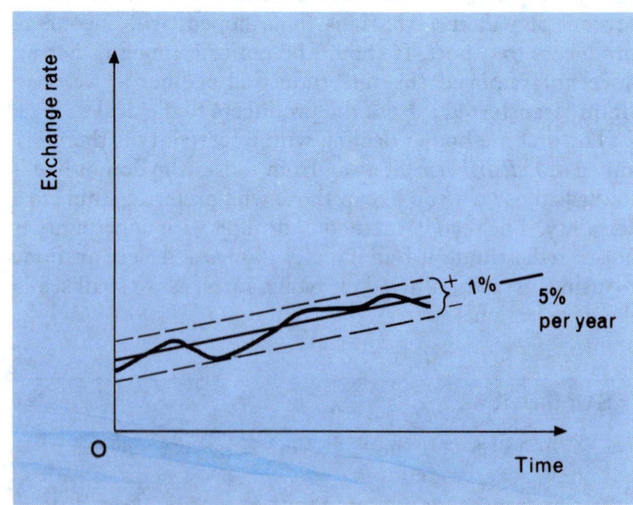

Figure 22.4 The 'snake in the tube' or 'tunnel'.

In terms of the expansion of world trade, the Bretton Woods system was a spectacular success from 1945 to 1971. Trade expanded at an average rate of over 10 per cent per annum, and the UK found it necessary to change its fixed exchange rate only twice in 26 years by agreed devaluations, in 1949 and 1967.

This success in maintaining fixed rates was achieved at a price. The UK found that, while export trade expanded, so did the level of imports and often at a faster rate. As we saw in Chapter 20, the UK visible balance has often been in deficit. Successive British governments had to restrain domestic demand in order to maintain the fixed exchange rate, i.e. restrict the supply of pounds going on to the foreign exchanges. This was the so-called **stop–go policy**.

Although the UK did maintain its fixed rates, the cost in terms of lost growth may have been considerable. Eventually, with ever-growing pressures on exchange rates, the increasing complexity of trade and the reluctance of governments to allow domestic policy to be dictated by exchange rate policy, the Bretton Woods system broke down and a period of floating exchange rates began in 1971.

The dirty float

Allowing exchange rates to float means allowing the market to determine the level of the exchange rate. Thus when the pattern of world demand changes the exchange rate will change, and this will lead to uncertainty and risk. When the movements of investment capital are considered, significant and rapid exchange rate movements are possible.

Governments have therefore continued to intervene in the foreign exchange markets when the exchange rate has moved too rapidly or too much. Often such intervention is unannounced, so that it is not possible to see if exchange rate movements are due to market conditions or intervention. Unannounced intervention is known as a **dirty float**.

The UK has maintained foreign exchange reserves which have been used to stabilize the exchange rate. Changes in the exchange rate of the pound against the US dollar and in the UK foreign exchange reserves are shown in Table 22.2. Note that some of the UK reserves are held in gold, and when the dollar is devalued the dollar value of UK gold reserves will rise.

We can see from the table that immediately after the Second World War (1945–8) the exchange rate was held at $4.03 per £1. The devaluation in 1949 brought the exchange rate down to $2.8 per £1. This was more or less held until 1967, when sterling was again devalued to about $2.4 per £1. After 1972 the pound was floated. This is apparent from the fluctuations thereafter.

The sharp drop in the UK reserves between 1988 and 1989 can be taken as an indication of the Bank of England's support for the pound in the foreign exchanges. Similarly, the steady rise in reserves during the few years preceding 1988 could indicate attempts by the authorities to hold down the exchange value of the pound.

SUMMARY

1. Exchange rate risks can also be reduced for exporters by the government entering the foreign exchange market.
2. The government will buy pounds when there is a surplus of them and will sell pounds when there is a shortage of them.

Table 22.2 $:£ exchange rates and UK reserves, 1945–90

Year	Exchange rate ($:£)	Reserves ($ million)	Year	Exchange rate ($:£)	Reserves ($ million)
1945	4.030	2,476	1968	2.394	2,421
1946	4.030	2,696	1969	2.390	2,528
1947	4.030	2,079	1970	2.396	2,827
1948	4.030	1,856	1971	2.440	6,582
1949	3.680	1,688	1972	2.502	5,646
1950	2.800	3,300	1973	2.453	6,476
1951	2.800	2,335	1974	2.340	6,789
1952	2.790	1,846	1975	2.220	5,429
1953	2.810	2,518	1976	1.805	4,129
1954	2.810	2,762	1977	1.746	20,557
1955	2.792	2,120	1978	1.920	15,694
1956	2.796	2,133	1979	2.122	22,538
1957	2.794	2,273	1980	2.328	27,476
1958	2.810	3,069	1981	2.025	23,347
1959	2.809	2,736	1982	1.749	16,997
1960	2.808	3,231	1983	1.516	17,817
1961	2.802	3,318	1984	1.336	15,694
1962	2.808	2,806	1985	1.2976	15,543
1963	2.800	2,658	1986	1.4672	21,923
1964	2.793	2,315	1987	1.6392	44,326
1965	2.796	3,004	1988	1.7796	51,685
1966	2.793	3,100	1989	1.6383	38,645
1967	2.795	2,694	1990	1.7864	38,464

Source: *Financial Statistics.*

3. To do this, it will hold gold and foreign exchange reserves.
4. By 'mopping up' excess supplies and excess demands, the government can prevent the exchange rate from changing.
5. This is called a fixed exchange rate. Before 1914 currencies were linked to gold; from 1945 until 1971 they were linked to the US$ under the Bretton Woods system.
6. When the intervention by the government is partial, we have a dirty float.

Exchange rates and hot money

Part of the explanation for the variability of the UK exchange rate can be ascribed to something other than the exchange requirement of importers and exporters. Foreigners buy UK goods and services, but they also lend to the UK and borrow from it. Thus some of the demand for sterling will be to finance trade (current account), but some will be to finance loans (capital account).

To see how this works, imagine a UK company (or the government) trying to borrow pounds in the UK. An American with spare funds (in dollars) may think that the interest rate being offered by the UK borrower is very attractive. In order to lend pounds to the UK borrower the American must first convert dollars into pounds. This is done on the international money market. This demand for pounds will bid up the price of pounds despite there having been no movement in the goods and services traded.

Now it turns out that quite small differences in interest rates between countries can induce quite large capital flows. Forecasts of changing exchange rates, e.g. a fall in the value of the pound, may also induce such capital movements in order to avoid a loss following a depreciation. This **hot money** moving between countries can and does cause large and rapid fluctuations in exchange rates, fluctuations which may prevent the exchange rate from working well for the current account. If, for example, hot money is flowing into the UK then the exchange rate will rise. This will make British goods comparatively expensive and foreign goods comparatively cheap. British manufacturers are then faced with falling orders at home and abroad.

Part of the decline in British manufacturing has been blamed on too high an exchange rate: a rate held up by capital inflows and by revenues from sales of North Sea oil to foreigners. The system which was supposed to be a self-correcting current account system turns out to be disrupted by large movements of loans on the capital account.

After the dirty float

So many things can influence exchange rates that individual governments have found it difficult to prevent exchange rates from fluctuating by intervention in the markets. This is because the size of the currency flows in the foreign exchange markets are so large that the authorities cannot bring enough pressure to bear.

In an attempt to stabilize exchange rate movements, the most powerful industrial nations, the 'Group of 7' (the USA, Japan, the UK, France, Canada, Italy and Germany) have attempted to co-operate, intervening in the markets to support each other's currencies. This has not been completely successful as domestic policy sometimes overrides agreements, and misunderstandings lead to uncoordinated action.

Another solution is to return to a form of fixed exchange rates. However, the difficulty of all nations reaching agreement and the huge increase in capital flows makes a world-wide system unlikely. A solution favoured within the European Community is a system of semi-fixed rates within the EC. This is known as the exchange rate mechanism of the **European Monetary System (EMS)**. Some would go further and solve the exchange rate problem with a common European currency. In the next chapter we look at these and other international co-operative ventures.

SUMMARY

1. Foreigners demand sterling to buy UK goods and also to lend to UK borrowers.
2. The amount they want to lend depends on UK interest rates.
3. Foreign money exchanged for pounds so that foreigners can chase high UK interest rates is called hot money.
4. The influence of hot money on exchange rates is powerful and more volatile than that due to the demand for goods.
5. Governments have tried to co-operate to reduce exchange rate movements and the UK has now joined a form of fixed exchange rate system, the exchange rate mechanism of the European Monetary System.

Exam Preparation and Practice

MULTIPLE-CHOICE QUESTIONS

1. When a country allows the exchange value of its currency to move in accordance with market forces which of the following is it operating?
A Dirty float.
B Forward market.
C Fixed exchange rate.
D Floating exchange rate.

2. In a three-country exchange rate system £1 = $2, $2 = 1 franc. What is the £:franc (F) exchange rate?
A £1 = 1F
B £1 = 2F
C £2 = 1F
D £3 = 1F

3. In a fixed exchange rate system, if the market exchange value of a currency rises above its agreed rate then the government could do any of the following to correct this EXCEPT:
A Reduce interest rates.
B Apply for a revaluation.
C Buy foreign currency with its own currency.
D Tighten domestic monetary policy.

4. If the UK government wishes to see the exchange rate of the pound sterling appreciate on the foreign exchange market, it might instruct the Bank of England to:
A increase sales of sterling on the foreign exchange market.
B increase short-term interest rates.
C repay a loan to the International Monetary Fund.
D relax any existing exchange rate controls on the export of capital.

(AEB)

5.

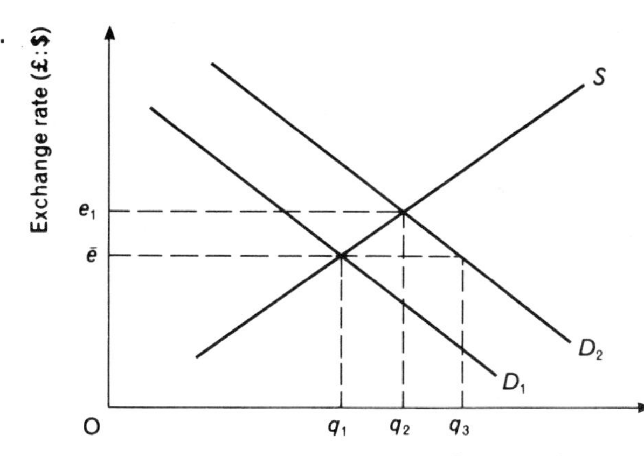

The diagram shows the pound:dollar exchange rate, which is fixed at $\bar{e}$ under an international agreement. If the demand curve for pounds moves to D_2, the government could restore the agreed rate by:
A Selling q_3-q_1 pounds on the foreign exchange markets.
B Raising interest rates.
C Buying q_3-q_1 pounds on the foreign exchange markets.
D Selling q_2-q_1 pounds on the foreign exchange markets.

EXERCISES

1. The diagram below shows the demand and supply schedules for the pound against the dollar. The initial demand curve for pounds is D_1 and the initial supply curve is S_1. Starting from the initial equilibrium in each case, find the exchange rate and the quantity of pounds traded after each of the following events.
(a) A rise in the popularity of British goods in the USA.
(b) A rise in the popularity of American goods in the UK.
(c) A fall in popularity of American goods in the UK combined with a rise in the popularity of UK goods in the USA.
(d) A fall in UK interest rates relative to interest rates in the rest of the world.
(e) A change in the opinion of speculators so that they expect a rise in the UK exchange rate in the medium term.

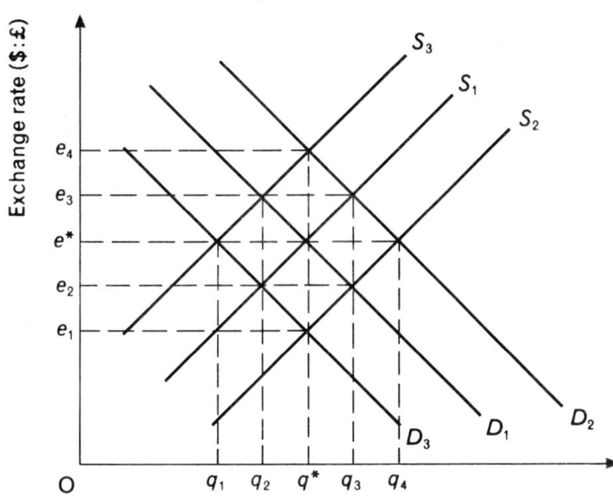

2. A manufacturer of cars exports to Australia. The domestic price of cars is £8,000. The present exchange rate is A\$2.2:£1, but is highly variable. The price of cars is fixed in Australian dollars at the time of export and payment is made 3 months later.

The manufacturer receives an order for 20 cars and the price is fixed at A\$17,600 each, to be paid in 90 days.
(a) What does the manufacturer receive in £ sterling if the exchange rate in 3 months' time is:
(i) A\$1.70:£1
(ii) A\$2.10:£1
(iii) A\$2.40:£1?
(b) If the manufacturer agrees to make a forward contract to sell his Australian dollars in 3 months' time and is offered a rate of A\$2.30, how much will he receive in £ sterling in 3 months' time?
(c) If the exchange rate is in fact A\$1.70:£1 in 3 months' time, what has the manufacturer lost and who has gained?
(d) Why is the manufacturer likely to be prepared to take out the forward contract despite the potential loss of revenue shown in (c)?

3. (a) If the £:\$ exchange rate is £1:\$4 and the value of the dollar is fixed at \$35 an ounce, what is the sterling value of 1 ounce of gold?
(b) If in the same fixed exchange rate system the French franc is set at £1:10F what is:
(i) the \$:Ffranc exchange rate;
(ii) the value of 1 ounce of gold in French francs?

4. The diagram below shows the demand and supply curves for sterling on the foreign exchange market.

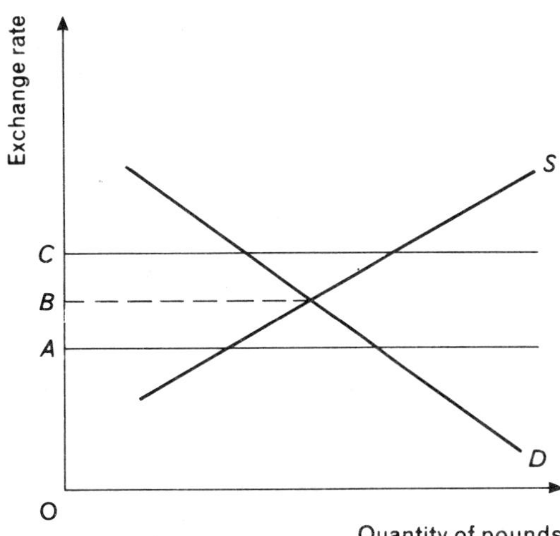

(a) What is the market exchange rate?
(b) If the exchange rate is 'fixed' at *OC*, what are the consequences for:
(i) the UK's foreign exchange reserves;
(ii) UK exporters;
(iii) UK domestic borrowers (assuming there are no restrictions on the movement of capital)?
(c) Could the exchange rate of *OC* be maintained indefinitely if the free-market rate remained as it is?

DATA-RESPONSE QUESTION

1. 'In Britain there is an obvious connection between a strong pound and the reduction in inflation. But a strong pound has its costs. Net exports are less than they would otherwise be, and the high interest rates required to keep sterling strong dampen domestic activity. These considerations suggest some fiscal stimulus – lower taxes or higher public spending – to offset high interest rates and a strong pound.'

(Source: S. Brittan, 'No magic rule for setting budget deficits', *The Financial Times*, 28 November 1985.)

(a) Carefully explain the 'obvious connection between a strong pound and the reduction in inflation'. **(6 marks)**

(b) Examine in more detail the 'costs' of a strong pound. **(7 marks)**

(c) Explain why high interest rates were 'required to keep sterling strong'. **(3 marks)**

(d) Why does the author suggest a fiscal stimulus to offset high interest rates and a strong pound? **(4 marks)**

(LON.)

23 The EC and other international organizations

In this chapter we will discuss:

1. The efforts of nations to co-operate on matters of trade.
2. How the European Community (EC) works and affects its member nations.
3. The development of a new fixed exchange rate system for the EC.

Introduction

We have seen that international trade is partly an exercise in co-operation and partly an exercise in competition.

It is an exercise in competition in that the increased output has to be allocated among trading nations. The central concept here is the terms of trade.

It is an exercise in co-operation in that, through trade, each country can specialize in the production of those goods in which it has a comparative advantage. By specializing in this way it is possible to increase production everywhere.

Reasons for co-operation

Tariffs and trade wars

We saw that one way of encouraging the terms of trade to move in our favour is by imposing a tax (a **tariff**) on imported goods.

It is certainly true that a tariff can improve our terms of trade provided no one else responds by imposing a tariff on their imports (i.e. our exports). Since we would both then have imposed tariffs, we would have discouraged imports and would therefore have reduced the level of international trade below that possible with free trade. This in turn implies that there will be less specialization and hence lower world production. Indeed it is possible to impose such high tariffs that international trade falls to zero. World production then returns to the level of production possible under autarky.

Import restrictions

These arguments in favour of free trade (zero tariffs) underpin many of the policies which gave rise to international organizations for trade co-operation. But as we have seen in Chapter 14 there are also other views concerning the benefits of trade.

The Keynesian model of the economy, for example, is based on the belief that output is determined by aggregate demand. It is therefore necessary to keep aggregate demand up to full-employment level. One element of aggregate demand is exports and one loss of aggregate demand is imports. This depressing effect of imports on aggregate demand has led some economists to argue in favour of import restrictions. This is particularly true of some modern Keynesians. They would like to expand aggregate demand by running a budget deficit and impose import controls in order to prevent this demand flowing abroad.

This kind of argument is similar in effect to that of the mercantalists. It is as if there were just so much aggregate demand available in the world and we should keep as much of it as possible for ourselves.

Beggar my neighbour

Arguments of this kind lead to the idea that we can 'export' our unemployment. By buying fewer foreign goods and selling more overseas, we can find employment for our own citizens at the expense of higher unemployment abroad. This kind of competition is an attempt to get more aggregate demand rather than an attempt to improve our terms of trade. But like the terms of trade argument, it does lead to the imposition of tariffs.

Trade co-operation is necessary here in order that the attempts to export unemployment (a 'beggar my neighbour' policy) will not result in mutually harmful outcomes. One possibility, for example, is that in times of high unemployment any one country will be wary of expanding home aggregate demand in the belief that it would result in a balance of trade deficit. The increased demand might go abroad to improve employment in other countries rather than at home. In these circumstances the trading partners could mutually agree to expand their home economies simultaneously. This co-ordination of expansion policies would nullify any imbalance of trade effects since both countries would now want more imports.

To the extent that each country's own internal economic policies are constrained by their external consequences, it is clearly advantageous to engage in some formal arrangement for co-operation.

Some international organizations

GATT

The widest scheme for encouraging free trade is the **General Agreement on Tariffs and Trade (GATT)**, which was put into effect in 1948. Since its inception there have been seven completed 'rounds' of talks and an eighth is under way. Each of these rounds has been aimed at agreeing some further reduction of trade restrictions and each has its own name. The sixth round, 1964–7, was called the Kennedy round. The seventh, 1973–9, was called the Tokyo round. The earlier rounds have focused mainly on tariff barriers; the eighth round, the Uruguay round, is trying to reach agreement on non-tariff barriers and agricultural subsidies. (Examples of such barriers are discussed at length in Chapter 24.) The eventual aim of GATT is to free international trade completely by the gradual reduction of existing impediments to trade on a worldwide basis.

EC

A somewhat less ambitious attempt at weakening trade restrictions (and harmonizing national economic policies) is the **European Community** – the EC. This was set up by the Treaty of Rome, signed in 1957 by the foreign ministers of France, West Germany, Italy, Belgium, Holland and Luxemburg.

It is possible that economic co-operation may one day lead to a united Europe. However, the original emphasis of the Treaty of Rome was on the reduction of trade barriers between members ('the Six') and the adoption of a common tariff against all non-members.

Article 3(a) states an aim as:

> the elimination, as between Member States, of customs duties and of quantitative restriction on the import and export of goods, and of all other measures having equivalent effect.

and 3(b):

> the establishment of a common customs tariff and of a common commercial policy towards third countries

and 3(c):

> the abolition, as between Member States, of obstacles to freedom of movement for persons, services and capital.

The Six made some progress in these aims over the years and resisted several unsuccessful attempts by the UK to join them. However, in 1973 Denmark, Ireland and the UK joined the Six. Greece joined in 1982 and Spain and Portugal joined in 1986. We will return to the EC later in this chapter.

EFTA

Between the formation of the EC and its subsequent expansion to include Denmark, Ireland and the UK, a parallel customs union was agreed between Austria, Denmark, Norway, Portugal, Sweden, Switzerland and the UK. This was called the European Free Trade Association (EFTA), created in 1960 and known as the 'Outer Seven' (the EC being known as the 'Inner Six'). Finland is an associate of EFTA and Iceland became a full member in 1970.

Since the UK and Denmark joined the EC, the membership of EFTA has been six full members and one associate member (Finland). The EC, on the other hand, now has a membership of twelve.

Comecon

Even before the emergence of the EC and EFTA, the Eastern Europeans had formed themselves into a Council for Mutual Economic Assistance (Comecon). The agreement in 1949 was originally between Albania, Bulgaria, Czechoslovakia, Hungary, Poland, Romania and the USSR. Albania left in 1961, but East Germany, Mongolia, Cuba and Vietnam subsequently joined.

Comecon, like the EC and EFTA, is aimed at trade co-operation but it also used to be concerned with the co-ordination of national economic plans. This was an important aspect of Comecon because its members had dispensed with the price mechanism as a means of co-ordinating internal and external economic decisions. They used instead the system of central planning bureaux. When forming their plans it was clearly advantageous for each country to know what its principal trading partners were hoping to achieve, particularly with respect to imports and exports. An exchange of information at an early stage of the plan was therefore mutually beneficial, and it is this exchange of information which Comecon was designed to achieve. Following the recent fall of Soviet planning, the future of Comecon is difficult to predict. Hungary, Poland and Czechoslovakia all wish to join the EC.

OECD

In 1948 a number of countries signed the convention which set up the Organization for European Economic Co-operation. This was replaced by the extended Organization for Economic Co-operation and Development (OECD) in 1961. Membership of the OECD comprises Australia, Austria, Belgium, Canada, Denmark, Finland, France, West Germany, Greece, Iceland, Ireland, Italy, Japan, Luxemburg, Holland, New Zealand, Portugal, Spain, Sweden, Switzerland, Turkey, the UK and the USA. This is clearly a much larger affair than those organizations concerned with purely European countries. Nevertheless one aim of the OECD is the freeing of international trade.

The European Community (EC)

The size of the EC may be gleaned from the data given in Table 23.1. Here we can see that, as far as population is concerned, the EC is larger than the world's two most powerful nations: the USA and the former USSR. In terms of economic output the EC produces slightly less than the USA but, although the figures for the USSR are not available, probably rather more than the USSR.

Table 23.1 The EC, USA and USSR compared

	EC	USA	USSR
Land area (000 sq. km)	2,250	9,400	22,400
Population (000s)	323,700	243,800	283,100
Population density (per sq. km)	144	26	13
Working population (000s)	142,060	121,602	131,300
Gross domestic product (milliard ECUs)	3,721.2	3,903.5	–
Gross domestic product per head	11,495	16,011	–
Imports (ECUs)	829,134	351,599	90,484
Exports (ECUs)	829,911	219,038	93,398

Note: All data for 1987.
Source: *Europe in Figures 1989/90* and *Eurostat*.

What is starkly different between the three is the degree of 'openness' of the economies. Almost 25 per cent of the EC's GDP is traded, but less than 10 per cent of that for the USA and an even smaller percentage for the USSR. The comparative openness of the EC would tend to imply that Europeans would be rather more concerned with trade policy than would the USA or the USSR.

The GDP of the EC may be almost as high as that of the USA, but it is important to know how that GDP is distributed *among* member nations. This is shown in Table 23.2. The dispersion is very great, with the richest countries having more than twice the per capita income of the poorest. Spain, Ireland, Greece and Portugal are all below the EC average. As we have seen in Chapter 19, however, it is not necessary for trading partners to be equally rich in order for trade to be mutually beneficial.

The range of incomes between the richest and the poorest was about the same in 1981, although Spain and Portugal were not then members of the EC. However, the rankings did change between those years. The main changes are Denmark's rise from 6th to 2nd (although it held this position in 1977) and Belgium's fall from 4th to 8th. The UK has improved its position from 7th to 5th and now achieves an above average position.

What is of interest to the economist is whether the institutions and policies of the EC have affected the overall prospects of the Community and/or the distribution of its benefits among member countries. It is the question of distribution that is most contentious.

Table 23.2 Distribution of per capita GDP (at market prices) among EC member states, 1987

	ECUs	1981 ranking
1. Luxemburg	18,313	1
2. Denmark	16,606	6
3. West Germany	16,580	2
4. France	15,951	3
5. UK	15,383	7
6. Holland	15,258	5
7. Italy	15,242	8
8. Belgium	14,712	4
9. Spain	10,807	–
10. Ireland	9,381	9
11. Greece	7,928	10
12. Portugal	7,838	–
USA	22,806	
Japan	16,368	

Source: *Eurostat*.

Common agricultural policy

The most economically significant aspect of the EC is the **common agricultural policy (CAP)**. From the division of the EC budget shown in Table 23.3, it is apparent that 62 per cent of it is concerned with agriculture.

Unlike all of the other international co-operative institutions, the CAP is not based on the theory of international trade. Article 3(d) of the Treaty of Rome states as an aim:

> the adoption of a common policy in the sphere of agriculture.

When the CAP was formed in 1965 it listed five well-defined aims:

1. To increase agricultural productivity.
2. To ensure a fair standard of living for the agricultural community.
3. To stabilize markets.
4. To assure availability of supplies.
5. To maintain reasonable prices to consumers.

These five aims make it clear that, at least as far as the CAP is concerned, the EC is not concerned only with the establishment of a common tariff against third parties, or with the reduction of tariffs between member countries. What is being aimed at here is price and income stability in agriculture. The CAP grew out of a set of long-established

Table 23.3 Division of the EC budget, 1989

	Milliard ECUs	% of budget
Agriculture and fisheries	28,250	62.0
Regional policy and transport	4,416	9.6
Social policy	3,358	7.3
Administration	2,216	4.6
Research, energy and technology	1,610	3.5
Development co-operation	552	1.2
Miscellaneous	5,428	11.8

Source: *Europe in Figures 1989/90*.

agricultural policies operated by member states. The CAP was aimed at harmonizing these national policies into a single, common policy.

The CAP has been criticized for causing overproduction and high prices within Europe. The strongest critics have been in the UK because it is largely a manufacturing country and pays more into the EC agriculture budget than its farmers receive back. This said, prior to entry into the EC the UK government had a policy dating back to the First World War of subsidizing farm incomes. So it is only the scale of the subsidy, not the principle, that most argue about.

The special nature of agricultural prices and incomes

The need for these special policies in agriculture arises from the fact that agriculture has two special characteristics, a combination of which can result in highly fluctuating prices and incomes.

First, the demand for agricultural products is inelastic. The demand curve is, of course, downward sloping, so that if prices fall more food will be bought. In comparatively rich countries, like those of the EC, most people have enough to eat and so are unlikely to expand their demand for food greatly as it becomes cheaper. On the other hand, when food prices rise it is not possible to cut consumption by very much. Food will be one of the last things to be cut when times are hard. Thus large price changes have little effect on the quantity demanded.

The second distinctive characteristic of agricultural products is that the supply is greatly influenced by such extraneous things as the weather. This imparts a degree of variation to agricultural production far greater than that of more 'controlled' sections of industry, such as manufacturing. This is illustrated in Figure 23.1.

In the diagram the supply curve S represents the amounts farmers would *plan* to produce at various prices. If, for example, the price of barley rose then farmers would plant more barley. In the case illustrated, at price P_p farmers plan to grow quantity q_p. Unfortunately, poor weather conditions could result in only q_1 tonnes of barley coming to crop (the actual supply curve S_1 is different from the anticipated S) and this results in price P_1. The inelastic nature of agricultural demand means that the small shortfall in barley production causes a proportionately larger rise in price, and this in turn causes a rise in farmers' income. The income of farmers therefore goes up in years of poor harvests.

Should there be a good harvest then we can imagine barley production being q_2, which implies a price of P_2. This proportionately larger fall in price than rise in output means that farm incomes will fall in years of good harvests.

Stabilizing farm incomes

The question addressed by the CAP is: how can these fluctuations in farm incomes and prices be controlled? In Chapter 5 we saw that if a market demand curve has an elasticity of unity throughout its length then the total revenue of an industry is the same at all prices (that is, price × quantity always equals the same figure). A possible solution is therefore to impose a demand curve with constant unitary elasticity on farm produce.

In Figure 23.2 a demand curve with constant elasticity (A) is superimposed on the original curves from Figure 23.1. At any point on demand curve A the total income of farmers is the same as when the price charged is P_p and quantity supplied is q_p, that is $P_p \times q_p$. When harvests are poor, say q_1 is produced, instead of price P_1 being charged, price P_{A1} is imposed. This price may be enforced by law, since at price P_{A1} quantity q_{d1} is demanded. Alternatively, to avoid a black market the authorities could supply the deficit ($q_{d1} - q_1$) from stock.

By supplying the quantity $q_{d1} - q_1$ the EC can avoid legislation or enforcement agencies; the market will achieve

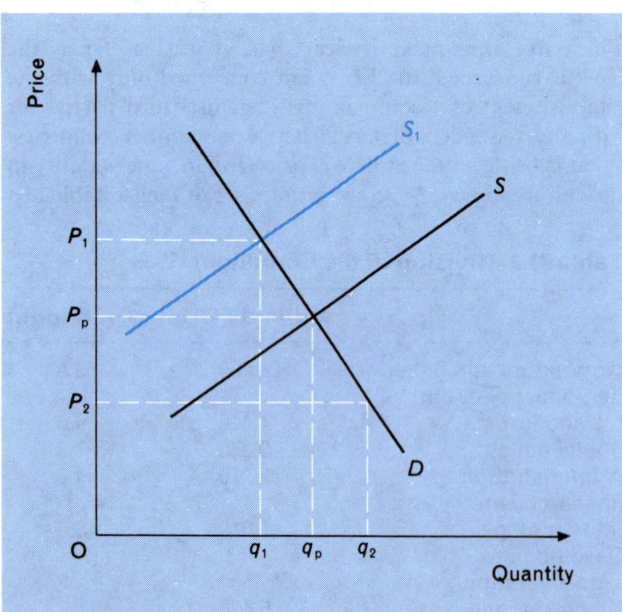

Figure 23.1 Effect of the weather on farm incomes.

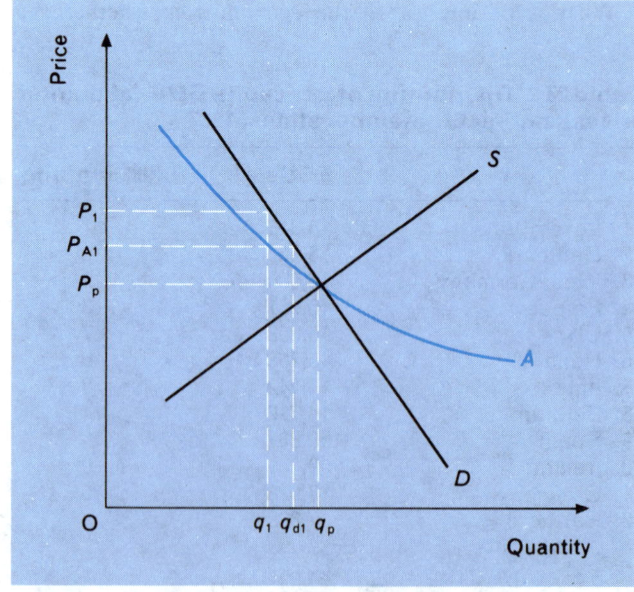

Figure 23.2 Intervening in the market to maintain farm incomes and moderate price fluctuations.

the same result. The aim of smoothing out farm price fluctuations is achieved. P_{A1} is lower than P_1 and, as the new price lies on the demand curve A, farm incomes are also stable.

In times of good harvests the reverse case holds. The authorities buy up surplus supplies to move the market on to demand curve A. Prices do not drop as low as they would otherwise and farm incomes remain constant. Farm prices do fluctuate in this system, but not as much as they otherwise would in a free market.

Import levies, export subsidies and intervention

The CAP maintains, or rather seeks to maintain, a reasonable and stable level of prices for European farmers in three ways: by imposing levies on imports; by paying export subsidies; and by buying up excess home supplies.

1. The import levy is designed to ensure that, whatever the world price of agricultural produce might be, such goods cannot be imported into the EC at a price less than the 'reasonable' price level previously decided. This reasonable price level is called the **target price**. If world prices are 10 per cent below that target price then a 10 per cent import levy is imposed. The import levy is calculated daily and hence keeps up to date with movements in world and target prices.

It is possible, of course, that at the target price there will be an excess supply – more sellers than buyers. If this is the case then national intervention agencies must step in and buy up the excess in order to prevent the price falling any more than 8 per cent below target price. This is the so-called **intervention price** and is effectively the minimum price which farmers could receive within the EC.

2. Furthermore, if world price is below intervention price then farmers would not export their surplus produce but would prefer to sell to the intervention agency. The intervention agency therefore stands in danger of building up huge stocks of produce, many of which are perishable. In order to limit the quantities of surplus agricultural production held by these agencies, the CAP allows an export subsidy to be paid to farmers so that they are indifferent as between selling to the intervention agency or exporting.

The CAP begins to look more like a managed economy than the outcome of a free-trade organization.

3. The EC solution to the problems of price and income stability obviously involves someone holding stocks of agricultural produce: stocks which are sometimes high (in times of good harvests) and sometimes very low, possibly zero (in times of bad harvests). What is important is to set the curve A so that on balance the surpluses of good harvests *equal* the deficits of poor harvests. In that way the size of the stocks held by intervention agencies does not get out of hand.

If, for example, the curve A were to be above the market-clearing price (Figure 23.3) then farmers' incomes are being held too high and planned output (q_{sp}) (on average) will exceed planned consumption (q_{dp}). This means that stocks of agricultural produce will rise over time, thus creating wine lakes and butter mountains.

In order to correct this it is necessary to reduce target prices and thereby encourage consumption and reduce production. Those who produce these goods are of course very reluctant to agree to this, and France particularly, which has a great deal of agricultural produce, tries to keep prices up.

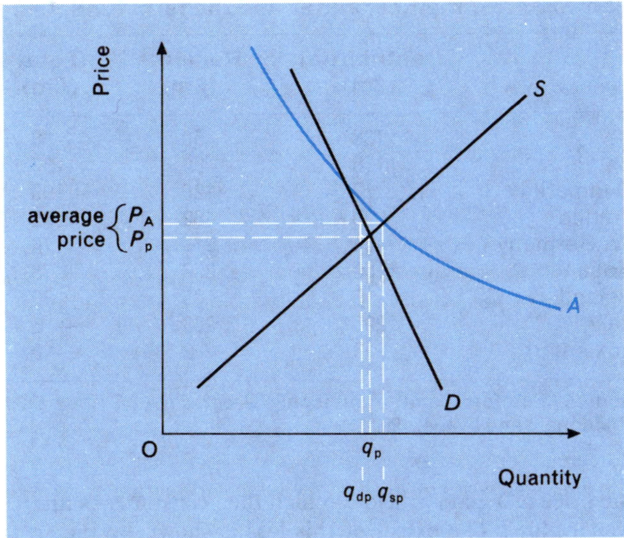

Figure 23.3 Setting farm incomes too high.

Costs of the CAP

Another part of our economic theory will help us here. Keeping price above market price deprives consumers of some of their possible consumer surplus and gives producers more producer surplus. This is illustrated in Figure 23.4.

Let us assume for the moment that harvests turn out as planned so that we have no additional complication of supply being disrupted by poor weather. Market price in Figure 23.4 (P_m) would give rise to production and consumption of q_m. However, if the price is held too high (say, at intervention price P_1) then q_s is produced, but only q_d is consumed.

When we looked at cost–benefit analysis we saw that if

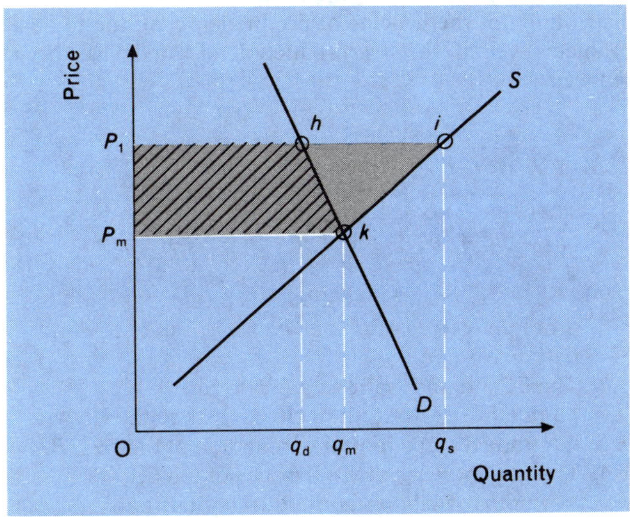

Figure 23.4 Costs of the CAP.

Table 23.4 EC member states and the farm fund, 1981

	Contribution (£m)	Receipts (£m)	Total (£m)
UK	138	50	−88
Belgium	116	80	−36
Denmark	17	126	+109
France	390	482	+92
W. Germany	456	277	−179
Holland	150	288	+78
Ireland	5	35	+30
Italy	299	283	−16
Luxemburg	3	2.5	−0.5

Source: Barnford and Robinson, *Geography of the EC*, Macdonald and Evans, 1983.

the price of a good is held too high then consumers suffer a welfare loss. The extent of this loss is shown by the area above the original or market price up to the new price and between the vertical axis and the demand curve. This is the area $P_m khP_1$ in Figure 23.4.

Producers will receive additional revenue, producer surplus. In this case the producer surplus is equal to the consumer surplus lost, plus the area above the supply curve between the market price P_m and the new price P_1, and to the right of the demand curve. This is shown by the area $P_m kiP_1$. The producer surplus is paid for partly by the consumer (the lost consumer surplus) and partly by the authorities, in this case the EC agriculture budget.

The CAP is contentious because of the question of who pays for the extra producer surplus, shown by area *hki*, in Figure 23.4. If each country contributed roughly the same amount as their farmers gained then presumably few governments would feel aggrieved. However, this is not the case. The UK and Germany, both primarily producers of manufactured goods, are net contributors to the EC agriculture budget, while France, Holland and Denmark show a net gain. Table 23.4 shows each member country's contribution to and income from the EC farm budget. In recent years action has been taken to reduce the vast surpluses of the CAP – for example, milk quotas have been imposed to reduce the milk lake. However, the redistribution of the benefits of production continue to be a problem even if the overproduction of goods has been reduced.

SUMMARY

1. There are a number of organizations that attempt to promote co-operation in and greater freedom of trade.
2. The EC is one organization that attempts to promote co-operation between a group of trading nations.
3. The EC member nations are in terms of population and output of similar size to the USA, but trade a much higher percentage of their GDP.
4. The common agricultural policy of the EC attempts to stabilize agricultural prices and maintain farm incomes.
5. Those members who produce a great deal of agricultural produce seem to be able to keep the terms of trade within the EC in their favour. They do this by keeping the price of their goods high and by imposing tariffs on suppliers from outside the EC.
6. Thus the EC is drawn together by the potential gains of belonging to a customs union.
7. The EC is not the only international organization aimed at moderating international competition. The European Free Trade Association (EFTA) and Comecon are similar in that they promote co-operation among a select few countries at the expense of the rest.

National currencies and the European currency unit

We have seen that the CAP seeks to stabilize market prices and farmers' incomes. But there are 12 different currencies in the EC and their relative values change through devaluations and revaluations. This means that if a price is fixed in Deutschmarks then any revaluation of the mark in terms of other currencies would cause sudden price changes when expressed in francs, pounds, krona, etc. Prices and incomes would be stable for the Germans but unstable everywhere else.

One way of lessening this problem is to express the target price in terms of a 'basket' of currencies rather than in terms of any single currency.

To see how this works, imagine a common market in which there are only three different currencies (as opposed to our more complicated market which has 12 separate currencies). Let these three currencies be called marks, francs and pounds. There will, of course, be an international money market for these currencies in which exchange rates between them will be established. Let us assume that one pound exchanges for 2 marks or 2 francs. This implies that one mark equals one franc.

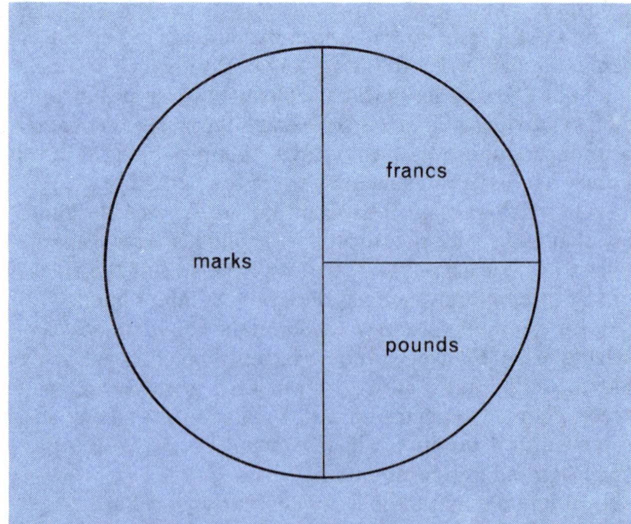

Figure 23.5 A basket of currencies.

Having set this somewhat simplified scene, it remains only to choose a particular basket of currencies to act as a unit of account (UA). One possible basket would comprise 50 per cent marks, 25 per cent francs and 25 per cent pounds. Figure 23.5 represents such a 'basket'.

Now we can work out the exchange rate between this basket (the UA) and marks, between the UA and francs, and between the UA and pounds. Take first the exchange rate between UAs and marks. We know from the definition of the UA that:

1 UA = 0.5m + 0.25f + 0.25£

We also know that 1f = 1m and £1 = 2m. Thus:

1 UA = 0.5m + 0.25m + 2 × 0.25m
1 UA = 1.25m

Therefore one unit of account (UA) is equal to 1.25 marks. Thus, for example, if the target price of wheat is 100 UAs per tonne then a German farmer would receive 125 marks per tonne.

We can do the same exercise for francs.

1 UA = 0.5m + 0.25f + 0.25£
and 1m = 1f and £1 = 2f
therefore 1 UA = 0.5f + 0.25f + 2 × 0.25f
therefore 1 UA = 1.25f

Thus the franc exchanges for units of account at the same rate as marks do (1:1.25). This is to be expected since we know that francs exchange for marks at a rate of one for one. The French farmer would therefore receive 125 francs for each tonne of wheat.

Finally, we can do the same for pounds.

1 UA = 0.5m + 0.25f + 0.25£
and 1m = £0.5 and 1f = £0.5
thus 1 UA =
£0.5 × 0.5 + £0.25 × 0.5 + £0.25
1 UA = £0.25 + £0.125 + £0.25
1 UA = £0.625

Thus the British farmer will receive £62.50 for a tonne of wheat.

If any of these three currencies is devalued then the exchange rates between *all* currencies and the unit of account will change.

Consider, for example, the case in which the mark is revalued to equal 2 francs or £1. We can now recalculate the three exchange rates between marks and UAs; francs and UAs; and pounds and UAs.

First for marks:

1 UA = 0.5m + 0.25f + £0.25
1f = 0.5m and £1 = 1m
therefore 1 UA = 0.5m + 0.25 × 0.5m + 0.25m
therefore 1 UA = 0.875m

Thus 100 UAs will now equal 87.5 marks

For francs:

1 UA = 0.5m + 0.25f + £0.25
and 1m = 2f and £1 = 2f
therefore 1 UA = 2 × 0.5f + 0.25f + 2 × 0.25f
therefore 1 UA = 1.75f

Thus 100 UAs will now be worth 175 francs

Finally for pounds:

1 UA = 0.5m + 0.25f + £0.25
and 1m = £1 and 1f = £0.5
therefore 1 UA = £0.5 + £0.25 × 0.5 + £0.25
therefore 1 UA = £0.875

Thus 100 UAs will equal £87.50.

This final result is again as expected since 1m = £1 on international money markets, so it must be true that the exchange rate between UAs and marks is the same as that between UAs and pounds.

The ECU

The net result of all this is that the price of agricultural products in the EC is defined in terms of a unit of account called the **European currency unit (ECU)**. This unit of account is defined as a particular basket of EC currencies. Even when the ECU price remains unchanged, variations in exchange rates between national currencies will still cause changes in prices expressed in national currencies. The variations caused in this way, however, are smaller than those which would result if target prices were expressed in terms of pounds or francs – or indeed in any other single currency.

To illustrate this final point, consider our previous example when the mark was revalued from 0.5m = £1 to 1m = £1. We saw then that the target price for wheat (100 UAs per tonne) translated into 125f, 125m and £62.50 before revaluation. After revaluation that target price stayed as 100 UAs but became equal to 87.5m, 175f and £87.50.

If the target price is expressed in marks then the price of wheat going to German farmers will remain at 100 marks no matter what the exchange rate is. The price of wheat going to French farmers, however, will go from 100f (before revaluation) down to 50f (after revaluation).

Similarly for UK farmers: before revaluation of the mark they received £50 per tonne, but after revaluation they will receive £100 per tonne.

These changes are summarized in Table 23.5. The first

Table 23.5 Effect of revaluation on farm prices

	TP = 100 UAs			TP = 100m		
	ER1	ER2	(%)	ER1	ER2	(%)
Franc	125.0	175.0	+40	100	50	−50
Pound price	62.5	87.5	+40	50	100	+100
Mark price	125.0	87.5	−30	100	100	0

Table 23.6 Conversion rates in ECUs, 1988 (1 ECU = yearly average shown)

	Conversion rate of 1 ECU
Belgium	43.43
Luxemburg	43.43
Denmark	7.95
West Germany	2.07
Greece	167.58
Portugal	170.06
France	7.04
Holland	2.33
Ireland	0.78
Italy	1,537.33
Spain	137.60
United Kingdom	0.66
United States	1.18
Japan	151.46

Source: *Europe in Figures 1989/90.*

Table 23.7 Composition of the ECU

Currency	Amount	Weight (%)
Belgian franc	3.431	8.1
French franc	1.332	19.4
Italian lira	151.8	10.1
Dutch florin	0.2198	9.6
German Deutschmark	0.6242	30.5
Danish krone	0.1976	2.5
Irish punt	0.008552	1.1
Spanish peseta	6.885	5.3
Greek drachma	1.44	0.7
Sterling	0.08784	11.9
Portuguese escudo	1.04741	0.8
		100.0

Note: These amounts have applied since Sept. 1989; weights are based on exchange rates at 20 April 1990.
Source: Bank of England.

column shows the price per tonne in francs, pounds and marks when the target price is 100 UAs. The second column shows what happens after revaluation of the mark. The third column shows the percentage changes in prices due to the revaluation. The next three columns tell the same story for the case when prices are fixed in marks. Both the UK and France suffer bigger price changes in the second case than in the first.

Of course, this example is rather extreme. It is unlikely that any currency is going to be revalued by 100 per cent. The actual exchange rates between various currencies in 1988 and the ECU are shown in Table 23.6, and the relative sizes of the actual basket are shown in Table 23.7.

The European Monetary System

In recent years the **European Monetary System (EMS)** has taken on more and more importance within Europe. The original aim of the EMS was to keep exchange rate variations between EC member states to a minimum and so promote trade.

The motivation for the creation of the EMS came from a period of highly unstable floating exchange rates between 1973 and 1979. The view of the other European states on floating exchange rates was never as enthusiastic as that of the UK government, and so in 1979, for a variety of national reasons, the EMS was created.

The EMS can be thought of as a Bretton Woods type of system. Each member country agreed to keep its currency within certain limits relative to a central rate. In place of the US dollar the central rate was set against the ECU. The original system saw currencies allowed to drift by up to 2.25 per cent from the central rate before action had to be taken (with the exception of the Italian lira, which was allowed a band of 6 per cent). A system of mutual support between central banks was also set up to allow short-term lending of foreign reserves.

As with the Bretton Woods system, devaluations were allowed, but only as a last resort and after consultation with and agreement of the other EMS nations.

EMS today

The simple attempt to reduce exchange rate fluctuations was only the start for the EMS. Today it has far greater ambitions and represents an attempt to promote monetary stability in Europe.

The maintenance of exchange rates within agreed limits is known as the exchange rate mechanism (ERM) of the EMS. Other aspects of the system include the ECU discussed earlier and credit facilities for member nations. Significantly, the EMS also represents an attempt at closer co-ordination of the economic policies of EC nations.

In the simplest terms, for countries to fix their exchange rates relative to one another they must ensure that conditions within their country do not diverge too greatly from those of the countries with which they have aligned their currency. This is because, while exchange rates within the ERM may be stable, the individual currencies are still traded for currencies outside the ERM. For example, the Dutch florin is traded against the Deutschmark within defined bands, but aginst the US dollar it floats freely.

To maintain the agreed exchange rate with the Deutschmark, the Dutch authorities must keep domestic interest rates and inflation in line with those of Germany, or the markets will cause the exchange rate to move outside its agreed limits. Also investors outside the ERM will find one of the currencies more attractive than the other and cause further movements. The implication of the ERM is that the Dutch florin must move against the US dollar in roughly the same way and to about the same degree as the Deutschmark. Thus Holland must pursue similar monetary policies to those of Germany.

In effect, the ERM is based around the Deutschmark as the strongest currency in the system. Germany is a strong, low-inflation economy. As Belgium, for example, has effectively tied its franc to the Deutschmark it has accepted the need to keep its inflation at German levels. This is seen as a strong and effective incentive to pursue an anti-inflation policy. Indeed, since its inception the inflation rates of countries participating in the ERM have fallen significantly.

The UK did not join the ERM until October 1990, but it

did participate in discussions on EMS matters. The principal UK objection appeared to be that joining the ERM would mean surrendering the right to pursue an independent monetary policy. For example, if the UK joined at an agreed exchange rate and its inflation rate was significantly higher than other ERM members then the exchange rate for the pound would depreciate. This would force the UK authorities to take action to keep the pound within the agreed limits and follow a tight monetary policy in order to bring down inflation. This might conflict with other interests, such as the political needs of a party nearing a general election.

The Delors report

The enthusiasm shown for the EMS in Europe is due to the desire for monetary stability in the sense of both exchange rates and inflation. In fact it is widely recognized in the capitals of the EC that independent monetary policy can have only a limited effect on national monetary conditions.

The economies of Europe are extremely 'open', in that a high share of GDP is traded and there are now few remaining restraints on the movement of capital. Thus the ability to pursue a monetary policy that differs from other nations is remote. Setting interest rates higher than competitors leads to a massive flow of funds into the currency (**hot money**) and so causes an appreciation of the exchange rate. This in turn leads to the country's goods becoming uncompetitive in world markets. It is therefore necessary to adopt broadly similar policies to one's trading partners.

This argument in turn suggests that a successful anti-inflation policy must be carried out internationally. Co-

Table 23.8 European Monetary System: bilateral central rates and intervention points

		BLF	DKR	DM	FF	HFL	IRL	LIT	PTA	UKL
	+		18.9143	4.95900	16.6310	5.58700	1.85100	3710.20	334.619	1.74510
100 BLF	=...	100	18.4938	4.84837	16.2608	5.46286	1.80981	3627.64	315.143	1.64352
	−		18.0831	4.74000	15.8990	5.34150	1.76950	3546.90	296.802	1.54790
	+	553.000		26.8100	89.9250	30.2100	10.0087	20062.0	1809.40	9.43610
100 DKR	=...	540.723	100	26.2162	87.9257	29.5389	9.78604	19615.4	1704.05	8.88687
	−	528.700		25.6300	85.9700	28.8825	9.56830	19179.0	1604.90	8.36970
	+	2109.50	390.160		343.050	115.2350	38.1825	76540.0	6901.70	35.9970
100 DM	=...	2062.55	381.443	100	335.386	112.6730	37.3281	74821.7	6500.00	33.8984
	−	2016.55	373.000		327.920	110.1675	36.4964	73157.0	6121.70	31.9280
	+	628.970	116.320	30.4950		34.3600	11.3830	22817.0	2057.80	10.7320
100 FF	=...	614.977	113.732	29.8164	100	33.5953	11.1299	22309.1	1938.06	10.1073
	−	601.295	111.200	29.1500		32.8475	10.8825	21813.0	1825.30	9.5191
	+	1872.15	346.240	90.7700	304.440		33.8868	67912.0	6125.30	31.9450
100 HFL	=...	1830.54	338.537	88.7526	297.661	100	33.1293	66405.3	5768.83	30.0853
	−	1789.85	331.020	86.7800	291.040		32.3939	64928.0	5433.10	28.3340
	+	56.5115	10.4511	2.74000	9.18900	3.08700		2050.03	184.892	0.964240
1 IRL	=...	55.2545	10.2186	2.67894	8.98480	3.01848	1	2004.43	174.131	0.908116
	−	54.0250	9.99130	2.61900	8.78500	2.95100		1959.84	163.997	0.855260
	+	28.1930	5.21400	1.36700	4.58450	1.54000	0.510246		92.2400	0.481050
1,000 LIT	=...	27.5661	5.09803	1.33651	4.48247	1.50590	0.498895	1000	86.6726	0.453053
	−	26.9530	4.98500	1.30650	4.38300	1.47250	0.487799		81.8200	0.426690
	+	33.6930	6.23100	1.63300	5.47850	1.84050	0.609772	1222.30		0.553740
100 PTA	=...	31.7316	5.86837	1.53847	5.15981	1.73345	0.574281	1151.11	100	0.521514
	−	29.8850	5.52600	1.44900	4.85950	1.63250	0.540858	1084.10		0.491160
	+	64.6050	11.9479	3.13200	10.50550	3.52950	1.16920	2343.62	203.600	
1 UKL	=...	60.8451	11.2526	2.95000	9.89389	3.32389	1.10118	2207.25	191.750	1
	−	57.3035	10.5976	2.77800	9.31800	3.13050	1.03710	2078.79	180.590	
1 ECU	=...	42.4032	7.84195	2.05586	6.89509	2.31643	0.767417	1538.24	133.631	0.696904

Note: The table shows the amount of the currency in the top row against the currency in the left-hand column. In each cell the central rate and the upper and lower limits are given. Thus, for example, the central rate between the French and Belgian francs is 16.2608 FF per 100 BLF (or, alternatively, 614.977 BLF per 100 FF). The Greek drachma and Portuguese escudo do not participate in the exchange mechanism; the notional central rates for these currencies are respectively DRA 205.311 and ESC 178.735 to the ECU.
BLF = Belgian franc; DKR = Danish krone; DM = Deutschmark; FF = French franc; HFL = Dutch florin; IRL = Irish punt; LIT = Italian lira; PTA = Spanish peseta; UKL = UK pound.
Source: *Eurostat*.

operation prevents one country's efforts from being dissipated by others. The next aim of the EMS is to formalize this co-operation even more.

The Delors report, published in April 1989, calls for **European monetary union (EMU)**. This envisages the eventual creation of a European central bank and a single European currency. Monetary policy would then be handled on a Europe-wide basis and the need for exchange rates between EC countries would be abolished.

Delors sees three stages in the creation of EMU. The first is for all EC countries to join the exchange rate mechanism of the EMS. At present Greece and Portugal do not participate in the ERM and until they do the second stage cannot be entered. The UK and Spain have recently joined the ERM and Italy has allowed the narrowing of the lira's margins for variation to 2.25 per cent, Spain and the UK have been allowed 6 per cent margins for a transitional period. The central rates and intervention points of the ERM are shown in Table 23.8 on the previous page.

Although the currencies are allowed their 2.25 or 6 per cent margins, this does not imply that each currency can vary by this amount against every currency in the ERM. Rather a currency has to remain within its margin against all of the others, which means effectively that, for example, the pound must always be within 6 per cent of its agreed band with the weakest or strongest currency in the ERM. Case Study 23.1 shows how in a single month the pound went from the weakest to the second strongest currency in the ERM, while its DM exchange rate moved only from DM2.9041 to DM2.9660.

Stage 3 of the Delors plan would result in the 'locking together' of European exchange rates and the possible creation of a single European currency and a European central bank. The advent of 1992 (see Chapter 24) and the single European market has led to intense debate on how fast the EC can and should proceed towards stage 3. The UK has made it clear that at present it wishes to proceed no further than stage 1.

Arguments for and against EMU

The debate about whether or not the UK should join the EMS is over. But whether the EC should proceed to stage 3 of the Delors report is still open to question. Far more questions are being asked in the UK than elsewhere. For example, in 1989 Mrs Thatcher lost both her Chancellor, Nigel Lawson, and her personal economic adviser, Prof. Allan Walters, who disagreed violently on this point. (Mr Lawson wanted to join the ERM, but opposed EMU; Prof. Walters favours EMU, but not the ERM.) It is possible that the UK will not participate in EMU and so will be left out of the process altogether.

The arguments in favour of EMU can be summarized as follows. First, it will remove exchange rate uncertainty and the need to convert currencies in order to trade within the Community. Secondly, the economies of Europe will be tied to the low-inflation German economy. Thirdly, an independent European central bank, on the lines of the German Bundesbank, would be free from political control, and supporters argue that it could pursue effective anti-inflation policies as the situation demanded.

It is further argued that the ERM will mean that workers and trade unions will have to limit their wage demands to those which can be justified by productivity increases. Previously, a wage rise that exceeded productivity improvements would lead to inflationary price rises, but the loss of

Case Study 23.1 Spain leads the way

The Bank of Spain's cut of 0.2 of a percentage point in one of its key money market rates, for the thrice-monthly auction of certificates, could have been more crucial than sterling's rate against the mark for the cut in British interest rates 45 minutes later.

Under the rules of the European exchange-rate mechanism, each government must hold its currency within $2\frac{1}{4}$ per cent either side of its central rate against each of the other eight, rather than any single standard such as the European currency unit. Only Spain and Britain, the most recent entrants, are allowed a 6 per cent range.

Spain has the highest interest rates in the system and the strongest currency, so sterling's lowest permissible point is against the peseta. Sterling's band is normally taken as between DM2.78 and DM3.13, since the mark is the most important currency in the system. The immediate permitted low is about DM2.88 and the high (constrained by the weakness of the French franc) about DM3.08. In practice, as soon as the marginal cut in Spanish rates were announced, the peseta moved slightly ahead, for the same reasons as the pound did, making it slightly more risky for British rates to be cut. After sterling also recovered in relief at the extent of the cut, the peseta was still about 5.5 per cent ahead of its central rate against sterling.

Selling pressure switched to the franc, on the supposition that it was France's turn to cut rates. Sterling, despite being backed by the second highest interest rates in the system, has been the weakest ERM currency since the Gulf war started.

In the afternoon, however, sterling edged above its central rate against the franc, making the French currency the weakest in the system for a short time. In terms of the league table, they are separated only by goal difference.

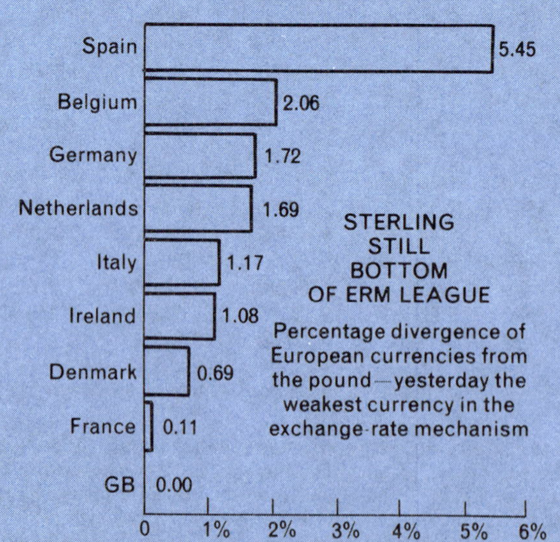

Pound moves up to second place in ERM

The pound had climbed past the Italian lira to second from the top of the European exchange-rate mechanism by the close of trade in London after extending its gains against the mark, rising above DM2.9800 at best.

With the financial markets resigned to having to wait until well into next month for a fresh base rate cut, dealers see scope for the pound to renew its rise against the weaker German currency after the long Easter weekend. After European markets closed, however, sterling eased to third place behind the lira.

An advance closer towards DM3, a level the pound last reached in the days immediately after ERM entry last October, now looks possible, although some currency analysts regard DM2.9800 as a strong resistance point.

The backwash of the dollar's strong climb against the mark has benefited the pound within the ERM, but has pushed it lower on the cross-rate against the dollar. Foreign exchange markets were quiet later in the day as dealers squared their books before the weekend. The pound closed in London at DM2.9660, just below its previous finish. Having been 1.73 cents lower at one stage, sterling regained ground to end at

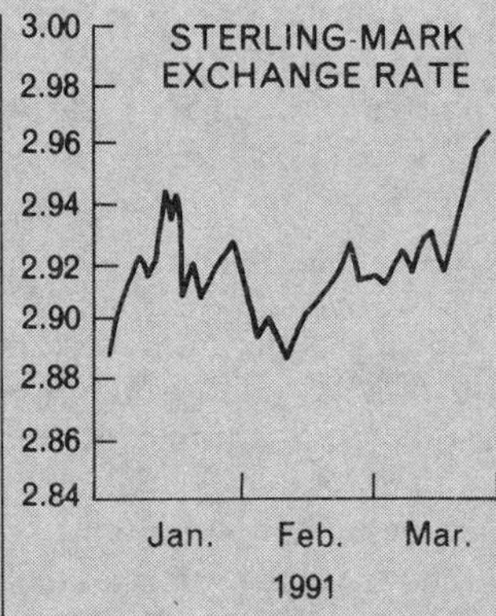

$1.7365, down more than half a cent.

The pound closed 0.2 of a point higher at 92.4 on its trade-weighted index, still well below the 96.5 it stood at on ERM entry. Market rates eased slightly, with the benchmark three-month rate $\frac{1}{16}$ lower at $12\frac{3}{8}$ per cent.

Keith Skeoch, chief economist at James Capel, said the pound's rise reflected the greater credibility the authorities now enjoyed in the markets. He added that Budget signals and remarks this week from Robin Leigh-Pemberton, Governor of the Bank of England, had reinforced market conviction about policy.

Uncertainty over how the Bundesbank will move on interest rates at its policy-setting council session next Thursday, and the prospect of an American easing after next Friday's unemployment data, are reasons why the British authorities would want to wait before moving on rates.

Some analysts believe the Treasury is waiting for April 12, publication date for the retail price figures for March, which are expected to show annual inflation slowing further.

Ian Harnett, chief economist at Strauss Turnbull, said the government was happy to have the pound in the upper half of its ERM bands, and would not want to lower the base rates prematurely, only to have to put them up again.

Weekly data on notes in circulation showed a 5 per cent rise in the week to March 27 year-on-year, pointing to annual growth in M0, the narrow money supply measure, slowing to 2.5 per cent in March. After jumping 2 pfennigs to DM1.72, the dollar eased to end less than half a pfennig up at DM1.7070.

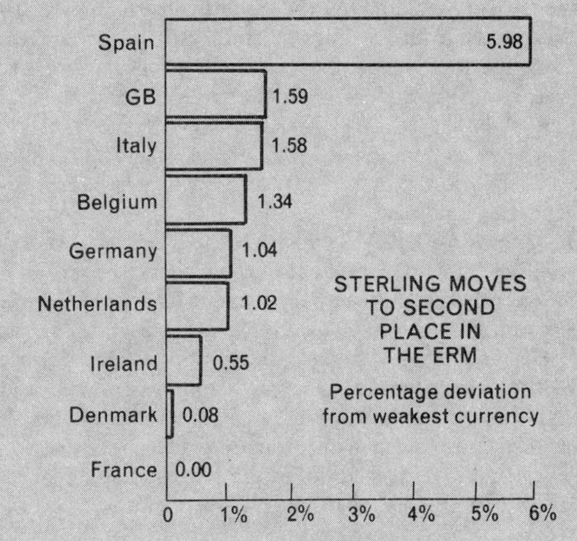

1. To what extent do the articles support the view that ERM membership means the UK cannot have an independent monetary policy?

2. Does the movement of the pound in the ERM mean that the 'fixed' nature of the ERM is only an illusion and will eventually end?

Source: Colin Narbrough, *The Times*, March 1990

competitiveness that this would cause could be offset by depreciation of the exchange rate. As this option does not exist in the ERM without severe difficulty, and does not exist at all in EMU, then a 'new realism' in wage bargaining would emerge and inflationary pressures would be reduced when workers realized that they really would be pricing themselves out of jobs.

The doubts about ERM and EMU are many. The principal UK objection is that the right to use independent monetary policy would be lost. Member countries would still have the right to use fiscal policy within their own borders (in the same way as US states can raise taxes), but the loss of sovereignty seems an important political barrier.

The creation of EMU would make inflation within a single country meaningless. This is because there would be a single currency and so monetary policy could be applied only on a Europe-wide basis. Therefore only European inflation would be monitored. The European central bank would have to keep all of Europe competitive, but would regional differences emerge? It is claimed that tying the UK to Germany would keep the UK competitive, but this may not work. If UK wages rise faster than productivity increases then UK workers may be priced out of work. Within the UK Wales has been operating in a currency union with England for centuries, yet is has chronically depressed areas. Could this happen in Europe?

The loss of the ability to correct domestic problems by allowing the exchange rate to change would be lost for ever. This does not mean that domestic problems cannot be solved, but the solutions may take longer and be more painful in terms of local unemployment.

Perhaps the most significant obstacle to the Delors plan is the need to find agreement. There now appear to be 13 players, the 12 member nations and the EC Commission (of which Delors is President). The Commission wishes to see a rapid transition to stage 3 of the Delors report. The various member states have differing views of the speed of transition, and of exactly what the ultimate goal is.

There are various views on the type of currency that will finally emerge. The UK favours a 'hard ECU', which will circulate with the existing domestic currencies. People will then be free to choose which they use. The Commission appears to favour an EC currency to replace the existing national currencies.

A major problem that has emerged is pinning down exactly what stage 2 of the Delors plan is. This transitionary phase has no adequate definition and many commentators admit to not knowing exactly what it means. Thus the starting point and destination have been defined, but the route between them remains vague. Even the agreements reached so far are likely to be changed, especially with the now 'Euro-enthusiastic' Major government in the UK having greater authority in the negotiations.

Finally, there is the question of what level the currencies are tied together at. As West Germany is finding after its merger with East Germany, the rate of conversion is critical. Setting aside the feelings of those who must convert their savings to the new currency, the problems for the economy can be considerable. If the rate of exchange is set too high then the country gains a competitive advantage, but this may lead to upward pressure on wages and cause inflation. Too low a rate of exchange will overvalue consumer money holdings.

The question of EMU will be settled in the next few years, either with or without the participation of the UK. So far we can say that the EMS and ERM have been a success and, as we shall see in Chapter 24, the single European market offers great opportunities for the future. There is no reason why the UK *must* join in with EMU, but if it does not then it will retain all of the problems of exchange rate variation with its main trading partners. It may even find itself locked out of the biggest single market in the world, a prospect that holds few attractions.

The World Bank and the International Monetary Fund (IMF)

The World Bank and the IMF are both agencies of the United Nations. The International Bank for Reconstruction and Development, to give the World Bank its full name, was set up in 1945 after the 1944 Bretton Woods agreement. Its purpose is to facilitate inter-country loans. Member countries contribute to the Bank's capital according to certain economic criteria, the most important of which is the national income of the member country. The Bank can, however, borrow from private sources and generally act as a bank by offering advice and expertise to customers and members. Unlike most UK banks, however, the World Bank lends 'long' – usually over about 30 years. The interest rate depends upon the cost of raising funds.

The IMF was also established in 1945 following the Bretton Woods agreement. Its principal aim is the management of international exchange rates. Initially this was done through a system of fixed exchange rates. Each country's currency was linked to the US dollar and was expected to remain within ± 1 per cent of that exchange rate. Since the dollar was convertible into gold at a fixed rate, this fixed system of dollar rates was equivalent to a gold exchange rate.

In order to 'manage' these exchange rates within the ± 1 per cent limits it was necessary that each member country could enter the foreign exchange markets as a buyer of its currency when its price was falling (devaluing) and as a seller when its price was rising (revaluing). In order to buy one's own currency one must have foreign currencies (gold and foreign currency reserves). The IMF provided a pool of such reserves by attracting a quota from each member. This quota was the amount of its own currency it contributed to the IMF and depended on the country's national income and other economic indicators.

This common pool of currencies could then be drawn on by countries who found it necessary to support their currencies on the international money markets and yet had no (or low) reserves. The maximum amount they could get from the IMF (their 'tranche') was twice their quota. Should the maintenance of a particular exchange rate prove impossible, then the realignment of currencies could be negotiated through the IMF.

A new reserve asset (apart from gold and national currencies) was introduced in 1969 when the IMF developed its own unit of account. It was called the **special drawing right (SDR)**. This is similar to the European currency unit (ECU) in that it comprises a basket of currencies. The SDR basket contains five currencies: the dollar, the pound, the franc, the mark and the yen. Claims on the IMF and indebtedness to it are now expressed in SDRs rather than gold or dollars.

The introduction of the SDR was timely because in 1972 the fixed exchange rate regime was abandoned. From 1972 onwards exchange rates were to be freer to follow market forces, and countries were no longer obliged to support their currencies on international money markets.

The IMF is therefore no longer concerned with the somewhat tight control over exchange rates, but much more with orderly exchange rates and the valuation of international indebtedness.

SUMMARY

1. The EC uses a special unit of account to administer the common agricultural policy, the European currency unit. The ECU, as a weighted average of all EC currencies, is more stable than any one currency, so fluctuations in prices are lower.
2. The European Monetary System aims to reduce exchange rate fluctuations between the currencies of EC states. The Delors plan hopes to develop the EMS into a new fixed exchange rate system and eventually into European monetary union.
3. In the UK there are doubts about the desirability of closer monetary co-operation.
4. A somewhat broader view than the EC is taken by organizations such as the OECD, the World Bank, the IMF and the GATT. These aim not so much at benefiting a few at the expense of the rest, but rather at mutual benefits for all.

Case Study 23.2 Fine-tuning with a crowbar

As the chancellor stood up to make his annual speech at the Mansion House last Thursday, the pound fell below DM2.95, the government lost the Eastbourne by-election and the other 11 members of the European Community agreed on a date for monetary union – with Britain or without it.

These four events were not unconnected. After the dangerous decision to enter the exchange rate mechanism at a deliberately overvalued rate, confidence in the government's economic policies was at a low ebb by Thursday, not only in the City and in Europe but also among the British public. Yet the main message of John Major's Mansion House speech was that the government's economic philosophy remained irrevocably fixed: the overriding objective was to eradicate inflation; this would be achieved by making a cast-iron commitment to a pre-announced financial target, in this case a strong pound.

Unfortunately for Mr Major, the number of true believers in this approach seems to be dwindling daily. Yet confidence has been the alpha and omega of Mrs Thatcher's economic philosophy ever since the Seventies, when Sir Keith Joseph introduced her to the 'rational expectations' school of monetarists. These people argued that inflation could be rapidly and relatively painlessly reduced by any government that could convince economic decision-makers of its implacable determination to stick to monetary targets. Once workers, managers and investors realised the government would not bail them out by printing money, they would give up their inflationary habits. The newly virtuous behaviour would be rapidly rewarded with stable prices and steady growth.

In the dark days of 1981, the faith in rational expectations took on the comical intensity of desperation. I well remember one of the Treasury's advisers arguing privately that Mrs Thatcher's fanatical media image would be a boon for economic policy: 'If people think she's mad, they'll finally believe that she will stop at nothing to hit the monetary targets.'

But it was not to be. The Resolute Approach was fine for winning wars against Argentina and beating Arthur Scargill. But as a way of managing a modern economy it simply did not work. It was not just in Britain but, even more importantly, in America that single-target monetarism was gradually abandoned in favour of a pragmatic type of interest and exchange rate management. This had more similarities to traditional Keynesian demand management than to the inflexibility of rational expectations.

Given the past experience of pragmatic changes in the government's economic policies, to say nothing of the imminence of a general election, it is by no means rational for people to believe that sterling will never be devalued simply because the government has joined the ERM. As for the chancellor's attempts to assure the markets that he will not cut interest rates until it is 'safe' to do so, this only feeds the misgivings.

There is a fundamental contradiction between the old monetarist promise to put economic policy-making on anti-inflationary autopilot and the constant references to refined personal judgements on the state of the economy made not only by the British chancellor, but by every other leading policy maker around the world these days. The fact is that seat-of-the-pants fine-tuning has returned with a vengeance not only in Britain and America, but also in Germany and Japan.

There is, however, a crucial element missing from the new type of economic fine-tuning, especially as it is practised in the Anglo-Saxon countries. While the intellectual content of monetarism has been effectively abandoned, the political commitment to using monetary policies alone has remained. The tax and credit policies that were a vital part of the economic toolbox in the Keynesian period of demand management have been deliberately thrown away. As a result, the policymakers in Britain and America have had only two policy instruments – interest rates and exchange rates – to try to influence a multiplicity of objectives, including inflation, unemployment and the balance of payments. On closer inspection, even these two instruments proved to be tied together in an awkward fashion, since interest and exchange rates have an extremely close interaction in a world without exchange controls.

As long as monetarist thinking was in the ascendant, this did not seem a problem. For the core of the monetarist belief was that controlling inflation should be the government's sole macroeconomic concern. One instrument, whether monetary targets, interest rates or exchange rates, should be sufficient to hit this target. But few are willing to accept this abdication of responsibility any longer, either in the electorate or the financial markets. Whether he likes it or not, the chancellor is once again expected to fine-tune the British economic engine to achieve satisfactory performance on inflation, employment and the balance of payments, all at the same time. To do this, he will need the whole toolbox of fiscal, monetary and credit policies. The crowbar of a fixed exchange rate will not be enough.

1. Does the author oppose the ERM or just the government's domestic policy?

2. Is it possible to 'fine tune' an economy as open as the UK?

Source: Anatole Kaletsky, *The Times*, 22 October 1990

Exam Preparation and Practice

MULTIPLE-CHOICE QUESTIONS

1. If the Dutch florin is revalued against the ECU then:
   A Goods priced in florins will now require more ECUs to purchase them.
   B Goods priced in florins will now require fewer ECUs to purchase them.
   C The florin is devalued against all other currencies in the ECU basket.
   D Dutch inflation is higher than in other countries with currencies in the ECU basket.

2. The exchange rate mechanism of the European Monetary System is:
   A A floating exchange rate system.
   B A fixed exchange rate system.
   C An institution to provide foreign exchange loans to countries in temporary balance of payments deficit.
   D The European central bank.

3. Special drawing rights are an attempt to
   A increase the amount of money customers can withdraw on demand from their bank accounts.

B facilitate the effectiveness of government monetary policy by withdrawing liquidity from the banking system.
C expand the amount of international liquidity.
D provide extra government assistance to firms setting up in depressed areas.

(AEB)

Answer key

Where there are three numbered alternatives

A	B	C	D	E
1, 2, 3 Correct	1, 2 Correct	2, 3 Correct	1 Correct	3 Correct

Where there are four numbered alternatives

A	B	C	D	E
1, 2 and 3 Correct	1 and 3 Correct	2 and 4 Correct	4 only Correct	1 and 4 Correct

4. The General Agreement on Tariffs and Trade has as its aim:
1 The reduction of tariff barriers.
2 The elimination of non-tariff barriers.
3 The strengthening of customs unions.

5. The common agricultural policy of the European Community has among its aims:
1 To keep food prices to the customer to a minimum.
2 To maintain the incomes of farmers.
3 To produce a surplus for use in Third World aid.
4 To stabilize prices in agricultural markets.

6. The European Monetary System features:
1 Set bands within which currencies may fluctuate against other member currencies.
2 Central banks committed to intervene if currencies are in danger of going outside predetermined limits.
3 An agreed rate of growth of the money supply of each member country.

(AEB)

EXERCISES

1. The following diagram shows the demand curve for wheat (D_w), the planned supply curve for wheat (S_p) and the actual supply curve for wheat (S_a) due to fine weather conditions. The government has decided to maintain farm incomes at the level that farmers would receive if the market supply curve was S_p (i.e. £20 × 150 tonnes).

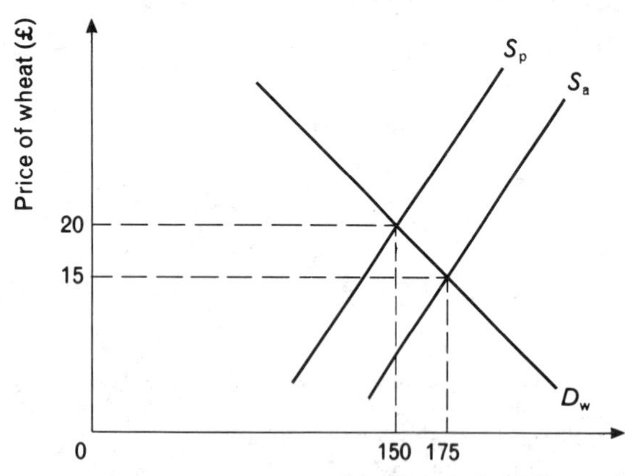

(a) What would be the effect of the actual supply conditions on farm incomes if the free market was allowed to operate?
(b) What price (to the nearest pound) would the government have to offer farmers to maintain their incomes at the planned level?
(c) If the price in (b) is guaranteed by the government, what will be the effect on the demand and supply of wheat, and what action would this force the government to take?
(d) If the world price of wheat is £12 a tonne, what would the authorities need to do to maintain their guaranteed price?

2. In the following diagram the curves D_w and S_w represent the market demand and supply curves for wheat. The government has guaranteed a price of £25 a tonne.

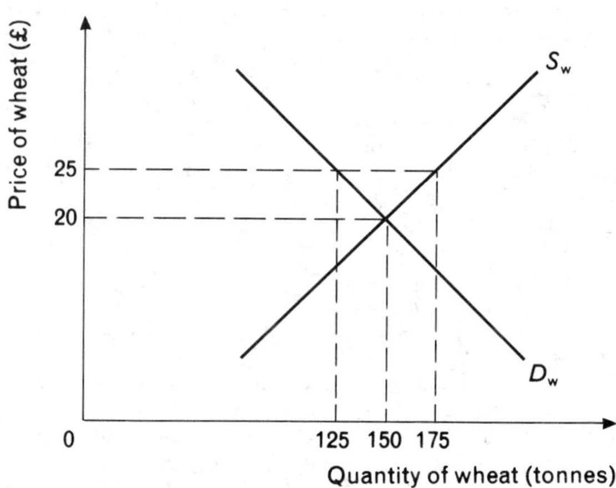

(a) What is the value of consumer surplus lost?
(b) What is the value of producer surplus gained by farmers?
(c) Who pays the difference between the consumer surplus lost and the producer surplus gained?

3. Imagine that Britain, France and Germany operate a customs union with a common agricultural policy. Farm prices are fixed against a composite currency unit (CCU). The CCU is made up of a basket of the three currencies: 1 CCU = 1/3£+1/6Ff+1/2DM. The present exchange rates are: £1:1f, £1:2DM.
(a) What is the f:DM exchange rate?
(b) What is 1 CCU worth in each currency of the customs union?
(c) The target price of wheat is 20 CCU a tonne. How much does a farmer in each country receive per tonne of wheat in his own currency?
(d) The French franc is devalued, so that £1:2f, 1f:1DM and £1:2DM What is the CCU now worth in terms of each currency?
(e) The target price of wheat is kept at 20 CCU per tonne. How much does a farmer in each country receive per tonne of wheat in his own currency?
(f) If the CCU did not exist and the target price of wheat was set at 15f per tonne, what price per tonne would farmers receive in their own currencies:
  (i) before the French franc devaluation;
  (ii) after the French franc devaluation?

DATA-RESPONSE QUESTION

1.

The European Monetary System

European monetary circles were dominated last week by a vigorous debate between the French and the West Germans on the future of the European Monetary System (EMS). The French have advanced three main proposals about the operation of the EMS. They are that:

1. The EMS currencies should be managed jointly against the dollar and the yen.
2. There should be agreed targets for monetary growth in each member country, underpinning the

agreed set of exchange rates.

3. Member states should accept equal responsibility for defending agreed parities, and there should be unlimited credit facilities between central banks available to be drawn long before a weak currency hits its "floor".

The French case boils down to this: the EMS should be more than just a "deutschmark zone". As Paris sees it, when under the present arrangements, exchange rates start getting out of line, the burden of adjustment falls entirely on the countries with the weaker currencies. They have to adopt more restrictive policies to keep their exchange rates within the agreed margins, whilst the strong currency countries generally sit tight. So although the system is biased against inflation, it is also biased against growth, and this at a time of chronic unemployment.

With their currencies tied to the deutschmark, countries like France have had to try and match West Germany's inflation performance, and, to the extent they have failed, the periodic realignment of exchange rates have not been sufficient to maintain the competitiveness of French industry. France has suffered a ferocious squeeze, which has certainly solved its inflation problem, but at the cost of a growth rate scarcely half that of Britain's over the past five years. In view of their EMS commitments they have no means of breaking away, as the British did in 1986 by means of a 25% devaluation of sterling against the deutschmark.

If member countries accepted equal responsibility for preserving agreed exchange rates, a weakening of the franc against the deutschmark would be countered by both French and West German central banks, which would lead to an expansion of the German money supply at the same time as a restriction of the French. Hence the deflationary bias of the system would be removed.

Source: *Adapted from an article by Christopher Smallwood in The Sunday Times, 13 September 1987*

(a) Explain what is meant by the terms "agreed parities" (line 13) and the "floor" (line 16) as used in the passage. *(4 marks)*

(b) Why is it that "the burden of adjustment falls entirely on the countries with the weaker currencies" (lines 20 to 22) under an exchange rate system such as the European Monetary system? *(7 marks)*

(c) How has membership of the European Monetary System contributed to the relatively slow growth of the French economy over the past five years? *(7 marks)*

(d) Why would the proposals made by the French (lines 7 to 16) help to remove "the deflationary bias" (line 47) of the European Monetary System? *(7 marks)*

(AEB)

PART V

CURRENT ISSUES

24 1992: The single European market

In this chapter we will discuss:

1. The nature of the changes proposed by the EC known as '1992'.
2. The economic implications of the proposed changes.
3. The potential microeconomic and macroeconomic gains of 1992 and the potential costs.

Introduction

By the end of 1992 the European Community will have put into law a series of directives that will mean that, as far as business is concerned, the customers of the 12 member nations will be one market. This means that in 1993 it should be just as easy for a firm in Jarrow to sell to a customer in Milan or to the Italian government as it always was for it to sell to a customer in Southampton or to the British government.

Perhaps the most surprising feature in all this is that pre-1992 it was difficult for firms in one EC country to operate in other EC member states. For many years the EC was known as the 'Common Market', but it appears that despite the removal of tariff barriers there remained many physical, technical and fiscal barriers to trade which effectively protected firms in their domestic markets.

The Single European Act aims to change all this and create a genuinely common market in Europe by sweeping away the non-tariff barriers which have survived since the Treaty of Rome in 1957. The European Commission has estimated that this market integration will lead to a rise of at least 4 per cent in European GDP, a downward effect on inflation equivalent to −6.1 per cent, the creation of 1.8 million new jobs, a beneficial effect on member government budgets equivalent to 2.2 per cent of Community GDP and an improvement in the EC balance of trade with the rest of the world equivalent to 1 per cent of EC GDP. The Commission stresses that these are conservative estimates!

What is 1992?

A brief review of inter-state trade within the European Community

The European Community was established in 1957 by the signing of the Treaty of Rome. The six members at that time (France, West Germany, Italy, Belgium, the Netherlands and Luxemburg) agreed to form a customs union for trade between themselves. This meant that trade between member states was not subject to any tariffs, and this principle was extended to the nations who joined subsequently.

The establishment of the customs union led to a substantial increase in trade between the member states, as economic theory would predict. The example of the United Kingdom is illustrated by Figure 24.1. Since 1973, when the UK joined the EC, the share of UK trade that is done with other EC members has risen from just over one-quarter to half of all foreign transactions.

This spectacular rise in trading activity within Europe cannot, however, be put down to 'free trade' in its pure form. Despite the abolition of intra-EC tariffs, there remain many barriers to trade. These non-tariff barriers include customs red-tape at national borders, which causes expensive delays, various national regulations that do not conform to other EC countries' standards, and protection of domestic industries from foreign competition by national governments.

The idea of 1992

When the EC was formed some member states had the idea of it eventually leading to a 'United States of Europe' – complete political and economic integration. The momentum for this in the early years was quite rapid, but with the enlargement of the community and the increasing number of regulations coming out of Brussels the purpose was lost. 1992 is designed to regenerate the drive towards European integration by sweeping aside all of the non-tariff barriers.

The enthusiasm of member states for the creation of a single market has been mixed, but a major breakthrough was achieved when the right of 'veto' was lost and replaced by majority voting. This meant that no one state could block the whole procedure as it had been able to in the past. All 12 states have now passed a Single European Act committing themselves to market integration by 31 December 1992. It is argued that some never fully understood the implications of their acceptance and that others (e.g. the UK) will not participate fully, but 1992 is a reality whether the individual European states like it or not.

The implications of 1992 go far beyond the integration of markets, for it will require both governments and business

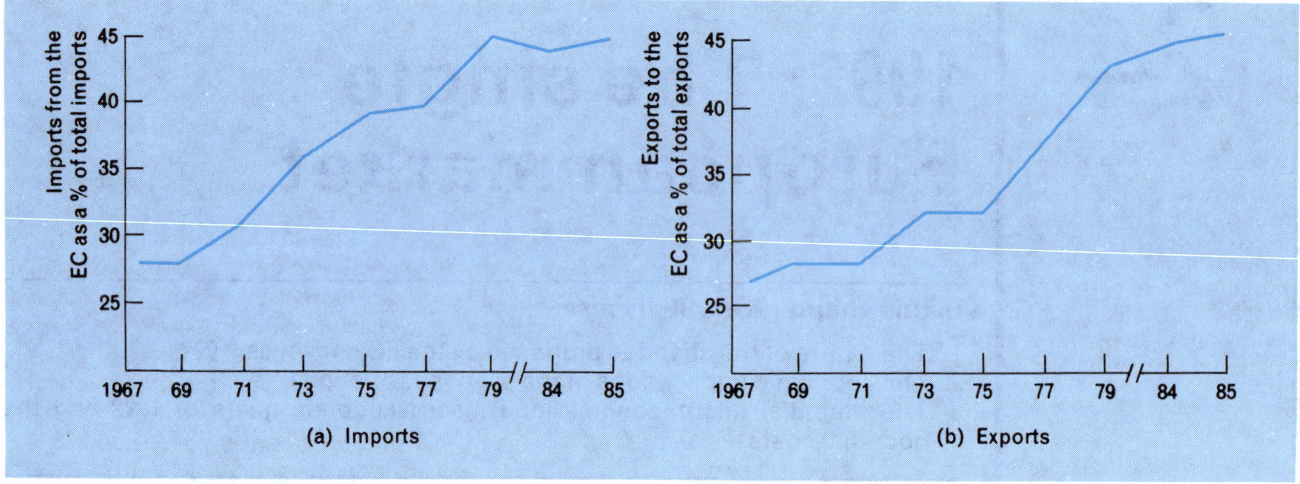

Figure 24.1 UK trade with the Community, 1967–85.

to respond. Governments will find that they must co-operate with each other on economic policy. Business will find that, unless it prepares for the open market, others will reap the massive advantages that it will bring. We can now look specifically at the barriers which are to be removed.

The non-tariff barriers

The Cecchini report identifies three types of barrier that must be eliminated for the single market to come into being;

1. Physical barriers.
2. Technical barriers.
3. Fiscal barriers.

It also sets out the gains to be made from the elimination of these barriers, which it describes in the following terms: 'the picture is one of debilitating costs which, if not crippling European business at home, ensure that they step out to confront global competition with lead weights round both feet'. The basis for this view will become clear later.

Physical barriers

Physical barriers are such things as border stoppages and customs controls with their attendant paperwork. Cecchini estimates that border controls cost industry approximately ECU 8 billion per year in lost time and extra expenditure. There are further costs of ECU 4.5–15 billion per year in trade that is simply not entered into because of the difficulties involved. Small firms are thought to be particularly badly affected as they pay a higher percentage of their trade value in costs.

An illustration of the waste that border controls cause is the familiar long queues at Italian customs posts, where two different sets of customs officials carry out essentially the same checks. The Cecchini report quotes an example of two 1,200 km journeys – one within the UK, and one from London to Milan. Ignoring rest periods and the Channel crossing time, it takes 36 hours to complete the journey within the UK, but 58 hours to go from London to Milan. Thus customs and border procedures add up to 50 per cent to transport costs.

Technical barriers

Technical barriers are many and varied. They range from simple safety requirements to the restriction of competition for government contracts.

In a survey to establish how firms ranked the importance of various barriers the difference in national standards was revealed to be one of the most acute problems. The sort of thing that firms complain about are the different health and safety standards of different countries. For example, the temperature that the side of an electric cooker can reach (an obvious and desirable safety precaution for young children) is different in various EC states. A manufacturer must either make several different models or just one to the highest safety specification. Either way costs are higher, in the first case due to a loss of potential economies of scale, and in the second because of the extra cost of inputs. Producing only at the highest standard also allows manufacturers in one country to undercut them by producing only for their own country's lower standard, another potential loss of scale economies.

Further problems arise with various national standards bodies, such as the British Standards Institute (BSI). The BSI sets standards which, while not compulsory, have great influence in the UK and none elsewhere. EC countries do not recognize each other's standards and this leads to expensive retesting in each state. How much easier if, having been passed safe in one country, a good is deemed to have done so in all, i.e. if there is mutual recognition.

This is precisely what the 1992 directives allow. After 1992 if a drug is passed safe for use in France the company producing it is saved the cost of expensive clinical tests in the other 11 EC member states. Table 24.1 from the Cecchini report summarizes the costs of divergent technical standards.

The procurement (purchasing and acquisition) of resources by governments is another significant technical barrier. At present 7 to 10 per cent of EC GDP is spent by governments on procurement, yet only 0.14 per cent of GDP is spent by the procuring government with firms outside its own borders. The Cecchini report estimates that savings equivalent to ECU 21.5 billion could be made by governments buying from the cheapest source, and by the lowering of prices due to genuine competition.

Table 24.1 A typology of costs resulting from divergent standards and regulations

For companies
- duplication of product development
- loss of potential economies of manufacturing scale
- competitive weakness on world markets and vulnerability on European markets as companies operate from a narrow national base

For public authorities
- duplication of certification and testing costs
- not getting value for money in public purchasing, whose non-competitive nature is often reinforced by national standards and certification

For consumers
- direct costs borne by companies and governments mean higher prices
- direct and larger losses due to industry's competitive weakness and inefficient structure

Fiscal barriers

Fiscal barriers are those which apply to the capital markets and those which arise from differences in rates of taxation, such as VAT.

The freedom of firms and people to move capital around has increased, although some EC countries do still operate exchange controls. But VAT rates do vary, as do excise duties. This presents significant paperwork problems as tax is paid in one country on entry and reclaimed on exit. And some countries favour their own industries by their excise duties. For example, the duty on wine in the UK is more severe than that on beer. The UK produces little wine, but a great quantity of beer.

The other problem in the financial sector is the inability of a financial institution of one country to trade in another. This has led to wide differences in the costs of financial services between countries. It is, for example, much more expensive to borrow money to buy a house in the UK than in other EC states. It is suggested that free competition across Europe will, by its presence, bring costs roughly into line. This would be a move towards the cheapest service.

The non-tariff barriers are therefore significant. Before we proceed to discuss the benefits to be gained for the EC as a whole, we can look at how 1992 will affect one industry. The following section is taken directly from the Cecchini report.

The benefits of 1992 to the automobile industry

Overview

Contributing almost 6 per cent of valued-added in EC manufacturing and employing 7 per cent of its workforce, the automobile industry is by any standards a key sector of the European economy. In 1985, EC manufacturers accounted for about 40 per cent of world passenger car output. Yet a range of barriers, including divergent technical regulations and massive tax differences, continue to fragment the Community market and impede the rational organization of a Europe-wide industry supplying it. Overall cost of the impediments signalled in the White Paper, or the savings which would over time result from their removal, in particular through economies of scale, is estimated at ECU 2.6 billion, or 5 per cent of the industry's unit costs.

These are the essential conclusions of the research report which was based, inter alia, on a detailed survey of auto manufacturers and suppliers. A particular focus of the report was how the post-1992 integrated market would impact on two key phases of industry activity – design and engineering, and manufacturing and assembly. Clearing away the regulatory diversity enabling industry to gear up these functions for the challenge of the 1990s is given additional incentive by the Community's market potential. By 1987, the EC had already overtaken the US to become the world's largest single car market.

A single market – but only in name

The trouble is that the world's largest single car market is single only in name. The range of obstacles hindering its effective integration, and likewise the matching rationalization of supply, provide a quintessential roll-call of Common Market disunity. This list, for reasons of space, is outlined here in abridged form:

fiscal barriers:
- taxation levels on car sales different in virtually all EC countries, ranging from 12 per cent in Luxemburg to some 200 per cent in Denmark and Greece;
- divergent policies on the refunding of VAT for company purchases of vehicles;
- distortion of competitive conditions by excessive aid to 'national champion' companies (grants, loans, equity injections, debt write-offs);
- use of fiscal incentives in some countries (Netherlands, Germany, Luxemburg and Denmark) to encourage sales of vehicles built to differing emission and noise standards.

physical barriers:
- documentary and inspection requirements at intra-EC borders, with attendant delays resulting in loss of time and money in the shipping of components;
- differences in communications standards between EC member states which impede co-operation in vehicle development and production.

technical barriers:
- lack of single EC-wide type approval procedure, requiring costly and time-consuming duplication of cars and tests;
- unique national vehicle equipment requirements, e.g. side repeater flasher lights in Italy, reclining driver's seat in West Germany, right-hand drive and dim-dip lighting in the UK, yellow headlamp bulbs in France, and unique rear reflectors in Germany.

Outlook for cost savings

Creating real European home market conditions by removing such regulatory barriers – a key example being the absence of full EC type approval should accelerate current trends in industrial reorganization and technological change both in car and component manufacturing.

However, the challenge is not just the removal of obstacles but, in addition, the circumstances which allow these barriers to lead to such great price differences. In this respect the situation is particularly aggravated when divergent national standards are compounded by distribution arrangements which tend to segment the market.

Getting maximum gains from an integrated EC car market also depends on developments in other areas. Thus a fully-integrated telecom sector and elimination of border red-tape would do much to facilitate the auto industry's component trade.

For 90 auto components surveyed, the research found that the European supply industry is providing many of the major components at rates far under 500,000 sets per annum. Sizeable economies of scale could be achieved if this level were reached. Sub-optimal production arises partly because carmakers are awarding the supply of a single part or assembly to several suppliers, and partly because of too many car models. A key economy of scale for European motor manufacturing would be the reduction in the number of car-platforms needed. Platforms are vehicle floor-plan designs to which common components are attached in the areas of running gear, suspension, and steering, and which, through relatively little changes, can be used for different car models. Today 30 platforms are used in the EC for passenger volume cars produced by the six majors (VW, Volvo, Renault, Fiat, Ford and GM), but in the fully integrated market conditions sought for 1992 this could be reduced to 21 involving platform-sharing between several manufacturers.

Market integration, with gains of this sort, will result in savings in unit costs of around 5 per cent, according to the research, or just over ECU 2.6 billion for Community manufacturers taken together. This saving is forecast to be partly attributable to direct cost reductions as a result of abolishing EC barriers, but in particular to economies of scale resulting from platform reductions.

Looked at through another prism, the overall ECU 2.6 billion figure can be expressed in terms of savings in respectively variable and fixed costs. Dominating the variable cost savings of almost ECU 900m is an estimated gain of ECU 826m in labour costs. This reflects a dramatic improvement in labour productivity, itself a result of the rationalized organization of output. Savings of ECU 1.7 billion in fixed costs are broken down as follows:

Savings in fixed costs in the automobile sector

Savings in fixed costs	ECU million
• tooling	571.7
• engineering	700.7
• warranty provision	175.3
• administration/finance	213.3
• advertising	42.3

To these gains must be added the potential increase in sales resulting from price reductions. It has been estimated that the EC's demand for cars might increase by around half a million units simply as a result of the drop in prices linked to the removal of barriers sought by the White Paper.

SUMMARY

1. '1992' is an attempt to create a single market in Europe, so that all producers and consumers can trade on equal terms anywhere in the EC.
2. The Single European Act will abolish all non-tariff barriers to trade within the EC, and so allow freer trade.
3. There are three types of non-tariff barrier:
   (a) Physical barriers such as border customs controls.
   (b) Technical barriers such as national safety standards.
   (c) Fiscal barriers such as different VAT rates for the same goods in different countries.
4. The removal of non-tariff barriers will lower the costs of trade and so lead to an expansion of trade, output and employment.

Economic theory and 1992

The creation of a single market in 1992 is essentially a **supply-side measure**. The aim is to create conditions in which the economy can work more easily – that is, without unnecessary interference. Supply-side measures have become more popular with national governments in recent years and are now as important as fiscal and monetary policy in the eyes of many. There are four areas of economic theory that we can employ to explain the advantages of 1992: the theory of comparative advantage, economies of scale, the effect of making an imperfect market more competitive, and the theory of demand.

Comparative advantage

In Chapter 19 we saw how, if countries specialize in the production of goods in which they have a **comparative advantage**, the overall production of goods rises and the average cost of production falls. We need not repeat these arguments here. The point is that the removal of non-tariff barriers allows countries to move towards the position where they can exploit their comparative advantage.

At present some European countries contain firms with higher costs than firms producing similar goods in other EC countries. And at present the non-tariff barriers must be making imported goods more expensive than those produced domestically. Following the removal of these barriers the goods of the country with the comparative advantage will be able to enter the others at a lower price. Thus countries will be forced to specialize in the goods in which they have a comparative advantage, to the benefit of the consumers of Europe.

Economies of scale

Unless there are constant returns to scale, the gains due to comparative advantage will be reinforced by the gain of

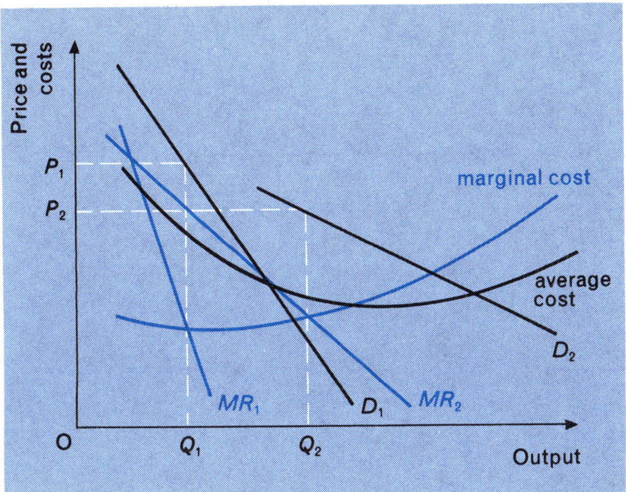

Figure 24.2 Realizing economies of scale.

economies of scale. As we saw in Chapter 3, it is often the case that the average cost of production will fall as a firm's output rises. This may be due to increased buying power leading to more generous discounts, more efficient use of capital and other factors, or managerial economies. These **economies of scale** will result in further price reductions and so still more benefits to the consumer. This process is illustrated in Figure 24.2.

In Figure 24.2 the firm originally faces the demand curve D_1, which is the demand from the firm's domestic market and the export market allowed by the present non-tariff barriers. Post-1992 the firm faces demand curve D_2, which is considerably to the right of D_1 because of the greater opportunities the firm has in the rest of the EC. When the firm faced demand curve D_1 it maximized profit by producing output OQ_1 and charging price OP_1. With the opening up of the market, the new profit-maximizing output is OQ_2 and the firm therefore charges OP_2.

Greater competition

Finally we can consider the benefits of greater competition because all firms will be able to compete across the EC equally, including for the contracts of foreign EC governments. The previously protected position of domestic industry will give way to genuine competition and the price of goods and services will be competed down.

The process that will cause this fall in prices is the movement of previously imperfect markets (oligopolies) towards a less imperfect one. Nobody is suggesting that EC markets are about to become perfectly competitive, but they will be closer to this than previously. This is reflected in Figure 24.2, which shows that the demand curve D_2 has a shallower slope than D_1. The greater competition that firms face in the single market suggests a relatively more elastic demand curve.

More demand

A further benefit from the general lowering of prices caused by all three of the above effects is to cause a rise in demand. As real prices fall, consumers will wish to buy more. This will lead to an overall rise in output (as opposed to a rearrangement of the centres of production) and so will cause a rise in the employment levels in the EC.

Finally, the fall in the cost levels of EC industry will allow them to compete more effectively in world markets. This will also bring about a rise in demand for EC goods, and so lead to a further rise in output and employment.

There are costs to balance against these gains. The most important of these are the adjustment costs – as the most efficient industries exploit their comparative advantages, others decline. While the overall level of employment and output will rise, there will be areas of the EC that lose out. The process of change can be very painful and it will be necessary to compensate certain regions. The Cecchini report suggests that the gains to the budgets of member governments will more than fund the extra regional aid required.

SUMMARY

1. 1992 is a supply-side measure – it aims to allow markets to work more efficiently.
2. 1992 will allow EC economies to gain in four areas:
   (a) By specialization in areas where they have a comparative advantage.
   (b) By reaping economies of scale due to higher production levels.
   (c) By cost reductions due to greater competition.
   (d) By the general fall in costs and prices, which will lead to higher demand and hence employment.
3. Following 1992 EC industries will be in a stronger position to compete in international markets.
4. There will be an adjustment cost following 1992 as less efficient industries decline, causing regional (structural) unemployment. It is estimated (by the Cecchini report) that the overall effect will be a higher level of EC employment.

Estimating the effects of 1992

The Cecchini report provides details of various studies of how the implementation of the 1992 measures will affect the economy of Europe. A most interesting aspect of the studies is their measurement of the gains to be made, which they approach from two angles – the microeconomic gains and the macroeconomic gains. Looking at both approaches allows us to see more clearly how 1992 will affect Europe. It is also a topical piece of applied economics and shows us how economic theory can be turned to real world problems.

Microeconomic gains

The microeconomic analysis draws attention to the gains in consumer surplus, the widening of product choice (a

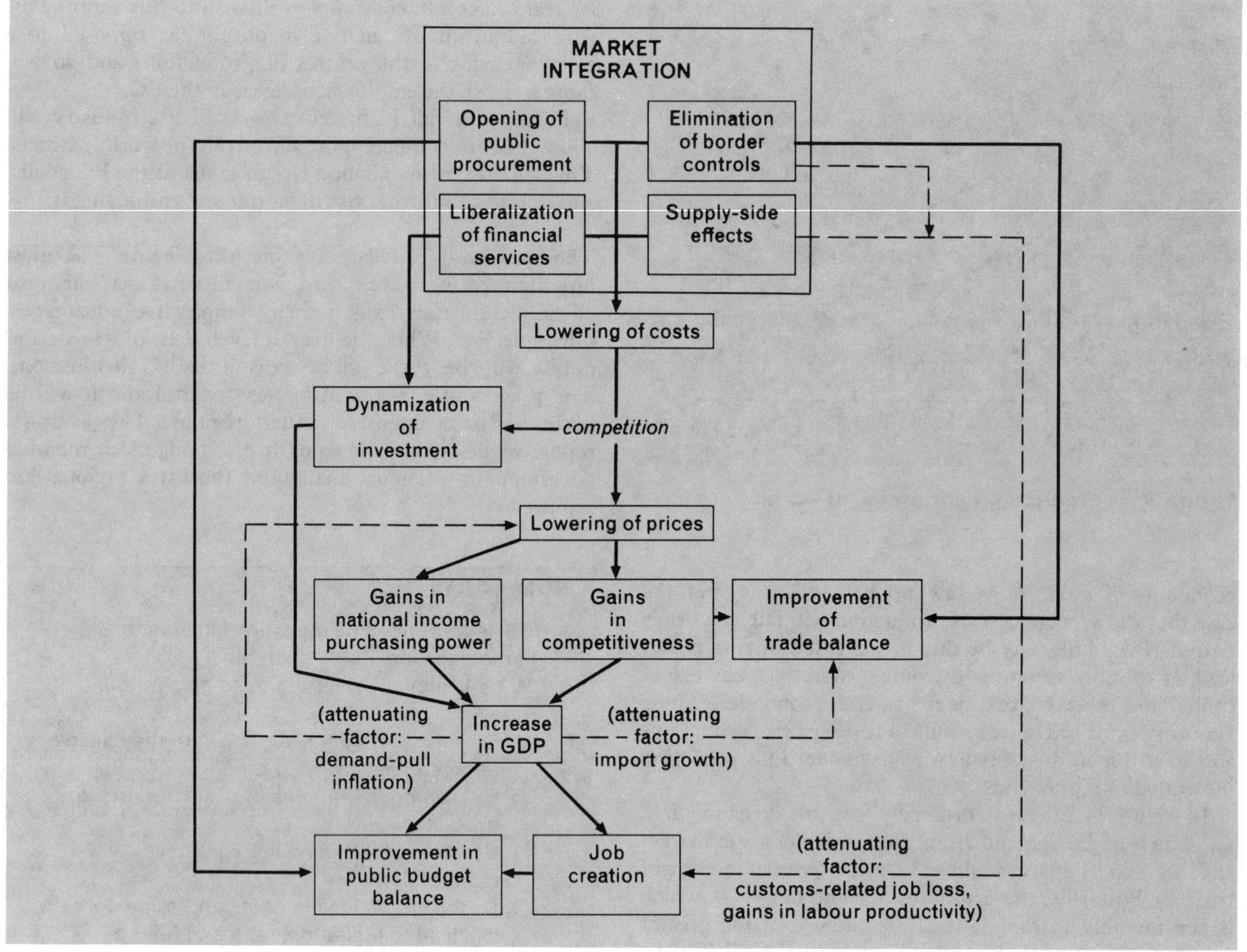

Figure 24.3 Flow-chart of microeconomic effects triggered by EC market integration.

welfare gain), the fall in prices due to economies of scale and comparative advantage, and the elimination of **X-inefficiency** (see Chapter 6 for a discussion of X-inefficiency).

Figure 24.3 is a flow chart of the microeconomic changes that 1992 will induce. The starting point is the removal of non-tariff barriers at the top centre of the diagram. There are two immediate effects: a reduction in costs due to the removal of barriers; and an increase in competition as domestic markets are exposed to a greater number of potential sellers.

The increase in competitive pressures has three effects, two of which feed into firms' price–cost margins. The direct effect of increased competition is to squeeze margins, but they also cause firms to cut out inefficiencies (X-inefficiency) and this allows at least a partial recovery of these margins after a time period. The third effect of competitive pressure is to cause firms to restructure. This may mean stopping production of a good altogether, moving sites and most importantly searching for more efficient methods and new products (technical progress and innovation). The restructuring and innovation then feed into the end result of fuller exploitation of economies of scale and comparative advantage. This third effect takes the longest time, and the full advantage will not be felt for years after 1992.

Now, following the impact of lower costs due to the removal of non-tariff barriers, we see there is another improvement in gross profit margins. This feeds into prices, which are lowered, and leads to an increase in domestic demand (demand curves slope downwards). More goods are then produced, and the increase in production allows greater economies of scale and the exploitation of comparative advantage. The full effect of this process will again not all be realized at once – the EC can expect to reap the rewards over a period of a few years. Once the advantages have fed through, however, they are permanent and should allow further growth on the basis of the competitive position of European firms.

The Cecchini report uses a four-step process to estimate the value of the microeconomic gain as detailed above. This is reproduced in Table 24.2. The mid-point estimate of gains in Table 24.2 is ECU 216 billion at 1988 prices, or 5.3 per cent of EC GDP. This is equivalent to £145 billion or US$263 billion. To put these figures into perspective, £145 billion (at 1990 prices) is approximately 75 per cent of total UK government annual expenditure. Moreover, these are only the direct effects and do not take account of 'the overall

Table 24.2 Potential gains in economic welfare for the EC resulting from completion of the internal market

	Billion ECUs	% of GDP
Step 1		
Gains from removal of barriers affecting trade	8–9	0.2–0.3
Step 2		
Gains from removal of barriers affecting overall production	57–71	2.0–2.4
Gains from removing barriers (sub-total)	65–80	2.2–2.7
Step 3		
Gains from exploiting economies of scale more fully	61	2.1
Step 4		
Gains from intensified competition reducing business inefficiencies and monopoly profits	46	1.6
Gains from market integration (sub-total)	62[1]–107	2.1[1]–3.7
Total		
For 7 member states at 1985 prices	127–187	4.3–6.4
For 12 member states at 1988 prices	174–258	4.3–6.4
Mid-point of above	216	5.3

Notes: [1]This alternative estimate for the sum of steps 3 and 4 cannot be broken down between the two steps.
The ranges for certain lines represent the results of using alternative sources of information and methodologies. The seven member states (Germany, France, Italy, United Kingdom, Benelux) account for 88% of the GDP of the EC twelve. Extrapolation of the results in terms of the same share of GDP for the seven and twelve member states is not likely to overestimate the total for the twelve. The detailed figures in the table relate only to the seven member states because the underlying studies mainly covered those countries.
Source: European Commission.

dynamics to be unleashed by the creation of a European home market' (Cecchini report, p. 85).

Macroeconomic gains

The macroeconomic analysis is based around the beneficial effects of 1992 on the now traditional constraints to growth in European countries, namely government budget deficits, inflation, unemployment and the external balance. All four constraints will be eased by market integration, and so the scope for growth will be improved.

Figure 24.4 shows a flow chart of the macroeconomic effects of 1992. At the top of the chart, four initial benefits of integration are shown, each of which has in addition to

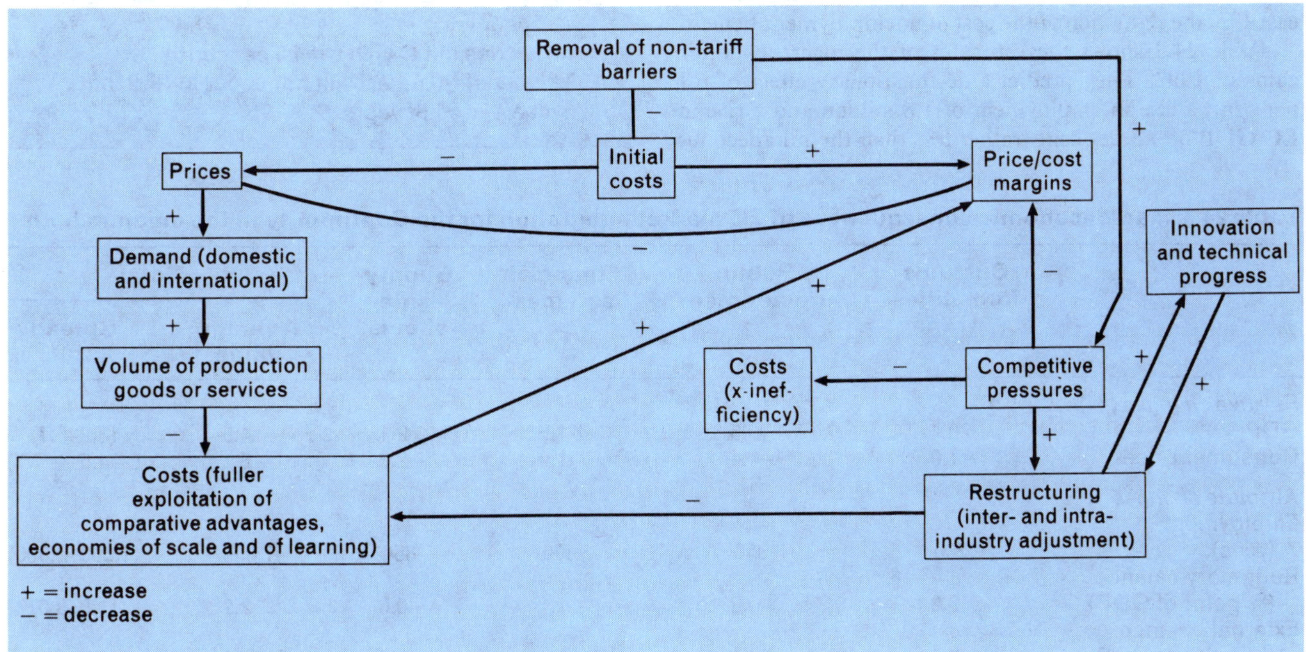

Figure 24.4 Principal macroeconomic mechanisms activated in the course of completing the internal market.

their combined effect on costs and prices an independent influence on the economies of the EC.

The effect of lower costs and so prices has already been followed through in terms of domestic output. In addition, Figure 24.4 shows the beneficial effect on the balance of trade caused by lower export prices. For individual EC economies there will also be an improvement in the terms of trade, as the prices of imports from other EC countries fall. An improvement in the terms of trade means that a country must give fewer exports in return for a given amount of imports. It is then better off in real terms because the country can consume more than before.

The chart also shows that there are negative factors to be considered. First, the growth of output will create inflationary (demand-pull) pressures within the economy, which will partially offset the predicted fall in prices. However, the estimates provided by the Commission suggest that price falls will outweigh inflationary pressure (see Table 24.3). Secondly, the rise in real GDP in Europe will lead to higher demand for goods from outside the EC. This will dampen the improvement in the balance of trade.

The price effects of integration will be reinforced by several other effects. The removal of border controls will cause a direct improvement in the balance of trade, although the overall gain in employment will be mitigated by the diminished need for customs officials. The freeing of the financial markets will allow firms to invest more easily in EC countries, and to use the cheapest financial services (the cost of which should be competed down in any case). This should lead to a more dynamic investment programme with a long-term beneficial effect on output and employment. Finally, the removal of local bias in the awarding of government contracts will cause the cost of public procurement to fall. This implies that member governments' budget deficits will fall (surpluses rise), giving greater scope for public investment or tax cuts. The public purse should also be eased by the reduction in the cost of unemployment benefit.

Table 24.3 shows the estimates of the macroeconomic gains of 1992. They predict a de-inflationary effect of 6.1 per cent, a rise in employment of 1.8 million and a rise in EC GDP of 4.5 per cent (rather less than the microeconomic estimate of 5.3 per cent).

The gains of 1992 are not necessarily immediate; it will take time for European firms to adjust to the new climate. Overall the 1992 measures should make Europe more efficient and more able to compete in world markets. The need to compete is seen as essential if US and Japanese firms are not to take the lion's share of future industrial markets. Indeed, one of the gambles of 1992 is that European firms will be quick enough to take advantage of the new situation for, while non-EC firms will still face tariff and non-tariff barriers, their costs are already lower in many cases.

SUMMARY

1. There are two ways to assess the gains from 1992 – by microeconomic effects and by macroeconomic effects.
2. The microeconomic gains from 1992 are:
   (a) A widening of consumer choice.
   (b) Reaping economies of scale.
   (c) The reduction of X-inefficiency.
   (d) Greater competitive pressures.
3. The Cecchini report estimates the microeconomic gains of 1992 as equivalent to 5.3 per cent of EC GDP.
4. The macroeconomic benefits of 1992 stem from four sources:
   (a) The opening of public procurement.
   (b) The elimination of border controls.
   (c) The liberalization of financial services.
   (d) Supply-side effects.
5. The Cecchini report estimates the macroeconomic gains from 1992 as:
   (a) A downward effect on inflation of 6.1 per cent.
   (b) A rise in overall employment by 1.8 million people.
   (c) A rise in EC GDP of 4.5 per cent.
6. The benefits of 1992 will not occur in 1992, but over a period of years.

Table 24.3 Macroeconomic consequences of EC market integration for the Community in the medium term

	Customs formalities	Public procurement	Financial services	Supply-side effects[1]	Total	
					Average value	Spread
Relative changes (%)						
GDP	0.4	0.5	1.5	2.1	4.5	(3.2–5.7)
Consumer prices	−1.0	−1.4	−1.4	−2.3	−6.1	(−4.5−−7.7)
Absolute changes						
Employment (000s)	200	350	400	850	1,800	(1,300–2,300)
Budgetary balance (% point of GDP)	0.2	0.3	1.1	0.6	2.2	(1.5–3.0)
External balance (% point of GDP)	0.2	0.1	0.3	0.4	1.0	(0.7–1.3)

Note: [1]Based on a scenario which includes the supply-side effects estimated by the consultants, economies of scale in manufacturing industry and competition effects (monopoly rent, X-inefficiency).
Source: HERMES (EC Commission and national teams) and INTERLINK (OECD) economic models.

Case Study 24.1 Advantage, Greece

Economists love working out how much the European Community will gain from the 1992 project. Which members will gain the most?

The official analysis of the economic effects of the 1992 project – the Cecchini report – said that removing the European Community's barriers to internal trade and investment would raise the EC's output by between $2\frac{1}{2}\%$ and $6\frac{1}{2}\%$ compared with what would otherwise have happened. But it did not try to calculate how this increase would be split among the 12 members – or whether some might actually lose. Answering that question turns out to be difficult. A new paper by Mr Damien Neven of INSEAD, in the latest issue of *Economic Policy*, makes an interesting, if inconclusive, stab at it.

The gains from project 1992 will come through several channels. Producers will have easier access to a bigger market, which should make it easier to reap economies of scale. They will also face tougher competition, and this, too, should push down costs – partly by encouraging specialisation in activities where producers have an international comparative advantage. (A country can have a comparative advantage at producing something even if it makes everything less efficiently than its competitors do; in that case its comparative advantage lies in producing the goods and services it makes least inefficiently.)

Consumers everywhere will benefit from all these effects, Mr Neven agrees. But some producers will not. Competition and specialisation may force them to shrink their businesses, or perhaps go under altogether. The pattern of that adjustment will decide the winners and losers (if any). Mr Neven ponders this question, asking how much of a difference project 1992 will make.

A good starting-point is to look at the existing pattern of specialisation. Mr Neven sifts through a mound of numbers with extraordinary diligence. What he finds, by and large, is not much specialisation. All the countries make and trade just about everything.

There are some exceptions. Britain and Holland are tobacco-processors to the Community; Portugal and Greece are big net exporters of shoes and clothing. And within the broad industrial groups examined by Mr Neven, further specialisation no doubt lurks. For instance, trade in food between Britain and France is roughly in balance; France's net exports of wine (one presumes) outweigh its net imports of other foods. In all, though, most trade is within industries, as opposed to between industries.

Slicing the data another way, Mr Neven divides 29 industries into broad classes, according to whether they are intensive in their use of labour, capital, human capital (measured by R&D spending) and natural resources. He then calculates the trade balance of each EC country in each class of industries. A big trade surplus (in relation to the country's total production within that class) would be a sure sign of specialisation.

Ireland, it seems, has something of a comparative advantage in human capital. So do West Germany and France.

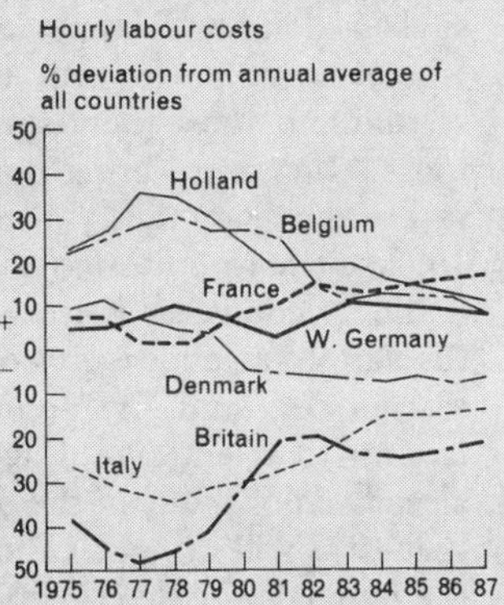

Hourly labour costs

% deviation from annual average of all countries

Holland
Belgium
France
W. Germany
Denmark
Britain
Italy

+50 40 30 20 10 0 −10 20 30 40 50

1975 76 77 78 79 80 81 82 83 84 85 86 87

Portugal and Greece, unsurprisingly, are strongly specialised in labour-intensive production. Spain, surprisingly, is less so. Britain does not appear to be particularly good or bad at anything. In general, as before, the countries of northern Europe (the EC excluding Greece, Portugal and Spain) are economic generalists.

Mr Neven therefore concludes that – for most of the EC, anyway – 1992 is going to go phut. Since trade is already fairly free within Europe, he reckons, any scope for efficient specialisation would already have made itself apparent; if it had, you could then have argued that entirely free trade would have allowed even more. But it seems there is little scope for efficient specialisation. A Euro-optimist might wonder about the circularity of that argument. The question is whether there will be more specialisation after 1992; the fact that there has been little of it so far is suggestive, but settles nothing.

So Mr Neven looks again, this time for opportunities to specialise that have yet to be exploited. In a free-trade Europe the price of labour, land, capital and other factors of production should eventually be more or less the same in all countries. If wages (for labour of a given quality) are lower in Greece, say, trade should push the economy towards labour-intensive production. That will drive wages together across the Community. The same goes for other factors of production. This convergence does not require labour (or the other factors) to be mobile; trade by itself should do the trick.

Wages are strikingly low in both Greece and Portugal; they are low in Spain, too, but the gap there is smaller. This suggests that there may still be some barriers to trade. If so, the 1992 project will spur more efficiently in the production of Greece and Portugal, especially, and wages there will start to rise.

In the rest of the EC, labour costs have been converging for the past ten years (see chart). Mr Neven estimates that the variation of wages among northern EC countries is no greater than the variation within them. Furthermore, country-by-country wage differences are no greater in industries (such as foodstuffs and pharmaceuticals) that are affected by barriers to trade than in the others. This suggests that trade barriers are not the reason for the wage differences that do exist, and that markets are now fairly competitive in northern Europe. Britain is an exception here. Its wages are low in the industries affected by other countries' trade barriers. In those industries, it therefore stands to gain higher exports and higher wages when the barriers come down.

What about economies of scale? This, potentially, is another source of gain from 1992. Countries with lots of small firms (which should be able to grow efficiently after 1992) stand to gain more than countries where firms, on average, are already large (and where the scope for future economies of scale is therefore less).

The size of firms in the 29 industries across the EC is remarkably similar. So while there may well be too many firms in every industry in the EC, no one country is likely to gain any more than the next. The exception is Spain, where firms are much smaller than the EC average. (Greece may well be another exception, but it has no reliable data.) Spain stands to gain from economies of scale as well as from its comparative advantage in labour-intensive production.

The 1992 project is for consumers everywhere. If Mr Neven is right, however, the lion's share of benefits for producers will go to southern Europe.

1. Does the work of Neven suggest that there will be no overall effects on EC GDP after 1992?

2. How would you expect the effect on labour to differ between Italy and Britain on the one hand and France and Belgium on the other?

Source: *The Economist*, 21 April 1990

Case Study 24.2 UK to block VAT plan

The government is expected to block a proposal for a minimum value-added tax rate of 15 per cent across the European Community. The move by Norman Lamont, the chancellor, will fuel further the row over Britain's commitment to Europe.

Mr Lamont's resistance to the proposal, expected to be made clear at a meeting of EC finance ministers today, will be a severe blow to the European Commission, which views VAT harmonisation as central in its plans for a barrier-free EC market after next year. If rates are not harmonised, the commission believes countries will keep border controls to limit shopping in lower-tax states.

On his last visit to Luxembourg, early last month, Mr Lamont made it clear that he viewed VAT regulation from Brussels as an attack on sovereignty.

British officials in Brussels yesterday said they believed an imposed minimum VAT level was an administrative burden on a system that could be self-governing through market forces. One official described the proposals as Brussels-style meddling 'at its starkest'.

Christiane Scrivener, the EC's tax commissioner, believes she has the backing of the other 11 EC members. She said last week: 'When a fruit is ripe, what happens if you don't eat it? It becomes rotten. Now the package is ripe to pass. You can't make it better than it is.'

A spokeswoman for Mme Scrivener said the other EC member states had compromised their positions to try to accommodate Britain in the VAT proposals. She said: 'I honestly don't think Norman Lamont knows what's good for his country. It's difficult to understand. First we had to convince the other states to accept the UK approach and then when it's done, they [Britain] turn round and reject this sort of pragmatism.'

The 15 per cent rate is the idea of Luxembourg, which currently holds the six-month rotating EC presidency. The plan also proposes a minimum 5 per cent reduced VAT level for certain 'necessary' goods and services, and a 'super reduced' rate of zero per cent, as applied by Britain at the moment to food, children's clothing and other products. The rates would come into effect for an undefined transitional period from January, 1993.

At present, standard VAT rates in the EC range from 12 per cent in Spain and Luxembourg, 17.5 per cent in Britain, to 22 per cent in Denmark and 23 per cent in Ireland.

On monetary union, Mr Lamont said yesterday that Britain would want to approach the issue of the single currency 'rather cautiously' to make sure any agreement would allow Parliament to vote on the issue.

Jacques Delors, EC president, said yesterday that Britain was not being offered a 'two speed' deal on a single European currency but a delay while its Parliament decided.

1. In your judgement, does the article suggest that the hopes of the EC for 1992 are overoptimistic?

Source: Tom Walker, *The Times*, 3 June 1991

Some final considerations of 1992

Anyone reading official EC reports on 1992 cannot fail to be struck by their tremendous optimism for the future. Even so some believe that the figures reported here are an underestimate. Baldwin has suggested that by ignoring 'second round' effects and externalities the Cecchini report has underestimated by half the rise in the value of output.

If this optimism is to be fulfilled, several hurdles must be overcome, firstly achieving the full co-operation of member governments and secondly inducing firms to respond.

The open market will insist on EC countries fully opening their markets to the products and workers of other member states. Thus the UK government must look upon the tender of a Belgian firm for a contract in the same light as a tender from a firm in Newcastle upon Tyne. Will the UK government be able to forget the implications of the contract for employment in north-east England? At present there are European Community rules about fair competition between firms and about government subsidies. The UK government found itself able to flout these rules by giving a 'hidden subsidy' to British Aerospace when it purchased the state motor car producer Austin-Rover. Who is to say that EC governments will not find ways of continuing to favour domestic producers?

The openness of Europe post-1992 will mean that the actions of one EC government will have much more wide-ranging influence on its neighbours. There will, therefore, be a much greater need for co-ordinated and consistent economic policies within the EC to prevent one nation's policies working directly against another's. It is also expected that the open market will bring about greater fluctuations of exchange rates between European currencies. Both of these factors call for a stronger exchange rate mechanism within the European Monetary system. The Delors plan has gone further and called for an eventual economic and political union of the EC, with one central bank, one currency and eventually one government.

The Delors plan is based on a belief that a single European state is desirable and that 1992 is just the first phase of such a union. Some member governments have no such vision of Europe and oppose further integration wholeheartedly. Indeed, the UK not only opposes the second and subsequent stages of the Delors plan, it is also most reluctant to bring its VAT system into line with the rest of the Community, thus defeating one of the objects of 1992 (the harmonization of tax rates).

The second fear is the ability of business to respond to the supply-side measures of 1992. As was stated in the last section, US and Japanese firms are not handicapped by having to operate in fragmented markets and therefore already enjoy many of the benefits of large-scale production that 1992 will bring. EC firms must be quick to respond to the new favourable conditions in Europe if they are not to lose out to foreign rivals.

It is not clear how well firms understand the opportunities that are about to be presented to them. Large firms have certainly been warned and governments have done their best to alert their populations by advertising campaigns. In the UK these have been reinforced by various voluntary bodies such as the CBI and the Institute of Directors. There is no certainty that the message has got through, however, and the experience of the Cranfield Institute is that the effect of their £4,000-a-day seminars on the subsequent behaviour of the participants is often undetectable! If such behaviour is typical following such a large and direct expense, we can only wait and see what 1992 brings.

In conclusion then 1992 offers great opportunities to European business and promises to assist the long-term welfare and competitiveness of the EC. There is, however, no certainty about the distribution of the benefits throughout the Community, and there are some doubts about the ability of both governments and business to respond to the challenge.

SUMMARY

1. The success of 1992 depends upon all countries fully participating, and governments regarding foreign and domestic bids on a genuinely equal basis.
2. The greater openness of EC economies after 1992 will require much closer economic policy co-operation between member governments.
3. It is not clear that industry has fully understood the implications of 1992 and so the envisaged benefits may not emerge, or may accrue only to the better informed.

Exam Preparation and Practice

MULTIPLE-CHOICE QUESTIONS

1. Which of the following is **not** a 'non-tariff' barrier?
   A Customs posts.
   B A tax on imported wheat.
   C Domestic safety standards.
   D Differing VAT rates.

2. Which of the following is **not** an example of a microeconomic gain from the single European market?
   A Reduction of X-inefficiency.
   B Greater innovation and technical progress.
   C Higher profit margins.
   D Improving balance of trade.

Answer key

Where there are four numbered alternatives

A	B	C	D	E
1, 2 and 3 Correct	1 and 3 Correct	2 and 4 Correct	4 only Correct	1 and 4 Correct

3. The creation of the single market in the EC (1992) will:
   1 Reduce non-tariff barriers.
   2 Allow European firms to reach economies of scale.
   3 Reduce the costs of firms that trade within the EC.
   4 Allow easier access to European markets by US firms.

25 Green economics

In this chapter we will discuss:

1. What is green economics?
2. The nature of non-renewable and stock-renewable resources.
3. The environmental problems of economic growth in a world of finite resources.
4. How economics might provide some answers to green problems.

Introduction

Green economics is a shorthand way of indicating not so much a separate branch of economics, but a way of doing economics which takes into account a much broader view of society than has traditionally been the case. You will remember that in the introduction economics was described as a study of how society or individuals within it organize the production and distribution of material wealth. It is the claim of free-enterprise economists that the untrammelled price mechanism will lead to the most efficient use of resources and, by encouraging and rewarding innovation, will result in economic growth.

These are big claims, but there is more to it than that. As well as efficiency and growth, the free-enterprise system is said to yield additional benefits of a non-economic kind almost as side effects. It is also claimed that there are hidden costs associated with free-enterprise systems, and these costs are at least partly economic costs. Green economics asks that we take these side effects more seriously than we have done in the past – efficiency and growth are all very well, but at what cost and to what end?

We can group the issues into three broad categories: sustainability, environment and equity.

Sustainability

Economic growth is an established fact, but only for a small minority of the world's people. As the growing economies get bigger and bigger, they make greater and greater demands on the world's resources. This is most clearly seen in their demand for fuels. Fuels are needed to drive the wheels of industry, to fire the engines of our transport systems and our agricultural machinery, and to feed our central heating systems and our motor cars. These fuels are made up of oil, coal, wood, peat and natural gas with just a small amount of nuclear energy – electricity, remember, is generated from these base fuels and is not a separate source of energy.

The question which occupies more and more of our thoughts is whether we can go on increasing our use of fuels as we have in the past, and whether we can genuinely invite the rest of mankind to join us in our energy consumption through economic development, or whether we are in for a rude awakening when they run out. That is to say, is the path we have followed for so long sustainable?

Non-renewable resources

The basic problem with **non-renewable resources** is that the earth receives just so much energy each year from the sun. Some of this energy heats the land and sea, some is absorbed by plant life and some is reflected back into space. Over millions of years this energy 'income' has been saved up by the natural processes of plants and has been 'stored' as coal, oil, gas, etc. – the so-called hydrocarbon fuels. Our science has allowed us to unlock these storage vaults and plunder the stock of energy for our own immediate needs.

We have, in other words, been living beyond our energy income, and simple housekeeping rules will tell us that we sooner or later have to learn to live within our incomes. In so far as our economic growth has been mere profligacy, when the fuel stocks run out not only will we stop growing but we will return to that standard of living which is compatible with our energy income. Growth would then not be sustainable, and neither is there a zero growth option – we would suffer a precipitate decline in living standards.

Figure 25.1 shows how the world has increased its use of non-renewable oil stocks in the last 100 years. You will see that we are using up this energy source at an ever-increasing rate.

This scenario can be illustrated with a simple farming example. Imagine a family working its farm with horse and human muscle power and only natural manures, pesticides, fungicides and weedkillers. They work long hours for very little food, and manage to support four adults and two children. Along comes the hydrocarbon revolution and they dispense with horses, etc. and start to use tractors together with fertilizers, pesticides, fungicides and weedkillers all derived from oil and coal. Output increases dramatically and they can now have more leisure and enough food to support six adults and four children.

They claim to have found the secret of success and invite their neighbours to adopt the same techniques. Then the oil and coal run out or become so difficult to get more and more of their working lives are spent in mines and on oil wells. The food supply falls, the higher population can no longer

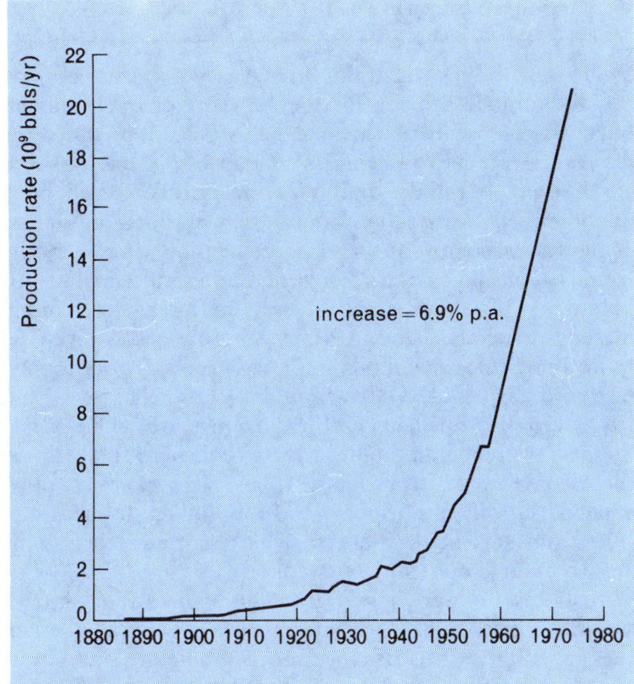

Figure 25.1 World production of crude oil, 1880–1980.

be supported and two adults and two children have to leave the farm.

If this change from a high-energy economy to a low-energy economy comes about slowly enough then the population size could adjust to its new sustainable size by 'natural wastage', but if it were sudden then the adjustment would be very painful indeed and the political consequences dire.

There have been broadly two responses to this situation: first, that we should seek alternatives to oil and coal; and secondly, that we should develop techniques which economize on these fixed stocks. The former response has led us in two very different directions. On the one hand there is the high-tech solution of using nuclear power, which, not having been stored up from the past energy incomes, is virtually limitless. On the other hand there is the very low-tech solution which advocates the wider use of wave power and windmills. Which of these paths to pursue is a matter for much debate and, as we shall see below, raises a number of other issues too.

The link between exhaustible resources and economic growth is forged by arguing that our economic growth has come about only as a result of our plundering the earth's energy storerooms. There is some truth in this and it is certainly the case that we have used up a lot of our resources, but that is not the whole story. It is equally possible to argue that the main driving force has been not our profligate use of fuels, but our improved technical knowledge. That is, we have learned how to do things better.

The technology argument goes like this. On our farm we learned that by planting turnips in rows rather than by simply broadcasting the seeds we could get harvests forty times as large. And as we learned more and more about agriculture and about manufacturing, our productivity continued to increase. In this way, by learning how to do things more efficiently we can have more leisure and bigger families, and this improved productivity lasts for ever. Having learned these things, we can invite our neighbours to share our knowledge with no cost to ourselves and no risk of a sudden reversal in productivity. Technology is our salvation, not by providing us with more fuel as in the case of the nuclear power industry, but by showing us how to do better with less fuel.

Any development which relies on the use of hydrocarbon fuels (or any other such endowment, like metal ores) is doomed to failure no matter how small its use of these materials may be. This is because we have a fixed stock of them and any use of them, however small, must eventually exhaust our supplies.

Stock-renewable resources

There is a slightly less pressing problem with other kinds of natural endowment. If we consider for a moment the cropping of fish from our rivers and from the seas, it is apparent that every year there will be a fresh crop of fish available. The stock is not fixed for all time, but is replenished with every passing year. If we are careful about how much we harvest, we can keep on harvesting every year for ever. If we take too much – say we take too many cod from the North Sea – then there will be fewer cod left in the sea to breed and so the stock will fall. If we take the same amount in the following year, there will be even fewer to breed from and the stock will fall still further. Eventually overfishing will lead to the extinction of cod altogether. Figure 25.2 shows how overfishing has led to a decline in the Pacific Coast sardine fishing industry.

The problem here then is to find the level of use which will leave the stock unchanged from year to year. This level of use is sustainable – any higher rate of use would be unsustainable in that it would lead to the exhaustion of the stock.

Thus if we develop some new way of fishing (say, using sonar devices to find the fish) then we get an immediate

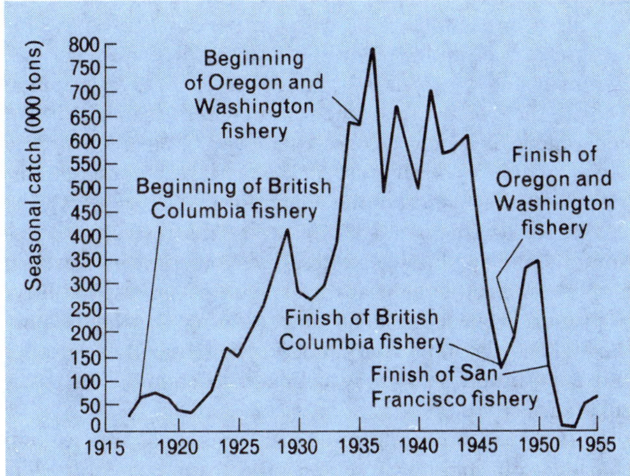

Figure 25.2 Total catch of Pacific sardines, 1915–55.

benefit and this looks like economic growth. But if we are now overfishing then the immediate benefit will eventually give way not only to a loss of the initial improvement, but to a subsequent loss of fish altogether.

Allowing for natural resource depletion and for stock regeneration raises important questions about the sustainability of our recent rates of growth, and indeed about the sustainability of our current level of output. But there is another aspect of sustainability which has little to do with resource management.

Instability

One of the ways we have advanced economically – particularly in the production of food – has been by the selection and breeding of high-yield seed stock. This partly constituted the Green Revolution, which was to bring relief to the starving millions in Asia by replacing traditional rice varieties with new super rice (see Chapter 26). There can be no doubt that yields have increased, but the worry is that by replacing a rich variety of seeds with just one type of seed we are putting all our eggs in one basket. If anything happens to destroy or harm that particular type of seed then all harvests will be lost. Had we stuck to the multitude of lower yielding varieties, some might have been destroyed and others harmed, but we would still have had some harvest and some seed stocks to plant next year.

The kind of shock envisaged may be an attack by a particular strain of fungus, a severe drought, a late summer or any one of the many vagaries of mother nature. The question being raised here is: just how robust is our economy (particularly our food supply) in resisting such shocks? How sustainable is it when things go wrong? Are we sacrificing long-term robustness (sustainability) for short-term growth?

These then are the three broad issues concerning sustainability. The first is the recognition that so far our economic growth has been fed from the storehouse of nature. No matter how sparingly we use our non-renewable resources, we must eventually run out of them. To what extent can we continue to grow, continue to invite other countries to join us in growth and even continue to maintain our current living standards in the face of exhaustible resources?

The second issue is to do with our use of stock-renewable resources. We can indeed crop these resources for ever and ever provided we are careful not to overcrop. Overcropping leads to the exhaustion of the resource in the same way that non-renewable resources are exhausted. Can we maintain our growth rates or our current output levels while remaining within this overcropping constraint?

The third issue is less clear cut and addresses the question of stability. To what extent have our past increases in crop yields been bought at the expense of harvest stability? We can improve harvests by concentrating planting on only the highest-yielding variety, but we then lose other varieties and expose ourselves to appalling risks should that particular variety fail.

So far we are dealing only with problems, and we will consider solutions to these and other problems later. The next set of problems also arise from growth and these are the environmental issues.

Environment

We have seen how the drains on our natural resources may impose limits to growth. Production requires the inputs of oil, coal, iron ore, bauxite, etc., all of which are provided by nature (i.e. are part of 'land' as a factor of production) and all of which are limited. But nature is involved in production in other ways too. Almost every production process generates waste products. The generation of electricity from coal or oil generates smoke and other more malign air pollutants. The production of meat by intensive farming methods generates 'slurry'. Many other processes give rise to unwanted noxious fluids – nitrates leached from highly fertilized farmland, DDT from insect repellants, CFCs from aerosol propellants and lead from petrol engines. In the past we relied on mother nature to dispose freely of all these unwanted byproducts. The gases were simply expelled into the atmosphere and the liquids drained into rivers and seas in the hope that nature would cleanse or absorb them at no cost to ourselves.

In a sense we were quite right in our expectations, but as we grew bigger and bigger, and as more countries joined in the growth race, nature became overwhelmed and was simply incapable of dealing with all our waste. The air pollution led to the destruction of trees, the threat of rising temperatures as the ozone layer was damaged and an increase in respiratory diseases and skin problems. The water pollution reduced rivers to a lifeless stream of evil-smelling fluids which could not be safely entered, let alone drunk from. In other words, our production activities were giving us more and more goods to consume but were taking a large and growing toll on our environment.

The consequences of some of these changes cannot be foreseen with any certainty, but we can see what has happened to date and we can use these observations to look at some of the likely future results. What we see and what we can foresee leads an increasing number to question the wisdom of pursuing economic growth. Some advocate zero growth – stay as we are, if we can, until we see more clearly the consequences of our choices. Some advocate returning to a level of living which is compatible with nature – learn once again to live in harmony with it rather than master it with science and technology.

Many years ago Kenneth Boulding warned that we were working with the wrong view of mother earth. We thought of progress like a journey across the prairie with fresh frontiers unfolding before us each day. He called this the prairie or cowboy view of nature. We could throw our trash aside and use whatever we found because tomorrow we would be somewhere else – what we did today need never concern us. Boulding suggested that a more appropriate way of viewing the world was as if it were a spaceship – he called this spaceship earth. On this spaceship we have only so much water and so much air. To keep going we have to ensure the constant recycling of these life-giving assets. If we ruin the recycling plant today then tomorrow we will have no water to drink and no air to breathe. Furthermore, if we throw down an old tin can today we could well cut ourselves on it tomorrow – our past stays with us.

Growth in a prairie world is quite a different thing from growth in a spaceship world. The Green lobby or 'Greens' maintain that we must learn to think in these latter terms and that the change is a matter of some urgency. We have to cut down on our use of non-renewable resources and, where possible, learn to recycle as much of them as we can. Metals, for example, can be used over and over again if we are careful to collect up old tin cans, scrapped motor cars, refrigerators, etc. Unfortunately, not all non-renewable resources are recyclable. Fuels, for example, cannot be reused – once you have burned the oil or coal it stays burnt. Economy of use rather than recycling is the only policy here. Even with recyclable resources there are some losses with each cycle and so economy of use has a role to play.

Equity

The equity issues are to do with the distribution of the costs and benefits of using up natural resources. They fall into two categories: first, the distribution among the current inhabitants of this planet; and secondly, the distribution between all the current inhabitants and all the future inhabitants.

As to the distribution among current inhabitants, there is a widely held view that it is the rich developed nations that benefit from the raw materials and fuels supplied to them by the poorer nations. The extraction of iron ores and copper and bauxite from the developing nations is under the control of multinational firms, since they have provided the capital for the operations. These firms are charged in law with promoting the interests of their shareholders. They therefore tend to promote the interests of the rich countries and so the poor feel exploited. The local labour is abundant and therefore poorly paid, and environmental damage is inflicted which the host nation is unable or reluctant to oppose.

Where the resource is under the control of the host country some attempt can be made to get the best price for it in international markets. In many cases, however, the markets are dominated by the buyers rather than the sellers, and commodity prices are low enough to ensure that the buyers (rich countries) get the lion's share of the benefits.

In one particular case the sellers seem to have most market power. Oil is an internationally traded commodity which is supplied largely by developing nations. By forming themselves into a **cartel** and presenting a common front to the market, the suppliers can dictate prices to the rest of the world and ensure that most of the benefits of their oil accrue to their own nationals rather than to the citizens of the buying countries. As is well known, most oil producing and exporting countries (members of OPEC) are not industrialized countries but nevertheless have some of the highest per capita incomes in the world. Market power is therefore clearly a major factor in the distribution of the benefits of resource use, and it is not clear that market power is evenly distributed.

As far as the distribution between the current and future generations of earthlings is concerned, there is no obvious way of assessing what would constitute equity. We do not know the tastes and preferences of our successors, nor do we know what kind of technology or population they will have. They by definition are not around yet and so cannot vote or make their wishes known through the market.

Most people would want to say that we should leave some oil and some fish, etc. for future generations, but it is a difficult case to argue logically. These are people we do not know and will never meet. Why should we care in any way about their welfare? Why, indeed, should we do without something ourselves so as to leave something for them? This is a somewhat extreme position, but it has been put forward. The more realistic question is: if we are to make a sacrifice for the benefit of future generations, how much of a sacrifice should we make?

One rather moral argument is that we hold the planet in trust and that it is not ours to do with as we please. At minimum we should try to ensure a continuing standard of living. On this basis and for want of a better rule we could decide to leave the world no worse off when we leave it than it was when we arrived here. This leads to intergenerational equality in terms of productive wealth and pleasantness of environment. If we use up some oil then we compensate by providing future generations with slightly more man-made capital – some roads or some factories. Taken together the remaining natural resources and the man-made resources yield a standard of living similar to that enjoyed by our generation.

To recapitulate the issues. First there was the problem of sustainability. In part this raises the issue of how we can continue producing at present rates – let alone continue growing at our present rates – when we are making higher and higher demands on strictly limited non-renewable resources and on vulnerable stock-renewable resources. It also raises a second issue of stability or resilience to shocks. Can our highly specialized, high-yielding seed varieties survive natural or man-made shocks, or will a sudden drought or flash flood wipe out the entire harvest and seed stock?

The second problem was the damage we are doing to our environment. Growth not only raids nature's storehouse of assets (accrued over millions of years) in a profligate way, but it also requires nature to absorb more and more waste products like smoke, CFCs, slurry and leached fertilizers. It is becoming increasingly clear that nature cannot withstand this abuse, and we shall have to find alternative waste disposal systems or reduce output to levels which can be absorbed by nature.

The third problem was that of equity. The earth has just so much productive potential and so a way must be found for allocating that productive potential among all those currently on earth and between the current population and all future populations. This involves two types of question. First, we have to decide who will get what – should we allow those currently living in the developed countries to 'take' the bulk of this wealth, or should we spread it around? These are 'goal setting', subjective questions and, like most subjective issues, they involve value judgements. Most people seem to feel that the current distribution is unfair to the poorer countries and that market power plays a part in this. Most people too feel that we should take care to leave the world in as good a state as we found it. That is to say, unknown and unborn generations should be considered when we decide how to use the earth's productive potential. However, this is a difficult point to argue since it is all a matter of opinion. Economists have no more authority to pronounce on these issues than anyone else.

If we could decide what we wanted to do, we would then be faced with the problem of how to achieve it. How can we ensure that future generations get the amount of wealth prescribed? These are not subjective issues but objective ones, and they require some technical expertise from economists who study systems of distribution.

SUMMARY

1. Green economics is not a separate branch of economics, but the application of economics to environmental problems.
2. There are three basic problems to address:
   (a) Sustainability.
   (b) Environment.
   (c) Equity.
3. Sustainability raises the issue of how we can continue producing at present rates and make higher demands on strictly limited non-renewable resources and on vulnerable stock-renewable resources?
4. Sustainability raises a second issue of stability or resilience to shocks, such as a disease that affects the new high-yield seed varieties.
5. The environment problem arises from growth, which not only raids nature's storehouse of assets but also requires nature to absorb more and more waste products like CFCs and leached fertilizers.
6. The equity problem concerns how the earth's productive potential can be divided among all those currently on earth and between the current population and all future populations.
7. Answers to these problems involve making choices. Most people seem to feel that the current distribution is unfair to the poorer countries. Most people too feel that we should take care to leave the world in as good a state as we found it.

Green issues and the price mechanism

Both the positive and normative problems with which we ended the last section present great difficulties. There is disagreement among economists as how best to solve them. Those committed to the free-enterprise system argue that the price mechanism not only will decide how these resources should be allocated but, if working properly, will also serve to allocate these resources in the same efficient way that it allocates all other resources.

In the case of exhaustible resources, for example, it is argued that as they become scarcer and scarcer their prices will rise. Consumers will use less of them and producers will seek and find substitutes for them. An important feature of this solution is that there would be a gradual adjustment as the finite resources ran out. Their scarcity would not lead to a catastrophic plunge into negative growth and mass starvation.

Market failure

Other economists argue that the market is incapable of working in these cases. There are two well-known features of the natural resource market which lead it to malfunction. First, it is a clear case of an incomplete market. For markets to work in the way predicted by economic theorists, they must take account of the preferences of all the parties concerned. All the suppliers and all the demanders must have access to the market and by casting their votes (buying particular items) must be able to determine how the resources will be allocated. As we have already seen, however, the natural resource allocation problem involves future generations – demanders and suppliers who are not yet born. These 'voters', being absent, are disenfranchised and are unable to influence the market.

The market is therefore incomplete, and those economic agents who do not currently have access to the market but who nevertheless have an interest in its outcome have to be represented by others. The obvious agent for this duty is our elected government. The government has the long-term interests of the country at heart, and has the power to override the market. By putting a tax on oil, for example, it could dissuade current consumers from using so much of it and hence leave some for future generations. The effect of placing a tax on a particular good was discussed in Chapter 5.

The second unusual feature of the natural resource market is what is technically called 'the problem of the commons'. Imagine a reserve of oil lying under land owned by two or three farmers. Each farmer drills down into the oil and begins pumping it out. They all know that there is a finite amount of oil in the well and that as it becomes scarcer it will become more valuable. Each farmer may therefore want to make the oil last for a long time and pass on the well to descendants. This would mean pumping less now in order to pump longer. But if one of the three farmers continues to pump at the fastest rate then the others will not only forgo future oil revenues but lose some current income too. Thus each farmer may want to ration out the oil and receive a high price, but knowing that the others may grab what they can while the grabbing is good, they too pump with no thought for the future.

The resource is 'common' to all the farmers, and although it is in their joint interest to use it sparingly, it is their individual interest to get out as much as they can as soon as they can.

Some remedies

One solution is to vest the ownership in one family and allow that family to bequeath their wealth to their offspring. Since families typically co-operate and do bear the welfare of their descendants in mind, there would be the possibility of preserving the resource. This is one rationale for the institution of private property on a fairly wide scale. If all the land in England were common land on which everyone had grazing rights then it would be in no one's interest to try to improve the land or leave it fallow. If one farmer withdrew sheep from a hillside and spread fertilizer in the hope that the land would recover and grow better grass then other farmers could continue to graze and take the benefit without the trouble or expense. Commons therefore usually get overused to the point of extinction. The fish in the sea are common property, and this has led to overfishing to such an extent that some stocks are in danger of disappearing altogether. If there was a way of vesting all the whales in the ownership of one person then there would be the power and the incentive to ensure that stocks did not run out. Private property and the right to make bequests constitute one of the ways in which society deals with these problems.

A second solution is to allow only the state to own natural resources. This is direct control and means that the rate of depletion is planned by central planners rather than organized via market forces. There is little evidence that the planners of Eastern Europe were careful with their natural resources, and indeed they may have been more profligate than those in capitalist countries. But this experience should not be taken to rule out the state solution completely. Because it has worked badly in some places and at some times does not imply that it is always so. One of the great benefits of the state solution is that the revenue from the sale or use of the resources goes to the whole population rather than only to those chosen to be the owners. This is no small matter, since millions and millions of pounds are made from the ownership of nature's gifts. Some economists have argued that, even when the private property solution is chosen, there should be heavy taxes on incomes from 'land'. This would preserve the resource through the operation of the market, but would not generate huge incomes for those in ownership.

The third solution is for those who commonly own a resource to come to some agreement to act in unison for their common good. The technical name for this is a cartel. Instead of sellers competing with each other to yield the market price, they collude to set a much higher price, discourage buyers and save some of their resources for later sale. The best-known example of this is the cartel of the oil producing and exporting countries (OPEC). Members of OPEC agree each to supply a certain amount of oil per year on to the world market. By controlling quantity they drive up price and get a better current deal and a better future deal too. The effect on crude oil prices in 1974 and 1979 was very dramatic and boosted the economies of the OPEC countries by huge margins. Of course, since the oil price is so high, there are those in the cartel who would like to sell more than their quota and there has to be some way of disciplining them. Nevertheless when it works cartelization is very effective indeed.

These then are three ways of addressing the problem of sustainability and intergenerational equity: private monopoly property rights over land and bequests; nationalization; and cartelization. There remains the problem of intra-generational equity, the division of the spoils between those who currently inhabit the earth.

Again some economists argue that the price mechanism will do the job – those with most to offer will get high rewards, and those with little to offer will get less. Competition between buyers ensures that no seller is undervalued, and competition between sellers ensures that no buyer is forced to pay more than the fair price. By 'fair' they mean, of course, that price which emerges from freely competing agents in a coercion-free competitive market.

The case for some alternative to the price mechanism rests on two points: first, that the markets are not competitive and are biased in favour of the richer countries; and secondly, that the free operation of the market gives rise to too much fluctuation in the incomes of the poor countries. If a poor country relies on the export of a single commodity for its foreign exchange earnings, any year-on-year changes in its price will play havoc with its earnings and hence its ability to service its debt and buy the imports necessary for its economy to maintain its current level of output.

This has led to the replacement of the pure market system by agreements between producers and consumers to try to stabilize the incomes of the poorer countries at a fair level.

An export revenue stabilization scheme (STABEX) is part of the Lomé Convention set up between the EC and 52 African, Caribbean and Pacific (ACP) developing countries. It guarantees a specific level of income on selected exports from ACP to the EC. Similar agreements exist even between rich countries. The common agricultural policy (CAP) of the EC aims at stabilizing the incomes of commodity producers in the EC (i.e. the farmers) at a reasonable level.

The central issue here, then, is the extent to which we should rely on the free operation of the market system to bring about a sustainable and equitable use of the earth's productive potential. Economists not surprisingly disagree. Some argue for little or no interference in the price mechanism, while others argue for its complete replacement. Many others lie somewhere between these extremes.

There remain the environmental issues: the use of the atmosphere, rivers and seas as free disposal dumps for noxious and unpleasant waste materials. These are costs of economic growth which are borne by the world at large, but do not enter the accounts of their perpetrators. This leads to the failure of the market to capture all the costs (and benefits) associated with any particular productive activity, so that decisions made via the market are not those which we would all on balance prefer. These costs and benefits being outside the market are technically referred to as **externalities**.

Where there are externalities there will be market failure. Some environmentalists have argued that we should decide politically not to allow any such pollution – we should simply say that no one may discharge any noxious substance into the air or the water, or bury it in the land. This somewhat extreme position is countered by those who believe that stopping pollution entirely would yield some benefits but at an enormous (unjustifiable) cost. Stopping all pollution would lead to a substantial fall in our living standards, since many of the products and processes which we currently depend upon or enjoy would be impossible without some pollution.

What is wanted, then, is not the minimum amount of pollution (even zero pollution) but the optimum amount of pollution. This again raises two questions: what is optimal, and how do we attain it? These questions are receiving more and more political attention, and their high public profile has led governments to take them very seriously. Economists have developed techniques for aiding governments in the formulation of environmental policies. We have seen in Chapter 7 how **cost–benefit analysis**, the leading methodology for dealing with externalities, does offer ways of quantifying many of these effects.

Having used CBA to value the externalities, the government then imposes taxes on various activities which reflect their external cost (subsidies reflect external benefits). Thus the post-tax prices do reflect the true costs and benefits of each process and, when these adjustments are made, the market system can be allowed to operate as before. Producers decide how much to pollute given the costs of so doing, and consumers decide what to buy given the full costs of the alternatives before them.

Conclusions

This chapter has dealt with a number of issues which are

Case Study 25.1 What price posterity?

As a politician, you must decide between two road-safety schemes. One will save 100 lives this year; the other 160 in 1996. Both cost the same; both must start now. Which do you choose?

Your answer reveals the rate at which you discount the value of human life. Economists generally assume that most people value jam today more highly than the same quantity of jam tomorrow. People would rather fill a need now than later. The level of real interest rates reflects this preference. Savers require compensation for postponing consumption. The returns on an investment must be high enough to make up for spending forgone today. The higher the discount rate, the bigger the return has to be.

Those who choose to save 100 lives straight away implicitly apply a discount rate of over 10%; choosing 160 lives in 1996 implies a discount rate of under 10%. A macabre exercise? On the contrary. The fact that people are willing to pay to reduce risks shows that they set an implicit value on human life – although they may pay far more to reduce the risk, say, of terrorist attack than of falling off a ladder.

Now some economists at the University of Maryland are studying the way people trade off a life saved today against one saved tomorrow. One of them, Maureen Cropper, with Paul Portney of Resources for the Future, asked 1,000 Maryland households about their attitudes to saving life. The replies suggest that, on average, people discount future lives saved at 8.6% a year if the time horizon is 25 years, and at 3.4% a year if it is 100 years. Put simply, that means they would be as willing to save the life of one person today as eight people in 25 years' time or 28 people in 100 years' time.

Such questions particularly intrigue environmental economists. The cost–benefit arithmetic, of which discount rates are an integral part, often discourages environmentally sound projects, because:

- Environmental benefits may be under valued because the market puts no price on them. Houses erected on a beauty spot have a value easily established in the marketplace; the lovely view does not.
- The consequences of some environmental decisions are irreversible. A dirty river may be cleaned up; but a species, once extinct, is gone for good.
- An environmental investment may mean the avoidance of a risk that may arise in the distant future. Banning ozone-gobbling chlorofluorocarbons should eventually repair the hole in the ozone layer. Might such a hole, left to grow, bring sudden catastrophe a century hence? And how should you identify the cost of such uncertainty?
- Environmental decisions frequently involve a long gap between incurring the cost and reaping the benefit. Rain-forest trees take years to grow; nitrates in soil may take 40 years to seep into water supplies. Sometimes the gap is so long that one generation incurs the spending and its grandchildren reap the benefit. Thus measures to curb greenhouse gases must be taken now to prevent climate change by the end of the next century.

Discounting the grandchildren

Faced with such problems, deeper-green economists throw in the sponge. Environmental decisions are different from other kinds, they argue. It is silly to claim that money in the bank can ever be a substitute for – say – the rain forest, as discounting appears to imply. If the concept of the discount rate is to be applied at all, then it should be a special low rate. Surely, they argue, environmental investment has more in common with health or education than with investing in a new factory. By spending money on education, parents may demonstrate that they favour a negative discount rate: they put their children before themselves.

Conventional economists worry that special treatment for the environment may lead to perverse results. It may encourage too much investment, of the wrong sort as well as the right. After all, applying an extra-low discount rate to forestry projects might, in central Africa, preserve rain forests; in Britain the same soft-hearted approach has meant conifers planted on moors and peat bogs.

Better, say these economists, to try to solve some of the problems of conventional discount rates. After all, society is constantly making trade-offs that imply preferences – including preferences between money in the bank and rain forests. A first step should be to improve the measurement of the value people put on the environment (a technique stoutly defended in a lecture this week by David Pearce of University College, London, to the Royal Society of Arts).

Put a proper value on an environmental 'good', and the balance between costs and benefits will start to look greener. Even the amount people will pay to avoid an irreversible decision may be captured. If, *reductio ad absurdum*, saving the African elephant cost the world's entire national product each year, the animal would be doomed. In the same way, though with more difficulty, uncertainty and risk could be valued, by building in an insurance premium.

These adjustments may make it possible to choose among green projects that have their effect in the next 30 or 40 years. But even conventional economists feel uneasy about applying such techniques to decisions that affect future generations. To do so means assuming that this generation can accurately predict the preferences of posterity. There is also something awkward about discounting benefits that arise a century hence. For, even at a modest discount rate, no investment will look worthwhile.

Real-world politicians will not use discounting to decide whether to tackle global warming or species extinction. Such decisions will be political. But, having once decided to go ahead, they may then use discounting to choose a route. Solar power or energy conservation? Afforestation or extractive reserves? Discounting will be more use as a way to rank green projects than to decide whether to undertake them in the first place.

1. Do you believe 'discount rates' can really be applied to human life?
2. Does the 'conventional' approach give consumers the right to choose the planet's destruction as an equally valid option?

Source: *The Economist*, 23 March 1991

increasingly attracting the attention of the public and of politicians. The reliance on markets to solve all our economic problems cannot be entirely defended when issues of sustainability and equity are considered. There is reason to suppose that markets fail to bring about the best of all possible outcomes when they are incomplete, uncompetitive and unstable, when they try to deal with property held in common ownership, or when they reflect only some of the costs and benefits of the possible production scenarios.

These shortcomings of the free-market system are not trivial. It cannot be argued that on the whole the market system works very well and we must put up with those few cases in which it fails us. The survival of large numbers of the world's population and the future of the planet itself are in the balance.

All is not gloom and doom, however. If we are aware of the problems and have the will to address them, we can take steps to improve matters. It would be claiming too much to say that economists have already solved these problems, but they have begun solving them. A number of approaches have been suggested and are being rapidly introduced into the policies of the major political institutions both at national and international levels.

SUMMARY

1. The free-market mechanism is unlikely to solve environmental problems because the market is incomplete – many of those it concerns have yet to be born!
2. As many natural resources are 'common' property, they are liable to abuse because conservation by one agent still allows exploitation by others.
3. Possible solutions are:
   (a) Taxing the use of resources.
   (b) Passing the resources into private ownership.
   (c) Nationalizing the resources.
   (d) Organizing the owners of the resources into cartels.
4. The oceans and rivers remain waste-dumping grounds. The existence of externalities means that this problem is unlikely to be eliminated by the market. Agreeing satisfactory levels for such environmental damage is difficult – what is the optimal level of pollution?
5. Cost–benefit analysis is one way in which economists can suggest solutions that balance the desire to maintain our standard of living against the need to preserve the planet.

Exam Preparation and Practice

MULTIPLE-CHOICE QUESTIONS

1. Which of the following is a sustainable (stock-renewable) source of energy?
A Coal.
B Oil.
C Gas.
D Wave power.

2. Which of the following is a suitable policy to conserve non-renewable resources?
A Stop using them.
B Reduce the rate of consumption.
C Develop more efficient techniques for their use.
D Increase their price.

Answer key

Where there are three numbered alternatives

A	B	C	D	E
1, 2, 3	1, 2	2, 3	1	3
Correct	Correct	Correct	Correct	Correct

3. Which of the following is a problem of 'green economics'?
1 The use of fossil fuels.
2 The stock of small whales in the sea.
3 The reduction of the number of seed varieties.

4. The market is not necessarily a good way of deciding how to settle green issues because:
1 Governments interfere in the price mechanism.
2 Future generations have no market power.
3 Markets do not reflect social costs.

26 Development economics

In this chapter we will discuss:

1. The nature of developing economies.
2. A comparison of developing countries with developed countries.
3. The ways developing countries can improve their position.
4. Why many developing countries have failed to catch up with the developed countries.

Introduction

We saw in Chapter 2 that economic growth is a fact of life that most of us take for granted. Every year from time immemorial we have become materially better and better off, so that ordinary men and women today live more luxuriously than did kings and queens of yore. This is one of the remarkable and little understood features of life as we know it. Even more remarkable is the fact that not all societies 'progress' in this way.

Some societies, such as the Aboriginals and the Amerindians, appear to have been in a 'steady state' for many centuries. Each year, each decade and each century closely resembles its predecessor. These societies were regarded by the classical economists as primitive in the sense that they had not yet mastered nature with science, had no written language and were organized in small groups of only a few families. These criteria for being civilized are our criteria, however, and leave out of account the rich cultural and social achievements of other societies and their ability to live in harmony with nature.

Other steady-state societies, such as China and India, were certainly not primitive in this sense. They had indeed reached high levels of social organization, had written languages and were very large communities. However, they had somehow stopped developing in the economic sense. Their standards of living were very low compared with ours, had been that way for many centuries and showed no signs of improving.

They are graphic examples of the kind of society which some early economists predicted for all of us. According to these economists all economies would eventually reach a steady state at which the vast majority of the population lived in abject poverty. Any improvement in their material condition would prove at best temporary as it would lead to an increased birth rate and a decreased death rate. The population would therefore grow until all the improvement had been eaten up and we were back at starvation level. Deprivation and starvation would then stabilize the population by increasing the death rate and decreasing the birth rate. This was the kind of prediction (backed up with watertight reasoning) which led to economics becoming known as the 'dismal science'.

One of the principal proponents of this view was the Revd Thomas Malthus, who argued that without some self-control our natural fecundity would inevitably lead to situations in which the population would grow until forcibly constrained by war, pestilence or famine.

For us this prediction has turned out to be false. Population did not expand anything like fast enough to undo all the progress we had made in production and distribution. But for India and China the prediction had more force. Not only did their output remain fairly static, but their populations grew until the 'dismal' conditions of Malthus came to pass.

If we took a head count of those for whom Malthus was correct and of those for whom Malthus was wrong then we would have to conclude that in the vast majority of cases he was correct. In 1987 there were 3,870 million people showing that he was correct and only 745 million showing that he was wrong – a majority of 5 to 1.

This minority of 745 million is, however, very important. It shows that there is nothing logically necessary about the Malthus scenario – if he can be wrong about 745 million people then he certainly is not infallible. It is demonstrably possible for us to escape grinding poverty, and if some can do it then why not all? This is one of the questions addressed by **development economics**.

The nature of developing economies

In both the 'primitive' and the steady-state kinds of community the material standards of living are very low indeed compared with those of modern developed economies. Since the developed countries seem to be continuing to develop at increasing rates, this gap is growing all the time.

To illustrate this imagine two countries starting off with the same GNP of, say, £100m. One country grows at 2.5 per cent per year and the other remains in steady state. In 5 years' time they will have GNPs of £113m and £100m respectively; after 10 years, £128m and £100m; after 20 years, £164m and £100m; and after 28 years, £200m and £100m. Thus the growing economy outstrips the steady state economy in bigger and bigger steps and, with a modest growth rate of 2.5 per cent per year, doubles its output in less than 30 years.

If we divide the world roughly into these two types of economy – the developed/rich on the one hand and the steady state/poor on the other – we can say that **growth economics** deals with the behaviour of the former and **development economics** deals with the latter.

Basically, development economics deals with the problems of being poor and getting started on the growth path. It concerns both the developed and the steady-state economies because, as communications have improved and as travel has become easier, the developed and the undeveloped worlds have become more and more aware of each other. The rich began to feel that they should do something to help the poor, and some of the poor, having seen the way the rich lived, were no longer quite so content with what little they had.

Development planning

Which of these states of society (growing and rich or steady-state and poor) is to be preferred remains a matter for debate. It does seem, however, that most people want to join the affluent few and are prepared to make sacrifices to do so – note, for example, the persistence of illegal immigrants crossing the Rio Grande to escape Mexican poverty and enjoy American affluence.

On the other hand, those who would reject materialism and cling to their tried and traditional ways of living seem to lack the power to stem the rising tide of Euroculture, with its religious and economic imperialism. The Indians of South America, for example, have given every indication of wanting to be left as they are, but more and more of their lands are being taken over for farming, roads and mining operations. They are reduced to pleading for understanding and having their case argued for them by well-known westerners, such as Sting. This of itself betrays their lack of power over their own destinies.

Economic development is sometimes imposed on a community by its own leaders rather than by outsiders. Community leaders may override the wishes of the majority of their subjects and seek to develop their societies in the belief that they will be shown in retrospect to have made a wise decision. At its most basic this represents one more example of governments interfering in the economic lives of their citizens.

Indeed, one of the features of development economics which marks it out from growth economics is the tendency for development to be very much in the hands of state planners, who take power away from the markets and override the price mechanism. Growth economics tends to take the price mechanism for granted and explain how growth is promoted by its free operation. This, you will remember, was the question addressed by Adam Smith in his *Enquiry into the Nature and Causes of the Wealth of Nations* and which gave rise to his identification of the price mechanism as the invisible hand guiding economies to respond to consumers, to be efficient and to grow.

The suspension of the price mechanism was clearly most pronounced in Communist countries, which mistrusted it for many reasons. Growth in these countries could not come about via the price mechanism because no such price mechanism was allowed to exist. Typically, these countries devised five-year plans and 'great leaps forward' where all the ingredients for growth were provided via state planners and were mixed according to their instructions.

This imposed huge costs on the citizenry in the USSR, for example, where the movement of populations, the suppression of recalcitrant groups and the collectivization of agriculture led to famine and mass deaths. These are indeed high costs to pay for economic progress, but the Soviet Union did emerge from a feudal society to become in only 50 years a world power with nuclear weapons and the technology to put a man into space. In China similar draconian measures were taken. The population programme, for example, meant that couples were simply forbidden to have more than one child. The state rather than the individual was the primary unit, and the state controlled almost every aspect of life.

In less centrally controlled countries, such as India, the government is equally committed to development but maintains the free-enterprise system and tries to work through the operation of the price mechanism rather than by diktat. It tries, for example, to persuade people to cut down on family size by education programmes and economic incentives, such as offering free transistor radios to those who volunteer for sterilization. Which of these two models of economic development (or which mixture of them) is most suited to any particular country is a matter of debate, but a commitment to development will involve some degree of interference into the free market.

Social indicators

Another of the distinguishing features of development economics is that it tries to take account of a number of 'social indicators' rather than concentrating solely on gross national product per capita. Other social indicators of economic development typically include: decreases in the infantile mortaility rate; decreases in the proportion of the population working in agriculture; increases in life expectancy; increases in literacy levels; more equality of income distribution; more physicians per thousand population; and higher calorie consumption per capita. All these are taken as indicators of an improving economy.

Some of these social indicators are given in Table 26.1 for four regions: Africa, Asia, Emena and Latin America. In each case the country with the lowest per capita GNP in that region is given first, then the regional average and then the highest per capita GNP country in the region.

In Africa, for example, the poorest country is Ethiopia with an annual per capita income of only $120! The average throughout Africa is $410 and that of the richest African country (South Africa) is $1,890 – more than fifteen times the income of Ethiopians. The proportion of the labour force engaged in agriculture is only 17 per cent in South Africa, but 80 per cent in Ethiopia (four times as much). The infant mortality rate is twice as high in the poorer country, and its calorie consumption is only 60 per cent of

Table 26.1 Some social indicators for developing and developed economies

Country and region	Population (m) 1987	GNP ($US per capita) 1987	% of labour in agriculture		Infant mortality (deaths per 1,000)		Calories per capita		Primary school enrolment[1] (%)	
			1965	1980	1965	1986	1965	1985	1965	1985
Ethiopia	44.8	120	86	80	165	129	1,832	1,704	11	36
Africa	485.8	410	77	70	158	107	2,136	2,153	45	–
S. Africa	33.3	1,890	32	17	124	68	2,643	2,926	90	–
Butan	1.3	150	95	92	–	143	2,904	2,477	7	25
Asia	2,495.0	400	76	69	114	63	2,043	2,389	79	107
Hong Kong	5.5	8,260	6	2	27	11	2,502	2,692	103	105
Yemen[2]	2.3	420	54	41	196	134	1,999	2,255	23	66
Emena[3]	512.1	1,510	55	41	127	72	2,451	2,925	75	87
UAE	1.5	15,680	21	5	103	33	2,672	3,652	–	99
Haiti	6.2	360	77	70	178	111	2,007	1,784	50	78
Latin America	404.6	1,730	45	33	96	48	2,459	2,697	98	108
Trinidad	1.2	4,220	20	10	42	29	2,497	2,915	93	95

Notes:
1. In this table and Table 26.2 the numbers enrolling for primary school education, expressed as a percentage of primary age schoolchildren, sometimes exceed 100% because some older people enrol as well.
2. Peoples Democratic Republic.
3. Eastern Mediterranean and North Africa.

that of the South Africans. Much the same pattern applies for the other regions too.

Throughout Table 26.1 there is remarkable consistency between the social indicators. High GNP usually occurs with high calorie intakes, high primary school enrolment, low percentage of labour force in agriculture and low infant mortality rate.

Although they tend to be correlated it is not obvious exactly how the indicators are related to each other. They may cause each other or may be caused by some other, as yet unidentified circumstance. For example, primary school education may increase as a result of increasing income, or income may increase as a result of wider primary school education. It may even be the case that they are mutually dependent. Increasing education leads to increasing income, which in turn leads to increasing education and so on – a kind of virtuous circle. It is the aim of development planners to precipitate such upward spirals.

Regions and resources

Within each region there are obviously huge differences in income, so there seems to be no geographical common denominator. It is therefore wrong to think in terms of a North–South divide. There are pockets of wealth amid poverty, and pockets of poverty amid wealth. The extremely high income of the United Arab Emirates (UAE) is almost entirely due to oil revenues, and this makes the UAE one of the richest countries in the world on a per capita basis. Its citizens have ten times the average income of Emena. Similarly for South Africa and Hong Kong – each has a far higher income per head than its region's average.

It is also apparent that the resources (natural endowments) of these countries play no obvious role in explaining their diversity in income. It is true that the UAE has enormous income from oil (a natural endowment), but Hong Kong has no natural endowment and South Africa has no greater endowment than some other African states – yet South Africa and Hong Kong are far richer than better endowed countries.

Income levels

Since neither regions nor natural resource levels are a sensible way of grouping these countries together, and since GNP seems to be correlated with other indicators of development, it would seem reasonable to group countries according to their GNPs.

It is customary to form them into three broad groups: low income countries (LICs); middle income countries (MICs); and industrialized market economies (IMEs). This is done in Table 26.2. The first two rows, the LICs and the MICs, taken together in row 3 constitute the so-called developing countries (DCs). They are also called the Third World (the developed countries are the 'first' world and the eastern Communist bloc is the 'second' world). More accurately they have been labelled the less developed countries (LDCs), as opposed to the underdeveloped countries (UDCs). It is felt less offensive, however, to use the term 'developing countries'. The fourth row shows the industrialized market economies, to which the developing countries aspire.

Returning to the first two rows, we see that the LICs have about twice the population of the MICs and about a fifth of their per capita income, so even within the developing countries there is a wide disparity of performance. These disparities pale into insignificance, however, when compared with those between the developing countries and the industrialized market economies. DCs have five times the population of IMEs, but only five-hundredths of their per capita GNP.

This may seem merely a difference in the degree of

Table 26.2 Developing and developed countries by income level

	Population (m) 1987	GNP ($US per capita) 1987	% of labour in agriculture		Infant mortality (deaths per 1,000)		Calories per capita		Primary school enrolment (%)	
			1965	1980	1965	1986	1965	1985	1965	1985
LICs	2,544.8	280	77	71	122	95	2,049	2,332	62	100
MICs	1,324.9	1,580	56	44	107	62	2,350	2,710	85	104
DCs	3,869.7	730	71	63	118	81	2,123	2,440	73	101
IMEs	745.7	14,580	14	7	24	11	3,137	3,357	–	101
China	1,068.7	300	81	61	90	39	2,034	2,620	89	124
India	797.1	300	73	70	150	86	2,100	2,126	74	92

Note: LICs = low income countries (including China and India); MICs = middle income countries; DCs = developing countries; IMEs = industrial market economics.

development, but it is a difference in degree so large as to be a difference in kind. That is to say, the problems faced by developing countries are different in kind from those of the developed world. The UK may lament its poor economic performance compared with that of Japan and Germany, and may try to take steps to attain the same kind of growth rates as those countries have enjoyed over the last 40 years, but the UK's position is not dire. It is not faced with famine and disease, and it is not in a steady state – the UK is growing, and every year sees its citizens better and better off. The problems facing developing countries are different in kind from those facing laggards in the developed world.

SUMMARY

1. Western economies are used to periods of prolonged economic growth. This is not true of the developing economies, which have often experienced centuries of no growth.
2. The prediction of Malthus, that population growth would lead to a return to a subsistence culture, has come true for five-sixths of the world's population.
3. Development economics deals with the problems of poor countries trying to grow.
4. Economic development is often imposed on countries by its leaders. This can mean that development planning involves a great deal of government control, if not central direction.
5. Development is usually accompanied by the following features:
   (a) Falling infant mortality.
   (b) A falling proportion of the population employed in agriculture.
   (c) Rising life expectancy.
   (d) Increasing literacy levels.
   (e) More equality of income distribution.
   (f) Rising calorie consumption per capita.
6. There are vast differences in the incomes and resources of countries. Thus developing countries face vastly different problems from the developed world and from each other.

Factors of production in developing economies

We saw in Chapter 1 that the amount of output an economy produces depends on its factors of production (land, labour and capital) and the efficiency with which those factors are applied to production. In order to seek explanations of lack of development it therefore seems reasonable to examine differences in factors and differences in efficiency.

Labour and land

We can see from Table 26.2 that there is no shortage of labour in developing countries. Indeed, there seems to be a surplus of labour with many unemployed or disguised unemployed (i.e. employed in the most mundane and unproductive of tasks, such as 'minding' parked cars). If there is such need for food and shelter, why is so much labour apparently wasted in this way?

Labour on its own, of course, can do very little. In order to grow food there must be land too. Remember that 'land' includes all natural endowments like seeds and water, as well as the soil in which things grow. There can be little doubt that some developing countries have insufficient farmland for their population size together with uncertain or insufficient rainfall. What is certain is that when nature misbehaves it will disrupt the harvests of the developing countries far more than those of the developed. Furthermore, the failure of a harvest may be uncomfortable for a rich country, but it is a disaster for those already on the brink of starvation.

These periodic disasters in poor countries attract our attention and tend to give the impression that the problem is one of overpopulation – that the population is too large for the land and is making too many demands on it. This impression is sometimes quite correct and population control is certainly a big factor in economic development, but this is by no means everywhere the case. One of the fastest growing developed economies (Japan) has an extremely high population density (310 persons per square kilometre) and few natural resources, whereas one of the poorer African countries (Nigeria) has a much lower population density (90 persons per square kilometre) and many natural resources.

Our response to these 'natural' disasters is twofold. First, there is an immediate need to be satisfied, and food, clothing, fuel and medicines are given to the victims by concerned individuals through charities (Band Aid, Oxfam, War on Want, etc.) and by governments. Secondly, there is the longer-term issue of preventing repetition of these disasters by encouraging the country to develop. But if land shortage is not the root cause, what other factor is there to consider?

Capital

The third factor of production is capital, and there is no doubt that developed countries have far more capital than the developing countries. As we have seen, capital is a produced means of production – some current output is devoted to improving future production rather than being eaten up as immediate consumption. The provision of capital therefore requires some current consumption to be forgone, and this is painful – even fatal – for very poor countries. How can they invest some current output when their people are already starving?

There seem to be several ways forward. First, they could invest anyway and sacrifice some of their current population so that future generations will be sufficiently well off to invest. Secondly, they could borrow from the rich countries. These borrowings would have to be paid back over time, but if wisely invested the borrowed funds should generate sufficient revenues to pay off the debt and its interest payments and still yield something for the borrowing country. Borrowings have been a major source of funds for the developing nations and comes through a variety of agencies.

There is an international market for loans, and individuals or firms who wish to participate in this market are typically organized through banks. Firms in the developing countries can apply to banks for investment funds as can firms in developed countries. The interest rates charged by the lenders will depend on the perceived risks of the project. Some banks see the developing world as more risky than the developed world from which they themselves have sprung, especially if repayment depends on uncertain harvests and uncertain commodity prices.

Sometimes banks require firm assurances that their loans will eventually be repaid. This leads to the governments of developing countries underwriting these debts. The banks believe that sovereign states do not go bankrupt and can be relied on always to pay their debts. This underwriting of debts by governments then allows firms in the developing countries to borrow at a lower interest rate than would otherwise have been possible.

On a more political level, the World Bank acts for countries in the same way that commercial and merchant banks act for individuals. Deposits by member countries are lent out to developing countries (and other countries too). The World Bank – or, more properly, the International Bank for Reconstruction and Development (IBRD) – was set up in 1945 at the same time as the International Monetary Fund (IMF). The reconstruction aspect of its work was primarily concerned with rebuilding the European economies after the Second World War. With the completion of that reconstruction the development aspect came to dominate.

The World Bank lends only to governments (or to projects for which the host government guarantees the loan), but it does so in circumstances in which private funds are unlikely to be on offer. The World Bank's principal creditors are Germany, the United States, Japan, Switzerland and Saudi Arabia.

But the World Bank does more than simply respond to proposals from developing countries. It also conducts its own research on likely projects, negotiates with borrowers and monitors the progress of each project. In this regard the World Bank oversees the projects financed by the United Nations Development Programme and works closely with the African Development Bank, the Arab Fund for Economic and Social Development, the European Development Fund and the Inter-American Development Bank.

In 1956 another agency of the United Nations – the International Finance Corporation – was set up. It is affiliated to the World Bank, but it is legally separate and makes its loans without the requirement that they be underwritten by the borrower's government. A little later, in 1960, the UN set up the International Development Association. It too is affiliated to but separate from the World Bank, and it is charged with improving the infrastructure of developing countries. By infrastructure is meant the roads, railways and airports, etc. which are vital for the workings of a modern economy and the exploitation of natural resources. The financial returns from this type of investment take many years to materialize, so these loans are usually made on much more favourable terms than those of the World Bank. The principal need not be repaid for many years and the interest charges are well below World Bank rates.

The total outstanding debt of all developing countries has been growing steadily (see Table 26.3). In 1988 37 per cent of it was held by Latin America and the Caribbean, 18 per cent by East Asia and the Pacific, and only 8 per cent by South Asia.

The ratio of debt to income can be calculated for 1987 by dividing total debt ($1,292 billion) by total population (3.87 billion) to yield a per capita debt in the developing countries of $334 – that is, $334 for every man, woman and child in the developing countries. From Table 26.2 we see that the income per head in developing countries is $730. Taken

Table 26.3 Total debt of developing countries, 1982–90 (US$ billion)

Year	1982	1983	1984	1985	1986	1987	1988	1989	1990
Total debt	839	905	936	1,041	1,146	1,292	1,284	1,290[1]	1,319[1]

Note:
1. Estimates.
1 billion = 1,000,000,000.

together these figures suggest that the debt to income ratio in 1987 was 45.7 per cent. This means that the average family in the developing countries owes almost half its annual income!

These debts were entered into in the belief that output would grow fast enough to meet the repayments (both principal and interest) and leave some benefit to the borrowing country – that is why some debt was underwritten by the governments of those countries. Unfortunately, things turned out differently.

Not all the borrowed funds were invested wisely. It is widely believed that some were used to finance armaments and prestige projects rather than revenue-generating developments. And some projects, which under reasonable assumptions about harvests, mining operations and commodity prices would have proved profitable, turned out badly in the face of adverse price movements. There will always be risks in any investment project, but in the case of the developing countries the poor borrowers were asked to bear all the risks and the rich lenders tried to ensure that their position was secured against government guarantees.

Typically, the debts had to be repaid in the currency of the lender. This meant that, in order to meet their repayments, the debtors had to earn foreign exchange. This in turn meant exporting enough to earn that foreign currency, and in many cases developing countries could compete in international markets in only a few basic commodities. This is tantamount to putting all one's eggs in one basket – any failure of price or output leads to a drying up of foreign exchange and means that debt service payments simply cannot be made. The level of indebtedness therefore increases as unpaid interest is added to the original debt, which continues to grow with no benefit to the debtor.

For largely domestic reasons connected with the government's attempts to control inflation, UK interest rates rose steeply in the late 1970s. Those developing countries which had borrowed from UK banks were completely unable to meet their interest payments out of increased revenues. Far from the borrowed funds yielding a surplus to the developing countries, the debts actually made them worse off. This is a graphic example of how economically interdependent we all are, and how important the economic policy of one country is to the welfare or even survival of others.

Table 26.4 shows the aggregate net transfers to the developing countries between 1980 and 1988. These are grants and new loans from private and official sources less interest payments. It is clear from these figures that, taken together, the developing countries did receive extra funds from 1980 to 1984, and during those years they could spend more than they earned. But since then the developing countries have actually been net losers, paying out more than they received each year. This meant that not even their already low incomes were available for their own uses. Already hungry, and in some cases starving, the poor were asked to tighten their belts to pay the high interest rates demanded by the rich.

The position is now so bad that many borrowing countries are simply unable to meet the interest payments on their loans, let alone repay the principal. The debts which were thought to be as safe as the Bank of England are no longer safe and there is a strong possibility that only a part of the debt will ever be repaid. Because of this some UK banks have written down the book value of their loans to developing countries by hundreds of millions of pounds. A £100m loan may now be worth only £50m, since that is the most the debtor can possibly afford to repay in the foreseeable future.

This inability of developing countries to repay their debts is a major problem facing both the private institutions which lent to them and the World Bank. How can the poor countries build up their capital stock if they have no funds to spare, and if loans (even generous loans) lead to the disastrous outcomes for both the lenders and the borrowers which recent experience suggests?

All that remains is using the existing factors (land, labour and capital) more efficiently.

SUMMARY

1. The problem of underdevelopment is due not to a lack of land or labour, but to a lack of capital.
2. Many developing countries experience periodic disasters which prompt emergency aid.
3. Developing countries find it difficult to build up their capital stock because they cannot afford to save.
4. Developing countries can borrow the capital they require from a variety of sources such as western commercial banks, the World Bank or the International Development Association.
5. Many developing countries have been unable to meet the interest payments on their development loans because of:
   (a) Rising interest rates.
   (b) Falling export commodity prices.
   (c) Poor revenue-generating investment of the loans.
6. The level of developing countries' debt is 45.7 per cent of their income.

Technology

We saw in Chapter 2 that the major influence on the growth rate is the application of increased knowledge. We have learned how to make better use of what land we have, by selective breeding of seed stocks and by using fertilizers and pesticides. In the western economies this application of knowledge extends well beyond agriculture, and huge gains in productivity have also been achieved in manufacturing and service industries.

Table 26.4 Aggregate net transfers, 1980–88 (US$ billion, at 1986 prices)

Year	1980	1981	1982	1983	1984	1985	1986	1987	1988
Aggregate net transfers	65.7	84.5	58.9	41.6	19.4	−0.7	−1.9	−9.9	−9.8

As far as developing countries are concerned, it is the agricultural sector which predominates. Indeed, we have already seen that one indicator of development is the percentage of the labour force in agriculture. Most developed countries began with almost everyone working in agriculture (the agrarian or primary stage of development) and gradually moved into the manufacturing or secondary phase as workers left the countryside and came into towns to work in the factories. The third (tertiary) phase of development is the expansion of the service sector at the expense of manufacturing.

The switch of workers from agriculture to manufacturing implies a big increase in the productivity of our agricultural sector, and indeed this is well documented in our history books. Similarly, the switch to services implies large productivity increases in manufacturing. This too has attracted much attention – particularly from those seeking to explain the differences in the growth rates of the developed world.

Some countries are trying to follow this three-stage development programme by concentrating on improving their food production. They have used seeds and planting methods developed in the first world to do this. This transfer of agricultural technology to developing countries has been called the Green Revolution and there can be no doubt that it has greatly improved yields – in some cases by 300 per cent. What this offers is relief from immediate starvation and some breathing space during which the manufacturing phase can be promoted. The danger is that population will catch up with the increased food supply too quickly, and so population control will again become an issue.

The entry of the developing countries into the secondary (manufacturing) phase of development has tended to follow the same pattern as that of agriculture, i.e. importing technology from the developed world. The problem with this is that what suits a developed economy may not suit a developing economy.

The kind of technology in use in developed countries tends to reflect the fact that there is plenty of capital available, but that labour is expensive. In other words, we tend to use labour-saving/capital-using production techniques. But these are entirely inappropriate for countries with huge underused labour forces and very little capital. Not only that, but the successful operation of modern techniques often requires a host of other services and skills, such as clean conditions and highly skilled repair staff. Some attempts to transfer our technology to other countries have therefore ended, like borrowing, in failure.

This has led to the accent being put more and more on appropriate technology. Our scientific knowledge can be used to improve the lot of developing countries, but it has to suggest solutions which meet the conditions in those countries.

Not all developing countries followed the agrarian–manufacturing–service route to development. Japan, Korea and Hong Kong were remarkably successful in leapfrogging intermediate stages and going for the highest levels of technical achievement. Japan particularly, having been dragged out of isolation by American gunboats in 1886, decided to take on the developed world at its own game and assiduously discovered all it could about western institutions, industries and armed forces. At first the Japanese tried simply to copy best practice and to learn from western mistakes. Having done so, they have now overtaken the west and it is Japan that now operates the latest best practice.

Conclusions

Development economics was once the great hope of the developing world. What it promised was entry of the very poor into the rich man's club, and this entry could be engineered by following certain well-understood rules. In the event most of these promises have remained unfulfilled and some have turned into nightmares.

Having identified capital shortage as the main constraint on development, the solution of loans and World Bank oversight of capital projects has led to even worse conditions for the poor of the developing world and has hung the millstone of debt around the neck of their already burdened economies.

Technology transfer was also attempted, and this too had somewhat mixed results. The insensitive imposition of inappropriate solutions to the perceived problems of the developing countries led to wastage and frustration.

These results have led a major development economist to argue that development economics had not lived up to, and indeed never would live up to, its initial promise: In his presidential address to the Development Studies Association in 1982 Albert Hirschman said:

> Development economics is a comparatively young area of inquiry. It was born just about a generation ago, as a subdiscipline of economics, with a number of other sciences looking on both skeptically and jealously from a distance . . . [O]ur subdiscipline had achieved its considerable lustre and excitement through the implicit idea that it could slay the dragon of backwardness virtually by itself or, at least, that its contribution to this task was central. We now know that this is not so.

SUMMARY

1. There are three stages of development:
   (a) The agrarian or primary stage.
   (b) The manufacturing or secondary stage.
   (c) The tertiary stage.
2. The transfer of agricultural technology from the developed world to the developing world has led to the Green Revolution.
3. The technology transferred to the developing world has tended to be labour saving when the developing world requires labour-intensive technology.
4. Many of the attempts to help the developing world have ended in failure.

Exam Preparation and Practice

MULTIPLE-CHOICE QUESTIONS

1. Which of the following would **not** be a good indicator of the standard of living of people in a Third World country?
   A The literacy rate.
   B The infant mortality rate.
   C Average life expectancy.
   D Income per head in US dollars.

2. Typically, less developed countries lack one factor of production in sufficient **quantity**. This is:
   A Land.
   B Labour.
   C Capital.
   D Entrepreneurs.

Answer key

Where there are three numbered alternatives

A	B	C	D	E
1, 2, 3	1, 2	2, 3	1	3
Correct	Correct	Correct	Correct	Correct

3. Which of the following must be achieved for a Third World country to develop into an industrialized society?
   1 A rise in agricultural productivity.
   2 An average propensity to consume of less than 1.
   3 A loan from the World Bank.

APPENDIX I Essay writing in examinations

Our aim in this section is to discuss how you might approach writing essays in examinations. We are not trying to provide model answers, or suggest that the essay structures are the ones the examiner had in mind when the question was set. Rather it is our aim to help you to develop an essay-writing technique based on the information to be found in *Modern Economics*.

In particular we must emphasize that the examination boards which set the questions we have used as examples are not in any way responsible for, and have not been consulted on, the answers given here. Students should realize that an alternative answer, quite different in emphasis to our illustrations, may also score well. At the request of the boards a disclaimer is reproduced at the end of each possible answer.

Most of the students who read this book will do so with a view to passing an examination. It is no small step to move from the book to the examination paper. Most students will know enough economics at least to attempt an answer. Many students will know enough economics to gain a very good mark. The main problem is not therefore a shortage of knowledge – quite the opposite. The main problem is to *select those items* from one's store of knowledge which are appropriate to any particular question. In setting a question an examiner is inviting the student to demonstrate a command over some part of the syllabus.

In choosing which items to offer as an answer to any particular question, the student reveals quite a lot about his or her understanding of the subject. If the examiner invites a demonstration of the student's grasp of macroeconomics, it would be somewhat revealing if the student began setting out the theory of rent. The first problem therefore is to identify the *part of the syllabus* to be dealt with. There are, to the practised eye, a number of clues given in each question, and in what follows some such clues are identified in questions from past A-level examination papers.

Having decided the part of the syllabus to be examined, it is then necessary to demonstrate a grasp of the technical aspects and an understanding of their significance. There is usually no clear cut-off between what should be dealt with and what should not. There is a whole range of relevant points to be made, from the absolutely central point to the many peripheral points. This degree of importance should be reflected in the space given. Main points may require one or two paragraphs, whereas minor points may simply appear as a list or as asides. By mentioning them the student shows an awareness of some of the finer points and an understanding that they are only peripheral to the question under consideration.

The techniques of deducing the appropriate part of economic theory, weighting those items which are dealt with and deciding what to omit cannot be directly taught. It comes with practice and hence it is vitally important for students to use what they have learned. This can be done by attempting to answer past A-level questions, and a number are included here for convenience.

At first it will seem impossibly difficult. The question may leave the student with absolutely no idea at all as to how to proceed. But with perseverence the technique is gradually learned so that it becomes almost automatic. That is why when the desperate student gives up trying to find an answer and seeks help from a teacher, the answer seems so obvious. The teacher almost unconsciously does the selection process and guides the student into a particular area of economics which the student knows well but did not recognize as being relevant.

In what follows, then, the selection process is spelled out by offering a commentary on how some particular questions may be analysed. Having outlined the first thoughts about the question, a possible response is offered. These examples are *not* intended to be model answers; they are intended to demonstrate a technique – the questions being considered are being used as demonstrations. Learning a technique will allow the student to demonstrate how much, or how little, he or she knows.

Allocating your time

When confronted with an examination paper, you must allow time for three activities:

1. Reading the paper and selecting the questions you will answer.
2. Planning your answers.
3. Writing your answers.

Let us suppose that you are required to write four essays in three hours, with each question carrying equal marks. (We shall discuss the problems of different papers later.)

It is important that you are familiar with the style of paper that you will be confronted with, so look at past papers to ensure that you are. When you are familiar with the style of paper, it should be possible to select in five minutes or so three of the four questions you will answer. It is wise to leave the choice of the last question until the end. You may be running out of time and need to write a very short answer, so it must be a question where you can earn quick marks.

From here you must plan your answers. There are two ways of proceeding:

1. To plan three answers immediately.
2. To plan the first essay, write it, then plan the next, etc.

How you proceed is up to you, but there is an advantage to method 1 which may not be obvious. Method 1 allows you to get the basic outlines of your essay down while your mind is still fresh. Then, when you have completed one essay, you can quickly clear your mind of the previous line of thought and switch to the new essay by scanning the plan. You may want to refine your plan at this stage – you probably will – but you avoid the problems of having to start on a new subject from scratch having spent over half an hour intensely involved in another one.

Whether you choose method 1 or 2, you must take *at least* five minutes to plan each answer. This avoids the howlers made by many candidates, such as not answering the question asked, or starting an essay only to discover that you can only answer the first part. Following our advice means that you will use at least 25 minutes choosing and planning the questions you will answer. This leaves 2 hours and 35 minutes for actually writing your answers, or almost 39 minutes a question. You must aim to write all you need in about this time. (Practice is vital in this respect, and if you are studying alone you should set yourself past questions and answer them in the appropriate time limit.)

If the examination requires you to answer five questions in three hours then the time for writing answers is reduced to 30 minutes. Obviously the scope or depth of answer required will be less.

We will now look in turn at each of the three activities we have identified.

Reading the paper and selecting the questions

Of course, you will want to answer the questions to which you are able to give the best answers. There are dangers, however. Many candidates have produced good answers to the wrong question by writing at length on an area of economics which they know well. Unfortunately, the question asked for something different, but the candidate has seen something in the question and has written all about that and only that. Let us say the question was this:
'Under conditions of perfect competition there will be only one price charged by firms, but in the case of a single supplier there may be more than one price.' Explain this statement. (London, June 1988)

Careful reading of the question shows that it requires you to explain how a monopolist (a single supplier) can charge many prices (discriminating monopoly) when many small firms all charge the same price. So just writing about, say, perfect competition would gain only some marks. The answer is that it is most profitable for the firms involved for the pattern described to emerge, and candidates must explain why.

Reading this section you may feel that we have made a trivial point. But experience shows that many candidates do get the wrong end of the stick. Therefore read the questions carefully and pause to decide what the question requires of you.

Two questions on the paper will probably leap out at you as being exactly what you want to write about – good. The others must be selected to gain you maximum marks. Some boards indicate how marks are allocated between parts of the questions, but others do not and so you must guess (ask your teacher's advice on this because knowing the division of marks allows you to weight your answer appropriately). It is usually a bad idea to attempt a question where you can only answer a minor part. Answering a question where you can write something about all of the parts of a question usually scores more highly. A possible exception to this arises when you are running out of time and have only, say, 20 minutes to answer the last question. You can then look for a question where you can answer one part (preferably the first) really well and quickly.

Planning your answers

A good plan is essential and can reduce answering the question to a matter of simply expanding the plan.

We can divide essay planning into three tasks:

1. Deciding on what is the relevant economics to include.
2. Organizing the selected material into an appropriate sequence to answer the question.
3. Asking yourself 'Does my plan answer the question asked?'

Task 1 requires you to pick out the relevant economic theory from what you have learned. The selection of material is important not only for what you put in, but also for what you leave out. In the essay about perfect competition and discriminating monopoly, you will know a lot about perfect competition that you simply will not have time to include.

Some people like to write down all of the things they can think of at this stage and then discard irrelevant material as they organize it into a logical order. In this case you might write something like Figure E1. PC, of course, means perfect competition – you do not need to write this out for your plan. The crucial decision for this plan was to realize that the relevant material regarding single suppliers was about discriminating monopoly. A candidate might think this way:

1. What does 'single supplier' mean? Answer: monopoly.
2. Pure monopoly usually means charging a profit-maximizing price.
3. Are there any conditions under which a monopolist charges more than one price? Answer: yes, a discriminating monopolist who can split markets into separate units.

A little thought puts you on the right track.

The scheme gets most of the basic ideas down, the detail of the two models and the need to compare them. Such a plan takes little time to write, but has no organization. So where do you start?

Some candidates never follow task 1 with task 2, or task 2 may simply involve numbering the points in Figure E1. (This *may* be all that is needed.) For the essay we have considered, we will construct a more ordered plan to combine with Figure E1.

The question clearly requires a brief exposition of perfect competition and discriminating monopoly. Writing time for

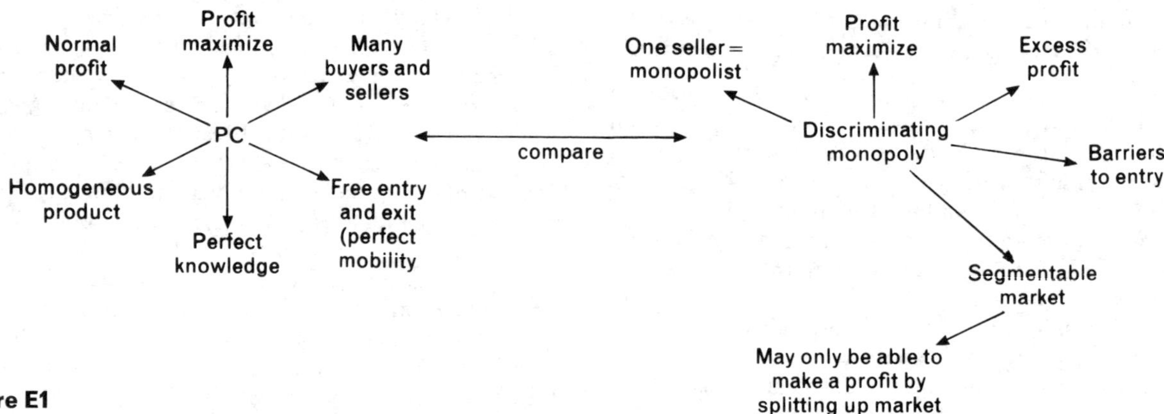

Figure E1

London Board essays is 30 minutes, so the descriptions must be kept brief to allow time for a comparison between the two models. So to Figure E1 add Figure E2.

Figure E2 uses the assumptions of Figure E1, but Figure E2 has allowed the candidate to order the essay and will allow the candidate to see what he or she wishes to write. This way, it is also possible to see if you are spending too much time on one section – the whole of the essay is set out here, which helps to keep the whole task in perspective, and as each part is written, detail can be adjusted accordingly. Notice that there are two sketch diagrams in our plan – diagrams usually make an essay much clearer and in the case of this essay they are essential.

In the description of perfect competition we have chosen to show how one firm's price is related to the market and so will draw a diagram similar to Figure 6.10. This is important as the question asks about market prices, not just the way a single firm sets its price.

For the description of discriminating monopoly we have chosen to include some examples (you will find them discussed in Chapter 6). You may comment that electricity supply, for example, is not a discriminating monopoly because anyone can buy cheap-rate electricity.

Figures E1 and E2 will not take long to compile. Now you must ask yourself 'Does my plan answer the question asked?' (task 3).

Look again at the question and the plan. Is perfect competition and discriminating monopoly covered by the plan. Have you left anything out? This essay is a reasonably straightforward question once you have realized that the single supplier with many prices is a discriminating monopolist. We can therefore pass this plan.

What if the answer to the question posed by task 3 is no? Well, you have saved yourself a lot of time. You can either adjust the plan by further thought, or if necessary abandon the plan and move to another essay. Either way you will probably gain more marks than otherwise. It is much worse to write for 20 minutes before you discover your mistake (worse still, if you only realize what has happened after the exam).

Some essay answers

'*Under conditions of perfect competition there will only be one price charged by firms, but in the case of a single supplier there may be more than one price.*' *Explain this statement.* (London, June 1988)

Firms operating under conditions of perfect competition and those who are monopolists (a single supplier of a good) are both assumed to be aiming to maximize profit. Under

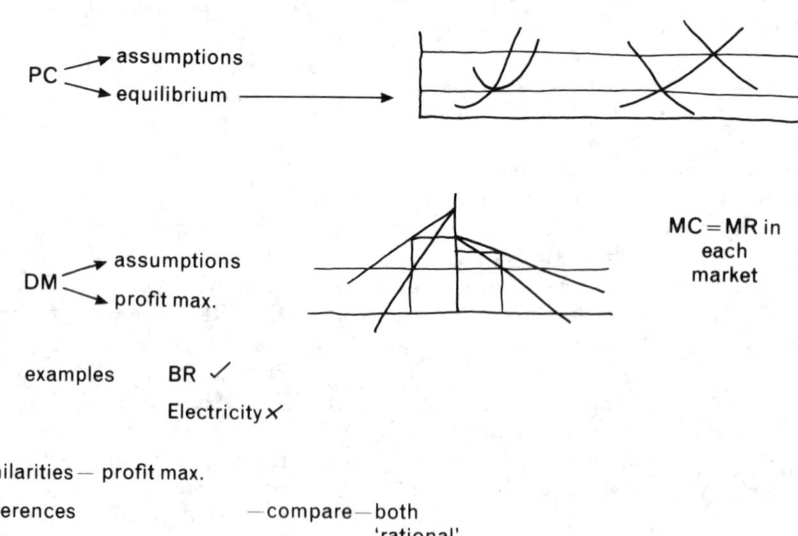

Figure E2

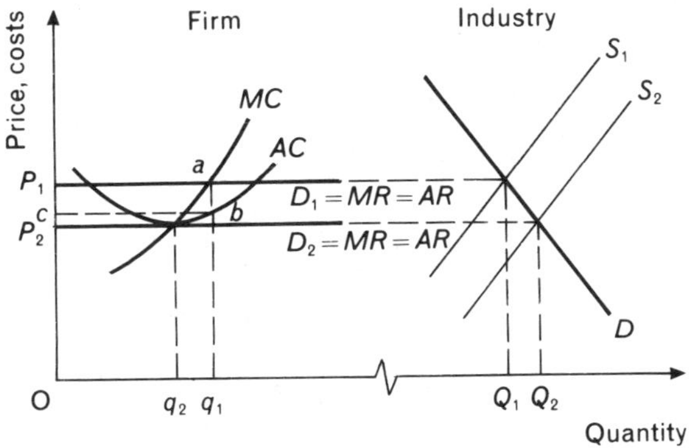

Figure E3

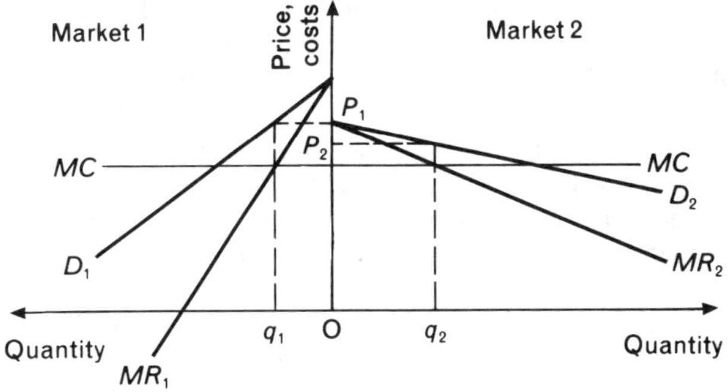

Figure E4

conditions of perfect competition there are many suppliers of the same product and they all charge the same price, yet it can be quite rational for a monopolist to charge various prices.

Under perfect competition all firms are price takers. There are very many firms supplying a homogeneous product to many consumers, each having perfect knowledge of the market, and firms have freedom to leave or enter the industry at will due to the perfect mobility of factors of production. This situation leads firms to compete with each other to the point where only normal profits are earned, and this is shown in Figure E3.

If the initial supply curve is S_1 then the representative firm shown on the left of the diagram is earning excess profits of P_1abc by equating marginal revenue to marginal cost and charging price P_1. Other firms will realize excess profits are available in this market and enter the industry. This will continue until market supply is given by supply curve S_2, where all firms will be earning only normal profits, i.e. they are operating at a point where price equals average cost, although this is also the profit-maximizing position.

This is the inevitable resting place of the market given perfect knowledge, where all consumers shun a firm charging more than the market price, and freedom of entry. Thus in order to compete all firms must be able to offer the same price, P_2, and at that point be efficient enough to earn normal profits. Each of the many firms in the industry charges the same price.

A monopolist also wishes to maximize profits. Because a monopolist is the only supplier it faces the market demand curve which is downward sloping. Like the perfectly competitive firm it equates marginal cost to marginal revenue. If the market is made up of just one sector, say the market for salt in the UK, then the firm charges one price and maximizes profits. In this case the monopolist will earn excess profits, but there is no force for change because there is no freedom of entry to the market.

However, the monopolist may not be supplying just one market. It may be that the good is supplied to several, quite separate groups of consumers. If these groups cannot exchange information and cannot trade with one another then it is possible to increase profits by maximizing profits in each market segment. This is done by equating marginal cost to the marginal revenue gained in each market.

Let us suppose that the monopolist supplies two quite separate groups and the demand curves are shown in Figure E4.

The monopolist could charge just one price, but by equating marginal cost to marginal revenue in each market a greater overall profit may be earned. If, for simplicity, we assume marginal cost to be constant and the same in each market segment then the monopolist charges P_1 in market 1 and P_2 in market 2.

The result can only hold when the two markets are completely separate and no trade is possible between the two segments. The only other condition that must apply for this strategy to yield a greater profit than charging a single price is that the elasticities of demand, and so marginal revenues, must be different in each market. For example, the electricity boards charge customers different prices for electricity at night (Economy 7) than during the day. However, this monopoly supplier of electricity is not discriminating because anybody may take advantage of Economy 7 power. British Rail are discriminating between very young and old people on one hand and 25 to 65 year olds on the other because the latter cannot take advantage of a Railcard offer.

Thus a single supplier may charge more than one price. It may charge a different price in every different isolated segment of the market. Yet in an industry with many firms, all charge the same price. Each market form contains profit-maximizing, rational firms; the differences are usually those of size, barriers to entry and the degree to which consumers can trade between themselves.

(The University of London Schools Examinations Board accepts no responsibility whatsoever for the accuracy or method of working in the answer given.)

What determines a firm's demand for a factor of production? With reference to the factor labour, is demand alone sufficient to determine labour's wage? (Cambridge, June 1986)

The question is about the behaviour of firms and so is about an aspect of microeconomics. In particular, it is about how much a firm will pay for its factor inputs, and specifically for labour.

This is another two part-question, but there is no guidance on how many marks are allocated to each. Although this is only our guess, the first part should carry most of the marks. The first part is about some core economics, while the second part is about its application. Thus a sound base of theory must be laid down and should attract good marks. We shall assume that at least 60 per cent of the marks of this question go to the first part.

In the planning stage you should note that the question asks about a firm's demand for all factors of production, and so you should start with a general point about how firms try to maximize profits from their mix of factor inputs. An explanation of marginal productivity theory should then follow, and here you could use labour as an example. This is both easier and a good way of linking with the second part of the essay.

In the second part you must demonstrate that you can apply theory. You should ask yourself 'what other factors affect the wage rate besides demand?'. Certainly there is supply, human capital, trade unions and even old-fashioned discrimination. To mention many factors will take too long, so you should endeavour to demonstrate principles and give examples, rather than try to explain every possible influence.

A possible answer

Firms take factor inputs and combine them in a way that allows them to produce a product while maximizing profit.

The demand for any factor input (land, labour and capital) is a derived demand. It is derived from the demand for the final product. If the demand for the firm's product falls, so does the firm's demand for factor inputs. The firm will combine the factor inputs it does require so it satisfies the profit-maximizing condition, where marginal cost (*MC*) equals marginal revenue (*MR*). This is done by employing each variable factor up to the point where the marginal cost of employing the factor is equal to the addition to total revenue due to employing the last unit of the factor.

This can be shown by reference to labour. In the short-run it may be the only variable factor; other factors can only respond to changing circumstances in the long run.

The marginal cost of employing labour in a perfect market is the wage rate. The marginal revenue of employing labour is known as the marginal revenue product of labour (*MRP*). The marginal revenue product is the marginal physical product of labour (*MPP*) multiplied by the price of the product produced. The marginal physical product curve and the marginal revenue product curves for a firm are shown in Figure E5. They are downward sloping, reflecting diminishing marginal returns.

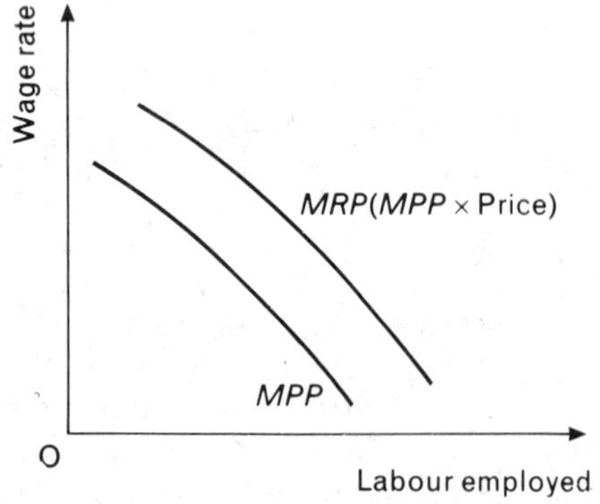

Figure E5

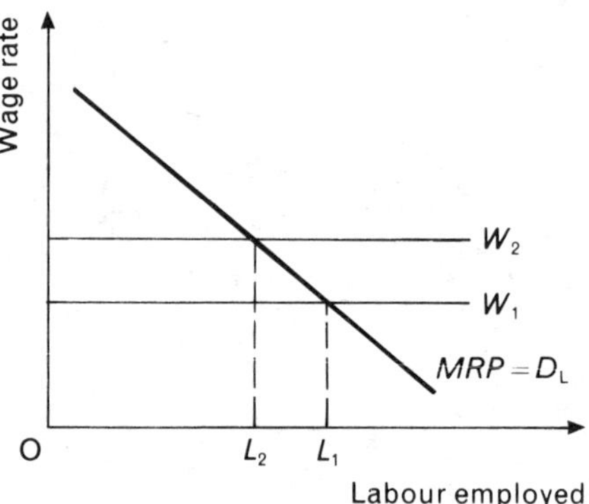

Figure E6

The marginal revenue product curve is the firm's demand curve for labour, and this is shown in Figure E6. As the wage rate varies, the firm employs labour where MRP = wage rate. The wage rate is the supply curve of labour, and so the firm goes to the point where the demand and supply curves intersect.

As the wage rate rises from W_1 to W_2, the firm reduces the amount of labour it employs from L_1 to L_2. The workers are paid exactly the value of their marginal product.

In this case the amount of labour employed depends on the wage rate, which is fixed, and the position of the *MRP* curve. The *MRP* curve will vary its position according to the price of the final product and the productivity of labour. Thus a higher price or improved productivity, due to better training or more capital for example, moves the MRP curve to the right and, *ceteris paribus*, more labour is employed. This is shown in Figure E7. This analysis can be extended to all factors, although the adjustment process may take longer than for labour.

From this discussion we can say that a firm's demand for a factor by a profit-maximizing firm depends on the marginal revenue product of the factor and the marginal cost of the factor. However, markets are not always perfect and so the situation where demand is so dominant may not occur.

Any restriction of the supply of labour will cause the wage rate of labour to vary according to the quantity employed, i.e. the wage rate is no longer given. If a firm is a monopsonist, or if trade unions can successfully restrict the supply of a particular type of labour, then firms will face an upward-sloping supply curve of labour. In the case of trade

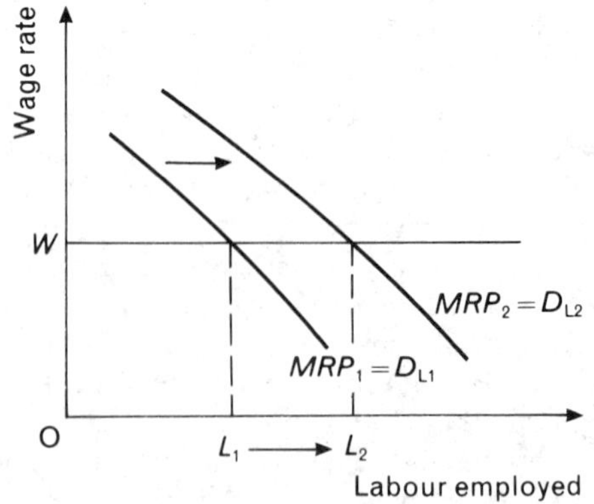

Figure E7

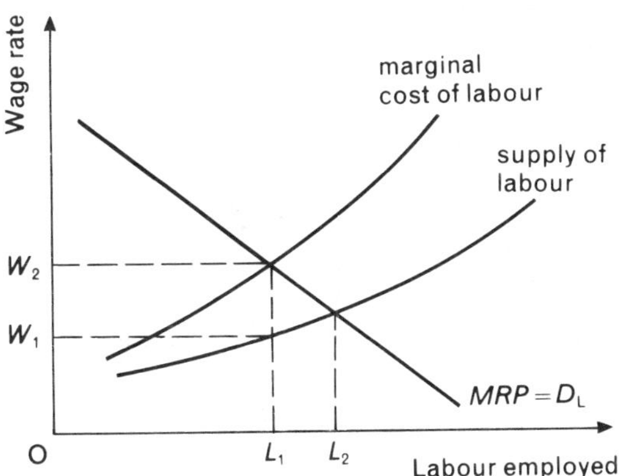

Figure E8

unions, any restriction of the supply of labour will lead to a higher wage rate, but fewer workers will be employed. The degree to which this happens will depend on how well the trade union really can restrict supply in the short and long run.

The final wage rate will also depend on the bargaining strength of the employers. Consider Figure E8. The supply of labour curve is upward sloping, which implies that the marginal cost of employing labour is higher than the supply price of the factor (because all workers are paid the same as the marginal worker). The firm or industry will employ OL_1 workers to maximize profit, but OL_1 workers are available at wage rate OW_1. The firm could afford to pay up to wage rate OW_2, the exact wage paid can lie anywhere between the two, and employment could be up to OL_2 workers, all depending on the relative strength of trade unions and employers.

Educational background also plays a part. People with degrees gain much better paid jobs than those with just A levels. This may mean they are more productive and are rightly paid more as their *MRP* is greater. However, it may be that employers are just taking qualifications as a signal, and that the productivity of the better paid is little different from that of the less well paid. This is then a matter of perception, and it can have an important influence on the decisions of employers. Similar cases can be made for the wages of women and black workers who, on average, are paid less than white males.

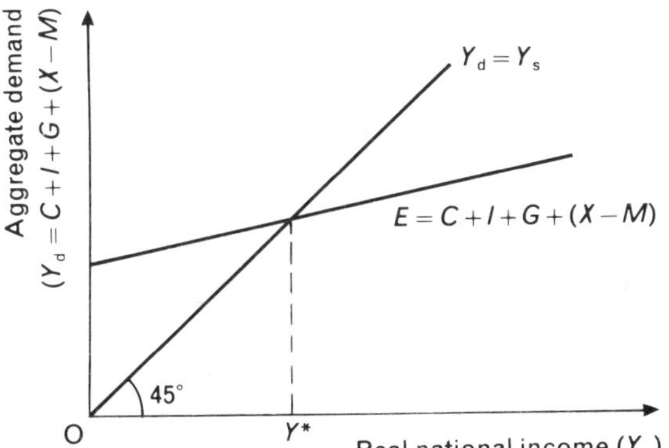

Figure E9

Thus we can conclude that demand is a very important determinant of the wage paid to labour, but in imperfect markets supply considerations are important, as can be other, 'non-economic' factors.

(The University of Cambridge Local Examinations Syndicate bears no responsibility for the example answers to questions taken from its past question papers which are contained in this publication.)

This essay, like many, could lead to you writing a book given sufficient time. You must keep a careful eye on the clock and design your answer to fit the time allowed – hence the summary discussion of discrimination, the principle of perception having already been established.

How can a government use fiscal policy in an attempt to change the level of aggregate demand? (60)
Examine the problems which the government might encounter in pursuing this objective. (40)
(London, January 1989)
(Figures in brackets refer to the allocation of marks, i.e. 60 per cent to the first part, 40 per cent to the second.)

This question should suggest to you that for the first part you should discuss Keynesian determination of national output. Indeed, it is generally true that you should first consider the Keynesian approach to *any* macroeconomics question at A level as this is the way the various syllabuses are weighted, even though this may no longer reflect the body of contemporary economic opinion.

The key words here are 'fiscal policy' and 'aggregate demand'. In Chapter 14 we show how fiscal policy – the manipulation of government spending and taxation – could influence the level of aggregate demand and so the level of national income (output) and employment. The most favoured way of answering this question is by the use of diagrams showing the components of aggregate demand as in Figure E9.

It is also possible to use the algebra of this system only, or *IS/LM* analysis, but we shall adopt the most straightforward approach.

The second part of the question, which carries 40 per cent of the marks, gives a great deal of scope to show that you are aware of the implications of government policies and how economic variables relate to one another. But it does not give you much time, so you must be selective. Two important areas to discuss will be the problem of inflation (using the Phillips curve) and the balance of payments constraint which may arise. Notice that discussion of the possible government borrowing requirement and its effects on interest rates is used to link the two parts of the question – the result of first planning the answer.

A possible answer

Fiscal policy is the manipulation of aggregate demand by governments by changing their own spending (G) and/or taxation (T). Up to the middle of the 1970s fiscal policy as suggested by Keynesian economists dominated government economic policy.

The economy can be thought of as a 'circular flow' of

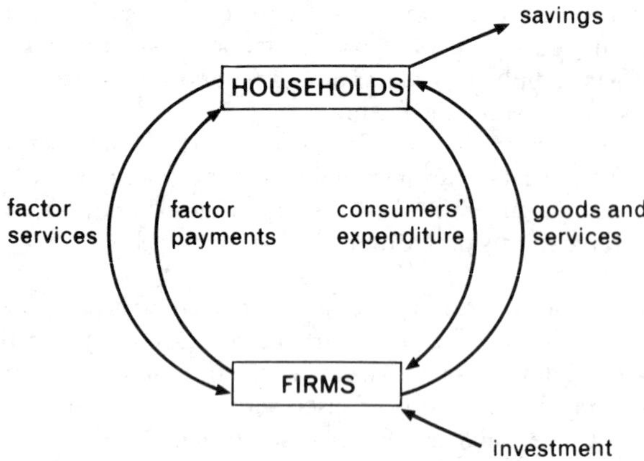

Figure E10

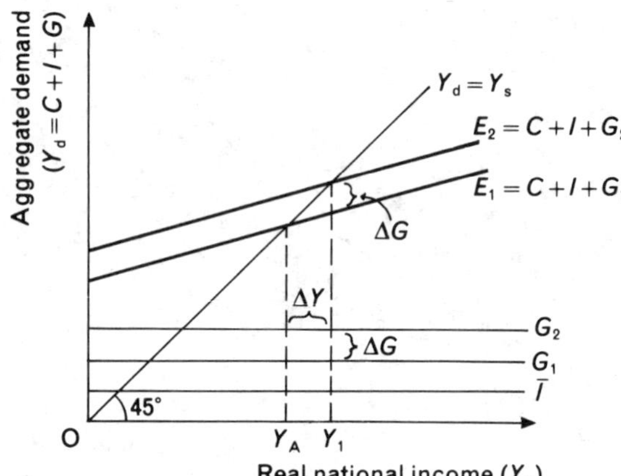

Figure E12

payments, and in the simplest example it can be represented in Figure E10.

If we assume that households own all factors of production then this represents a simple closed economy. The level of output (firms' production) depends on the demands of households for goods and services, which in turn depends on their income.

There is no reason why the level of demand need be sufficient to employ all factors of production, so unemployment may occur. This may be due to withdrawals from the circular flow such as savings, but whatever the reason it would be possible to employ more people if aggregate demand was higher. One way of achieving this would be for the government to spend more or tax less – that is, injecting demand into the circular flow or reducing withdrawals from it.

We can explain this with the use of a model. Let $Y =$ national income in a closed economy.

$$Y = C + I + G$$

where

$C =$ consumption expenditure
$I =$ investment expenditure
$G =$ government expenditure

$C = c(1-t)Y$, i.e. a percentage (c) of after-tax income is consumed and the rest is saved. I and G are determined outside of the system and so are fixed with regard to Y.

If G or I rise then aggregate demand also rises and so does output (national income). Figure E11 shows an economy in equilibrium.

The expenditure function is the sum of C, I and G. The economy is in equilibrium where income (Y) equals expenditure (E), which is where the expenditure function crosses the 45° line. National income is therefore Y_A.

Suppose that Y_A is a level of output where unemployment exists. The government may wish to reduce unemployment and so may increase its own spending, which will cause aggregate demand to rise. This is shown in Figure E12.

In the diagram, government spending rises from G_1 to G_2, which causes the expenditure function to shift from E_1 to E_2. This leads to a rise in national income, from Y_A to Y_1, and a higher level of output implies a lower level of unemployment. In the diagram, the change in national income, ΔY, is greater than the change in government spending, ΔG. This is due to the 'multiplier effect'. The multiplier occurs because the extra government spending is passed on in further consumption spending by those who receive it, and this process continues until all of the increase in G is withdrawn from the circular flow. The value of the multiplier is $\dfrac{1}{s+ct}$ where $s =$ the marginal propensity to save and $t =$ the marginal propensity to tax.

The government may also change the tax rate and so increase or decrease disposable income. This will directly

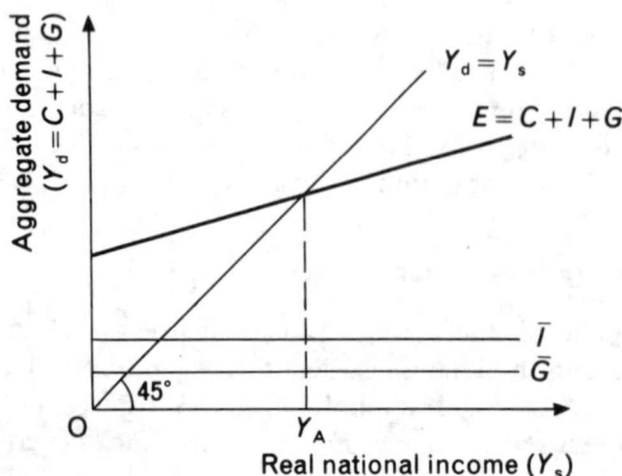

Figure E11

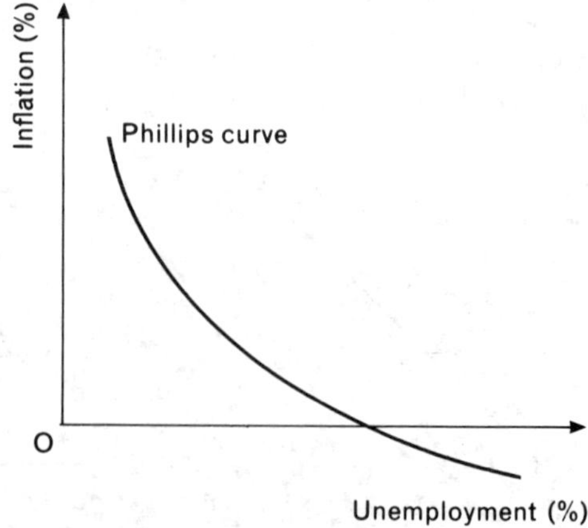

Figure E13

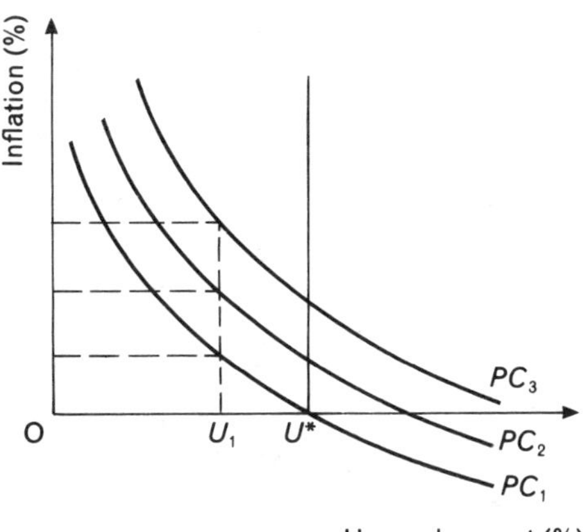

Figure E14

affect consumption ($C = c(1-t)Y$), but instead of shifting, the expenditure function changes its slope, the result still being a change in the level of national income.

Whichever way the government tries to influence aggregate demand, it will have an implication for the government budget. If spending (G) is increased with no increase in taxation then the government may find it has a budget deficit which it must finance by borrowing. The difference between total government spending and revenue is known as the public-sector borrowing requirement (PSBR), although in some recent years the UK government has run a budget surplus. The need to raise finance can affect the money markets, forcing up the rate of interest and so reducing private investment, which will reduce aggregate demand. This will partly offset the rise in national income that was the aim of the change in fiscal policy. This is an example of 'crowding out'.

Another problem may be inflation, which can occur if the level of aggregate demand exceeds the level of output the economy can produce, leading to an 'inflationary gap'. This said, the Phillips curve suggests that the lower the level of unemployment, the higher the level of inflation (Figure E13).

In recent years the Phillips curve relationship was broken down, but it is suggested that the curve shifts as inflationary expectations rise when unemployment is held below its 'natural rate' (Figure E14). If the government holds the level of unemployment at U_1 by fiscal policy, the Phillips curve shifts progressively outwards, leading to ever higher inflation.

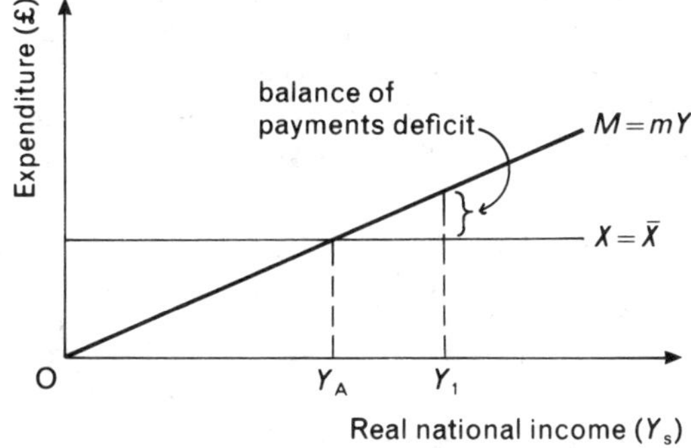

Figure E15

A further problem is known as the 'balance of payments constraint'. The demand for exports is fixed with respect to national income, but the demand for imports is a function of disposable income. Thus raising national income from Y_A to Y_1 may lead to a balance of payments deficit (Figure E15).

Such a deficit is a problem in itself and may also lead to downward pressure on the exchange rate, causing rising import prices or pressure for a change in the pound's position in the European exchange rate mechanism.

In conclusion fiscal policy can be a powerful tool of economic policy, but may lead to other economic problems.

(The University of London Schools Examinations Board accepts no responsibility whatsoever for the accuracy or method of working in the answer given.)

At the end of the essay I have referred to possible consequences for the exchange rate. It is impossible to divorce macroeconomic policy from the external economy and you should endeavour to link the two whenever appropriate.

The diagrams are labelled here as they are in the main text, but you may use abbreviations once you have clearly defined a term. For example, you could write RNI on the axis for real national income as long as you have first used real national income (RNI), this will save time.

Outline a theory of interest rate determination. Discuss whether, when demand in the economy is low, falling interest rates are a sign of further depression or possible recovery in economic activity. (JMB, June 1983)

This question is clearly addressing part of the macroeconomics section of the book. Interest rates are nationally or even internationally determined, and the reference to 'demand' and 'depression' are all the clues needed.

The question implies that there is more than one theory of interest rate determination. It is worthwhile just thinking of some possible candidates before deciding which is more appropriate. Three spring immediately to mind: the Keynesian liquidity preference theory; the classical loanable funds theory; and the view that in an open economy interest rates are determined in the world as a whole and that each (small) country takes them as 'given'.

Of these three the last might be worth a brief mention but clearly offers insufficient material for an A-level examination answer. This leaves two possibilities – liquidity preference and loanable funds.

The choice between these may be a free one – the student simply makes a choice and goes ahead. This choice cannot be avoided by covering both theories because the question clearly asks for *a* theory. In these circumstances it is essential to look at the rest of the question to see if any further clue is given. The mention of 'demand' and 'depression' suggests that a Keynesian approach is the more appropriate. In classical models, output should settle down at that corresponding to the 'natural rate of employment'. The interest rate merely determines how output is divided between current consumption and investment (savings).

The most likely approach is therefore that of Keynes. It requires an account of liquidity preference theory, which is quite lengthy even when only its bare bones are set out.

Thus there will be little time for relating interest to the level of demand. This final part of the essay will therefore be much shorter than the first. It is as well, nevertheless, to bear in mind what this paragraph will say, since the rest of the answer should lead up to it. In the Keynesian model which is well away from full employment (as the question says), interest rates would be high if there were a shortage of liquidity and low if there were a surplus. They will fall if money supply is increased, and if this encouraged investment then aggregate demand would increase and a recovery would begin. If, however, the fall in interest rates was due to a fall in the demand for money then a further depression is indicated.

A possible answer

There are three possible theories for the determination of interest rates: (1) in a small 'open' economy they may be determined entirely by the rest of the world and the economy simply takes them as 'given'; (2) the classical theory, which is based on the supply of and demand for loanable funds; and (3) the Keynesian theory, which is based on the liquidity preference approach.

According to Keynesian theory, money may be used both as a medium of exchange and as a store of value. Its use as a medium of exchange means that as the nominal value of output increases so will the amount of money necessary to act as a medium of exchange. This is shown by the quantity equation:

$$M_T V = PY$$

where V is the velocity of circulation and is assumed constant
M_T is the amount of money demanded as a medium of exchange
and PY is the nominal value of national output.

This is the only demand for money in classical theory. Keynes identified three motives for holding money: for transactions (as above), as a precaution and for speculation.

If we assume that only two assets can act as a store of value – money and bonds – then the speculative demand for money is the desire to hold money for this function. Bonds yield a rate of interest whereas money does not, and so holding money involves a sacrifice – lost interest. However, the price of bonds fluctuates and in the case of consols the price of bonds varies inversely with the rate of interest, i.e. when the rate of interest rises the price of bonds fall.

People will therefore decide to hold some of their wealth in the form of money due to the uncertain price of bonds. If all one's wealth were held as bonds and the interest rate doubled then the value of the bonds would be halved. Also if the wealth-holder needed some cash it would be difficult to sell the bonds.

The difficulty of encashing an asset and the uncertainty of its value together determine its liquidity. Money is perfectly liquid, but bonds are illiquid. Interest is paid to persuade wealth-holders to give up the liquidity of money and hold illiquid bonds. This is the liquidity preference theory of interest. As the interest rate increases, more wealth-holders will prefer bonds to money and so the demand for money will fall. The relationship between interest and the demand for money as a store of value is

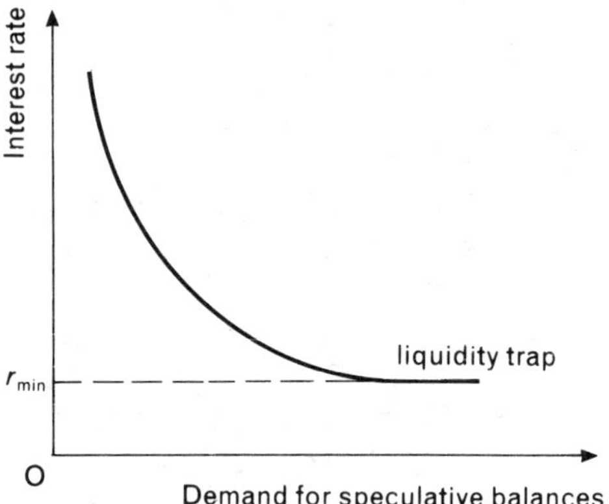

Figure E16

called a liquidity preference schedule, and it is downward sloping as shown in Figure E16.

The amount of money available as a store of value depends upon the amount issued by the government. Thus it is the interaction of the liquidity preference of wealth-holders and the supply of money that determines interest rates. If the government issues more money then more is available as a store of value. The rate of interest falls as the economy moves down the liquidity preference schedule to the right. Similarly, a desire to hold less money as a store of value will cause the liquidity preference schedule to shift to the left, again causing interest rates to fall.

Falling interest rates in a depression can be a good sign. Certainly firms will feel able to invest more as the rate of interest falls, and this will cause aggregate demand to rise. The operation of the multiplier will cause any new investment to have an increased effect on national income and so there will be a rise in consumer spending. A recovery can begin.

An alternative view is that the depression is worsening when interest rates fall. Keynes pointed out that in a depression the economy is likely to be in the 'liquidity trap'. Here demand and national income are so low that a great proportion of the money stock is not required for transactions. Falling interest rates therefore show that the liquidity trap has not yet been reached and output may be continuing to fall.

The liquidity preference theory of interest suggests that interest is determined by the supply of and demand for money. The interest rate will fall when money supply is increased or when nominal output falls. The former indicates a recovery of the economy whereas the latter indicates further decline. Thus movements of the interest rate alone cannot be used as an indicator of economic health.

(The Joint Matriculation Board is in no way responsible for the accuracy of the answer given here.)

This is a rather long answer and requires a great deal of thought about what should be included and what should be excluded. There is no time to define money or to say much about bonds. It would be easy and unwise to spend too much time trying to spell out every part of the relevant economic theory. A plan is therefore essential. It is also important to keep in mind where the answer is going – what is the final point to be made. This focuses one's mind and discourages unnecessary detours. It is a difficult question to answer under examination conditions.

'The balance of payments always balances and thus has no significance.' Discuss. (London, January 1984)

This question is brief and to the point. The words 'balance of payments' could possibly be construed to mean any balance sheet exercise, but the definite article which precedes them clearly indicates the UK's balance of payments. This further indicates that of the three areas of economics (microeconomics, macroeconomics and international trade) this question is aimed at international trade. Furthermore, since it deals only with financial flows (payments), there is no need to explore the theory relating to real trade (e.g. the pure theory of international trade).

What is wanted here then is a definition of the balance of payments, an explanation of why the account always balances and finally an appraisal of the claim that, being balanced, it has no significance.

A possible answer

The balance of payments is the record of the financial transactions between one country and the rest of the world. It is divided into two parts: the current account and the capital account.

The current account records payments made by the UK for its imports of goods and services and the payments made to the UK for its exports of goods and services. The import and export of goods is called 'visible trade' and when the value of imported goods exceeds the value of exports there is a balance of trade deficit. When the reverse is true there is a balance of trade surplus.

Any imbalance in the balance of trade could be offset by an equal and opposite imbalance in the values of the imports and exports of services. This is called 'invisible trade'. Thus a deficit on visible trade (balance of trade deficit) could be partially, totally or more than offset by a surplus on invisible trade. If the visible deficit is only partially offset by the invisible surplus then the combined accounts (the current account) will be in overall deficit too.

If this were the case then the total value of goods and services imported by the UK would exceed the total value of goods and services exported by the UK.

Any deficit (surplus) on current account could be offset by a surplus (deficit) on capital account. The capital account records the payments made by UK citizens to buy *assets* abroad (foreign bonds, stocks and shares) and the payments made by foreigners to buy UK assets. Thus the UK invests abroad and lends abroad and foreigners invest in the UK and lend to the UK.

If the UK is lending and investing more abroad than foreigners are lending and investing here then payments out will exceed payments in and the capital account will be in deficit.

If the sum of capital account and current account yields a deficit (payments abroad exceed payments from abroad) then this deficit has to be financed. The extra payments abroad have to be provided by someone. Conversely, if there is a surplus then the extra payments from abroad must be absorbed by someone.

The extra payments paid abroad have to be in foreign currencies since their recipients do not use pounds sterling for normal transactions. Thus a deficit would lead to an outflow, from the UK, of gold and foreign currencies (typically provided by the UK government). In the case of a surplus there will be an inflow of gold and foreign currencies and these will, again typically, find their way to the UK government. The provision (and absorption) of gold and foreign currencies by the UK government to meet deficits (surpluses) on capital and current accounts is included in the balance of payments accounts and (since it always equals the imbalance of current and capital accounts) the balance of payments must always balance. When incomplete information or unrecorded trade occurs, the difference between the current and capital accounts is expressed in a 'balancing item'.

This result does not, however, imply that the accounts are irrelevant. The composition of the account is important and has great significance for economic health.

First, if the current account is in surplus then the capital account can be in deficit. Therefore the UK can invest more abroad than is being invested by foreigners in the UK: there is a net acquisition of assets by the UK. This should eventually lead to higher incomes from abroad in the form of interest and profits.

If the capital and current accounts, taken together, are in deficit then the gap would have to be provided for out of gold and foreign currency reserves. These reserves would eventually be exhausted and so some action is necessary to correct the deficit.

The current account deficit could be eased in two ways. The government could reduce aggregate demand and hence reduce imports (which fall as aggregate demand falls). Alternatively, it could allow (or engineer) a fall in the exchange rate (a devaluation of the pound). This would encourage exports and discourage imports. These policies (deflation and devaluation) will therefore either reduce UK production (and hence employment) or increase the cost of UK imports or both. Neither policy is therefore likely to be popular.

The capital account deficit could be eased by increasing the rate of interest in the UK. This would make UK assets more attractive to investors than foreign assets. Thus more foreigners would lend to the UK and fewer UK citizens would lend abroad. These increased interest rates would have some detrimental effects on the UK economy since investment in new capital would be discouraged and, via the multiplier, this would reduce output and employment. This too would be unpopular.

Therefore, although the balance of payments always balances, it is not irrelevant. The composition of the account is important, and imbalances within its subsections lead to economic policies and consequences which are of great importance.

(The University of London Schools Examinations Board accepts no responsibility whatsoever for the accuracy or method of working in the answer given.)

This answer deals at length with the claim made in the question that the balance of payments always balances.

This is intended to demonstrate to the examiner a good grasp of the accounts and their components.

The second part of the answer deals with the claim that the account is irrelevant. This part of the answer is intended to show some knowledge of the significance of the accounts, and that the student can make use of macroeconomics too in spelling out some of the main points.

Distinguish between social and private costs. Examine the problems that arise if there is a divergence between social and private costs. (AEB, November 1982)

This question refers to subject matter covered in two parts of *Modern Economics*. We discussed the nature of costs in the chapters on microeconomics. Private costs are those we described as the costs of factor inputs. We also discussed the problem of social costs or externalities which fall on those other than the consumers and producers of a good as a market failure. Finally in Part V we discussed green economics, which showed us examples of social costs and the problems of resource allocation that these create.

When writing this essay you should ensure that the first part gives a clear but concise account of social and private costs. The second part calls for a clear statement of the problems that might emerge from social and private costs diverging. Here it is important to state first what would happen if they did not. You can then compare the two situations and draw some conclusions. Examples are important to this essay. You can then show you are aware of current concerns and are able to apply economic theory to the real world.

You can also consider the problems of dealing with the situation that arises when social and private costs diverge. This will enable you to show your knowledge of possible policy measures and cost–benefit analysis as a way of assessing the problem.

A possible answer

In mixed economies most, and in free-enterprise economies all, decisions on what, how and for whom to produce are made by the price mechanism. The interaction of demand and supply determines prices. This gives all the necessary information to consumers and producers so that they can maximize utility and profits respectively.

According to supporters of the market system, this will lead to an allocatively efficient use of scarce resources for the economy as a whole. This was described by Adam Smith as an 'invisible hand' guiding self-interested individuals to act in a way that caused the economy to move to an optimum allocation of resources. However, this result relies on the assumption that private costs and benefits reflect all costs and benefits.

Private costs are those incurred by firms in the production of an output, e.g. wages and rent. In perfect markets we know that the sum of firms' marginal cost curves is the industry supply curve and so reflects the costs of production. The demand curve reflects the benefits consumers gain from consuming the good.

The supply and demand curves accurately reflect the costs or benefits of the producers and consumers, but some

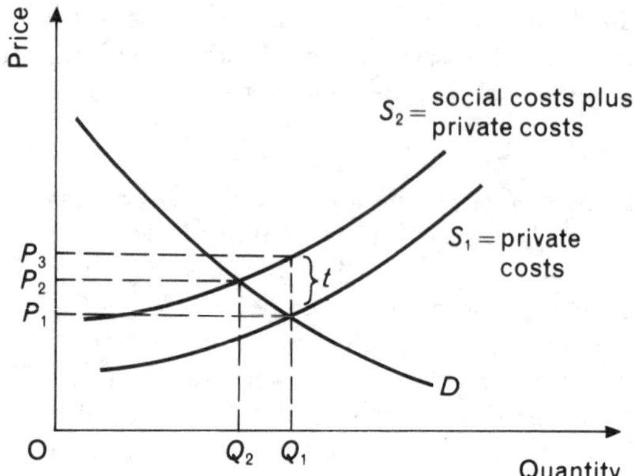

Figure E17

products impose costs on others also. Costs imposed upon society regardless of their consumption of the good are known as 'social costs' or 'externalities'. If there are no social costs then markets allocate resources efficiently. However, if there are social costs then an individual market allocates resources only as those in the market desire and not as society as a whole would wish. This is shown in Figure E17.

If there are no social costs – then the quantity of the good produced (OQ_1) at price OP_1 is allocatively efficient. If there are social costs then a free market will produce the same quantity at the same price, but the true cost to society is OP_3 per unit. This may represent the cost of cleaning up pollution caused by the product, or just the reduced quality of life from, say, living near a noisy airport.

If we add the social costs caused by the product to the private costs, this gives us supply curve S_2. If these costs are fully taken into account then only OQ_2 units will be produced at price OP_2. Social costs can include pollution, noise, the spoiling of areas of natural beauty and the using up of resources, denying their use to future generations.

In free markets there is no way of passing these costs on and so fossil fuels are used up, but their price reflects only the costs of extraction and not the damage done to the environment. In this sense the market has failed.

The problems that arise are therefore those of resource allocation, and deciding how to correct these are not easy matters. From Figure E17 it would seem that the imposition of a tax equal to the amount t would solve the problem. This would mean that the market price did reflect the full costs of production, but it would not solve the problem of how large the social costs really are.

It is by no means clear what the costs of pollution are. For many years the only apparent cost of pollution from motor cars was blackened buildings, but it now appears that people's health and the atmosphere have been severely affected. Even if we know what the social effects are, how can they be measured so that a monetary value can be put on them and market prices adjusted? One method is to move to central planning, but the method favoured by economists is cost–benefit analysis.

The problems of applying cost–benefit analysis to a particular market failure are by no means easy to solve. There may well be strong disagreements about how bad the pollution actually is. Some people, for example, might be much more sensitive to smoke or noise than others. The problem is to bring all these views together into an objective measure of costs. Further problems arise when the costs of a particular decision are borne by one section of the community while the benefits are enjoyed by another. This occurs, for example, when an airport is built. Those who live in the flight path suffer the noise pollution, but everyone else enjoys holidays abroad. The difficulty is to compare the benefits enjoyed by the holiday-makers with the costs borne by the residents.

We may conclude that when there are social costs in addition to private costs the market does not allocate resources efficiently. Correcting this in itself creates problems, not the least of which is identifying the social costs and benefits involved.

(The Associated Examination Board is in no way responsible for the accuracy of the answer suggested here.)

Essay bank

The essays in this section are included to show you the range and type of question asked at A level and to provide you with a set of questions on which to practise your essay technique.

Microeconomics

Production

Why might a firm's average cost curve be U-shaped (a) in the short run and (b) in the long run? Will a firm that sets price equal to marginal cost make greater or less than normal profits when its average costs are rising? (Oxford, June 1986)

Define concisely total, average and marginal costs. Explain the relationship between the three types of cost. Should a firm cease production if it cannot cover its average costs? (London, June 1987)

Distinguish between fixed and variable costs. To what extent are the price and output decisions of a firm affected by the existence of fixed costs? (Oxford and Cambridge, June 1990)

Explain and illustrate how a cost-minimising firm should determine the combination of factors of production. (Oxford and Cambridge, June 1989)

Consumers

(a) Define an inferior good and give an example.
(b) Define a Giffen good and give an example.
(c) Explain carefully, for each of the above, the relationship between the price of the good and the quantity purchased by the consumer. (Cambridge, November 1985)

Why are demand curves thought to be normally downward sloping?
Why is this not always the case? (London, June 1982)

Distinguish between the income and substitution effects of a price change for (a) a normal good and (b) a Giffen good. (Cambridge, November 1986)

What is meant by the term 'utility'?
In an economy in which there exist products that have bad effects, or in which there is persuasive advertising, is it possible for consumers to maximise its welfare? (JMB, June 1989)

Determination of prices

(a) What are the likely consequences for price and output of an increase in demand for a firm's product?
(b) What are the likely consequences for price and output of an increase in demand for an industry's product? (Cambridge, November 1987)

Why is it important to take elasticities into account when using supply and demand curves to analyse economic problems? (AEB, November 1990)

'Water, which is essential to life, costs little, whereas diamonds, which are not, are expensive.' Why is this so? (Oxford and Cambridge, July 1982)

What factors are likely to influence the individual market demand for local bus services?
The Price Elasticity of Demand for local bus travel is approximately 0.4. What are the commercial and social implications of this for the policy of cutting (or not raising) bus fares in order to maintain a local service? (JMB, June 1982)

Consider briefly the main determinants of the demand for a product. What factors govern the size and nature of the Price and Income Elasticities of Demand in the cases of
(a) an individual's demand for salt?
(b) consumers' demand for holidays?
(c) industrial demand for aluminium? (Oxford, June 1989)

Market structure

(a) What factors account for the emergence of monopoly power? (6)
(b) Explain how a monopolist may be able to earn profits greater than 'normal profits'. (7)
(c) Consider the possible social advantages and disadvantages of monopoly situations. (7) (WJEC, June 1984)

Why does perfect competition provide the optimum allocation of resources? (Oxford and Cambridge, June 1986)

What types of market structure might give rise to the following, and why?
(a) low prices; (b) high profits; (c) advertising. (Oxford, June 1988)

'The only realistic theories of the firm are to be found under the heading of Oligopoly.' Discuss. (Oxford and Cambridge, S level, 1989)

(a) What is a monopoly?

(b) How do the price charged by a monopolist and the output produced differ from the price and output of a competitive firm? Explain your reasoning. (Cambridge, November 1987)

Market failure

In what circumstances would cost–benefit analysis be used to evaluate capital project proposals?
What difficulties are likely to be encountered in the application of cost–benefit analysis? (AEB, November 1983)

Why do governments intervene in markets to alter the working of the price mechanism?
Evaluate the long and short term consequences of such intervention in the market for agricultural produce. (JMB, June 1988)

What is meant by an optimal allocation of resources?
Under what conditions might market forces result in an optimal allocation of resources? (AEB, June 1989)

Would an optimal allocation of resources be ensured if all firms were to set prices at marginal costs of production? (Oxford and Cambridge, S level, June 1989)

Outline and comment on the case for the public provision of some goods and services. (Oxford and Cambridge, June 1987)

Comparative systems

Explain the basis on which economists, in classifying economic systems, distinguish between 'market' and 'command' economies.
On what basis, if any, is it possible to say which type of economy is superior? (JMB, June 1987)

Outline the essential differences between free market and centrally planned economies.
Discuss the economic problems which may arise in the transition of the Eastern European economies to the free market system. (JMB, June 1991)

Factor markets

'Unless someone has repealed the law of supply and demand, I am afraid that the higher the price that is asked for labour, the less labour will be employed' (the Rt. Hon. Norman Tebbit MP, Secretary of State for Employment). Explain and critically assess this statement. (AEB, June 1989)

What determines the demand for a person's services?
Using UK examples, to what extent are the earnings of the highest paid demand determined? (Cambridge, June 1989)

'Low pay is related directly to low productivity.' Discuss. (Cambridge, June 1991)

Explain, giving examples, what is meant by 'economic rent'.
Why is it argued that taxes should be levied on economic rents? (London, June 1983)

Macroeconomics

National income

A country's national income statistics are often interpreted as an index of the economic welfare of its citizens. Consider some of the limitations of using national income statistics for this purpose. (WJEC, June 1984)

Discuss the relationship between unemployment and government expenditure. (London, June 1982)

Why might an increase in Gross National Product measured at constant market prices be a misleading indicator of an increase in economic welfare? (Oxford, June 1988)

Money

What is money?
Explain what acts as money in the UK at present. (JMB, June 1982)

What determines the demand for money?
How is the demand affected by inflation? (London, June 1982)

Define money and outline how its forms may vary with the level of development of an economy. Discuss why there are so many measures of the money supply in the UK. (JMB, June 1988)

National output determination

(a) Define carefully the terms 'injections' into and 'withdrawals' from the circular flow of income. (5)
(b) Discuss the main categories of injections and withdrawals that can be identified in the economy. (10)
(c) Explain the significance of these concepts in the Keynesian theory of income and employment determination. (10) (WJEC, June 1984)

What is meant by fiscal policy?
How might it be used to increase the level of activity in an economy? (Oxford and Cambridge, June 1987)

Show that an economy is in equilibrium when injections equal withdrawals.
Why is it necessary to distinguish between planned and actual levels of injections and withdrawals? (Oxford and Cambridge, June 1987)

Discuss the possible economic effects which might result from a significant increase in public expenditure financed by increased taxation. (AEB, November 1989)

Inflation, unemployment and macroeconomic policy

'Inflation is caused by excess demand and sustained by expectations.' Discuss. (AEB, June 1987)

Why might a government consider control of the money supply to be an essential component of economic policy? (London, June 1987)

Explain the meaning of the term 'demand for money'.
Compare the Keynesian and Monetarist views of the demand for money and indicate their respective policy implications. (JMB, June 1989)

Explain what is meant by the 'natural rate' of unemployment.
Evaluate the likely effects on the economic performance of the British economy of policies designed to reduce the natural rate. (JMB, June 1988)

Argue the case for and against an incomes policy. Might such a policy help to reduce unemployment in the UK? (Oxford, June 1988)

(a) How, in principle, can the Government use fiscal policy to influence the level of unemployment? (15)
(b) What arguments have been advanced against the use of government policy of this sort? (10) (WJEC, June 1989)

Compare the relative costs of unemployment and inflation to the economy. Can policy-makers choose the level of unemployment and inflation in the economy? (JMB, June 1985)

The open economy

Trade

What is meant by the term 'comparative' and 'absolute' advantage in production?
To what extent do these concepts explain the types of goods a country exports and imports? (London, June 1984)

(a) Explain how countries gain from specialisation and international trade.
(b) Why, then, do countries restrict free trade? (Cambridge, June 1988)

(a) What are a country's 'terms of trade'?
(b) How, and why, may changes in the terms of trade affect domestic living standards? (Cambridge, November 1985)

Balance of payments and exchange rates

'The balance of payments always balances and thus has no significance.' Discuss. (London, June 1984)

Explain what is meant by a floating exchange rate system.
How, if at all, will a fall in the external value of sterling affect (a) Britain's current balance and (b) the overall balance of payments? (JMB, June 1984)

Consider the arguments for and against a system of fixed exchange rates. (London, June 1983)

'A lower exchange rate for sterling must improve the United Kingdom Balance of Payments and raise output because competitiveness improves.' Discuss. (Oxford, June 1986)

(a) Discuss whether a balance of payments deficit poses problems for the United Kingdom economy.
(b) Critically compare different ways in which a balance of payments deficit may be reduced. (AEB, November 1990)

Current issues

EC and 1992

Discuss the possible economic effects upon member countries resulting from the creation of a Single European Market within the European Economic Community in 1992. (AEB, November 1990)

'EEC policies to support the prices received by producers of agricultural products cannot be justified by any criteria of economic efficiency or distributional justice.' Consider this view. (WJEC, June 1990)

Compare the alternative ways open to the Government to influence the level of economic activity.
Explain what effect, if any, membership of the ERM has upon the Government's choice of policy instruments. (JMB, June 1991)

Assess critically the argument that the introduction of a common currency within the European Community will increase trade and growth within the Community without any adverse economic consequences. (JMB, June 1991)

Green economics

The general public is becoming more aware of so-called 'green issues'. As an economist explain the causes and effects of externalities and comment on policies to deal with such problems in the light of this growing awareness. (Cambridge, S level, June 1991)

Economic development

'A high level of investment by itself will not be enough to ensure economic development.' Discuss this view. (Cambridge, November 1990)

'As with all externalities, the proper way to treat them is to make those who cause environmental damage pay for it.' Discuss (Oxford and Cambridge, June 1990)

Compiled by Sean Collins

APPENDIX II Answers to multiple-choice questions

Chapter 1

1. C
2. C
3. A
4. A
5. B
6. C

Chapter 2

1. C
2. D
3. A
4. A
5. D
6. B
7. E
8. A

Chapter 3

1. C
2. D
3. B
4. C
5. D
6. C
7. A
8. B
9. D
10. E
11. C

Chapter 4

1. A
2. A
3. C
4. B
5. D
6. B
7. C
8. B
9. E
10. E
11. D

Chapter 5

1. D
2. B
3. C
4. D
5. C
6. B
7. B
8. B
9. A
10. B
11. D
12. E
13. A
14. C
15. B
16. D
17. C
18. E
19. D
20. A
21. C
22. B
23. B
24. A
25. E
26. C
27. A
28. B
29. A
30. B

Chapter 6

1. A
2. D
3. C
4. D
5. D
6. B
7. D
8. C
9. C
10. A
11. A
12. C
13. E
14. C

Chapter 7

1. A
2. C
3. D
4. C
5. C

Chapter 8

1. C
2. A
3. B
4. C
5. B
6. C
7. A

Chapter 9

1. C
2. B
3. C
4. A
5. D
6. D
7. B
8. A
9. D
10. B
11. B
12. B
13. C
14. B

Chapter 10

1. C
2. C
3. D
4. A
5. A

Chapter 12

1. C
2. C
3. D
4. C
5. B
6. A
7. D
8. C
9. A
10. C
11. B
12. B

Chapter 13

1. C
2. C
3. D
4. B
5. C
6. A
7. E
8. B
9. A
10. D

Chapter 14

1. D
2. C
3. B
4. B
5. A
6. C
7. A
8. E
9. A
10. C
11. B
12. B
13. A
14. A
15. E
16. B
17. C
18. B

Chapter 15

1. C
2. D
3. C
4. B
5. B

Chapter 16

1. D
2. B
3. B
4. C
5. A
6. D
7. D
8. A
9. E

Chapter 17

1. A
2. E
3. C
4. B
5. E
6. A

Chapter 18

1. B
2. D
3. C
4. B
5. C
6. A
7. C
8. A
9. D
10. D
11. B
12. C

Chapter 19

1. D
2. B
3. A
4. C
5. D
6. A
7. C
8. A
9. B
10. D
11. E

Chapter 20

1. C
2. B
3. A
4. C
5. C
6. B
7. E

Chapter 21

1. D
2. A
3. C
4. B
5. B

Chapter 22

1. D
2. B
3. D
4. B
5. A

Chapter 23

1. A
2. B
3. C
4. B
5. C
6. B

Chapter 24

1. B
2. D
3. A

Chapter 25

1. D
2. A
3. A
4. C

Chapter 26

1. D
2. C
3. B

APPENDIX

III Glossary of terms

absolute advantage: in international trade, a country will specialize in the production of those goods and services which it can produce more cheaply/more profitably than other countries. *See also* comparative advantage.

accelerator: the principle that aggregate investment is a function of the change in real national output. The extent of the effect of the accelerator on national income depends on the degree of spare capacity, the expectations of entrepreneurs and the value of the multiplier.

***ad valorem* tax:** a tax imposed on goods and services according to their value. It is usually expressed as a percentage of value and not a fixed sum. *See also* specific tax.

aggregate demand: the sum of all expenditures for the economy. In an open economy this is the sum of consumers' expenditure, investment expenditure, government expenditure and net exports.

aggregate demand curve: the sum of all expenditure at differing aggregate price levels.

aggregate supply: the sum of the output of all goods and services for an economy. Imports are also an element of aggregate supply.

aggregate supply curve: the sum of the output of all goods and services at differing aggregate price levels.

appreciation: occurs when the value of something increases. In the foreign exchange markets, an appreciation of sterling occurs when the £ rises in value against other currencies, as a result of the free interplay of the forces of supply and demand. It is the opposite of depreciation.

arbitrage: the process of buying and selling foreign currencies, often simultaneously, in order to take profitable advantage of any disparity of prices that may occur. The effect of arbitrage is to rectify the imbalance in prices in the market. Arbitrageurs can operate in markets other than the foreign exchange market: for example, in commodity markets.

asset: something of value. Companies express what they own as assets on a balance sheet.

autarky: a situation of self-sufficiency. In the case of a country no international trade takes place and so there is no distinction between what is produced and what is consumed.

automatic stabilizers: features of an economic system that react in the opposite direction to the business cycle without the need for a policy initiative. For example, in a recession unemployment benefit payments rise, partly offsetting the loss of earned income and so reducing the effect on aggregate consumption.

autonomous consumption: *see* consumption function.

average cost (or average total cost): the cost per unit produced. It is calculated by dividing total costs of production by the number of units produced. As total cost = fixed + variable cost, it follows that average cost = average fixed + average variable cost.

average propensity to consume (APC): the proportion of total disposable household income used for consumption. It is found by dividing consumption by total disposable income. That which is not consumed is saved, so the average propensity to save plus the average propensity to consume = 1.

average revenue: the revenue received per unit sold. It is calculated by dividing total revenue by the number of units sold.

backward integration: *see* vertical integration.

balance of payments: a record of a country's financial transactions with the rest of the world. This set of accounts is usually produced annually, and comprises the following:

1. *Current account* – records income received from or paid abroad and expenditure on goods (visibles) and services (invisibles) exported and imported. The balance of trade = visible exports – visible imports. The invisible trade balance = invisible exports – invisible imports.
2. *Capital account* – records inflows and outflows of currency due to international dealings in financial assets, such as investments and loans.
3. Due to the difficulty in recording international transactions a balancing item is introduced equal to the difference between the sum shown on the current account and the sum shown on the capital account.

   Taken together these three items always equal zero, so the balance of payments always balances.

balanced budget: a situation where government expenditure = government revenue from taxation and other sources. *See also* fiscal policy.

bankers' balance at the Bank of England: the deposits of commercial banks at the Bank of England. By law, commercial banks are required to hold 0.45 per cent of their liabilities in this form.

barriers to entry: obstacles which prevent the entry of new firms into an industry. These barriers can arise due to legal reasons (e.g. patents), extensive advertising by existing firms, the existence of low-cost firms enjoying advanced internal economies of scale, etc. Sometimes barriers are the result of natural monopoly.

barter: a process of exchange which does not involve a medium of exchange (money). It is the direct exchange of goods for other goods.

base year: the date which a statistical series takes as its point of reference, i.e. changes are measured from that year.

black economy: a term which refers to that economic activity (production, exchange and consumption) which is not officially declared and therefore goes unrecorded in national income calculations.

black market: trade that is carried on outside of official markets. It usually takes place where a restricted rationed market exists and official prices are set such as in wartime Britain or a command economy.

bonds: the term used for debt issued by the government or companies which pays a fixed sum in interest each year. Bonds issued by the government are known as 'gilts'. *See also* consols.

budget: a financial statement made by the Chancellor of the Exchequer, traditionally in March/April each year, in which plans for government income and expenditure are announced. It is the formal statement of the government's intentions regarding fiscal policy.

budget constraint (budget line): a graphical construction which, by relating the consumer's income to the relative prices of commodities available, indicates the constraint upon the consumer's total expenditure on these commodities. The consumer can afford to purchase any combination of commodities providing that it lies within the budget constraint line.

budget deficit: a situation where government revenue (from taxation, etc.) is insufficient to pay for planned expenditure. The shortfall is met from borrowing, officially designated the PSBR (public sector borrowing requirement).

budget surplus: a situation where government revenue (from taxation, etc.) exceeds the sum necessary to finance government expenditure. It is the opposite of a budget deficit.

building society: a financial institution that provides long-term loans (mortgages) by lending the funds of its members. Recent changes in the operations of building societies have made them very similar to banks, and this has prompted the use of a measure of the money supply that includes their deposits as one of the main monetary indicators (M4).

business cycles: the fluctuation of real national output. Typically, market economies and mixed economies do not grow at a constant rate: faster periods of growth are called booms, slower periods or declines are called recessions or depressions.

capacity point: the level of output at which a firm is producing at the lowest point on its short-run average cost curve.

capital: one of the factors of production. It is wealth, in the form of machinery, premises, stocks, etc., which is devoted to the production of further wealth.

capital account: *see* balance of payments.

capital consumption: *see* depreciation.

capitalist economy: *see* free-enterprise economy.

cartel: a market organization where firms in an industry co-operate, and agree to fix prices and market shares. An example of such an arrangement would be OPEC. *See also* oligopoly.

central bank: a bankers' bank and lender of the last resort. In the UK the central bank is the Bank of England. It is charged with overseeing the banking system and acting on behalf of the Treasury to manage the money supply and national debt.

central planning bureau (CPB): the central planning authority of a command or planned economy. The CPB allocates resources and sets production targets, prices and distribution patterns. *See also* planned economy.

ceteris paribus: means 'all other things remaining equal'. The assumption allows economists to study the response to just one variable.

circular flow of income: describes the process whereby income received by households (in the form of wages, interest, rent and profits), earned in the process of production, flows back to firms in the form of expenditure on their output. This expenditure stimulates further production, which yet again leads to income being earned by households. Injections such as more consumption, investment, exports and government expenditure, will increase the size of this flow. Leakages in the form of savings, taxation and expenditure on imports will reduce the size of the flow.

circulating capital: capital that changes its form during the productive process, e.g. raw materials.

closed economy: a hypothetical model which makes the simplifying assumption that an economy does not engage in international trade. In other words, there are no exports or imports.

collusion: co-operation between firms on pricing and output decisions. This is usually an attempt to avoid competition and maximize joint profits. It is illegal in many countries.

collusive oligopoly: *see* oligopoly.

command economy: *see* planned economy.

commercial bank: a financial institution that safeguards depositors' money and makes loans for profit. Commercial banks have the ability to 'create' money through loans as only a proportion of deposits are required for everyday use.

common agricultural policy (CAP): the agricultural support scheme of the European Community. The CAP attempts to maintain farm incomes and guarantee supply.

comparative advantage, theory of: world output will be increased if countries specialize in the production of those goods and services to which their resources are comparatively best suited. Comparative advantage exists when a country has a lower opportunity cost than another country in the production of a particular good. It is not essential that a country enjoys an absolute advantage before international specialization and trade can occur to the benefit of all nations.

competition: a market phenomenon which is represented by a continuum, with pure monopoly (no competition) at one extreme and perfect competition at the other.

competitive oligopoly: *see* oligopoly.

complementary goods: two goods are said to be complements when an increase in the price of one causes a decrease in the consumption of both.

concentration ratio: the percentage of total output in an industry due to the largest few firms. The four-firm concentration ratio is found by dividing the output of the four largest firms in an industry by total industry output and expressing this as a percentage.

consols: a type of government security which pays a fixed sum of money every year, but is issued for an indefinite period. Maturity occurs only when the government decides to redeem the security (consolidated stock).

constant prices: these are used when comparing figures from different years. All prices are converted to their purchasing power equivalent in the base year, so that real rather than nominal values may be observed.

constant returns to scale: a long-run situation where an increase in production or output results in an equal proportionate increase in total cost. In other words, a 10 per cent increase in output results in a 10 per cent increase in total cost. It follows, therefore, that average cost remains the same (constant) as output increases.

consumer equilibrium: the point at which a consumer is maximizing utility from his or her chosen bundle of goods with a given income.

consumer sovereignty: the belief that the power of consumers' demand, exercised in the free market, will determine what goods and services are produced and in what quantities. Some economists argue that this power is insignificant in today's modern industrial economy, dominated by large firms who, it is argued, themselves determine what to produce.

consumer surplus: the difference between the maximum sum that consumers would be willing to pay to consume a certain amount of a product, and the sum that they actually do pay. It is measured by the area under the demand curve and above the price line.

consumption: the using up of goods and services by households.

consumption function: represents the relationship between aggregate consumption expenditure and the level of disposable income. It indicates what will happen to the level of consumption as the level of income changes.

cost–benefit analysis: this is essentially a method of project appraisal, whereby all the costs and benefits (i.e. private and social, monetary and non-monetary) of a particular project, over different time periods, and between different groups are considered in order to determine whether or not the project is justified.

cost-push inflation: a theory of inflation stating that inflationary pressures are caused by increases in costs of production – notably increases in incomes (such as wages) which are not matched by increases in productivity. 'Imported inflation' is another element of cost-push caused by increases in the price of imported raw materials.

costs of inflation: these depend on whether or not inflation is anticipated. Costs of anticipated inflation are relatively small (menu costs and shoe-leather costs). Unanticipated inflation causes a breakdown in the efficiency of the price system, redistribution of real income and wealth, and uncertainty which can lead to lower output and employment. Inflation may lead to a loss of international competitiveness.

counter-cyclical policy: *see* demand management policy.

credit multiplier: a mechanism through which an initial increase in deposits at a commercial bank will generate a multiple increase in total deposits and lending. The size of this multiple is determined by the size of the cash reserve retained by the bank in order to meet day-to-day demands for cash by customers. The larger the cash reserve, the smaller the multiplier and the eventual increase in deposits and lending.

cross-price elasticity of demand: the sensitivity or responsiveness of the demand for one commodity to changes in the price of another commodity. Goods which are in joint demand (complements) have a negative cross elasticity, and goods in competitive demand (substitutes) have a positive cross elasticity of demand.

crowding out: a term applied to the situation where government activity causes a reduction in private-sector activity. The most common example occurs where increased government spending (fiscal policy) causes interest rates to rise and this produces an offsetting fall in investment.

current account: *see* balance of payments.

customs union: an arrangement between certain countries to adopt a policy of free trade among themselves, but with a common external tariff barrier affecting any goods imported from other countries.

cyclical unemployment: unemployment arising due to short-run deficient aggregate demand in the economy. It usually occurs during the 'downswing' phase of the trade cycle.

deadweight loss: the loss of consumer surplus due to the restriction of output or raising of price, but not transferred to any other economic agent.

decreasing returns to scale: a situation in which an increase in production or output (say, 10 per cent) leads to a more than proportionate increase in total cost (i.e. in excess of 10 per cent). Thus, as output rises, average cost rises. *See also* 'law of diminishing returns'.

deflationary gap (output gap): occurs when the actual level of real national income (output) is below the full employment level. It is equivalent to the difference between actual (planned) expenditure at the full employment level of national income and the level of aggregate demand necessary to achieve full employment.

demand: the amount of a particular good or service that all consumers are willing and able to buy at a given price, at a given moment in time.

demand curve: this represents the amounts of a good or service that consumers would purchase at different prices, at a given moment in time with all other prices and incomes fixed.

demand for money: the total amount of money held by all individuals and groups in the economy for any purpose. The opportunity cost of holding money is the rate of interest that could have been earned had bonds been held instead. Three possible motives for holding money were identified by Keynes: the demand for transactions, for precaution and for speculation. The first two varied with the level of national income, the last with the rate of interest.

demand management policy: government policy designed to regulate the level of economic activity by manipulating the components of aggregate demand, i.e. consumption, investment, etc. *See also* stop–go policy.

demand-pull inflation: inflationary pressures caused by excess aggregate demand in the economy, for goods and services in general.

demerit goods: a good the consumption of which leads to undesirable consequences on society and possibly the consumer. *See also* externalities.

depreciation: generally, this refers to the phenomenon whereby the value of an asset diminishes over time. In the foreign exchange markets it is a situation in which the value of a currency, expresssed in terms of another currency, falls as a result of the operation of market forces (i.e. supply and demand) in a system of freely fluctuating exchange rates. *See also* appreciation.

depression (recession): a fall in the level of economic activity. A popular definition of recession is a fall in the absolute level of GDP for two successive quarters, although the term is often applied to a slowdown in the rate of growth. Long recessions are also called depressions. Contrary to the assertions of the press, there is no official definition.

deregulation: the removal of state controls or rules from an industry so that market forces have a greater role to play. *See also* supply-side economics.

derived demand: the demand for a factor of production by firms due to the demand for the firm's product, i.e. the demand for factors of production is derived from the demand for goods and services.

devaluation: a situation in which the foreign exchange value of a currency is lowered, under a system of fixed exchange rates, upon the direction of the government. Its effects are the same as for depreciation; it is the cause that differs. *See also* revaluation.

development economics: the study of economic growth and development in less developed countries (LDCs).

diminishing marginal utility: as consumption of one good rises, the amount of satisfaction a consumer derives from the last unit consumed will decline. In simple terms, 'the more you have, the less you want'.

direct tax: a tax which is imposed on income received (e.g. wages and salaries, interest, rent and profit) and on capital. Some examples are income tax, corporation tax, capital gains and capital transfer taxes.

dirty float: this situation occurs when, although a freely floating exchange rate system is supposed to be in operation, the monetary authorities intervene in order to influence the market price of their currency.

discount houses: a financial institution that borrows from commercial banks 'at call' and buys bonds that have only a short time to maturity.

discriminating monopoly: *see* price discrimination.

diseconomies of scale: a situation where the long-run average cost curve of a firm is rising.

disintermediation: the deliberate diversion of business by financial institutions away from areas subject to controls by the monetary authorities; also known as Goodhart's Law.

disposable income: refers to income received after all compulsory deductions (such as income tax, and national insurance) have been made. It is the amount actually available for spending.

distribution of income: the way income is distributed among people. It is possible to look at how income and wealth are distributed among types of factors of production (classes) – the functional distribution of income or distribution among households.

division of labour: a situation in which the production of a good is divided into a number of separate and distinct tasks, with an individual worker concentrating on performing one, or a small number, of these. It is a form of specialization of labour.

dumping: the disposal of goods on a foreign market at below the cost of manufacture. This may be the result of subsidizing a domestic industry to protect employment and so producing unwanted goods, or attempting to undermine foreign producers in their own country.

duopoly: an oligopolistic market structure, which exists when total supply is accounted for by only two producers.

economic growth: the growth of the productive potential of the economy as defined by the outward movement of the production possibility frontier. Measuring economic growth is difficult and it is therefore usually taken as the rate of change of real output.

economic rent: the reward or income received by a factor of production in excess of its transfer earnings (i.e. over and above that amount necessary to keep it in its existing employment). The economic rent received by the entrepreneur, for example, would be excess profit.

economies of concentration: advantages which arise due to the concentration of industry within a particular area. These advantages (such as improved infrastructure and the growth of ancillary services) are enjoyed by all firms situated within the area. *See also* external economies of scale.

economies of scale: *see* internal economies and external economies of scale.

efficiency: economists refer to two types of efficiency: productive efficiency; and allocative efficiency. Productive efficiency is achieved when factor inputs are employed in a least-cost combination. Allocative is achieved when resources are allocated so that no reallocation is possible without making someone worse off (also known as Pareto efficiency).

elastic demand: *see* price elasticity of demand.

elasticity of demand: *see* price/income/cross-price elasticity of demand.

elasticity of supply: the responsiveness or sensitivity of supply to changes in price. Supply is said to be relatively elastic when a given change in price causes a more than proportionate change in supply. Conversely, a relatively inelastic supply is where a less than proportionate change in supply is the result of a price change.

Engel curve: a curve depicting changes in consumption for a particular good or service as a result of changes in income when all prices are held constant.

entrepreneur: the person responsible for initiating and controlling the process of production, and bearing the associated risks.

entry forestalling: the attempt by a firm, often a monopoly, to prevent firms from entering the market and so competing away excess profits. *See also* barriers to entry.

equilibrium: a situation where there is no internal force for change. In economics it is usually used to refer to a state where demand equals supply either in a product market, e.g. the demand and supply of jam, or for the economy as a whole, e.g. planned investment and planned saving.

European Community (EC): the organization of European communities established by the Treaty of Rome in 1957. The EC is effectively a customs union with external tariff barriers. In addition to economic co-operation, in recent years the EC has tried to form a common foreign policy. Members as of 1992: Belgium, Holland, Luxemburg, Denmark, Germany, France, Italy, Spain, Portugal, UK, Ireland, Greece.

European currency unit (ECU): a 'basket' of currencies of countries belonging to the European Community, which serves as a unit of account. In effect, it serves the same purpose within the EC as SDRs do between IMF member countries.

European Monetary System (EMS): a co-operative arrangement between most European Community countries. The exchange rate mechanism of the EMS imposes limits on the exchange rate fluctuations of member currencies.

excess profit: the return accruing to the entrepreneur in excess of normal profit. In other words, profit received over and above that which is necessary to just keep the entrepreneur in an industry.

exchange rate: the price of a currency expressed in terms of other currencies.

expectations-augmented Phillips curve: an adaptation of the Phillips curve which states that views of future inflation need not always remain the same. Upward revisions of inflationary expectations lead to the upward shifting of the Phillips curve and so for any given level of unemployment a higher rate of inflation emerges.

external economies of scale: the advantage of lower unit costs of production that accrue to one firm due to the reaping of internal economies of scale by another, which are passed on in the form of lower input (material) costs.

externalities: the social costs incurred, and the social benefits enjoyed, by the community as the result of an economic transaction, i.e. those costs and benefits not experienced by the parties to the transaction and thus not included in market prices.

factors of production: those resources which are utilized in the production of goods and services. They can be categorized under the main headings of land, labour and capital, although enterprise or entrepreneurship is often included as well.

fiat money: token money in the form of notes and coins, the use of which is enforced by a state declaration that it should be considered as legal tender.

firm: an organization, usually owned privately by an entrepreneur, where factors of production are brought together to produce an output for profit.

fiscal policy: any change in government expenditure and/or revenue, designed to influence the level of activity in the economy as a whole. It is sometimes referred to as budgetary policy.

fixed capital: capital that does not change its form during the productive process, e.g. lathes.

fixed cost: costs of production which do not vary in direct relation to the level of output. In other words, as output increases or decreases, fixed costs remain unchanged. They are sometimes incurred in advance of production and apply only in the short run.

fixed exchange rate: where the rate at which a country's currency exchanges for other currencies is determined by the national governments rather than by market forces. In other words, it is the opposite of floating exchange rates.

floating exchange rate: a situation in the foreign exchange market where the rate at which one currency exchanges for another is determined by the interaction of the forces of supply and demand.

foreign exchange market: where the currencies of countries are traded. Under floating exchange rate regimes it is here that exchange rates are determined.

foreign exchange reserves: the stock of foreign currency, gold and special drawing rights held by the central bank.

forward integration: *see* vertical integration.

forward markets (or forward currency exchange): these markets exist in order to reduce the uncertainty involved under a regime of floating exchange rates. A contract is made for the purpose of buying or selling a certain amount of a foreign currency at a given future date, and at an agreed rate of exchange. When the specified date arrives, the deal must take place at the agreed rate, regardless of what the current market rate may be.

free-enterprise economy: an economy in which productive resources are privately owned, and which are allocated through the unfettered operation of the price mechanism. It is characterized by the attitude of *laissez-faire* – i.e. non-interference by the state in economic matters – and, therefore, it is the opposite of a planned economy.

free good: a commodity whose consumption or production involves no opportunity cost. An example of a free good is fresh air.

free trade: an international trading situation in which the free movement of goods and services between countries is not constrained by the imposition of tariffs, quotas or any other restriction. It is the opposite of protected trade (or protectionism).

frictional unemployment: unemployment of a temporary nature which arises as a result of the movement of labour between occupations and/or regions.

full employment: this occurs when all members of the working population are either in work or able to secure work at existing wage rates. For this to be possible, the number of unfilled vacancies must equal, or slightly exceed, the number unemployed. In a dynamic economy, some minimum amount of unemployment is both inevitable and desirable at any given time, if resources are to move from declining to expanding sectors of the economy.

funding: the process of changing government debt from short-term, liquid debt into long-term, illiquid debt.

GATT (General Agreement on Tariffs and Trade): an international organization which, via a series of 'rounds', seeks to negotiate reductions in tariff and other trade barriers. Its ultimate aim is to achieve completely free trade in the world economy.

Giffen good: an inferior good for which the income effect will dominate or offset the substitution effect, resulting in an upward-sloping demand curve.

gilt-edged securities: includes all securities issued by the British government. They are considered a safe purchase as the holder is sure that the government will not default.

gold standard: under this mechanism, each national currency had a gold price and was convertible into gold. Internal money supply was, therefore, determined by the government's gold reserves. As gold was the common denominator for all currencies, the rate of exchange between them was fixed. Moreover, the gold standard led to automatic corrections of any disequilibrium in the balance of payments.

green economics (environmental economics): that branch of economics which applies the techniques of economics to environmental problems such as pollution and the use of non-renewable resources.

gross domestic product (GDP): a figure showing the total output of goods and services produced within the domestic economy within a given period of time, usually one year.

gross investment: *see* investment.

gross national product (GNP): the total output of goods and services produced both at home and abroad by the factors of production owned by the residents of a country. GDP + net property income from abroad = GNP.

horizontal integration: the joining together of two or more firms operating at the same stage of production and within the same industry. An example would be the merger of two retailing chains.

hot money: money which is transferred between the financial centres of the world in order to take advantage of the higher interest rates offered in one country than in another or to make a speculative capital gain.

household: consumers acting individually or in a group to buy goods and services.

human capital: the store of experience and skill in people that has been built up by education and training. Investing in human capital increases the productivity of labour.

imperfect competition (or imperfect market): a situation where the conditions of perfect competition are not fulfilled. A firm operating under conditions of imperfect competition faces a downward-sloping demand curve and so has some degree of monopoly power. Its price is always greater than its marginal cost of production. *See also* monopoly, oligopoly, monopolistic competition.

income effect: the effect of a change in real income on the consumption of a particular good or service. The effect will depend on whether the good in question is an inferior good or a normal good.

income elasticity of demand: the responsiveness or sensitivity of demand for a particular good or service to changes in real income. Income elastic demand is where a change in income causes a more than proportionate change in the amount demanded. Income inelastic demand is where a change in income causes a less than proportionate change in the amount demanded. Zero income elasticity is where a change in income has no effect on the level of demand. Negative income elasticity is where a change in the level of real income leads to a change in demand in the opposite direction (e.g. an increase in income results in a fall in the amount demanded). *See also* normal and inferior goods.

incomes policy: *see* prices and incomes policy.

increasing returns to scale: where an increase in a firm's output results in a less than proportionate increase in the firm's costs, i.e. average cost will fall.

indicative planning: the attempt by government to guide markets towards certain goals by producing and publishing non-binding plans. These plans indicate opportunities and hope to co-ordinate responses without direct intervention.

indifference curve: a graphical construction showing all the possible combinations of goods that will yield the consumer an identical level of utility or satisfaction. Thus the consumer is 'indifferent' as to which of the particular combinations he or she receives.

indirect tax: a tax which is levied upon a good or service, sometimes referred to as an expenditure tax or an outlay tax. Examples of indirect taxes are value added tax, customs duties and excise duties.

inelastic demand: *see* price elasticity of demand.

infant industry: a newly established and developing industry which is accorded government protection, usually in the form of a tariff barrier, to enable its growth until it is able to withstand foreign competition.

inferior good: a good which has a negative income elasticity.

inflation: a persistent and significant rise in the general level of prices, the result of which is a fall in the value of money. *See also* demand-pull and cost-push inflation.

inflationary gap: occurs when the actual level of real national income (output) is greater than the full employment level. It is equivalent to the difference between actual (planned) expenditure at the full employment level of national income and the level of aggregate demand necessary to achieve full employment.

injections: *see* circular flow of income.

integration: the merging or amalgamation of two or more firms into one firm. *See also* vertical/horizontal/lateral integration.

interest rate: *see* structure of interest rates.

internal economies of scale: advantages accruing to an individual firm, usually in the form of lower unit costs, due to increases in the scale of its operations. These economies can be categorized under various headings according to the sphere in which they arise, e.g. technical economies, managerial economies, marketing economies, financial economies.

International Monetary Fund (IMF): set up in 1944 at the Bretton Woods conference to manage the international exchange rate regime.

intervention price: the price at which the authorities responsible for administering the common agricultural policy (within the EC) enter the market and purchase excess supply, in order to support the price of the product in question. The intervention price is fixed at a level slightly below the target price for each commodity.

investment: that part of current output which, rather than being consumed, is devoted to further production. It includes expenditure on capital goods such as machinery and plant, and on net additions to stocks. Gross investment represents investment before allowing for depreciation/capital consumption. Net investment = gross investment minus depreciation.

invisibles: services and intangible items that are traded. Examples of invisibles are banking and insurance, shipping, civil aviation, interest, profits and dividends. *See also* balance of payments.

involuntary unemployment: a term largely associated with the work of J.M. Keynes. It refers to unemployment which arises due to deficient aggregate demand in the economy. Thus people are unemployed through no fault of their own; it is the fault of the failure of effective demand in the economic system.

***IS/LM*:** a system of macroeconomic analysis that links the goods market, the money market and the labour market. With *IS/LM* analysis it is possible to compare and contrast monetarist and Keynesian views on the effectiveness of policy.

isocost line: a graphical construction representing all points where different combinations of factors of production incur the same cost.

isoquant: a line which represents all the combinations of the factors of production which will produce the same quantity of output.

J curve: the pattern that a country's balance of trade may follow after a depreciation of that country's currency. The trade balance initially worsens then improves, showing an elongated 'J' when the trade balance is mapped against time.

Keynesian economics: the economics of those who follow the views first put forward by J.M. Keynes in *The General Theory of Employment, Interest and Money* in 1936. Keynes suggested that the classical view of the economy, where prices always adjusted so that markets cleared, was wrong and that it was possible for the economy to settle down into an equilibrium with substantial unemployment.

Keynesian multiplier: a process which occurs automatically when the economy is in a position of macroeconomic disequilibrium due to change in one of the components of aggregate demand. Any change in one of these components will cause a larger change in the level of total income and employment. The ratio of the change in total income to the change in one component of aggregate demand is called the multiplier. *See also* multiplier.

kinked demand curve model: a model which seeks to explain the behaviour of firms engaged in oligopolistic competition. The demand curve facing the firm at price levels above the existing price is seen to be relatively elastic, as rivals are unlikely to follow the price rise of one firm. At price levels below the existing price, demand is expected to be relatively inelastic, as the price reduction of one firm is likely to be followed by the others. As a result, the demand curve based on these expectations will be kinked at the existing price.

labour: all human effort, of a physical and mental nature, that is devoted to the production of goods and services. The reward/income received by labour for its part in the productive process takes the form of wages and salaries.

***laissez-faire*:** *see* free-enterprise economy.

land: all the gifts of nature which people use in the production of goods and services. The reward/income received by land is rent.

lateral integration: the joining together of two or more firms which are currently engaged in completely different industries, usually for the purpose of diversifying production. An example would be the merger of a retail chain organization and a brewery.

law of diminishing returns: occurs in the short-run when successive units of a variable factor of production are applied to the fixed factors, changes in output will eventually diminish. Marginal returns will diminish first, followed by average returns.

leakages: *see* circular flow of income.

legal tender: all bank notes and coins (up to certain maximum amounts) are classed as legal tender because a person is under a legal obligation to accept such currency in settlement of debts.

liability: something of value held by one person or company but owned by another. It is therefore liable for repayment.

liquidity: the ease and certainty with which an asset can be converted into cash. Perfect liquidity is cash itself.

liquidity preference: the desire by individuals to hold assets in the form of cash or non-interest-bearing bank deposits, rather than in the form of securities. Keynes identified three motives which explain this demand for money (as active and idle balances) – the transactions, precautionary and speculative motives.

liquidity preference theory: this maintains that the rate of interest is determined by the interaction of the demand for money (i.e. liquidity preference) and the supply of money.

loanable funds theory: this maintains that interest rates are determined by the interaction of the demand for and the supply of loanable funds, i.e. funds which are available for lending.

long run: the period of time when all factors of production are variable.

Lorenz curve: a graphical representation of the relationship between cumulative income and cumulative households. The Lorenz curve will show the degree of inequality of the distribution of income and this can be summarized in a Gini coefficient.

macroeconomics: that aspect of economics which is concerned with aggregates or the sum of all individual actions, e.g. the determination of the general level of wages, aggregate demand, national income, etc.

managed float: *see* dirty float.

marginal cost: the addition to total cost due to producing one extra unit.

marginal cost pricing: the process of determining a monopolist's output at the point where price and marginal cost are equal (and not necessarily where $MR = MC$ as is assumed under the traditional theory for explaining price and output decision making).

marginal physical product (of labour): the change in total output (in volume terms) due to the employment of an additional unit of labour.

marginal propensity to consume (MPC): the amount of additional consumption resulting from an extra unit of income. The marginal propensity to consume plus the marginal propensity to save = 1.

marginal revenue: the addition to total revenue due to selling one extra unit of output.

marginal revenue product (of labour): the addition to total revenue arising from the employment of one extra unit of labour. Marginal revenue product = marginal physical product × price.

marginal utility: the change in total utility/satisfaction resulting from a change in consumption of one extra unit of a good, the consumption of all other goods remaining the same.

market: any mechanism by which buyers and sellers are kept in close, often immediate, contact with one another. It is not necessarily a physical place; it can exist via telephone or computer links.

market clearing: the price at which all that is supplied to market is demanded. It is where the demand and supply curves intersect.

market failure: a situation where the market is unable to allocate resources efficiently. An example is the market's inability to take account of social costs.

Marshall–Lerner condition: in order for depreciation/devaluation or appreciation/revaluation to result in the elimination of a balance of payments disequilibrium, it is necessary for the combined price elasticities of demand for exports and imports to be greater than unity (i.e. greater than 1).

Medium-term financial strategy (MTFS): the government framework for setting monetary growth and PSBR targets from 1980 to 1985. By announcing targets up to five years in advance, it was hoped to reduce inflationary expectations.

mercantilism: the seventeenth-century belief that international trade is a competition with the most successful exporting much while importing little. The mercantilist judges success by the amount of gold and foreign currency built up by a nation.

merger: the amalgamation or joining together of two or more firms, resulting in the formation of a single organization.

merit good: a good that is socially desirable, but because it is not provided by the market in sufficient quantities the government intervenes in the economy in order to ensure that everyone receives a particular good or service. Examples of merit goods are education and health care.

microeconomics: that aspect of economics concerned with the behaviour of individuals in their role as consumers and/or producers, e.g. the determination of wages for teachers, the determination of the price of apples, etc.

minimum efficient scales (MES): the lowest level of production at which average costs are low enough to allow a firm to compete in the market. *See also* increasing returns to scale.

mixed economy: an economic system comprising aspects of both free-market and centrally planned economies. In other words, resources are owned both by private individuals and by the state, and are allocated partly by the price mechanism and partly by central direction.

monetarists: those who believe that the economy is essentially self-regulating and that any deviation from the natural rate of employment and output is due to interference in the free-market process. Milton Friedman, an influential member of the monetarist school, stated the view that 'inflation is always and everywhere a monetary phenomenon', meaning that inflation is due to excess monetary growth.

monetary base: the quantity of notes and coins circulating in the non-bank private sector, plus the amount held by the clearing banks in the form of cash in the tills, and as balances at the Bank of England.

monetary policy: an attempt, by changing the liquidity of government debt, to influence the level of economic activity via changes in the cost of credit (i.e. the rate of interest) or the availability of credit (i.e. the money supply).

money: any material which is generally acceptable in exchange for goods and services, and in the settlement of debts.

money income (or nominal income): the income received by a person measured in money terms, i.e. in £s and pence.

money supply (or money stock): the amount of money which is in an economy at any given time. Owing to the difficulty of providing one universally acceptable definition of this term, there are various measures of the money supply such as M0 and M4 which take account of different aspects of money in its widest sense.

monopolistic competition: a market with free entry and exit, but with each firm producing a slightly differentiated product. Freedom of entry means that profits are competed down to normal profits, while each firm faces a downward-sloping demand curve. *See also* imperfect competition.

monopoly: market situation where one firm accounts for the output of the entire industry. *See also* imperfect competition.

Monopolies and Mergers Commission: the government-appointed agency which investigates the competition implications of a proposed takeover or merger or existing practice in cases referred to it by the Secretary of State for Trade and Industry.

monopsony: a market situation in which there exists only one buyer.

multiplier effect: the measure of the effect on real national income of a change in some component of aggregate demand. For example, if investment rises by £100 and real national income rises by £200 as a result, the multiplier is 2. Formally, the multiplier is defined as 1 divided by the marginal propensity to withdraw.

national debt: the total amount owed as a result of government borrowing, largely from the British people, over the years. It is the accumulated public debt at any given time. The PSBR in one year is the addition to this debt.

national income: the total amount of goods and services, measured in money terms, which are produced in a given time by the factors of production, owned by the residents of a particular country.

nationalization: the process of taking an industry into state ownership and under state control. This is usually achieved by passing legislation which makes compulsory the transfer of the ownership of the means of production to the state.

natural monopoly: a market situation in which the production of a good or service is most efficiently undertaken by just one firm, owing to the existence of economies of scale over a range of output which is large in relation to market demand.

natural rate of unemployment: a situation in which the labour market is in equilibrium (the demand for and supply of labour are equal) and any unemployment that exists at this rate is voluntary. This is because the unemployed are not prepared to work at the going wage rate.

net investment: *see* investment.

net present value (NPV): the benefit from an investment discounted over time.

non-accelerating inflation rate of unemployment (NAIRU): also known as the long-run Phillips curve and often taken as an indicator of the natural rate of unemployment. It is the level of unemployment that is consistent with a stable level of inflation. Any attempt to stimulate effective demand, to reduce unemployment below this level, will raise inflationary pressures in the economy and increase the rate of inflation every year.

non-price competition: the attempt by firms to gain market share without dropping prices. Advertising to increase brand loyalty, free gifts and introductory offers are all examples.

non-renewable resources: resources that, once used, cannot be replaced, such as coal, oil and iron ore.

non-tariff barriers: restrictions on international trade that do not rely on specific import taxes. Examples include physical barriers such as customs posts and technical barriers such as national safety standards.

normal good: a good which has a positive income elasticity of demand. In other words, as real income rises, the demand for the good also rises.

normal profit: some minimum level of return which is just enough to keep the entrepreneur in business. If normal profit is not achieved, the entrepreneur will leave the industry in the long run. As a result, normal profit is included in calculations of total costs.

normative economics: that branch of economics concerned with statements of what ought to be, rather than what actually is. *See also* positive economics.

oligopoly: a situation in which the market comprises only a few firms, or a few dominant firms. Competitive oligopoly occurs when the firms compete with one another, either on the basis of price (price competition) or via non-price competition, such as product differentiation. Collusive oligopoly occurs when the firms agree to co-operate rather than compete. This usually results in fixing prices and output quotas. *See also* cartels.

open economy: one that trades with other countries. An open economy is open to the competition of other countries.

open-market operations: the sale or purchase of government securities by the Bank of England in order to influence the money supply. *See also* monetary policy.

opportunity cost (or real cost): the cost of satisfying a want expressed in terms of the next best alternative forgone, e.g. the real cost of work is the leisure time forgone.

paradox of thrift: saving is held to be good by tradition. In the Keynesian system saving is a leakage from the circular flow and so extra savings lead to lower output and employment.

Pareto optimum: allocative efficiency. *See also* economic efficiency.

perfect competition: a market in which there is free entry and exit, perfect mobility of factors and a large number of relatively small producers, all of whom are price takers.

perfect market: a market in which there are a large number of relatively small buyers and sellers, so that no one buyer or seller can influence the market price by altering its individual demand or supply. Price is determined by market demand and supply, with each firm selling as much or as little as it likes at that price.

Phillips curve: an empirical relationship, noted by Professor A.W. Phillips of the London School of Economics, between the rates of change of money wages on the one hand, and of unemployment on the other.

planned economy (or command economy): an economic system under which decisions about what to produce and in what quantities, and how to organize production, are determined by a centralized authority, which then allocates resources accordingly. It is the opposite of a free-enterprise economy.

positive economics: that branch of economics concerned with statements, the validity of which can be tested by reference to known 'facts', independent of any value judgement. *See also* normative economics.

poverty: the state where a person or household has an income below that where they can fully participate in their own society. Exact definitions are difficult and the 'poverty line' is therefore sometimes defined as the level of state income support.

present value: the value today of some payment or receipt in the future. Present value is found by dividing the sum in the future by 1 plus the rate of interest raised to the power of the number of years into the future that the sum will be received (paid), i.e. $(1+r)^n$ where $r =$ the rate of interest and $n =$ the number of years into the future. Net present value is found by deducting the present value of all receipts from the present value of payments.

price: the exchange value of a good or service which is measured in money terms.

price discrimination (or discriminating monopoly): the practice of a firm charging different prices to different consumers for the same good or service.

price elasticity of demand: the sensitivity or responsiveness of demand to changes in price. Completely inelastic demand is where a given change in price has no effect upon the amount demanded. Infinitely elastic demand is where demand for a good or service is so sensitive that if price changes nothing is demanded. Relatively elastic demand is where a given change in price causes a more than proportionate change in the amount demanded. Relatively inelastic demand is where a given change in prices causes a less than proportionate change in the amount demanded. Unit elasticity of demand is where a given change in price causes a proportionate change in the amount demanded.

price leadership: a market situation in which the price change of one firm (the price leader) is intentionally adopted by other firms, the price takers or price followers.

price rigidity: an observable phenomenon whereby the price of a particular good or service remains unchanged over long periods of time, despite changing market conditions. One attempt to explain this phenomenon is provided by the kinked demand curve theory.

price taker: an economic agent who has no influence on the market price and so only decides to trade or not at that price, e.g. a perfectly competitive firm.

prices and incomes policy: a policy under which the government attempts to limit the rate of increase in prices and money incomes, in order to reduce inflationary pressures in the economy.

private costs: the cost of production actually incurred by a firm, i.e. costs of labour, capital and land inputs. *See also* social costs.

privatization: the process of transferring a nationalized industry, such as British Telecom, or a state-owned firm, such as British Petroleum, into private ownership.

producer surplus: the difference between what the producer actually receives from the sale of a given output, and the minimum amount it would have been prepared to accept for the output.

product differentiation: the process by which a firm creates real or perceived differences between its product and those of its rivals. This is achieved mainly by branding and advertising, and the effect is to reduce the degree to which one product is seen by consumers as a substitute for another.

production function: this indicates the amount of a particular good or service that can be produced, in a given time period, by various combinations of the factors of production employed, assuming a given state of technical knowledge.

production possibility frontier/boundary: a line showing the total amount of one product (or product category) that can be produced given the output of another product (or category), assuming the full employment of all an economy's resources. It also shows the opportunity cost of producing more of one product, in terms of the amount of the other product that must be forgone.

productivity: in general terms, productivity is the output of a particular good or service per unit of input, e.g. the productivity of labour is output per man-hour.

profit: the reward earned by the entrepreneur in the process of production. It is calculated by subtracting total costs from total revenue.

profit maximization: assumed to be the goal of entrepreneurs in the traditional theory of a firm. It is achieved where marginal cost = marginal revenue. Doubts about profit maximization as a goal have arisen due to the separation of owners from managers in modern firms (the divorce of ownership and control), and alternative maximands such as sales revenue, output and utility have been suggested.

progressive taxation: a system of taxation under which the average rate of tax rises as income rises, with the result that those on higher incomes pay a greater proportion of tax compared to those on lower incomes.

proportional taxation: a system of taxation under which the average rate of tax remains the same as income rises, so that all taxpayers pay the same proportion of their income in taxes. A proportional tax is sometimes called a 'flat rate' tax.

protectionism: the imposition of tariffs and other restrictions on free international trade, in order to protect home industry and employment.

public good: a good that has to be consumed collectively because the benefit arising from consumption is diffuse and indiscriminate. An example is external defence, which benefits everyone. Since no one can be excluded from its benefits, the usual practice of having to pay for what you receive will no longer hold – everyone benefits whether they pay or not and it has to be provided 'free' and be paid for out of the tax revenue of the state.

public-sector borrowing requirement (PSBR): the amount the government has to borrow, in order to finance a budget deficit. When the government raises more in taxation than it spends, it repays debt. There is then a public-sector debt repayment (PSDR).

public utilities: publicly owned natural monopolies which provide 'essential' services such as gas, electricity and water. Many are now privatized, but they are highly regulated.

pure monopoly: an extreme market situation in which total supply of a good is attributed to only one firm. In other words, the firm is the industry.

quantity theory of money: the quantity of money (M_s) multiplied by its velocity of circulation (V) is equal to national output (Y_o) multiplied by the average level of prices (P). Hence the equation $M_s \times V = Y_o \times P$. One interpretation of this equation is that if V and Y_o are unchanged, an increase in M_s will result in an increase in the average price level (i.e. inflation). The original theory stated that $M_s \times V = P \times T$, where T is equal to the number of transactions. This was also known as the Fisher equation.

quasi rent: this refers to a situation in which economic rent is earned in the short run only. In the long run, it is likely to be competed away by the entry of new firms into the industry.

quota: a physical restriction upon the amount of a particular good or service that can be imported or exported, usually within a given period of time.

rational expectations: a hypothesis that economic agents will not make systematic or repeated errors; rather they will use economic theory and all relevant available data to form expectations. An implication of rational expectations is the ineffectiveness of monetary and fiscal policy.

real cost: *see* opportunity cost.

real income: the actual purchasing power (in terms of the goods and services that could be bought) of a given money income. Changes in real income arise through changes in the level of money income and/or changes in the value of money, as measured by the average price level.

regressive taxation: a system of taxation under which the average rate of tax falls as income rises, with the result that those on lower incomes pay a greater proportion of their income as tax compared to those on higher incomes.

renewable resources: those natural resources which are capable of regeneration and are not, therefore, finite. Fish stocks, for example, will be replaced if carefully harvested.

replacement ratio: the percentage of a person's income he or she receives as unemployment and other benefits when out of work.

research and development (R & D): the attempt to discover and refine new ideas and processes. Research may be basic or applied. Basic research is undertaken for its own sake; applied research is carried out with a commercial objective. Development is the refinement and improvement of existing ideas, processes and products. Basic research is often funded by the public sector.

reserve assets: liquid assets held by a bank in order to meet customs requests for withdrawals or the requirements of the central bank. *See also* credit multiplier.

retail price index (RPI): the most common measure of inflation. The RPI is constructed from a weighted average of prices of a 'basket' of goods and services representative of consumer expenditure.

restrictive practices: a variety of practices, conducted by one firm or a group of firms (e.g. cartels), which are designed to reduce the level of competition from other firms in the market.

revaluation: a situation in which the foreign exchange value of a currency is raised, under a system of fixed exchange rates, upon the direction of the government. Its effects, which are the opposite of devaluation, are the same as for currency appreciation.

Robinson Crusoe economy: a situation where the entire economy consists of a simple worker and decision maker such as Robinson Crusoe on his desert island. Robinson had only to make choices about his own labour and so the consequences of his actions only affected him (his utility).

savings: income which is not devoted to the consumption of goods and services in the current period.

Say's Law: propounded by the French economist J.B. Say, it maintains that 'supply will create its own demand'. In other words, an increase in production (supply) will generate factor incomes (effective demand) just sufficient to buy the very output produced.

scarcity: this arises because nature does not provide all of the goods and services human beings would like to consume. As wants exceed resources, this gives rise to market prices which indicate how much consumers want a good. *See also* opportunity cost.

seasonal unemployment: unemployment which is caused by seasonal fluctuations in the demand for particular goods and/or services. It is most common in the tourist industry, but also exists in agriculture and the construction industry.

short run: the period of time when at least one factor of production is fixed in supply. A firm may add to those factors that are not fixed, but will experience diminishing returns.

social costs: costs that arise from economic decisions which affect others but are not paid for by the producer or consumer (private costs). An example is pollution. *See also* externalities.

special deposits: a device employed by the monetary authorities in order to control the rate of growth of credit creation and the money supply. The authorities freeze the commercial banks' deposits of liquid assets at the Bank of England. The main use of this weapon has been to mop up excess liquidity in order to increase the effectiveness of other measures, such as open-market operations.

special drawing rights (SDRs): a unit of account used by international governments and their central banks. It is a form of international liquidity created by the International Monetary Fund for member countries, and its value is fixed in relation to a 'basket' of 16 major currencies. Its value was once fixed to the official gold price – hence the reference to SDRs as 'paper gold'.

specialization: *see* division of labour.

specific tax: a tax in the form of a set amount of money, levied on a particular good or service, irrespective of the value (i.e. price) of the product, e.g. a tax of 70p on a packet of cigarettes. *See also ad valorem* tax.

spot market: a market in which the commodity being bought and sold is immediately available – i.e. on the spot – at the agreed and current market price. It is the opposite of a forward market.

stagflation: a situation in which the economy is experiencing high unemployment and inflation simultaneously.

standard of living: generally defined as 'the amount of goods and services that a person can afford to consume in a given time period'. A typical measure, therefore, is real income per capita. Such a definition, however, fails to take account of other aspects of 'economic welfare', such as the utility derived from voluntary activities, social costs and benefits, changes in leisure, etc.

stock (inventories): most firms hold supplies of raw materials, work in progress and finished goods. Stock allows smooth and continuous production. Stocks of finished goods are usually the first variable to indicate rising or falling sales levels.

The Stock Exchange: the market in which shares (stock) in public limited companies (PLCs) are traded. The average price of shares is shown by index numbers such as the Financial Times 100 (FTSE).

stop–go policy: the use of demand management techniques, in the post-war years, to stimulate the economy when unemployment threatened (go), and to reduce demand (stop) when the balance of payments subsequently moved into deficit. This resulted in an uneven pattern of economic growth.

structural unemployment: unemployment caused by a decline in the demand for the product of a particular industry (or industries). It commonly occurs in the 'staple' industries, such as shipbuilding and textiles, with the emergence of new, modern industries, reflecting a changing pattern of demand, typical in advanced, dynamic economies.

structure of interest rates: a term which recognizes that no single rate of interest exists in the market. Instead, diverse financial institutions offer different rates to different types of borrower or saver. Lending rates, for example, will be affected by such factors as the size, duration and purpose of the loan, and the security (if any) that can be offered.

subsidy: a payment, usually made by government, to reduce the market price of a product. It is a negative tax, used most frequently to reduce food prices.

substitute: a good or service that is purchased in place of another. Technically, goods are substitutes when an increase in the price of one causes an increase in the consumption of the other. *See also* complementary goods.

substitution effect: the effect on consumption of a price change when the consumer's real income is maintained at its original level. A fall in the price of a particular product will cause consumers to buy more of it, as it will now be cheaper (*ceteris paribus*) than other goods. Similarly, a rise in the price of a product will lead to a decline in the amount consumers will demand, as they will switch to cheaper substitutes – depending on the closeness of these substitutes.

supply: the amount of a particular good or service that producers are willing and able to offer for sale at a given price, at a given moment in time.

supply curve: this indicates the amount of a particular good or service that producers will offer for sale at each and every price, at a given moment in time.

supply-side economics: this is based on the view that it is possible to influence aggregate supply and so national output and employment by the use of microeconomic policy, such as income tax cuts and labour training schemes.

takeover: when one firm buys the shares of another without the consent of the present board of directors.

target price: the price fixed in respect of every agricultural product, under the common agricultural policy of the EC, which will yield farmers a reasonable rate of return, and help to stabilize the price of foodstuffs.

tariff: a tax or duty that is imposed on imported goods. Tariffs may be general (i.e. on all imported goods) or selective (i.e. only on certain types of good, or goods from certain countries). They may be imposed on an *ad valorem* basis or as a specific duty. *See also* protectionism.

taxation: the legal imposition of a charge by government on its citizens. Taxation of individuals may be directly placed on incomes or indirectly placed on goods and paid in the purchase price. Companies and capital are also taxed. *See also* direct tax and indirect tax.

technological progress: the process where human knowledge advances, allowing greater productive efficiency or possibilities. It may take the form of making existing products more cheaply, or finding new products.

technological unemployment: unemployment that arises when investment in mechanized and automated techniques of production displace the labour input.

terms of trade: a measurement of the price of imports compared to the price of exports. Terms of trade will change, therefore, given any change in the price of either imported or exported goods.

total cost: the sum of all the factor incomes (wages, interest, rent and normal profit) incurred in the process of production. Total costs = fixed costs + variable costs.

total revenue: total receipts from the sale of a good or service at any given time. Total revenue = number of units sold × price.

trade union: an organization of labourers that seeks to promote the interest of workers through better conditions and pay.

transfer earnings: the minimum return necessary to keep a factor in its existing employment. An example of transfer earnings is normal profit. Any payment in excess of this minimum return is called economic rent.

transfer payments: income received as a result of a redistribution between different groups, rather than in return for any contribution to national output or income. Examples are pensions, student grants and other social payments.

transmission mechanism: the process by which changes in the money supply affect real output and the price level. The disagreement on how the transmission mechanism works is an important distinction between monetarist and Keynesian views.

Treasury bill: short-term government securities issued by the Treasury. They are issued usually for a period of about three months.

underemployment: a situation in which factors of production are in employment but are not being used to their full capacity. It would be possible, therefore, to produce the same output with fewer resources. Underemployment of labour is often called overmanning.

unemployment: *see* involuntary unemployment and voluntary unemployment.

utility: the satisfaction derived from the consumption of a good or service at a given time.

value added: the difference between the sum cost of inputs into a process (materials, components, etc.) and the selling price.

variable cost: the cost of employing variable factors of production which will, therefore, vary in direct relation with output: the greater output is, the higher variable cost will be. When there is no output, variable cost will be zero.

velocity of circulation: the frequency with which the money stock changes hands in a given time period. In the quantity theory of money, velocity of circulation is represented by V so $M \times V = P \times Y$, and so V represents the income velocity of circulation. In the Fisher equation $M \times V = P \times T$, V represents the transactions velocity of circulation. The difference arises because Y represents current output, whereas T represents transactions and so includes transactions of second-hand goods.

vertical integration: the joining together of two or more firms in the same industry, but at different stages of production. Forward vertical integration is when a firm merges with another at a later stage of production, e.g. a shoe manufacturer merges with a chain of shoe shops. Backward vertical integration is when a firm merges with another at an earlier stage of production, e.g. a shoe manufacturer merges with a firm involved in tanning leather.

visibles: tangible items or goods, usually referred to in relation to international trade and the balance of payments. *See also* invisibles.

voluntary unemployment: unemployment arising because people are not prepared to work at existing wage rates. *See also* natural rate of unemployment and involuntary unemployment.

wages councils: government-appointed bodies which set minimum wages in areas where trade union organization is weak or difficult.

wealth: includes all assets that exist at any given time – i.e. real assets (in the form of goods) and financial assets – which can command a market value when transferred to another.

working population: potentially all those above school-leaving age and below retiring age who are capable of working. In practice it is measured as those who are employed, self-employed, claiming benefit or in the forces.

X-inefficiency: managerial and technical inefficiency which causes costs to be higher than the minimum attainable. It is associated with situations of restricted competition and when goals other than profit maximization are pursued by managers. *See also* profit maximization.

E.M. Gilman's glossary from first edition, revised and extended by Mark Russell and Paul Lewis

Index